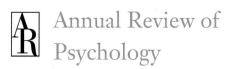

Annual Review of
Psychology

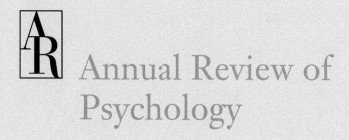

Annual Review of Psychology

Volume 67, 2016

Susan T. Fiske, *Editor*

Princeton University

Daniel L. Schacter, *Associate Editor*

Harvard University

Shelley E. Taylor, *Associate Editor*

University of California, Los Angeles

www.annualreviews.org • science@annualreviews.org • 650-493-4400

Annual Reviews

4139 El Camino Way • P.O. Box 10139 • Palo Alto, California 94303-0139

Annual Reviews
Palo Alto, California, USA

International Standard Serial Number: 0066-4308
International Standard Book Number: 978-0-8243-0267-2
Library of Congress Control Number: 50013143

All Annual Reviews and publication titles are registered trademarks of Annual Reviews.

⊚ The paper used in this publication meets the minimum requirements of American National Standards for Information Sciences—Permanence of Paper for Printed Library Materials, ANSI Z39.48-1992.

Annual Reviews and the Editors of its publications assume no responsibility for the statements expressed by the contributors to this *Annual Review*.

TYPESET BY APTARA
PRINTED AND BOUND BY SHERIDAN BOOKS, INC., CHELSEA, MICHIGAN

Introduction

Psychology is not in crisis, contrary to popular rumor. Every few decades, critics declare a crisis, point out problems, and sometimes motivate solutions. When we were graduate students, psychology was in "crisis," raising concerns about whether it was scientific enough. Issues of measurement validity, theoretical rigor, and realistic applicability came to the fore. Researchers rose to the challenges, and psychological science soldiered on.

This decade, the crisis implicates biomedical, social, and behavioral sciences alike, and the focus is replicability. First came a few tragic and well-publicized frauds; fortunately, they are rare—though never absent from science conducted by humans—and they were caught. Now the main concern is some well-publicized failures to replicate, including some large-scale efforts to replicate multiple studies, for example in social and cognitive psychology. National panels will convene and caution scientists, reviewers, and editors to uphold standards. Graduate training will improve, and researchers will remember their training and learn new standards.

All this is normal science, not crisis. A replication failure is not a scientific problem; it is an opportunity to find limiting conditions and contextual effects. Of course studies don't always replicate.

Annual Reviews provides an additional remedy that is also from the annals of normal science: the expert, synthetic review article. As part of the cycle of discovery, novel findings attract interest, programs of research develop, scientists build on the basic finding, and inevitably researchers discover its boundary conditions and limiting mechanisms. Expert reviewers periodically step in, assess the state of the science—including both dead ends and well-established effects—and identify new directions. Crisis or no crisis, the field develops consensus about the most valuable insights. As editors, we are impressed by the patterns of discovery affirmed in every Annual Review article.

Susan T. Fiske, Princeton, New Jersey
Daniel L. Schacter, Cambridge, Massachusetts
Shelley E. Taylor, Los Angeles, California

Annual Review of
Psychology

Volume 67, 2016

Contents

Indexes

Errata

An online log of corrections to *Annual Review of Psychology* articles may be found at
http://www.annualreviews.org/errata/psych

Related Articles

From the ***Annual Review of Law and Social Science***, Volume 11 (2015)

From the *Annual Review of Public Health*, Volume 35 (2014)

Thomas F. Pettigrew

In Pursuit of Three Theories: Authoritarianism, Relative Deprivation, and Intergroup Contact

Thomas F. Pettigrew

Department of Psychology, University of California, Santa Cruz, Santa Cruz, California 95064; email: pettigr@ucsc.edu

Annu. Rev. Psychol. 2016. 67:1–21

First published online as a Review in Advance on September 10, 2015

The *Annual Review of Psychology* is online at psych.annualreviews.org

This article's doi: 10.1146/annurev-psych-122414-033327

Keywords

prejudice, authoritarianism, relative deprivation, intergroup contact, Gordon Allport, Samuel Stouffer

Abstract

Throughout my career, I have pursued three theories related to intergroup prejudice—each with a different mentor. Each theory and its supporting research help us to understand prejudice and ways to ameliorate the problem. This autobiographical review article summarizes some of the advances in these three areas during the past six decades. For authoritarianism, the article advocates removing political content from its measurement, linking it with threat and dismissive-avoidant attachment, and studying how authoritarians avoid intergroup contact. Increased work on relative deprivation made possible an extensive meta-analysis that shows the theory, when appropriately measured, has far broader effects than previously thought. Increased research attention to intergroup contact similarly made possible a meta-analysis that established the pervasive effectiveness of intergroup contact to reduce prejudice under a wide range of conditions. The article closes by demonstrating how the three theories relate to each other and contribute to our understanding of prejudice and its reduction.

Contents

GETTING STARTED

My discovery of social psychology remains a vivid memory. It was a crisp February morning in 1950 when I began an introductory course in the subject at the University of Virginia. There were then no social psychologists in the psychology department. But the course was ably taught by a leading expert in hearing, Willard Thurlow.

The course text was the venerable *Theory and Problems of Social Psychology* (Kretch & Crutchfield 1948). It featured two intriguing chapters on prejudice—one on racial prejudice and a second on "how to eliminate this prejudice among our people." Because of my deep concerns about southern race relations, this subject was of enormous interest to me. Since my initial ambition to be an architect had not worked out (I could not draw!), I knew immediately that I had found the field in which to specialize.

Two books impressed me. Gunnar Myrdal's (1944) 1,500-page *An American Dilemma* provided a sociological perspective on the South's racial situation. And *The Authoritarian Personality* (TAP; Adorno et al. 1950) provided a psychological perspective. But while Myrdal's tome accurately reflected my experiences growing up in racially segregated Richmond, Virginia, the theory of the authoritarian personality seemed incomplete to me. I knew many Virginians—foremost among them my soft-spoken, equalitarian father—who largely conformed to the region's racial norms but did not at all fit the authoritarian mold. TAP contained no southern samples and simply assumed that greater authoritarianism explained the white South's elevated racism.

Something was missing when the theory was applied to the white South. The answer was supplied by Myrdal's landmark volume. The South's tortured racial history—slavery, a lost war, poverty, and intense racial segregation—had shaped discriminatory norms to which Southerners of both races had had to conform for decades. To be sure, authoritarianism played a role, but so did conformity to entrenched racially discriminatory norms that characterized southern society. Both the personality and social structural levels of analysis are necessary to understand intergroup prejudice—a theme that underlies virtually all my work throughout my career.

Thurlow was the first of my three mentors who encouraged my interests. Somehow he knew that Gordon Allport was writing a book on prejudice. So he recommended that I apply to Harvard University for doctoral work. Such timely mentoring can redirect your life, and I remain grateful for Thurlow's guidance. Unaware of how arrogant it appeared, I mentioned in my Harvard application to the Social Relations Department that I wanted to work with Allport on prejudice; otherwise I was not interested in attending. Fortunately, Allport was in charge of graduate admissions, and my naive impertinence did not prove fatal. Harvard's social psychology doctoral program gave me the singular opportunity to work with Allport, a warm mentor and influential psychologist (Pettigrew 1969, 1990, 1999, 2015a), as well as Samuel Stouffer, an inspiring sociological social psychologist (Pettigrew 2015b). Fortunately, my graduate years, 1952–1956, covered the period that Nichols (1998) has called the "peak years" of Harvard's old Social Relations Department.

In 1952, race relations was not a privileged specialty. I was the object of concern among my fellow doctoral students. They urged me to choose another field, as race relations offered few jobs and little research support. But my southern experiences with racial injustice had fired my desire to be a social psychologist, so these limitations seemed irrelevant. The scene changed in 1954 when the US Supreme Court ruled against racial segregation in public schools. Suddenly, my peers became interested in the topic, and their concerns diminished.

The three theories that have guided my career all relate to prejudice. The first two—authoritarianism and relative deprivation—explain and predict prejudice. The third theory—intergroup contact—constitutes social psychology's most important contribution to reducing prejudice.

AUTHORITARIANISM

I entered Harvard with my thesis topic already selected—the role of authoritarianism in southern race relations. Both Allport and Stouffer encouraged me to pursue this topic. It was an exciting time to be working with them. Not only was Allport (1954) writing his classic book on prejudice, but Stouffer was developing his important work on American attitudes toward the virulent Senator Joseph McCarthy—*Communism, Conformity and Civil Liberties* (Stouffer 1955).

Both teachers shaped my doctoral thesis (Pettigrew 1958, 1959). From Allport, I learned how to cast my contentions in sharper conceptual focus. From Stouffer, I learned how to test them on probability samples with survey methods. In the summer of 1955, I set out with Charles Lamont, my undergraduate assistant and undaunted friend, to sample door-to-door white racial opinions in small towns in the South and North. To deter trouble, I put Virginia license plates on my old Chevrolet. And Stouffer got official interviewer certification papers from a national survey agency for us to identify ourselves to local police departments.

In the most deep-South community sampled—Moultrie, Georgia—the tension was palpable. In May 1955, the Supreme Court had followed its historic desegregation ruling with a vague "all deliberate speed" order. The white South, quite deliberate but rarely speedy, interpreted this order as a sign of weakness. Resistance groups called White Citizens' Councils—basically middle-class Ku Klux Klans—soon mobilized in such towns as Moultrie.

As a consequence, the survey schedule had to minimize recognition of its purpose. Following Stouffer's advice, we asked the white respondents what they considered to be the most important problem facing the nation. With the school desegregation issue so salient, most respondents named it as the most important. If they did not, we asked for the second most important problem—if need be, the third. By then, the entire sample had named racial issues. Thus, we introduced the racial attitude questions as a subject they themselves had raised.

Our results supported normative theory. The mean levels of authoritarianism were not significantly different between the southern and northern samples. As expected, the authoritarian scores predicted anti-black attitudes equally well in the two regions—showing its validity at the individual level of analysis. But at the macro level, the scores could not explain the great differences in prejudice between the regions. Middleton (1976) later followed up this work with a national sample, and he both replicated and extended these results.

In 1956, Allport obtained a grant for me to accompany him for a half-year visit to a social science center in Durban, South Africa. Although I could obtain only university student respondents, I replicated the American results with one difference. Afrikaners were on average more authoritarian as well as more prejudiced than other white South Africans. Nonetheless, conformity to rigorously enforced racist norms remained central (Pettigrew 1958). These and other findings have led me to embrace normative theory throughout my career (Pettigrew 1991a).

During the "cognitive revolution," interest in authoritarianism declined precipitously in North America. Only after Altemeyer (1981) introduced his right-wing authoritarianism (RWA) scales did interest return. But throughout these decades, I continued to include a measure of authoritarianism when studying prejudice of all types in the United States, South Africa, and Western Europe. And it never failed to be a major predictor of prejudice at the individual level of analysis. When Sidanius & Pratto (1999) introduced their measure of social dominance orientation (SDO), I began to include it also in my studies.

My success with authoritarianism measures is consistent with that of others around the world. Few relationships in social science are as stable and virtually universal as the link between authoritarianism and prejudice. This is not to claim that the relationship is invariant; normative and situational variables can substantially moderate the link (Baier et al. 2016; Pettigrew 1959, 2000; Reynolds et al. 2001; Sales 1973).

Despite its many conceptual and methodological problems, authoritarianism has proven to be a durable theory (Pettigrew 2016). But several problems have long troubled me. First, the F and RWA scales contain blatantly political content. Does this not confound the results with political conservatism? Second, how does authoritarianism develop, and how does it relate to other established personality syndromes? Third, what is the role of threat in authoritarianism? Could threat be a critical contextual component for the acting out of authoritarian behavior? Finally, how does authoritarianism influence such prejudice-reducing remedies as intergroup contact? Recent work sheds light on each of these concerns.

Political Confounding

Given the overlap of the F and RWA scales with political conservatism, critics justifiably challenge the finding that authoritarianism routinely correlates positively with conservatism. Purely personality measures of authoritarianism are needed now to complement these political attitude assessments. This would eliminate the political content of RWA scales and address the debate between those who view authoritarianism as a personality syndrome and others who view it as a political ideology. However, there is no necessary conflict between these two perspectives. Authoritarianism begins early in life as a personality orientation that later typically leads to a particular political ideology. Moreover, just because situational and societal factors influence authoritarianism does not mean it cannot be considered a personality variable. Other personality syndromes are also socially influenced.

Oesterreich (2005) has begun to address these issues in what, hopefully, will become a focus of future research. By using directly opposed statements (e.g., "I like changes" versus "I don't like changes") from which to choose, Oesterreich balanced his personality scale of authoritarianism. His 23-item scale attained a 0.84 alpha with a large representative sample of German voters. These items cover a range of authoritarian personality characteristics: insecurity ("I feel uncomfortable in new and unfamiliar situations"), conformity and submission ("I have no problems following orders, even when I am not convinced of their necessity"), a focus on strength ("I admire dominant people"), a need for closure ("I am irritated by people who call well-established things into question"), and resistance to new experience ("I don't like to be confronted with new ideas").

The success of this attempt to measure authoritarianism with purely personality indicators is signified by its solid relationships with such correlates of authoritarianism as prejudice and right-wing extremism (Oesterreich 2005). The further development of such personality-based indicators of authoritarianism would greatly benefit future research.

The Development of Authoritarianism

Twin studies have revealed a significant level of heritability in authoritarianism (Ludeke & Krueger 2013, McCourt et al. 1999), and Altemeyer (1996) found strong correlations between the authoritarianism levels of young adults and their parents.

But what about the relationships between authoritarianism and other established personality features that could shed light on the development of authoritarianism? The fact that security issues are critical for authoritarians suggests links between authoritarianism and attachment theory. Indeed, several investigators have noted this possibility, and its potential importance deserves emphasis.

Hopf (1992, 1993) draws explicit connections between authoritarianism and avoidant attachment. She found that lower-status German adolescents who were high on avoidant attachment articulated the most extreme authoritarian views. And though TAP stressed displacement of hostility from a stern father, Hopf (1992, 1993) notes that 7 of the 20 men classified as authoritarian by Frenkel-Brunswik had experienced the death of their mothers as young children, compared to none of the nonauthoritarians (Fisher's exact test, $p < 0.005$). In contrast to TAP, Ackerman & Jahoda (1950) emphasized parental rejection and found rejection by one or both parents to be common among their sample of anti-Semites. Van IJzendoorn (1997) gave a sample of American university students the Adult Attachment Scale (AAS) and the RWA. He found that students who scored high on avoidant attachment scored highest on authoritarianism, whereas those who scored high on the secure and anxious attachment dimensions scored lowest.

General descriptions of avoidants often read as if they were direct quotations from TAP. Hence, Main et al. (1985) found that avoidant adults idealized their parents but could not provide clear, episodic memories to support their unrealistically glowing assessments—precisely what TAP found for those scoring high on authoritarianism.

Worldwide research results support the linkage between avoidant attachment and authoritarianism. In India, Hassen (1987), in a study of 400 Muslim teenagers, found that parental rejection correlated positively with both authoritarianism and prejudice. In Italy, Roccato & Ricolfi (2005) noted that members of an extreme right-wing political party scored high on measures of authoritarianism, social dominance orientation, and avoidant attachment and low on secure attachment. In Germany, Oesterreich (2005) used three items that tap avoidant attachment in his authoritarianism scale: "I don't like to meet new people," "I try to avoid contact with people who are different," and "I feel uncomfortable with people I do not know."

Not all studies support the avoidant–authoritarian link. Several papers, all using convenience samples of American undergraduate subjects, have actually shown small negative correlations between various avoidance measures and right-wing authoritarianism (Gormley & Lopez 2010, Thornhill & Fincher 2007, Weber & Federico 2007).

Avoidant attachment orientation is one of three orientations delineated by Ainsworth and colleagues (1978): secure, anxious, and avoidant (Mikulincer & Shaver 2007). These attachment "styles" are best thought of as continuous and interrelated dimensions rather than as exclusive "types" (Fraley & Waller 1998). In broad strokes, secure individuals neither avoid nor are especially anxious about close relationships. Anxious individuals typically seek close relationships with others but are highly anxious about them. Avoidants simply attempt to avoid close relationships. Prototype items for each style are (a) secure: "It is easy for me to become emotionally close to others"; (b) anxious: "I worry a lot about my relationships"; and (c) avoidant: "I find it difficult to trust others completely."

Later, Bartholomew (1990; Bartholomew & Horowitz 1991) separated the avoidant style into two distinct groupings: dismissive-avoidants and fearful-avoidants. Both styles harbor negative views of others, but they differ in their views of the self. Dismissive-avoidants tend to value independence and feel self-sufficient. A prototypical item is, "I prefer not to depend on others or have others depend on me." By contrast, fearful-avoidants report less self-esteem and self-acceptance. They are more likely to have suffered a serious loss of or rejection by a primary caregiver in early life. A prototypical item is, "I sometimes worry that I will be hurt if I allow myself to become too dependent on others." This division within the avoidant style may well help to explain some of the differences found in its relationship with authoritarianism.

In a further exploration of the avoidant–authoritarianism link, Jost Stellmacher, German and American colleagues, and I (manuscript in preparation) have conducted three quite different studies. The first is a secondary analysis of a national probability survey of German citizens. We found a strong relationship among the 2,400 respondents between authoritarianism and a four-item measure of avoidant attachment with controls for age, education, and sex. The second study of American university students replicated this finding with a more extensive measure of avoidant attachment, but it uncovered no relationship between authoritarianism and anxious attachment. A third study examined 219 German respondents with a still more extensive questionnaire using the online platform Unipark (**http://www.unipark.de**). The respondents in this unrepresentative sample varied widely in age but were generally highly educated. This study again found a significant correlation between avoidance and authoritarianism. Authoritarians are disproportionally found among both types of avoidants.

However, the most interesting findings of our studies are the moderators and mediators that shape the relationship. Thus, the first study found that the link between the two variables is strongly moderated by contact with outgroups. Those with more such contact revealed a significantly smaller relationship between avoidant attachment and authoritarianism. The third study found that openness to experience—often shown to be an underlying component of authoritarianism (e.g., Ekehammar et al. 2004)—acts as a significant mediator of the avoidant–authoritarian link. More detailed work on this promising link between authoritarianism and attachment theory is clearly indicated.

The Role of Threat in Authoritarianism

Threat is often intertwined with authoritarianism. An analysis of a 2004 probability sample of 1,153 German citizens (Pettigrew & Tropp 2011, pp. 155–156, 196–200) uncovered ties between authoritarianism and two types of threat in predicting anti-Muslim prejudice. Individual threat is measured by four items emphasizing personal feelings: "Foreigners living here threaten *my* personal freedom and rights. . .*my* personal economic situation. . .*my* personal way of life. . .and *my* personal security" – in short, "*they*" are threatening "*me*."

Collective threat involves the ingroup: "Foreigners living here threaten *our* freedom and rights. . .*our* prosperity. . .*our* culture. . .and *our* security" – in short, "*they*" are threatening "*us*." These threat factors mediate much of the association between authoritarianism and anti-Muslim prejudice. Although authoritarianism is strongly and positively related to both types of threat, it is the perception of collective threat that is most highly associated with prejudice. Moreover, the effect of individual threat is almost entirely mediated by collective threat.

That collective, rather than individual, threat drives much of the association between authoritarianism and prejudice is consistent with the emphasis on group identification for authoritarians of both Duckitt (1989) and Stellmacher & Petzel (2005). It is also consistent with the findings of Sales (1973) and others that show how authoritarianism is influenced by societal-level threat factors (Baier et al. 2016; Pettigrew 1959, 2000; Reynolds et al. 2001). Further research in this area should focus on how threat shapes the social context for authoritarians to act out their beliefs.

How Does Authoritarianism Influence Such Prejudice-Reducing Remedies as Intergroup Contact?

Many assume that authoritarians are highly resistant to efforts to reduce prejudice. But consider intergroup contact. Hodgson and colleagues (2009) and others (Pettigrew & Tropp 2011) have shown that intergroup contact has the potential to reduce prejudice among authoritarians significantly. This may seem surprising, as it counters the view of TAP (Adorno et al. 1950, p. 973). Yet this result fits with many findings that show that intergroup contact potentially can alter numerous factors closely related to authoritarianism: anxiety, group attributions, individual and collective threat, meta-stereotypes, SDO, stereotype threat, trust, forgiveness, empathy, perspective taking, knowledge of the outgroup, ingroup identification, political tolerance, and perceptions of outgroup variability (Pettigrew & Tropp 2011).

In *The Nature of Prejudice*, Allport (1954, p. 279) viewed authoritarianism as a personality barrier to diminishing prejudice via intergroup contact. Because Allport had a narrow research base to rely on at mid-century, this conclusion was based on a single study. Mussen (1950) studied the racial attitudes of white boys at an interracial camp. He found that boys with equalitarian-like traits evinced diminished racial prejudice after their interracial experience, whereas those with authoritarian-like traits had become more prejudiced. But this early finding may not be the exception it appears. Mussen did not use a direct measure of authoritarianism, nor did he have a direct measure of contact. It seems likely that the authoritarian white campers were threatened by the presence of the black campers and simply avoided contact with them.

This is the critical point. Authoritarianism *is* a barrier to positive intergroup contact effects by restricting the willingness to participate in the contact in the first place. Only when authoritarians do have the contact can contact lessen prejudice. Attaining the intergroup contact is the problem.

German survey data illustrate the point (Pettigrew & Tropp 2011, pp. 210–11). Three selection processes are delineated. First, 341 of the 1,377 sample members did not live in a neighborhood with foreigners. But the mere presence of foreigners does not guarantee intergroup contact—the second selection process. Indeed, 25% of the German respondents who lived in mixed areas reported no contact with their foreign neighbors. Finally, intergroup contact does not ensure that intergroup friendship will develop—and such friendships are a major means for contact to diminish prejudice (Davies et al. 2011, Pettigrew & Tropp 2011). This last contact selection process removes 18% of the German respondents who have neighborhood contact but no foreign friends.

Regression tests for the predictors of these three processes reveal how authoritarianism consistently blocks intergroup contact (Pettigrew & Tropp 2011, pp. 210–12). Although age, gender, and prior prejudice are also involved, only authoritarianism is significantly and negatively related to all three processes. German authoritarians are less likely than nonauthoritarians to be living in an area with foreigners, less likely to have contact with them even when they do live in such an area, and less likely to make friends with those foreigners with whom they have neighborhood contact. Moreover, authoritarians in the survey significantly more often view their contact with outgroups as superficial, involuntary, and with a resident foreigner of unequal status—violations of Allport's (1954) facilitating factors for maximum contact effects.

Thus, authoritarians carefully avoid resident foreigners at multiple levels. Contact effects can be as successful with authoritarians as with others, but authoritarians are far less likely to have such contact.

RELATIVE DEPRIVATION

To study a second theory involving prejudice, I am indebted to Samuel Stouffer, my Harvard methodology mentor. One of the most influential social psychologists in sociology's history, he introduced the concept of relative deprivation (RD). Together with Paul Lazarsfeld, Stouffer fashioned the probability survey into a refined research instrument for social science. He also directed three of the major social science projects of the mid-twentieth century: Myrdal's (1944) *An American Dilemma* (Stouffer headed the study after Myrdal returned to his native Sweden when it was threatened in World War II); *The American Soldier* series on US Army morale (Stouffer 1962, Stouffer et al. 1949), which Stouffer directed throughout World War II; and the survey study of McCarthyism published during that dark episode in American political history (Stouffer 1955).

Stouffer was an inspiring but unorthodox teacher; he could not have been more different in style from the somewhat shy, formal, and reserved Allport. Instruction from Stouffer was informal and empirical. Intensely engrossed in his work, he taught by example. Students followed him from office to computing room and back, absorbing as best they could his excitement and "feel" for survey analysis. To this day, I have never lost the sense of excitement and curiosity in analyzing survey data instilled by these memorable occasions. If a member of his survey analysis seminar offered an interesting hypothesis, he would leap up and exclaim, "Let's test it!" Then he would lead the class to the machine room and start stuffing the survey data cards into the old IBM 101 counter, sorter, and printer.

Origins of the Relative Deprivation Concept

Stouffer eschewed sociology's penchant for "grand theory." Consistent with his empirical emphasis, he believed in close-to-the-data reasoning and middle-level concepts. The most famous illustration of Stouffer's talent for middle-range concepts comes from the *American Soldier* studies (Stouffer 1962, Stouffer et al. 1949). Stouffer devised RD as a post hoc explanation for the study's well-known anomalies.

For example, he found that the military police were more satisfied with their slow promotions than the Air Corpsmen were with their rapid promotions. This apparent puzzle assumes the wrong comparison. Immediate comparisons, Stouffer reasoned, were the salient referents: The military police compared their promotions with other military police—not with Air Corpsmen whom they rarely encountered. Satisfaction is relative to the available comparisons we have. RD became a useful social science concept because social judgments are shaped not only by absolute standards but also by standards set by social comparisons (Pettigrew 1967, 1978, 2015b; Smith et al. 2012; Walker & Smith 2002).

Following Stouffer, RD can be defined as a judgment that one or one's ingroup is disadvantaged compared to a relevant referent; this judgment invokes feelings of angry resentment. In addition to the fundamental feature that the concept operates at the level of individuals, RD involves three psychological processes: (*a*) People first make cognitive comparisons, (*b*) they next make cognitive appraisals that they or their ingroup are disadvantaged, and finally (*c*) these disadvantages are seen as unfair and arouse angry resentment. If any one of these three requirements is missing, RD is not operating (Smith et al. 2012).

Thus defined, RD is a social psychological concept *par excellence*. It postulates a subjective state that shapes emotions, cognitions, and behavior. It connects the individual with the interpersonal and intergroup levels of analysis. It melds easily with other social psychological processes to provide more integrative theory—a prime disciplinary need (Pettigrew 1991b). RD challenges conventional wisdom about the leading importance of absolute deprivation. And it has proven useful throughout the social sciences.

Development of the Theory

Many social psychological theories burn hot then suddenly cool. But RD and related ideas have simmered slowly on a back burner for two-thirds of a century. Merton (1957) enlarged the idea within a reference group framework. Building on this framework, Davis (1959) provided a mathematical model of RD. This work led me to point out that RD was but one of a large family of concepts and theories that employed relative comparisons in both sociology and psychology (Pettigrew 1967).

Runciman (1966) broadened the RD construct by his invaluable distinction between egoistic (individual) and fraternal (group) RD. People can believe that they are unfairly personally deprived [individual RD (IRD)] or that a social group to which they belong and identify is unfairly deprived [group RD (GRD)]. Feelings of GRD should be associated with group-serving attitudes and behavior such as collective action and outgroup prejudice, whereas IRD should be associated with such individual-serving attitudes and behavior as academic achievement and property crime.

Many psychological publications have since expanded the theory and linked RD with a host of other concepts and theories (Albert 1977, Crosby 1976, Mark & Folger 1984, Olson et al. 1986, Suls & Miller 1977, Walker & Smith 2002). But the study and application of RD has progressed less well in sociology and political science. Gurr (1970) wrote a widely cited book titled *Why Men Rebel* that largely ignores social psychological work and the fact that RD is a phenomenon of individuals—not societies. He employed such gross macro-level measures of RD as economic and political indices of whole societies. Although *Why Men Rebel* uncovered interesting findings, it is not an RD study. As a result, justified criticism of this work in the social movement field mistakenly cast RD as of little value (Pettigrew 2015b).

The Ecological Fallacy

A classic ecological fallacy occurs when micro-level phenomena, such as RD, are erroneously assumed from macro phenomena (Pettigrew 1996, 2006; Robinson 1950). It is a fallacy because macro units are usually too broad to determine individual data, and individuals have unique properties that cannot be inferred from macro data. Indeed, the central thrust of RD theory is that individual responses are often different from those that are expected of the macro category. Given contrasting comparisons, the rich can be dissatisfied and the poor content—just the opposite from what their macro income characteristics would indicate. The ecological fallacy has seriously stymied the development of RD theory in its application to social movement theory (Pettigrew 2015b).

In short, RD makes the claim that absolute levels of deprivation of individuals only partly determine feelings of dissatisfaction and injustice. Imagined counterfactuals, past experiences, and comparisons with similar others also strongly influence such feelings. RD describes these subjective evaluations by individuals, and it offers an elegant way to explain numerous paradoxes (Tyler & Smith 1998). Thus, RD explains why there is often little relationship between objective standards of living and satisfaction with one's income (Strumpel 1976): The objectively disadvantaged are often satisfied with receiving low levels of societal resources, whereas the objectively advantaged are often dissatisfied with high levels of societal resources (Martin 1986, Pettigrew 1964). RD models suggest that the objectively disadvantaged often compare themselves to others in the same situation or worse, whereas the objectively advantaged often compare themselves to those who enjoy even more advantages.

Two Relative Deprivation Problems

Two problems account for the discrepancies in results found in RD research. First, in *The American Soldier*, Stouffer did not measure RD directly; rather, as noted previously, he inferred it as a post hoc explanation for surprising results. This failure to initiate a prototype measure has led to literally hundreds of diverse and often conflicting measures that have bedeviled RD research.

Worse, many of the measures purporting to tap RD do not meet the concept's basic features. One prevalent example involves the Cantril-Kilpatrick Self-Anchoring Scale (Cantril 1965). This measure has respondents place themselves on a 10-step ladder, with the top rung labeled as the best possible life and the bottom rung as the worst possible life. This scale measures discrepancies between people's attainments and aspirations. But it does not measure discrepancies between their expectations as to what they want and deserve and their current situation, and how they feel about these discrepancies (Smith et al. 2012). Thus, this measure emphasizes RD's cognitive component at the expense of its affective component.

Second, Stouffer offered a concept, not a testable theory. This problem, too, has impeded development of RD. Only recently have full-fledged theories emerged that allow direct testing and falsification. In the 1980s, Heather Smith (then a doctoral student at the University of California, Santa Cruz and now a professor at Sonoma State University) and I decided that what was needed was a meta-analysis of the far-flung research literature that employed the concept (Smith et al. 2012). It took 25 years of an off-and-on effort to complete the Herculean task.

Meta-Analytic Tests of Relative Deprivation

Our first task was to clear the underbrush that had sprung up due to the absence of a precise theoretical and measurement model. We used inclusion criteria that ensured that RD was being tested, and a huge 76% drop-off occurred. Although we initially secured 860 studies that purported to study RD, only 210 met our modest criteria and entered the meta-analysis. Failing to exclude these marginal studies has been a major problem in the past for qualitative RD reviews that did not employ strict inclusion rules. As a consequence, their criticism of RD typically involved studies that did not actually assess RD.

Our second task was to ascertain the mean effect sizes for the entire RD literature as of January 2010. The 210 separate studies we located included 293 independent samples, 421 nonindependent tests, and 186,073 respondents. Three different checks indicated that our tests were not altered by a publication bias that favored positive results (for details, see Smith et al. 2012). The mean effect sizes that emerged were highly statistically significant but small: +0.106 for studies, +0.144 for samples, and +0.134 for tests.

Why such small RD effects? We examined three hypotheses for an explanation. First, our affect hypothesis predicts that stronger RD effects will emerge when people are angry over their perceived disadvantage. One can detect a personal or group disadvantage but believe that it is justified, as system justification research has repeatedly shown (Jost et al. 2004). Indeed, experiments show that system-justifying beliefs act as a moderator for both IRD and GRD. Subjects with these beliefs show smaller RD effects (Osborne & Sibley 2013). Hence, feelings of anger and resentment are basic to the RD formulation.

Our second proposition involves the fit hypothesis. We predicted that RD effects will be larger when the levels of analysis between RD and the dependent variable are the same (Walker & Pettigrew 1984). Put differently, we contend that RD effects are reduced when IRD is used to predict group-level phenomena and GRD is used to predict individual-level phenomena.

Our third test is methodological. The research quality hypothesis holds that the more rigorous studies will yield larger effects. If the major effects of RD were found among the poorest conducted studies—as with the effects of psychotherapy for adult depression (Cuijpers et al. 2010)—one would question RD's predictive power. But we predicted the opposite—that the most rigorous RD studies would reveal the largest effects. We defined quality in terms of the reliability of both the RD and dependent variables.

The Meta-Analytic Results

Figure 1 provides the overall results by showing the percentages of variance accounted for by subsets of the tests. For bar A, the RD tests that were conducted worst had none of our three desirable characteristics and yielded an r of +0.079. Bar B shows a mean r of +0.134 for all 421 tests. Bar C shows a mean r of +0.165 for those tests that did tap affect but had neither reliable measures nor a fit between the levels of analysis of RD and the outcome variable. Bar D shows a

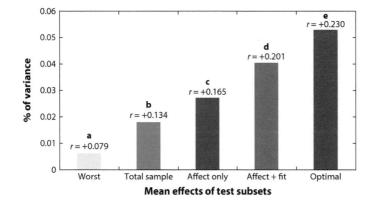

Figure 1

Mean effects of test subsets by percentage of variance explained. Adapted with permission from Smith et al. (2012).

mean r of +0.201 when the tests boast both fit and an affect measure but lack reliable measures. Finally, bar E records the results of the optimal tests. It reveals a mean r of +0.230 when all three of our conditions are met—reliable measures that tap affect and have the same level of analysis between RD and the dependent variable. Furthermore, direct statistical tests of our three hypotheses are all significant at the 0.05 level (Smith et al. 2012). These results solidly support the importance of RD when it is tested appropriately.

The Range of Dependent Variables

Similar results were also found for four broad types of dependent variables (Pettigrew 2015b): (*a*) Internal states include psychological stress and physical health; (*b*) individual behaviors encompass both normative (e.g., church activities) and nonnormative (e.g., bullying) actions; (*c*) intergroup attitudes consist of prejudice measures and variables tapping stereotypes, nationalism, and ingroup identification; and (*d*) collective behaviors range from self-reported rioting to a readiness to join strikes and endorse violent politics.

Tested rigorously with reliable measures that tap angry resentment against dependent variables of similar scope, these meta-analytic results demonstrate that RD can be a useful theory in a wide variety of domains of central interest to social psychology.

Universality of the Relative Deprivation Phenomena

Our meta-analysis also addresses a question too seldom raised by social psychology—whether its findings are universal. Positive results were recorded from 30 different nations with widely contrasting respondents, societies, and cultures (Smith et al. 2012).

Relative Versus Objective Deprivation

One limiting possibility is that RD effects may simply reflect absolute deprivation. Relevant research does not support this possibility. We located 26 studies that allow a direct comparison of relative and absolute deprivation (Smith et al. 2012). All 26 used income as the objective measure of deprivation. In terms of the percentage of variance explained, the mean effects of RD are more than twice that of absolute deprivation. These data supply yet another reason why macro-level measures of objective deprivation cannot be used to gauge the perceived RD of individuals.

INTERGROUP CONTACT

Just as Thurlow had known, Allport (1954, 1958) was starting to write his classic volume *The Nature of Prejudice* as I arrived at Harvard in 1952. He wrote most of the book at his summer cabin near Lincoln, Maine. While at Harvard, he concentrated on his teaching and extensive administrative duties. But he did work occasionally on the book in Cambridge, and I served as his "go-for" assistant—not for coffee but rather for books from Widener Library.

Allport's book appeared in a hardbound edition in 1954. Issued by a small, local publisher, it had only modest sales. Not until the 1958 paperback edition, issued by a major publisher and reduced 40% in size, did its sales swell and its influence mount.

I committed the volume virtually to memory as soon as it appeared. Two chapters particularly caught my attention. Chapter 17 on conformity bolstered my theory about the white South's anti-black prejudice. Chapter 16 on intergroup contact offered a means of reducing prejudice and coincided with my own experience as a white American who often found himself in African

American settings. I became so interested in intergroup contact that I chose to take my doctoral special examination on the subject. The test was administered and graded by Allport himself, who became my third and major mentor.

Four Key Factors and Their Problems

Prior to the 1950s, most writers held that intergroup contact exacerbated prejudice and conflict (e.g., Baker 1934). But there was scant relevant research. In his chapter 16, Allport partly followed an earlier analysis by the eminent sociologist Robin Williams (1947). The chapter mentions many pertinent points, yet its broad and discursive nature made it difficult to prepare for the examination. So I boiled the text down to four key factors that enabled intergroup contact to reduce prejudice: (*a*) equal status between the groups within the situation, (*b*) common goals, (*c*) cooperation between groups, and (*d*) authority support for the contact.

Allport approved of my synthesis, and I continued to use it in later publications (e.g., Pettigrew 1971). But there are three limitations to this approach. First, like any list, it does not do full justice to Allport's rich discussion. Second, it is a "positive factors" approach that later research has shown to be too restrictive. Allport, writing during a tense racial era, assumed that intergroup contact typically failed to reduce prejudice. So he sought to make explicit positive factors that were necessary for contact to diminish prejudice.

In turn, this "necessary factors" approach led to a third problem (Pettigrew 1986). During the decades following the publication of Allport's volume, writers repeatedly added further factors that they presumed to be required for intergroup contact to have positive results. As the laundry list of necessary conditions accumulated, the theory was in danger of becoming meaningless. The ever-increasing list of "necessary" conditions rapidly excluded the majority of the world's intergroup situations and rendered the theory trivial. Social psychologists were concentrating on avoiding type I errors (false positives) while ignoring type II errors (false negatives).

The 1960s and 1970s witnessed increasing attention to contact theory as its policy implications became evident. I found it useful as the basis for expert testimony in support of racial school desegregation in legal cases in Springfield, Massachusetts, in Los Angeles, and in Norfolk and Richmond, Virginia (Pettigrew 1979).

A Needed Meta-Analysis

To test the theory thoroughly, I long wanted to review the research on intergroup contact. But there were too few studies to analyze and inadequate review methods. By the 1990s, however, the contact literature had expanded substantially and meta-analysis—a vast improvement over qualitative reviews—had been developed. So Linda Tropp (then a doctoral student at the University of California, Santa Cruz and now a professor at the University of Massachusetts at Amherst) and I decided the time had arrived to conduct a thorough review of intergroup contact research (Pettigrew & Tropp 2000, 2006, 2008, 2011).

Once again, it took years to gather a near-complete collection of the extensive contact-prejudice research. We uncovered a total of 515 studies with 713 independent samples and 1,351 nonindependent tests that met our inclusion rules. (For a complete listing of these studies, see Pettigrew & Tropp 2011.) The research spans from 1941 through 2000 and contains responses from more than 250,000 participants, with 51% of the samples focused on racial or ethnic target groups.

Several conclusions emerged. First, the average effect for all studies was $r = -0.21$ (Cohen's $d = 0.43$). Like that found for RD, this is a solid, average effect size for meta-analyses in social psychology (Richard et al. 2003). Larger effect sizes are rare in meta-analyses because they typically include a wide variety of research formats, analyses, contexts, and subjects.

This average effect size cannot be explained away by participant selection, publication bias, sampling biases, or poorly conducted research. Like the RD results, the most rigorous studies tend to provide the largest effects. This phenomenon is repeated in 21st-century research. Recent work is more rigorously executed and yields larger contact effects than earlier work (Pettigrew & Tropp 2008).

We found that the positive effects of intergroup contact are not confined to just those outgroup members who directly participated in the contact. The primary generalization typically extends from the immediate outgroup members who participated in the contact to the entire outgroup. This effect is enhanced when the contact situation makes participants' group identities salient (Brown & Hewstone 2005). The effects of contact also extend to situations different from the original contact situation (Cook 1984).

Furthermore, our review uncovered evidence for the universality of intergroup contact phenomena across varied settings, age cohorts, and 38 countries throughout the world. We also found significant contact effects for groups that differ in race, ethnicity, nationality, sexual orientation, and physical and mental disabilities. Of course, there is variability in these effects. For example, studies repeatedly show that the effects for majority groups tend to be significantly larger than those for minority groups (Tropp & Pettigrew 2005). Yet the positive trend is remarkably consistent. The universality of the intergroup contact phenomenon suggests that there is a basic underlying process. This process may reflect the fact that familiarity generally leads to liking—the mere exposure effect (Zajonc 1968).

An important theoretical finding of the meta-analysis is that the four factors I gleaned from Allport's contact chapter were facilitating, but not necessary, factors for contact's constructive effects (Pettigrew & Tropp 2006, 2011). Studies featuring none of the key factors still tend to yield positive effects of contact on prejudice, though generally smaller than those of other studies.

Intergroup Contact Effects Spread Broadly

There is even an extended contact effect (Wright et al. 1997). Just having an ingroup friend who has an outgroup friend tends to improve attitudes toward the outgroup. Vicarious contact of various types, such as television viewing, book reading, and imagined contact, can erode prejudice and ease the anxiety that often accompanies interracial contact (Fujioka 1999; Gómez & Huici 2008; Graves 1999; Herek & Capitanio 1997; Schiappa et al. 2005, 2006; Turner et al. 2007, experiments 2 and 3; Vezzali et al. 2012). Part of this process involves the perception of norm changes and part is mediated by a positive change in meta-stereotypes—what you believe the outgroup thinks of your ingroup (Gómez & Huici 2008, Vorauer et al. 1998). These indirect contact effects are especially important for those who live in segregated areas without outgroup friends (Christ et al. 2010).

Macro-Level Implications of Intergroup Contact

Another significant finding is that extensive intergroup contact in an area can improve the area's intergroup norms. Using multilevel analyses of seven large surveys across three continents, Christ and his coworkers (2014) demonstrated that intergroup norms significantly improved following intergroup contact. This finding is especially noteworthy, for it is rare that changes at the meso level of analysis (contact) have been shown to change norms at the macro level (Pettigrew 1997).

This new normative change finding helps to explain a longstanding conflict in studies of ethnic diversity. A half-century ago, I and others typically found that racial prejudice and discrimination were greatest in those areas of the racially segregated South that had the highest proportion of black citizens—an apparent threat effect (Blalock 1967, Pettigrew 1957, Pettigrew & Campbell 1960, Pettigrew & Cramer 1959). But these studies all took place in areas with strict segregation. We failed to see that these negative effects of diversity could be offset by the greater intergroup contact that can ensue if there are no structural barriers to the contact. These dual effects of diversity— greater threat and greater contact—have now often been demonstrated (e.g., Pettigrew et al. 2010; Wagner et al. 2003, 2006).

Unfortunately, Putnam (2007), in a much-publicized paper, repeated this mistake (Pettigrew & Tropp 2011, pp. 164–67). Without controlling for either intergroup contact or neighborhood segregation, he found that intergroup diversity increased intergroup distrust. But Uslaner (2012; see also Rothwell 2010, 2012), using the same survey data set but carefully controlling for segregation, found in repeated analyses that it was neighborhood segregation and not diversity per se that related to intergroup distrust. The Putnam paper offers a striking example of the importance of omitted variables in social science analyses.

Growth in Intergroup Contact Research

The research literature on intergroup contact has exploded—from only 30 publications before 1960 to more than 400 since 2000. Longitudinal studies provide the most compelling support for the theory (Binder et al. 2009, Christ et al. 2010, Eller & Abrams 2004, Levin et al. 2003). Especially impressive is the longitudinal research conducted by Sidanius and colleagues (2008). This study's five data points reveal the evolving pattern of interracial roommate effects over a four-year period.

In 1998, I published a tentative theory of intergroup contact in the *Annual Review of Psychology* (Pettigrew 1998). Next, Brown & Hewstone (2005) provided an intensive review of the many moderating and mediating factors involved in intergroup contact's effects. During the past three decades, these two British investigators have tirelessly contributed significant research and analyses on the theory. Smaller, more focused meta-analyses reveal that two mediators in particular account for contact's reduction in prejudice: optimal contact reduces anxiety about intergroup interaction while it induces empathy and perspective taking (Pettigrew & Tropp 2008). Continued progress in the area is detailed in *Advances in Intergroup Contact* (Hodson & Hewstone 2013).

Contact's potential for diminishing prejudice extends even to outgroups not involved in the contact—the secondary transfer effect (STE; Pettigrew 2009). A growing array of research supports the STE (Lolliot et al. 2013). Tausch and her international colleagues (2010) ruled out three alternative explanations for STEs—prior contact with the secondary outgroup, socially desirable responding, and prior attitudes. In addition, they found strong STEs in cross-sectional studies conducted in Cyprus, Northern Ireland, and Texas and in a longitudinal study conducted in Northern Ireland. Finally, these analyses uncovered strong evidence for attitude generalization.

Another investigation employed a large sample drawn from eight European countries to examine the relationship between intergroup contact with immigrants and attitudes toward primary (immigrants) and secondary (homosexuals and Jews) outgroups (Schmid et al. 2012). Intergroup contact not only directly related with decreasing primary outgroup prejudice but also indirectly with decreasing secondary outgroup prejudice via attitude generalization. These relationships occurred primarily for individuals low in social dominance orientation.

Vezzali & Giovannini (2012) studied 175 Italian high school students. With the effects of prior contact statistically controlled, contact with immigrants improved attitudes toward them. And this attitude change generalized to improved attitudes toward the disabled and homosexuals as well. Intergroup attitudes, intergroup anxiety, and perspective taking all played mediating roles.

In Arizona, STEs have even been found for imagined contact with illegal immigrants (Harwood et al. 2014). These effects were found especially for groups that bore some similarity to the target group—Mexican Americans, legal immigrants, Asian Americans, and homeless people.

Extended, vicarious, and secondary transfer effects make it clear that intergroup contact effects spread broadly—a vital point for social policy.

What About Negative Contact?

Recent research on contact theory has explored the potential of negative contact to increase prejudice. Using Australian and American samples, Barlow and colleagues (2012) found that the quantity of negative contact related more closely to increased prejudice than the quantity of positive contact related to reduced prejudice. They regarded their results as reflecting greater category salience of negative contact. But other research with German samples fails to replicate this result and finds positive contact effects to be significantly stronger (Christ et al. 2008; Pettigrew & Tropp 2011, chapter 12). This discrepancy in findings may simply reflect contrasting empirical measures.

But the German data paint a more complex picture. First, there is far more positive than negative contact, save in special situations of open conflict. This fact helps to explain why the contact meta-analysis could locate only 21 studies (4%) reporting negative effects of contact (Pettigrew & Tropp 2006, 2011). Second, although these studies show that positive contact's correlation with reduced prejudice (-0.47) is much larger than that of negative prejudice enhancing prejudice ($+0.28$), the strongest link (-0.49) is achieved by considering both types simultaneously—positive contact minus negative contact. Indeed, those German respondents who report both positive and negative contact with foreign residents demonstrate almost as much acceptance of immigrants as those reporting only positive contact. Positive contact acts as a buffer against the detrimental effects of negative contact. This conclusion was confirmed in later research conducted in Northern Ireland, Cyprus, and Arizona (Paolini et al. 2014). Although more attention to negative contact is needed, it must be considered together with positive contact.

PREDICTING PREJUDICE WITH ALL THREE THEORIES

Considered separately, all three of my favorite theories help to explain prejudice. But do they continue to predict prejudice when considered together and with other important predictors? A 2002 national probability survey of German citizens offers an answer by including 16 major predictors of prejudice against resident foreigners (Pettigrew et al. 2007, model 7; Pettigrew & Tropp 2011, pp. 157–58). In addition to measures of our three theories, the regression includes such standard prejudice predictors as SDO, age, gender, education, and political conservatism as well as two economic measures. As expected, the largest predictors are SDO, authoritarianism, and positive contact (a lone negative correlate of prejudice). But following these "big three," GRD ranks together with political inefficacy (a close correlate of RD) as the next most important and highly significant predictors of anti-immigrant prejudice in Germany. Thus, our three theories are among the top five predictors, each adding significantly to the prediction of prejudice even when 13 other predictors are included in the regression.

Figure 2 provides a structural equation model involving measures of the three theories together with the previously described measure of collective threat in predicting German prejudice against foreign residents. Note that the direct authoritarianism path to prejudice is sharply reduced by the mediation achieved by positive associations with GRD and collective threat and its negative association with positive contact. Observe, too, that the powerful collective threat scale mediates the links of all three key predictors with prejudice.

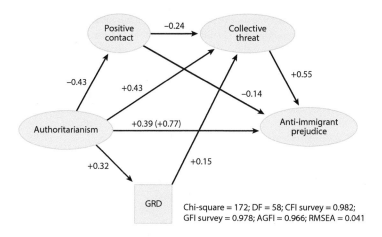

Figure 2

Four major predictors of prejudice. Based on data from the 2004 GRE (Group-Focused Enmity) German probability survey (Heitmeyer 2005). Abbreviations: AGFI, adjusted goodness of fit index; DF, degrees of freedom; GRD, group relative deprivation; RMSEA, root mean squared error of approximation.

One Final Note

The three theories that I have pursued throughout my career all contribute to our understanding of prejudice. While all three help predict prejudice, contact theory offers a means for diminishing prejudice. The worldwide significance of these findings is enhanced by their apparent universalism across widely contrasting subjects, targets, cultures, and nations—30 nations in the RD meta-analysis, and 38 nations in the contact meta-analysis. As always, the progress that has been made in all three domains raises further questions for future research.

The reader will undoubtedly have noticed that I have relied heavily on German data throughout this article. This is the result of Professor Wilhelm Heitmeyer (2002, 2003, 2005) of Bielefeld University generously allowing me to analyze his rigorous phone surveys of the German population. These surveys provided the richest data on intergroup prejudice that I have ever analyzed. In addition, I have had the opportunity of working for many years with Professor Ulrich Wagner and his many talented doctoral students at Philipps University in Marburg, Germany. Together we all analyzed these survey data and became close friends. All retired researchers should be as fortunate as I to have access to such colleagues and data at the close of their careers.

DISCLOSURE STATEMENT

The author is not aware of any affiliations, memberships, funding, or financial holdings that might be perceived as affecting the objectivity of this review.

LITERATURE CITED

Ackerman NW, Jahoda M. 1950. *Anti-Semitism and Emotional Disorder*. New York: Harper & Row
Adorno TW, Frenkel-Brunswik E, Levinson DJ, Sanford RN. 1950. *The Authoritarian Personality*. New York: Harper & Row
Ainsworth MDS, Blehar MC, Waters E, Wall S. 1978. *Patterns of Attachment*. Hillsdale, NJ: Erlbaum
Albert S. 1977. Temporal comparison theory. *Psychol. Rev.* 84:485–503
Allport GW. 1954. *The Nature of Prejudice*. Reading, MA: Addison-Wesley. Hardcover ed.
Allport GW. 1958. *The Nature of Prejudice*. Garden City, NY: Doubleday Anchor. Paperback ed.

Altemeyer B. 1981. *Right-Wing Authoritarianism*. Winnipeg, Can.: Univ. Manitoba Press

Altemeyer B. 1996. *The Authoritarian Specter*. Cambridge, MA: Harvard Univ. Press

Baier D, Hadjar A, Boehnke K. 2016. Authoritarianism in an everyday context: dispositional, situational, or what? See Funke et al. 2016. In press

Baker PE. 1934. *Negro-White Adjustment*. New York: Assoc. Press

Barlow FK, Paolini S, Pedersen A, Hornsey MJ, Radke HRM, et al. 2012. The contact caveat: Negative contact predicts increased prejudice more than positive contact predicts reduced prejudice. *Personal. Soc. Psychol. Bull.* 38:1629–43

Bartholomew K. 1990. Avoidance of intimacy. *J. Soc. Pers. Relatsh.* 7:147–78

Bartholomew K, Horowitz LM. 1991. Attachment styles among young adults. A test of a four-category model. *J. Personal. Soc. Psychol.* 61:226–244

Binder J, Zagefka H, Brown R, Funke F, Kessler T, et al. 2009. Does contact reduce prejudice or does prejudice reduce contact? A longitudinal test of the contact hypothesis amongst majority and minority groups in three European countries. *J. Personal. Soc. Psychol.* 96:843–56

Blalock HM. 1967. Per cent non-white and discrimination in the South. *Am. Sociol. Rev.* 22:677–82

Brown R, Hewstone M. 2005. An integrative theory of intergroup contact. *Adv. Exper. Soc. Psychol.* 37:255–343

Cantril H. 1965. *The Pattern of Human Concerns*. New Brunswick, NJ: Rutgers Univ. Press

Christ O, Hewstone M, Tausch N, Wagner U, Voci A, et al. 2010. Direct contact as a moderator of extended contact effects: cross-sectional and longitudinal impact on outgroup attitudes, behavioral intentions, and attitude certainty. *Personal. Soc. Psychol. Bull.* 36:1723–38

Christ O, Schmid K, Lolliot S, Swart H, Stolle D, et al. 2014. Contextual effect of positive intergroup contact on outgroup prejudice. *PNAS* 111(11):3996–4000

Christ O, Ullrich J, Wagner U. 2008. *The joint effects of positive and negative intergroup contact on attitudes and attitude strength*. Paper presented at annu. meet. Eur. Assoc. Exper. Soc. Psychol., Opatija, Croatia

Cook SW. 1984. Cooperative interaction in multiethnic contexts. In *Groups in Contact*, ed. N Miller, MB Brewer, pp. 155–85. Orlando, FL: Academic. 316 pp.

Crosby F. 1976. A model of egotistical deprivation. *Psychol. Rev.* 83:85–113

Cuijpers P, van Straten A, Bohlmeijer E, Hollon S, Andersson G. 2010. The effects of psychotherapy for adult depression are overestimated. *Psychol. Med.* 40:211–23

Davies K, Tropp L, Aron A, Pettigrew TF, Wright SC. 2011. Cross-group friendships and intergroup attitudes: a meta-analytic review. *Personal. Soc. Psychol. Rev.* 15:332–51

Davis JA. 1959. A formal interpretation of the theory of relative deprivation. *Sociometry* 22:280–96

Duckitt J. 1989. Authoritarianism and group identification. *Polit. Psychol.* 10:63–84

Ekehammar B, Akrami N, Gylje M, Zakrisson I. 2004. What matters most to prejudice: Big Five personality, social dominance orientation, or right-wing authoritarianism? *Eur. J. Personal.* 18:463–82

Eller A, Abrams D. 2004. Come together: longitudinal comparisons of Pettigrew's reformulated intergroup contact model and the common ingroup identity model in Anglo-French and Mexican-American contexts. *Eur. J. Soc. Psychol.* 34:229–56

Fraley RC, Waller NG. 1998. Adult attachment patterns. In *Attachment Theory and Close Relationships*, ed. JA Simpson, WS Rhodes, pp. 77–114. New York: Guilford

Fujioka Y. 1999. Television portrayals and African-American stereotypes. *J. Mass Commun. Q.* 76:52–75

Funke F, Petzel T, Cohrs C, Duckitt J, eds. 2016. *Perspectives on Authoritarianism*. Berlin, Ger.: Verlag Sozialwissenschaften. In press

Gómez A, Huici C. 2008. Vicarious intergroup contact and role of authorities in prejudice reduction. *Span. J. Psychol.* 11:103–14

Gormley B, Lopez FG. 2010. Authoritarian and homophobic attitudes: gender and adult attachment style differences. *J. Homosex.* 57:525–38

Graves SB. 1999. Television and prejudice reduction: When does television as a vicarious experience make a difference? *J. Soc. Issues* 55:707–27

Gurr TR. 1970. *Why Men Rebel*. Princeton, NJ: Princeton Univ. Press

Harwood J, Paolini S, Joyce N, Rubin M, Arroyo A. 2014. Secondary transfer effects from imagined contact. *Br. J. Soc. Psychol.* 50:180–89

Hassen MK. 1987. Parental behavior, authoritarianism and prejudice. *Manas* 34:41–50

Heitmeyer W, ed. 2002. *Deutsche Zustände*. Folge 1 [*The German Situation*. Part 1]. Frankfurt am Main, Ger.: Suhrkamp Verlag. 303 pp.

Heitmeyer W, ed. 2003. *Deutsche Zustände*. Folge 2 [*The German Situation*. Part 2.]. Frankfurt am Main, Ger.: Suhrkamp Verlag. 315 pp.

Heitmeyer W, ed. 2005. *Deutsche Zustände*. Folge 3 [*The German Situation*. Part 3]. Frankfurt am Main, Ger.: Suhrkamp Verlag. 315 pp.

Herek GM, Capitanio JP. 1997. AIDS stigma and contact with persons with AIDS: effects of direct and vicarious contact. *J. Appl. Soc. Psychol.* 27:1–36

Hodson G, Harry H, Mitchell A. 2009. Independent benefits of contact and friendship on attitudes toward homosexuals among authoritarians and highly identified heterosexuals. *Eur. J. Soc. Psychol.* 35:509–25

Hodson G, Hewstone M. 2013. *Advances in Intergroup Contact*. New York: Psychol. Press

Hopf C. 1992. Authoritarians and their families: qualitative studies on the origins of authoritarian dispositions. In *Strength and Weakness: The Authoritarian Personality Today*, ed. WF Stone, G Lederer, R Christie, pp. 119–43. New York: Springer-Verlag. 277 pp.

Hopf C. 1993. Rechtsextremismus und Beziehungserfahrungen [Right-wing extremism and relational experiences]. *Z. Soziol.* 22:449–63

Jost JT, Banaji MR, Nosek B. 2004. A decade of system justification theory. *Polit. Psychol.* 25:881–919

Kretch D, Crutchfield RS. 1948. *Theory and Problems of Social Psychology*. New York: McGraw-Hill

Levin S, Van Laar C, Sidanius J. 2003. The effects of ingroup and outgroup friendships on ethnic attitudes in college. *Group Process. Intergroup Relat.* 6:76–92

Lolliot S, Schmid K, Hewstone M, Al Ramiah A, Tausch N, Swart H. 2013. Generalized effects of intergroup contact: the secondary transfer effect. See Hodson & Hewstone 2013, pp. 81–112

Ludeke SG, Krueger RF. 2013. Authoritarianism as a personality trait: evidence from a longitudinal behavior genetic study. *Personal. Individ. Differ.* 55:480–84

Main M, Kaplan N, Cassidy J. 1985. Security in infancy, childhood, and adulthood. *Monogr. Soc. Res. Child Dev.* 50:6–104

Mark, MM, Folger R. 1984. Responses to relative deprivation. *Rev. Personal. Soc. Psychol.* 5:182–218

Martin J. 1986. The tolerance of injustice. See Olson et al. 1986, pp. 217–42

McCourt K, Bouchard TJ Jr, Lykken DT, Tellegen A, Keyes M. 1999. Authoritarianism revisited: genetic and environmental influences examined in twins reared apart and together. *Personal. Individ. Differ.* 27:985–1014

Merton R. 1957. *Social Theory and Social Structure*. Glencoe, IL: Free Press. Rev. ed.

Middleton R. 1976. Regional differences in prejudice. *Am. Sociol. Rev.* 41:94–117

Mikulincer M, Shaver PR. 2007. *Attachment in Adulthood*. New York: Guilford

Mussen PH. 1950. Some personality and social factors related to changes in children's attitudes toward Negroes. *J. Abnorm. Soc. Psychol.* 45:423–41

Myrdal G. 1944. *An American Dilemma*. New York: Harper & Row

Nichols LT. 1998. Social relations undone: disciplinary divergence and departmental politics at Harvard, 1946–1970. *Am. Sociol.* 29:83–107

Oesterreich D. 2005. Flight into security: a new approach and measure of the authoritarian personality. *Polit. Psychol.* 26:275–97

Olson J, Herman CP, Zanna MP, eds. 1986. *Relative Deprivation and Social Comparison. The Ontario Symposium*, Vol. 4. Hillsdale, NJ: Erlbaum

Osborne D, Sibley CG. 2013. Through rose-colored glasses: System-justifying beliefs dampen the effects of relative deprivation on well-being and political mobilization. *Personal. Soc. Psychol. Bull.* 39:991–1004

Paolini S, Harwood J, Rubin M, Husnu S, Joyce N, et al. 2014. Positive and extensive intergroup contact in the past buffers against the disproportionate impact of negative contact in the present. *Eur. J. Soc. Psychol.* 44:548–62

Pettigrew TF. 1957. Demographic correlates of border-state desegregation. *Am. Soc. Rev.* 22:683–89

Pettigrew TF. 1958. Personality and sociocultural factors in intergroup attitudes: a cross-national comparison. *J. Confl. Resolut.* 2:29–42

Pettigrew TF. 1959. Regional differences in anti-Negro prejudice. *J. Abnorm. Soc. Psychol.* 59:28–36

Pettigrew TF. 1964. *A Profile of the Negro American.* New York: Van Nostrand

Pettigrew TF. 1967. Social evaluation theory: convergences and applications. In *Nebraska Symposium on Motivation, 1967*, ed. D Levine, pp. 241–311. Lincoln: Univ. Neb. Press

Pettigrew TF. 1969. Gordon Willard Allport, 1897–1967. *J. Personal. Soc. Psychol.* 12:1–5

Pettigrew TF. 1971. *Racially Separate or Together?* New York: McGraw-Hill

Pettigrew TF. 1978. Three issues in ethnicity: boundaries, deprivations, and perceptions. In *Major Social Problems*, ed. M Yinger, R Cutler, pp. 25–49. New York: Basic Books

Pettigrew TF. 1979. Tensions between the law and social science. In *Schools and the Courts: Desegregation*, Vol. I, pp. 23–44. Eugene: Univ. OR ERIC Clgh. Educ. Manag.

Pettigrew TF. 1986. The contact hypothesis revisited. In *Contact and Conflict in Intergroup Encounters*, ed. M Hewstone, R Brown, pp. 169–95. Oxford, UK: Blackwell

Pettigrew TF. 1990. A bold stroke for personality a half-century ago. *Contemp. Psychol.* 35:533–36

Pettigrew TF. 1991a. Normative theory in intergroup relations. *Psychol. Dev. Soc.* 3:3–16

Pettigrew TF. 1991b. Toward unity and bold theory: Popperian suggestions for two persistent problems of social psychology. In *The Future of Social Psychology*, ed. C Stephan, W Stephan, TF Pettigrew, pp. 13–27. New York: Springer-Verlag

Pettigrew TF. 1996. *How to Think Like a Social Scientist.* New York: HarperCollins

Pettigrew TF. 1997. Personality and social structure: social psychological contributions. In *Handbook Personality Psychology*, ed. R Hogan, JA Johnson, SR Briggs, pp. 417–38. San Diego, CA: Academic. 987 pp.

Pettigrew TF. 1998. Intergroup contact theory. *Annu. Rev. Psychol.* 49:65–85

Pettigrew TF. 1999. Gordon Willard Allport: a tribute. *J. Soc. Issues* 55(3):415–27

Pettigrew TF. 2000. Placing authoritarianism in social context. *Polit. Groups Individ.* 8:5–20

Pettigrew TF. 2006. Commentary: the advantages of multi-level approaches. *J. Soc. Issues* 62:615–20

Pettigrew TF. 2009. Secondary transfer effect of contact: Do intergroup contact effects generalize to non-contacted outgroups? *Soc. Psychol.* 40:55–65

Pettigrew TF. 2015a. Allport, Gordon W (1897–1967). In *International Encyclopedia of the Social and Behavioral Sciences*, ed. JD Wright. pp. 562–65. Oxford, UK: Elsevier. 2nd ed.

Pettigrew TF. 2015b. Samuel Stouffer and relative deprivation. *Soc. Psychol. Q.* 78:7–24

Pettigrew TF. 2016. The indestructible theory. See Funke et al. 2016. In press

Pettigrew TF, Campbell EQ. 1960. Faubus and segregation: an analysis of Arkansas voting. *Public Opin. Q.* 24:436–47

Pettigrew TF, Cramer MR. 1959. The demography of desegregation. *J. Soc. Issues* 15:61–71

Pettigrew TF, Tropp LR. 2000. Does intergroup contact reduce prejudice? Recent meta-analytic findings. In *Reducing Prejudice and Discrimination: Social Psychological Perspectives*, ed. S Oskamp, pp. 93–114. Mahwah, NJ: Erlbaum

Pettigrew TF, Tropp LR. 2006. A meta-analytic test of intergroup contact theory. *J. Personal. Soc. Psychol.* 90:1–33

Pettigrew TF, Tropp LR. 2008. How does intergroup contact reduce prejudice? *Eur. J. Soc. Psychol.* 38:922–34

Pettigrew TF, Tropp LR. 2011. *When Groups Meet: The Dynamics of Intergroup Contact.* New York: Psychol. Press

Pettigrew TF, Wagner U, Christ O. 2007. Who opposes immigration? *Du Bois Rev.* 4:19–39

Pettigrew TF, Wagner U, Christ O. 2010. Population ratios and prejudice: modeling both contact and threat effects. *J. Ethn. Migr. Stud.* 36:635–50

Putnam R. 2007. *E pluribus unum:* diversity and community in the 21st century. *Scand. Pol. Stud.* 30:137–74

Reynolds KJ, Turner JC, Haslam SA, Ryan MK. 2001. The role of personality and group factors in explaining prejudice. *J. Exp. Soc. Psychol.* 37:427–34

Richard FD, Bond CF Jr, Stokes-Zoota JJ. 2003. One hundred years of social psychology quantitatively described. *Rev. Gen. Psychol.* 7:331–63

Robinson WS. 1950. Ecological correlations and the behavior of individuals. *Am. Sociol. Rev.* 15:351–57

Roccato M, Ricolfi L. 2005. On the correlation between right-wing authoritarianism and social dominance orientation. *Basic Appl. Soc. Psychol.* 27:187–200

Rothwell JT. 2010. Trust in diverse, integrated cities: a revisionist perspective. *Brookings Inst. Work. Pap. Ser.* Washington, DC: Brookings Inst.

Rothwell JT. 2012. The effects of racial segregation on trust and volunteering in U.S. cities. *J. Urban Stud.* 49:2109–36

Runciman WG. 1966. *Relative Deprivation and Social Justice*. London, UK: Routledge & Kegan Paul

Sales S. 1973. Threat as a factor in authoritarianism. *J. Personal. Soc. Psychol.* 28:44–57

Schiappa E, Gregg P, Hewes DE. 2005. The parasocial contact hypothesis. *Commun. Monogr.* 72:92–115

Schiappa E, Gregg P, Hewes DE. 2006. Can one TV show make a difference? *Will & Grace* and the parasocial contact hypothesis. *J. Homosex.* 51:15–37

Schmid K, Hewstone M, Kuepper B, Zick A, Wagner U. 2012. Secondary transfer effects of intergroup contact. *Soc. Psychol. Q.* 75:28–51

Sidanius J, Levin S, Van Laar C, Sears DO. 2008. *The Diversity Challenge: Social Identity and Intergroup Relations on the College Campus*. New York: Russell Sage Found. 448 pp.

Sidanius J, Pratto F. 1999. *Social Dominance*. Cambridge, UK: Cambridge Univ. Press. 403 pp.

Smith H, Pettigrew TF, Pippin G, Bialosiewicz S. 2012. Relative deprivation: a theoretical and meta-analytic critique. *Personal. Soc. Psychol. Rev.* 16:203–32

Stellmacher J, Petzel T. 2005. Authoritarianism as a group phenomenon. *Polit. Psychol.* 26:245–74

Stouffer SA. 1955. *Communism, Conformity and Civil Liberties*. New York: Doubleday

Stouffer SA. 1962. *Social Research to Test Ideas*. New York: Free Press

Stouffer SA, Suchman EA, DeVinney LC, Starr SA, Williams RM. 1949. *The American Soldier*, Vol. 1. Princeton, NJ: Princeton Univ. Press

Strumpel B, ed. 1976. *Economic Means for Human Needs*. Ann Arbor, MI: Inst. Soc. Res.

Suls JM, Miller RL, eds. 1977. *Social Comparison Processes*. New York: Halsted Press

Tausch N, Hewstone M, Kenworthy JB, Psaltis C, Schmid K, et al. 2010. Secondary transfer effects of intergroup contact. *J. Personal. Soc. Psychol.* 99:282–302

Thornhill R, Fincher CL. 2007. What is the relevance of attachment and life history to political values? *Evol. Human Behav.* 28:215–22

Tropp LR, Pettigrew TF. 2005. Relationships between intergroup contact and prejudice among minority and majority status groups. *Psychol. Sci.* 16:651–57

Turner RN, Crisp RJ, Lambert E. 2007. Imagining intergroup contact can improve intergroup attitudes. *Group Process. Intergroup Relat.* 10:427–41

Tyler TR, Smith HJ. 1998. Social justice and social movements. In *Handbook of Social Psychology*, Vol. 2, ed. D Gilbert, ST Fiske, G Lindzey, pp. 595–629. New York: McGraw Hill. 4th ed. 1,085 pp.

Uslaner EM. 2012. *Segregation and Mistrust: Diversity, Isolation, and Social Cohesion*. New York: Cambridge Univ. Press. 284 pp.

Van IJzendoorn MH. 1997. Attachment, emergent morality, and aggression. *Int. J. Behav. Dev.* 21:703–27

Vezzali L, Giovannini D. 2012. Secondary transfer effect of intergroup contact. *J. Community Appl. Soc. Psychol.* 22:125–44

Vezzali L, Stathi S, Giovannini D. 2012. Indirect contact through book reading. *Psychol. Schools* 49:148–62

Vorauer JD, Main KJ, O'Connell GB. 1998. How do individuals expect to be viewed by members of lower status groups? *J. Personal. Soc. Psychol.* 75:917–37

Wagner U, Christ O, Pettigrew TF, Stellmacher J, Wolf H. 2006. Prejudice and minority proportion: contact instead of threat effects. *Soc. Psychol. Q.* 69:380–90

Wagner U, van Dick R, Pettigrew TF, Christ O. 2003. Ethnic prejudice in East and West Germany: the explanatory power of intergroup contact. *Group Process. Intergroup Relat.* 6:22–36

Walker I, Pettigrew TF. 1984. Relative deprivation theory: an overview and conceptual critique. *Br. J. Soc. Psychol.* 23:301–10

Walker I, Smith HJ, eds. 2002. *Relative Deprivation*. New York: Cambridge Univ. Press. 390 pp.

Weber C, Federico CM. 2007. Interpersonal attachment and patterns of ideological belief. *Polit. Psychol.* 28:389–416

Williams RM Jr. 1947. *The Reduction of Intergroup Tensions*. New York: Soc. Sci. Res. Counc. 153 pp.

Wright SC, Aron A, McLaughlin-Volpe T, Ropp SA. 1997. The extended contact effect. *J. Personal. Soc. Psychol.* 73:73–90

Zajonc RB. 1968. Attitudinal effects of exposure. *J. Personal. Soc. Psychol.* 9:1–27

Drug Addiction: Updating Actions to Habits to Compulsions Ten Years On

Barry J. Everitt and Trevor W. Robbins

Department of Psychology and Behavioural and Clinical Neuroscience Institute, University of Cambridge, Cambridge CB2 3EB, United Kingdom; email: bje10@cam.ac.uk, twr2@cam.ac.uk

Annu. Rev. Psychol. 2016. 67:23–50

First published online as a Review in Advance on August 7, 2015

The *Annual Review of Psychology* is online at psych.annualreviews.org

This article's doi: 10.1146/annurev-psych-122414-033457

Keywords

striatum, prefrontal cortex, insula, inhibitory control, endophenotype, vulnerability

Abstract

A decade ago, we hypothesized that drug addiction can be viewed as a transition from voluntary, recreational drug use to compulsive drug-seeking habits, neurally underpinned by a transition from prefrontal cortical to striatal control over drug seeking and taking as well as a progression from the ventral to the dorsal striatum. Here, in the light of burgeoning, supportive evidence, we reconsider and elaborate this hypothesis, in particular the refinements in our understanding of ventral and dorsal striatal mechanisms underlying goal-directed and habitual drug seeking, the influence of drug-associated Pavlovian-conditioned stimuli on drug seeking and relapse, and evidence for impairments in top-down prefrontal cortical inhibitory control over this behavior. We further review animal and human studies that have begun to define etiological factors and individual differences in the propensity to become addicted to drugs, leading to the description of addiction endophenotypes, especially for cocaine addiction. We consider the prospect of novel treatments for addiction that promote abstinence from and relapse to drug use.

Contents

INTRODUCTION

The understanding of drug addiction has perhaps made most progress when conceived in terms of its underlying neuropsychological processes. Classic ideas of Pavlovian conditioning, positive reinforcement, opponent motivational processes, and cognitive control have all been shown to play a role not only in explaining apparently bizarre behavioral symptoms of drug abusers but also in relating the behavior to underlying dysfunctional neural networks. In our last major review of this area, more than a decade ago, we summarized the relevance of then-recent advances in specifying mechanisms of instrumental conditioning that produced both goal-directed behavior and stimulus-response habit learning (Everitt & Robbins 2005). We surmised that habits could be the building blocks of compulsive drug seeking. Compulsive behavior can be defined as the maladaptive persistence of responding despite adverse consequences (Dalley et al. 2011), and so clearly other factors must be involved. At the time, we suggested that aversive motivational states, as in withdrawal phenomena (Koob & LeMoal 1997), drug-induced sensitization (Robinson & Berridge 1993), and a loss of top-down inhibitory response control (Jentsch & Taylor 1999, Robbins & Everitt 1999) might all be contributory factors. One of the aims of this review is to re-examine the relative importance of these factors in the light of recent empirical evidence in experimental studies of both animals and humans. Pavlovian conditioning also evidently contributes to substance abuse and has formed the basis of attempts at remediation through extinction-based behavioral therapy; early work established the importance of such conditioning to both withdrawal and relapse to drug-seeking behavior, with the subjective correlate of craving (Tiffany 1990).

One of the current challenges to the field is indeed to understand how Pavlovian and instrumental conditioning processes interact during the course of drug abuse to produce compulsive behavior. One clue may reside in the importance of so-called Pavlovian-instrumental transfer (PIT), by which a conditioned stimulus (CS) exerts motivational influences on the expression of instrumental behavior. An important route by which such transfer occurs may also be the development of conditioned reinforcing properties of such CSs; in other words, the possibility that behavior may be maintained, especially over delays between drug taking, by the presentation of cues associated with drug-taking experiences, contingent upon responding

(Arroyo et al. 1998, Goldberg 1973). A further complication is the effect a drug itself has on such conditioned rewarding stimuli not only associated with drugs themselves but also with other positive reinforcers (e.g., Taylor & Robbins 1984). An exciting source of converging support has been the gradual identification of key neural systems underpinning these processes and interactions.

This approach has proved to be entirely contemporary in the face of two widely differing approaches to understand mental disorders, including addiction, exemplified by the new edition of the American Psychiatric Association's *Diagnostic and Statistical Manual of Mental Disorders* (DSM-5; Am. Psychiatr. Assoc. 2013) on the one hand, and the Research Domain Criteria (RDoC) project of the National Institutes of Health (Cuthbert 2014) on the other. The DSM method depends on a symptom-based categorization of mental disorders; the RDoC approach by contrast is dimensional, eschewing clinically expressed symptoms for objectively demonstrated deficits in neurobehavioral systems. Our own approach, and that of others, is intermediate between these two extremes: We seek to understand the symptomatic phenomena of drug addiction and abuse in terms of underlying neurobehavioral and neurocognitive systems. This enterprise appears to have borne some fruit; it is remarkable that the DSM-5 has abandoned former definitions of addiction in terms of substance dependence (a theoretically loaded term used in deference to stigmatizing views of the word addiction). A system of different substance use disorders of varying severity, culminating in addiction, is now defined according to the expression of a criterion number from a set of 11 basic symptoms (Am. Psychiatr. Assoc. 2013). In fact, although expressions of dependence, craving, and tolerance are among this set of symptoms, definitions of the majority of the set clearly reflect different aspects of compulsive behavior and failures of control. We thus take some encouragement for the field in continuing this neuroscientific program of investigation, which was begun in earnest in the 1990s, notably with the human neuroimaging work of Volkow and others, and is still gathering momentum.

LEARNING THEORY ACCOUNTS OF ADDICTION

From the initial important demonstration of the key role played by the mesolimbic dopamine (DA) system in the reinforcing—or rewarding—effects of addictive drugs (Roberts & Koob 1982, Wise 2008), neuroadaptations in nucleus accumbens function following repeated use have remained a major focus of cellular and molecular theories of addiction (Nestler 2004), as well as theories incorporating psychological mechanisms, including Pavlovian incentive motivational processes enhanced by incremental adaptations to repeated drug use (sensitization) (Leyton & Vezina 2014, Robinson & Berridge 1993) or opponent processes engaged by withdrawal (Koob & LeMoal 1997, Wikler 1965). However, it rapidly became apparent that responses to drugs can acquire motivational significance by being associated with environmental stimuli through Pavlovian conditioning (Gawin & Kleber 1986, O'Brien et al. 1998) and that these drug-associated CSs exert a marked influence on the instrumental behaviors of drug seeking and use (Everitt et al. 2001), induce subjective craving states, and precipitate relapse long into abstinence (Childress et al. 1999, Garavan et al. 2000, Grant et al. 1996).

As a result, concepts of addiction incorporating learning theory accounts of Pavlovian conditioning mechanisms (Everitt et al. 2001, Robinson & Berridge 1993, Saunders & Robinson 2013, Stewart et al. 1984) and, more recently, instrumental learning mechanisms (Everitt et al. 2001, Everitt & Robbins 2005, Robbins & Everitt 1999), have become more prominent. We have now reached a remarkable juncture at which learning theory accounts of addiction dominate the literature, whether based on motivational or hedonic mechanisms (Kalivas & Volkow 2005, Koob & Volkow 2010) or more sophisticated and evidence-based Pavlovian and instrumental learning mechanisms and interactions between them (Belin et al. 2009, Everitt & Robbins 2005, Hogarth et al. 2010, Saunders & Robinson 2013). Moreover, this theoretical advance is compatible with an increasing focus on neuronal plasticity processes, such as long-term potentiation and long-term depression (Grueter et al. 2012, Hyman et al. 2006, Kauer & Malenka 2007, Luescher & Malenka 2011).

INSTRUMENTAL LEARNING AND ADDICTION

Our theorizing focused on the fact that the general concept of positive reinforcement conflates at least two different processes identified by contemporary analyses of instrumental conditioning with conventional reinforcers (Dickinson 1985, Dickinson & Balleine 1994): (*a*) a declarative associative process based upon knowledge of the relationship between instrumental behavior, or action (A) and its outcome (O), taking the form of intentional goal-directed actions maintained by a representation of the goal (A-O association), which, if devalued, results in markedly decreased instrumental responding; and (*b*) a stimulus-response (S-R) process by which a reinforcer strengthens an association between the response and the contextual and discrete stimuli present at the time of reinforcement. Instrumental behavior dependent on this associative structure takes the form of a habit that is elicited by the CSs independently of the value of the goal, such that its devaluation has little or no effect on instrumental seeking responses. These instrumental learning processes are generally engaged in parallel, but under some conditions (e.g., a degraded relationship between A and O, or after much repetition) the S-R habit response dominates so that instrumental behavior acquires autonomy and is elicited outside conscious awareness, persistent and resistant to extinction. Habits are not in themselves pathological, being an efficient mode of information processing, but carried to excess under certain circumstances become maladaptive (Robbins & Everitt 1999). The notion of transition and the imbalance between goal-directed and habitual drug seeking is central to our hypothesis but is insufficient in itself to explain compulsive drug seeking (Everitt & Robbins 2005, Robbins et al. 2008).

IMBALANCE BETWEEN GOAL-DIRECTED AND HABITUAL BEHAVIOR

There are now several demonstrations of habitual drug seeking behavior in animals, as well as neurobehavioral data in humans addicted to drugs, that indicate the dominant engagement of habit systems in the brain. However, a challenge for the field has been unambiguously to demonstrate S-R control over the seeking of intravenously self-administered drugs using the conventional techniques of reinforcer devaluation (through specific satiety or lithium chloride–induced malaise) or response contingency degradation that are readily achievable with ingestive reinforcers (Everitt 2014, Everitt & Robbins 2013). Such demonstrations underpin the somewhat counterintuitive conclusion that not all instrumental behavior is necessarily goal directed unless the performance of the behavior itself has become reinforcing. Descriptions of drug seeking by humans in motivational terms of "liking" and "wanting" may thus represent to some extent *post hoc* rationalizations of behavioral urges that we earlier characterized as "must do!" responses (Everitt & Robbins 2005).

Early demonstrations of the rapid resistance to devaluation of oral cocaine or alcohol (Dickinson et al. 2002, Miles et al. 2003) have been independently confirmed in the responding of rats for alcohol (Corbit et al. 2012) and for the intravenous (i.v.) self-administration of nicotine (Clemens et al. 2014). Using a novel method in which cocaine-seeking responses on one lever gave access to a second, "taking" lever delivering i.v. cocaine, we showed that devaluation achieved by extinguishing specifically the taking link of the chain reduced seeking early in training, which confirmed that it was goal directed (Olmstead et al. 2001). This demonstration was later confirmed and extended by Zapata et al. (2010), who showed additionally that cocaine-seeking behavior became insensitive to devaluation, i.e., habitual, after extended training (Zapata et al. 2010). This effect of extended training to promote habitual drug seeking has further been shown in rats self-administering nicotine (Clemens et al. 2014).

Alcohol-dependent human subjects also exhibit overreliance on S-R representations, as shown in a computer-based task distinguishing between goal-directed and habitual control (Sjoerds et al. 2013). In fact, observations in humans and animals indicate that even noncontingent (i.e., not self-administered) addictive drug exposure can tip the balance between A-O and S-R associative mechanisms to favor the latter. Thus, for humans undergoing instrumental training for chocolate reward, noncontingent alcohol administration attenuated goal-directed control over chocolate choice and accelerated habit learning (Hogarth et al. 2013). In rats, noncontingent alcohol exposure accelerated the development of habitual control over natural reward seeking (Corbit et al. 2012), whereas repeated noncontingent amphetamine treatment resulted in extremely rapid development of habitual control over responding for sucrose (Nelson & Killcross 2006). Even posttraining cocaine administration was able to facilitate habitual responding for a natural reward (Schmitzer-Torbert et al. 2014). Hence, exposure to addictive drugs may impair the ability of outcome representations to control responding, leading to the dominant control over behavior by S-R contingencies. It is also possible that addictive drugs directly enhance habit learning for both drug and natural rewards (Everitt & Robbins 2013, Hogarth et al. 2013).

Major advances in understanding the neural basis of the transition from goal-directed to habitual drug seeking, as well as PIT and conditioned reinforcement, have depended on data from the response of animals and humans to food rewards. The goal-directed system in both rats and humans depends on interactions between the medial prefrontal cortex (mPFC) and the posterior dorsomedial striatum (pDMS) (Shiflett et al. 2010, Yin et al. 2005). In contrast, the habit system implicates the anterior dorsolateral striatum (aDLS), or putamen in humans, and perhaps motor cortical areas (Balleine & O'Doherty 2010, Yin et al. 2004). Significantly, electrophysiological data from animals learning and performing a T-maze, food-reinforced task have revealed a transition from activity in the DMS during acquisition and early performance that decreased with overtraining to be dominated by DLS activity mediating habitual performance (Thorn et al. 2010). The transition from goal-directed to habitual drug seeking maps well onto this conceptual landscape.

There is now considerable evidence that the aDLS is gradually engaged to underlie well-established, habitual drug seeking (Barker & Taylor 2014, Belin et al. 2009, Everitt 2014, Everitt & Robbins 2013). Initial observations of dorsal striatal DA release during the performance of a well-trained cocaine-seeking task (Ito et al. 2002) and decreases of such responding by intra-DLS DA receptor blockade (in the absence of effects in the nucleus accumbens) (Vanderschuren et al. 2005) have been reinforced by recent studies (Corbit et al. 2012, Zapata et al. 2010), but with the additional finding that aDLS DA receptor blockade earlier during acquisition of cocaine-seeking behavior was ineffective (Murray et al. 2012). Thus, the aDLS is not required for initial cocaine seeking, when it is goal directed, but gradually becomes dominant in the control over this behavior when it is well established and habitual (Murray et al. 2012). By contrast, DA receptor blockade in the pDMS impaired the acquisition of cocaine seeking when goal directed but had no effect after extended training (Murray et al. 2012). Zapata et al. (2010) additionally showed that well-trained cocaine seeking depended on the aDLS and that its inactivation reinstated sensitivity to devaluation—that is, rendered it goal directed.

The hypothesized devolution in control over alcohol seeking was further shown to proceed from the DMS to DLS (Corbit et al. 2012), with habitual responding depending on DLS α-amino-3-hydroxy-5-methyl-4-isoxazolepropionic acid (AMPA) and DA D2 receptors (Corbit et al. 2014). Other neurobiological data sit well with the recruitment by chronic drug exposure of DLS cellular adaptations. Prolonged but not brief stimulant self-administration alters cellular plasticity markers in DLS neurons in rats (Jedynak et al. 2007) as well as striatal DA D2 receptors and metabolic markers in monkeys that spread from ventral to dorsal striatum after months, but not weeks, of cocaine self-administration (Letchworth et al. 2001). The escalation of cocaine intake after extended access is causally associated with specific micro-RNAs in the dorsal striatum (Jonkman & Kenny 2013), and chronic alcohol vapor exposure in mice facilitated DLS-dependent neuronal plasticity and learning suggested to be related to the progression to alcoholism (DePoy et al. 2013).

In humans, too, neuroimaging and behavioral studies have revealed the importance of dorsal striatal processes in individuals addicted to drugs. Cue-induced cocaine craving was associated with increased DA release and metabolic activity in the dorsal striatum (Garavan et al. 2000, Volkow et al. 2006). Alcohol-dependent subjects presented with alcohol-related CSs showed a shift in activation from the ventral to the dorsal striatum when compared to recreational alcohol drinkers (Vollstaedt-Klein et al. 2010). An overreliance on S-R habit learning in alcohol-dependent individuals was associated with the decreased activation of areas of the brain implicated in A-O, goal-directed learning, such as the ventromedial PFC and anterior putamen, but with the increased activation of the posterior putamen that mediates habit learning (Sjoerds et al. 2013). In human subjects engaged in learning a virtual maze task that could dissociate spatial and S-R response navigational strategies, response learners had increased dorsal striatal gray matter volume and activity measured using functional magnetic resonance imaging (fMRI), whereas spatial learners had increased hippocampal gray matter and activity. Furthermore, response learners had greater use of abused substances in comparison with spatial learners, including double the lifetime alcohol consumption, a greater number of cigarettes smoked, and a greater lifetime use of cannabis (Bohbot et al. 2013). Cocaine-dependent individuals and their non-cocaine-abusing siblings had a significantly enlarged left putamen (Ersche et al. 2011a, 2013a), suggesting that greater dorsal striatal (putamen) volume may be associated with a predisposition to acquire drug-seeking and -taking habits (see below).

TRANSITION FROM VENTRAL TO DORSAL STRIATUM

Our emphasis on shifts within dorsal striatal instrumental learning systems has deflected detailed consideration of the contribution of ventral striatal (nucleus accumbens)–mediated processes by which addictive drugs exert their reinforcing effects as Pavlovian unconditioned stimuli (Di Chiara & Imperato 1988, Ikemoto & Wise 2004) as well as their conditioned associations, for example, as PIT and expressed in instrumental responding as conditioned reinforcement (Cardinal et al. 2002, Corbit & Balleine 2005, Hall et al. 2001). However, it is evident that not only is there a shift of control within the dorsal striatum, but that ventral striatal processes initially recruit and eventually become dominated by—yet continue to influence—the dorsal striatum. Thus, we (Everitt & Robbins 2005) hypothesized that the intrastriatal shift in the control over drug seeking and taking might have a neuroanatomical basis in the circuitry that connects the ventral to the dorsal striatum via recurrent connections with midbrain DA neurons (Haber et al. 2000).

Recent evidence for this scheme has depended on a novel procedure to disconnect ventral from dorsal striatum by combining a specific unilateral lesion of the nucleus accumbens core with contralateral DLS DA receptor blockade, thereby disabling this system bilaterally (Belin & Everitt 2008). This disconnection reduced well-established habitual cocaine seeking at a time point previously shown to depend on the aDLS, but importantly had no effect on a newly acquired instrumental seeking response. That processing in the nucleus accumbens core can indeed influence DA transmission in the aDLS was further demonstrated using in vivo voltammetry in rats self-administering cocaine in which late-developing, drug CS-evoked DA transients in the aDLS were completely prevented by a specific nucleus accumbens core (NAcbC) lesion (Willuhn et al. 2012). Remarkably, functional coupling between the ventral and the dorsal striatum has also been shown in former heroin addicts, together with decreased functional coupling between the striatum and the PFC (Xie et al. 2014). Neurocomputational models of addiction have successfully incorporated this concept (Dezfouli et al. 2009, Piray et al. 2010), which may be linked to earlier notions of a reinforcement learning model, which assigns the role of critic to the nucleus accumbens that modulates the actor role over action selection assigned to the dorsal striatum (O'Doherty et al. 2004). Repeated drug taking may result in a failure of the critic properly to direct action selection by the actor, thus rendering choices and actions rigid and independent of the value of outcomes (Belin et al. 2013).

Ventral striatal mediation of drug-associated conditioned reinforcement and PIT also depends upon its afferents from the amygdala (Cardinal et al. 2002). However, the neural circuitry by which the amygdala influences habitual instrumental behavior in the DLS is unclear, since it does not project there directly. The two main routes by which amygdala-DLS interactions could occur are (a) via glutamatergic basolateral amygdala (BLA) projections to the NAcbC, which can thereby influence the spiraling dopaminergic circuitry linking the core with the DLS, and (b) via the central amygdala (CeN) projections directly to the substantia nigra pars compacta that dopaminergically innervates the DLS. The latter amygdala CeN-DLS system has been shown functionally to be important for Pavlovian conditioned orienting (Han et al. 1997) and for the acquisition of food-reinforced habits (Lingawi & Balleine 2012). By disconnecting either the BLA or the CeN from the DLS (by combining a unilateral lesion of either the CeN or BLA with infusion of a DA receptor antagonist into the contralateral aDLS), Murray and colleagues (2013) have demonstrated the functional importance of this polysynaptic and indirect circuitry in the acquisition and maintenance of cue-controlled cocaine-seeking habits. Moreover, it was further shown electrophysiologically that activation of the BLA can both up- and downregulate cortically driven aDLS medium spiny neuron activity via its projections to the NAcbC (Belin-Rauscent et al. 2013).

MODULATORS OF HABIT

The strength and persistence of habits can be modulated by motivational processes. Drug-associated CSs can retrieve representations of a drug's identity and, through specific PIT, elicit and potentiate instrumental responses for the same drug outcome (Hogarth et al. 2013). Through general PIT, CSs can retrieve the drug's affective value and hence a motivational state that is similar to that elicited by the drug itself, but which has a general excitatory effect on responses for both the same and other goals. Although both forms of PIT can readily be demonstrated for ingestive rewards (Cardinal & Everitt 2004, Saunders & Robinson 2013) including alcohol (Milton et al. 2012), we previously drew attention to the fact that neither effect had been seen in individuals' responding for i.v. drug reinforcement (Everitt & Robbins 2005), though some reports of this effect have appeared more recently (reviewed by Saunders & Robinson 2013). Hogarth and colleagues (2013) have in particular pointed out that early in training, drug CSs can indeed retrieve the drug's specific identity to produce specific transfer effects, whereas extended exposure to drugs, including their self-administration, results in such CSs failing to retrieve the drug's specific identity, instead retrieving the drug's affective value to exert a general PIT effect on drug seeking. Such a shift from specific to general PIT can therefore explain the effect of drug CSs in an addicted individual's environment to potentiate habitual drug responding during delays to drug reinforcement that are bridged by either the same or other CSs acting as conditioned reinforcers of drug-seeking responses. Indeed, it has been shown that CS-potentiated smoking in humans was unaffected by satiety and therefore independent of the current incentive value of the drug (cigarette puffs), instead reflecting a general motivational enhancement of habitual drug use (Hogarth et al. 2010). This account is neurally compatible with the shift from DMS- to DLS-dependent mechanisms recruited by Pavlovian CS processing in the nucleus accumbens via the spiraling dopaminergic circuitry linking ventral and dorsal striatum (Belin et al. 2009, Everitt & Robbins 2013).

Negative emotional states, such as those instantiated by stress, can also influence habit learning. Thus, rats subjected to chronic stress rapidly developed insensitivity to outcome value and were relatively impervious to changes in A-O contingency. These changes biased rats toward habitual behavioral strategies and resulted in atrophy of the mPFC and the associative striatum and hypertrophy of the DLS (Dias-Ferreira et al. 2009). An intriguing possibility, then, is that drug withdrawal stress that is known to result in raised reward thresholds and long-term changes in hedonic state (Koob 2008) may, through activation of stress systems in the amygdala (Koob 2008), also influence the development of S-R drug-seeking habits by facilitating its coupling with the DLS (Lingawi & Balleine 2012, Murray et al. 2013). Indeed, instrumental avoidance learning, which presumably contributes to withdrawal-motivated negative reinforcement, becomes impervious to extinction and may resemble compulsive habits in OCD (Gillan et al. 2015).

Incremental responses to addictive drugs and drug-associated CSs that collectively reflect the process of sensitization are widely assumed to lead to a pathological motivation for drugs, or drug wanting (Kalivas & Volkow 2005, Robinson & Berridge 1993). The phenomenon of sensitization has now clearly been demonstrated in humans exposed relatively few times to amphetamine, leading to very long-lasting enhancements in striatal DA responses to both drugs and drug CSs (Leyton 2007, Leyton & Vezina 2014, Vezina & Leyton 2009). One consequence of this process is that drug CSs, through their enhanced ability to increase DA release in the ventral striatum, may lead to subjective craving states and what might be assumed to be a voluntary urge to seek and take drugs (Leyton & Vezina 2014). Paradoxically, long-term drug use in humans is associated with decreased striatal dopaminergic function both in terms of reduced D2 DA receptors and DA release (a hypodopaminergic state), including lower craving responses to drug cues (Volkow et al. 2007). This paradox may be resolved by considering individual differences in the propensity to attribute incentive salience to drug-associated CSs and hence the marked variation in craving responses to drug cues in addicted individuals (Saunders & Robinson 2013). However, the enhanced DA transmission underlying sensitization is not restricted to the ventral striatum but is also seen in the dorsal striatum and is associated with the potentiated expression of motor stereotypies. The latter depend upon the dorsal striatum (Kelly et al. 1975) and are putatively a form of compulsive responding. Stimulant sensitization may therefore lead both to potentiated motivational and Pavlovian associative processes and a parallel enhancement of S-R learning mediated by upregulation of DA in the ventral and dorsal striatum, respectively.

FROM HABIT TO COMPULSION

Compulsive drug seeking despite negative consequences is now a major criterion of substance use disorder. However, the fact that not everyone initially or recreationally taking drugs ultimately exhibits compulsive drug seeking (Anthony et al. 1994) has provided a challenge for its experimental investigation. This challenge has recently been met by the demonstration that in rats (as in humans), about 20% exhibit compulsive drug seeking despite adverse consequences, but only after chronic drug use (Belin et al. 2008, Deroche-Gamonet et al. 2004, Pelloux et al. 2007).

Thus in the three-criteria addiction model (Belin et al. 2008, Deroche-Gamonet et al. 2004), 20% of rats having self-administered cocaine for 100, but not 40, days continued to respond for cocaine despite receiving mild footshock punishment; they also persisted in responding when a CS signaled that cocaine was unavailable and showed increased motivation for cocaine. Contemporaneously, we modified our previously established cocaine seeking-taking chained schedule (Olmstead et al. 2001) to introduce unpredictable footshock punishment and therefore required rats to risk these adverse consequences when seeking the opportunity to take cocaine (Pelloux et al. 2007). After a brief cocaine history, all rats stopped seeking cocaine when the punishment contingency was introduced (i.e., they abstained from drug use), but after a long history of cocaine self-administration, some 20% of rats continued to seek cocaine (i.e., were compulsive) (Pelloux et al. 2007). The compulsive cocaine seeking was not necessarily associated with increased motivation for the drug nor with impaired fear conditioning. The extent of exposure to cocaine, rather than the degree of conditioning through Pavlovian pairings of CS and drug, was further shown to be a critical factor in determining the development of cocaine seeking under punishment (Jonkman et al. 2012b). Compulsive cocaine seeking in a vulnerable subgroup of rats has now been demonstrated in different strains of rats and in different laboratories (Belin et al. 2008, Cannella et al. 2013, Chen et al. 2013, Deroche-Gamonet et al. 2004, Pelloux et al. 2007) using three-criteria or seeking-under-threat-of-punishment procedures.

Initial neural investigation of compulsive cocaine seeking revealed the involvement of a discrete aDLS domain specifically in punished, but not unpunished, cocaine seeking (Jonkman et al. 2012a), thus identifying a link to the neural basis of drug-seeking habits. Pelloux and colleagues (2012) also showed reduced levels of serotonin (5-HT) utilization across prefrontal cortical areas, as well as decreased DA utilization in the dorsal striatum, selectively in compulsive but not in noncompulsive rats, despite a very similar history of cocaine exposure. It was demonstrated that the low levels of 5-HT utilization were causal in compulsive cocaine seeking by showing that forebrain 5-HT depletion, or systemic treatment with a 5-HT2C receptor antagonist, after a short cocaine history, when none of the rats were compulsive, resulted in increased levels of seeking under punishment. Of translational interest was that treatment with a serotonin-selective 5-HT reuptake inhibitor, citalopram, dose-dependently reduced compulsive seeking in rats that had developed this behavior after a long drug-taking history (Pelloux et al. 2012).

In replicating our observation of a compulsive cocaine-seeking subpopulation of rats after a long history of cocaine exposure, Chen and colleagues (2013) showed that in vivo optogenetic stimulation of the prelimbic cortex decreased compulsive cocaine seeking in compulsive animals, whereas the 80% subpopulation of rats that had suppressed their cocaine seeking during punishment subsequently increased their cocaine seeking under punishment (i.e., became compulsive) after optogenetic inhibition of the prelimbic cortex. These data (Chen et al. 2013, Jonkman et al. 2012a, Pelloux et al. 2012), together with the demonstration of anaplasticity in NAcb neurons in three-criteria "addicted" rats (Kasanetz et al. 2010), suggest altered corticostriatal mechanisms and disrupted top-down or inhibitory control in compulsive cocaine seeking.

ADDICTION AND TOP-DOWN CONTROL

Addiction to drugs has long been presumed in the popular imagination to represent a failure of will by which the addict's propensity to seek and take drugs is not appropriately regulated by volitional processes (Leshner 1997). Whilst this view is controversial and has been held by some to impede progress in the biological understanding and treatment of addiction, the past decade has seen increasing evidence, via a range of neuroimaging modalities, of changes in brain structure and function in addicted individuals that illuminate its underlying motivational control processes. This evidence has been paralleled by enhanced interest in the role of cortical processes in the regulation of conditioned behavior, including drug seeking and taking as well as their underlying Pavlovian and instrumental processes, in experimental animals.

Although the emphasis has been on the role of limbic-striatal mechanisms, these have increasingly been considered in the context of neural circuits involving cortical, and especially prefrontal, regions. A general theme has been that loss of fronto-executive inhibitory control produces a dominance of subcortically mediated responding, including S-R habit learning, potentially exacerbating the drive to compulsive behavior (Jentsch & Taylor 1999, Robbins & Everitt 1999). However, a range of processes, including attention, memory, and other aspects of executive function besides inhibitory control, are mediated by cortically dominant circuits. For example, apparent loss of control could result not only from exacerbated habitual behavior, but also from an impairment of goal-directed behavior, with the consequent imbalance favoring habit learning. Important questions have been the degree to which such processes contribute to addiction and the extent to which they result from chronic drug taking, or are present premorbidly, and hence represent predispositions leading to susceptibility to substance use disorders.

A previous review (Robbins et al. 2008) surveyed the results of more than 20 studies using structural MRI of substance abusers, including abusers of stimulant drugs, nicotine, opiates, cannabis, and alcohol. Results were variable, but the general trend was of loss of cortical gray matter volume and white matter in alcoholics, sometimes globally (Fein et al. 2002) but often in specific regions, for example, especially in frontal and parietal regions, the dorsal hippocampus (Jang et al. 2007, Mechtcheriakov et al. 2007), and striatum (Sullivan et al. 2005). There are also reported losses in the cingulate cortex and PFC in nicotine smokers (Brody et al. 2004, Gallinat et al. 2006).

Findings in stimulant (methamphetamine or cocaine) abusers were relatively consistent, often including loss of prefrontal or cingulate gray matter in combination with increases in the basal ganglia (i.e., caudate, putamen, globus pallidus). The latter are especially relevant in the context of the S-R habit hypothesis advanced previously (Everitt & Robbins 2005), which would predict greater changes in the putamen relative to the caudate.

Focusing on stimulants, Ersche and colleagues (2013b) performed a voxel-based meta-analysis of 16 suitable magnetic resonance structural imaging studies comprising 494 stimulant-dependent individuals and 428 controls. These investigators concluded that gray matter decreased significantly in stimulant-dependent individuals in four cortical regions: the insula, ventromedial PFC, inferior frontal gyrus, and pregenual anterior cingulate gyrus, as well as the anterior thalamus. These reductions in these five areas concur well with the regions commonly implicated using perfusion methods and metabolic imaging (e.g., with positron emission tomography). Volkow & Fowler (2000) made the seminal observation that striatal D2 DA receptor downregulation is related to orbitofrontal cortex (OFC) hypometabolism—clearly implicating the OFC as a component of fronto-striatal circuitry that is modulated by striatal DA. Ersche et al. (2012a) supplemented these studies by demonstrating loss of white matter in chronic stimulant abusers in such structures as the frontal lobes.

The key questions arising from such analyses, whether of stimulant or other substance use disorders, are the nature of the functions that these regions mediate and the origin of the reductions. These can be addressed by means of correlation with salient epidemiological, clinical, and neuropsychological assessments; by reference to studies of effects of cortical brain damage; and by the design of studies utilizing fMRI.

In general, the changes in frontal brain function are consistent with impairments in decision-making cognition in chronic drug abusers (Rogers et al. 1999), and these impairments resemble in some ways the effects of frontal lesions in clinical patients (see also Bechara et al. 2001, Clark et al. 2008). Deficits in decision making can be due to disruption of several distinct contributory processes. The ventromedial PFC (and medial OFC) is implicated in reward-related processing in fMRI studies (both in the anticipation of reward and in its reinforcing outcome). Damage to the ventromedial PFC in humans causes impairments in the assessment of value and choice outcomes, as well as gross impairments in decision-making tasks such as the Iowa Gambling Task and the Cambridge Gambling Task (Bechara et al. 2001, Clark et al. 2008). Functional imaging of stimulant and opiate abusers has shown changes in the way the OFC is activated during risky decision making (Ersche et al. 2005). The consequent deficits in decision-making cognition are of considerable clinical importance, as they evidently exacerbate the general functional difficulties of chronic drug abusers, whether these difficulties are caused by the drugs themselves or pre-existing dispositions. Impairments in the representation of goals at the cortical level may also lead to the "narrowing" of options open to chronic drug abusers and thus help to determine the compulsive focus on drug-seeking behavior.

The possibility that the insula was implicated in processing the visceral sequelae of drug taking (helping to translate sensations into subjective feelings) was raised by Everitt & Robbins (2005), and the past decade has seen a large increase in studies of the role of the insula in addiction (Paulus & Stewart 2014). The insular cortex may play an ancillary role in effective decision making via its mediation of hypothetical somatic markers that contribute to affective states influencing risky choice behavior (Clark et al. 2008, Verdejo-Garcia & Bechara 2009). Somatic markers are essentially interoceptive Pavlovian cues that can both elicit conditioned responses and contribute to PIT. Such cues, as well as more readily identified exteroceptive CSs, are well known to elicit drug-seeking behavior and concomitant subjective craving, as well as aversive withdrawal phenomena, both mediated in part via limbic-striatal circuitry including the amygdala. This may explain the remarkable observation of a blockade of craving in nicotine-dependent individuals following damage to the insula caused, for example, by strokes (Naqvi et al. 2007). A subsequent analysis of neuroimaging studies by Naqvi & Bechara (2009) has provided broad support for this original observation over a number of drug classes, including nicotine, cocaine, alcohol, and heroin. Of the 16 studies examined, the insula was the only brain region to be consistently activated by urges to seek drugs, although the anterior cingulate and OFC were often activated, too. Animal studies involving inactivation of the insula have suggested a causal role in an animal model of craving (Contreras et al. 2007).

The somatic marker hypothesis of addiction (Naqvi & Bechara 2010, Verdejo-Garcia et al. 2006) thus essentially seeks to explain core aspects of addiction in terms of an aberrant emotional or homeostatic guidance of decision making that leads to craving and impulsive behavior (i.e., relapse). The insula clearly plays an important role in the functioning of neural circuitry linking to limbic and striatal (i.e., the nucleus accumbens) structures, thus also providing a powerful source of motivational Pavlovian influences over instrumental choice, including craving. However, we doubt that the insula exerts the crucial lack of control over instrumental behavior that is evident in addictive individuals.

Interoception is often linked to notions of awareness and insight, although these notions are not synonymous. The lack of insight, often attributed to addicted individuals as well as individuals with other neuropsychiatric disorders, is problematic, for example, when assessing the adverse consequences of drug taking, including impaired social behavior. A lack of conscious awareness may be symptomatic of habitual behavior, which, by its nature, is implicit and autonomous. It is also consistent with generalized impairments in goal-directed behavior or instrumental control over actions, which may signal the lack of agency generally associated with mPFC function (Balleine & O'Doherty 2010). Error processing especially implicates sectors of the anterior cortex, and hence its dysfunction would promote unawareness of error feedback. A recent review has speculated on the nature of the neural networks contributing to insight that probably include the insula and anterior cingulate cortex (Goldstein et al. 2009). It should be noted that those hypotheses that postulate self-medication by drug abusers, for example, to alleviate withdrawal syndromes or amotivational/avolitional states such as reward deficiency, would appear to be opposed to these notions of impaired insight.

In addition to impairments in decision making, drug abusers are commonly impaired in several facets of "cold" executive function, including working memory, cognitive flexibility, and response inhibition (Friedman et al. 2006, Ornstein et al. 2000, Rogers & Robbins 2001). Of these, impairments of inhibitory response control are of obvious interest as potentially leading to relapse, impulsivity, and compulsion (Morein-Zamir & Robbins 2014).

In humans, the anterior cingulate and inferior frontal cortex (especially in the right hemisphere) are generally considered to be cortical components of a neural circuit mediating inhibitory response control, which also includes the striatum, subthalamic nucleus, and supplementary motor cortex. The impairments are most often quantified in terms of go/no-go or stop-signal reaction time performance (Aron et al. 2014) but may have an obvious influence on decision making, especially decision making involving conflict or the need to reflect on information processing. Disruptions in the activity of this network may therefore lead to forms of impulsive behavior that occur when a subject is unable to cancel an initiated response. Such impulsive behavior may also occur in attention-deficit/hyperactivity disorder as well as in drug abuse (Robbins et al. 2012). fMRI studies showing impaired go/no-go responding in parallel with underactivation of PFC circuitry in stimulant abusers have also revealed, rather surprisingly and significantly, remediation both in terms of activation and behavioral performance following cocaine treatment within the scanner (Garavan et al. 2008)—suggestive of a possible therapeutic role for catecholamine agents and not inconsistent with the so-called self-medication hypothesis. The enhancement of inhibitory control may have arisen as a direct consequence of catecholamine-induced modulation of PFC functioning or alternatively as a reduction of a hypothetical withdrawal state, although it is evident that stimulant drugs can enhance similar performance in healthy volunteers (de Wit et al. 2000, Fillmore et al. 2005).

In another study with therapeutic implications, attention to drug cues that normally elicit craving in stimulant drug abusers was associated with activation of the (left) inferior frontal cortex and was remediated in some patients by treatment with a D2 DA receptor agonist (Ersche et al. 2011b). Other aspects of impulsivity that depend, for example, on the temporal discounting of reward (and hence tolerance to reward delay) may implicate additional cortico-striatal circuitry that targets the nucleus accumbens (Dalley et al. 2011).

In animal studies, there has been considerable research on the role of fronto-striatal circuitry in mediating inhibitory control in the special case of relapse into drug seeking/taking. The often-used extinction-reinstatement model is based on the fact that extinction (in this case of instrumental responding, not Pavlovian CS extinction) is a form of inhibitory control over learned associations. The mechanisms known to mediate the extinction of Pavlovian fear, which include the mPFC (comprising the prelimbic and infralimbic cortex in rodents), have similarly been implicated, along with the nucleus accumbens (especially the core subregion), in the recovery, renewal, or reinstatement of self-administration behavior after a period of extinction (Kalivas & McFarland 2003). However, it is possible that the role of the mPFC is not limited to extinction alone, but may represent more general behavioral regulatory roles, including the balance between goal-directed and habitual behavior (see above).

Inhibitory control may also be recruited in the regulation of compulsive behavior, which can be defined as the maladaptive persistence of responding (Dalley et al. 2011). If the substrate of compulsive behavior is in part habitual, the precise neural circuitry mediating inhibitory control is less clear but may also implicate such structures as the lateral and medial OFC. Thus, reversal learning, which involves the suppression of perseverative tendencies in parallel with new learning, appears to depend on OFC projections (Chudasama & Robbins 2003, Dias et al. 1996) to the dorsomedial striatum (Castañé et al. 2010, Clarke et al. 2008) as well as interactions with other regions of the striatum, including the putamen (Groman et al. 2013). Such reversal learning for monetary reward can be quite seriously impaired in human drug abusers (Ersche et al. 2008) as well as in monkeys exposed to chronic cocaine administration (Jentsch et al. 2002). Functional connectivity studies of chronic stimulant abusers, in parallel with studies of patients with obsessive-compulsive disorder (OCD), have shown that frontal zones of connectivity including the OFC are correlated in both cases with measures of compulsivity [the Yale-Brown Obsessive Compulsive Scale (Y-BOCS) and the Obsessive Compulsive Drug Use Scale (OCDUS)] in the stimulant abusers (Meunier et al. 2012). Such studies encourage the notion that compulsivity associated with a neural circuit regulated by the OFC may be a general construct of neuropsychiatric disorders, including addiction. These cortical regions are also implicated in the production of compulsive stimulant drug seeking in rats that results in adverse consequences such as electric footshock (Chen et al. 2013; Pelloux et al. 2012, 2013).

These aspects of impaired executive function are clearly relevant to addiction, but their precise causal role remains unclear. They may form part of a general cognitive-deficit syndrome, including other impairments (for example, in memory), that has profound implications for rehabilitation. Thus, to what extent are cortical changes associated with such cognitive changes irreversible or subject to recovery with abstinence? Alternatively, a subset of the deficits may not only exacerbate the drive to compulsive behavior but also may be present in the drug abuser prior to drug exposure; in other words, some deficits may play a causal role in addiction. Specifically, the loss of top-down control may represent a critical step by which habits gain control over behavior due to an imbalance with goal-directed behavior, and the performance of these habits may become less subject to cognitive or inhibitory control imposed by the PFC, with dysregulated, perseverative behavior being a prominent consequence. A critical question then becomes the precise timing of changes in top-down control from the PFC during the hypothesized devolution of control from ventral to dorsal striatum. As discussed in the next section, these important issues of causality and development of addiction are now beginning to be addressed in both human and animal studies.

ETIOLOGICAL FACTORS AND INDIVIDUAL DIFFERENCES: ADDICTION ENDOPHENOTYPES

Dissecting causality in studies of addiction is especially difficult because of multiple factors: genetics, early experience, acute pharmacological actions of abused drugs, potential neurotoxic effects of the drugs themselves as well as the effects of withdrawal, and long-term chronic effects of relapse and abstinence. Such difficulties are highlighted by problems of interpretation of some of the most seminal findings in the field: downregulation of D2 DA receptors in chronic cocaine, methamphetamine, and alcohol abusers (e.g., Volkow et al. 2007). Are such changes causes or consequences of drug abuse? This general question can be posed of virtually all studies of drug abusers in the absence of prospective data on their preabuse state, but it is in fact difficult to address. The common finding of impulsivity in drug abusers might also reflect a premorbid condition that actually contributes to drug seeking rather than resulting from it.

One useful approach in neuropsychiatry has been to determine intermediate phenotypes or endophenotypes (Gottesman & Gould 2003). Endophenotypes are core characteristics, for example, behavioral or neural, found in first-degree relatives as well as their drug-abusing proband. Generally, expression of the characteristic is intermediate between that of the proband and healthy controls. Endophenotypes are commonly interpreted as reflecting genetic influences, but of course it is entirely plausible that they arise from common environmental, for example, familial, effects.

Moreover, the most parsimonious interpretation of an endophenotype is that it cannot have arisen from drug taking because it is pre-existing; nonetheless, it could itself be further influenced by subsequent drug exposure.

Addiction Endophenotypes in Experimental Animals

The obvious difficulties of studying the period of pre-exposure to drugs of abuse in human participants do not, of course, apply to experimental animals. Consequently, the field has recently been stimulated by many studies of neurobehavioral characteristics of rodents and nonhuman primates that are predictive of the propensity to take drugs. One of the original studies identified a group of high-reactive (HR) rats that were susceptible to i.v. self-administration of low doses of d-amphetamine based on their levels of locomotor activity in a novel situation (Piazza et al. 1989). Originally, these rats were suggested to be sensation seeking, although it is not quite clear on what theoretical basis this dimension was invoked. They exhibited a number of neurobiological changes, including paradoxical susceptibility to stress; increases in the corticosteroid response to novelty were paralleled by a propensity to corticosterone self-administration (Piazza et al. 1993). Subsequently, the importance of stress as a candidate endophenotype for stimulant abuse was highlighted by studies in monkeys (Morgan et al. 2002) and exposure to social defeat stress in rodents (Covington & Miczek 2005).

Recent studies have focused on the trait of impulsivity [measured as excessive premature responses in a test of sustained attention, the 5-choice serial reaction time task (5-CSRTT)], finding that high impulsives exhibited escalation and greater intake of cocaine in a binge-access paradigm (Dalley et al. 2007). These high-impulsive rats also exhibited, prior to any cocaine experience, reductions in D2/3 receptor binding in the ventral but not dorsal striatum, analogous to what had been shown in chronic stimulant abusers (Volkow et al. 2007) and also in rhesus monkeys subsequently exhibiting high levels of stimulant self-administration (Nader et al. 2010). High-impulsive rats were not, however, high reactive and further differed from that phenotype in showing compulsive cocaine administration when risking punishment through mild electric footshock (Belin et al. 2008). Hence, high impulsivity was hypothetically linked to compulsive drug seeking; however, the important issue remains as to whether this is indeed a causal association.

The high-impulsive rat phenotype has been subsequently refined. These rats do not exhibit obvious alterations in appetitive Pavlovian conditioning (autoshaping or sign tracking) and are not especially susceptible to novelty stress or anxiety (Molander et al. 2011) or to impairments on the rodent stop-signal reaction time task, another index of impulsive action (Robinson et al. 2009). They do, however, exhibit steeper reward discounting compared to controls, enhanced intake of nicotine or sucrose, and a mild preference for novelty (see review by Dalley et al. 2011). Other studies (Perry & Carroll 2008) have also shown that changes in the temporal discounting of reward, sometimes defined as impulsive choice, can be predictive of future drug self-administration. Most recently, a similar high-impulsive phenotype based on premature responding in the 5-CSRTT has been shown in the ethanol-preferring B6 strain of mice (Sanchez-Roige et al. 2014), although the high-impulsive rat does not exhibit binge self-administration of heroin (McNamara et al. 2010), indicating that this relationship does not exist for all major drugs of abuse.

Although high impulsivity in rodents predicts vulnerability to compulsive cocaine seeking, whereas high reactivity in rats mainly alters initial responsivity to stimulants, these are not the only rodent behavioral endophenotypes to confer susceptibility to stimulant drug effects. Escalation of cocaine intake has also been reported in highly anxious rats, as measured by their tendency to avoid open arms of the elevated plus maze (Dilleen et al. 2012), and in novelty-preferring rats, as indexed by their choice of a novel side of a test chamber (Belin et al. 2011). Moreover, risky behavior in a decision-making task (Mitchell et al. 2014), associated with lower striatal D2 mRNA expression, led to enhanced adult intake of cocaine. The experience of cocaine self-administration also enhanced risky decision making in adults; perhaps these rats would have also exhibited compulsive cocaine self-administration despite adverse consequences, but this has not yet been tested. High-impulsive rats exhibit mild tendencies for novelty preference in several contexts, but the propensity for impulsivity is only weakly related to novelty preference (Molander et al. 2011). Thus, impulsivity is dissociable from other candidate endophenotypes of novelty preference and anxiety, as well as sensation seeking, suggested for the HR rat.

The picture has been further complicated by a program of genetic selective inbreeding leading to the production of HR and low-reactive (LR) rats (indexed by locomotor hyperactivity in novel settings) that also exhibit differential behavioral sequelae of appetitive Pavlovian conditioning. HR rats tend to orient to discrete cues predictive of food (sign trackers), whereas LR rats tend to approach a food magazine directly (goal trackers) (Flagel et al. 2011, 2014). Similar to findings in earlier work on HR rats, they exhibit greater sensitivity to stimulant-induced sensitization and greater self-administration as well as a greater propensity to relapse (as indexed by extinction reinstatement) and evidence for enhanced motivation for cocaine. However, the propensity of HR rats for compulsive stimulant seeking has not yet been investigated in detail. Their tendency to impulsivity is equivocal; they display increased motor impulsivity [as measured by overresponding on a differential reinforcement of lower rates of behavior (DRL) schedule] but decreased temporal discounting of reward (Flagel et al. 2014).

Overall, it would appear that the response to stimulants and the propensity to compulsive stimulant seeking, although clearly interactive to some extent, may be differentially affected by a range of trait-like influences in rodents. Impulsivity, risk taking, novelty preference, locomotor activity, and anxiety may all be reflected in these responses, to different degrees. Their influence on other forms of drug taking may also differ; there are some indications that responses to nicotine and alcohol may be similarly affected to responses to stimulants such as cocaine. The overlapping influence of the various endophenotypes probably reflects subtle differences in underlying neural networks, which almost certainly center on the nucleus accumbens (Dalley et al. 2011).

Thus, the neuroendophenotype of the high-impulsive rats is associated with specific changes in D2/3 receptor autoradiography and DAT immunocytochemistry in the nucleus accumbens shell as well as with gray matter reduction in the nucleus accumbens core (Caprioli et al. 2014, Dalley et al. 2011). There is no evidence from in vivo microdialysis studies of altered presynaptic levels of accumbens DA (Dalley et al. 2007). Recent work is characterizing differential electrophysiological activity in these regions between high and low impulsives (Donnelly et al. 2014). There are also concomitant changes in top-down influences of the anterior cingulate and mPFC and bottom-up regulatory monoaminergic projections (Dalley et al. 2011).

The nucleus accumbens is also a major focus for changes (e.g., in DA function) in HR rats as well as in high-impulsive rats. However, both outbred and inbred HR rats are hyperdopaminergic in terms of response to systemic DA D2 agonists such as quinpirole, fast-scan cyclic voltammetry, and an increased proportion of high-affinity D2 receptors (with no changes in total D2 binding) (Flagel et al. 2014). Rats classified as high impulsives on the basis either of 5-CSRTT or delayed discounting performance also exhibit differential patterns of DA release in the nucleus accumbens. There is apparently greater release in the nucleus accumbens shell and lower release in the core in the 5-CSRTT high impulsives, and lower DA release in both subregions in steep-discounting rats (Diergaarde et al. 2008). High impulsives (5-CSRTT) are also hypersensitive to quinpirole, but the nature of this effect differs between the shell and core subregions. Clearly, a full understanding of the possible differences between these various trait-like characteristics must depend on a systematic comparison using the same methods to assess DA function. However, it does appear that different modulations of DA function in the nucleus accumbens result in subtly different behavioral phenotypes that participate in different stages of the development of compulsive stimulant self-administration, including its initiation, development, and maintenance. The analysis of rodent endophenotypes for other drugs of abuse has not perhaps proceeded to such an intensive degree as for stimulants, but it promises to do so in the future.

The ultimate test of the validity of these candidate endophenotypes would be to demonstrate that their amelioration leads also to reductions in compulsive drug use. Amelioration of high impulsivity has been reported for rats chronically self-administering cocaine (Dalley et al. 2007) and for experimenter-administered methylphenidate, the D2/3 receptor agonist quinpirole or atomoxetine (Fernando et al. 2012). Methylphenidate also caused an upregulation of D2/3 receptors in high-impulsive rats but the opposite neural (and behavioral) effects in controls (Caprioli et al. 2014). Such ameliorative effects may also depend on noradrenergic mechanisms, as the selective noradrenaline reuptake blocker atomoxetine was effective whether administered systemically (Robinson et al. 2008) or into the shell of the nucleus accumbens (Economidou et al. 2012). The implications of these findings for the treatment of substance use disorders remains to be explored in detail, although it is of interest that relapse from punishment-induced suppression of cocaine self-administration is especially significant for high-impulsive rats and that this disinhibition is susceptible to blunting by systemic atomoxetine (Economidou et al. 2009).

Endophenotypes for Human Substance Use Disorders

Identifying reliable endophenotypes for addiction would benefit the field in several ways: (*a*) More accurate phenotypes may lead to more successful searches for genome-wide association and candidate genes, (*b*) stratification of clinical populations would lead to more sensitive clinical trials, (*c*) endophenotypes may allow predictions of future vulnerability to substance use disorders, and (*d*) as previously discussed, defining endophenotypes also enables a limited analysis to be performed of possible etiological factors in addiction.

Some of the animal work reviewed above has inspired a fresh look at possible human equivalents. This has been facilitated in the area of impulsivity, where several objective measures can be implemented in both humans and experimental animals, including the serial reaction time task, the stop-signal reaction time task, and temporal discounting of reward (Dalley et al. 2011). A recent example has been the finding that not only chronic stimulant abusers exhibit deficits in tests of inhibitory control such as the stop-signal reaction time task, but also their nondrug-abusing siblings, as compared to controls (Ersche et al. 2012a, 2013b). These deficits were correlated with the degree of white matter loss in frontal regions in siblings as well as stimulant abusers. There were also changes in siblings in such regions as the amygdala and putamen, both of which had greater volume. However, regions of gray matter loss in probands, including the OFC and anterior insula, did not show any change in the relatives. These changes may well occur as a consequence of stimulant drug taking, especially as some of the changes (e.g., in the OFC) were related to duration of drug use as well as to measures of compulsive behavior (Ersche et al. 2011a). This is consistent with longitudinal findings in rhesus monkeys exposed to cocaine self-administration (Porrino et al. 2010). Thus, study of possible endophenotypes may help to chart the progression of changes in brain structure and function over the course of addiction.

Recreational stimulant abusers who take the drugs regularly without fulfilling DSM criteria for stimulant dependence provide informative comparisons. These individuals exhibited increased gray matter volume in the OFC, anterior cingulate, and insula, suggestive of possible resilience to the compulsive drug-seeking characteristic of addiction. These individuals seem unlikely to be at an earlier point on a trajectory to drug dependence; the results highlight how individual neurobiological differences may drastically affect outcome after drug abuse (Ersche et al. 2013b).

An alternative approach is prospective: Is it possible to detect markers of future drug abuse in adolescent populations? The IMAGEN project, in which 2,000 healthy adolescents aged 14 years were screened for brain structure, functional brain imaging, neuropsychological test performance, drug-taking history, and genomics, has addressed this question. One finding pertinent to the impulsivity endophenotype is that the neural circuits activated by the stop-signal reaction time task do have some predictive associations with incipient drug taking propensity at that age (Whelan et al. 2012). Thus, activity in lateral orbital frontal circuits during successful response inhibition was directly related to self-reported experimentation with alcohol and nicotine. Moreover, as the drug use extended to illicit substances, there was also a significant relationship with hyperactivity in right inferior frontal and anterior cingulate circuits known to mediate successful stop-signal reaction time task performance.

Independent studies have shown that chronic cocaine users exhibit hypoactivity in the same regions, and so from this cross-sectional perspective there may be a gradual evolution of the activity of this region. Further evidence is provided by the important observation that the siblings of chronic stimulant abusers exhibit hyperactivity of similar circuits (Morein-Zamir et al. 2013), suggesting that this activity may be initially compensatory, hypothetically resisting craving or the temptation to seek drugs, only later showing reductions. This is of course highly speculative, and longitudinal studies of adolescent drug users are now clearly required. Moreover, other candidate endophenotypes in humans should be examined to establish their validity and utility. An alternative way of addressing the issue of loss of top-down control is to examine the neural changes occurring during successful abstinence as well as over the long term (Garavan et al. 2013).

PROSPECTS FOR NEW TREATMENTS OF ADDICTION

Despite major advances in understanding the neuropsychological and molecular mechanisms involved in drug addiction, few if any new medications have been introduced clinically, in particular those that might prevent relapse and prolong periods of abstinence. The considerable interest in preventing relapse by diminishing the impact of drug-associated CSs on craving and drug seeking has led to the preclinical identification of novel pharmacological treatments (reviewed in Everitt 2014), but there is little evidence to suggest that they will reach the stage of clinical trials and regulatory approval. There is some optimism that repurposing already approved medications, such as those used in the treatment of impulsive and compulsive disorders, may result in novel proabstinence treatments (Everitt 2014), but a challenge for this treatment approach is the requirement for frequent, perhaps daily, dosing and attendant problems of side effects and compliance.

However, there has been a recent resurgence of interest in psychological approaches to diminishing the impact of drug CSs on relapse. Cue exposure therapy—that is, extinction of the CS through repeated nonreinforced presentations—has been frequently attempted, but a meta-analysis of a substantial literature has indicated that overall it results in little benefit (Myers & Carlezon 2012), in part because of the contextual specificity of extinction learning (Conklin & Tiffany 2002); however, the view is perhaps less pessimistic for alcoholics (Glautier et al. 1994, MacKillop & Lisman 2008, Stasiewicz et al. 2007). Attempts to enhance drug CS extinction with the glutamate receptor agonist D-cycloserine, following demonstrations of enhanced Pavlovian fear extinction (Davis 2002, Lee et al. 2006b), have also generally been unsuccessful (Myers & Carlezon 2012) and may even result in an increase, not a decrease, in craving elicited by later exposure to the CS (Price et al. 2013), an explanation for which is discussed below.

A new approach to treatment with great potential involves targeting memory reconsolidation, the process set in motion by the reactivation of a memory by presenting drug CSs but insufficiently to engage extinction learning. This reactivation causes the memory trace to become labile in the brain, a state from which it must be restabilized through de novo protein synthesis in order to persist. The phenomenon has long been known (Lewis 1979) but was relatively ignored until its rediscovery through the demonstration that conditioned fear memory reconsolidation could be prevented by intra-amygdala protein synthesis inhibition in conjunction with memory reactivation (Nader et al. 2000). Subsequently, fear memory reconsolidation was shown to require expression of the immediate-early gene *zif268* (Lee et al. 2004), intracellular signaling molecules (Tronson & Taylor 2007), and activity at *N*-methyl-D-aspartate (NMDA) receptors (Lee et al. 2006b) and β-adrenergic receptors (Debiec & Ledoux 2004).

Against this background, we investigated whether drug memories might undergo reconsolidation. This was a major challenge because, unlike Pavlovian fear conditioning that requires only one or two CS-unconditioned stimulus pairings, instrumental drug self-administration must take place repeatedly, involving hundreds of CS-drug pairings, for a drug CS alone to elicit drug seeking and relapse (Lee & Everitt 2007). We showed that a small number of cocaine CS presentations in rats that had self-administered the drug daily for two weeks of more (several hundred cocaine-CS pairings) could indeed reactivate and destabilize the memory, such that knockdown of *zif268* in the amygdala prevented reconsolidation as assessed by a major decrease in the subsequent ability of the CS to act as a conditioned reinforcer and support cocaine seeking or to precipitate relapse (Lee et al. 2005).

There has been considerable focus on the neurochemical mechanisms that initiate or modulate drug memory reconsolidation, both to link them to intracellular signaling pathways (Barak et al. 2014, Miller & Marshall 2005, Milton et al. 2008a) and also to identify therapeutic leads (Milton & Everitt 2010). NMDA receptor or β-adrenoceptor antagonists given at memory reactivation can prevent cocaine or alcohol memory reconsolidation, with the result that drug CSs have a much reduced capacity or no capacity to elicit drug seeking or relapse when presented subsequently (Lee et al. 2006a; Milton 2013; Milton et al. 2008a,b). Heroin conditioned-withdrawal memories similarly undergo reconsolidation following reactivation (Hellemans et al. 2006). Moreover, Pavlovian associations underlying sign tracking, PIT, and conditioned reinforcement (the main properties of drug CSs involved in maintaining drug seeking and precipitating relapse) also undergo NMDA- or β-adrenoceptor-dependent reconsolidation, indicating that these Pavlovian influences on drug seeking and relapse can all be diminished by a single or few treatments given at a CS-drug memory reactivation (Milton 2013, Milton & Everitt 2010).

Memory retrieval does not always labilize the memory trace in the brain, and this likely explains failures to see reconsolidation blockade when amnestic drugs are given in association with retrieval under some conditions (Milton et al. 2012). Especially important is the finding that fear (Lee et al. 2006b) and drug memory (Lee et al. 2009) reconsolidation can be enhanced by NMDA receptor agonism at reactivation, thereby potentiating the impact of the CS at subsequent test. This may explain the paradoxical effect of D-cycloserine to increase craving to later presentations of a cocaine CS—the opposite of the intended effect to enhance drug CS extinction (Price et al. 2013). This should remind us that we are far from being able to specify precisely the conditions under which memory is destabilized to undergo reconsolidation and to delineate this from those conditions under which extinction is engaged. Reconsolidation and extinction are dissociable and mutually exclusive processes in terms of their molecular basis (Merlo et al. 2014) and are bidirectionally modulated by NMDA receptor agonism and antagonism (Lee et al. 2006b).

Therapeutically, targeting reconsolidation of drug memories as a means of reducing the propensity for drug CSs to elicit craving and relapse has the obvious advantage that only single, or very few, drug treatments in association with drug memory retrieval are needed. Furthermore, reconsolidation blockade appears not to be context dependent, so therapy in the clinic could be effective in the addict's environment. Additionally, problems of compliance that come with daily and long-term treatments would be avoided, and the single or few drug treatments could take place during psychological therapy sessions, such as cognitive behavioral or cue-exposure therapies. A promising place to begin overdue clinical studies would be β-adrenoceptor antagonist treatment at drug memory reactivation, since these drugs are clinically approved and safe.

A surprising observation may, however, suggest that the story is not over for cue exposure therapy. If fear extinction is carried out soon after a brief memory reactivation in both rats and humans, the fear memory is not only extinguished but also seemingly erased, as it does not spontaneously recover or renew, which it does after extinction alone (Monfils et al. 2009, Schiller et al. 2010). Thus, if repeated or long-term exposure to a CS occurs during the time window (approximately four hours) when reconsolidation takes place following brief memory reactivation, extinction becomes much more effective in diminishing the memory—so-called superextinction. In an ambitious combined animal and human study, it has been shown that a superextinction protocol can impair cocaine and heroin memories in rats having self-administered the drugs, and also in a heroin-dependent inpatient population (Xue et al. 2012). In the addicted individuals, the treatment sessions involved memory reactivation by viewing a brief video featuring drug taking, followed after a short delay by longer exposure to the same video (extinction). At subsequent test, there was both decreased autonomic reactivity and craving following cue exposure and a significant decrease in relapse up to six months later. This remains the only study of its kind and clearly requires replication, but like reconsolidation-based approaches, it suggests great promise of psychological treatments to prevent relapse and promote abstinence from drug use.

DISCLOSURE STATEMENT

B.J.E. received a research grant from GlaxoSmithKline. T.W.R. is a consultant for and receives royalties from Cambridge Cognition; is a consultant for and received a research grant from Eli Lilly; received a research grant from GlaxoSmithKline; is a consultant for and received a research grant from Lundbeck; and is a consultant for Teva, Shire Pharmaceuticals, and Otsuka.

ACKNOWLEDGMENTS

First and foremost, we acknowledge the major contribution of the many postdoctoral and graduate researchers in our laboratory, as well as of our collaborators, during the past 30 years. We dedicate this review to the memory of one of those postdoctoral researchers, Daina Economidou, who tragically died in December 2012. We have received generous and long-term support from the Medical Research Council for the research on drug addiction summarized here: B.J.E., T.W.R., and A. Dickinson, G9537555 (1996–2001) and G9537855 (2001–2006); B.J.E., T.W.R., A. Dickinson, and J. Dalley, G0600196 (2006–2011); B.J.E., T.W.R., J. Dalley, and A. Milton, G1002231 (2011–2016); J. Dalley, T.W.R., B.J.E., T. Fryer, J.-C. Baron, and F. Airbirhio, G0701500 (2008–2012); K. Ersche, E. Bullmore, and T.W.R., G0701497 (2008–2011); and J. Dalley, B.J.E., and T.W.R., G0802729 (2009–2011). Finally, we apologize to many colleagues for not citing original papers in this review due to strict reference number limitations imposed by the *Annual Review of Psychology*.

LITERATURE CITED

Am. Psychiatr. Assoc. 2013. *Diagnostic and Statistical Manual of Mental Disorders*. Washington, DC: Am. Psychiatr. Publ. 5th ed.

Anthony JC, Warner LA, Kessler RC. 1994. Comparative epidemiology of dependence on tobacco, alcohol, controlled substances, and inhalants: basic findings from the national comorbidity survey. *Exp. Clin. Psychopharmacol.* 2:244–68

Aron AR, Robbins TW, Poldrack RA. 2014. Inhibition and the right inferior frontal cortex: one decade on. *Trends Cogn. Neurosci.* 18(4):177–85

Arroyo M, Markou A, Robbins TW, Everitt BJ. 1998. Acquisition, maintenance and reinstatement of intravenous cocaine self-administration under a second-order schedule of reinforcement in rats: effects of conditioned cues and unlimited access to cocaine. *Psychopharmacology* 140:331–44

Balleine BW, O'Doherty JP. 2010. Human and rodent homologies in action control: corticostriatal determinants of goal-directed and habitual action. *Neuropsychopharmacology* 35:48–69

Barak S, Liu F, Neasta J, Ben Hamida S, Janak PH, Ron D. 2014. Erasure of alcohol-associated memories by mTORC1 inhibition prevents relapse. *Alcohol* 48:176–76

Barker JM, Taylor JR. 2014. Habitual alcohol seeking: modeling the transition from casual drinking to addiction. *Neurosci. Biobehav. Rev.* 47:281–94

Bechara A, Dolan S, Denburg N, Hindes A, Anderson SW, Nathan PE. 2001. Decision-making deficits, linked to a dysfunctional ventromedial prefrontal cortex, revealed in alcohol and stimulant abusers. *Neuropsychologia* 39:376–89

Belin D, Belin-Rauscent A, Murray JE, Everitt BJ. 2013. Addiction: failure of control over maladaptive incentive habits. *Curr. Opin. Neurobiol.* 23:564–72

Belin D, Berson N, Balado E, Piazza PV, Deroche-Gamonet V. 2011. High-novelty-preference rats are predisposed to compulsive cocaine self-administration. *Neuropsychopharmacology* 36:569–79

Belin D, Everitt BJ. 2008. Cocaine seeking habits depend upon dopamine-dependent serial connectivity linking the ventral with the dorsal striatum. *Neuron* 57:432–41

Belin D, Jonkman S, Dickinson A, Robbins TW, Everitt BJ. 2009. Parallel and interactive learning processes within the basal ganglia: relevance for the understanding of addiction. *Behav. Brain Res.* 199:89–102

Belin D, Mar AC, Dalley JW, Robbins TW, Everitt BJ. 2008. High impulsivity predicts the switch to compulsive cocaine-taking. *Science* 320:1352–55

Belin-Rauscent A, Simon M, Everitt BJ, Benoit-Marand M, Belin D. 2013. Corticostriatal interaction subserving incentive habits. *Behav. Pharmacol.* 24:1.4

Bohbot VD, Del Balso D, Conrad K, Konishi K, Leyton M. 2013. Caudate nucleus-dependent navigational strategies are associated with increased use of addictive drugs. *Hippocampus* 23:973–84

Brody AL, Mandelkern MA, Jarvik ME, Lee GS, Smith EC, et al. 2004. Differences between smokers and nonsmokers in regional gray matter volumes and densities. *Biol. Psychiatry* 55:77–84

Cannella N, Halbout B, Uhrig S, Evrard L, Corsi M, et al. 2013. The mGluR2/3 agonist LY379268 induced anti-reinstatement effects in rats exhibiting addiction-like behavior. *Neuropsychopharmacology* 38:2048–56

Caprioli D, Sawiak SJ, Merlo E, Theobald DEH, Spoelder M, et al. 2014. Gamma aminobutyric acidergic and neuronal structural markers in the nucleus accumbens core underlie trait-like impulsive behavior. *Biol. Psychiatry* 75:115–23

Cardinal RN, Everitt BJ. 2004. Neural and psychological mechanisms underlying appetitive learning: links to drug addiction. *Curr. Opin. Neurobiol.* 14:156–62

Cardinal RN, Parkinson JA, Hall J, Everitt BJ. 2002. Emotion and motivation: the role of the amygdala, ventral striatum, and prefrontal cortex. *Neurosci. Biobehav. Rev.* 26:321–52

Castañé A, Theobald DEH, Robbins TW. 2010. Selective lesions of the dorsomedial striatum impair serial spatial reversal learning in rats. *Behav. Brain Res.* 210:74–83

Chen BT, Yau H-J, Hatch C, Kusumoto-Yoshida I, Cho SL, et al. 2013. Rescuing cocaine-induced prefrontal cortex hypoactivity prevents compulsive cocaine seeking. *Nature* 496:359–62

Childress AR, Mozley PD, McElgin W, Fitzgerald J, Reivich M, O'Brien CP. 1999. Limbic activation during cue-induced cocaine craving. *Am. J. Psychiatry* 156:11–18

Chudasama Y, Robbins TW. 2003. Dissociable contributions of the orbitofrontal and infralimbic cortex to Pavlovian autoshaping and discrimination reversal learning: further evidence for the functional heterogeneity of the rodent frontal cortex. *J. Neurosci.* 23:8771–80

Clark L, Bechara A, Damasio H, Aitken MRF, Sahakian BJ, Robbins TW. 2008. Differential effects of insular and ventromedial prefrontal cortex damage on risky decision-making. *Brain* 131:1311–22

Clarke HF, Robbins TW, Roberts AC. 2008. Lesions of the medial striatum in monkeys produce perseverative impairments during reversal learning similar to those produced by lesions of the orbitofrontal cortex. *J. Neurosci.* 28:10972–82

Clemens KJ, Castino MR, Cornish JL, Goodchild AK, Holmes NM. 2014. Behavioral and neural substrates of habit formation in rats intravenously self-administering nicotine. *Neuropsychopharmacology* 39:2584–93

Conklin CA, Tiffany ST. 2002. Applying extinction research and theory to cue-exposure in addiction treatments. *Addiction* 97:155–67

Contreras M, Ceric F, Torrealba F. 2007. Inactivation of the interoceptive insula disrupts drug craving and malaise induced by lithium. *Science* 318:655–58

Corbit LH, Balleine BW. 2005. Double dissociation of basolateral and central amygdala lesions on the general and outcome-specific forms of Pavlovian-instrumental transfer. *J. Neurosci.* 25:962–70

Corbit LH, Nie H, Janak PH. 2012. Habitual alcohol seeking: time course and the contribution of subregions of the dorsal striatum. *Biol. Psychiatry* 72:389–95

Corbit LH, Nie H, Janak PH. 2014. Habitual responding for alcohol depends upon both AMPA and D2 receptor signaling in the dorsolateral striatum. *Front. Behav. Neurosci.* 8:301

Covington HE, Miczek KA. 2005. Intense cocaine self-administration after episodic social defeat stress, but not after aggressive behavior: dissociation from corticosterone activation. *Psychopharmacology* 183:331–40

Cuthbert BN. 2014. The RDoC framework: facilitating transition from ICD/DSM to dimensional approaches that integrate neuroscience and psychopathology. *World Psychiatry* 13:28–35

Dalley JW, Everitt BJ, Robbins TW. 2011. Impulsivity, compulsivity, and top-down cognitive control. *Neuron* 69:680–94

Dalley JW, Fryer TD, Brichard L, Robinson ESJ, Theobald DEH, et al. 2007. Nucleus accumbens D2/3 receptors predict trait impulsivity and cocaine reinforcement. *Science* 315:1267–70

Davis M. 2002. Role of NMDA receptors and MAP kinase in the amygdala in extinction of fear: clinical implications for exposure therapy. *Eur. J. Neurosci.* 16:395–98

de Wit H, Crean J, Richards JB. 2000. Effects of d-amphetamine and ethanol on a measure of behavioural inhibition in humans. *Behav. Neurosci.* 114:830–37

Debiec J, Ledoux JE. 2004. Disruption of reconsolidation but not consolidation of auditory fear conditioning by noradrenergic blockade in the amygdala. *Neuroscience* 129:267–72

DePoy L, Daut R, Brigman JL, MacPherson K, Crowley N, et al. 2013. Chronic alcohol produces neuroadaptations to prime dorsal striatal learning. *PNAS* 110:14783–88

Deroche-Gamonet V, Belin D, Piazza PV. 2004. Evidence for addiction-like behavior in the rat. *Science* 305:1014–17

Dezfouli A, Piray P, Keramati MM, Ekhtiari H, Lucas C, Mokri A. 2009. A neurocomputational model for cocaine addiction. *Neural Comput.* 21:2869–93

Di Chiara G, Imperato A. 1988. Drugs abused by humans preferentially increase synaptic dopamine concentrations in the mesolimbic system of freely moving rats. *PNAS* 85:5274–78

Dias R, Robbins TW, Roberts AC. 1996. Dissociation in prefrontal cortex of affective and attentional shifts. *Nature* 380:69–72

Dias-Ferreira E, Sousa JC, Melo I, Morgado P, Mesquita AR, et al. 2009. Chronic stress causes frontostriatal reorganization and affects decision-making. *Science* 325:621–25

Dickinson A. 1985. Actions and habits: the development of behavioural autonomy. *Philos. Trans. R. Soc. B* 308:67–78

Dickinson A, Balleine BB. 1994. Motivational control of goal-directed action. *Anim. Learn. Behav.* 22:1–18

Dickinson A, Wood N, Smith JW. 2002. Alcohol seeking by rats: action or habit? *Q. J. Exp. Psychol. B* 55:331–48

Diergaarde L, Pattij T, Poortvliet I, Hogenboom F, de Vries W, et al. 2008. Impulsive choice and impulsive action predict vulnerability to distinct stages of nicotine seeking in rats. *Biol. Psychiatry* 63:301–8

Dilleen R, Pelloux Y, Mar AC, Molander A, Robbins TW, et al. 2012. High anxiety is a predisposing endophenotype for loss of control over cocaine, but not heroin, self-administration in rats. *Psychopharmacology* 222:89–97

Donnelly NA, Holtzman T, Rich PD, Nevado-Holgado AJ, Fernando AB, et al. 2014. Oscillatory activity in the medial prefrontal cortex and nucleus accumbens correlates with impulsivity and reward outcome. *PLOS ONE* 9(10):e111300

Economidou D, Pelloux Y, Robbins TW, Dalley JW, Everitt BJ. 2009. High impulsivity predicts relapse to cocaine-seeking after punishment-induced abstinence. *Biol. Psychiatry* 65:851–56

Economidou D, Theobald DEH, Robbins TW, Everitt BJ, Dalley JW. 2012. Norepinephrine and dopamine modulate impulsivity on the five-choice serial reaction-time task through opponent actions in the shell and core sub-regions of the nucleus accumbens. *Neuropsychopharmacology* 37:2057–66

Ersche KD, Barnes A, Jones PS, Morein-Zamir S, Robbins TW, Bullmore ET. 2011a. Abnormal structure of frontostriatal brain systems is associated with aspects of impulsivity and compulsivity in cocaine dependence. *Brain* 134:2013–24

Ersche KD, Bullmore ET, Craig KJ, Shabbir SS, Abbott S, et al. 2010. Influence of compulsivity of drug abuse on dopaminergic modulation of attentional bias in stimulant dependence. *Arch. Gen. Psychiatry* 67:632–44

Ersche KD, Fletcher PC, Lewis SJ, Clark L, Stocks-Gee G, et al. 2005. Abnormal frontal activations related to decision-making in current and former amphetamine and opiate dependent individuals. *Psychopharmacology* 180:612–23

Ersche KD, Jones PS, Williams GB, Smith DG, Bullmore ET, Robbins TW. 2013a. Distinctive personality traits and neural correlates associated with stimulant drug use versus familial risk of stimulant dependence. *Biol. Psychiatry* 74:137–44

Ersche KD, Jones PS, Williams GB, Turton AJ, Robbins TW, Bullmore ET. 2012a. Abnormal brain structure implicated in stimulant drug addiction. *Science* 335:601–4

Ersche KD, Roiser JP, Abbott S, Craig KJ, Mueller U, et al. 2011b. Response perseveration in stimulant dependence is associated with striatal dysfunction and can be ameliorated by a D-2/3 receptor agonist. *Biol. Psychiatry* 70:754–62

Ersche KD, Roiser JP, Robbins TW, Sahakian BJ. 2008. Chronic cocaine but not chronic amphetamine use is associated with perseverative responding in humans. *Psychopharmacology* 197:421–31

Ersche KD, Turton AJ, Chamberlain SR, Mueller U, Bullmore ET, Robbins TW. 2012b. Cognitive dysfunction and anxious-impulsive personality traits are endophenotypes for drug dependence. *Am. J. Psychiatry* 169:926–36

Ersche KD, Williams GB, Robbins TW, Bullmore ET. 2013b. Meta-analysis of structural brain abnormalities associated with stimulant drug dependence and neuroimaging of addiction vulnerability and resilience. *Curr. Opin. Neurobiol.* 23:615–24

Everitt BJ. 2014. Neural and psychological mechanisms underlying compulsive drug seeking habits and drug memories—indications for novel treatments of addiction. *Eur. J. Neurosci.* 40:2163–82

Everitt BJ, Dickinson A, Robbins TW. 2001. The neuropsychological basis of addictive behaviour. *Brain Res. Rev.* 36:129–38

Everitt BJ, Robbins TW. 2005. Neural systems of reinforcement for drug addiction: from actions to habits to compulsion. *Nat. Neurosci.* 8:1481–89

Everitt BJ, Robbins TW. 2013. From the ventral to the dorsal striatum: devolving views of their roles in drug addiction. *Neurosci. Biobehav. Rev.* 37:1946–54

Fein G, Di Sclafani V, Cardenas VA, Goldmann H, Tolou-Shams M, Meyerhoff DJ. 2002. Cortical gray matter loss in treatment-naive alcohol dependent individuals. *Alcohol Clin. Exp. Res.* 26:558–64

Fernando AB, Economidou D, Theobald DEH, Zou MF, Newman AH, et al. 2012. Modulation of high impulsivity and attentional performance in rats by selective direct and indirect dopaminergic and noradrenergic receptor agonists. *Psychopharmacology* 219:341–52

Fillmore MT, Rush CR, Hays L. 2005. Cocaine improves inhibitory control in a human model of response conflict. *Exp. Clin. Psychopharmacol.* 3:327–35

Flagel SB, Clark JJ, Robinson TE, Mayo L, Czuj A, et al. 2011. A selective role for dopamine in stimulus-reward learning. *Nature* 469:53–63

Flagel SB, Waselus M, Clinton SM, Watson SJ, Akil H. 2014. Antecedents and consequences of drug abuse in rats selectively bred for high and low response to novelty. *Neuropharmacology* 76:425–36

Friedman NP, Miyake A, Corley RP, Young SE, DeFries JC, Hewitt JK. 2006. Not all executive functions are related to intelligence. *Psychol. Sci.* 17(2):172–79

Gallinat J, et al. 2006. Smoking and structural brain deficits: a volumetric MR investigation. *Eur. J. Neurosci.* 24:1744–50

Garavan H, Hester R, Whelan R. 2013. The neurobiology of successful abstinence. *Curr. Opin. Neurobiol.* 23:668–74

Garavan H, Kaufman JN, Hester R. 2008. Acute effects of cocaine on the neurobiology of cognitive control. *Philos. Trans. R. Soc. B* 363:3267–76

Garavan H, Pankiewicz J, Bloom A, Cho JK, Sperry L, et al. 2000. Cue-induced cocaine craving: neuroanatomical specificity for drug users and drug stimuli. *Am. J. Psychiatry* 157:1789–98

Gawin FH, Kleber HD. 1986. Abstinence symptomatology and psychiatric diagnosis in cocaine abusers: clinical observations. *Arch. Gen. Psychiatry* 43:107–13

Gillan CM, Apergis-Schoute AM, Morein-Zamir S, Urcelay GP, Sule A, et al. 2015. Functional neuroimaging of avoidance habits in obsessive-compulsive disorder. *Am. J. Psychiatry* 172:284–93

Glautier S, Drummond C, Remington B. 1994. Alcohol as an unconditioned stimulus in human classical conditioning. *Psychopharmacology* 116:360–68

Goldberg SR. 1973. Comparable behavior maintained under fixed-ratio and second-order schedules of food presentation, cocaine injection or d-amphetamine injection in the squirrel monkey. *J. Pharmacol. Exp. Ther.* 186:18–30

Goldstein RZ, Craig ADB, Bechara A, Garavan H, Childress AR, et al. 2009. The neurocircuitry of impaired insight in drug addiction. *Trends Cogn. Sci.* 13:372–80

Gottesman II, Gould TD. 2003. The endophenotype concept in psychiatry: etymology and strategic intentions. *Am. J. Psychiatry* 160:636–45

Grant S, London ED, Newlin DB, Villemagne VL, Xiang L, et al. 1996. Activation of memory circuits during cue-elicited cocaine craving. *PNAS* 93:12040–45

Groman SM, James AS, Seu E, Crawford MA, Harpster SN, Jenstch JD. 2013. Monoamine levels within the orbitofrontal cortex and putamen interact to predict reversal learning performance. *Biol. Psychiatry* 73:756–62

Grueter BA, Rothwell PE, Malenka RC. 2012. Integrating synaptic plasticity and striatal circuit function in addiction. *Curr. Opin. Neurobiol.* 22:545–51

Haber SN, Fudge JL, McFarland NR. 2000. Striatonigral pathways in primates form an ascending spiral from the shell to the dorsolateral striatum. *J. Neurosci.* 20:2369–82

Hall J, Parkinson JA, Connor TM, Dickinson A, Everitt BJ. 2001. Involvement of the central nucleus of the amygdala and nucleus accumbens core in mediating Pavlovian influences on instrumental behaviour. *Eur. J. Neurosci.* 13:1984–92

Han JS, McMahan RW, Holland P, Gallagher M. 1997. The role of an amygdalo-nigrostriatal pathway in associative learning. *J. Neurosci.* 17:3913–19

Hellemans KG, Everitt BJ, Lee JL. 2006. Disrupting reconsolidation of conditioned withdrawal memories in the basolateral amygdala reduces suppression of heroin seeking in rats. *J. Neurosci.* 26:12694–99

Hogarth L, Balleine BW, Corbit LH, Killcross S. 2013. Associative learning mechanisms underpinning the transition from recreational drug use to addiction. *Addict. Rev.* 1282:12–24

Hogarth L, Dickinson A, Duka T. 2010. The associative basis of cue-elicited drug taking in humans. *Psychopharmacology* 208:337–51

Hyman SE, Malenka RC, Nestler EJ. 2006. Neural mechanisms of addiction: the role of reward-related learning and memory. *Annu. Rev. Neurosci.* 29:565–98

Ikemoto S, Wise RA. 2004. Mapping of chemical trigger zones for reward. *Neuropharmacology* 47:190–201

Ito R, Dalley JW, Robbins TW, Everitt BJ. 2002. Dopamine release in the dorsal striatum during cocaine-seeking behavior under the control of a drug-associated cue. *J. Neurosci.* 22:6247–53

Jang DP, Namkoong K, Kim JJ, Park S, Kim IY, et al. 2007. The relationship between brain morphometry and neuropsychological performance in alcohol dependence. *Neurosci. Lett.* 428:21–26

Jedynak JP, Uslaner JM, Esteban JA, Robinson TE. 2007. Methamphetamine-induced structural plasticity in the dorsal striatum. *Eur. J. Neurosci.* 25:847–53

Jentsch JD, Olausson P, De la Garza R, Taylor JR. 2002. Impairments of reversal learning and response perseveration after repeated, intermittent cocaine administrations to monkeys. *Neuropsychopharmacology* 26:183–90

Jentsch JD, Taylor JR. 1999. Impulsivity resulting from frontostriatal dysfunction in drug abuse: implications for the control of behavior by reward-related stimuli. *Psychopharmacology* 146:373–90

Jonkman S, Kenny PJ. 2013. Molecular, cellular, and structural mechanisms of cocaine addiction: a key role for microRNAs. *Neuropsychopharmacology* 38:198–211

Jonkman S, Pelloux Y, Everitt BJ. 2012a. Differential roles of the dorsolateral and midlateral striatum in punished cocaine seeking. *J. Neurosci.* 32:4645–50

Jonkman S, Pelloux Y, Everitt BJ. 2012b. Drug intake is sufficient, but conditioning is not necessary for the emergence of compulsive cocaine seeking after extended self-administration. *Neuropsychopharmacology* 37:1612–19

Kalivas PW, McFarland K. 2003. Brain circuitry and the reinstatement of cocaine-seeking behavior. *Psychopharmacology* 168:44–56

Kalivas PW, Volkow ND. 2005. The neural basis of addiction: a pathology of motivation and choice. *Am. J. Psychiatry* 162:1403–13

Kasanetz F, Deroche-Gamonet V, Berson N, Balado E, Lafourcade M, et al. 2010. Transition to addiction is associated with a persistent impairment in synaptic plasticity. *Science* 328:1709–12

Kauer JA, Malenka RC. 2007. Synaptic plasticity and addiction. *Nat. Rev. Neurosci.* 8:844–58

Kelly PH, Seviour PW, Iversen SD. 1975. Amphetamine and apomorphine responses in the rat following 6-OHDA lesions of the nucleus accumbens septi and corpus striatum. *Brain Res.* 94:507–22

Koob GF. 2008. A role for brain stress systems in addiction. *Neuron* 59:11–34

Koob GF, LeMoal M. 1997. Drug abuse: hedonic homeostatic dysregulation. *Science* 278:52–58

Koob GF, Volkow ND. 2010. Neurocircuitry of addiction. *Neuropsychopharmacology* 35:217–38

Lee JLC, Di Ciano P, Thomas KL, Everitt BJ. 2005. Disrupting reconsolidation of drug memories reduces cocaine-seeking behavior. *Neuron* 47:795–801

Lee JLC, Everitt BJ. 2007. Reactivation-dependent amnesia: disrupting memory reconsolidation as a novel approach for the treatment of maladaptive memory disorders. In *Research and Perspectives in Neurosciences. Memories: Molecules and Circuits*, ed. Y Christen, B Bontempi, AJ Silva, pp. 83–98. Paris: Fondation Ipsen

Lee JLC, Everitt BJ, Thomas KL. 2004. Independent cellular processes for hippocampal memory consolidation and reconsolidation. *Science* 304:839–43

Lee JLC, Gardner RJ, Butler VJ, Everitt BJ. 2009. D-cycloserine potentiates the reconsolidation of cocaine-associated memories. *Learn. Mem.* 16:82–85

Lee JLC, Milton AL, Everitt BJ. 2006a. Cue-induced cocaine seeking and relapse are reduced by disruption of drug memory reconsolidation. *J. Neurosci.* 26:5881–87

Lee JLC, Milton AL, Everitt BJ. 2006b. Reconsolidation and extinction of conditioned fear: inhibition and potentiation. *J. Neurosci.* 26:10051–56

Leshner AI. 1997. Addiction is a brain disease, and it matters. *Science* 278:45–47

Letchworth SR, Nader MA, Smith HR, Friedman DP, Porrino LJ. 2001. Progression of changes in dopamine transporter binding site density as a result of cocaine self-administration in rhesus monkeys. *J. Neurosci.* 21:2799–807

Lewis DJ. 1979. Psychobiology of active and inactive memory. *Psychol. Bull.* 86:1054–83

Leyton M. 2007. Conditioned and sensitized responses to stimulant drugs in humans. *Prog. Neuropsychopharmacol. Biol. Psychiatry* 31:1601–13

Leyton M, Vezina P. 2014. Dopamine ups and downs in vulnerability to addictions: a neurodevelopmental model. *Trends Pharmacol. Sci.* 35:268–76

Lingawi NW, Balleine BW. 2012. Amygdala central nucleus interacts with dorsolateral striatum to regulate the acquisition of habits. *J. Neurosci.* 32:1073–81

Luescher C, Malenka RC. 2011. Drug-evoked synaptic plasticity in addiction: from molecular changes to circuit remodeling. *Neuron* 69:650–63

MacKillop J, Lisman SA. 2008. Effects of a context shift and multiple context extinction on reactivity to alcohol cues. *Exp. Clin. Psychopharmacol.* 16:322–31

McNamara R, Dalley JW, Robbins TW, Everitt BJ, Belin D. 2010. Trait-like impulsivity does not predict escalation of heroin self-administration in the rat. *Psychopharmacology* 212:453–64

Mechtcheriakov S, Brenneis C, Egger K, Koppelstaetter F, Schocke M, Marksteiner J. 2007. A widespread distinct pattern of cerebral atrophy in patients with alcohol addiction revealed by voxel-based morphometry. *J. Neurol. Neurosurg. Psychiatry* 78:610–14

Merlo E, Milton AL, Goozee ZY, Theobald DE, Everitt BJ. 2014. Reconsolidation and extinction are dissociable and mutually exclusive processes: behavioral and molecular evidence. *J. Neurosci.* 34:2422–31

Meunier D, Ersche KD, Craig KJ, Fornito A, Merlo-Pich E, et al. 2012. Brain functional connectivity in stimulant drug dependence and obsessive-compulsive disorder. *NeuroImage* 59:1461–68

Miles FJ, Everitt BJ, Dickinson A. 2003. Oral cocaine seeking by rats: action or habit? *Behav. Neurosci.* 117:927–38

Miller CA, Marshall JF. 2005. Molecular substrates for retrieval and reconsolidation of cocaine-associated contextual memory. *Neuron* 47:873–84

Milton AL. 2013. Drink, drugs and disruption: memory manipulation for the treatment of addiction. *Curr. Opin. Neurobiol.* 23:706–12

Milton AL, Everitt BJ. 2010. The psychological and neurochemical mechanisms of drug memory reconsolidation: implications for the treatment of addiction. *Eur. J. Neurosci.* 31:2308–19

Milton AL, Lee JL, Butler VJ, Gardner R, Everitt BJ. 2008a. Intra-amygdala and systemic antagonism of NMDA receptors prevents the reconsolidation of drug-associated memory and impairs subsequently both novel and previously acquired drug-seeking behaviors. *J. Neurosci.* 28:8230–37

Milton AL, Lee JL, Everitt BJ. 2008b. Reconsolidation of appetitive memories for both natural and drug reinforcement is dependent on β-adrenergic receptors. *Learn. Mem.* 15:88–92

Milton AL, Schramm MJ, Wawrzynski JR, Gore F, Oikonomou-Mpegeti F, et al. 2012. Antagonism at NMDA receptors, but not beta-adrenergic receptors, disrupts the reconsolidation of Pavlovian conditioned approach and instrumental transfer for ethanol-associated conditioned stimuli. *Psychopharmacology* 219:751–61

Mitchell MR, Weiss VG, Beas BS, Morgan D, Bizon JL, et al. 2014. Adolescent risk taking, cocaine self-administration and striatal dopamine signalling. *Neuropsychopharmacology* 39:955–62

Molander AC, Mar A, Norbury A, Steventon S, Moreno M, et al. 2011. High impulsivity predicting vulnerability to cocaine addiction in rats: some relationship with novelty preference but not novelty reactivity, anxiety or stress. *Psychopharmacology* 215:721–31

Monfils MH, Cowansage KK, Klann E, LeDoux JE. 2009. Extinction-reconsolidation boundaries: key to persistent attenuation of fear memories. *Science* 324:951–55

Morein-Zamir S, Jones PS, Bullmore ET, Robbins TW, Ersche KD. 2013. Prefrontal hypoactivity associated with impaired inhibition in stimulant-dependent individuals but evidence for hyperactivation in their unaffected siblings. *Neuropsychopharmacology* 38:1945–53

Morein-Zamir S, Robbins TW. 2014. Fronto-striatal circuits in response inhibition: relevance to addiction. *Brain Res.* doi: 10.1016/j.brainres.2014.09.012

Morgan D, Grant KA, Gage HD, Mach RH, Kaplan JR, et al. 2002. Social dominance in monkeys: dopamine D2 receptors and cocaine self-administration. *Nat. Neurosci.* 5:169–74

Murray JE, Belin D, Everitt BJ. 2012. Double dissociation of the dorsomedial and dorsolateral striatal control over the acquisition and performance of cocaine seeking. *Neuropsychopharmacology* 37:2456–66

Murray JE, Belin D, Everitt BJ. 2013. Basolateral and central nuclei of the amygdala are required for the transition to dorsolateral striatal control over habitual cocaine seeking. *51st Annu. Meet. Am. Coll. Neuropsychopharmacol.*, abstract M221, Hollywood, FL

Myers KM, Carlezon WA Jr. 2012. D-cycloserine effects on extinction of conditioned responses to drug-related cues. *Biol. Psychiatry* 71:947–55

Nader K, Schafe GE, LeDoux JE. 2000. Fear memories require protein synthesis in the amygdala for reconsolidation after retrieval. *Nature* 406:722–26

Nader M, Czoty PW, Gould RW, Riddick NV. 2010. Characterising organism X environment interactions in non-human primate models of addiction: PET imaging studies of dopamine D2 receptors. In *The Neurobiology of Addiction: New Vistas*, ed. TW Robbins, BJ Everitt, DJ Nutt, pp. 187–202. Oxford, UK: Oxford Univ. Press

Naqvi NH, Bechara A. 2009. The hidden island of addiction; the insula. *Trends Neurosci.* 32:56–67

Naqvi NH, Bechara A. 2010. The insula and drug addiction: an interoceptive view of pleasure, urges, and decision-making. *Brain Struct. Funct.* 214:435–50

Naqvi NH, Rudrauf D, Damasio H, Bechara A. 2007. Damage to the insula disrupts addiction to cigarette smoking. *Science* 315:531–34

Nelson A, Killcross S. 2006. Amphetamine exposure enhances habit formation. *J. Neurosci.* 26:3805–12

Nestler EJ. 2004. Molecular mechanisms of drug addiction. *Neuropharmacology* 47:24–32

O'Brien CP, Childress AR, Ehrman R, Robbins SJ. 1998. Conditioning factors in drug abuse: Can they explain compulsion? *J. Psychopharmacol.* 12:15–22

O'Doherty J, Dayan P, Schultz J, Deichmann R, Friston K, Dolan RJ. 2004. Dissociable roles of ventral and dorsal striatum in instrumental conditioning. *Science* 304:452–54

Olmstead MC, Lafond MV, Everitt BJ, Dickinson A. 2001. Cocaine seeking by rats is a goal-directed action. *Behav. Neurosci.* 115:394–402

Ornstein TJ, Iddon JL, Baldacchino AM, Sahakian BJ, London M, et al. 2000. Profiles of cognitive dysfunction in chronic amphetamine and heroin abusers. *Neuropsychopharmacology* 23:113–26

Paulus MP, Stewart JL. 2014. Interoception and drug addiction. *Neuropharmacology* 76:342–50

Pelloux Y, Dilleen R, Economidou D, Theobald D, Everitt BJ. 2012. Reduced forebrain serotonin transmission is causally involved in the development of compulsive cocaine seeking in rats. *Neuropsychopharmacology* 37:2505–14

Pelloux Y, Everitt BJ, Dickinson A. 2007. Compulsive drug seeking by rats under punishment: effects of drug taking history. *Psychopharmacology* 194:127–37

Pelloux Y, Murray JE, Everitt BJ. 2013. Differential roles of the prefrontal cortical subregions and basolateral amygdala in compulsive cocaine seeking and relapse after voluntary abstinence in rats. *Eur. J. Neurosci.* 38:3018–26

Perry JL, Carroll ME. 2008. The role of impulsive behavior in drug abuse. *Psychopharmacology* 200:1–26

Piazza PV, Deminière JM, Le Moal M, Simon H. 1989. Factors that predict individual vulnerability to amphetamine self-administration. *Science* 245:1511–13

Piazza PV, Deroche V, Deminiere JM, Maccari S, LeMoal M, Simon H. 1993. Corticosterone in the range of stress levels possesses reinforcing properties: implications for sensation-seeking behaviors. *PNAS* 90(24):11738–42

Piray P, Keramati MM, Dezfouli A, Lucas C, Mokri A. 2010. Individual differences in nucleus accumbens dopamine receptors predict development of addiction-like behavior: a computational approach. *Neural Comput.* 22:2334–68

Porrino LJ, Hanlon CA, Gill KE, Beveridge TJR. 2010. Parallel studies of neural and cognitive impairment in humans and monkeys. In *The Neurobiology of Addiction: New Vistas*, ed. TW Robbins, BJ Everitt, DJ Nutt, pp. 241–56. Oxford, UK: Oxford Univ. Press

Price KL, Baker NL, McRae-Clark AL, Saladin ME, DeSantis SM, et al. 2013. A randomized, placebo-controlled laboratory study of the effects of D-cycloserine on craving in cocaine-dependent individuals. *Psychopharmacology* 226:739–46

Robbins TW, Ersche KD, Everitt BJ. 2008. Drug addiction and the memory systems of the brain. *Addict. Rev.* 1141:1–21

Robbins TW, Everitt BJ. 1999. Drug addiction: bad habits add up. *Nature* 398:567–70

Robbins TW, Gillan CM, Smith DG, de Wit S, Ersche KD. 2012. Neurocognitive endophenotypes of impulsivity and compulsivity: towards dimensional psychiatry. *Trends Cogn. Sci.* 16:81–91

Roberts DC, Koob GF. 1982. Disruption of cocaine self-administration following 6-hydroxydopamine lesions of the ventral tegmental area in rats. *Pharmacol. Biochem. Behav.* 17:901–4

Robinson ESJ, Eagle DM, Economidou D, Theobald DEH, Mar AC, et al. 2009. Behavioural characterisation of high impulsivity on the 5-choice serial reaction time task: specific deficits in "waiting" versus "stopping." *Behav. Brain Res.* 196:310–16

Robinson ESJ, Eagle DM, Mar AC, Bari A, Banerjee G, et al. 2008. Similar effects of the selective noradrenaline reuptake inhibitor atomoxetine on three distinct forms of impulsivity in the rat. *Neuropsychopharmacology* 33:1028–37

Robinson TE, Berridge KC. 1993. The neural basis of drug craving: an incentive-sensitization theory of addiction. *Brain Res. Rev.* 18:247–91

Rogers RD, Everitt BJ, Baldacchino A, Blackshaw AJ, Swainson R, et al. 1999. Dissociable deficits in the decision-making cognition of chronic amphetamine abusers, opiate abusers, patients with focal damage to prefrontal cortex, and tryptophan-depleted normal volunteers: evidence for monoaminergic mechanisms. *Neuropsychopharmacology* 20:322–39

Rogers RD, Robbins TW. 2001. Investigating the neurocognitive deficits associated with chronic drug misuse. *Curr. Opin. Neurobiol.* 11:250–57

Sanchez-Roige S, Baro V, Trick L, Peña-Oliver Y, Stephens DN, Duka T. 2014. Exaggerated waiting impulsivity associated with human binge drinking and high alcohol consumption in mice. *Neuropsychopharmacology* 39:2919–27

Saunders BT, Robinson TE. 2013. Individual variation in resisting temptation: implications for addiction. *Neurosci. Biobehav. Rev.* 37:1955–75

Schiller D, Monfils MH, Raio CM, Johnson DC, LeDoux JE, Phelps EA. 2010. Preventing the return of fear in humans using reconsolidation update mechanisms. *Nature* 463:49–54

Schmitzer-Torbert N, Apostolidis S, Amoa R, O'Rear C, Kaster M, et al. 2014. Post-training cocaine administration facilitates habit learning and requires the infralimbic cortex and dorsolateral striatum. *Neurobiol. Learn. Mem.* 118:105–12

Shiflett MW, Brown RA, Balleine BW. 2010. Acquisition and performance of goal-directed instrumental actions depends on ERK signaling in distinct regions of dorsal striatum in rats. *J. Neurosci.* 30:2951–59

Sjoerds Z, de Wit S, van den Brink W, Robbins TW, Beekman ATF, et al. 2013. Behavioral and neuroimaging evidence for overreliance on habit learning in alcohol-dependent patients. *Transl. Psychiatry* 3:e337

Stasiewicz PR, Brandon TH, Bradizza CM. 2007. Effects of extinction context and retrieval cues on renewal of alcohol-cue reactivity among alcohol-dependent outpatients. *Psychol. Addict. Behav.* 21:244–48

Stewart J, de Wit H, Eikelboom R. 1984. The role of unconditioned and conditioned drug effects in the self-administration of opiates and stimulants. *Psychol. Rev.* 91:251–68

Sullivan EV, Deshmukh A, De Rosa E, Rosenbloom MJ, Pfefferbaum A. 2005. Striatal and forebrain nuclei volumes: contribution to motor function and working memory deficits in alcoholism. *Biol. Psychiatry* 57:768–76

Taylor JR, Robbins TW. 1984. Enhanced behavioural control by conditioned reinforcers following microinjections of d-amphetamine into the nucleus accumbens. *Psychopharmacology* 84:405–12

Thorn CA, Atallah H, Howe M, Graybiel AM. 2010. Differential dynamics of activity changes in dorsolateral and dorsomedial striatal loops during learning. *Neuron* 66:781–95

Tiffany ST. 1990. A cognitive model of drug urges and drug-use behavior: role of automatic and nonautomatic processes. *Psychol. Rev.* 97:147–68

Tronson NC, Taylor JR. 2007. Molecular mechanisms of memory reconsolidation. *Nat. Rev. Neurosci.* 8:262–75

Vanderschuren LJ, Di Ciano P, Everitt BJ. 2005. Involvement of the dorsal striatum in cue-controlled cocaine seeking. *J. Neurosci.* 25:8665–70

Verdejo-Garcia A, Perez-Garcia M, Bechara A. 2006. Emotion, decision-making and substance dependence: a somatic-marker model of addiction. *Curr. Neuropharmacol.* 4:17–31

Verdejo-Garcia A, Bechara A. 2009. A somatic marker theory of addiction. *Neurosci. Biobehav. Rev.* 56:48–62

Vezina P, Leyton M. 2009. Conditioned cues and the expression of stimulant sensitization in animals and humans. *Neuropharmacology* 56:160–68

Volkow ND, Fowler JS. 2000. Addiction, a disease of compulsion and drive: involvement of the orbitofrontal cortex. *Cereb. Cortex* 10:318–25

Volkow ND, Fowler JS, Wang GJ, Swanson JM, Telang F. 2007. Dopamine in drug abuse and addiction: results of imaging studies and treatment implications. *Arch. Neurol.* 64:1575–79

Volkow ND, Wang GJ, Telang F, Fowler JS, Logan J, et al. 2006. Cocaine cues and dopamine in dorsal striatum: mechanism of craving in cocaine addiction. *J. Neurosci.* 26:6583–88

Vollstaedt-Klein S, Wichert S, Rabinstein J, Buehler M, Klein O, et al. 2010. Initial, habitual and compulsive alcohol use is characterized by a shift of cue processing from ventral to dorsal striatum. *Addiction* 105:1741–49

Whelan R, Conrod PJ, Poline J-P, Lourdusamy A, Banaschewski T, et al. 2012. Adolescent impulsivity phenotypes characterized by distinct brain networks. *Nat. Neurosci.* 15:920–25

Wikler A. 1965. Conditioning factors in opiate addiction and relapse. In *Narcotics*, ed. DI Willner, GG Kassenbaum, pp. 7–21. New York: McGraw-Hill

Willuhn I, Burgeno LM, Everitt BJ, Phillips PEM. 2012. Hierarchical recruitment of phasic dopamine signaling in the striatum during the progression of cocaine use. *PNAS* 109:20703–8

Wise RA. 2008. Dopamine and reward: the anhedonia hypothesis 30 years on. *Neurotox. Res.* 14:169–83

Xie C, Shao Y, Ma L, Zhai T, Ye E, et al. 2014. Imbalanced functional link between valuation networks in abstinent heroin-dependent subjects. *Mol. Psychiatry* 19:10–12

Xue Y-X, Luo Y-X, Wu P, Shi H-S, Xue L-F, et al. 2012. A memory retrieval-extinction procedure to prevent drug craving and relapse. *Science* 336:241–45

Yin HH, Knowlton BJ, Balleine BW. 2004. Lesions of dorsolateral striatum preserve outcome expectancy but disrupt habit formation in instrumental learning. *Eur. J. Neurosci.* 19:181–89

Yin HH, Ostlund SB, Knowlton BJ, Balleine BW. 2005. The role of the dorsomedial striatum in instrumental conditioning. *Eur. J. Neurosci.* 22:513–23

Zapata A, Minney VL, Shippenberg TS. 2010. Shift from goal-oriented to habitual cocaine seeking after prolonged experience in rats. *J. Neurosci.* 30:15457–63

Remembering Preservation in Hippocampal Amnesia

Ian A. Clark and Eleanor A. Maguire

Wellcome Trust Center for Neuroimaging, Institute of Neurology, University College London, London WC1N 3BG, United Kingdom; email: ian.clark@ucl.ac.uk, e.maguire@ucl.ac.uk

Annu. Rev. Psychol. 2016. 67:51–82

First published online as a Review in Advance on September 10, 2015

The *Annual Review of Psychology* is online at psych.annualreviews.org

This article's doi:
10.1146/annurev-psych-122414-033739

Keywords

hippocampus, memory, navigation, deficits, neuropsychology, scene construction

Abstract

The lesion-deficit model dominates neuropsychology. This is unsurprising given powerful demonstrations that focal brain lesions can affect specific aspects of cognition. Nowhere is this more evident than in patients with bilateral hippocampal damage. In the past 60 years, the amnesia and other impairments exhibited by these patients have helped to delineate the functions of the hippocampus and shape the field of memory. We do not question the value of this approach. However, less prominent are the cognitive processes that remain intact following hippocampal lesions. Here, we collate the piecemeal reports of preservation of function following focal bilateral hippocampal damage, highlighting a wealth of information often veiled by the field's focus on deficits. We consider how a systematic understanding of what is preserved as well as what is lost could add an important layer of precision to models of memory and the hippocampus.

Contents

OVERVIEW

MTL: medial temporal lobe

Working memory: the transient holding online of information

Recognition memory: the ability to recognize previously encountered events, objects, or people

Familiarity: the feeling that an event was previously experienced, but without recollection of the associated details or context

Autobiographical memory: memory of our personal past experiences

Semantic memory: general and world knowledge

Memory is fundamental to everyday cognition. Consequently, a key goal of cognitive psychology and neuropsychology is to understand how memories are formed, represented, and recollected. Studies of patients with damage to a particular brain region, the hippocampus, have been pivotal in illuminating the organization of the memory system by showing, for example, that memory is not a unitary phenomenon. The importance of the hippocampus for memory was first formally demonstrated nearly 60 years ago by patient HM (Scoville & Milner 1957). Removal of HM's medial temporal lobe (MTL, which includes the hippocampi) for the relief of intractable seizures left him with profound amnesia, unable to recall any new personal experiences (episodic/autobiographical memories), and presurgical autobiographical memories were also compromised to a degree. Nevertheless, HM's cognition did not collapse; he retained an above-average IQ, apparently intact perceptual and language capabilities, and aspects of his memory—working memory and procedural learning—were also preserved. Furthermore, although elements of his recognition memory were impaired, his familiarity was not, and although his autobiographical memory was affected, his semantic memory for the same time periods was intact (Augustinack et al. 2014).

Scoville & Milner (1957) appreciated that HM's cognitive and memory profile had two equally important components—what was impaired and what was preserved—and that only by considering both could the structure of memory and its functional anatomy be properly understood. In the decades since the case of HM was first reported there has been a wealth of studies investigating patients with damage to the MTL, including those with focal lesions to the hippocampi (reviewed in Spiers et al. 2001, Winocur & Moscovitch 2011). However, this work has predominantly focused on patients' deficits. Indeed, even HM's purportedly preserved abilities have been questioned in recent years, with visual perception (Lee et al. 2012) and working memory (Ranganath & Blumenfeld 2005) reported to be impaired in patients with focal bilateral hippocampal damage. In other work, the remit of the hippocampus has been extended beyond autobiographical memory to include spatial navigation (Maguire et al. 1998, 2006; O'Keefe & Dostrovsky 1971; O'Keefe &

Nadel 1978) and imagining the future (Hassabis et al. 2007b), with deficits in these domains also apparent following hippocampal lesions.

Consequent upon the dominance of the lesion-deficit model in neuropsychology, consideration of preserved functions has been eclipsed by the field's emphasis on unearthing impairments. We believe this narrow focus could impede our ability to achieve a full understanding of hippocampal functionality and the organization of memory and related cognition. It is not that the field is devoid of evidence relating to the intact abilities of patients with hippocampal damage, but rather that what is there is piecemeal and has not been considered in its totality. Our main aim in this article is to redress the balance by collating some of the evidence that exists in the literature concerning preservation of function in the context of bilateral hippocampal damage. We then consider how a systematic understanding of what is preserved as well as what is lost could be used to inform a theoretically enriched understanding of memory and its neural substrates.

We focus primarily on patients with putative focal bilateral hippocampal damage. Where relevant, mention is made of animal work, patients with less focal hippocampal lesions, and functional magnetic resonance imaging (fMRI) studies.

WHY IS PRESERVATION PROBLEMATIC?

Before examining the pertinent empirical data, it is interesting to first consider why preservation has failed to achieve parity with reports of deficits in patients with bilateral hippocampal damage. As noted, neuropsychological research is traditionally based on the lesion-deficit model. The logic here is if a patient cannot do X, then the execution of X must depend upon the lesioned area. Investigations are therefore aimed at highlighting cognitive impairments following brain damage by finding statistically significant performance differences between patients and matched healthy participants, usually leading to conclusions about the necessity of a brain region for a specific task or function. Here preservation runs into its first problem. The usual analysis employed within psychology is that of null hypothesis significance testing. This test asks, at the simplest level, whether two means are different from each other. Finding a significant result (often with a threshold of $p < 0.05$—a deficit in function) lends itself to a simple conclusion—that the means of patients and control subjects are different. However, a nonsignificant or "null" result (typically $p > 0.05$—preservation of function) is not typically regarded as the reverse conclusion. Null results can occur for multiple reasons, for example, type II errors (accepting a false null hypothesis), low study power (the probability of correctly rejecting the null hypothesis when it is false), and poor experimental design.

Problems with preservation do not end there, as further issues arise in relation to interpreting the results. If, following hippocampal damage, some aspects of cognition are preserved, the simplest assumption is that the hippocampus is not required for those tasks to be performed. However, there are other potential explanations for preservation. First, brain structure and function are not fixed. Environmental stimulation or memory encoding can alter the structure of the brain; for example, when trainee taxi drivers learn the layout of ~25,000 streets around London, this is associated, within subjects, with increased gray matter volume in the posterior hippocampus (Woollett & Maguire 2011). Second, brain regions are not always selective in their responsivity—in the congenitally blind, visual areas have been found to activate during fMRI studies of braille reading (i.e., tactile inputs) and verbal memory (Amedi et al. 2003). As such, it is possible that following damage to the hippocampus, other brain regions may be able to compensate to some degree. This may be particularly relevant in developmental amnesia (Vargha-Khadem et al. 1997), where early life insult to the hippocampi may lead to a reorganization of function within the brain.

It is also uncertain to what extent remnant tissue contributes to cognitive tasks. It is typically assumed in neuropsychology that damage to brain structures of the extent usually observed in patients with hippocampal damage could in effect equate to a near-complete loss of functionality. That is, as stated by Gold & Squire (2005), "These observations suggest that a reduction in hippocampal volume of approximately 40%, as estimated from MRI scans, likely indicates the nearly complete loss of hippocampal neurons. The tissue collapses with the result that the hippocampus is markedly reduced in volume, but the tissue does not disappear entirely. Thus, a loss of approximately 40% of hippocampal volume as measured from MRI scans should not be taken to mean that 60% of the hippocampus remains functional" (pp. 84–85). However, several fMRI studies conducted with patients have shown that even where hippocampal tissue volume is reduced by 50%, it nevertheless activates during successful performance on tasks that are thought to be hippocampal dependent (e.g., Maguire et al. 2001, 2010a; Mullally et al. 2012a). Preservation may thus, in some cases, be supported by remnant portions of the hippocampus that are still functional.

People also differ in the strategies they employ to perform a task. These different cognitive styles and strategies can influence the brain networks engaged (Sanfratello et al. 2014), and this could be expressed in different patterns of preservation following brain damage. Further, the brain contains degeneracy; that is, many-to-one structure-function relationships (Price & Friston 2002). As such, and related to the use of different cognitive strategies and plasticity, preservation of function following lesions does not necessarily mean that the damaged region is never involved in a particular cognitive process.

So there is much to muddy the waters in preservation, and it is perhaps not surprising, therefore, that journal editors and individual scientists have long been wary of null results (Ferguson & Heene 2012, Rosenthal 1979) and concomitant conclusions regarding preservation of function. It should be noted that preserved performance on one task observed in the context of impaired performance on a second task within the same experimental design can temper some of the above concerns, although these single dissociations are not without their own interpretive issues (Dunn & Kirsner 2003).

DEFICITS ARE ALSO DIFFICULT

Studies investigating deficits are not, however, immune from problems either. They are also susceptible to type I errors (incorrect rejection of the null hypothesis) and poor experimental design. One of the most contentious issues is in relation to study power and sample size. It is often the case in neuropsychology that single patients are studied and compared to a small group of control subjects. This substantially raises the likelihood of type I errors and also makes it difficult to gauge the generalizability of findings. Discussion of these important issues is beyond the scope of this article, but see Rosenbaum et al. (2014) for recent consideration of these matters.

Beyond statistical issues, interpretation of deficits is not straightforward. In patients with bilateral hippocampal damage, the accusation is sometimes leveled that the lesions are not truly focal to the hippocampus and that damage to other areas might have contributed to the impairment, thus making conclusions specific to the hippocampus impossible (e.g., Kim et al. 2015, Squire et al. 2010). It has been further suggested that pathology arising from limbic encephalitis (LE) is invariably more diffuse compared with etiologies such as anoxia (Kim et al. 2015, Squire et al. 2010). However, postmortem studies of certain types of LE document highly selective hippocampal damage (Dunstan & Winer 2006, Khan et al. 2009, Park et al. 2007). On the other hand, patients who have been described as having selective hippocampal damage from non-LE pathologies can have wider brain damage (e.g., Kim et al. 2015: patient DA, heroin overdose, bilateral globus pallidus lesions; patient KE, toxic shock syndrome, basal ganglia lesions). We therefore believe that arguments about the selectivity of lesions are specious because many pathological processes produce widespread brain damage, but only those rare patients with apparently selective hippocampal lesions are typically included in studies where the prime or sole interest is in the hippocampus (e.g., Mullally et al. 2012b).

Even where high-resolution MRI scanning of patients' brains has been undertaken and subsequent painstaking measurement of hippocampus and other regions confirm the circumscribed nature of the lesions, covert pathology that is undetectable using current technologies might be present. Indeed, even when a more remote brain area has not itself been directly damaged, diaschisis may have occurred—this is a sudden loss or change of function in a portion of the brain connected to a distant damaged brain area (e.g., Campo et al. 2012). For example, studies in rats using immediate-early gene imaging as a marker of neuronal activity found that lesions in the anterior thalamic nuclei and hippocampus both produce marked retrosplenial cortex (RSC) dysfunction (Albasser et al. 2007, Jenkins et al. 2004). This finding suggests that the functional impact of hippocampal lesions could be exacerbated by distal dysfunctions in RSC. These lesions had little or no effect on RSC cell numbers (Jenkins et al. 2004, Poirier & Aggleton 2009), so that seemingly intact cytoarchitecture (that might appear normal on an MRI scan) was combined with a functional abnormality. In humans also, focal brain lesions have been found to disrupt network organization across the brain during fMRI scanning (Gratton et al. 2012, Hayes et al. 2012).

The lesion-deficit model encourages conclusions about the necessity of a brain area for a specific function. But no brain region is an island, and so at best this is an oversimplification. Thus, even when strenuous efforts are made to confirm the circumscribed nature of hippocampal lesions in the context of a deficit (including subsequently at postmortem, e.g., Zola-Morgan et al. 1986), this must always be caveated by the possibility that the function in question may not be solely the domain of the hippocampus.

WHY BOTHER TESTING PATIENTS?

Given the difficulties outlined above, one might well question the usefulness of testing patients at all. We firmly believe in the value of neuropsychological research; it has been transformative for the field of memory and continues to hold its own even in these days of functional neuroimaging (Rorden & Karnath 2004). In fact, our aim in highlighting the issues faced by patient studies is to make the point that examining or theorizing about preservation is no more flawed or inappropriate than is postulating about deficits. Importantly, neuropsychology is constantly striving to improve its methods (for more on this, see Rosenbaum et al. 2014). For instance, complementing neuropsychological studies with fMRI in healthy control subjects helps to establish convergent evidence (e.g., Hassabis et al. 2007a,b). Similarly, conducting fMRI scanning on the patients themselves (during tasks they are able to perform) is becoming more common, and this can provide clues about the potential functionality of remnant tissue (Maguire et al. 2010a,b; Mullally et al. 2012a). Moreover, detailed statistical and methodological reporting can overcome some of the concerns associated with null results (see sidebar Interpretation of Null Results). The interpretation of deficits arising after bilateral hippocampal lesions has also benefitted from meta-analyses and in-depth reviews (Kessels et al. 2001, Spiers et al. 2001, Squire 1992, Winocur & Moscovitch 2011), which have included some consideration of preservation, specifically in the domain of learning (Cohen 1984, Schacter & Graf 1986). As far as we are aware, however, there have been no reviews of preservation of function across multiple domains.

Therefore, after a brief overview of hippocampal anatomy and extant theoretical frameworks, in the subsequent sections we consider a range of cognitive functions with which the hippocampus has been associated, starting with two of the classics, navigation and autobiographical memory.

INTERPRETATION OF NULL RESULTS

Although it is not statistically possible to accept the null hypothesis, meaningful conclusions can still be made from null findings. Interpretation does, however, require further reporting of the data, including effects sizes and confidence intervals as well as the usual p-values (e.g., Aberson 2002). Although this is recommended in the most recent edition (sixth) of the *Publication Manual of the American Psychological Association* (Am. Psychol. Assoc. 2010), it is not yet common practice. Effect sizes provide a standardized measure of the extent of the difference between two means (e.g., Cohen's *d*) or the proportion of variance explained (e.g., eta-squared or r^2). If effect sizes are very small, then differences between groups are likely to be nonsignificant even with greater experimental power. Confidence intervals around means and effect sizes measure the deviation around these variables—small confidence intervals that largely overlap suggest high similarity between groups; large confidence intervals or smaller regions of overlap suggest possible differences given greater sensitivity and power. Thus, more detailed description of the results, including where possible the data for each patient and every control subject, can increase the interpretability of the statistics leading to a null result.

Naturally we refer to deficits, but our prime focus is on highlighting those functions that seem to be completely intact as well as instances where pockets of preservation have been observed within the context of an overarching impairment. Although not exhaustive, this survey reveals some unexpected abilities, new angles on extant beliefs, and surprising gaps in our knowledge.

HIPPOCAMPAL ANATOMY

The hippocampus is a brain structure thought to be common to all mammals (West 1990) and is located in the MTL of each hemisphere (**Figure 1**). The hippocampal formation consists of two laminae rolled up inside each other. One formation is termed the hippocampus proper or *cornu ammonis*; it is subdivided according to differences in cellular structure into subfields named CA1, CA2, CA3, and CA4. The other lamina is the dentate gyrus. The entorhinal cortex mediates connections to and from the hippocampus; there are also direct connections between hippocampus and subcortical regions via the fornix. In rodents, the hippocampus runs along a dorsal-ventral axis, corresponding to a posterior-anterior axis in humans. Different parts of this axis have distinct connections to other regions of the brain, suggesting potential functional differentiation between dorsal and ventral hippocampus—an idea that receives support from a range of empirical data (e.g., Fanselow & Dong 2010, Maguire et al. 2000, Moser & Moser 1998, Poppenk et al. 2013, Strange et al. 2014).

The hippocampus in humans is susceptible to a range of common pathologies including Alzheimer's disease, epilepsy, limbic encephalitis, and stroke. The typical etiologies that gave rise to the focal bilateral hippocampal damage (as far as can be determined with current techniques) in the patients we consider here are anoxia, ischemia, and some forms of limbic encephalitis (**Figure 2**).

THEORIES OF HIPPOCAMPAL FUNCTION

An in-depth description of theories of hippocampal function is beyond the scope of this review, and these theories are amply covered elsewhere (Eichenbaum & Cohen 2014, Konkel & Cohen 2009, Maguire & Mullally 2013, O'Keefe & Nadel 1978, Squire & Zola-Morgan 1991). Here we

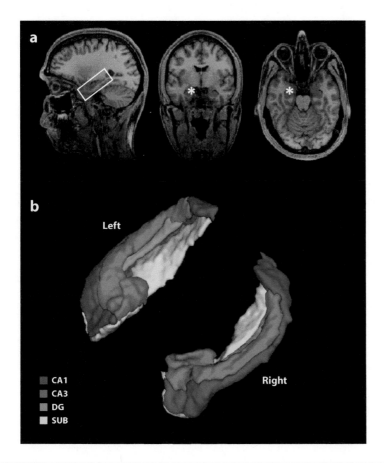

Figure 1

The anatomy of the human hippocampus. (*a*) The structural magnetic resonance imaging scan of a healthy individual in sagittal view (within the white box), coronal view, and axial view, where the left hippocampus is indicated with a white asterisk, and the right hippocampus is free to view. (*b*) A 3-D rendering of two hippocampi, with the subfields color-coded. Abbreviations: CA1, *cornu ammonis* subfield 1; CA3, *cornu ammonis* subfield 3; DG, dentate gyrus; SUB, subiculum.

briefly mention the main theories and their germane points, reserving further elaboration for the relevant sections below.

O'Keefe & Dostrovsky (1971) discovered that cells in the hippocampus encode the location of a rat in its environment. Each place cell fires when the rat enters the cell's preferred area (its place field) irrespective of where the rat is looking. These findings were formalized into the cognitive map theory (O'Keefe & Nadel 1978), which proposes that the hippocampus in rats and other mammals, including humans, provides a world-centered or allocentric spatial framework, as opposed to a framework where space is egocentric and represented relative to the observer him/herself. Allocentric spatial representations facilitate flexible navigation strategies as well as potentially provide a spatial scaffold upon which episodic/autobiographical memories can be built.

An alternative view of the relationship between spatial and episodic memory is offered by the relational theory, which argues that the primary function of the hippocampus is not spatial but should instead be thought of as the representation of associations between disparate elements (Cohen & Eichenbaum 1993, Eichenbaum 2004). Specifically, this theory posits the existence

Allocentric space: a world-centered spatial framework of the environment

Egocentric space: space is represented relative to the observer him/herself

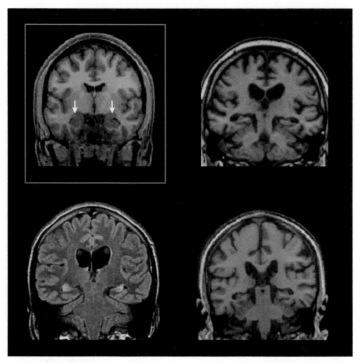

Figure 2

Examples of bilateral hippocampal damage in three patients. Within the upper left green box is a coronal section from a healthy brain, with the two hippocampi indicated by white arrows. The three other images show coronal sections from patients with damage to the two hippocampi.

of three elemental cognitive processes that are all mediated by the hippocampus—associative representation, sequential organization, and relational networking. According to this view, these fundamental properties can fully account for the spatial processing found within the hippocampus and are flexible enough to explain possible nonspatial hippocampal processes. Relational theory has parallels with other models, including the constructive episodic simulation hypothesis (Schacter & Addis 2007, Schacter et al. 2012), which suggests that the hippocampus and connected brain regions flexibly recombine elements of existing episodic memories to create new (e.g., future) scenarios, and another theory that emphasizes the hippocampal role in binding objects and contexts (Ranganath 2010).

By contrast, Hassabis & Maguire (2007, 2009; see also Maguire & Mullally 2013) have proposed that a primary function of the hippocampus is to support a process called scene construction. This is defined as the process of mentally generating and maintaining a complex and coherent scene. A scene is a spatially coherent representation of the world, small or large scale, within which an individual can potentially operate, for example, a scene of your local park or of your desktop. Scene construction necessitates the retrieval and integration of the relevant components of the scene from modality-specific cortex, which are then bound into a spatially coherent scene representation. Notably, this concept is flexible enough to account for both newly imagined scenes and retrieved episodic memories, as this core process is held to be involved in both. The authors argue that scene construction may also be critical for other functions, such as spatial navigation and planning for the future. Scene construction theory and the constructive episodic simulation hypothesis (Schacter

Scene:
a spatially coherent representation of the world, small or large scale, within which we can potentially operate

& Addis 2007, Schacter et al. 2012) are consistent with a large body of evidence suggesting that episodic memory is not simply a perfect record of past events, but instead should be considered more of a reconstructive process (Bartlett 1932, Conway & Pleydell-Pearce 2000, Schacter et al. 1998). Scene construction theory differs from the cognitive map theory in placing the creation and representation of scenes at the center of hippocampal processing, although space is important to both views.

As well as theoretical positions focusing on the nature of the information being processed by the hippocampus, some theories have considered the timescale of hippocampal involvement in memory. There is general agreement that episodic/autobiographical memories depend on the hippocampus during initial encoding (Scoville & Milner 1957). However, the role of the hippocampus in supporting such memories when they are more remote is contentious. The standard model of consolidation argues that memories (semantic and autobiographical) become less dependent on the hippocampus, eventually eschewing the need for its involvement altogether during retrieval (Marr 1971, Squire 1992, Squire & Wixted 2011, Teyler & DiScenna 1985). Alternative theories, in particular the multiple trace theory (and also the scene construction theory), propose instead that the hippocampus is necessary for retrieving vivid, contextually rich, and detailed autobiographical memories in perpetuity (Nadel & Moscovitch 1997, Winocur & Moscovitch 2011), whereas semantic information is consolidated over time such that hippocampal involvement is no longer necessary for retrieval.

The array of views outlined above demonstrates that, although a great deal is known about the hippocampus, there is still not wide agreement on the information it represents, the processes it performs, and the timescale of its involvement. By collating here instances of preserved function in the context of hippocampal damage, we hope to contribute to a more fully rounded view of the hippocampus, but also to examine whether consideration of preservation can help to reconcile, or adjudicate between, these theoretical views of hippocampal function.

NAVIGATION

Animal work points to a key role for the hippocampus in allocentric spatial navigation (O'Keefe & Dostrovsky 1971, O'Keefe & Nadel 1978). Studies in humans also support the idea of a spatial function for the hippocampus. For instance, increased gray matter volume in the posterior hippocampus is observed in individuals who have to learn very large and complex spatial layouts (Maguire et al. 2000, Woollett & Maguire 2011). During fMRI scanning, the hippocampus is engaged when subjects are mentally or virtually navigating (Spiers & Maguire 2006), and intracranial recording from electrodes implanted in the hippocampi of patients being considered for epilepsy surgery show navigation-related responses (Ekstrom et al. 2003).

Neuropsychological studies also appear to confirm the necessity of the hippocampus for spatial memory and navigation. Patients with MTL lesions have difficulty learning visual (Milner 1965), tactile (Corkin 1965), and in situ (Astur et al. 2002) mazes. The latter has also been found following focal hippocampi damage (Goodrich-Hunsaker et al. 2010). As in the rat literature, the spatial impairments are typically interpreted as being allocentric in nature (Holdstock et al. 2000).

Although patient studies have also confirmed that hippocampal damage prevents the spatial learning of new environments (Maguire et al. 2006, Rosenbaum et al. 2000, Teng & Squire 1999), evidence suggests the hippocampus is not essential for the recall of remotely learned spatial memories. Patient EP (who had extensive damage to his medial and anterior temporal lobes), although unable to learn new environments, had preserved ability to navigate in an environment he had learned many years prior to his illness (Teng & Squire 1999). He was able to describe routes between his home and local places, between different local locations, and between locations when some streets were blocked, and he was able to determine the direction (by pointing) to particular landmarks when in a specific location. Another patient, KC (who also had widespread brain damage including the hippocampi), demonstrated a similar pattern of results (Rosenbaum et al. 2000). These two cases speak against the idea of the hippocampus being necessary for allocentric spatial tasks (as proposed by the cognitive mapping theory) and, moreover, imply that remote spatial memories are not hippocampal dependent (discordant with the multiple trace and scene construction theories).

However, it has been argued that the environments that EP and KC recalled with such accuracy had highly regular, predictable, grid-pattern layouts that may have been overlearned and therefore did not require true allocentric spatial processing (Spiers & Maguire 2007). Interesting in itself is the fact that some spatial layouts could lend themselves, over time and with extensive experience, to becoming more akin to semantic information and so not require the hippocampus for retrieval. The data from EP and KC therefore highlight that, just as with memory in general, spatial memory may also fractionate along hippocampal-dependent (allocentric) and non-hippocampal-dependent (semantic) lines. But what aspect of navigation is actually impaired in the context of focal hippocampal damage, and is it correct to let the cognitive mapping theory off the hook, so to speak, by interpreting EP and KC's preservation as akin to preserved semantic knowledge?

Another patient has extended our understanding further. TT was a licensed London taxi driver of long standing who suffered primary damage to his hippocampi (Maguire et al. 2006). TT, as with other patients with hippocampal damage, could not learn new environments. But how accurate was his knowledge of and navigation in London, a city noted for its chaotic, unpredictable, and complex layout? Compared to matched London taxi driver controls, TT could recognize and describe in detail London landmarks, and he had accurate representations of their spatial relationships and the absolute distances between them. Furthermore, he could place landmarks on a map of London and could point to the location of landmarks with high accuracy. TT could also navigate through (virtual reality) London using main artery or "A" roads. Thus, with more focal hippocampal damage and a more complex environment than EP and KC, patient TT also showed remarkably preserved allocentric spatial ability. It is therefore incorrect to say, as is often the case in the literature, that the hippocampus is essential for navigation in its entirety. These three cases show that characterizing hippocampal function in terms of allocentricity alone may not be adequate. Moreover, these findings also suggest that representations of basic relationships between landmarks, and binding or combining of information, can occur without the hippocampus at least for material learned prior to the lesions being sustained (Eichenbaum & Cohen 2014, Konkel & Cohen 2009).

Interestingly, TT became lost when navigation depended on the complex network of London's smaller roads (Maguire et al. 2006). This is unlikely to be explained by a lack of detailed knowledge of London, which TT undoubtedly possessed. Instead, TT may not have been able to visualize in advance where he needed to turn off the A roads onto the smaller roads. Indeed, TT was also significantly impaired at imagining scenes (Hassabis et al. 2007b). The data from TT also show that the hippocampus remains necessary for spatial navigation even in environments learned long ago, but in a specific way that might involve visualizing scenes of key points in the environment.

AUTOBIOGRAPHICAL MEMORY, SEMANTIC MEMORY, AND TIME

Although navigation is a function shared across species, research into the human hippocampi has also focused on memory processes that are not easily accessible in nonhumans. In particular, investigators have examined episodic or autobiographical memory, which concerns memories of our personal past experiences, and semantic memory, which refers to general knowledge (see Tulving 1972, 2002). Patients with focal bilateral hippocampal damage are consistently reported to be unable to form lasting memories of new autobiographical events, and this is widely accepted by all theoretical models of hippocampal function. There is less agreement about whether patients can acquire new semantic information (Mishkin et al. 1998, Squire & Zola 1998, Tulving & Markowitsch 1998). Impairments in both recall and recognition for news events, famous faces, and whether famous individuals were living or dead have been found in patients with selective hippocampal damage (e.g., Reed & Squire 1998). By contrast, patient YR could recognize famous people and events that came to prominence after her hippocampal damage and could categorize famous people regarding the nature of their fame. She was impaired, however, at categorizing events and dating names and events (Holdstock et al. 2002). The status of semantic learning post hippocampal lesion is therefore not clear.

By contrast, semantic memory for information learned prelesion is preserved (e.g., Andelman et al. 2010, Lee et al. 2005b, Winocur & Moscovitch 2011), and again most theoretical positions accept that semantic information can be retrieved without the hippocampus. However, the question of whether the hippocampus is required for recalling remote autobiographical memories is hotly debated. Two patterns emerge from the literature. Some patients suffer complete loss of autobiographical memories across all time points—recent and remote (e.g., Cipolotti et al. 2001, Maguire et al. 2006, Viskontas et al. 2000). Others experience a temporal gradient, typically with recent memories lost and then preserved autobiographical memories that are more remote (e.g., Squire & Zola 1998). How remote the memories need to be before they are preserved is not clearcut, with some patients reported to have intact autobiographical memories stretching back decades (Bayley et al. 2003, Kapur & Brooks 1999, Kirwan et al. 2008). In reviewing the neuropsychological literature, Winocur & Moscovitch (2011) estimate that there is equal support across cases reported in the literature for hippocampal damage to be associated with complete loss of autobiographical memories on the one hand and preservation of more remote memories on the other.

Several possible reasons for these differing patterns have been proposed. For example, it is likely that many of our autobiographical memories become less detailed and more like semantic memories over time (so-called semanticization). This could explain the apparent preservation of remote autobiographical memory in some patients (Winocur & Moscovitch 2011). It could also be the case that those patients with more extensive loss of remote autobiographical memories had more widespread and covert damage (e.g., Reed & Squire 1998). However, neither of these explanations is adequate to account for the contrary evidence. Autobiographical memory and consolidation are of central importance to memory neuroscience because they speak fundamentally to the type of information the hippocampus represents and, by inference, the timescale of its involvement and the processes involved. Yet elucidation of the neuropsychology seems deadlocked.

The fMRI studies of healthy participants have more often supported the view that the hippocampus is necessary for retrieving vivid autobiographical memories in perpetuity (Gilboa et al. 2004, Maguire et al. 2001, Maguire & Frith 2003, Ryan et al. 2001). Of course, fMRI shows brain areas that are involved in, but not whether they are necessary for, a task. Recently, Bonnici et al. (2012) used a different type of method to analyze fMRI data acquired during autobiographical memory recall. Multivoxel pattern analysis (MVPA) can be used to establish whether information about a memory is represented in the pattern of fMRI activity across voxels in the hippocampus (Chadwick et al. 2012). Bonnici et al. (2012) found that information about both recent (two-week-old) and remote (ten-year-old) autobiographical memories (matched across factors such as vividness and detail) was represented in the anterior hippocampus (MVPA classification accuracies were significantly above chance for the two types of memories and were not significantly different from each other). On the other hand, in the posterior hippocampus (and ventromedial prefrontal cortex), classification accuracies were significantly higher for remote memories than recent memories. Further examination revealed that the posterior hippocampal findings were specific to subregion CA3 and the dentate gyrus (Bonnici et al. 2013).

These results suggest that some kind of change has indeed taken place between recent and remote autobiographical memories, and this is reflected not only in a change in hippocampal-cortical involvement, but also within the hippocampus itself—which is not predicted by any theory. The anterior hippocampus may perform a function that is common to both recent and remote memories (perhaps scene construction; Zeidman et al. 2014), whereas remote memories require more of whatever process is going on in the posterior hippocampus—perhaps the reinstatement of the spatial context (Woollett & Maguire 2011). More generally, these data indicate that the mixed pattern of preserved or impaired remote autobiographical memory observed within the neuropsychological literature may depend on the location and extent of the damage within the hippocampus itself.

The precise role of the hippocampus in autobiographical memory is crucial to resolve, and going forward we believe that using fMRI with patients with hippocampal damage could reveal information about the functionality of remaining hippocampal tissue and its location, as can techniques such as MVPA. What are urgently needed are longitudinal fMRI studies that follow autobiographical memory representations over long time periods (i.e., years) to examine if and how memory traces change over time and concomitant neural responses. These are very challenging fMRI studies to conduct, however, and there are none that we are aware of in the literature to date.

Implicit in autobiographical memory is the notion of time—memories can be recent or from far back in time, and we can also project ourselves forward in time (so-called mental time travel) (Tulving 1972, 2002). Neurons that appear to respond to time have been found in the rodent hippocampus (MacDonald et al. 2011), although an fMRI study in humans found that frontal and parietal cortices, but not the hippocampus, supported mental time travel (Nyberg et al. 2010). Time, however, can be construed in different ways, and an in-depth discussion of time is beyond the scope of this article (for reviews, see Eichenbaum 2014, Hassabis & Maguire 2007). However, it is interesting to consider some instances of preserved time-related processing.

We know, for example, that patients with bilateral hippocampal damage can do basic tasks, such as arrange pictures into a sequence to make a logical story, and are able to recombine elements in narratives to ensure that a logical story unfolds (Mullally & Maguire 2014). Although patients have lost the ability to recall their past (and imagine the future; see Imagination section), they still understand the concept of time (Craver et al. 2014b). For example, patient KC, who has widespread damage that includes the hippocampi bilaterally, performed comparably to control participants in being willing to trade a smaller, sooner reward for a larger, delayed reward (temporal discounting; Kwan et al. 2012). If his concept of time was impaired, we would expect him to always choose the reward in the present regardless of the value of a future reward. Furthermore, KC made decisions that would affect future rewards in the same way as control participants made decisions, demonstrating that although he could not imagine future experiences, he could, on some level, still travel in time (Craver et al. 2014a).

EMOTION AND THEORY OF MIND

Even though patients with bilateral hippocampal damage cannot form new autobiographical memories, they can still be affected emotionally by events over time. Although fear (Bechara et al. 1995) and eyeblink (Gabrieli et al. 1995) conditioning were unaffected following bilateral hippocampal lesions, explicit memory for the conditioning was lost. Additionally, after viewing emotional film clips (either happy or sad), patients' mood remained inducted even though they could not remember details of the film (Feinstein et al. 2010). Further, patients could produce as many emotional memories from before their lesion (the majority of which were positive) as could controls, and when memories were rated on emotional intensity by independent raters, ratings were equal to those of controls (Buchanan et al. 2005). On the other hand, when rated for emotional intensity by the patients themselves, memories were rated as less intense.

Yet, although patients with hippocampal damage seem to have retained emotional responses (i.e., the emotion generated when an event is happening), their anxiety response is impaired. For example, in response to a standardized stress test (public speaking), patients showed increased heart rate and affective responses, as did control participants, but no cortisol response—cortisol has been associated with anxiety (Buchanan et al. 2009). Additionally, in a virtual foraging environment, patients were not affected by changes in threat level, and they spent less time in the "safe place" and behaved less cautiously over time compared to controls despite explicit knowledge of the threat level (Bach et al. 2014). Thus, patients show reduced approach-avoidance behavior when there is a potential threat (i.e., anxiety, not fear). This differentiation in patients accords with findings described in the animal literature, suggesting a distinction between the brain circuitry involved in fear, which is thought to be processed by the amygdala, and anxiety, which is thought to be mediated by the hippocampus (Gray & McNaughton 2003, McHugh et al. 2004). Another study suggests that even though patients with hippocampal damage can experience emotions, their empathy—the ability to share and understand the feelings of others—is reduced. Questionnaire measures (completed by patients and family members) suggested lower trait empathy, and patients were unaffected by empathy inductions via auditory recording and written notes (Beadle et al. 2013).

The ability to empathize would seem to be related to theory of mind, which allows an individual to infer the mental states of others. Theory of mind has been reported as intact following hippocampal damage. Patient KC (and a second similar patient, ML), who had widespread damage that included the hippocampi bilaterally, performed at the same level as controls on a range of theory-of-mind tasks (Rosenbaum et al. 2007). This finding is interesting to consider in the light of the report of reduced empathy following hippocampal lesions (Beadle et al. 2013). Being able to logically understand what someone else knows, including their emotional state (as in theory of mind), may be different from fully experiencing someone else's emotional state (as in empathy). Support for this difference comes from a study examining counterfactual (CF) thinking, where patients with focal bilateral hippocampal pathology showed intact high-level causal inference, which allowed them to logically infer the thoughts and emotional state of a protagonist in an emotional event without needing to simulate or experience the event or emotions (Mullally & Maguire 2014). In a way, this distinction could be considered similar to that between semantic and episodic memory. It is also interesting to note that when healthy participants were presented with a situation depicting another individual in difficulty, imagining themselves helping the person (episodic simulation) or recalling an event from their past where they helped another (episodic memory) led to increased prosocial intentions (Gaesser & Schacter 2014). That is, engaging elements of episodic processing to help fully experience the event rather than just observing it boosted participants' empathy, thus suggesting a link between episodic memory and empathy.

Overall, therefore, basic emotional processing and the ability to feel emotions "in the moment" as well as to logically infer in factual terms the thoughts and feelings of others appear to be preserved in patients with bilateral hippocampal damage. What these patients cannot seem to do is imagine another person's situation in order to fully experience that person's emotions, which may not be a deficit in emotion per se, but rather an impairment of constructing another's situation.

Empathy: the ability to share and understand the feelings of others

Theory of mind: the ability to infer the mental states of others

RECOGNITION MEMORY

The recall or reexperiencing of autobiographical memories is often contrasted with recognition memory, which is the ability to recognize previously encountered events, objects, or people. It is typically subdivided into two component processes: recollection and familiarity, often referred to as remembering and knowing, respectively. Recollection is the retrieval of contextual details associated with the previously experienced event. By contrast, familiarity is the feeling that the event was previously experienced, but without recollection of the associated details or context (for reviews, see Gardiner & Parkin 1990, Tulving & Thomson 1973, Yonelinas 2002).

The role of the hippocampus in recognition memory is hotly debated. Some researchers suggest that all recognition memory (with the exception of faces; see below) requires the hippocampus (e.g., Smith et al. 2014a). Others believe that recollection is dependent on the hippocampus, but familiarity is not (Brown & Aggleton 2001, Eichenbaum et al. 2007). Another view is that hippocampal involvement is stimulus dependent, being required for recognition of across-domain pairs of items (e.g., a picture and a sound) but not single items or within-domain (e.g., picture-picture) pairs (e.g., Mayes et al. 2007).

This is an entrenched debate, and as with autobiographical memory, there is neuropsychological evidence from patients with focal hippocampal damage to support each perspective. We cannot do justice to this substantial literature in our limited space here, and others have written eloquently and at length about it elsewhere (Brown & Aggleton 2001, Eichenbaum et al. 2007, Yonelinas 2002). Therefore we limit ourselves to making just a few observations.

One consistent result is that of preserved face recognition (Aggleton & Shaw 1996, Bird & Burgess 2008, Mayes et al. 2004, Smith et al. 2014a), although this may only be at short delays (Smith et al. 2014a). In an exceptionally thorough examination of recognition memory across different types of stimuli (including words, faces, buildings, and objects), patient YR's forced choice, Yes/No, and intra-item associations, as well as associations between items of the same category, were preserved (Mayes et al. 2004). YR was impaired only on recognition tests for associations between items of different kinds (e.g., words and faces), a finding that has been replicated (e.g., Holdstock et al. 2005, Konkel et al. 2008).

The consistent finding of preserved face recognition may seem at odds with YR's impaired recognition of associations across domains. However, a face—in contrast to other complex stimuli—is thought to be processed as a whole entity and not as multiple component parts (e.g., Tsao & Livingstone 2008). An interesting contrast to faces is that of scenes. Scene stimuli are complex stimuli in that they are made up of multiple features. Unlike faces, however, scenes are thought to be processed by combining each individual feature. Notably, despite preserved ability to recognize faces, patients with focal hippocampal damage are typically impaired at recognizing scenes (Taylor et al. 2007).

Thus, preserved recognition memory following hippocampal damage may occur for two reasons: first, if a familiarity process can be used and not a recollective one (Eichenbaum et al. 2007); second, provided the internal representation of a spatially coherent scene/context is not required (Lee et al. 2012, Maguire & Mullally 2013, Zeidman et al. 2014).

WORKING MEMORY

When performing a number of the above tasks, working memory may be engaged. Working memory is the transient holding online of information; for example, maintaining stimuli in mind to decide upon whether they are old or new at short delays. Working memory has traditionally been regarded as immune from hippocampal damage. Indeed, standard tests of working memory (e.g., digit span) are preserved following such damage (e.g., Andelman et al. 2010, Goodrich-Hunsaker & Hopkins 2009, Hopkins et al. 2004, Victor & Agamanolis 1990, Warren et al. 2012).

Experimental tests of working memory also indicate preservation. The eye movements of patients with hippocampal damage had patterns similar to those of control participants when shown a manipulated scene soon after the original, a finding that suggests spared working memory (Ryan et al. 2000, Ryan & Cohen 2004). Further, during the spatial exploration of masked scenes (the scene could be seen only through a moveable window), patients with hippocampal damage were able to successfully relocate to their original start location from the goal object within each trial (Yee et al. 2014). Additionally, working memory in patients has been shown to be preserved for single objects or single locations (Olson et al. 2006a,b).

However, other investigations suggest that working memory might not be completely hippocampal independent (e.g., Ranganath & Blumenfeld 2005, Yonelinas 2013). Although working memory is preserved for single items, more complex associations that require combining elements together led to impaired working memory, for object-location (Olson et al. 2006a,b), face-scene, and object-scene (Hannula et al. 2006, 2015) relations as well as for topographical stimuli (Hartley et al. 2007). Moreover, magnetoencephalography work suggests increased hippocampal theta synchronicity with occipital and temporal regions during working memory maintenance of scenes (Cashdollar et al. 2009).

Thus, working memory seems to be preserved following hippocampal damage for single items and locations. However, impairments are reported when more complex stimuli, typically involving scenes, are used.

VERBAL MEMORY

Although debates rage about hippocampal contributions to some of the memory types outlined above, one form of memory is invariably compromised by bilateral hippocampal lesions: verbal memory. Patients cannot recall lists of single words (Buchanan et al. 2005), word-pair associates (Cipolotti et al. 2006), and verbal narratives (Barense et al. 2007). Why might this be the case, given that single words do not require any associative binding, and none of this verbal material appears to involve allocentric processing, object-context binding, or the internal construction of scenes?

Standardized verbal memory tests (e.g., the Warrington Word Recognition Memory Test, the Wechsler Memory Scale word-pair associates and logical memory subtests, and the Rey Auditory Verbal Learning Test) all use concrete words that represent specific imaginable items (Paivio 1969). One speculation offered by Maguire & Mullally (2013) is that people may automatically use imagery, such as scenes, during encoding and retrieval of concrete verbal material. For instance, we might visualize the scene within which a story is unfolding, or we might place the items described in word pairs in a simple scene together. Despite the rise and fall of imagery-based memory theories across the decades (Paivio 1969), evidence suggests that visual imagery not only boosts pair-associate recall in healthy participants but also enables patients with left temporal lobectomies to partially compensate for their verbal memory deficits (Jones 1974). If verbal memory tasks routinely benefit from the use of imagery-based mnemonic strategies, and if hippocampal amnesic patients have difficulty imagining scenes (Hassabis et al. 2007b), they would be disadvantaged on such tasks. This, then, gives rise to the clear prediction that the patients should be less impaired when learning and recalling abstract words.

Abstract words typically represent ideas and concepts and, as such, they are much less imageable. From the literature, it is surprisingly difficult to ascertain whether memory for abstract words is preserved following focal bilateral hippocampal damage, as most tests and studies have used concrete, imageable words. In contrast, in patients who had unilateral temporal lobectomies for the relief of intractable epilepsy, abstract words have been examined. Patients with right temporal lobectomy were found to have impaired memory for concrete word pairs but preserved memory for abstract word pairs in comparison with controls (Jones-Gotman & Milner 1978; see also Jones-Gotman 1979). Moreover, whereas greater hippocampal lesion extent was associated with a bigger drop in performance on concrete word pairs, lesion size had no effect on abstract word-pair performance.

Further work suggests that imageability may be key to understanding this pattern of preservation and impairment (Jones-Gotman 1979). Patients and control participants were presented with a list of mixed concrete and abstract words. They were asked to visualize some words and to pronounce others; after a delay, they had to recall the word list. Patients with right temporal lobectomy performed comparably to control participants for both concrete and abstract words when the words were previously pronounced, but their performance was inferior on both abstract and concrete words when the words were previously visualized. A greater extent of hippocampal lesion was associated with impaired performance on visualized concrete words but had no relationship with the other conditions. Imageability of words therefore seems to be important to understanding the relationship between words and the hippocampus. In further support of this theory, Gold et al. (2006) and Kirwan et al. (2010) found that patients with bilateral hippocampal damage were impaired at both word recognition and recall with mixed concrete and abstract words. However, for the abstract words these investigators explicitly required the patients to learn by imagining an indoor or outdoor scene, which likely explains their impairment, given that patients with hippocampal damage are unable to imagine scenes (Andelman et al. 2010, Hassabis et al. 2007b, Mullally et al. 2012a, Race et al. 2011, Rosenbaum et al. 2009).

It could be that abstract words simply require greater effort and memory search to develop a representational image (Kieras 1978) but thereafter are processed like concrete words. If this is the case, then a significant overlap should exist in the brain networks supporting the processing of concrete and abstract words in neuroimaging studies of healthy participants. However, extant data show differences in the brain networks for processing abstract and concrete words (e.g., Binder et al. 2005, Wang et al. 2013).

The majority of hippocampal theories have a visuospatial bias (Bird et al. 2012, Maguire & Mullally 2013, Moscovitch et al. 2006, O'Keefe & Nadel 1978, Ranganath 2010, Schacter & Addis 2009). Accounting for verbal memory deficits is therefore challenging. If, however, there is a distinction between abstract and concrete memoranda, and processing of the former is preserved following bilateral hippocampal lesions, this would have important implications for understanding and conceptualizing hippocampal processing. It is therefore surprising that abstract verbal material has featured so little across the decades of research involving patients with bilateral hippocampal damage. This gap in our knowledge clearly needs to be addressed.

LEARNING

As observed previously, the acquisition of new episodic information, such as autobiographical events, is compromised in the context of bilateral hippocampal damage, whereas reports are mixed concerning the preservation of semantic learning. Patients who sustained their bilateral hippocampal damage very early in life display instances of preserved learning and other interesting features (see sidebar Developmental Amnesia). However, our main focus here is in asking whether patients whose bilateral hippocampal damage occurred in adulthood can learn and retain any kind of new information. There is an extensive literature on preserved priming and implicit learning in amnesia that we cannot cover here, and so we refer the reader to a recent review (Reber

DEVELOPMENTAL AMNESIA

Developmental amnesia (DA) occurs following a hypoxic/ischemic incident perinatally or in early childhood that results in bilateral hippocampal pathology (Gadian et al. 2000; Vargha-Khadem et al. 1997, 2003). A distinguishing feature of DA compared to hippocampal damage sustained in adulthood is that the content of semantic memory and world knowledge, which is rich and age appropriate, has been learned after the onset of hippocampal pathology. This contrasts with the autobiographical memory of those with DA, which is impaired. This memory pattern may indicate that semantic learning is hippocampal independent, although reorganization of the developing brain in the presence of hippocampal damage could be a contributing factor. Also in contrast to adult patients (e.g., Hassabis et al. 2007b), individuals with DA appear to have preserved ability to imagine fictitious and future scenes (Cooper et al. 2011, Hurley et al. 2011, Maguire et al. 2010b). However, this seems to rely on their intact semantic and world knowledge—individuals with DA describe it as an effortful process and one where they are unable to actually visualize the scenes in their mind's eye. Moreover, unlike control participants, the remnant hippocampal tissue in well-characterized DA patient Jon was not significantly activated while he constructed scenes during fMRI (Mullally et al. 2014).

2013). We limit this section to reflections on other aspects of preserved learning that have not received such extensive coverage.

Patient HM displayed some implicit learning; for example, his motor skills improved on a tapping task and two tracking tasks (where a drum rotated and he was required to keep contact with a specified track with just one hand or with both hands simultaneously), even though he had no memory of previously performing the tasks (Corkin 1968). Implicit learning has also been shown for digit, spatial location, word, and pseudo-word sequences (e.g., Gagnon et al. 2004) and for procedural learning, including geometric figure tracing, weaving, and pouring liquid into multiple containers from a height (Cavaco et al. 2004). Long-lasting priming (up to seven days) involving verbal material (e.g., word stem completion and word pairs) and object naming has also been reported in patients (Schacter et al. 1993, Tulving & Schacter 1990). By contrast, mixed results have been reported for visuospatial search, in which participants had to locate a rotated "T" within a display of rotated "L" distractors. Results originally suggested that patients showed no priming (Chun & Phelps 1999), but a later study suggested otherwise (Manns & Squire 2001). Thus, priming over a more complex scene display may be reduced in comparison with priming for single items.

Some elements of probabilistic learning are also preserved in patients with bilateral hippocampal damage. This preservation concerns tasks in which the associations between stimuli and responses are probabilistic; thus, information from a single trial is not reliable, nor is it as relevant as information accrued across many trials. During initial learning trials, learning rates have been reported as equal between patients and controls (Knowlton et al. 1996, Reber et al. 1996). However, after continuous training (e.g., more than 50 learning trials), controls began to outperform patients (Knowlton et al. 1994), possibly because controls begin to use more complex strategies to learn outcomes (Meeter et al. 2006). However, although initial learning could take place, when outcome probabilities were changed, patients did not change their responses, suggesting an impairment in flexibly using the acquired knowledge (Shohamy et al. 2008).

By contrast, another study found that probabilistic learning in patients was impaired across the board (Hopkins et al. 2004). In this study, while patients' scores remained at approximately the same level as previously reported, control participants' scores increased to much higher levels. Further, when a similar paradigm—but deterministic learning and configural (i.e., combined) elements—was used, patients were impaired compared to control participants (Kumaran et al. 2007). Two patients in this latter study showed better learning than the other patients, suggesting that they had some ability to combine information; however, on debriefing the patients indicated that although they had formed associations between outcomes and individual combined patterns, they could not relate the patterns to each other. Thus, it seems that even when some basic elements of associative learning are retained, the ability to integrate and use this information may be lost in the context of hippocampal damage.

Another type of learning, collaborative learning or learning within a common ground, has been found to be intact following bilateral hippocampal lesions (Duff et al. 2006). Over time, patients needed to use fewer words to generate labels for abstract objects when describing them to a known partner. Further, this label knowledge was retained at six months. However, the patients could not remember the objects themselves—although the shortened labels created in common ground were retained, the objects needed to be present for the patients to describe them (Rubin et al. 2011).

In another examination of associative learning, patients with damage to the hippocampus and wider MTL learned (and retained at one week) arbitrary associations via fast mapping despite impairment on a matched standard association task (Merhav et al. 2014, Sharon et al. 2011). Fast mapping is the process by which children rapidly acquire new words (Carey & Bartlett 1978) and involves actively discovering associations instead of deliberate learning. However, two other studies failed to find preserved learning following fast mapping (Smith et al. 2014b, Warren & Duff 2014). The reasons for this disparity are not clear, and more work on fast mapping is required to better understand the parameters within which such learning might be possible.

In summary, patients with bilateral hippocampal damage are able to form arbitrary associations, particularly when learning is implicit. Yet patients typically do not remember how or where the information was obtained, nor can they flexibly use the acquired information. The knowledge therefore seems to lack a backdrop or a context, and a time or place—a theme that runs through several hippocampal theories (Buzsaki & Moser 2013, Eichenbaum & Cohen 2014, Maguire & Mullally 2013).

VISUAL PERCEPTION

The hippocampus receives a large number of inputs from multiple sensory modalities and in particular from vision (Felleman & Van Essen 1991). It may be that preserved or impaired cognitive functions could in fact arise from a basic processing level, namely that of visual perception. Traditionally, visual perception has been reported as preserved following hippocampal damage (Scoville & Milner 1957; see also Lee et al. 2005b, Spiers et al. 2001). Moreover, a series of studies suggests that focal bilateral hippocampal damage predominantly leaves visual discrimination abilities intact for material such as faces, single objects, abstract art, and colors. There is one exception: Patients could not discriminate between scenes (Graham et al. 2006; Lee et al. 2005a,b).

Hippocampal engagement during the perception and discrimination of scenes has been shown in fMRI studies of healthy participants (Barense et al. 2010, Lee et al. 2008, Mundy et al. 2012). Zeidman et al. (2014) recently investigated the hippocampal response to visually perceiving scenes, constructing scenes in the imagination, and maintaining scenes in working memory. They found extensive hippocampal activation for perceiving scenes and a circumscribed area of anterior medial hippocampus common to scene perception and scene construction (**Figure 3**). Hippocampal activity was significantly lower for maintaining scenes in working memory. Further evidence from patients and from fMRI in healthy participants suggests that the hippocampus is engaged in

Fast mapping: the process by which children rapidly acquire new words, whereby new associations are discovered and not deliberately learned

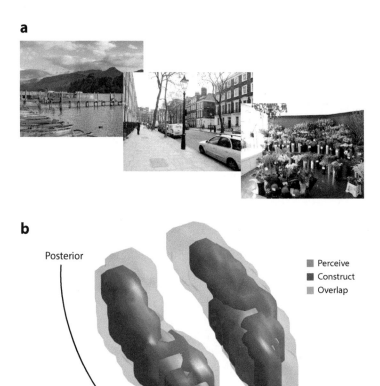

a

b

Posterior

Anterior   Right

Left

- Perceive
- Construct
- Overlap

Figure 3

Scene processing and the hippocampus. (*a*) Examples of scenes used in the scene-viewing condition of Zeidman et al.'s (2014) functional magnetic resonance imaging study. (*b*) A schematic of the two hippocampi from that study indicating activity associated with viewing scenes and constructing scenes in the mind's eye, and an area in anterior medial hippocampus of maximal overlap in the activity associated with these two conditions.

perception when discriminating strength-based perception (the global entity) but not state-based perception (local visual features; Aly et al. 2013), highlighting region CA1 in particular (Elfman et al. 2014).

However, patients have also been reported to have preserved visual perception and stimulus discrimination regardless of the stimuli used (Kim et al. 2011, Shrager et al. 2006). These authors suggest that impairments in visual perception observed elsewhere are in fact due to discrimination ability not improving over time as in control participants, overloading of working memory, or long-term memory-encoding deficits (Kim et al. 2011, Knutson et al. 2012). Zeidman et al. (2014) recently described how differences across the patient scene perception literature could be reconciled. They propose that whether scene perception is preserved or impaired in patients with hippocampal lesions may depend on whether a task requires an internal model of a spatially coherent scene to be constructed. We elaborate further on this idea below.

IMAGINATION

When, in 1992, HM was asked what he believed he would do tomorrow, he replied, "Whatever is beneficial" and appeared to have "no database to consult when asked what he would do the next day, week, or in years to come" (S. Corkin, personal communication; cited in de Vito & Della Sala 2011). Similar anecdotal evidence of problems in imagining the future was reported in patient KC (Rosenbaum et al. 2005, Tulving 1985; see also patient DB in Klein et al. 2002). Hassabis et al. (2007b) formally tested a group of patients with more focal bilateral hippocampal pathology and found they were unable to imagine personal future scenarios and fictitious scenes. They reported that their attempted scenes were spatially fragmented. Providing the scene elements to the patients did not improve their performance. Subsequently, this scene construction deficit was replicated across different laboratories and in different sets of patients with hippocampal damage (Andelman et al. 2010, Mullally et al. 2012b, Race et al. 2011, Rosenbaum et al. 2009), with the exception of one study in which scene construction ability was reported to be preserved (Squire et al. 2010). It is notable that the patients in this latter study did not exhibit pervasive autobiographical memory loss (see also Kirwan et al. 2008). As such, this finding in fact provides further support for the scene construction theory, which posits that if patients have intact autobiographical memory, then they should also have preserved scene construction ability, because the former depends on the latter (Maguire & Mullally 2013; see also Maguire & Hassabis 2011 and Mullally et al. 2012a). Hippocampal engagement during scene construction/simulation tasks has been confirmed in fMRI studies of healthy participants (Addis et al. 2007, Hassabis et al. 2007a). Interestingly, Hassabis et al. (2007b) found that one patient with bilateral hippocampal damage could construct scenes, and during fMRI this was associated with significant activation of the remnant tissue of his right hippocampus (Mullally et al. 2012a).

Although the inability to imagine fictitious or future scenes is striking, it is equally informative to consider related preservations. Patients with hippocampal damage were able to imagine single isolated objects and could list relevant associated items; they simply could not visualize them in a coherent scene (Hassabis et al. 2007b, Mullally et al. 2012a). Patients tested by Mullally et al. (2012b) and Race et al. (2013) could richly describe pictures of scenes that were put in front of them, which in the latter study included forming detailed narrative descriptions of scene images, suggesting that basic scene perception was intact. This seems at odds with the findings of impaired scene perception described in the previous section.

Further clues about the role of the hippocampus in scene processing come from the study of boundary extension (BE) (Intraub & Richardson 1989). BE is a cognitive phenomenon whereby people erroneously remember seeing more of a scene than was present in the sensory input; it occurs because when we view a scene, we implicitly extrapolate beyond the borders to form an extended representation of that scene. In the absence of the original visual input, this extended scene is remembered instead of the original input, causing a memory error. BE is a robust and consistent effect and, of note, only occurs in relation to scenes and not single isolated objects (Gottesman & Intraub 2002), a dissociation that mirrors the imagination dichotomy observed in patients with hippocampal damage (Hassabis et al. 2007b).

Mullally et al. (2012b) found that patients with focal bilateral hippocampal damage had significantly attenuated BE. They did not extrapolate as much as controls beyond the view in scenes they were shown, and this paradoxically led to significantly better memory for the scenes compared to the control participants (for other examples of paradoxical facilitation following brain lesions, see Kapur 2011). BE depends on the ability to imagine beyond the view in a scene, and having lost this ability, the patients were then less susceptible to the BE effect. An fMRI study of healthy participants confirmed the engagement of the hippocampus during BE (Chadwick et al. 2013).

Mullally et al. (2012b) showed patients a picture of a scene and asked them to imagine what might be beyond the view. Although patients could generate as many context-appropriate details as control participants and could associate them with each other and the context, they made significantly fewer spatial references and were unable to visualize the extended scenes in their mind's eye.

Kim et al. (2015) recently tested most of the same patients who were examined by Squire et al. (2010) and have reported that these patients showed normal BE, thus disputing the idea that the hippocampus is required for scene construction. They also questioned the degree of hippocampal volume loss reported in Mullally et al.'s (2012b) patients. In fact, Kim et al. (2015) made a factual error on this latter point. They incorrectly claimed that two of Mullally et al.'s (2012b) patients had hippocampal volume loss greater than 70%. As stated by Mullally et al. (2012b), the volumes were reduced to (not by) 68.7% to 78.33% of normal, rendering redundant their arguments about this point.

Concerning their BE findings, it is not surprising that Kim et al. (2015) found normal BE in their patients, given that BE depends upon scene construction ability, which was shown to be intact in these patients (Squire et al. 2010). Moreover, Kim et al. (2015) changed critical elements in how BE was tested, which may have fostered null results (see Maguire et al. 2015). Critically, BE weakens as stimulus view widens (Hubbard et al. 2010). To enhance sensitivity to group differences, in Mullally et al. (2012b) very tight close-ups were selected for the BE drawing task (objects filled 43.4% of the space). By contrast, Kim et al. (2015) used more wide-angled photographs (objects filled 30.2% of the space), thus reducing the ability to distinguish group differences. In addition, Kim et al. (2015) more than doubled the number of trials typical for this method (Mullally et al. 2012b; see also Hubbard et al. 2010). This raises concerns, given that such trial limitations were used to minimize intertrial effects on memory. Kim et al.'s (2015) experiment 2b is especially surprising because participants were explicitly discouraged from selecting the correct ("the same") response, thus biasing the experiment away from finding attenuated BE and consequently, once again, restricting the opportunity for detecting group differences. We therefore believe that the patients tested in Squire et al. (2010) and Kim et al. (2015), who were without pervasive autobiographical memory deficits, and features of the testing in both studies may go some way toward accounting for the anomalies between their results and others in the literature.

One other apparent preservation is relevant to consider here. We often engage in counterfactual (CF) thinking, which involves reflecting on what might have been. Creating alternative versions of reality seems to have parallels with recollecting the past and imagining the future (for more on CF thinking, see Schacter et al. 2015). Given that these are impaired in patients with hippocampal damage, we might predict that CF thinking would be compromised following hippocampal damage. Testing nonpersonal CF thinking, Mullally & Maguire (2014) found that patients could deconstruct reality, add in and recombine elements, and change relations between temporal sequences of events, enabling them to determine plausible alternatives of complex episodes. However, a difference between the patients and control participants emerged in the patients' subtle avoidance of CF simulations that required the construction of an internal spatial representation. These findings suggest that mental simulation in the form of nonepisodic CF thinking does not seem to depend upon the hippocampus unless there is the added requirement for construction of a coherent spatial scene within which to play out scenarios.

In summary, it may be that healthy individuals are never passively perceiving scenes because the BE effect, underpinned by scene construction, always occurs and engages the hippocampus. Thus, without a model of a scene being constructed in the hippocampus, the scene currently in view can only be comprehended in isolation and cannot be extended beyond its borders or in one's imagination. It is for this reason Zeidman et al. (2014) proposed that scene perception tasks that require the generation of an internal model of a scene (as is typically required in scene discrimination tasks) are dependent upon the hippocampus. Maguire & Mullally (2013) go further and suggest that any task or any aspect of cognition that requires an internal model of a scene will be adversely affected by bilateral hippocampal lesions.

THEORETICAL IMPLICATIONS AND CONCLUSIONS

Here we surveyed the literature across numerous cognitive tasks to collate instances of preserved, and even facilitated, performance in patients with focal bilateral hippocampal damage. What is striking in the first instance is the nature of the preservations. For example, we are accustomed to reading in the literature that navigation is impaired in patients with focal bilateral hippocampal damage, but this kind of sweeping statement belies the facts. In terms of environments learned prelesion, only one specific aspect of navigation seems to be impaired, whereas performance on the majority of tasks assessing even high-level allocentric spatial memory and knowledge are all intact. In other instances, a lack of empirical studies precludes a proper evaluation of hippocampal involvement. Verbal memory is a case in point, held to be a paradigmatic example of impairment following hippocampal lesions, and yet there is a dearth of studies examining patients' ability to learn abstract verbal memoranda. Given such gaps in our knowledge and accepting that theories are formulated on more than neuropsychological evidence alone, how do the theoretical accounts we outlined earlier hold up when the preservations described here are considered?

Rather than focusing on specific instances of preservation and their implications for each theory, it is perhaps more useful to ask whether any clear or unifying themes emerge from the data as a whole. By concentrating on commonalities across different aspects of memory and cognition, we can to some degree guard against the interpretational issues summarized at the outset.

We believe that the patterns of preservation noted here help isolate a core problem that patients with focal bilateral hippocampal damage face. They cannot construct a spatially coherent model of the world. In other words, they are unable to construct internal representations of scenes. They seem unable to visualize in advance when to make turnings onto smaller roads during navigation, they cannot reconstruct scenes of past events or imagine scenes in the future, they are impaired at constructing another person's situation to experience that person's emotions, and they have deficits in recognition memory and working memory, specifically for scenes. Their learning is devoid of a context, and their perception—specifically of scenes—is compromised when internal models of scenes need to be generated. They show attenuated BE, leaving them access to only what is in front of their eyes.

Considering current theories, we believe the scene construction theory can best account for the patterns of impairment and preservation across these functional domains (Hassabis & Maguire 2007, 2009; Maguire & Mullally 2013). A purely allocentric account (O'Keefe & Nadel 1978) or a purely associative/relational model (Konkel et al. 2008) are not completely satisfactory given that patients appear to retain aspects of these abilities in some shape or form. Viewing the core function of the hippocampus as constructing spatially coherent scenes helps to explain the role of the hippocampus in a diversity of cognitive functions that extend beyond memory. As noted by Maguire & Mullally (2013), the hippocampus is not solely responsible for all of these functions, but rather it contributes a key ingredient—scene construction. This is why considering preservations is vital for aiding interpretation; the many aspects of navigation and memory that are preserved following hippocampal damage make sense because they do not require the internal construction of scenes. We note that at this time the scene construction theory has not been tested directly in relation to all the preservations and deficits that follow hippocampal damage. This in particular applies to verbal memory, although the majority of hippocampal theories have a similar visuospatial bias (Bird et al. 2012, Maguire & Mullally 2013, Moscovitch et al. 2006, O'Keefe & Nadel 1978,

Ranganath 2010, Schacter & Addis 2009), and accounting for verbal memory deficits is a universal challenge. We also appreciate that others have different views and have noted that the reader may wish to take into account evidence purported to speak against the scene construction theory (e.g., Kim et al. 2015, Squire et al. 2010).

Finally, we acknowledge that we are stakeholders in the scene construction theory and that others with divergent views may come to different conclusions after reflecting on the patterns of preservation we have collated here. We welcome debates that consider all of the evidence. Overall, our hope is that people take preservations into account to a greater extent in their empirical studies and their theoretical models of the hippocampus and memory, that they begin to make principled predictions about preservations as well as deficits, and that the findings surveyed here stimulate new questions about the old issues of what the hippocampus does and how memory works.

SUMMARY POINTS

1. Neuropsychological studies are dominated by the lesion-deficit model, and preservation of function following brain damage receives less attention.

2. Considering preservation of function following focal bilateral hippocampal damage could help to inform, refine, or refute extant models of the hippocampus and memory.

3. We collated evidence across a range of functional domains concerning preservations following focal bilateral hippocampal lesions.

4. Although not exhaustive, this review revealed some unexpected abilities, new angles on extant beliefs, and surprising gaps in our knowledge.

5. Overall, when considered in their totality, the data appear to suggest that patients with hippocampal damage cannot construct spatially coherent models, or scenes, of the world, and this may explain their pattern of performance across disparate aspects of cognition.

6. We believe that the scene construction theory may be best able to account for the preservations and deficits that arise from focal bilateral hippocampal damage.

FUTURE ISSUES

1. Presentation of neuropsychological data would be improved by routine reporting of effect sizes and confidence intervals and by showing all data from each participant. In this way, preservations in particular can be interpreted more accurately.

2. Scanning patients using fMRI could provide insights into the functionality of remnant hippocampal tissue and aid in interpreting preservations.

3. Researchers should make principled predictions about preservations as well as deficits when assessing patients with focal bilateral hippocampal damage.

4. Putting a spotlight on preservations has revealed gaps in our knowledge, for example, concerning verbal memory, that need to be pursued.

5. If we understand more about preservation following hippocampal damage, we may be better placed to approach rehabilitation in a more efficacious way in the future.

6. We believe that the scene construction theory is currently in the best position to account for the patterns of preservation and impairments observed following focal bilateral hippocampal damage. But how is scene construction realized by the hippocampus, and what are the mechanisms involved?

DISCLOSURE STATEMENT

The authors are not aware of any affiliations, memberships, funding, or financial holdings that might be perceived as affecting the objectivity of this review.

ACKNOWLEDGMENTS

Support for the authors came from a Wellcome Trust Principal Research Fellowship to E.A.M. The authors thank Narinder Kapur for helpful discussions, and Sinéad Mullally and Helene Intraub for their contributions to the discussion of boundary extension.

LITERATURE CITED

Aberson C. 2002. Interpreting null results: improving presentation and conclusions with confidence intervals. *J. Artic. Support Null Hypothesis* 1:36–42

Addis DR, Wong AT, Schacter DL. 2007. Remembering the past and imagining the future: common and distinct neural substrates during event construction and elaboration. *Neuropsychologia* 45:1363–77

Aggleton JP, Shaw C. 1996. Amnesia and recognition memory: a re-analysis of psychometric data. *Neuropsychologia* 34:51–62

Albasser MM, Poirier GL, Warburton EC, Aggleton JP. 2007. Hippocampal lesions halve immediate-early gene protein counts in retrosplenial cortex: distal dysfunctions in a spatial memory system. *Eur. J. Neurosci.* 26:1254–66

Aly M, Ranganath C, Yonelinas AP. 2013. Detecting changes in scenes: The hippocampus is critical for strength-based perception. *Neuron* 78:1127–37

Amedi A, Raz N, Pianka P, Malach R, Zohary E. 2003. Early "visual" cortex activation correlates with superior verbal memory performance in the blind. *Nat. Neurosci.* 6:758–66

Am. Psychol. Assoc. 2010. *Publication Manual of the American Psychological Association*. Washington, DC: Am. Psychol. Assoc.

Andelman F, Hoofien D, Goldberg I, Aizenstein O, Neufeld MY. 2010. Bilateral hippocampal lesion and a selective impairment of the ability for mental time travel. *Neurocase* 16:426–35

Astur RS, Taylor LB, Mamelak AN, Philpott L, Sutherland RJ. 2002. Humans with hippocampus damage display severe spatial memory impairments in a virtual Morris water task. *Behav. Brain Res.* 132:77–84

Augustinack JC, van der Kouwe AJW, Salat DH, Benner T, Stevens AA, et al. 2014. H.M.'s contributions to neuroscience: a review and autopsy studies. *Hippocampus* 24:1267–86

Bach DR, Guitart-Masip M, Packard PA, Miró J, Falip M, et al. 2014. Human hippocampus arbitrates approach-avoidance conflict. *Curr. Biol.* 24:541–47

Barense MD, Gaffan D, Graham KS. 2007. The human medial temporal lobe processes online representations of complex objects. *Neuropsychologia* 45:2963–74

Barense MD, Henson RNA, Lee ACH, Graham KS. 2010. Medial temporal lobe activity during complex discrimination of faces, objects, and scenes: effects of viewpoint. *Hippocampus* 20:389–401

Bartlett FC. 1932. *Remembering: A Study in Experimental and Social Psychology*. Cambridge, UK: Cambridge Univ. Press

Bayley PJ, Hopkins RO, Squire LR. 2003. Successful recollection of remote autobiographical memories by amnesic patients with medial temporal lobe lesions. *Neuron* 38:135–44

Beadle JN, Tranel D, Cohen NJ, Duff MC. 2013. Empathy in hippocampal amnesia. *Front. Psychol.* 4:69

Bechara A, Tranel D, Damasio H, Adolphs R, Rockland C, Damasio A. 1995. Double dissociation of conditioning and declarative knowledge relative to the amygdala and hippocampus in humans. *Science* 269:1115–18

Binder J, Westbury C, McKiernan K, Possing E, Medler D. 2005. Distinct brain systems for processing concrete and abstract concepts. *J. Cogn. Neurosci.* 17:905–17

Bird CM, Bisby JA, Burgess N. 2012. The hippocampus and spatial constraints on mental imagery. *Front. Hum. Neurosci.* 6:142

Bird CM, Burgess N. 2008. The hippocampus supports recognition memory for familiar words but not unfamiliar faces. *Curr. Biol.* 18:1932–36

Bonnici HM, Chadwick MJ, Lutti A, Hassabis D, Weiskopf N, Maguire EA. 2012. Detecting representations of recent and remote autobiographical memories in vmPFC and hippocampus. *J. Neurosci.* 32:16982–91

Bonnici HM, Chadwick MJ, Maguire EA. 2013. Representations of recent and remote autobiographical memories in hippocampal subfields. *Hippocampus* 23:849–54

Brown MW, Aggleton JP. 2001. Recognition memory: What are the roles of the perirhinal cortex and hippocampus? *Nat. Rev. Neurosci.* 2:51–61

Buchanan TW, Tranel D, Adolphs R. 2005. Emotional autobiographical memories in amnesic patients with medial temporal lobe damage. *J. Neurosci.* 25:3151–60

Buchanan TW, Tranel D, Kirschbaum C. 2009. Hippocampal damage abolishes the cortisol response to psychosocial stress in humans. *Horm. Behav.* 56:44–50

Buzsaki G, Moser EI. 2013. Memory, navigation and theta rhythm in the hippocampal-entorhinal system. *Nat. Neurosci.* 16:130–38

Campo P, Garrido MI, Moran RJ, Maestú F, García-Morales I, et al. 2012. Remote effects of hippocampal sclerosis on effective connectivity during working memory encoding: a case of connectional diaschisis? *Cereb. Cortex* 22:1225–36

Carey S, Bartlett E. 1978. Acquiring a single new word. In *Proc. Stanf. Child Lang. Conf.* 15:17–29

Cashdollar N, Malecki U, Rugg-Gunn FJ, Duncan JS, Lavie N, Duzel E. 2009. Hippocampus-dependent and -independent theta-networks of active maintenance. *PNAS* 106:20493–98

Cavaco S, Anderson SW, Allen JS, Castro-Caldas A, Damasio H. 2004. The scope of preserved procedural memory in amnesia. *Brain* 127:1853–67

Chadwick MJ, Bonnici HM, Maguire EA. 2012. Decoding information in the human hippocampus: a user's guide. *Neuropsychologia* 50:3107–21

Chadwick MJ, Mullally SL, Maguire EA. 2013. The hippocampus extrapolates beyond the view in scenes: an fMRI study of boundary extension. *Cortex* 49:2067–79

Chun MM, Phelps EA. 1999. Memory deficits for implicit contextual information in amnesic subjects with hippocampal damage. *Nat. Neurosci.* 2:844–47

Cipolotti L, Bird C, Good T, Macmanus D, Rudge P, Shallice T. 2006. Recollection and familiarity in dense hippocampal amnesia: a case study. *Neuropsychologia* 44:489–506

Cipolotti L, Shallice T, Chan D, Fox N, Scahill R, et al. 2001. Long-term retrograde amnesia . . . the crucial role of the hippocampus. *Neuropsychologia* 39:151–72

Cohen NJ. 1984. Preserved learning capacity in amnesia: evidence for multiple memory systems. In *Neuropsychology of Memory*, ed. LR Squire, N Butters, pp. 83–103. New York: Guilford

Cohen NJ, Eichenbaum H. 1993. *Memory, Amnesia and the Hippocampal System*. Cambridge, MA: MIT Press

Conway MA, Pleydell-Pearce CW. 2000. The construction of autobiographical memories in the self- memory system. *Psychol. Rev.* 107:261–88

Cooper JM, Vargha-Khadem F, Gadian DG, Maguire EA. 2011. The effect of hippocampal damage in children on recalling the past and imagining new experiences. *Neuropsychologia* 49:1843–50

Corkin S. 1965. Tactually-guided maze learning in man: Effects of unilateral cortical excisions and bilateral hippocampal lesions. *Neuropsychologia* 3:339–51

Corkin S. 1968. Acquisition of motor skill after bilateral medial temporal-lobe excision. *Neuropsychologia* 6:255–65

Craver CF, Cova F, Green L, Myerson J, Rosenbaum RS, et al. 2014a. An Allais paradox without mental time travel. *Hippocampus* 24:1375–80

Craver CF, Kwan D, Steindam C, Rosenbaum RS. 2014b. Individuals with episodic amnesia are not stuck in time. *Neuropsychologia* 57:191–95

de Vito S, Della Sala S. 2011. Predicting the future. *Cortex* 47:1018–22

Duff MC, Hengst J, Tranel D, Cohen NJ. 2006. Development of shared information in communication despite hippocampal amnesia. *Nat. Neurosci.* 9:140–46

Dunn JC, Kirsner K. 2003. What can we infer from double dissociations? *Cortex* 39:1–7

Dunstan EJ, Winer JB. 2006. Autoimmune limbic encephalitis causing fits, rapidly progressive confusion and hyponatraemia. *Age Ageing* 35:536–37

Eichenbaum H. 2004. Hippocampus: cognitive processes and neural representations that underlie declarative memory. *Neuron* 44:109–20

Eichenbaum H. 2014. Time cells in the hippocampus: a new dimension for mapping memories. *Nat. Rev. Neurosci.* 15:732–44

Eichenbaum H, Cohen NJ. 2014. Can we reconcile the declarative memory and spatial navigation views on hippocampal function? *Neuron* 83:764–70

Eichenbaum H, Yonelinas AR, Ranganath C. 2007. The medial temporal lobe and recognition memory. *Annu. Rev. Neurosci.* 30:123–52

Ekstrom AD, Kahana MJ, Caplan JB, Fields TA, Isham EA, et al. 2003. Cellular networks underlying human spatial navigation. *Nature* 425:184–88

Elfman KW, Aly M, Yonelinas AP. 2014. Neurocomputational account of memory and perception: thresholded and graded signals in the hippocampus. *Hippocampus* 24:1672–86

Fanselow MS, Dong H-W. 2010. Are the dorsal and ventral hippocampus functionally distinct structures? *Neuron* 65:7–19

Feinstein JS, Duff MC, Tranel D. 2010. Sustained experience of emotion after loss of memory in patients with amnesia. *PNAS* 107:7674–79

Felleman DJ, Van Essen DC. 1991. Distributed hierarchical processing in the primate cerebral cortex. *Cereb. Cortex* 1:1–47

Ferguson CJ, Heene M. 2012. A vast graveyard of undead theories: publication bias and psychological science's aversion to the null. *Perspect. Psychol. Sci.* 7:555–61

Gabrieli JDE, McGlinchey-Berroth R, Carrillo MC, Gluck MA, Cermak LS, Disterhoft JF. 1995. Intact delay-eyeblink classical conditioning in amnesia. *Behav. Neurosci.* 109:819–27

Gadian DG, Aicardi J, Watkins KE, Porter DA, Mishkin M, Vargha-Khadem F. 2000. Developmental amnesia associated with early hypoxic–ischaemic injury. *Brain* 123:499–507

Gaesser B, Schacter DL. 2014. Episodic simulation and episodic memory can increase intentions to help others. *PNAS* 111:4415–20

Gagnon S, Foster J, Turcotte J, Jongenelis S. 2004. Involvement of the hippocampus in implicit learning of supra-span sequences: the case of SJ. *Cogn. Neuropsychol.* 21:867–82

Gardiner J, Parkin A. 1990. Attention and recollective experience in recognition memory. *Mem. Cogn.* 18:579–83

Gilboa A, Winocur G, Grady CL, Hevenor SJ, Moscovitch M. 2004. Remembering our past: functional neuroanatomy of recollection of recent and very remote personal events. *Cereb. Cortex* 14:1214–25

Gold JJ, Smith CN, Bayley PJ, Shrager Y, Brewer JB, et al. 2006. Item memory, source memory, and the medial temporal lobe: concordant findings from fMRI and memory-impaired patients. *PNAS* 103:9351–56

Gold JJ, Squire LR. 2005. Quantifying medial temporal lobe damage in memory-impaired patients. *Hippocampus* 15:79–85

Goodrich-Hunsaker NJ, Hopkins RO. 2009. Word memory test performance in amnesic patients with hippocampal damage. *Neuropsychology* 23:529–34

Goodrich-Hunsaker NJ, Livingstone SA, Skelton RW, Hopkins RO. 2010. Spatial deficits in a virtual water maze in amnesic participants with hippocampal damage. *Hippocampus* 20:481–91

Gottesman CV, Intraub H. 2002. Surface construal and the mental representation of scenes. *J. Exp. Psychol.: Hum. Percept. Perform.* 28:589–99

Graham KS, Scahill VL, Hornberger M, Barense MD, Lee ACH, et al. 2006. Abnormal categorization and perceptual learning in patients with hippocampal damage. *J. Neurosci.* 26:7547–54

Gratton C, Nomura EM, Pérez F, D'Esposito M. 2012. Focal brain lesions to critical locations cause widespread disruption of the modular organization of the brain. *J. Cogn. Neurosci.* 24:1275–85

Gray J, McNaughton N. 2003. *The Neuropsychology of Anxiety*. Oxford, UK: Oxford Univ. Press

Hannula DE, Tranel D, Allen JS, Kirchhoff BA, Nickel AE, Cohen NJ. 2015. Memory for items and relationships among items embedded in realistic scenes: disproportionate relational memory impairments in amnesia. *Neuropsychology* 29:126–38

Hannula DE, Tranel D, Cohen NJ. 2006. The long and the short of it: relational memory impairments in amnesia, even at short lags. *J. Neurosci.* 26:8352–59

Hartley T, Bird CM, Chan D, Cipolotti L, Husain M, et al. 2007. The hippocampus is required for short-term topographical memory in humans. *Hippocampus* 17:34–48

Hassabis D, Kumaran D, Maguire EA. 2007a. Using imagination to understand the neural basis of episodic memory. *J. Neurosci.* 27:14365–74

Hassabis D, Kumaran D, Vann SD, Maguire EA. 2007b. Patients with hippocampal amnesia cannot imagine new experiences. *PNAS* 104:1726–31

Hassabis D, Maguire EA. 2007. Deconstructing episodic memory with construction. *Trends Cogn. Sci.* 11:299–306

Hassabis D, Maguire EA. 2009. The construction system of the brain. *Philos. Trans. R. Soc. B* 364:1263–71

Hayes SM, Salat DH, Verfaellie M. 2012. Default network connectivity in medial temporal lobe amnesia. *J. Neurosci.* 32:14622–29

Holdstock JS, Mayes AR, Cezayirli E, Isaac CL, Aggleton JP, Roberts N. 2000. A comparison of egocentric and allocentric spatial memory in a patient with selective hippocampal damage. *Neuropsychologia* 38:410–25

Holdstock JS, Mayes AR, Gong QY, Roberts N, Kapur N. 2005. Item recognition is less impaired than recall and associative recognition in a patient with selective hippocampal damage. *Hippocampus* 15:203–15

Holdstock JS, Mayes AR, Isaac CL, Gong Q, Roberts N. 2002. Differential involvement of the hippocampus and temporal lobe cortices in rapid and slow learning of new semantic information. *Neuropsychologia* 40:748–68

Hopkins RO, Myers CE, Shohamy D, Grossman S, Gluck M. 2004. Impaired probabilistic category learning in hypoxic subjects with hippocampal damage. *Neuropsychologia* 42:524–35

Hubbard TL, Hutchison JL, Courtney JR. 2010. Boundary extension: findings and theories. *Q. J. Exp. Psychol.* 63:1467–94

Hurley NC, Maguire EA, Vargha-Khadem F. 2011. Patient HC with developmental amnesia can construct future scenarios. *Neuropsychologia* 49:3620–28

Intraub H, Richardson M. 1989. Wide-angle memories of close-up scenes. *J. Exp. Psychol.: Learn. Mem. Cogn.* 15:179–87

Jenkins TA, Vann SD, Amin E, Aggleton JP. 2004. Anterior thalamic lesions stop immediate early gene activation in selective laminae of the retrosplenial cortex: evidence of covert pathology in rats? *Eur. J. Neurosci.* 19:3291–304

Jones MK. 1974. Imagery as a mnemonic aid after left temporal lobectomy: contrast between material-specific and generalized memory disorders. *Neuropsychologia* 12:21–30

Jones-Gotman M. 1979. Incidental learning of image-mediated or pronounced words after right temporal lobectomy. *Cortex* 15:187–97

Jones-Gotman M, Milner B. 1978. Right temporal-lobe contribution to image-mediated verbal learning. *Neuropsychologia* 16:61–71

Kapur N, ed. 2011. *The Paradoxical Brain*. Cambridge, UK: Cambridge Univ. Press

Kapur N, Brooks DJ. 1999. Temporally-specific retrograde amnesia in two cases of discrete bilateral hippocampal pathology. *Hippocampus* 9:247–54

Kessels RPC, de Haan EHF, Kappelle LJ, Postma A. 2001. Varieties of human spatial memory: a meta-analysis on the effects of hippocampal lesions. *Brain Res. Rev.* 35:295–303

Khan NL, Jeffree MA, Good C, Macleod W, Al-Sarraj S. 2009. Histopathology of VGKC antibody-associated limbic encephalitis. *Neurology* 72:1703–5

Kieras D. 1978. Beyond pictures and words: alternative information-processing models for imagery effect in verbal memory. *Psychol. Bull.* 85:532–54

Kim S, Dede AJO, Hopkins RO, Squire LR. 2015. Memory, scene construction, and the human hippocampus. *PNAS* 112:4767–72

Kim S, Jeneson A, van der Horst AS, Frascino JC, Hopkins RO, Squire LR. 2011. Memory, visual discrimination performance, and the human hippocampus. *J. Neurosci.* 31:2624–29

Kirwan CB, Bayley PJ, Galván VV, Squire LR. 2008. Detailed recollection of remote autobiographical memory after damage to the medial temporal lobe. *PNAS* 105:2676–80

Kirwan CB, Wixted JT, Squire LR. 2010. A demonstration that the hippocampus supports both recollection and familiarity. *PNAS* 107:344–48

Klein SB, Loftus J, Kihlstrom JF. 2002. Memory and temporal experience: the effects of episodic memory loss on an amnesic patient's ability to remember the past and imagine the future. *Soc. Cogn.* 20:353–79

Knowlton BJ, Mangels JA, Squire LR. 1996. A neostriatal habit learning system in humans. *Science* 273:1399–402

Knowlton BJ, Squire LR, Gluck MA. 1994. Probabilistic classification learning in amnesia. *Learn Mem.* 1:106–20

Knutson AR, Hopkins RO, Squire LR. 2012. Visual discrimination performance, memory, and medial temporal lobe function. *PNAS* 109:13106–11

Konkel A, Cohen NJ. 2009. Relational memory and the hippocampus: representations and methods. *Front. Neurosci.* 3:166–74

Konkel A, Warren DE, Duff MC, Tranel D, Cohen NJ. 2008. Hippocampal amnesia impairs all manner of relational memory. *Front. Hum. Neurosci.* 2:15

Kumaran D, Hassabis D, Spiers HJ, Vann SD, Vargha-Khadem F, Maguire EA. 2007. Impaired spatial and non-spatial configural learning in patients with hippocampal pathology. *Neuropsychologia* 45:2699–711

Kwan D, Craver CF, Green L, Myerson J, Boyer P, Rosenbaum RS. 2012. Future decision-making without episodic mental time travel. *Hippocampus* 22:1215–19

Lee ACH, Buckley MJ, Pegman SJ, Spiers H, Scahill VL, et al. 2005a. Specialization in the medial temporal lobe for processing of objects and scenes. *Hippocampus* 15:782–97

Lee ACH, Bussey TJ, Murray EA, Saksida LM, Epstein RA, et al. 2005b. Perceptual deficits in amnesia: challenging the medial temporal lobe "mnemonic" view. *Neuropsychologia* 43:1–11

Lee ACH, Scahill VL, Graham KS. 2008. Activating the medial temporal lobe during oddity judgment for faces and scenes. *Cereb. Cortex* 18:683–96

Lee ACH, Yeung L-K, Barense MD. 2012. The hippocampus and visual perception. *Front. Hum. Neurosci.* 6:91

MacDonald CJ, Lepage KQ, Eden UT, Eichenbaum H. 2011. Hippocampal "time cells" bridge the gap in memory for discontiguous events. *Neuron* 71:737–49

Maguire EA, Burgess N, Donnett JG, Frackowiak RSJ, Frith CD, O'Keefe J. 1998. Knowing where and getting there: a human navigation network. *Science* 280:921–24

Maguire EA, Frith CD. 2003. Lateral asymmetry in the hippocampal response to the remoteness of autobiographical memories. *J. Neurosci.* 23:5302–7

Maguire EA, Gadian DG, Johnsrude IS, Good CD, Ashburner J, et al. 2000. Navigation-related structural change in the hippocampi of taxi drivers. *PNAS* 97:4398–403

Maguire EA, Hassabis D. 2011. Role of the hippocampus in imagination and future thinking. *PNAS* 108:E39

Maguire EA, Intraub H, Mullally SL. 2015. Scenes, spaces and memory traces: What does the hippocampus do? *Neuroscientist.* doi: 10.1177/1073858415600389

Maguire EA, Kumaran D, Hassabis D, Kopelman MD. 2010a. Autobiographical memory in semantic dementia: a longitudinal fMRI study. *Neuropsychologia* 48:123–36

Maguire EA, Mullally SL. 2013. The hippocampus: a manifesto for change. *J. Exp. Psychol.: Gen.* 142:1180–89

Maguire EA, Nannery R, Spiers HJ. 2006. Navigation around London by a taxi driver with bilateral hippocampal lesions. *Brain* 129:2894–907

Maguire EA, Vargha-Khadem F, Hassabis D. 2010b. Imagining fictitious and future experiences: evidence from developmental amnesia. *Neuropsychologia* 48:3187–92

Maguire EA, Vargha-Khadem F, Mishkin M. 2001. The effects of bilateral hippocampal damage on fMRI regional activations and interactions during memory retrieval. *Brain* 124:1156–70

Manns JR, Squire LR. 2001. Perceptual learning, awareness, and the hippocampus. *Hippocampus* 11:776–82

Marr D. 1971. Simple memory: a theory for archicortex. *Philos. Trans. R. Soc. B* 262:23–81

Mayes A, Montaldi D, Migo E. 2007. Associative memory and the medial temporal lobes. *Trends Cogn. Sci.* 11:126–35

Mayes AR, Holdstock JS, Isaac CL, Montaldi D, Grigor J, et al. 2004. Associative recognition in a patient with selective hippocampal lesions and relatively normal item recognition. *Hippocampus* 14:763–84

McHugh SB, Deacon RMJ, Rawlins JNP, Bannerman DM. 2004. Amygdala and ventral hippocampus contribute differentially to mechanisms of fear and anxiety. *Behav. Neurosci.* 118:63–78

Meeter M, Myers CE, Shohamy D, Hopkins RO, Gluck MA. 2006. Strategies in probabilistic categorization: results from a new way of analyzing performance. *Learn. Mem.* 13:230–39

Merhav M, Karni A, Gilboa A. 2014. Neocortical catastrophic interference in healthy and amnesic adults: a paradoxical matter of time. *Hippocampus* 24:1653–62

Milner B. 1965. Visually-guided maze learning in man: effects of bilateral hippocampal, bilateral frontal, and unilateral cerebral lesions. *Neuropsychologia* 3:317–38

Mishkin M, Vargha-Khadem F, Gadian DG. 1998. Amnesia and the organization of the hippocampal system. *Hippocampus* 8:212–16

Moscovitch M, Nadel L, Winocur G, Gilboa A, Rosenbaum RS. 2006. The cognitive neuroscience of remote episodic, semantic and spatial memory. *Curr. Opin. Neurobiol.* 16:179–90

Moser M-B, Moser EI. 1998. Functional differentiation in the hippocampus. *Hippocampus* 8:608–19

Mullally SL, Hassabis D, Maguire EA. 2012a. Scene construction in amnesia: an fMRI study. *J. Neurosci.* 32:5646–53

Mullally SL, Intraub H, Maguire EA. 2012b. Attenuated boundary extension produces a paradoxical memory advantage in amnesic patients. *Curr. Biol.* 22:261–68

Mullally SL, Maguire EA. 2014. Counterfactual thinking in patients with amnesia. *Hippocampus* 24:1261–66

Mullally SL, Vargha-Khadem F, Maguire EA. 2014. Scene construction in developmental amnesia: an fMRI study. *Neuropsychologia* 52:1–10

Mundy ME, Downing PE, Graham KS. 2012. Extrastriate cortex and medial temporal lobe regions respond differentially to visual feature overlap within preferred stimulus category. *Neuropsychologia* 50:3053–61

Nadel L, Moscovitch M. 1997. Memory consolidation, retrograde amnesia and the hippocampal complex. *Curr. Opin. Neurobiol.* 7:217–27

Nyberg L, Kim ASN, Habib R, Levine B, Tulving E. 2010. Consciousness of subjective time in the brain. *PNAS* 107:22356–59

O'Keefe J, Dostrovsky J. 1971. The hippocampus as a spatial map. Preliminary evidence from unit activity in the freely-moving rat. *Brain Res.* 34:171–75

O'Keefe J, Nadel L. 1978. *The Hippocampus as a Cognitive Map.* Oxford, UK: Clarendon

Olson IR, Moore KS, Stark M, Chatterjee A. 2006a. Visual working memory is impaired when the medial temporal lobe is damaged. *J. Cogn. Neurosci.* 18:1087–97

Olson IR, Page K, Moore KS, Chatterjee A, Verfaellie M. 2006b. Working memory for conjunctions relies on the medial temporal lobe. *J. Neurosci.* 26:4596–601

Paivio A. 1969. Mental imagery in associative learning and memory. *Psychol. Rev.* 76:241–63

Park DC, Murman DL, Perry KD, Bruch LA. 2007. An autopsy case of limbic encephalitis with voltage-gated potassium channel antibodies. *Eur. J. Neurol.* 14:e5–6

Poirier GL, Aggleton JP. 2009. Post-surgical interval and lesion location within the limbic thalamus determine extent of retrosplenial cortex immediate-early gene hypoactivity. *Neuroscience* 160:452–69

Poppenk J, Evensmoen HR, Moscovitch M, Nadel L. 2013. Long-axis specialization of the human hippocampus. *Trends Cogn. Sci.* 17:230–40

Price CJ, Friston KJ. 2002. Degeneracy and cognitive anatomy. *Trends Cogn. Sci.* 6:416–21

Race E, Keane MM, Verfaellie M. 2011. Medial temporal lobe damage causes deficits in episodic memory and episodic future thinking not attributable to deficits in narrative construction. *J. Neurosci.* 31:10262–69

Race E, Keane MM, Verfaellie M. 2013. Losing sight of the future: impaired semantic prospection following medial temporal lobe lesions. *Hippocampus* 23:268–77

Ranganath C. 2010. A unified framework for the functional organization of the medial temporal lobes and the phenomenology of episodic memory. *Hippocampus* 20:1263–90

Ranganath C, Blumenfeld RS. 2005. Doubts about double dissociations between short- and long-term memory. *Trends Cogn. Sci.* 9:374–80

Reber PJ. 2013. The neural basis of implicit learning and memory: a review of neuropsychological and neuroimaging research. *Neuropsychologia* 51:2026–42

Reber PJ, Knowlton BJ, Squire LR. 1996. Dissociable properties of memory systems: differences in the flexibility of declarative and nondeclarative knowledge. *Behav. Neurosci.* 110:861–71

Reed JM, Squire LR. 1998. Retrograde amnesia for facts and events: findings from four new cases. *J. Neurosci.* 18:3943–54

Rorden C, Karnath H-O. 2004. Using human brain lesions to infer function: a relic from a past era in the fMRI age? *Nat. Rev. Neurosci.* 5:812–19

Rosenbaum RS, Gilboa A, Levine B, Winocur G, Moscovitch M. 2009. Amnesia as an impairment of detail generation and binding: evidence from personal, fictional, and semantic narratives in K.C. *Neuropsychologia* 47:2181–87

Rosenbaum RS, Gilboa A, Moscovitch M. 2014. Case studies continue to illuminate the cognitive neuroscience of memory. *Ann. N. Y. Acad. Sci.* 1316:105–33

Rosenbaum RS, Köhler S, Schacter DL, Moscovitch M, Westmacott R, et al. 2005. The case of K.C.: contributions of a memory-impaired person to memory theory. *Neuropsychologia* 43:989–1021

Rosenbaum RS, Priselac S, Köhler S, Black SE, Gao F, et al. 2000. Remote spatial memory in an amnesic person with extensive bilateral hippocampal lesions. *Nat. Neurosci.* 3:1044–48

Rosenbaum RS, Stuss DT, Levine B, Tulving E. 2007. Theory of mind is independent of episodic memory. *Science* 318:1257

Rosenthal R. 1979. The file drawer problem and tolerance for null results. *Psychol. Bull.* 86:638–41

Rubin RD, Brown-Schmidt S, Duff MC, Tranel D, Cohen NJ. 2011. How do I remember that I know you know that I know? *Psychol. Sci.* 22:1574–82

Ryan JD, Althoff RR, Whitlow S, Cohen NJ. 2000. Amnesia is a deficit in relational memory. *Psychol. Sci.* 11:454–61

Ryan JD, Cohen NJ. 2004. Processing and short-term retention of relational information in amnesia. *Neuropsychologia* 42:497–511

Ryan L, Nadel L, Keil K, Putnam K, Schnyer D, et al. 2001. Hippocampal complex and retrieval of recent and very remote autobiographical memories: evidence from functional magnetic resonance imaging in neurologically intact people. *Hippocampus* 11:707–14

Sanfratello L, Caprihan A, Stephen JM, Knoefel JE, Adair JC, et al. 2014. Same task, different strategies: how brain networks can be influenced by memory strategy. *Hum. Brain Mapp.* 35:5127–40

Schacter DL, Addis DR. 2007. Constructive memory: the ghosts of past and future. *Nature* 445:27

Schacter DL, Addis DR. 2009. On the nature of medial temporal lobe contributions to the constructive simulation of future events. *Philos. Trans. R. Soc. B* 364:1245–53

Schacter DL, Addis DR, Hassabis D, Martin VC, Spreng RN, Szpunar KK. 2012. The future of memory: remembering, imagining, and the brain. *Neuron* 76:677–94

Schacter DL, Benoit RG, De Brigard F, Szpunar KK. 2015. Episodic future thinking and episodic counterfactual thinking: intersections between memory and decisions. *Neurobiol. Learn. Mem.* 117:14–21

Schacter DL, Chiu CY, Ochsner KN. 1993. Implicit memory: a selective review. *Annu. Rev. Neurosci.* 16:159–82

Schacter DL, Graf P. 1986. Preserved learning in amnesic patients: perspectives from research on direct priming. *J. Clin. Exp. Neuropsychol.* 8:727–43

Schacter DL, Norman KA, Koutstaal W. 1998. The cognitive neuroscience of constructive memory. *Annu. Rev. Psychol.* 49:289–318

Scoville WB, Milner B. 1957. Loss of recent memory after bilateral hippocampal lesions. *J. Neurol. Neurosurg. Psychiatry* 20:11–21

Sharon T, Moscovitch M, Gilboa A. 2011. Rapid neocortical acquisition of long-term arbitrary associations independent of the hippocampus. *PNAS* 108:1146–51

Shohamy D, Myers CE, Hopkins RO, Sage J, Gluck MA. 2008. Distinct hippocampal and basal ganglia contributions to probabilistic learning and reversal. *J. Cogn. Neurosci.* 21:1820–32

Shrager Y, Gold JJ, Hopkins RO, Squire LR. 2006. Intact visual perception in memory-impaired patients with medial temporal lobe lesions. *J. Neurosci.* 26:2235–40

Smith CN, Jeneson A, Frascino JC, Kirwan CB, Hopkins RO, Squire LR. 2014a. When recognition memory is independent of hippocampal function. *PNAS* 111:9935–40

Smith CN, Urgolites ZJ, Hopkins RO, Squire LR. 2014b. Comparison of explicit and incidental learning strategies in memory-impaired patients. *PNAS* 111:475–79

Spiers HJ, Maguire EA. 2006. Thoughts, behaviour, and brain dynamics during navigation in the real world. *NeuroImage* 31:1826–40

Spiers HJ, Maguire EA. 2007. The neuroscience of remote spatial memory: a tale of two cities. *Neuroscience* 149:7–27

Spiers HJ, Maguire EA, Burgess N. 2001. Hippocampal amnesia. *Neurocase* 7:357–82

Squire LR. 1992. Memory and the hippocampus: a synthesis from findings with rats, monkeys, and humans. *Psychol. Rev.* 99:195–231

Squire LR, van der Horst AS, McDuff SGR, Frascino JC, Hopkins RO, Mauldin KN. 2010. Role of the hippocampus in remembering the past and imagining the future. *PNAS* 107:19044–48

Squire LR, Wixted JT. 2011. The cognitive neuroscience of human memory since H.M. *Annu. Rev. Neurosci.* 34:259–88

Squire LR, Zola SM. 1998. Episodic memory, semantic memory, and amnesia. *Hippocampus* 8:205–11

Squire LR, Zola-Morgan S. 1991. The medial temporal lobe memory system. *Science* 253:1380–86

Strange BA, Witter MP, Lein ES, Moser EI. 2014. Functional organization of the hippocampal longitudinal axis. *Nat. Rev. Neurosci.* 15:655–69

Taylor KJ, Henson RNA, Graham KS. 2007. Recognition memory for faces and scenes in amnesia: dissociable roles of medial temporal lobe structures. *Neuropsychologia* 45:2428–38

Teng E, Squire LR. 1999. Memory for places learned long ago is intact after hippocampal damage. *Nature* 400:675–77

Teyler TJ, DiScenna P. 1985. The role of hippocampus in memory: a hypothesis. *Neurosci. Biobehav. Rev.* 9:377–89

Tsao DY, Livingstone MS. 2008. Mechanisms of face perception. *Annu. Rev. Neurosci.* 31:411–37

Tulving E. 1972. Episodic and semantic memory. In *Organization of Memory*, ed. E Tulving, pp. 381–403. New York: Academic

Tulving E. 1985. Memory and consciousness. *Can. Psychol.* 26:1–12

Tulving E. 2002. Episodic memory: from mind to brain. *Annu. Rev. Psychol.* 53:1–25

Tulving E, Markowitsch HJ. 1998. Episodic and declarative memory: role of the hippocampus. *Hippocampus* 8:198–204

Tulving E, Schacter D. 1990. Priming and human memory systems. *Science* 247:301–6

Tulving E, Thomson DM. 1973. Encoding specificity and retrieval processes in episodic memory. *Psychol. Rev.* 80:352–73

Vargha-Khadem F, Gadian DG, Watkins KE, Connelly A, Van Paesschen W, Mishkin M. 1997. Differential effects of early hippocampal pathology on episodic and semantic memory. *Science* 277:376–80

Vargha-Khadem F, Salmond CH, Watkins KE, Friston KJ, Gadian DG, Mishkin M. 2003. Developmental amnesia: effect of age at injury. *PNAS* 100:10055–60

Victor M, Agamanolis D. 1990. Amnesia due to lesions confined to the hippocampus: a clinical-pathologic study. *J. Cogn. Neurosci.* 2:246–57

Viskontas IV, McAndrews MP, Moscovitch M. 2000. Remote episodic memory deficits in patients with unilateral temporal lobe epilepsy and excisions. *J. Neurosci.* 20:5853–57

Wang J, Baucom LB, Shinkareva SV. 2013. Decoding abstract and concrete concept representations based on single-trial fMRI data. *Hum. Brain Mapp.* 34:1133–47

Warren DE, Duff MC. 2014. Not so fast: Hippocampal amnesia slows word learning despite successful fast mapping. *Hippocampus* 24:920–33

Warren DE, Duff MC, Magnotta V, Capizzano AA, Cassell MD, Tranel D. 2012. Long-term neuropsychological, neuroanatomical, and life outcome in hippocampal amnesia. *Clin. Neuropsychol.* 26:335–69

West MJ. 1990. Stereological studies of the hippocampus: a comparison of the hippocampal subdivisions of diverse species including hedgehogs, laboratory rodents, wild mice and men. *Prog. Brain Res.* 83:13–36

Winocur G, Moscovitch M. 2011. Memory transformation and systems consolidation. *J. Int. Neuropsychol. Soc.* 17:766–80

Woollett K, Maguire EA. 2011. Acquiring "the Knowledge" of London's layout drives structural brain changes. *Curr. Biol.* 21:2109–14

Yee LTS, Warren DE, Voss JL, Duff MC, Tranel D, Cohen NJ. 2014. The hippocampus uses information just encountered to guide efficient ongoing behavior. *Hippocampus* 24:154–64

Yonelinas AP. 2002. The nature of recollection and familiarity: a review of 30 years of research. *J. Mem. Lang.* 46:441–517

Yonelinas AP. 2013. The hippocampus supports high-resolution binding in the service of perception, working memory and long-term memory. *Behav. Brain Res.* 254:34–44

Zeidman P, Mullally SL, Maguire EA. 2014. Constructing, perceiving, and maintaining scenes: hippocampal activity and connectivity. *Cereb. Cortex*. doi: 10.1093/cercor/bhu266

Zola-Morgan S, Squire LR, Amaral DG. 1986. Human amnesia and the medial temporal region: enduring memory impairment following a bilateral lesion limited to field CA1 of the hippocampus. *J. Neurosci.* 6:2950–67

Beyond Words: How Humans Communicate Through Sound

Nina Kraus[1,2,3,4] and Jessica Slater[1,2]

[1]Auditory Neuroscience Laboratory, Departments of [2]Communication Sciences,
[3]Neurobiology and Physiology, [4]Otolaryngology, Northwestern University, Evanston,
Illinois 60208; www.brainvolts.northwestern.edu; email: nkraus@northwestern.edu

Annu. Rev. Psychol. 2016. 67:83–103

First published online as a Review in Advance on
September 11, 2015

The *Annual Review of Psychology* is online at
psych.annualreviews.org

This article's doi:
10.1146/annurev-psych-122414-033318

Keywords

speech, music, rhythm, learning, neural plasticity, auditory processing

Abstract

Every day we communicate using complex linguistic and musical systems, yet these modern systems are the product of a much more ancient relationship with sound. When we speak, we communicate not only with the words we choose, but also with the patterns of sound we create and the movements that create them. From the natural rhythms of speech, to the precise timing characteristics of a consonant, these patterns guide our daily communication. By examining the principles of information processing that are common to speech and music, we peel back the layers to reveal the biological foundations of human communication through sound. Further, we consider how the brain's response to sound is shaped by experience, such as musical expertise, and implications for the treatment of communication disorders.

Contents

INTRODUCTION

The human relationship with sound is much deeper and more ancient than our relationship with words. The intoxicating sophistication and precision of modern languages can blind us to more fundamental aspects of auditory processing that underlie everyday communication. Yet a great deal of communicative power lies beneath the surface of words, and our modern languages and musical systems reflect how humans evolved in a world of sound (see **Figure 1**). Sound is created by physical movement, from the crunch of leaves underfoot, to the vibrations of vocal cords and

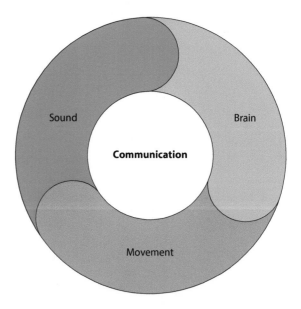

Figure 1

Our modern communication systems are the product of our ancient relationship with sound, rooted in the physical world.

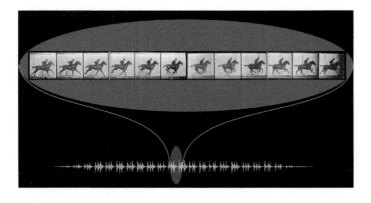

Figure 2

Sound provides an inventory of motion: The repeating movements of a galloping horse create repeating patterns in the resulting sound wave. Original images of a horse galloping by Eadweard Muybridge. Figure created by Adam Trefonides.

violin strings. The ability to make sense of sound helps us to construct accurate representations of our world, based on what we know about how sounds are produced. Just as a movie sound engineer will use sound effects to inform us about what is happening off camera (e.g., the wail of a siren or the door-slam of a departing lover), the sounds we hear as we navigate our daily lives create a dynamic map of objects around us and how they are moving in space. Sound extends our perceptual reach beyond the boundaries of our visual field. Though we can close our eyes or shift our gaze, our ears remain open, providing input from all directions. Auditory information therefore plays an important role in guiding our other senses, such as when we hear a sound and turn our head to look. Sound provides a kind of connective tissue, ensuring the continuity of our experience over time and choreographing the focus of our senses.

Sounds emanating from a single source share common characteristics and exhibit distinctive patterns that link them to their physical origin: The pitch and timbre of a sound are dependent on the resonant characteristics of an object, so a sequence of sounds with similar pitch and timbre implies a common source. If sounds are produced regularly in time, this may suggest an object in motion (see **Figure 2**). Leaves crunching with regularity and increasing volume may signal the approach of an animate leaf-crunching entity, such as a predator. The combination of loudness and rate of leaf crunching tells us about the size of the potential predator, how fast it is approaching, and, ultimately, which way to run.

Our brains are therefore performing constant computations to determine the underlying physicality of the sounds we hear, combining inputs from both ears and seeking out patterns that might inform us of approaching danger. When we communicate through sound, we are not only producing and perceiving acoustic signals; we are also exchanging detailed inventories of motion. Although the nuanced functions of modern language may seem far removed from a literal map of objects in space, knowing how a sound is produced can facilitate perception; for example, the mechanical properties of the human vocal apparatus place inherent constraints on the sound sequences likely to be generated in the course of a human utterance. Our motor planning and production systems possess implicit knowledge about which patterns of speech are most likely to be produced, based on the motor sequences required to produce them. Numerous studies have demonstrated that brain regions involved in speech production are activated when listening to speech (Watkins et al. 2003, Wilson et al. 2004), supporting the idea that "Speech is processed both as a sound and as an action" (Scott & Johnsrude 2003, p. 105). Given the close ties between speech and physical gesture, it is unsurprising that the brain integrates both sound and movement to understand a communicative act. Further, processing speech as an action may help in situations where there is not a clear one-to-one mapping between sound and meaning. For example, a given phoneme can give rise to very different acoustic forms depending on the sounds that come before or after it and the characteristic articulation patterns of the individual talker. Putting the sound into an articulatory context may facilitate correct categorization of the phoneme despite acoustic ambiguity. Lack of physical context may also explain why the development of effective speech recognition technology has presented such a challenge. As the philosopher Wittgenstein (1953) stated, "If a lion could talk, we could not understand him," emphasizing that meaningful communication requires some degree of common experience between the communicators in order to understand the origin of the signal, how it was produced, and therefore what it means.

Our natural environments are complex, and there may be many inputs competing for our attention. Patterns help guide attention and streamline processing by grouping elements together into coherent objects. For example, timing cues play an important role in grouping sounds into an auditory object (Andreou et al. 2011, Shamma et al. 2011). Timing patterns must be integrated across multiple timescales, from the microsecond timing that helps us distinguish the crunch of leaves from the snap of a branch, to the slower rhythm of footsteps. Auditory information is also integrated with input from other modalities such as vision (Musacchia et al. 2008, Schutz & Lipscomb 2007). For example, the well-known McGurk effect is a demonstration of how conflicting visual information influences the perception of a sound: A video presenting repeated utterances of the syllable [ba] is dubbed on to the lip movements for [ga], resulting in normal-hearing adults perceiving a hybrid percept, the syllable [da] (McGurk & MacDonald 1976). Perception therefore involves not only identifying the presence of some kind of regularity or structure, but also integration of inputs across modalities and weighing between alternatives such that the "best fit" candidate wins out—in the case of the McGurk effect, the resulting percept is a compromise between conflicting alternatives. Both the immediate context of a sound and a perceiver's accumulated experience with sound over the course of a lifetime can shape how each new sound is interpreted.

In summary, our ancient relationship with sound is grounded in the physical world. The way that our brains evolved to make sense of sound is driven by how its physicality affects us and how our own physicality produces sound. As a result, our brains are constantly searching for patterns, particularly the kinds of patterns that tell us something about the physical world. The patterns our brains seek out determine how we group acoustic features together to form meaningful objects and streams, and these patterns are integral to the complex communication systems we use every day. Importantly, we are not disembodied listeners: Production and perception are entangled, and this entanglement is evident in the neural circuitry that supports our perception of sound (Kraus et al. 2015).

In the remaining sections of this review, we focus on how communication is guided by patterns, considering both statistical patterns and temporal patterns (see **Figure 3**). We then examine underlying biological mechanisms and how the interaction between production and perception is reflected in the brain. We pay particular attention to how these processing mechanisms relate to everyday communication skills such as reading and how their biological foundations are shaped by experience, including musical expertise.

PATTERNS AND PREDICTION

Statistical Learning

One way the human brain makes sense of incoming sounds is by keeping track of statistical patterns and making predictions based on those patterns. For example, exposure to English quickly reveals

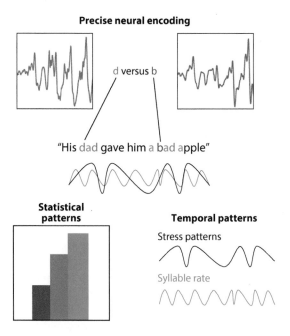

Figure 3

During speech perception, the brain is processing patterns across multiple timescales. Precise neural encoding of fine-timing features helps a listener differentiate one consonant from another; statistical characteristics and temporal patterns guide perception and help form predictions about what is coming next.

that the sound "th" is very likely to be followed by "a" but very unlikely to be followed by "p." By aggregating the probabilities of sound relationships over time, statistical learning enables a listener to discern meaningful structure in sound (Saffran et al. 1996). Predictions are constantly updated and corrected as further information comes in, and the timeframe over which statistical patterns are accrued can range from a short period of exposure (several minutes in an experimental setting) to a lifetime of experience, for example with a native language. Statistical learning has been observed even in infants and is considered a key mechanism underlying the natural acquisition of language (Saffran et al. 1996).

Sensitivity to environmental statistics is encoded throughout the auditory pathway and is not specific to humans: There is evidence that neurons adjust their firing rates in response to the sound-level statistics of their environment in individual auditory cortex neurons of rats (Ulanovsky et al. 2004), and from recordings in the auditory midbrain of guinea pigs (Dean et al. 2005, 2008). Statistics-based adaptation of firing rates has also been demonstrated in the rat thalamus (Antunes et al. 2010) and inferior colliculus (Malmierca et al. 2009), and even in the auditory nerve of anaesthetized cats (Wen et al. 2009). In the case of sound level, this statistical adaptation functions as a gain control, allowing the organisms to maximize their dynamic sensitivity within the parameters of the environment they are in. In a similar way, neurons can adjust their firing to the more complex statistical patterns of a language or musical system. Neonates less than 2 days old were able to pick up on statistical patterns in an artificial language to which they were exposed for one hour during sleep (Teinonen et al. 2009), reinforcing that humans seem to be innately wired with complex pattern detection mechanisms that do not even require active attention. An experiment assessing statistical learning abilities in cotton-top tamarins revealed that these nonhuman primates are also capable of probability-based pattern detection (Hauser et al. 2001). However, a later study determined that human infants were better able to learn the complex grammatical structures that are characteristic of human language (Saffran et al. 2008), whereas the cotton-top tamarins were only able to learn simple grammars, suggesting that species may differ in the degree of sophistication of these statistical learning mechanisms.

Statistical learning is not limited to the auditory domain, with infants also demonstrating sensitivity to statistical patterns in sequences of visual stimuli (Kirkham et al. 2002). It is interesting to note that the basal ganglia, which play an important role in the generation of movement patterns such as walking, are also involved in pattern learning (Kotz et al. 2009), including the acquisition of linguistic and musical grammar (Conway & Pisoni 2008, Ettlinger et al. 2011, Ullman 2001). Whereas the dorsal pathway of the basal ganglia is associated with sensorimotor planning, the ventral pathway plays an important role in reward-based behavior. Although the extent of overlap between the various functions of the basal ganglia remains an active area of research, there is increasing evidence that neural circuitry previously associated with motor planning may in fact serve a broader function in pattern detection and prediction, for cognitive as well as motor action (Graybiel 2005, Schubotz 2007). The reward-based circuitry also introduces an important chemical ingredient for learning, in the form of the neurotransmitter dopamine. Further insight into probability-based learning is provided by examples in which an explicit reward is provided for a particular task: As the brain starts to build predictions based on experience, reward pathways are activated not only by a reward itself, but also in anticipation of likely reward (Knutson et al. 2001), with the degree of activation reflecting the statistical probabilities derived from prior experience (Morris et al. 2006). Dopamine therefore provides a chemical mechanism by which probability can be tracked within the brain and facilitate pattern-based prediction of future events.

Statistical learning mechanisms can themselves be shaped by experience. For example, there is evidence that musical expertise results in improved implicit learning abilities for both musical and linguistic structures (Ettlinger et al. 2011, François & Schön 2011, Skoe et al. 2013b), and musicians were better able to pick up statistical patterns in a novel Morse code–based language (Shook et al. 2013). Short-term musical training has also been shown to improve the ability to parse a speech stream into words (François et al. 2013). Receptivity to statistical learning seems to shift over the course of development; for example, while infants are able to differentiate metrical categories from another musical culture, adults only respond to those present in their own culture (Hannon & Trehub 2005). This suggests that as experience accumulates over a lifetime, the nervous system may maximize its efficiency in processing the most relevant distinctions at the cost of being able to adapt to new ones.

In summary, it has been suggested that the ability of neuronal populations to adapt their firing to statistical properties reflects a fundamental organizing principle of the nervous system, allowing an organism to function in dynamic environments (Kvale & Schreiner 2004, Tallal & Gaab 2006). The nervous system is able to encode patterns derived from the statistical features of incoming information and make predictions based on these patterns that guide both perception and action.

Temporal Patterns

In addition to aggregating probabilities over a period of time, the nervous system is also highly sensitive to how events are structured in time. Put simply, while statistical patterns allow prediction of what is likely to come next, temporal patterns indicate when something is likely to occur. As we know from the experience of listening to unfamiliar languages, separating a continuous stream of speech into meaningful units is no simple task. In addition to the statistical patterns discussed above, temporal patterns can also help a listener to discern the meaningful structure of speech (Cunillera et al. 2006, Cutler & Butterfield 1992, Nakatani & Schaffer 1978). In fact, there is evidence that stress patterns in speech outweigh statistical cues for determining word boundaries when conflicting cues are pitted against each other (Johnson & Jusczyk 2001).

The ability to anticipate based on temporal patterns brings significant processing advantages. For example, the dynamic attending theory purports that the brain may modulate attention over time, such that attention is maximized when important events are most likely to occur (Large & Jones 1999). In other words, the brain synchronizes its activity with the temporal structures present in its environment and increases processing efficiency by allocating resources when they are most likely to be needed.

The effectiveness of this strategy has been demonstrated experimentally; for example, once a temporal pattern is established (e.g., via a repeating tone), linguistic discrimination judgments are made more rapidly if the target sound fits into the established temporal structure rather than deviating from it (Cason & Schön 2012, Quene & Port 2005). Similarly, timing regularities in a speech stream may result in a listener developing temporal expectancies, and these expectancies can influence how subsequent sounds are processed based on whether those sounds align with the expected timing or not (Pitt & Samuel 1990, Quene & Port 2005, Roncaglia-Denissen et al. 2013, Schmidt-Kassow & Kotz 2008). Further, a study by Morillon and colleagues (2014) revealed that moving a finger silently to a reference beat improved the separation of on-beat auditory target tones from distractors, suggesting that the allocation of attention over time was locked to the rhythmic motor activity.

Sensitivity to durational patterns is particularly important for understanding speech under degraded listening conditions (Slater & Kraus 2015, Smith et al. 1989), and violations of expectation can also influence processing. For example, prolonging the duration of less predictable words can help a listener recognize them in a novel context (Turk & Shattuck-Hufnagel 2014). It is important to note that patterns therefore provide a framework that can modulate processing in two ways, either by emphasizing the importance of elements that are consistent with the pattern or by drawing attention to elements that do not fit the pattern. Both sides of the coin are reflected in neural processing, with certain brain responses signaling deviation from expectation (for example, the mismatch negativity, which is enhanced in response to a deviant stimulus; Näätänen 1995), and others reflecting conformity to a pattern (for example, the enhanced subcortical response to speech sounds in a regular versus unpredictable context; Parbery-Clark et al. 2011). Our nuanced relationship with patterns—especially the tension between conformity and deviation—is integral to how we communicate, and it has been proposed that much of the emotional power of music stems from the creation (and violation) of temporal expectations within a predictable framework (Huron 2006).

Links with reading ability. The previous section emphasized that temporal patterns play an important role in guiding auditory perception. Although it is not always intuitive to think of reading as an auditory skill, typically developing children derive their first internal representations of linguistic meaning by parsing the sounds of speech. Effective parsing mechanisms are therefore critical to the development of accurate phonemic representations, which can later be mapped to the orthographic representations of written language.

The ability to make use of rhythmic cues when perceiving speech has been linked to reading skills (for review, see Tierney & Kraus 2013b). A recent study by Woodruff Carr et al. (2014) compared preschoolers who could synchronize to a beat with those who could not: Those who could synchronize had better prereading skills, such as the ability to separate words into their individual sounds, than those who were unable to synchronize. The good synchronizers also had more precise neural encoding of the temporal modulations in speech (Woodruff Carr et al. 2014), suggesting that one of the fundamental mechanisms common to language skills and synchronization ability may be the precision with which the nervous system can encode temporal features. This is discussed further in the next section.

Impaired rhythmic abilities have been linked with language disorders such as dyslexia (Corriveau & Goswami 2009, Overy et al. 2003, Thomson & Goswami 2008), and a study assessing metric perception showed that performance strongly predicted reading ability and phonologic awareness across a population of normal and dyslexic subjects (Huss et al. 2010). These findings have led to the development of rhythm-based interventions to address reading difficulties such as dyslexia, with some success (Bhide et al. 2013; Overy 2000, 2003). However, the various studies demonstrating links between rhythm-related skills and language skills have assessed a wide variety of rhythmic skills, and the rhythm-based interventions have each trained different skills. A clearer understanding of the connections between specific aspects of rhythmic processing and language skills could lead to more accurate diagnosis and better targeted treatment approaches for language problems that are associated with rhythmic deficits. It is also important to note that links between rhythm and language skills across a population do not necessarily mean that training the former can improve the latter in an individual. Further longitudinal studies are needed to better understand the impact of training and to determine whether training that specifically targets certain rhythmic skills is indeed more effective than developing these skills within the context of broader musical training or using other auditory training approaches.

Distinct components of rhythm processing. A great deal remains to be learned about how rhythmic subskills relate with one another, and researchers have proposed various ways of categorizing them. Many rhythm-related activities involve the synchronization of movement to sound, such as tapping to a simple metronome or to the beat of a piece of music. Tapping accurately to a metronome involves perceiving the regular pattern, anticipating the next beat, and coordinating movement accordingly, as well as updating the motor plan based on any discrepancy between the produced movement and the target sound. Tasks involving the production of movement may yield different outcomes than those involving perceptual judgment alone, because humans have been shown to adapt their movements to timing perturbations that are below the threshold of perception (Repp 2000); in other words, individuals may adjust their tapping to a timing perturbation of 15 ms yet report that they did not perceive any shift. Some rhythmic tasks also rely more heavily on memory than others; for example, discriminating between complex rhythmic sequences involves maintaining one sequence in memory to compare with the next.

Tapping to the beat of music involves an additional layer of processing, since a listener must first extract the underlying pulse of the music and then synchronize with that pulse. Moving to the beat of music is something that comes naturally to most people, even young children, but beat and metrical structure are ultimately perceptual constructs. For example, the same piece of music could induce a different metrical percept in different listeners or under different conditions, and metrical structure can be perceived even when individual accented beats are absent (for example, in a syncopated melody) (Iversen et al. 2009). Tasks also differ in terms of complexity and predictability: Musical examples can be extremely complex yet still arranged around a roughly isochronous and predictable beat, whereas speech does not generally adhere to an isochronous framework. It is important to note, however, that live musical performance does contain significant timing fluctuations and more complex temporal patterns, closer to the free-flowing rhythms of speech (Palmer 1997, Repp 1992), and these subtle timing cues contribute greatly to the expressive quality of music (Ashley 2002). Despite the tempo fluctuations of live performances, listeners have no difficulty perceiving the underlying pulse of music; in fact, it has been suggested that beat perception may be helped by this natural timing variability (Rankin et al. 2009). This ability is thought to rely upon the entrainment of neural oscillators to the beat, and this self-sustaining "internal beat" can be tolerant to minor variations and syncopations that may be present in the actual acoustic signal (Large & Snyder 2009, Nozaradan 2014, Nozaradan et al. 2012). Although the temporal patterns of natural speech seem less predictable than the beat of music, it is perhaps easier than one might expect to speak in unison with another speaker, even when the content is unfamiliar (Cummins 2013). This may reflect the close integration of auditory and motor systems, which may facilitate prediction based on articulatory and phrasing cues. Further explication of these nonperiodic aspects of timing and synchronization is a promising line of research that may provide important insight into the links between music and speech (Cummins 2013, Patel 2010).

As discussed previously, the tension between conformity and deviation is an important component of how the brain processes sound, and this tension is especially relevant to rhythm and temporal processing. Whereas the extraction of beat and metrical structure requires tolerance of minor timing variations, other elements of musical communication—such as expressive timing or coordination between players in an ensemble—require direct responses to those same minor variations. Experimentally, participants may be directed to perform specific tasks that isolate different aspects of rhythmic processing, such as beat-based tasks in which timing information is perceived in relation to an underlying beat (for example, detecting whether a target sound is on or off the beat), and duration-based tasks, which involve the perception of absolute timing information (such as determining whether two tones are of the same length) (Merchant et al. 2015). However, in more natural settings the brain must constantly find its own balance between latching onto stability and structure versus detecting and responding to deviations. The resulting interaction between the brain's internal time keeping and its ability to respond to incoming sounds is reflected in the neural circuitry underlying rhythm perception. The so-called motor regions that were discussed above, in the context of their role in pattern detection and perception, are actively involved in rhythm perception (Zatorre et al. 2007). These areas include the basal ganglia, frontal cortex, cerebellum, and midbrain, and because these areas are so highly interconnected, attempts to attach specific functions to distinct areas have met with limited success. However, it is thought that the basal ganglia play a particular role in generating internal representations of beat and metrical structure, whereas the cerebellum is important for coordinating precise motor movements and in tracking durations and timing in complex sound sequences (Grahn 2012, Grube et al. 2010, Merchant et al. 2015). These interconnected systems work together, integrating the big-picture patterns with the fine details, striving for the optimal balance between stability and flexibility.

The important role of motor areas in rhythmic processing is further emphasized by studies showing that movement influences metrical perception in both infants and adults. In the initial study with infants (Phillips-Silver & Trainor 2005), an experimenter bounced the infants on different beats of a rhythm pattern during a training period. The rhythm pattern had ambiguous metrical structure, and the training period specifically emphasized one of the two possible metrical structures. How the babies were bounced during the training phase influenced their subsequent listening preferences when they listened to two auditory versions of the rhythm patterns: The infants preferred to listen to the auditory version with intensity accents that matched the beats on which they had been bounced. There was no such effect when babies observed bouncing but were not bounced themselves, confirming that the effect was due to movement rather than visual input (Phillips-Silver & Trainor 2005). A follow-up study with adults (Phillips-Silver & Trainor 2007) involved participants bouncing to the beat of an auditory rhythm pattern by bending their knees, either emphasizing a waltz- or march-like metrical structure. After this training period, participants listened to auditory versions of the same sequences with increased intensities on certain beats, to match either the waltz or march form. As with the infant study, the bouncing pattern during the training period influenced how the participants perceived the subsequent auditory patterns, with participants reporting greater similarity when the auditory patterns matched their bouncing patterns than when they did not (Phillips-Silver & Trainor 2007).

Research from our laboratory has focused on identifying distinct areas of rhythmic ability that are linked with reading ability. Interestingly, this work has revealed that rhythmic skills may in fact be broken down into distinct rhythmic "intelligences" that do not necessarily pattern together, and the broad connections observed between rhythm skills and reading ability may in fact reflect multiple underlying mechanisms. In particular, the ability to remember and reproduce rhythmic sequences is not necessarily linked to the ability to synchronize accurately to an auditory stimulus and adjust to fine timing perturbations, yet both abilities track with reading skills (Tierney & Kraus 2015). This distinction emphasizes that both music and language involve meaningful information at different timescales, and that effective communication involves integration across these timescales, with both fine temporal precision and sensitivity to rhythmic patterns playing a role.

COMMUNICATION THROUGH SOUND: BIOLOGICAL FOUNDATIONS

Precise Timing in the Auditory System

The auditory system, capable of much finer temporal resolution than other sensory systems, is specialized for timing (Griffiths et al. 2001). Highly efficient neural coding strategies have evolved across species to handle the microsecond timing sensitivity necessary for tasks such as sound localization (Mauk & Buonomano 2004), and in humans, precise encoding of temporal features is especially important for speech perception because the most meaningful parts of the signal are carried by the fastest-changing components, namely the consonants. The ability to encode these subtle timing characteristics is critical to developing accurate phonologic representations and therefore essential for the development of strong reading skills, with more precise subcortical timing linked to better reading abilities (Banai et al. 2009, Hornickel et al. 2009); reading difficulties are associated with less consistent timing in neural responses to speech (Hornickel & Kraus 2013). The ability to synchronize accurately with a metronome involves timing precision on the order of milliseconds (Madison & Merker 2004, Repp 2000, Thaut & Kenyon 2003), which in turn relies heavily on the precision and consistency of neural timing (Tierney & Kraus 2013a, 2014). Research with adolescents reveals that the ability to synchronize with a beat is associated with more consistent subcortical neural timing in the auditory system in response to speech sounds (Tierney & Kraus 2013a) as well as better cognitive and linguistic skills (Tierney & Kraus 2013c) (see **Figure 4**). These outcomes have led to the hypothesis that it may be the precise neural timing involved in entrainment to a beat that at least in part underpins the converging evidence that reading skills are strengthened by musical training, specifically by improving phonological awareness (reviewed in Tierney & Kraus 2014).

Vocal Learning: The Auditory-Motor Connection?

In humans, sound plays a uniquely important role in the coordination of fine motor control, as is reflected in the ability to synchronize to much faster auditory sequences than visual (Repp 2003) and less variability when tapping to an auditory signal than to a visual stimulus (Chen et al. 2002, Hove et al. 2012, Kolers & Brewster 1985, Patel et al. 2005). Interestingly, this auditory advantage does not exist in other species, such as macaque monkeys (Zarco et al. 2009), despite their ability to accurately perceive timing intervals. In other words, synchronization skills require not only

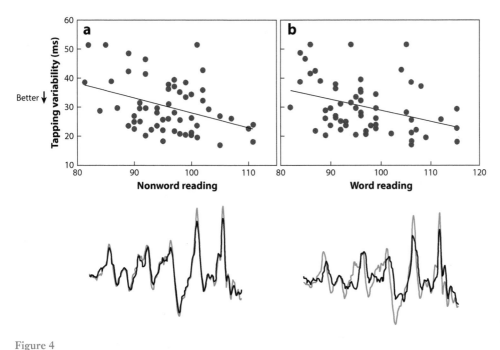

Figure 4

Synchronization to a metronome requires precise temporal encoding in the auditory system, which is also critical to the development of reading skills. (*Top*) Children who tap less variably to a beat have better reading skills. (*Bottom*) Less variable tappers (*a*) have less trial-to-trial variability in their neural response to the speech syllable /da/ than more variable tappers (*b*). Red and black waveforms represent two averages from the same recording session. Figure adapted with permission from Tierney & Kraus (2013a,b).

the precise encoding of sound, but also particular connections between the auditory and motor systems to allow that temporal precision to guide movement. In fact, the ability to synchronize to a regular beat is surprisingly rare in the animal kingdom (Patel et al. 2009). Nonhuman primates, such as monkeys, can perceive durations very accurately, yet extensive efforts to train monkeys to synchronize to an auditory stimulus have been notably unsuccessful (Merchant & Honing 2013, Zarco et al. 2009). Integration between auditory and motor systems is especially strong in vocal learning species, such as songbirds, which are not only able to mimic sounds in their environment but are also able to learn the underlying rules (e.g., grammar) of a sound system and create new sounds based on those rules. Coactivation of comparable motor and auditory brain regions has been observed in both humans and songbirds during vocal learning tasks (Brown et al. 2004), and it has been proposed that the auditory-motor feedback loops that evolved to support vocal learning may also underlie the ability to synchronize to a beat. Individual cases, such as the report of beat-keeping abilities in a sea lion (Cook et al. 2013), leave this a matter of continuing research, since sea lions have not previously been identified as a vocal learning species; however, other pinnipeds such as seals are known to be vocal learners. It may therefore be the vocal learning status of the sea lion that needs to be updated rather than the hypothesized connection between vocal learning and the ability to keep a beat (Patel & Iversen 2014). Furthermore, the common ground between vocal learning and beat synchronization may lie not only in connections between auditory and motor regions, but also more specifically in the motor areas involved in learning and generating patterns (e.g., the basal ganglia), since it is the ability to generate novel utterances based on inherent rules that distinguishes vocal learners from other species capable of vocalizations and vocal mimicry.

This is supported by converging evidence for a specific genetic factor, the *FOXP2* transcription factor gene, that is expressed in the basal ganglia circuitry of vocal learning species (for a review, see Fisher & Scharff 2009).

Neural Synchrony and Multiple Timescales

The brain must integrate information across multiple timescales at once, from the fine timing distinctions between consonant sounds to the longer-scale patterns of syllable rate and stress patterns. Integrating these streams of information into a coherent percept relies heavily on working memory, which determines the capacity for retaining sequences in memory and the scope of pattern matching that can be attempted. Neural oscillations may play an important role in coordinating activity across brain regions and across timescales because they allow the brain to "entrain" to various aspects of temporal structure (Giraud & Poeppel 2012). The cerebral hemispheres show specialization for fast versus slow timing characteristics, based on lateralization of oscillatory activity at different frequency bands (Belin et al. 1998, Poeppel 2003). Better reading abilities have been linked to stronger lateralization of relevant timing rates within the speech signal, such as right-hemispheric specialization for the slower syllable rate of speech (Abrams et al. 2009, Goswami 2011). The left-hemispheric specialization that supports rapid acoustic processing is linked to the precision of subcortical encoding of speech sounds, suggesting that accurate timing in the auditory brainstem is a fundamental ingredient in processing the fast acoustic properties of speech that are critical to the development of reading skills (Abrams et al. 2006, Tierney & Kraus 2013b). Neuronal entrainment is therefore happening simultaneously on multiple timescales, mirroring the multiple timescales of information that unfold in a spoken or musical phrase. Nested rates of brain activity can concurrently synchronize to different stimulus features, and increased coherence between different frequencies of neural oscillations (for example, theta and gamma bands) has been observed during short-term memory tasks (Schack et al. 2002) as well as during a task involving adaptation of speech movement based on auditory feedback (Sengupta & Nasir 2015). Coordination of pattern extraction and prediction across these timescales is therefore important not only for the efficient allocation of neural resources but also for learning. When this coordination breaks down, there can be behavioral consequences; for example, abnormal oscillatory patterns have been associated with reading impairments, such as dyslexia (Abrams et al. 2009, Goswami 2011, Heim et al. 2011, Nagarajan et al. 1999), and may contribute to the impaired multisensory integration that is common in dyslexics (Facoetti et al. 2010, Goswami 2011).

In summary, temporal patterns play an important role in guiding perception and are reflected in the rhythms of neural activity. Links between rhythmic skills and language-related skills, including reading, indicate some degree of common processing between these domains. Although there is still much to be understood about how various aspects of rhythmic processing relate with one another, there is evidence that at least two distinct areas of rhythmic skill are related with reading ability: first, the ability to distinguish fine timing characteristics, and second, the ability to remember and reproduce rhythmic sequences. A recurring theme throughout this review is that our experience of sound is rooted in the physical world, that sound is rooted in movement, and that our motor systems play an essential role in our perception of the inherent structure of sound. In the next section, we consider how these mechanisms can be shaped by experience.

THE IMPRINT OF EXPERIENCE

As we have already emphasized, our perception of communication sounds is influenced not only by acoustic features and immediate context, but also by our accumulated experience with sound over the course of a lifetime. Each new speech utterance presents a new processing challenge: Much of our processing of sound happens automatically, without conscious attention, and this automatic processing is finely tuned by experience.

Automatic Sound Processing: Our Lab's Approach

The auditory system is a distributed but integrated system, capable of dynamic modulation of signal processing as well as long-term tuning of sensory function with experience. In our view, cognitive and sensory processing should not be viewed as distinct; rather, they are melded together through experience because what we have paid attention to in the past will shape our automatic response to new sounds in the present (Kraus & White-Schwoch 2015).

The auditory midbrain is an information-processing hub in which cortical and sensory inputs converge (Bajo et al. 2009, Nelken 2008, Suga & Ma 2003). Direct connections exist between the auditory midbrain and brain regions important for motor control and coordination, including the cerebellum, basal ganglia, and premotor cortex (Casseday et al. 2002). Investigation of the evoked auditory brainstem response to complex sounds (cABR, of which the inferior colliculus is a primary generator) has proved a fruitful approach in exploring experience-based plasticity (Skoe & Kraus 2010). The cABR preserves stimulus characteristics with great fidelity. By comparing stimulus and response characteristics in both time and frequency domains, it is possible to assess the neural representation of fundamental characteristics such as pitch, timing, and timbre. The cABR reflects experience with sound (Bidelman et al. 2011, Kraus & Chandrasekaran 2010, Krishnan et al. 2005, Tzounopoulos & Kraus 2009) and therefore provides an objective biologic snapshot of sound processing in an individual (Kraus 2011). This approach has been used to develop early biomarkers of language development (White-Schwoch et al. 2015) as well as to explore how auditory processing is shaped by expertise, such as musical experience, and impairment, such as dyslexia and autism (reviewed in Kraus & Nicol 2014).

The Musician Signature

Experience does not shape auditory processing with a simple volume knob effect; rather, it selectively enhances relevant components and attenuates irrelevant inputs (Kraus & White-Schwoch 2015). What is relevant to any given individual will determine the focus of his or her experience and, over time, this accumulated experience results in distinct "neural signatures" of expertise (Kraus & Nicol 2014). For example, the brain response of musicians can be tuned in to the specific timbre of the instrument they play, such that the familiar timbre produces a larger response than does the sound of another instrument (Strait et al. 2012). The style of musical playing can also affect automatic processing of sound, as shown by jazz musicians demonstrating greater sensitivity to subtle acoustic variations in their preattentive brain responses in comparison with musicians of other genres (Vuust et al. 2012). However, some of the effects of experience are more general and can transfer to other domains. Converging evidence suggests that the ability to parse a complex auditory scene can be strengthened by musical practice, and there are numerous examples of musical expertise conferring advantages for speech processing (Patel 2011). For example, the neural representation of fine timing characteristics is more precise in musicians than in nonmusicians: Musicians show greater neural differentiation of contrastive consonant sounds than do nonmusicians across the life span (Parbery-Clark et al. 2012c, Strait et al. 2013), and this has been demonstrated longitudinally in elementary school children following two years of music training (Kraus et al. 2014; reviewed in Kraus & Strait 2015). Furthermore, musicians' subcortical encoding of sound is influenced by statistical predictability (Parbery-Clark et al. 2011, Skoe et al.

2013b), suggesting that musical experience may strengthen the ability of the nervous system to benefit from underlying patterns in sound in both musical and linguistic contexts.

Recent work indicates that just a few years of musical training in childhood can influence the neural encoding of sound in adulthood, years after the training has ceased (Skoe & Kraus 2012, White-Schwoch et al. 2013), emphasizing that past experience with sound can shape automatic sound processing in the present, even many years later. It is proposed that the observed enhancements in the neural encoding of sound may be driven in a top-down manner by strengthened cognitive function, such as enhanced working memory and attention, which help to tune sensory function based on prior experience and specific task demands (Ahissar et al. 2009, Conway et al. 2009, Kraus & Chandrasekaran 2010, Kraus et al. 2012, Kraus & White-Schwoch 2015, Nelken & Ulanovsky 2007). This results in more effective targeting of neural resources and better synchronization of underlying neural activity, thereby promoting more consistent and robust neural responses (Krizman et al. 2012, Parbery-Clark et al. 2012b, Skoe & Kraus 2013, Tierney et al. 2015). For example, when listeners are presented with two concurrent speech streams and asked to attend to one and ignore the other, their neural responses to the attended stream are more consistent from trial to trial than the responses to ignored speech, demonstrating that attention can help to coordinate firing across populations of neurons (Strait & Kraus 2011). Neural processing advantages in musicians are linked to behavioral advantages in everyday communication tasks, such as understanding speech in a noisy background. Musicians across the life span demonstrate superior speech-in-noise perception and auditory working memory compared with nonmusician peers (for a review, see Strait & Kraus 2013, Swaminathan et al. 2015, Zendel et al. 2015), and improved speech-in-noise perception was observed longitudinally in elementary school children following two years of music class (Slater et al. 2015). Recent work reveals that the ability to perceive speech in noise is correlated with performance on a rhythm perception task (Slater & Kraus 2015), emphasizing that temporal patterns are especially important for following speech under difficult listening conditions.

Clinical and Educational Implications

Understanding the fundamental mechanisms by which humans process communication sounds not only is interesting from a theoretical perspective but also has great utility in clinical and educational settings. Many of the same aspects of neural processing that are strengthened in auditory experts, such as musicians, are found to be deficient in populations with language-related disorders (for a review, see Tierney & Kraus 2013b), suggesting that training and remediation that appropriately target underlying mechanisms could be effective in treating individuals with language-based deficits. Furthermore, the biological benefits of musical expertise may counteract some of the natural declines in neural processing associated with aging (Parbery-Clark et al. 2009, 2012a) as well as the negative impact on neural function that may result from living in poverty (Skoe et al. 2013a). Longitudinal studies have demonstrated positive effects of school-based music training on the neural processing of speech (Kraus & Strait 2015) and have revealed that neural processing of speech can be strengthened by short-term training in children with language-based learning problems (for a review, see Kraus & Hornickel 2012). The potential role of music-based interventions for the treatment of language disorders is a continuing area of research.

CONCLUSIONS

In this review we have emphasized that the sophisticated systems of modern communication are rooted in our more ancient relationship with sound. This relationship is grounded in the physical world and is reflected in the patterns that our brains seek out as we try to make sense of the sounds we hear. These patterns also provide a framework for communicating with others, and there is close integration between our ability to produce as well as perceive communication sounds. The same neural networks involved in generating the movements to produce sound are also intimately involved in the perception and prediction of underlying patterns. Therefore, communication is not simply the transfer of sound signals from one person to another but rather is an interaction between physical entities. Evidence indicates that when two individuals synchronize their movements, this increases affiliation between them and promotes bonding (Cirelli et al. 2012, Hove & Risen 2009, Launay et al. 2013). The inherent rhythms of music and speech facilitate interpersonal synchrony by allowing us to predict what is coming next and align our movements with others (Phillips-Silver et al. 2010). From the dyadic exchange between mother and child (Censullo et al. 1985) to conversational turn-taking (Auer et al. 1999) and improvisational jazz (Berkowitz 2010), these patterns in time not only streamline information processing, they also help us to connect.

An important aspect of synchrony is that it is a natural signature of emotion, since the potent neural chemistry of emotion can trigger activation across multiple brain regions within a very short space of time (Scherer 2013) and may stem from the basic signaling mechanisms underlying fight or flight behavior. Interpersonal synchrony may build upon this foundation such that synchronized activity with another person implies shared emotion, and it has been suggested that synchrony may foster social bonds between individuals by blurring the perceived boundary between self and other (Tarr et al. 2014). In a sense, this blurring of boundaries between self and other is what communication is all about: Words may scratch the surface, but sound can move us beyond words.

FUTURE ISSUES

1. Understanding how different timescales of information are integrated in the brain will be an important area of future research.

2. Identifying distinct components of rhythmic processing will be important for understanding connections between music and language skills.

3. Longitudinal studies will be important to assess whether rhythm-based training can improve language skills within an individual.

4. Identifying biological markers of communication deficits will allow for more effective treatment and early intervention.

5. Motor regions of the brain may play a broader role in pattern-based behavior than previously thought.

6. Further investigation of dynamic synchrony, for example, two people speaking in unison, may help reveal predictive mechanisms important for speech.

DISCLOSURE STATEMENT

The authors are not aware of any affiliations, memberships, funding, or financial holdings that might be perceived as affecting the objectivity of this review.

ACKNOWLEDGMENTS

Research by the authors is supported by NSF BCS-1057556, NSF BCS-0921275, NSF SMA-1015614, NSF BCS-1430400, the Mathers Foundation, the National Association of Music Merchants (NAMM), the Interactive Metronome, and the Hugh Knowles Hearing Center. We thank Trent Nicol for comments on a previous version of this manuscript and Adam Trefonides for contributions to the figures.

LITERATURE CITED

Abrams DA, Nicol T, Zecker S, Kraus N. 2009. Abnormal cortical processing of the syllable rate of speech in poor readers. *J. Neurosci.* 29:7686–93

Abrams DA, Nicol T, Zecker SG, Kraus N. 2006. Auditory brainstem timing predicts cerebral asymmetry for speech. *J. Neurosci.* 26:11131–37

Ahissar M, Nahum M, Nelken I, Hochstein S. 2009. Reverse hierarchies and sensory learning. *Philos. Trans. R. Soc. B* 364:285–99

Andreou L-V, Kashino M, Chait M. 2011. The role of temporal regularity in auditory segregation. *Hear. Res.* 280:228–35

Antunes FM, Nelken I, Covey E, Malmierca MS. 2010. Stimulus-specific adaptation in the auditory thalamus of the anesthetized rat. *PLOS ONE* 5:e14071

Ashley R. 2002. Do[n't] change a hair for me: the art of jazz rubato. *Music Percept.* 19:311–32

Auer P, Couper-Kuhlen E, Müller F. 1999. *Language in Time: The Rhythm and Tempo of Spoken Interaction.* Oxford, UK: Oxford Univ. Press

Bajo VM, Nodal FR, Moore DR, King AJ. 2009. The descending corticocollicular pathway mediates learning-induced auditory plasticity. *Nat. Neurosci.* 13:253–60

Banai K, Hornickel J, Skoe E, Nicol T, Zecker S, Kraus N. 2009. Reading and subcortical auditory function. *Cereb. Cortex* 19:2699–707

Belin P, Zilbovicius M, Crozier S, Thivard L, Fontaine A, et al. 1998. Lateralization of speech and auditory temporal processing. *J. Cogn. Neurosci.* 10:536–40

Berkowitz AL. 2010. *The Improvising Mind: Cognition and Creativity in the Musical Moment.* New York: Oxford Univ. Press

Bhide A, Power A, Goswami U. 2013. A rhythmic musical intervention for poor readers: a comparison of efficacy with a letter-based intervention. *Mind Brain Educ.* 7:113–23

Bidelman GM, Gandour JT, Krishnan A. 2011. Cross-domain effects of music and language experience on the representation of pitch in the human auditory brainstem. *J. Cogn. Neurosci.* 23:425–34

Brown S, Martinez MJ, Hodges DA, Fox PT, Parsons LM. 2004. The song system of the human brain. *Cogn. Brain Res.* 20:363–75

Cason N, Schön D. 2012. Rhythmic priming enhances the phonological processing of speech. *Neuropsychologia* 50:2652–58

Casseday JH, Fremouw T, Covey E. 2002. The inferior colliculus: a hub for the central auditory system. In *Integrative Functions in the Mammalian Auditory Pathway*, ed. D Oertel, AN Popper, RR Fay, pp. 238–318. New York: Springer

Censullo M, Lester B, Hoffman J. 1985. Rhythmic patterning in mother-newborn interaction. *Nurs. Res.* 34:342–46

Chen Y, Repp BH, Patel AD. 2002. Spectral decomposition of variability in synchronization and continuation tapping: comparisons between auditory and visual pacing and feedback conditions. *Hum. Mov. Sci.* 21:515–32

Cirelli LK, Wan SJ, Trainor LJ. 2014. Fourteen-month-old infants use interpersonal synchrony as a cue to direct helpfulness. *Philos. Trans. R. Soc. B* 369:20130400

Conway CM, Pisoni DB. 2008. Neurocognitive basis of implicit learning of sequential structure and its relation to language processing. *Ann. N. Y. Acad. Sci.* 1145:113–31

Conway CM, Pisoni DB, Kronenberger WG. 2009. The importance of sound for cognitive sequencing abilities: the auditory scaffolding hypothesis. *Curr. Dir. Psychol. Sci.* 18:275–79

Cook P, Rouse A, Wilson M, Reichmuth C. 2013. A California sea lion (*Zalophus californianus*) can keep the beat: motor entrainment to rhythmic auditory stimuli in a non vocal mimic. *J. Comp. Psychol.* 127:412–27

Corriveau KH, Goswami U. 2009. Rhythmic motor entrainment in children with speech and language impairments: tapping to the beat. *Cortex* 45:119–30

Cummins F. 2013. Joint speech: the missing link between speech and music? *Percepta: J. Musical Cogn.* 1:17–32

Cunillera T, Toro JM, Sebastián-Gallés N, Rodríguez-Fornells A. 2006. The effects of stress and statistical cues on continuous speech segmentation: an event-related brain potential study. *Brain Res.* 1123:168–78

Cutler A, Butterfield S. 1992. Rhythmic cues to speech segmentation: evidence from juncture misperception. *J. Mem. Lang.* 31:218–36

Dean I, Harper NS, McAlpine D. 2005. Neural population coding of sound level adapts to stimulus statistics. *Nat. Neurosci.* 8:1684–89

Dean I, Robinson BL, Harper NS, McAlpine D. 2008. Rapid neural adaptation to sound level statistics. *J. Neurosci.* 28:6430–38

Ettlinger M, Margulis EH, Wong PC. 2011. Implicit memory in music and language. *Front. Psychol.* 2:211

Facoetti A, Trussardi AN, Ruffino M, Lorusso ML, Cattaneo C, et al. 2010. Multisensory spatial attention deficits are predictive of phonological decoding skills in developmental dyslexia. *J. Cogn. Neurosci.* 22:1011–25

Fisher SE, Scharff C. 2009. *FOXP2* as a molecular window into speech and language. *Trends Genet.* 25:166–77

François C, Chobert J, Besson M, Schön D. 2013. Music training for the development of speech segmentation. *Cereb. Cortex* 23:2038–43

François C, Schön D. 2011. Musical expertise boosts implicit learning of both musical and linguistic structures. *Cereb. Cortex* 21:2357–65

Giraud A-L, Poeppel D. 2012. Cortical oscillations and speech processing: emerging computational principles and operations. *Nat. Neurosci.* 15:511–17

Goswami U. 2011. A temporal sampling framework for developmental dyslexia. *Trends Cogn. Sci.* 15:3–10

Grahn JA. 2012. Neural mechanisms of rhythm perception: current findings and future perspectives. *Top. Cogn. Sci.* 4:585–606

Graybiel AM. 2005. The basal ganglia: learning new tricks and loving it. *Curr. Opin. Neurobiol.* 15:638–44

Griffiths TD, Uppenkamp S, Johnsrude I, Josephs O, Patterson RD. 2001. Encoding of the temporal regularity of sound in the human brainstem. *Nat. Neurosci.* 4:633–37

Grube M, Lee K-H, Griffiths TD, Barker AT, Woodruff PW. 2010. Frontiers: Transcranial magnetic theta-burst stimulation of the human cerebellum distinguishes absolute, duration-based from relative, beat-based perception of subsecond time intervals. *Front. Psychol.* 1:171

Hannon EE, Trehub SE. 2005. Metrical categories in infancy and adulthood. *Psychol. Sci.* 16:48–55

Hauser MD, Newport EL, Aslin RN. 2001. Segmentation of the speech stream in a non-human primate: statistical learning in cotton-top tamarins. *Cognition* 78:B53–64

Heim S, Friedman JT, Keil A, Benasich AA. 2011. Reduced sensory oscillatory activity during rapid auditory processing as a correlate of language-learning impairment. *J. Neurolinguist.* 24:538–55

Hornickel J, Kraus N. 2013. Unstable representation of sound: a biological marker of dyslexia. *J. Neurosci.* 33:3500–4

Hornickel J, Skoe E, Nicol T, Zecker S, Kraus N. 2009. Subcortical differentiation of stop consonants relates to reading and speech-in-noise perception. *PNAS* 106:13022–27

Hove MJ, Iversen JR, Zhang A, Repp BH. 2012. Synchronization with competing visual and auditory rhythms: Bouncing ball meets metronome. *Psychol. Res.* 77:388–98

Hove MJ, Risen JL. 2009. It's all in the timing: Interpersonal synchrony increases affiliation. *Soc. Cogn.* 27:949–60

Huron DB. 2006. *Sweet Anticipation: Music and the Psychology of Expectation.* Cambridge, MA: MIT Press

Huss M, Verney JP, Fosker T, Mead N, Goswami U. 2010. Music, rhythm, rise time perception and developmental dyslexia: Perception of musical meter predicts reading and phonology. *Cortex* 47:674–89

Iversen JR, Repp BH, Patel AD. 2009. Top-down control of rhythm perception modulates early auditory responses. *Ann. N. Y. Acad. Sci.* 1169:58–73

Johnson EK, Jusczyk PW. 2001. Word segmentation by 8-month-olds: when speech cues count more than statistics. *J. Mem. Lang.* 44:548–67

Kirkham NZ, Slemmer JA, Johnson SP. 2002. Visual statistical learning in infancy: evidence for a domain general learning mechanism. *Cognition* 83:B35–42

Knutson B, Adams CM, Fong GW, Hommer D. 2001. Anticipation of increasing monetary reward selectively recruits nucleus accumbens. *J. Neurosci.* 21:RC159

Kolers PA, Brewster JM. 1985. Rhythms and responses. *J. Exp. Psychol.: Hum. Percept. Perform.* 11:150–67

Kotz SA, Schwartze M, Schmidt-Kassow M. 2009. Non-motor basal ganglia functions: a review and proposal for a model of sensory predictability in auditory language perception. *Cortex* 45:982–90

Kraus N. 2011. Listening in on the listening brain. *Phys. Today* 64:40–45

Kraus N, Chandrasekaran B. 2010. Music training for the development of auditory skills. *Nat. Rev. Neurosci.* 11:599–605

Kraus N, Hornickel J. 2012. Meaningful engagement with sound for strengthening communication skills. In *Auditory Processing Disorders: Assessment, Management and Treatment*, ed. D Geffner, D Ross-Swain, pp. 693–717. San Diego: Plural

Kraus N, Nicol T. 2014. The cognitive auditory system: the role of learning in shaping the biology of the auditory system. In *Perspectives on Auditory Research*, ed. AN Popper, RR Fay, pp. 299–319. New York: Springer Sci.+Bus. Media

Kraus N, Slater J, Thompson EC, Hornickel J, Strait DL, et al. 2014. Music enrichment programs improve the neural encoding of speech in at-risk children. *J. Neurosci.* 34:11913–18

Kraus N, Strait DL. 2015. Emergence of biological markers of musicianship with school-based music instruction. *Ann. N. Y. Acad. Sci.* 1337:163–69

Kraus N, Strait DL, Parbery-Clark A. 2012. Cognitive factors shape brain networks for auditory skills: spotlight on auditory working memory. *Ann. N. Y. Acad. Sci.* 1252:100–7

Kraus N, White-Schwoch T. 2015. Unraveling the biology of auditory learning: a cognitive-sensorimotor-reward framework. *Trends Cogn. Sci.* In press

Krishnan A, Xu Y, Gandour J, Cariani P. 2005. Encoding of pitch in the human brainstem is sensitive to language experience. *Brain Res. Cogn. Brain Res.* 25:161–68

Krizman J, Marian V, Shook A, Skoe E, Kraus N. 2012. Subcortical encoding of sound is enhanced in bilinguals and relates to executive function advantages. *PNAS* 109:7877–81

Kvale MN, Schreiner CE. 2004. Short-term adaptation of auditory receptive fields to dynamic stimuli. *J. Neurophysiol.* 91:604–12

Large EW, Jones MR. 1999. The dynamics of attending: how people track time-varying events. *Psychol. Rev.* 106:119–59

Large EW, Snyder JS. 2009. Pulse and meter as neural resonance. *Ann. N. Y. Acad. Sci.* 1169:46–57

Launay J, Dean RT, Bailes F. 2013. Synchronization can influence trust following virtual interaction. *Exp. Psychol.* 60:53–63

Madison G, Merker B. 2004. Human sensorimotor tracking of continuous subliminal deviations from isochrony. *Neurosci. Lett.* 370:69–73

Malmierca MS, Cristaudo S, Pérez-González D, Covey E. 2009. Stimulus-specific adaptation in the inferior colliculus of the anesthetized rat. *J. Neurosci.* 29:5483–93

Mauk MD, Buonomano DV. 2004. The neural basis of temporal processing. *Annu. Rev. Neurosci.* 27:307–40

McGurk H, MacDonald J. 1976. Hearing lips and seeing voices. *Nature* 264:746–48

Merchant H, Grahn J, Trainor L, Rohrmeier M, Fitch WT. 2015. Finding the beat: a neural perspective across humans and non-human primates. *Philos. Trans. R. Soc. Lond. B* 370:20140093

Merchant H, Honing H. 2013. Are non-human primates capable of rhythmic entrainment? Evidence for the gradual audiomotor evolution hypothesis. *Front. Neurosci.* 7:274

Morillon B, Schroeder CE, Wyart V. 2014. Motor contributions to the temporal precision of auditory attention. *Nat. Commun.* 5:5255

Morris G, Nevet A, Arkadir D, Vaadia E, Bergman H. 2006. Midbrain dopamine neurons encode decisions for future action. *Nat. Neurosci.* 9:1057–63

Musacchia G, Strait D, Kraus N. 2008. Relationships between behavior, brainstem and cortical encoding of seen and heard speech in musicians and non-musicians. *Hear. Res.* 241:34–42

Näätänen R. 1995. The mismatch negativity: a powerful tool for cognitive neuroscience. *Ear Hear.* 16:6–18

Nagarajan S, Mahncke H, Salz T, Tallal P, Roberts T, Merzenich MM. 1999. Cortical auditory signal processing in poor readers. *PNAS* 96:6483–88

Nakatani LH, Schaffer JA. 1978. Hearing "words" without words: prosodic cues for word perception. *J. Acoust. Soc. Am.* 63:234–45

Nelken I. 2008. Processing of complex sounds in the auditory system. *Curr. Opin. Neurobiol.* 18:413–17

Nelken I, Ulanovsky N. 2007. Mismatch negativity and stimulus-specific adaptation in animal models. *J. Psychophysiol.* 21:214–23

Nozaradan S. 2014. Exploring how musical rhythm entrains brain activity with electroencephalogram frequency-tagging. *Philos. Trans. R. Soc. Lond. B* 369:20130393

Nozaradan S, Peretz I, Mouraux A. 2012. Selective neuronal entrainment to the beat and meter embedded in a musical rhythm. *J. Neurosci.* 32:17572–81

Overy K. 2000. Dyslexia, temporal processing and music: the potential of music as an early learning aid for dyslexic children. *Psychol. Music* 28:218–29

Overy K. 2003. Dyslexia and music. From timing deficits to musical intervention. *Ann. N.Y. Acad. Sci.* 999:497–505

Overy K, Nicolson RI, Fawcett AJ, Clarke EF. 2003. Dyslexia and music: measuring musical timing skills. *Dyslexia* 9:18–36

Palmer C. 1997. Music performance. *Annu. Rev. Psychol.* 48:115–38

Parbery-Clark A, Anderson S, Hittner E, Kraus N. 2012a. Musical experience offsets age-related delays in neural timing. *Neurobiol. Aging* 33:1483.e1–4

Parbery-Clark A, Anderson S, Hittner E, Kraus N. 2012b. Musical experience strengthens the neural representation of sounds important for communication in middle-aged adults. *Front. Aging Neurosci.* 4:30

Parbery-Clark A, Skoe E, Kraus N. 2009. Musical experience limits the degradative effects of background noise on the neural processing of sound. *J. Neurosci.* 29:14100–7

Parbery-Clark A, Strait D, Kraus N. 2011. Context-dependent encoding in the auditory brainstem subserves enhanced speech-in-noise perception in musicians. *Neuropsychologia* 49:3338–45

Parbery-Clark A, Tierney A, Strait DL, Kraus N. 2012c. Musicians have fine-tuned neural distinction of speech syllables. *Neuroscience* 219:111–19

Patel AD. 2010. *Music, Language, and the Brain.* New York: Oxford Univ. Press

Patel AD. 2011. Why would musical training benefit the neural encoding of speech? The OPERA hypothesis. *Front. Psychol.* 2:142

Patel AD, Iversen JR. 2014. The evolutionary neuroscience of musical beat perception: the Action Simulation for Auditory Prediction (ASAP) hypothesis. *Front. Syst. Neurosci.* 8:57

Patel AD, Iversen JR, Bregman MR, Schulz I. 2009. Studying synchronization to a musical beat in nonhuman animals. *Ann. N. Y. Acad. Sci.* 1169:459–69

Patel AD, Iversen JR, Chen Y, Repp BH. 2005. The influence of metricality and modality on synchronization with a beat. *Exp. Brain Res.* 163:226–38

Phillips-Silver J, Aktipis CA, Bryant GA. 2010. The ecology of entrainment: foundations of coordinated rhythmic movement. *Music Percept.* 28:3–14

Phillips-Silver J, Trainor LJ. 2005. Feeling the beat: Movement influences infant rhythm perception. *Science* 308:1430

Phillips-Silver J, Trainor LJ. 2007. Hearing what the body feels: auditory encoding of rhythmic movement. *Cognition* 105:533–46

Pitt MA, Samuel AG. 1990. The use of rhythm in attending to speech. *J. Exp. Psychol.: Hum. Percept. Perform.* 16:564–73

Poeppel D. 2003. The analysis of speech in different temporal integration windows: cerebral lateralization as "asymmetric sampling in time." *Speech Commun.* 41:245–55

Quene H, Port RF. 2005. Effects of timing regularity and metrical expectancy on spoken-word perception. *Phonetica* 62:1–13

Rankin SK, Large EW, Fink PW. 2009. Fractal tempo fluctuation and pulse prediction. *Music Percept.* 26:401–13

Repp BH. 1992. Diversity and commonality in music performance: an analysis of timing microstructure in Schumann's "Traumerei." *J. Acoust. Soc. Am.* 92:2546–68

Repp BH. 2000. Compensation for subliminal timing perturbations in perceptual-motor synchronization. *Psychol. Res.* 63:106–28

Repp BH. 2003. Rate limits in sensorimotor synchronization with auditory and visual sequences: the synchronization threshold and the benefits and costs of interval subdivision. *J. Mot. Behav.* 35:355–70

Roncaglia-Denissen MP, Schmidt-Kassow M, Kotz SA. 2013. Speech rhythm facilitates syntactic ambiguity resolution: ERP evidence. *PLOS ONE* 8:e56000

Saffran J, Hauser M, Seibel R, Kapfhamer J, Tsao F, Cushman F. 2008. Grammatical pattern learning by human infants and cotton-top tamarin monkeys. *Cognition* 107:479–500

Saffran JR, Aslin RN, Newport EL. 1996. Statistical learning by 8-month-old infants. *Science* 274:1926–28

Schack B, Vath N, Petsche H, Geissler H-G, Möller E. 2002. Phase-coupling of theta-gamma EEG rhythms during short-term memory processing. *Int. J. Psychophysiol.* 44:143–63

Scherer K. 2013. The evolutionary origin of multimodal synchronization in emotional expression. *J. Anthropol. Sci.* 91:1–16

Schmidt-Kassow M, Kotz SA. 2008. Entrainment of syntactic processing? ERP-responses to predictable time intervals during syntactic reanalysis. *Brain Res.* 1226:144–55

Schubotz RI. 2007. Prediction of external events with our motor system: towards a new framework. *Trends Cogn. Sci.* 11:211–18

Schutz M, Lipscomb S. 2007. Hearing gestures, seeing music: Vision influences perceived tone duration. *Perception* 36:888–97

Scott SK, Johnsrude IS. 2003. The neuroanatomical and functional organization of speech perception. *Trends Neurosci.* 26:100–7

Sengupta R, Nasir SM. 2015. Redistribution of neural phase coherence reflects establishment of feedforward map in speech motor adaptation. *J. Neurophysiol.* 113:2471–79

Shamma SA, Elhilali M, Micheyl C. 2011. Temporal coherence and attention in auditory scene analysis. *Trends Neurosci.* 34:114–23

Shook A, Marian V, Bartolotti J, Schroeder SR. 2013. Musical experience influences statistical learning of a novel language. *Am. J. Psychol.* 126:95–104

Skoe E, Kraus N. 2010. Auditory brain stem response to complex sounds: a tutorial. *Ear Hear.* 31:302–24

Skoe E, Kraus N. 2012. A little goes a long way: how the adult brain is shaped by musical training in childhood. *J. Neurosci.* 32:11507–10

Skoe E, Kraus N. 2013. Musical training heightens auditory brainstem function during sensitive periods in development. *Front. Psychol.* 4:622

Skoe E, Krizman J, Kraus N. 2013a. The impoverished brain: disparities in maternal education affect the neural response to sound. *J. Neurosci.* 33:17221–31

Skoe E, Krizman J, Spitzer E, Kraus N. 2013b. The auditory brainstem is a barometer of rapid auditory learning. *Neuroscience* 243:104–14

Slater J, Kraus N. 2015. The role of rhythm in perceiving speech in noise: a comparison of percussionists, vocalists and non-musicians. *Cogn. Process.* In press

Slater J, Skoe E, Strait DL, O'Connell S, Thompson E, Kraus N. 2015. Music training improves speech-in-noise perception: longitudinal evidence from a community-based music program. *Behav. Brain Res.* 291:244–52

Smith MR, Cutler A, Butterfield S, Nimmo-Smith I. 1989. The perception of rhythm and word boundaries in noise-masked speech. *J. Speech Hear. Res.* 32:912–20

Strait DL, Chan K, Ashley R, Kraus N. 2012. Specialization among the specialized: Auditory brainstem function is tuned in to timbre. *Cortex* 48:360–62

Strait DL, Kraus N. 2011. Can you hear me now? Musical training shapes functional brain networks for selective auditory attention and hearing speech in noise. *Front. Psychol.* 2:113

Strait DL, Kraus N. 2013. Biological impact of auditory expertise across the life span: musicians as a model of auditory learning. *Hear. Res.* 308:109–21

Strait DL, O'Connell S, Parbery-Clark A, Kraus N. 2013. Musicians' enhanced neural differentiation of speech sounds arises early in life: developmental evidence from ages 3 to 30. *Cereb. Cortex* 24:2512–21

Suga N, Ma X. 2003. Multiparametric corticofugal modulation and plasticity in the auditory system. *Nat. Rev. Neurosci.* 4:783–94

Swaminathan J, Mason CR, Streeter TM, Best V, Kidd G Jr., Patel AD. 2015. Musical training, individual differences and the cocktail party problem. *Sci. Rep.* 5:11628

Tallal P, Gaab N. 2006. Dynamic auditory processing, musical experience and language development. *Trends Neurosci.* 29:382–90

Tarr B, Launay J, Dunbar RI. 2014. Music and social bonding: "self-other" merging and neurohormonal mechanisms. *Front. Psychol.* 5:1096

Teinonen T, Fellman V, Näätänen R, Alku P, Huotilainen M. 2009. Statistical language learning in neonates revealed by event-related brain potentials. *BMC Neurosci.* 10:21

Thaut MH, Kenyon GP. 2003. Rapid motor adaptations to subliminal frequency shifts during syncopated rhythmic sensorimotor synchronization. *Hum. Mov. Sci.* 22:321–38

Thomson JM, Goswami U. 2008. Rhythmic processing in children with developmental dyslexia: Auditory and motor rhythms link to reading and spelling. *J. Physiol.* 102:120–29

Tierney A, Kraus N. 2013a. The ability to move to a beat is linked to the consistency of neural responses to sound. *J. Neurosci.* 33:14981–88

Tierney A, Kraus N. 2013b. Music training for the development of reading skills. *Progress in Brain Research. Changing Brains: Applying Brain Plasticity to Advance and Recover Human Ability*, ed. MM Merzenich, M Nahum, TM Van Vleet, 207:209–21. Amsterdam: Elsevier

Tierney A, Kraus N. 2014. Auditory-motor entrainment and phonological skills: precise auditory timing hypothesis (PATH). *Front. Hum. Neurosci.* 8:949

Tierney AT, Kraus N. 2013c. The ability to tap to a beat relates to cognitive, linguistic, and perceptual skills. *Brain Lang.* 124:225–31

Tierney A, Kraus N. 2015. Evidence for multiple rhythmic skills. *PLOS ONE.* In press

Tierney AT, Krizman J, Kraus N. 2015. Music training alters the course of adolescent auditory development. *PNAS* 112:10062–67

Turk A, Shattuck-Hufnagel S. 2014. Timing in talking: What is it used for, and how is it controlled? *Philos. Trans. R. Soc. B* 369:20130395

Tzounopoulos T, Kraus N. 2009. Learning to encode timing: mechanisms of plasticity in the auditory brainstem. *Neuron* 62:463–69

Ulanovsky N, Las L, Farkas D, Nelken I. 2004. Multiple time scales of adaptation in auditory cortex neurons. *J. Neurosci.* 24:10440–53

Ullman MT. 2001. A neurocognitive perspective on language: the declarative/procedural model. *Nat. Rev. Neurosci.* 2:717–26

Vuust P, Brattico E, Seppänen M, Näätänen R, Tervaniemi M. 2012. Practiced musical style shapes auditory skills. *Ann. N. Y. Acad. Sci.* 1252:139–46

Watkins KE, Strafella AP, Paus T. 2003. Seeing and hearing speech excites the motor system involved in speech production. *Neuropsychologia* 41:989–94

Wen B, Wang GI, Dean I, Delgutte B. 2009. Dynamic range adaptation to sound level statistics in the auditory nerve. *J. Neurosci.* 29:13797–808

White-Schwoch T, Woodruff Carr K, Anderson S, Strait DL, Kraus N. 2013. Older adults benefit from music training early in life: biological evidence for long-term training-driven plasticity. *J. Neurosci.* 33:17667–74

White-Schwoch T, Woodruff Carr K, Thompson EC, Anderson S, Nicol T, et al. 2015. Auditory processing in noise: a preschool biomarker for literacy. *PLOS Biol.* 13:e1002196

Wilson SM, Saygin AP, Sereno MI, Iacoboni M. 2004. Listening to speech activates motor areas involved in speech production. *Nat. Neurosci.* 7:701–2

Wittgenstein L. 1953. *Philosophical Investigations.* Oxford, UK: Blackwell

Woodruff Carr K, White-Schwoch T, Tierney AT, Strait DL, Kraus N. 2014. Beat synchronization predicts neural speech encoding and reading readiness in preschoolers. *PNAS* 111:14559–64

Zarco W, Merchant H, Prado L, Mendez JC. 2009. Subsecond timing in primates: comparison of interval production between human subjects and rhesus monkeys. *J. Neurophysiol.* 102:3191–202

Zatorre RJ, Chen JL, Penhune VB. 2007. When the brain plays music: auditory–motor interactions in music perception and production. *Nat. Rev. Neurosci.* 8:547–58

Zendel BR, Tremblay CD, Belleville S, Peretz I. 2015. The impact of musicianship on the cortical mechanisms related to separating speech from background noise. *J. Cogn. Neurosci.* 27:1044–59

Episodic Memory and Beyond: The Hippocampus and Neocortex in Transformation

Morris Moscovitch,[1,2,3] Roberto Cabeza,[4] Gordon Winocur,[2,5,6] and Lynn Nadel[7]

[1]Department of Psychology, University of Toronto, Toronto, Ontario M5S 3G3, Canada; email: momos@psych.utoronto.ca

[2]Rotman Research Institute, Baycrest Center, Toronto, Ontario, M6A 2E1 Canada

[3]Department of Psychology, Baycrest Center, Toronto, Ontario M6A 2E1, Canada

[4]Center for Cognitive Neuroscience, Duke University, Durham, North Carolina 27708; email: cabeza@duke.edu

[5]Department of Psychology, Trent University, Peterborough, Ontario K9J 7B8, Canada

[6]Department of Psychiatry, University of Toronto, Toronto, Ontario M5T 1R8, Canada; email: gwinocur@research.baycrest.org

[7]Department of Psychology and Cognitive Science Program, University of Arizona, Tucson, Arizona 85721; email: nadel@u.arizona.edu

Annu. Rev. Psychol. 2016. 67:105–34

The *Annual Review of Psychology* is online at psych.annualreviews.org

This article's doi: 10.1146/annurev-psych-113011-143733

Keywords

episodic memory, frontal cortex, hippocampus, parietal cortex, schema, transformation

Abstract

The last decade has seen dramatic technological and conceptual changes in research on episodic memory and the brain. New technologies, and increased use of more naturalistic observations, have enabled investigators to delve deeply into the structures that mediate episodic memory, particularly the hippocampus, and to track functional and structural interactions among brain regions that support it. Conceptually, episodic memory is increasingly being viewed as subject to lifelong transformations that are reflected in the neural substrates that mediate it. In keeping with this dynamic perspective, research on episodic memory (and the hippocampus) has infiltrated domains, from perception to language and from empathy to problem solving, that were once considered outside its boundaries. Using the component process model as a framework, and focusing on the hippocampus, its subfields, and specialization along its longitudinal axis, along with its interaction with other brain regions, we consider these new developments and their implications for the organization of episodic memory and its contribution to functions in other domains.

Contents

INTRODUCTION

The concept of episodic memory, according to Tulving (1983, 2002), refers to a declarative memory that contains information specific to the time and place of acquisition (what laypeople may call an autobiographical episode), as distinguished from semantic memory, which is concerned with knowledge not tied to its context of acquisition. Recollection, a process that enables one to relive episodes, is associated with autonoetic consciousness, a subjective sense of time and of the self as the one who experienced the episode and possesses the memory. By contrast, the process of knowing enables one to recognize an event or stimulus as familiar without locating it in time and place. Familiarity-based memory is associated with noetic consciousness, or at least with a much reduced autonoetic consciousness. Because these events and processes are what researchers studying episodic memory mean to capture in a laboratory setting, Tulving referred to the single, unrelated trials that are the typical memoranda of laboratory experiments as events (or mini-events) embedded within the larger episode of the laboratory experiment. For an event to qualify as an episodic memory, details of the event and of the place in which it occurred must be present at retrieval, accompanied by autonoetic consciousness that enables reexperiencing [James 1950 (1890), p. 658; Tulving 1983, 2002; see Rubin & Umanath 2015 for a critique and alternative].

Tulving's formulation still governs much of the research on episodic memory and the brain, but the introduction of new topics, modes of inquiry, more naturalistic approaches and technologies has added great variety to the landscape. It is this altered landscape that we wish to capture in our review. Because it is considered central to our understanding of the brain basis of episodic memory, the hippocampus (HPC) serves as the hub of our article, much as it is considered the hub of regions dealing with episodic memory. The article focuses on four parts: (*a*) the role the HPC plays in representing the various aspects and attributes of episodic memory; (*b*) other structures that are implicated in different aspects of episodic memory and its transformation to gist and semantics; (*c*) the contribution of the HPC and episodic memory to nonepisodic memory functions such as priming, short-term memory (STM), and semantics and to nonmnemonic functions such as perception, problem solving, decision making, and language; and finally, and briefly, (*d*) the functional and structural connectivity between the HPC and other regions and networks implicated in episodic memory.

In the interest of space and timeliness, we favored the most recent references and reviews over early empirical papers. All figures accompanying the review can be downloaded by following the **Supplemental Material link** in the online version of this article or at the Annual Reviews home page at **http://www.annualreviews.org/**. We regret that owing to space limitations we could not cover in detail, and sometimes not at all, many topics relevant to episodic memory, such as emotion, reward, individual differences, and lifespan development.

COMPONENT PROCESSES AND DYNAMIC HIERARCHIES

We use a component process model as our framework. Building on Tulving's ideas, and the acknowledged role of the HPC in memory, Moscovitch & Winocur (1992; also Moscovitch 1992) proposed that at encoding the HPC obligatorily binds together into a memory trace or engram (Dudai 2012, Josselyn et al. 2015, Tonegawa et al. 2015) those neural elements in the medial temporal lobe (MTL) and neocortex that give rise to the multimodal, multidomain representations that constitute the content of a conscious experience. The experience includes the accompanying phenomenological awareness and reflects a process involving the network interactions that make up the experience itself (Moscovitch 1995). In this view, consciousness, or the phenomenology of experience, is inextricably linked to episodic memory. The episodic memory trace or engram consists of a bound ensemble of HPC-neocortical neurons with a sparsely coded HPC component. This is envisioned as a spatial scaffold or matrix (Nadel 2008, O'Keefe & Nadel 1978) that acts as a pointer or index (Teyler & Rudy 2007) to neocortical components that together represent the totality of the experience, including not only the perceptual, emotional, and conceptual details that form the content of the experience, but also the processes that imbue it with a sense of autonoetic consciousness. Because HPC binding is obligatory, storage is random, and only close temporal contiguity, or close contiguity with a reinstated context, determines the elements that are bound to each other.

At retrieval, the HPC-neocortical ensemble is reactivated in a two-stage recollection process by an internal or external cue. The first involves a rapid and unconscious interaction between the cue and HPC (ecphory), which in turn reactivates the neocortical traces bound with it. The process may end here or proceed to the second stage. In the second stage, which is slower and conscious, cortical processes operate on the output of the first stage to reinstate the conscious experience of the episode (Moscovitch 2008). Because the HPC-mediated operations, once initiated, are obligatory, control processes at encoding and retrieval, mediated by prefrontal cortex (PFC) and related structures, operate on the information delivered to the HPC and on the output from it to make memory intelligent and goal directed.

Hippocampus, Neocortical Connections, and Specialization Along Its Long Axis

The HPC sits at the top of a hierarchy of largely cortical systems (the ventral and dorsal streams) in which later stages integrate information from previous ones, building more complex representations in the process and influencing the operation of earlier stages through back projections (Nadel & Peterson 2013) [**Supplemental Figure 1** (follow the **Supplemental Material link** in the online version of this article or at **http://www.annualreviews.org/**)].

Receiving its input from the entorhinal cortex, which in turn receives its input from the perirhinal cortex (PRC) and the parahippocampal cortex (PHC), the HPC integrates information about complex object representations from the PRC and view-specific scene representations from the PHC into a view-invariant representation that "frames the spatial relations among the various parts of the environment " (Nadel & Peterson 2013, p. 1248) and locates those parts and their features within that spatial frame (Bird & Burgess 2008, Hassabis & Maguire 2009, Nadel 2008). HPC-mediated memories are said to reflect relational associations (Eichenbaum et al. 2007, Olsen et al. 2012), in that both the separate elements of some event and their relation retain their distinctiveness.

This framework focuses primarily on representational inputs to the HPC from the posterior neocortex, and it says nothing about HPC connections to anterior structures such as the amygdala (emotion), anterior temporal cortex (semantics), and PFC [schemas and working memory (WM)]. These structures play different, but important, roles in episodic memory through their interaction with the HPC. We will pay some attention below to the relation of the HPC to the ventromedial PFC (vmPFC). Readers interested in the interactions between HPC and lateral frontal cortex during encoding and retrieval should refer to Simons & Spiers (2003) and Anderson & Huddleston (2012), and to Talmi (2013) on amygdala and emotion.

The HPC creates the same kind of representation throughout its length, but at different scales. At the posterior end, its representations capture detailed information about local spatiotemporal aspects of an experienced event based on input from the posterior neocortex. At the anterior end, its representations capture global aspects of an event (i.e., the general context and the emotion and meaning attached to it) based also on interactions with the anterior neocortex. Thus, these two types of HPC representation arise primarily from differences in input-output connections along the long axis of the HPC (Poppenk et al. 2013, Strange et al. 2014) [**Supplemental Figure 2** (follow the **Supplemental Material link** in the online version of this article or at **http://www.annualreviews.org/**)]. This framework sets the stage for investigating the contribution of various HPC subfields to episodic memory (see below) and for understanding how memories are transformed from detailed representations to schematic ones at both functional and neurological levels (Penfield & Mathieson 1974).

Memory Transformation

As Bartlett (1932) noted, memory representations are not static entities but change throughout an individual's life with time and experience. As we discuss in the sections that follow, some memories retain their highly detailed specificity and, as the data suggest, continue to rely on the

HPC and remain recollective; others are transformed through forgetting or schematization, so that they lose details and retain only the gist or familiarity; and others become incorporated into a semantic network and acquire its properties. The latter cases rely more on neocortical structures, with the vmPFC and anterior temporal lobe prominent among them. In some cases, specific and gist-like representations can coexist, leading to dynamic interactions and to the dominance of one memory over the other or to the conversion of one type to the other, depending on circumstances. The neural instantiation of these memories corresponds to their functional representation, in accordance with what we believe is a general principle in cognitive neuroscience: Representations that differ from one another must necessarily be mediated by different structures (collections of neurons), and representations mediated by different structures must necessarily differ in some fundamental way from one another. This principle, which we call functional-neural isomorphism (F-NI), helps account for patterns of HPC-neocortical involvement during memory consolidation.

Process-Specific Alliances

Not all components of the HPC nor of the neocortical (and other) structures with which they interact are activated at the same time or in all tasks. Instead, we conceive of subsets of components forming temporary process-specific alliances (PSAs) whose composition is determined by the moment-to-moment demands of a task. Whereas the posterior neocortical components, in conjunction with the posterior hippocampus (pHPC), determine the local, spatio-perceptual aspects of the experience, anterior components of the HPC, in conjunction with the anterior temporal lobe, PFC, and amygdala, represent conceptual and emotional aspects. The PSAs also include control structures that regulate encoding and retrieval. All these memory components can interact with components earlier and later in the hierarchy, and in other domains, such as language, planning, and decision making, leading to the involvement of the HPC, and by inference episodic memory, in nonmnemonic functions (see below).

The updated component process model makes the following assumptions:

1. During perception, sensory information is progressively bound into feature clusters in early sensory regions, into integrated objects and contexts in late sensory and cortical MTL regions, and into complex events binding objects with their spatiotemporal contexts together with the feeling (phenomenology) of experience in the HPC.

2. The same regions remain active for a while due to top-down modulation from the PFC, which allows the persistence of object and context representations, as well as unified event representations, within WM.

3. During encoding, a fraction of transient representations in WM are transformed to a long-lasting format in the cortex and HPC. The HPC representation points to the location of cortical memory traces (HPC-cortex PSA). This encoding process is supported by schematic relational processes in the vmPFC [aHPC-vmPFC PSA; anterior hippocampus (aHPC)] and semantic processes in the ventrolateral PFC (vlPFC) (vlPFC-MTL PSA) and anterior temporal cortex.

4. Finally, during retrieval, access to the integrated event representation in HPC leads to the reactivation of the MTL and posterior cortices, hence to cortical memory traces (HPC-cortex PSA) (stage 1) and to the awareness of the recovered memories, involving regions such as the ventral parietal cortex (VPC) (HPC-VPC PSA) (stage 2). As in the case of encoding processes, these retrieval processes are supported by control processes mediated by the PFC. Oscillatory mechanisms are assumed to contribute to all these four groups of processes.

PERCEPTUAL (LOCAL) DETAILS AND EVENT (GLOBAL) ELEMENTS

Episodic Details and Representations

It is generally agreed that patients with extensive bilateral damage manifest a global anterograde amnesia that affects acquisition, retention, and retrieval of all episodic memories. This includes the particular details of the event as well as its theme and general structure, though it is the episodic details that are most severely affected. When damage is more restricted, confined to small portions of the HPC, or unilateral, the relative sparing of acquisition of gist and semantic memory compared to episodic memory is more noticeable (Winocur & Moscovitch 2011, Winocur et al. 2010).

To measure these aspects of autobiographical memory retrieval, Levine et al. (2002) created the Autobiographical Interview (AI), whose scoring distinguishes between different internal details that are unique to the event (perception, emotions, locations) and capture episodic aspects of it, and external details, which are not unique to the event and capture more semantic aspects. Administering the AI to patients with unilateral temporal lobe epilepsy or lobectomy that included the HPC, St-Laurent et al. (2014) found that memory for perceptual details was most affected; memory for more global details, such as the story elements that comprise the series of events within an episode, was also impaired, but not as severely; and memory for external details was preserved. Using the AI, or a variety of similar tests such as the Autobiographical Memory Inventory (Kopelman et al. 1989) and the Test Episodique de Mémoire du Passé autobiographique (TEMPau) task (Piolino et al. 2009), investigators found the same pattern of impaired episodic but relatively spared semantic aspects of autobiographical memory in patients with MTL lesions or dysfunction, regardless of etiology (transient epilepsy, ischemic attacks, degenerative disorders such Alzheimer's disease, amnesic variant of minimal cognitive impairment, later stages of frontotemporal dementia, and psychiatric and mood disorders; reviewed in Piolino et al. 2009, Viard et al. 2012, Winocur & Moscovitch 2011).

In functional magnetic resonance imaging (fMRI) studies of autobiographical memory, HPC activation has been shown to be modulated by the number of details or the vividness of the recalled autobiographical event, which is correlated with internal details (Sheldon & Levine 2013; reviewed in Cabeza & St. Jacques 2007, Svoboda et al. 2006, Winocur & Moscovitch 2011). It is noteworthy that HPC sensitivity to details and vividness was also observed when recollecting generic and often repeated events such as family dinners (Addis et al. 2004); this is consistent with findings from patients and suggests a general HPC propensity for representing details (Rosenbaum et al. 2009, Rubin & Umanath 2015).

Film clips provide more experimental control than tests of autobiographical memory, yet they retain a naturalistic quality. The pattern of results obtained with clips in patients with MTL lesions (St-Laurent et al. 2014), compared to HPC activation in healthy controls in fMRI studies, was similar to that obtained on recall of autobiographical episodes (Ben-Yakov & Dudai 2011, Furman et al. 2012, Maguire & Mullally 2013) [**Supplemental Figure 3** (follow the **Supplemental Material link** in the online version of this article or at **http://www.annualreviews.org/**)].

Although the use of more naturalistic stimuli has grown, by far the largest majority of studies use unrelated stimuli as the method of choice in studying episodic memory, sometimes presented in arbitrary contexts and tested almost exclusively by recognition. It is reassuring, therefore, that similar regions are activated when laboratory memory studies emphasize recollection (but not familiarity), whether measured subjectively, by asking individuals to rate the extent to which the item evoked the experience at study (recollection or know response), or objectively, by asking individuals to recognize elements of the context in which the stimulus appeared (source memory) (Skinner & Fernandes 2007). Known as the recollective network, these regions overlap substantially with those activated during recall of vivid, autobiographical memories (Cabeza & St. Jacques 2007, Rugg & Vilberg 2013, Svoboda et al. 2006) and include HPC, PHC, medial prefrontal cortex (mPFC), VPC (angular gyrus), and retrosplenial cortex/posterior cingulate [**Supplemental Figure 4** (follow the **Supplemental Material link** in the online version of this article or at **http://www.annualreviews.org/**)]. As with more naturalistic tests, the degree of HPC activation is associated with the amount of detail that is retrieved (Rugg & Vilberg 2013) or its contextual specificity (Cohn et al. 2009, Sadeh et al. 2012), but not with memory strength, even when great care is taken to equate recollection and familiarity with strength (Migo et al. 2012, Montaldi & Mayes 2011; but see Squire & Wixted 2011).

With respect to performance in patients with MTL lesions that include the HPC, Montaldi & Mayes (2011) and Yonelinas (2013) concluded that even when overall accuracy, an index of strength, is equated, memory under conditions associated with recollection is selectively impaired compared to memory based on familiarity (for counterarguments, see Dede et al. 2013, Squire & Wixted 2011). By contrast, familiarity-based memory is impaired and recollection is preserved following PRC lesions that spare the HPC (Bowles et al. 2010).

As we noted earlier, recollection, mediated by the HPC, depends on relational yet flexible associations among disparate (random) and distinct (separable) elements (for reviews, see Eichenbaum et al. 2007, Olsen et al. 2012, Yonelinas 2013). When associations lose their relational nature and become unitized (e.g., combining the words fire and dog into firedog), HPC involvement as inferred from lesion (Quamme et al. 2007) and fMRI (Haskins et al. 2008) is diminished or lost.

Spatial Details and Representations

Because all autobiographical events unfold in a particular spatial context, it has been argued that spatial context has a privileged status in episodic memory, consistent with the HPC's role in spatial memory and navigation (Buzsaki & Moser 2013, Nadel 2008). The scene construction hypothesis holds that the HPC is necessary for constructing coherent scenes that provide the scaffold or framework for supporting memory for events (Hassabis & Maguire 2009). Studies of patients with HPC lesions and functional neuroimaging studies in healthy people show that constructing coherent scenes is dependent on the HPC (Maguire & Mullally 2013). Moreover, there is great overlap among brain regions and networks activated on spatial tasks and on episodic memory tasks, even when the latter do not have an obvious spatial component (Spreng et al. 2009). Robin et al. (2015), however, found that even when narratives lack information about spatial location, participants spontaneously add them at encoding or recall, which may account for some of the overlap.

There is evidence that memory for events is facilitated by familiar spatial information (e.g., Robin & Moscovitch 2014), and that regions sensitive to memory for events interact with regions sensitive to spatial memory in the HPC even at the single-cell level (Miller et al. 2013). In a study that suggests the primacy of spatial over event memory in the HPC, Chadwick et al. (2010) had participants recall in detail film clips in which two different events occurred in two distinct spatial locations. Using multivariate pattern analysis (MVPA) to differentiate neurally the retrieved memories from one another, they found that classification accuracy for distinct episodes was significantly better than chance only in the HPC. When required to classify the clips with regard to differences in location as compared to event content, only locations could be classified accurately, and then only in the HPC.

Temporal Details and Representations

Time is a central aspect of episodic memory. Events unfold in time just as they unfold in space. However, evidence for a hippocampal role in forming, maintaining, and retrieving temporal associations, as well as relating them to events, is controversial: Some consider time to be a derived property, whereas others consider temporal coding to be a core function or property of the HPC (Dalla Barba & La Corte 2013, Davachi & Dubrow 2015, Eichenbaum 2014, Howard & Eichenbaum 2013).

There are at least three aspects of temporal processing that have been addressed in the literature (Schacter et al. 2012): (*a*) the temporal tag or signal associated with different moments in the unfolding of an event, which can also code for duration; (*b*) the coding for the temporal order of elements within and across episodes; and (*c*) the subjective sense of time, so that we can identify our experience of the memory as occurring in the near or distant past or future.

To account for the first two aspects, based on evidence from time cells (Eichenbaum 2014), investigators have proposed a hippocampal mechanism that could construct a scale-invariant representation of time over hundreds of seconds; this could serve as the contextual/neuronal background in which events are embedded via association (Howard & Eichenbaum 2013). This model can account both for temporal order effects in memory and for the reduction in temporal precision with temporal distance. Davachi & Dubrow (2015) noted that contiguity as a determinant of temporal order is better for elements within an event or segment than across them, pointing to an important role for event segmentation. They also note that learning a sequence through repeated presentations may rely on pattern completion, with one item serving as a cue for eliciting replay of the associated elements. Although both proposals are broadly consistent with the temporal contiguity aspects of the component process model, it remains to be explained why, in general, memory for temporal information is very poor in comparison to memory for spatial information.

Memory for duration and temporal order across very short intervals such as milliseconds, and across long intervals such as minutes, hours, or days, seems to depend on information and strategies mediated by extrahippocampal structures (Davachi & Dubrow 2015, Moscovitch 1992), among them the cerebellum, PFC, posterior parietal cortex (PPC) (Danckert et al. 2007), and basal ganglia. The cognitive processes and neural mechanisms that underlie our subjective sense of time as past, present, or future are even less well understood, though some have proposed that the HPC plays a crucial role. The growing interest in the temporal aspects of memory will hopefully stimulate research that will add to our meager knowledge of them and resolve some of the controversies.

INTRAHIPPOCAMPAL SPECIALIZATION

Memory Precision, Pattern Separation, and Hippocampus Subfields

Although there is ample evidence that relational associations account for our ability to recollect the details of an episode, a number of studies suggest that the precision, or high resolution, of those memories is a critical component even for recognition of single items such as faces, as long as the items are complex and the targets are distinguished from similar lures after a long delay (Craik 1986, Smith et al. 2014a, Yonelinas 2013). To account for this sensitivity to complexity and precision, investigators have pointed to a fundamental computational mechanism, called orthogonalization, instantiated in the organization and operation of the projections between two hippocampal subfields, the dentate gyrus (DG) and CA3. This orthogonalization, or pattern separation that is dependent on DG, yields distinct representations that enable memory precision between items (or collections of items) with overlapping features (Hunsaker & Kesner 2013, Norman 2010) [**Supplemental Figure 5** (follow the **Supplemental Material link** in the online version of this article or at **http://www.annualreviews.org/**)]. The efficiency of pattern separation should determine the precision of the memory and the number of separable details held in memory (Poppenk et al. 2013).

Recent advances in high-resolution fMRI have allowed investigators to test these ideas more directly. Bakker et al. (2008) found that DG/CA3 (which were considered together because they could not be delineated separately) showed the greatest sensitivity to tests of memory discrimination between highly similar items (which they presumed depended on pattern separation). CA1, on the other hand, showed a linear response and tracked the similarity matrix, indicating that the more similar the items were, the more likely they were to be coded as the same. Pattern separation was related to recollection (Kim & Yassa 2013) in younger adults. Older adults showed a reduction in DG/CA3 responsivity to pattern separation but normal CA1 responses, consistent with their poorer ability to distinguish targets from similar foils at recognition (Yassa et al. 2011). Importantly, the extent of HPC involvement in distinguishing between target and lures may depend on whether the differences between them are relational or based on single features (Aly et al. 2013, Yonelinas 2013).

The same involvement of HPC subfields is evident in distinguishing among more naturalistic stimuli. Precision of episodic recall of film clips, as measured by the extent to which participants could rate the clips as different, was related to the size and activity of the CA3 region (Chadwick et al. 2014) [**Supplemental Figure 6** (follow the **Supplemental Material link** in the online version of this article or at **http://www.annualreviews.org/**)]. Comparable findings were reported by Bonnici et al. (2013) for autobiographical memories in the pHPC, where remote, but not recent, memories could be distinguished from one another only in DG and CA3.

By contrast, CA1 is presumed to collate information generated through pattern completion in CA3 and to deliver it back to the entorhinal cortex after having compared it with the current perceptual input. CA1, therefore, can act as a match-mismatch detector and facilitate the laying down of new memories and retrieval of old ones (Ben-Yakov et al. 2014). Selective damage to CA1, therefore, leads to extensive episodic memory loss (Bartsch et al. 2011, Zola-Morgan et al. 1986).

SPECIALIZATION ALONG THE LONGITUDINAL AXIS OF THE HIPPOCAMPUS

The distribution of the hippocampal subfields is not uniform along the longitudinal axis (Malykhin et al. 2010). DG/CA3 ratios are higher in the pHPC than in the aHPC, with greater CA1 proliferation in the anterior portion. This would suggest more powerful pattern separation capabilities in the pHPC than in the aHPC, a notion that fits well with recent work demonstrating greater precision and detail in the grain of HPC representations and reduced receptive field size of place cells as one moves from anterior to posterior regions (Strange et al. 2014). Neuroanatomical (Aggleton 2012) and connectivity analysis during resting state (Ranganath & Ritchey 2012) showed that the pHPC is preferentially connected to perceptual regions in the posterior neocortex, whereas the aHPC is preferentially connected to anterior regions, such as the vmPFC and the lateral temporal cortex extending into the temporal pole and the amygdala, which are associated with the processing of schemas, semantic information, and social and emotional cues, respectively. These connectivity patterns could conspire to create unique aHPC and pHPC encoding and representational environments, with the aHPC coding information in terms of the general or global relations among entities, and the pHPC coding information in terms of precise positions within some continuous dimension (Poppenk et al. 2013) (**Supplemental Figure 2**).

The evidence generally supports the model (see Poppenk et al. 2013 for review). Whether on tests of autobiographical memory (Nadel et al. 2013) or on laboratory tests of spatial memory

(Evensmoen et al. 2015), aHPC activity is associated with the general locations where events occurred or coarse map-like representations of those locations, whereas activity in the pHPC is associated with local details or finer-grained maps (for comparable results in rodents see review in Preston & Eichenbaum 2013). Similar effects are found in studies of real-world navigation in a virtual environment. Greater aHPC activation is associated with increased distance between sequentially presented landmarks (Morgan et al. 2011), greater scale of the environment (Baumann & Mattingley 2013), and direction to goal, whereas pHPC activations are inversely correlated with distance to goal (Howard et al. 2014). Consistent with this model, and with the hypothesis that recollection is associated with memory for local details, Poppenk & Moscovitch (2011) found that individual differences in recollection were correlated with the size of the pHPC (and the pHPC/aHPC ratio), which in turn was related to the functional connectivity of the pHPC with posterior neocortical regions at rest.

With respect to autobiographical memory, our framework has much in common with Conway's (2009) nested hierarchical model, in which a conceptual frame provides contextualizing knowledge that helps locate and organize the local perceptual and spatial details that comprise the episode [**Supplemental Figure 7** (follow the **Supplemental Material link** in the online version of this article or at **http://www.annualreviews.org/**)]. Retrieving the frame of the episode or the lifetime period in which it occurred, which is a typical first step in constructing memory for an autobiographical episode, is often associated with aHPC and neocortical activation, whereas recovering and elaborating the perceptual details of the event is associated with pHPC activation (McCormick et al. 2013, St-Laurent et al. 2014; for review and other evidence, see Schacter et al. 2012).

Such differences are also observed when considering global and local aspects of a single object. The neural suppression that occurs when an object is repeated is seen in the DG/CA3 subfields of the aHPC, but when fine discrimination between targets and similar lures is required, then the pHPC is activated (Reagh et al. 2014).

Similarly, encoding novel events, or forming relational associations between random items, is associated with aHPC activation, possibly because such activities typically involve higher-order conceptual processing, whereas encoding familiar or repeated events relies less on such conceptual processes and more on attending to perceptual aspects of the event (Poppenk et al. 2013). Since repeated events also have a retrieval component, this formulation is consistent with evidence of differential aHPC and pHPC activation at encoding and retrieval (Kim 2015).

The global-local hypothesis of anterior-posterior HPC organization that we propose provides a plausible first approximation of functional organization along the long axis of the HPC with respect to episodic memory. Another virtue of this conception of aHPC function is that it serves as a bridge between detailed episodic representations that are dependent on the HPC and more schematic, gist-like representations that emerge as memories are transformed with time and experience (Preston & Eichenbaum 2013, Robin et al. 2015, Winocur & Moscovitch 2011) and become reliant on extrahippocampal structures, such as the vmPFC and anterior temporal lobe, that have strong aHPC connections.

MEMORY CONSOLIDATION, TRANSFORMATION, AND ASSIMILATION

Postencoding Consolidation

Episodic memory is dynamic, with significant transformations occurring throughout the memory's lifetime (Bartlett 1932, Dudai 2012). In accord with our model, and with the principle of F-NI, these transformations are accompanied by corresponding shifts in underlying neural structures that support different kinds of memory representations.

Studies of postencoding consolidation indicate that different processes are predictive of better memory for the studied material, such as a spike in HPC activity immediately after the end of an event (Ben-Yakov & Dudai 2011), event-specific reactivation of encoding processes during rest (Staresina et al. 2013), and increased connectivity between the HPC and structures specialized in processing associated stimuli measured at rest after a block of associative memory study trials (Tambini et al. 2010). Memory can be reduced by interference from other stimuli (Ben-Yakov et al. 2013) or enhanced by emotional stimuli (Dunsmoor et al. 2015) presented during this postencoding period.

Postencoding processes during sleep have complex effects on memories acquired during the previous day, and recent work suggests that their impact may be related to the type of memory examined as well as to the stages of sleep under study (Diekelman & Born 2010, Stickgold 2013). With respect to episodic memory, there is evidence that recollection can be preserved or degraded and transformed to familiarity, but the conditions that lead to one or the other outcome, and the neural mechanisms involved, have yet to be elucidated (Lewis & Durrant 2011).

Remote Memory

The issue of memory transformation lies at the heart of the debate on the neural representation of remote memory, in which changes can occur across weeks, years, and even decades (Nadel & Moscovitch 1997, Winocur & Moscovitch 2011). The observation that remote, compared to recent, memories appear to be relatively spared following damage to the MTL, and the HPC in particular, formed the foundation of the standard consolidation theory (SCT). This theory states that the HPC serves as a temporary memory structure needed only until memories are consolidated elsewhere, presumably in the neocortex, where they are retained and from where they can be retrieved. Although Penfield & Milner (1958) and Penfield & Mathieson (1974) noted that extra-HPC memories are generalized (gist-like) and fundamentally different from the detailed, specific memories mediated by the HPC, some versions of SCT did not make any distinction between the two types of memory. In other versions, all remote memories were assumed to be incorporated into a neocortical semantic or schematic network, leaving no HPC-mediated specific episodic memories behind (Frankland & Bontempi 2005, McClelland et al. 1995, Wang & Morris 2010).

Drawing on the work of previous investigators, Nadel & Moscovitch (1997) took issue with each of these interpretations and with evidence that all remote memories are spared following HPC damage. They noted that individuals can retain detailed remote episodic memories and that the HPC and related structures are needed for their retention and retrieval, no matter how old the memories are. Reactivation of old memories leads to the re-encoding and formation of a rich distributed network of multiple traces in the HPC, which provides some protection from small, but not large, HPC lesions. Gist-like (semanticized) memories of episodes as well as semantic memories, mediated as they are by other structures, would survive HPC damage under any circumstances. The multiple trace theory proposed by Nadel & Moscovitch (1997) links the type of memory representation (detailed versus gist-like/schematic/semantic) with the structure that mediates it (HPC versus neocortex), and it helps account for the different patterns of retrograde amnesia observed after HPC damage.

Building on ideas from multiple trace theory, Winocur & Moscovitch (2011; see also Winocur et al. 2010) proposed that some autobiographical and spatial memories in humans, as well as context-dependent memories in rodents, are transformed with time and experience from highly detailed, context-specific memories to less detailed, schematic memories that retain the gist of an experience or event or schematic representation of an environment, but not many particulars. These transformed memories are based on representations in extra-HPC structures and do not depend on the HPC. Insofar as memories remain detailed and retain their contextual specificity, they will continue to depend on representations encoded in the HPC, regardless of their age. Both types of representations can coexist and dynamically interact, so that a memory that has previously been manifested in a schematic rather than detailed form can regain its specificity with appropriate reminders and once again engage the HPC (Winocur et al. 2010, Winocur & Moscovitch 2011).

Appealing to the principle of F-NI, Winocur & Moscovitch (2011) reasoned that a memory that was once mediated by the HPC and is now mediated by the cortex must differ in accord with the processing and representational capabilities of these two structures. If the intricate architecture of the HPC is needed to perform the computations that are central to the retention and retrieval of precise, detailed, and relational representations of recent memories, it is difficult to see how comparable representations, only older, could be mediated solely by the neocortex, which lacks the requisite architecture.

The debate between adherents of each camp has continued for 20 years and has been reviewed extensively, so it will only be summarized here. Performance on tests of autobiographical memory that are especially sensitive to attributes that capture the essence of episodic memory—such as perceptual details, viewpoint specificity, vividness, judgments of recollection, and relational associations—suffers after HPC damage or dysfunction, regardless of etiology and of the amount of time passed since the memory was acquired. Unless the damage extends to extra-HPC regions, memories for gist or semantic aspects of personal experiences, public events, and well-known narratives such as bible stories and fairy tales are relatively well preserved (Winocur & Moscovitch 2011), though memory for details, even for well-known stories, may be compromised (Kwan et al. 2013, Verfaellie et al. 2014). The same is true of spatial memory: Memory for perceptual details needed to reexperience the environment (scene construction) is lost, whereas schematic memories sufficient for navigation are retained (Winocur & Moscovitch 2011).

Evidence from fMRI is consistent with this observation. Autobiographical memories that are detailed and vivid engage the HPC no matter how long ago they were acquired (Winocur & Moscovitch 2011). Importantly, the pattern of activation along the long axis of the HPC resembles that observed for recently acquired novel and familiar memories: More recent memories engage the aHPC and more remote ones engage the pHPC, and the distinction between recent and remote memories, and among the memories themselves, is mediated by the posterior DG/CA3 subfield (Bonnici et al. 2013). Likewise, connectivity of the HPC to other structures in the autobiographical memory network varies with vividness and remoteness (Furman et al. 2012, Sheldon & Levine 2013).

The same pattern of decreasing HPC and increasing neocortical activation with remoteness and accompanying loss of specificity or recollection is found in traditional laboratory tests of episodic memory with delays of one (Ritchey et al. 2015) to six weeks (Viskontas et al. 2009a; but see Nieuwenhuis & Takashima 2011 for different types of associative memories that may be schema dependent). Likewise, for remote spatial memory, studies suggest that what is preserved after HPC damage is a gist-like, schematic representation of the environment (essentially a coarse-grained map) that is adequate for navigation but not for conjuring up the kind of details that allow for reexperiencing the environment (Rosenbaum et al. 2000, Winocur & Moscovitch 2011). Consistent with this interpretation, HPC activation is found during mental navigation in a recently encountered environment but is diminished or absent when navigating in a familiar environment (Hirshhorn et al. 2012).

Proponents of the SCT argue that extensive retrograde amnesia for autobiographical events occurs only when lesions of the MTL extend beyond the HPC to include the temporal neocortex

(Squire & Wixted 2011). Although this explanation may account for deficits in remote memory in some patients, it cannot account for deficits in many others whose lesions are restricted to the HPC or its projections via the fornix (see review in Winocur & Moscovitch 2011), or to disruption restricted to CA1 fields in transient global amnesia (Bartsch et al. 2011). To account for fMRI results, proponents of the SCT have argued that HPC activity observed while recalling remote memories is related to the re-encoding of autobiographical memories retrieved from the neocortex rather than to the memories themselves (Squire & Wixted 2011). This critique is difficult to refute, though recent evidence of the different patterns of activation for recent and remote memories in the HPC and midline structures would argue against a simple re-encoding interpretation (Bonnici et al. 2013).

Recent and Remote Memory and Memory Transformation in Rodents

The most unequivocal evidence comes from studies of context-dependent (episodic) and context-independent (gist-like) memory in rodents, where considerable control can be exerted over the learning environment and over lesion location and extent. These data favor the transformation hypothesis. Longitudinal studies show a loss of contextual specificity of memories tested a month after acquisition compared to tests given shortly after learning (Winocur et al. 2010). This loss of context specificity is accompanied by a lesser dependence on the HPC and a higher dependence on the anterior cingulate cortex (ACC) or prelimbic cortex, the rodent homologue of the vmPFC in humans, as determined by both the effects of lesions and early gene expression (Frankland & Bontempi 2005, Winocur et al. 2010). Importantly, providing reminder cues in the long-delay condition a day prior to the test (Winocur et al. 2010) or periodically reactivating the context (de Oliveira Alvares et al. 2012) restore or maintain contextual specificity, rendering the memory once again HPC dependent and vulnerable to the effects of HPC lesions.

These findings provide a possible interpretation of system reconsolidation, a process whereby memories that once were believed to be consolidated in extra-HPC structures become labile once they are reactivated by a reminder (retrieval cue) and become vulnerable once again to the disruptive effects of HPC lesions, protein synthesis inhibitors, or synaptic interference (Dudai 2012, Nader & Hardt 2009, Wang & Morris 2010).

The fact that specificity and hippocampal dependence could be restored by reminders not only speaks to the dynamic nature of memory and against the SCT, but also suggests that some vestige of the original specific memory must be retained by the HPC. Evidence in support of this hypothesis comes from optogenetic studies in which temporary disruption of those CA1 cells that encoded the information leads to loss of contextual fear memories even at long delays (Goshen et al. 2011, Tanaka et al. 2014), just as CA1 disruption causes remote memory loss in humans (Bartsch et al. 2011). Recent studies in which cells that constitute the memory (engram) are labeled (tagged), reactivated, or suppressed support our hypothesis that long-term retention of context-dependent memories is mediated by neural ensembles in the HPC (Josselyn et al. 2015, Tonegawa et al. 2015).

Memory Transformation and the Ventromedial Prefrontal Cortex: Remote Memory and Schemas

The vmPFC seems to play a special role in mediating remote memories (Frankland & Bontempi 2005), but its precise nature is not clear. One promising clue to vmPFC function comes from the work of Tse, Morris, and collaborators (Tse et al. 2007; see Wang & Morris 2010) on schemas, which can be defined as "adaptable associative networks of knowledge extracted over multiple similar experiences" (Ghosh et al. 2014, p. 12057). Tse et al. (2007) showed that the vmPFC is crucial for assimilating new olfactory-location associations into a spatial schema, which is acquired over many exposures. As a result, the new associations become independent of the HPC more quickly, relying instead on the ACC/vmPFC.

Such results are interpreted according to a schema modification model (Dudai 2012, Wang & Morris 2010), which posits that schemas provide the organizing structures that influence memory formation and retrieval (Bartlett 1932) as well as interpretation of ongoing events. We propose that the vmPFC, with its reciprocal connections to the aHPC, could act as a hub binding the global context of events represented in the aHPC and general knowledge, including that about the self, into a schema that captures what is common to all such events (see also Benoit et al. 2014). A fundamental function of any schema is to make predictions about what one should expect to experience in a given context/situation/setting, to aid in interpreting events that occur there, and to enable one to notice new details that do not fit the schema. For example, one may have schemas of what kitchens are like and what one does in them. Walking into a strange kitchen may produce a novel episodic memory for the kitchen and for the local events that transpire there; schemas ensure that the experience of being in the kitchen is not in itself strange but relatively predictable.

Some investigators have suggested that the vmPFC is the consolidated (remote) memory homologue of the HPC, taking over its function. This notion runs counter to the F-NI principle. Our proposal is that the vmPFC and HPC may both deal with context, but of fundamentally different sorts. The HPC binds together local and global contextual information about a specific event or environment, whereas the vmPFC binds together what is common across similar events and possibly helps "decide" which among them is relevant for a particular task (Preston & Eichenbaum 2013).

A number of predictions follow from this hypothesis:

1. Insofar as retrieval is dependent on the vmPFC without HPC involvement, the retrieved memory will be gist-like or general, rather than detailed and specific. This appears to be the case in humans and rodents with HPC damage.

2. The vmPFC should interact with the aHPC to encode schematic information and to help retrieve detailed information via schema-related cues (for similar proposals, see Conway 2009, Preston & Eichenbaum 2013, van Kesteren et al. 2012). The vmPFC's role in retrieval becomes more prominent as local perceptual details mediated by the pHPC are degraded, making retrieval more dependent on the global aspects of the memory represented in the aHPC (Bonnici et al. 2013, Sheldon et al. 2013).

3. Damage to the vmPFC, therefore, should be more evident in tests of remote, rather than recent, memory, and vary inversely with the specificity of retrieval cues.

4. The vmPFC may be implicated more as structured events are transformed or when isolated events are experienced within a structured context, as in Tse et al.'s (2007) studies and Takashima et al.'s (2009) human analogue of them, but not when events are isolated and random as in many traditional laboratory experiments.

5. Following vmPFC damage, schema formation and representation may itself be impaired, so that what delineates a schema (e.g., what one does in a kitchen) is distorted, nebulous, or overinclusive (Ghosh et al. 2014). Consequently, individuals with vmPFC damage may experience the present, and reexperience the past, through the lens of distorted or misapplied schemas, and this may contribute to confabulation, a memory disorder characterized by the production of patently false information about autobiographical episodes, personal semantics, historical events, and common narratives (Gilboa & Verfaellie 2010, Moscovitch & Winocur, 2002, Schnider 2008, Shallice & Cooper 2012).

Interim Summary

Memories for recent events draw on interactions between schemas, semantics, and perceptual aspects of an experience, mediated in part by different regions in the anterior and posterior neo-cortex. These are bound together in relational representations mediated by the pHPC for local details and the aHPC for global context, accounting for the specificity characteristic of episodic memory (Craik 1986). Over time, detailed information about local aspects of the event become degraded or lost, and our memory reports come to rely on more global aspects mediated by the aHPC in conjunction with schema-related information mediated by the vmPFC. The latter helps determine performance when the HPC is entirely lost. Damage to the vmPFC leads to deficient and distorted use of schemas in memory, perception, and reasoning.

CONSCIOUSNESS, THE HIPPOCAMPUS, AND THE LATERAL AND POSTERIOR PARIETAL CORTEX

Consciousness is a defining feature of episodic memory, as evidenced by the fact that performance on a variety of implicit or nondeclarative tests can be normal in patients with MTL damage and severe episodic memory deficits (Moscovitch et al. 1993). These findings suggest the following conclusions: (*a*) The HPC, and by implication recollection, does not contribute to normal perfor-mance on nonepisodic memory tasks such as priming; (*b*) the HPC can only process consciously apprehended information; and (*c*) consciousness invariably accompanies the retrieval of the de-tailed information that underlies recollection. In the last decade, each of these conclusions has been challenged and effectively overturned.

The two-stage model of recollection predicts that priming for relational associations should be preserved insofar as it draws on information underlying the first rapid, nonconscious stage of recollection mediated by the HPC. Recent studies show that priming of relational associations, measured by manual reaction times (Schacter et al. 2004) or eye movements (Hannula & Ranganath 2009), is accompanied by HPC activation, is impaired in people with HPC damage (Olsen et al. 2012), and is more robust for items that are subsequently judged to be recollected than for familiar ones (Sheldon & Moscovitch 2010). Going one step further, Henke and collaborators showed that the HPC encodes information presented subliminally as long as it is relational (Henke 2010).

The Ventral Posterior Parietal Cortex and Subjective Aspects of Memory (Autonoetic Consciousness)

Consistent with our component process model, studies on nonconscious memory suggest that engagement of the HPC is not sufficient for explicit recollection or episodic memory, and that other structures also need to be recruited. Structures in the frontoparietal network are among the possible candidates. Here we focus on the PPC, since it has been the object of much debate concerning its role in episodic memory.

Activation of the PPC, particularly on the left, often accompanies memory retrieval on laboratory tests of recognition and autobiographical memory (Cabeza & St. Jacques 2007, Rugg & Vilberg 2013, Svoboda et al. 2006). Of the two major divisions of the PPC, dorsal parietal cortex (DPC) and VPC, the VPC is associated with successful recollection, source monitoring, and high-confidence responses, whereas the DPC is associated with familiarity and low-confidence responses (for other differences between the two divisions, see Cabeza et al. 2012) [**Supplemental Figure 8** (follow the **Supplemental Material link** in the online version of this article or at **http://www.annualreviews.org/**)].

A number of hypotheses have been proposed to account for VPC involvement in episodic memory, and recent reviews have discussed extensively their merits and deficiencies (Berryhill 2012, Cabeza et al. 2012, Rugg & Vilberg 2013). Here, we focus on the hypothesis that the VPC is implicated in the apprehension of the subjective qualities of memory (Simons et al. 2010). This hypothesis accounts not only for the reduced and less detailed recollections of patients with VPC lesions that can be ameliorated by cuing (Berryhill 2012, Davidson et al. 2008), but also for the low confidence the patients have in their memory even when source accuracy is high (Hower et al. 2014, Simons et al. 2010), an outcome that can be produced in normal people by deactivating the VPC with theta burst stimulation (Yazar et al. 2014). These findings raise the possibility that the VPC, perhaps via its interactions with the frontal cortex, is an essential component for enabling autonoetic consciousness. It is interesting in this regard that VPC activation accompanies memories that come to mind involuntarily, either when they are elicited by a cue (Hall et al. 2014) or when they overcome active suppression (Benoit et al. 2014). It is also noteworthy that the VPC has been associated with functions that are the hallmarks of autonoetic consciousness: WM and attention, time perception, feelings of intentionality, and a sense of self associated with theory of mind (ToM) (see Berryhill 2012, Cabeza et al. 2012). As noted, the VPC is also linked with the PFC (Prebble et al. 2013), another region that is associated with ToM (Mitchell 2009) and whose damage, or disconnection, can lead to reduced recollection and deactivation of the VPC (Levine et al. 2009).

These findings suggest a dissociation between successful retrieval of the content of episodic memories and the phenomenological experience that accompanies successful retrieval. It remains to be determined whether the diminished autonoetic consciousness associated with VPC and PFC damage or disconnection results from an impaired postretrieval process that, as part of the second stage of recollection, attributes phenomenological experience to a detailed memory, or whether it results from loss of the "consciousness feature" of the HPC-neocortical engram, which VPC codes much as inferior temporal structures code for perceptual features.

BREAKING DOWN BORDERS AND CONQUERING DOMAINS

Following the introduction of the concept of episodic memory in 1972, much research has focused on how to distinguish episodic memory from other cognitive functions in general, and in particular from other forms of memory, at both the functional and neural levels. Given the widespread connections of the HPC (Aggleton 2012, Ranganath & Ritchey 2012) and its position in the component process model, the isolation and encapsulation of episodic memory could not be sustained. The last decade has seen an imperialist encroachment of episodic memory and the HPC into various domains, from perception to imagination, and from decision making to food regulation (Robinson et al. 2013, Rozin et al. 1998). We highlight four of these domains and consider how they relate to our model (see also Rubin et al. 2014).

The Hippocampus, Perception, and Working Memory

The idea that the HPC sits at the end of a perceptual hierarchy, receiving input from lower levels and projecting back to them, suggests that HPC influence should be felt in perception and WM, thereby eroding the hard and fast distinction between long-term memory (LTM), perception, and WM. According to the hierarchical representation model (HRM; Lee et al. 2012), the HPC's role at the top of the hierarchy and the role of the structures below it are defined strictly not in terms of memory or perception, but rather (or also) in terms of the representations they support, consistent with the component process model. Insofar as the HPC represents relational information among separable entities, or even among features in single complex stimuli, perceptual discrimination based on such features activates the HPC and is impaired in people with HPC damage (Lee et al. 2012, Yonelinas 2013).

Drawing on their theory stating that the HPC is implicated in scene construction, Mullally et al. (2012) showed that boundary extension—the normal tendency to reconstruct a scene with a larger background than actually was presented—was markedly diminished in patients with HPC lesions compared to controls, even when stimuli were presented as briefly as 200 ms [**Supplemental Figure 9** (follow the **Supplemental Material link** in the online version of this article or at **http://www.annualreviews.org/**)]. In subsequent neuroimaging studies, Chadwick et al. (2013) showed that boundary extension is accompanied by hippocampal activation that, in turn, projects down the hierarchy to levels in the visual cortex.

HPC has also been shown to be implicated in STM and WM, especially if precision and relational binding are required (Olsen et al. 2012, Yonelinas 2013). Binding errors in reporting information in STM in people with HPC damage (Pertzov et al. 2013) and matching a target array of items on a screen with a test array presented shortly afterward was shown to be associated with HPC activation and to be reduced in people with medial temporal/HPC damage (Nichols et al. 2006, Olson et al. 2006; but see Talmi et al. 2005) or atrophy; the reduction was correlated with the extent of posterior hippocampal atrophy for location and with perirhinal atrophy for objects (Das et al. 2015). Performance on all the tests was correlated with estimates of recollection, whereas only performance on the object test was correlated with familiarity.

Though such developments blur the boundaries between LTM, WM, and perception, obliterating them would obscure the striking differences one sees clinically: Patients with HPC lesions rarely complain of perceptual or WM deficits but always complain of episodic memory deficits, whereas the reverse is true of people with damage to levels that are lower in the hierarchy. Capitalizing on this observation, Squire and collaborators (e.g., Kim et al. 2015, Squire & Wixted 2011) presented evidence showing that if the lesions were confined to the HPC and the tests did not implicate LTM, then perception and STM/WM was normal in patients with HPC lesions (see also Baddeley et al. 2010 and rebuttal in Clark & Maguire 2016; Maguire et al. 2015).

To counter this negative evidence, and the arguments based on it, Yonelinas (2013) and Lee et al. (2012) have argued, in accord with the HRM, that the complexity of the items and the precision of the discrimination determine HPC involvement on tests of perception and STM/WM. Moreover, it is likely that susceptibility to interference increases as one moves up the hierarchy, and hence the impact on memory is more keenly felt when higher levels are damaged. The component process model and the F-NI principle are consistent with either account, and the resolution of the debate rests on the question of whether HPC-mediated relational processing applies only to memory or also to perception (see also Clark & Maguire 2016, Maguire et al. 2015).

Episodic Simulation, Problem Solving, Empathy, and Decision Making

One of the most striking findings in recent years points to the large overlap in processes and structures involved in retrieving episodic memories, imagining future personal events, and constructing scenes, thereby propelling the HPC into domains it had not occupied previously (Addis & Schacter 2011, Buckner 2010, Maguire & Mullally 2013, Schacter et al. 2012, Viard et al. 2012). Because HPC-based memories are relational, their elements could be recombined to form new associations, which together with constructive processes dependent on the pHPC (Gaesser et al. 2013) would create new scenarios (Romero & Moscovitch 2012) and construct new scenes (Hassabis & Maguire 2009) in the service of current needs. Addis, Schacter, and colleagues referred to this as episodic simulation, a cognitive operation that draws on processes similar to episodic memory to create imagined events [see Maguire & Mullally (2013), who argue that scene construction is the fundamental process].

Recent studies have shown that episodic simulation can lead to better social problem solving (Sheldon et al. 2011), greater empathy (Ciaramelli et al. 2013), and more willingness to help people in distress (Gaesser & Schacter 2014); in all cases, performance was related to the vividness or level of detail of the simulation. HPC damage or deterioration with aging leads to a drop in problem-solving performance (Sheldon et al. 2011) and reduces empathy in general (Beadle et al. 2013, Davidson et al. 2012), whereas training on recovery of episodic details improves problem solving (Madore & Schacter 2014). On the other side of the coin, vivid negative images associated with past events and conjured spontaneously in social situations contribute to social anxiety (Moscovitch et al. 2013).

Episodic simulation also influences decision making, as illustrated on tests of temporal discounting (i.e., the tendency to discount rewards if they are delayed). Benoit et al. (2011) showed that temporal discounting can be reduced by imagining in detail how one would spend the money in the future as compared to merely thinking conceptually about its usefulness; the extent of the reduction is related to vmPFC activation and its functional connectivity with the HPC. Consistent with the fMRI results, Palombo et al. (2015) showed that episodic simulation is ineffective in reducing the normal tendency for temporal discounting in people with amnesia associated with MTL damage (Kwan et al. 2013), because their capacity for simulation is compromised.

Whereas episodic simulation depends on conscious processes, unconscious stage-one associative processes mediated by the HPC likely underlie performance on tests of associative inference. In such tests, participants are shown overlapping pairs of items (e.g., AB and BC) and learn to associate A with C though they never co-occur. Shohamy & Wagner (2008) showed that this effect is mediated by the HPC and occurs at encoding without the participant's awareness, such that when BC is presented, the common element, B, reactivates the previously learned association, AB, and integrates both with C, a process they termed integrative encoding. This accords with the principle of obligatory binding of elements occurring in close temporal contiguity. Similar processes influence reward-based decisions in which a stimulus (A) acquires value through its secondary association (B) with monetary reward (C) (Wimmer & Shohamy 2012). The degree to which A comes to be associated with C is determined also by its interaction with schema-related processes in the vmPFC and its intrinsic resting-state connectivity with the HPC (Gerraty et al. 2014). Similar processes may underlie performance on tests of second-order conditioning in rats (Gilboa et al. 2014) and transitive inference in rats and humans who are presented with overlapping stimulus pairs in which one member of the pair is rewarded (e.g., A > B, B > C, C > D) and participants must infer how it is related to the other items (Preston & Eichenbaum 2013). If the latter task is solved by forming relational associations, then the HPC is necessary, but if it is solved by unitization, then it can be performed without recourse to the HPC but may still be dependent on the vmPFC and PRC (Ryan et al. 2013).

Such effects cannot be said to be related to full-blown episodic memory, which is defined as being associated with autonoetic consciousness, but should rather be related to operations of pattern separation, pattern completion, and associative binding that operate outside of conscious awareness but presumably underlie both episodic memory and these types of associative learning, in accord with the two-stage model of recollection and HPC activation. Consistent with this observation, Reber & Henke (2012) showed that associative inference based on integrative encoding can be attained even when AB and BC items are presented subliminally.

Language and Semantic Memory

Language processing was considered to be preserved in amnesia, at least as far as core phonological, syntactic, and semantic aspects were concerned (Corkin 2013). By and large, this view has not changed, though it is fair to say that it has not been thoroughly explored either. However, in accord with the principle of F-NI, language and semantic memory should be no different than any other function if they draw on processes and representations mediated by the HPC. These are most evident in pragmatic uses of language, particularly in complex social discourse, which requires such HPC-mediated processes as the "flexible use of relational memory representations dredged from the past, and inserted appropriately into the flow of speech, or created rapidly in the present and incorporated effortlessly into the context that forms the common ground of social discourse" (Duff & Brown-Schmidt 2012). Discourse analysis reveals that such functions are aberrant or impoverished in amnesic patients (Race et al. 2015). The paucity of the experiential aspects of episodic memory in patients with HPC damage is revealed in their greater than normal selection of the definite over indefinite article and the diminished use of the historical present, a figure of speech in which a past event is referred in the present tense (e.g., Yesterday, I saw a fire; the fireman *goes* into the house, *battles* the flames…) and whose frequency of usage is correlated with the number of internal details in their narrative (Park et al. 2011).

As with language, insofar as semantic memory is informed by detailed, precise information about autobiographical events and allocentric spatial representations, it will be influenced by episodic memory representations mediated by the HPC. Evidence from studies of patients with amnesia and with semantic dementia suggests that people, places, public events, and even common objects and their names can be imbued with autobiographical significance (AS) in the sense that they automatically (either with or without conscious awareness) conjure up recollective information that facilitates naming, recognition, and semantic judgments. Consistent with the component process model, this AS advantage is lost in people with MTL damage (for review, see Renoult et al. 2012).

Renoult et al. (2015) used event-related potentials to explore this phenomenon further. When names of famous and nonfamous people were presented to participants in a nonepisodic fame-judgment task, they found that the amplitude of the N400 varied with the amount of the semantic, but not episodic, knowledge participants had about the people, whereas the reverse was true for the late positive component over the parietal electrode, which is sensitive to recollection.

These sets of findings suggest a novel interpretation of reports by Quiroga and collaborators (see review in Quiroga 2012), who found that single cells in the human HPC, which they named concept cells, respond selectively and invariantly to representations of famous people across modalities. Viskontas et al. (2009b), however, noted that the majority of the cells respond to people who are personally familiar to the patient. As in studies on AS, the pictures or names presented to the patients may automatically have evoked a recollective process, and therefore referring to the cells as AS or episodic cells would be equally appropriate.

The contribution of HPC-mediated episodic memory processes is also evident in tests of semantic fluency. Impaired performance on tests of semantic fluency following temporal lobe lesions has been shown to be related to HPC damage and not exclusively to lateral temporal damage as was once believed (Greenberg et al. 2009). This interpretation is supported by recent evidence from fMRI showing that HPC activation is associated specifically with the generation of episodic information from which semantic exemplars are derived, presumably by imagining personal experiences (e.g., evoking one's kitchen if required to name kitchen utensils) when the most common exemplars are exhausted (Sheldon & Moscovitch 2012). Similarly, in a free association task to single words, responses become more idiosyncratic presumably because they are derived from personal episodic memories, whereas in patients with MTL lesions, the responses are fewer and less idiosyncratic because they rely more on semantic memory (Sheldon et al. 2013). Consistent with this finding is a report by Addis et al. (2015) showing that performance on tests of divergent thinking is related to one's ability to construct episodic simulations and can be enhanced by inducing episodic specificity (Madore et al. 2015).

Although previously acquired semantic memory, stripped of episodic aspects, can be relatively spared in HPC patients, the acquisition of new vocabulary, though possible without the HPC, is laborious and poor (see Corkin 2013), but only if it depends on forming explicit relational associations between the target item and its name. Acquisition is relatively preserved, however, through fast mapping, an indirect associative procedure in which the participant discovers (infers) the association between the item and its name (Sharon et al. 2011). This fast mapping process may depend on rapid assimilation of the item to pre-existing schemas or semantic memory networks mediated by neocortex (Coutanche & Thompson-Schill 2015, Sharon et al. 2011). Item-name associations learned through fast mapping, however, are prone to catastrophic interference (Merhav et al. 2014). The reverse pattern, of better acquisition through the explicit route and poor fast mapping, is seen in patients with anterior temporal lesions that include the perirhinal cortex (Merhav et al. 2015, Sharon et al. 2011), suggesting that this structure may help mediate fast mapping. Not all attempts to replicate these fast-mapping results, however, have been successful (e.g., Smith et al. 2014b). The reasons for the discrepancies will need to be elucidated if we are to gain a better understanding of the neural mechanisms mediating fast mapping (Coutanche & Thompson-Schill 2015).

The evidence we reviewed indicates that episodic memory, as mediated by the HPC, contributes more to language and semantics than classical views on dissociable multiple memory systems would lead us to believe. As with perception and WM, we do not wish to end by obliterating distinctions that we believe are still useful; rather, based on our component process model, we propose that the systems are much more interactive than we once thought, enabling episodic memory and the HPC to influence functions outside their traditional domain. This interactive approach is increasingly evident in neuroimaging research, with its current emphasis on networks and on structural and functional connectivity among nodes in those networks.

PROCESS-SPECIFIC ALLIANCES SUPPORTING EPISODIC MEMORY

The individual brain regions discussed in the previous sections cannot support episodic memory unless they interact with each other and with other regions. In functional neuroimaging studies, these interactions can be indirectly measured as covariation in activity, or functional connectivity. Functional connectivity can be investigated at the level of large-scale networks, such as the default mode network (Andrews-Hanna 2012), or at the level of small networks that are assembled to mediate a specific cognitive operation and rapidly disassembled when the operation is no longer needed. To postulate one of these PSAs (Cabeza & Moscovitch 2013), there should be evidence that (*a*) all regions in the PSA are associated with the process they are assumed to mediate, (*b*) each region is associated with a complementary suboperation of this process, and (*c*) the regions communicate with each other in general and during the process of interest. There are many examples of PSAs that contribute to episodic memory and fulfill these criteria; here, we mention only two.

The first example is the PSA between the pHPC and VPC during recollective retrieval. Consistent with the first criterion, meta-analyses of event-related fMRI studies have strongly linked these regions to retrieval success and recollection (Cabeza et al. 2012). During retrieval, the pHPC and VPC show a recollection-related activity pattern, whereas a very different pattern emerges in the aHPC (e.g., Daselaar et al. 2006) [**Supplemental Figure 10** (follow the **Supplemental Material link** in the online version of this article or at **http://www.annualreviews.org/**)]. In keeping with the second criterion, the pHPC has been linked to the recovery of episodic memory details and the VPC to the complementary process of operating on the recovered information (Cabeza et al. 2012). Finally, fulfilling the third criterion, the pHPC and VPC have direct white-matter connections and interact very closely during rest and during episodic recollection (Cabeza et al. 2012).

Another example is the PSA between the HPC and domain-specific posterior cortices during encoding and retrieval. Consistent with the first criterion, activity in domain-specific cortices has been associated with successful encoding of relevant stimuli and with the reactivation of this information during retrieval (Danker & Anderson 2010). Second, HPC lesions yield global memory deficits, whereas cortical damage yields domain-specific memory deficits. Finally, the HPC and domain-specific cortices are anatomically linked, and there is evidence that they are functionally connected during rest (Schlichting & Preston 2014) and during successful encoding and retrieval processes (e.g., Ritchey et al. 2013) [**Supplemental Figure 11** (follow the **Supplemental Material link** in the online version of this article or at **http://www.annualreviews.org/**)].

Given that PSAs are rapidly assembled and disassembled, they require a mechanism that can quickly control communication between distant brain regions, and the most likely candidate is neuronal oscillations. There is abundant evidence that oscillations, particularly those in gamma (40–100 Hz) and theta (4–8 Hz) frequencies, control PSAs during episodic encoding and retrieval (Nyhus & Curran 2010). During encoding, gamma phase synchronization helps bind perceptual features into objects in posterior cortices (Engel et al. 1991), and gamma-theta coupling helps integrate objects into events in the HPC and posterior cortices (Jensen & Lisman 2005). In animal studies, HPC theta has been linked to successful spatial learning (Ekstrom et al. 2001) and to long-term potentiation (Hyman et al. 2003). In human studies, successful encoding has been associated with both gamma (Osipova et al. 2006) and theta (Long et al. 2014) frequencies in the HPC and posterior cortices. The coupling is assumed to be controlled by the PFC, and as WM load increases, theta power increases in frontal-midline electroencephalography (EEG) electrodes (frontal-midline theta) (Jensen & Tesche 2002). Moreover, an intracranial EEG study found phase-amplitude coupling between theta and beta-gamma when faces were maintained in WM (Axmacher et al. 2010).

During retrieval, access to a fraction of the HPC representation of the original event is assumed to cause reinstatement of the associated theta cycle, which triggers the reinstatement of the nested gamma cycles and their associated cortical representations (Jensen & Lisman 2005). In keeping with this hypothesis, human studies have found greater gamma and theta (Osipova et al. 2006) power in the HPC and posterior cortices for correct old responses than for new ones. There is evidence of greater gamma power for remember than for know responses in several scalp locations (Burgess & Ali 2002). One of these locations is the parietal cortex, consistent with the aforementioned PSA between the pHPC and the VPC.

In sum, the HPC can only support episodic memory if it interacts very closely with other regions. Each episodic process is mediated by a transient collaboration between regions mediating complementary operations, or PSA, consistent with our component process model. PSAs require a mechanism that can rapidly turn on and off interactions among distant regions, such as neural oscillations in gamma and theta frequencies (Johnson & Knight 2015), and our understanding of these PSAs may help distinguish between recurrent retrieval and re-encoding processes (Ben-Yakov et al. 2014).

CONCLUSION

Since its inception, the scientific study of memory has been influenced by the research program of its pioneers. Ebbinghaus [1964 (1885)] wished to study memory's essence, isolated from the influence of any other mental function. Bartlett (1932), on the other hand, saw memory as inextricably tied to other mental functions, and often operating in their service. To accomplish his goals, Ebbinghaus used nonsense syllables as memoranda, whereas Bartlett used complex verbal and pictorial stimuli. Given Ebbinghaus's memoranda, memory could only be seen as strengthened or lost (forgotten). Memory for Bartlett's material, on the other hand, could also be transformed with time and experience to reflect the cultural and personal schemas of the person. Memory is the only topic covered in Ebbinghaus's classical book, whereas Bartlett's reads like a book in social psychology. Indeed, Bartlett eschewed the word memory since it implied something static, preferring instead to title his book *Remembering* to reflect an active, adaptive, and changing process akin to other actions we perform. In this regard, his view was closer to that of James [1950 (1890)], who was concerned with the phenomenology of memory and had a functionalist approach to psychology. Although this review has discussed elements of all three perspectives, it has focused especially on Bartlett's and James's. At this time, it would be surprising if it were otherwise, given how interactive brain regions are with one another and how new technological advances drive this point home. We should take care, however, not to lose sight of the trees while our attention is directed toward the interactive forest.

DISCLOSURE STATEMENT

The authors are not aware of any affiliations, memberships, funding, or financial holdings that might be perceived as affecting the objectivity of this review.

ACKNOWLEDGMENTS

The writing of this article and some of the research reported herein were supported by grants to M.M. and G.W. from the Canadian Institutes for Health Research (grant MGP 6694) and from the Natural Sciences and Engineering Research Council of Canada; to L.N. from NIH, NSF, and the LuMind Foundation; and to R.C. from NIH-NIA (AG19731). The authors gratefully acknowledge the support of the following people: Nick Hoang in preparing the manuscript; Yadin Dudai, Jessica Robin, and Talya Sadeh for their helpful comments; and Dan Schacter for his suggestions, encouragement, and patience.

LITERATURE CITED

Addis DR, Moscovitch M, Crawley AP, McAndrews MP. 2004. Recollective qualities modulate hippocampal activation during autobiographical memory retrieval. *Hippocampus* 14:752–62

Addis DR, Pan L, Musicaro R, Schacter DL. 2015. Divergent thinking and constructing episodic simulations. *Memory*. In press

Addis DR, Schacter DL. 2011. The hippocampus and imagining the future: Where do we stand? *Front. Hum. Neurosci.* 5:173

Aggleton JP. 2012. Multiple anatomical systems embedded within the primate medial temporal lobe: implications for hippocampal function. *Neurosci. Biobehav. Rev.* 36:1579–96

Aly M, Ranganath C, Yonelinas AP. 2013. Detecting changes in scenes: The hippocampus is critical for strength-based perception. *Neuron* 78:1127–37

Anderson MC, Huddleston E. 2012. Towards a cognitive and neurobiological model of motivated forgetting. *Neb. Symp. Motiv.* 58:53–120

Andrews-Hanna JR. 2012. The brain's default network and its adaptive role in internal mentation. *Neuroscientist* 18:251–70

Axmacher N, Henseler MM, Jensen O, Weinreich I, Elger CE, Fell J. 2010. Cross-frequency coupling supports multi-item working memory in the human hippocampus. *PNAS* 107:3228–33

Baddeley A, Allen R, Vargha-Khadem F. 2010. Is the hippocampus necessary for visual and verbal binding in working memory? *Neuropsychologia* 48:1089–95

Bakker A, Kirwan CB, Miller M, Stark CE. 2008. Pattern separation in the human hippocampal CA3 and dentate gyrus. *Science* 319:1640–42

Bartlett FC. 1932. *Remembering: A Study in Experimental and Social Psychology.* Cambridge, UK: Cambridge Univ. Press

Bartsch T, Dohring J, Rohr A, Jansen O, Deuschl G. 2011. CA1 neurons in the human hippocampus are critical for autobiographical memory, mental time travel, and autonoetic consciousness. *PNAS* 108:17562–67

Baumann O, Mattingley JB. 2013. Dissociable representations of environmental size and complexity in the human hippocampus. *J. Neurosci.* 33:10526–33

Beadle JN, Tranel D, Cohen NJ, Duff MC. 2013. Empathy in hippocampal amnesia. *Front. Psychol.* 4:69

Ben-Yakov A, Dudai Y. 2011. Constructing realistic engrams: Poststimulus activity of hippocampus and dorsal striatum predicts subsequent episodic memory. *J. Neurosci.* 31:9032–42

Ben-Yakov A, Eshel N, Dudai Y. 2013. Hippocampal immediate poststimulus activity in the encoding of consecutive naturalistic episodes. *J. Exp. Psychol.: Gen.* 142:1255–63

Ben-Yakov A, Rubinson M, Dudai Y. 2014. Shifting gears in hippocampus: temporal dissociation between familiarity and novelty signatures in a single event. *J. Neurosci.* 34:12973–81

Benoit RG, Gilbert SJ, Burgess PW. 2011. A neural mechanism mediating the impact of episodic prospection on farsighted decisions. *J. Neurosci.* 31:6771–79

Benoit RG, Szpunar KK, Schacter DL. 2014. Ventromedial prefrontal cortex supports affective future simulation by integrating distributed knowledge. *PNAS* 111:16550–55

Berryhill ME. 2012. Insights from neuropsychology: pinpointing the role of the posterior parietal cortex in episodic and working memory. *Front. Integr. Neurosci.* 6:31

Bird CM, Burgess N. 2008. The hippocampus and memory: insights from spatial processing. *Nat. Rev. Neurosci.* 9:182–94

Bonnici HM, Chadwick MJ, Maguire EA. 2013. Representations of recent and remote autobiographical memories in hippocampal subfields. *Hippocampus* 23:849–54

Bowles B, Crupi C, Pigott S, Parrent A, Wiebe S, et al. 2010. Double dissociation of selective recollection and familiarity impairments following two different surgical treatments for temporal-lobe epilepsy. *Neuropsychologia* 48:2640–47

Buckner RL. 2010. The role of the hippocampus in prediction and imagination. *Annu. Rev. Psychol.* 61:27–48

Burgess AP, Ali L. 2002. Functional connectivity of gamma EEG activity is modulated at low frequency during conscious recollection. *Intl. J. Psychophysiol.* 46:91–100

Buzsaki G, Moser EI. 2013. Memory, navigation and theta rhythm in the hippocampal-entorhinal system. *Nat. Neurosci.* 16:130–38

Cabeza R, Ciaramelli E, Moscovitch M. 2012. Cognitive contributions of the ventral parietal cortex: an integrative theoretical account. *Trends Cogn. Sci.* 16:338–52

Cabeza R, Moscovitch M. 2013. Memory systems, processing modes, and components: functional neuroimaging evidence. *Perspect. Psychol. Sci.* 8:49–55

Cabeza R, St. Jacques P. 2007. Functional neuroimaging of autobiographical memory. *Trends Cogn. Sci.* 11:219–27

Chadwick MJ, Bonnici HM, Maguire EA. 2014. CA3 size predicts the precision of memory recall. *PNAS* 111:10720–25

Chadwick MJ, Hassabis D, Weiskopf N, Maguire EA. 2010. Decoding individual episodic memory traces in the human hippocampus. *Curr. Biol.* 20:544–47

Chadwick MJ, Mullally SL, Maguire EA. 2013. The hippocampus extrapolates beyond the view in scenes: an fMRI study of boundary extension. *Cortex* 49:2067–79

Ciaramelli E, Bernardi F, Moscovitch M. 2013. Individualized theory of mind (iToM): when memory modulates empathy. *Front. Psychol.* 4:4

Clark IA, Maguire EA. 2016. Remembering preservation in hippocampal amnesia. *Annu. Rev. Psychol.* 67:51–82

Cohn M, Moscovitch M, Lahat A, McAndrews MP. 2009. Recollection versus strength as the primary determinant of hippocampal engagement at retrieval. *PNAS* 106:22451–55

Conway MA. 2009. Episodic memories. *Neuropsychologia* 47:2305–13

Corkin S. 2013. *Permanent Present Tense: The Unforgettable Life of the Amnesic Patient, H.M.* New York: Basic Books

Coutanche MN, Thompson-Schill SL. 2015. Rapid consolidation of new knowledge in adulthood via fast mapping. *Trends Cogn. Sci.* 19:486–88

Craik FIM. 1986. A functional account of age differences in memory. In *Human Memory and Cognitive Capabilities*, ed. F Klix, H Hagendorf, pp. 409–22. Amsterdam: North-Holland

Dalla Barba G, La Corte V. 2013. The hippocampus, a time machine that makes errors. *Trends Cogn. Sci.* 17:102–4

Danckert J, Ferber S, Pun C, Broderick C, Striemer C, et al. 2007. Neglected time: impaired temporal perception of multisecond intervals in unilateral neglect. *J. Cogn. Neurosci.* 19:1706–20

Danker JF, Anderson JR. 2010. The ghosts of brain states past: Remembering reactivates the brain regions engaged during encoding. *Psychol. Bull.* 136:87–102

Das SR, Mancuso L, Olson IR, Arnold SE, Wolk DA. 2015. Short-term memory depends on dissociable medial temporal lobe regions in amnestic mild cognitive impairment. *Cereb. Cortex*. In press

Daselaar SM, Fleck M, Dobbins IG, Madden DJ, Cabeza R. 2006. Effects of healthy aging on hippocampal and rhinal memory functions: an event-related fMRI study. *Cereb. Cortex* 16:1771–82

Davachi L, Dubrow S. 2015. How the hippocampus preserves order: the role of prediction and context. *Trends Cogn. Sci.* 19:92–99

Davidson PS, Anaki D, Ciaramelli E, Cohn M, Kim ASN, et al. 2008. Does parietal cortex support episodic memory? Evidence from focal lesion patients. *Neuropsychologia* 46:1743–55

Davidson PS, Drouin H, Kwan D, Moscovitch M, Rosenbaum RS. 2012. Memory as social glue: close interpersonal relationships in amnesic patients. *Front. Psychol.* 3:531

de Oliveira Alvares L, Einarsson EO, Santana F, Crestani AP, Haubrich J, et al. 2012. Periodically reactivated context memory retains its precision and dependence on the hippocampus. *Hippocampus* 22:1092–95

Dede AJ, Wixted JT, Hopkins RO, Squire LR. 2013. Hippocampal damage impairs recognition memory broadly, affecting both parameters in two prominent models of memory. *PNAS* 110:6577–82

Diekelmann S, Born J. 2010. The memory function of sleep. *Nat. Rev. Neurosci.* 11:114–26

Dudai Y. 2012. The restless engram: Consolidations never end. *Annu. Rev. Neurosci.* 35:227–47

Duff MC, Brown-Schmidt S. 2012. The hippocampus and the flexible use and processing of language. *Front. Hum. Neurosci.* 6:69

Dunsmoor JE, Murty VP, Davachi L, Phelps EA. 2015. Emotional learning selectively and retroactively strengthens memories for related events. *Nature* 520:345–48

Ebbinghaus H. 1964 (1885). *Memory: A Contribution to Experimental Psychology*. New York: Dover

Eichenbaum H. 2014. Time cells in the hippocampus: a new dimension for mapping memories. *Nat. Rev. Neurosci.* 15:732–44

Eichenbaum H, Yonelinas AP, Ranganath C. 2007. The medial temporal lobe and recognition memory. *Annu. Rev. Neurosci.* 30:123–52

Ekstrom AD, Meltzer J, McNaughton BL, Barnes CA. 2001. NMDA receptor antagonism blocks experience-dependent expansion of hippocampal "place fields." *Neuron* 31:631–38

Engel AK, Kreiter AK, Konig P, Singer W. 1991. Synchronization of oscillatory neuronal responses between striate and extrastriate visual cortical areas of the cat. *PNAS* 88:6048–52

Evensmoen HR, Ladstein J, Hansen TI, Moller JA, Witter MP, et al. 2015. From details to large scale: The representation of environmental positions follows a granularity gradient along the human hippocampal and entorhinal anterior-posterior axis. *Hippocampus* 25:119–35

Frankland PW, Bontempi B. 2005. The organization of recent and remote memories. *Nat. Rev. Neurosci.* 6:119–30

Furman O, Mendelsohn A, Dudai Y. 2012. The episodic engram transformed: Time reduces retrieval-related brain activity but correlates it with memory accuracy. *Learn. Mem.* 19:575–87

Gaesser B, Schacter DL. 2014. Episodic simulation and episodic memory can increase intentions to help others. *PNAS* 111:4415–20

Gaesser B, Spreng RN, McLelland VC, Addis DR, Schacter DL. 2013. Imagining the future: evidence for a hippocampal contribution to constructive processing. *Hippocampus* 23:1150–61

Gerraty RT, Davidow JY, Wimmer GE, Kahn I, Shohamy D. 2014. Transfer of learning relates to intrinsic connectivity between hippocampus, ventromedial prefrontal cortex, and large-scale networks. *J. Neurosci.* 34:11297–303

Ghosh VE, Moscovitch M, Melo Colella B, Gilboa A. 2014. Schema representation in patients with ventromedial PFC lesions. *J. Neurosci.* 34:12057–70

Gilboa A, Sekeres M, Moscovitch M, Winocur G. 2014. Higher-order conditioning is impaired by hippocampal lesions. *Curr. Biol.* 24:2202–7

Gilboa A, Verfaellie M. 2010. Telling it like it isn't: the cognitive neuroscience of confabulation. *J. Int. Neuropsychol. Soc.* 16:961–66

Goshen I, Brodsky M, Prakash R, Wallace J, Gradinaru V, et al. 2011. Dynamics of retrieval strategies for remote memories. *Cell* 147:678–89

Greenberg DL, Keane MM, Ryan L, Verfaellie M. 2009. Impaired category fluency in medial temporal lobe amnesia: the role of episodic memory. *J. Neurosci.* 29:10900–8

Hall SA, Rubin DC, Miles A, Davis SW, Wing EA, et al. 2014. The neural basis of involuntary episodic memories. *J. Cogn. Neurosci.* 26:2385–99

Hannula DE, Ranganath C. 2009. The eyes have it: Hippocampal activity predicts expression of memory in eye movements. *Neuron* 63:592–99

Haskins AL, Yonelinas AP, Quamme JR, Ranganath C. 2008. Perirhinal cortex supports encoding and familiarity-based recognition of novel associations. *Neuron* 59:554–60

Hassabis D, Maguire EA. 2009. The construction system of the brain. *Philos. Trans. R. Soc. Lond. B* 364:1263–71

Henke K. 2010. A model for memory systems based on processing modes rather than consciousness. *Nat. Rev. Neurosci.* 11:523–32

Hirshhorn M, Grady C, Rosenbaum RS, Winocur G, Moscovitch M. 2012. The hippocampus is involved in mental navigation for a recently learned, but not a highly familiar environment: a longitudinal fMRI study. *Hippocampus* 22:842–52

Howard MW, Eichenbaum H. 2013. The hippocampus, time, and memory across scales. *J. Exp. Psychol.: Gen.* 142:1211–30

Howard LR, Javadi AH, Yu Y, Mill RD, Morrison LC, et al. 2014. The hippocampus and entorhinal cortex encode the path and Euclidean distances to goals during navigation. *Curr. Biol.* 24:1331–40

Hower KH, Wixted J, Berryhill ME, Olson IR. 2014. Impaired perception of mnemonic oldness, but not mnemonic newness, after parietal lobe damage. *Neuropsychologia* 56:409–17

Hunsaker MR, Kesner RP. 2013. The operation of pattern separation and pattern completion processes associated with different attributes or domains of memory. *Neurosci. Biobehav. Rev.* 37:36–58

Hyman JM, Wyble BP, Goyal V, Rossi CA, Hasselmo ME. 2003. Stimulation in hippocampal region CA1 in behaving rats yields long-term potentiation when delivered to the peak of theta and long-term depression when delivered to the trough. *J. Neurosci.* 23:11725–31

James W. 1950 (1890). *Principles of Psychology*, Vol. 1. New York: Dover

Jensen O, Lisman JE. 2005. Hippocampal sequence-encoding driven by a cortical multi-item working memory buffer. *Trends Neurosci.* 28:67–72

Jensen O, Tesche CD. 2002. Frontal theta activity in humans increases with memory load in a working memory task. *Eur. J. Neurosci.* 15:1395–99

Johnson EL, Knight RT. 2015. Intracranial recordings and human memory. *Curr. Opin. Neurobiol.* 31:18–25

Josselyn SA, Kohler S, Frankland PW. 2015. Finding the engram. *Nat. Rev. Neurosci.* 16:521–34

Kandel ER, Dudai Y, Mayford MR. 2014. The molecular and systems biology of memory. *Cell* 157:163–86

Kim H. 2015. Encoding and retrieval along the long axis of the hippocampus and their relationships with dorsal attention and default mode networks: the HERNET model. *Hippocampus* 25(4):500–10

Kim J, Yassa MA. 2013. Assessing recollection and familiarity of similar lures in a behavioral pattern separation task. *Hippocampus* 23:287–94

Kim S, Dede AJO, Hopkins RO, Squire LR. 2015. Memory, scene construction, and the human hippocampus. *PNAS* 112:4767–72

Kopelman MD, Wilson BA, Baddeley AD. 1989. The autobiographical memory interview: a new assessment of autobiographical and personal semantic memory in amnesic patients. *J. Clin. Exp. Neuropsychol.* 11:724–44

Kwan D, Craver CF, Green L, Myerson J, Rosenbaum RS. 2013. Dissociations in future thinking following hippocampal damage: evidence from discounting and time perspective in episodic amnesia. *J. Exp. Psychol.: Gen.* 142:1355–69

Lee AC, Yeung LK, Barense MD. 2012. The hippocampus and visual perception. *Front. Hum. Neurosci.* 6:91

Levine B, Svoboda E, Hay JF, Winocur G, Moscovitch M. 2002. Aging and autobiographical memory: dissociating episodic from semantic retrieval. *Psychol. Aging* 17:677–89

Levine B, Svoboda E, Turner GR, Mandic M, Mackey A. 2009. Behavioral and functional neuroanatomical correlates of anterograde autobiographical memory in isolated retrograde amnesic patient M.L. *Neuropsychologia* 47:2188–96

Lewis PA, Durrant SJ. 2011. Overlapping memory replay during sleep builds cognitive schemata. *Trends Cogn. Sci.* 15:343–51

Long NM, Burke JF, Kahana MJ. 2014. Subsequent memory effect in intracranial and scalp EEG. *NeuroImage* 84:488–94

Madore KP, Addis DR, Schacter DL. 2015. Creativity and memory: effects of an episodic-specificity induction on divergent thinking. *Psychol. Sci.* 26:1461–68

Madore KP, Schacter DL. 2014. An episodic specificity induction enhances means-end problem solving in young and older adults. *Psychol. Aging* 29:913–24

Maguire EA, Intraub H, Mullally SL. 2015. Scenes, spaces, and memory traces: What does the hippocampus do? *Neuroscientist.* In press

Maguire EA, Mullally SL. 2013. The hippocampus: a manifesto for change. *J. Exp. Psychol.: Gen.* 142:1180–89

Malykhin NV, Lebel RM, Coupland NJ, Wilman AH, Carter R. 2010. In vivo quantification of hippocampal subfields using 4.7 T fast spin echo imaging. *NeuroImage* 49:1224–30

McClelland JL, McNaughton BL, O'Reilly RC. 1995. Why there are complementary learning systems in the hippocampus and neocortex: insights from the successes and failures of connectionist models of learning and memory. *Psychol. Rev.* 102:419–57

McCormick C, St-Laurent M, Ty A, Valiante TA, McAndrews MP. 2013. Functional and effective hippocampal-neocortical connectivity during construction and elaboration of autobiographical memory retrieval. *Cereb. Cortex* 25:1297–305

Merhav M, Karni A, Gilboa A. 2014. Neocortical catastrophic interference in healthy and amnesic adults: a paradoxical matter of time. *Hippocampus* 24(12):1653–62

Merhav M, Karni A, Gilboa A. 2015. Not all declarative memories are created equal: fast mapping as a direct route to cortical declarative representations. *NeuroImage.* 117:80–92

Migo EM, Mayes AR, Montaldi D. 2012. Measuring recollection and familiarity: improving the remember/know procedure. *Conscious. Cogn.* 21:1435–55

Miller JF, Neufang M, Solway A, Brandt A, Trippel M, et al. 2013. Neural activity in human hippocampal formation reveals the spatial context of retrieved memories. *Science* 342:1111–14

Mitchell JP. 2009. Inferences about mental states. *Philos. Trans. R. Soc. Lond. B* 364:1309–16

Montaldi D, Mayes AR. 2011. Familiarity, recollection and medial temporal lobe function: an unresolved issue. *Trends Cogn. Sci.* 15:339–40

Morgan LK, Macevoy SP, Aguirre GK, Epstein RA. 2011. Distances between real-world locations are represented in the human hippocampus. *J. Neurosci.* 31:1238–45

Moscovitch DA, Chiupka CA, Gavric DL. 2013. Within the mind's eye: Negative mental imagery activates different emotion regulation strategies in high versus low socially anxious individuals. *J. Behav. Ther. Exp. Psychiatry* 44:426–32

Moscovitch M. 1992. Memory and working-with-memory: a component process model based on modules and central systems. *J. Cogn. Neurosci.* 4:257–67

Moscovitch M. 1995. Recovered consciousness: a hypothesis concerning modularity and episodic memory. *J. Clin. Exp. Neuropsychol.* 17:276–90

Moscovitch M. 2008. The hippocampus as a "stupid," domain-specific module: implications for theories of recent and remote memory, and of imagination. *Can. J. Exp. Psychol.* 62:62–79

Moscovitch M, Vriezen ER, Goshen-Gottstein Y. 1993. Implicit tests of memory in patients with focal lesions or degenerative brain disorders. In *The Handbook of Neuropsychology*, Vol. 8, ed. F Boller, J Grafman, pp. 133–73. Amsterdam: Elsevier Sci.

Moscovitch M, Winocur G. 1992. Frontal lobes and memory. In *The Encyclopedia of Learning and Memory: A Volume in Neuropsychology*, ed. LR Squire, pp. 182–87. New York: Macmillan

Moscovitch M, Winocur G. 2002. The frontal cortex and working with memory. In *The Frontal Lobes*, ed. DT Stuss, RT Knight, pp. 188–209. Oxford, UK: Oxford Univ. Press

Mullally SL, Intraub H, Maguire EA. 2012. Attenuated boundary extension produces a paradoxical memory advantage in amnesic patients. *Curr. Biol.* 22:261–68

Nadel L. 2008. Hippocampus and context revisited. In *Hippocampal Place Fields: Relevance to Learning and Memory*, ed. S Mizumori, pp. 3–15. Oxford, UK: Oxford Univ. Press

Nadel L, Hoscheidt S, Ryan LR. 2013. Spatial cognition and the hippocampus: the anterior-posterior axis. *J. Cogn. Neurosci.* 25:22–28

Nadel L, Moscovitch M. 1997. Memory consolidation, retrograde amnesia and the hippocampal complex. *Curr. Opin. Neurobiol.* 7:217–27

Nadel L, Peterson MA. 2013. The hippocampus: part of an interactive posterior representational system spanning perceptual and memorial systems. *J. Exp. Psychol.: Gen.* 142:1242–54

Nader K, Hardt O. 2009. A single standard for memory: the case for reconsolidation. *Nat. Rev. Neurosci.* 10:224–34

Nichols EA, Kao YC, Verfaellie M, Gabrieli JD. 2006. Working memory and long-term memory for faces: evidence from fMRI and global amnesia for involvement of the medial temporal lobes. *Hippocampus* 16:604–16

Nieuwenhuis IL, Takashima A. 2011. The role of the ventromedial prefrontal cortex in memory consolidation. *Behav. Brain Res.* 218:325–34

Norman KA. 2010. How hippocampus and cortex contribute to recognition memory: revisiting the complementary learning systems model. *Hippocampus* 20:1217–27

Nyhus E, Curran T. 2010. Functional role of gamma and theta oscillations in episodic memory. *Neurosci. Biobehav. Rev.* 34:1023–35

O'Keefe J, Nadel L. 1978. *The Hippocampus as a Cognitive Map*. Oxford, UK: Oxford Univ. Press

Olsen RK, Moses SN, Riggs L, Ryan JD. 2012. The hippocampus supports multiple cognitive processes through relational binding and comparison. *Front. Hum. Neurosci.* 6:146

Olson IR, Page K, Moore KS, Chatterjee A, Verfaellie M. 2006. Working memory for conjunctions relies on the medial temporal lobe. *J. Neurosci.* 26:4596–601

Osipova D, Takashima A, Oostenveld R, Fernandez G, Maris E, Jensen O. 2006. Theta and gamma oscillations predict encoding and retrieval of declarative memory. *J. Neurosci.* 26:7523–31

Palombo DJ, Keane MM, Verfaellie M. 2015. The medial temporal lobes are critical for reward-based decision making under conditions that promote episodic future thinking. *Hippocampus* 25:345–53

Park L, St-Laurent M, McAndrews MP, Moscovitch M. 2011. The immediacy of recollection: the use of the historical present in narratives of autobiographical episodes by patients with unilateral temporal lobe epilepsy. *Neuropsychologia* 49:1171–76

Penfield W, Mathieson G. 1974. Memory: autopsy findings and comments on the role of hippocampus in experiential recall. *Arch. Neurol.* 31:145–54

Penfield W, Milner B. 1958. Memory deficit produced by bilateral lesions in the hippocampal zone. *AMA Arch. Neurol. Psychiatry* 79:475–97

Pertzov Y, Miller TD, Gorgoraptis N, Caine D, Schott JM, et al. 2013. Binding deficits in memory following medial temporal lobe damage in patients with voltage-gated potassium channel complex antibody-associated limbic encephalitis. *Brain* 136:2474–85

Piolino P, Desgranges B, Eustache F. 2009. Episodic autobiographical memories over the course of time: cognitive, neuropsychological and neuroimaging findings. *Neuropsychologia* 47:2314–29

Poppenk J, Evensmoen HR, Moscovitch M, Nadel L. 2013. Long-axis specialization of the human hippocampus. *Trends Cogn. Sci.* 17:230–40

Poppenk J, Moscovitch M. 2011. A hippocampal marker of recollection memory ability among healthy young adults: contributions of posterior and anterior segments. *Neuron* 72:931–37

Prebble SC, Addis DR, Tippett LJ. 2013. Autobiographical memory and sense of self. *Psychol. Bull.* 139:815–40

Preston AR, Eichenbaum H. 2013. Interplay of hippocampus and prefrontal cortex in memory. *Curr. Biol.* 23:R764–73

Quamme JR, Yonelinas AP, Norman KA. 2007. Effect of unitization on associative recognition in amnesia. *Hippocampus* 17:192–200

Quiroga RQ. 2012. Concept cells: the building blocks of declarative memory functions. *Nat. Rev. Neurosci.* 13:587–97

Race E, Keane MM, Verfaellie M. 2015. Sharing mental simulations and stories: hippocampal contributions to discourse integration. *Cortex* 63:271–81

Ranganath C, Ritchey M. 2012. Two cortical systems for memory-guided behaviour. *Nat. Rev. Neurosci.* 13:713–26

Reagh ZM, Watabe J, Ly M, Murray E, Yassa MA. 2014. Dissociated signals in human dentate gyrus and CA3 predict different facets of recognition memory. *J. Neurosci.* 34:13301–13

Reber TP, Henke K. 2012. Integrating unseen events over time. *Conscious. Cogn.* 21:953–60

Renoult L, Davidson PS, Palombo DJ, Moscovitch M, Levine B. 2012. Personal semantics: at the crossroads of semantic and episodic memory. *Trends Cogn. Sci.* 16:550–58

Renoult L, Davidson PS, Schmitz E, Park L, Campbell K, et al. 2015. Autobiographically significant concepts: more episodic than semantic in nature? An electrophysiological investigation of overlapping types of memory. *J. Cogn. Neurosci.* 27:57–72

Ritchey M, Montchal ME, Yonelinas AP, Ranganath C. 2015. Delay-dependent contributions of medial temporal lobe regions to episodic memory retrieval. *eLife* 4:e05025

Ritchey M, Wing EA, LaBar KS, Cabeza R. 2013. Neural similarity between encoding and retrieval is related to memory via hippocampal interactions. *Cereb. Cortex* 23:2818–28

Robin J, Hirshhorn M, Rosenbaum RS, Winocur G, Moscovitch M, Grady CL. 2015. Functional connectivity of hippocampal and prefrontal networks during episodic and spatial memory based on real-world environments. *Hippocampus* 25:81–93

Robin J, Moscovitch M. 2014. The effects of spatial contextual familiarity on remembered scenes, episodic memories, and imagined future events. *J. Exp. Psychol.: Learn. Mem. Cogn.* 40:459–75

Robin J, Wynn J, Moscovitch M. 2015. The spatial scaffold: the effects of spatial context on memory for events. *J. Exp. Psychol.: Learn. Mem. Cogn.* In press

Robinson E, Aveyard P, Daley A, Jolly K, Lewis A, et al. 2013. Eating attentively: a systematic review and meta-analysis of the effect of food intake memory and awareness on eating. *Am. J. Clin. Nutr.* 47:728–42

Romero K, Moscovitch M. 2012. Episodic memory and event construction in aging and amnesia. *J. Mem. Lang.* 67:270–84

Rosenbaum RS, Gilboa A, Levine B, Winocur G, Moscovitch M. 2009. Amnesia as an impairment of detail generation and binding: evidence from personal, fictional, and semantic narratives in K.C. *Neuropsychologia* 47:2181–87

Rosenbaum RS, Priselac S, Köhler S, Black SE, Gao F, et al. 2000. Remote spatial memory in an amnesic person with extensive bilateral hippocampal lesions. *Nat. Neurosci.* 3:1044–48

Rozin P, Dow S, Moscovitch M, Rajaram S. 1998. What causes humans to begin and end a meal? A role for memory for what has been eaten, as evidenced by a study of multiple meal eating in amnesic patients. *Psychol. Sci.* 9:392–96

Rubin DC, Umanath S. 2015. Event memory: a theory of memory for laboratory, autobiographical, and fictional events. *Psychol. Rev.* 122:1–23

Rubin RD, Watson PD, Duff MC, Cohen NJ. 2014. The role of the hippocampus in flexible cognition and social behavior. *Front. Hum. Neurosci.* 8:742

Rugg MD, Vilberg KL. 2013. Brain networks underlying episodic memory retrieval. *Curr. Opin. Neurobiol.* 23:255–60

Ryan JD, Moses SN, Barense M, Rosenbaum RS. 2013. Intact learning of new relations in amnesia as achieved through unitization. *J. Neurosci.* 33:9601–13

Sadeh T, Maril A, Goshen-Gottstein Y. 2012. Encoding-related brain activity dissociates between the recollective processes underlying successful recall and recognition: a subsequent-memory study. *Neuropsychologia* 50:2317–24

Schacter DL, Addis DR, Hassabis D, Martin VC, Spreng RN, Szpunar KK. 2012. The future of memory: remembering, imagining, and the brain. *Neuron* 76:677–94

Schacter DL, Dobbins IG, Schnyer DM. 2004. Specificity of priming: a cognitive neuroscience perspective. *Nat. Rev. Neurosci.* 5:853–62

Schlichting ML, Preston AR. 2014. Memory reactivation during rest supports upcoming learning of related content. *PNAS* 111:15845–50

Schnider A. 2008. *The Confabulating Mind: How the Brain Creates Reality.* Oxford, UK: Oxford Univ. Press

Shallice T, Cooper R. 2012. The organisation of mind. *Cortex* 48:1366–70

Sharon T, Moscovitch M, Gilboa A. 2011. Rapid neocortical acquisition of long-term arbitrary associations independent of the hippocampus. *PNAS* 108:1146–51

Sheldon S, Levine B. 2013. Same as it ever was: Vividness modulates the similarities and differences between the neural networks that support retrieving remote and recent autobiographical memories. *NeuroImage* 83:880–91

Sheldon S, McAndrews MP, Moscovitch M. 2011. Episodic memory processes mediated by the medial temporal lobes contribute to open-ended problem solving. *Neuropsychologia* 49:2439–47

Sheldon S, Moscovitch M. 2012. The nature and time-course of medial temporal lobe contributions to semantic retrieval: an fMRI study on verbal fluency. *Hippocampus* 22:1451–66

Sheldon S, Romero K, Moscovitch M. 2013. Medial temporal lobe amnesia impairs performance on a free association task. *Hippocampus* 23:405–12

Sheldon SA, Moscovitch M. 2010. Recollective performance advantages for implicit memory tasks. *Memory* 18:681–97

Shohamy D, Wagner AD. 2008. Integrating memories in the human brain: hippocampal-midbrain encoding of overlapping events. *Neuron* 60:378–89

Simons J, Peers P, Mazuz Y, Berryhill M, Olson I. 2010. Dissociation between memory accuracy and memory confidence following bilateral parietal lesions. *Cereb. Cortex* 20:479–85

Simons JS, Spiers HJ. 2003. Prefrontal and medial temporal lobe interactions in long-term memory. *Nat. Rev. Neurosci.* 4:637–48

Skinner EI, Fernandes MA. 2007. Neural correlates of recollection and familiarity: a review of neuroimaging and patient data. *Neuropsychologia* 45:2163–79

Smith CN, Jeneson, Frascino JC, Kirwan CB, Hopkins RO, Squire LR. 2014a. When recognition memory is independent of hippocampal function. *PNAS* 111:9935–40

Smith CN, Urgolites ZJ, Hopkins RO, Squire LR. 2014b. Comparison of explicit and incidental learning strategies in memory-impaired patients. *PNAS* 111:475–79

Spreng RN, Mar RA, Kim AS. 2009. The common neural basis of autobiographical memory, prospection, navigation, theory of mind, and the default mode: a quantitative meta-analysis. *J. Cogn. Neurosci.* 21:489–510

Squire LR, Wixted JT. 2011. The cognitive neuroscience of human memory since H.M. *Annu. Rev. Neurosci.* 34:259–88

Staresina BP, Alink A, Kriegeskorte N, Henson RN. 2013. Awake reactivation predicts memory in humans. *PNAS* 110:21159–64

Stickgold R. 2013. Parsing the role of sleep in memory processing. *Curr. Opin. Neurobiol.* 23:847–53

St-Laurent M, Moscovitch M, Jadd R, McAndrews MP. 2014. The perceptual richness of complex memory episodes is compromised by medial temporal lobe damage. *Hippocampus* 24:560–76

Strange BA, Witter MP, Lein ES, Moser EI. 2014. Functional organization of the hippocampal longitudinal axis. *Nat. Rev. Neurosci.* 15:655–69

Svoboda E, McKinnon MC, Levine B. 2006. The functional neuroanatomy of autobiographical memory: a meta-analysis. *Neuropsychologia* 44:2189–208

Takashima A, Nieuwenhuis IL, Jensen O, Talamini LM, Rijpkema M, Fernandez G. 2009. Shift from hippocampal to neocortical centered retrieval network with consolidation. *J. Neurosci.* 29:10087–93

Talmi D. 2013. Enhanced emotional memory: cognitive and neural mechanisms. *Curr. Dir. Psychol. Sci.* 22:430–36

Talmi D, Grady CL, Goshen-Gottstein Y, Moscovitch M. 2005. Neuroimaging the serial position curve: a test of single-store versus dual-store models. *Psychol. Sci.* 16:716–23

Tambini A, Ketz N, Davachi L. 2010. Enhanced brain correlations during rest are related to memory for recent experiences. *Neuron* 65:280–90

Tanaka KZ, Pevzner A, Hamidi AB, Nakazawa Y, Graham J, Wiltgen BJ. 2014. Cortical representations are reinstated by the hippocampus during memory retrieval. *Neuron* 84(2):347–54

Teyler TJ, Rudy JW. 2007. The hippocampal indexing theory and episodic memory: updating the index. *Hippocampus* 17:1158–69

Tonegawa S, Pignatelli M, Roy DS, Ryan TJ. 2015. Memory engram storage and retrieval. *Curr. Opin. Neurobiol.* 35:101–9

Tse D, Langston RF, Kakeyama M, Bethus I, Spooner PA, et al. 2007. Schemas and memory consolidation. *Science* 316:76–82

Tulving E. 1983. *Elements of Episodic Memory*. Oxford, UK: Clarendon

Tulving E. 2002. Episodic memory: from mind to brain. *Annu. Rev. Psychol.* 53:1–25

van Kesteren MT, Ruiter DJ, Fernandez G, Henson RN. 2012. How schema and novelty augment memory formation. *Trends Neurosci.* 35:211–19

Verfaellie M, Bousquet K, Keane MM. 2014. Medial temporal and neocortical contributions to remote memory for semantic narratives: evidence from amnesia. *Neuropsychologia* 61:105–12

Viard A, Desgranges B, Eustache F, Piolino P. 2012. Factors affecting medial temporal lobe engagement for past and future episodic events: an ALE meta-analysis of neuroimaging studies. *Brain Cogn.* 80:111–25

Viskontas IV, Carr VA, Engel SA, Knowlton BJ. 2009a. The neural correlates of recollection: Hippocampal activation declines as episodic memory fades. *Hippocampus* 19:265–72

Viskontas IV, Quiroga RQ, Fried I. 2009b. Human medial temporal lobe neurons respond preferentially to personally relevant images. *PNAS* 106:21329–34

Wang SH, Morris RG. 2010. Hippocampal-neocortical interactions in memory formation, consolidation, and reconsolidation. *Annu. Rev. Psychol.* 61:49–79

Wimmer GE, Shohamy D. 2012. Preference by association: how memory mechanisms in the hippocampus bias decisions. *Science* 338:270–73

Winocur G, Moscovitch M. 2011. Memory transformation and systems consolidation. *J. Int. Neuropsychol. Soc.* 17:766–80

Winocur G, Moscovitch M, Bontempi B. 2010. Memory formation and long-term retention in humans and animals: convergence towards a transformation account of hippocampal-neocortical interactions. *Neuropsychologia* 48:2339–56

Yassa MA, Lacy JW, Stark SM, Albert MS, Gallagher M, Stark CE. 2011. Pattern separation deficits associated with increased hippocampal CA3 and dentate gyrus activity in nondemented older adults. *Hippocampus* 21:968–79

Yazar Y, Bergstrom ZM, Simons JS. 2014. Continuous theta burst stimulation of angular gyrus reduces subjective recollection. *PLOS ONE* 9:e110414

Yonelinas AP. 2013. The hippocampus supports high-resolution binding in the service of perception, working memory and long-term memory. *Behav. Brain Res.* 254:34–44

Zola-Morgan S, Squire LR, Amaral DG. 1986. Human amnesia and the medial temporal region: enduring memory impairment following a bilateral lesion limited to field CA1 of the hippocampus. *J. Neurosci.* 6:2950–67

Counterfactual Thought

Ruth M.J. Byrne

School of Psychology and Institute of Neuroscience, Trinity College Dublin, University of Dublin, Ireland; email: rmbyrne@tcd.ie

Annu. Rev. Psychol. 2016. 67:135–57

First published online as a Review in Advance on September 14, 2015

The *Annual Review of Psychology* is online at psych.annualreviews.org

This article's doi: 10.1146/annurev-psych-122414-033249

Keywords

imagination, reasoning, decision-making, regret, blame, moral judgment

Abstract

People spontaneously create counterfactual alternatives to reality when they think "if only" or "what if" and imagine how the past could have been different. The mind computes counterfactuals for many reasons. Counterfactuals explain the past and prepare for the future, they implicate various relations including causal ones, and they affect intentions and decisions. They modulate emotions such as regret and relief, and they support moral judgments such as blame. The loss of the ability to imagine alternatives as a result of injuries to the prefrontal cortex is devastating. The basic cognitive processes that compute counterfactuals mutate aspects of the mental representation of reality to create an imagined alternative, and they compare alternative representations. The ability to create counterfactuals develops throughout childhood and contributes to reasoning about other people's beliefs, including their false beliefs. Knowledge affects the plausibility of a counterfactual through the semantic and pragmatic modulation of the mental representation of alternative possibilities.

Contents

THE COUNTERFACTUAL IMAGINATION

There is an allure to imagining how things could have turned out differently. We spontaneously create counterfactual alternatives to reality when we think "if only . . . " or "what if . . . " and imagine how the past could have been different. In this article, I consider three key issues: what the mind computes to create counterfactuals, how the mind creates counterfactuals, and how knowledge modulates the plausibility of counterfactuals.

WHAT THE MIND COMPUTES TO CREATE COUNTERFACTUALS

The mind computes counterfactuals for diverse reasons. At one end of the counterfactual spectrum, imagined alternatives entertain and amuse us in fantasy and fiction, and they flourish in literature, film, and theater. At the other end, counterfactuals support logical, mathematical, and scientific reason, and they underpin complex deductions. In between these endpoints, counterfactuals serve several key purposes: They explain the past, prepare for the future, modulate emotional experience, and support moral judgments.

Explanations of the Past

Counterfactuals justify, defend, and excuse the past. For example, some politicians and media personalities responded to reports that American soldiers tortured and abused prisoners in the Abu Ghraib prison in Iraq by arguing that the treatment of prisoners would have been worse under former Iraqi president Saddam Hussein, a counterfactual defense that has been found to increase people's tolerance for human rights violations (e.g., Markman et al. 2008). Counterfactuals excuse poor performance, by denying effort or resources, for example, "If I had had more time . . .", and they justify bad outcomes by denying control, for example, "If I had known . . ." (e.g., Markman & Tetlock 2000, McCrea 2008, Tyser et al. 2012). They manage impressions and derogate actions in various situations, from political rhetoric to accident safety reports (e.g., Catellani & Covelli 2013, Morris & Moore 2000).

Counterfactual: an imagined alternative to reality about the past, sometimes expressed as "if only . . ."

Counterfactual explanations also imbue the past with personal meaning—a sense of purpose and coherence—by influencing judgments that certain pivotal events were "meant to be" (e.g., Kray et al. 2010, Waytz et al. 2015). When people think about life events, such as their college or friendship choices, they judge their choices to have added meaning to their lives far more when they imagine how things could have turned out differently, compared to those who do not imagine how things could have turned out differently (e.g., Kray et al. 2010). Counterfactual explanations achieve their impact by identifying or implying relations of many different sorts, including causal, intentional, deontic, spatial, temporal, and inferential relations, but the link between counterfactuals and causes has received special attention (e.g., Spellman & Mandel 1999).

Counterfactuals and causes. On the one hand, counterfactual and causal thoughts are clearly entwined. For example, people judged that a painkiller caused a runner to experience a side effect of fatigue and lose a race when they knew about an alternative drug with no side effects. They imagined that if the runner had taken the other painkiller, she would not have experienced the side effects. But when the alternative drug also led to side effects, they judged that the painkiller had less causal impact on the outcome. They imagined that even if the runner had taken the other painkiller, she still would have experienced the side effects (e.g., McCloy & Byrne 2002). Philosophical analyses since the time of Hume and Mill have suggested that a causal relation, for example, "Heating the water to 100°C caused it to boil," appears to implicitly evoke a contrast between reality and a counterfactual alternative, for example, "If the water had not been heated to 100°C then it would not have boiled" (e.g., Nickerson 2015).

But on the other hand, the content of counterfactual and causal thoughts often differs. Suppose a drunk driver swerved across the road and crashed into Mr. Jones who was driving home by an unusual route. People identify the cause of the accident as the drunk driver swerving across the road, but they create counterfactuals such as, "If only Mr. Jones had driven home by his usual route, the accident wouldn't have happened" (e.g., Mandel & Lehman 1996). Causal explanations tend to refer to strong causes that covary with the outcome, such as the drunk driver, whereas counterfactuals consider how to prevent an outcome by removing enabling causes such as Mr. Jones's route (e.g., Byrne 2005, Frosch & Byrne 2012). Events often have several causes, and one cause can preempt or supersede another (e.g., Hilton & Schmeltzer 2015, Kominsky et al. 2015).

Counterfactual explanations require more cognitive effort than causal ones (e.g., Byrne 2005, 2007). When people reflect on a past event, they spontaneously offer about twice as many causal explanations that describe the facts as they happened, for example, "I didn't meet new people because I didn't go to the party," compared to counterfactual thoughts that refer to an imagined alternative, for example, "If I had gone to the party I would have met new people" (e.g., McEleney & Byrne 2006). But counterfactuals are particularly useful for identifying causes when experiments are not possible, such as in reflections on one's own past or in historical analyses, for example, "If all states in the twentieth century had been democracies, there would have been fewer wars" (e.g., Tetlock & Belkin 1996).

Not all counterfactuals are about causes, and counterfactuals that imply a causal relation differ in systematic ways from counterfactuals that identify other sorts of relations, such as intentions. For example, counterfactuals about a cause-effect sequence unpick the cause. Suppose Paul did not study and got poor marks. When people read about a cause, such as a shortage of library staff, that led to an effect, such as the library closed early, they imagine an alternative to the cause, for example, "If only there had not been a shortage of library staff..." (e.g., Walsh & Byrne 2007; see also Wells et al. 1987). In contrast, counterfactuals about a reason-action sequence unpick the action. When people read about a reason, such as Paul wanted to meet some old friends, that led to an action, such as he went to a party, they imagine an alternative to the action, for example, "If only Paul had not gone to the party . . ." (e.g., Walsh & Byrne 2007; see also Juhos et al. 2015).

Preparations for the Future

Some counterfactuals explain the past, whereas others help people prepare for the future. For example, when people try to solve puzzles, they create counterfactual explanations that excuse their performance, such as, "Things would have been better for me if the allocated time were longer," but they create prefactuals to prepare for future attempts by considering how they could control the outcome, such as, "Things will be better for me next time if I concentrate more" (e.g., Ferrante et al. 2013). Counterfactuals help people to prepare for the future in several ways, such as in the formation of intentions and in supporting future decisions.

Counterfactuals affect the formation of intentions. Aviation pilots in a near-miss accident spontaneously imagine how things could have turned out differently, for example, "If I had understood the controller's words accurately, I wouldn't have initiated the inappropriate landing attempt," and they form specific plans and intentions to prevent a recurrence of the event (e.g., Morris & Moore 2000). People spontaneously create thoughts about how things could have turned out better after they play a blackjack game, for example, "If I'd gotten the 2, I would have beaten the dealer," and those who believe they will have the opportunity to play the game again create more counterfactuals than those who do not (e.g., Markman et al. 1993). People who create an upward counterfactual and imagine how things could have turned out better formulate intentions to carry out activities that will ensure a better outcome in the future, compared to those who create a downward counterfactual and imagine how things could have turned out worse, or who do not imagine how things could have turned out differently (e.g., Markman et al. 2008, Roese 1997). When people think about how their performance on an anagram task could have turned out better, for example, "I could have performed better than I did if I had tried more and different combinations of letters," they persist for longer in trying to solve subsequent anagrams compared to people who think about how their performance could have been worse. Their performance also improves, in part by changing thoughts about useful strategies (e.g., Markman et al. 2008).

Such preparatory counterfactuals help people to learn from mistakes and to prevent similar bad outcomes in the future by providing a roadmap to transition from the current situation to a different future situation (e.g., Epstude & Roese 2008). People who imagine a counterfactual alternative about the recent past are primed to read quickly an intention about the near future based on it (e.g., Smallman & McCulloch 2012). Results from functional magnetic resonance imaging (fMRI) studies show that episodic counterfactual thoughts not only recruit the same core network brain regions as the episodic recollection of specific past experiences, but also similar brain regions as the imagining of future good events or thinking about intentions and goals (e.g., Schacter et al. 2015, Van Hoeck et al. 2013; see also Barbey et al. 2011). When people imagine how things could turn out better, their intentions are affected in many important practical situations, such as stopping smoking (e.g., Page & Colby 2003). Counterfactuals that prepare for the future are useful in the formation of subgoals in artificial intelligence systems (e.g., Ginsberg 1986).

Counterfactuals support decision making. Counterfactuals also help to prepare for the future by influencing decisions. Thoughts about how things could have turned out differently if a different decision had been made often lead to regret for choices for which the person was personally responsible (e.g., Zeelenberg & Pieters 2007). Regret aversion leads to ameliorative action (e.g., Epstude & Roese 2008). For example, when people experience regret following a bad outcome

Prefactual: an imagined alternative to reality about the future

Upward counterfactual: an imagined alternative about how things could have been better

Downward counterfactual: an imagined alternative about how things could have been worse

from their choice of provider for various sorts of services such as train or airplane travel, they switch to another provider (e.g., Zeelenberg & Pieters 2007; see also Ma & Roese 2014). Children as young as 7 years more often switch to a different choice when they experience regret about their choice after they discover that a nonchosen alternative would have led to a better outcome, compared to children who do not experience regret (e.g., O'Connor et al. 2014). The development of the influence of regret on decision making continues into late childhood and adolescence (e.g., Habib et al. 2012). Even some nonhuman primates appear to make choices influenced by counterfactual outcomes (e.g., Santos & Rosati 2015). Too much choice can lead people to be dissatisfied with their actual choice because of its many counterfactual alternatives, and it may be necessary to suppress or discount some of the counterfactuals (e.g., Hafner et al. 2012).

Emotional Experiences

The comparison of reality to a counterfactual alternative amplifies negative emotions such as regret, guilt, and shame, as well as positive emotions such as relief, satisfaction, and sympathy (e.g., Kahneman & Miller 1986). Counterfactuals modulate emotional experiences. For example, tourists who survived the 2004 tsunami in Southeast Asia spontaneously created thoughts about how things could have been worse far more than thoughts about how things could have been better, and they viewed themselves as lucky survivors rather than unlucky victims (e.g., Teigen & Jensen 2011). Counterfactual comparisons affect the experience of relief after near misses (e.g., Sweeny & Vohs 2012; see also Larsen et al. 2004).

People tend to imagine how things could have turned out differently after good events—near misses, lucky wins, and successes, as well as after bad events—tragic accidents, deaths, and failures, but they do so more often after bad events (e.g., Sanna & Turley 1996). Most people tend to imagine how things could have been better rather than worse, depending on various factors such as how long ago the events occurred (e.g., Rim & Summerville 2014). They tend to consider it more likely that bad events in their own past could have had a good outcome rather than that good events could have had a bad outcome (e.g., De Brigard et al. 2013). A counterfactual comparison can even make an objectively better outcome appear worse, for example, Olympic silver medalists were judged to look more unhappy at the moment when they discovered they had come in second compared to bronze medalists when they discovered they had come in third (e.g., Medvec et al. 1995; see also McGraw et al. 2005). Thoughts about how things could have been better may help prepare for the future by forming intentions to improve, but at an affective cost—they can lead people to experience negative emotions (e.g., Epstude & Roese 2008).

Differences in the specific content of counterfactual thoughts can accentuate different emotions. Guilt is amplified when people imagine how an outcome could have turned out differently as a result of a change to their actions, for example, "My friend wouldn't have argued with me if I hadn't given my telephone number to her boyfriend," whereas shame is amplified when they imagine instead a change to their personality, for example, "My friend wouldn't have argued with me if I weren't such a disloyal person" (e.g., Niedenthal et al. 1994). Guilt and self-blame are amplified in prisoners who engage in counterfactual thoughts about their capture, conviction, and sentencing (e.g., Mandel & Dhami 2005). Similarly, counterfactual thoughts amplify regret rather than disappointment when people imagine changes to their actions for choices for which they are responsible (e.g., Zeelenberg & Pieters 2007; see also Nicolle et al. 2011). Most people readily retrieve regrets from their autobiographical memories (e.g., Davison & Feeney 2008, Gilovich & Medvec 1995, Morrison & Roese 2011). Some regrets are for lost opportunities, and others persist when there are potential future opportunities for corrective action (e.g., Beike et al. 2009, Roese & Summerville 2005). Children begin to experience regret between approximately 5 and 7 years of age; they subsequently develop an understanding of it and can predict when others will experience it (e.g., O'Connor et al. 2014, Weisberg & Beck 2010). Later still, they begin to anticipate future regret and develop strategies to avoid it, such as not seeking out information about the outcomes of nonchosen options (e.g., Guttentag & Ferrell 2008).

Counterfactuals can also deflect negative feelings. For example, when opportunities for future action do not exist, people imagine how things could have been worse, as the tourists after the 2004 tsunami did, which can provide consolation (e.g., Epstude & Roese 2008, McMullen & Markman 2000, Teigen & Jensen 2011). People also inhibit counterfactuals about large losses more than small losses, and such self-censorship can provide the solace that the outcome appeared to be inevitable (e.g., Tykocinski & Steinberg 2005). The construction of counterfactuals about how things could have been worse, and the inhibition of counterfactuals, helps people to feel better, but at a cost—people do not benefit from the preparatory effects of counterfactual thoughts, such as learning from mistakes (e.g., Epstude & Roese 2008, McMullen & Markman 2000).

Counterfactual thoughts can become dysfunctional. Left unchecked, counterfactual thoughts can become dysfunctional. Regret is associated with depression, and people who report being severely depressed imagine alternatives to life events that appear unreasonable to others (e.g., Markman & Miller 2006, Roese et al. 2009). Regret and counterfactual thoughts are also associated with anxiety (e.g., Kocovski et al. 2005, Roese et al. 2009). Most people imagine how things might have turned out differently after traumatic life events, such as bereavements, illnesses, accidents, or assaults (e.g., Callander et al. 2007, Davis et al. 1995, Epstude & Jonas 2015). Their well-being is affected by these thoughts, for example, people who experience the death of a child or partner in a car accident and who continue to create counterfactuals in the months and years after the event experience most distress (e.g., Davis et al. 1995). The frequency of counterfactual thoughts and the symptoms of posttraumatic stress disorder are correlated (e.g., El Leithy et al. 2006).

Individuals differ in their tendency to imagine how things could have been different. People who are prone to daydreaming and fantasy show a greater propensity to engage in counterfactual thinking (e.g., Bacon et al. 2013), and so do people with a strong belief in free will (e.g., Alquist et al. 2015). Individuals also differ in their tendency to imagine that things could have been better rather than that they could have been worse (e.g., Rye et al. 2008). These differences occur as a result of enduring personality characteristics, such as self-esteem, as well as transient factors, such as mood (e.g., Sanna et al. 1999).

Moral Judgments

The comparison of reality to a counterfactual alternative can act as a powerful social glue that supports moral judgments such as blame ascriptions. On the one hand, counterfactuals and blame ascriptions are clearly entwined. Counterfactuals have long been used to determine legal culpability in "but for" arguments, such as that an injury would not have happened except for the defendant's conduct. When people listen to a lawyer suggesting a counterfactual about an attack in which changes to the victim's behavior change the outcome, they ascribe higher blame to the victim and lower blame to the attacker. Conversely, when changes to the victim's behavior do not change the outcome, they ascribe higher blame to the attacker and lower blame to the victim (e.g., Branscombe et al. 1996). Judgments of sympathy and compensation for victims, and punishment for perpetrators, are affected by how readily a counterfactual can be imagined (e.g., Macrae et al. 1993; see also Goldinger et al. 2003).

Conversely, people do not imagine an alternative to an action that leads to a bad outcome when the action conforms to a moral norm or obligation. Suppose Steven arrives home too late to save his dying wife because he was delayed by several events, such as visiting his elderly parents, getting stuck in a traffic jam, and so on. People do not tend to imagine an alternative to the morally constrained action and wish, "If only Steven hadn't called in on his parents" (e.g., McCloy & Byrne 2000; see also Walsh & Byrne 2007). Violating a norm is associated with blame (e.g., Malle et al. 2014). Counterfactuals modulate blame by interrogating whether the event was preventable—the actor could have done something differently, and whether there was an obligation to prevent it—the actor should have done something differently (e.g., Malle et al. 2014). For example, when people hear about a doctor who prescribed a drug for a patient who had an allergic reaction to it and died, they blame the doctor and judge he should pay compensation. They do so when he could have done something differently—when there was another drug that he could have prescribed. And they do so when he should have done something differently—when he should have checked the patient's records to see whether she had allergies (e.g., Alicke et al. 2008).

But on the other hand, the content of counterfactuals and blame ascriptions sometimes differs, just as the content of counterfactuals and causal thoughts sometimes differs (e.g., Walsh & Byrne 2007). Consider Joe, who failed to pick up his son from school. Joe's neighbor brought his son home instead, and on the way the boy was injured when a drunk driver crashed into them. People imagine how things could have turned out differently by changing Joe's behavior. But they assign more fault—blame, responsibility, and causality—to the drunk driver than to Joe (e.g., N'gbala & Branscombe 1995). They ascribe blame to the strong cause, the drunk driver, whereas they imagine alternatives to the enabling cause, Joe's failure (e.g., Byrne 2005). Counterfactuals impact moral judgments by identifying or implying relations of many different sorts, not only causal relations but also deontic and intentional relations.

Counterfactuals and judgments about intentions. Counterfactuals influence judgments about other people's intentions (e.g., Knobe 2010, Pellizzoni et al. 2010). Imagine a chairman who starts a new program that will help increase profits but will also harm the environment. The chairman wants to make as much profit as he can and does not care about harming the environment. People judge that the chairman intentionally harmed the environment, even though it was a side effect of his goal. Imagine instead that the new program will help increase profits and will help the environment. The chairman wants to make as much profit as he can and does not care about helping the environment. People judge that the chairman did not intentionally help the environment (e.g., Knobe 2003). The effect also occurs for nonmoral side effects and for violations of nonmoral norms (e.g., Guglielmo & Malle 2010, Uttich & Lombrozo 2010). The difference between the harmful side effect and the helpful side effect is that for the harmful side effect, the chairman makes a choice between two options, pursuing his goals or meeting a moral norm of protecting the environment. In contrast, for the helpful side effect, the chairman does not choose between two options, he just learns that what he wants to do has a good side effect. Counterfactuals amplify judgments of intentionality: When people imagine how the outcome could have turned out differently, they judge that the chairman intended to harm the environment even more than when they do not imagine an alternative (e.g., Ndubuisi & Byrne 2013).

Counterfactuals also influence how people judge the morality of their own intentions. People feel moral not only when they think about virtuous things that they did, but also when a counterfactual alternative is available about immoral things that they did not do (e.g., Effron et al. 2012). People who identified a white suspect of a crime believed that others would view them more positively when the counterfactual alternative was a black suspect rather than a white one. They subsequently judged ambiguous actions as not racist, such as a woman walking alone at night who sees a black man coming toward her and crosses the street. The foregone immoral counterfactual alternative to their earlier action seems to license subsequent dubious behavior (e.g., Effron et al. 2012).

Semifactual: an imagined alternative that results in the same outcome as reality, sometimes expressed as "even if…"

Counterfactuals and moral dilemmas. Counterfactuals affect decisions about whether it is appropriate to violate a moral principle (e.g., Bucciarelli et al. 2008). Suppose Mark is on a runaway train about to kill five men on the track. He can hit a switch to change tracks, which will save the five men, but his action will lead to the death of a man on the other track. Most people judge that it is morally appropriate for Mark to act. But suppose instead Mark is on a railway bridge above a runaway train that is about to kill five men on the track. He can push a nearby stranger off the bridge onto the tracks, which will save the five men, but his action will lead to the death of the stranger. Most people judge that it is not morally appropriate for Mark to act (e.g., Greene et al. 2004). Some moral dilemmas, such as the one about pushing a stranger, evoke emotional reactions more than others, such as the one about hitting a switch, but people can provide reasoned justifications for their decisions in both versions (e.g., Gubbins & Byrne 2014; see also Royzman et al. 2011). They readily create a counterfactual alternative to imagine what they could have done to avoid the worst outcome, in which five people died, for the version that requires hitting a switch. But they take longer to imagine what they could have done to avoid the worst outcome, in which five people died, in the version about pushing the stranger (e.g., Migliore et al. 2014).

The mind has evolved the ability to imagine alternatives to reality, which confers many advantages. The loss of counterfactual thinking following injury to the prefrontal cortex is devastating (see Impairments of Imagination sidebar). Counterfactual thoughts help people to explain the past, prepare for the future, modulate emotional experience, and make moral judgments. The process of computing counterfactuals is primarily an automatic, unconscious one, although people can sometimes intervene to deliberately create or suppress counterfactuals. What the mind computes and why people create counterfactuals constrains how the mind creates counterfactuals, to which we now turn.

HOW THE MIND CREATES COUNTERFACTUALS

An algorithm to specify the mental representations and cognitive processes that create counterfactuals takes as input the relevant facts of the actual event and produces as output a counterfactual alternative. The intervening processes change aspects of the mental representation of the facts to create a second mental representation, the counterfactual alternative.

Dual Possibilities

The computational mechanisms underlying counterfactual reasoning maintain and update two representations, the imagined alternative and the known or presupposed reality. When people read a counterfactual such as, "If there had been roses in the shop, there would have been lilies," they are primed to read quickly the conjunction "There were no roses and there were no lilies" as well as the conjunction "There were roses and there were lilies" (e.g., Santamaria et al. 2005). They consider that someone uttering the counterfactual means to imply "There were no roses" and "There were no lilies" (e.g., Thompson & Byrne 2002). People make inferences from counterfactuals that they otherwise find difficult from ordinary conditionals. For example, they make the modus tollens inference from "There were no lilies" to "Therefore there were no roses" (e.g., Byrne & Tasso 1999). They do so for various linguistic forms such as, "There would have been roses only if there had been lilies" (e.g., Egan et al. 2009). They make different inferences from "if only" counterfactuals compared to "even if" semifactuals, such as, "Even if there had been roses, there still would have been lilies" (e.g., Moreno-Rios et al. 2008). A counterfactual inducement such as, "If you had hit your sister, I would have grounded you" continues to have illocutionary force for the future as an ongoing threat (e.g., Egan & Byrne 2012).

IMPAIRMENTS OF IMAGINATION

The many problems that counterfactuals solve are perhaps most evident when the ability to create them is lost. Injury to the prefrontal cortex can result in an impairment of one or more of the computational processes that are required for counterfactual thinking. The loss of counterfactual thinking has devastating consequences. Some of the well-known deficits associated with prefrontal impairment, such as a failure to learn from mistakes and insensitivity to the consequences of decisions, as well as atypical regret and blame experiences, may result from an impairment in counterfactual thinking (e.g., Gomez Beldarrain et al. 2005, McNamara et al. 2003).

Individuals with injuries to the orbitofrontal or dorsolateral prefrontal cortex show an absence of spontaneous counterfactual expressions. For example, when healthy adults talk about a bad event from their past for a few minutes, they usually spontaneously mention a few ways in which it could have turned out differently, but individuals with injuries to the prefrontal cortex rarely mention alternatives (e.g., Gomez Beldarrain et al. 2005). Similar impairments occur in individuals with prefrontal cortex damage as a result of advanced Parkinson's disease (e.g., McNamara et al. 2003) or schizophrenia (e.g., Hooker et al. 2000, Roese et al. 2008). Such impairments have an impact on preparing for the future. For example, counterfactual impairments affect the formation of intentions. Individuals with schizophrenia who imagine a counterfactual alternative about the past are not primed to read a related intention about the future, unlike healthy individuals (e.g., Roese et al. 2008). Counterfactual impairments also affect decision making. fMRI results show activity in various brain regions including the medial orbitofrontal cortex when healthy adults experience regret on comparing the outcome of a gamble with a counterfactual nonobtained outcome (e.g., Coricelli et al. 2005). In contrast, individuals with lesions to the orbitofrontal cortex do not report experiencing regret and do not appear to anticipate regret to avoid bad outcomes on subsequent gambles (e.g., Camille et al. 2004). Analogous results are observed for individuals with obsessive-compulsive disorder (e.g., Gillan et al. 2014). The Counterfactual Inference Test contains items based on norms for the sorts of counterfactuals that most people tend to create (e.g., Hooker et al. 2000). It shows that people who have acquired injuries to the prefrontal cortex do not tend to create the same sorts of counterfactuals as healthy individuals do (e.g., Hooker et al. 2000, McNamara et al. 2003).

The subjunctive grammatical mood and words such as "would have," or "could have" as well as "if only" are important linguistic cues to counterfactuality. However, the subjunctive mood is not necessary or sufficient to indicate counterfactuality, and it can be communicated in languages such as Chinese that do not typically rely on such linguistic markers (e.g., Yeh & Gentner 2005). Some subjunctive conditionals are not interpreted as counterfactual. Obligations, such as "If the nurse had cleaned up the blood, then she would have had to wear rubber gloves," communicate the presupposition that the nurse did not clean up blood, but not that the nurse did not have to wear rubber gloves, nor that she did not wear them (e.g., Quelhas & Byrne 2003).

Real-world conflicts and "as if" simulation. For counterfactuals to help prepare for the future, they require not only a simulation of a possible alternative as if it were true but also an evaluative comparison of the alternative to the current reality to work out the difference between the two (e.g., Markman & McMullen 2003). Counterfactuals activate areas of the medial prefrontal cortex related to conflict detection (e.g., Van Hoeck et al. 2013; see also Barbey et al. 2011). People must resolve the conflict between the real world and the imagined counterfactual alternative, which can lead to an initial brief disruption in the immediate comprehension of a counterfactual (e.g., Ferguson & Sanford 2008). For example, people read a counterfactual, such as "If cats were vegetarians, they would be cheaper for owners to look after," and then read information consistent with the counterfactual and inconsistent with real-world knowledge, such as "Families could feed their cat a bowl of carrots, and it would gobble it down happily." Eye-tracking measures show that they look at "carrots" for as long when they are primed by the counterfactual as when they are primed by an ordinary conditional about the real world. This result indicates that they envisage both the real world and the counterfactual alternative (e.g., Ferguson & Sanford 2008; see also Ferguson et al. 2008). The initial disruption by reality is rapidly resolved, and later measures indicate an immersion in the counterfactual alternative.

When the counterfactual context supports an immediate "as if" simulation, no disruption by real-world knowledge occurs (e.g., Nieuwland & Martin 2012). People read causal sentences, such as "Because NASA developed its Apollo Project, the first country to land on the moon was...", that contained a false word (Russia) or a true one (America). The false word elicits a larger brain response than the true one in the N400, a peak recorded in event-related potentials around 400 milliseconds after the word, which indicates early semantic processing. The same effect occurs even for a counterfactual, such as "If NASA had not developed its Apollo Project, the first country to land on the moon would have been...", when it ends with a word people consider to be false in the counterfactual context (America) or a word they consider to be true (Russia) (e.g., Nieuwland & Martin 2012).

For some counterfactuals, people dwell experientially on the imagined alternative; for example, they vividly envisage being hit by a truck after a near-miss experience and become transported into the alternative and simulate it as if it were true (e.g., Markman & McMullen 2003, Markman et al. 2008). In fact, counterfactual simulations can be mistaken for remembered events. When people select an action from a pair, such as clapping hands or snapping fingers, and then recall the action they performed or else imagine they had performed the other action, they falsely remember performing the action they had counterfactually imagined more than actions they had not imagined (e.g., Gerlach et al. 2014). Older adults do so more than younger ones (e.g., Gerlach et al. 2014). The simulation of a counterfactual activates sensory motor processes. People listened to counterfactuals that referred to movements toward or away from them, such as "If I had been far away from the basket, I would have passed the ball to another player," and they responded by pressing a key that required them to move their hand toward or away from them. The length of time to respond is affected by whether there is a match or a mismatch between the movement word and the movement response, just as it is for causal assertions (e.g., De Vega & Urritia 2011).

When people imagine how episodes from their past could have been better or worse, fMRI results show that the likely counterfactuals activate the same core brain network as episodic recollections, whereas unlikely counterfactuals require more imaginative work (e.g., De Brigard et al. 2013). Similarly, people visually read or aurally heard some real-world information such as, "The motor is switched off today," and they considered counterfactuals such as "If the motor had been switched on today, would it have burned fuel?" or ordinary conditionals such as "If the motor was switched on yesterday, did it burn fuel?" The fMRI results show greater activation for the counterfactuals in areas associated with increased mental imagery (e.g., Kulakova et al. 2013; see also Barbey et al. 2011). People may simulate an imagined alternative to reality by constructing mental models (e.g., Byrne & Johnson-Laird 2009, Johnson-Laird & Byrne 2002). They construct parsimonious mental representations because of the limitations of human working memory, and they tend to envisage possibilities that are true or are assumed temporarily to be true. They keep track of the epistemic status of their models as real or imagined (e.g., Byrne 2005, Johnson-Laird & Byrne 2002).

The Development of Counterfactual Thought

Children's appreciation of counterfactual alternatives to reality begins to make its first appearance as early as 2 years of age, when they begin to engage in pretend play, temporarily suspending their commitment to reality and adopting the perspective of a pretend situation (e.g., Harris et al. 1996). But counterfactual reasoning requires a further cognitive feat, to compare the known or supposed facts to the imagined alternative. Children aged 2 years can identify which toy horse "almost" fell off a table when one galloped right to the edge and the other stopped before reaching the edge. But when one horse galloped right off the table and fell, and the other stopped before reaching the edge, even 3- and 4-year-olds do not identify correctly which one almost fell (e.g., Beck & Guthrie 2011, Harris et al. 1996). Children aged 3 and 4 years have difficulties envisaging multiple possibilities. When they observe a mouse sliding down a slide that splits into two alternative tracks, they are correct in their answers to counterfactual questions such as "What if it had gone the other way—where would it be?" but experience more difficulty on open counterfactual questions such as "Could it have gone anywhere else?" (e.g., Beck et al. 2006). The accomplishment of counterfactual thinking continues to be refined throughout the childhood years. Children as young as 3 and 4 years make the correct counterfactual inference when they are told that a doll made a floor dirty with her shoes and are asked whether the floor would be dirty if she had taken her shoes off (e.g., Harris et al. 1996). But children aged 6 years and older make errors when they cannot rely on general assumptions and have to envisage alternative possibilities to take into account the specifics of what actually happened (e.g., Rafetseder et al. 2013).

The development of counterfactual and false belief reasoning. The development of counterfactuals is important for the development of a theory of mind and the understanding that other people can have false beliefs (e.g., Riggs et al. 1998). From their first months through to adolescence, children exhibit an emerging and increasingly nuanced appreciation that other people's mental states—their beliefs, desires, and knowledge—may differ from their own. Consider a story about Sally and Anne, who are in the kitchen. Sally places some chocolate in the cupboard and she leaves. Anne takes the chocolate and moves it to the fridge. Sally returns. When 3-year-olds are asked where Sally will look for the chocolate, they tend to say she will look in the fridge; 4- and 5-year-olds tend to say she will look in the cupboard (e.g., Wimmer & Perner 1983). Counterfactuals such as "If Anne had not moved the chocolate, where would it be?" are a key ingredient in reasoning about false beliefs such as "Where does Sally think the chocolate is?" (e.g., Riggs et al. 1998). Children make correct counterfactual inferences earlier than correct false-belief inferences (e.g., Perner et al. 2004). Understanding false beliefs is correlated with counterfactual thinking even when age, verbal intelligence, and other linguistic factors are controlled (e.g., Guajardo et al. 2009). The two sorts of inferences activate similar brain areas (e.g., Van Hoeck et al. 2014). Children with autism spectrum disorders have difficulties with both sorts of inferences (e.g., Grant et al. 2004). Even children with high-functioning autism spectrum disorders create counterfactuals that differ from those of typically developing children (e.g., Begeer et al. 2009). Counterfactual and false-belief reasoning both require executive function skills, including working memory skills (e.g., to simulate two mental representations simultaneously), inhibitory control skills (e.g., to suppress attention to the mental representation of reality), and representational flexibility skills (e.g., to consider different perspectives on the same situation) (e.g., Beck et al. 2011, Drayton et al. 2011).

The mechanisms underlying counterfactual reasoning sustain alternative mental representations—the known or presupposed facts and the imagined counterfactual possibility. The sorts of changes people make to the representation of the facts to create the imagined alternative depend on the content and the contextual information that they have included in the mental representation of the facts, to which we now turn.

TRUTH AND LOGIC

Counterfactuals can be true or false, but how to establish their truth is a nontrivial matter (e.g., Nickerson 2015). A counterfactual such as "If kangaroos had no tails they would topple over" conveys that its "if" part is false—kangaroos do have tails, and that it's "then" part is false—kangaroos do not topple over (e.g., Lewis 1973). All counterfactuals have a false "if" part and a false "then" part, and thus the truth of a counterfactual cannot be a function of the truth of its components. A major advance in logical analyses of counterfactuals was the proposal that the meaning of a counterfactual depends on its truth in a possible world, one that is the same as this world except that the counterfactual is true in it (e.g., Stalnaker 1968). Counterfactuals require a consideration of the possible world that is most similar to the actual world (e.g., Lewis 1973).

But people do not have the cognitive capacity to consider all of the potentially infinite sets of possible worlds, and they cannot compare all of the counterfactual alternatives that can be constructed for any set of facts (e.g., Byrne 2005, Johnson-Laird & Byrne 2002). Moreover, ideas of a possible world that is as close as possible to actuality are slippery (e.g., Kratzer 2012, Williamson 2007). The attraction of counterfactuals such as "If Oswald had missed his target, Kennedy would not have been shot" is that they appeal to an imagined world that appears "only a muscle twitch away" from the actual one, where history has been minimally rewritten (e.g., Tetlock & Belkin 1996). But establishing what counts as a minimal change may be intractable—even a tiny change to one aspect of reality can have major consequences, and objectively small changes may be of significant psychological magnitude (e.g., Kahneman & Miller 1986). In fact, people judge counterfactual alternatives that they imagined to episodes from their past to be less plausible when they simulate them repeatedly. Even though the counterfactuals become more detailed and more easily constructed, the repeated simulations highlight further discrepancies between reality and the counterfactual (e.g., De Brigard et al. 2013).

HOW KNOWLEDGE MODULATES THE PLAUSIBILITY OF COUNTERFACTUALS

The mind constructs counterfactuals that are plausible—reasonable, believable, and acceptable. Their plausibility may be challenged, for example, by the discovery of further information or by others with different opinions, and the counterfactual may be augmented or abandoned (see Truth and Logic sidebar). An algorithm to simulate the processes that create counterfactuals will have the goal to produce plausible ones. Semantic and pragmatic knowledge modulates the representation of the facts upon which a counterfactual is based.

Counterfactual "Fault Lines"

Some aspects of reality seem to be more mutable than others. People tend to change their mental representation of the facts of an event, such as a car accident, by creating an additive counterfactual that adds something extra to the event, such as "If only he had worn a seatbelt," rather than by creating a subtractive counterfactual that deletes something about the event, such as "If only he had not gone out" (e.g., Epstude & Roese 2008, Kahneman & Tversky 1982a). A striking discovery is that most people tend to imagine the very same sorts of counterfactuals. People zoom in on similar fault lines in their representation of reality (e.g., Kahneman & Tversky 1982a), as the following examples illustrate.

1. Exceptions: People create a counterfactual by changing an exceptional event to be normal. Suppose Mr. Jones left the office at his usual time but drove home by an unusual route and was killed by a truck that crashed into his car at an intersection. Most people imagine things could have turned out differently if he had gone home by his usual route. Suppose

Additive counterfactual: an imagined alternative in which something extra is added to the representation of reality

Subtractive counterfactual: an imagined alternative in which something is deleted from the representation of reality

Fault lines: aspects of the representation of reality that people zoom in on when they imagine an alternative to it

instead that the accident happened when Mr. Jones left the office earlier than usual but was driving home by his usual route. Most people imagine that things could have turned out differently if he had left at his usual time (e.g., Kahneman & Tversky 1982a). One practical consequence of this exceptionality effect is that people feel more sympathy toward a victim who was mugged and judge that the perpetrator should be punished more harshly when the victim was on the way home by an unusual route rather than by the usual route (e.g., Macrae et al. 1993).

2. Controllable events: People create a counterfactual in which they change an event within their own control. Suppose Steven arrives home too late to save his dying wife because he was delayed by several events, some within his control such as stopping for a beer at a bar, and some outside his control such as a traffic jam. People imagine things could have been different if Steven had not stopped at the bar—they mentally undo the controllable event more than the uncontrollable one (e.g., Girotto et al. 1991). A practical consequence of this controllability effect is that people who experience the death of a spouse or child in a traffic accident, in which it is established that their loved one was not to blame, tend to focus on their own behavior, for example, "If only I had not let him go to the store that night," rather than on the other driver's behavior (e.g., Davis et al. 1995).

3. Actions: People create a counterfactual in which they change an action. Consider Lisa, who has shares in company A, thinks about switching to Company B, and decides to do so. She loses $1,000. Consider also Jenny, who has shares in Company B, thinks about switching to Company A, but decides to stay where she is. She also loses $1,000. People judge that Lisa, who acted, feels worse (e.g., Kahneman & Tversky 1982b). A practical consequence of this action effect is that when people consider the risks from a vaccination and the risks from an illness, they sometimes decide not to vaccinate against the illness, even when the risks of a bad outcome from the vaccine are smaller than the risks from the illness. They prefer to do nothing, even when inertia also leads to change (e.g., Ritov & Baron 1990).

4. Recent events: People create a counterfactual in which they change the most recent event in a temporal sequence of independent events. Imagine a game in which two people toss a coin, and if they toss the same face coin they will both win $1,000. Alicia goes first and tosses heads, Laura goes second and tosses tails, and so they both lose. People imagine that the second player, Laura, will feel more guilt and be blamed more (e.g., Miller & Gunasegaram 1990). The temporal order effect occurs for sequences of more than two events (e.g., Segura et al. 2002). It has practical implications; for example, counterfactuals about sports events, or about historical events, tend to focus on the "last chance" juncture (e.g., Tetlock & Belkin 1996).

There are several alternative explanations for the extraordinary consensus in the creation of counterfactuals.

Alternative Explanations

The plausibility of a counterfactual depends on the influence of content and context in the mental representation of the facts, from which the counterfactual is constructed.

Probability and causal models. One view is that people zoom in on fault lines in their representation of reality, such as exceptions or controllable events, because these fault lines correspond to events that are most likely to change the outcome (e.g., Petrocelli et al. 2011). For example, people were told about a game in which a contestant must choose to open one of three doors, and behind one there is a person. If the contestant chooses the door that the person is behind, they must answer correctly a trivia question asked by the person. Sam chose door 3 and did not

Exceptionality effect: the tendency to imagine an alternative by changing exceptional events to be normal

Controllability effect: the tendency to imagine an alternative by changing a controllable event rather than an uncontrollable one

Action effect: the tendency to imagine an alternative by changing an action rather than an inaction

Temporal order effect: the tendency to imagine an alternative by changing the most recent event rather than earlier events

win—the person was behind door 2. People considered the counterfactual "If Sam had chosen door 2, then he would have won." The "if" part, "if Sam had chosen door 2," either had a high likelihood—Sam had wavered between door 2 and door 3, or a low likelihood—Sam's favorite number was 3. The "then" part, "then he would have won," either had a high likelihood—the trivia question was on a topic Sam knew about, or a low likelihood—the question was on a topic Sam knew nothing about. People attributed more responsibility and negative affect to Sam when the "if" part had a high likelihood and the "then" part had a high likelihood given the "if" part; that is, when Sam nearly chose door 2 and when he knew a lot about the trivia topic (e.g., Petrocelli et al. 2011). Judgments of the probability of a counterfactual can appear to be linked to judgments of its conditional probability (e.g., Over et al. 2007).

A related idea is that the causal facts determine a counterfactual's probability, and Bayes nets capture patterns of conditional probability information about how events within a causal system depend on their immediate causes (e.g., Sloman & Lagnado 2005). Counterfactuals are instructions to make a mini-surgery modification to a causal model (e.g., Pearl 2013). Consider a simple causal device that consists of four components, A, B, C, and D, in which A or B cause C—either alone is sufficient to cause C—and C causes D. On this view a counterfactual such as "If C hadn't operated, component A would still have operated' is plausible because an intervention on C, so that it is not operating, prunes the causal model to remove links into C, but the values of the other variables remain as they are. Yet when people were told about such a causal device, they judged that if C had not operated, A would not have operated, presumably because they reasoned that in the case in which C is not operating, neither A nor B could be operating (e.g., Rips 2010). They did not create minimal changes by assuming an intervention changed only the most recent event in the causal system before the counterfactual antecedent, leaving events leading to the counterfactual's antecedent to happen as they did (e.g., Rips 2010). Similarly, in causal sequences of life events, people do not intervene on the most recent event. Consider Mary, who is delayed on her way to a sale by a series of causally related events, for example, she had to wait while people crossed a pedestrian crossing, which then caused her to be held up in a subsequent traffic jam. People do not imagine how things could have been different by undoing the most recent event in such a causal sequence. Instead they imagine the very first cause in the causal sequence had not occurred (e.g., Wells et al. 1987; see also Segura et al. 2002).

The counterfactuals people create do not appear to be guided by likelihood. Consider the story about Mr. Jones, who left the office at his usual time but drove home by an unusual route and was killed by a truck that crashed into his car at an intersection. The most improbable event is two cars being in exactly the same place at the same time, and yet no one imagines an alternative to this unlikely event (e.g., Kahneman & Tversky 1982a). People also do not seem to interpret ordinary conditionals in terms of their probability (e.g., Goodwin 2014, Johnson-Laird et al. 2015). And the spontaneous counterfactuals of the tourists who survived the 2004 tsunami in Southeast Asia did not change the most improbable event, that they would happen to take their Christmas vacation in the one holiday resort in the world that suffered a major natural disaster at that time (e.g., Teigen & Jensen 2011).

Alternative possibilities. Another view is that people zoom in on the fault lines because they provide readily available alternative possibilities (e.g., Kahneman & Tversky 1982a). The availability of alternatives is determined by factors such as norms; for example, an exception recruits from memory its corresponding norm. Hence, people change exceptions to be normal, rather than changing normal events to be exceptional (e.g., Kahneman & Miller 1986).

A counterfactual is plausible when semantic and pragmatic knowledge ensures that the representation of the facts, upon which the counterfactual is based, includes alternative possibilities.

Consider Lisa, who switched shares from company A to Company B. The mental representation includes not only the current facts—Lisa has shares in Company B, but also the previous, now counterfactual, possibility—Lisa had shares in Company A. The mental representation provides a ready-made counterfactual alternative, if only Lisa had stayed with Company A. Now consider Jenny, who stayed with shares in Company B. The mental representation includes the current facts—Jenny has shares in Company B, but the past situation was the same as the current one, and so the mental representation does not include a second possibility. The mental representation does not provide a ready-made counterfactual alternative (e.g., Byrne & McEleney 2000). As a result, people judge that Lisa, who acted, feels worse (e.g., Kahneman & Tversky 1982b).

A test of this account is that each of the observed fault lines is eliminated when the mental representation of reality explicitly includes different alternative possibilities, as the following examples illustrate.

1. Exceptional and normal events: People do not change exceptions to be normal when they read a story about a gambler who usually chose a medium bet from the possible set of small, medium, or large bets, but this time chose a small bet. They imagine "If only he had chosen the large bet..." when the representation of the facts includes the information that the large bet led to a better outcome. They change the exceptional event to be exceptional in a different way, rather than to be normal (e.g., Dixon & Byrne 2011).

2. Controllable and uncontrollable events: People do not change controllable events when they experience the event rather than read about it. When people choose between envelopes that contain an easy or difficult sum, and fail to solve the sum within the given time, they imagine "If only I had been able to use pen and paper..." or "If only I had had more time...." They mentally undo uncontrollable constraints of the situation rather than the envelope choice within their control, unlike people who read about the situation (e.g., Girotto et al. 2007). Observers behave like actors, not like readers—they too imagine alternatives outside the player's control (e.g., Pighin et al. 2011).

3. Actions and inactions: People do not change actions when they take a long-term perspective on events. When people read about college choices that turned out badly, they judged that the individual who acted would feel worse in the short term, but the individual who did not act would feel worse in the long term (e.g., Gilovich & Medvec 1995). They imagine alternatives to an inaction from a long-term perspective when it has unknown consequences; for example, the outcome from the foregone opportunity to switch colleges is unknown. But they imagine alternatives to an action even from a long-term perspective when the inaction has known consequences; for example, for investments, the outcome of a foregone opportunity is known (e.g., Byrne & McEleney 2000). They also regret inactions rather than actions when they imagine how episodes from their own past could have turned out differently; for example, they regret missed educational opportunities, not spending enough time with their family and friends, and not pursuing hobbies (e.g., Gilovich & Medvec 1995, Morrison & Roese 2011).

4. Recent events: People do not change the most recent event when the context provides an alternative to the first event. For example, people read that the first player in the coin toss game tossed heads, but there was a technical hitch and the game was restarted; this time the first player tossed tails and the second player tossed heads. People imagined a counterfactual in which the first player had tossed heads (e.g., Byrne et al. 2000). Likewise, people read a description of the coin toss game, which included an illustration such as that both players must toss the same face coin; for example, both players must toss heads. When they read that the first player tossed tails, the opposite of the illustration, and the second player tossed

heads, they changed the first event rather than the most recent event (e.g., Walsh & Byrne 2004).

Each of the observed fault lines can be eliminated when the representation of reality explicitly includes different alternative possibilities. The discovery provides some support for the idea that a counterfactual is plausible when semantic and pragmatic knowledge ensures that the representation of the facts, upon which the counterfactual is based, includes alternative possibilities.

Between the ages of 6 and 8 years, around the time when children are gaining some mastery at envisaging alternative possibilities, they begin to create counterfactuals that zoom in on the fault lines (e.g., Meehan & Byrne 2005). The tendency to do so is robust across cultures, even though the content of counterfactual thoughts reflects cultural priorities (e.g., Chen et al. 2006). Our everyday counterfactual thoughts tend to be firmly rooted in reality: We rarely imagine fantastical counterfactuals, such as that our neighbor would not have been killed when his car crashed if only people were immortal. The remarkable regularities in the counterfactuals that most people create reflect the role of semantic and pragmatic knowledge in modulating the representation of the facts upon which a counterfactual is based.

CONCLUSIONS

Beckett's assertion in *Malone Dies*—"I could die today, if I wished, merely by making a little effort, if I could wish, if I could make an effort"—pits the power of the imagination against pale reality. The mind has the competence to compute counterfactuals that serve many purposes, to explain the past and prepare for the future, and to modulate emotional experiences and moral judgments. The architecture of cognition imposes limitations on the nature of the counterfactuals that people create. Counterfactuals are limited by working memory restrictions on the nature and complexity of the alternative possibilities that can be envisaged. Their plausibility is susceptible to the vagaries of content and context. The extent to which specific counterfactuals serve well the many purposes for which they are designed depends on the quality of the knowledge that people access and include in their mental representation of reality. Episodic counterfactuals about how events could have been different in our own past are as vulnerable to distortion as the autobiographical memories on which they are based. Second-order counterfactuals, about how another person will imagine how events could have been different, exhibit many frailties of perspective taking. Notwithstanding these limitations on performance, counterfactuals free our minds from facts to allow a consideration of myriad other possibilities.

SUMMARY POINTS

1. The mind computes counterfactual alternatives to reality for many reasons. Counterfactuals explain the past by implying causal and other sorts of relations. They prepare for the future by affecting the formation of intentions and by influencing decision making.

2. Counterfactuals modulate emotional experiences, including negative emotions such as regret and guilt as well as positive emotions such as relief and sympathy. They can become dysfunctional, for example, in depression and anxiety and after traumatic events.

3. Counterfactuals support moral judgments about blame and responsibility. They affect judgments about other people's intentions, and they influence the resolution of moral dilemmas.

4. The mind computes counterfactuals by changing aspects of the mental representation of the facts to create a second mental representation corresponding to an imagined alternative. The mechanisms underlying counterfactual reasoning maintain and update two mental representations, of reality and its imagined alternative.

5. The ability to create counterfactuals develops throughout childhood. It relies on the development of working memory skills for simulating multiple possibilities as well as inhibitory control skills for suppressing attention to the mental representation of reality. Counterfactual thoughts support the development of reasoning about other people's beliefs, including their false beliefs.

6. People create counterfactuals that are plausible. They exhibit remarkable regularities in the alternatives to reality that they create. Most people zoom in on the same pivotal junctures or fault lines in their representation of reality to create a counterfactual alternative to it.

7. Semantic and pragmatic knowledge modulates the possibilities that people consider, based on their mental representation of reality, from which they create a plausible counterfactual alternative.

FUTURE ISSUES

1. Most research has examined "if only" thoughts, how people imagine the ways in which alternative antecedents could have led to a counterfactual outcome. Comparatively little research has examined "what if" thoughts, how people imagine alternative consequences that could have followed from a counterfactual starting point. Are "what if" thoughts like "if only" thoughts?

2. Most research has focused on counterfactual thoughts about the past—about what would have, could have, or should have happened. Do prefactual thoughts about the future—about what might, can, or should happen—share the same characteristics?

3. The computation of counterfactuals has been examined in various systems in artificial intelligence. But there are as yet few computational simulations of theories of the mental representations and cognitive processes that people rely on when they create counterfactuals.

DISCLOSURE STATEMENT

The author is not aware of any affiliations, memberships, funding, or financial holdings that might be perceived as affecting the objectivity of this review.

ACKNOWLEDGMENTS

I would like to thank Sarah Beck, Alicia Byrne Keane, Kai Epstude, Heather Ferguson, Vittorio Girotto, Geoff Goodwin, Jordan Grafman, Phil Johnson-Laird, Mark Keane, Josh Knobe, Bertram Malle, Teresa McCormack, Neal Roese, and Clare Walsh for generously providing very helpful comments on an earlier draft of this article.

LITERATURE CITED

Alicke MD, Buckingham J, Zell E, Davis T. 2008. Culpable control and counterfactual reasoning in the psychology of blame. *Personal. Soc. Psychol. Bull.* 34:1371–81

Alquist JL, Ainsworth SE, Baumeister RF, Daly M, Stillman TF. 2015. The making of might-have-beens: effects of free will belief on counterfactual thinking. *Personal. Soc. Psychol. Bull.* 41(2):268–83

Bacon AM, Walsh CR, Martin L. 2013. Fantasy proneness and counterfactual thinking. *Personal. Individ. Differ.* 54(4):469–73

Barbey AK, Krueger F, Grafman J. 2011. Architecture of counterfactual thought in the prefrontal cortex. In *Predictions in the Brain: Using Our Past to Generate a Future*, ed. M Bar, pp. 40–57. New York: Oxford Univ. Press

Beck SR, Carroll DJ, Brunsdon VEA, Gryg CK. 2011. Supporting children's counterfactual thinking with alternative modes of responding. *J. Exp. Child Psychol.* 108:190–202

Beck SR, Guthrie C. 2011. Almost thinking counterfactually: children's understanding of close counterfactuals. *Child Dev.* 82(4):1189–98

Beck SR, Robinson EJ, Carroll DJ, Apperly IA. 2006. Children's thinking about counterfactuals and future hypotheticals as possibilities. *Child Dev.* 77.2:413–26

Begeer S, Terwogt MM, Lunenburg P, Stegge H. 2009. Additive and subtractive counterfactual reasoning of children with high-functioning autism spectrum disorders. *J. Autism Dev. Disord.* 39.11:1593–97

Beike DR, Markman KD, Karadogan F. 2009. What we regret most are lost opportunities: a theory of regret intensity. *Personal. Soc. Psychol. Bull.* 35.3:385–97

Branscombe NR, Owen S, Garstka TA, Coleman J. 1996. Rape and accident counterfactuals: Who might have done otherwise and would it have changed the outcome? *J. Appl. Soc. Psychol.* 26.12:1042–67

Bucciarelli M, Khemlani S, Johnson-Laird PN. 2008. The psychology of moral reasoning. *Judgm. Decis. Mak.* 3(2):121–39

Byrne RMJ. 2005. *The Rational Imagination: How People Create Alternatives to Reality*. Cambridge, MA: MIT Press

Byrne RMJ. 2007. Précis of *The Rational Imagination: How People Create Alternatives to Reality*. *Behav. Brain Sci.* 30:439–53

Byrne RMJ, Johnson-Laird PN. 2009. "If" and the problems of conditional reasoning. *Trends Cogn. Sci.* 13:282–87

Byrne RMJ, McEleney A. 2000. Counterfactual thinking about actions and failures to act. *J. Exp. Psychol.: Learn. Mem. Cogn.* 26:1318–31

Byrne RMJ, Segura S, Culhane R, Tasso A, Berrocal P. 2000. The temporality effect in counterfactual thinking about what might have been. *Mem. Cogn.* 28:264–81

Byrne RMJ, Tasso A. 1999. Deductive reasoning with factual, possible, and counterfactual conditionals. *Mem. Cogn.* 27.4:726–40

Callander G, Brown GP, Tata P, Regan L. 2007. Counterfactual thinking and psychological distress following recurrent miscarriage. *J. Reprod. Infant Psychol.* 25(1):51–65

Camille N, Coricelli G, Sallet J, Pradat-Diehl P, Duhamel JR, Sirigu A. 2004. The involvement of the orbitofrontal cortex in the experience of regret. *Science* 304(5674):1167–70

Catellani P, Covelli V. 2013. The strategic use of counterfactual communication in politics. *J. Lang. Soc. Psychol.* 32(4):480–89

Chen J, Chiu CY, Roese NJ, Tam KP, Lau IYM. 2006. Culture and counterfactuals: on the importance of life domains. *J. Cross-Cult. Psychol.* 37(1):75–84

Coricelli G, Critchley HD, Joffily M, O'Doherty JP, Sirigu A, Dolan RJ. 2005. Regret and its avoidance: a neuroimaging study of choice behavior. *Nat. Neurosci.* 8.9:1255–62

Davis CG, Lehman DR, Wortman CB, Silver RC, Thompson SC. 1995. The undoing of traumatic life events. *Personal. Soc. Psychol. Bull.* 21:109–24

Davison IM, Feeney A. 2008. Regret as autobiographical memory. *Cogn. Psychol.* 57.4: 385–403

De Brigard F, Addis DR, Ford JH, Schacter DL, Giovanello KS. 2013. Remembering what could have happened: neural correlates of episodic counterfactual thinking. *Neuropsychologia* 51(12):2401–14

De Brigard F, Szpunar KK, Schacter DL. 2013. Coming to grips with the past effect of repeated simulation on the perceived plausibility of episodic counterfactual thoughts. *Psychol. Sci.* 24(7):1329–34

De Vega M, Urrutia M. 2011. Counterfactual sentences activate embodied meaning: an action sentence compatibility effect study. *J. Cogn. Psychol.* 23:962–73

Dixon J, Byrne RMJ. 2011. "If only" counterfactual thoughts about exceptional actions. *Mem. Cogn.* 39.7:1317–31

Drayton S, Turley-Ames KJ, Guajardo NR. 2011. Counterfactual thinking and false belief: the role of executive function. *J. Exp. Child Psychol.* 108.3:532–48

Effron DA, Miller DT, Monin B. 2012. Inventing racist roads not taken: the licensing effect of immoral counterfactual behaviors. *J. Personal. Soc. Psychol.* 103(6):916–32

Egan S, Byrne RMJ. 2012. Inferences from counterfactual threats and promises. *Exp. Psychol.* 59(4):227–35

Egan S, Garcia-Madruga J, Byrne RMJ. 2009. Indicative and counterfactual "only if" conditionals. *Acta Psychol.* 132(3):240–49

El Leithy S, Brown GP, Robbins I. 2006. Counterfactual thinking and posttraumatic stress reactions. *J. Abnorm. Psychol.* 115(3):629–35

Epstude K, Jonas KJ. 2015. Regret and counterfactual thinking in the face of inevitability: the case of HIV positive men. *Soc. Psychol. Personal. Sci.* 6:157–63

Epstude K, Roese NJ. 2008. The functional theory of counterfactual thinking. *Personal. Soc. Psychol. Rev.* 12(2):168–92

Ferguson HJ, Sanford AJ. 2008. Anomalies in real and counterfactual worlds: an eye- movement investigation. *J. Mem. Lang.* 58:609–26

Ferguson HJ, Sanford AJ, Leuthold H. 2008. Eye-movements and ERPs reveal the time course of processing negation and remitting counterfactual worlds. *Brain Res.* 1236:113–25

Ferrante D, Girotto V, Stragà M, Walsh C. 2013. Improving the past and the future: a temporal asymmetry in hypothetical thinking. *J. Exp. Psychol.: Gen.* 142(1):23–27

Frosch CA, Byrne RMJ. 2012. Causal conditionals and counterfactuals. *Acta Psychol.* 14:54–66

Gerlach KD, Dornblaser DW, Schacter DL. 2014. Adaptive constructive processes and memory accuracy: consequences of counterfactual simulations in young and older adults. *Memory* 22(1):145–62

Gillan CM, Morein-Zamir S, Kaser M, Fineberg NA, Sule A, et al. 2014. Counterfactual processing of economic action-outcome alternatives in obsessive-compulsive disorder. *Biol. Psychiatry* 75(8):639–46

Gilovich T, Medvec VH. 1995. The experience of regret: what, when, and why. *Psychol. Rev.* 102:379–95

Ginsberg ML. 1986. Counterfactuals. *Artif. Intell.* 30.1:35–79

Girotto V, Ferrante D, Pighin S, Gonzalez M. 2007. Postdecisional counterfactual thinking by actors and readers. *Psychol. Sci.* 18:510–15

Girotto V, Legrenzi P, Rizzo A. 1991. Event controllability in counterfactual thinking. *Acta Psychol.* 78:111–33

Goldinger SD, Kleider HM, Azuma T, Beike DR. 2003. "Blaming the victim" under memory load. *Psychol. Sci.* 14(1):81–85

Gomez Beldarrain M, Garcia-Monco JC, Astigarraga E, Gonzalez A, Grafman J. 2005. Only spontaneous counterfactual thinking is impaired in patients with prefrontal cortex lesions. *Cogn. Brain Res.* 24.3:723–26

Goodwin GP. 2014. Is the basic conditional probabilistic? *J. Exp. Psychol.: Gen.* 143:1214–41

Grant CM, Riggs KJ, Boucher J. 2004. Counterfactual and mental state reasoning in children with autism. *J. Autism Dev. Disord.* 34(2):177–88

Greene JD, Nystrom LE, Engell AD, Darley JM, Cohen JD. 2004. The neural bases of cognitive conflict and control in moral judgment. *Neuron* 44:389–400

Guajardo NR, Parker J, Turley-Ames K. 2009. Associations among false belief understanding, counterfactual reasoning, and executive function. *Br. J. Dev. Psychol.* 27(3):681–702

Gubbins E, Byrne RM. 2014. Dual processes of emotion and reason in judgments about moral dilemmas. *Think. Reason.* 20(2):245–68

Guglielmo S, Malle BF. 2010. Can unintended side effects be intentional? Resolving a controversy over intentionality and morality. *Personal. Soc. Psychol. Bull.* 36(12):1635–47

Guttentag R, Ferrell J. 2008. Children's understanding of anticipatory regret and disappointment. *Cogn. Emot.* 22.5:815–32

Habib M, Cassotti M, Borst G, Simon G, Pineau A, et al. 2012. Counterfactually mediated emotions: a developmental study of regret and relief in a probabilistic gambling task. *J. Exp. Child Psychol.* 112(2):265–74

Hafner RJ, White MP, Handley SJ. 2012. Spoilt for choice: the role of counterfactual thinking in the excess choice and reversibility paradoxes. *J. Exp. Soc. Psychol.* 48(1):28–36

Harris PL, German TP, Mills P. 1996. Children's use of counterfactual thinking in causal reasoning. *Cognition* 61:233–59

Hilton D, Schmeltzer C. 2015. A matter of detail: matching counterfactuals to actual cause in pre-emption scenarios. Manuscript under review

Hooker C, Roese NJ, Park S. 2000. Impoverished counterfactual thinking is associated with schizophrenia. *Psychiatry* 63(4):326–35

Johnson-Laird PN, Byrne RMJ. 2002. Conditionals: a theory of meaning, pragmatics, and inference. *Psychol. Rev.* 109:646–78

Johnson-Laird PN, Khemlani SS, Goodwin GP. 2015. Logic, probability, and human reasoning. *Trends Cogn. Sci.* 19(4):201–14

Juhos C, Quelhas AC, Byrne RMJ. 2015. Reasoning about intentions: counterexamples to reasons for actions. *J. Exp. Psychol.: Learn. Mem. Cogn.* 41(1):55–76

Kahneman D, Miller DT. 1986. Norm theory: comparing reality to its alternatives. *Psychol. Rev.* 93.2:136–53

Kahneman D, Tversky A. 1982a. The simulation heuristic. In *Judgment Under Uncertainty: Heuristics and Biases*, ed. D Kahneman, P Slovic, A Tversky, pp. 201–8. New York: Cambridge Univ. Press

Kahneman D, Tversky A. 1982b. The psychology of preferences. *Sci. Am.* 246.1:160–73

Knobe J. 2003. Intentional action and side-effects in ordinary language. *Analysis* 63:190–93

Knobe J. 2010. Person as scientist, person as moralist. *Behav. Brain Sci.* 33:353–65

Kocovski NL, Endler NS, Rector NA, Flett GL. 2005. Ruminative coping and post-event processing in social anxiety. *Behav. Res. Ther.* 43(8):971–84

Kominsky JF, Phillips J, Gerstenberg T, Lagnado D, Knobe J. 2015. Causal superseding. *Cognition* 137:196–209

Kratzer A. 2012. *Modals and Conditionals: New and Revised Perspectives*. New York: Oxford Univ. Press

Kray LJ, George LG, Liljenquist KA, Galinsky AD, Tetlock PE, Roese NJ. 2010. From what might have been to what must have been: Counterfactual thinking creates meaning. *J. Personal. Soc. Psychol.* 98.1:106–18

Kulakova E, Aichhorn M, Schurz M, Kronbichler M, Perner J. 2013. Processing counterfactual and hypothetical conditionals: an fMRI investigation. *NeuroImage* 72:265–71

Larsen JT, McGraw AP, Mellers BA, Cacioppo JT. 2004. The agony of victory and thrill of defeat: mixed emotional reactions to disappointing wins and relieving losses. *Psychol. Sci.* 15(5):325–30

Lewis D. 1973. *Counterfactuals*. Oxford, UK: Blackwell

Ma J, Roese NJ. 2014. The maximizing mindset. *J. Consum. Res.* 41:71–92

Macrae CN, Milne AB, Griffiths RJ. 1993. Counterfactual thinking and the perception of criminal behaviour. *Br. J. Psychol.* 84.2:221–26

Malle BF, Monroe AE, Guglielmo S. 2014. A theory of blame. *Psychol. Inq.* 25(2):147–86

Mandel DR, Dhami MK. 2005. "What I did" versus "what I might have done": effect of factual versus counterfactual thinking on blame, guilt, and shame in prisoners. *J. Exp. Soc. Psychol.* 41.6:627–35

Mandel DR, Lehman DR. 1996. Counterfactual thinking and ascriptions of cause and preventability. *J. Personal. Soc. Psychol.* 71.3:450–63

Markman KD, Gavanski I, Sherman SJ, McMullen MN. 1993. The mental simulation of better and worse possible worlds. *J. Exp. Soc. Psychol.* 29.1:87–109

Markman KD, McMullen MN. 2003. A reflection and evaluation model of comparative thinking. *Personal. Soc. Psychol. Rev.* 7(3):244–67

Markman KD, McMullen MN, Elizaga RA. 2008. Counterfactual thinking, persistence, and performance: a test of the reflection and evaluation model. *J. Exp. Soc. Psychol.* 44(2):421–28

Markman KD, Miller A. 2006. Depression, control, and counterfactual thinking: functional for whom? *J. Soc. Clin. Psychol.* 25:210–27

Markman KD, Mizoguchi N, McMullen MN. 2008. "It would have been worse under Saddam": implications of counterfactual thinking for beliefs regarding the ethical treatment of prisoners of war. *J. Exp. Soc. Psychol.* 44(3):650–54

Markman KD, Tetlock PE. 2000. I couldn't have known: accountability, foreseeability, and counterfactual denials of responsibility. *Br. J. Soc. Psychol.* 39:313–25

McCloy R, Byrne RMJ. 2000. Counterfactual thinking about controllable actions. *Mem. Cogn.* 28:1071–78

McCloy R, Byrne RMJ. 2002. Semifactual "even if" thinking. *Think. Reason.* 8:41–67

McCrea SM. 2008. Self-handicapping, excuse making, and counterfactual thinking: consequences for self-esteem and future motivation. *J. Personal. Soc. Psychol.* 95:274–92

McEleney A, Byrne RMJ. 2006. Spontaneous causal and counterfactual thoughts. *Think. Reason.* 12:235–55

McGraw AP, Mellers BA, Tetlock PE. 2005. Expectations and emotions of Olympic athletes. *J. Exp. Soc. Psychol.* 41(4):438–46

McMullen MN, Markman KD. 2000. Downward counterfactuals and motivation: the wake-up call and the Pangloss effect. *Personal. Soc. Psychol. Bull.* 26(5):575–84

McNamara P, Durso R, Brown A, Lynch A. 2003. Counterfactual cognitive deficit in persons with Parkinson's disease. *J. Neurol. Neurosurg. Psychiatry* 74(8):1065–70

Medvec VH, Madey SF, Gilovich T. 1995. When less is more: counterfactual thinking and satisfaction among Olympic medalists. *J. Personal. Soc. Psychol.* 69(4):603

Meehan JE, Byrne RMJ. 2005. Children's counterfactual thinking: the temporal order effect. In *Proceedings of the 27th Annual Conference of the Cognitive Science Society*, ed. BG Bara, L Barsalou, M Bucciarelli, pp. 1467–73. Mahwah, NJ: Erlbaum

Migliore S, Curcio G, Mancini F, Cappa SF. 2014. Counterfactual thinking in moral judgment: an experimental study. *Front. Psychol.* 5:451

Miller DT, Gunasegaram S. 1990. Temporal order and the perceived mutability of events: implications for blame assignment. *J. Personal. Soc. Psychol.* 59(6):1111–18

Moreno-Rios S, Garcia-Madruga J, Byrne RMJ. 2008. Semifactual "even if" reasoning. *Acta Psychol.* 128:197–209

Morris MN, Moore PC. 2000. The lessons we (don't) learn: counterfactual thinking and organizational accountability after a close call. *Adm. Sci. Q.* 45:737–65

Morrison M, Roese N. 2011. Regrets of the typical American: findings from a nationally representative sample. *Soc. Psychol. Personal. Sci.* 2:576–83

N'gbala A, Branscombe NR. 1995. Mental simulation and causal attribution: when simulating an event does not affect fault assignment. *J. Exp. Soc. Psychol.* 31:139–62

Ndubuisi B, Byrne RMJ. 2013. Intentionality and choice. In *Proceedings of the 35th Annual Conference of the Cognitive Science Society*, ed. M Knauff, M Pauen, N Sebanz, I Wachsmuth, pp. 1970–75. Austin, TX: Cogn. Sci. Soc.

Nickerson R. 2015. *Conditional Reasoning*. Oxford, UK: Oxford Univ. Press

Nicolle A, Bach DR, Frith C, Dolan RJ. 2011. Amygdala involvement in self-blame regret. *Soc. Neurosci.* 6.2:178–89

Niedenthal PM, Tangney JP, Gavanski I. 1994. "If only I weren't" versus "if only I hadn't": distinguishing shame and guilt in counterfactual thinking. *J. Personal. Soc. Psychol.* 67.4:585–95

Nieuwland MS, Martin AE. 2012. If the real world were irrelevant, so to speak: the role of propositional truth-value in counterfactual sentence comprehension. *Cognition* 122.1:102–9

O'Connor E, McCormack T, Feeney A. 2014. Do children who experience regret make better decisions? A developmental study of the behavioral consequences of regret. *Child Dev.* 85(5):1995–2010

Over DE, Hadjichristidis C, Evans JSTB, Handley SJ, Sloman SA. 2007. The probability of causal conditionals. *Cogn. Psychol.* 54:62–97

Page CM, Colby PM. 2003. If only I hadn't smoked: the impact of counterfactual thinking on a smoking-related behavior. *Psychol. Mark.* 20(11):955–76

Pearl J. 2013. Structural counterfactuals: a brief introduction. *Cogn. Sci.* 37(6):977–85

Pellizzoni S, Girotto V, Surian L. 2010. Beliefs and moral valence affect intentionality attributions: the case of side effects. *Rev. Philos. Psychol.* 1(2):201–9

Perner J, Sprung M, Steinkogler B. 2004. Counterfactual conditionals and false belief: a developmental dissociation. *Cogn. Dev.* 19(2):179–201

Petrocelli JV, Percy EJ, Sherman SJ, Tormala ZL. 2011. Counterfactual potency. *J. Personal. Soc. Psychol.* 100(1):30–46

Pighin S, Byrne RMJ, Ferrante D, Gonzalez M, Girotto V. 2011. Counterfactual thoughts about experienced, observed, and narrated events. *Think. Reason.* 17(2):197–211

Quelhas AC, Byrne RMJ. 2003. Reasoning with deontic and counterfactual conditionals. *Think. Reason.* 9(1):43–65

Rafetseder E, Schwitalla M, Perner J. 2013. Counterfactual reasoning: from childhood to adulthood. *J. Exp. Child Psychol.* 114.3:389–404

Riggs KJ, Peterson DM, Robinson EJ, Mitchell P. 1998. Are errors in false belief tasks symptomatic of a broader difficulty with counterfactuality? *Cogn. Dev.* 13(1):73–90

Rim S, Summerville A. 2014. How far to the road not taken? The effect of psychological distance on counterfactual direction. *Personal. Soc. Psychol. Bull.* 40(3):391–401

Rips LJ. 2010. Two causal theories of counterfactual conditionals. *Cogn. Sci.* 34(2):175–221

Ritov I, Baron J. 1990. Reluctance to vaccinate: omission bias and ambiguity. *J. Behav. Decis. Mak.* 3:263–77

Roese NJ. 1997. Counterfactual thinking. *Psychol. Bull.* 121(1):133–48

Roese NJ, Epstude KAI, Fessel F, Morrison M, Smallman R, et al. 2009. Repetitive regret, depression, and anxiety: findings from a nationally representative survey. *J. Soc. Clin. Psychol.* 28(6):671–88

Roese NJ, Park S, Smallman R, Gibson C. 2008. Schizophrenia involves impairment in the activation of intentions by counterfactual thinking. *Schizophr. Res.* 103(1–3):343–44

Roese NJ, Summerville A. 2005. What we regret most . . . and why. *Personal. Soc. Psychol. Bull.* 31(9):1273–85

Royzman EB, Goodwin GP, Leeman RF. 2011. When sentimental rules collide: "norms with feelings" in the dilemmatic context. *Cognition* 121(1):101–14

Rye MS, Cahoon MB, Ali RS, Daftary T. 2008. Development and validation of the counterfactual thinking for negative events scale. *J. Personal. Assess.* 90(3):261–69

Sanna LJ, Turley KJ. 1996. Antecedents to spontaneous counterfactual thinking: effects of expectancy violation and outcome valence. *Personal. Soc. Psychol. Bull.* 22(9):906–19

Sanna LJ, Turley-Ames KJ, Meier S. 1999. Mood, self-esteem, and simulated alternatives: thought-provoking affective influences on counterfactual direction. *J. Personal. Soc. Psychol.* 76(4):543–58

Santamaria C, Espino O, Byrne RMJ. 2005. Counterfactual and semifactual conditionals prime alternative possibilities. *J. Exp. Psychol.: Learn. Mem. Cogn.* 31:1149–54

Santos LR, Rosati AG. 2015. The evolutionary roots of human decision making. *Annu. Rev. Psychol.* 66:321–47

Schacter DL, Benoit RG, De Brigard F, Szpunar KK. 2015. Episodic future thinking and episodic counterfactual thinking: intersections between memory and decisions. *Neurobiol. Learn. Mem.* 117:14–21

Segura S, Fernandez-Berrocal P, Byrne RMJ. 2002. Temporal and causal order effects in counterfactual thinking. *Q. J. Exp. Psychol.* 55:1295–305

Sloman SA, Lagnado DA. 2005. Do we "do"? *Cogn. Sci.* 29:5–39

Smallman R, McCulloch KC. 2012. Learning from yesterday's mistakes to fix tomorrow's problems: when functional counterfactual thinking and psychological distance collide. *Eur. J. Soc. Psychol.* 42(3):383–90

Spellman BA, Mandel DR. 1999. When possibility informs reality: counterfactual thinking as a cue to causality. *Curr. Dir. Psychol. Sci.* 8.4:120–23

Stalnaker RC. 1968. "A theory of conditionals." In *Studies in Logical Theory*, ed. N Rescher, pp. 98–112. Oxford, UK: Basil Blackwell

Sweeny K, Vohs KD. 2012. On near misses and completed tasks: the nature of relief. *Psychol. Sci.* 23:464–68

Teigen KH, Jensen TK. 2011. Unlucky victims or lucky survivors? Spontaneous counterfactual thinking by families exposed to the tsunami disaster. *Eur. Psychol.* 16(1):48–57

Tetlock PE, Belkin A, eds. 1996. *Counterfactual Thought Experiments in World Politics: Logical, Methodological and Psychological Perspectives*. Princeton, NJ: Princeton Univ. Press

Thompson V, Byrne RMJ. 2002. Reasoning counterfactually: making inferences about things that didn't happen. *J. Exp. Psychol.: Learn. Mem. Cogn.* 28:1154–70

Tykocinski OE, Steinberg N. 2005. Coping with disappointing outcomes: retroactive pessimism and motivated inhibition of counterfactuals. *J. Exp. Soc. Psychol.* 41(5):551–58

Tyser MP, McCrea SM, Knuepfer K. 2012. Pursuing perfection or pursuing protection? Self-evaluation concerns and the motivational consequences of counterfactual thinking. *Eur. J. Soc. Psychol.* 42:372–82

Uttich K, Lombrozo T. 2010. Norms inform mental state ascriptions: a rational explanation for the side-effect effect. *Cognition* 116(1):87–100

Van Hoeck N, Begtas E, Steen J, Kestemont J, Vandekerckhove M, Van Overwalle F. 2014. False belief and counterfactual reasoning in a social environment. *NeuroImage* 90:315–25

Van Hoeck N, Ma N, Ampe L, Baetens K, Vandekerckhove M, Van Overwalle F. 2013. Counterfactual thinking: an fMRI study on changing the past for a better future. *Soc. Cogn. Affect. Neurosci.* 8:556–64

Walsh CR, Byrne RMJ. 2004. Counterfactual thinking: the temporal order effect. *Mem. Cogn.* 32:369–78

Walsh CR, Byrne RMJ. 2007. How people think "if only . . ." about reasons for actions. *Think. Reason.* 13.4:461–83

Waytz A, Hershfield HE, Tamir DI. 2015. Mental simulation and meaning in life. *J. Personal. Soc. Psychol.* 108(2):336–55

Weisberg DP, Beck SR. 2010. Children's thinking about their own and others' regret and relief. *J. Exp. Child Psychol.* 106(2):184–91

Wells GL, Taylor BR, Turtle JW. 1987. The undoing of scenarios. *J. Personal. Soc. Psychol.* 53(3):421–30

Williamson T. 2007. Philosophical knowledge and knowledge of counterfactuals. *Grazer Philos. Stud.* 74.1:89–124

Wimmer H, Perner J. 1983. Beliefs about beliefs: representation and constraining function of wrong beliefs in young children's understanding of deception. *Cognition* 13(1):103–28

Yeh D, Gentner D. 2005. Reasoning counterfactually in Chinese: picking up the pieces. In *Proceedings of the Twenty-seventh Annual Meeting of the Cognitive Science Society*, pp. 2410–15. Mahwah, NJ: Erlbaum

Zeelenberg M, Pieters R. 2007. A theory of regret regulation 1.0. *J. Consum. Psychol.* 17(1):3–18

Psychological Reasoning in Infancy

Renée Baillargeon,[1] Rose M. Scott,[2] and Lin Bian[1]

[1]Department of Psychology, University of Illinois, Champaign, Illinois 61820;
email: rbaillar@illinois.edu, linbian2@illinois.edu

[2]Psychological Sciences, University of California, Merced, California 95343;
email: rscott@ucmerced.edu

Annu. Rev. Psychol. 2016. 67:159–86

First published online as a Review in Advance on September 17, 2015

The *Annual Review of Psychology* is online at psych.annualreviews.org

This article's doi:
10.1146/annurev-psych-010213-115033

Keywords

infant cognition, psychological reasoning, theory of mind, rationality, agency, mental states, false beliefs, implicit reasoning

Abstract

Adults routinely make sense of others' actions by inferring the mental states that underlie these actions. Over the past two decades, developmental researchers have made significant advances in understanding the origins of this ability in infancy. This evidence indicates that when infants observe an agent act in a simple scene, they infer the agent's mental states and then use these mental states, together with a principle of rationality (and its corollaries of efficiency and consistency), to predict and interpret the agent's subsequent actions and to guide their own actions toward the agent. In this review, we first describe the initial demonstrations of infants' sensitivity to the efficiency and consistency principles. We then examine how infants identify novel entities as agents. Next, we summarize what is known about infants' ability to reason about agents' motivational, epistemic, and counterfactual states. Finally, we consider alternative interpretations of these findings and discuss the current controversy about the relation between implicit and explicit psychological reasoning.

Contents

INTRODUCTION

Over the past two decades, numerous reports have presented evidence that psychological reasoning, the ability to make sense of agents' intentional actions, emerges early in infancy (0–2 years of age). This evidence supports the mentalistic view that human infants are born equipped with a psychological-reasoning system that provides them with a skeletal explanatory framework for reasoning and learning about agents' actions (e.g., Baillargeon et al. 2015, Baron-Cohen 1995, Johnson 2005, Leslie 1994, Premack & Premack 1995, Scott et al. 2015b, Spelke & Kinzler 2007). When infants observe an agent act in a simple scene, their psychological-reasoning system enables them (*a*) to infer the mental states that underlie the agent's actions and (*b*) to use these mental states, together with a principle of rationality, to predict and interpret the agent's subsequent actions and to guide their own actions toward the agent. The rationality principle dictates that, all other things being equal, agents will act rationally; corollaries of the principle include efficiency (agents will expend as little effort as possible to achieve their goals) and consistency (agents will act in a manner consistent with their mental states) (e.g., Baillargeon et al. 2015, Dennett 1987, Gergely et al. 1995).

In our review, we first describe the initial demonstrations of infants' sensitivity to the efficiency and consistency principles. We then examine how infants identify novel entities as agents. Next, we summarize what is known about infants' ability to reason about agents' motivational states (e.g., goals and dispositions), epistemic states (e.g., knowledge and ignorance), and counterfactual states (e.g., false beliefs and pretense). Finally, we consider alternative interpretations of these results and discuss the current controversy about the relation between implicit and explicit psychological reasoning. In the limited space available, we could not include recent findings on infants' sociomoral reasoning (for reviews, see Baillargeon et al. 2014, 2015; Bloom 2013; Hamlin 2013). Nevertheless, it should be stressed that these findings provide additional support for those reviewed here: Infants could not predict or evaluate social interactions among novel entities without first identifying these entities as agents and determining what goals they are pursuing and what information is available to them (e.g., Hamlin et al. 2007, Johnson et al. 2010, Meristo & Surian 2013, Sloane et al. 2012). Our review highlights these foundational psychological-reasoning building blocks.

THE RATIONALITY PRINCIPLE

The initial investigations to address (implicitly or explicitly) infants' sensitivity to the rationality principle used the violation-of-expectation method, a prevalent looking-time method that takes advantage of infants' natural tendency to look longer at events that violate, as opposed to confirm, their current expectations (e.g., Luo & Baillargeon 2005b, Stahl & Feigenson 2015, Wang et al. 2004).

Efficiency

The first demonstration that infants are sensitive to the efficiency principle came from experiments by Gergely and Csibra using a novel detour task (e.g., Csibra 2008, Csibra et al. 2003, Gergely et al. 1995). Infants ages 6 to 12 months first received familiarization trials in which an agent had to move around or over an obstacle to reach a target. In the test trials, the obstacle was removed, and the agent traveled to the target either in a straight line (new-path event) or along the same detour path as before (old-path event). Infants looked reliably longer at the old-path than at the new-path event, suggesting that they (*a*) attributed to the agent the goal of reaching the target and (*b*) expected the agent to pursue this goal efficiently, in accordance with the efficiency principle: With the obstacle removed, a more efficient path to the target became possible, and infants detected a violation when the agent ignored this shorter path and followed the same path as before. These conclusions were supported by a control condition identical to the experimental condition except that in the familiarization trials the obstacle stood behind the agent and thus no longer blocked access to the target; nevertheless, the agent used the same detour path as in the experimental condition. Infants looked about equally at the two test events, suggesting that they could not generate a rational explanation for the agent's behavior in the familiarization trials (i.e., why did the agent detour en route to the target?), and they therefore held no expectation about the agent's actions in the test trials. These findings have been replicated in many laboratories (e.g., Brandone & Wellman 2009, Kamewari et al. 2005, Sodian et al. 2004).

Additional investigations indicated that infants expect efficiency not only in the length of the path used to reach a target (they expect a shorter as opposed to a longer path), but also in the number of actions performed to obtain an object (they expect a shorter as opposed to a longer means-end action sequence; e.g., Scott & Baillargeon 2013, Southgate et al. 2008). Finally, infants consider mental as well as physical effort in judging efficiency (Scott & Baillargeon 2013). In an experiment with 16-month-olds, an agent saw an experimenter cover two identical toys with a transparent and an opaque cover (a small screen then hid the transparent cover from the infants, so that neither toy was visible to them). Although both toys were physically equally accessible to the agent, infants expected her to reach for the toy that was visible to her and hence mentally more accessible. Together, these results indicate that infants' understanding of efficiency is highly abstract and encompasses both physical and mental effort.

Consistency

The first demonstration that infants are sensitive to the consistency principle came from experiments by Woodward using a novel preference task (e.g., Woodward 1998, 1999). Infants ages 5 to 12 months first received familiarization trials in which an agent faced two different objects, object A and object B; in each trial, the agent reached for and grasped object A. In the test trials, the objects' positions were switched, and the agent reached for either object A (old-object event) or object B (new-object event). Infants looked reliably longer at the new-object than at the old-object event, suggesting that they (*a*) attributed to the agent a preference or liking for object A, as the agent always chose it over object B, and (*b*) expected the agent to continue acting on this preference in the test trials, in accordance with the consistency principle. This finding has been replicated in many laboratories (e.g., Luo & Baillargeon 2005a, Martin et al. 2012, Spaepen & Spelke 2007).

Subsequent investigations introduced two variations of the preference task that reinforced its conclusions. In one variation, only object A was present in the familiarization trials; object B was not added until the test trials (e.g., Bíró et al. 2011, Luo & Baillargeon 2005a, Song et al. 2014). Infants now looked equally at the two test events: Because no choice information was available in the familiarization trials, infants had no basis for gauging the agent's disposition toward object A (i.e., did the agent reach for it because of a positive disposition toward it or because it was the only object present?); as a result, infants could form no expectation about which object the agent would choose in the test trials. The other variation was identical to the original preference task except that new object C replaced object B in the test trials (e.g., L. Bian and R. Baillargeon, manuscript in preparation; Robson & Kuhlmeier 2013). Infants looked longer at the new- than at the old-object event, and this effect was eliminated when only object A was present in the familiarization trials. Thus, when the agent repeatedly chose object A over object B, infants attributed to the agent an enduring positive disposition toward object A, and they expected this disposition to be maintained even in the presence of a new object.

Consistency Trumps Efficiency

When efficiency and consistency are pitted against one another, infants expect consistency to prevail. After an agent demonstrates a preference for object A over object B in the familiarization trials, infants expect the agent to reach for object A in the test trials even when physical constraints are added so that a longer, more effortful means-end action sequence is required to retrieve it than object B (Scott & Baillargeon 2013). Infants thus expect consistency to trump efficiency, at least in situations where the effort required to obtain a preferred object is not much greater than that required to obtain a nonpreferred object.

IDENTIFYING AGENTS

The findings summarized in the preceding section indicate that infants in the first year of life are already capable of sophisticated psychological reasoning about agents' actions. But whom do infants view as agents? Do infants initially interpret the actions of only human agents and gradually extend their action understanding to nonhuman agents? Or do infants reason from an early age about the actions of nonhuman agents? The available evidence supports the latter possibility: Positive results have been obtained using nonhuman agents (e.g., boxes and geometric shapes) with infants as young as 3 to 6 months (a) in detour, preference, and other psychological-reasoning tasks (e.g., Csibra 2008, Luo 2011b, Schlottmann & Ray 2010) and (b) in sociomoral-reasoning tasks (e.g., Hamlin et al. 2007, 2010, Hamlin & Wynn 2011). These findings naturally raise the question of how infants identify novel nonhuman entities as agents.

Internal Control

One early hypothesis about how infants identify novel agents involved self-propulsion: Perhaps any entity that can move on its own is viewed as agentive (e.g., Baron-Cohen 1995, Leslie 1994, Premack 1990). In time, however, it became clear that this hypothesis was incorrect. Instead, infants seem to identify a novel entity as an agent if it gives sufficient evidence that it has internal control over its actions (i.e., that it chooses when and how to act). This evidence can come in a variety of guises.

Detecting and responding purposely to changes. When a change occurs in a scene, a novel entity is categorized as an agent if it gives evidence that it detects this change and responds to it in a goal-directed manner (a goal-directed action is performed to achieve a particular outcome, such as a communicative or an instrumental outcome). In a series of experiments, Johnson and her colleagues (Johnson et al. 2007b, Shimizu & Johnson 2004) tested 12-month-olds using a preference task in which the "agent" was an oval entity covered with green fiberfill. When the entity simply approached and rested against object A in the familiarization trials, infants did not view the entity as agentive and looked equally at the new- and old-object test events (making clear that self-propulsion alone does not constitute evidence of agency, nor does repeating a single, fixed action that could be described as a goal-directed action). Positive results were obtained, however, if the entity first interacted with an experimenter in a "conversation": the experimenter spoke in English and the entity responded with varying beeps. Because the entity gave evidence that it detected and responded purposely to the experimenter's utterances (as though pursuing a communicative goal), infants perceived it as agentive. Additional results indicated that infants did not view the entity as an agent if (a) the experimenter spoke but the entity remained silent (suggesting that it was not merely seeing the experimenter talk to the entity that led infants to view it as agentive) or (b) if the entity beeped but the experimenter remained silent (suggesting that it was not merely observing the entity produce varying beeps that led infants to view it as an agent; variable self-generated behavior, if it appears random, does not constitute evidence of agency). In converging experiments using an attention-following task, Johnson et al. (2008) found that after observing the oval entity turn toward one of two targets, 14- to 15-month-olds turned in the same direction if the entity first conversed with an experimenter (agent condition) but not if it beeped and the experimenter remained silent (nonagent condition).

The preceding results have been replicated and extended in other laboratories (e.g., Beier & Carey 2014, Deligianni et al. 2011). In one attention-following task, for example, 12- to 13-month-olds perceived a rounded brown entity as agentive if it responded with beeps when the experimenter clapped his hands playfully toward it, but not if it first responded with beeps when the experimenter clapped two sticks toward it with a neutral expression (Beier & Carey 2014). This negative result suggests that mere turn-taking does not provide sufficient evidence for agency: The entity must demonstrate that it can not only detect events in its environment, but also respond to them in a goal-directed manner, as when participating in a conversation or a playful interaction. When the experimenter clapped sticks and the entity beeped in response, infants were unable to interpret its actions as goal directed, and they therefore did not identify it as an agent.

In the preceding experiments, the novel entity interacted with a human experimenter; in other experiments, no experimenter was involved, and infants viewed the entity as agentive if it gave evidence that it detected and responded purposely to changes in the scene (e.g., the introduction of objects, a change to the size of an obstacle, or the approach of another entity; Bíró et al. 2007, Hernik & Southgate 2012, Luo & Baillargeon 2005a, Schlottmann et al. 2012). In one preference task, for example, 5-month-olds first saw a box move back and forth at the center of an apparatus (Luo & Baillargeon 2005a). Next, object A and object B were added, and the box approached and rested against object A. Infants interpreted the change in the box's behavior as evidence that it was agentive; as a result, they attributed to the box a preference for object A, and they looked longer when it approached object B in the test trials. Interestingly, this effect was eliminated if a long handle was attached to the box, with the end of the handle protruding through the sidewall of the apparatus; it was then unclear whether the box had autonomous control over its actions, and infants no longer viewed it as an agent.

Choosing goals or means. When no change occurs in a scene, infants may still perceive a novel entity as agentive if it gives evidence that it is choosing either which target to approach or which (efficient) path to follow to a target. In preference tasks, 6- and 12-month-olds viewed a novel entity as agentive (as evidenced by their looking longer at the new-object event in the test trials) if it "turned" toward object A before approaching it in the familiarization trials, as though choosing it as its goal object (Johnson et al. 2007b, Schlottmann & Ray 2010). In a detour task, Csibra (2008) familiarized 6-month-olds with an event in which a box had to move around an obstacle to reach a target. Infants viewed the box as agentive (as evidenced by their looking longer at the old-path event in the test trials) if it detoured randomly around the left or the right side of the obstacle across the familiarization trials, as though choosing its path in each trial. In contrast, infants did not identify the box as an agent if it approached the target using the same fixed path around the obstacle in every familiarization trial. This negative result provides further evidence that for infants, self-propulsion and the repeated production of a single, fixed action that could be described as a goal-directed action do not provide sufficient evidence for agency (from an adult perspective, a mechanical device such as a ceiling fan would show these same abilities).

Self-Propelled Objects, Agents, and Animals

Although self-propulsion is not sufficient for infants to identify a novel entity as an agent, it could still be necessary for them to do so. Are infants able to view inert objects as agents, as adults are (e.g., the Magic Mirror in the Snow White fairy tale)? This question has received little experimental attention to date, but preliminary evidence suggests that infants identify an inert object as an agent if it demonstrates autonomous control over its communications (e.g., if it beeps when object A, but not object B, is revealed; Baillargeon et al. 2009). This initial evidence, paired with the results reviewed in the preceding section and additional findings on infants' expectations about self-propelled objects and animals (e.g., Baillargeon et al. 2009, Leslie 1994, Luo et al. 2009, Newman et al. 2008, Setoh et al. 2013), suggests three conclusions. First, self-propulsion and agency are distinct concepts for infants: An object may be self-propelled without being agentive, and it may be agentive without being self-propelled. A self-propelled object has an internal source of physical energy that allows it to exert or resist physical forces; an agentive object has mental states that give it control over its actions. Second, objects that are both self-propelled and agentive are categorized as animals and endowed with additional, biological properties such as innards. In a series of experiments, 8-month-olds detected a violation when a novel entity that was both self-propelled and agentive was revealed to be hollow, but they detected no such violation when the entity was only self-propelled, only agentive, or neither self-propelled nor agentive (Setoh et al. 2013). Third, these various results suggest that at least three core causal-reasoning systems (and their associated concepts) operate seamlessly to guide infants' responses to novel entities: the physical-reasoning system (energy), the psychological-reasoning system (mental states), and the biological-reasoning system (innards). As Keil (1995) emphasized, these early abstract causal understandings are very shallow and divorced of all mechanistic detail; nevertheless, they play a critical role in orienting infants to construe entities and their causal powers effectively.

Predictive Cues

We have seen that infants identify a novel entity as an agent if it gives evidence of internal control over its actions. This identification process may be relatively slow, however, so it makes sense that infants would also use their discrimination and categorization abilities to learn which perceptual cues predict agency.

Because most of the agentive entities infants encounter in daily life are humans and nonhuman animals (henceforth animals), predictive cues for agency will include motion cues (e.g., biological motion), morphological cues (e.g., having a face, a humanoid form, or a four-legged form), and surface-texture cues (e.g., having fur). Not surprisingly, given their intense interest in humans and animals (e.g., LoBue et al. 2013), infants rapidly begin to learn these cues and to use them in identifying novel agents (e.g., Arterberry & Bornstein 2002, Johnson et al. 2001, Kamewari et al. 2005, Setoh et al. 2013, Träuble & Pauen 2011, Yoon & Johnson 2009). In a detour task, for example, 6.5-month-olds identified a humanoid robot as an agent even though it followed the same fixed path around the obstacle in each familiarization trial (Kamewari et al. 2005). Similarly, in attention-following tasks, 12-month-olds turned in the same direction as a point-light human in an upright position (Yoon & Johnson 2009) or as a novel rounded entity with a face and fur (Johnson et al. 2001).

ATTRIBUTING MOTIVATIONAL STATES

The initial findings of Gergely, Csibra, and Woodward (reviewed previously) indicated that infants can attribute to agents motivational states such as goals and dispositions. Subsequent research has extended these findings in several directions, as summarized below.

Goals

By their first birthday, infants can infer a variety of goals, including inspecting, reaching, obtaining, or displacing an object; comforting, helping, hindering, chasing, or hitting an agent; and giving a toy to an agent or stealing a toy from an agent (Csibra et al. 2003; Hamlin & Wynn 2011; Johnson et al. 2007a, 2010; Király et al. 2003; Kuhlmeier et al. 2003; Luo & Baillargeon 2005a; Premack & Premack 1997; Woodward 1998). Moreover, infants understand not only single goal-directed actions, but also more complex means-end action sequences. In a preference task with 12-month-olds, for example, object A and object B rested inside separate containers, and in each familiarization trial the agent opened object A's container in order to retrieve it (Woodward & Sommerville 2000). In the test trials, the objects switched containers, and the agent grasped either the old (old-container event) or the new (new-container event) container and paused. Infants looked longer at the old- than at the new-container event, suggesting that they attributed to the agent a preference for object A and understood that her intermediate actions on its container merely served her overarching goal of obtaining object A. As was found in detour tasks, infants demonstrated sensitivity to the efficiency principle in their interpretations of the agent's means-end actions: If object A stood next to (as opposed to inside) its container in the familiarization trials, infants could no longer make sense of the agent's inefficient actions (i.e., why did she first open the container next to object A?), and they held no expectation about her actions in the test trials (see also Bíró et al. 2011).

Infants also demonstrate their ability to identify goals in imitation tasks. For example, infants are more likely to imitate actions that are marked as intentional ("There!") than actions that are marked as accidental ("Woops") (e.g., Carpenter et al. 1998, Olineck & Poulin-Dubois 2005); they are equally likely to reproduce intended outcomes after watching successful or incomplete demonstrations (e.g., Meltzoff 1995, Olineck & Poulin-Dubois 2009); and they are more likely to reproduce goal-relevant than goal-irrelevant action components (e.g., Brugger et al. 2007, Carpenter et al. 2005).

Although infants can understand a variety of goals, there are of course situations where they will fail to identify an agent's particular goal, for a variety of reasons. In some cases, infants may simply lack the relevant knowledge to infer the goal of a novel action. We can easily imagine that infants may be nonplussed when they first observe a parent listen to a cell phone, point a remote key at a car, or lick a fingertip before turning a page; infants may appreciate that the parent is acting purposely but be uncertain about what outcomes these actions are meant to achieve. In line with this analysis, 9-month-olds failed at a preference task in which an agent placed the back of her hand against object A in the familiarization trials instead of grasping it; because infants could not infer the goal of this baffling back-of-hand action, they looked equally at the new- and old-object events (Woodward 1999). Several investigations have taken advantage of this negative result to examine what experiences might lead infants to view the back-of-hand action as a goal-directed action (e.g., Bíró et al. 2014, Király et al. 2003; for similar investigations with other novel actions, see, e.g., Gerson & Woodward 2012, 2013). In one experiment, for example, an experimenter and 12-month-olds first took turns lifting Velcro-covered blocks using a Velcro band worn on the back of their hands (Bíró et al. 2014). After this training session, infants received a preference task in which an agent wearing a similar Velcro band produced back-of-hand actions, without lifting the objects. Results were positive, suggesting that the training session helped infants view the agent's back-of-hand actions as goal directed; as a result, infants attributed to the agent a preference for the object she repeatedly chose, and they expected her to maintain this preference in the test trials, in accordance with the consistency principle.

In other cases, infants may possess the relevant knowledge to identify an agent's goal but have difficulty doing so because the scene does not provide sufficient information to guide or support their reasoning. In one imitation task, for example, 16-month-olds first watched an experimenter demonstrate the use of a novel T-shaped rake to retrieve a toy out of reach (Esseily et al. 2013). When encouraged to do the same, infants showed some success only if the experimenter had first made clear the goal of her actions by stretching her arm and hand toward the out-of-reach toy, as though vainly trying to grasp it. In other investigations, 3-month-olds succeeded at detour and preference tasks only if they were first primed to focus on the goal of the agent's actions (e.g., Skerry et al. 2013, Sommerville et al. 2005). In one investigation, for example, infants in the experimental condition first received a brief play session in which they wore Velcro mittens (adapted from Needham et al. 2002) that allowed them to pick up Velcro-covered toys by swiping at them (Skerry et al. 2013). Next, infants received a detour task involving videotaped events: In the familiarization trials, an agent wearing a similar Velcro mitten reached over a barrier to get a toy and then paused; in the test trials, the barrier was removed and the agent reached for the toy either in a straight line (new-path event) or using the same arching action as before (old-path event). Infants looked longer at the old- than at the new-path event; in contrast, infants who wore mittens without Velcro during the play session, or who did not receive a play session, looked about equally at the two events. Together, these results suggest that the experimental play session, where swipes brought about observable outcomes, helped infants focus on and extract the goal of the agent's actions in the detour task. Once infants had identified this goal, they expected the agent to pursue it efficiently, in accordance with the efficiency principle. Although the young infants in this experiment were unable to focus on the agent's goal without an appropriate priming experience (see also Gerson & Woodward 2014, Sommerville et al. 2005), it is unlikely that such an experience is always necessary, as positive results have been obtained with 3-month-olds in tasks involving richer or less minimal actions (e.g., Hamlin et al. 2010, Luo 2011b).

Finally, in situations where infants succeed in identifying an agent's goal, they expect the agent's subsequent actions to abide not only by the efficiency principle, as we have seen, but also by the consistency principle. First, infants detect a violation if an agent changes goal for no apparent reason. Thus, after watching familiarization trials in which a large circle chased a small circle in a scene, 12-month-olds detected a consistency violation in the test trials if the large circle caught up with the small circle and continued moving past it, as though ignoring it, instead of stopping against it (Csibra et al. 2003). Second, infants detect a violation if an agent shows an inappropriate emotional reaction following the attainment of a goal (Skerry & Spelke 2014). After watching a circle successfully jump over an obstacle to reach a target, 8- and 10-month-olds detected a consistency violation if the circle displayed a negative emotional reaction (frowning, crying, and rocking) as opposed to a positive emotional reaction (smiling, giggling, and bouncing).

Preferences

Modifications of the preference task have yielded many additional insights into infants' ability to attribute preferences. First, when watching an agent repeatedly choose object A over object B in the familiarization trials, infants attribute to the agent not simply a preference for that object in particular, but rather a preference for that object category in general (Spaepen & Spelke 2007). Thus, after seeing an agent repeatedly choose a black female doll over an orange dump truck (or the reverse), 12-month-olds attributed to the agent a preference for dolls (or trucks), and they expected the agent to reach for the toy from the preferred category even when new toys (a white male doll and a red tow truck) were used in the test trials.

Second, infants can use not only unvarying-choice information (i.e., the agent always chooses object A over object B), but also other types of information to attribute a preference to an agent. One type is emotional information: If an agent emotes positively toward one toy but negatively toward another toy, infants attribute to the agent a preference for the first toy (e.g., Barna & Legerstee 2005, Egyed et al. 2013). Another type is statistical information: If an agent chooses only toy ducks from a box that contains mostly toy frogs, infants infer that the agent prefers the ducks (e.g., Gweon et al. 2010, Kushnir et al. 2010). Yet another type is effort information: If an agent faces a single toy but has to go to some effort to obtain it in each familiarization trial (e.g., has to open a container or detour around an obstacle to retrieve it), infants conclude that the agent must have a positive disposition toward the toy. As might be expected, only rational effort matters: Infants do not attribute a positive disposition if the agent's effortful actions are inefficient because the toy stands next to the container or the detour is wider than necessary (e.g., Bíró et al. 2011, Hernik & Southgate 2012). A final type of information, equifinality information, may constitute a special case of effort information: If an agent faces a single toy and approaches it in every familiarization trial even though the toy's position keeps changing (suggesting that the agent is willing to adjust its actions as needed to contact the toy), infants again conclude that the agent has a liking for the toy (Luo 2011b).

Third, infants recognize that preferences are attributes of individual agents: Mommy prefers white wine, but daddy prefers beer; big sister Jane is fond of sports, but big brother Karl likes video games. Thus, after watching familiarization trials in which agent A demonstrates a preference for object A over object B, infants age 9 months and older hold no expectation about which of the two objects a new agent, agent B, will prefer (e.g., Buresh & Woodward 2007, Henderson & Woodward 2012). An important exception is that infants do generalize preferences demonstrated in "pedagogical" contexts to other agents (Csibra & Gergely 2009). In an experiment with 18-month-olds (Egyed et al. 2013), agent A emoted positively toward object A and negatively toward object B, and then she left the room. Next, agent B arrived and asked the infants to give her one of the objects. If agent A used ostensive-communicative signals (e.g., looked at, smiled at, and greeted the infants) before and during her emotional displays, infants (a) interpreted these displays as pedagogical encounters aimed at teaching them the properties of the objects, (b) inferred that object A was pleasing but object B was not, and (c) expected agent B to share the same knowledge and preference and so gave her object A.

Fourth, in addition to preferences for objects (e.g., dolls), infants can attribute other types of preferences to agents. One type involves preferences for particular activities. After seeing an agent slide different objects, one at a time, forward and backward on an apparatus floor, 9- and 13-month-olds attributed to the agent a predilection for sliding objects, and they expected the agent to select a slidable over an unslidable object in the test trials (Song & Baillargeon 2007, Song et al. 2005). Another type of preference is for particular colors. After seeing that an agent preferred a red toy pepper over a black cup, and a red toy pyramid over a yellow toy house, 16-month-olds attributed to the agent a preference for red objects, and they expected the agent to select a new red object over a new green object in the test trials (Luo & Beck 2010). In recent experiments, 16-month-olds failed to attribute a color preference to an agent who consistently reached for a red football over a yellow football, no doubt because both toys belonged to the same object category (Mou et al. 2014). However, if infants saw the agent choose the red football over the yellow football in three familiarization trials, and then they saw the agent choose the yellow football over a green football in the next three familiarization trials, they concluded that the agent had an ordered set of preferences, and they expected the agent to prefer the red football over the green football when presented with both in the test trials.

Emotional States

To date, there has been little attention to the question of whether infants understand that emotions and moods, like goals and dispositions, can motivate agents' actions in a scene. As adults, we readily understand that an angry boy may kick rocks in his path or that a teenager looking forward to a date may sing happily in the shower. At what age do infants begin to understand that emotions may motivate (as opposed to simply accompany) actions? Such understanding appears to be present at least by the second year of life (Hepach & Westermann 2013). In one experiment, 14-month-olds saw two agents who were at times angry or happy perform actions that were either congruent or incongruent with their current moods. Infants showed greater sympathetic activity (as measured by pupil dilation) when an agent in an angry mood gently patted a toy or when an agent in a happy mood hit the toy.

Predicting Others' Actions

As evidence steadily accumulated that infants could infer agents' motivational states, researchers began to ask whether infants could use these states not only to interpret but also to predict agents' actions (e.g., Henrichs et al. 2014, Hunnius & Bekkering 2010, Kanakogi & Itakura 2011). As Brandone et al. (2014) stated, "a *prospective* intentional stance is fundamental to interpreting actions in real-time social situations and thus to interacting seamlessly with others" (p. 23).

The use of eye-tracking methodology has made it possible to examine in great detail under what conditions infants produce predictive looks that reflect their understanding of agents' motivational states. With this methodology, infants have been found to correctly anticipate agents' actions in detour tasks (e.g., Bíró 2013) and in preference tasks (e.g., Cannon & Woodward 2012, Kim & Song 2015). In one preference task, for example, 11-month-olds received four trials, each of which had three phases involving different movie clips (Cannon & Woodward 2012). In the familiarization phase, object A and object B rested in the top and bottom right corners of the monitor; a hand entered from the left, moved straight across the scene, and deflected just past midline to grasp object A. This event was repeated three times. In the next phase, the object's positions were switched. In the test phase, the hand moved as before but paused just past midline. Infants were more likely to make their first look from the hand to object A, suggesting that they attributed to the agent a preference for this object and anticipated that the agent would reach for it again.

Analyses of infants' brain activity during preference tasks also provide evidence of predictive psychological reasoning (Southgate & Begus 2013). In one experiment, 9-month-olds watched videotaped events while their sensorimotor-cortex activation was measured using electroencephalography (EEG). Infants first received familiarization trials in which an agent's hand consistently reached for and grasped object A as opposed to object B. Next, infants received several test trials; each included a baseline period (a moving screensaver) and a static anticipatory period in which either object A or object B was present and the hand rested in front of it. Comparison of the baseline and static periods showed greater motor activation during the test trials involving object A. Thus, infants anticipated that the agent would reach when preferred object A was present, but they showed no such anticipation when object B was present.

Making Sense of Irrational Actions

We have seen that when an agent produces irrational actions (e.g., makes an unnecessary detour while approaching a target or opens a container before grasping a toy next to it), infants hold no expectation about the agent's subsequent actions. But are there situations where infants succeed in generating explanations for apparently irrational actions? Research on this question has focused on pedagogical cues and situational constraints.

Pedagogical cues. Infants interpret inefficient actions differently when the actions are accompanied by pedagogical signals. Király et al. (2013) built on a puzzling finding from an imitation task by Meltzoff (1988): After watching a model activate a light-box by touching it with his forehead, 14-month-olds were more likely to reproduce this action one week later than were control infants. Why did the infants imitate this inefficient head action instead of using the more efficient approach of touching the light-box with their hands? Király et al. (2013) speculated that the ostensive-communicative cues that accompanied the model's demonstrations signaled to the infants that he was attempting to teach them the conventional use of this novel object. To examine this speculation, Király and colleagues tested 14-month-olds in two conditions. In the communicative condition, a model provided ostensive-communicative signals (e.g., she looked at and spoke to the infants) before and between her head actions on the light-box. In the noncommunicative condition, the model performed the same demonstrations without interacting with the infants. After a 10-minute delay, infants in both conditions were presented with the light-box for 20 seconds. Although all infants first used their hands to activate the light-box, 65% of the infants in the communicative condition also attempted at least once to perform the head action (this effect was replicated in another experiment with a one-week delay); in contrast, only 29% of the infants in the noncommunicative condition did so. The authors concluded that the head action, when accompanied by pedagogical cues, was "learned as a culturally relevant novel instrumental means that ought to be used to operate the novel artifact" (Király et al. 2013, p. 482).

Situational constraints. Infants make use of situational constraints to generate explanations for actions that would otherwise violate the efficiency principle. In another imitation task with a light-box, Gergely et al. (2002) found that 14-month-olds were less likely to reproduce a model's head action one week later if her hands were occupied during the demonstration (the model wrapped herself in a blanket that she held with both hands) than if her hands were free (the model wore the blanket loosely and laid her hands on either side of the light-box). Infants thus attended to the constraints affecting the model's actions: When her hands were occupied, they interpreted her inefficient head action simply as an expedient, alternative means of activating the light-box. Similar results have been obtained in other laboratories (e.g., Paulus et al. 2011, Pinkham & Jaswal 2011, Schwier et al. 2006).

Infants also attend to situational constraints to make sense of actions that appear to violate the consistency principle. Luo (2010) built on a puzzling finding from a preference task by Woodward (2003): When an agent simply looked intently at object A (as opposed to object B) in the familiarization trials, without grasping it, 12-month-olds still succeeded in attributing to the agent a preference for object A, but 7- and 9-month-olds did not (i.e., they looked equally at the new- and old-object test events). One possible interpretation of this negative result was that the younger infants detected a consistency violation: If the agent wanted object A, as her attentional behavior suggested, why did she not take it, since it was within her reach and there was no obstacle in her way? In line with this interpretation, Luo (2010) found that 8-month-olds succeeded in attributing a preference for object A to the agent if the scene was modified to provide an explanation for her failure to reach: Either her hands were occupied holding the two handles of a sippy cup or she sat behind a small window that only allowed her to look at the objects. These results suggest that whereas 8-month-olds are in the habit of reaching for interesting objects within easy reach and interpret others' actions accordingly, 12-month-olds have learned (perhaps via parental admonitions during their expanding locomotor forays) that one may sometimes look at, but not touch, interesting objects.

ATTRIBUTING EPISTEMIC STATES

When interpreting an agent's actions in a scene, do infants consider not only the agent's motivation, but also the knowledge the agent possesses or lacks about the scene? To address this question, researchers have explored infants' ability to reason about epistemic states such as knowledge and ignorance. A critical issue has been whether infants (*a*) are fundamentally egocentric and as such incapable of attributing to an agent a representation of a scene that differs from their own or (*b*) are nonegocentric and able to recognize, at least in some situations, that an agent's knowledge about a scene may be less complete than their own.

Keeping Track of What Objects Agents Can See or Have Seen

Do infants attend to what objects an agent can or cannot see, and has or has not seen, and expect the agent to know about the seen objects but to be ignorant about the unseen objects? To shed light on these questions, several experiments have used preference tasks in which object B is hidden from the agent—but not the infants—during the familiarization trials; the rationale is that if infants realize that the agent can see object A but not object B, they should perform as infants typically do when only object A is present in the familiarization trials (Kim & Song 2015, Luo & Baillargeon 2007, Luo & Johnson 2009). In one experiment, 12-month-olds were assigned to an ignorance or a knowledge condition (Luo & Baillargeon 2007). In the familiarization trials of the ignorance condition, the agent sat centered behind a transparent screen and an opaque screen; object A stood in front of the transparent screen, and object B stood in front of the opaque screen (object B was thus visible to the infants but not the agent). In each familiarization trial, the agent reached around the transparent barrier and grasped object A. In the test trial, the screens were removed, the objects' positions were switched, and the agent reached for either object A (old-object event) or object B (new-object event). The knowledge condition was identical except that before the familiarization trials the agent placed object B in front of the opaque screen herself and thus knew of its presence there. Infants in the knowledge condition looked longer if shown the new-object as opposed to the old-object event, whereas infants in the ignorance condition looked equally at the two events. Thus, infants took into account the agent's knowledge when interpreting her actions during the familiarization trials. When the agent knew both objects were present, infants interpreted her repeated actions on object A as demonstrating a preference for that object. In contrast, when the agent was ignorant about object B's presence in the scene, infants realized that her actions on object A could not be interpreted as signaling a preference (i.e., she might be reaching for object A simply because she thought it was the only object present).

These findings were subsequently extended to 6-month-olds (Kim & Song 2015, Luo & Johnson 2009). For example, in an anticipatory-looking task modeled after that of Luo & Baillargeon (2007), Kim & Song (2015) found that infants in the knowledge condition anticipated that the agent would reach for object A in the test trial, whereas infants in the ignorance condition showed no such anticipation. These results indicate that at least by 6 months of age, infants are nonegocentric: If an agent's representation of a scene is incomplete relative to their own, they use the agent's representation to predict and interpret the agent's actions.

By the second year of life, infants also use the agent's representation to guide their own actions in the scene. For example, Tomasello & Haberl (2003) found that when an agent requested one of three objects excitedly, 12- and 18-month-olds gave her the one she had not seen previously, suggesting that they kept track of which objects the agent had experienced during the testing session. Repacholi et al. (2008) also reported that after watching an agent angrily scold an experimenter for playing with an "irritating" toy, 18-month-olds were more likely to play with the toy if the agent did not look at them (e.g., if she read a magazine) than if she looked at them directly.

Finally, infants in the second year of life realize that just as they may see an object that an agent cannot see, an agent may see an object that they themselves cannot see (e.g., Chow et al. 2008, Moll & Tomasello 2004). For example, Moll & Tomasello (2004) found that when an agent looked behind an opaque barrier with expressions of excitement, 12- and 18-month-olds crawled or walked forward to peek around the barrier and see what the agent could see.

Keeping Track of What Events Agents Have Seen

Infants keep track of what events an agent has or has not witnessed in a scene, and they attribute appropriate epistemic states to the agent: They expect an agent who has witnessed an event to know about it, and they expect an agent who has not witnessed an event to be ignorant about it. For example, if an agent is present while an experimenter hides a preferred toy in one of two boxes, infants ages 6 to 18 months expect the agent to know the toy's location and to search the correct box, and they detect a violation if the agent searches the incorrect box instead (e.g., Z. He and R. Baillargeon, manuscript in preparation; Scott & Baillargeon 2009; Song & Baillargeon 2008; Surian et al. 2007). Conversely, if the agent is absent while the toy is hidden, infants expect the agent to be ignorant about the toy's location and to search either box at random (Z. He and R. Baillargeon, manuscript in preparation; Scott & Baillargeon 2009). These results provide additional evidence that infants are nonegocentric and realize that an agent may know less about a scene than they do. In addition, these results make clear that infants expect agents to act in a manner consistent with both their motivational and epistemic states: An agent who wants her preferred toy and knows its location should search that location, in accordance with the consistency principle.

By the second year of life, infants use the knowledge available to an agent not only to interpret but also to predict the agent's actions (e.g., Meristo et al. 2012, Surian & Geraci 2012). In one anticipatory-looking task, for example, 17-month-olds watched events in which a triangle chased a circle, which finally hid in one of two boxes (Surian & Geraci 2012). When the triangle witnessed this hiding event, infants anticipated that it would approach the correct box to find the circle. Finally, infants' understanding of an agent's epistemic states also guides their own actions toward the agent. Thus, infants age 12 months and older spontaneously pointed to inform an agent about the current location of an object if she was absent when it was moved to a new location (Liszkowski et al. 2006) or if she was looking away when it fell to the floor (Liszkowski et al. 2008).

Evaluating Irrational Agents: The Case of Epistemic Unreliability

We saw previously that when an agent acts irrationally (e.g., performs an unnecessary detour en route to a target), infants typically hold no expectation about the agent's subsequent actions. In some cases, infants may simply conclude that they lack sufficient information to understand the agent's actions. In other cases, however, infants may evaluate the agent as irrational and withhold future expectations, both in the original context in which the irrational action occurred as well as in new contexts; for infants as for adults, it is difficult to predict the actions of irrational agents or to trust new information they impart. Evidence for this second possibility comes from tasks on epistemic unreliability, which contrast reliable agents who act in accordance with their epistemic states and unreliable agents who do not.

In a series of unreliable-looker tasks, Poulin-Dubois and her colleagues tested whether 14- to 16-month-olds who saw an agent act in a manner inconsistent with her epistemic states in a first context would then hold no expectation about her behavior in a second context. In the first context, the agent expressed excitement ("Wow!") when looking inside a bucket that either contained a toy (reliable-looker condition) or was empty (unreliable-looker condition). The second context was adapted from prior tasks and varied across experiments, but in each case infants held expectations for the actions of the reliable but not the unreliable looker. Thus, infants were more likely to peek around a barrier after watching the reliable looker express excitement as she looked behind the barrier (Chow et al. 2008); they were more likely to detect a violation if the reliable looker failed to use her knowledge of an object's location when searching for it (Poulin-Dubois & Chow 2009); and they were more likely to activate a light-box with their foreheads after watching the reliable looker perform this novel inefficient action (Poulin-Dubois et al. 2011).

In an unreliable-user task, Zmyj et al. (2010) first showed 14-month-olds events in which an agent used everyday objects in either the typical manner (reliable-user condition; e.g., putting sunglasses on his nose and using a toothbrush to brush his teeth) or an atypical manner (unreliable-user condition; e.g., putting sunglasses on his foot and using a toothbrush to brush his hand). Next, the agent activated a light-box with his forehead, and infants in the reliable-user condition were more likely to imitate this novel inefficient action than were infants in the unreliable-user condition.

Finally, unreliable-labeler tasks take advantage of the fact that infants in the second year of life already know labels for many familiar objects (e.g., Begus & Southgate 2012, Brooker & Poulin-Dubois 2013, Koenig & Woodward 2010, Krogh-Jespersen & Echols 2012). In one task, for example, 18-month-olds first watched an agent label familiar objects either correctly (reliable-labeler condition) or incorrectly (unreliable-labeler condition). Infants were more likely to learn a novel label and to imitate a novel inefficient action taught by the reliable labeler as opposed to the unreliable labeler (Brooker & Poulin-Dubois 2013). Similarly, 16-month-olds were more likely to point to novel objects—as though requesting information about these objects (Kovács et al. 2014b)—if faced with a reliable as opposed to an unreliable labeler (Begus & Southgate 2012).

The preceding results suggest two broad conclusions. First, infants evaluate an agent who acts in a manner inconsistent with her epistemic states as irrational: They are less likely to seek information from her, to learn novel words and actions from her, or to detect a violation when she acts irrationally in a new context. This evaluation appears to be psychological rather than sociomoral in nature: 18-month-olds were equally likely to help a reliable or an unreliable labeler by bringing closer an object out of reach (Brooker & Poulin-Dubois 2013). Second, the preceding results extend our understanding of the consistency principle. Until now, our discussion of consistency violations has focused on situations where an agent with a demonstrated goal or preference suddenly deviated from it, for no apparent reason. What the research on epistemic unreliability makes clear is that in assessing consistency, infants bring to bear what they have learned from their social environments about how agents typically react to situations, use or label objects, and so on. Thus, an agent who emotes positively over an empty bucket, puts sunglasses on her foot, or labels a ball as a shoe is an agent who violates the consistency principle, given shared societal norms and conventions (for an interesting exception showing infants' sensitivity to humor cues, see Hoicka & Wang 2011).

ATTRIBUTING COUNTERFACTUAL STATES

The evidence reviewed in the preceding section indicates that beginning in the first year of life, infants recognize that agents may at times be ignorant about some aspect of a scene. But what happens when agents are not merely ignorant but hold false beliefs about a scene? Are infants able to reason about counterfactual states such as false beliefs?

For many years, it was widely assumed that the ability to attribute false beliefs did not emerge until about 4 years of age (e.g., Gopnik & Astington 1988, Wellman et al. 2001, Wimmer & Perner 1983). The evidence for this conclusion came primarily from elicited-prediction tasks in which children were asked to predict the behavior of an agent who held a false belief about a scene. In a classic task (Baron-Cohen et al. 1985), children listened to a story enacted with props: Sally hid a marble in a basket and then left; in her absence, Anne moved the marble to a nearby box; Sally then returned, and children were asked where she would look for her marble. Most 4-year-olds answered correctly and pointed to the basket (where Sally falsely believed the marble was); in contrast, most 3-year-olds pointed to the box (where the marble actually was), suggesting that they did not yet understand that Sally would hold a false belief about the marble's location.

Over the past decade, the conclusion that false-belief understanding does not emerge until the preschool years has been called into question by steadily accumulating evidence that children in the third, second, and even first year of life demonstrate such understanding when tested with other types of false-belief tasks (e.g., Baillargeon et al. 2010, 2015). Positive results have now been obtained with infants in spontaneous-response and elicited-intervention tasks. In both types of tasks, infants watch a scene in which an agent comes to hold a false belief. In spontaneous-response tasks, infants are asked no test question; instead, their spontaneous responses to the unfolding scene are measured. In elicited-intervention tasks, infants are asked a test question that prompts them to perform some action for the mistaken agent.

Spontaneous-Response False-Belief Tasks

The first spontaneous-response task with infants used the violation-of-expectation method and examined whether 15-month-olds would expect an agent to act in accordance with her false belief about a toy's location (Onishi & Baillargeon 2005). Infants first received familiarization trials in which an agent hid a toy in a green as opposed to a yellow box. Next, infants received one of four different belief-induction trials that resulted in the agent believing, truly or falsely, that the toy was in the green or the yellow box: In the knowledge-green condition, the agent watched as the yellow box moved a short distance and then returned to its original position; in the false-belief-green condition, the agent was absent when the toy moved from the green box into the yellow box; in the knowledge-yellow condition, the agent saw the toy move into the yellow box; and finally, in the false-belief-yellow condition, the agent watched as the toy moved into the yellow box, but was absent when it returned to the green box. In the test trial, the agent reached into either the green or the yellow box and then paused. In each condition, infants expected the agent to act on the information available to her, whether it was true or false; thus, infants in the knowledge-green and false-belief-green conditions expected the agent to reach into the green box, whereas infants in the knowledge-yellow and false-belief-yellow conditions expected her to reach into the yellow box. In each case, infants detected a consistency violation when the agent searched the other box.

The results of Onishi & Baillargeon (2005) have been confirmed and extended in many other spontaneous-response tasks. First, infants' reasoning about false beliefs about location (like their reasoning about other mental states) is highly context sensitive. For example, infants expect an agent not to hold a false belief about an object's location (*a*) if she wears a see-through as opposed to an opaque blindfold while the object is moved (Senju et al. 2011), (*b*) if she can see part of the object in its new location when she returns (Surian et al. 2007), (*c*) if she is given relevant information (e.g., "The ball is in the cup!"), as opposed to irrelevant information (e.g., "I like the cup!"), about the object's new location (Song et al. 2008), and (*d*) if the object rolls down a beam to its new location because the agent tipped the beam with her hand while looking away (Träuble et al. 2010).

Second, infants understand not only false beliefs about the location of an object, but also false beliefs about the presence, properties, and identity of an object (e.g., Scott & Baillargeon 2009, Scott et al. 2010, Song & Baillargeon 2008, Southgate & Vernetti 2014). In a task on identity (Scott & Baillargeon 2009), for example, 18-month-olds first received familiarization trials in which an agent faced a one-piece penguin that did not come apart and a disassembled two-piece penguin. In each trial, the agent hid a small key in the bottom piece of the two-piece penguin and then assembled it; once assembled, the two-piece penguin was identical to the one-piece penguin. In the test trials, while the agent was absent, an experimenter assembled the two-piece penguin, placed it under a transparent cover, and then placed the one-piece penguin under an opaque cover. The agent then returned with her key and reached for either the transparent or the opaque cover and then paused. Infants expected the agent to reach for the opaque cover and looked longer when she reached for the transparent cover instead (this looking pattern reversed if the agent witnessed the experimenter's actions). These results indicated that infants expected the agent (*a*) to mistake the penguin visible under the transparent cover for the one-piece penguin (because the two-piece penguin had always been disassembled at the start of the familiarization trials) and hence (b) to falsely conclude that the disassembled two-piece penguin was hidden under the opaque cover (because both penguins were always present in the familiarization trials). Infants thus attributed to the agent not just one but two interlocking false beliefs.

Third, infants take into account an agent's false belief(s) not only to interpret the agent's actions (e.g., to understand why the agent approaches the wrong location to find a desired object), but also to predict the agent's actions and to guide their own actions toward the agent. In anticipatory-looking tasks, 17- to 25-month-olds spontaneously anticipated that an agent who believed an object was in location A (when it was in fact in location B or had been removed from the scene) would search location A for the object (e.g., Meristo et al. 2012, Senju et al. 2011, Southgate et al. 2007, Surian & Geraci 2012). In anticipatory-pointing tasks, 18-month-olds spontaneously pointed to inform a mistaken agent that an object had been moved to a new location (Knudsen & Liszkowski 2012a) or that an aversive object had been placed at the location she falsely believed held her desired object (Knudsen & Liszkowski 2012b).

Fourth, the evidence that infants represent others' false beliefs now extends to the first year of life (e.g., Kovács et al. 2010, Luo 2011a, Southgate & Vernetti 2014). In a looking-time task, for example, 7-month-olds first received familiarization trials in which a Smurf agent placed a self-propelled ball in front of an occluder; the ball then moved behind the occluder, which was lowered to reveal the ball. In the test trials, infants saw a knowledge and a false-belief event. In the knowledge event, the agent again introduced the ball and watched as it first moved behind the occluder and then exited the scene; finally, the occluder was lowered to reveal no ball. The false-belief event was identical except that the agent left after the ball moved behind the occluder and returned only after the ball had exited the scene. Infants looked longer at the false-belief than at the knowledge event, and this effect was eliminated if the occluder was not lowered at the end of the events. These and other results indicated that when watching the false-belief event, infants expected the agent (a) to falsely believe the ball was still present behind the occluder and hence (b) to be surprised by the ball's disappearance and perhaps also to generate an explanation for it (as do 6-month-olds when a self-propelled object slips out of view to a new location; Luo et al. 2009). Evidence that young infants can not only interpret but also predict the actions of mistaken agents comes from an EEG experiment that measured 6-month-olds' sensorimotor cortex activation as they watched false-belief events (Southgate & Vernetti 2014). Compared to a baseline period, infants showed motor activation when an agent falsely believed a box contained a ball, but they showed no motor activation when the agent falsely believed the box contained no ball. Infants thus anticipated that the agent would search for the ball when she falsely believed it was present, but not when she falsely believed it was absent.

Fifth, evidence of false-belief understanding has also been obtained with toddlers in the third year of life (ages 2 to 3 years) using various spontaneous-response tasks (e.g., He et al. 2011, 2012; Scott et al. 2012). Importantly, some of these tasks have been highly verbal, with linguistic demands comparable to those of elicited-prediction tasks (He et al. 2012, Scott et al. 2012). In one violation-of-expectation task, for example, 2.5-year-olds watched a typical Sally-Anne scene along with an adult "subject" who was then asked where Sally would look for her toy when she returned (Scott et al. 2012). Children looked longer when the "subject" responded incorrectly and pointed to the toy's current as opposed to original location. Similarly, in a preferential-looking task, 2.5-year-olds listened to a false-belief story, accompanied by a picture book, about a character named Emily and her apple (Scott et al. 2012). In the final double-page of the book, one picture showed Emily searching for her apple where she falsely believed it to be (original-location picture), and the other picture showed Emily searching for her apple in its current location (current-location picture). Upon hearing the final line of the story, which stated that Emily was looking for her apple, children looked preferentially at the original-location picture, suggesting that they represented Emily's false belief and understood how it would guide her actions. These results make clear that the reason why young children fail at elicited-prediction tasks but succeed at spontaneous-response tasks is not simply that the former are highly verbal whereas the latter are not; young children succeed even at highly verbal spontaneous-response false-belief tasks.

Finally, positive results have been obtained using nonverbal and highly verbal spontaneous-response false-belief tasks not only with young Western children, but also with 22- to 40-month-old children from three traditional non-Western societies: a Salar community in northwest China, a predominantly Shuar community in southeastern Ecuador, and a Yasawan community in northwest Fiji (Barrett et al. 2013).

Elicited-Intervention False-Belief Tasks

In elicited-intervention false-belief tasks, infants are asked a test question, but this question does not require them to predict the behavior of a mistaken agent. Instead, they are prompted to perform an action such as retrieving or selecting an object for the agent; for infants to succeed, their actions must be guided by an understanding of the agent's false belief. In the helping task of Buttelmann et al. (2009), an experimenter first showed 18-month-olds how to lock and unlock two lidded boxes; the boxes were left unlocked. Next, a male agent entered the room, hid a toy in one of the boxes, and then left. While he was gone, the experimenter moved the toy to the other box and locked both boxes. When the agent returned, he tried to open the box where he had hidden his toy, without success, and then sat centered behind the boxes. When prompted to help the agent ("Go on, help him!"), most infants approached the box the agent had not acted on, suggesting that they understood he wanted his toy and falsely believed it was still in its original location (when the agent witnessed the toy's transfer, infants inferred that he wanted to open the empty box, and they approached that box instead).

In the referential-communication task of Southgate et al. (2010), 17-month-olds watched as an agent hid two distinct objects in two lidded boxes and then left; in her absence, an experimenter switched the objects. When the agent returned, she pointed to one of the boxes and said it contained a "sefo." The agent then opened the two boxes and asked infants, "Can you get the sefo for me?" Most infants approached the box the agent had not pointed to, suggesting that they understood the agent held a false belief about which object was in which box and intended to label the other object as the sefo. Similar results were obtained when the agent simply pointed to one of the boxes, said she wanted to play with the object in it, and asked the infants, "Can you get it for me?"

In addition to false beliefs about location, elicited-intervention tasks have been used to examine infants' understanding of false beliefs about contents and identity (Buttelmann et al. 2014, 2015). In an unexpected-contents task (Buttelmann et al. 2014), 18-month-olds and an agent first encountered three "block boxes" that each contained a block. Next, in the agent's absence, infants learned that a fourth block box actually contained a spoon. When the agent returned and reached vainly for the fourth block box, infants were shown a block and a spoon and asked to give one to the agent. Similarly, in a deceptive-identity task (Buttelmann et al. 2015), 18-month-olds and an agent first encountered an object that appeared to be a toy duck. Next, in the agent's absence, infants learned that the object was actually a brush. When the agent returned and reached vainly for the object, infants were shown a (nondeceptive) toy duck and a brush and asked to give one to the agent. In each task, infants correctly selected the object that matched the agent's false belief (i.e., the block and the duck, respectively); this pattern reversed if the agent remained present during the relevant demonstrations.

HOW SHOULD EARLY PSYCHOLOGICAL REASONING BE CHARACTERIZED?

We have argued, based on the findings presented in this review, that early psychological reasoning is mentalistic: Infants attribute to agents motivational, epistemic, and counterfactual mental states, and they use these mental states—together with the principle of rationality—to predict, interpret, and evaluate agents' actions and to guide their own actions toward the agents. Several alternative interpretations have been offered for these findings.

Alternative Interpretations

According to some views, infants are not yet capable of genuine psychological reasoning. In the low-level-process view, infants represent events in psychological-reasoning experiments "as colours, shapes, and movements, rather than as actions on objects by agents" (Heyes 2014, p. 648), and their responses are driven by perceptual novelty and other low-level domain-general processes. In the behavioral-rule view, infants do perceive agents acting on objects, but their expectations about agents are statistical rather than causal. In everyday life, infants gather information, in the form of statistical regularities or behavioral rules, about how agents typically behave in specific situations (e.g., an agent will search for an object where it was last seen); infants then apply these rules to interpret or predict agents' actions (e.g., Perner 2010, Ruffman 2014). Given the wealth of findings available today, these views seem unlikely. Infants' psychological reasoning is highly context sensitive, and a myriad of low-level processes or behavioral rules would be needed to explain all these findings. It seems more plausible to grant infants an abstract capacity for making sense of agents' actions (for further discussion, see Baillargeon et al. 2015, Carruthers 2013, Jacob 2015, Scott 2014).

According to the teleological view, young infants do engage in psychological reasoning and abide by a principle of rationality, but their reasoning is at first nonmentalistic and reality based. More specifically, (a) infants deal exclusively with physical variables such as situational constraints and end-states (infants do not attribute goals to agents, but simply track the outcomes they achieve), and (b) infants are egocentric and cannot entertain a representation of reality that is different from their own (Gergely & Csibra 2003, Gergely et al. 1995). The recent evidence that even young infants appreciate that an agent may be ignorant or mistaken about some aspect of a scene is inconsistent with the teleological view, or at least suggests that psychological reasoning is already mentalistic by the first half birthday.

According to the minimalist view, infants' psychological-reasoning system is mentalistic from the start, but the range of mental states it can handle is sharply limited. In particular, the system cannot represent false beliefs and other counterfactual states, although it can track belief-like states or "registrations" that are sufficient for success at many spontaneous-response and elicited-intervention tasks (e.g., Apperly & Butterfill 2009, Butterfill & Apperly 2013). Upon encountering an object, an agent registers its location and properties; by tracking this registration (even if its contents become outdated), infants can predict the agent's actions. For example, if an agent hides an object in one location and in her absence the object is moved to another location, infants can anticipate that the agent, upon returning to the scene, will search for the object where she last registered it. According to the minimalist view, infants' psychological-reasoning system presents a number of "signature" limits, which include (a) an inability to represent false beliefs about identity (these require taking into account not only *what* objects are registered but also *how* they are registered), and (b) an inability to reason about a complex, interlocking set of mental states that interact causally (e.g., Apperly & Butterfill 2009, Butterfill & Apperly 2013, Low et al. 2014, Low & Watts 2013). However, there is reason to doubt both of these limits: Infants have now been found to attribute false beliefs about identity in several tasks, and success at these tasks typically requires reasoning about an interlocking, causally coherent set of motivational, epistemic, and counterfactual states (e.g., Buttelmann et al. 2015, Scott & Baillargeon 2009, Scott et al. 2015a, Song & Baillargeon 2008). For example, recent experiments examined whether 17-month-olds could reason about the actions of a deceptive agent who sought to implant in another agent a false belief about the identity of an object (Scott et al. 2015a). In each experiment, a thief attempted to secretly steal a desirable rattling toy during its owner's absence by substituting a less desirable silent toy. Infants realized that this substitution could be effective only if the silent toy was visually identical to the rattling toy and the owner did not routinely shake her toy when she returned; when these conditions were met, infants expected the owner to be deceived and to mistake the silent toy for the rattling toy she had left behind. These results suggest that infants in the second year of life can reason not only about the actions of agents who hold false beliefs about identity, but also about the actions of agents who seek to implant such false beliefs, providing strong support for the mentalistic view that an abstract capacity to represent and reason about false beliefs is already present in infancy.

Implicit and Explicit Psychological Reasoning

What does implicit mean? Infants' psychological reasoning is often characterized as implicit, but different investigators mean different things by this term. One meaning (akin to sham) refers to processes that mimic more advanced, explicit processes but do not, in fact, involve the same concepts (e.g., if infants represented that "an object and another object" were in a box, they would have only an implicit understanding of the concept "two," as this concept would not figure in any way in their reasoning). Another meaning of the term implicit (akin to unconscious) refers to reasoning that occurs without explicit awareness of either the processes at work or the contents they generate. Yet another meaning of the term implicit (akin to intuitive) refers to reasoning that occurs without conscious awareness of the processes involved but can be accompanied by awareness of the contents generated.

Given the evidence reviewed in this article, the intuitive meaning of the term implicit comes closest to describing infants' psychological reasoning. As Vierkant argued, it is unlikely that infants in false-belief tasks who produce actions such as retrieving, selecting, and pointing to objects are unaware of these actions: "There might well be some false-belief understanding that cannot yet be deliberated about by a child, but which can nevertheless inform the fully consciously controlled actions of that child.... The child makes a conscious choice, and this choice turns out to be an appropriate one, because it was influenced by the child's false-belief understanding.... The behavior is not controlled by an unconscious zombie system . . . but by a conscious agent" (Vierkant 2012, p. 154).

Explicit reasoning does not supplant intuitive reasoning. Like infants, older children and adults routinely engage in intuitive reasoning about others' actions (e.g., Brown-Schmidt et al. 2008, German & Cohen 2012, Kovács et al. 2010, Senju et al. 2009); unlike infants, however, older children and adults are also capable of explicit psychological reasoning. First, they can consciously deliberate about others' actions and verbalize their understanding of these actions (e.g., they can explain that Sally will go to the basket because she thinks her marble is still there; Amsterlaw & Wellman 2006, Bartsch & Wellman 1989). Second, they develop a folk theory of psychology (just as they develop folk theories of astronomy and biology; e.g., Carey 1985, Vosniadou & Brewer 1992), which enables them to think and talk about theoretical concepts such as false beliefs (e.g., Gopnik & Wellman 1994, Leslie 2000).

There is currently a heated debate about how explicit psychological reasoning develops, how it relates to implicit psychological reasoning (in children and in adults), and whether its emergence is what makes possible children's success at elicited-prediction false-belief tasks (e.g., when a 4-year-old points to the correct location in such a task, this action is certainly consciously controlled, but does it necessarily reflect an explicit reasoning process?). These issues represent the new frontier in the research on early psychological reasoning, and findings from behavioral and neuroscientific methods are producing new insights (e.g., Hyde et al. 2015, Kovács et al. 2014a). One other approach is also yielding thought-provoking results: Over the past few years, researchers have begun to conduct longitudinal studies exploring the continuity of psychological reasoning from infancy to childhood (e.g., Aschersleben et al. 2008, Thoermer et al. 2012, Wellman et al. 2008, Yamaguchi et al. 2009). Although results have been somewhat variable due to small samples, several studies have reported significant correlations involving false-belief understanding. In a recent study, for example, performance in an anticipatory-looking task at age 18 months predicted performance in various elicited-prediction tasks at 50 months (Sodian et al. 2015). These results not only point to substantial continuity in early psychological reasoning, but also raise important questions about individual differences and the factors responsible for them.

Finally, in light of the preceding discussion, it may be clearer why in this review we chose to refer to infants' ability to infer others' mental states as "psychological reasoning" rather than as "theory of mind," as is often the case. We prefer the term psychological reasoning for two reasons (see also Schaafsma et al. 2015). First, this term underscores the deep similarities between infants' psychological reasoning and their reasoning in other core domains of causal reasoning, such as physical and sociomoral reasoning (e.g., Baillargeon et al. 2013, 2015). Second, the term theory of mind sometimes fosters the assumption that the acquisition of a folk theory of psychology is the primary endpoint of development in this domain and allows an explicit form of reasoning to supplant a more intuitive form of reasoning. As we have just seen, intuitive psychological reasoning persists throughout life, and its relation to explicit psychological reasoning is far from being completely understood.

CONCLUSION

The extensive evidence reviewed in this article indicates that from a very early age, psychological reasoning is mentalistic in nature. Upon observing an agent act in a scene, infants attempt to infer the agent's motivational, epistemic, and counterfactual states; infants then use these mental states, together with the principle of rationality, to predict and interpret the agent's subsequent actions and to guide their own actions toward the agent. Much remains to be discovered about how infants' ability to infer and reason about others' mental states improves with age, about the maturation of the brain networks that underlie this ability, and about the various factors that contribute to individual differences in neurotypical and other populations. Nevertheless, it seems clear that this core domain of causal reasoning depends on a content-rich, adaptive, neurocomputational system that begins to operate early in life (Cosmides & Tooby 2013).

DISCLOSURE STATEMENT

The authors are not aware of any affiliations, memberships, funding, or financial holdings that might be perceived as affecting the objectivity of this review.

ACKNOWLEDGMENTS

We wish to thank Shelley Taylor and Lisa Dean for their suggestions, support, and patience, as well as Andrei Cimpian, Melody Buyukozer Dawkins, Cynthia Fisher, Gerald DeJong, Francesco Margoni, and Francisca Ting for helpful comments.

LITERATURE CITED

Amsterlaw J, Wellman HM. 2006. Theories of mind in transition: a microgenetic study of the development of false belief understanding. *J. Cogn. Dev.* 7:139–72

Apperly IA, Butterfill SA. 2009. Do humans have two systems to track beliefs and belief-like states? *Psychol. Rev.* 116:953–70

Arterberry ME, Bornstein MH. 2002. Infant perceptual and conceptual categorization: the roles of static and dynamic stimulus attributes. *Cognition* 86:1–24

Aschersleben G, Hofer T, Jovanovic B. 2008. The link between infant attention to goal-directed action and later theory of mind abilities. *Dev. Sci.* 11:862–68

Baillargeon R, He Z, Setoh P, Scott, RM, Sloane S, Yang DYJ. 2013. False-belief understanding and why it matters: the social-acting hypothesis. In *Navigating the Social World: What Infants, Children, and Other Species Can Teach Us*, ed. MR Banaji, SA Gelman, pp. 88–95. New York: Oxford Univ. Press

Baillargeon R, Scott RM, He Z. 2010. False-belief understanding in infants. *Trends Cogn. Sci.* 14:110–18

Baillargeon R, Scott RM, He Z, Sloane S, Setoh P, et al. 2015. Psychological and sociomoral reasoning in infancy. In *APA Handbook of Personality and Social Psychology: Vol. 1. Attitudes and Social Cognition*, ed. M Mikulincer, PR Shaver, E Borgida, JA Bargh, pp. 79–150. Washington, DC: Am. Psychol. Assoc.

Baillargeon R, Setoh P, Sloane S, Jin K, Bian L. 2014. Infant social cognition: psychological and sociomoral reasoning. In *The Cognitive Neurosciences*, ed. MS Gazzaniga, GR Mangun, pp. 7–14. Cambridge, MA: MIT Press. 5th ed.

Baillargeon R, Wu D, Yuan S, Li J, Luo Y. 2009. Young infants' expectations about self-propelled objects. In *The Origins of Object Knowledge*, ed. B Hood, L Santos, pp. 285–352. Oxford, UK: Oxford Univ. Press

Barna J, Legerstee M. 2005. Nine- and twelve-month-old infants relate emotions to people's actions. *Cogn. Emot.* 19:53–67

Baron-Cohen S. 1995. *Mind Blindness: An Essay on Autism and Theory of Mind*. Cambridge, MA: MIT Press/Bradford Books

Baron-Cohen S, Leslie AM, Frith U. 1985. Does the autistic child have a "theory of mind"? *Cognition* 21:37–46

Barrett HC, Broesch T, Scott RM, He Z, Baillargeon R, et al. 2013. Early false-belief understanding in traditional non-Western societies. *Proc. R. Soc. B* 280:20122654

Bartsch K, Wellman H. 1989. Young children's attribution of action to beliefs and desires. *Child Dev.* 60:946–64

Begus K, Southgate V. 2012. Infant pointing serves an interrogative function. *Dev. Sci.* 15:611–17

Beier JS, Carey S. 2014. Contingency is not enough: Social context guides third-party attributions of intentional agency. *Dev. Psychol.* 50:889–902

Bíró S. 2013. The role of the efficiency of novel actions in infants' goal anticipation. *J. Exp. Child Psychol.* 116:415–27

Bíró S, Csibra G, Gergely G. 2007. The role of behavioral cues in understanding goal-directed action in infancy. *Prog. Brain Res.* 164:303–22

Bíró S, Verschoor S, Coalter E, Leslie AM. 2014. Outcome producing potential influences twelve-month-olds' interpretation of a novel action as goal-directed. *Infant Behav. Dev.* 37:729–38

Bíró S, Verschoor S, Coenen L. 2011. Evidence for a unitary goal concept in 12-month-old infants. *Dev. Sci.* 14:1255–60

Bloom P. 2013. *Just Babies: The Origins of Good and Evil*. New York: Crown

Brandone AC, Horwitz SR, Aslin RN, Wellman HM. 2014. Infants' goal anticipation during failed and successful reaching actions. *Dev. Sci.* 17:23–34

Brandone AC, Wellman HM. 2009. You can't always get what you want: Infants understand failed goal-directed actions. *Psychol. Sci.* 20:85–91

Brooker I, Poulin-Dubois D. 2013. Is a bird an apple? The effect of speaker labeling accuracy on infants' word learning, imitation, and helping behaviors. *Infancy* 18:E46–68

Brown-Schmidt S, Gunlogson C, Tanenhaus MK. 2008. Addressees distinguish shared from private information when interpreting questions during interactive conversation. *Cognition* 107:1122–34

Brugger A, Lariviere LA, Mumme DL, Bushnell EW. 2007. Doing the right thing: infants' selection of actions to imitate from observed event sequences. *Child Dev.* 78:806–24

Buresh JS, Woodward AL. 2007. Infants track action goals within and across agents. *Cognition* 104:287–314

Buttelmann D, Carpenter M, Tomasello M. 2009. Eighteen-month-old infants show false belief understanding in an active helping paradigm. *Cognition* 112:337–42

Buttelmann D, Over H, Carpenter M, Tomasello M. 2014. Eighteen-month-olds understand false beliefs in an unexpected-contents task. *J. Exp. Child Psychol.* 119:120–26

Buttelmann F, Suhrke J, Buttelmann D. 2015. What you get is what you believe: Eighteen-month-olds demonstrate belief understanding in an unexpected-identity task. *J. Exp. Child Psychol.* 131:94–103

Butterfill S, Apperly IA. 2013. How to construct a minimal theory of mind. *Mind Lang.* 28:606–37

Cannon E, Woodward AL. 2012. Infants generate goal-based action predictions. *Dev. Sci.* 15:292–98

Carey S. 1985. *Conceptual Change in Childhood*. Cambridge, MA: MIT Press

Carpenter M, Call J, Tomasello M. 2005. Twelve- and 18-month-olds copy actions in terms of goals. *Dev. Sci.* 8:F13–20

Carpenter M, Nagell K, Tomasello M. 1998. Social cognition, joint attention, and communicative competence from 9 to 15 months of age. *Monogr. Soc. Res. Child Dev.* 63:1–143

Carruthers P. 2013. Mindreading in infancy. *Mind Lang.* 28:141–72

Chow V, Poulin-Dubois D, Lewis J. 2008. To see or not to see: Infants prefer to follow the gaze of a reliable looker. *Dev. Sci.* 11:761–70

Cosmides L, Tooby J. 2013. Evolutionary psychology: new perspectives on cognition and motivation. *Annu. Rev. Psychol.* 64:201–29

Csibra G. 2008. Goal attribution to inanimate agents by 6.5-month-old infants. *Cognition* 107:705–17

Csibra G, Bíró S, Koós O, Gergely G. 2003. One-year-old infants use teleological representations of actions productively. *Cogn. Sci.* 27:111–33

Csibra G, Gergely G. 2009. Natural pedagogy. *Trends Cogn. Sci.* 13:148–53

Deligianni F, Senju A, Gergely G, Csibra G. 2011. Automated gaze-contingent objects elicit orientation following in 8-months-old infants. *Dev. Psychol.* 47:1499–503

Dennett DC. 1987. *The Intentional Stance*. Cambridge, MA: MIT Press

Egyed K, Király I, Gergely G. 2013. Communicating shared knowledge in infancy. *Psychol. Sci.* 24:1348–53

Esseily R, Rat-Fischer L, O'Regan K, Fagard J. 2013. Understanding the experimenter's intention improves 16-month-olds' observational learning of the use of a novel tool. *Cogn. Dev.* 28:1–9

Gergely G, Bekkering H, Király I. 2002. Rational imitation in preverbal infants. *Nature* 415:755

Gergely G, Csibra G. 2003. Teleological reasoning in infancy: the naïve theory of rational action. *Trends Cogn. Sci.* 7:287–92

Gergely G, Nádasdy Z, Csibra G, Bíró S. 1995. Taking the intentional stance at 12 months of age. *Cognition* 56:165–93

German TC, Cohen AS. 2012. A cue-based approach to "theory of mind": re-examining the notion of automaticity. *Br. J. Dev. Psychol.* 30:45–58

Gerson SA, Woodward AL. 2012. A claw is like my hand: Comparison supports goal analysis in infants. *Cognition* 122:181–92

Gerson SA, Woodward AL. 2013. The goal trumps the means: Highlighting goals is more beneficial than highlighting means in means-end training. *Infancy* 18:289–302

Gerson SA, Woodward AL. 2014. Learning from their own actions: the unique effect of producing actions on infants' action understanding. *Child Dev.* 85:264–77

Gopnik A, Astington JW. 1988. Children's understanding of representational change and its relation to the understanding of false belief and the appearance-reality distinction. *Child Dev.* 59:26–37

Gopnik A, Wellman HM. 1994. The theory theory. See Hirschfeld & Gelman 1994, pp. 257–93

Gweon H, Tenenbaum JB, Schulz LE. 2010. Infants consider both the sample and the sampling process in inductive generalization. *PNAS* 107:9066–71

Hamlin JK. 2013. Moral judgment and action in preverbal infants and toddlers: evidence for an innate moral core. *Curr. Dir. Psychol. Sci.* 22:186–93

Hamlin JK, Wynn K. 2011. Young infants prefer prosocial to antisocial others. *Cogn. Dev.* 26:30–39

Hamlin JK, Wynn K, Bloom P. 2007. Social evaluation by preverbal infants. *Nature* 450:557–59

Hamlin JK, Wynn K, Bloom P. 2010. Three-month-olds show a negativity bias in their social evaluations. *Dev. Sci.* 13:923–29

He Z, Bolz M, Baillargeon R. 2011. False-belief understanding in 2.5-year-olds: evidence from violation-of-expectation change-of-location and unexpected-contents tasks. *Dev. Sci.* 14:292–305

He Z, Bolz M, Baillargeon R. 2012. 2.5-year-olds succeed at a verbal anticipatory-looking false-belief task. *Br. J. Dev. Psychol.* 30:14–29

Henderson AME, Woodward AL. 2012. Nine-month-old infants generalize object labels, but not object preferences across individuals. *Dev. Sci.* 15:641–52

Henrichs I, Elsner C, Elsner B, Wilkinson N, Gredebäck G. 2014. Goal certainty modulates infants' goal-directed gaze shifts. *Dev. Psychol.* 50:100–7

Hepach R, Westermann G. 2013. Infants' sensitivity to the congruence of others' emotions and actions. *J. Exp. Child Psychol.* 115:16–29

Hernik M, Southgate V. 2012. Nine-month-old infants do not need to know what the agent prefers in order to reason about its goals: on the role of preference and persistence in infants' goal-attribution. *Dev. Sci.* 15:714–22

Heyes C. 2014. False belief in infancy: a fresh look. *Dev. Sci.* 17:647–59

Hirschfeld LA, Gelman SA, eds. 1994. *Mapping the Mind: Domain Specificity in Cognition.* New York: Cambridge Univ. Press

Hoicka E, Wang S. 2011. Fifteen-month-old infants match vocal cues to intentional actions. *J. Cogn. Dev.* 12:299–314

Hunnius S, Bekkering H. 2010. The early development of object knowledge: a study of infants' visual anticipations during action observation. *Dev. Psychol.* 46:446–54

Hyde DC, Aparicio Betancourt M, Simon CE. 2015. Human temporal-parietal junction automatically tracks other's beliefs: an fNIRS study. *Hum. Brain Mapp.* In press

Jacob P. 2015. A puzzle about belief-ascription. In *Mind and Society: Cognitive Science Meets the Social Sciences,* ed. B Kaldis. Berlin: Springer. In press

Johnson SC. 2005. Reasoning about intentionality in preverbal infants. In *The Innate Mind:* Vol. 1. *Structure and Contents,* ed. P Carruthers, S Laurence, S Stich, pp. 254–71. Oxford, UK: Oxford Univ. Press

Johnson SC, Bolz M, Carter E, Mandsanger J, Teichner A, Zettler P. 2008. Calculating the attentional orientation of an unfamiliar agent in infancy. *Cogn. Dev.* 23:24–37

Johnson SC, Booth A, O'Hearn K. 2001. Inferring the goals of a nonhuman agent. *Cogn. Dev.* 16:637–56

Johnson SC, Dweck CS, Chen FS, Stern HL, Ok S-J, Barth ME. 2010. At the intersection of social and cognitive development: internal working models of attachment in infancy. *Cogn. Sci.* 34:807–25

Johnson SC, Ok S-J, Luo Y. 2007a. The attribution of attention: nine-month-olds' interpretation of gaze as goal-directed action. *Dev. Sci.* 10:530–37

Johnson SC, Shimizu YA, Ok S-J. 2007b. Actors and actions: the role of agent behavior in infants' attribution of goals. *Cogn. Dev.* 22:310–22

Kamewari K, Kato M, Kanda T, Ishiguro H, Hiraki K. 2005. Six-and-a-half-month-old children positively attribute goals to human action and to humanoid-robot motion. *Cogn. Dev.* 20:303–20

Kanakogi Y, Itakura S. 2011. Developmental correspondence between action prediction and motor ability in early infancy. *Nat. Commun.* 2:341

Keil FC. 1995. The growth of causal understandings of natural kinds: modes of construal and the emergence of biological thought. In *Causal Cognition,* ed. A Premack, D Sperber, pp. 234–67. Oxford, UK: Oxford Univ. Press

Kim E, Song H. 2015. Six-month-olds actively predict others' goal-directed actions. *Cogn. Dev.* 33:1–13

Király I, Csibra G, Gergely G. 2013. Beyond rational imitation: learning arbitrary means actions from communicative demonstrations. *J. Exp. Child Psychol.* 116:471–86

Király I, Jovanovic B, Prinz W, Aschersleben G, Gergely G. 2003. The early origins of goal attribution in infancy. *Conscious. Cogn.* 12:752–69

Knudsen B, Liszkowski U. 2012a. Eighteen- and 24-month-old infants correct others in anticipation of action mistakes. *Dev. Sci.* 15:113–22

Knudsen B, Liszkowski U. 2012b. 18-month-olds predict specific action mistakes through attribution of false belief, not ignorance, and intervene accordingly. *Infancy* 17:672–91

Koenig MA, Woodward AL. 2010. Sensitivity of 24-month-olds to the prior inaccuracy of the source: possible mechanisms. *Dev. Psychol.* 46:815–26

Kovács ÁM, Kuehn S, Gergely G, Csibra G, Brass M. 2014a. Are all beliefs equal? Implicit belief attributions recruiting core brain regions of theory of mind. *PLOS ONE* 9:e106558

Kovács ÁM, Tauzin T, Téglás E, Gergely G, Csibra G. 2014b. Pointing as epistemic request: 12-month-olds point to receive new information. *Infancy* 19:543–57

Kovács ÁM, Téglás E, Endress AD. 2010. The social sense: susceptibility to others' beliefs in human infants and adults. *Science* 330:1830–34

Krogh-Jespersen S, Echols CH. 2012. The influence of speaker reliability on first versus second label learning. *Child Dev.* 83:581–90

Kuhlmeier V, Wynn K, Bloom P. 2003. Attribution of dispositional states by 12-month-olds. *Psychol. Sci.* 14:402–8

Kushnir T, Xu F, Wellman HM. 2010. Young children use statistical sampling to infer the preferences of other people. *Psychol. Sci.* 21:1134–40

Leslie AM. 1994. ToMM, ToBy, and agency: core architecture and domain specificity. See Hirschfeld & Gelman 1994, pp. 119–48

Leslie AM. 2000. How to acquire a "representational theory of mind." In *Metarepresentations: A Multidisciplinary Perspective*, ed. D Sperber, pp. 197–223. Oxford, UK: Oxford Univ. Press

Liszkowski U, Carpenter M, Striano T, Tomasello M. 2006. Twelve- and 18-month-olds point to provide information for others. *J. Cogn. Dev.* 7:173–87

Liszkowski U, Carpenter M, Tomasello M. 2008. Twelve-month-olds communicate helpfully and appropriately for knowledgeable and ignorant partners. *Cognition* 108:732–39

LoBue V, Bloom Pickard M, Sherman K, Axford C, DeLoache JS. 2013. Young children's interest in live animals. *Br. J. Dev. Psychol.* 31:57–69

Low J, Drummond W, Walmsley A, Wang B. 2014. Representing how rabbits quack and competitors act: limits on preschoolers' efficient ability to track perspectives. *Child Dev.* 85:1519–34

Low J, Watts J. 2013. Attributing false beliefs about object identity reveals a signature blind spot in humans' efficient mind-reading system. *Psychol. Sci.* 24:305–11

Luo Y. 2010. Do 8-month-old infants consider situational constraints when interpreting others' gaze as goal-directed action? *Infancy* 15:392–419

Luo Y. 2011a. Do 10-month-old infants understand others' false beliefs? *Cognition* 121:289–98

Luo Y. 2011b. Three-month-old infants attribute goals to a non-human agent. *Dev. Sci.* 14:453–60

Luo Y, Baillargeon R. 2005a. Can a self-propelled box have a goal? Psychological reasoning in 5-month-old infants. *Psychol. Sci.* 16:601–8

Luo Y, Baillargeon R. 2005b. When the ordinary seems unexpected: evidence for incremental physical knowledge in young infants. *Cognition* 95:297–328

Luo Y, Baillargeon R. 2007. Do 12.5-month-old infants consider what objects others can see when interpreting their actions? *Cognition* 105:489–512

Luo Y, Beck W. 2010. Do you see what I see? Infants' reasoning about others' incomplete perceptions. *Dev. Sci.* 13:134–42

Luo Y, Johnson SC. 2009. Recognizing the role of perception in action at 6 months. *Dev. Sci.* 12:142–49

Luo Y, Kaufman L, Baillargeon R. 2009. Young infants' reasoning about events involving inert and self-propelled objects. *Cogn. Psychol.* 58:441–86

Martin A, Onishi KH, Vouloumanos A. 2012. Understanding the abstract role of speech in communication at 12 months. *Cognition* 123:50–60

Meltzoff AN. 1988. Infant imitation after a 1-week delay: long-term memory for novel acts and multiple stimuli. *Dev. Psychol.* 24:470–76

Meltzoff AN. 1995. Understanding the intentions of others: re-enactment of intended acts by 18-month-old children. *Dev. Psychol.* 31:838–50

Meristo M, Morgan G, Geraci A, Iozzi L, Hjelmquist E, et al. 2012. Belief attribution in deaf and hearing infants. *Dev. Sci.* 15:633–40

Meristo M, Surian L. 2013. Do infants detect indirect reciprocity? *Cognition* 129:102–13

Moll H, Tomasello M. 2004. 12- and 18-month-old infants follow gaze to spaces behind barriers. *Dev. Sci.* 7:F1–9

Mou Y, Province JM, Luo Y. 2014. Can infants make transitive inferences? *Cogn. Psychol.* 68:98–112

Needham A, Barrett T, Peterman K. 2002. A pick-me-up for infants' exploratory skills: early simulated experiences reaching for objects using "sticky mittens" enhances young infants' object exploration skills. *Infant Behav. Dev.* 25:279–95

Newman GE, Herrmann P, Wynn K, Keil FC. 2008. Biases towards internal features in infants' reasoning about objects. *Cognition* 107:420–32

Olineck KM, Poulin-Dubois D. 2005. Infants' ability to distinguish between intentional and accidental actions and its relation to internal state language. *Infancy* 8:91–100

Olineck KM, Poulin-Dubois D. 2009. Infants' understanding of intention from 10 to 14 months: interrelations among violation of expectancy and imitation tasks. *Infant Behav. Dev.* 32:404–15

Onishi KH, Baillargeon R. 2005. Do 15-month-old infants understand false beliefs? *Science* 308:255–58

Paulus M, Hunnius S, Vissers M, Bekkering H. 2011. Imitation in infancy: rational or motor resonance? *Child Dev.* 82:1047–57

Perner J. 2010. Who took the cog out of cognitive science? Mentalism in an era of anti-cognitivism. In *Cognition and Neuropsychology: International Perspectives on Psychological Science*, ed. PA Frensch, R Schwarzer, pp. 241–61. Hove, UK: Psychol. Press

Pinkham AM, Jaswal VK. 2011. Watch and learn? Infants privilege efficiency over pedagogy during imitative learning. *Infancy* 16:535–44

Poulin-Dubois D, Brooker I, Polonia A. 2011. Infants prefer to imitate a reliable person. *Infant Behav. Dev.* 34:303–9

Poulin-Dubois D, Chow V. 2009. The effect of looker's past reliability on infants' reasoning about beliefs. *Dev. Psychol.* 45:1576–82

Premack D. 1990. The infant's theory of self-propelled objects. *Cognition* 36:1–16

Premack D, Premack AJ. 1995. Origins of human social competence. In *The Cognitive Neurosciences*, ed. MS Gazzaniga, pp. 205–18. Cambridge, MA: MIT Press

Premack D, Premack AJ. 1997. Infants attribute value +/− to the goal-directed actions of self-propelled objects. *J. Cogn. Neurosci.* 9:848–56

Repacholi BM, Meltzoff AN, Olsen B. 2008. Infants' understanding of the link between visual perception and emotion: "If she can't see me doing it, she won't get angry." *Dev. Psychol.* 44:561–74

Robson SJ, Kuhlmeier VA. 2013. *Selectivity promotes 9-month-old infants to encode the goals of others.* Paper presented at Bienn. Meet. Soc. Res. Child Dev., April, Seattle, WA

Ruffman T. 2014. To belief or not belief: children's theory of mind. *Dev. Rev.* 34:265–93

Schaafsma SM, Pfaff DW, Spunt RP, Adolphs R. 2015. Deconstructing and reconstructing theory of mind. *Trends Cogn. Sci.* 19:65–72

Schlottmann A, Ray ED. 2010. Goal attribution to schematic animals: Do 6-month-olds perceive biological motion as animate? *Dev. Sci.* 13:1–10

Schlottmann A, Ray ED, Surian L. 2012. Emerging perception of causality in action-and-reaction sequences from 4 to 6 months of age: Is it domain-specific? *J. Exp. Child Psychol.* 112:208–30

Schwier C, van Maanen C, Carpenter M, Tomasello M. 2006. Rational imitation in 12-month-old infants. *Infancy* 10:303–11

Scott RM. 2014. Post hoc versus predictive accounts of children's theory of mind: a reply to Ruffman. *Dev. Rev.* 34:300–4

Scott RM, Baillargeon R. 2009. Which penguin is this? Attributing false beliefs about object identity at 18 months. *Child Dev.* 80:1172–96

Scott RM, Baillargeon R. 2013. Do infants really expect others to act efficiently? A critical test of the rationality principle. *Psychol. Sci.* 24:466–74

Scott RM, Baillargeon R, Song H, Leslie A. 2010. Attributing false beliefs about non-obvious properties at 18 months. *Cogn. Psychol.* 61:366–95

Scott RM, He Z, Baillargeon R, Cummins D. 2012. False-belief understanding in 2.5-year-olds: evidence from two novel verbal spontaneous-response tasks. *Dev. Sci.* 15:181–93

Scott RM, Richman JC, Baillargeon R. 2015a. Infants understand deceptive intentions to implant false beliefs about identity: new evidence for early mentalistic reasoning. *Cogn. Psychol.* 82:32–56

Scott RM, Roby E, Smith M. 2015b. False-belief understanding in the first years of life. In *The Routledge Handbook of the Philosophy of the Social Mind*, ed. J Kiverstein. Oxford, UK: Routledge. In press

Senju A, Southgate V, Snape C, Leonard M, Csibra G. 2011. Do 18-month-olds really attribute mental states to others? A critical test. *Psychol. Sci.* 22:878–80

Senju A, Southgate V, White S, Frith U. 2009. Mindblind eyes: an absence of spontaneous theory of mind in Asperger syndrome. *Science* 325:883–85

Setoh P, Wu D, Baillargeon R, Gelman R. 2013. Young infants have biological expectations about animals. *PNAS* 110:15937–42

Shimizu YA, Johnson SC. 2004. Infants' attribution of a goal to a morphologically unfamiliar agent. *Dev. Sci.* 7:425–30

Skerry AE, Carey SE, Spelke ES. 2013. First-person action experience reveals sensitivity to action efficiency in prereaching infants. *PNAS* 110:18728–33

Skerry AE, Spelke ES. 2014. Preverbal infants identify emotional reactions that are incongruent with goal outcomes. *Cognition* 130:204–16

Sloane S, Baillargeon R, Premack D. 2012. Do infants have a sense of fairness? *Psychol. Sci.* 23:196–204

Sodian B, Kristen SE, Licata M. 2015. *The longitudinal relation of implicit and explicit false belief understanding.* Presented at Bienn. Meet. Soc. Res. Child Dev., Philadelphia, PA

Sodian B, Schoeppner B, Metz U. 2004. Do infants apply the principle of rational action to human agents? *Infant Behav. Dev.* 27:31–41

Sommerville JA, Woodward AL, Needham A. 2005. Action experience alters 3-month-old infants' perception of others' actions. *Cognition* 96:B1–11

Song H, Baillargeon R. 2007. Can 9.5-month-old infants attribute to an agent a disposition to perform a particular action on objects? *Acta Psychol.* 124:79–105

Song H, Baillargeon R. 2008. Infants' reasoning about others' false perceptions. *Dev. Psychol.* 44:1789–95

Song H, Baillargeon R, Fisher C. 2005. Can infants attribute to an agent a disposition to perform a particular action? *Cognition* 98:B45–55

Song H, Baillargeon R, Fisher C. 2014. The development of infants' use of novel verbal information when reasoning about others' actions. *PLOS ONE* 9:e92387

Song H, Onishi KH, Baillargeon R, Fisher C. 2008. Can an agent's false belief be corrected by an appropriate communication? Psychological reasoning in 18-month-old infants. *Cognition* 109:295–315

Southgate V, Begus K. 2013. Motor activation during the prediction of nonexecutable actions in infants. *Psychol. Sci.* 24:828–35

Southgate V, Chevallier C, Csibra G. 2010. Seventeen-month-olds appeal to false beliefs to interpret others' referential communication. *Dev. Sci.* 16:907–12

Southgate V, Johnson MH, Csibra G. 2008. Infants attribute goals even to biomechanically impossible actions. *Cognition* 107:1059–69

Southgate V, Senju A, Csibra G. 2007. Action anticipation through attribution of false belief by two-year-olds. *Psychol. Sci.* 18:587–92

Southgate V, Vernetti A. 2014. Belief-based action prediction in preverbal infants. *Cognition* 130:1–10

Spaepen E, Spelke E. 2007. Will any doll do? 12-month-olds' reasoning about goal objects. *Cogn. Psychol.* 54:133–54

Spelke ES, Kinzler KD. 2007. Core knowledge. *Dev. Sci.* 10:89–96

Stahl AE, Feigenson L. 2015. Observing the unexpected enhances infants' learning and exploration. *Science* 348:91–94

Surian L, Caldi S, Sperber D. 2007. Attribution of beliefs by 13-month-old infants. *Psychol. Sci.* 18:580–86

Surian L, Geraci A. 2012. Where will the triangle look for it? Attributing false beliefs to geometric shapes at 17 months. *Br. J. Dev. Psychol.* 30:30–44

Thoermer C, Sodian B, Vuori M, Perst H, Kristen S. 2012. Continuity from an implicit to an explicit understanding of false belief from infancy to preschool age. *Br. J. Dev. Psychol.* 30:172–87

Tomasello M, Haberl K. 2003. Understanding attention: 12- and 18-month-olds know what is new for other persons. *Dev. Psychol.* 39:906–12

Träuble B, Marinović V, Pauen S. 2010. Early theory of mind competencies: Do infants understand others' beliefs? *Infancy* 15:434–44

Träuble B, Pauen S. 2011. Cause or effect: What matters? How 12-month-old infants learn to categorize artifacts. *Br. J. Dev. Psychol.* 29:357–74

Vierkant T. 2012. Self-knowledge and knowing other minds: the implicit/explicit distinction as a tool in understanding theory of mind. *Br. J. Dev. Psychol.* 30:141–55

Vosniadou S, Brewer WF. 1992. Mental models of the earth: a study of conceptual change in childhood. *Cogn. Psychol.* 24:535–85

Wang S, Baillargeon R, Brueckner L. 2004. Young infants' reasoning about hidden objects: evidence from violation-of-expectation tasks with test trials only. *Cognition* 93:167–98

Wellman HM, Cross D, Watson J. 2001. Meta-analysis of theory of mind development: the truth about false belief. *Child Dev.* 72:655–84

Wellman HM, Lopez-Duran S, LaBounty J, Hamilton B. 2008. Infant attention to intentional action predicts preschool theory of mind. *Dev. Psychol.* 44:618–32

Wimmer H, Perner J. 1983. Beliefs about beliefs: representation and constraining function of wrong beliefs in young children's understanding of deception. *Cognition* 13:103–28

Woodward AL. 1998. Infants selectively encode the goal object of an actor's reach. *Cognition* 69:1–34

Woodward AL. 1999. Infants' ability to distinguish between purposeful and non-purposeful behaviors. *Infant Behav. Dev.* 22:145–60

Woodward AL. 2003. Infants' developing understanding of the link between looker and object. *Dev. Sci.* 6:297–311

Woodward AL, Sommerville JA. 2000. Twelve-month-old infants interpret action in context. *Psychol. Sci.* 11:73–77

Yamaguchi M, Kuhlmeier VA, Wynn K, VanMarle K. 2009. Continuity in social cognition from infancy to childhood. *Dev. Sci.* 12:746–52

Yoon J, Johnson SC. 2009. Biological motion displays elicit social behavior in 12-month-olds. *Child Dev.* 80:1069–75

Zmyj N, Buttelmann D, Carpenter M, Daum MM. 2010. The reliability of a model influences 14-month-olds' imitation. *J. Exp. Child Psychol.* 106:208–20

Socioemotional, Personality, and Biological Development: Illustrations from a Multilevel Developmental Psychopathology Perspective on Child Maltreatment

Dante Cicchetti

Institute of Child Development, University of Minnesota, Minneapolis, Minnesota 55455;
email: cicchett@umn.edu

Annu. Rev. Psychol. 2016. 67:187–211

The *Annual Review of Psychology* is online at
psych.annualreviews.org

This article's doi:
10.1146/annurev-psych-122414-033259

Keywords

developmental analysis, developmental psychopathology principles,
gene–environment interaction, social experience and neurobiological
development, stage-salient issues, randomized control trial interventions,
RCTs, resilience

Abstract

Developmental theories can be affirmed, challenged, and augmented by incorporating knowledge about atypical ontogenesis. Investigations of the biological, socioemotional, and personality development in individuals with high-risk conditions and psychopathological disorders can provide an entrée into the study of system organization, disorganization, and reorganization. This article examines child maltreatment to illustrate the benefit that can be derived from the study of individuals subjected to nonnormative caregiving experiences. Relative to an average expectable environment, which consists of a species-specific range of environmental conditions that support adaptive development among genetically normal individuals, maltreating families fail to provide many of the experiences that are required for normal development. Principles gleaned from the field of developmental psychopathology provide a framework for understanding multilevel functioning in normality and pathology. Knowledge of normative developmental processes provides the impetus to design and implement randomized control trial (RCT) interventions that can promote resilient functioning in maltreated children.

Contents

INTRODUCTION

Child maltreatment represents a pathogenic relational environment that confers significant risk for maladaptation across psychological and biological domains of development. The deleterious sequelae accompanying child maltreatment not only result in adverse consequences during infancy and childhood, but also often initiate a negative developmental cascade that continues throughout the life course. The proximal environment involving the nuclear family as well as more distal factors associated with the culture and community more broadly transact to undermine normal psychological and biological developmental processes in children who have experienced child maltreatment (Cicchetti & Toth 2015).

DEFINITIONAL CONSIDERATIONS

The National Society for the Prevention of Cruelty to Children defines maltreatment as "all forms of physical and/or emotional ill-treatment, sexual abuse, neglect or negligent treatment, or commercial or other exploitation, resulting in actual or potential harm to the child's health, survival, development or dignity in the context of a relationship of responsibility, trust, or power" (Butchart et al. 2006, p. 9).

A fundamental difficulty inherent in the investigation of child maltreatment is that the range of phenomena covered by the term is quite varied. In terms of the subtypes of maltreatment, neglect involves failure to provide for the child's basic physical needs for adequate food, clothing, shelter, and medical treatment. In addition to inadequate attention to physical needs, forms of this subtype include lack of supervision, moral-legal neglect, and educational neglect. Emotional maltreatment involves extreme thwarting of children's basic emotional needs for psychological safety and security, acceptance and self-esteem, and age-appropriate autonomy. Examples of emotional maltreatment of increasing severity include belittling and ridiculing the child, showing extreme negativity and hostility, exposing the child to severe marital violence, abandoning the child, and making suicidal or homicidal threats. Physical abuse involves the nonaccidental infliction of physical injury on the child (e.g., bruises, welts, burns, choking, broken bones). Injuries range from minor and temporary to permanently disfiguring. Finally, sexual abuse involves attempted or actual sexual contact between the child and the caregiver for purposes of the caregiver's sexual satisfaction or financial benefit by forced prostitution. Events range from exposure to pornography or adult sexual activity, to sexual touching and fondling, to forced intercourse with the child.

The Maltreatment Classification System (MCS) (Manly 2005) was developed for coding official records; it captures not only subtypes of maltreatment, but also dimensions such as severity, frequency/chronicity, perpetrator(s), and developmental periods during which maltreatment occurred. The timing of maltreatment (i.e., early onset, early and recent, or recent only) may play an important role in developmental outcomes. The MCS has been used in more than 50 research laboratories in both the United States and Europe and has demonstrated excellent psychometric properties.

Because extensive research information is required if it is to be useful in making policy decisions, researchers must be able to communicate their findings and compare their results across laboratories and across samples. Standardizing and unifying definitions of child maltreatment are fundamental steps toward improving research and hence the knowledge base about abuse and neglect. Systematized definitions are also crucial to ensure the provision of consistent and adequate services to children in need.

DEVELOPMENTAL ANALYSIS

A developmental analysis is essential for tracing the roots, etiology, and nature of maladaptation so that interventions may be timed and guided as well as developmentally appropriate (Toth et al. 2013). In addition, a developmental analysis proves useful for uncovering the compensatory mechanisms—biological, psychological, and social-contextual—that may be used to promote resilient functioning despite the experience of significant adversity (Masten & Cicchetti 2016).

A developmental analysis strives to examine the prior sequences of adaptation or maladaptation in development that have contributed to a given outcome in a particular developmental period. Because developmental psychology assumes a life-span view of developmental processes and aims to delineate how prior development influences later development, a major issue in the discipline is how to determine continuity in the quality of adaptation across developmental time. The same behaviors in different developmental periods may represent quite different levels of adaptation. For example, behaviors indicating competence within a developmental period may indicate incompetence within subsequent developmental periods. Normative behaviors manifested early in development may indicate maladaptation when exhibited at a later time. The manifestation of competence in different developmental periods is rarely indicated by isomorphism in behavior presentation.

PRINCIPLES OF DEVELOPMENTAL PSYCHOPATHOLOGY

A focus on the boundary between normal and abnormal development is central to the field of developmental psychopathology (Cicchetti & Toth 2009, Rutter 2013). Such a perspective emphasizes not only how the study of normal development can inform the understanding of maladaptation and psychopathology, but also how the investigation of risk and pathology can enhance our comprehension of normal development. The investigation of developmental processes in maltreated children can make important contributions to our understanding of the processes underlying normal development. It contributes precision to developmental theory, and it challenges and impels scholars to critically examine extant developmental theories in the light of knowledge about maladaptation, psychopathology, and resilience.

Conversely, to grasp the deviances in a developing system, one must also possess an accurate description of the system itself. To comprehend how abnormalities are transmitted from one developmental level to another, one must first know how the normal transitions from one level of functioning to another take place. Only by understanding the total ongoing development of normal systems is it possible to comprehend developmental deviations as adaptational irregularities of those systems.

Developmental psychopathology is not primarily the study of disorders. That is not to say that the field does not seek to enhance our understanding of psychopathology; however, the central focus of developmental psychopathology is the elucidation of developmental processes and how they function as indicated and elaborated by the examination of extremes in developmental outcome. Such extremes contribute substantial diversity to the possible outcomes in development, thereby enhancing our understanding of developmental processes.

Additionally, developmental psychopathologists are interested in variations in the continuum between the mean and the extremes. These variations may represent individuals who currently are not divergent enough to be considered disordered, but who may progress to further extremes as development continues. Such individuals may be vulnerable to developing future disordered outcomes. Diversity in process and outcome are hallmarks of the developmental psychopathology perspective. The principles of equifinality and multifinality derived from general systems theory are relevant in this regard (von Bertalanffy 1968). Equifinality refers to the observation that a diversity of paths may lead to the same outcome. In contrast, multifinality suggests that any one component may function differently depending on the organization of the system in which it operates (Cicchetti & Rogosch 1996). For example, research in molecular genetics suggests that maltreated children's risk for psychopathology is not inevitable. Gene–environment interaction (G × E) occurs when the effect of exposure to an environmental pathogen (such as child maltreatment; Karg et al. 2011) on a behavioral, health, or biological phenotype is conditional upon a person's genotype or, conversely, when the genotype's effect is moderated by the environment. Specific examples of G × E on (child maltreatment) developmental outcomes are provided in later sections in this article.

A central tenet of developmental psychopathology is that individuals may move between pathological and nonpathological forms of functioning. Adaptive coping mechanisms may be at work even in the presence of pathology (Cicchetti 2010, Masten 2014). Thus, it is only through the consideration of both adaptive and maladaptive processes that it becomes possible to define the presence, nature, and boundaries of the underlying psychopathology. Furthermore, investigators in the field of developmental psychopathology are invested in comprehending how individuals achieve competent adaptation despite experiencing great adversity or prolonged trauma. They also emphasize the importance of understanding the functioning of individuals who, after diverging onto deviant developmental pathways, resume positive functioning and achieve adequate adaptation.

Following advances in the comprehension of developmental processes in both typical and atypical development, research in the field has increasingly incorporated a multilevel approach and an interdisciplinary perspective (Cicchetti & Natsuaki 2014, Pellmar & Eisenberg 2000). To understand typical and atypical development as well as resilience in their full complexity, one must examine and integrate all levels of analysis. Each level both informs and constrains the others. Because the influence of levels on one another is almost always bidirectional, no component, subsystem, or level of organization possesses causal privilege in the developmental system (Thelen & Smith 1998).

THE CASE OF CHILD MALTREATMENT

What happens to individual development when there are severe disturbances in the child-rearing environment? How do these atypical, unexpected organism–environment interactions and transactions influence socioemotional, personality, and neurobiological development?

The investigation of maltreated children affords an opportunity to examine environmental experiences that are far beyond the range of what is normatively encountered. By studying child maltreatment, we can learn more about how typical and atypical environments influence biological and psychological development. An examination of models focusing on average expectable environments and probabilistic epigenesis will enhance our understanding of the processes and mechanisms associated with individual development in the face of severe environmental challenge.

ORGANIZATIONAL PERSPECTIVE

Much of the research conducted on the effects of child maltreatment has been guided by the organizational perspective on development, a powerful theoretical framework for conceptualizing a lifespan approach to risk and resilience as well as normal development. The organizational perspective sees development not as a series of tasks that need to be accomplished and that subsequently decrease in importance; rather, development is conceived as comprising a number of age- and stage-relevant tasks from infancy through adulthood. Although the salience of these tasks may wane in relation to newly emerging issues, the tasks remain important to adaptation over time (Sroufe 2013). A hierarchical picture of adaptation emerges in which the successful resolution of an issue salient at an early stage increases the probability of subsequent successful adjustment. As each new stage-salient issue comes to the fore, opportunities for growth and consolidation as well as challenges and new vulnerabilities arise. These tasks include the development of emotion regulation, the formation of attachment relationships, the development of an autonomous self, the formation of effective peer relationships, and successful adaptation to school. To our knowledge, little research has been conducted on the stage-salient issues of adolescence and emerging adulthood in child maltreatment, such as autonomous self-development, forming close relationships within and across gender, and deriving a cohesive sense of self-identity. These latter issues deserve future attention.

Because each stage-salient issue is also a lifelong task that is integrated and coordinated with each subsequent issue, no one is ever completely inoculated against or totally doomed to maladaptive and/or psychopathological outcomes. Individuals are continuously affected by new socioemotional and biological experiences. Thus, changes in the biological and socioemotional conditions in their homes and in their courses of adaptation—positive or negative—remain possible throughout the life span. Despite this possibility, however, prior adaptation does place constraints on subsequent adaptation. In particular, the longer an individual persists along a maladaptive pathway, the more difficult it is to reclaim a normal developmental trajectory.

This article examines how maltreated children resolve the central developmental tasks of infancy and childhood. Due to space constraints, the focus herein is on the stage-salient issues of emotion, emotion recognition, and emotion regulation; attachment; self-development; and peer relationships.

EMOTION, EMOTION RECOGNITION, AND EMOTION REGULATION

Theorizing about emotional development without considering the deviations that might be expected from prominent and pervasive intra- and extra-organismic disturbances, as well as the transactions among them, would result in an incomplete and ambiguous portrayal of the developmental process. The central function of the emotions system is to motivate and organize behavior. The emotions system is composed of separable components involving dedicated neural processes, expressive behaviors, and subjective experiences or feeling states. Although the emotions system and the cognitive system are highly interactive and have reciprocal causal relations, each system has a degree of independent functioning. The independence is greatest in early childhood and declines thereafter as system intercoordination increases. From this perspective, a central tenet of emotion regulation is the intercoordination of the emotions and cognitive systems. Problems of intersystem communication cause regulation failures, and this dysregulation brings about affective-cognitive products that are maladaptive to particular situations (Calkins & Perry 2016). Emotion regulation is critical both in initiating, motivating, and organizing adaptive behavior and in preventing stressful levels of negative emotions and maladaptive behavior.

A major advantage of investigating emotional development in maltreated children is that whereas the basic emotional environment experienced by most typically developing nonmaltreated children may be so invariant that environmental/experiential influences are overlooked (Pollak et al. 2000), the emotional experiences of maltreated children enable researchers to parse the relative contributions of experience and learning versus innate predispositions. In comparison with nonmaltreating parents, maltreating parents exhibit less positive emotion and more negative emotion, including episodes of intense hostility and interpersonal threat (Cicchetti & Valentino 2006). Moreover, maltreating parents are more likely to isolate themselves and their families from others, thereby minimizing the number of nonparental models of emotional communication to whom their children are exposed. Because brain development occurs most rapidly during the first years of life (Stiles 2008), these aberrant emotional experiences may result in neuropathological connections that undermine effective expression, perception/recognition, regulation, processing, and understanding of emotion (Cicchetti 2002, Cicchetti & Ng 2014).

Divergences in the emotional expression of maltreated children have been observed as early as in infants 3 months of age: Severely physically abused infants have exhibited increased rates of fearfulness, anger, and sadness during mother–infant interactions (Cicchetti & Ng 2014). The early expression of fear and anger is a particularly salient finding, considering that the normative development of these affects does not typically occur until approximately 7–9 months of age (Sroufe 1996). In contrast, neglected infants displayed an attenuated range of emotional expression and an increased duration of negative affect compared to nonmaltreated infants.

Early malevolent care may accelerate the development of negative affect circuitry in the brains of maltreated infants. This may be accomplished by excessive synaptic pruning of the positive affect neural circuits as a result of inadequate or insufficient early positive experiences by abused babies. The accelerated development of negative affect circuitry may be the groundwork for the negativity bias (Ayoub et al. 2006) manifested by abused children in behavioral and psychophysiological studies of attention to facial expressions and in studies of social information processing (see below for empirical examples of negativity bias). Thus, maltreated children may be at risk for developing differential developmental pathways to emotion dysregulation very early in life.

Accurate emotion recognition is critical because it represents the early use of social cues on which children's subsequent interpretations and behavioral responses will depend. The identification of basic emotions from both facial and contextual clues is normatively mastered by the preschool years. Unfortunately, maltreated children evince lower accuracy in recognizing emotions than nonmaltreated children, even after controlling for receptive linguistic ability (Pollak et al. 2000).

Developmentally, early information processing limitations require children to focus their attention on the most salient aspects of their environment (Bjorklund 1997). For children who are physically abused, displays of anger may signal imminent threat. Consequently, Pollak and colleagues (2000) hypothesized that 3- to 5-year-old physically abused children would exhibit an increased sensitivity to anger-related cues, perhaps also resulting in decreased attention to other types of emotional cues. Confirming this hypothesis, they found that physically abused preschoolers perceived angry faces as more salient and distinctive relative to other emotions (e.g., sadness, fear, disgust, happiness) on a perceptual scaling task, whereas nonmaltreated comparison children did not show this pattern. Moreover, when physically abused children were instructed to match facial expressions to emotional situations, they demonstrated a lower threshold for detecting anger compared to demographically comparable nonmaltreated children. Further studies have confirmed this heightened vigilance to anger in physically abused children: Compared to nonmaltreated children, physically abused children display broader perceptual category boundaries for detecting anger (Pollak & Kistler 2002), they require less visual information to perceive angry facial expressions (Pollak & Sinha 2002), and they recognize anger earlier in the formation of the facial expression when fewer cues are available (Pollak et al. 2009).

Psychophysiological studies also provide evidence that physically abused children allocate more attentional resources to the detection of anger but respond similarly to nonmaltreated children when attending to happy and fearful faces. Specifically, measurement of cognitive event-related brain potentials (ERPs) indicates that school-aged maltreated children display larger P3b amplitude when their attention is directed toward angry targets as opposed to happy or fearful ones (Pollak et al. 1997). This pattern of response appears to be specific to anger rather than to negative emotions such as fear (Pollak et al. 2001). P3b amplitude varies as a function of task relevance and has been used to clarify specific cognitive operations such as the evaluation of stimulus significance (Johnson 1993). It may also be reflective of processes involved in the updating of mental representations in working memory. In general, such psychophysiological processes serve to maintain representations of one's environment by highlighting events that are significant.

A study examining the neural correlates of facial affect processing in 15-month-old maltreated and nonmaltreated infants revealed differences between the two groups on three ERP components: P1, P260, and Nc. Findings for the P260 waveform were consistent with previous ERP findings in older maltreated children, revealing a hyperresponsivity to angry relative to happy facial affect in maltreated infants. However, the findings for P1 and Nc waveforms indicated a hyperresponsivity to relative novelty, whereby the maltreated infants had greater amplitude in response to happy facial affect, whereas nonmaltreated infants had greater responsivity to angry faces. The results provided further support for the hypothesis that the experience of maltreatment and the predominately negative emotional tone in maltreating families alter the functioning of neural systems associated with the processing of facial emotion. In particular, the findings suggest that at this early stage in the development of facial affect recognition, novelty of facial emotion is especially salient. These results exemplify the importance of early preventive interventions focused on emotion for children who have experienced maltreatment early in life.

An increased sensitivity to anger might be adaptive for physically abused children, as it would allow for hypervigilant detection of imminent harm; however, successful regulation includes the capacity for flexibility and control over attention. The failure of regulatory capacities that enable flexibility and control makes what is adaptive in the maltreating home maladaptive when generalized to more normative social contexts (Pollak 2008). Pollak & Tolley-Schell (2003) posited that early experiences of abuse may alter the development of perceptual systems by decreasing the minimum amount of threat-related stimulation needed to engage focused attention on the threat-inducing stimuli. If physically abused children respond more quickly and/or strongly to signals of threat, then disengaging attention away from anger may be problematic. Using a selective attention paradigm with an emotional component, Pollak & Tolley-Schell (2003) employed both physiological and behavioral measures to assess 8- to 11-year-old children's orienting reaction and response time during valid trials, and children's disengagement reaction and response time during invalid trials. Psychophysiological data confirmed the hypothesis that physically abused children demonstrate a selective increase in ERP response (as measured by P3b) on invalid angry trials, providing evidence that increased attentional resources are required to disengage from previously cued angry faces only. Physically abused children also demonstrated faster reaction times in the valid angry condition, consistent with the notion that abused children orient rapidly to cues primed by anger. There were no differences, however, in physically abused children's psychophysiological responses or reaction times to happy trials, providing further support for a specific or differential deficit involving attentional processing of anger.

At subsequent developmental periods, physically abused children may manifest social information–processing deficits and difficulties with peer relationships. Social information–processing biases that are prevalent among abused children's relations with peers indicate that maltreated children are more, rather than less, likely to respond to angry or aggressive emotional cues (Dodge et al. 1997, Teisl & Cicchetti 2008). Such social information–processing biases are consistent with the attentional biases exhibited by abused children in response to expressions of anger (Pollak & Tolley-Schell 2003).

Behavioral and psychophysiological evidence of maltreated children's differential processing of affective information suggests that early experiences influence subsequent emotional development and shape the implicated brain circuitry. The effects observed among maltreated children may reflect experience-dependent processes that involve the fine-tuning of attention, learning, perceptual, and memory systems that facilitate the rapid identification of anger (Pollak 2008).

Emotion regulation is a developmentally acquired process that emerges from increasing differentiation and hierarchical integration of biological and psychological systems. Emotion regulation evolves as a function of both intrinsic features and extrinsic socioemotional experiences within the context of early parent–child interactions. At the biological level, important intra-organismic factors for the development of emotion regulation include individual differences in genotypic variation, organizational changes in the structure and function of the central nervous system, cerebral hemispheric lateralization, and the development of neurotransmitter systems. Extra-organismically, children's emotional experiences, expressiveness, and arousal are influenced by caregivers' response to and tolerance of affect (Sroufe 1996). Parents' socialization of affect displays during early interpersonal exchanges serves as the model through which aspects of emotion regulation may be learned.

Defined as the monitoring, evaluating, and modifying of emotional reactions for the purpose of attaining individual goals, emotion regulation optimizes one's adaptive engagement with the environment (Thompson et al. 2008). Because the ability to autonomously regulate one's emotions is thought to emerge from early parent-child relations (Sroufe 1996), maltreatment poses a serious risk to children's development of emotion regulation. An unpredictable and disorganized environment, such as the one found in maltreating homes (Cicchetti & Toth 2005), would make children particularly vulnerable to frequent negative emotional experiences, including anger, frustration, reactivity, and irritability from caregivers. Consequently, maltreated children are likely to experience overwhelming emotional arousal that leads to difficulties managing and processing negative emotions.

Thus, child maltreatment represents a significant threat to the optimal development of affective processing abilities. Given the severe disturbances in the average expectable environment provided by maltreating caregivers, considerable evidence has mounted to demonstrate the detrimental effects of maltreatment on children's emotional development and regulation. Moreover, in accord with the organizational perspective on development, adequate emotion regulation serves as a foundation for the successful development of the subsequent stage-salient issues of forming secure attachment relationships, an autonomous and coherent self-system, and effective relationships with peers. By contrast, early failures of emotion regulation increase the probability that a child will develop insecure and disorganized attachment relationships, self-system impairments, and difficulties with peers. These repeated developmental disruptions create a profile of relatively enduring vulnerability factors that places maltreated children at high risk for future maladaptation (Cicchetti & Toth 2015).

The early maladaptive processing of stimuli that contributes to affective regulatory problems may lay the foundation for future difficulties in modulating affect. A number of cross-sectional investigations have corroborated the prediction, emanating from the organizational perspective, that maltreated children are at increased risk of a developmental progression from affect regulation problems to behavioral dysregulation.

In an investigation of 4- to 6-year-old children, approximately 80% of maltreated preschoolers exhibited patterns of emotion dysregulation (i.e., undercontrolled/ambivalent and overcontrolled/unresponsive types) in response to witnessing interadult anger, compared to only 37% of the nonmaltreated comparison children. Undercontrolled/ambivalent emotion regulation patterns were associated with maternal reports of child behavior problems and were found to mediate the link between maltreatment and children's symptoms of anxiety or depression (Maughan & Cicchetti 2002). Findings such as these support a sensitization model whereby repeated exposure to anger and familial violence results in greater emotional reactivity.

During the school-age years, children continue to develop emotion regulation skills as they encounter increasing socialization demands from peers as well as from family. Shields & Cicchetti (1998) found that maltreated children were more verbally and physically assaultive than were the nonmaltreated comparison children, with physical abuse placing children at heightened risk for aggression. Maltreated children were also more likely than comparison children to exhibit the distractibility, overactivity, and poor concentration characteristic of children who experience deficits in attention modulation. Physically and sexually abused children also displayed attention disturbances suggestive of subclinical or nonpathological dissociation, including daydreaming, blank stares, and confusion. Deficits in emotion regulation were also evident, in that maltreated children were less likely than comparison children to show adaptive regulation and more likely to display emotional lability-negativity and contextually inappropriate expressions of emotion. Such pervasive deficits in maltreated children's regulatory capacities are cause for special concern, because the ability to modulate behavior, attention, and emotion underlies children's adaptive functioning in a number of key domains, including self-development, academic achievement, and interpersonal relationships (Cicchetti 1991, Shonk & Cicchetti 2001).

Shields & Cicchetti (1998) also demonstrated that impaired capacities for attention modulation contribute to emotion dysregulation in maltreated children. Specifically, attention deficits mediate maltreatment's effects on emotional lability-negativity, inappropriate affect, and attenuated emotion regulation. Attention processes that suggest subclinical or nonpathological dissociation also contribute to maltreated children's deficits in emotion regulation. Thus, abuse seems to potentiate disruptions in attention that result in a relative detachment from and unawareness of one's surrounding, as well as in hyperattunement and hyperreactivity to the social surrounding (Pollak & Tolley-Schell 2003, Rieder & Cicchetti 1989). Together, these deficits appear to compromise maltreated children's ability to regulate behavior and affect in social settings.

Romens & Pollak (2012) conducted an investigation of attention patterns for sad, depression-relevant cues in children with and without maltreatment experiences. They also assessed individual differences in attention related to reactivity to and regulation of a sad emotional state. The maltreated children exhibited an attention bias toward sad faces after experimental initiation of a sad emotional state. The subgroup of maltreated children who were ruminative manifested a relatively stable pattern of heightened attention to sad faces, regardless of emotional state. Consequently, it is conceivable that individual difference in emotion regulation may be utilized to identify which maltreated children may have an increased risk for depression (Romens & Pollak 2012). Relatedly, Shackman & Pollak (2014) found that physically abused children exhibited greater negative affect and more aggressive behavior compared to nonmaltreated children, and this relationship was mediated by children's allocation of attention to angry faces. These findings suggest that physical abuse leads to the dysregulation of both aggression and negative affect and that this increases the likelihood that physically abused children will develop externalizing behavior disorders.

Additional evidence suggests that emotional dysregulation may mediate the increased risk for bullying and victimization that has been noted among maltreated children (Shields & Cicchetti 2001), highlighting how the internalization of salient aspects of the early caregiving relationship may have maladaptive implications among these children. As maltreated children are victimized by parents, they may develop a working model of relationships as dangerous and malevolent that incorporates the roles of both bully and victim. These cognitive-affective structures may then guide behaviors and peer interactions, promoting atypical emotional responsiveness and coloring children's interpretations of the behavior of social partners. Supporting this hypothesis, Shields et al. (2001) found that 8- to 12-year-old maltreated children's narrative representations of their caregivers were more negative-constricted and less positive-coherent than those of nonmaltreated children. Maladaptive caregiver representations were associated with greater emotion dysregulation, aggression, and peer rejection, whereas positive-coherent representations were related to prosocial behaviors and peer preferences as indexed by peer rating and adult observation.

Furthermore, Kim-Spoon et al. (2013) investigated the longitudinal contributions of emotion regulation and emotional lability-negativity to internalizing symptomatology. A sample of over 300 maltreated ($N = 171$) and nonmaltreated ($N = 151$) children were followed from age 7 to 10 years. For both maltreated and nonmaltreated children, emotion regulation was a mediator between emotional lability-negativity and internalizing symptomatology, whereas emotional lability-negativity did not mediate the relation between emotion regulation and externalizing symptomatology. Early maltreatment was associated with high emotional lability-negativity (at age 7) that contributed to poor emotion regulation (at age 8), which in turn was predictive of increases in internalizing symptomatology (from age 8 to 9).

These findings suggest that emotion regulation and emotional lability-negativity may be important factors in identifying distinct pathways to child psychopathology. Specifically, low emotional lability-negativity and adaptive emotion regulation appear to play protective roles in the development of internalizing symptomatology. These findings also suggest that emotion regulation is an important mediational process between emotional lability-negativity and internalizing symptomatology. Therefore, improving emotion regulation skills in children is likely to be an effective strategy to impede the subsequent development of internalizing symptomatology. The results also imply that emotion regulation can be targeted to reduce the deleterious effects of increased emotional lability-negativity after early maltreatment experiences, thus preventing internalizing symptomatology.

FORMATION OF ATTACHMENT RELATIONSHIPS

The establishment of a secure attachment relationship between an infant and his or her caregiver represents a primary task during the first year of life. Attachment theorists have posited that as development proceeds, a secure attachment relationship provides a base from which to explore and, ultimately, contribute to the integration of cognitive, socioemotional, and behavioral capacities that influence ongoing and future relationships as well as the understanding of the self (Bowlby

1969, Sroufe 1990). Children construct internal working models of their attachment figures out of their interactions with their caregiver, their own actions, and the feedback they receive from these interactions. Once organized, these internal working models tend to operate outside of conscious awareness and are thought to be relatively resistant to change. Children formulate their conceptions of how acceptable or unacceptable they are in the eyes of their attachment figures (i.e., their self-image) based on their interactional history with their primary caregivers. Maltreated children experience distortions of the caregiving environment in which internal working models develop. Exposed to insensitive and pathological care, maltreated children develop negative expectations regarding the availability and trustworthiness of others, as well as mental representations of the self as incompetent and unworthy (Stronach et al. 2011).

Maltreated children are especially at risk for developing insecure disorganized (Type D) attachments (see Cyr et al. 2010 for a meta-analysis). Estimates of the manifestations of disorganized attachment among maltreated children range from 80% to over 90%. In the strange situation paradigm (Ainsworth et al. 1978), Type D infants demonstrate inconsistent and disorganized strategies for coping with separations from and reunions with their caregivers (Hesse & Main 2006). In addition, infants with disorganized attachments display bizarre behaviors such as freezing, stilling, and stereotypies, as well as contradictory behavior directed toward their attachment figures (e.g., approaching their parents with head averted).

A number of explanations have been proffered to account for the preponderance of disorganized attachment relationships between maltreated children and their primary caregivers. Because inconsistent care is a hallmark of maltreating families, some investigators have hypothesized that the combination of insensitive overstimulation and insensitive understimulation may lead to the contradictory behaviors observed among maltreated infants classified as Type D. According to Hesse & Main (2006), attachment disorganization is caused by frightened and frightening parental behavior, which is thought to have its origins in unresolved parental trauma. Maltreating behaviors are arguably among the most frightening parenting behaviors, placing children in an irresolvable paradox in which their attachment figures are simultaneously their source of safety and their source of fear.

Genetic variation also has been explored as a contributor to the development of disorganized attachment; however, little consistent evidence has emerged for a candidate gene main effect on attachment disorganization (see Lujik et al. 2011). For example, among maltreated children, Cicchetti et al. (2011) found that neither the serotonin transporter gene (5-HTT) nor the dopamine receptor D4 gene (DRD4) were associated with disorganized attachment. They concluded that the anomalous aspects of maltreating parents may be so robust that they overpower the potential effect of genetic variation in the etiological pathway to attachment disorganization (Cicchetti et al. 2011). In contrast, a recent investigation of over 700 Norwegian children who were not maltreated revealed that the *catechol-O-methyltransferase Val158Met* genotype moderated the effect of disorganized attachment on the social development of 4- to 6-year-old children.

Although attachment is conceptualized as an important stage-salient developmental task during the first year of life, attachment security continues to exert its influence on development across the life span. First, substantial stability in insecure and disorganized patterns of attachment has been observed among maltreated children (Barnett et al. 1999). Second, disorganized attachment initiates a maladaptive trajectory that heightens the risk for future relational dysfunction as well as various forms of psychopathology (Hesse & Main 2006). Finally, in a recent 22-year longitudinal investigation of the influence of early infant attachment to the mother on emotion regulation in adulthood, attachment status at 18 months predicted neural responding during the regulation of positive affect 20 years later (Moutsiana et al. 2014). These findings demonstrate the powerful influence that early disturbances in attachment can exert across the life span.

DEVELOPMENT OF AN AUTONOMOUS SELF

The development of an integrated sense of self typically occurs in the toddler years, arising from the successful resolution of previous stage-salient tasks, such as early emotion regulation and the formation of a secure attachment relationship. Early caregiving experiences serve as the basis for the development of representational models of the attachment figure as well as corresponding and coherent representational models of the self and of the self in relation to others (Fonagy et al. 2007). As discussed above, many maltreated infants fail to develop an organized pattern of attachment, increasing the probability of subsequent perturbations in representational development. Indeed, maltreated children show disruptions in many aspects of the self-system.

Aberrations in self-development have been observed as early as in children 18 months of age, as demonstrated by investigations of visual self-recognition. On the mirror-rouge paradigm, infants and toddlers examine their rouge-altered noses in a mirror. Maltreated and nonmaltreated children are comparable in their capacity to recognize themselves; however, differences emerge with respect to their affective responses. Specifically, maltreated toddlers are more likely than nonmaltreated comparison children to display neutral or negative emotions upon viewing their images in a mirror (Schneider-Rosen & Cicchetti 1991). This finding may be interpreted as reflecting negative feelings about the self in maltreated youngsters. Negative self-system processes continue to be evident in the preschool period. Additionally, maltreated children's narrative representations of parents and of self are more negative than those of nonmaltreated children (Toth et al. 2013). Moreover, physically abused children possess more grandiose self-representations. These variations by subtype may reflect differences in maltreating experiences. For example, grandiose self-representations may reflect a coping process to maintain personal control in an adverse and threatening home environment, whereas negative self-representations may develop from the chronic absence of attention and validation in a neglecting home.

A recent investigation of the mediating role of self-system processes in physically abused 4- to 7-year-old children identified subgroups of abused children that differed in their internal working models of relationships (Hawkins & Haskett 2014). These differences were related to child adjustment, with children who had more positive and fewer negative representations evidencing fewer internalizing or externalizing behavior problems.

Research among school-age maltreated children provides further evidence of self-system deviation. Relative to teacher ratings, younger maltreated children overestimate their own sense of social competence and peer acceptance. These children may be engaging in defensive processing in order to increase their sense of competence (Cicchetti & Toth 2015). In fact, research indicated that the development of a grandiose self, as reflected by inflated social self-efficacy, may serve as a protective factor in the link between maltreatment and internalizing symptomatology. However, as maltreated children mature, they tend to underestimate their competence and are rated by teachers as having lower self-esteem (Cicchetti & Toth 2015).

In another examination of self-system processes in maltreated children, Bennett et al. (2010) studied shame proneness in child neglect. Shame is a highly negative and psychically painful state in which the individual perceives the entire self as defective (Lewis 1995). Bennett et al. (2010) found that neglected children reported more shame proneness and more depressive symptomatology than nonmaltreated comparison children. Prior investigations of heterogeneous groups of physically abused, sexually abused, and neglected children found elevated levels of shame. Thus, the findings of Bennett et al. (2010) extended work on shame to a group of neglected children and are consistent with the results of these earlier studies.

Finally, maltreated children are at risk for developing dissociative features and dissociation, perhaps the most severe deficit in the integration of the self (Macfie et al. 2001a,b; Toth et al.

2011; Valentino et al. 2008). Dissociation is a disruption in the normal integration of consciousness, memory, identity, emotion, perception, body representation, motor control, and behavior (Am. Psychiatr. Assoc. 2013). Dissociation interferes with the normal development of the self and healthy functioning in core areas of development, predicting lack of sense of self-agency; low self-esteem; poor abilities in symbolic thinking, peer competence, and affect modulation; and attention problems (Carlson et al. 2009).

The link between maltreatment and dissociation has been observed across a wide age range, from preschoolers to adults. Among preschoolers, physical and sexual abuse appear to be the most robustly related to dissociative features, with physical abuse emerging as particularly salient for the development of dissociation at clinical levels. From a developmental perspective, the timing and chronicity of traumatic experiences are key to understanding their impact on self-system functioning (Carlson et al. 2009). Furthermore, longitudinal research indicates that fragmentation in self-organization has been found in sexually abused adolescent girls, who demonstrated deviant splitting between positive and negative self-references (Calverley et al. 1994).

PEER RELATIONSHIPS

Theories inspired by an organizational perspective on development have suggested that the negative relational patterns acquired in a maltreating environment become incorporated into the structures that are pertinent for successful peer relations. Within the context of their early caregiving experiences, maltreated children may develop negative expectations regarding the self and others, as well as a concept of relationships as involving victimization and coercion. These internalizations lead to the selection and structuring of later social interactions so that they recreate and validate familiar relationship patterns. Research supports this conceptualization of continuity in relational functioning, because maltreated children have been shown to exhibit a broad range of difficulties in the peer domain.

With regard to peer relations, maltreated children appear to traverse one of two general developmental pathways: (a) withdrawal from peer interactions or (b) heightened aggression toward peers. In addition to these two generally diverging pathways, a subgroup of maltreated and non-maltreated children has been identified who demonstrate both aggressive and withdrawn behaviors (Cicchetti & Toth 2015). Among maltreated children, those who evidence high aggression and high withdrawal demonstrate lower social effectiveness than nonmaltreated youngsters. This unusual pattern of interaction with peers is consistent with the attachment history of maltreated children, which may be related to disorganized representational models and may result in disturbances in social encounters. By revealing indications of a response predisposition to both fight and flight, maltreated children's interactions with peers lend support to the notion that these children have internalized both sides of their relationships with their caregivers. Thus, maltreated children's representational models may have elements of both the victim and the victimizer, and these models may be enacted in peer relationships (Banny et al. 2013).

The effects of maltreatment on disrupted peer group functioning may be explained by perturbations in cognitive and emotional processes. With regard to social information processing, physically abused children make errors in encoding social cues, exhibit biases toward attributing hostile intent, generate more aggressive responses, and positively evaluate aggression as an appropriate response (Teisl & Cicchetti 2008). These deficits, in turn, mediate the association between physical abuse and aggression in the peer context. Whereas maladaptive social cognition emerges as a salient explanatory factor for physically abused children, emotion dysregulation appears to play an integral role in the link between maltreatment and aggression for all maltreated groups. Poor emotion regulation also mediates the association between maltreatment and victimization by peers.

PERSONALITY ORGANIZATION AND PERSONALITY DISORDERS

Maltreatment has also been implicated in the etiology of personality disorders. Given that personality disorders do not emerge spontaneously at the age of 18, the cut-off established in the psychiatric nomenclature, researchers have begun to adopt a developmental psychopathology approach to identify early precursors and processes that confer vulnerability to later personality pathology (Cicchetti & Crick 2009a,b).

Consistent with this approach, Rogosch & Cicchetti (2005) found that maltreated children exhibit higher mean levels of potential precursors to borderline personality disorder (e.g., emotional lability, conflictual relationships with adults and peers, relational aggression, self-harm) than do nonmaltreated children comparisons. In a prospective investigation of personality organization, Rogosch & Cicchetti (2004) found that 6-year-old maltreated children exhibited lower agreeableness, conscientiousness, and openness to experience as well as higher neuroticism than did nonmaltreated children. Analysis of personality clusters revealed that the majority of nonmaltreated children were represented in the adaptive gregarious and reserved personality clusters, whereas maltreated children largely accounted for the makeup of less adaptive personality profiles (i.e., undercontroller, overcontroller, and dysphoric). Furthermore, longitudinal stabilities were observed across ages 7, 8, and 9, suggesting continuity in maltreated children's personality liabilities.

In a longitudinal investigation of the effects of child maltreatment on subsequent personality processes, Kim et al. (2009) followed maltreated and nonmaltreated children between the ages of 6 and 10 years:

> Growth mixture modeling indicated multifinality in personality development depending on the risk status (i.e., maltreated versus nonmaltreated). Two trajectory classes of ego resiliency were identified for maltreated children; those who showed a declining trajectory exhibited greater maladjustment. In contrast, three trajectory classes of ego control were identified for nonmaltreated children; the subgroups showing increases in ego undercontrol or dramatic changes from high ego undercontrol to high ego overcontrol exhibited poor adjustment. Experiencing multiple maltreatment subtypes and physical/sexual abuse were related to higher levels of ego undercontrol and externalizing symptomatology, whereas early onset of maltreatment was associated with the low and decreasing trajectory of ego resiliency and higher levels of internalizing symptomatology. The findings suggest that ego resiliency and ego control, personality processes related to self-regulation, may be important factors in identifying distinct pathways to later personality disorders as well as pathways to resilient functioning. (Kim et al. 2009, p. 889)

In a landmark epidemiological study, Caspi and colleagues (2002) followed a large sample of male children from birth to adulthood to ascertain why some maltreated children grow up to develop antisocial personality disorder, whereas others do not. Results revealed that a functional polymorphism in the promoter region (where gene transcription is initiated) of the monoamine oxidase A (*MAOA*) gene moderated the effect of child maltreatment. The *MAOA* gene is located on the X chromosome and encodes the *MAOA* enzyme, which metabolizes neurotransmitters such as norepinephrine, serotonin, and dopamine, rendering them inactive. Maltreated children with the genotype conferring high *MAOA* activity were significantly less likely to develop antisocial behavior problems than maltreated children with the low-activity *MAOA* genotype. In addition, maltreatment and nonmaltreatment groups did not differ on *MAOA* activity, suggesting a lack of an evocative G × E correlation as an explanation for their findings. Many, but not all, subsequent studies have been successful in replicating Caspi and colleagues' original findings and in extending them downward to samples of children and adolescents (Kim-Cohen et al. 2006).

Weder et al. (2009) examined a G × E interaction of *MAOA* genotype and maltreatment in children residing in foster care. The maltreated children represented the extreme on a continuum of adversity. They were assessed at a highly stressful time, shortly after they had been removed from their parents' care because they had been physically abused. A total trauma index score was derived based on exposure to physical abuse, sexual abuse, domestic violence, multiple out-of-home placements, and community violence. Scores were rated from mild to moderate to extreme. Weder et al. (2009) detected a significant interaction between exposure to moderate levels of trauma and the low-activity *MAOA* genotype in conferring increased risk for aggression. Children who were exposed to extreme levels of trauma had high aggression scores regardless of *MAOA* genotype. Extreme levels of aggression appear to overshadow the effects of *MAOA* genotype, especially when traumatized children are experiencing acute stress. The findings of Weder and colleagues are consistent with those of Caspi et al. (2002).

As in Caspi et al.'s (2002) original study, Cicchetti et al. (2012) conducted an investigation to examine a G × E interaction of *MAOA* genotype and maltreatment in school-age boys showing early signs of antisocial behavior. For lifetime antisocial behaviors, Cicchetti et al. (2012) did not find *MAOA* to contribute to models of antisocial behavior as reported by peers or adults beyond the influence of maltreatment effects. The G × E interaction effect was significant. Among nonmaltreated boys, those with low-activity *MAOA* genotypes had significantly higher observer-reported symptoms of antisocial behavior than those with high-activity *MAOA* genotypes. Moreover, maltreated boys in the low-activity *MAOA* group had higher self-reported antisocial behavior than nonmaltreated boys. A similar pattern of findings was observed for child self-report of antisocial behavior in the past six months, as the G × E interaction was significant. Specifically, maltreated boys with low-activity *MAOA* genotypes had higher recent antisocial behavior than those with high-activity genotypes. No significant differences were found among nonmaltreated boys based on the *MAOA* genotype group. Furthermore, maltreated boys with low-activity *MAOA* genotypes had higher-level self-reported antisocial symptoms than nonmaltreated boys. The risk for antisocial behavior associated with child maltreatment was reduced among boys with high-activity *MAOA* genotypes. The findings of Cicchetti et al. (2012) are consistent with those reported by Caspi et al. (2002) and Weder et al. (2009).

Byrd & Manuck (2014) conducted a meta-analysis of studies testing the interaction of *MAOA* genotype and childhood adversities/maltreatment on antisocial outcomes in predominately non-clinical samples. Consistent with the findings of Caspi et al. (2002), for males early maltreatment predicted antisocial outcomes more strongly for low-activity, relative to high-activity, *MAOA* genotype. For females, in contrast, *MAOA* did not interact with early life adversities, and maltreatment alone predicted antisocial behavior in females who had the high-activity *MAOA* genotype.

In a related study, Cicchetti et al. (2014) conducted an investigation in which

...gene-environment-gender effects in predicting child borderline personality disorder among maltreated and nonmaltreated low-income children (*N* = 1,051) were examined. Adult-, peer-, and self-report assessments of borderline precursor indicators were obtained, as well as child self-report on the Borderline Personality Features Scale for Children. Genetic variants of the oxytocin receptor genotype (*OXTR*) and the *FK505* binding protein 5 gene *CATT* haplotype were investigated. Children who self-reported high levels of borderline personality symptomatology were differentiated by adults, peers, and additional self-reports on indicators of emotional instability, conflictual relationships with peers and adults, preoccupied attachment, and indicators of self-harm and suicide ideation. Maltreated children also were more likely to evince many of these difficulties relative to nonmaltreated children. A series of analyses of covariance, controlling for age and ancestrally informative markers, indicated significant Maltreatment x Gene x Gender three-way interactions. Consideration of the maltreatment parameters of subtype, onset, and recency expanded understanding of variation among maltreated children. The three-way interaction effects demonstrated differential patterns among girls and boys. Among girls the gene-environment interaction was more consistent with a diathesis-stress model (Gottesman & Shields 1972), whereas among boys a differential-sensitivity to the environment (Belsky et al. 2007, Ellis et al. 2011) interaction effect was indicated. Moreover, the genetic variants associated with greater risk for higher borderline symptomatology, dependent on maltreatment experiences, were opposite in girls compared to boys. The findings have important implications for understanding variability in early predictors of borderline personality pathology. (p. 831)

EFFECTS OF MALTREATMENT ON NEUROBIOLOGICAL DEVELOPMENT AND FUNCTIONING

There has been a burgeoning of interest in conducting neuroimaging research to comprehend how early adverse experiences such as child maltreatment exert their effects on the developing brain (Hostinar et al. 2014). Multiple brain regions and neural circuits are disrupted by the experience of child abuse and neglect (Cicchetti & Toth 2015). The aberrant neural circuitry most likely contributes to the variability in phenotype (i.e., multifinality) observed in maltreated individuals. Scholars have conducted research on the effects of child maltreatment on neurobiological development for nearly two decades. There is now growing evidence that child maltreatment affects specific regions of the brain (Hart & Rubia 2012, McCrory et al. 2010). The pathways most affected in maltreated children and adolescents are predominately in fronto-limbic networks. These comprise the prefrontal cortex (PFC), including the orbitofrontal cortex and anterior cingulate cortex, and the amygdala (but not the hippocampus, which may show a volume reduction in emerging adulthood) (Hart & Rubia 2012, McCrory et al. 2010, Teicher et al. 2012). A recent investigation provides preliminary evidence that the amygdala may have a sensitive period in adolescence (Pechtel et al. 2014). A very consistent finding in maltreated children and adolescents is structural abnormalities of the corpus callosum and the cerebellum (Rinne-Albers et al. 2013, Teicher et al. 2004); most typically these are volume and area reductions. Additionally, diffusion tensor imaging studies have revealed deficits in structural connectivity between the anterior cingulate cortex and the dorsolateral, orbitofrontal, and ventromedial PFC (Hart & Rubia 2012), thereby suggesting abnormalities in prefrontal brain networks.

In terms of functional MRI, investigations suggest that maltreatment experiences are associated with hypoactivity in the PFC of the dorsolateral and ventromedial PFC. The atypical activation in these brain regions occurs during response inhibition, working memory, and emotion processing tasks (Hart & Rubia 2012).

CHILD MALTREATMENT AND RESILIENCE

In some individuals, deviations from the average expectable environment increase the likelihood to develop maladaptive functioning, whereas other individuals demonstrate positive adaptation in the face of the same challenges. Resilience is conceived as a dynamic developmental process encompassing the attainment of positive adaptation despite exposure to significant threat, severe adversity, or trauma, which typically constitute major assaults on the processes underlying biological and psychological development (Luthar et al. 2000, Masten & Cicchetti 2015, Southwick et al. 2014). Resilience is not a magical phenomenon (Masten 2014). The same developmental cascades that can amplify maladaptive outcomes over time can perpetuate or amplify positive outcomes when the individual benefits from some combination of experiences and/or biological propensities that tip the initial balance toward adaptive outcomes (Cicchetti 2013).

The occurrence of resilient outcomes in maltreated children points out that self-righting tendencies in human development may be strong, even in the face of deviance and failure in the environment (Cicchetti 2013, Masten 2014). At one level, different parts of the brain may attempt to compensate for the negative influences; at another, maltreated individuals may seek out new experiences in areas where they possess strengths. Because plasticity is a central feature of the mammalian brain, early neurobiological anomalies or aberrant experiences should not be considered as determining the ultimate fate of the maltreated child (Cicchetti & Curtis 2006). Discovering how maltreated children develop and function resiliently despite their multitudes of adverse experiences offers promise for informing the design, implementation, and multilevel evaluation of prevention and intervention trials (Luthar & Cicchetti 2000).

To provide an illustration of socioemotional and personality pathways to resilience in maltreated children, a three-year longitudinal study conducted in a summer camp context (Cicchetti & Rogosch 2012) found that ego resiliency and moderate ego control, as well as self-system variables, predicted resilient functioning in maltreated children; in contrast, ego resiliency, perceived emotional availability of the mother, and relationship quality with camp counselors were significantly more likely to be predictive of resilient functioning in nonmaltreated children from comparably low socioeconomic backgrounds. This study utilized a composite measure of resilience that included multimethod, multi-informant assessments of competent peer relations, school success, and low levels of internalizing and externalizing psychopathology. Relationships were more central to developing resilient outcomes in nonmaltreated children, whereas self-system processes and personality characteristics were more central to resilient outcomes in maltreated children. Thus, self-reliance, personal conviction, and self-confidence, in concert with interpersonal reserve, may bode well for the development of resilient adaptation in maltreated children.

In addition to psychosocial predictors of resilience, a number of biological variables also have been shown to be predictive of resilient functioning. These include neuroendocrine regulation and left hemispheric activation asymmetry (see Cicchetti 2013 for an elaboration). To our knowledge, there has been only one molecular genetic study of resilient functioning in maltreated children. To examine the processes underlying the development of resilience at the molecular genetic level of analysis, Cicchetti & Rogosch (2012) identified a multicomponent index of resilient function. They selected four theoretically and empirically informed candidate genes that have been found to be related to behaviors associated with resilient functioning—*5-HTTLPR*, *CRHR1*, *DRD4-521C/T*, and *OXTR*—and investigated genetic variants in each of these genes.

Maltreatment consistently exerted a strong, adverse main effect on resilient functioning; however, more of the gene variants of the four respective genes were shown to have a main effect on resilience. In contrast, $G \times E$ effects were obtained and a similar pattern emerged for all four genes: A particular genotype was found to differentiate strongly between levels of resilient function in maltreated and nonmaltreated children. Contrary to the typical $G \times E$ studies on psychopathology, the results of the Cicchetti & Rogosch (2012) investigation revealed that genetic variation had a negligible effect in predicting resilient functioning in the maltreated group, whereas genotypic variation was shown to contribute to higher resilient functioning in nonmaltreated children when they possessed a particular genotype relative to maltreated children with the same genotype.

Cicchetti & Rogosch's (2012) findings suggest that the genes included in their investigation appear to be minimally related to resilient functioning in maltreated children for each of the genes examined. Genetic variation had a stronger impact on resilient functioning among the nonmaltreated children who also resided in stressful poverty-laden environments. Accordingly, it appears that the powerful main effects of maltreatment on resilience may have overshadowed any potential contribution of genetics to resilient functioning in abused and neglected children.

TRANSLATIONAL IMPLICATIONS

The quintessential goal of the field of prevention science is to intervene in the course of development to ameliorate or eliminate the emergence of maladaptation or psychopathology. Developmental psychopathology, with its focus on the dialectic between the study of normality and pathology, is in a unique position to provide an important theoretical foundation for prevention science (Ialongo et al. 2006, Inst. Med. 1994).

Developmental psychopathologists who adhere to an organizational perspective direct prevention science to focus on the progressive organization of developmental competencies and incompetencies in the course of epigenesis, with the goal of structuring preventive interventions (Ialongo et al. 2006). To effect change in the course of development and avert psychopathological outcomes, preventive interventions informed by an organizational perspective should focus on promoting competence and reducing ineffective resolution of the stage-salient issues that emerge at different developmental periods in ontogenesis. Adopting the approach emphasized by organizational theorists may help achieve the deflection of maladaptation onto more adaptive developmental pathways, thereby enhancing the individual's greater likelihood of subsequent successful adaptation (Masten 2014, Masten & Cicchetti 2016). Inherent in the organizational perspective is the importance of early intervention, before developmental liabilities may become consolidated (Toth et al. 2013).

The findings of randomized control trial (RCT) interventions also possess important implications for developmental theory. As developmental experiments, randomized control prevention trials provide a wealth of information about the processes of typical and atypical development (Howe et al. 2002, Ialongo et al. 2006). The translation of developmental theory into the design and implementation of preventive interventions and the results of these trials must form a circular link back to the conceptual framework to advance both developmental theory and future randomized intervention trials. If a randomized prevention trial is able to alter the developmental course and to reduce the risk of the disorder or negative outcome, its results can contribute to our understanding of developmental processes (Howe et al. 2002). Conversely, if the reduction of a targeted risk factor does not appear to have altered the pathogenic process, then that risk factor should not be viewed as a causal agent but may be a marker of atypical development (Kraemer et al. 1997).

Cicchetti et al. (2006) conducted a theoretically informed RCT for maltreating mothers and their 1-year-old infants. One-year-old infants from maltreating families ($N = 137$) and their mothers were randomly assigned to one of three intervention conditions: (*a*) child-parent psychotherapy (CPP), (*b*) psychoeducational parenting intervention (PPI), and (*c*) community standard (CS) controls. A fourth group of infants from nonmaltreating families ($N = 52$) and their mothers served as an additional low-income normative comparison (NC) group. At baseline, mothers in the maltreatment group, relative to mothers in the nonmaltreatment group, reported greater abuse and neglect in their own childhoods, more insecure relationships with their own mothers, more maladaptive parenting attitudes, more parenting stress, and lower family support, and they were observed to evince lower maternal sensitivity. Infants in the maltreatment groups had significantly higher rates of disorganized attachment than infants in the NC group. In a postintervention follow-up at age 26 months, children in the CPP and PPI groups demonstrated substantial increases in secure attachment, whereas increases in secure attachment were not found for the CS and NC groups. Moreover, disorganized attachment continued to predominate in the CS group. These results were maintained when intent-to-treat analyses were conducted.

Interestingly, and somewhat surprisingly, both CPP, a relational intervention, and PPI, a nonrelational intervention, were found to be equally efficacious in fostering secure attachment and in reducing disorganized attachment in infants from maltreating families (Cicchetti et al. 2006). However, in a one-year longitudinal follow-up examining the sustained efficacy of these intervention models, only CPP was found to be efficacious in continuing to promote security of attachment over time (Pickreign-Stronach et al. 2013). These findings suggest that, in cases of extremely maladaptive parenting, more intensive models of interventions that go beyond parent skills training (such as CPP) may be necessary.

The translation of knowledge from the field of developmental psychopathology into the conduct of this clinical trial underscores the importance of broadening such efforts. The results of this RCT are both gratifying and sobering. The fact that plasticity is possible during infancy and that even the most disorganized form of attachment is modifiable in extremely dysfunctional mother-child dyads offers significant hope for thousands of young children and their families. By fostering secure attachment, costlier interventions such as foster care placement, special education services, residential treatment, and incarceration can be averted. Unfortunately, these results also shed light on the harsh reality of the ineffectiveness of services currently being provided in many communities.

An area of paramount importance to move the field forward involves the elucidation of underlying biological processes that are influenced by child maltreatment and of how they may be affected by intervention or moderate treatment effects (Cicchetti & Toth 2015). Given the presence of diverse forms of psychopathology in individuals with histories of child maltreatment (Cicchetti & Valentino 2006), future research will need to disentangle the effects of maltreatment from psychiatric comorbidity when evaluating structural and functional brain anomalies. Although considerably more basic research on neuroimaging in maltreated populations, particularly children and adolescents, is needed, the importance of neuroimaging assessments into RCTs could provide information on the potential malleability of the brain to psychosocial interventions.

Determining the multiple levels at which change is engendered through RCTs will provide insight into the mechanisms of change, the extent to which neural plasticity may be promoted, and the interrelations between biological and psychological processes in the development of maladaptation, psychopathology, and resilience in maltreated children. It would thus be possible to conceptualize efficacious resilience-promoting interventions as examples of experience-dependent neural plasticity (Cicchetti & Curtis 2006). If assessments of biological systems are routinely incorporated into the measurement armamentaria employed in resilience-promoting interventions, then we will be in a position to discover whether the nervous system can be modified by experience (Cicchetti & Gunnar 2008).

FUTURE ISSUES

1. It is of paramount importance that rigorous and precise definitions of maltreatment experiences be incorporated into all investigations of child maltreatment etiology, sequelae, and intervention.

2. Most investigations of the consequences of child maltreatment have examined neurobiological and psychological systems separately. The time has come to conduct longitudinal research that examines biological and psychological systems concurrently over developmental time.

3. It remains to be discovered whether the neurobiological structural and/or functional difficulties displayed by many abused and neglected children are irreversible or, if reversible, whether there are sensitive periods when neural plasticity is more likely to occur. Because the brain is a dynamic, self-organizing system that is mutable, future neuroimaging research should strive to ascertain whether the brain structure and functioning of resilient maltreated children differ from those of resilient nonmaltreated children.

4. Although some progress in this area has occurred, it is imperative that future research continues to examine mediators that contribute to our understanding of the mechanisms that underlie both the developmental sequelae of maltreatment and intervention efficacy.

5. Despite rapid, promising advances, our understanding of the genetic moderation of intervention outcome, particularly for maltreated children, remains in its infancy. Most interventions have strived to change the environment with no consideration for genetic involvement. Thus, interventions targeting both gene and environment are in a nascent state, and such work must occur more frequently in the future.

6. Research on $G \times E$ and on epigenetics needs to incorporate, as well as emphasize, a developmental perspective (i.e., $G \times E \times D$). Genes may influence how environmental experience affects the developmental process, and this may operate differently at various developmental periods. Moreover, the effects of genes and experience at a particular period may be influenced by the effects of prior development. Environments may affect the timing of genetic effects and gene expression. In addition, there are experience effects on the epigenome, and these also may operate differently across the course of development.

7. Prevention and intervention strive to alter the environment in order to bring about positive outcomes. Research on epigenetics suggests that prevention and intervention may also change the epigenome and that this could result in improved outcomes. If researchers are to understand the processes through which early adverse experiences such as child maltreatment impart maladaptation, psychopathology, or resilience, then it is critical that genetic variation (functional polymorphisms) and epigenetic modifications be examined.

8. Genetic effects on intervention efficacy may happen in a number of ways (Belsky & van IJzendoorn 2015). Are some individuals, based on genetic variation, more susceptible to the positive effects of intervention? Are particular interventions more effective on particular individuals based on genetic differences (i.e., should interventions match genotype groups)? Does intervention affect DNA methylation, resulting in changes in gene expressions? DNA methylation changes in response to experience could lead to the design of both prevention and intervention strategies that alter the expression of genes to promote healthy physical and mental outcomes. Given that the demethylated epigenome is transmitted to the next generation, it will be important to determine if decreased child maltreatment risk through efficacious intervention would alter the epigenome, which in turn would result in a less risky epigenome being transmitted to the next generation.

DISCLOSURE STATEMENT

The author is not aware of any affiliations, memberships, funding, or financial holdings that might be perceived as affecting the objectivity of this review.

ACKNOWLEDGMENTS

Work on this article was supported by grants from the National Institute of Drug Abuse (DA 177741, DA 12903), the National Institute of Mental Health (MH 083979, MH 091070), and the Spunk Fund, Inc.

LITERATURE CITED

Ainsworth MDS, Blehar MC, Waters E, Wall S. 1978. *Patterns of Attachment: A Psychological Study of the Strange Situation.* Hillsdale, NJ: Erlbaum

Am. Psychiatr. Assoc. 2013. *Diagnostic and Statistical Manual of Mental Disorders.* Washington, DC: Am. Psychiatr. Publ. 5th ed.

Ayoub CC, O'Connor E, Rappolt-Schlichtmann G, Fischer KW, Rogosch FA, et al. 2006. Cognitive and emotional differences in young maltreated children: a translational application of dynamic skill theory. *Dev. Psychopathol.* 3(18):679–706

Banny A, Cicchetti D, Rogosch FA, Crick NR, Oshri A. 2013. Vulnerability to depression: a moderated mediation model of the roles of child maltreatment, peer victimization, and genetic variation among children from low-SES backgrounds. *Dev. Psychopathol.* 25:599–614

Barnett D, Ganiban J, Cicchetti D. 1999. Maltreatment, negative expressivity, and the development of Type D attachments from 12- to 24-months of age. *Monogr. Soc. Res. Child Dev.* 64:97–118

Belsky J, Bakermans-Kranenburg MJ, van IJzendoorn MH. 2007. For better and for worse: differential susceptibility to environmental influences. *Curr. Dir. Psychol. Sci.* 16:300–4

Belsky J, van IJzendoorn MH, eds. 2015. What works for whom? Genetic moderation of intervention efficacy. *Dev. Psychopathol.* 27(1, Spec. Issue):1–162

Bennett DS, Sullivan MW, Lewis M. 2010. Neglected children, shame proneness, and depressive symptoms. *Child Maltreat.* 15(4):305–14

Bjorklund DF. 1997. The role of immaturity in human development. *Psychol. Bull.* 122:153–69

Bowlby J. 1969. *Attachment.* New York: Basic Books

Butchart A, Putney H, Furniss T, Kahane T. 2006. *Preventing Child Maltreatment: A Guide to Taking Action and Generating Evidence.* Geneva: World Health Organ.

Byrd AL, Manuck SB. 2014. *MAOA*, childhood maltreatment, and antisocial behavior: meta-analysis of a gene–environment interaction. *Biol. Psychiatry* 75(1):9–17

Calkins SD, Perry NB. 2016. The development of emotion regulation: implications for child adjustment. In *Developmental Psychopathology*, Vol. 4, ed. D Cicchetti. New York: Wiley. 3rd ed. In press

Calverley RM, Fischer KW, Ayoub C. 1994. Complex splitting of self-representations in sexually abused adolescent girls. *Dev. Psychopathol.* 6:195–213

Carlson EA, Yates TM, Sroufe LA. 2009. Dissociation and development of the self. In *Dissociation and the Dissociative Disorders: DSM-V and Beyond*, ed. PF Dell, J O'Neill, E Somer, pp. 39–52. New York: Routledge

Caspi A, McClay J, Moffitt T, Mill J, Martin J, Craig IW. 2002. Role of genotype in the cycle of violence in maltreated children. *Science* 297:851–54

Cicchetti D. 1991. Fractures in the crystal: developmental psychopathology and the emergence of the self. *Dev. Rev.* 11:271–87

Cicchetti D. 2002. The impact of social experience on neurobiological systems: illustration from a constructivist view of child maltreatment. *Cogn. Dev.* 17:1407–28

Cicchetti D. 2010. Resilience under conditions of extreme stress: a multilevel perspective. *World Psychiatry* 9:1–10

Cicchetti D. 2013. Resilient functioning in maltreated children: past, present, and future perspectives. *J. Child Psychol. Psychiatry* 54:402–22

Cicchetti D, Crick NR, eds. 2009a. Precursors of and diverse pathways to personality disorder in children and adolescents, part 1. *Dev. Psychopathol.* 21(3, Spec. Issue). Cambridge, UK: Cambridge Univ. Press

Cicchetti D, Crick NR, eds. 2009b. Precursors of and diverse pathways to personality disorder in children and adolescents, part 2. *Dev. Psychopathol.* 21(4, Spec. Issue). Cambridge, UK: Cambridge Univ. Press

Cicchetti D, Curtis WJ. 2006. The developing brain and neural plasticity: implications for normality, psychopathology, and resilience. In *Developmental Psychopathology: Developmental Neuroscience*, Vol. 2, ed. D Cicchetti, DJ Cohen, pp. 1–64. New York: Wiley. 2nd ed.

Cicchetti D, Gunnar MR. 2008. Integrating biological processes into the design and evaluation of preventive interventions. *Dev. Psychopathol.* 20(3):737–43

Cicchetti D, Natsuaki MN, eds. 2014. Multilevel developmental perspectives toward understanding internalizing disorders: current research and future directions. *Dev. Psychopathol.* 26(4 Pt. 2, Spec. Issue). Cambridge, UK: Cambridge Univ. Press

Cicchetti D, Ng R. 2014. Emotional development in maltreated children. In *Children and Emotion: New Insights into Developmental Affective Sciences*, ed. KH Lagattuta, pp. 29–41. Basel, Switz.: Karger

Cicchetti D, Rogosch FA. 1996. Equifinality and multifinality in developmental psychopathology. *Dev. Psychopathol.* 8:597–600

Cicchetti D, Rogosch FA. 2012. Gene by environment interaction and resilience: effects of child maltreatment and serotonin, corticotropin releasing hormone, dopamine, and oxytocin genes. *Dev. Psychopathol.* 24:411–27

Cicchetti D, Rogosch FA, Hecht KF, Crick NR, Hetzel S. 2014. Moderation of maltreatment effects on childhood borderline personality symptoms by gender and oxytocin receptor and FK506 binding protein 5 genes. *Dev. Psychopathol.* 26(3):831–49

Cicchetti D, Rogosch FA, Thibodeau EL. 2012. The effects of child maltreatment on early signs of antisocial behavior: genetic moderation by tryptophan hydroxylase, serotonin transporter, and monoamine oxidase A genes. *Dev. Psychopathol.* 24:907–28

Cicchetti D, Rogosch FA, Toth SL. 2006. Fostering secure attachment in infants in maltreating families through preventive interventions. *Dev. Psychopathol.* 18(3):623–50

Cicchetti D, Rogosch FA, Toth SL. 2011. The effects of child maltreatment and polymorphisms of the serotonin transporter and dopamine D4 receptor genes on infant attachment and intervention efficacy. *Dev. Psychopathol.* 23:357–72

Cicchetti D, Toth SL. 2005. Child maltreatment. *Annu. Rev. Clin. Psychol.* 1:409–38

Cicchetti D, Toth SL. 2009. The past achievements and future promises of developmental psychopathology: the coming of age of a discipline. *J. Child Psychol. Psychiatry* 50:16–25

Cicchetti D, Toth SL. 2015. Child maltreatment. In *Handbook of Child Psychology and Developmental Science*, Vol. 3: *Socioemotional Processes*, ed. RM Lerner, ME Lamb, pp. 515–63. New York: Wiley. 7th ed.

Cicchetti D, Valentino K. 2006. An ecological transactional perspective on child maltreatment: failure of the average expectable environment and its influence upon child development. In *Developmental Psychopathology*, Vol. 3, ed. D Cicchetti, DJ Cohen, pp. 129–201. New York: Wiley. 2nd ed.

Cyr C, Euser EM, Bakermans-Kranenburg MJ, van IJzendoorn MH. 2010. Attachment security and disorganization in maltreating and high-risk families: a series of meta-analyses. *Dev. Psychopathol.* 22:87–108

Dodge K, Pettit G, Bates JE. 1997. How the experience of early physical abuse leads children to become chronically aggressive. In *Rochester Symposium on Developmental Psychopathology*, Vol. 8, ed. D Cicchetti, SL Toth, pp. 263–88. Rochester, NY: Univ. Rochester Press

Ellis BJ, Boyce WT, Belsky J, Bakermans-Kranenburg MJ, van IJzendoorn MH. 2011. Differential susceptibility to the environment: an evolutionary-neurodevelopmental theory. *Dev. Psychopathol.* 23:7–28

Fonagy P, Gergely G, Target M. 2007. The parent-infant dyad and the construction of the subjective self. *J. Child Psychol. Psychiatry* 48(3–4):288–328

Gottesman I, Shields J. 1972. *Schizophrenia and Genetics: A Twin Study Vantage Point*. New York: Academic

Hart H, Rubia K. 2012. Neuroimaging of child abuse: a critical review. *Front. Hum. Neurosci.* 6:52

Hawkins AL, Haskett ME. 2014. Internal working models and adjustment of physically abused children: the mediating role of self-regulatory abilities. *J. Child Psychol. Psychiatry* 55(2):135–43

Hesse E, Main M. 2006. Frightened, threatening, and dissociative parental behavior in low-risk samples: description, discussion, and interpretations. *Dev. Psychopathol.* 18:309–44

Hostinar CE, Sullivan RM, Gunnar MR. 2014. Psychobiological mechanisms underlying the social buffering of the hypothalamic-pituitary-adrenocortical axis: a review of animal models and human studies across development. *Psychol. Bull.* 140:256–82

Howe GW, Reiss D, Yuh J. 2002. Can prevention trials test theories of etiology? *Dev. Psychopathol.* 14:673–94

Ialongo N, Rogosch FA, Cicchetti D, Toth SL, Buckley J, et al. 2006. A developmental psychopathology approach to the prevention of mental health disorders. In *Developmental Psychopathology*, Vol. 1, ed. D Cicchetti, DJ Cohen, pp. 968–1018. New York: Wiley. 2nd ed.

Inst. Med. 1994. *Reducing Risks for Mental Disorders: Frontiers for Preventative Intervention Research*. Washington, DC: Natl. Acad. Press

Johnson R. 1993. On the neural generators of the P300 component of the even-related potential. *Psychophysiology* 30:90–97

Karg K, Burnmeister M, Shedden K, Sen S. 2011. The serotonin transporter promoter variant (5-HTTLPR), stress, and depression meta-analysis revisited: evidence of genetic moderation. *Arch. Gen. Psychiatry* 68:444–54

Kim JE, Cicchetti D, Rogosch FA, Manly JT. 2009. Child maltreatment and trajectories of personality and behavioral functioning: implications for the development of personality disorder. *Dev. Psychopathol.* 21(3):889–912

Kim-Cohen J, Caspi A, Taylor A, Williams B, Newcombe R, et al. 2006. *MAOI*, maltreatment, and gene-environment interaction predicting children's mental health: new evidence and a meta-analysis. *Mol. Psychiatry* 11:903–13

Kim-Spoon J, Rogosch FA, Cicchetti D. 2013. A longitudinal study of emotion regulation, emotion lability/negativity, and internalizing symptomatology in maltreated and nonmaltreated children. *Child Dev.* 84:297–312

Kraemer HC, Kazdin AE, Offord DR, Kessler RC, Jensen PS, Kupfer DJ. 1997. Coming to terms with the terms of risk. *Arch. Gen. Psychiatry* 54:337–43

Lewis M. 1995. *Shame: The Exposed Self.* New York: Free Press

Luijk MPCM, Roisman GI, Haltigan JD, Tiemeier H, Booth-LaForce C, et al. 2011. Dopaminergic, serotonergic, oxytonergic candidate genes associated with infant attachment security and disorganization? In search of man and interaction effects. *J. Child Psychol. Psychiatry* 52:1295–307

Luthar SS, Cicchetti D. 2000. The construct of resilience: implications for intervention and social policy. *Dev. Psychopathol.* 12:857–85

Luthar SS, Cicchetti D, Becker B. 2000. The construct of resilience: a critical evaluation and guidelines for future work. *Child Dev.* 71:543–62

Macfie J, Cicchetti D, Toth SL. 2001a. Dissociation in maltreated versus nonmaltreated preschool-aged children. *Child Abuse Negl.* 25:1253–67

Macfie J, Cicchetti D, Toth SL. 2001b. The development of dissociation in maltreated preschool-aged children. *Dev. Psychopathol.* 13:233–54

Manly JT. 2005. Advances in research definitions of child maltreatment. *Child Abuse Negl.* 29(5):425–39

Masten AS. 2014. *Ordinary Magic: Resilience in Development.* New York: Guilford

Masten AS, Cicchetti D. 2016. Resilience in development: progress and transformation. In *Developmental Psychopathology*, Vol. 4, ed. D Cicchetti. New York: Wiley. 3rd ed. In press

Maughan A, Cicchetti D. 2002. The impact of child maltreatment and interadult violence on children's emotion regulation abilities. *Child Dev.* 7:1525–42

McCrory E, De Brito SA, Viding E. 2010. The neurobiology and genetics of maltreatment and adversity. *J. Child Psychol. Psychiatry* 51:1079–95

Moutsiana C, Fearon P, Murray L, Cooper P, Goodyer I, et al. 2014. Making an effort to feel positive: Insecure attachment in infancy predicts the neural underpinnings of emotion regulation in adulthood. *J. Child Psychol. Psychiatry* 55:999–1008

Pechtel P, Lyons-Ruth K, Anderson CM, Teicher MH. 2014. Sensitive periods of amygdala development: the role of maltreatment in preadolescence. *NeuroImage* 97:236–44

Pellmar TC, Eisenberg L. 2000. *Bridging Disciplines in the Brain, Behavioral, and Clinical Sciences.* Washington, DC: Natl. Acad. Press

Pickreign-Stronach ES, Toth SL, Rogosch FA, Cicchetti D. 2013. Preventive interventions and sustained attachment security in maltreated children: a 12-month follow-up of a randomized controlled trial. *Dev. Psychopathol.* 26:919–30

Pollak SD. 2008. Mechanisms linking early experience and the emergence of emotions: illustrations from the study of maltreated children. *Curr. Dir. Psychol. Sci.* 17:370–75

Pollak SD, Cicchetti D, Hornung K, Reed A. 2000. Recognizing emotion in faces: developmental effects of child abuse and neglect. *Dev. Psychol.* 36:679–88

Pollak SD, Cicchetti D, Klorman R, Brumaghim J. 1997. Cognitive brain event-related potentials and emotion processing in maltreated children. *Child Dev.* 68:773–87

Pollak SD, Kistler DJ. 2002. Early experience is associated with the development of categorical representations for facial expressions of emotion. *PNAS* 99:9072–76

Pollak SD, Klorman R, Thatcher JE, Cicchetti D. 2001. P3b reflects maltreated children's reactions to facial displays of emotion. *Psychophysiology* 38:267–74

Pollak SD, Messner M, Kistler DJ, Cohn JF. 2009. Development of perceptual expertise in emotion recognition. *Cognition* 110:242–47

Pollak SD, Sinha P. 2002. Effects of early experience on children's recognition of facial displays of emotion. *Dev. Psychol.* 38:784–91

Pollak SD, Tolley-Schell SA. 2003. Selective attention to facial emotion in physically abused children. *J. Abnorm. Psychol.* 112(3):323–38

Rieder C, Cicchetti D. 1989. Organizational perspective on cognitive control functioning and cognitive-affective balance in maltreated children. *Dev. Psychol.* 25:382–93

Rinne-Albers MA, van der Wee NJ, Lamers-Winkelman F, Vermeiren RR. 2013. Neuroimaging in children, adolescents and young adults with psychological trauma. *Eur. Child Adolesc. Psychiatry* 22(12):745–55

Rogosch FA, Cicchetti D. 2004. Child maltreatment and emergent personality organization: perspectives from the five-factor model. *J. Abnorm. Psychol.* 32:123–45

Rogosch FA, Cicchetti D. 2005. Child maltreatment, attention networks, and potential precursors to borderline personality disorder. *Dev. Psychopathol.* 17(4):1071–89

Romens SE, Pollak SD. 2012. Emotion regulation predicts attention bias in maltreated children at-risk for depression. *J. Child Psychol. Psychiatry* 53(2):120–27

Rutter M. 2013. Developmental psychopathology: a paradigm shift or just a relabeling? *Dev. Psychopathol.* 25:1201–13

Schneider-Rosen K, Cicchetti D. 1991. Early self-knowledge and emotional development: visual self-recognition and affective reactions to mirror self-image in maltreated and nonmaltreated toddlers. *Dev. Psychol.* 27:481–88

Shackman JE, Pollak SD. 2014. Impact of physical maltreatment on the regulation of negative affect and aggression. *Dev. Psychopathol.* 26(4 Pt. 1):1021–33

Shields A, Cicchetti D. 1998. Reactive aggression among maltreated children: the contributions of attention and emotion dysregulation. *J. Clin. Child Psychol.* 27:381–95

Shields A, Cicchetti D. 2001. Parental maltreatment and emotion dysregulation as risk factors for bullying and victimization in middle childhood. *J. Clin. Child Psychol.* 30:349–63

Shields A, Ryan RM, Cicchetti D. 2001. Narrative representations of caregivers and emotion dysregulation as predictors of maltreated children's rejection by peers. *Dev. Psychol.* 37:321–37

Shonk SM, Cicchetti D. 2001. Maltreatment, competency deficits, and risk for academic and behavioral maladjustment. *Dev. Psychol.* 37:3–14

Southwick SM, Bonanno GA, Masten AS, Panter-Brick C, Yehuda R. 2014. Resilience definitions, theory, and challenges: interdisciplinary perspectives. *Eur. J. Psychotraumatol.* 5:25338

Sroufe LA. 1990. An organizational perspective on the self. In *The Self in Transition: Infancy to Childhood*, ed. D Cicchetti, M Beeghly, pp. 281–307. Chicago: Univ. Chicago Press

Sroufe LA. 1996. *Emotional Development: The Organization of Emotional Life in the Early Years*. New York: Cambridge Univ. Press

Sroufe LA. 2013. The promise of developmental psychopathology: past and present. *Dev. Psychopathol.* 25:1215–24

Stiles J. 2008. *The Fundamentals of Brain Development: Integrating Nature and Nurture*. Cambridge, MA: Harvard Univ. Press

Stronach EP, Toth SL, Rogosch FA, Oshri A, Manly JT, Cicchetti D. 2011. Child maltreatment, attachment organization and internal representations of mother and mother-child relationships. *Child Maltreat.* 16:137–45

Teicher MN, Anderson CM, Polcari A. 2012. Childhood maltreatment is associated with reduced volume in the hippocampal subfields CA3, dentate gyrus, and subiculum. *PNAS* 109(9):E563–72

Teicher MN, Dumont N, Ito Y, Vaituzis AC, Giedd J, Andersen S. 2004. Childhood neglect is associated with reduced corpus callosum area. *Biol. Psychiatry* 15:80–85

Teisl M, Cicchetti D. 2008. Physical abuse, cognitive and emotional processes, and aggressive/disruptive behavior problems. *Soc. Dev.* 16(1):1–23

Thelen E, Smith LB. 1998. Dynamic systems theories. In *Handbook of Child Psychology*, Vol. 1: *Theoretical Models of Human Development*, ed. W Damon, R Lerner, pp. 563–634. New York: Wiley

Thompson RA, Lewis MD, Calkins SD. 2008. Reassessing emotion regulation. *Child Dev. Perspect.* 2:124–31

Toth SL, Gravener-Davis JA, Guild DJ, Cicchetti D. 2013. Relational interventions for child maltreatment: past, present, future perspectives. *Dev. Psychopathol.* 25(4 Pt. 2):1601–17

Toth SL, Pickreign-Stronach ES, Rogosch FA, Caplan R, Cicchetti D. 2011. Illogical thinking and thought disorder in maltreated children. *J. Am. Acad. Child Adolesc. Psychiatry* 50:659–68

Valentino K, Cicchetti D, Toth SL, Rogosch FA. 2008. True and false recall and dissociation among maltreated children: the role of self-schema. *Dev. Psychopathol.* 20:213–32x

von Bertalanffy L. 1968. *General System Theory: Foundations, Development, Applications*. New York: George Braziller

Weder N, Yang BZ, Douglas-Palumberi H, Massey J, Krystal JH, et al. 2009. *MAOA* genotype, maltreatment, and aggressive behavior: the changing impact of genotype at varying levels of trauma. *Biol. Psychiatry* 65:417–24

The Affective Neuroscience of Aging

Mara Mather

Davis School of Gerontology, University of Southern
California, Los Angeles, California 90089; email: mara.mather@usc.edu

Annu. Rev. Psychol. 2016. 67:213–38

First published online as a Review in Advance on
October 2, 2015

The *Annual Review of Psychology* is online at
psych.annualreviews.org

This article's doi:
10.1146/annurev-psych-122414-033540

Keywords

aging, emotion, affective neuroscience, amygdala, ventromedial prefrontal
cortex

Abstract

Although aging is associated with clear declines in physical and cognitive
processes, emotional functioning fares relatively well. Consistent with this
behavioral profile, two core emotional brain regions, the amygdala and ventromedial prefrontal cortex, show little structural and functional decline in
aging, compared with other regions. However, emotional processes depend
on interacting systems of neurotransmitters and brain regions that go beyond these structures. This review examines how age-related brain changes
influence processes such as attending to and remembering emotional stimuli, regulating emotion, and recognizing emotional expressions, as well as
empathy, risk taking, impulsivity, behavior change, and attentional focus.

Contents

INTRODUCTION

Aging is a multifaceted process that involves interacting brain regions and neurotransmitter systems that are not uniformly affected by aging. As should be expected given the variability in vulnerability to aging among brain regions and systems, some everyday abilities decline more than others in normal aging. Emotion is a fascinating domain within the study of aging because emotional functions show less decline in normal aging than many other processes, and in some cases, are as or more effective in older adults than in younger adults. In this article, I first review brain regions and neurotransmitter systems that play important roles in emotion and how these fare in aging. I then review age differences in various emotional tasks and processes and what is known about how they relate to age-related brain changes.

THE FATE OF EMOTION-RELATED BRAIN REGIONS AND MONOAMINERGIC NEUROTRANSMITTER SYSTEMS IN NORMAL AGING

Prefrontal Cortex

In the 1990s, a frontal theory of aging emerged, accounting for older adults' cognitive deficits by the greater decline in prefrontal than in other brain regions in aging (West 1996). But when it came to affect, the prefrontal theory of aging did not make sense. For instance, after a tamping iron destroyed part of the lower middle section of the prefrontal cortex (in the ventromedial prefrontal

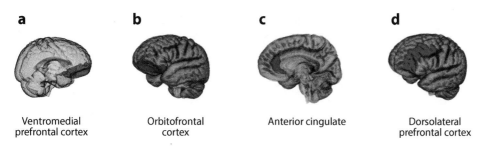

a
Ventromedial
prefrontal cortex

b
Orbitofrontal
cortex

c
Anterior cingulate

d
Dorsolateral
prefrontal cortex

Figure 1

Subdividing the prefrontal cortex is not simple, and boundaries are not always agreed upon. However, in terms of understanding the aging and emotion literature, several subregions are important. (*a*) First, the ventromedial prefrontal cortex (vmPFC) is the medial portion of the prefrontal cortex from the lower half of the prefrontal cortex, demarcated at the genu (or "knee" in Latin) of the corpus callosum. (*b*) The orbitofrontal cortex is the "floor" of the frontal cortex, which is found just above the eye orbits. (*c*) The anterior cingulate cortex is the medial portion of the prefrontal cortex that is adjacent to the corpus callosum. The vmPFC overlaps with the medial part of the orbitofrontal cortex and typically includes the ventral portion of the anterior cingulate (Clark et al. 2008). (*d*) Although the dorsolateral prefrontal region is often defined as the middle frontal gyrus covering the lateral part of Brodmann areas 9 and 46 (e.g., Murray & Ranganath 2007), some studies examining age differences in anatomical volume define it more broadly to include superior, middle, and inferior frontal gyri spanning from the most dorsomedial point of the cortex down to the lateral orbital sulcus (e.g., Lövdén et al. 2013).

cortex or vmPFC; see **Figure 1a**) of the famous lesion patient Phineas Gage, he lost the ability to control his emotions. Yet despite age-related prefrontal decline, emotional control impairments are not associated with normal aging.

Indeed, a striking contrast exists between the emotional behavior of older adults and that of patients with vmPFC lesions. In many cases, vmPFC damage is associated with impulsive aggression, violence, and anger (Grafman et al. 1996). Older adults, on the other hand, tend to be less prone to outbursts or feelings of anger than younger adults (Birditt & Fingerman 2005, Charles & Carstensen 2008, Phillips et al. 2006), and partner aggression is lower among older than younger adults (O'Leary & Woodin 2005). Another characteristic of vmPFC lesions in patients is the loss of ability to maintain secure attachments (Damasio et al. 1990). In contrast, deficits in attachment processes are not associated with aging—instead, attachment anxiety is lower among older than younger adults (Chopik et al. 2013).

Phillips & Della Sala (1998) were the first to propose that the frontal theory of aging needed to be revised to accommodate such discrepancies. They proposed that dorsolateral prefrontal regions subserving fluid intelligence decline more in normal aging than do orbitofrontal regions associated with emotional contributions to social behavior and decision making (see **Figure 1b**). They subsequently tested a modified version of their theory with vmPFC as the critical preserved region using a battery of tasks selected to tap either vmPFC or dorsolateral PFC (dlPFC) and found that age-related impairments were significantly more pronounced on the dlPFC tasks (MacPherson et al. 2002).

Subsequent findings that vmPFC declined in volume significantly less than dlPFC supported this hypothesis regarding differential rates of decline. For instance, an analysis aggregating across six different samples with a total of 883 participants found that highly significant negative correlations existed between age and cortical thickness in the superior, middle, and inferior frontal gyri but not in the anterior cingulate cortices or in vmPFC (**Figure 2**; Fjell & Walhovd 2010).

Thus, the pattern of emotion-related findings and the structural data make a compelling case for relatively preserved vmPFC in aging. However, it should be noted that researchers using the

vmPFC:
ventromedial
prefrontal cortex

dlPFC: dorsolateral
prefrontal cortex

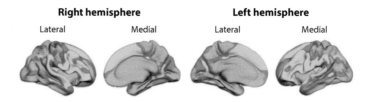

Right hemisphere

Lateral   Medial

Left hemisphere

Lateral   Medial

Figure 2

Brain regions shown in yellow are those that exhibited the largest decline in cortical thickness with age across a sample of 883 participants ranging in age from 18 to 94 (Fjell et al. 2009b).

Iowa Gambling Task, delay discounting, or facial emotion recognition as part of task batteries to assess ventromedial-dorsolateral distinctions in aging sometimes concluded that vmPFC functions are also significantly impaired in aging (Baena et al. 2010, Lamar & Resnick 2004). As addressed in later sections, it is problematic to assume that these particular tasks depend on vmPFC.

Amygdala

The amygdala abuts the anterior end of the hippocampus (**Figure 3**) and is a collection of nuclei that have somewhat distinct roles but together play a key role in emotion. In particular, the amygdala helps detect potentially emotionally relevant stimuli—relevant because they are novel, pose a threat, or are goal relevant—and then modulates other brain systems to enhance attention and memory for those stimuli. It is clearly involved in anxiety and fear but also plays a part in positive affect and motivation.

Findings regarding the structural integrity of the amygdala suggest that it is better maintained in aging than are most other regions, although findings are not entirely consistent. In some structural magnetic resonance imaging (MRI) studies, the amygdala shows no significant differences in volume across the adult lifespan, in the context of decline in other structures (Jernigan et al. 2001, Jiang et al. 2014, Li et al. 2014, Shen et al. 2013). A postmortem study also showed no significant decrease in volume with age (Brabec et al. 2010). Some studies reveal age-associated declines in amygdala volume that are less marked than in other brain regions (Good et al. 2001, Grieve et al.

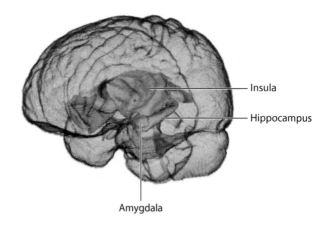

Insula

Hippocampus

Amygdala

Figure 3

Locations of the left amygdala, hippocampus, and insula; the right amygdala, hippocampus, and insula are shown in the background.

2005, Kalpouzos et al. 2009, Long et al. 2012), whereas others show notable negative associations between amygdala volume and age (Allen et al. 2005b, Curiati et al. 2009, Fjell et al. 2013b, Mu et al. 1999, Walhovd et al. 2005).

There are also conflicting findings among longitudinal studies. Amygdala and hippocampal volumes showed similarly significant declines when assessed using an automated program (FreeSurfer; Fjell et al. 2009a) that held up when those who converted to Alzheimer's disease three to four years later were excluded (Fjell et al. 2013a). In contrast, in two studies using hand tracing, no longitudinal amygdala decline was detected (Cherbuin et al. 2011, Frodl et al. 2008).

Differences across studies may have to do with methods used to assess amygdala volume (e.g., FreeSurfer may not be accurate for the amygdala; Morey et al. 2009) or differences in the people assessed. On balance across the cross-sectional and longitudinal studies, the evidence suggests there is some decline in the amygdala but that it is often less pronounced than that found in other regions such as the hippocampus, a region involved in memory processes adjacent to the amygdala.

One issue to keep in mind is that for the amygdala, bigger is not necessarily better. Greater amygdala volume can be associated with having had stressful experiences (Tottenham et al. 2010), and stressed people show reduced amygdala gray matter density after a stress-reduction program (Hölzel et al. 2009). On the other hand, among both younger and older adults, greater amygdala volume is associated with the size and complexity of one's social network (Bickart et al. 2011).

Furthermore, the intrinsic integrity of a brain region will have little impact without connections to other brain regions. Initial findings regarding the effects of aging on amygdala connectivity are intriguing. Resting-state functional MRI reveals that the functional connectivity density of an amygdala-based network increases with age, in contrast with age-related functional connectivity density decreases in nodes of other networks (such as the default mode network and dorsal attention network; Tomasi & Volkow 2012).

Prefrontal-amygdala functional connectivity may reflect PFC regulation of anxiety and other emotional responses. Among older adults, amygdala connectivity with vmPFC (see **Figure 1**) during processing of emotion stimuli is associated with more positive memories (Sakaki et al. 2013), less negative evaluation of pictures (St. Jacques et al. 2010), and a more normative decline in cortisol over the course of a day (Urry et al. 2006). Thus, for older adults, medial PFC-amygdala functional connectivity during rest seems to be associated with more positive emotions or stress profiles, and thus far, there is no evidence for declines in functional connectivity for the amygdala (instead, the reverse is seen; Tomasi & Volkow 2012).

The role of structural connectivity in older adults' emotional well-being is less clear. Among younger adults, trait anxiety scores have been linked with the structural integrity of the uncinate fasciculus, a white matter tract that connects the amygdala to ventrolateral PFC. Some studies find that better structural integrity predicts lower anxiety, whereas others report the opposite relationship (for a review, see Clewett et al. 2014). The uncinate fasciculus shows decreased white matter intensity in normal aging (Burzynska et al. 2010, Davis et al. 2009). If this plays a causal role in anxiety, one should see increased prevalence of anxiety with age that is not accounted for by other risk factors. This is not the case: In population-based studies, there is no positive association with age and anxiety (Beekman et al. 1998, Schaub & Linden 2000). Consistent with this, in a study that examined the relationship of anxiety to the amygdala-ventral PFC in those aged 19 to 85 (with connectivity assessed for all of ventral PFC rather than just the uncinate fasciculus), better white matter structural integrity of the amygdala-ventral PFC pathway was not associated with lower anxiety either across the whole group or when age was accounted for (Clewett et al. 2014). One interesting possibility is that amygdala-vmPFC structural connectivity may promote negative emotional processing among younger adults but positive emotional processing among older adults (Ford & Kensinger 2014).

Functional neuroimaging indicates that, in older adults, the amygdala still activates robustly to novel salient stimuli, such as novel faces (Wright et al. 2007, 2008). As I review in the later section on age-related positivity effects, other studies have found age-related shifts in the type of emotional stimuli to which the amygdala activates most strongly. In this section, the evidence reviewed indicates that the amygdala shows relatively little decline in structure or function in normal aging.

Insula

The insula is a cortical area found within the sulcus separating the temporal lobe from the parietal and frontal lobes that receives interoceptive sensory information from the internal milieu of the body and helps regulate autonomic nervous system activity. It is involved in many aspects of emotion, including pain sensation, self-related and empathic feelings, and risk and uncertainty processing.

Findings regarding adult age differences in insula volume vary. Cross-sectional studies using manual tracing find a moderate negative association with age that is not always significant (Allen et al. 2005a, Raz et al. 2010). Allen and colleagues argued that findings of more marked insula decline from voxel-based morphometry studies (Good et al. 2001, Tisserand et al. 2004) may result from data-smoothing artifacts at the border of the insula.

There have not been many longitudinal studies of insular volume, but findings from two studies using similar tracing methods differed somewhat. In one study, there was a significant decline between the first and second assessment but not between the second and third assessment (Raz et al. 2010); in the other, the insula showed substantially more shrinkage longitudinally but was also identified as the brain region with the most individual differences in longitudinal change across those studied (Persson et al. 2014). This high degree of individual difference in change may also help explain differences in findings across studies.

Consistent with the structural declines seen in the insula, older adults are less aware of visceral sensations than are younger adults (for a review, see Mather 2012). Older adults are also less vulnerable to pain associated with visceral pathology even though they are more vulnerable to neuropathic pain (Gagliese 2009). Research is needed to test whether there are direct relationships between age-related declines in structure and in sensation.

The insula also serves as the hub in a resting-state network known as the salience network. The salience network responds to behaviorally relevant stimuli and facilitates dynamic interactions among other large-scale networks (Menon & Uddin 2010). Resting-state functional MRI (fMRI) studies reveal age-related declines in functional connectivity within the salience network (He et al. 2014, Meier et al. 2012, Onoda et al. 2012) and between the frontoinsular cortex and other resting-state networks (He et al. 2014).

Thus, in summary, current evidence indicates the insula is a region that shows moderate age-related decline with notable individual differences.

Dopaminergic Influences

To understand emotional processing, it is important to also consider the role of neurotransmitter systems. Two that have critical roles in emotional processing and that have been identified as showing significant age-related changes are dopamine and norepinephrine. These two neurotransmitters have similar structures and interacting effects on cognition. However, they also have distinct roles.

Dopamine has received much attention for its effects on reward processing and is also important for learning, attention, and movement control. Midbrain dopamine neurons typically activate briefly following unpredicted rewards. This response codes a prediction error, or the difference between obtained and predicted reward value (Schultz 2013). These signals provide powerful tools to support learning about various states, rules, and sequences in the world.

LC: locus coeruleus

Aging affects the dopaminergic system (for a review, see Li & Rieckmann 2014). Dopaminergic neurons and dopamine transporters decrease in density, and positron emission tomography markers of dopamine system function show associations between these declines and executive function among older adults (Bäckman et al. 2010). Genes associated with dopaminergic system function are more strongly associated with individual differences in working memory and executive functions in late than in early life, suggesting that age-related decline in dopamine function makes genetic variation more influential (Colzato et al. 2013, Li et al. 2013, Nagel et al. 2008, Störmer et al. 2012).

Noradrenergic Influences

The locus coeruleus (LC) is a small nucleus in the brainstem that is the primary source of the brain's noradrenaline. Its neurons fire at different rates, depending on whether one is alert or drowsy, and respond rapidly to arousing stimuli, such as loud noises and threatening stimuli. Although the LC is small, its neurons have particularly long axons and so can infuse large regions of the brain with noradrenaline whenever arousal increases.

The literature on age-related structural changes in the LC is mixed. For instance, in one study, postmortem counts of LC neurons decreased 40% across a 60-year period (Vijayashankar & Brody 1979), whereas in another study using different methods, younger and older nondemented adults showed no difference in LC neuron count or size (Mouton et al. 1994). A key factor is that both Alzheimer's and Parkinson's diseases target the LC, and in these disorders, LC damage occurs long before symptoms are marked enough to lead to a diagnosis (e.g., Braak et al. 2011).

Individual differences in both LC structure and noradrenaline levels are associated with cognitive function. In a postmortem study, neuronal density in the LC was more strongly correlated with cognitive decline in the few years right before death than was neuronal integrity in the ventral segmental area, substantial nigra, or dorsal raphe nucleus (Wilson et al. 2013). In vivo, LC integrity (as assessed by structural imaging optimized to show the LC neuromelanin deposits) is correlated with verbal IQ scores (Clewett et al. 2015). In addition, higher levels of cerebrospinal fluid noradrenaline are associated with poorer cognitive performance (Wang et al. 2013).

RELATIONS BETWEEN EMOTIONAL PROCESSING IN AGING AND BRAIN FUNCTION

In the previous sections, I outlined how key brain regions and neurotransmitter systems contributing to emotional functioning fare in normal aging. In the next sections, I turn to the question of how specific aspects of emotional behavior might relate to these age-related changes in the brain.

Positivity Effect

In 2003, we reported an age-by-valence interaction in attention (Mather & Carstensen 2003) and memory (Charles et al. 2003). Relative to younger adults, older adults focused more on positive and less on negative stimuli, a pattern that became known as the age-related positivity effect (Mather & Carstensen 2005). Many subsequent (but not all) studies found similar effects, and a recent meta-analysis of 100 studies indicated that the age-by-valence interaction is a reliable effect in memory and in attention (Reed et al. 2014).

Older adults' positivity effect could help maintain better moods (e.g., Isaacowitz et al. 2009b) and thereby help explain how longitudinal studies show that levels of negative affect tend to decrease whereas positive affect either tends to increase slightly or shows less decrease than negative affect with increasing age, at least until individuals are in their 70s (Carstensen et al. 2011, Charles et al. 2001, Gruenewald et al. 2008). But does the positivity effect actually result from emotion-regulation processes? Or is it just a serendipitous side effect of age-related decline in brain mechanisms (in particular the amygdala) that support noticing and remembering negative, potentially threatening information (Cacioppo et al. 2011)?

As reviewed previously, the amygdala does not show marked decline among healthy older adults, either in structure or function. Furthermore, it is relatively more responsive to positive than negative stimuli in older adults compared with younger adults (Erk et al. 2008, Ge et al. 2014, Kehoe et al. 2013, Leclerc & Kensinger 2011, Mather et al. 2004, Waldinger et al. 2011; but see Moriguchi et al. 2011 for no age-by-valence effects in the amygdala). Thus, the amygdala does not stop responding to emotional stimuli in later life, but instead shifts the valence to which it is most responsive.

Other findings regarding the positivity effect also do not fit an amygdala decline account. The amygdala draws attention to emotionally salient stimuli and helps create more long-lasting memory traces of those stimuli. Like younger adults, older adults show an advantage in noticing and detecting potentially threatening or arousing stimuli (Hahn et al. 2006, Knight et al. 2007, LaBar et al. 2000, Leclerc & Kensinger 2008b, Mather & Knight 2006), suggesting intact amygdala detection functionality. When stimuli are presented in pairs and looking patterns are assessed, the positivity effect in visual attention does not emerge until after the first look or detection of the stimuli, at a point when controlled processes can exert an influence (Isaacowitz et al. 2009a, Knight et al. 2007), suggesting that a key component of the age-related positivity effect is that older adults are more likely to disengage from negative stimuli. Consistent with this, younger adults are significantly slower to disengage from negative than positive distractors, whereas older adults are slightly better at disengaging from negative than positive distractors (Hahn et al. 2006) or no-longer-relevant stimuli (Ashley & Swick 2009).

Also arguing against the amygdala-decline account are findings that the age-by-valence positivity effect interactions in memory and pleasantness ratings are stronger for low- than high-arousal emotional words (Kensinger 2008, Streubel & Kunzmann 2011). Likewise, younger and older adults showed similar amygdala activation in response to high-arousal negative stimuli, but for low-arousal negative stimuli older adults showed decreased amygdala activity compared with younger adults, along with increased activity in the anterior cingulate cortex (Dolcos et al. 2014). Greater anterior cingulate cortex activity was associated with less negative ratings of low-arousal negative pictures for older but not for younger adults (for similar links between vmPFC/anterior cingulate activity and rating intensity, see also Ge et al. 2014). Thus, across studies, older adults' memory, ratings, and amygdala activity resembles that of younger adults more when stimuli arousal is high than when it is low.

The positivity effect modulation by arousal fits with a regulation account of the age difference, as once someone has reacted to a stimulus, emotion regulation tends to be more difficult and less successful for higher-arousal stimuli (Sheppes 2014). Thus, if older adults generally attempt to regulate their responses to emotional stimuli after processing them, the biggest age differences should be seen for those stimuli that offer the highest opportunity for modulation by regulatory strategies: negative or positive stimuli that are not so arousing.

Consistent with a regulatory account, compared with younger adults, older adults tend to show a greater increase in prefrontal activation for emotional than neutral stimuli (for reviews, see Mather 2012, Nashiro et al. 2012a, St. Jacques et al. 2009). In particular, vmPFC and adjacent anterior cingulate cortex seem to play an especially important role in maintaining older adults' well-being. Greater activity in these regions (in tandem with less activity in the amygdala) during processing negative emotional stimuli has been linked with greater positivity, better emotional stability, and a better diurnal stress profile among older adults (Dolcos et al. 2014, Sakaki et al. 2013, Urry et al. 2006, Williams et al. 2006). Likewise, there are links between well-being and responses in these regions during processing of positive stimuli. During a cueing task, older adults were more distracted than younger adults by task-irrelevant positive faces (but not by sad or fearful faces) and showed greater activity in anterior cingulate in response to the distracting positive faces than did younger adults (Brassen et al. 2011). This anterior cingulate activity was associated with greater emotional stability.

Across studies, it seems clear that activity in these medial frontal cortex regions is associated with age differences in positivity, but it is not as clear when older adults will show greater or less activity than younger adults. Whereas studies using the International Affective Picture System images or emotional faces have found greater medial PFC activation to negative than positive stimuli among older compared with younger adults (Leclerc & Kensinger 2011, Williams et al. 2006), studies using words or object images have found age-related reversals in vmPFC regions in the opposite direction: Older adults show more medial PFC activity during processing positive than negative stimuli and vice versa for younger adults (Leclerc & Kensinger 2008a, 2010, 2011). Medial PFC could be employed both to engage more deeply with positive stimuli (for instance, by relating it to oneself) and to reinterpret or to distract oneself from negative stimuli. Thus, it may vary across stimuli sets (and also depend on orienting instructions) whether the desire to disengage from negative stimuli or to engage with positive stimuli is the stronger driving motivation during the session.

Behavioral studies provide further support for the notion that older adults engage prefrontal resources in order to help increase positivity and/or diminish negativity of attention and memory by showing that higher executive function is associated with higher positivity among older adults but not younger adults (Isaacowitz et al. 2009b, Knight et al. 2007, Mather & Knight 2005, Petrican et al. 2008, Sasse et al. 2014, Simón et al. 2013; but see Foster et al. 2013 for conflicting findings).

Why might older adults be more likely than younger adults to deploy cognitive resources to regulate emotions? Socioemotional selectivity theory posits that everyone has some sense of time left in life and that as time is perceived as more limited, people prioritize emotional goals more (Carstensen et al. 2006), which in turn should lead to more focus on regulating emotion when confronted with emotional stimuli (Kryla-Lighthall & Mather 2009). One prediction from this perspective that has not received support is that one's perceived time left in life should predict the positivity effect (Demeyer & De Raedt 2013, Foster et al. 2013). However, individual differences in depression and optimism likely also influence perceived time left in life and should be associated with a lower positive-to-negative ratio in attention and memory. This opposing correlation could obscure the effects of any concurrent lifespan changes. Thus, manipulations of time perspective provide a cleaner way to examine if there is a relationship between time perspective and the positivity effect. Indeed, studies manipulating time perspective have shown that shifting to a more limited time perspective increases positivity in emotion perception (Kellough & Knight 2012) and memory (S.J. Barber, P.C. Opitz, B. Martins, M. Sakaki, and M. Mather, manuscript in preparation).

In summary, the age-related positivity effect cannot be accounted for by age-related amygdala decline. The effect is often associated with age-related differences in how medial PFC responds to positive versus negative stimuli, which is consistent with a regulatory account.

Emotion Regulation

The aging and emotion regulation literature can be confusing because researchers who focus on everyday outcomes and behaviors portray older adults as being better at regulating emotions, yet in the laboratory, when they are given a structured emotion-regulation task, there is no clear evidence of greater emotion-regulation skill among older adults (for reviews, see Mather 2012, Mather & Ponzio 2015, Silvers et al. 2013). How can we reconcile these different perspectives? First, insofar as older adults focus more on emotional goals, they should allocate more resources to regulate emotions throughout their everyday lives, which should improve emotional outcomes. In other words, older adults may be chronic emotion regulators, whereas younger adults are more sporadic (e.g., Mather & Johnson 2000). Second, different emotion-regulation strategies rely on different brain regions, and older adults may compensate for lateral prefrontal declines by shifts in their go-to or preferred emotion-regulation strategy. Thus, laboratory-based experiments may fail to capture the regulatory strategies that older adults use in their everyday lives. Indeed, there is an age difference in preferences such that with greater age, people tend to prefer distraction more and reappraisal less (Scheibe et al. 2015).

Reappraisal (involving changing one's interpretation of an emotional stimulus) is a cognitively demanding strategy that, in younger adults, tends to recruit dorsal and lateral PFC regions as well as the posterior parietal lobe but does not typically recruit the vmPFC (Buhle et al. 2013). In two neuroimaging studies, older adults activated left ventrolateral PFC less than younger adults when reappraising to diminish the impact of negative emotional pictures (Opitz et al. 2012, Winecoff et al. 2011). Across two regulation strategies (reappraisal and distraction), older adults showed less dlPFC activity for regulation trials than younger adults showed (Allard & Kensinger 2014). Thus, one pattern now seen across a few studies is less lateral PFC activity during instructed emotion regulation for older than younger adults. Also, older adults are less effective than younger adults at disengaging brain regions associated with the default mode network during reappraisal (Martins et al. 2014).

On the one hand, older adults' preference for using distraction rather than reappraisal is surprising given that selective attention shares some dlPFC mechanisms with working memory, and declines in working memory are one hallmark of aging. Also, older adults are less effective at avoiding being distracted by external salient stimuli (Madden et al. 2014). Yet voluntary attention shifting, or top-down attention, shows little influence of age (Greenwood et al. 1993, Madden 2007). Parietal cortex plays a key role in top-down attention, and fewer age differences tend to be seen in functional activity in parietal cortex than in other regions during cognitive tasks (Spreng et al. 2011). Well-maintained voluntary control over attention selection may make distraction an attractive emotion-regulation option for older adults. In particular, older adults do well at using expectations or cues to guide subsequent attention (Madden 2007), which suggests that preparing to implement distraction when given a cue that something emotional is about to occur would be a particularly effective strategy for older adults. In contrast, without an external cue, proactive control is likely a computationally costly strategy for lateral PFC (Braver et al. 2014) and so may not be effective for older adults.

Recognizing Others' Emotions

Emotions are conveyed in many ways, but faces are often the most specific and clear signal of emotions. Both face identity (Germine et al. 2011) and emotion-recognition abilities (Ruffman et al. 2008) decline with age. One question is whether the age-related declines in recognizing emotions are just a function of some of the general declines in face processing. For instance, brain imaging studies reveal that older adults show less neural specialization for faces in the ventral visual cortex (Goh et al. 2010) and declines in the contributions of fusiform face area to identifying and remembering faces (Dennis et al. 2008, Grady et al. 2000). In addition, the white matter tracts passing through the right fusiform gyrus are more reduced in their structural integrity among older adults than white matter more generally, and the integrity of these tracts is associated with the ability to discriminate two similar faces (Thomas et al. 2008).

However, the emotion deficits cannot be explained simply by declines in general face-processing abilities because aging has a different impact on the ability to recognize different emotions (Ruffman et al. 2008). Older adults tend to be worse than younger adults at identifying fear and sadness and sometimes also anger. In contrast, they show little impairment at recognizing happiness, surprise, and disgust. Indeed, they sometimes are better than younger adults at recognizing disgust.

What might explain the finding that older adults show no impairment and instead even better disgust recognition than younger adults? The recognition and experience of disgust is more closely linked with the insula than any other brain region. Thus, older adults' ability to recognize others' disgust expressions suggests age-related maintenance or even increased insular involvement in face processing. Consistent with this, older adults showed more insular cortex activity than younger adults during successful encoding of fearful faces (Fischer et al. 2010) and during rating emotions (Keightley et al. 2007). However, it is hard to reconcile better insula function in late life with the age-related declines seen in the insula (as described in the insula section above).

A more plausible possibility is that age-related shifts in general face-processing strategies cause the selective enhancement in disgust recognition. Compared with younger adults, older adults are less likely to look at someone's eyes and more likely to look at their mouth or nose (Circelli et al. 2013, Firestone et al. 2007, Heisz & Ryan 2011, Murphy & Isaacowitz 2010, Sullivan et al. 2007, Wong et al. 2005) and are worse than younger adults at detecting configural changes in the eye region than in the mouth/nose region of the face (Chaby et al. 2011, Slessor et al. 2013). The age difference in top-bottom bias is seen for both neutral and emotional faces but not for scenes (Circelli et al. 2013).

Research with younger adults indicates that fear, sadness, and anger are more recognizable from the top half of the face, whereas happiness and (especially) disgust are more recognizable from the bottom half of the face (Calder et al. 2000). Surprise showed no strong top-bottom bias (Calder et al. 2000). These differences correspond with the pattern of impairment/lack thereof for older adults' emotion recognition. Indeed, among older adults, looking more at the top half of a face predicted better recognition of anger, fear, and sadness, whereas looking more at the bottom half of a face predicted better recognition of disgust, and happiness and surprise showed no significant relationship (Wong et al. 2005).

If intact perception of facial disgust expressions is due to a general shift in face-processing mechanisms and not to a stronger influence of brain regions specialized for perceiving disgust, then perception of disgust should not be selectively maintained in aging in other sensory modalities. This appears to be the case, as aging is associated with impairments in perceiving which emotion others express verbally, and disgust is as impaired as the other emotions (e.g., Lambrecht et al. 2012).

These age-related shifts in face processing may stem from changes in the brain networks involved in face processing. A network of brain regions contributes to perceiving and interpreting eye gaze, including the superior temporal sulci, the medial prefrontal cortex, and the amygdala. Existing research does not provide sufficient information to indicate whether a particular component of this network involved in processing eye gaze is particularly affected in aging. The one fMRI study to compare younger and older adults while they categorized emotion from pictures of eyes had a small sample and did not find the typical behavioral impairments among the older adults (Castelli et al. 2010).

In summary, aging is associated with declines in recognizing facial expressions of some emotions more than others and a slight improvement in recognizing disgust. These shifts do not appear to be due to selective declines in brain regions more involved in perceiving one emotion than another (if such segregation exists; for arguments against it, see Lindquist et al. 2012) but instead are due to changes in how older adults process faces. Such face-processing changes may be due to age-related changes in the structure and function of face-processing regions, but clear brain linkages have yet to be established.

Empathy

To successfully navigate the social world, it is important not just to recognize what emotions others are experiencing, but also to be able to predict how the emotion will influence their actions. To make such predictions, we rely on both the capacity to personally share (and thereby simulate) the emotions of others and the ability to understand how the perspective of others may differ from our own. These affective and cognitive aspects of empathy rely on dissociable neural circuits and so may be affected differently by aging.

Current models suggest that the insula is involved in simulating the feelings of others via embodied representations of their emotional states (e.g., Bernhardt & Singer 2012). On the other hand, the cognitive aspects of empathy (requiring theory of mind) rely on a neural network including the medial prefrontal cortex, posterior superior temporal sulcus, temporoparietal junction, and temporal pole (Bzdok et al. 2012).

Self-reported assessments of empathy show either no age-related differences in empathy (Diehl et al. 1996, Eysenck et al. 1985) or declines (Chen et al. 2014, Phillips et al. 2002, Schieman & Van Gundy 2000). When emotional and cognitive empathy are distinguished using separate subscales, cognitive but not affective empathy is lower among older than younger adults (Bailey et al. 2008, Beadle et al. 2012; but see Khanjani et al. 2015). A limitation of these studies is their cross-sectional design. A study that examined both cross-sectional and longitudinal age effects found that older cohorts tended to report less empathy but that there was no decline in self-reported empathy in individuals over a 12-year period, suggesting that cross-sectional findings of age differences in empathy may be due to cohort rather than age effects (Grühn et al. 2008). Considered together, these self-reported findings provide little clear evidence of age-related decline in empathy.

Going beyond self-report measures by using measures of emotion perception, emotion congruency with the speaker, and sympathetic body and facial responses, one study found that older adults tended to be more perceptive and empathic for a more self-relevant social loss theme than for a life transition theme, and older adults performed as well as or better than younger adults for this theme (Richter & Kunzmann 2011). Thus, as in other domains, older adults perform quite well when given self-relevant contexts (Hess 2005).

Theory-of-mind tests tap some of the processes needed for cognitive empathy. As outlined in the previous section, older adults are less likely to attend to eyes than are younger adults. They also tend to be impaired at a common theory-of-mind test using pictures of eyes (Bailey et al. 2008, Khanjani et al. 2015, Phillips et al. 2002, Slessor et al. 2007), although their impairment also extends to inferring age and gender based on eyes (Slessor et al. 2007), so it does not seem to be emotion specific. Likewise, when given stories testing the ability to make theory-of-mind inferences about the beliefs of others, older adults are impaired, but they tend to be similarly impaired at making inferences about physical or mechanical causation (German & Hehman 2006, Happé et al. 1998, Slessor et al. 2007; but see Maylor et al. 2002 for conflicting findings). These studies suggest that age-related impairments in cognitive empathy likely stem from broader impairments in cognitive function (Moran 2013). Consistent with this, older adults showed less activation in the dorsomedial

PFC than did younger adults while performing three different mentalizing tasks (Moran et al. 2012), whereas there were no consistent age differences in activity within the regions typically associated with cognitive empathy.

Another fMRI study compared younger, middle-aged, and older adults' responses to brief animations of hands or feet in painful or nonpainful situations and in dyads or alone (Chen et al. 2014). Across age groups, there was a significant effect of social context, with greater activity in the medial prefrontal cortex, posterior superior temporal sulcus, posterior cingulate cortex, and fusiform gyrus in the dyad trials. In contrast, in the right anterior insula, the response to seeing others in pain (compared with no pain) decreased across age groups, with older adults showing no significant effect. However, such changes were not significantly associated with insular gray matter changes (Chen et al. 2014), suggesting that structural volume in itself is not a strong predictor. Older adults also showed less insula activation in comparison with younger adults when offered unfair divisions of money in an ultimatum game study (Harlé & Sanfey 2012). These findings suggest that insula is less involved in interpreting social situations among older than younger adults.

In summary, initial evidence suggests that older adults show less involvement of the insula in situations in which one might simulate the feelings of others, and some evidence also suggests that although they show similar cognitive-empathy brain networks, decreased involvement of brain regions such as dlPFC that support executive function more generally may contribute to declines in making inferences about the mental states of others. Self-reported empathy scales do not necessarily reflect these changes.

Iowa Gambling Task

As mentioned previously, research using behavioral tasks to discriminate dlPFC from either ventromedial or orbital PFC in contributing to age differences has yielded mixed results (Baena et al. 2010, Lamar & Resnick 2004, MacPherson et al. 2002). A key issue that has not been fully appreciated is that the tasks used to tap vmPFC function also rely on other regions in the PFC and elsewhere. In this and the next section, I focus on the two decision tasks that have received the most attention in the aging literature and discuss what can and what cannot be gleaned from the current findings about the neural underpinnings.

The Iowa Gambling Task demonstrated that patients with vmPFC lesions have deficits in decision making that relate to impaired integration of emotional signals (Bechara et al. 1996). When given this gambling task, patients with vmPFC lesions are less likely to learn to avoid decks of cards that typically yield positive outcomes but occasionally lead to a large loss. Yet the vmPFC's role in making decisions and the underlying mechanisms of the Iowa Gambling Task have been the subjects of much debate (e.g., Buelow & Suhr 2009, Maia & McClelland 2004).

Despite uncertainty about what processes it taps, the Iowa Gambling Task has been the most highly utilized task to probe for adult age differences in decision making, and across studies, older adults are more impaired at avoiding the risky decks in this task (Mata et al. 2011). But does this impairment reflect vmPFC impairment? Not necessarily. Patients with dlPFC lesions also show deficits on the Iowa Gambling Task (Fellows & Farah 2005a), which suggests that impairments in working memory that allow ongoing information to be updated and integrated may contribute to declines in performance on the task among some older adults.

Indeed, there are indications that older adults' impairments on the task relate to impairments in learning from the decks over time. First of all, older adults' deficits tend to be stronger in later blocks than in initial ones (Denburg et al. 2005, Zamarian et al. 2008), with impairments sometimes seen in the later blocks even when there is no overall main effect of age (Baena et al. 2010, Isella et al. 2008). This pattern suggests a learning deficit. Also, older adults show more recency effects and more rapid forgetting in the task (Wood et al. 2005). Thus, impairments in memory processes may account for the age impairments in this task seen in some studies.

The Iowa Gambling Task has also revealed an emotional difference across age groups even when performance is equivalent. Whereas younger adults weighted previous losses more heavily than previous wins in their card deck choices, older adults weighted wins and losses evenly (Wood et al. 2005). In addition, healthy younger adults typically produce larger anticipatory skin conductance responses before selecting from a "bad" than a "good" deck in the task (Bechara et al. 1996). In contrast, older adults who completed the task successfully showed the opposite pattern, with larger anticipatory skin conductance responses before selecting from a good than a bad deck (Denburg et al. 2006). These findings indicate that the emotional nature of decision strategies in this task shift with age to focus more on the positive than on the negative outcomes, a shift seen in other contexts as well, such as during decision search (Löckenhoff & Carstensen 2007, Mather et al. 2005), deciding among risky gambles (Mather et al. 2012), and anticipating wins or losses (Nielsen et al. 2008).

Delay Discounting

Would you prefer $10 now or $15 in a month? Given evidence that vmPFC lesions lead to impulsive behavior (Berlin et al. 2004), one might think that vmPFC should help people be more patient and wait for delayed rewards instead of taking less valuable immediate rewards. But although patients with vmPFC lesions are less likely than controls to think about distant future events, they do not show differences in how much they value present versus future monetary rewards on a delay discounting task (Fellows & Farah 2005b). Thus vmPFC seems to influence how likely one is to think about one's own distant future rather than how much one values rewards in the future.

Older adults typically show less delay discounting than younger adults (Eppinger et al. 2012, Green et al. 1994, Reimers et al. 2009), although such differences can be reduced by controlling for income levels (Green et al. 1996). In addition, the animal literature shows consistent decreases in delay discounting with age (e.g., Roesch et al. 2012, Simon et al. 2010), although a critical difference is that delay discounting tasks for animals require the animal to learn about the delays and rewards via repeated experience. With humans, most delay discounting tasks simply describe the amount of money and delay in text format on each trial and do not present outcomes until the end of the session. One interesting finding is that when two options differ only in delay (and not in reward amount), older rats are impaired at learning to avoid the longer delay option, but that when the two options differ in reward amount (and not in delay), they are not impaired (Roesch et al. 2012). Thus, learning about differences in time duration may be more impaired in aging than is learning about differences in amount (cf. Zanto et al. 2011).

Among healthy participants between the ages of 63 and 93, those with greater structural thickness in the vmPFC exhibited less delay of gratification (Drobetz et al. 2014). Likewise, in rats trained in the delay discounting task before lesioning, orbitofrontal lesions resulted in less impulsive choices of a smaller-sooner reward over a larger-later reward than did sham lesions (Winstanley et al. 2004). Thus, the orbitofrontal cortex may help integrate information about the delay into the representation of value for an option. Failure to integrate that information makes the delayed option seem more attractive, and older adults may be impaired at this integration of time delay information into value estimations.

However, in initial functional neuroimaging studies with humans, there was no indication that vmPFC changes are associated with delay discounting changes in aging. For instance, in two fMRI studies, there were no significant age differences in medial PFC regions associated with temporal discounting (Eppinger et al. 2012, Samanez-Larkin et al. 2011). Furthermore, in a study of 123 older adults, functional connectivity between fronto-insular seed regions and PFC did not differ for those older adults with high versus low delay discounting (Han et al. 2013). Thus, further work is needed to evaluate the role of vmPFC in age differences in delay discounting.

Studies also suggest a role for other neural systems. For instance, the same study with the negative structural correlation with vmPFC found that greater dlPFC cortical surface area predicted greater delay of gratification (Drobetz et al. 2014). Also, younger adults showed significantly greater striatal activation when choosing immediate over delayed choice options, whereas older adults showed no significant difference (Eppinger et al. 2012, Samanez-Larkin et al. 2011), suggesting that age-related reductions in dopaminergic reward sensitivity may be involved. In the next section, we review age-related changes in dopaminergic influences over reward processing.

Reward Processing

Dopaminergic coding of reward prediction error seems to be disrupted in older adults. Older adults show reduced prediction error–related activity in the vmPFC and ventral striatum (a region that encompasses the nucleus accumbens and is involved in reward processing) in tasks requiring learning about which response to make to specific stimuli (Eppinger et al. 2013, Samanez-Larkin et al. 2014). Older adults also show impairments on behavioral reward learning tasks (e.g., Mell et al. 2005), especially those involving more computationally demanding model-based strategies (Worthy et al. 2014). Both the prediction error signal in the ventral striatum and probabilistic reward learning performance are enhanced when older adults receive the dopamine precursor levodopa (Chowdhury et al. 2013).

Age-related impairments may be specific to situations in which reward prediction errors support learning, because in other contexts older and younger adults show similar influences of reward. In older adults, striatal regions still respond robustly to rewarding outcomes (e.g., Samanez-Larkin et al. 2014, Schott et al. 2007, Vink et al. 2015). Recognition and source memory are enhanced by positive compared with negative feedback (Eppinger et al. 2010, Mather & Schoeke 2011) and by reward anticipation (Spaniol et al. 2014) in older adults as much as in younger adults. Task reaction times are also speeded up by potential rewards as much for older as younger adults (Vink et al. 2015).

Emotion and Behavior Change

Why do we have emotions, in particular negative emotions? One overarching potential function of emotions is to trigger behavior change (Frijda & Parrott 2011, Oatley & Johnson-Laird 1987). Yet emotions often enhance learning associations (Mather 2007). Thus, strong emotion during learning a contingency (e.g., whenever I select this option, I get a reward) could impair later behavior change that requires suppressing the learned association.

Reversal learning research indicates that orbitofrontal brain regions are critical for updating knowledge about choice outcomes and so should support flexible behavior. Yet although orbitofrontal lesions alone impair performance, when there is a concurrent amygdala lesion, orbitofrontal lesions no longer impede learning contingency reversals (Stalnaker et al. 2007). This suggests that orbitofrontal cortex facilitates flexible updating by opposing amygdala stabilization of the prior contingency. Consistent with the notion that orbitofrontal cortex works against amygdala-strengthening emotional associations, orbitofrontal activity is greater during reversal of emotional than neutral outcomes, with negative functional connectivity seen between orbitofrontal cortex and amygdala (Nashiro et al. 2012b). Older adults show effects of emotion that are similar to those of younger adults both in an fMRI reversal task (Nashiro et al. 2013b) and when updating simple associations between stimuli (Nashiro et al. 2013a), suggesting that prefrontal-amygdala interactions mediating flexible updating remain intact in later life.

Being able to flexibly change behavior may also depend on the LC and the noradrenaline it releases (Aston-Jones & Cohen 2005). Not much is known yet about how age-related changes in the LC-noradrenaline system might relate to the likelihood of exploring new options versus remaining fixated on current choices, but it is an interesting avenue for future research, especially given findings of less exploratory behavior (Mata et al. 2013) and less information seeking during decision making (Mather 2006) among older than younger adults.

Arousal and Cognitive Selectivity

As outlined in the recent Glutamate Amplifies Noradrenergic Effects model (Mather et al. 2015), the LC increases the selectivity of processing through a variety of mechanisms, including shunting blood flow and metabolic resources to highly active regions and away from other regions. At local synapses, norepinephrine interacts with the brain's primary excitatory neurotransmitter, glutamate, to amplify activity at the most highly active neurons while inhibiting activation elsewhere. These modulatory effects of the LC are especially potent in moments of high emotional arousal, when people tend to focus on whatever is most salient and ignore the rest. Thus, noradrenaline prepares the brain for targeted action by supporting processing in brain regions that are most highly active at that moment. This model accounts for findings that arousal increases the selectivity of attention and memory, favoring salient and high-priority items (e.g., Lee et al. 2014, Sakaki et al. 2014). Initial evidence indicates that older adults show similar enhancement of bottom-up salience under arousal (Sutherland & Mather 2015) but that arousal does not increase selectivity for older adults; instead, it broadly enhances processing of both low- and high-priority items (T.H. Lee, S.G. Greening, A. Ponzio, D. Clewett, and M. Mather, manuscript in preparation).

CONCLUSIONS

Emotion processes depend on interacting systems of neurotransmitters and specific brain regions. Changes with age in these systems vary in nature and in degree.

The amygdala and the vmPFC, two brain regions that play key roles in emotion processing, show less structural and functional decline with age in comparison with many other brain regions. In addition, they show shifts in processing that support favoring positive over negative stimuli in attention and memory. Although older adults do perform differently than younger adults on tests that have previously been identified with the vmPFC, such as facial emotion expression recognition and the Iowa Gambling Task performance, the differences in performance are better explained by factors other than age-related vmPFC decline, such as a reduced focus on eyes during face processing and declines in dlPFC working memory and learning processes.

The insula shows both structural and functional decline in aging that initial evidence suggests may be linked to age-related changes in empathic processes. Yet despite the role of the insula in feelings of disgust, older adults tend to recognize disgusted facial expressions as well or better than younger adults, potentially due to their greater focus on noses and mouths rather than eyes when looking at faces.

Age-related decline in the dopaminergic system is associated with impaired reward prediction error computation, but when new learning is not involved, reward anticipation and response are well maintained in aging.

The noradrenergic system is vulnerable to pathology that slowly progresses throughout the lifespan and may trigger a compensatory release of noradrenaline. Older adults often show as much of an arousal response to emotional stimuli as younger adults, but this arousal seems to have less of a targeted effect on cognitive processing.

In general, shifts in the relative efficacy of different brain systems may contribute to changes in the strategies older adults use to cope with difficult emotional situations and to maintain effective emotional processing. The relative lack of decline in core emotion-related brain regions likely plays a key role in explaining older adults' well-maintained emotional functioning, in particular the ability to maintain positive affect and minimize negative affect in everyday life.

SUMMARY POINTS

1. Amygdala and vmPFC structure and function are relatively well maintained in healthy aging.

2. Increased vmPFC activity (along with decreased amygdala activity) in older adults confronted with negative stimuli is associated with better everyday emotional outcomes.

3. Age-related declines in lateral PFC may be related to shifts in preferred emotion-regulation strategies.

4. Selective sparing of recognition of facial disgust along with declines in recognition of fear, sadness, and anger is better accounted for by changes in general face-processing strategies than by aging effects on specific brain regions.

5. Although reward-learning processes are impaired among older adults, responses to rewarding outcomes are maintained.

6. Potential age-related decreases in insular contributions to interoception and simulating the emotions of others deserve further examination.

7. For both older and younger adults, emotion interferes with updating associations via amygdala-PFC interactions.

DISCLOSURE STATEMENT

The author is not aware of any affiliations, memberships, funding, or financial holdings that might be perceived as affecting the objectivity of this review.

ACKNOWLEDGMENTS

I thank Rico Velasco for assistance in creating figures using 3D Slicer (**http://www.nitrc.org/projects/slicer/**) and the National Institutes of Health for support from grants RO1AG025340, R01AG038043, and R21AG048463.

LITERATURE CITED

Allard ES, Kensinger EA. 2014. Age-related differences in neural recruitment during the use of cognitive reappraisal and selective attention as emotion regulation strategies. *Front. Psychol.* 5:296

Allen JS, Bruss J, Brown CK, Damasio H. 2005a. Methods for studying the aging brain: volumetric analyses versus VBM. *Neurobiol. Aging* 26:1275–78

Allen JS, Bruss J, Brown CK, Damasio H. 2005b. Normal neuroanatomical variation due to age: the major lobes and a parcellation of the temporal region. *Neurobiol. Aging* 26:1245–60

Ashley V, Swick D. 2009. Consequences of emotional stimuli: age differences on pure and mixed blocks of the emotional Stroop. *Behav. Brain Funct.* 5:14

Aston-Jones G, Cohen JD. 2005. An integrative theory of locus coeruleus-norepinephrine function: adaptive gain and optimal performance. *Annu. Rev. Neurosci.* 28:403–50

Bäckman L, Lindenberger U, Li SC, Nyberg L. 2010. Linking cognitive aging to alterations in dopamine neurotransmitter functioning: recent data and future avenues. *Neurosci. Biobehav. Rev.* 34:670–77

Baena E, Allen PA, Kaut KP, Hall RJ. 2010. On age differences in prefrontal function: the importance of emotional/cognitive integration. *Neuropsychologia* 48:319–33

Bailey PE, Henry JD, Von Hippel W. 2008. Empathy and social functioning in late adulthood. *Aging Ment. Health* 12:499–503

Beadle JN, Paradiso S, Kovach C, Polgreen L, Denburg NL, Tranel D. 2012. Effects of age-related differences in empathy on social economic decision-making. *Int. Psychogeriatr.* 24:822–33

Bechara A, Tranel D, Damasio H, Damasio AR. 1996. Failure to respond autonomically to anticipated future outcomes following damage to prefrontal cortex. *Cereb. Cortex* 6:215–25

Beekman AT, Bremmer MA, Deeg DJ, Van Balkom AJ, Smit JH, et al. 1998. Anxiety disorders in later life: a report from the Longitudinal Aging Study Amsterdam. *Int. J. Geriatr. Psychiatry* 13:717–26

Berlin H, Rolls E, Kischka U. 2004. Impulsivity, time perception, emotion and reinforcement sensitivity in patients with orbitofrontal cortex lesions. *Brain* 127:1108–26

Bernhardt BC, Singer T. 2012. The neural basis of empathy. *Annu. Rev. Neurosci.* 35:1–23

Bickart KC, Wright CI, Dautoff RJ, Dickerson BC, Barrett LF. 2011. Amygdala volume and social network size in humans. *Nat. Neurosci.* 14:163–64

Birditt KS, Fingerman KL. 2005. Do we get better at picking our battles? Age group differences in descriptions of behavioral reactions to interpersonal tensions. *J. Gerontol. Ser. B Psychol. Sci. Soc. Sci.* 60:P121–28

Braak H, Thal DR, Ghebremedhin E, Del Tredici K. 2011. Stages of the pathologic process in Alzheimer disease: age categories from 1 to 100 years. *J. Neuropathol. Exp. Neurol.* 70:960–69

Brabec J, Rulseh A, Hoyt B, Vizek M, Horinek D, et al. 2010. Volumetry of the human amygdala—an anatomical study. *Psychiatry Res. Neuroimaging* 182:67–72

Brassen S, Gamer M, Buchel C. 2011. Anterior cingulate activation is related to a positivity bias and emotional stability in successful aging. *Biol. Psychiatry* 70:131–37

Braver TS, Krug MK, Chiew KS, Kool W, Westbrook JA, et al. 2014. Mechanisms of motivation—cognition interaction: challenges and opportunities. *Cogn. Affect. Behav. Neurosci.* 14:443–72

Buelow MT, Suhr JA. 2009. Construct validity of the Iowa gambling task. *Neuropsychol. Rev.* 19:102–14

Buhle JT, Silvers JA, Wager TD, Lopez R, Onyemekwu C, et al. 2013. Cognitive reappraisal of emotion: a meta-analysis of human neuroimaging studies. *Cereb. Cortex* 24(11):2981–90

Burzynska AZ, Preuschhof C, Bäckman L, Nyberg L, Li S-C, et al. 2010. Age-related differences in white matter microstructure: region-specific patterns of diffusivity. *NeuroImage* 49:2104–12

Bzdok D, Schilbach L, Vogeley K, Schneider K, Laird AR, et al. 2012. Parsing the neural correlates of moral cognition: ALE meta-analysis on morality, theory of mind, and empathy. *Brain Struct. Funct.* 217:783–96

Cacioppo JT, Berntson CG, Bechara A, Tranel D, Hawkley LC. 2011. Could an aging brain contribute to subjective well-being? The value added by a social neuroscience perspective. In *Social Neuroscience: Toward Understanding the Underpinnings of the Social Mind*, ed. A Todorov, ST Fiske, D Prentice, pp. 249–62. New York: Oxford Univ. Press

Calder AJ, Young AW, Keane J, Dean M. 2000. Configural information in facial expression perception. *J. Exp. Psychol.: Hum. Percept. Perform.* 26:527–51

Carstensen LL, Mikels JA, Mather M. 2006. Aging and the intersection of cognition, motivation and emotion. In *Handbook of the Psychology of Aging*, ed. JE Birren, KW Schaie, pp. 343–62. San Diego, CA: Academic. 6th ed.

Carstensen LL, Turan B, Scheibe S, Ram N, Ersner-Hershfield H, et al. 2011. Emotional experience improves with age: evidence based on over 10 years of experience sampling. *Psychol. Aging* 26:21–33

Castelli I, Baglio F, Blasi V, Alberoni M, Falini A, et al. 2010. Effects of aging on mindreading ability through the eyes: an fMRI study. *Neuropsychologia* 48:2586–94

Chaby L, Narme P, George N. 2011. Older adults' configural processing of faces: role of second-order information. *Psychol. Aging* 26:71–79

Charles ST, Carstensen LL. 2008. Unpleasant situations elicit different emotional responses in younger and older adults. *Psychol. Aging* 23:495–504

Charles ST, Mather M, Carstensen LL. 2003. Aging and emotional memory: the forgettable nature of negative images for older adults. *J. Exp. Psychol.: Gen.* 132:310–24

Charles ST, Reynolds CA, Gatz M. 2001. Age-related differences and change in positive and negative affect over 23 years. *J. Personal. Soc. Psychol.* 80:136–51

Chen Y-C, Chen C-C, Decety J, Cheng Y. 2014. Aging is associated with changes in the neural circuits underlying empathy. *Neurobiol. Aging* 35:827–36

Cherbuin N, Sachdev PS, Anstey KJ. 2011. Mixed handedness is associated with greater age-related decline in volumes of the hippocampus and amygdala: the PATH through life study. *Brain Behav.* 1:125–34

Chopik WJ, Edelstein RS, Fraley RC. 2013. From the cradle to the grave: age differences in attachment from early adulthood to old age. *J. Personal.* 81:171–83

Chowdhury R, Guitart-Masip M, Lambert C, Dayan P, Huys Q, et al. 2013. Dopamine restores reward prediction errors in old age. *Nat. Neurosci.* 16:648–53

Circelli KS, Clark US, Cronin-Golomb A. 2013. Visual scanning patterns and executive function in relation to facial emotion recognition in aging. *Aging Neuropsychol. Cogn.* 20:148–73

Clark L, Bechara A, Damasio H, Aitken MRF, Sahakian BJ, Robbins TW. 2008. Differential effects of insular and ventromedial prefrontal cortex lesions on risky decision-making. *Brain* 131:1311–22

Clewett D, Bachman S, Mather M. 2014. Age-related reduced prefrontal-amygdala structural connectivity is associated with lower trait anxiety. *Neuropsychology* 28:631–42

Clewett D, Lee TH, Greening S, Ponzio A, Margalit E, Mather M. 2015. Neuromelanin marks the spot: identifying a locus coeruleus biomarker of cognitive reserve in healthy aging. *Neurobiol. Aging.* In press

Colzato LS, Van Den Wildenberg WP, Hommel B. 2013. The genetic impact (C957T-DRD2) on inhibitory control is magnified by aging. *Neuropsychologia* 51:1377–81

Curiati P, Tamashiro J, Squarzoni P, Duran F, Santos L, et al. 2009. Brain structural variability due to aging and gender in cognitively healthy elders: results from the São Paulo Ageing and Health Study. *Am. J. Neuroradiol.* 30:1850–56

Damasio AR, Tranel D, Damasio H. 1990. Individuals with sociopathic behavior caused by frontal damage fail to respond autonomically to social stimuli. *Behav. Brain Res.* 41:81–94

Davis SW, Dennis NA, Buchler NG, White LE. 2009. Assessing the effects of age on long white matter tracts using diffusion tensor tractography. *NeuroImage* 46:530–41

Demeyer I, De Raedt R. 2013. Attentional bias for emotional information in older adults: the role of emotion and future time perspective. *PLOS ONE* 8:e65429

Denburg NL, Recknor EC, Bechara A, Tranel D. 2006. Psychophysiological anticipation of positive outcomes promotes advantageous decision-making in normal older persons. *Int. J. Psychophysiol.* 61:19–25

Denburg NL, Tranel D, Bechara A. 2005. The ability to decide advantageously declines prematurely in some normal older persons. *Neuropsychologia* 43:1099–106

Dennis NA, Hayes SM, Prince SE, Madden DJ, Huettel SA, Cabeza R. 2008. Effects of aging on the neural correlates of successful item and source memory encoding. *J. Exp. Psychol.: Learn. Mem. Cogn.* 34:791–808

Diehl M, Coyle N, Labouvie-Vief G. 1996. Age and sex differences in strategies of coping and defense across the life span. *Psychol. Aging* 11:127–39

Dolcos S, Katsumi Y, Dixon RA. 2014. The role of arousal in the spontaneous regulation of emotions in healthy aging: a fMRI investigation. *Front. Psychol.* 5:681

Drobetz R, Hänggi J, Maercker A, Kaufmann K, Jäncke L, Forstmeier S. 2014. Structural brain correlates of delay of gratification in the elderly. *Behav. Neurosci.* 128:134–45

Eppinger B, Herbert M, Kray J. 2010. We remember the good things: age differences in learning and memory. *Neurobiol. Learn. Mem.* 93:515–21

Eppinger B, Nystrom LE, Cohen JD. 2012. Reduced sensitivity to immediate reward during decision-making in older than younger adults. *PLOS ONE* 7:e36953

Eppinger B, Schuck NW, Nystrom LE, Cohen JD. 2013. Reduced striatal responses to reward prediction errors in older compared with younger adults. *J. Neurosci.* 33:9905–12

Erk S, Walter H, Abler B. 2008. Age-related physiological responses to emotion anticipation and exposure. *NeuroReport* 19:447–52

Eysenck SB, Pearson PR, Easting G, Allsopp JF. 1985. Age norms for impulsiveness, venturesomeness and empathy in adults. *Personal. Individ. Differ.* 6:613–19

Fellows LK, Farah MJ. 2005a. Different underlying impairments in decision-making following ventromedial and dorsolateral frontal lobe damage in humans. *Cereb. Cortex* 15:58–63

Fellows LK, Farah MJ. 2005b. Dissociable elements of human foresight: a role for the ventromedial frontal lobes in framing the future, but not in discounting future rewards. *Neuropsychologia* 43:1214–21

Firestone A, Turk-Browne NB, Ryan JD. 2007. Age-related deficits in face recognition are related to underlying changes in scanning behavior. *Aging Neuropsychol. Cogn.* 14:594–607

Fischer H, Nyberg L, Backman L. 2010. Age-related differences in brain regions supporting successful encoding of emotional faces. *Cortex* 46:490–97

Fjell AM, McEvoy L, Holland D, Dale AM, Walhovd KB. 2013a. Brain changes in older adults at very low risk for Alzheimer's disease. *J. Neurosci.* 33:8237–42

Fjell AM, Walhovd KB. 2010. Structural brain changes in aging: courses, causes and cognitive consequences. *Rev. Neurosci.* 21:187–221

Fjell AM, Walhovd KB, Fennema-Notestine C, McEvoy LK, Hagler DJ, et al. 2009a. One-year brain atrophy evident in healthy aging. *J. Neurosci.* 29:15223–31

Fjell AM, Westlye LT, Amlien I, Espeseth T, Reinvang I, et al. 2009b. High consistency of regional cortical thinning in aging across multiple samples. *Cereb. Cortex* 19:2001–12

Fjell AM, Westlye LT, Grydeland H, Amlien I, Espeseth T, et al. 2013b. Critical ages in the life course of the adult brain: nonlinear subcortical aging. *Neurobiol. Aging* 34:2239–47

Ford JH, Kensinger EA. 2014. The relation between structural and functional connectivity depends on age and on task goals. *Front. Hum. Neurosci.* 8:307

Foster SM, Davis HP, Kisley MA. 2013. Brain responses to emotional images related to cognitive ability in older adults. *Psychol. Aging* 28:179–90

Frijda NH, Parrott WG. 2011. Basic emotions or ur-emotions? *Emot. Rev.* 3:406–15

Frodl T, Jäger M, Smajstrlova I, Born C, Bottlender R, et al. 2008. Effect of hippocampal and amygdala volumes on clinical outcomes in major depression: a 3-year prospective magnetic resonance imaging study. *J. Psychiatry Neurosci.* 33:423–30

Gagliese L. 2009. Pain and aging: the emergence of a new subfield of pain research. *J. Pain* 10:343–53

Ge R, Fu Y, Wang D, Yao L, Long Z. 2014. Age-related alterations of brain network underlying the retrieval of emotional autobiographical memories: an fMRI study using independent component analysis. *Front. Hum. Neurosci.* 8:629

German TP, Hehman JA. 2006. Representational and executive selection resources in "theory of mind": evidence from compromised belief-desire reasoning in old age. *Cognition* 101:129–52

Germine LT, Duchaine B, Nakayama K. 2011. Where cognitive development and aging meet: face learning ability peaks after age 30. *Cognition* 118:201–10

Goh JO, Suzuki A, Park DC. 2010. Reduced neural selectivity increases fMRI adaptation with age during face discrimination. *NeuroImage* 51:336–44

Good CD, Johnsrude IS, Ashburner J, Henson RNA, Friston KJ, Frackowiak RSJ. 2001. A voxel-based morphometric study of ageing in 465 normal adult human brains. *NeuroImage* 14:21–36

Grady CL, McIntosh AR, Horwitz B, Rapoport SI. 2000. Age-related changes in the neural correlates of degraded and nondegraded face processing. *Cogn. Neuropsychol.* 17:165–86

Grafman J, Schwab K, Warden D, Pridgen A, Brown H, Salazar A. 1996. Frontal lobe injuries, violence, and aggression: a report of the Vietnam Head Injury Study. *Neurology* 46:1231–38

Green L, Fry AF, Myerson J. 1994. Discounting of delayed rewards: a life-span comparison. *Psychol. Sci.* 5:33–36

Green L, Myerson J, Lichtman D, Rosen S, Fry A. 1996. Temporal discounting in choice between delayed rewards: the role of age and income. *Psychol. Aging* 11:79–84

Greenwood PM, Parasuraman R, Haxby JV. 1993. Changes in visuospatial attention over the adult lifespan. *Neuropsychologia* 31:471–85

Grieve SM, Clark CR, Williams LM, Peduto AJ, Gordon E. 2005. Preservation of limbic and paralimbic structures in aging. *Hum. Brain Mapp.* 25:391–401

Gruenewald TL, Mroczek DK, Ryff CD, Singer BH. 2008. Diverse pathways to positive and negative affect in adulthood and later life: an integrative approach using recursive partitioning. *Dev. Psychol.* 44:330–43

Grühn D, Rebucal K, Diehl M, Lumley M, Labouvie-Vief G. 2008. Empathy across the adult lifespan: longitudinal and experience-sampling findings. *Emotion* 8:753–65

Hahn S, Carlson C, Singer S, Gronlund SD. 2006. Aging and visual search: automatic and controlled attentional bias to threat faces. *Acta Psychol.* 123:312–36

Han SD, Boyle PA, Yu L, Fleischman DA, Arfanakis K, Bennett DA. 2013. Ventromedial PFC, parahippocampal, and cerebellar connectivity are associated with temporal discounting in old age. *Exp. Gerontol.* 48:1489–98

Happé FG, Winner E, Brownell H. 1998. The getting of wisdom: theory of mind in old age. *Dev. Psychol.* 34:358–62

Harlé KM, Sanfey AG. 2012. Social economic decision-making across the lifespan: an fMRI investigation. *Neuropsychologia* 50:1416–24

He X, Qin W, Liu Y, Zhang X, Duan Y, et al. 2014. Abnormal salience network in normal aging and in amnestic mild cognitive impairment and Alzheimer's disease. *Hum. Brain Mapp.* 35:3446–64

Heisz JJ, Ryan JD. 2011. The effects of prior exposure on face processing in younger and older adults. *Front. Aging Neurosci.* 3:15

Hess TM. 2005. Memory and aging in context. *Psychol. Bull.* 131:383–406

Hölzel BK, Carmody J, Evans KC, Hoge EA, Dusek JA, et al. 2009. Stress reduction correlates with structural changes in the amygdala. *Soc. Cogn. Affect. Neurosci.* 5:11–17

Isaacowitz DM, Allard ES, Murphy NA, Schlangel M. 2009a. The time course of age-related preferences toward positive and negative stimuli. *J. Gerontol. Ser. B Psychol. Sci. Soc. Sci.* 64:188–92

Isaacowitz DM, Toner K, Neupert SD. 2009b. Use of gaze for real-time mood regulation: effects of age and attentional functioning. *Psychol. Aging* 24:989–94

Isella V, Mapelli C, Morielli N, Pelati O, Franceschi M, Appollonio IM. 2008. Age-related quantitative and qualitative changes in decision making ability. *Behav. Neurol.* 19:59–63

Jernigan TL, Archibald SL, Fennema-Notestine C, Gamst AC, Stout JC, et al. 2001. Effects of age on tissues and regions of the cerebrum and cerebellum. *Neurobiol. Aging* 22:581–94

Jiang J, Sachdev P, Lipnicki DM, Zhang H, Liu T, et al. 2014. A longitudinal study of brain atrophy over two years in community-dwelling older individuals. *NeuroImage* 86:203–11

Kalpouzos G, Chételat G, Baron J-C, Landeau B, Mevel K, et al. 2009. Voxel-based mapping of brain gray matter volume and glucose metabolism profiles in normal aging. *Neurobiol. Aging* 30:112–24

Kehoe EG, Toomey JM, Balsters JH, Bokde AL. 2013. Healthy aging is associated with increased neural processing of positive valence but attenuated processing of emotional arousal: an fMRI study. *Neurobiol. Aging* 34:809–21

Keightley ML, Chiew KS, Winocur G, Grady CL. 2007. Age-related differences in brain activity underlying identification of emotional expressions in faces. *Soc. Cogn. Affect. Neurosci.* 2:292–302

Kellough JL, Knight BG. 2012. Positivity effects in older adults' perception of facial emotion: the role of future time perspective. *J. Gerontol. Ser. B Psychol. Sci. Soc. Sci.* 67:150–58

Kensinger EA. 2008. Age differences in memory for arousing and nonarousing emotional words. *J. Gerontol. Ser. B Psychol. Sci. Soc. Sci.* 63:P13–18

Khanjani Z, Mosanezhad JE, Hekmati I, Khalilzade S, Etemadi NM, et al. 2015. Comparison of cognitive empathy, emotional empathy, and social functioning in different age groups. *Aust. Psychol.* 50:80–85

Knight M, Seymour TL, Gaunt JT, Baker C, Nesmith K, Mather M. 2007. Aging and goal-directed emotional attention: Distraction reverses emotional biases. *Emotion* 7:705–14

Kryla-Lighthall N, Mather M. 2009. The role of cognitive control in older adults' emotional well-being. In *Handbook of Theories of Aging*, ed. V Berngtson, D Gans, N Putney, M Silverstein, pp. 323–44. New York: Springer. 2nd ed.

LaBar KS, Mesulam MM, Gitelman DR, Weintraub S. 2000. Emotional curiosity: Modulation of visuospatial attention by arousal is preserved in aging and early-stage Alzheimer's disease. *Neuropsychologia* 38:1734–40

Lamar M, Resnick SM. 2004. Aging and prefrontal functions: dissociating orbitofrontal and dorsolateral abilities. *Neurobiol. Aging* 25:553–58

Lambrecht L, Kreifelts B, Wildgruber D. 2012. Age-related decrease in recognition of emotional facial and prosodic expressions. *Emotion* 12:529–39

Leclerc CM, Kensinger EA. 2008a. Age-related differences in medial prefrontal activation in response to emotional images. *Cogn. Affect. Behav. Neurosci.* 8:153–64

Leclerc CM, Kensinger EA. 2008b. Effects of age on detection of emotional information. *Psychol. Aging* 23:209–15

Leclerc CM, Kensinger EA. 2010. Age-related valence-based reversal in recruitment of medial prefrontal cortex on a visual search task. *Soc. Neurosci.* 5:560–76

Leclerc CM, Kensinger EA. 2011. Neural processing of emotional pictures and words: a comparison of young and older adults. *Dev. Neuropsychol.* 36:519–38

Lee TH, Sakaki M, Cheng R, Velasco R, Mather M. 2014. Emotional arousal amplifies the effects of biased competition in the brain. *Soc. Cogn. Affect. Neurosci.* 9:2067–77

Li S-C, Papenberg G, Nagel IE, Preuschhof C, Schröder J, et al. 2013. Aging magnifies the effects of dopamine transporter and D2 receptor genes on backward serial memory. *Neurobiol. Aging* 34:358.e1–10

Li S-C, Rieckmann A. 2014. Neuromodulation and aging: implications of aging neuronal gain control on cognition. *Curr. Opin. Neurobiol.* 29:148–58

Li W, Tol MJ, Li M, Miao W, Jiao Y, et al. 2014. Regional specificity of sex effects on subcortical volumes across the lifespan in healthy aging. *Hum. Brain Mapp.* 35:238–47

Lindquist KA, Wager TD, Kober H, Bliss-Moreau E, Barrett LF. 2012. The brain basis of emotion: a meta-analytic review. *Behav. Brain Sci.* 35:121–43

Löckenhoff CE, Carstensen LL. 2007. Aging, emotion, and health-related decision strategies: Motivational manipulations can reduce age differences. *Psychol. Aging* 22:134–46

Long X, Liao W, Jiang C, Liang D, Qiu B, Zhang L. 2012. Healthy aging: an automatic analysis of global and regional morphological alterations of human brain. *Acad. Radiol.* 19:785–93

Lövdén M, Schmiedek F, Kennedy KM, Rodrigue KM, Lindenberger U, Raz N. 2013. Does variability in cognitive performance correlate with frontal brain volume? *NeuroImage* 64:209–15

MacPherson SE, Phillips LH, Della Sala S. 2002. Age, executive function, and social decision making: a dorsolateral prefrontal theory of cognitive aging. *Psychol. Aging* 17:598–609

Madden DJ. 2007. Aging and visual attention. *Curr. Dir. Psychol. Sci.* 16:70–74

Madden DJ, Parks EL, Davis SW, Diaz MT, Potter GG, et al. 2014. Age mediation of frontoparietal activation during visual feature search. *NeuroImage* 102:262–74

Maia TV, McClelland JL. 2004. A reexamination of the evidence for the somatic marker hypothesis: what participants really know in the Iowa gambling task. *PNAS* 101:16075–80

Martins B, Ponzio A, Velasco R, Kaplan J, Mather M. 2014. Dedifferentiation of emotion regulation strategies in the aging brain. *Soc. Cogn. Affect. Neurosci.* 10:840–47

Mata R, Josef AK, Samanez-Larkin GR, Hertwig R. 2011. Age differences in risky choice: a meta-analysis. *Ann. N. Y. Acad. Sci.* 1235:18–29

Mata R, Wilke A, Czienskowski U. 2013. Foraging across the life span: Is there a reduction in exploration with aging? *Front. Neurosci.* 7:53

Mather M. 2006. A review of decision-making processes: weighing the risks and benefits of aging. In *When I'm 64*, ed. LL Carstensen, CR Hartel, pp. 145–73. Washington, DC: Natl. Acad. Press

Mather M. 2007. Emotional arousal and memory binding: an object-based framework. *Perspect. Psychol. Sci.* 2:33–52

Mather M. 2012. The emotion paradox in the aging brain. *Ann. N. Y. Acad. Sci.* 1251:33–49

Mather M, Canli T, English T, Whitfield SL, Wais P, et al. 2004. Amygdala responses to emotionally valenced stimuli in older and younger adults. *Psychol. Sci.* 15:259–63

Mather M, Carstensen LL. 2003. Aging and attentional biases for emotional faces. *Psychol. Sci.* 14:409–15

Mather M, Carstensen LL. 2005. Aging and motivated cognition: the positivity effect in attention and memory. *Trends Cogn. Sci.* 9:496–502

Mather M, Clewett D, Sakaki M, Harley CW. 2015. Norepinephrine ignites local hot spots of neuronal excitation: how arousal amplifies selectivity in perception and memory. *Behav. Brain Sci.* In press

Mather M, Johnson MK. 2000. Choice-supportive source monitoring: Do our decisions seem better to us as we age? *Psychol. Aging* 15:596–606

Mather M, Knight M. 2005. Goal-directed memory: the role of cognitive control in older adults' emotional memory. *Psychol. Aging* 20:554–70

Mather M, Knight M, McCaffrey M. 2005. The allure of the alignable: younger and older adults' false memories of choice features. *J. Exp. Psychol.: Gen.* 134:38–51

Mather M, Knight MR. 2006. Angry faces get noticed quickly: Threat detection is not impaired among older adults. *J. Gerontol. Ser. B Psychol. Sci. Soc. Sci.* 61:P54–57

Mather M, Mazar N, Gorlick M, Lighthall NR, Ariely D. 2012. Risk preferences and aging: the "certainty effect" in older adults' decision making. *Psychol. Aging* 27:801–16

Mather M, Ponzio A. 2015. Emotion and aging. In *Handbook of Emotions*, ed. LF Barrett, M Lewis, J Haviland-Jones. New York: Guilford. 4th ed. In press

Mather M, Schoeke A. 2011. Positive outcomes enhance incidental learning for both younger and older adults. *Front. Neurosci.* 5:129

Maylor EA, Moulson JM, Muncer AM, Taylor LA. 2002. Does performance on theory of mind tasks decline in old age? *Br. J. Psychol.* 93:465–85

Meier TB, Desphande AS, Vergun S, Nair VA, Song J, et al. 2012. Support vector machine classification and characterization of age-related reorganization of functional brain networks. *NeuroImage* 60:601–13

Mell T, Heekeren HR, Marschner A, Wartenburger I, Villringer A, Reischies FM. 2005. Effect of aging on stimulus-reward association learning. *Neuropsychologia* 43:554–63

Menon V, Uddin LQ. 2010. Saliency, switching, attention and control: a network model of insula function. *Brain Struct. Funct.* 214:655–67

Moran JM. 2013. Lifespan development: the effects of typical aging on theory of mind. *Behav. Brain Res.* 237:32–40

Moran JM, Jolly E, Mitchell JP. 2012. Social-cognitive deficits in normal aging. *J. Neurosci.* 32:5553–61

Morey RA, Petty CM, Xu Y, Hayes JP, Wagner HR, et al. 2009. A comparison of automated segmentation and manual tracing for quantifying hippocampal and amygdala volumes. *NeuroImage* 45:855–66

Moriguchi Y, Negreira A, Weierich M, Dautoff R, Dickerson BC, et al. 2011. Differential hemodynamic response in affective circuitry with aging: an fMRI study of novelty, valence, and arousal. *J. Cogn. Neurosci.* 23:1027–41

Mouton PR, Pakkenberg B, Gundersen HJG, Price DL. 1994. Absolute number and size of pigmented locus coeruleus neurons in young and aged individuals. *J. Chem. Neuroanat.* 7:185–90

Mu Q, Xie J, Wen Z, Weng Y, Shuyun Z. 1999. A quantitative MR study of the hippocampal formation, the amygdala, and the temporal horn of the lateral ventricle in healthy subjects 40 to 90 years of age. *Am. J. Neuroradiol.* 20:207–11

Murphy NA, Isaacowitz DM. 2010. Age effects and gaze patterns in recognising emotional expressions: an in-depth look at gaze measures and covariates. *Cogn. Emot.* 24:436–52

Murray LJ, Ranganath C. 2007. The dorsolateral prefrontal cortex contributes to successful relational memory encoding. *J. Neurosci.* 27:5515–22

Nagel IE, Chicherio C, Li S-C, Von Oertzen T, Sander T, et al. 2008. Human aging magnifies genetic effects on executive functioning and working memory. *Front. Hum. Neurosci.* 2:1

Nashiro K, Sakaki M, Huffman D, Mather M. 2013a. Both younger and older adults have difficulty updating emotional memories. *J. Gerontol. Ser. B Psychol. Sci. Soc. Sci.* 68:224–27

Nashiro K, Sakaki M, Mather M. 2012a. Age differences in brain activity during emotion processing: reflections of age-related decline or increased emotion regulation? *Gerontology* 58:156–63

Nashiro K, Sakaki M, Nga L, Mather M. 2012b. Differential brain activity during emotional versus non-emotional reversal learning. *J. Cogn. Neurosci.* 24:1794–805

Nashiro K, Sakaki M, Nga L, Mather M. 2013b. Age-related similarities and differences in brain activity underlying reversal learning. *Front. Integr. Neurosci.* 7:37

Nielsen L, Knutson B, Carstensen LL. 2008. Affect dynamics, affective forecasting, and aging. *Emotion* 8:318–30

O'Leary KD, Woodin EM. 2005. Partner aggression and problem drinking across the lifespan: How much do they decline? *Clin. Psychol. Rev.* 25:877–94

Oatley K, Johnson-Laird PN. 1987. Towards a cognitive theory of emotions. *Cogn. Emot.* 1:29–50

Onoda K, Ishihara M, Yamaguchi S. 2012. Decreased functional connectivity by aging is associated with cognitive decline. *J. Cogn. Neurosci.* 24:2186–98

Opitz PC, Rauch LC, Terry DP, Urry HL. 2012. Prefrontal mediation of age differences in cognitive reappraisal. *Neurobiol. Aging* 33:645–55

Persson N, Ghisletta P, Dahle CL, Bender AR, Yang Y, et al. 2014. Regional brain shrinkage over two years: individual differences and effects of pro-inflammatory genetic polymorphisms. *NeuroImage* 103:334–48

Petrican R, Moscovitch M, Schimmack U. 2008. Cognitive resources, valence, and memory retrieval of emotional events in older adults. *Psychol. Aging* 23:585–94

Phillips LH, Della Sala S. 1998. Aging, intelligence, and anatomical segregation in the frontal lobes. *Learn. Individ. Differ.* 10:217–43

Phillips LH, Henry J, Hosie J, Milne A. 2006. Age, anger regulation and well-being. *Aging Ment. Health* 10:250–56

Phillips LH, MacLean RDJ, Allen R. 2002. Age and the understanding of emotions: neuropsychological and sociocognitive perspectives. *J. Gerontol. Ser. B Psychol. Sci. Soc. Sci.* 57:P526–30

Raz N, Ghisletta P, Rodrigue KM, Kennedy KM, Lindenberger U. 2010. Trajectories of brain aging in middle-aged and older adults: regional and individual differences. *NeuroImage* 51:501–11

Reed AE, Chan L, Mikels JA. 2014. Meta-analysis of the age-related positivity effect: age differences in preferences for positive over negative information. *Psychol. Aging* 29:1–15

Reimers S, Maylor EA, Stewart N, Chater N. 2009. Associations between a one-shot delay discounting measure and age, income, education and real-world impulsive behavior. *Personal. Individ. Differ.* 47:973–78

Richter D, Kunzmann U. 2011. Age differences in three facets of empathy: performance-based evidence. *Psychol. Aging* 26:60–70

Roesch MR, Bryden DW, Cerri DH, Haney ZR, Schoenbaum G. 2012. Willingness to wait and altered encoding of time-discounted reward in the orbitofrontal cortex with normal aging. *J. Neurosci.* 32:5525–33

Ruffman T, Henry JD, Livingstone V, Phillips LH. 2008. A meta-analytic review of emotion recognition and aging: implications for neuropsychological models of aging. *Neurosci. Biobehav. Rev.* 32:863–81

Sakaki M, Fryer K, Mather M. 2014. Emotion strengthens high-priority memory traces but weakens low-priority memory traces. *Psychol. Sci.* 25:387–95

Sakaki M, Nga L, Mather M. 2013. Amygdala functional connectivity with medial prefrontal cortex at rest predicts the positivity effect in older adults' memory. *J. Cogn. Neurosci.* 25:1206–24

Samanez-Larkin GR, Mata R, Radu PT, Ballard IC, Carstensen LL, McClure SM. 2011. Age differences in striatal delay sensitivity during intertemporal choice in healthy adults. *Front. Neurosci.* 5:126

Samanez-Larkin GR, Worthy DA, Mata R, McClure SM, Knutson B. 2014. Adult age differences in frontostriatal representation of prediction error but not reward outcome. *Cogn. Affect. Behav. Neurosci.* 14:672–82

Sasse LK, Gamer M, Büchel C, Brassen S. 2014. Selective control of attention supports the positivity effect in aging. *PLOS ONE* 9:e104180

Schaub R, Linden M. 2000. Anxiety and anxiety disorders in the old and very old—results from the Berlin Aging Study (BASE). *Compr. Psychiatry* 41:48–54

Scheibe S, Sheppes G, Staudinger UM. 2015. Distract or reappraise? Age-related differences in emotion-regulation choice. *Emotion.* In press

Schieman S, Van Gundy K. 2000. The personal and social links between age and self-reported empathy. *Soc. Psychol. Q.* 63:152–74

Schott BH, Niehaus L, Wittmann BC, Schutze H, Seidenbecher CI, et al. 2007. Ageing and early-stage Parkinson's disease affect separable neural mechanisms of mesolimbic reward processing. *Brain* 130:2412–24

Schultz W. 2013. Updating dopamine reward signals. *Curr. Opin. Neurobiol.* 23:229–38

Shen J, Kassir MA, Wu J, Zhang Q, Zhou S, et al. 2013. MR volumetric study of piriform-cortical amygdala and orbitofrontal cortices: the aging effect. *PLOS ONE* 8:e74526

Sheppes G. 2014. Emotion regulation choice: theory and findings. In *Handbook of Emotion Regulation*, ed. JJ Gross, pp. 126–39. New York: Guilford. 2nd ed.

Silvers JA, Buhle JT, Ochsner KN, Silvers J. 2013. The neuroscience of emotion regulation: basic mechanisms and their role in development, aging, and psychopathology. *Handb. Cogn. Neurosci.* 1:52–78

Simon NW, Lasarge CL, Montgomery KS, Williams MT, Mendez IA, et al. 2010. Good things come to those who wait: attenuated discounting of delayed rewards in aged Fischer 344 rats. *Neurobiol. Aging* 31:853–62

Simón T, Suengas AG, Ruiz-Gallego-Largo T, Bandrés J. 2013. Positive bias is a defining characteristic of aging to the same extent as declining performance. *Int. J. Psychol.* 48:704–14

Slessor G, Phillips LH, Bull R. 2007. Exploring the specificity of age-related differences in theory of mind tasks. *Psychol. Aging* 22:639–43

Slessor G, Riby DM, Finnerty AN. 2013. Age-related differences in processing face configuration: the importance of the eye region. *J. Gerontol. Ser. B Psychol. Sci. Soc. Sci.* 68:228–31

Spaniol J, Schain C, Bowen HJ. 2014. Reward-enhanced memory in younger and older adults. *J. Gerontol. Ser. B Psychol. Sci. Soc. Sci.* 69:730–40

Spreng RN, Wojtowicz M, Grady CL. 2011. Reliable differences in brain activity between young and old adults: a quantitative meta-analysis across multiple cognitive domains. *Neurosci. Biobehav. Rev.* 34:1178–94

St. Jacques PL, Bessette-Symons B, Cabeza R. 2009. Functional neuroimaging studies of aging and emotion: fronto-amygdalar differences during emotional perception and episodic memory. *J. Int. Neuropsychol. Soc.* 15:819–25

St. Jacques PL, Dolcos F, Cabeza R. 2010. Effects of aging on functional connectivity of the amygdala during negative evaluation: a network analysis of fMRI data. *Neurobiol. Aging* 31:315–27

Stalnaker TA, Franz TM, Singh T, Schoenbaum G. 2007. Basolateral amygdala lesions abolish orbitofrontal-dependent reversal impairments. *Neuron* 54:51–58

Störmer VS, Passow S, Biesenack J, Li S-C. 2012. Dopaminergic and cholinergic modulations of visual-spatial attention and working memory: insights from molecular genetic research and implications for adult cognitive development. *Dev. Psychol.* 48:875–89

Streubel B, Kunzmann U. 2011. Age differences in emotional reactions: arousal and age-relevance count. *Psychol. Aging* 26:966–78

Sullivan S, Ruffman T, Hutton SB. 2007. Age differences in emotion recognition skills and the visual scanning of emotion faces. *J. Gerontol. Ser. B Psychol. Sci. Soc. Sci.* 62:P53–60

Sutherland MR, Mather M. 2015. Negative arousal increases stimulus priority in older adults. *Exp. Aging Res.* 41:259–71

Thomas C, Moya L, Avidan G, Humphreys K, Jung KJ, et al. 2008. Reduction in white matter connectivity, revealed by diffusion tensor imaging, may account for age-related changes in face perception. *J. Cogn. Neurosci.* 20:268–84

Tisserand DJ, Van Boxtel MP, Pruessner JC, Hofman P, Evans AC, Jolles J. 2004. A voxel-based morphometric study to determine individual differences in gray matter density associated with age and cognitive change over time. *Cereb. Cortex* 14:966–73

Tomasi D, Volkow N. 2012. Functional connectivity density and the aging brain. *Mol. Psychiatry* 17:471–71

Tottenham N, Hare TA, Quinn BT, McCarry TW, Nurse M, et al. 2010. Prolonged institutional rearing is associated with atypically large amygdala volume and difficulties in emotion regulation. *Dev. Sci.* 13:46–61

Urry HL, Van Reekum CM, Johnstone T, Kalin NH, Thurow ME, et al. 2006. Amygdala and ventromedial prefrontal cortex are inversely coupled during regulation of negative affect and predict the diurnal pattern of cortisol secretion among older adults. *J. Neurosci.* 26:4415–25

Vijayashankar N, Brody H. 1979. Quantitative study of the pigmented neurons in the nuclei locus coeruleus and subcoeruleus in man as related to aging. *J. Neuropathol. Exp. Neurol.* 38:490–97

Vink M, Kleerekooper I, Van Den Wildenberg WP, Kahn RS. 2015. Impact of aging on frontostriatal reward processing. *Hum. Brain Mapp.* 36:2305–17

Waldinger RJ, Kensinger EA, Schulz MS. 2011. Neural activity, neural connectivity, and the processing of emotionally valenced information in older adults: links with life satisfaction. *Cogn. Affect. Behav. Neurosci.* 11:426–36

Walhovd KB, Fjell AM, Reinvang I, Lundervold A, Dale AM, et al. 2005. Effects of age on volumes of cortex, white matter and subcortical structures. *Neurobiol. Aging* 26:1261–70

Wang LY, Murphy RR, Hanscom B, Li G, Millard SP, et al. 2013. Cerebrospinal fluid norepinephrine and cognition in subjects across the adult age span. *Neurobiol. Aging* 34:2287–92

West RL. 1996. An application of prefrontal cortex function theory to cognitive aging. *Psychol. Bull.* 120:272–92

Williams LM, Brown KJ, Palmer D, Liddell BJ, Kemp AH, et al. 2006. The mellow years? Neural basis of improving emotional stability over age. *J. Neurosci.* 26:6422–30

Wilson RS, Nag S, Boyle PA, Hizel LP, Yu L, et al. 2013. Neural reserve, neuronal density in the locus coeruleus, and cognitive decline. *Neurology* 80:1202–8

Winecoff A, Labar KS, Madden DJ, Cabeza R, Huettel SA. 2011. Cognitive and neural contributors to emotion regulation in aging. *Soc. Cogn. Affect. Neurosci.* 6:165–76

Winstanley CA, Theobald DE, Cardinal RN, Robbins TW. 2004. Contrasting roles of basolateral amygdala and orbitofrontal cortex in impulsive choice. *J. Neurosci.* 24:4718–22

Wong B, Cronin-Golomb A, Neargarder S. 2005. Patterns of visual scanning as predictors of emotion identification in normal aging. *Neuropsychology* 19:739–49

Wood S, Busemeyer J, Koling A, Cox CR, Davis H. 2005. Older adults as adaptive decision makers: evidence from the Iowa gambling task. *Psychol. Aging* 20:220–25

Worthy D, Cooper J, Byrne K, Gorlick M, Maddox WT. 2014. State-based versus reward-based motivation in younger and older adults. *Cogn. Affect. Behav. Neurosci.* 14:1208–20

Wright CI, Dickerson BC, Feczko E, Negeira A, Williams D. 2007. A functional magnetic resonance imaging study of amygdala responses to human faces in aging and mild Alzheimer's disease. *Biol. Psychiatry* 62:1388–95

Wright CI, Negreira A, Gold AL, Britton JC, Williams D, Barrett LF. 2008. Neural correlates of novelty and face-age effects in young and elderly adults. *NeuroImage* 42:956–68

Zamarian L, Sinz H, Bonatti E, Gamboz N, Delazer M. 2008. Normal aging affects decisions under ambiguity, but not decisions under risk. *Neuropsychology* 22:645–57

Zanto TP, Pan P, Liu H, Bollinger J, Nobre AC, Gazzaley A. 2011. Age-related changes in orienting attention in time. *J. Neurosci.* 31:12461–70

Gene × Environment Determinants of Stress- and Anxiety-Related Disorders

Sumeet Sharma,[1,2] Abigail Powers,[1] Bekh Bradley,[1,3] and Kerry J. Ressler[1,2]

[1]Department of Psychiatry and Behavioral Sciences, Emory University School of Medicine, Atlanta, Georgia 30322

[2]McLean Hospital, Harvard Medical School, Belmont, Massachusetts 02478, email: kressler@mclean.harvard.edu

[3]Atlanta VA Medical Center, US Department of Veterans Affairs, Decatur, Georgia 30033

Annu. Rev. Psychol. 2016. 67:239–61

First published online as a Review in Advance on October 6, 2015

The *Annual Review of Psychology* is online at psych.annualreviews.org

This article's doi: 10.1146/annurev-psych-122414-033408

Keywords

anxiety, depression, posttraumatic stress disorder, stress, trauma, epigenetics, gene-by-environment interaction, genome-wide association study

Abstract

The burgeoning field of gene-by-environment (G × E) interactions has revealed fascinating biological insights, particularly in the realm of stress-, anxiety-, and depression-related disorders. In this review we present an integrated view of the study of G × E interactions in stress and anxiety disorders, including the evolution of genetic association studies from genetic epidemiology to contemporary large-scale genome-wide association studies and G × E studies. We convey the importance of consortia efforts and collaboration to gain the large sample sizes needed to move the field forward. Finally, we discuss several robust and well-reproduced G × E interactions and demonstrate how epidemiological identification of G × E interactions has naturally led to a plethora of basic research elucidating the mechanisms of high-impact genetic variants.

Contents

INTRODUCTION

In the study of mental health, the complex interplay of experience, environment, and genetics in both health and disease makes it challenging to interpret the contribution of any particular genetic variant to disease. The disciplines of psychology and psychiatry, perhaps more than any other fields of medicine, are faced with understanding diseases of incredible complexity, from the genetics underpinning neural circuits and hormonal signaling, to the influence of environment-dependent experience on shaping these pathways, to the way biological processes create the mind. These challenges have led to the application of genetic association studies to mental health diseases. By necessity, the complexity of cognitive and emotional disorders, and the crucial role of the environment in these diseases, has quickly led to the study of gene-by-environment (G × E) interactions in mental health. In this review we focus on G × E interactions in stress- and anxiety-related disorders, but we also present a broad overview of genetic association studies.

The fifth edition of the *Diagnostic and Statistical Manual of Mental Disorders* (DSM-5; Am. Psychiatr. Assoc. 2013) has drawn a distinction between stress and anxiety, separating trauma- and stressor-related disorders [e.g., posttraumatic stress disorder (PTSD), acute stress disorder] from anxiety disorders (e.g., generalized anxiety disorder, phobias, panic attack). However, representing fear and anxiety along a continuum with shared symptomology may paint a more accurate picture (Craske et al. 2009). Furthermore, for PTSD, comorbidity with other psychiatric disorders may be the rule rather than the exception (Brady et al. 2000). Depressive disorders may also be better defined in relation to stress and anxiety, as evidenced by the diagnostic comorbidity of both PTSD and anxiety disorders with depression, and the well-established relationship between early life stress and the development of depression. At present it is unclear whether individuals with comorbid disorders exhibit a unique disease etiology as compared to individuals with just one disorder, or whether the comorbidity of stress, anxiety, and depression is simply a product of the diagnostic criteria we use to identify each of these disorders.

In addition to discussing genetic associations and robust G × E findings, below we also consider the disease selection criteria and environmental measures used in genetic association studies. Because sample size is the primary hindrance to achieving significant genetic associations, studies may tend to group together subjects that have distinct diseases in an effort to maximize statistical power. We focus primarily on PTSD as the disease outcome, because it is the best-studied stress and anxiety disorder; however, we also consider depression because of the association between stress and depression, and the insightful G × E studies that have confirmed this outcome.

In this review of G × E associations in stress and anxiety disorders, we outline the progress from the origins of genetic epidemiology to the genome-wide association studies (GWAS) and G × E studies of today. Though we do not cover every facet of genetic association studies, we aim to convey the continuity of this field and lay out a logical path moving forward. We also present the theory underpinning genetic association studies and the challenges that have arisen from these fundamentals. Finally, we discuss specific G × E examples to illustrate how findings are validated and how basic neurobiology research has dovetailed with genetic association studies to understand the biology underlying genetic variants identified in G × E studies.

AN OVERVIEW OF GENETIC ASSOCIATION STUDIES

Genetic Epidemiology

Understanding G × E studies requires an overview of genetic association approaches in general and of the progress in the field. The first step in studying disease genetics is determining the heritability of a particular disorder, which has historically been carried out through epidemiological studies. One of the earliest studies of psychiatric heritability was conducted in 1911, when Canon and Rosanoff used family pedigrees to search for patterns of Mendelian inheritance in psychiatric patients (Zhang 2011). This was a precursor to large-scale genetic epidemiology studies (e.g., twin-, family-, adoption-, and other population-based studies) that have provided a necessary first step in establishing heritability and exploring genetic interactions in stress and anxiety disorders. A meta-analysis from Hettema et al. (2001) examined family and twin studies for panic disorder, generalized anxiety disorder, phobias, and obsessive-compulsive disorder. Each disorder was found to be heritable, with odds ratios from familial studies of 4–6, and heritability estimates from twin studies of 0.43 for panic disorder and 0.32 for generalized anxiety disorder (Hettema et al. 2001). For PTSD, twin studies estimate heritability at 0.3–0.4 (Cornelis et al. 2010). These genetic epidemiology studies, together with others, have established the influence of genetic inheritance on the development of PTSD, and other stress and anxiety disorders. Once heritability is established, the next step is to identify specific genetic regions associated with disease, which is what linkage approaches aim to accomplish. But before we delve into specific approaches, we need to explore what genetic variants might contribute to disease and what kinds of associations are theoretically possible.

Hypotheses of Genetic Association Studies

A genetic variant is any portion of an individual's DNA sequence that differs from the reference human genome sequence. The majority of genetic association studies focus on single nucleotide polymorphisms (SNPs) as the source of genetic variation, so we concentrate on these. However, chromosomal rearrangements (duplications, deletions, inversions, and translocations) can also be quite common, and SNP-based GWAS can be extended to query copy number variation (McCarroll 2008, Mills et al. 2011). Evolutionary models of complex diseases posit that both common variation and rare variation in the genome contribute to disease (Cichon et al. 2009). A common SNP is defined to have a minor allele frequency (MAF) of at least 5%, whereas a rare variant is defined by a MAF of 1% or less; at the extreme, a rare variant may only be present in a single individual. The MAF is defined as the frequency of the least common allele in a population.

The common disease–common variant hypothesis posits that some portion of disease heritability must lie in common variants, and it assumes that testing SNPs in enough cases and controls can collectively identify common SNPs with small individual effects on disease status. It is more challenging to draw statistically significant conclusions about rare variants, as their prevalence is very low; however, the 1000 Genomes Project and other large-scale efforts have allowed us to query SNPs with a MAF in the population as low as 0.01% (Schizophr. Work. Group Psychiatr. Genom. Consort. 2014). The rich catalog of human variation that has been produced by the HapMap Project and the 1000 Genomes Project has greatly contributed to the advancement of genetic association studies (Abecasis et al. 2012, Int. HapMap Consort. 2003). To understand how the efforts of large consortia are essential to progress in the field of genetic association, we first briefly discuss the mechanism of genetic association studies.

Genome-Wide Association Studies: Basic Tenets

The purpose of GWAS is to identify loci in the genome where genetic variation is associated with the presence of disease. These disease-associated variants are thought to increase the risk of developing the related disorder (Hirschhorn et al. 2002), but mechanistic studies are required to confirm the influence of a genetic variant on disease pathophysiology. In contrast to G × E studies, GWAS query the main effect of a genetic variant. The statistical definition of a main effect is the effect of an independent variable on a dependent variable, averaging across all other independent variables involved. In GWAS terms, that is equivalent to determining the association of a particular genetic variant with a disease or an endophenotype measure, averaging across all other variables. G × E studies are an extension of GWAS, wherein G × E studies also consider the environment as a variable. In a G × E framework, the environment can be considered the pathogenic or etiologic factor, and the genetic variant is contributing to the susceptibility to that environmental pathogen (Kim-Cohen et al. 2006). However, G × E studies and GWAS are similar in that the same limitations of genetic association studies are present in both—namely, the limitation posed by our ability to measure variation in the genome.

At present, measuring SNPs is by far the most cost-effective manner to genotype individuals. Efforts by industry and large consortia have made genotyping an individual much cheaper. In particular, Illumina and the Psychiatric Genomics Consortium (PGC) have collaborated to produce the PsychArray, a SNP genotyping array that can be purchased for ~$100 and contains ~600,000 probes to test for common variants and SNPs specific for psychiatric disorders.

It is assumed that most genetic susceptibility to a disease is acquired through a de novo mutation in an ancestor. As a consequence of meiotic crossover, the disease-causing mutation is inherited along with the surrounding DNA sequence as this mutation is passed down to successive generations (**Figure 1**) (Ardlie et al. 2002). Identifying a particular genetic variant (such as a SNP) that is inherited along with one such inherited block of DNA (referred to as a haplotype) allows us to determine the presence of that haplotype by testing only that SNP (tag SNP; **Figure 1**). We can use the association of tag SNPs with disease to infer that the haplotype linked with the tag SNP is associated with disease, and that within that haplotype there is a genetic variant driving disease etiology or susceptibility. This nonrandom association of genetic variants within haplotypes is called linkage disequilibrium (LD), and it is the basic principle that underlies genetic association studies (Cichon et al. 2009).

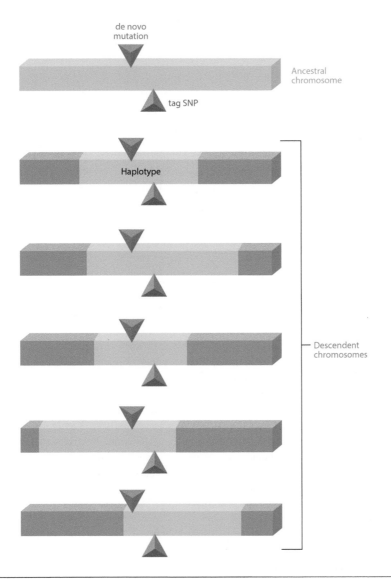

Figure 1

A schematic demonstration of linkage disequilibrium. The top chromosome represents an ancestor, where a de novo mutation (*red triangle*) first appears. This mutation is passed down to descendent chromosomes, but it is inherited along with the nearby ancestral DNA sequence (haplotype). The linkage of alleles that lie within a haplotype is referred to as linkage disequilibrium. One such allele that is highly linked to the haplotype is chosen to be a tag single nucleotide polymorphism (tag SNP) (*green triangle*).

A critical point in understanding GWAS is the determination of which SNPs are used for analysis, given that there are tens of millions of SNPs within the genome. Tag SNPs are not necessarily disease-causal, or disease-related mutations; they simply act as proxies for the haplotypes with which they segregate and are co-inherited. A process called imputation allows us to infer SNPs in a genotyped individual by comparing the individual's haplotype structure with that of reference genomes. In other words, the distribution of haplotypes in the patient genome is compared to fully sequenced reference genomes with the same (or similar) haplotype structure, and

FUTURE OF GENOME SEQUENCING

Emerging whole-genome sequencing technologies are likely to reduce the cost of whole-genome sequencing to a point where large-scale sequencing approaches can be used to directly genotype patients in studies of genetic association. Complete sequences will allow the full evaluation of rare variants, common variants, and chromosomal rearrangements as well as their association with disease. To fully characterize repetitive DNA sequences and chromosomal rearrangements, sequencing technologies need to be able to sequence long stretches of DNA. Second-generation sequencing platforms can produce a range of read lengths, with an upper limit of approximately 1 kb. However, it is difficult to map shorter reads to very repetitive regions of the genome because there are often not enough unique base pairs for a confident alignment. To achieve longer read lengths, a variety of unique approaches and technologies are being developed. Emerging methodologies such as third-generation sequencing technologies utilizing single-molecule visualization methods and engineered proteins, and computational programs that generate long reads from shorter reads, in silico, are paving the way toward this goal.

SNPs are inferred based on the sequence of the reference genome. The imputation process is also crucial for comparison of multiple data sets and meta-analyses, as it allows SNPs to be "called" (or determined) independent of the specific tag SNPs utilized in the array (Halperin & Stephan 2009).

For these reasons, the richness of the reference data sets is integral to progress in all types of genetic association studies. The HapMap Project and 1000 Genomes Project have sequenced multiple individuals from major global populations to catalog haplotypes and high-fidelity tag SNPs. SNP calling depends on imputation, and imputation is only as effective as the reference genomes are complete. The latest schizophrenia GWAS mega-analysis used the 1000 Genomes Project reference panel to call variants with MAFs as low as 0.01. Richer reference data sets may allow us to probe for less-frequent alleles in the population. New sequencing technologies will greatly enhance studies of genetic association (see sidebar Future of Genome Sequencing). Sequencing cases and controls directly will allow us to identify rare variation and its contribution to disease. Moving forward, large-scale consortia-based efforts will continue to be crucial to progress in psychiatry-specific genetic association studies.

Genome-Wide Association Studies: Consortia Efforts and Statistical Power

The need for greater statistical power in psychiatric genetics led to the formation of the PGC. As in other disciplines of biomedical research, it quickly became apparent that many variants identified through GWAS are of very small effect size—i.e., their contribution to disease is small. Thus, discovering these variants of small effect requires very large samples. Logue et al. (2015) calculated that tens of thousands of subjects will be required to discover disease-associated SNPs with MAFs of 5–20% in the population (**Figure 2**). The PGC has facilitated collaborative efforts in studies of genetic association for schizophrenia, bipolar disorder, and major depressive disorder (MDD), among others. Schizophrenia represents the major GWAS success in psychiatry so far. To date, the latest schizophrenia GWAS meta-analysis has revealed over 108 loci as being genome-wide significant (Schizophr. Work. Group Psychiatr. Genom. Consort. 2014). An association at a genome-wide significance level means that a genetic variant is associated with cases over controls, with $p < 5 \times 10^{-8}$, based on a conservative multiple test correction of $p = 0.05$ divided by 1 million SNP tests. This p-value is based on statistical estimates assuming that all common SNPs have been tested. Although other nonfrequentist statistical measures (Bayesian approaches) have been

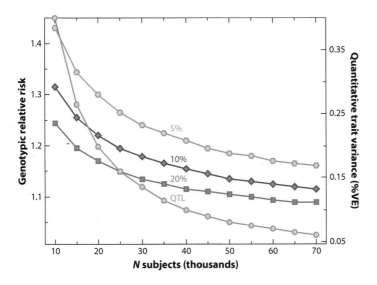

Figure 2

Sample size calculation as a function of power: an example calculation demonstrating the sample sizes necessary to achieve 80% power for case-control and quantitative-trait association analyses, for SNPs with MAFs of 5%, 10%, and 20% that have relative risks between 1.1 and 1.4. Calculation assumes PTSD prevalence of 15%, additive model, a type I error rate of 5×10^{-8}, and perfect LD between marker and trait allele for MAF >5%. Calculations were based on a 1:3 PTSD case-control ratio for quantitative traits such as PTSD symptoms. Abbreviations: LD, linkage disequilibrium; MAF, minor allele frequency; PTSD, posttraumatic stress disorder; QTL, quantitative trait locus; SNP, single nucleotide polymorphism; VE, environmental variance.

used that also have merit (Sham & Purcell 2014), the majority of studies to date utilize significance testing with p-values as the measure of statistical significance. In this review we refer to genome-wide significance in GWAS for those variants that reach the p-value threshold of 5×10^{-8}.

Success in GWAS for stress- and anxiety-related disorders has been limited. To date, five independent GWAS for PTSD have been carried out and replicated. These studies identified both genes [*RORA*, *COBL*, *TLL1* (a long noncoding RNA), and *PRTFDC1*] and intergenic regions as significant hits, and other studies have begun to show the association of these loci with functional intermediate phenotypes (Almli et al. 2015, Guffanti et al. 2013, Logue et al. 2013, Nievergelt et al. 2015, Xie et al. 2013). Each study also replicated the association of the identified SNP in these genes with PTSD in an independent cohort. However, only a subset of these hits achieved genome-wide significance. This points to a need for greater sample sizes. The PTSD working group of the PGC is moving toward a huge GWAS effort of over 10,000 cases and 40,000 trauma-exposed controls (Logue et al. 2015), with the possibility of reaching even 100,000 total samples within the next few years. This effort will be the first large-scale GWAS for PTSD. It may replicate the findings from previous studies with smaller cohorts, and it may identify more genome-wide significant SNPs associated with PTSD. Taken together, such works offer the best hope for determining the overall genetic architecture underlying mental disorders including PTSD. However, genetic association studies should first answer the important question of how much effort the field should invest into searching for main effects with GWAS versus focusing on G × E studies. G × E studies offer both the promise of better understanding and discovering of environmental pathogens, and the hope of determining genetic risks that are not observable when examining only main effects.

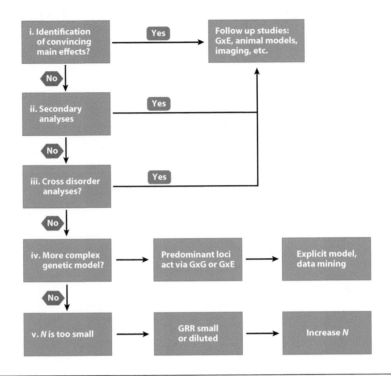

Figure 3

A proposed workflow for genetic association efforts put forward by the PGC. Abbreviations: G × E, gene-by-environment; G × G, gene-by-gene; GRR, genotypic relative risk; GWAS, genome-wide association study; PGC, Psychiatric Genomics Consortium.

Gene-by-Environment Interactions: Rationale

In 2009, the Psychiatric GWAS Consortium Steering Committee (a subset of the PGC) laid out a proposed workflow for genetic association studies (**Figure 3**) (Psychiatr. GWAS Consort. Steer. Comm. 2009). The rationale behind genetic association studies has been clear for decades and G × E efforts follow naturally in the progression of GWAS analyses. The next step in the study of genetic association is to identify disease-causal genetic variants by determining how these variants influence the susceptibility or resilience of an individual to particular environmental pathogens. In stress- and anxiety-related disorders, environmental measures generally include instruments that query levels of overall trauma, childhood trauma, and other stressful experiences. Disease status, as determined by physician diagnosis, can also be used as a variable in G × E studies.

The decision tree in **Figure 3** is the path for a hypothetical within-disorder GWAS mega-analysis. For PTSD, mega-analyses have not been carried out as of yet, but smaller GWAS analyses have already discovered genome-wide significant SNPs. There is debate over whether G × E studies should be pursued for variants that have not been found to have a significant main effect in GWAS analyses. There are two points to consider here: G × E analyses may uncover hidden interactions that are not discovered in GWAS, and the sample size limitation for PTSD GWAS, at present, may prevent us from investigating targets because of a perceived lack of significance. However, even with the caveat of small sample sizes, main effect loci have been discovered, and the path forward should certainly involve studies of G × E. Note, however, that of the remaining possibilities in **Figure 3**, cross-disorder analyses and more complex genetic models may still be true for genes involved in stress- and anxiety-related disorders. As we discuss

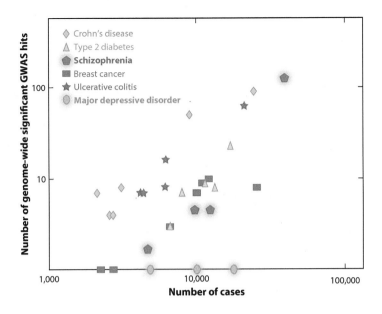

Figure 4

Genome-wide association study (GWAS) power has increased with greater sample sizes across many diseases, except for major depressive disorder. The graph demonstrates progress in GWAS for a variety of diseases, including schizophrenia and major depressive disorder. For all disorders except major depression, increased sample sizes have resulted in more genome-wide significant GWAS hits (y axis, GWAS single nucleotide polymorphisms discovered with a p-value $< 5 \times 10^{-8}$; x axis, number of cases used in each study).

below, cross-disorder analyses are still an important consideration, and a more complex model based on G × E interactions is yielding new insights.

Another strong argument for pursuing G × E studies comes from the latest GWAS for MDD. Although this GWAS had approximately 9,000 cases and controls, no SNPs achieved genome-wide significance (Ripke et al. 2013). Increased sample sizes for MDD have not resulted in greater significance for SNPs, whereas in schizophrenia and other diseases adding more subjects clearly resulted in more genome-wide significant SNPs associated with disease (**Figure 4**). One interpretation is that depression is etiologically heterogeneous, and cases with a stronger genetic component are diluted by cases with more environmental contribution. Another interpretation is that MDD is not strongly influenced by genetic variation. Larger sample sizes to sufficiently power experiments and find genome-wide significant SNPs may be a costly endeavor, and they may not yield any associations we expect; on the other hand, G × E offers the possibility to leverage more sophisticated measures of environmental influence to identify the contributions of both genetics and environment to the development of psychiatric disease. PTSD, as an example of a stress disorder, has yet to be explored at a deep level in GWAS; however, smaller studies have already identified and replicated genome-wide significant associations in GWAS and significant G × E associations, and larger pursuits are under way.

GWAS provide an unbiased approach by evaluating common variations across the genome to identify risk loci. For polygenic disorders, multiple variants likely work together to form the genetic contribution to a disorder. However, studying genetic variants alone does not address the environmental component we know to be critically important in psychiatric disease. Moreover, as evidenced by GWAS for MDD, increasing sample sizes to search for main effects may not lead to improved variant detection as it did for schizophrenia, making the search for G × E interactions more relevant. In reality, increasing the sample sizes of GWAS studies will translate to increased sample sizes for G × E approaches, as long as care is taken to obtain additional information of environmental measures in a clinical setting.

Gene-by-Environment Interactions: Basic Tenets and Limitations

The study of G × E interactions speaks to a question at the core of mental health and the study of human disease in general: To what extent do individual genetic variation and environmental context influence the etiology of disease? The conception of G × E represents the realization that for many disorders, the effect of an external stimulus—be it an infectious agent, cancer, or physical or psychological trauma—depends on the unique genetic makeup of each individual. In the realm of stress and anxiety disorders, genetic variation may predispose individuals to resilience or susceptibility to environmental stressors, which may then result in the development of psychiatric disorders. This also means that without exposure to those environmental stressors, the negative outcome may not occur; thus, it is the interaction between genes and environment that is critical for the expression of the phenotype of interest.

G × E interactions represent our understanding of the shared influence that genes and the environment play in the development of mental disorders. Statistically, an interaction between two variables means that the outcome (disease) depends on both variables. For example, without knowing the genetic variants present in an individual, it is impossible to know the relative risk for development of PTSD in the aftermath of a traumatic event; vice versa, without knowing what traumatic experiences the individual has encountered, it is impossible to know whether he or she will develop PTSD based on genetics alone. Thus, both components must be known to evaluate the etiology of disease.

The potential bias of G × E correlation is also an important consideration. Genetic variation and environmental influences may not be independent entities; that is, an individual's genetics may predispose him or her to seek out particular environments. For example, an individual predisposed to high levels of anxiety may find himself or herself engaging in substance abuse in order to alleviate anxiety symptoms temporarily. Thus, the environment may be correlated with the genotype and therefore not be an independent variable. Such correlations are deeply embedded biases that have to be tolerated in human studies of G × E interaction. However, the identification of such correlations may lead to improved models for discovery of G × E interactions (Dick 2011).

One can conceive of two general forms for SNP-based G × E interactions (**Figure 5**) (Dick 2011). In the first case (**Figure 5a**), a fan-shaped interaction, the presence of a risk allele increases the probability of disease negligibly at baseline; however, as the individual experiences increased environmental risk, these risk alleles translate to a much higher probability of disease. In a second model (**Figure 5b,c**), a crossover interaction indicates that a particular SNP may not only be deleterious, but its influence depends on the environmental risk exposure. In **Figure 5b**, the so-called risk allele actually is protective in a low-risk environment (as compared to the wild type); disease probability is increased as environmental risk is increased. Meanwhile, individuals with none of these risk alleles have an increased probability of disease when the environmental risk is low but a decreased probability of disease in a high-risk environment. These complex interactions demonstrate that certain genetic variants can play very different roles depending on the environmental context in which they evolved, and the definition of risk allele and normal allele may not be so clear-cut.

The level of environmental loading at which crossing over occurs is likely variable; however, the importance of these models is in the biology they convey. To truly understand the effect of a genetic variant, one must take into account the full gamut of environments from positive to negative. A bias

a

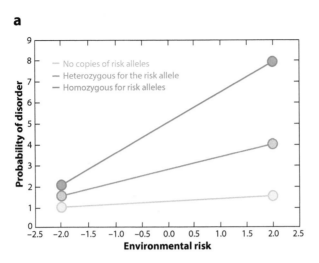

b

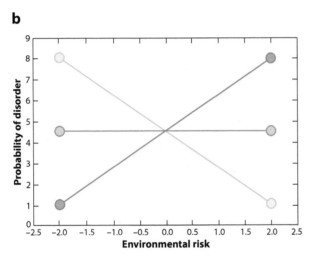

c

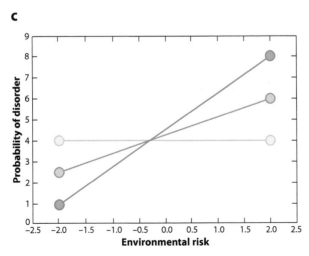

Figure 5

Three simple types of gene-by-environment (G × E) interactions: (*a*) a fan-shaped interaction, (*b*) a crossover interaction with the wild-type alleles demonstrating an increased probability of disease in low-risk environments and a decreased probability of disease in high risk-environments, and (*c*) a crossover interaction with the wild-type allele posing no increased or decreased risk.

in our data sets today is the focus on negative environmental measures. This bias arises from our interest in asking disease-relevant biological questions. However, as **Figure 5b** and **5c** show, it is conceivable that alleles that predispose someone to disease in a high-risk environment may also be beneficial by reducing susceptibility to disease in a low-risk environment. In the absence of more explicit measures of positive environment, in addition to negative risk factors, a full understanding of how a genetic variant interacts with the environment will be difficult, particularly with respect to resilience. However, some studies are starting to address this question more directly. For example, Dunn et al. (2014) used a measure of post-traumatic growth to find a SNP in the *RGS2* gene that conferred resilience among Hurricane Katrina victims.

Major criticisms of $G \times E$ studies center on their lack of reproducibility, positive-results bias, insufficient sample sizes, and improper design of the statistical models used. These concerns suggest that the false positive rate in $G \times E$ studies may be much higher than we suspect, which harkens back to the days of candidate gene findings, many of which failed replication when subject to unbiased GWAS analyses (Zannas & Binder 2014). Keller (2014) put forth a fundamental criticism of the linear models used to eliminate confounding variables. In the vast majority of $G \times E$ studies to date, confounders are entered as covariates in a general linear model; however, to properly control for the impact of confounders, a covariate $\times$ environment term and a covariate $\times$ gene term must be included in the same model. This demonstrates that fundamental approaches to $G \times E$ are maturing, and the development of genome-wide approaches to $G \times E$ will help us evaluate the significance of current findings in a more rigorous, unbiased manner. Recent nonlinear statistical approaches to whole-genome $G \times E$ and GWAS analytic methods are making progress (Almli et al. 2014). Issues of power and sample size require consortia efforts, and we should pay attention to the standardization of environmental measures; however, advances in fundamental statistical methodologies should be applied to all future studies and reanalyses of past studies. This points to the need for closer communication between neuroscientists and statistical geneticists. In light of the increased attention to $G \times E$ approaches, some journals have laid out strict criteria for publication, which is an excellent step to improve the false positive rate of published findings (Hewitt 2012).

DEFINING ENVIRONMENTS AND PHENOTYPES IN STUDIES OF GENETIC ASSOCIATION

Environment

A countless number of possible factors can influence mental health outcomes. In particular, certain clinically measured environmental factors have been shown to be important risk factors for many psychiatric conditions. For example, exposure to trauma and significant stressful life events are well-established risk factors for the development of many major mental disorders, including depression, anxiety disorders, PTSD, and substance use disorders (Brewin et al. 2000, Hettema et al. 2005, Kilpatrick et al. 2003). Important considerations in studies of $G \times E$ include the measurement of these environmental factors and the scaling of these measures in calculations.

Very often, the primary method for measuring environmental variables is self-report questionnaires. Questionnaires provide a quick, inexpensive approach for assessing a wide range of constructs for researchers. However, there are a number of limitations to the use of self-report instruments. The most important issue is whether the questionnaire is valid and fully captures the construct of interest in the study. Self-report questionnaires are also limited to the information remembered and willingly provided by the individual. Retrospective biases, as well as social desirability and response bias, are all factors that affect the information obtained through questionnaires. An alternative to self-report questionnaires is the use of structured or semistructured clinical interviews conducted by trained research interviewers (or clinicians), which provide a more thorough assessment of psychiatric symptoms. Again, these instruments are limited to the information provided by the individual, but additional questioning and expertise by the interviewer often allow clarification of the construct under study and reduce the chance to code symptoms incorrectly due to ambiguous wording of questions. Standardized clinical interviews, although often more valid than self-report questionnaires, are much more expensive and more lengthy to administer, and therefore they limit the feasibility of large-scale data collection.

The developmental stage in which environmental factors occur also affects risk. With regard to trauma, for example, research has shown that early exposure to trauma or abuse in childhood is particularly detrimental and leads to a wide range of negative mental health outcomes, putting individuals at risk for psychopathology and related outcomes (e.g., suicide, psychiatric hospitalization) (Gillespie et al. 2009, MacMillan et al. 2001, McLaughlin et al. 2010). More generally, childhood adversity (e.g., abuse, parental loss, negative family environment) is a risk factor for depression, anxiety disorders, personality disorders, and other diseases (Carr et al. 2013, Heim & Nemeroff 2001, Kendler et al. 1992). Therefore, both the presence of certain environmental factors and the time at which they occur are of critical importance in the context of psychiatric risk. Questions about developmental effects are difficult to dissect in an epidemiological context, but as we discuss below, animal models provide a powerful outlet to evaluate the influence of genetic variants throughout development.

Today as well as in the future, it will be important for G × E studies to be standardized to allow for large-scale comparisons. The methods and instruments used by researchers vary dramatically across studies, sometimes making it difficult to compare findings across samples. Variation in the type of scaling used to measure any given environmental factor (e.g., dichotomous response versus Likert scale) also changes how a construct is evaluated and can often inhibit the ability to make adequate comparisons across groups. Collaboration will be crucial for standardization of environmental measures across institutions, and efforts by the PGC have paved the way to facilitate these large-scale coordinated efforts.

Outcome Measures in Genetic Studies

The outcome measure of genetic association studies can be a disease diagnosis, but it can also be an intermediate phenotype or endophenotype, an independent measure that correlates with a disease, such as amygdala reactivity. Just as the definition of the environmental component requires careful design, so too does the definition of the outcome being investigated. Querying disease directly has been the mainstay of genetic association studies; however, intermediate phenotypes such as fear-potentiated startle, stress/anxiety questionnaires, and neuroimaging (such as amygdala activation) are also methods used to understand how genetic variation influences behavioral physiology (Stein et al. 2008). These intermediate phenotypes or endophenotypes define the outcome more narrowly than a potentially broad disease category, and the association of a genetic variant with an endophenotype points to a more specific consequence of that variant. Endophenotypes can be used in both GWAS and G × E studies.

A deeper consideration is the true nosology of a mental health disorder. Definitions from the DSM are explicitly designed to provide the most clinical utility. However, the striking comorbidities of mental health patients raise an important question: At a genetic level, are any two comorbid psychiatric disorders truly distinct, or is there a shared etiology? As we discussed in the introduction, stress, anxiety, and depression can be conceived of as a spectrum; however, this may not be reflected in the DSM criteria that define diseases clinically. In 2013, the Psychiatric Genomics Consortium Cross-Disorder Group endeavored to leverage GWAS data to investigate the shared genetics between major psychiatric disorders for which GWAS have been carried out (Cross-Disord. Group Psychiatr. Genom. Consort. 2013). This study demonstrated that schizophrenia and bipolar disorder, schizophrenia and MDD, attention-deficit/hyperactivity disorder and MDD, and bipolar disorder and MDD share a detectable genetic variation. These findings suggest that certain genetic variants may play a role in the etiology of multiple disorders, and the high comorbidity may be a consequence of this shared susceptibility. On the opposite end of the spectrum, our current disease categories may be too broad, and patients with heterogeneous etiologies are being lumped together in genetic association studies. This is supported by recent work by the CONVERGE consortium, in which two loci were associated with depression, at genomewide significance, in a phenotypically homogeneous cohort of severely depressed Chinese women (CONVERGE consort. 2015).

The primary diseases studied by the PGC possess the most complete GWAS data sets. However, as more diseases are studied and more comprehensive GWAS data sets become available, cross-disorder and subgroup analyses can become more comprehensive and may reveal new outcome measures and genomewide significant loci to be investigated.

GENE-BY-ENVIRONMENT INTERACTIONS

Many studies of G × E interactions use stress, anxiety, or PTSD measures; however, only a few have been robustly replicated. Rather than presenting the full gamut of findings, we lay out what is known about three genes in which variants have been robustly associated with depression-, stress- and anxiety-related G × E interactions: the serotonin transporter promoter (*5-HTTLPR*) polymorphism, the brain-derived neurotropic factor (*BDNF*) *Val66Met* polymorphism, and the *FK506 binding protein 5* (*FKBP5*) polymorphism. We recognize that a great deal of literature exists for mechanistic function of the *5-HTTLPR* and the *BDNF Val66Met* polymorphisms; however, due to space limitations we focus on presenting the epidemiological evidence connecting these two well-established variants to disease, and we emphasize the often conflicting reports that emerge, even for these now well-established associations. For *FKBP5* we present a more comprehensive picture of the variant, from discovery to pathophysiological mechanism—a feat achieved from epidemiological research as well as cell culture and animal-model studies.

Serotonin Transporter Promoter Polymorphism (*5-HTTLPR*)

Several studies and meta-analyses have shown that the *5-HTTLPR* (*5-HTT* gene-linked polymorphic region) variant moderates the relationship between stressful life events and depression. One of the first G × E interactions to be discovered, this variant largely became the testing ground for the concept, with many studies designed to replicate this finding and much debate as to whether this is a true G × E interaction. The *5-HTTLPR* polymorphism is a variation in the number of repeats in the promoter region of the serotonin reuptake transporter (*SLC6A4*); these GC-rich, 20- to 23-bp-long repeat elements are generally studied in the context of the short (*S*) allele (14 repeats) and the long (*L*) allele (16 repeats). We refer to individuals with two copies of the short allele as *SS*, individuals with one copy of the short allele and one copy of the long allele as *SL*, and individuals with two copies of the long allele as *LL*. Homozygous *S* allele carriers, in combination with increased exposure to stressful life events, are predictive of depression (Bogdan et al. 2014, Caspi et al. 2003, Karg et al. 2011). There is also evidence of increased stress reactivity among

5-HTTLPR SS allele carriers. However, these findings remain mixed and suggest that only main stressful life events affect the development of depression (Gillespie et al. 2005, Risch et al. 2009).

Findings are also mixed regarding G × E interactions in predicting risk for PTSD, with some evidence suggesting that the specific population studied may affect the results. Numerous studies have shown SS 5-HTTLPR genotype in combination with trauma exposure of various types to be a risk factor for PTSD across both civilian and veteran populations (Holman et al. 2011, Kolassa et al. 2010, Mercer et al. 2012, Wang et al. 2011, Xie et al. 2009). Moreover, among adult hurricane survivors, Kilpatrick et al. (2007) found that SS allele carriers had significantly greater risk for the development of PTSD following exposure to the hurricane only in the presence of low social support. However, recent evidence in two African American samples showed that the SS 5-HTTLPR allele was associated with lower PTSD re-experiencing and hyperarousal symptoms among individuals exposed to childhood emotional abuse, suggesting that two S alleles could be a protective factor against the development of PTSD symptoms in the presence of childhood abuse (Walsh et al. 2014). This supports evidence from Xie et al. (2012) showing an interaction between childhood maltreatment and one or two copies of the S allele in the 5-HTTLPR genotype in predicting PTSD, but only among European American adults; this G × E interaction was not found in African American adults. Other research with European adults has shown that the LL 5-HTTLPR genotype interacts with trauma exposure to predict increased risk for PTSD (Grabe et al. 2009). Also, in a study of 41 motor vehicle accident survivors, the LL 5-HTTLPR genotype showed an interaction with trauma exposure to predict chronic PTSD (Thakur et al. 2009). These studies thus suggest that the S allele may be protective in certain populations. To complicate things further, some studies have found no evidence of an effect of 5-HTTLPR on risk for PTSD in the face of stressful or traumatic events (Mellman et al. 2009, Sayin et al. 2010). The 5-HTTLPR SS allele was associated with higher likelihood of suicide attempt in African American substance-dependent males, but only in the presence of high levels of reported child abuse (Roy et al. 2007). A recent meta-analysis examined the association between 5-HTTLPR and panic disorder and found no evidence of a relationship (Blaya et al. 2007); however, G × E associations were not examined.

With regard to intermediate phenotypes, within a sample of ethnically diverse college undergraduates, those homozygous for the S allele, who reported higher levels of childhood maltreatment showed significantly higher levels of anxiety sensitivity compared to heterozygotes or homozygous L carriers. Anxiety sensitivity can be seen as an intermediate phenotype for anxiety and depressive disorders (Stein et al. 2008). Alternatively, another study found that the LL genotype interacted with childhood maltreatment to predict increased anxiety sensitivity in a sample of healthy adults (Klauke et al. 2011), again highlighting how mixed the results are in G × E 5-HTTLPR studies. Other evidence from a college sample using daily monitoring techniques to assess daily stress and anxiety levels found that individuals with at least one S 5-HTTLPR allele showed heightened levels of anxious mood in the presence of increased daily stressors (Gunthert et al. 2007).

BDNF Val66Met Polymorphism (V66M)

Brain-derived neurotrophic factor (BDNF) is perhaps the best-studied protein in neuroscience, given its integral role in neural development and function. A wealth of literature describes *BDNF*'s role at a molecular and behavioral level, but more recently, epidemiological G × E studies have also elucidated interactions between the Met allele at amino acid position 66 and stress in promoting anxiety and depression. Early in the study of G × E, a three-way interaction among *V66M*, *5-HTTLPR*, and maltreatment history was shown to predict depression in a cohort of 196 adult cases and controls (Kaufman et al. 2006). A 2010 study followed up on this finding, investigating whether this three-way interaction could be observed in an adolescent cohort; however, there was no detected association among *V66M*, *5-HTTLPR*, and maltreatment on adolescent depression (Nederhof et al. 2010). In 2012, a study of 780 pairs of Chinese adolescent twins investigated this three-way interaction, finding that *V66M*, *5-HTTLPR*, and maltreatment did indeed associate with adolescent depression symptoms (Chen et al. 2012). These studies of variable outcomes highlight the power of consortium approaches and the increased statistical power they afford, but their results may be confounded by the fact that they were performed in different populations around the world. Endophenotype approaches have found that an interaction between *V66M* and early life stress is associated with smaller hippocampal and amygdala volumes, elevated heart rate, and reduced working memory (Gatt et al. 2009).

FK506 Binding Protein-5 Polymorphism (FKBP5)

In 2008, an interaction between SNPs in *FKBP5* and early childhood trauma (*FKBP5* × childhood trauma) was found to influence the severity of adult PTSD symptoms in a population of urban, low-socioeconomic-status African Americans (Binder et al. 2008). A subsequent study replicated this finding in a larger cohort of subjects of African descent (Xie et al. 2010). Another study investigating G × E interactions in chronic pain patients in Pennsylvania demonstrated that the interaction between *FKBP5* genotype and total trauma exposure is associated with PTSD (Boscarino et al. 2012). No main effect for *FKBP5* genotype and PTSD was detected in any of the preceding studies. Interestingly, adult trauma did not interact with *FKBP5* genotype to influence PTSD symptoms, whereas follow-up studies have consistently reported the interaction of childhood trauma and *FKBP5* to be significant. This suggests a developmental window in which environmental risk creates a long-lasting molecular alteration in the *FKBP5* pathway, which influences the development of PTSD in adulthood. Subsequent molecular analyses of *FKBP5* have yielded insight as to how this memory may be maintained by epigenetic mechanisms (Klengel et al. 2013) (see **Figure 6** and sidebar Overview of Epigenetics and Chromatin Conformation).

OVERVIEW OF EPIGENETICS AND CHROMATIN CONFORMATION

The regulation of transcription (the production of RNA from DNA) is highly coordinated. Transcription factors (TFs) orchestrate how RNA polymerase II transcribes mRNA. Many TFs bind to specific DNA sequences. The composition and distribution of these sequences hardwire epigenetic and transcription factor binding profiles, and variants in these motifs affect how strongly transcription factors are able to bind. DNA can also be physically modified, changing the physical properties of the DNA and the strength with which TFs can bind to it. 5-methylcytosine (5-mC) results from the addition of a methyl group to the 5-position on a cytosine ring, and 5-mC deposition in some transcription factor motifs has been shown to alter the binding efficacy of transcription factors to those motifs.

The conformation of chromatin refers to the stretches of linear DNA that are in contact with one another. The purpose of the interaction between these distal DNA sequences is to allow enhancer or inhibitory elements, which can increase or decrease, respectively, the rate of Pol II transcription to differentially regulate gene expression. The GR-sensitive intron 2 enhancer in *FKBP5* is an example of this.

Klengel et al. (2013) assert that 5-mC reduction in intron 7 of *FKBP5* is propagated through childhood, dependent on early life stress. This 5-mC reduction results in increased *FKBP5* mRNA expression and a lasting alteration in the homeostatic balance of the HPA axis, which shapes the potential for future posttraumatic stress disorder psychopathology.

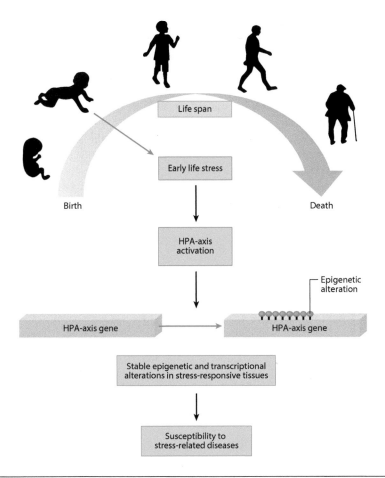

Figure 6

Development and G × E interactions. There are developmental windows in which trauma and stress have particular influence on epigenetic signaling, thus propagating the effects through an individual's life span. The HPA axis, in particular, is modified by early life stress, as evidenced by G × E interactions identified in *FKBP5*. Abbreviations: G × E, gene-by-environment; HPA, hypothalamic-pituitary-adrenal.

The *FKBP5* × childhood trauma interaction has also been shown to influence a variety of other psychiatric disorders and traits including depression, schizophrenia, aggression, psychosis, and suicide attempts (Appel et al. 2011, Collip et al. 2013, Dackis et al. 2012, Roy et al. 2010, Zimmermann et al. 2011). These diverse associations can be understood by the fundamental molecular role *FKBP5* plays in regulating glucocorticoid signaling in the cell. *FKBP5* exerts an inhibitory effect on *glucocorticoid receptor (GR)*-mediated signaling, acting in an ultrashort feedback loop of the hypothalamic-pituitary-adrenal (HPA) axis. *FKBP5* is a co-chaperone in the heat shock protein 90 (*Hsp90*) steroid receptor complex. *FKBP5* binding to the *Hsp90* complex results in reduced binding affinity of glucocorticoids to *GRs*, and overexpression of *FKBP5* reduces *GR*-mediated signaling. Furthermore, *FKBP5* is rapidly induced by glucocorticoids in a number of tissues, including brain and peripheral blood. Thus, *GR*-mediated signaling upregulates *FKBP5*, a negative regulator of glucocorticoid signaling, resulting in rapid negative feedback of the stress response at the cellular level. Anatomically, *FKBP5* expression is strongest in brain regions associated with stress and anxiety responses, including the hippocampus, the amygdala, and the paraventricular nucleus (Zannas & Binder 2014).

The most understood variants in *FKBP5* are *rs3800373*, *rs9296158*, and *rs1360780* (rs designations are used to identify specific SNPs). These SNPs lie in strong linkage disequilibrium within a haplotype that covers the entire gene. Work by Klengel et al. (2013) unraveled the molecular implications of *rs1360780*. This variant was chosen for its proximity to a *GR* element (Lee et al. 2013), a short DNA motif that binds *GRs*, in intron 2 of *FKBP5*. The risk allele of *rs1360780* is A/T, and the protective allele is C/G. Klengel et al. (2013) showed that the A/T allele enhances expression of *FKBP5*, and that this effect is mediated by differential interaction between intron 2 and the transcription start site (**Figure 7c,d**). Given that the *GRE* in intron 2 is responsive to glucocorticoid signaling, the risk allele is thought to enhance the effects of *GR* signaling on *FKBP5* transcription

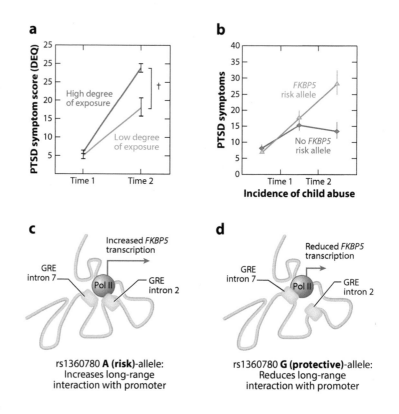

Figure 7

Examples of gene-by-environment (G × E) effects in posttraumatic stress disorder (PTSD). (*a*) An example of an environmental exposure as a function of time post-trauma, illustrating the severity of PTSD symptoms two to four weeks after a campus shooting by degree of exposure. The graph shows the mean PTSD symptom score [Distressing Event Questionnaire (DEQ)] at time 1 and time 2 (± standard error). A sum ranging from 0 to 2 for positive responses to high-exposure events is classified as a low degree of exposure. (*b*) An example of G × E exposure as a function of level of childhood trauma exposure, in which an *FKBP5* risk allele (*tan line*) is associated with heightened adult PTSD symptoms following high burdens of childhood trauma compared to the protective allele (*purple line*). (*c*) The risk allele of the *rs1360780* SNP in intron 2 of *FKBP5* increases the transcriptional output of RNA polymerase II (Pol II) at the transcription start site by increasing the long-distance interactions between the GRE containing intron 2 and the promoter, thus increasing the production of *FKBP5* mRNA. (*d*) The protective allele reduces the interaction between intron 2 and the promoter, reducing the production of *FKBP5* mRNA.

by bringing this distal transcriptional enhancer in close proximity to the promoter, therefore curbing the ultrashort HPA axis feedback loop in which *FKBP5* participates. This prolonged homeostatic perturbation results in lasting alterations in the neural circuits governing stress and anxiety.

CONCLUSIONS AND FUTURE DIRECTIONS

The robust G × E interactions we have described above are all involved in major signaling systems in development and neural function. However, an important point is that tens, if not hundreds to thousands, of different genes and gene loci are likely involved in genetic heritability, underlying part of the risk for stress- and anxiety-related disorders. These genetic risks are likely interacting with different aspects of the environment, such that some may interact with level of trauma exposure, e.g., *5-HTTLPR* and *BDNF*, whereas others may be particularly sensitive to the time of developmental exposure, as suggested by the finding that HPA-axis genes *FKBP5* and *CRHR1* interact with childhood trauma, but less so with adult trauma exposure. Still other gene pathways likely interact with sex hormones to provide differential sex effects (e.g., *ADCYAP1R1*), and others interact with physical toxin exposure (e.g., lead or mercury). The ways in which the environment may differentially integrate with genomic information are extremely varied. Larger-scale studies and studies combining consortia-level GWAS with environmental factors are likely to provide the most important paths to new discovery.

As our understanding of the complexity of genome regulation will continue to expand, so too will our appreciation for a greater understanding of quantitative measurements of exposure, with psychological trauma in particular. Additionally, we must understand which outcome measures best represent the effects of stress and trauma exposure, be they categorical diagnostic outcomes, continuous symptom-level outcomes, comorbid outcomes, and intermediate or endophenotypes outcomes such as physiological or brain imaging–based measures. Despite their complexity, advances in our understanding of G × E interactions will eventually further our knowledge of the biology of the brain and the mind. Such progress will also allow for a better understanding of how the environment—the world around us—creates both mental health and mental illness.

DISCLOSURE STATEMENT

The authors are not aware of any affiliations, memberships, funding, or financial holdings that might be perceived as affecting the objectivity of this review. The contents of this review do not reflect the views of the Department of Veterans Affairs of the United States government.

ACKNOWLEDGMENTS

This work was primarily supported by the National Institutes of Mental Health (MH071537 and MH096764 to K.J.R.; HD071982 to B.B.; and MH102890 to A.P.). Support was also received from the Emory University and Grady Memorial Hospital General Clinical Research Center, NIH National Centers for Research Resources (M01RR00039), the Howard Hughes Medical Institute (K.J.R.), and the Steven and Alexandra Cohen Foundation (CRM). We are grateful to the staff and participants from the Grady Trauma Project for their time and effort in supporting this research.

LITERATURE CITED

Abecasis GR, Auton A, Brooks LD, DePristo MA, Durbin RM, et al. 2012. An integrated map of genetic variation from 1,092 human genomes. *Nature* 491:56–65

Almli LM, Duncan R, Feng H, Ghosh D, Binder EB, et al. 2014. Correcting systematic inflation in genetic association tests that consider interaction effects: application to a genome-wide association study of posttraumatic stress disorder. *JAMA Psychiatry* 71:1392–99

Almli LM, Stevens J, Smith AK, Kilaru V, Qian M, et al. 2015. Genome-wide identified risk variant for PTSD is a methylation quantitative trait locus and confers decreased cortical activation to fearful faces. *Am. J. Med. Genet. B: Neuropsychiatr. Genet.* 168:327–36

Am. Psychiatr. Assoc. 2013. *Diagnostic and Statistical Manual of Mental Disorders.* Washington, DC: Am. Psychiatr. Publ. 5th ed.

Appel K, Schwahn C, Mahler J, Schulz A, Spitzer C, et al. 2011. Moderation of adult depression by a polymorphism in the FKBP5 gene and childhood physical abuse in the general population. *Neuropsychopharmacology* 36:1982–91

Ardlie KG, Kruglyak L, Seielstad M. 2002. Patterns of linkage disequilibrium in the human genome. *Nat. Rev. Genet.* 3:299–309

Binder E. 2014. Molecular mechanisms of gene × environment interaction in stress-related psychiatric disorders. NIH Videocasting Postcasting video, 49:53. Posted Febr. 24, 2014. **http://videocast.nih.gov/ summary.asp?Live=13688&bhcp=1**

Binder EB, Bradley RG, Liu W, Epstein MP, Deveau TC, et al. 2008. Association of FKBP5 polymorphisms and childhood abuse with risk of posttraumatic stress disorder symptoms in adults. *JAMA* 299:1291–305

Blaya C, Salum GA, Lima MS, Leistner-Segal S, Manfro GG. 2007. Lack of association between the serotonin transporter promoter polymorphism (5-HTTLPR) and panic disorder: a systematic review and meta-analysis. *Behav. Brain Funct.* 3:41

Bogdan R, Agrawal A, Gaffrey MS, Tillman R, Luby JL. 2014. Serotonin transporter-linked polymorphic region (5-HTTLPR) genotype and stressful life events interact to predict preschool-onset depression: a replication and developmental extension. *J. Child Psychol. Psychiatry* 55:448–57

Boscarino JA, Erlich PM, Hoffman SN, Zhang X. 2012. Higher FKBP5, COMT, CHRNA5, and CRHR1 allele burdens are associated with PTSD and interact with trauma exposure: implications for neuropsychiatric research and treatment. *Neuropsychiatr. Dis. Treat.* 8:131–39

Brady KT, Killeen TK, Brewerton T, Lucerini S. 2000. Comorbidity of psychiatric disorders and posttraumatic stress disorder. *J. Clin. Psychiatry* 61(Suppl. 7):22–32

Brewin CR, Andrews B, Valentine JD. 2000. Meta-analysis of risk factors for posttraumatic stress disorder in trauma-exposed adults. *J. Consult. Clin. Psychol.* 68:748–66

Carr CP, Martins CMS, Stingel AM, Lemgruber VB, Juruena MF. 2013. The role of early life stress in adult psychiatric disorders: a systematic review according to childhood trauma subtypes. *J. Nerv. Ment. Dis.* 201:1007–20

Caspi A, Sugden K, Moffitt TE, Taylor A, Craig IW, et al. 2003. Influence of life stress on depression: moderation by a polymorphism in the 5-HTT gene. *Science* 301:386–89

Chen J, Li X, McGue M. 2012. Interacting effect of BDNF Val66Met polymorphism and stressful life events on adolescent depression. *Genes Brain Behav.* 11:958–65

Cichon S, Craddock N, Daly M, Faraone SV, Gejman PV, et al. 2009. Genomewide association studies: history, rationale, and prospects for psychiatric disorders. *Am. J. Psychiatry* 166:540–56

Collip D, Myin-Germeys I, Wichers M, Jacobs N, Derom C, et al. 2013. FKBP5 as a possible moderator of the psychosis-inducing effects of childhood trauma. *Br. J. Psychiatry* 202:261–68

CONVERGE consort. 2015. Sparse whole-genome sequencing identifies two loci for major depressive disorder. *Nature* 523:588–91

Cornelis MC, Nugent NR, Amstadter AB, Koenen KC. 2010. Genetics of post-traumatic stress disorder: review and recommendations for genome-wide association studies. *Curr. Psychiatry Rep.* 12:313–26

Craske MG, Rauch SL, Ursano R, Prenoveau J, Pine DS, Zinbarg RE. 2009. What is an anxiety disorder? *Depression Anxiety* 26:1066–85

Cross-Disord. Group Psychiatr. Genom. Consort. 2013. Genetic relationship between five psychiatric disorders estimated from genome-wide SNPs. *Nat. Genet.* 45:984–94

Dackis MN, Rogosch FA, Oshri A, Cicchetti D. 2012. The role of limbic system irritability in linking history of childhood maltreatment and psychiatric outcomes in low-income, high-risk women: moderation by FK506 binding protein 5 haplotype. *Dev. Psychopathol.* 24:1237–52

Dick DM. 2011. Gene-environment interaction in psychological traits and disorders. *Annu. Rev. Clin. Psychol.* 7:383–409

Dunn EC, Solovieff N, Lowe SR, Gallagher PJ, Chaponis J, et al. 2014. Interaction between genetic variants and exposure to Hurricane Katrina on post-traumatic stress and post-traumatic growth: a prospective analysis of low income adults. *J. Affect. Disord.* 152–154:243–49

Gatt JM, Nemeroff CB, Dobson-Stone C, Paul RH, Bryant RA, et al. 2009. Interactions between BDNF Val66Met polymorphism and early life stress predict brain and arousal pathways to syndromal depression and anxiety. *Mol. Psychiatry* 14:681–95

Gillespie CF, Bradley B, Mercer K, Smith AK, Conneely K, et al. 2009. Trauma exposure and stress-related disorders in inner city primary care patients. *Gen. Hosp. Psychiatry* 31:505–14

Gillespie NA, Whitfield JB, Williams B, Heath AC, Martin NG. 2005. The relationship between stressful life events, the serotonin transporter (5-HTTLPR) genotype and major depression. *Psychol. Med.* 35:101–11

Grabe HJ, Spitzer C, Schwahn C, Marcinek A, Frahnow A, et al. 2009. Serotonin transporter gene (SLC6A4) promoter polymorphisms and the susceptibility to posttraumatic stress disorder in the general population. *Am. J. Psychiatry* 166:926–33

Guffanti G, Galea S, Yan L, Roberts AL, Solovieff N, et al. 2013. Genome-wide association study implicates a novel RNA gene, the lincRNA AC068718.1, as a risk factor for post-traumatic stress disorder in women. *Psychoneuroendocrinology* 38:3029–38

Gunthert KC, Conner TS, Armeli S, Tennen H, Covault J, Kranzler HR. 2007. Serotonin transporter gene polymorphism (5-HTTLPR) and anxiety reactivity in daily life: a daily process approach to gene-environment interaction. *Psychosom. Med.* 69:762–68

Halperin E, Stephan DA. 2009. SNP imputation in association studies. *Nat. Biotechnol.* 27:349–51

Heim C, Nemeroff CB. 2001. The role of childhood trauma in the neurobiology of mood and anxiety disorders: preclinical and clinical studies. *Biol. Psychiatry* 49:1023–39

Hettema JM, Neale MC, Kendler KS. 2001. A review and meta-analysis of the genetic epidemiology of anxiety disorders. *Am. J. Psychiatry* 158:1568–78

Hettema JM, Prescott CA, Myers JM, Neale MC, Kendler KS. 2005. The structure of genetic and environmental risk factors for anxiety disorders in men and women. *Arch. Gen. Psychiatry* 62:182–89

Hewitt JK. 2012. Editorial policy on candidate gene association and candidate gene-by-environment interaction studies of complex traits. *Behav. Genet.* 42:1–2

Hirschhorn JN, Lohmueller K, Byrne E, Hirschhorn K. 2002. A comprehensive review of genetic association studies. *Genet. Med.* 4:45–61

Hoffmann A, Spengler D. 2014. DNA memories of early social life. *Neuroscience* 264:64–75

Holman EA, Lucas-Thompson RG, Lu T. 2011. Social constraints, genetic vulnerability, and mental health following collective stress. *J. Trauma. Stress* 24:497–505

Int. HapMap Consort. 2003. The International HapMap Project. *Nature* 426:789–96

Karg K, Burmeister M, Shedden K, Sen S. 2011. The serotonin transporter promoter variant (5-HTTLPR), stress, and depression meta-analysis revisited: evidence of genetic moderation. *Arch. Gen. Psychiatry* 68:444–54

Kaufman J, Yang BZ, Douglas-Palumberi H, Grasso D, Lipschitz D, et al. 2006. Brain-derived neurotrophic factor-5-HTTLPR gene interactions and environmental modifiers of depression in children. *Biol. Psychiatry* 59:673–80

Keller MC. 2014. Gene × environment interaction studies have not properly controlled for potential confounders: the problem and the (simple) solution. *Biol. Psychiatry* 75:18–24

Kendler KS, Neale MC, Kessler RC, Heath AC, Eaves LJ. 1992. Childhood parental loss and adult psychopathology in women: a twin study perspective. *Arch. Gen. Psychiatry* 49:109–16

Kilpatrick DG, Koenen KC, Ruggiero KJ, Acierno R, Galea S, et al. 2007. The serotonin transporter genotype and social support and moderation of posttraumatic stress disorder and depression in hurricane-exposed adults. *Am. J. Psychiatry* 164:1693–99

Kilpatrick DG, Ruggiero KJ, Acierno R, Saunders BE, Resnick HS, Best CL. 2003. Violence and risk of PTSD, major depression, substance abuse/dependence, and comorbidity: results from the National Survey of Adolescents. *J. Consult. Clin. Psychol.* 71:692–700

Kim-Cohen J, Caspi A, Taylor A, Williams B, Newcombe R, et al. 2006. MAOA, maltreatment, and gene–environment interaction predicting children's mental health: new evidence and a meta-analysis. *Mol. Psychiatry* 11:903–13

Klauke B, Deckert J, Reif A, Pauli P, Zwanzger P, et al. 2011. Serotonin transporter gene and childhood trauma—a G × E effect on anxiety sensitivity. *Depression Anxiety* 28:1048–57

Klengel T, Binder EB. 2015. FKBP5 allele-specific epigenetic modification in gene by environment interaction. *Neuropsychopharmacology* 40:244–46

Klengel T, Mehta D, Anacker C, Rex-Haffner M, Pruessner JC, et al. 2013. Allele-specific FKBP5 DNA demethylation mediates gene–childhood trauma interactions. *Nat. Neurosci.* 16:33–41

Kolassa I, Ertl V, Eckart C, Glöckner F, Kolassa S, et al. 2010. Association study of trauma load and SLC6A4 promoter polymorphism in posttraumatic stress disorder: evidence from survivors of the Rwandan genocide. *J. Clin. Psychiatry* 71:543–47

Lee SH, Ripke S, Neale BM, Faraone SV, Purcell SM, et al. 2013. Genetic relationship between five psychiatric disorders estimated from genome-wide SNPs. *Nat. Genet.* 45:984–94

Logue MW, Amstadter AB, Baker DG, Duncan L, Koenen KC, et al. 2015. The Psychiatric Genomics Consortium Posttraumatic Stress Disorder Workgroup: Posttraumatic stress disorder enters the age of large-scale genomic collaboration. *Neuropsychopharmacology* 40:2287–97

Logue MW, Baldwin C, Guffanti G, Melista E, Wolf EJ, et al. 2013. A genome-wide association study of post-traumatic stress disorder identifies the retinoid-related orphan receptor alpha (RORA) gene as a significant risk locus. *Mol. Psychiatry* 18(8):937–42

MacMillan HL, Fleming JE, Streiner DL, Lin E, Boyle MH, et al. 2001. Childhood abuse and lifetime psychopathology in a community sample. *Childhood* 158(11):1878–83

Major Depressive Disord. Work. Group Psychiatr. GWAS Consort. 2013. A mega-analysis of genome-wide association studies for major depressive disorder. *Mol. Psychiatry* 18(4):497–511

McCarroll SA. 2008. Extending genome-wide association studies to copy-number variation. *Hum. Mol. Genet.* 17:R135–42

McLaughlin KA, Conron KJ, Koenen KC, Gilman SE. 2010. Childhood adversity, adult stressful life events, and risk of past-year psychiatric disorder: a test of the stress sensitization hypothesis in a population-based sample of adults. *Psychol. Med.* 40:1647–58

Mellman TA, Alim T, Brown DD, Gorodetsky E, Buzas B, et al. 2009. Serotonin polymorphisms and post-traumatic stress disorder in a trauma exposed African American population. *Depression Anxiety* 26:993–97

Mercer KB, Orcutt HK, Quinn JF, Fitzgerald CA, Conneely KN, et al. 2012. Acute and posttraumatic stress symptoms in a prospective gene × environment study of a university campus shooting. *Arch. Gen. Psychiatry* 69:89–97

Mills RE, Walter K, Stewart C, Handsaker RE, Chen K, et al. 2011. Mapping copy number variation by population-scale genome sequencing. *Nature* 470:59–65

Nederhof E, Bouma EM, Oldehinkel AJ, Ormel J. 2010. Interaction between childhood adversity, brain-derived neurotrophic factor val/met and serotonin transporter promoter polymorphism on depression: the TRAILS study. *Biol. Psychiatry* 68:209–12

Nievergelt CM, Maihofer AX, Mustapic M, Yurgil KA, Schork NJ, et al. 2015. Genomic predictors of combat stress vulnerability and resilience in U.S. Marines: A genome-wide association study across multiple ancestries implicates PRTFDC1 as a potential PTSD gene. *Psychoneuroendocrinology* 51:459–71

Psychiatr. GWAS Consort. Steer. Comm. 2009. A framework for interpreting genome-wide association studies of psychiatric disorders. *Mol. Psychiatry* 14:10–17

Ripke S, Wray NR, Lewis CM, Hamilton SP, Weissman MM, et al. 2013. A mega-analysis of genome-wide association studies for major depressive disorder. *Mol. Psychiatry* 18:497–511

Risch N, Herrell R, Lehner T, Liang K-Y, Eaves L, et al. 2009. Interaction between the serotonin transporter gene (5-HTTLPR), stressful life events, and risk of depression: a meta-analysis. *JAMA* 301:2462–71

Roy A, Gorodetsky E, Yuan Q, Goldman D, Enoch MA. 2010. Interaction of FKBP5, a stress-related gene, with childhood trauma increases the risk for attempting suicide. *Neuropsychopharmacology* 35:1674–83

Roy A, Hu X-Z, Janal MN, Goldman D. 2007. Interaction between childhood trauma and serotonin transporter gene variation in suicide. *Neuropsychopharmacology* 32:2046–52

Sayin A, Kucukyildirim S, Akar T, Bakkaloglu Z, Demircan A, et al. 2010. A prospective study of serotonin transporter gene promoter (5-HTT gene linked polymorphic region) and intron 2 (variable number of tandem repeats) polymorphisms as predictors of trauma response to mild physical injury. *DNA Cell Biol.* 29:71–77

Schizophr. Work. Group Psychiatr. Genom. Consort. 2014. Biological insights from 108 schizophrenia-associated genetic loci. *Nature* 511:421–27

Sham PC, Purcell SM. 2014. Statistical power and significance testing in large-scale genetic studies. *Nat. Rev. Genet.* 15:335–46

Stein MB, Schork NJ, Gelernter J. 2008. Gene-by-environment (serotonin transporter and childhood maltreatment) interaction for anxiety sensitivity, an intermediate phenotype for anxiety disorders. *Neuropsychopharmacology* 33:312–19

Thakur GA, Joober R, Brunet A. 2009. Development and persistence of posttraumatic stress disorder and the 5-HTTLPR polymorphism. *J. Trauma. Stress* 22:240–43

Walsh K, Uddin M, Soliven R, Wildman DE, Bradley B. 2014. Associations between the SS variant of 5-HTTLPR and PTSD among adults with histories of childhood emotional abuse: results from two African American independent samples. *J. Affect. Disord.* 161:91–96

Wang Z, Baker DG, Harrer J, Hamner M, Price M, Amstadter A. 2011. The relationship between combat-related posttraumatic stress disorder and the 5-HTTLPR/rs25531 polymorphism. *Depression Anxiety* 28:1067–73

Xie P, Kranzler HR, Farrer L, Gelernter J. 2012. Serotonin transporter 5-HTTLPR genotype moderates the effects of childhood adversity on posttraumatic stress disorder risk: a replication study. *Am. J. Med. Genet. B: Neuropsychiatr. Genet.* 159:644–52

Xie P, Kranzler HR, Poling J, Stein MB, Anton RF, et al. 2009. Interactive effect of stressful life events and the serotonin transporter 5-HTTLPR genotype on posttraumatic stress disorder diagnosis in 2 independent populations. *Arch. Gen. Psychiatry* 66:1201–9

Xie P, Kranzler HR, Poling J, Stein MB, Anton RF, et al. 2010. Interaction of FKBP5 with childhood adversity on risk for post-traumatic stress disorder. *Neuropsychopharmacology* 35:1684–92

Xie P, Kranzler HR, Yang C, Zhao H, Farrer LA, Gelernter J. 2013. Genome-wide association study identifies new susceptibility loci for posttraumatic stress disorder. *Biol. Psychiatry* 74:656–63

Zannas AS, Binder EB. 2014. Gene-environment interactions at the FKBP5 locus: sensitive periods, mechanisms and pleiotropism. *Genes Brain Behav.* 13:25–37

Zhang H. 2011. Statistical analysis in genetic studies of mental illnesses. *Stat. Sci.* 26:116–29

Zimmermann P, Bruckl T, Nocon A, Pfister H, Binder EB, et al. 2011. Interaction of FKBP5 gene variants and adverse life events in predicting depression onset: results from a 10-year prospective community study. *Am. J. Psychiatry* 168:1107–16

Automaticity: Componential, Causal, and Mechanistic Explanations

Agnes Moors[1,2]

[1] Research Group of Quantitative Psychology and Individual Differences; Centre for Social and Cultural Psychology, University of Leuven, 3000 Leuven, Belgium; email: Agnes.Moors@ppw.kuleuven.be

[2] Department of Experimental Clinical and Health Psychology, Ghent University, 9000 Ghent, Belgium

Annu. Rev. Psychol. 2016. 67:263–87

First published online as a Review in Advance on August 28, 2015

The *Annual Review of Psychology* is online at psych.annualreviews.org

This article's doi: 10.1146/annurev-psych-122414-033550

Keywords

conscious, control, attention, representation, practice, complexity

Abstract

The review first discusses componential explanations of automaticity, which specify non/automaticity features (e.g., un/controlled, un/conscious, non/efficient, fast/slow) and their interrelations. Reframing these features as factors that influence processes (e.g., goals, attention, and time) broadens the range of factors that can be considered (e.g., adding stimulus intensity and representational quality). The evidence reviewed challenges the view of a perfect coherence among goals, attention, and consciousness, and supports the alternative view that (*a*) these and other factors influence the quality of representations in an additive way (e.g., little time can be compensated by extra attention or extra stimulus intensity) and that (*b*) a first threshold of this quality is required for unconscious processing and a second threshold for conscious processing. The review closes with a discussion of causal explanations of automaticity, which specify factors involved in automatization such as repetition and complexity, and a discussion of mechanistic explanations, which specify the low-level processes underlying automatization.

Contents

INTRODUCTION

Automaticity is a central phenomenon in psychology. The scientific explanation of a phenomenon typically spans the following stages: (*a*) the choice of a provisional demarcation or working definition of the phenomenon; (*b*) development of an explanation, which links the to-be-explained phenomenon (explanandum) to an explaining fact (explanans); (*c*) testing of the explanation in empirical research; and (*d*) if the explanation is sufficiently supported, entering of the explanans in the definition of the phenomenon, which is now a scientific definition (Bechtel 2008).[1] This logic can be applied to automaticity as well. Starting point are descriptions of the phenomena of automaticity as they are experienced by laypeople in daily life, either in the form of a list of features or a list of prototypical exemplars. As an illustration of features, people tend to call a process or behavior automatic when it seems to run by itself, while their mind is elsewhere, when they are unable to prevent or stop it, and/or when it happens fast. Examples of prototypical automatic processes include reflexes or emergency reactions (e.g., eye blinking, retracting one's hand from a hot stove, and vigilant attention shifts), skilled processes (e.g., riding a bike, typing, and playing the piano), and impulsive processes (e.g., lashing out in anger, eating the bowl of nuts in front of you, and compulsive thoughts).

Starting from this provisional demarcation, theorists have proposed componential, causal, and mechanistic explanations for automaticity. A componential explanation unpacks the components of automaticity and specifies the relations among them. A causal explanation of the automaticity of a process specifies the factors involved in the transition of a process from nonautomatic to automatic, also called automatization. A mechanistic explanation of the automaticity of a process specifies the low-level processes underlying automatization. Both componential and mechanistic explanations span different levels of analysis (Bechtel 2008, Marr 1982). It is useful to distinguish between

---

[1] For an example from chemistry, water (explanandum), provisionally demarcated with superficial features (e.g., clear, odorless fluid, falling out of the sky) has been explained by linking it to H_2O (explanans). Abundant empirical confirmation of this explanation has eventually led to a redefinition of water as H_2O.

an observable level, a set of hidden levels, and a brain level: On the observable level, a process is described as the transition from an observable input to an observable output. On the hidden levels, the process is decomposed into subprocesses, which can themselves be described in terms of their inputs and outputs. Intermediate, hidden inputs and outputs are called representations. Each of the subprocesses can be decomposed in even finer-grained subprocesses, until, at the ultimate stages of decomposition, they correspond to brain processes. This article discusses existing proposals for componential, causal, and mechanistic explanations of automaticity and reviews the empirical evidence in their favor or against them.

Control: *A* has control over *X* when *A* has a goal about *X* and the goal causes fulfillment of the goal

COMPONENTIAL EXPLANATIONS

Automaticity has been decomposed into a number of components, called automaticity features. Examples are: uncontrolled in the promoting and counteracting sense, unconscious, efficient, and fast. Authors vary with regard to the features they put forward and the relations they assume among them. Some theorists focus on efficiency (Shiffrin 1988), others emphasize lack of control (Posner & Snyder 1975), and still others include the entire list (Bargh 1994). Given the divergence among authors, it is best to always specify the features one has in mind when calling a process automatic.

This section starts with a brief demarcation of the listed features (i.e., components) and a specification of their ingredients (i.e., subcomponents; for an in-depth analysis and a more extensive list of features, see Moors & De Houwer 2006a). It goes on to argue that features are not intrinsic to processes but point at conditions under which processes can occur (Bargh 1992), or more generally, factors that can influence processes. This opens the door for considering the role of factors that do not traditionally belong to the automaticity concept. After describing these factors, the section discusses possible relations among them and reviews the empirical evidence in favor of or against these relations.

Features

Un/controlled. A process is controlled by a person when three ingredients are in place: (*a*) The person has a goal about the process, that is, a representation of a desired state; (*b*) the desired state occurs; and (*c*) there is a causal relation between the goal and the occurrence of the desired state. Goals can be of the promoting kind (i.e., the goal to engage in a process) or of the counteracting kind (e.g., to prevent, change, or interrupt the process). Accordingly, a process can be controlled in the promoting sense (i.e., caused by the goal to engage in it) or in the counteracting sense (i.e., counteracted by the goal to counteract it). Another word for controlled in the promoting sense is intentional. A process is uncontrolled if one (or more) of the three ingredients is lacking: The goal is absent, the desired state does not occur, or the causal relation is absent.

Un/conscious. Philosophers traditionally distinguish two ingredients of consciousness: (*a*) an aboutness aspect, denoting the content of consciousness (e.g., the apple in front of me, a prejudice toward someone), and (*b*) a phenomenal aspect, denoting the subjective quality or "what it is like" to be conscious of something (e.g., what it is like to see the redness of the apple or to entertain the prejudice; Block 1995). If a process is conceptualized as the transition between an input and an output, being conscious of a process boils down to being conscious of the input, the output, and the transition from one to the other. A process is unconscious when one or more of these three elements is missing.

Non/efficient. A process is called efficient versus nonefficient if it requires little (or no) versus a substantial amount of attentional capacity (Shiffrin 1988). The ingredient at stake is attentional capacity or the amount of attention. In addition to quantity, attention also has a quality or direction, which is partly independent from quantity: Directing and allocating attention requires some amount of attention (Konstantinou & Lavie 2013), but it may not require a lot.

Fast/slow. A process is fast versus slow when it requires little versus much time or when it has a short versus long duration. The ingredient at stake here is time or duration. The duration of a process should not be conflated with the duration of its input. A fleeting stimulus may trigger a slow process, and an enduring stimulus may trigger a fast process.

Like efficiency, speed is most naturally considered as a gradual feature. The feature controlled can be considered to be a gradual feature as well: A goal can be partially or entirely reached. The gradual nature of consciousness is debated: Some findings favor a continuous transition from unconscious to conscious processing (Moutoussis & Zeki 2002, Nieuwenhuis & De Kleijn 2011), whereas others favor a discontinuous one (Sergent & Dehaene 2004).

Extending the Range of Factors

The view defended here is that non/automaticity features are not intrinsic to processes, but point at conditions under which processes occur or at factors that influence their occurrence (Bargh 1992). Thus, a process is uncontrolled in the promoting sense if it is not caused by the goal to engage in the process, uncontrolled in the counteracting sense if it is not counteracted by the goal to do so, unconscious if it occurs in the absence of consciousness (of the input, the output, and/or the transition from input to output), efficient if it occurs when attentional capacity is scarce, and fast if it occurs in a short time interval.

One could argue that the range of factors that can influence the occurrence of processes goes beyond those that are traditionally covered by the automaticity concept. In principle, any aspect of the experimental procedure (and beyond) can influence processing, but researchers tend to focus on those factors that generalize across experiments and from which they expect a high explanatory power. Factors can be organized in a taxonomy according to at least six combinable axes (see **Figure 1**): (*a*) procedural versus nonprocedural, (*b*) current versus prior, (*c*) person versus stimulus (and person × stimulus), (*d*) physical versus mental (and mind dependent), (*e*) absolute versus relative, and (*f*) occurrent versus dispositional. A brief clarification of these notions now follows.

(*a*) Procedural factors are induced by the procedure of an experiment (e.g., the stimulus set); nonprocedural factors are not (e.g., a participant's personality). (*b*) Current factors are present here and now; prior factors were present in a prior part of the procedure or at a time before that (e.g., learning history). (*c, d*) Next are person and stimulus factors. Person factors can be physical (e.g., fatigue, genetic makeup) or mental. Examples of mental person factors are the presence and availability of a stimulus representation (in long-term memory) and the level and duration of its activation (in working memory). It is useful to distinguish at least three types of representations: goals (i.e., representations of desired stimuli), expectations (i.e., representations of expected stimuli), and mere stimulus representations (i.e., representations of stimuli that are neither desired nor expected). Other mental person factors are the amount and direction of attention. Attention can be directed to a spatial location, a time window, the input of a process (an external stimulus or feature, or an internal representation), the output of a process (an internal representation or an external response), or the process itself (i.e., the transition from input to output). Stimulus factors can be physical or mind dependent. Physical stimulus factors comprise current factors such as duration and intensity (subsuming factors such as contrast, luminance, size, and movement), or

	Mental	Physical	Mind dependent
Stimulus		**Prior** Recency Frequency **Current** Intensity Duration Abrupt onset Novelty	**Current** Un/expectedness Novelty/familiarity Goal in/congruence
Person	**Prior/current** Quality of representation: Goal　Expectation　Mere representation	**Prior/current** Neurophysiological and behavioral responses	
Stimulus × person		**Prior** Overt selection history Reward history	**Prior** Processing history

Figure 1

Examples of procedural factors (cf. *a*) that fit into the intersections of the following axes: stimulus versus person versus stimulus × person (cf. *c*), mental versus physical versus mind dependent (cf. *d*), and current versus prior (cf. *b*).

prior factors, such as frequency or repetition (i.e., the number of times the stimulus was presented before) and recency (i.e., whether the stimulus was presented recently). Mind-dependent stimulus factors are ones that depend in part on the mental state of the participant. Examples are goal in/congruence (i.e., mis/match with a goal, which together form goal relevance or significance; Bernstein & Taylor 1979), un/expectedness (i.e., mis/match with an expectation), and novelty[2]/familiarity (i.e., mis/match with a mere representation; Öhman 1992).[3] Some physical factors refer to the interaction between person and stimuli, such as a person's selection and reward history (Awh et al. 2012). (*e*) All stimulus factors can be absolute or relative. For instance, it makes sense to consider a stimulus' intensity relative to that of other stimuli or to consider a representation's activation level relative to that of other representations. Novelty is often relative to a certain context rather than absolute. (*f*) Finally, most factors are occurrent, referring to actual states (e.g., the activation level of a representation), but some are dispositional, expressing a potential state (e.g., availability and accessibility of a representation).

The proposed taxonomy goes beyond the classical top-down versus bottom-up distinction in several ways. Top-down factors correspond to mental person factors and bottom-up factors to physical stimulus factors. More than a few researchers (e.g., Awh et al. 2012, Theeuwes 2010), however, have extended the category of bottom-up factors with mind-dependent stimulus factors such as unexpectedness and salience (i.e., the capacity of a stimulus to stand out or capture attention; Itti 2007). Yet these factors may be better characterized as referring to the interaction between bottom-up and top-down (Corbetta & Schulman 2002). Moreover, several other factors, such as selection and reward history, fall outside the bottom-up versus top-down divide (Awh et al. 2012). Another problem is the often-made supposition that bottom-up influences are automatic whereas

Goal in/congruence: mis/match of a stimulus with a goal

Un/expectedness mis/match of a stimulus with an expectation

Novelty/familiarity: mis/match of a stimulus with any mere representation (i.e., mind-dependent stimulus factor); "novel" can also mean "never presented" (i.e., physical stimulus factor)

Stimulus intensity: physical stimulus factor subsuming contrast, luminance, size, and movement

---

[2] Novelty can also refer to a purely physical stimulus factor, in which case "novel" means "never presented."

[3] Some authors mention the emotional character of stimuli as a factor (Pourtois et al. 2013), but this often can be unpacked as goal relevance, threat value, negativity, valence, or arousal (Sander et al. 2003).

top-down influences are not, although it is rarely specified what is meant by automatic in this context.

A further remark is that mind-dependent stimulus factors have to be manipulated via physical stimulus factors. The latter can be considered as physical counterparts of the former, and the former as mind-dependent counterparts of the latter. For instance, familiarity and accessibility can be considered as mind-dependent counterparts of frequency and recency, respectively. In a similar vein, dispositional factors can be translated in an occurrent counterpart. This is what happens when accessibility is translated in the quality of a representation and when availability of a representation is translated in the existence of a memory trace leading to a representation. The insight that physical and mind-dependent factors can be counterparts of each other helps explain why debates about whether the source of certain effects is physical (e.g., abrupt onset) or mind dependent (e.g., unexpected) are largely pointless. Thus, the multiple-axis taxonomy proposed here not only allows for a larger degree of precision and exhaustivity in the number of factors considered compared to the bottom-up versus top-down dichotomy, but also helps to reveal pseudo discussions.[4]

Relations Among Features/Factors

Now that the features of non/automaticity have been situated within a broader range of factors, the groundwork is laid for examining the relations among these features. At one end of the spectrum is the view that there is perfect coherence among all automaticity features (e.g., uncontrolled, unconscious, efficient, and fast) and among all nonautomaticity features (e.g., controlled, conscious, nonefficient, and slow). This view has various origins. The first origin is ideas of conceptual overlap among features. Examples are the idea that consciousness is an ingredient of "true" control (e.g., Prinz 2004) and that consciousness coincides with attention (e.g., O'Regan & Noë 2001). The second source is ideas about implicational relations (i.e., of necessity and sufficiency) among features or factors. Examples are the ideas that goals are necessary and sufficient for attention (Folk et al. 1992), that attention is necessary and sufficient for consciousness (e.g., De Brigard & Prinz 2010), and that consciousness is necessary for control (e.g., Uleman 1989).

At the other end of the spectrum are proponents of a decompositional view, who argue that the idea of perfect coherence is based on shaky grounds (e.g., Bargh 1992, Moors & De Houwer 2006a, Shiffrin 1988). Each of the sources of the perfect coherence view can be challenged. First, features can be defined in nonoverlapping ways, as is clear from the definitions of control, consciousness, attention, and speed presented in the previous paragraphs. Second, there may be implicational relations among factors (some factors may be necessary *or* sufficient for other factors), but the question is whether these are one-to-one relations (whether one factor is both necessary *and* sufficient for another factor).

To demonstrate that one factor A is necessary for another factor B, one should demonstrate that in all instances in which A is absent, B is absent as well. Because investigating all instances is impossible, researchers often come up with one or more instances in which A and B are both absent, and generalize the conclusions about the necessity of A for B in these instances to all other instances. To demonstrate that A is not necessary for B requires finding only one instance in which A is absent but B is present or one instance in which another condition C is sufficient.

---

[4]On a meta-scientific scale, this proposal fits in the general approach to organize any set of phenomena (whether they are factors, processes, or even theories) according to multiple combinable axes instead of into a limited number of categories and to resist accepting untested assumptions of the unity of these categories.

To demonstrate that A is sufficient for B requires demonstrating that in all instances in which A is present, B is present as well. Again, because investigating all instances is impossible, researchers collect one or more instances in which both A and B are present and generalize the conclusions about the sufficiency of A for B in these instances to all other instances. To demonstrate that A is not sufficient for B requires finding only one instance in which A is present and B is absent or one instance in which another condition C is necessary. The next sections review the empirical evidence pertaining to the implicational relations among goals, attention, and consciousness (the ingredients of the features un/controlled, non/efficient, and un/conscious). Is it warranted to maintain that (*a*) goals are necessary and sufficient for attention, (*b*) attention is necessary and sufficient for consciousness, and (*c*) consciousness is necessary and sufficient for goals?

From Goals to Attention

This section reviews empirical research pertaining to the influence, necessity, and sufficiency of goals for attention.

Influence of goals on attention. The claim that goals influence attention can be split into the subclaims that (*a*) the content of goals influences the direction of attention and (*b*) the strength of goals influences the amount of attention. Evidence for the first type of influence (content on direction) is abundant (see Awh et al. 2012, Hommel 2010). Spatial cuing studies show that the goal to respond to a target (presence or feature) combined with information about the likely location of the target (provided by a cue that reliably predicts this location) leads to the directing of attention to that location (e.g., Posner 1980). Other studies show that the goal to respond to a target feature (e.g., color) leads to the directing of attention to that feature across space. If the target is defined by a conjunction of features (e.g., color plus location), attention is also directed to nontargets that have feature overlap with the target (e.g., color). This is illustrated by a study of Folk & Remington (1998) in which the task to respond to red targets in one of four boxes increased attention to red (compared to white) dots surrounding the boxes before the targets were presented. In other studies, it is shown that attention is directed to stimuli or features that are relevant not to a current goal but rather to a previous goal or a goal that applies in a different context (e.g., a different type of trials). Vogt et al. (2010) alternated spatial cuing trials with goal trials in which participants had to respond to the words "ship" and "field." They found that attention measured during the spatial cuing trials was directed to the words that were relevant during the goal trials but irrelevant during the spatial cuing trials. Dijksterhuis & Aarts (2010) reviewed studies showing that attention also can be directed by unconscious goals. All of the above-cited studies are concerned with the influence of the goal to respond to a particular stimulus/feature[5] (e.g., red versus green) on the direction of attention. A different line of research is concerned with the influence of the goal to perform a particular action (e.g., grasping versus reaching) on the direction of attention. Müsseler & Hommel (1997) found that the instruction to reach versus grasp an oddball stimulus was facilitated when the oddball was defined in terms of its location (relevant for reaching) versus its size (relevant for grasping).

The second type of influence (strength on amount) is demonstrated in studies in which stronger goals led to stronger attentional bias effects (Engelmann et al. 2009, Libera & Chelazzi 2006). Using a dot-probe task, Mogg et al. (1998) observed that hungry participants attended more to food-related words than neutral words in comparison with nonhungry participants.

---

[5] A stimulus can be considered as a collection of features.

Necessity of goals for attention. If instances can be found in which attention is directed by factors other than goals, it can be concluded that goals are not necessary for the directing of attention. Studies using visual search and spatial cuing showed that early attention can be directed by abrupt onsets (Enns et al. 2001, Mulckhuyse & Theeuwes 2010) and by other ways to render stimuli unexpected (Posner et al. 1980). In visual search studies, the observation that the selection of a target defined by color, size, motion, or orientation was not delayed by increasing the number of distractors surrounding it indicates that these features were processed efficiently (i.e., without requiring much attention) and that they guided or directed attention (Wolfe & Horowitz 2004). These and many other studies purport to show that abrupt onsets and other physical stimulus factors are the initial guides of attention and that they are able to override the influence of goals (Belopolsky et al. 2010, Theeuwes 2010). The picture emerging in these studies is that goals can at best adjust the size of the attention window in early stages, but that most of their influence kicks in later (through recurrent feedback processes; Theeuwes 2010). It is further argued that most so-called early influences of goals on attention conceal effects of repetition or selection history (Awh et al. 2012). For instance, the effect found in the study of Folk & Remington (1998) can equally well be explained by repetition priming because the target was kept constant across trials. In stark contrast with this stimulus capture view, proponents of the contingent capture view provide evidence that early effects of abrupt onsets depend in fact on current task goals (e.g., Wu et al. 2014; see also Lamy & Kristjánsson 2013). For instance, in many visual search studies, participants were instructed (and hence presumably had the goal) to search for deviant (or other) stimuli. Thus, it cannot be concluded that the physical features found to guide attention in these studies were sufficient for doing so (Folk et al. 1992). The controversy has led some researchers to adopt a reconciling position, according to which both types of factors contribute to the early directing of attention in an additive way (Kastner & Ungerleider 2000, Pourtois et al. 2013, Wolfe et al. 2003). Lamy & Kristjánsson (2013), for instance, acknowledge the dramatic role of the selection history but still point at studies that provide evidence for the unconfounded influence of goals (e.g., Irons et al. 2012).

In sum, there is debate about whether physical stimulus factors such as abrupt onsets can be sufficient for the directing of attention, but it is clear that selection and reward history independent of current goals can influence attention, which means that at least current goals are not necessary.

Sufficiency of goals for attention. With regard to the sufficiency of goals for attention, it is useful to distinguish between attention search and attention allocation. Attention search can be understood as the directing of attention across the perceptual field while keeping the representation of a stimulus/feature active (Awh et al. 2006). Attention allocation can be understood as the directing of attention to a specific stimulus/feature, a specific location, or a specific time window. Goals may be sufficient for attention search and spatial and temporal attention allocation, but it seems safe to assume that stimulus/feature-based attention allocation also requires the presence of a stimulus with some duration and intensity and with one or more specific features.

In sum, the arguments and empirical evidence reviewed above support the ideas that (*a*) goals do influence attention; (*b*) goals are not necessary for attention, given that other factors seem sufficient in some instances; and (*c*) goals may be sufficient for some forms of attention (attention search and spatial and temporal attention allocation) but not for others (stimulus/feature-based attention allocation).

From Attention to Consciousness

This section reviews empirical research pertaining to the influence, necessity, and sufficiency of attention for conscious processing.

Influence of attention on consciousness. The claim that attention has an influence on consciousness can be split into the subclaims that (*a*) the direction of attention influences the content of consciousness and (*b*) the amount of attention spent on something (stimulus/process) increases the likelihood that it becomes conscious. Evidence for the first type of influence (direction on content) comes from effects known as inattentional blindness (i.e., an unexpected stimulus with a high intensity and long duration fails to reach consciousness when attention is directed to another stimulus; e.g., Mack & Rock 1998) and change blindness (i.e., a change in a visual pattern does not become conscious when attention is not focused on the changing part; e.g., Rensink et al. 1997). Evidence for the second type of influence (quantity on likelihood) comes from effects known as the attentional blink (i.e., a stimulus fails to reach consciousness when attention is consumed by another stimulus that is presented about 200 ms earlier; Raymond et al. 1992) and load-induced blindness (i.e., the threshold for consciousness of a stimulus increases when attentional capacity is consumed by a secondary task; Macdonald & Lavie 2008).

Necessity of attention for consciousness. The idea that attention influences consciousness is uncontroversial, but there is debate about whether it is also necessary for consciousness. A first position is that attention is necessary for all conscious processes, leaning on the metaphor of attention as the spotlight in the theater of consciousness or the gate to a global workspace or working memory in which consciousness is possible (Baars 1988, De Brigard & Prinz 2010, Kouider & Dehaene 2007). A second position is that top-down attention is necessary for some conscious processes or effects (e.g., full reportability, consciousness of unexpected and unfamiliar stimuli; cf. inattentional blindness) but not others (e.g., partial reportability, consciousness of familiar stimuli or the gist of stimuli, pop-out effect in visual search tasks, and iconic memory; Koch & Tsuchiya 2007, van Boxtel et al. 2010). Note that these authors do not exclude the necessity of bottom-up attention for the latter type of conscious effects. A third position is that attention is necessary for one type of consciousness (access consciousness) but not another (phenomenal consciousness; Block 1995, Bronfman et al. 2014).

The empirical effects listed above (inattentional blindness, change blindness, attentional blink, load-induced blindness, and full reportability) all indicate that the absence of attention leads to an absence of consciousness. Critics have argued that the studies merely show an absence of reportability, which may not indicate an absence of consciousness (e.g., inattentional blindness) but rather an absence of memory (i.e., inattentional amnesia; Wolfe 1999). Prinz (2010) objected that in inattentional blindness studies, participants report seeing nothing, whereas in typical forgetting studies (e.g., Sperling 1960), participants do report seeing something but cannot report what it is. Even if the empirical effects do show genuine absence of consciousness, however, they at best demonstrate that attention is necessary in some instances but not that it is necessary in all instances, which (as explained above) is beyond empirical reach.

To show that attention is not necessary for consciousness, it is enough to find one instance in which attention is absent but consciousness is still present. van Boxtel et al. (2010) reviewed inattentional blindness studies in which participants were still conscious (i.e., not blind) of the gist of the unattended stimuli. This and other evidence has been criticized on the grounds that attention was not really absent in these studies or that consciousness was not really present (overestimated because of forced choice awareness measures; e.g., Prinz 2010). Another argument for the idea that attention is not necessary for consciousness comes from studies showing that attention and consciousness rely on separate neural pathways and are therefore part of separate systems. For instance, some authors have linked attention to a dorsal vision-for-action pathway and consciousness to a central vision-for-perception pathway (Milner & Goodale 1995, Vorberg et al. 2003). Reliance on different neural pathways indicates that attention and consciousness are different things, but it does not exclude dependence of one on the other (Tapia et al. 2013). Moreover, more recent accounts take it that both pathways are for action, the ventral pathway for action planning and the dorsal pathway for action adjustment, and that cross talk between them is crucial (Hommel 2010).

Sufficiency of attention for consciousness. Several theorists (e.g., Kouider & Dehaene 2007) subscribe to the view that attention is not sufficient for consciousness of a stimulus because other factors are necessary, such as certain levels of stimulus intensity and duration. This is obvious for some forms of attention but less so for other forms. Searching for a stimulus or directing one's attention to a location or a temporal window is not sufficient for becoming conscious of a stimulus; the stimulus also has to be present, which means that it has to have some duration and some intensity. Stimulus-based attention allocation, on the other hand, already presupposes the presence of a stimulus with some duration and intensity, which is why it is less obvious that this type of attention would not be sufficient for consciousness of the stimulus (for related arguments, see De Brigard & Prinz 2010).

To show that attention is sufficient for consciousness, one should show that in all instances in which attention is present, consciousness is present as well. Examining all instances in which attention is present is impossible. Standard empirical practice consists in accumulating evidence for instances in which both attention and consciousness are present and generalizing them to all other instances. Another strategy is searching for flaws in studies purporting to show that attention is not sufficient for consciousness (e.g., Prinz 2011).

To demonstrate that attention is not sufficient for consciousness, one should find one instance in which attention is present and consciousness is absent. A first line of evidence comes from studies in which manipulation of the direction of attention modulated unconscious processing. This has been shown for temporal (Kiefer & Brendel 2006), spatial (Kentridge et al. 2008; Sumner et al. 2006; Tapia et al. 2011, 2013), and feature-based attention (Kanai et al. 2006, Schmidt & Schmidt 2010, Spruyt et al. 2012, Tapia et al. 2010). In these studies, directing attention to the time window, location, and/or feature of a subliminal stimulus occasioned or improved processing of that stimulus, but not up to a point that the stimulus became conscious. Other findings show the modulating influence of the amount of available attention on unconscious processing (Martens & Kiefer 2009). For instance, Pessoa et al. (2002) reported that the manipulation of attention load led to more or less activity in subcortical structures, such as the amygdala, and this activity was taken as evidence of unconscious processing.

Another piece of evidence comes from studies in which unconscious stimuli influenced the spatial, feature-based, or stimulus-based direction of attention (see reviews by Mulckhuyse & Theeuwes 2010 and van Boxtel et al. 2010). For instance, Jiang et al. (2006) showed that participants directed their attention to subliminal pictures of male or female nudes depending on their sexual preference, thereby producing a spatial cuing effect: faster reaction times to targets preceded by a relevant unconscious nude cue than targets not preceded by such a cue.

The evidence reviewed in this section supports the ideas that (*a*) attention does influence consciousness, (*b*) attention is not necessary for all types of consciousness, and (*c*) attention is not sufficient for consciousness, given that other factors appear to be necessary in some instances.

From Consciousness to Goals

It is often assumed that implementation of the goal to engage in a process (as in control in the promoting sense) requires a conscious stimulus input (e.g., Shallice 1988) and that implementation of a counteracting goal (as in control in the counteracting sense) requires consciousness of the process (e.g., Dehaene & Naccache 2001). Several findings contradict these assumptions. A first line of research shows that conscious goals can be applied to unconscious input. Several studies report that a conscious promoting goal or task can be misapplied to unconscious stimuli (e.g., Ansorge & Neumann 2005, Kunde et al. 2003, Tapia et al. 2010). For instance, Van Opstal et al. (2010) found that same-different judgments of target pairs (numbers: 3-3) were also conducted on preceding masked prime pairs (letters: a-A). Martens et al. (2011) found that a conscious task set (e.g., perceptual versus semantic), independent of a specific task (e.g., press left for square and right for circle), influenced processing of unconscious stimuli. Other studies reported that conscious counteracting goals were successfully applied to unconscious processes operating on unconscious stimuli (e.g., Jáskowski et al. 2003). For instance, Verwijmeren et al. (2013) found that the conscious warning about subliminal advertising diminished its impact on subsequent choice behavior.

A second line of research shows that unconscious goals can be applied to conscious input. Lau & Passingham (2007; see also Mattler 2003) reported faster target responses when the instructed target task and an unconsciously primed target task were the same than when they were different (e.g., phonological versus semantic judgment). This makes the case for promoting goals. The case for counteracting goals is made by van Gaal et al. (2008, 2009), who found that a subliminal cue signaling the participant to stop responding (stop cue) or to refrain from responding (no-go cue) resulted in actual stopping or delayed responses. Although this line of research does not contradict the assumption that control requires a conscious input, it does show that unconscious control is possible (at least under certain conditions; Hassin 2013, Kiefer 2012, Kunde et al. 2012).

A handful of studies combine the features of both lines of research, demonstrating an impact of unconscious goals on unconscious input. Ric & Muller (2012) presented a masked instruction to add (versus represent) numbers, followed by two masked flanker numbers, again followed by a number or letter target. If the target was a number and corresponded to the sum of the flankers, classification of the target was facilitated, but only when the masked instruction was to add numbers.

In sum, the evidence reviewed above indicates that (*a*) implementation of a (conscious or unconscious) promoting goal does not require a conscious stimulus input, and (*b*) implementation of a counteracting goal does not require a conscious process.

Alternative Set of Relations Among Factors

Taken together, the empirical evidence reviewed above does not support the idea that goals, attention, and consciousness stand in a one-to-one relation. This goes against the perfect coherence view. The evidence suggests an alternative set of relations, convergent with several contemporary proposals (e.g., Cleeremans & Jiménez 2002, Kiefer 2012, Kouider & Dehaene 2007, Kunde et al. 2012, Pourtois et al. 2013). This alternative set of relations imposes a different way of thinking about automaticity and has important implications for the diagnosis of a process as automatic.

The starting point is the premise that all information processes require an input of sufficient quality. The nature of this input depends on the type of process considered. A first type of process takes the raw stimulus as its input and hence requires a stimulus of sufficient quality. Examples of first-type processes are the formation of a new stimulus representation and the activation of an already existing representation. (In the latter example, an additional condition is the existence and availability of the stimulus representation.) A second type of process takes a stimulus representation as its input and hence requires a stimulus representation with sufficient quality. Examples of second-type processes are the spreading of activation from the stimulus representation to associated representations and processes that use the stimulus representation in some other way. But what are stimulus quality and representational quality made out of? Stimulus quality subsumes

Representational quality: mental person factor subsuming intensity, duration, and distinctiveness of a representation

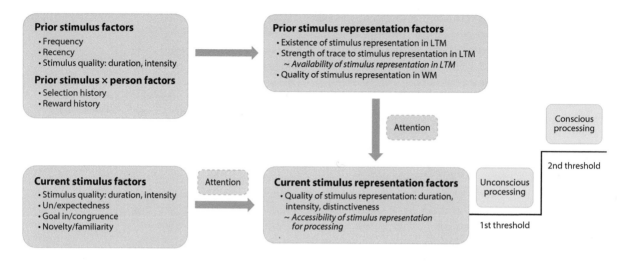

Figure 2

Factors hypothesized to influence representational quality.

factors such as stimulus intensity and duration. Representational quality subsumes factors such as the level and duration of its activation and possibly other factors such as distinctiveness (see Cleeremans & Jiménez 2002).

Representational quality can be influenced by various factors, which can be organized in the following sets: (*a*) current stimulus factors, both physical ones (e.g., stimulus quality subsuming stimulus intensity and duration) and mind-dependent ones (e.g., goal in/congruence, un/expectedness, and novelty/familiarity); (*b*) prior stimulus factors (e.g., frequency and recency) and prior stimulus × person factors (e.g., selection and reward history); (*c*) prior stimulus representation factors, such as the existence, availability, and quality of prior stimulus representations (goals, expectations, and mere representations); and (*d*) the amount and direction of attention. The current representational quality itself fits in a set that can be named current stimulus representation factors. It is closely tied to accessibility: High-quality representations are accessible for application in further processing and behavior (see **Figure 2**).

As to the relations between these sets, it may be hypothesized that prior stimulus (× person) factors (e.g., frequency, recency, selection history, and reward history) influence prior stimulus representation factors (e.g., the existence, availability, and quality of goals, expectations, and mere representations). These prior stimulus representation factors, in turn, may influence the quality of current stimulus representations, and so may current stimulus factors (e.g., intensity, duration, goal in/congruence, un/expectedness, novelty/familiarity). Attention has been hypothesized to either moderate (i.e., influence) or mediate (i.e., be necessary for) the latter two influences.

The picture drawn so far suggests that the factors influencing current representational quality are cumulative: If one of the factors is low, other factors may compensate so that the quality nevertheless reaches the threshold required to trigger processing. For instance, the short duration of a stimulus may be compensated by an increase in its intensity, the amount of attention directed to it, and/or the amount of preactivation from goals, expectations, or mere representations (or vice versa). Consciousness has a special status: Rather than being a primary codeterminant[6] of

---

[6]Note that consciousness can be a secondary codeterminant of representational quality via recurrent processing.

representational quality, consciousness is better conceived of as the result of an additional increase in representational quality up to a second threshold. In other words, representational quality must reach a first threshold to allow for unconscious processing and a second threshold to allow for conscious processing (Cleeremans & Jiménez 2002). To elaborate on this picture, different types of (conscious and unconscious) processes (e.g., sensory versus semantic) may require somewhat different thresholds of representational quality, and it may also be fruitful to consider thresholds for access and maintenance in working memory and for transfer to long-term memory. The exact position of all these thresholds is an empirical matter, but the upshot is this: Some factors may be low (e.g., short stimulus duration) and others high (e.g., high amount of attention), but their summed influence on the representational quality may suffice to trigger unconscious or conscious processing. This is at odds with a perfect coherence view, which assumes that processes are either high on all factors or low on all factors (e.g., fast processes are also ones that are efficient and remain unconscious). The next sections review empirical evidence pertaining to (a) the influences of various factors on current representational quality, (b) the additivity of these influences, and (c) the increasing thresholds of representational quality from unconscious to conscious processes.

Factors Influencing Representational Quality

This section provides examples of empirical evidence for the influence of prior stimulus (× person) factors, prior stimulus representation factors, and current stimulus factors on the quality of the current stimulus representation, as well as evidence for the role of attention in these influences. The quality of a stimulus representation is inferred from (a) neural activity in regions known to code for the stimulus (or regions feeding into these) or (b) behavioral performance on various tasks thought to be mediated by representational quality.

Prior stimulus (× person) factors. The frequent and/or recent presentation of stimuli has been shown to improve processes and behavior based on these stimuli, as illustrated by increased priming effects due to repetition (Atas et al. 2013) and expertise (Kiesel et al. 2009), and the increased likelihood of using a frequently or recently presented adjective in a subsequent unrelated person judgment (Higgins 1996). An increase in current representational quality has been taken to be one of several mediators of this influence. A possible scenario is that the frequent presentation of a stimulus installs a stimulus representation (existence) and/or reinforces the memory trace leading to an existing one (availability). Each stimulus presentation also temporarily increases the quality of the representation. Thus, if a stimulus was recently presented, the representation of the stimulus has an increased quality, which allows (a) it to be accessed and applied in subsequent processing or (b) an additional presentation of the stimulus to benefit from the preactivation. On a neural level, recent functional magnetic resonance imaging studies (e.g., Müller et al. 2013) report that the repetition of initially novel, low-quality stimuli leads to an increase followed by a decrease in neural activity in regions coding for the stimuli (inverse U-shaped function). This has been taken to reflect the formation or optimizing of stimulus representations, starting with a strengthening phase and followed by a sharpening phase with more robust or more synchronous firing (Müller et al. 2013, Ranganath & Rainer 2003).

Prior stimulus representation factors. Prior stimulus representation factors include the existence, availability, and quality of prior stimulus representations, such as goals, expectations, and mere representations. Evidence for the influence of prior representation factors on current representational quality comes from studies in which the goal to respond to a stimulus feature (and probably also the expectation to encounter the feature) increased the baseline firing of neurons coding for that feature, even in the absence of a stimulus (e.g., Serences & Boynton 2007).

Current stimulus factors: physical and mind dependent. Evidence for an influence of physical stimulus factors on representational quality comes from psychophysical studies showing an influence of luminance, contrast, and stimulus duration on neural activity and priming effects (e.g., Kouider & Dehaene 2007, Schmidt et al. 2006, Tzur & Frost 2007).

Mind-dependent stimulus factors also influence representational quality. This is suggested by studies in which masked priming effects only occurred when the primes were part of an expected range of stimuli (Kiesel et al. 2006; see also Kiefer 2012). Other lines of research report that unexpected (abrupt) and novel stimuli boost their neural representations (e.g., Müller et al. 2013) with the help of neuromodulators (e.g., acetylcholine, noradrenaline, and dopamine) known to be involved in the recruitment of attention and the strengthening of memory traces (Lisman et al. 2011, Ranganath & Rainer 2003). Similar neural-boosting effects have been registered for valenced or goal-relevant stimuli (Cunningham & Zelazo 2007, Pourtois et al. 2013, Sander et al. 2003). Behavioral evidence for the influence of goal relevance on representational quality comes from studies showing that (subliminal and other) stimuli were better or only capable of producing certain effects when they were relevant for a goal or task [e.g., priming effects (Ansorge & Neumann 2005, Tapia et al. 2010) and implicit learning (Eitam & Higgins 2010, Hassin 2013, Kiefer 2012, Kunde et al. 2012)]. For instance, subliminal drink advertisements only affected consumption when participants were thirsty (Karremans et al. 2006).

One question that arises is how it is possible that both matches (e.g., goal-congruent, expected, and familiar stimuli) and mismatches (e.g., goal-incongruent, unexpected, and novel stimuli) with prior representations can increase the quality of current representations. A first piece of the puzzle is that matches can surf on the prior activation of the stimulus representation on which they subsist. If one wants, expects, or thinks about an apple, the representation of an apple is already active and the subsequent encounter with an apple (match) simply adds to this activation. This does not hold for mismatches, which suggests that a different (or additional) mechanism underlies their influence on current representational quality: Goal-incongruent, unexpected, and novel stimuli are all potentially goal relevant (Öhman 1992). This may induce a call on the entire system to recruit extra resources for boosting the stimulus representation (e.g., via attention; Eitam & Higgins 2010, Öhman 1992).

Attention. The idea that attention influences representational quality is inherent in the view that one of the functions of attention is to enhance, amplify, sensitize, or boost processing (e.g., Dehaene & Naccache 2001, Kiefer 2012, Pourtois et al. 2013). Selection, another cited function of attention, is not independent from enhancement. The representation of a stimulus that gets selected is relatively more enhanced than the representations of competing stimuli, although the absolute level of enhancement may vary greatly. Selection is related to the direction of attention, whereas enhancement is related to its quantity.

There is abundant evidence that attention driven by various sources (e.g., abrupt onsets, goals, and goal-relevant stimuli) influences representational quality; in other words, that attention moderates the influence of these sources on representational quality. Studies show that spatial attention driven by abrupt onsets and goals increases (or optimizes) neural activity and improves perceptual performance in contrast detection and selection tasks (see Carrasco 2011, Kiefer 2012). Similarly, feature-based attention increases the neural activity in cortical areas coding for those features and improves perceptual performance inside and outside the focus of attention (see Carrasco 2011,

Maunsell & Treue 2006). Pourtois et al. (2013) reviewed evidence that attention driven by fearful faces (exemplifying threat value, arousal, negative valence, and/or goal relevance) enhances neural activity in areas coding for faces and improves low-level perceptual performance.

Three remarks are in place. First, improved perceptual performance can rely on increased neural activity and/or increased external noise reduction (see Carrasco 2011), but both neural mechanisms may contribute to an increase in representational quality considered on a higher level of analysis (Pourtois et al. 2013). Second, Ling & Carrasco (2006) suggested an inverse U-shaped relation between attention and representational intensity, starting with enhancement and followed by adaptation after sustained attention. Third, some researchers (e.g., Pourtois et al. 2013) take increased neural activity in certain sensory areas as the neural signature of attention, thus blurring the distinction between attention and representational quality and perhaps even jeopardizing the viability of the attention concept altogether.

The studies listed above suggest a moderating role of attention. Another line of research has explicitly addressed the mediating role of attention; that is, whether attention is necessary for processing. This has been the topic of controversy between early and late selection models. Early models only allow the preattentive processing of simple sensory features (Broadbent 1958), whereas late models allow the entire meaning of stimuli to be processed before attention (Deutsch & Deutsch 1963). To demonstrate preattentive and hence attentionless processing of a feature (e.g., sensory, semantic, valence), one must show that the feature is processed (i.e., leakage of the feature through the attention filter) while attention to it is absent (i.e., no slippage of attention toward the feature; Lachter et al. 2004). Irrelevant feature tasks (e.g., priming, Stroop, and flanker) examine whether processing occurs of a feature that is irrelevant for the task and hence presumably not attended to. Another way to demonstrate attentionless processing of a feature is to show that the manipulation of attention (present versus absent) does not affect the quality or speed of this processing. In a spatial cuing task, for instance, a cue steers attention toward a location in which the target does or does not appear. If processing of the target is unaffected by whether it was validly or invalidly cued, it is taken to be independent of spatial attention. Evidence for the preattentive processing of semantic features with both methods is mixed (Lachter et al. 2004, McCann et al. 1992). Critics have argued that in these methods, focused or diffuse attention toward the irrelevant feature (in irrelevant-feature tasks) or uncued location (in cuing tasks) was not entirely prevented (e.g., because stimulus durations still allowed for covert attention shifts; Lachter et al. 2004) and was sometimes even encouraged (e.g., in tasks with unpredictable target locations, participants have to move attention across the entire perceptual field). Conversely, if attentional modulation of the effects does occur, this may indicate that processing of the feature of interest required attention, but it may also indicate that the influence of the feature on responding required attention (McCann et al. 1992, Moors et al. 2010). Finally, these studies can at best demonstrate that attention is necessary for processing in some instances, but not that attention is necessary overall.

Additivity of Factors Influencing Representational Quality

In the masked priming literature, the idea is pervasive that stimulus intensity, time, and attention influence the quality of the stimulus representation (as measured by the magnitude of the priming effect) in a compensatory manner (Kiefer et al. 2011, p. 61). Tzur & Frost (2007) parametrically manipulated luminance and stimulus onset asynchrony (SOA; time between prime onset and mask onset) and observed that an increase in luminance compensated for a decrease in SOA in determining the priming effect. In a study by Schmidt et al. (2006), the increase in priming with increasing SOA was steeper for high-contrast than low-contrast primes, which suggests an additive

Stimulus onset asynchrony (SOA): time between the onsets of two stimuli (e.g., prime and mask)

effect of contrast and SOA. A trade-off between attention and SOA is suggested by Bruchmann et al.'s (2011) finding that unattended stimuli with a long duration and that are unmasked can be conscious, whereas attended stimuli with a short duration and that are masked remain unconscious. Reynolds et al.'s (2000) observation that the contrast of unattended stimuli must be 50% higher than that of attended stimuli provides evidence for the additivity of attention and stimulus intensity. Using a spatial cuing task, Risko et al. (2011) found that repeated words suffered less from a lack of spatial attention than did nonrepeated words, supporting the idea that repetition and attention compensate each other. Some studies provide support for the additivity of different types of attention, such as spatial and feature-based attention (e.g., Hayden & Gallant 2009); attention driven by goals, abrupt onsets, and/or emotional faces (Brosch et al. 2011, Cave & Wolfe 1990); and attention directed to stimuli with a conjunction of features (e.g., horizontal and red; Andersen et al. 2008). In its most radical form, the additivity assumption takes it that no factor is necessary by itself but can be compensated by other factors. A weaker interpretation is that some factors can be compensated up to some point, but they cannot be entirely absent.

Increasing Thresholds of Representational Quality from Unconscious to Conscious Processing

The idea that the representational quality must be higher for conscious than for unconscious processing (Cleeremans & Jiménez 2002) is reflected in the use of backward masking to render stimuli unconscious. Backward masking reduces the exposure time and in this way presumably truncates the representational quality (Kouider & Dehaene 2007). Behavioral studies confirm that increasing the SOA between primes and masks increases the visibility of the primes (Charles et al. 2013, Lau & Passingham 2006, Vorberg et al. 2003). Neurophysiological studies report correlations between the strength of the neural responses evoked by a stimulus and conscious detection of the stimulus (e.g., Kouider et al. 2007, Macknik & Livingstone 1998, Mathewson et al. 2009, Moutoussis & Zeki 2002).

The idea that unconscious and conscious processes require different thresholds of representational quality does not imply that this is the only difference between both types of processes. Priming studies reporting (single and double) dissociations between priming effects (indicating prime processing) and masking effects (indicating prime consciousness) at the same SOA range have been explained by invoking various extra mechanisms: consolidation or working memory encoding (Kiefer et al. 2011), attention-mediated availability to working memory encoding (Prinz 2011), and recurrent processing (Lamme & Roelfsema 2000). This leaves us with two scenarios: Representational quality is only one among several conditions for consciousness, or the extra representational quality is what allows the extra mechanisms to kick in (Mathewson et al. 2009).

In conclusion, the empirical data reviewed resonate well with the view that unconscious and conscious processing must be fueled by external or internal factors and that several of these factors are interchangeable. The factors covered by the traditional automaticity concept (goals, attention, and time) do not have a special status in this respect. Before discussing the implications of this view for the diagnosis of processes as automatic, the review zooms in on the causal and mechanistic explanations of automaticity proposed in the literature.

CAUSAL AND MECHANISTIC EXPLANATIONS

A causal explanation of the automaticity of a process links the automaticity features of the process (explanandum) to causal factors (explanans). In other words, these are factors involved in the development toward automaticity, or short, automatization. Two major causal factors that have been identified are hard-wired makeup and practice, and they have served as a basis to distinguish two types of automatic processes. Hard-wired automatic processes come with a number of innate automaticity features. Learned automatic processes have acquired their position on several automaticity dichotomies as a result of practice (Treisman et al. 1992). Practice involves the repetition of the same procedure over the same stimuli (consistent data practice) or over varying stimuli (consistent procedure practice; Carlson & Lundy 1992). Consistent data practice increases the automaticity of processes tied to specific stimuli. Consistent procedure practice builds up the automaticity of processes independent of specific stimuli. Practice can range from a single repetition to a very elaborate number of repetitions (Spelke et al. 1976). Practice corresponds to the factor repetition or frequency, which has been hypothesized to exert its influence via the strengthening of representational quality. This hypothesis brings us to the territory of mechanistic explanations.

A mechanistic explanation of the automaticity of a process specifies the subprocesses at lower levels of analysis responsible for automatization; that is, the transition of the process from a (more) nonautomatic to a (more) automatic state. Here, only learned automatic processes are considered because innate automatic ones are not supposed to make such a transition. There are two proposals for low-level processes involved in the automatization of processes. Logan (1988) proposed that the automatization of a high-level process (e.g., calculation) is based on a shift from the low-level process of algorithm computation (defined by Logan as multistep memory retrieval) to the low-level process of single-step memory retrieval. After sufficient repetition of the same chain of steps going from the same input to the same output, a direct association is formed between the input and the output, such that the presentation of the input alone directly activates the output. Anderson (1992; see also Tzelgov et al. 2000), however, proposed that the automatization of a high-level process can be based on the strengthening of algorithms or procedures, next to the strengthening of declarative facts. If the same procedure is repeatedly applied (on the same or different stimuli), it gets stored in procedural memory so that it can be directly retrieved and applied thereafter. If the stimuli also remain the same, input-output relations are formed as well and stored in declarative memory.

The distinction between single-step memory retrieval and algorithm-computation or procedure application is reminiscent of that between associative and rule-based processes in dual-process models of reasoning and decision making (Sloman 1996). These models typically follow Logan's (1988) view that nonautomatic (high-level) processes are based on (low-level) rule-based processes, whereas automatic (high-level) processes are based on (low-level) associative processes. It is notoriously difficult to conceptually and empirically distinguish between rule-based and associative processes (Hahn & Chater 1998, Moors 2014, Moors & De Houwer 2006b). For instance, both processes can explain generalization toward new stimuli (Smith & Lerner 1986). This complicates empirical research designed to test whether rule-based processes can be automatic in addition to associative ones (cf. Hélie et al. 2010). Despite these difficulties, Logan (1988) not only proposed to explain but also to define automaticity in terms of direct memory retrieval (automatic processes are ones based on direct memory retrieval). It could be argued that by doing this, he prematurely entered an insufficiently tested explanation of automaticity into the scientific definition of this phenomenon (see Bechtel 2008).

Another factor that has been mentioned as influencing automatization is the complexity of a process. Complexity refers to the number of steps that must be followed (vertical complexity) or the number of units of information that must be integrated at a single time (horizontal complexity). The received view is that simple but not complex processes can be automatic. This view is contradicted by recent studies showing that complex information integration can be fast, unintentional, and even unconscious (see reviews by Hassin 2013, Mudrik et al. 2014). For instance, Mudrik et al. (2011) used a continuous flash suppression method to keep pictures below the threshold of awareness. They found that pictures broke faster through the suppression when they depicted a mismatch between an object and the context (e.g., a watermelon in a basketball game) than when

Rule-based process: mental process in which the output is produced by the application of a rule to an input

Associative process: mental process in which the output is produced by the activation of a memory trace leading to a previously stored output

they did not (e.g., a basketball in a basketball game). This suggests that integration of the stimuli with their context occurred before they broke into consciousness. Other illustrations of unconscious information integration have been reported in decision research (e.g., Bechara et al. 1997), categorization (Hélie et al. 2010), similarity judgments (Van Opstal et al. 2010), and arithmetic (Ric & Muller 2012). Although several researchers now believe that some forms of information integration can occur unconsciously, they do think there are limits. Mudrik et al. (2014) argued that unconscious information integration is not possible for novel information and when the temporal and spatial distance between the to-be-integrated elements is too large. Other authors hold that rules can be applied to subliminal input only if the rule was set in advance (e.g., Kiefer 2012). Based on the additivity view defended here, it could be tested whether some of those limits may be shifted when other factors, such as the goal relevance of the stimuli, is increased (see Hassin 2013).

CONCLUSION

The research reviewed does not support the traditional view of perfect coherence between the ingredients of the most often mentioned features of non/automaticity: goals, attention, and consciousness. The evidence suggests an alternative picture in which the quality of the input determines processing, with the factors feeding into this quality capable of compensating each other, and with less quality needed for unconscious than conscious processing. Although the evidence reviewed here already goes some way in supporting these assumptions, future research is needed to test them in a more systematic way.

The alternative view has important implications for the diagnosis of the automaticity of specific processes (e.g., evaluation, decision making, and information integration). Given that automaticity is a gradual notion, conclusions about automaticity can at best be relative. Rather than studying whether a process is automatic, one can study whether it is more automatic than other ones. But this is not all. Building on the assumptions that every process requires an input of sufficient quality, and that several factors can contribute to this quality in a cumulative manner, comparing processes with regard to a single factor (e.g., amount of attention) is not very informative. For instance, if one process requires less attention than another one, this may be because the first has a more intense stimulus input, which compensates for the lack of attention. Proponents of the perfect coherence view sometimes argue that generalizing the conclusions of necessity and sufficiency reached in some instances to all other instances is an inference to the best explanation. This argument is jeopardized, however, if the instances in which evidence for necessity and sufficiency were obtained were ones in which compensating factors were absent or low. For instance, it is possible that in studies in which attention was found to be necessary for consciousness, other factors that could have contributed to the representational quality necessary for consciousness (e.g., prior goals, repetition) were low. Thus, if the aim is to compare the automaticity of two processes, it is best to map the network of factors required for both processes to operate, or alternatively, to compare the processes with regard to a single factor while keeping all other factors equal. This not only asks for a parametric approach, in which factors are gradually manipulated (Mudrik et al. 2014, Schmidt et al. 2011), but also for an approach in which the relations between several parametrically operationalized factors are outlined.

SUMMARY POINTS

1. Componential explanations of automaticity specify non/automaticity features such as un/conscious, un/intentional, non/efficient, and fast/slow as well as their interrelations.

2. Features of non/automaticity can be reframed as factors (e.g., goals, attention, time, consciousness) that influence the occurrence of processes. This opens the door for considering factors that are not traditionally included in the automaticity concept but that also influence the occurrence of processes.

3. Factors can be organized according to six independent axes: (*a*) procedural versus nonprocedural, (*b*) current versus prior, (*c*) person versus stimulus (and person × stimulus), (*d*) physical versus mental (and mind dependent), (*e*) absolute versus relative, and (*f*) occurrent versus dispositional. This taxonomy goes beyond the common top-down versus bottom-up dichotomy in several ways.

4. The view that there is perfect coherence among non/automaticity factors is challenged by empirical evidence against the assumptions that (*a*) goals are necessary and sufficient for attention, (*b*) attention is necessary and sufficient for consciousness, and (*c*) consciousness is necessary and sufficient for goals.

5. Evidence is reviewed in support of the alternative view that (*a*) most of the listed factors influence the quality of representations (which form the input of many processes), (*b*) they do so in an additive way (such that the lack of one factor can be compensated by the excess of another factor), and (*c*) a first threshold of this quality is required for unconscious processing and a second threshold for conscious processing.

6. Factors influencing representational quality (which is itself a current representation factor) can be organized into current stimulus factors, prior stimulus factors, and prior representation factors. Attention may be considered as a mediator or moderator of some of these influences.

7. Processes cannot be diagnosed as automatic or nonautomatic but rather as more or less automatic than other processes. However, given the additivity assumption, comparing two processes according to a single feature or factor of automaticity is not very informative, unless all other factors are kept equal. If this is not possible, it is best to map the entire network of factors required for both processes to operate.

8. Causal explanations of automaticity specify factors involved in automatization such as repetition and complexity, and mechanistic explanations specify low-level processes underlying automatization, such as direct memory retrieval and the strengthening of procedures.

FUTURE EFFORTS

Instead of comparing processes with regard to the entire network of factors they require to operate, the focus may be shifted to comparing processes with regard to the amount of representational quality they require. Future efforts may concentrate on ways to measure representational quality.

DISCLOSURE STATEMENT

The author is not aware of any affiliations, memberships, funding, or financial holdings that might be perceived as affecting the objectivity of this review.

ACKNOWLEDGMENTS

Preparation of this review was supported by Methusalem grant BOF09/01M00209 of Ghent University. The author thanks Jan De Houwer for commenting on a previous draft and for the years of support.

LITERATURE CITED

Andersen SK, Hillyard SA, Müller MM. 2008. Attention facilitates multiple stimulus features in parallel in human visual cortex. *Curr. Biol.* 18(13):1006–9

Anderson JR. 1992. Automaticity and the ACT* theory. *Am. J. Psychol.* 105:165–80

Ansorge U, Neumann O. 2005. Intentions determine the effect of nonconsciously registered visual information: evidence for direct parameter specification in the metacontrast dissociation. *J. Exp. Psychol.: Hum. Percept. Perform.* 31:762–77

Atas A, Vermeiren A, Cleeremans A. 2013. Repeating a strongly masked stimulus increases priming and awareness. *Conscious. Cogn.* 22:1422–30

Awh E, Belopolsky AV, Theeuwes J. 2012. Top-down versus bottom-up attentional control: a failed theoretical dichotomy. *Trends Cogn. Sci.* 16(8):437–43

Awh E, Vogel EK, Oh SH. 2006. Interactions between attention and working memory. *Neuroscience* 139:201–8

Baars BJ. 1988. *A Cognitive Theory of Consciousness.* Cambridge, UK: Cambridge Univ. Press

Bargh JA. 1992. The ecology of automaticity: toward establishing the conditions needed to produce automatic processing effects. *Am. J. Psychol.* 105:181–99

Bargh JA. 1994. The four horsemen of automaticity: awareness, intention, efficiency, and control in social cognition. In *Handbook of Social Cognition*, vol. 1, ed. RS Wyer, TK Srull, pp. 1–40. Hillsdale, NJ: Erlbaum

Bechara A, Damasio H, Tranel D, Damasio AR. 1997. Deciding advantageously before knowing the advantageous strategy. *Science* 275:1293–95

Bechtel W. 2008. *Mental Mechanisms: Philosophical Perspectives on Cognitive Neuroscience.* London, UK: Routledge

Belopolsky AV, Schreij D, Theeuwes J. 2010. What is top-down about contingent capture? *Atten. Percept. Psychophys.* 72:326–41

Bernstein A, Taylor K. 1979. The interaction of stimulus information with potential stimulus significance in eliciting the skin conductance orienting response. In *The Orienting Reflex in Humans*, ed. H Kimmel, E van Olst, J Orlebeke, pp. 499–519. Hillsdale, NJ: Erlbaum

Block N. 1995. On a confusion about a function of consciousness. *Behav. Brain Sci.* 18:227–87

Broadbent D. 1958. *Perception and Communication.* London, UK: Pergamon Press

Bronfman ZZ, Brezis N, Jacobson H, Usher M. 2014. We see more than we can report: "cost free" color phenomenality outside focal attention. *Psychol. Sci.* 25:1394–403

Brosch T, Pourtois G, Sander D, Vuilleumier P. 2011. Additive effects of emotional, endogenous, and exogenous attention: behavioral and electrophysiological evidence. *Neuropsychologia* 49(7):1779–87

Bruchmann M, Hintze P, Mota S. 2011. The effects of spatial and temporal cueing on metacontrast masking. *Adv. Cogn. Psychol.* 7:132–41

Carrasco M. 2011. Visual attention: the past 25 years. *Vis. Res.* 51:1484–525

Carlson RA, Lundy DH. 1992. Consistency and restructuring in cognitive procedural sequences. *J. Exp. Psychol.: Learn. Mem. Cogn.* 18:127–41

Cave KR, Wolfe JM. 1990. Modeling the role of parallel processing in visual search. *Cogn. Psychol.* 22:225–71

Charles L, Van Opstal F, Marti S, Dehaene S. 2013. Distinct brain mechanisms for conscious versus subliminal error detection. *NeuroImage* 73:80–94

Cleeremans A, Jiménez L. 2002. Implicit learning and consciousness: a graded, dynamic perspective. In *Implicit Learning and Consciousness*, ed. RM French, A Cleeremans, pp. 1–40. Hove, UK: Psychol. Press

Corbetta M, Schulman GL. 2002. Controls of goal-directed and S-driven attention in the brain. *Nat. Neurosci.* 3:201–15

Cunningham WA, Zelazo PD. 2007. Attitudes and evaluations: a social cognitive neuroscience perspective. *Trends Cogn. Sci.* 11:97–104

De Brigard F, Prinz J. 2010. Attention and consciousness. *WIREs Cogn. Sci.* 1:51–59

Dehaene S, Naccache L. 2001. Towards a cognitive neuroscience of consciousness: basic evidence and a workspace framework. *Cognition* 79:1–37

Deutsch JA, Deutsch D. 1963. Attention: some theoretical considerations. *Psychol. Rev.* 70:80–90

Dijksterhuis A, Aarts H. 2010. Goals, attention, and (un)consciousness. *Annu. Rev. Psychol.* 61:467–90

Eitam B, Higgins ET. 2010. Motivation in mental accessibility: relevance of a representation (ROAR) as a new framework. *Personal. Soc. Psychol. Compass* 4:951–67

Engelmann JB, Damaraju E, Padmala S, Pessoa L. 2009. Combined effects of attention and motivation on visual task performance: transient and sustained motivational effects. *Front. Hum. Neurosci.* 3:1–17

Enns JT, Austen EL, Di Lollo V, Rauschenberger R, Yantis S. 2001. New objects dominate luminance transients in setting attentional priority. *J. Exp. Psychol.: Hum. Percept. Perform.* 27:1287–302

Folk CL, Remington R. 1998. Selectivity in distraction by irrelevant featural singletons: evidence for two forms of attentional capture. *J. Exp. Psychol.: Hum. Percept. Perform.* 24:847–58

Folk CL, Remington RW, Johnston JC. 1992. Involuntary covert orienting is contingent on attentional control settings. *J. Exp. Psychol.: Hum. Percept. Perform.* 18:1030–44

Hahn U, Chater N. 1998. Similarity and rules: Distinct? Exhaustive? Empirically distinguishable? *Cognition* 65:197–230

Hassin RR. 2013. Yes it can: on the functional abilities of the human unconscious. *Perspect. Psychol. Sci.* 8:195–207

Hayden BY, Gallant JL. 2009. Combined effects of spatial and feature-based attention on responses of V4 neurons. *Vis. Res.* 49(10):1182–87

Hélie S, Waldschmidt JG, Ash FG. 2010. Automaticity in rule-based and information-integration categorization. *Atten. Percept. Psychophys.* 72:1013–31

Higgins ET. 1996. Knowledge activation: accessibility, applicability, and salience. In *Social Psychology: Handbook of Basic Principles*, ed. ET Higgins, AW Kruglanski, pp. 133–68. New York: Guilford

Hommel B. 2010. Grounding attention in action control: the intentional control of selection. In *Effortless Attention: A New Perspective in the Cognitive Science of Attention and Action*, ed. BJ Bruya, pp. 121–40. Cambridge, MA: MIT Press

Irons JL, Folk CL, Remington RW. 2012. All set! Evidence of simultaneous attentional control settings for multiple target colors. *J. Exp. Psychol.: Hum. Percept. Perform.* 38(3):758–75

Itti L. 2007. Visual salience. *Scholarpedia* 2(9):3327

Jáskowski P, Skalska B, Verleger R. 2003. How the self controls its "automatic pilot" when processing of subliminal information. *J. Cogn. Neurosci.* 15:911–20

Jiang Y, Costello P, Fang F, Huang M, He S. 2006. Gender- and sexual orientation–dependent attentional effect of invisible images. *PNAS* 103(45):17048–52

Kanai R, Tsuchiya N, Verstraten FA. 2006. The scope and limits of top-down attention in unconscious visual processing. *Curr. Biol.* 16:2332–36

Karremans JC, Stroebe W, Claus J. 2006. Beyond Vicary's fantasies: the impact of subliminal priming and brand choice. *J. Exp. Soc. Psychol.* 42(6):792–98

Kastner S, Ungerleider LG. 2000. Mechanisms of visual attention in the human cortex. *Annu. Rev. Neurosci.* 23:315–41

Kentridge RW, Nijboer TC, Heywood CA. 2008. Attended but unseen: Visual attention is not sufficient for visual awareness. *Neuropsychologia* 46:864–69

Kiefer M. 2012. Executive control over unconscious cognition: attentional sensitization of unconscious information processing. *Front. Hum. Neurosci.* 6:61

Kiefer M, Ansorge U, Haynes J-D, Hamker F, Mattler U, et al. 2011. Neuro-cognitive mechanisms of conscious and unconscious visual perception: from a plethora of phenomena to general principles. *Adv. Cogn. Psychol.* 7:55–67

Kiefer M, Brendel D. 2006. Attentional modulation of unconscious "automatic" processes: evidence from event-related potentials in a masked priming paradigm. *J. Cogn. Neurosci.* 18:184–98

Reviews studies showing that preemptive control but not reactive control is possible on unconscious stimuli.

Kiesel A, Kunde W, Pohl C, Berner MP, Hoffmann J. 2009. Playing chess unconsciously. *J. Exp. Psychol.: Learn. Mem. Cogn.* 35:292–98

Kiesel A, Kunde W, Pohl C, Hoffmann J. 2006. Priming from novel masked stimuli depends on target set size. *Adv. Cogn. Psychol.* 2:37–45

Koch C, Tsuchiya N. 2007. Attention and consciousness: two distinct brain processes. *Trends Cogn. Sci.* 11:16–22

Konstantinou N, Lavie N. 2013. Dissociable roles of different types of working memory load in visual detection. *J. Exp. Psychol.: Hum. Percept. Perform.* 39:919–24

Kouider S, Dehaene S. 2007. Levels of processing during non-conscious perception: a critical review of visual masking. *Philos. Trans. R. Soc. B* 362:857–75

Kouider S, Dehaene S, Jobert A, Le Bihan D. 2007. Cerebral bases of subliminal and supraliminal priming during reading. *Cereb. Cortex* 17:2019–29

Kunde W, Kiesel A, Hoffmann J. 2003. Conscious control over the content of unconscious cognition. *Cognition* 88:223–42

Kunde W, Reuss H, Kiesel A. 2012. Consciousness and cognitive control. *Adv. Cogn. Psychol.* 8:9–18

Lachter J, Forster KI, Ruthruff E. 2004. Forty-five years after Broadbent 1958: still no identification without attention. *Psychol. Rev.* 111:880–913

Lamme VAF, Roelfsema PR. 2000. The distinct modes of vision offered by feedforward and recurrent processing. *Trends Neurosci.* 23:571–79

Lamy DF, Kristjánsson A. 2013. Is goal-directed attentional guidance just intertrial priming? A review. *J. Vis.* 13(3):14

Lau HC, Passingham RE. 2007. Unconscious activation of the cognitive control system in the human prefrontal cortex. *J. Neurosci.* 27(21):5805–11

Libera CD, Chelazzi L. 2006. Visual selective attention and the effects of monetary reward. *Psychol. Sci.* 17(3):222–27

Lin Z, Murray SO. 2013. Visible propagation from invisible exogenous cueing. *J. Vis.* 13(11):12

Ling S, Carrasco M. 2006. When sustained attention impairs perception. *Nat. Neurosci.* 9(10):1243–45

Lisman J, Grace AA, Duzel E. 2011. A neo-Hebbian framework for episodic memory; role of dopamine-dependent late LTP. *Trends Neurosci.* 34(10):536–47

Logan GD. 1988. Toward an instance theory of automatization. *Psychol. Rev.* 95:492–527

Macdonald JS, Lavie N. 2008. Load induced blindness. *J. Exp. Psychol.: Hum. Percept. Perform.* 34(5):1078–91

Mack A, Rock I. 1998. *Inattentional Blindness.* Cambridge, MA: MIT Press

Macknik SL, Livingstone MS. 1998. Neuronal correlates of visibility and invisibility in the primate visual system. *Nat. Neurosci.* 1:144–49

Marr D. 1982. *Vision: A Computational Investigation into the Human Representation and Processing of Visual Information.* New York: Freeman

Martens U, Ansorge U, Kiefer M. 2011. Controlling the unconscious: attentional task sets modulate subliminal semantic and visuo-motor processes differentially. *Psychol. Sci.* 22:282–91

Martens U, Kiefer M. 2009. Specifying attentional top-down influences on subsequent unconscious semantic processing. *Adv. Cogn. Psychol.* 5:56–68

Mathewson KE, Gratton G, Fabiani M, Beck DM, Ro T. 2009. To see or not to see: Prestimulus alpha phase predicts visual awareness. *J. Neurosci.* 29:2725–32

Mattler U. 2003. Priming of mental operations by masked stimuli. *Percept. Psychophys.* 65:167–87

Maunsell JHR, Treue S. 2006. Feature-based attention in visual cortex. *Trends Neurosci.* 6:295–346

McCann RS, Folk CL, Johnston JC. 1992. The role of spatial attention in visual word processing. *J. Exp. Psychol.: Hum. Percept. Perform.* 18:1015–29

Milner AD, Goodale MA. 1995. *The Visual Brain in Action.* Oxford, UK: Oxford Univ. Press

Mogg K, Bradley BP, Hyare H, Lee S. 1998. Selective attention to food-related stimuli in hunger: Are attentional biases specific to emotional and psychopathological states, or are they also found in normal drive states? *Behav. Res. Ther.* 36:227–37

Reviews studies showing that unconscious stimuli can trigger a response if a stimulus-response association was previously formed.

Much but not all evidence for the influence of goals on attention can be explained by intertrial priming.

Moors A. 2014. Examining the mapping problem in dual process models. In *Dual Process Theories of the Social Mind*, ed. JW Sherman, B Gawronski, Y Trope, pp. 20–34. New York: Guilford

Moors A, De Houwer J. 2006a. Automaticity: a theoretical and conceptual analysis. *Psychol. Bull.* 132:297–326

Moors A, De Houwer J. 2006b. Problems with dividing the realm of processes. *Psychol. Inq.* 17:199–204

Moors A, Spruyt A, De Houwer J. 2010. In search of a measure that qualifies as implicit: recommendations based on a decompositional view of automaticity. In *Handbook of Implicit Social Cognition: Measurement, Theory, and Applications*, ed. B Gawronski, KB Payne, pp. 19–37. New York: Guilford

Moutoussis K, Zeki S. 2002. The relationship between cortical activation and perception investigated with invisible stimuli. *PNAS* 99:9527–32

Mudrik L, Breska A, Lamy D, Deouell LY. 2011. Integration without awareness: expanding the limits of unconscious processing. *Psychol. Sci.* 22(6):764–70

Mudrik L, Faivre N, Koch C. 2014. Information integration without awareness. *Trends Cogn. Sci.* 18(9):488–96

Mulckhuyse M, Theeuwes J. 2010. Unconscious attentional orienting to exogenous cues: a review of the literature. *Acta Psychol.* 134(3):299–309

Müller NG, Strumpf H, Scholz M, Baier B, Melloni L. 2013. Repetition suppression versus enhancement—it's quantity that matters. *Cereb. Cortex* 23:315–22

Müsseler J, Hommel B. 1997. Blindness to response-compatible stimuli. *J. Exp. Psychol.: Hum. Percept. Perform.* 23:861–72

Nieuwenhuis S, De Kleijn R. 2011. Consciousness of targets during the attentional blink: a gradual or all-or-none dimension? *Atten. Percept. Psychophys.* 73:364–73

Öhman A. 1992. Orienting and attention: preferred preattentive processing of potentially phobic stimuli. In *Attention and Information Processing in Infants and Adults*, ed. BA Campbell, H Hayne, R Richardson, pp. 263–95. Hillsdale, NJ: Erlbaum

O'Regan JK, Noë A. 2001. A sensorimotor account of vision and visual consciousness. *Behav. Brain Sci.* 24:939–1031

Pessoa L, McKenna M, Gutierrez E, Ungerleider LG. 2002. Neural processing of emotional faces requires attention. *PNAS* 99:11458–63

Posner MI. 1980. Orienting of attention. *Q. J. Exp. Psychol.* 32:3–25

Posner MI, Snyder CR, Davidson BJ. 1980. Attention and the detection of signals. *J. Exp. Psychol.* 109(2):160–74

Posner MI, Snyder CRR. 1975. Attention and cognitive control. In *Information Processing and Cognition: The Loyola Symposium*, ed. RL Solso, pp. 153–75. Hillsdale, NJ: Erlbaum

Pourtois G, Schettino A, Vuilleumier P. 2013. Brain mechanisms for emotional influence on perception and attention: what is magic and what is not. *Biol. Psychol.* 92(3):492–512

Prinz J. 2004. *Gut Reactions: A Perceptual Theory of Emotion*. Oxford, UK: Oxford Univ. Press

Prinz J. 2010. When is perception conscious? In *Perceiving the World: New Essays on Perception*, ed. B Nanay, pp. 310–32. Oxford, UK: Oxford Univ. Press

Prinz J. 2011. Is attention necessary or sufficient for consciousness? In *Attention: Philosophical and Psychological Essays*, ed. C Mole, D Smithies, W Wu, pp. 174–204. Oxford, UK: Oxford Univ. Press

Ranganath C, Rainer G. 2003. Neural mechanisms for detecting and remembering novel events. *Nat. Rev. Neurosci.* 4:193–202

Raymond JE, Shapiro KL, Arnell KM. 1992. Temporary suppression of visual processing in an RSVP task: an attentional blink? *J. Exp. Psychol.: Hum. Percept. Perform.* 18:849–60

Rensink RA, O'Regan JK, Clark JJ. 1997. To see or not to see: the need for attention to perceive changes in scenes. *Psychol. Sci.* 8(5):368–73

Reynolds JH, Pasternak T, Desimone R. 2000. Attention increases sensitivity of V4 neurons. *Neuron* 37:853–63

Ric F, Muller D. 2012. Unconscious addition: when we unconsciously initiate and follow arithmetic rules. *J. Exp. Psychol.: Gen.* 141:222–26

Risko EF, Stolz JA, Besner D. 2011. Basic processes in reading: on the relation between spatial attention and familiarity. *Lang. Cogn. Process.* 26:47–62

In-depth analysis of the concepts un/intentional, un/controlled, goal in/dependent, non/autonomous, not/purely stimulus driven, non/efficient, un/conscious, and fast/slow.

Reviews evidence for unconscious information integration and suggests potential moderators such as distance and novelty.

Sander D, Grafman J, Zalla T. 2003. The human amygdala: an evolved system for relevance detection. *Rev. Neurosci.* 14:303–16

Schmidt F, Haberkamp A, Schmidt T. 2011. Dos and don'ts in response priming research. *Adv. Cogn. Psychol.* 7:120–31

Schmidt F, Schmidt T. 2010. Feature-based attention to unconscious shapes and colors. *Atten. Percept. Psychophys.* 72:1480–94

Schmidt T, Niehaus S, Nagel A. 2006. Primes and targets in rapid chases: tracing sequential waves of motor activation. *Behav. Neurosci.* 120:1005–16

Serences JT, Boynton GM. 2007. Feature-based attentional modulations in the absence of direct visual stimulation. *Neuron* 55:301–12

Sergent C, Dehaene S. 2004. Is consciousness a gradual phenomenon? Evidence for an all-or-none bifurcation during the attentional blink. *Psychol. Sci.* 15:720–28

Shallice T. 1988. Information-processing models of consciousness: possibilities and problems. In *Consciousness in Contemporary Science*, ed. AJ Marcel, E Bisiach, pp. 305–33. Oxford, UK: Oxford Univ. Press

Shiffrin RM. 1988. Attention. In *Stevens' Handbook of Experimental Psychology*, vol. 2, ed. RC Atkinson, RJ Hernstein, G Lindzey, RD Luce, pp. 739–11. New York: Wiley

Sloman SA. 1996. The empirical case for two systems of reasoning. *Psychol. Bull.* 119:3–22

Smith ER, Lerner M. 1986. Development of automatism of social judgements. *J. Personal. Soc. Psychol.* 50:246–59

Spelke ES, Hirst WC, Neisser U. 1976. Skills of divided attention. *Cognition* 4:215–30

Sperling G. 1960. The information available in brief visual presentations. *Psychol. Monogr.* 74:1–29

Spruyt A, De Houwer J, Everaert T, Hermans D. 2012. Unconscious semantic activation depends on feature-specific attention allocation. *Cognition* 122:91–95

Sumner P, Tsai PC, Yu K, Nachev P. 2006. Attentional modulation of sensorimotor processes in the absence of perceptual awareness. *PNAS* 103:10520–25

Tapia E, Breitmeyer BG, Broyles EC. 2011. Properties of spatial attention in conscious and nonconscious visual information processing. *Conscious. Cogn.* 20:426–31

Tapia E, Breitmeyer BG, Jacob J, Broyles EC. 2013. Spatial attention effects during conscious and nonconscious processing of visual features and objects. *J. Exp. Psychol.: Hum. Percept. Perform.* 39:745–56

Tapia E, Breitmeyer BG, Schooner CR. 2010. Role of task-directed attention in nonconscious and conscious response priming by form and color. *J. Exp. Psychol.: Hum. Percept. Perform.* 36:74–87

Theeuwes J. 2010. Top-down and bottom-up control of visual selection. *Acta Psychol.* 135:77–99

Treisman A, Vieira A, Hayes A. 1992. Automaticity and preattentive processing. *Am. J. Psychol.* 105:341–62

Tzelgov J, Yehene V, Kotler L, Alon A. 2000. Automatic comparisons of artificial digits never compared: learning linear ordering relations. *J. Exp. Psychol.: Learn. Mem. Cogn.* 26:103–20

Tzur B, Frost R. 2007. SOA does not reveal the absolute time course of cognitive processing in fast priming experiments. *J. Mem. Lang.* 56:321–35

Uleman JS. 1989. A framework for thinking intentionally about unintended thoughts. In *Unintended Thought*, ed. JS Uleman, JA Bargh, pp. 425–49. New York: Guilford

van Boxtel JJ, Tsuchiya N, Koch C. 2010. Consciousness and attention: on sufficiency and necessity. *Front. Psychol.* 1:217

van Gaal S, Ridderinkhof KR, Fahrenfort JJ, Scholte HS, Lamme VAF. 2008. Frontal cortex mediates unconsciously triggered inhibitory control. *J. Neurosci.* 28:8053–62

van Gaal S, Ridderinkhof KR, van den Wildenberg WPM, Lamme VAF. 2009. Dissociating consciousness from inhibitory control: evidence for unconsciously triggered response inhibition in the stop-signal task. *J. Exp. Psychol.: Hum. Percept. Perform.* 35:1129–39

Van Opstal F, Gevers W, Osman M, Verguts T. 2010. Unconscious task application. *Conscious. Cogn.* 19:999–1006

Verwijmeren T, Karremans JC, Benritte SF, Stroebe W, Wigboldus DHJ. 2013. Warning: You are being primed! The effect of a warning on the impact of subliminal ads. *J. Exp. Soc. Psychol.* 49:1124–29

Vogt J, De Houwer J, Moors A, Van Damme S, Crombez G. 2010. The automatic orienting of attention to goal-relevant stimuli. *Acta Psychol.* 134:61–69

Vorberg D, Mattler U, Heinecke A, Schmidt T, Schwarzbach J. 2003. Invariant time course of priming with and without awareness. In *Psychophysics Beyond Sensation: Laws and Invariants of Human Cognition*, ed. C Kaernbach, E Schröger, H Müller, pp. 271–88. Mahwah, NJ: Erlbaum

Wolfe JM. 1999. Inattentional amnesia. In *Fleeting Memories*, ed. V Coltheart, pp. 71–94. Cambridge, MA: MIT Press

Wolfe JM, Butcher SJ, Lee C, Hyle M. 2003. Changing your mind: on the contributions of top-down and bottom-up guidance in visual search for feature singletons. *J. Exp. Psychol.: Hum. Percept. Perform* 29:483–502

Wolfe JM, Horowitz TS. 2004. What attributes guide the deployment of attention and how do they do it? *Nat. Rev. Neurosci.* 5(6):495–501

Wu S-C, Remington RW, Folk CL. 2014. Onsets do not override top-down goals but they are responded to more quickly. *Atten. Percept. Psychophys.* 76:649–54

Psychology of Habit

Wendy Wood and Dennis Rünger

Department of Psychology, University of Southern California, Los Angeles,
California 90089-1061; email: wendy.wood@usc.edu, dennis.ruenger@gmail.com

Annu. Rev. Psychol. 2016. 67:289–314

First published online as a Review in Advance on
September 10, 2015

The *Annual Review of Psychology* is online at
psych.annualreviews.org

This article's doi:
10.1146/annurev-psych-122414-033417

Keywords

automaticity, dual-process models, goals, behavior change, model-free
learning

Abstract

As the proverbial creatures of habit, people tend to repeat the same behaviors
in recurring contexts. This review characterizes habits in terms of their cognitive, motivational, and neurobiological properties. In so doing, we identify
three ways that habits interface with deliberate goal pursuit: First, habits
form as people pursue goals by repeating the same responses in a given context. Second, as outlined in computational models, habits and deliberate goal
pursuit guide actions synergistically, although habits are the efficient, default
mode of response. Third, people tend to infer from the frequency of habit
performance that the behavior must have been intended. We conclude by
applying insights from habit research to understand stress and addiction as
well as the design of effective interventions to change health and consumer
behaviors.

Contents

INTRODUCTION

The yin and yang of the history of habits is closely tied to broader trends in the history of psychology. William James's (1890) view that "habit covers a very large part of life," necessitated that we "define clearly just what its limits are" (p. 104). Psychology complied, and the habit construct acquired specific meanings in the behaviorist traditions of Thorndike's (1898) law of effect, Hull's (1943) formalized drive theory, and Skinner's (1938) operant conditioning. However, these reinforcement-based models of habit were soon supplanted as the field embraced more purposive and cognitive perspectives. To Tolman (1948), repeated behaviors reflected learning of internal representations and maps, and Miller et al. (1960) argued that habits be replaced with information-processing mechanisms of goal pursuit. Accordingly, cognitive psychology and decision-making research in the 1960s and 70s developed largely separately from research on habit.

More recent theories have captured the complexity of action control and enabled integration of these opposing conceptualizations. The concept of automaticity (Shiffrin & Schneider 1977) and theories of dual information processing (Wason & Evans 1975) provided frameworks inclusive of habits and thoughtful decision making. Through procedural memory, habits could be cognitively represented as distinct from other types of implicit processes as well as from explicit, declarative memories (Squire & Zola-Morgan 1991). Reinforcement learning (RL) research with animals identified a behavioral criterion for detecting habit performance, involving insensitivity to changes in rewarding outcomes (Dickinson 1985), and neuroscience began to identify the brain regions and circuits involved in habitual behavior (Graybiel 1998). Social-cognitive approaches outlined a variety of ways in which habits interface with goals (Verplanken & Aarts 1999, Ouellette & Wood 1998), and computational models included goal pursuit and prospective planning as well as habit-like mechanisms of stimulus-driven or model-free action control (Cooper et al. 2014, Daw et al. 2005). Empirical fuel for the study of habit was provided by evidence of the high levels of repetition in daily activities (Khare & Inman 2006, Wood et al. 2002). Further framing these developments is the reading public's interest in understanding their own habits (e.g., Duhig 2012, Rubin 2015).

In this article, we take stock of the fast-growing research on habits. Our review is necessarily wide reaching, covering a variety of behavioral domains, cognitive tasks, and neuroscientific findings. We also consider animal learning research when relevant, given that habit learning mechanisms are largely conserved across mammalian species and do not appear to be degraded in humans or replaced by higher cortical functions (Bayley et al. 2005). Across these diverse research paradigms, the common elements are habit learning through repeated responding so as to form context-response associations in memory, and automated habit performance that is relatively insensitive to changes in the value or contingency of response outcomes. As we explain, these definitions of habit learning and performance capture the cognitive and neural mechanisms involved in habit memory and are reflected in characteristic patterns in habitual responding.

The schematic in **Figure 1** provides a framework for this review by depicting three ways in which habits interface with goals to guide behavior. Goals energize and direct action by defining a desired end state. In our three-pronged model, habits and goals interact through habit formation, habit performance, and inferences about the causes of behavior. First, goals influence habit formation via exposure by initially motivating people to repeat actions within particular performance contexts (see Habit Formation section). This is illustrated by the arrows from goal system to context cues and habitual response in **Figure 1**. Once habits form, context cues come to automatically activate the habit representation in memory (see Habit Automaticity section). Second, via activation or inhibition, people act on the habit in mind as well as on their prevailing goals (see Computational Models section). External factors such as stress and distraction influence the impact of these two processes by reducing the motivation or ability to deliberately pursue goals and increasing reliance on habits (see Factors that Shift the Balance Between Habits and Goals section). As outlined in dual-process frameworks, habits provide a sort of default response unless people are sufficiently motivated and able to tailor their behavior to current circumstances. Finally, through inference processes, people interpret their goals from observing their own frequent behavior, as reflected by the double-headed arrow in **Figure 1** between the habitual response and the goal system (see Inferences about the Causes of Habit Performance section). To conclude the

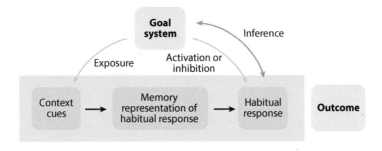

Figure 1

Schematic of three ways in which habits interface with deliberate goal pursuit: through initial repetition and exposure to contexts during habit formation (illustrated by the arrows from goal system to context cues and habitual response), through activation or inhibition of the habitual response, and through inferences about the probable causes of habit responding (reflected by the double-headed arrow between habitual response and goal system).

HABIT AUTOMATICITY

The terms habit and automaticity are sometimes used interchangeably. Like other automatic responses, habits are activated in memory in an autonomous fashion without requiring executive control (Evans & Stanovich 2013). Habits, however, are not synonymous with automaticity but are best understood as learned automatic responses with specific features (Wood et al. 2014). Two defining features of habit automaticity are (*a*) activation by recurring context cues and (*b*) insensitivity to short-term changes in goals (a.k.a., not goal dependent), including changes in the value of response outcomes and the response-outcome contingency. Additional features that apply to most habitual responses include speed and efficiency, limited thought, rigidity, and integration of sequences of responses that can be executed as a unit (Seger & Spiering 2011, Smith & Graybiel 2013). However, each of these additional features may not be assessed in all habit research paradigms. Instrumental learning studies, for example, often do not evaluate response speed, whereas learning of motor sequences in cognitive-experimental research is assessed primarily via changes in response latency.

Habits differ from other automatic, implicit processes including priming, classical conditioning, and nonassociative learning (Evans & Stanovich 2013, Squire & Zola-Morgan 1991). For example, the priming of goals, attitudes, or concepts can activate a range of responses, not only the repetition of a particular well-learned response (see Wood et al. 2014). Even strongly desired goals that stably characterize people's motives do not necessarily yield stability in the particular means of goal pursuit. In contrast, habit automaticity applies to a specific response. Furthermore, unlike habits, automated goals (e.g., implementation intentions) influence behavior primarily to the extent that they are consistent with people's explicit motivations (Sheeran et al. 2005).

Automatic Cuing of Habits

A variety of cues might trigger habit performance, including aspects of physical environments, other people, and preceding actions in a sequence. Once habits form, perception of the relevant context cues automatically activates the mental representation of the habitual response. Exposure to cues might be deliberate, as when sitting at a computer in order to activate thoughts of work. Or exposure can be inadvertent, as when a chance sighting of a fast-food outlet activates thoughts of eating. We assume that the memory representation of a habit response is cognitively richer than a mere motor program that controls response execution. Given that human cognition is based on integrated sensorimotor units (Hommel 2009), a habitual response will be represented in terms of response features as well as perceptual features. Specifically, the sensory feedback while making a response, which gives rise to the experience of performing the action, is included in the mental representation. As a consequence, a habit cue not only triggers a motor program, it also activates a multimodal representation, or thought, of the habitual response. Consistent with this view, Neal et al. (2012) found that runners with strong running habits automatically brought to mind thoughts of running and jogging when exposed to words designating the physical locations in which they typically ran.

Once habitual responses are activated, people can act on the response in mind without making a decision to do so. That is, habit performance follows relatively directly from the perception of context cues and thoughts about the behavior, reflecting the tight linkage between an internal action representation and the action itself (James 1890). For example, when students who frequently went to the sports stadium on campus were incidentally exposed to an image of the stadium, they raised their voices as they would habitually in that context, despite no change in their motivation to speak loudly (Neal et al. 2012). Also, in a study conducted in a local cinema, participants with stronger habits to eat popcorn at the movies consumed more than those with weak habits, even when they disliked the popcorn because it was stale and unpalatable (Neal et al. 2011). However, when in a campus meeting room watching music videos, participants with strong cinema-popcorn eating habits were guided by their preferences and ate little stale popcorn.

Habit performance is typified by the insensitivity to outcomes apparent in speaking loudly in a quiet laboratory setting and eating popcorn despite disliking it. This insensitivity has been demonstrated directly in instrumental learning experiments in which participants were first trained extensively to choose a reward to a certain image cue (e.g., Tricomi et al. 2009). Participants then ate as much of the reward as they desired, so that they did not want any more of that specific food. Nonetheless, when tested again, extensively trained participants in this paradigm continued to make the habitual but unwanted choice to the associated image (see also Hogarth et al. 2012b, Schwabe & Wolf 2010).

Triandis's (1977) early work on behavior prediction sparked social psychologists' interest in the idea that repeated behavior becomes more habitual and less dependent on goal pursuit. In prediction studies, behavioral intentions and habit strength (usually operationalized as frequency of past performance) are used to predict future performance. In a meta-analysis of 64 such studies, Ouellette & Wood (1998) found that intentions were stronger predictors of actions that were performed only occasionally (e.g., getting flu shots) than actions that could be repeated more regularly (e.g., wearing seat belts). Actions performed regularly apparently became habitual and persisted with little guidance from intentions (see also Gardner et al. 2011). In addition, habits and intentions interact in guiding daily variations in behavior. For example, on days when participants' intentions to engage in physical activity were weaker than usual, they fell back on their exercise habits and worked out only to the extent that exercise was habitual (Rebar et al. 2014). Also, in a longitudinal test, habit strength to donate blood determined the relation between intentions and actual donations (P. Sheeran, G. Godin, M. Conner, and M. Germain, unpublished data). That is, for participants with weak donation habits, increasingly favorable intentions predicted a greater number of future donations. However, as habit strength increased, the predictive power of intentions diminished, and participants with the strongest habits simply repeated their past donations without input from intentions.

When acting out of habit, the ready response in mind reduces deliberation and narrows focus even when some explicit decision making is required. In a multiattribute choice task involving a series of travel mode decisions, participants with stronger habits to ride a bike or drive their car conducted less extensive information searches, considered fewer action alternatives, and biased the searches toward their habitual choice (Aarts et al. 1997; see also Betsch et al. 2001). Experimentally enhancing attention to the decision process temporarily increased alternative choices, but the habitual choice reemerged with continued decisions (Verplanken et al. 1997). These results may in part reflect that the repeated activation of one response in a context reduces the cognitive accessibility of alternatives (Danner et al. 2007). Essentially, people with strong habits process information in ways that reduce the likelihood that they will consider acting otherwise.

Habit Automaticity and Deliberation About Action

Dual-process theories of decision making and judgment outline the mechanisms that lead people to respond automatically or to engage in deliberate information processing that draws on the limited-capacity resource of working memory (Evans & Stanovich 2013). From this view, people often act habitually in the interests of efficiency (Wood et al. 2014). When motivated and able to engage in deliberate goal pursuit, however, they might identify desired outcomes, set and initiate behavioral intentions, end actions, and evaluate outcomes (Gollwitzer & Brandstätter 1997).

Dual-process models in psychology often specify that automatic and deliberate systems interact through a default-interventionist architecture (Evans & Stanovich 2013) so that responses are largely habitual unless the deliberative system intervenes to impose an alternative. In contrast, reinforcement-learning computational models of routine behavior and decision making (see Computational Models section) often invoke the less psychologically plausible parallel-competitive form of dual-process architecture, in which planning proceeds in parallel with habitual control. As Evans & Stanovich (2013) point out, parallel processing assumes that a costly central executive is almost continuously ready to be engaged in planning and deliberation. More recently, some computational models have adapted a more default interventionist approach in which planning intervenes to alter habits only when necessary (e.g., Pezzulo et al. 2013). It is useful to note that, although we invoke the dual-process framework in this review, action control is influenced by more than two processes, including automated goal pursuit (Sheeran et al. 2005) as well as Pavlovian conditioning of incentive motivation (Balleine & O'Doherty 2010).

In summary, perception of habit cues automatically activates habit representations, and people typically carry out the habit in mind. Thus, behavior prediction studies reveal that people often act out of habit, even when it is in conflict with their intentions. In dual-process models depicting the ways that habits integrate with goals in guiding behavior, habits are a ready default unless people are motivated and able to intervene and engage in more deliberate goal pursuit.

HABIT FORMATION

Given that everyday habits develop as people go about pursuing life goals, habit formation is closely intertwined with goal pursuit. Nonetheless, an implication of the basic context-response mechanism underlying habits is that behavior becomes less responsive to current goals and planning as habit associations strengthen.

Habits develop through instrumental learning and build on the fundamental principle that rewarded responses are repeated (Thorndike 1898). When repeatedly pursuing a goal such as making coffee, people experience covariations between context cues (e.g., coffee filter) and actions (e.g., measure grounds) that lead to goal attainment. Daily life is full of such repetition. In experience-sampling research in which people recorded once per hour what they were thinking, feeling, and doing, about 43% of actions were performed almost daily and usually in the same context (Wood et al. 2002; see also Khare & Inman 2006). Particular actions, such as eating different types of food, also tend to be performed in particular physical locations (Liu et al. 2015). Typically, the learning of context-response associations is an unintended consequence of this repetition. Suggestive of this automaticity, participants in Wood et al.'s (2002) study often reported that they did not think about repeated behaviors during performance.

Associative and Reward Mechanisms in Habit Learning

Habits strengthen through associative and reward-learning mechanisms that capture the slow, incremental nature of habit formation. With each repetition, small changes occur in the cognitive and neural mechanisms associated with procedural memory. Through Hebbian learning, cognitive associations between context cues and a response are strengthened gradually so that people are prepared to repeat performance when the context cues are encountered again (called direct cuing by Wood & Neal 2007).

The strength of context-response associations is further modulated by the reward following the response. At a neural level, midbrain dopamine systems support this reinforcement process. By signaling reward prediction errors, or the discrepancy between an anticipated and actual reward, a phasic dopamine response acts as a teaching signal for habit learning in the striatum (Balleine & O'Doherty 2010). Specifically, the dopaminergic signal that is triggered by an unexpected change in reward magnitude works retroactively to stamp in associations between the still-active memory traces of the response and the cues in the performance context (Wise 2004). Thus, dopamine signals promote habit learning as people initially repeat responses to a reward, but the signals become less active with repetition, as the reward recurs.

In computational RL models, habit formation is conceptualized as the learning of value signals that represent the expected future rewards for the different response options in a given context and provide the basis for selecting an action (see Computational Models section). Value-based selection of habitual responses can be regarded as a form of motivated cuing (Wood & Neal 2007).

Another way in which habitual responding continues to be influenced by motivational processes is through context cues that have become associated with the reward that follows an action. As learned predictors of reward, such Pavlovian context cues can cause the habitual response to be performed with increased vigor (Balleine & O'Doherty 2010). Of note, the motivational effect of such Pavlovian predictors of rewarding outcomes is distinct from the motivational value of the outcome itself. Holland (2004), for example, found that responses extensively trained into habits were insensitive to changes in outcome value but continued to be influenced by reward-related cues.

A standard finding from animal learning is that habits develop most readily when rewards are provided on interval schedules, meaning that responses are rewarded only after a time has elapsed. Such rewards mimic natural resources that are replenished over time. With these schedules, changes in response rate during the time interval do not change the amount of reward delivered, thereby reducing the experience of instrumental contingency between the response and the reward (Dickinson 1985). Thus, interval rewards likely promote habit learning because context-response associations can form without including a representation of the goal or outcome of the action.

As a caveat to the principle that habits form from repetition, habits do not always emerge with complex tasks in which different response choices lead to different rewards. In animal research, even after extensive training at a task involving a lever press (yielding sucrose) or chain pull (yielding a food pellet), rats failed to form habits—they continued to be sensitive to reward value and ceased responding for one of these rewards after it had been paired with a toxin (Colwill & Rescorla 1985). Perhaps in an analogous fashion, decision making in humans impedes habit formation. In a repeated sequential choice task, participants failed to form habits to the extent that they spontaneously used a planning strategy and based their choices on the value and probability of response outcomes (Gillan et al. 2015). Similarly, habit formation was hindered when an instrumental task promoted planning compared with mapping of responses to cues (Liljeholm et al. 2015). It appears, then, that deliberative decision making is protective against habit formation even when people respond repeatedly to particular cues.

In summary, habits are likely to form from responses repeated contiguously with context cues, especially when responses are rewarded on an interval schedule. Under the influence of dopaminergic neural systems, habits form that are insensitive to current shifts in reward value and structure. However, planning and making deliberate choices during responding can hinder habit formation.

Measures of Habit Strength

Habitization is a process, with no clear demarcation point when strong habits have formed. Nonetheless, instrumental learning tasks provide a clear behavioral criterion. That is, habits have formed when participants continue to repeat a well-practiced response after the reward has been reduced in value (e.g., for food rewards, after consuming to satiety) or is no longer tied to the response (Dickinson 1985). In these paradigms, habitual responding is evaluated during a subsequent extinction phase (rewards withheld) in order to preclude additional learning based on the changed reward values.

Behavioral indicators of habit strength are captured in a variety of experimental paradigms beyond the simple motor responses often thought emblematic of habits. Habit strength has been manipulated in experimental paradigms involving word-association tasks (Hay & Jacoby 1996, Quinn et al. 2010), choice tasks involving pictorial and other judgment stimuli (de Wit et al. 2009, Gillan et al. 2015), two-stage decision-making tasks (Daw et al. 2011), and problem-solving tasks such as tower building (Patsenko & Altmann 2010). Strong habits also form as humans repeatedly navigate through virtual mazes (Marchette et al. 2011) and rats through actual mazes (Packard & Goodman 2013). Echoing insensitivity to reward, strong habits in these paradigms often emerge as errors, reflecting persistent responding despite task changes in the correct, rewarding outcome. Habits also emerge as chunked responses into a unit (Dezfouli & Balleine 2013, Graybiel 1998), which is related to the performance gains (reduced response time, increased accuracy) in many sequential learning tasks (e.g., Lungu et al. 2014). In addition, eye-tracking measures have been used to capture visual attention to task structures triggering habitual responses (Patsenko & Altmann 2010).

The strength of everyday habits is typically assessed from people's self-reports. One method is to combine self-reported ratings of behavioral frequency with ratings of the stability of the performance context, reflecting the logic that habits represent the repeated pairing of responses and recurring context cues (Galla & Duckworth 2015, Wood & Neal 2009). Using an alternative approach, the Self-Report Habit Index estimates habit strength from a questionnaire measure of the experience of automaticity and frequency of past performance (Verplanken & Orbell 2003), which has further been streamlined to measure only automaticity (Gardner 2015, Gardner et al. 2012). However, as Labrecque & Wood (2015) noted, experienced automaticity measures often fail to assess triggering contexts and may capture automation more generally, as opposed to habit automaticity that guides performance with limited input from current intentions. However, these measures can successfully capture habit strength when triggering cues are present (P. Lin, W. Wood, and J. Monterosso, unpublished data). Perhaps the most valid assessments of everyday habit strength involve reaction time measures of the accessibility of the habitual response given exposure to associated context cues (e.g., Neal et al. 2012).

In summary, assessments of habit formation rest most importantly on evidence that responses are insensitive to changes in rewarding outcomes. Habit formation has been documented in a variety of laboratory tasks using a variety of behavioral assays. For everyday habits, self-report assessments can capture habit strength, although direct assessment of context-response associations is probably most valid.

COMPUTATIONAL MODELS

Computational models offer detailed accounts of the cognitive processes that support habit learning and performance. We selectively focus on models that incorporate habit-like control systems as well as deliberate goal pursuit. Instead of making the simplified assumption that a behavior is either goal directed or habitual, these models explore how adaptive behavior can emerge from the interplay of different modes of action control. Competing ideas have been proposed about how the different action controllers work together to produce a response.

In Cooper et al.'s (2014) goal circuit (GC) model, goals structure the learning of habits and control their expression. The GC model is an artificial neural network composed of two interlinked habit and goal subnetworks. The habit system, which was originally proposed by Botvinick & Plaut

(2004), selects actions in a bottom-up manner based on the current stimulus environment and on internal feedback about the network's previous state. This response selection process is biased by input from the goal system. A habit develops gradually as the network repeats the same sequence of responses while learning to attain goals in a particular environment. Eventually, the habit system becomes capable of performing a sequence autonomously without goal input. In addition to guiding learning in the habit system, the goal network enables top-down control over habitual action sequences, as when a person deliberately overrides a habitual response.

Taatgen et al. (2008) developed a model within the ACT-R (adaptive control of thought–rational) cognitive architecture that shows how behavioral control shifts from an internal, declarative task representation to environmental cues when acquiring a new action routine. Initially, explicit task knowledge is used to control behavior in a goal-directed manner. With practice, explicit memory retrieval is gradually transformed into a process by which perceptual cues trigger the relevant action directly. This proceduralization of explicit knowledge accounts for performance improvements during skill learning. Additional learning is possible by combining stimulus-cued productions of sequences into a single new production. The creation of new, specialized knowledge structures or chunks that can be used more efficiently is a central element in cognitive theories of skill acquisition (Newell 1990).

In cognitive neuroscience, the prevalent theoretical perspective is that goal-directed actions and habits can be described by different classes of RL (Daw et al. 2005, Dolan & Dayan 2013). Goal-directed, or model-based, learning is a computationally demanding process of mental simulation and planning. Using this approach, an agent computes on the fly which action maximizes long-run cumulative reward. Habit formation, in contrast, relies on model-free RL involving trial-and-error learning to estimate and store the long-run values of actions that are available in the different states or contexts. Actions are then chosen based on the stored or cached action values, reflecting predictions about future reward. Model-free control lacks the flexibility of model-based learning because short-term changes in the reward value of an action outcome have only limited effect on the cached value. Thus, model-free RL theoretically captures a key property of habits—insensitivity to changes in reward. Both types of learning are driven by prediction errors, with model-based learning capturing the discrepancy between the current state and the expected one and model-free learning capturing the difference between predicted and experienced reward.

In an initial dual-system RL model, Daw et al. (2005) assumed a competitive, winner-take-all mechanism in which the habit system or the goal system gained control over action, depending on which system provided the more reliable estimates of action values. However, subsequent investigations favor a more dynamic integration in which both systems contribute to the computation of action values according to their relative reliabilities (Lee et al. 2014). A related proposal involves Bayesian model averaging that takes into account prediction accuracy and model complexity. In this view, with experience, goal-directed actions are replaced by habits because the habit system becomes increasingly reliable and favored over the computationally more complex goal-directed system (FitzGerald et al. 2014). Furthermore, it is likely that model-based judgments are implemented only selectively, given the psychological costs of planning (see Habit Automaticity and Deliberation About Action section). In recognition, a number of contingent RL systems engage model-based processing conditional on trade-offs between accuracy and efficiency (Keramati et al. 2011, Pezzulo et al. 2013).

Beyond integrating independently computed action values, some RL models assume a direct influence of deliberate planning on habit learning. For example, in Gershman et al.'s (2014) two-step decision task, participants changed their choice preferences in the first task step (believed to reflect model-free habit processing) after independently learning about second-step reward contingencies. To account for this finding, Gershman and colleagues argued that the model-based system simulated a complete two-step decision process, and the model-free system learned from the simulations. Similarly, Pezzulo et al. (2013) proposed that model-based planning can update and improve the value estimates of the model-free system. By enabling goals to influence the action values represented in habit learning, these models promote the formation of habits compatible with goals.

The RL approach can account not only for the insensitivity of habits to changes in reward value but also for the chunking feature of habit automaticity. Theories of hierarchical RL show that it can be advantageous to concatenate individual actions and treat the sequence as a single response unit or chunk (Botvinick & Weinstein 2014) because the faster responding enabled by chunking can lead to greater average reward (Keramati et al. 2011). The chunked units could be deployed in a goal-directed (Dezfouli & Balleine 2012) or model-free manner on the basis of the reward history (Botvinick et al. 2009).

Questions remain, however, about the appropriateness of equating model-free learning with habit processes. Dezfouli & Balleine's (2012) proposal that habits are action chunks that are acquired and controlled through model-based processes marks a radical departure from the common RL assumption that habits are the result of model-free learning. Even more significant, individual-difference studies have reported that the strength of model-free learning was unrelated to habit formation and insensitivity to the value of the task outcome (Friedel et al. 2014, Gillan et al. 2015). Instead, outcome insensitivity was greater among participants evidencing little model-based learning. It is possible that the standard two-stage RL decision task does not capture the process that produces outcome-insensitive habits, perhaps because participants have to choose between multiple outcomes with varying reward rates (see discussion in the Associative and Reward Mechanisms in Habit Learning section). Thus, model-free learning in these tasks might reflect other stimulus-driven strategies such as simple decision heuristics as well as habits. Future research on model-free processes may need to develop new experimental tasks to better capture habits.

In summary, habits form as a product of repeated behaviors in the service of goal pursuit. Learning in the habit system may proceed independently or be guided by the goal system. Recent theories suggest that rather than being independent action controllers, habit and goal systems integrate in ways that reflect the reliability of each system and the costs of planning. In some contingent RL models, the habit system serves as an efficient default, and people plan only when motivated and able.

NEUROBIOLOGY OF HABITS

From a dual-system perspective, a fundamental objective is to identify brain regions whose activity is uniquely associated with habitual and goal-directed behavior, respectively. Current neuroscientific research is guided, to an increasing extent, by the computational RL models that we discussed in the previous section. Thanks to the rapid advancement of functional neuroimaging with human subjects, it is now possible to relate computational dual-process models to brain functioning at increasingly fine-grained levels of analysis. The emerging picture is one of a neurocognitive system that integrates the computations of partially overlapping neural systems of habitual and goal-directed control.

Neural Systems Associated with Habits

Research conducted with rodents, monkeys, and humans has provided converging evidence that habitual and goal-directed behaviors are mediated by neural circuits that link cortical brain areas and the basal ganglia (BG), a collection of subcortical nuclei. These circuits are organized as anatomically separate reentrant loops, two of which are essential for deliberate and habitual responding (Burton et al. 2015, Yin & Knowlton 2006). The associative cortico-BG loop supports working memory functions and goal-directed actions and links the prefrontal cortex (PFC) with two striatal BG regions, the caudate nucleus and the anterior putamen. The sensorimotor loop underlies automatic, habitual behaviors and connects the somatosensory and motor cortex with the medial and posterior putamen. Though anatomically separate, the two loops can interact, for example, through spiraling dopaminergic connectivity (Haber et al. 2000).

Animal learning studies have demonstrated the importance of the sensorimotor loop for habitual responding. Rats do not acquire a lever-pressing habit when their dorsolateral striatum (DLS), the equivalent of the primate putamen, is lesioned prior to lever-press training for sucrose. Even after extended training, these rats continued to be goal directed and pressed the lever less frequently when sucrose was devalued (Yin et al. 2004). Furthermore, when the DLS was inactivated pharmacologically after a lever-pressing habit was acquired, outcome sensitivity was reinstated (Yin et al. 2006).

Suggesting that the DLS is involved in the chunking of individual actions into a sequence, electrical recordings from neurons in the DLS of rats exhibited a task-bracketing pattern of activity during habitual runs through a maze—high neuronal activity at the beginning and end of a run, with lower activity in-between. Task bracketing emerged when the learned behavior was still goal directed (Smith & Graybiel 2013), which indicates that habits develop in parallel with goal-directed learning but do not influence overt behavior early in training. By contrast, when goal-directed control is abolished by lesioning associated brain regions such as the rodent posterior dorsomedial striatum (DMS, corresponding to the caudate nucleus in primates) or the prelimbic medial PFC, behavior immediately comes under habitual control (Killcross & Coutureau 2003, Yin et al. 2005).

Neuroimaging research with human participants implicates similar networks of brain regions. Practicing sequences of finger movements for days or weeks decreased brain activation in areas associated with goal-directed control [e.g., premotor and prefrontal cortical areas, anterior cingulate cortex (ACC), and associative BG territories] and increased activation in the sensorimotor network, including the putamen (e.g., Lehéricy et al. 2005, Steele & Penhune 2010). Participants who developed a lever-pressing habit for potato chips and candy over three days of training showed similar increases in activity in the sensorimotor striatum (posterior putamen) both within practice days as well as across days (Tricomi et al. 2009). Neuroimaging studies of motor sequence learning further confirmed the role of the sensorimotor striatum in chunk formation, along with a frontoparietal network and the mediotemporal lobes (Lungu et al. 2014).

The sensorimotor loop is critical for habit learning, and an extended network of brain regions modulates its activity. Motivational influences on habit acquisition are mediated by ascending dopamine projections from the substantia nigra pars compacta to the dorsal striatum that modulate habit plasticity at corticostriatal synapses (Balleine & O'Doherty 2010). Lesioning this nigrostriatal pathway in rats disrupted habit formation (Faure et al. 2005). Habit acquisition also was impeded by lesions of the amygdala central nucleus, most likely due to its effect on substantia nigra pars compacta function (Lingawi & Balleine 2012). Finally, rodents' infralimbic cortex, a medial PFC region, directly participates in the formation of a habit and is required for its expression (Killcross & Coutureau 2003, Smith & Graybiel 2013).

Whether the sensorimotor loop is responsible for long-term habit storage remains unclear. After six months of practicing sequences of joystick movements, monkeys that had their sensorimotor loop disrupted pharmacologically were not impaired in the expression of sequence knowledge and still executed overlearned sequences faster and more accurately than random control sequences (Desmurget & Turner 2010). One explanation is that, with extensive practice, habit learning is consolidated in cortical brain areas (Atallah et al. 2007). This possibility fits Penhune & Steele's (2012) conclusion that long-term representations of learned skills are encoded in a network of motor cortical regions. In their research, delayed recall of a motor sequence engaged not the BG but rather cortical regions (primary motor and premotor cortices and parietal lobe). This idea is supported further by the finding that participants who practiced motor sequences for more than six weeks showed, late in training, neural specialization in cortical motor areas [primary motor and premotor cortices and the supplementary motor area (SMA)] (Wymbs & Grafton 2014).

In summary, converging evidence implicates the sensorimotor cortico-BG loop as the core neural substrate of habit learning and performance. Whether the BG are also required for the long-term retention of habits is a matter of current debate.

Neural Systems that Integrate Habit and Goal-Directed Action Control

Based on computational RL theory, a stream of neuroimaging research has evaluated performance in sequential decision tasks that elicit both habit-based (model-free) learning and prospective planning about outcomes (model based). The results are broadly consistent with the mapping of habitual and goal-directed control onto the associative and sensorimotor cortico-BG loops. For example, Wunderlich et al. (2012) related activity in the posterior putamen to cached action values (habits) that were acquired through extensive training, and activity in the anterior caudate nucleus was related to values used in model-based planning. Similarly, Lee et al. (2014) reported that the posterior putamen, SMA, dorsomedial PFC, and dorsolateral PFC encoded model-free action values, whereas model-based values were associated with activity in orbitofrontal cortex (OFC) and medial PFC as well as the ACC (see also de Wit et al. 2009, Valentin et al. 2007).

Recent dual-system RL models propose that response selection is based on action values represented in ventromedial prefrontal cortex (vmPFC) that are jointly determined by a model-free (habit) and prospective planning controllers (e.g., Daw et al. 2011). This integration of model-based and model-free value signals is thought to be conducted by an arbitrator associated with activity in the inferior lateral PFC, frontopolar cortex, and ACC (Lee et al. 2014). How exactly such an arbitrator regulates the contribution of each system is still largely unknown. According to one analysis, shifts in response strategy are achieved primarily by strengthening or inhibiting the influence of the model-free habit system (Lee et al. 2014). Other findings suggest dynamic changes in both the habit system and the goal system (Gremel & Costa 2013).

Consistent with the idea that habits develop as people pursue goals, recent evidence suggests that multiple brain regions participate in both goal-directed and habitual control. For example, Lee et al. (2014) found with the multi-step decision task that two regions, the SMA and dmPFC, represented both model-free and model-based values. Similarly, Gremel & Costa (2013) trained rats to lever press for sucrose using either a habitual or a goal-directed strategy. They reported that a large proportion of neurons in DLS, DMS, and OFC participated in both habitual and goal-directed responding, and that the relative engagement of neurons in these areas depended on the current response strategy.

In summary, research guided by RL theory has identified the neural substrates of model-based (goal-directed) and model-free (habitual) control. These neural systems are partially overlapping, and their computations are integrated by brain regions that regulate the relative influence of the two modes of behavioral control.

FACTORS THAT SHIFT THE BALANCE BETWEEN HABITS AND DELIBERATE GOAL PURSUIT

Given the cognitive and neural features that differentiate habitual responding from more deliberate pursuit of goals, action control proceeds by balancing these and other processes (e.g., Pavlovian

HABIT SLIPS

Habit slips, or errors of inadvertent habit performance, occur primarily when an intended action and a habit share a performance context or some action component (Norman 1981). In daily life, people appear to slip up by performing unwanted habits about six times a week, especially when their attention is diverted from the task at hand (Reason 1979). For example, habit slips underlie errors in responding to innocent-appearing email phishing attacks (Vishwanath 2015). In laboratory tests, habits were most likely to be performed inadvertently when goal-directed control was taxed by, for example, advanced age or performing a secondary task (e.g., de Wit et al. 2014, Ruh et al. 2010).

Moving beyond the truism that people make errors when not attending to what they are doing, research has identified several sources of habit slips. Slips arising from failures in planning reflect limits in motivation or knowledge about completion of task goals, and they are most likely at decision points such as the end-of-task subroutines (Norman 1981, Reason 1979). However, habit slips also emerge from failures in automated, habitual guides to performance, as when degraded representations of task context occur within a sequence of well-learned actions (Botvinick & Bylsma 2005). In still another analysis, habit slips arise from normal processing, especially open-loop action control in which habits are executed ballistically once they are launched, even when they are not the optimal response (Dezfouli et al. 2014, Orbell & Verplanken 2010). Thus, habit slips reflect failures to select the correct action through top-down control or bottom-up activation as well as ballistic habit performance.

conditioning; de Wit & Dickinson 2009). Tipping the balance between habits and goal pursuit are factors such as distraction (see Habit Slips sidebar), time pressure, limited task ability, or limited willpower (for a review, see Wood et al. 2014). These factors drive action control by pitting efficiency in processing against more effortful reliable processing (Evans & Stanovich 2013). That is, people act on strong habits when they lack the ability and motivation to engage the central executive in deliberation or, in RL terminology, when pressured by the time costs of model-based planning.

Considerable research reveals increased habit performance with impaired executive functioning. For example, when willpower was reduced by previously performing a taxing decision-making task, participants did not tailor their responses to their current circumstances but instead fell back on strongly habitual choices (Neal et al. 2013, Vohs et al. 2005). Also, when distracted by performing a demanding task, participants completing a categorization task increased the use of stimulus-response strategies over rule-based ones (Foerde et al. 2006), and participants completing a multistep decision task increased model-free responding (Otto et al. 2013a). Furthermore, in individual-difference paradigms, older adults and those with lower cognitive-control abilities were less able to leverage higher-order goal representations for model-based responding in order to modify habitual, model-free solutions to a variety of tasks (de Wit et al. 2014, Otto et al. 2015). In like manner, participants possessing low spatial perspective-taking ability, after practicing navigating a maze, used more habitual and less goal-directed navigation strategies (Marchette et al. 2011).

Stress and drug addiction are of particular interest because of the multiple routes by which they tip the balance toward habits and away from deliberate decision making. As we explain in the next sections, these factors not only impede executive processes but also perhaps promote habit learning.

Stress

Acute as well as chronic stress can increase people's reliance on habits (Schwabe & Wolf 2013). For example, participants exposed to a combination of physical and psychosocial stressors (immersing a hand into ice water while being monitored by a stranger and videotaped) after instrumental learning acted more habitually and were less sensitive to changes in the value of task rewards (Schwabe & Wolf 2010). This stress-induced shift toward habits is due in part to stress impeding deliberate action control. At the neural level, the shift toward habitual behavior was accompanied by decreased activity in OFC and medial PFC, brain regions associated with goal-directed learning (Schwabe et al. 2012). In sequential decision-making tasks, acute stress selectively attenuated deliberate, model-based control and promoted habit performance in vulnerable participants—those with low working-memory capacity (Otto et al. 2013b) or high levels of chronic stress (Radenbach et al. 2015). Similarly, in a study of visual classification learning, stressed participants were biased toward relying on a habit-linked procedural learning strategy at the expense of explicit learning (Schwabe & Wolf 2012). These results could reflect simply the breakdown of higher-order decision-making functions under stress, or stress could lead to a shift in the allocation of cognitive resources so that people fall back on habits and other strategies to prevent unreliable performance. From an RL perspective, stress shifts the balance toward habits over lengthy planning by increasing experienced time pressure (Doll et al. 2012).

Along with impeding deliberate thought, stress also might promote habit acquisition. Research with rodents suggests that stress can, under specific conditions, facilitate habit learning through mechanisms associated with dorsolateral striatal function (Dias-Ferreira et al. 2009). In humans, however, stress does not clearly affect habit formation. To isolate stress effects on habit learning, stress is induced before training, and learning is assessed after acute stress effects have dissipated so that these do not affect performance. Administering stress hormones led to improved learning in a simple stimulus-response task but had no effect on habit learning in a virtual radial maze (Guenzel et al. 2014a). Furthermore, a combination of pretraining physical and psychosocial stressors actually impaired habitual performance at maze navigation, albeit only in male participants (Guenzel et al. 2014b).

In summary, neurophysiological responses to stress increase habitual responding by impeding deliberate action control and, potentially, by promoting habit formation. More generally, stress research highlights the benefits of habits for rescuing performance. In support of this functional role, stressed participants' task performance was impaired to the extent that they attempted to engage goal-directed neural systems (Schwabe & Wolf 2013). Given the ready acquisition and performance of habits, they provide a useful default when threat and pressure derail more thoughtful responding.

Addiction

From a habit perspective, the path to drug addiction involves not a pathological motivation for drugs but rather a shift from goal-directed to habitual drug seeking and consumption (Everitt 2014, Hogarth et al. 2013). Initial drug seeking is voluntary and reflects the hedonic value of the drug. Through instrumental learning with drug rewards, context cues rapidly become associated with drug use. In addition, Pavlovian mechanisms contribute to the want for drugs and for cue-evoked cravings (Berridge 2007). These various learning mechanisms are involved in the cues that come to trigger drug seeking and consumption independently of the drug outcome, much as people repeat habits with limited sensitivity to goals and outcomes (Zapata et al. 2010). Phenomenologically, the addict no longer likes the drug yet uses it compulsively, often despite intentions to quit. Drug-outcome insensitivity is promoted further as repeated exposures build tolerance to rewarding drug effects.

Drug use promotes habit formation in part by impairing goal-directed control. In illustration, study participants who had consumed alcohol responded habitually and continued to choose chocolate in a repeated food-choice task despite having just eaten three chocolate bars (Hogarth et al. 2012a). Comparable findings have emerged with chronic addicts abstinent at test. For example, participants who were obese, obsessive-compulsive, or dependent on methamphetamine showed compromised goal-directed learning at a decision-making task, along with a maladaptive reliance on habits (Voon et al. 2015). Furthermore, these responses in chronic addicts were associated with neural markers of lower gray matter volumes in the caudate, medial OFC, and lateral PFC. Also, alcohol-dependent participants responded habitually after rewards had been devalued in an associative learning task, and greater reliance on habits was associated with reduced engagement of brain areas implicated in goal-directed action (vmPFC) and increased engagement of areas implicated in habit learning (posterior putamen; Sjoerds et al. 2013). Even when not under drug influence, simply being in the presence of cues repeatedly associated with drug exposure can disrupt goal-directed responding (Ostlund et al. 2010). In general, goal-directed impairments increasingly narrow addicts' behavioral repertoires onto drug habits by restricting their capacity for intentionally selecting alternative actions.

Drug use also promotes habit responding through neurobiological processes that sensitize users to the incentive properties of drugs. Drug rewards appear to engage habits more rapidly than other reinforcers (see review in Everitt 2014). Stimulants in particular accelerate and consolidate the development of drug use habits, speeding the neural shifts from associative to sensorimotor areas typically found with habit formation. The accelerated formation of habits hastens the transition from initial or occasional user to addict.

In summary, drug exposure hijacks the habit learning system by exerting a continuous pressure in favor of habitual, context-driven behavior and away from the evaluation of the outcomes of action. As a result of these habitual and deliberative processes, drug use escalates so that people ultimately seek drugs compulsively (Redish et al. 2008).

INFERENCES ABOUT THE CAUSES OF HABIT PERFORMANCE

People often are aware of their habitual responses although they are largely unaware of the cuing mechanism that activates habits. Given this limited introspective access, people's explanations for their habitual responses are largely post hoc accounts. According to classic social psychology theories, when internal cues to action are weak, ambiguous, or uninterpretable, people infer what their motivations must be from observing their behavior and the context in which it occurs (Bem 1972).

The simple frequency of habit performance plausibly implies strong, consistent underlying motives. Such inferences could be correct in an historical sense, because people might accurately remember the goals that initially guided habit formation. However, they will not be correct concerning current habit performance. In support of such an inference, participants with stronger habits were more certain about their behavioral intentions and perceived the behavior as guided more by their goals than were participants with weaker habits, when in fact the opposite was true— intentions and goals were particularly poor predictors of strongly habitual behaviors (Ji & Wood 2007, Neal et al. 2012). People infer that goals underlie a range of habitual behaviors, even habits of compulsive drug seeking and use. Everitt & Robbins (2005) suggested that addicts' experience of wanting a drug is not a precursor of consumption but rather a post hoc rationalization of compulsive drug-use habits. Similarly, obsessive-compulsive disorders may originate in excessive habit formation, with irrational threat beliefs then inferred to explain the compulsively repeated behaviors (Gillan & Robbins 2014). Although people infer intentionality for a wide variety of automatically cued responses, when internal cues are strong and unambiguous, causal inferences are unnecessary. Then, inconsistencies between habits and goals might just be labeled as such (e.g., "I can't help it, it's a habit").

The inference of motives behind habit performance is represented in some computational models as non-goal-mediated routine responding giving rise to goal representations. For example, in Sun et al.'s (2001) CLARION (Connectionist Learning with Adaptive Rule Induction Online) model, habitual responses that are controlled through bottom-up procedural knowledge can, over time, come to be represented in top-down rules via a rule extraction-refinement algorithm. In Cooper et al.'s (2014) goal circuit model, stimulus-driven habitual responses can activate goal representations that subsequently provide input to habits. In this way, active goals may be a consequence, rather than a precursor, of habitual action. From the perspective of RL models, this inference might occur through the model-based system adopting the values expressed in habit learning, perhaps to reduce computational overhead (Doll et al. 2012).

Goal inferences are sparked not only by the simple frequency of habit performance but also by the positive affect associated with many habits. Habits are likely to be favored due to the ease with which they can be performed compared with alternatives. Thus, consumers value using existing products and services over new ones because of the difficulty of learning new usage behaviors (e.g., computer program updates; Murray & Häubl 2007). Habits also are likely to be viewed positively due to the fluency or speed and ease of processing associated with frequently performed behaviors. High fluency is experienced as positive in part because it signals familiarity over uncertainty and success at processing and understanding, and this positive affect generalizes to evaluation of the activity (Reber et al. 2004). Habit inferences thus exploit a psychological calculus that favors what feels easy because it is well practiced over what feels more difficult because it is new. Being favorably disposed toward habits, people may infer that they intended to perform the response.

Although the inferences that follow habit performance may not be accurate descriptions of the mechanisms actually generating action, such inferences sometimes contribute to well-being. Repeated behaviors, such as students' choices of the same seat in a classroom, heighten feelings of comfort, confidence, and control despite that these choices might initially be random (Avni-Babad 2011). Furthermore, habit performance may promote coherence or comprehensibility of experiences and thus enhance meaning in life (S. Heintzelman and L. King, unpublished observation). However, inferences about habits are not always beneficial, and the transparency of habit knowledge to introspection can lead people to underestimate its usefulness. For example, when highly motivated to perform well, participants with good procedural knowledge at a task overrode their habits and responded thoughtfully, despite that this impaired task performance (L. Carden, W. Wood, D. Neal, and A. Pascoe, unpublished observation).

In summary, people may explain habit performance, even addictive habits, by inferring relevant goals and intentions. Despite being largely erroneous, the inference that habits were intended may seem intuitively plausible given response frequency. Also relevant, switching costs can discourage deviating from habits, and experienced fluency can increase liking for them.

CHANGING HABITS

Unwanted habits are at the root of many failed attempts at behavior change. Evidence comes from Webb & Sheeran's (2006) meta-analysis of 47 studies that successfully used persuasive appeals and other interventions to change participants' intentions. The changed intentions, however, only yielded change in behaviors that participants performed sporadically (e.g., course enrollment) and not in behaviors that could be repeated into habits (e.g., seat belt use). Even the largely effective implementation intentions, or if-then plans to act on intentions at particular times and places (Gollwitzer & Sheeran 2006), are not successful at controlling many strong habits (Maher & Conroy 2015, Webb et al. 2009).

From a habit perspective, difficulties in changing established behavior patterns do not reflect people's continuing desire to perform the old behavior or a failure of willpower. The central challenge is that old habits continue to be activated automatically by recurring environmental cues (J. Labrecque and W. Wood, unpublished observation; Walker et al. 2014). Even after new habits have been learned, old memory traces are not necessarily replaced (Bouton et al. 2011). Relapse can occur when old habit memories are activated by prior routines and other context cues.

Addressing the role of habit learning is a central challenge for the next generation of behavior change interventions (Marteau et al. 2012, Rothman et al. 2015). In response to this challenge, interventions can be designed to (*a*) impede the automated cueing of old, unwanted habits as well as (*b*) promote the repetition of a new, desired behavior into a habit.

Interventions to Impede Unwanted Habit Performance

To reduce interference from old habits, behavior change interventions can incorporate mechanisms of inhibition. In research investigating the spontaneous inhibition of unwanted habits in daily life, the most successful strategy involved thinking, "Don't do it," and being mindful of slip-ups (Quinn et al. 2010). This strategy also successfully controlled habit errors when participants were instructed to use it in an experimental task. As expected, it worked by enhancing cognitive control, not by decreasing habit strength (Quinn et al. 2010). Also effective is tying inhibitory plans to the cues that activate unwanted habits (e.g., "After dinner, I'll skip dessert as usual and substitute fruit"; Adriaanse et al. 2010).

Interference from old habits also can be reduced by changing cues in performance environments. Animal research suggests that habit performance is especially impaired when contexts shift, with goal-directed responding transferring more successfully across contexts (Thrailkill & Bouton 2015). One way to change habit cues is through managing exposure. For example, unhealthy eating habits can be curbed by increasing the salience or accessibility of healthy foods (Sobal & Wansink 2007). A study illustrated how people do this in daily life: At all-you-can-eat Chinese buffets, patrons with lower body mass index used chopsticks, chose small plates, put napkins on their laps, and sat with their sides or backs to the buffet (Wansink & Payne 2012). Another way that habit cues change is through naturally occurring life transitions, such as when people switch jobs or move house. Habit discontinuity interventions capitalize on this reduced exposure to cues that trigger old habits (Thøgersen 2012, Verplanken et al. 2008, Walker et al. 2014). Life transitions that alter habit cues can provide a window of opportunity to act on new intentions without competition from old habits (Wood et al. 2005).

Interventions to Promote Formation of Desired Habits

By encouraging the formation of new habits, behavior change interventions can be designed to habitize a new behavior so that it is maintained despite short-term desires and temptations. In an experiment illustrating how healthy habits can arm people against succumbing to food temptations (P.-Y. Lin, W. Wood, and J. Monterosso, unpublished data), participants learned in a computerized task to avoid chocolate (study 1) or to choose carrots (study 2). When later given options of eating unhealthy treats, participants continued to make habitual choices, at least when context cues automatically triggered the healthy habit. Also, echoing the factors that balance habits and goals, participants were most likely to act on their healthy habits when they lacked the willpower to deliberate about food choices.

Despite the promise of habit formation in maintaining desired behaviors, only a few interventions with nonclinical populations have built on the three pillars of habit formation–repetition in stable contexts with appropriate reward schedules (see Lally & Gardner 2013, Rünger & Wood 2015). The importance of repetition was illustrated in Lally et al.'s (2010) field experiment in which repetitions of a simple health behavior (e.g., walking after dinner) required from 18 days to as many as 254 days in the same context to become habitual and performed without thinking. For exercise, Kaushal & Rhodes (2015) estimated that going to the gym became automatic within six weeks, assuming visits of four times per week. Unfortunately, few health or other behavioral interventions have adapted interval reward schedules to facilitate habit formation (Burns et al. 2012). However, the importance of stable cues was demonstrated in interventions using tooth brushing to cue dental flossing and form flossing habits (e.g., Judah et al. 2013, Orbell & Verplanken 2010). The few interventions built on the three components of habit formation have yielded promising results for weight loss (Carels et al. 2014, Lally et al. 2008) and consumption of healthy food in families (Gardner et al. 2014).

Interestingly, in a habit formation intervention, electronic reminders to perform a desired behavior increased repetition but also impeded automaticity and learning of context-response associations (Stawarz et al. 2015). Perhaps reminders engaged deliberate decision making that impaired learning context–response associations (see Associative and Reward Mechanisms in Habit Learning section). More passive reminders in the form of physical signs, although helpful in prompting initial repetition and habit formation, ultimately lost potency over time (Tobias 2009).

Additional evidence of the utility of habit formation comes from interventions that did not specifically target habits. For example, forming gym-going habits enabled new members of a health club to sustain working out (Armitage 2005), and forming nonsmoking habits enabled former smokers to remain abstinent a year after the end of a smoking cessation program (Baldwin et al. 2006). In a study of regular exercisers, approximately 90% had a location or time cue to exercise, and exercising was more automatic for those who exercised in a routine way and were cued by a particular location (Tappe et al. 2013).

Research on self-control also suggests the usefulness of habits for maintaining desired behaviors. People with high trait self-control do not appear to attain goals through inhibition of problematic desires but instead through forming habits that allow them to achieve goals without experiencing unwanted temptations (Galla & Duckworth 2015, Hofmann et al. 2012). Trait self-control generally fosters proficiency at performing tasks that require automation (de Ridder et al. 2012). Nonetheless, everyone tends to fall back on performing habits—both good and bad—when they lack the capacity or motivation to make decisions to act in nonhabitual ways (Neal et al. 2013).

In summary, through combating unwanted habits and ensuring that desired behaviors are repeated in ways that promote habit formation, interventions can promote adoption of behaviors that endure over time. These interventions adapt the habit strategies that people with effective self-control use in their daily lives to ensure successful goal attainment.

CONCLUSION

The current state of the science on habits has provided the definition that James (1890) requested, overturned behaviorists' conceptions of simple stimulus-response associations, and placed habits within broader models of goal-directed action. Habits reflect associative learning and the formation of context-response associations in procedural memory. Once habits form, perception of the context automatically brings the response to mind, and people often carry out that response. As habits strengthen, they gradually become independent of the incentive value of their consequences, and neural activation shifts from associative toward sensorimotor cortico-striatal brain regions. When repeated in a sequence, habitual responses also may be chunked together and activated as a unit. In short, our review provides a framework for understanding, predicting, and changing that common component of everyday life in which behavioral control has been outsourced onto the context cues contiguous with past performance.

Although habits are largely insensitive to changes in goal structure and value, they interact in three different ways with deliberate goal pursuit. First, habits form in daily life as people pursue goals by repeating actions in particular performance contexts. Initially, goals and declarative task knowledge structure behavior. With repetition, responses and associated context cues are captured in procedural learning systems. Goals also may contribute to habit formation through heightening attention to certain stimuli and identifying the value of action outcomes. Given the profusion of direct and indirect connections between neural circuits underlying goal-directed and habitual (model-free) behaviors, goals can have a biasing influence on habit formation (Doll et al. 2012). Cross talk between habit systems and more deliberative action control, especially during habit formation, is consistent with an evolutionary history in which neural systems supporting more sophisticated planning capacities evolved on top of neural mechanisms associated with habits.

A second interface between goals and habits emerges after habits form. That is, habits provide an efficient baseline response that likely integrates with more effortful goal pursuit only when necessary, as when habits prove unreliable in a given context or when people are especially motivated and able to tailor responses to particular circumstances. Various factors impede people's ability to deliberate and thus tip the balance toward relying on habits, including time pressure, distraction, stress, and addiction. Addictive substances may in addition promote habit responding by accelerating habit learning.

A third way in which goals integrate with habits is through the explanations that people generate for their habits. Because habit cuing is inaccessible to introspection, people must infer the reasons for such responses. A plausible inference for repeated behaviors is strong, consistent underlying motivations and goals.

The research we reviewed highlights a number of advantages to acting habitually. For example, habit knowledge is protected from short-term whims and occasional happenings, given that habits form through incremental experience and do not shift readily with changes in people's goals and plans. Also, by outsourcing action control to environmental cues, people have a ready response when distraction, time pressure, lowered willpower, and stress reduce the capacity to deliberate about action and tailor responses to current environments. Furthermore, habit systems are smart in the sense that they enable people to efficiently capitalize on environmental regularities.

As we noted at the end of the present review, understanding habits is important from the applied perspective of human health and welfare. Drug addictions and other compulsions appear to co-opt habit processes and reduce people's capacity to purposively guide their behavior. Lifestyle habits of poor diet and limited exercise are major contributors to chronic diseases. By building on an understanding of habit mechanisms, addiction treatments as well as interventions to change lifestyle behaviors may successfully disrupt these unwanted habits and help people to form more effective habits that meet their goals for healthy, productive lives.

DISCLOSURE STATEMENT

The authors are not aware of any affiliations, memberships, funding, or financial holdings that might be perceived as affecting the objectivity of this review.

ACKNOWLEDGMENTS

The authors thank Peter Dayan, Sanne de Wit, Benjamin Gardner, Barbara Knowlton, David T. Neal, Yael Niv, Sheina Orbell, A. Ross Otto, Carol Seger, Kyle Smith, and Bas Verplanken for their thoughtful comments on an earlier version of the article. This article was made possible through the support of a grant from the John Templeton Foundation. The opinions expressed are those of the authors and do not necessarily reflect the Foundation's views.

LITERATURE CITED

Aarts H, Verplanken B, Van Knippenberg A. 1997. Habit and information use in travel mode choices. *Acta Psychol.* 96:1–14

Adriaanse MA, Oettingen G, Gollwitzer PM, Hennes EP, de Ridder DTD, de Wit JBF. 2010. When planning is not enough: fighting unhealthy snacking habits by mental contrasting with implementation intentions (MCII). *Eur. J. Soc. Psychol.* 40:1277–93

Armitage CJ. 2005. Can the theory of planned behavior predict the maintenance of physical activity? *Health Psychol.* 24:235–45

Atallah HE, Lopez-Paniagua D, Rudy JW, O'Reilly RC. 2007. Separate neural substrates for skill learning and performance in the ventral and dorsal striatum. *Nat. Neurosci.* 10:126–31

Avni-Babad D. 2011. Routine and feelings of safety, confidence, and well-being. *Br. J. Psychol.* 102:223–44

Baldwin AS, Rothman AJ, Hertel AW, Linde JA, Jeffery RW, et al. 2006. Specifying the determinants of the initiation and maintenance of behavior change: an examination of self-efficacy, satisfaction, and smoking cessation. *Health Psychol.* 25:626–34

Balleine BW, O'Doherty JP. 2010. Human and rodent homologies in action control: corticostriatal determinants of goal-directed and habitual action. *Neuropsychopharmacology* 35:48–69

Bayley PJ, Frascino JC, Squire LR. 2005. Robust habit learning in the absence of awareness and independent of the medial temporal lobe. *Nature* 436:550–53

Bem DJ. 1972. Constructing cross-situational consistencies in behavior: some thoughts on Alker's critique of Mischel. *J. Personal.* 40:17–26

Berridge KC. 2007. The debate over dopamine's role in reward: the case for incentive salience. *Psychopharmacology* 191:391–431

Betsch T, Haberstroh S, Glöckner A, Haar T, Fiedler K. 2001. The effects of routine strength on adaptation and information search in recurrent decision making. *Organ. Behav. Hum. Decis. Process.* 84:23–53

Botvinick MM, Bylsma LM. 2005. Distraction and action slips in an everyday task: evidence for a dynamic representation of task context. *Psychol. Bull. Rev.* 12:1011–17

Botvinick MM, Niv Y, Barto AC. 2009. Hierarchically organized behavior and its neural foundations: a reinforcement learning perspective. *Cognition* 113:262–80

Botvinick MM, Plaut DC. 2004. Doing without schema hierarchies: a recurrent connectionist approach to normal and impaired routine sequential action. *Psychol. Rev.* 111:395–429

Botvinick MM, Weinstein A. 2014. Model-based hierarchical reinforcement learning and human action control. *Philos. Trans. R. Soc. B* 369:20130480

Bouton ME, Todd TP, Vurbic D, Winterbauer NE. 2011. Renewal after the extinction of free operant behavior. *Learn. Behav.* 39:57–67

Burns RJ, Donovan AS, Ackermann RT, Finch EA, Rothman AJ, Jeffery RW. 2012. A theoretically grounded systematic review of material incentives for weight loss: implications for interventions. *Ann. Behav. Med.* 44:375–88

Burton AC, Nakamura K, Roesch MR. 2015. From ventral-medial to dorsal-lateral striatum: neural correlates of reward-guided decision-making. *Neurobiol. Learn. Mem.* 117:51–59

Carels RA, Burmeister JM, Koball AM, Oehlhof MW, Hinman N, et al. 2014. A randomized trial comparing two approaches to weight loss: differences in weight loss maintenance. *J. Health Psychol.* 19:296–311

Colwill RM, Rescorla RA. 1985. Postconditioning devaluation of a reinforcer affects instrumental responding. *J. Exp. Psychol.: Anim. Behav. Process.* 11:120–32

Cooper RP, Ruh N, Mareschal D. 2014. The goal circuit model: a hierarchical multi-route model of the acquisition and control of routine sequential action in humans. *Cogn. Sci.* 38:244–74

Danner UN, Vries NK, Aarts H. 2007. Habit formation and multiple means to goal attainment: Repeated retrieval of target means causes inhibited access to competitors. *Personal. Soc. Psychol. Bull.* 33:1367–79

Daw ND, Gershman SJ, Seymour B, Dayan P, Dolan RJ. 2011. Model-based influences on humans' choices and striatal prediction errors. *Neuron* 69:1204–15

Daw ND, Niv Y, Dayan P. 2005. Uncertainty-based competition between prefrontal and dorsolateral striatal systems for behavioral control. *Nat. Neurosci.* 8:1704–11

de Ridder DTD, Lensvelt-Mulders G, Finkenauer C, Stok FM, Baumeister RF. 2012. Taking stock of self-control: a meta-analysis of how trait self-control relates to a wide range of behaviors. *Personal. Soc. Psychol. Rev.* 16:76–99

de Wit S, Corlett PR, Fletcher PC, Dickinson A, Aitken MR. 2009. Differential engagement of the ventromedial prefrontal cortex by goal-directed and habitual behavior toward food pictures in humans. *J. Neurosci.* 29:11330–38

de Wit S, Dickinson A. 2009. Associative theories of goal-directed behaviour: a case for animal-human translational models. *Psychol. Res.* 73:463–76

de Wit S, van de Vijver I, Ridderinkhof KR. 2014. Impaired acquisition of goal-directed action in healthy aging. *Cogn. Affect. Behav. Neurosci.* 14:647–58

Desmurget M, Turner RS. 2010. Motor sequences and the basal ganglia: kinematics, not habits. *J. Neurosci.* 30:7685–90

Dezfouli A, Balleine BW. 2012. Habits, action sequences and reinforcement learning. *Eur. J. Neurosci.* 35:1036–51

Dezfouli A, Balleine BW. 2013. Actions, action sequences and habits: evidence that goal-directed and habitual action control are hierarchically organized. *PLOS Comp. Biol.* 9:e1003364

Dezfouli A, Lingawi NW, Balleine BW. 2014. Habits as action sequences: hierarchical action control and changes in outcome value. *Philos. Trans. R. Soc. B* 369:20130482

Dias-Ferreira E, Sousa JC, Melo I, Morgado P, Cerqueira JJ. 2009. Chronic stress causes frontostriatal reorganization and affects decision-making. *Science* 325:621–25

Dickinson A. 1985. Actions and habits: the development of behavioural autonomy. *Philos. Trans. R. Soc. B* 308:67–78

Dolan RJ, Dayan P. 2013. Goals and habits in the brain. *Neuron* 80:312–25

Doll BB, Simon DA, Daw ND. 2012. The ubiquity of model-based reinforcement learning. *Curr. Opin. Neurobiol.* 22:1075–81

Duhig C. 2012. *The Power of Habit: Why We Do What We Do in Life and Business.* New York: Random House

Evans J, Stanovich KE. 2013. Dual-process theories of higher cognition advancing the debate. *Perspect. Psychol. Sci.* 8:223–41

Everitt BJ. 2014. Neural and psychological mechanisms underlying compulsive drug seeking habits and drug memories—indications for novel treatments of addiction. *Eur. J. Neurosci.* 40:2163–82

Everitt BJ, Robbins TW. 2005. Neural systems of reinforcement for drug addiction: from actions to habits to compulsion. *Nat. Neurosci.* 8:1481–89

Faure A, Haberland U, Condé F, El Massioui N. 2005. Lesion to the nigrostriatal dopamine system disrupts stimulus-response habit formation. *J. Neurosci.* 25:2771–80

FitzGerald THB, Dolan RJ, Friston KJ. 2014. Model averaging, optimal inference, and habit formation. *Front. Hum. Neurosci.* 8:457

Foerde K, Knowlton BJ, Poldrack RA. 2006. Modulation of competing memory systems by distraction. *PNAS* 103:11778–83

Friedel E, Koch SP, Wendt J, Heinz A, Deserno L, Schlagenhauf F. 2014. Devaluation and sequential decisions: linking goal-directed and model-based behavior. *Front. Hum. Neurosci.* 8:587

Galla BM, Duckworth AL. 2015. More than resisting temptation: Beneficial habits mediate the relationship between self-control and positive life outcomes. *J. Personal. Soc. Psychol.* 109:508–25

Gardner B. 2015. A review and analysis of the use of "habit" in understanding, predicting and influencing health-related behaviour. *Health Psychol. Rev.* 9:277–95

Gardner B, Abraham C, Lally P, de Bruijn GJ. 2012. Towards parsimony in habit measurement: testing the convergent and predictive validity of an automaticity subscale of the Self-Report Habit Index. *Int. J. Behav. Nutr. Phys. Act.* 9:102

Gardner B, de Bruijn GJ, Lally P. 2011. A systematic review and meta-analysis of applications of the Self-Report Habit Index to nutrition and physical activity behaviours. *Ann. Behav. Med.* 42:174–87

Gardner B, Sheals K, Wardle J, McGowan L. 2014. Putting habit into practice, and practice into habit: a process evaluation and exploration of the acceptability of a habit-based dietary behaviour change intervention. *Int. J. Behav. Nutr. Phys. Act.* 11:135

Gershman SJ, Markman AB, Otto AR. 2014. Retrospective revaluation in sequential decision making: a tale of two systems. *J. Exp. Psychol.: Gen.* 143:182–94

Gillan CM, Otto AR, Phelps EA, Daw ND. 2015. Model-based learning protects against forming habits. *Cogn. Affect. Behav. Neurosci.* 15:523–36

Gillan CM, Robbins TW. 2014. Goal-directed learning and obsessive-compulsive disorder. *Philos. Trans. R. Soc. B* 369:20130475

Gollwitzer PM, Brandstätter V. 1997. Implementation intentions and effective goal pursuit. *J. Personal. Soc. Psychol.* 73:186–99

Gollwitzer PM, Sheeran P. 2006. Implementation intentions and goal achievement: a meta-analysis of effects and processes. In *Advances in Experimental Social Psychology*, Vol. 38, ed. MP Zanna, pp. 69–119. San Diego, CA: Elsevier

Graybiel AM. 1998. The basal ganglia and chunking of action repertoires. *Neurobiol. Learn. Mem.* 70:119–36

Gremel CM, Costa RM. 2013. Orbitofrontal and striatal circuits dynamically encode the shift between goal-directed and habitual actions. *Nat. Commun.* 4:2264

Guenzel FM, Wolf OT, Schwabe L. 2014a. Glucocorticoids boost stimulus-response memory formation in humans. *Psychoneuroendocrinology* 45:21–30

Guenzel FM, Wolf OT, Schwabe L. 2014b. Sex differences in stress effects on response and spatial memory formation. *Neurobiol. Learn. Mem.* 109:46–55

Haber SN, Fudge JL, McFarland NR. 2000. Striatonigrostriatal pathways in primates form an ascending spiral from the shell to the dorsolateral striatum. *J. Neurosci.* 20:2369–82

Hay JF, Jacoby LL. 1996. Separating habit and recollection: memory slips, process dissociations, and probability matching. *J. Exp. Psychol.: Learn. Mem. Cogn.* 22:1323–35

Hofmann W, Baumeister RF, Förster G, Vohs KD. 2012. Everyday temptations: an experience sampling study of desire, conflict, and self-control. *J. Personal. Soc. Psychol.* 102:1318–35

Hogarth L, Attwood AS, Bate HA, Munafò MR. 2012a. Acute alcohol impairs human goal-directed action. *Biol. Psychol.* 90:154–60

Hogarth L, Balleine BW, Corbit LH, Killcross S. 2013. Associative learning mechanisms underpinning the transition from recreational drug use to addiction. *Ann. NY Acad. Sci.* 1282:12–24

Hogarth L, Chase HW, Baess K. 2012b. Impaired goal-directed behavioural control in human impulsivity. *Q. J. Exp. Psychol.* 65:305–16

Holland PC. 2004. Relations between Pavlovian-instrumental transfer and reinforcer devaluation. *J. Exp. Psychol.: Anim. Behav. Proc.* 30:104–17

Hommel B. 2009. Action control according to TEC (theory of event coding). *Psychol. Res.* 73:512–26

Hull CL. 1943. *Principles of Behavior: An Introduction to Behavior Theory.* New York: Appleton-Century

James W. 1890. *The Principles of Psychology.* New York: H. Holt

Ji MF, Wood W. 2007. Purchase and consumption habits: not necessarily what you intend. *J. Consum. Psychol.* 17:261–76

Judah G, Gardner B, Aunger R. 2013. Forming a flossing habit: an exploratory study of the psychological determinants of habit formation. *Br. J. Health Psychol.* 18:338–53

Kaushal N, Rhodes RE. 2015. Exercise habit formation in new gym members: a longitudinal study. *J. Behav. Med.* 38:652–63

Keramati M, Dezfouli A, Piray P. 2011. Speed/accuracy trade-off between the habitual and the goal-directed processes. *PLOS Comp. Biol.* 7:e1002055

Khare A, Inman JJ. 2006. Habitual behavior in American eating patterns: the role of meal occasions. *J. Consum. Res.* 32:567–75

Killcross S, Coutureau E. 2003. Coordination of actions and habits in the medial prefrontal cortex of rats. *Cereb. Cortex* 13:400–8

Labrecque JS, Wood W. 2015. What measures of habit strength to use? Comment on Gardner 2014. *Health Psychol. Rev.* 9:303–10

Lally P, Chipperfield A, Wardle J. 2008. Healthy habits: efficacy of simple advice on weight control based on a habit-formation model. *Int. J. Obes.* 32:700–7

Lally P, Gardner B. 2013. Promoting habit formation. *Health Psychol. Rev.* 7:S137–58

Lally P, Van Jaarsveld CHM, Potts HWW, Wardle J. 2010. How are habits formed: modelling habit formation in the real world. *Eur. J. Neurosci.* 40:998–1009

Lee SW, Shimojo S, O'Doherty JP. 2014. Neural computations underlying arbitration between model-based and model-free learning. *Neuron* 81:687–99

Lehéricy S, Benali H, Van de Moortele PF, Pélégrini-Issac M, Waechter T, et al. 2005. Distinct basal ganglia territories are engaged in early and advanced motor sequence learning. *PNAS* 102:12566–71

Liljeholm M, Dunne S, O'Doherty JP. 2015. Differentiating neural systems mediating the acquisition versus expression of goal-directed and habitual behavioral control. *Eur. J. Neurosci.* 41:1358–71

Lingawi NW, Balleine BW. 2012. Amygdala central nucleus interacts with dorsolateral striatum to regulate the acquisition of habits. *J. Neurosci.* 32:1073–81

Liu JL, Han B, Cohen DA. 2015. Associations between eating occasions and places of consumption among adults. *Appetite* 87:199–204

Lungu OL, Monchi O, Albouy G, Jubault T, Ballarin E, et al. 2014. Striatal and hippocampal involvement in motor sequence chunking depends on the learning strategy. *PLOS ONE* 9:e103885

Maher JP, Conroy DE. 2015. Habit strength moderates the effects of daily action planning prompts on physical activity but not sedentary behavior. *J. Sport Exerc. Psychol.* 37:97–107

Marchette SA, Bakker A, Shelton AL. 2011. Cognitive mappers to creatures of habit: differential engagement of place and response learning mechanisms predicts human navigational behavior. *J. Neurosci.* 31:15264–68

Marteau TM, Hollands GJ, Fletcher PC. 2012. Changing human behavior to prevent disease: the importance of targeting automatic processes. *Science* 337:1492–95

Miller GA, Galanter E, Pribram KH. 1960. *Plans and the Structure of Behavior.* New York: Holt, Rinehart, & Winston

Murray KB, Häubl G. 2007. Explaining cognitive lock-in: the role of skill-based habits of use in consumer choice. *J. Consum. Res.* 34:77–88

Neal DT, Wood W, Drolet A. 2013. How do people adhere to goals when willpower is low? The profits (and pitfalls) of strong habits. *J. Personal. Soc. Psychol.* 104:959–75

Neal DT, Wood W, Labrecque JS, Lally P. 2012. How do habits guide behavior? Perceived and actual triggers of habits in daily life. *J. Exp. Soc. Psychol.* 48:492–98

Neal DT, Wood W, Wu M, Kurlander D. 2011. The pull of the past: When do habits persist despite conflict with motives? *Personal. Soc. Psychol. Bull.* 37:1428–37

Newell A. 1990. *Unified Theories of Cognition.* Cambridge, MA: Harvard Univ. Press

Norman DA. 1981. Categorization of action slips. *Psychol. Rev.* 88:1–15

Orbell S, Verplanken B. 2010. The automatic component of habit in health behavior: habit as cue-contingent automaticity. *Health Psychol.* 29:374–83

Ostlund SB, Maidment NT, Balleine BW. 2010. Alcohol-paired contextual cues produce an immediate and selective loss of goal-directed action in rats. *Front. Integr. Neurosci.* 4:19

Otto AR, Gershman SJ, Markman AB, Daw ND. 2013a. The curse of planning: dissecting multiple reinforcement-learning systems by taxing the central executive. *Psychol. Sci.* 24:751–61

Otto AR, Raio CM, Chiang A. 2013b. Working-memory capacity protects model-based learning from stress. *PNAS* 52:20941–46

Otto AR, Skatova A, Madlon-Kay S, Daw ND. 2015. Cognitive control predicts use of model-based reinforcement learning. *J. Cogn. Neurosci.* 27:319–33

Ouellette JA, Wood W. 1998. Habit and intention in everyday life: the multiple processes by which past behavior predicts future behavior. *Psychol. Bull.* 124:54–74

Packard MG, Goodman J. 2013. Factors that influence the relative use of multiple memory systems. *Hippocampus* 23:1044–52

Patsenko EG, Altmann EM. 2010. How planful is routine behavior? A selective-attention model of performance in the Tower of Hanoi. *J. Exp. Psychol.: Gen.* 139:95–116

Penhune VB, Steele CJ. 2012. Parallel contributions of cerebellar, striatal and M1 mechanisms to motor sequence learning. *Behav. Brain Res.* 226:579–91

Pezzulo G, Rigoli F, Chersi F. 2013. The mixed instrumental controller: using value of information to combine habitual choice and mental simulation. *Front. Psychol.* 4:92

Quinn JM, Pascoe A, Wood W, Neal DT. 2010. Can't control yourself? Monitor those bad habits. *Personal. Soc. Psychol. Bull.* 36:499–511

Radenbach C, Reiter AMF, Engert V, Sjoerds Z, Villringer A, et al. 2015. The interaction of acute and chronic stress impairs model-based behavioral control. *Psychoneuroendocrinology* 53:268–80

Reason JT. 1979. Actions not as planned: the price of automatization. In *Aspects of Consciousness*, ed. G Underwood, R Stevens, pp. 67–89. London: Academic

Rebar AL, Elavsky S, Maher JP, Doerksen SE, Conroy DE. 2014. Habits predict physical activity on days when intentions are weak. *J. Sport Exerc. Psychol.* 36:157–65

Reber R, Schwarz N, Winkielman P. 2004. Processing fluency and aesthetic pleasure: Is beauty in the perceiver's processing experience? *Personal. Soc. Psychol. Rev.* 8:364–82

Redish AD, Jensen S, Johnson A. 2008. A unified framework for addiction: vulnerabilities in the decision process. *Behav. Brain Sci.* 31:415–37

Rothman AJ, Gollwitzer PM, Grant AM, Neal DT, Sheeran P, Wood W. 2015. Hale and hearty policies: how psychological science can create and maintain healthy habits. *Perspect. Psychol. Sci.* In press

Rubin G. 2015. *Better than Before*. New York: Random House

Ruh N, Cooper RP, Mareschal D. 2010. Action selection in complex routinized sequential behaviors. *J. Exp. Psychol.: Hum. Percept. Perform.* 36:955–75

Rünger D, Wood W. 2015. Maintenance of healthy behaviors: forming and changing habits. In *Behavioral Economics and Public Health*, ed. C Roberto, I Kawachi. Oxford, UK: Oxford Univ. Press. In press

Schwabe L, Tegenthoff M, Höffken O, Wolf OT. 2012. Simultaneous glucocorticoid and noradrenergic activity disrupts the neural basis of goal-directed action in the human brain. *J. Neurosci.* 32:10146–55

Schwabe L, Wolf OT. 2010. Socially evaluated cold pressor stress after instrumental learning favors habits over goal-directed action. *Psychoneuroendocrinology* 35:977–86

Schwabe L, Wolf OT. 2012. Stress modulates the engagement of multiple memory systems in classification learning. *J. Neurosci.* 32:11042–49

Schwabe L, Wolf OT. 2013. Stress and multiple memory systems: from "thinking" to "doing." *Trends Cogn. Sci.* 17:60–68

Seger CA, Spiering BJ. 2011. A critical review of habit learning and the basal ganglia. *Front. Syst. Neurosci.* 5:1–9

Sheeran P, Webb TL, Gollwitzer PM. 2005. The interplay between goal intentions and implementation intentions. *Personal. Soc. Psychol. Bull.* 31:87–98

Shiffrin RM, Schneider W. 1977. Controlled and automatic human information processing: II. Perceptual learning, automatic attending and a general theory. *Psychol. Rev.* 84:127–90

Sjoerds Z, de Wit S, van den Brink W, Robbins TW, Beekman ATF, et al. 2013. Behavioral and neuroimaging evidence for overreliance on habit learning in alcohol-dependent patients. *Transl. Psychiatry* 3:e337

Skinner BF. 1938. *The Behavior of Organisms*. New York: Appleton-Century-Crofts

Smith KS, Graybiel AM. 2013. A dual operator view of habitual behavior reflecting cortical and striatal dynamics. *Neuron* 79:361–74

Sobal J, Wansink B. 2007. Kitchenscapes, tablescapes, platescapes, and foodscapes: influences of microscale built environments on food intake. *Environ. Behav.* 39:124–42

Squire LR, Zola-Morgan S. 1991. The medial temporal lobe memory system. *Science* 253:1380–86

Stawarz K, Cox AL, Blandford A. 2015. Beyond self-tracking and reminders: designing smartphone apps that support habit formation. In *Proc. 33rd annu. ACM Conf. Hum. Factors Comput.*, pp. 2653–62. New York: ACM

Steele CJ, Penhune VB. 2010. Specific increases within global decreases: a functional magnetic resonance imaging investigation of five days of motor sequence learning. *J. Neurosci.* 30:8332–41

Sun R, Merrill E, Peterson T. 2001. From implicit skills to explicit knowledge: a bottom-up model of skill learning. *Cogn. Sci.* 25:203–44

Taatgen NA, Huss D, Dickison D, Anderson JR. 2008. The acquisition of robust and flexible cognitive skills. *J. Exp. Psychol.: Gen.* 137:548–65

Tappe K, Tarves E, Oltarzewski J, Frum D. 2013. Habit formation among regular exercisers at fitness centers: an exploratory study. *J. Phys. Act. Health* 10:607–13

Thøgersen J. 2012. The importance of timing for breaking commuters' car driving habits. *Collegium* 12:130–40

Thorndike EL. 1898. Animal intelligence: an experimental study of the associative processes in animals. *Psychol. Monogr. Gen. Appl.* 2:1–109

Thrailkill EA, Bouton ME. 2015. Contextual control of instrumental actions and habits. *J. Exp. Psychol.: Anim. Learn. Cogn.* 41:69–80

Tobias R. 2009. Changing behavior by memory aids: a social psychological model of prospective memory and habit development tested with dynamic field data. *Psychol. Rev.* 116:408–38

Tolman EC. 1948. Cognitive maps in rats and men. *Psychol. Rev.* 55:189–208

Triandis HC. 1977. *Interpersonal Behavior*. Monterey, CA: Brooks/Cole Publ.

Tricomi E, Balleine BW, O'Doherty JP. 2009. A specific role for posterior dorsolateral striatum in human habit learning. *Eur. J. Neurosci.* 29:2225–32

Valentin VV, Dickinson A, O'Doherty JP. 2007. Determining the neural substrates of goal-directed learning in the human brain. *J. Neurosci.* 27:4019–26

Verplanken B, Aarts H. 1999. Habit, attitude, and planned behaviour: Is habit an empty construct or an interesting case of goal-directed automaticity? *Eur. Rev. Soc. Psychol.* 10:101–34

Verplanken B, Aarts H, Van Knippenberg A. 1997. Habit, information acquisition, and the process of making travel mode choices. *Eur. J. Soc. Psychol.* 27:539–60

Verplanken B, Orbell S. 2003. Reflections on past behavior: a self-report index of habit strength. *J. Appl. Soc. Psychol.* 33:1313–30

Verplanken B, Walker I, Davis A, Jurasek M. 2008. Context change and travel mode choice: combining the habit discontinuity and self-activation hypotheses. *J. Environ. Psychol.* 28:121–27

Vishwanath A. 2015. Examining the distinct antecedents of e-mail habits and its influence on the outcomes of a phishing attack. *J. Comput. -Mediat. Commun.* doi: 10.1111/jcc4.12126

Vohs KD, Baumeister RF, Ciarocco NJ. 2005. Self-regulation and self-presentation: regulatory resource depletion impairs impression management and effortful self-presentation depletes regulatory resources. *J. Personal. Soc. Psychol.* 88:632–57

Voon V, Derbyshire K, Rück C, Irvine MA, Worbe Y, et al. 2015. Disorders of compulsivity: a common bias towards learning habits. *Mol. Psychiatry* 20:345–52

Walker I, Thomas GO, Verplanken B. 2014. Old habits die hard: travel habit formation and decay during an office relocation. *Environ. Behav.* doi: 10.1177/0013916514549619

Wansink B, Payne CR. 2012. Eating behavior and obesity at Chinese buffets. *Obesity* 16:1957–60

Wason PC, Evans J. 1975. Dual processes in reasoning? *Cognition* 3:141–54

Webb TL, Sheeran P. 2006. Does changing behavioral intentions engender behavior change? A meta-analysis of the experimental evidence. *Psychol. Bull.* 132:249–68

Webb TL, Sheeran P, Luszczynska A. 2009. Planning to break unwanted habits: Habit strength moderates implementation intention effects on behaviour change. *Br. J. Soc. Psychol.* 48:507–23

Wise RA. 2004. Dopamine, learning and motivation. *Nat. Rev. Neurosci.* 5:483–94

Wood W, Labrecque JS, Lin PY, Rünger D. 2014. Habits in dual process models. In *Dual Process Theories of the Social Mind*, ed. JW Sherman, B Gawronski, Y Trope, pp. 371–85. New York: Guilford

Wood W, Neal DT. 2007. A new look at habits and the habit-goal interface. *Psychol. Rev.* 114:843–63

Wood W, Neal DT. 2009. The habitual consumer. *J. Consum. Psychol.* 19:579–92

Wood W, Quinn JM, Kashy DA. 2002. Habits in everyday life: thought, emotion, and action. *J. Personal. Soc. Psychol.* 83:1281–87

Wood W, Tam L, Witt MG. 2005. Changing circumstances, disrupting habits. *J. Personal. Soc. Psychol.* 88:918–33

Wunderlich K, Dayan P, Dolan RJ. 2012. Mapping value based planning and extensively trained choice in the human brain. *Nat. Neurosci.* 15:786–91

Wymbs NF, Grafton ST. 2014. The human motor system supports sequence-specific representations over multiple training-dependent timescales. *Cereb. Cortex.* doi: 10.1093/cercor/bhu144

Yin HH, Knowlton BJ. 2006. The role of the basal ganglia in habit formation. *Nat. Rev. Neurosci.* 7:464–76

Yin HH, Knowlton BJ, Balleine BW. 2004. Lesions of dorsolateral striatum preserve outcome expectancy but disrupt habit formation in instrumental learning. *Eur. J. Neurosci.* 19:181–89

Yin HH, Knowlton BJ, Balleine BW. 2006. Inactivation of dorsolateral striatum enhances sensitivity to changes in the action-outcome contingency in instrumental conditioning. *Behav. Brain Res.* 166:189–96

Yin HH, Ostlund SB, Knowlton BJ, Balleine BW. 2005. The role of the dorsomedial striatum in instrumental conditioning. *Eur. J. Neurosci.* 22:513–23

Zapata A, Minney VL, Shippenberg TS. 2010. Shift from goal-directed to habitual cocaine seeking after prolonged experience in rats. *J. Neurosci.* 30:15457–63

Media Effects: Theory and Research

Patti M. Valkenburg,[1] Jochen Peter,[1]
and Joseph B. Walther[2]

[1]Amsterdam School of Communication Research, University of Amsterdam,
Amsterdam 1012 WX, The Netherlands; email: p.m.valkenburg@uva.nl, j.peter@uva.nl

[2]Wee Kim Wee School of Communication and Information, Nanyang Technological
University, 637718 Singapore; email: jwalther@ntu.edu.sg

Annu. Rev. Psychol. 2016. 67:315–38

First published online as a Review in Advance on
August 19, 2015

The *Annual Review of Psychology* is online at
psych.annualreviews.org

This article's doi:
10.1146/annurev-psych-122414-033608

Keywords

media effects theory, selective exposure, media violence, computer-
mediated communication (CMC), mass communication, mass media,
meta-analysis

Abstract

This review analyzes trends and commonalities among prominent theories
of media effects. On the basis of exemplary meta-analyses of media effects and
bibliometric studies of well-cited theories, we identify and discuss five features of media effects theories as well as their empirical support. Each of these
features specifies the conditions under which media may produce effects on
certain types of individuals. Our review ends with a discussion of media
effects in newer media environments. This includes theories of computer-
mediated communication, the development of which appears to share a similar pattern of reformulation from unidirectional, receiver-oriented views,
to theories that recognize the transactional nature of communication. We
conclude by outlining challenges and promising avenues for future research.

Contents

INTRODUCTION

Research on the effects of media originated under the umbrella term "mass communication research." The last five reviews on the effects of media that appeared in the *Annual Review of Psychology* include the word "mass" in their titles (Liebert & Schwartzberg 1977, Roberts & Bachen 1981, Schramm 1962, Tannenbaum & Greenberg 1968, Weiss 1971). The concept of mass communication arose during the 1920s as a response to new opportunities to reach large audiences via the mass media: newspapers, radio, and film (McQuail 2010). However, "mass" refers not only to the size of the audience that mass media reach, but also to uniform consumption, uniform impacts, and anonymity, notions that are progressively incompatible with contemporary media use.

Since the 1980s, media use has become increasingly individualized and, with the advent of the Internet, has also taken a decidedly personalized character. This increase in individualization and personalization of media use has enabled a form of communication that Castells (2007) has called mass self-communication. Mass self-communication shares with mass communication the notions that messages are transmitted to potentially large audiences and that the reception of media content is self-selected: Media users select media content to serve their own needs, regardless of whether those needs match the intent of the generator of the content (McQuail 2010). However, whereas mass communication research focuses only on media reception processes, mass self-communication focuses on media reception and generation processes and, thus, on the effects of media generation on the generators themselves (Castells 2007).

The current coexistence of mass communication (e.g., via newspapers, radio, and television) with mass self-communication (e.g., via social media) is reflected in the structure and content of this article. The aim of this review is to assess the most important media effects theories that have emerged in the past four decades and to chart the development of media effects thinking from its roots in assumptions about unidirectional effects to contemporary recognition of complex reciprocal interactions. To do so, we do not aim to discuss each of the theories of media effects that has emerged successively. Instead, we start with a brief overview of approaches and their summary by way of several exemplary meta-analyses of media effects. We then organize our review around five important features of media effects theories, including their analytic implications

Media use: the intended or incidental selection of media types (e.g., TV, video games, the Internet), content (e.g., entertainment, advertising, news), and technologies (e.g., social media)

Media effects: the deliberate and nondeliberate short- and long-term within-person changes in cognitions (including beliefs), emotions, attitudes, and behavior that result from media use

and empirical support. Subsequently, we describe the effects of mass self-communication in the newer media environment. We briefly discuss the historical development of theories of computer-mediated communication (CMC), including the state of present-day CMC theories and research. We conclude by outlining challenges and promising avenues for future research.

Meta-Analyses of Media Effects

Research on the effects of media emerged between the 1920s and 1930s, but it became a prominent focus only at the end of the 1950s, after the introduction of television and the emergence of academic communication departments in Europe and the United States (but see Hovland et al. 1953, Katz & Lazarsfeld 1955, Lazarsfeld et al. 1948). These developments generated a proliferation of media effects theories and research, albeit initially—as in other social science disciplines—at a fairly basic level. By the 1980s, thousands of empirical studies had been published investigating the cognitive, emotional, attitudinal, and behavioral effects of media on children and adults (Potter 2012, Potter & Riddle 2007). Moreover, since the 1990s, a sizeable number of meta-analyses have synthesized the results of these empirical studies. **Table 1** presents a list of 20 examples of meta-analyses on media effects that have appeared in the past two decades. These meta-analyses were selected because together they cover the broad plenitude of media effects that have been investigated since the 1960s, ranging from the effects of exposure to media violence on aggression and of advertising on purchase behavior, to the effects of Internet use on political engagement and of Facebook use on loneliness.

Meta-analyses of media effects have typically yielded small to moderate effect sizes that lie between $r = 0.10$ and $r = 0.20$, with some deviations. For example, as **Table 1** shows, meta-analyses of the effects of violent computer games on aggressive behavior have reported effect sizes of $r = 0.08$ (Ferguson & Kilburn 2009), $r = 0.15$ (Sherry 2001), and $r = 0.19$ (Anderson & Bushman 2001, Anderson et al. 2010). Meta-analyses of the effects of health campaigns on health behavior have yielded effects sizes between $r = 0.04$ and $r = 0.15$ (Snyder et al. 2004), and those of the effects of media use on body dissatisfaction between $r = 0.08$ (Holmstrom 2004) and $r = 0.14$ (Grabe et al. 2008).

Although small to medium effect sizes are common in many disciplines (Valkenburg & Peter 2013b), several researchers have argued that the small media effects reported defy common sense because everyday experience offers many anecdotal examples of strong media effects (e.g., McGuire 1986). For example, even though a recent meta-analysis of studies into the effects of fear-provoking media on children's fright reactions yielded a small to moderate average effect on fear and anxiety ($r = 0.18$; Pearce & Field 2015), severe media-induced emotional reactions around the clinical threshold have been observed in small subgroups of children.

Such discrepancies in results are less contradictory than they seem at first sight. They suggest that there are strong individual differences in susceptibility to media effects. Meta-analyses of media effects typically focus on main effects or group-level moderator effects. As a result, they do not highlight more subtle yet potent individual differences (Pearce & Field 2015). In the past four decades, media effects theories have tried to specify the conditions under which media produce effects on certain individuals. There are several explanations of why media effects are limited when observed in large heterogeneous groups. These explanations are grounded in five specific features of media effects theories. Four of these features were identified earlier by Valkenburg & Peter (2013a), albeit in less detail. This review both complements and extends the Valkenburg & Peter analysis by adding more evidence and seeking parallels between the mass communication and mass self-communication literature.

Table 1 Exemplary meta-analyses of media effects

Study	Type of media use	Outcome	r
1. Wood et al. (1991)	Media violence	Aggression	0.13[a]
2. Paik & Comstock (1994)	Media violence	Antisocial behavior	0.31
3. Allen et al. (1995)	Exposure to nudity	Aggression	−0.14
	Violent pornography	Aggression	0.22
4. Anderson & Bushman (2001)	Video game use	Aggression	0.19
		Prosocial behavior	−0.16
5. Sherry (2001)	Violent video game use	Aggression	0.15
6. Snyder et al. (2004)	Health campaigns	Seat belt use	0.15
		Alcohol consumption	0.09
		Smoking	0.05
7. Marshall et al. (2004)	Television viewing	Fatness/physical activity	0.08/−0.13
	Video game use	Fatness/physical activity	0.13/−0.14
8. Mares & Woodard (2005)	Child use of positive media	Positive interaction	0.24
		Altruism	0.37
		Stereotype reduction	0.20
9. Wellman et al. (2006)	Tobacco use in media	Attitudes toward smoking	0.11[a]
		Smoking initiation	0.22
10. Desmond & Garveth (2007)	Exposure to advertising	Brand attitude	0.15
		Product selection	0.15
11. Barlett et al. (2008)	Media use	Male body esteem	−0.11
		Male body satisfaction	−0.10
12. Grabe et al. (2008)	Media use	Body satisfaction	−0.14
		Internalization of thin ideal	−0.19
		Eating behaviors/beliefs	−0.15
13. Savage & Yancey (2008)	Media violence/panel studies	Criminal aggression	0.12
	Media violence/experiment studies	Criminal aggression	0.06
14. Ferguson & Kilburn (2009)	Media violence	Aggression	0.08
15. Boulianne (2009)	Internet use	Political engagement	0.07
	Online news use	Political engagement	0.13
16. Anderson et al. (2010)	Video games	Aggression	0.19
17. Powers et al. (2013)	Video games (quasi/true experiments)	Spatial imagery	0.13/0.21[a]
		Executive function	0.21/0.08
18. Nikkelen et al. (2014)	Media use/media violence	ADHD-related behaviors	0.12/0.12
19. Song et al. (2014)	Facebook use	Loneliness	0.17
20. Pearce & Field (2015)	Exposure to scary television	Fear/anxiety	0.18

[a]Differing effect sizes (e.g., odds ratio, Cohen's *d*) were transformed to correlations (*r*).
Abbreviation: ADHD, attention-deficit/hyperactivity disorder.

FIVE FEATURES OF MEDIA EFFECTS THEORIES

The focus of this review is on micro-level media effects theories. Several bibliographic analyses have tried to document the state of the art of both micro- and macro-level media effects theories in the scholarly journals (Bryant & Miron 2004, Potter 2012, Potter & Riddle 2007). **Table 2** lists the micro-level media effects theories that have been identified as particularly well cited in these bibliographic studies. Valkenburg & Peter (2013a) have recently attempted to organize existing

Table 2 Well-cited micro-level media effects theories

Author(s)	Theory/model	Times cited[a]	Description
Lazarsfeld et al. (1948) Katz and Lazarsfeld (1955)	Two-step flow theory	6,161 4,789	Argues that media effects are indirect rather than direct and established through the personal influence of opinion leaders
Tichenor et al. (1970)	Knowledge gap theory	1,413	Discusses how mass media can increase the gap in knowledge between those of higher and lower socioeconomic status
McCombs & Shaw (1972)	Agenda-setting theory	6,390	Describes how news media can influence the salience of topics on the public agenda
Katz et al. (1973) Rosengren (1974)	Uses-and-gratifications theory	901 481	Attempts to understand why and how people actively seek out specific media to satisfy specific needs
Gerbner et al. (1980)	Cultivation theory	1,297	Argues that the more time people spend "living" in the television world, the more likely they are to believe the social reality portrayed on television
Berkowitz (1984)	Priming theory	677	Argues that media effects depend on the preconceptions that are already stored in human memory
Petty & Cacioppo (1986)	Elaboration likelihood model	5,086	Explains how mediated stimuli are processed (via either the central or peripheral route) and how this processing influences attitude formation or change
Entman (1993) Scheufele (1999)	Framing Framing as a theory of media effects	6,597 2,196	Discusses how the media draw attention to certain topics and place them within a field of meaning (i.e., frame), which in turn influences audience perceptions
Lang (2000)	Limited-capacity model	884	Analyzes how people's limited capacity for information processing affects their memory of, and engagement with, mediated messages
Bandura (2002)	Social cognitive theory of mass communication	1,360	Analyzes the psychological mechanisms through which symbolic communication through mass media influences human thought, affect, and behavior
Slater (2007)[b]	Reinforcing spiral theory	234	Argues that factors close to one's identity act as both a predictor and an outcome of media use

[a]Citations in Google Scholar (April 2015).
[b]Slater's (2007) theory did not show up as a well-cited theory in the bibliographic studies of Bryant & Miron (2004), Potter (2012), and Potter & Riddle (2007), but its citations increased considerably after those publications appeared.

micro-level media effects theories in terms of their basic assumptions. They observed that these theories differ substantially in how they conceptualize the media effects process. Some theories, particularly the earlier ones, focus primarily on unidirectional linear relationships between media use and certain outcomes (e.g., cultivation theory; Gerbner et al. 1980). Other, more comprehensive theories (e.g., Bandura 2009, Slater 2007) pay more attention to the interaction between media factors (media use, media processing) and nonmedia factors (e.g., disposition, social context). The existing media effects theories can be organized along the following five global features that address the relationships between both media factors and nonmedia factors and specify the boundary conditions of media effects.

Micro-level media effects theories: theories that base their observations and conclusions on individual media users rather than on groups, institutions, systems, or society at large

Feature 1: Selectivity of Media Use

A first feature of media effects theories that specifies the boundary conditions of media effects involves the selectivity paradigm. The two propositions of this paradigm are that (*a*) people only attend to a limited number of messages out of the constellation of messages that can potentially attract their attention, and (*b*) only those messages they select have the potential to influence them (Klapper 1960, Knobloch-Westerwick 2015, Rubin 2009). More than 60 years ago, researchers discovered that people do not randomly attend to media but rather focus on certain messages as a result of specific social or psychological needs or beliefs (Katz & Lazarsfeld 1955). For example, in their classic study of the 1940 US presidential election, Lazarsfeld et al. (1948) suggested that people often seek out political content that reinforces their beliefs while they avoid content that was meant to change their opinions. This insight led the researchers to conclude that the power of media to change attitudes or behavior is limited (Klapper 1960, Lazarsfeld et al. 1948).

The selectivity paradigm, so coined in the 1940s, has been further elaborated into two theoretical perspectives: uses-and-gratifications (Katz et al. 1973, Rosengren 1974, Rubin 2009) and selective exposure theory (Knobloch-Westerwick 2015, Zillmann & Bryant 1985). Both the uses-and-gratifications and selective exposure theory postulate that individuals select media in response to their needs or desires and that a variety of psychological and social factors guide and filter this selection. Both theories also propose that media use is a precursor to consequences (named obtained gratifications in uses-and-gratifications theory and media effects in selective exposure theory). An important difference between the two theories is that uses-and-gratifications theory conceptualizes media users as rational and aware of their selection motives, whereas selective exposure theory argues that media users are often not aware of, or at least not fully aware of, their selection motives. This difference in conceptualization of the media user has methodological consequences. For example, in line with the assumption that users can articulate their motives for using media, research based on the uses-and-gratifications theory mainly uses self-reports to gauge media use behavior. In contrast, research based on selective exposure theory typically uses unobtrusive observational methods of users' selective exposure to media (Knobloch-Westerwick 2015).

The selectivity approach emerged in the 1940s as a new paradigm that aimed to show that it is more relevant to investigate "what people do with the media" than "what media do to people" (Katz 1959, p. 2). Most of the early studies within this new paradigm conceptualized media use as the outcome; postexposure processes received less attention. In the past decade, however, the selectivity paradigm has become an integrated part of general media effects theories (e.g., social cognitive theory, Bandura 2009; conditional model of political communication effects, McLeod et al. 2009; reinforcing spiral model, Slater 2007; differential susceptibility to media effects model, Valkenburg & Peter 2013a). For the most part, these theories conceptualize media use as a mediator between antecedents and consequences of media effects. In other words, not the media but rather the media user is the center point in a process that may bring about a change, the media effect. This insight has important implications for media effects research. It means that individuals, by shaping their own selective media use (deliberately or not), also partly shape their own media effects. According to Valkenburg & Peter (2013a), three factors influence selective media use: dispositional, developmental, and social context factors.

Dispositional factors. Dispositions that may lead to selective media use range from more distal and stable factors (e.g., temperament, personality, gender) to more proximal and transient ones (e.g., beliefs, motivations, moods). Distal dispositions such as sensation seeking and trait aggression have been linked to watching violent, sexual, and frightening media; psychoticism (characterized by impulsiveness and nonconformism) to attraction to horror films; and need for cognition to exposure to various mainstream types of news (for reviews, see Knobloch-Westerwick 2006, Krcmar 2009, Oliver & Krakowiak 2009). Finally, women are more likely to watch soap operas, drama, and romance than men are, whereas men are more likely to select sports, horror, and action-adventure than females are (for more evidence, see Knobloch-Westerwick 2015, Oliver et al. 2006, Oliver & Krakowiak 2009).

The evidence of the effects of proximal dispositions on selective exposure is more complex. Since the work of Lazarsfeld et al. (1948) and Klapper (1960), the selectivity paradigm has predominantly been inspired by Festinger's (1957) cognitive dissonance theory, which argues that people typically avoid discomforting cognitive dissonance caused by information that is incompatible with their existing dispositions (e.g., beliefs, attitudes). To avoid or solve this state of dissonance, they may actively seek information that reinforces their dispositions, and they avoid potentially contradictory information that would exacerbate dissonance. However, although there is ample evidence for the notion that individuals seek congenial information (Hart et al. 2009), cognitive dissonance reduction is not as consistent a cause of selective exposure as it was previously assumed to be (Donsbach 2009, Hart et al. 2009, Smith et al. 2007). First, the seeking of congenial information seems to hold more consistently for political than for health messages (Hart et al. 2009, Knobloch-Westerwick 2015). Second, subsequent evidence showed that under specific conditions, people are willing or even eager to attend to uncongenial information, for example, when the perceived utility of information is great, when they are uncommitted to an attitude, or when the reliability of the offered information turns out to be poor (Hart et al. 2009).

In the realm of media entertainment, counterintuitive findings also challenged the consistency assumption. For example, when it comes to fearful and tragic entertainment, people often expose themselves to content that is inconsistent with their moods and existing values and that may even elicit uncomfortable reactions, such as fear and sadness. Several more recent theories have proposed plausible explanations for people's occasional attitude-inconsistent selective exposure to information and entertainment, for example, information-utility theory (Atkin 1973), mood management theory (Zillmann & Bryant 1985), and eudaimonia theory (Oliver 2008).

Developmental factors. As for development, research has shown that individuals typically prefer media content that is only moderately discrepant from their age-related comprehension schemata and experiences (e.g., Valkenburg & Cantor 2001). If they encounter media content that is too discrepant, they will allocate less attention to it or avoid it. This moderate-discrepancy hypothesis explains, for example, why (*a*) toddlers are mostly attracted to media with a slow pace, familiar contexts, and simple characters; (*b*) preschoolers typically choose a faster pace, more adventurous contexts, and more sophisticated characters; and (*c*) adolescents are the most avid users of social media and seek entertainment that presents humor based on taboos and irreverent or risky behavior (Valkenburg & Peter 2013a). Although developmentally related media preferences are most evident in childhood, they also extend to adulthood. For example, in comparison to younger adults, middle-aged and older adults more strongly prefer nonarousing, meaningful, and uplifting media content, whereas younger adults more strongly prefer arousing, violent, and frightening media (Mares et al. 2008, Mares & Sun 2010, Mares & Woodard 2006).

Social context factors. Most media effects theories recognize the importance of social context at the micro, meso, and macro level in encouraging or discouraging media use (Klapper 1960, Prior 2005, Slater 2007). Social influences can occur deliberately and overtly, when institutions, schools, or parents restrict or regulate media use (Nathanson 2001, Webster 2009). On the macro level, structural aspects of the media system (e.g., channel availability) can affect media choices

(Webster 2009), whereas on the micro level, adults can forbid children to watch violent content and encourage them to use educational media (Nathanson 2001).

Social influences can also occur more covertly, through an individual's perception of the prevailing norms in the groups to which they belong (e.g., family, peer clique, subcultures). This more subtle influence has received relatively little attention in the literature. The majority of research has focused on individual antecedents of media use, thereby ignoring the notion that selective media use also operates on the level of social identity (Harwood 1999), the part of our self-concept that we derive from our membership in a social group or groups (Taifel 1978). Selective exposure is most likely to occur when it is perceived to converge with the opinions, values, and norms in the social group(s) to which media users perceive themselves to belong.

People have a strong need to identify with group norms and to bolster their self-esteem by comparing their social identity to the norms and attitudes of relevant outgroups (Taifel & Turner 1979). Media offer individuals many opportunities to develop and maintain their social identities. They can use media to learn about ingroups and outgroups (e.g., age groups, ethnic groups; Harwood 1999). For example, adolescents often watch drama to learn social lessons about how people like themselves flirt or start and end relationships or which types of humor are appropriate (Valkenburg 2014). Hence, it is likely that media provide media users with "social identity gratifications" (Blumler 1985, Harwood 1999).

Feature 2: Media Properties as Predictors

A second feature of media effects theories that may specify the boundary conditions of media effects involves properties of media themselves. Three types of media properties may influence media effects: modality (e.g., text, auditory, visual, audiovisual), content properties (e.g., violence, fearfulness, type of character, argument strength), and structural properties (e.g., special effects, pace, visual surprises).

Modality. Since the early days of mass communication research, it has been common to study the differential effectiveness of modalities for information processing and learning. Marshall McLuhan (1964) is best known for his theory of the differential impact of modalities. By means of his aphorism, "The medium is the message," he argued that media affect individuals and society not by the content delivered but primarily by their modalities. Inspired by McLuhan's theories, a myriad of media comparison studies have tested whether information delivered via auditory or textual modalities encouraged learning, reading skills, or imagination more (or less) than information delivered through audiovisual media (e.g., Beentjes & van der Voort 1988, Greenfield et al. 1986). These media comparison studies largely lost their appeal in the new millennium, probably because they often failed to produce convincing results, especially when it comes to learning (Clark 2012). Many content and structural properties related to the presentation of information (e.g., difficulty, repetition, prompting) turned out to be more important for learning and information processing than modality (Clark 2012).

Due to advances in technology, in the new millennium research interest in the differential effects of media modalities has shifted to, for example, a comparison of the effects of interfaces that differ in their degree of interactivity on engagement, information processing, and learning (Sundar et al. 2015). Media comparison studies also started to focus on the differential effects of reading on paper versus screens (via tablets or e-readers) for learning and information processing (e.g., Mangen et al. 2013, Small et al. 2009). This rapidly growing literature has to date yielded small and inconsistent differences in favor of reading on paper (cf. Mangen et al. 2013, Rockinson-Szapkiw et al. 2013).

Content properties. The contribution of media content to guide selective exposure or to predict media effects has received relatively little attention on both the theoretical and the empirical levels. For example, in an edited book about selective exposure (Hartmann 2009), not a single chapter focused on specific media content that may trigger or enhance the likelihood of selective exposure. Likewise, a comprehensive edited volume on media effects contained no integrating theory on how media content may enhance or constrain media effects (Bryant & Oliver 2009). Although related fields (e.g., cinematography, advertising) have paid more attention to content properties that may attract attention or enhance effects (e.g., Boerman et al. 2011), media effects researchers typically assess the effectiveness of media content/messages from the psychological reactions they elicit (O'Keefe 2003, Slater et al. 2015). For example, in experiments investigating the differential effects of fear-provoking messages, the extent of fearfulness is typically evaluated via pretests or manipulation checks in which subjects' reactions are observed or surveyed (O'Keefe 2003). Such an effect-based approach, however, offers little understanding of the specific content/message properties that have evoked these states in media users.

The complexity faced in formulating a comprehensive theory of content properties that guide selective exposure is particularly challenging because the attractiveness and effectiveness of content are strongly contingent upon individual users or, at best, subtypes of users. After all, what keeps one's attention on media content is the result of a complex and intertwined set of dispositional, developmental, and social context factors. For example, the nature of characters, narratives, contexts, and humor that attract the attention of early adolescents may be unappealing or even distasteful to other age groups. Still, the literature reveals some notions about media content that may guide selective exposure. For example, it has often been found that people pay more attention to negative media content than to positive content, especially when it comes to news (Zillmann et al. 2004). These results are consistent with theories that argue that people are hardwired for attention to danger-conveying stimuli (Shoemaker 1996). People attach more weight to negative information because such information probably contrasts with their baseline positive reactions to social information (Fiske 2002), a phenomenon named the Pollyanna effect (Matlin & Stang 1978). Pratto & John's (1991) work on automatic vigilance, the human tendency to automatically direct more attention to negative than positive stimuli, has sometimes been used to explain individuals' selective exposure to negative news or to sad and frightening entertainment (Knobloch-Westerwick 2015).

Several different media effects theories have proposed content properties that may enhance media effects. For example, Bandura's (2009) social cognitive theory postulates that media depictions of rewarded behavior and attractive media characters enhance the likelihood of media effects. Priming theory (Berkowitz & Powers 1979) predicts that justified violence (i.e., violence portrayed as morally correct) enhances the likelihood of aggressive outcomes. Transportation theory (Green & Brock 2000, Green et al. 2004) and the extended elaboration likelihood model (Slater & Rouner 2002) propose that media messages embedded in engaging narratives lead to increased media effects. And the elaboration likelihood model (Petty & Cacioppo 1986) predicts that argument strength and/or the attractiveness and credibility of the source can enhance persuasive effects. However, despite these scattered attempts, an overarching theory of content properties that may either guide selective exposure or moderate media effects is still largely lacking. What Swanson (1987) observed about uses-and-gratifications theory still holds for the role of content properties in media effects research: "It remains essentially a conception of the audience's mass communication experience in which the role and importance of message content are not well understood" (p. 245).

Structural properties. Research has also identified structural properties of media (e.g., visual surprises, special effects, peculiar sounds) that may trigger our orienting reflex to media; this reflex has been argued to instigate selective exposure (Knobloch-Westerwick 2015). The orienting reflex is our immediate and automatic response to change in our environment, such as a bright flash of light or a sudden noise. It is accompanied by an attentional process that has been called stimulus-driven or transient attention (e.g., Corbetta & Shulman 2002). This type of attention contrasts with goal-directed or sustained attention, which is not driven by stimulus properties but rather is directed by the goals and experiences of the media user him- or herself.

Stimulus-driven automatic attention is already present in infants and is less contingent on audience factors than sustained attention is (Bradley 2009, Valkenburg & Vroone 2004). However, although stimulus-driven automatic attention can instigate selective exposure, it is unlikely a sufficient condition for sustained selective exposure. First, after repeated exposure to a novel or otherwise salient stimulus, people's attention toward it becomes weaker, even if the stimulus is strong (Bradley 2009). Second, selective exposure is primarily guided by the goals and experiences of media users, and hence it is more sensitive than stimulus-driven attention to dispositional, developmental, and social context differences in the media users.

Feature 3: Media Effects Are Indirect

A third feature of many media effects theories that may specify the boundary conditions of media effects is that most media effects are indirect rather than direct (e.g., McLeod et al. 2009, Petty & Cacioppo 1986). An indirect effect is one in which the influence of an independent variable (e.g., media use) on other variables (e.g., outcomes of media use) works via its influence on one or more intervening (mediating) variables. The conceptualization of indirect media effects is important for two reasons. First, intervening variables provide important explanations for how and why media effects occur, and therefore they can be helpful when designing prevention and intervention programs. Second, ignoring indirect effects can lead to a biased estimation of effects sizes in empirical research and thus of meta-analyses (Holbert & Stephenson 2003). After all, it is the combination of direct and indirect effects that makes up the total effect of an independent variable on a dependent variable. Thus, "if an indirect effect does not receive proper attention, the relationship between two variables of concern may not be fully considered" (Raykov & Marcoulides 2012, p. 7).

Media effects theories have identified three types of indirect effects. In the first type, which we discussed in the section about selectivity (Feature 1), media use itself acts as an intervening variable between pre-media-use variables (development, dispositions, and social context factors) and outcome variables. In the second type of indirect effects, the cognitive, emotional, and physiological processes that occur during and shortly after exposure act as mediators. It has often been posited and shown that the way in which individuals process media forms the route to media effects. For example, research based on the elaboration likelihood model (Petty & Cacioppo 1986) has found that attitude change is more enduring when a message leads to a high level of attention and elaboration (i.e., the central route). Anderson & Bushman's (2002) general aggression model predicts indirect effects of exposure to media violence on aggression through three response states: cognition, emotion, and arousal. Finally, experiments based on Zillmann's (1996) excitation-transfer model have demonstrated that residual arousal that results from media-induced sexual excitement can intensify positive (e.g., altruistic) and negative (e.g., anger, aggression) feelings and behavior.

The third type of indirect effects that has been identified conceptualizes postexposure variables that may themselves be dependent variables (e.g., attitudes and beliefs) as mediators of other postexposure variables. Especially in political and health communication, it has repeatedly been found that effects of media use on political and health behavior are mediated by certain beliefs and attitudes (Holbert & Stephenson 2003). For example, recent work in political communication increasingly conceptualizes the relationship between news media and voting behavior as indirect, mediated through various political beliefs and attitudes (McLeod et al. 2009). In addition, researchers focusing on agenda setting (McCombs & Shaw 1972), a theory that explains how news media influence the salience of topics on the public agenda by enhancing accessibility in the memories of the audience, have recently reconceptualized agenda setting as a mediator between exposure to news and subsequent political beliefs and attitudes (McCombs & Reynolds 2009).

Finally, theories of health communication via media campaigns also turned from direct associations between individuals' exposure to programs and health behavior, as seen in the 1980s, to a focus on indirect effects in the 1990s. The ultimate goal of most research-based health campaigns is to achieve a change in behaviors, such as reducing alcohol intake or quitting smoking (Hornik 2003). In addition, most theory-based health campaigns are grounded in the notion that the more researchers know about the intervening variables (i.e., the underlying mechanisms) between exposure to programs and a given health behavior, the better they can develop an effective campaign or intervention to reinforce or change that behavior (Fishbein & Cappella 2006). In their review of health communication theories, Fishbein & Cappella (2006) identified seven potential intervening variables that are worth considering in health campaigns, including beliefs about and attitudes toward the behavior and perceived norms concerning performance of the behavior. Identifying such variables is essential to understand not only the underlying mechanisms of media effects but also the true magnitude of these effects.

Feature 4: Media Effects Are Conditional

Models that propose conditional media effects share the notion that media effects can be enhanced or reduced by individual difference and social context variables. Several media effects theories recognize conditional media effects, including uses-and-gratifications theory (Rubin 2009), reinforcing spiral model (Slater 2007), the conditional model of political communication effects (McLeod et al. 2009), the elaboration likelihood model (Petty & Cacioppo 1986), and the differential susceptibility to media effects model (Valkenburg & Peter 2013a). For example, in the elaboration likelihood model, need for cognition—the tendency to enjoy effortful information processing—is seen as a moderator of media effects on attitudes.

Some theories have proposed that the same factors that can predispose media selection can also modify the direction or strength of the effects of media use (e.g., Bandura 2009, McLeod et al. 2009). Valkenburg & Peter (2013a) argued that dispositional, developmental, and social context factors have a double role in the media effects process: They not only predict media use, but in interaction with media properties they influence the way in which media content is processed. In other words, properties of media affect how media content is processed (i.e., property-driven processing), but the effects of this property-driven processing are contingent upon specific dispositions, developmental level, and social context factors of the media user.

As previously discussed, individuals have the tendency, at least to a certain extent, to seek out congenial media content (Hart et al. 2009, Klapper 1960); that is, content that does not deviate too much from their dispositions and developmental level and the norms that prevail in the social groups to which they belong. It is conceivable that these same factors can also moderate the way in which media content is processed. Qualitative critical audience research has often emphasized that audiences differ in their interpretations of media content (e.g., Hall 1980) and that these interpretations partly depend on gender, class, race, and age (e.g., Kim 2004). However, in social science–based media effects theories, such interactive influences on media processing have, to our knowledge, received less attention. There has been ample research on selective exposure and selective recall but less research on selective reception processes (Hart et al. 2009). Moreover, the scarce research that is available has mainly focused on cognitive processing of media content and less on emotional processing, despite the growing evidence that emotional processes, such as identification with characters and involvement in the narrative, are important routes to persuasion (e.g., Slater & Rouner 2002).

As for dispositions, research indicates that trait aggressiveness moderates media violence effects on cognitive processing (e.g., misinterpretation of ambiguous nonviolent acts) and emotional processing (e.g., a decreased empathy with characters; Bushman 1995, Krcmar 2009). A high need for cognition has been shown to moderate message effects on cognitive processing (Cacioppo et al. 1996, Shrum 2009). Trait empathy and need for affect can enhance emotional processing when watching sad or frightening films (Krcmar 2009, Oliver & Krakowiak 2009). Finally, bodily needs such as hunger may significantly alter the way in which individuals perceive food products presented on a screen. Such products may seem bigger when subjects are hungry than when they are not (McClelland & Atkinson 1948).

The moderating role of dispositional variables can be explained by the disposition-content congruency hypothesis (Valkenburg & Peter 2013a), which argues that dispositionally congruent media content may be processed faster and more efficiently than incongruent content because it can be assimilated more readily to the media user's existing cognitive schemata. Because congruent content requires less cognitive effort, it leaves more resources available for the processing of less salient content (Alba & Hutchinson 1987). Dispositionally congruent content can also affect emotional processing through processing fluency. Congruent content enhances the media users' experience of familiarity or at least their illusion of familiarity. This (illusion of) familiarity may in turn enhance positive affect and aesthetic pleasure, a process that has been named the hedonistic fluency hypothesis (Reber et al. 2004).

As for the moderating role of developmental level, research shows that, in comparison to older children and adults, younger children are less effective in investing cognitive effort during media use. They still lack the knowledge and experience to assimilate new information into their existing framework. They also show stronger physiological arousal reactions to violent and frightening media, even if this content is unrealistic (Valkenburg & Cantor 2001). Finally, whereas younger adults invest more cognitive effort in processing negative stimuli (e.g., mutilations; Mares et al. 2008), middle and older adults invest more cognitive effort in processing positive stimuli (e.g., babies, animals). As previously discussed, if individuals encounter media content that is too discrepant from these schemata and experiences, they will either avoid it or allocate less attention to it. Moderately discrepant media content, which is, by definition, partly familiar to a media user, is also likely to be processed more fluently. Such content can more easily be related to existing schemata than can fully discrepant content. As a result, it can activate more and more different nodes (e.g., emotions, cognitions) in people's semantic network (Valkenburg & Peter 2013a).

Social contexts can also modify the way in which we perceive media. When physical violence is accepted in families, children may learn to interpret media violence differently than do other children (Schultz et al. 2001), and they may become more susceptible to media effects on aggression (Fikkers et al. 2013). Moderating effects on cognitive and emotional processing also happen more covertly due to emotional contagion (McDonald 2009). Because media users are sensitive to others' attitudes, moods, and emotional reactions, their own cognitive and emotional responses can be intensified or dampened during shared media use. Valkenburg & Peter's (2013a) context-content convergence hypothesis posits that individuals are more susceptible to media messages if these messages converge with the values and norms in the social environment of the media user. In cultivation theory (Gerbner et al. 1980, p. 15), this phenomenon has been named resonance: When something experienced in the media is similar to one's social environment, it creates a double dose of the message, which enhances the likelihood of media effects.

Feature 5: Media Effects Are Transactional

A final feature of media effects theories that may specify the boundary conditions of media effects is that such effects are transactional (e.g., Anderson & Bushman 2002, Bandura 2009, Früh & Schönbach 1982, Slater 2007). Transactional theories assume reciprocal causal relationships between characteristics of the media users, their selective media use, factors in their environment, and outcomes of media (Bandura 2009). Transactional theories elaborate on the selectivity paradigm (Feature 1), which assumes that individuals, by selectively exposing themselves to media, in part shape their own media effects. Transactional models aim to explain how and why this occurs. They specify the boundaries of media effects by recognizing that media users can be influenced only by media content that they selectively use and selectively interpret.

Transactional media effects theories are usually quite complex and based on at least three assumptions. First, producers and receivers of media content/messages are connected through communication technologies (e.g., radio, television, Internet) and engage in transactions; that is, they exchange information and values with each other through communication technologies (Bauer 1964). These transactions between producers and receivers imply that communication technologies function as reciprocal mediators between these entities (Früh & Schönbach 1982). Second, both producers and receivers of media content/messages influence each other and, hence, both can change as a result of the media content/messages they produce or receive: Receivers can change as a result of their own selective media choices (see Feature 1) and selective perception processes (see Feature 4); producers can change because they learn from, or cater to, what they perceive to be audience needs and preferences (Webster 2009). Third, transactions can be distinguished as interpersonal, that is, the transactions between producers and receivers, and intrapersonal, that is, the transactions within the cognitive and affective systems of the producers or receivers themselves (cf. Früh & Schönbach 1982). Intrapersonal transactions may, for example, guide selective exposure to, and selective perception of, interpersonal transactions.

Transactional models of media effects see predictive paths both from media use to media outcomes, and from these outcomes to media use. Such paths have been conceptualized as dynamic (Früh & Schönbach 1982) or, more specifically, as a reinforcing spiral (Slater 2007). The depiction of reciprocal media-outcome relationships as a reinforcing spiral may imply a positive or negative feedback loop that ends in extreme media use and extreme levels on outcome variables (Slater 2015). However, transactional models assign a central moderating role to the social environment in which the producers and receivers are embedded. For example, Bandura (2009) assumes that humans have interactive agency, which means that they are neither entirely autonomous from their environment nor completely subject to environmental influences. Influences of media on individuals may therefore initially increase, but as a result of dispositional, developmental, or environmental forces, in time individuals will tend toward homeostasis (Slater 2015).

Transactional media effects have received little research attention. For example, none of the recent meta-analyses on media use and aggression have been able to include effect sizes for reciprocal relationships in their analyses despite the accumulation of longitudinal studies in the field (e.g., see the meta-analyses of Anderson et al. 2010, Ferguson & Kilburn 2009). This even holds for the relationship between media use and ADHD symptoms, which can be integral parts of one's identity and thus likely to predispose media use. Of about 40 empirical studies on the relationship between media use and ADHD symptoms, more than 95% conceptualize media use only as a cause and not as a result of these symptoms (Nikkelen et al. 2014).

However, other studies have pointed to transactional media effects. For example, Slater et al. (2003) found that exposure to violent media prospectively predicted aggressiveness, and aggressiveness prospectively predicted violent media content. Eveland et al. (2003) found that individuals' elaboration of television and print news messages was reciprocally related to their level of political knowledge. Such reciprocal relationships have also been found for sensation seeking and watching R-rated movies (Stoolmiller et al. 2010). Finally, adolescents who frequently watch pornography more often tend to see women as sex objects, which in turn increases their use of and emotional responses to this material (Peter & Valkenburg 2009).

MEDIA EFFECTS IN THE NEWER MEDIA ENVIRONMENT

Theories and research on the effects of individual or group behavior in computer-mediated environments emerged in the 1970s, long before the Internet became widespread. Unlike media effects research, which evolved from the study of mass communication, this strand of theory and research originated as a hybrid of interpersonal communication, teleconferencing, and organizational behavior, with a focus on how computer-mediated communication (CMC) affected interpersonal and group interaction. Theories of CMC have typically focused on discovering, and comparing, the psychological and behavioral effects of face-to-face communication to those of CMC. Alternatively, they studied how communicating online in large-scale networks of strangers differs from proximal interactions with known partners. CMC theories often centered on questions such as whether, and how, certain characteristics of CMC, such as anonymity or the lack of nonverbal (auditory or visual) cues, influence the quality of social interaction and the impressions CMC partners form of one another.

Computer-Mediated Communication Theories

The first generation of CMC theories, which have retrospectively been named cues-filtered-out theories, tried to compare the "lean" text-only applications such as email and online discussion boards with the presumably richer face-to-face communication (for a review, see Culnan & Markus 1987). They tried to explain why, for example, CMC fosters less socioemotional communication and more shallow impressions of communication partners and why depersonalization and anonymity due to CMC can lead to inhibited behavior, such as flaming. Well-known theories from that period are the media richness theory of Daft & Lengel (1986), the social presence theory of Short et al. (1976), and the lack of social context cues hypothesis of Sproull & Kiesler (1986).

As the Internet became widely adopted for personal use and popular accounts of supportive virtual communities garnered attention, the 1990s saw a new cluster of theories with less restrictive views of CMC. An influential theory from that period is Walther's (1992) social information processing theory, which explains how CMC partners gradually overcome the absence of nonverbal cues online by creatively employing verbal cues and interaction strategies (such as content and style variations and more direct personal questions and answers) to encode and decode social and emotional messages in CMC. In this way, with sufficient time and message exchanges, the level of impression development among communication partners and the intimacy of CMC can become comparable to that of face-to-face communication. An alternative approach, the social identification/deindividuation (SIDE) model, argues that text-only CMC, without physical appearance cues that signal the individual identities of partners, enhances the salience of a social identity at the expense of a personal identity (Postmes et al. 2000). The enhanced categorization of the self and others as members of groups in CMC causes participants to behave according to perceived group norms. As a result, CMC leads to more normative behavior than that of face-to-face groups.

Another influential approach from that period is Walther's (1996) hyperpersonal communication model, with the even more optimistic prediction that text-only messages can lead to more favorable impressions of a CMC partner and more intimacy than does face-to-face communication. According to the model, CMC message creation encourages communication partners to present themselves in optimal ways. By exploiting CMC's capacity for greater control over self-presentations, they can carefully craft their self-portrayals more nicely or attractively than they generally do, or are able to, in face-to-face interactions. Recipients of CMC communication, in turn, fill in the blanks in their impressions of their partners that the absence of audiovisual cues leaves open, which encourages them to idealize these partners. According to Walther, CMC can thereby even become hyperpersonal, that is, more intimate than offline communication.

Inspired by Walther's hyperpersonal communication theory, Valkenburg & Peter (2009) developed and tested the Internet-enhanced self-disclosure hypothesis among adolescents. They argued that the Web 2.0 technologies that arose in the new millennium are increasingly designed to encourage communication with existing friends. As a result, much of the time that adolescents spend with such technologies is used to maintain existing friendships, which may eventually enhance the closeness of these friendships. In several of their studies they found that, due to their limited audiovisual cues, social media may lead adolescents to perceive that the Internet provides a safe place to disclose intimate information to their friends. The more adolescents used social media, the more they disclosed themselves online to their friends. This enhanced online self-disclosure, in turn, stimulated the quality of their friendships, albeit only when adolescents used social media to communicate primarily with their existing friends and not when they used it primarily to chat with strangers (Valkenburg & Peter 2009, 2011).

The focus of early CMC theories on anonymity and limited nonverbal cues fit well through 2005, when CMC was predominantly text-based and typically took place in anonymous chat rooms and newsgroups between unacquainted communication partners. However, with the introduction of Web 2.0 applications such as Twitter (2006), Facebook (2006), WhatsApp (2009), and Instagram (2010), online communication has diversified, with many more audiovisual platforms as well as uses within existing relationships. People now actively use a variety of text-based and audiovisual communication channels. These developments have made it more difficult, and sometimes less relevant, to compare specific CMC applications with each other or with face-to-face communication. These changes in technologies call for changes in theories and research.

Mass Self-Communication and Expression Effects

In Web 2.0–based social applications, information is distributed multidirectionally in a network where audiences can vary from one to many. Importantly, Internet-based social communication enables everyone with an Internet connection to become a sender of information, that is, a content creator and a media source. Given that a considerable proportion of the information distributed via social media is personal and self-related, Castells (2007, p. 248), as discussed previously, has outlined a "new form of socialized communication" that he calls mass self-communication. Like mass communication, mass self-communication can potentially reach a global audience, but "it is self-generated in content, self-directed in emission," and it typically focuses on self-related information (Castells 2007, p. 248).

The concept of mass self-communication has important implications not only for media effects theories but also for CMC theories. Many, especially the older, CMC theories suffer from the same omissions as some older media effects theories. Both types of theories are often rooted in a reception model; that is, in the notion that certain properties of media or technologies (modality, content, structure) have a unidirectional impact on recipients. Even CMC theories, which are ostensibly theories that focus on the communication between two or more individuals, have often focused on the effects of certain CMC properties (i.e., anonymity, reduced nonverbal cues) on the recipients of these properties. Although media effects as well as CMC theories like to describe recipients as active in the sense that they have autonomy over the way they receive and interpret media or CMC properties, the assumed influence is unidirectional: from the media or technology to recipients. In fact, in both media effects and CMC theories, "effects" are often conceptualized as recipient effects.

The concept of mass self-communication does not deny the processes related to the reception of media content. However, its emphasis on the self-generated, self-directed, and self-focused character of Internet-based social communication draws our attention to the possible effects of content produced by the sender on him- or herself. Long before the advent of Web 2.0, observers noted that media users had become producers as well as consumers of information and entertainment, a phenomenon for which the now somewhat obsolete term "prosumers" was coined (Toffler 1980). This implies that, in terms of transactional media effects theories, CMC technology provides users not only a fast and easily accessible vehicle for interpersonal transactions, but also an increased opportunity for intrapersonal transactions; that is, transactions within the senders (and recipients) themselves. In other words, the production and distribution of content by a sender may affect not only its recipient(s), but also the sender him- or herself. This phenomenon, that our own behavior exerts influence on ourselves, has been recently referred to as an expression effect (Pingree 2007).

The study of expression effects is rather new in the field of media effects, and research into the mechanisms is still scarce. A plausible explanation for the occurrence of expression effects is based on the same need that guides selective media exposure—the need to be consistent. Bem's (1972) self-perception theory may be useful as a starting point. Like Festinger (1957), Bem suggests that people need to be consistent in their beliefs, attitudes, and behavior. Whereas the generally accepted belief is that cognitions and attitudes precede one's behavior, self-perception theory, in contrast, argues that individuals derive their cognitions, beliefs, and attitudes from their own prior overt behavior. They adapt their beliefs and attitudes by observing their own behavior in retrospect.

Several CMC studies have addressed expression effects. For example, Shah et al. (2005) found that online civic messaging—that is, the creation of political messages on the Internet—significantly influenced the senders' own civic engagement, and often more strongly than exposure to traditional news media. Gonzales & Hancock (2008) asked subjects to present themselves in either a public or private blog as either introverts or extraverts. They found that subjects later perceived themselves according to their introvert or extravert self-presentation, but only when their blogs were public. Such intrapersonal changes even appear to hold when the online self-presentation occurs through an avatar (a digital, graphical character that represents the CMC user in virtual worlds or games), a phenomenon that has been named the Proteus effect (Yee et al. 2009).

Other studies demonstrate ways in which expression and social effects combine. Valkenburg et al. (2006) found that adolescents' own behavior on social network sites is related to their self-esteem. Adolescents who created an online profile seemed to use feedback from their peers about these profiles to adjust and optimize their profiles, which was associated with more positive feedback. In this way, through improved feedback and their own communicative behavior, they managed to enhance their self-esteem. This result was extended by Walther et al. (2011a). Drawing on Gonzales & Hancock (2008), Walther et al. asked subjects to write blogs; half of the subjects were instructed to write as if they were introverts and the other half as extraverts. They showed that when CMC users received confirming feedback (from either a person or a computer program), it magnified the expression effect (i.e., the effect of their self-presentation on their own self-concept).

In summary, the scarce research into CMC research in general and expression effects in particular indicates that both intrapersonal (expression effects) and interpersonal (feedback) processes may affect the self-presentation and self-concepts of senders and recipients of mediated communication (Van Der Heide et al. 2013). In addition, both senders and recipients have specific dispositions that may prompt their media consumption, shape their attention to the messages that are exchanged, and affect their interpretation (Walther et al. 2011b). Future research should further explore the exact conditions that facilitate, and mechanisms that explain, expression effects. Future research should also attempt to understand whether and how expression effects occur, and for whom they particularly hold, so that interventions can be designed to mitigate negative effects (e.g., of comments on suicide or proanorexia sites) and encourage positive ones (e.g., comments on websites that encourage civic participation).

CONCLUSION

In this review, we have taken stock of the development of two subdisciplines of communication science: (mass) media effects and computer-mediated communication (CMC). We charted some notable parallels in conceptual thinking within these subdisciplines. First, both media effects and CMC research have found their roots in theories that conceptualize effects as powerful and direct processes, which have been metaphorically called a hypodermic needle or magic bullet in media effects theories and technological determinism in CMC. Second, in the course of time, both subdisciplines progressed from a unidirectional receiver-oriented view to transactional paradigms. Current theories in both subdisciplines acknowledge that individuals shape and are shaped by their own selective use of media or communication technologies.

Despite this apparent progression in theory formation, research into the uses and effects of the newest generation of communication technologies is still in its infancy. An important factor that hampers the field is that its object of study, media and technology, is a moving target, a phenomenon that is continuously subject to change while we try to understand it. Since the advent of Web 2.0, these changes have rapidly accelerated. The tools and applications that we study are often outdated by the time that articles about them are published. Another factor is that our understanding of the uses and effects of media and communication technologies develop in a variety of disparate disciplines and subdisciplines that until now have often largely ignored each other, which also hampers integrative theory formation and testing (Craig 1999).

An integration of mass media and CMC research is more opportune than ever, now that we spend several hours per day with social media, and mass media communication has turned into mass self-communication. Take a phenomenon such as social TV, the most obvious blending of a mass medium and CMC, in which many people simultaneously share their TV experience with other viewers via Twitter or Facebook and divide their attention between television and the comments of thousands of other viewers. Based on the context-congruence hypothesis, it is to be expected that comments from like-minded coviewers may enhance selective processing of media content and, hence, media effects. However, research on such phenomena is still scarce. There is an obvious need for research that compares the effects of social watching with watching alone and specifies the conditions under which user-generated comments affect viewers.

There are more important technological trends that may influence one or more of the five features of media effects theories identified in this review. First, communication technologies have become ever more mobile. They moved from our desk (desktop), to our bag (laptop), to our pocket (smartphone), which has significantly altered our media use (Feature 1). Not only has the time we spend with communication technologies increased significantly, but also our tendency to media multitask (i.e., the use of TV, radio, print, the Internet, or any other medium in conjunction with another). About 30% of the time adolescents spend with media now consists of media multitasking (Rideout et al. 2010). This development has important research implications. How do we, for example, validly measure media use if individuals spend one-third of their media use multitasking (Feature 1)? And how can we still validly estimate the effects of such scattered media use?

Not only may our media use be more selective, another trend is that the media messages we receive are increasingly more selected for us. Personalization of media lies at the core of the "de-massification of mass communication" because it further allows media users to select their own media content (Sundar et al. 2015, p. 60). Corporations such as Amazon, Netflix, and Google News increasingly attempt to personalize their content for each user in order to enhance engagement and shorten the distance between their products and website consumers. Personalization occurs through book or movie recommendations or by targeting information and advertising for individual users. Through personalization, corporations attempt to drive selective exposure (Feature 1) and help users find entertainment, information, or brands that they never knew existed but are likely to want. Research on personalization has rapidly emerged in the past few years. Preliminary evidence shows that personalization may increase the cognitive and emotional engagement of media users (Features 2 and 4), and by this route, it can enhance media effects (for an overview, see Sundar et al. 2015). Future research should address the underlying mechanisms and contingent conditions under which personalized media content may exert positive or negative transactional influences.

A final unmistakable trend in communication technologies that may enhance the likelihood of media effects is the increasing lifelike visualization in both mass communication and mass self-communication. Text-only CMC, which was still common around the start of the millennium, has been supplemented or even replaced by visual CMC (e.g., Instagram). Movies increasingly appear in 3D, and we will soon be able to experience virtual reality games or worlds by means of head-mounted devices such as Oculus Rift. Such display devices provide users with a strong degree of sensory richness because they make them think and feel that the environment responds to their actions and that users themselves are the source of changes to their environment (Sundar et al. 2015). Research into virtual reality or immersive virtual environments began in the past millennium, but recent technological advances are moving such technologies out of the research lab into our living room, where they can bring extremely engaging and vivid virtual worlds (Karutz & Bailenson 2015).

Research into the everyday experiences with such technologies is still scarce. Important questions are, for example, how the properties of such technologies may enhance emotional and cognitive involvement with vivid and lifelike characters and narratives (Features 2 and 4). And how may these properties further affect some of the canonical foci of (mass) media effects, such as learning, fear reactions, and aggression? These new developments may demand adjustments or refinements of theories and new ways of thinking. Providing answers to these questions and charting their implications for media effects research will make the task of the next contributors on this topic to the *Annual Review of Psychology* particularly interesting.

DISCLOSURE STATEMENT

The authors are not aware of any affiliations, memberships, funding, or financial holdings that might be perceived as affecting the objectivity of this review.

ACKNOWLEDGMENTS

This research was supported by a grant to the first author from the European Research Council under the European Union's Seventh Framework Program (FP7/2007–2013)/ERC grant agreement no. AdG09 249488-ENTCHILD.

LITERATURE CITED

Alba JW, Hutchinson JW. 1987. Dimensions of consumer expertise. *J. Consum. Res.* 13:411–54

Allen M, D'Alessio D, Brezgel K. 1995. A meta-analysis summarizing the effects of pornography II: aggression after exposure. *Hum. Commun. Res.* 22:258–83

Anderson CA, Bushman BJ. 2001. Effects of violent video games on aggressive behavior, aggressive cognition, aggressive affect, physiological arousal, and prosocial behavior: a meta-analytic review of the scientific literature. *Psychol. Sci.* 12:353–59

Anderson CA, Bushman BJ. 2002. Human aggression. *Annu. Rev. Psychol.* 53:27–51

Anderson CA, Shibuya A, Ihori N, Swing EL, Bushman BJ, et al. 2010. Violent video game effects on aggression, empathy, and prosocial behavior in eastern and western countries: a meta-analytic review. *Psychol. Bull.* 136:151–73

Atkin C. 1973. Instrumental utilities and information seeking. In *New Models for Mass Communication Research*, ed. P Clarke, pp. 205–42. Oxford, UK: Sage

Bandura A. 2002. Social cognitive theory of mass communication. In *Media Effects: Advances in Theory and Research*, ed. J Bryant, D Zillmann, pp. 121–53. Hillsdale, NJ: Erlbaum

Bandura A. 2009. Social cognitive theory of mass communication. See Bryant & Oliver 2009, pp. 94–124

Barlett CP, Vowels CL, Saucier DA. 2008. Meta-analyses of the effects of media images on men's body-image concerns. *J. Soc. Clin. Psychol.* 27:279–310

Bauer R. 1964. The obstinate audience: the influence process from the point of view of social communication. *Am. Psychol.* 19:319–28

Beentjes JWJ, van der Voort THA. 1988. Television's impact on children's reading skills: a review of research. *Read. Res. Q.* 23:389–413

Bem DJ. 1972. Self-perception theory. In *Advances in Experimental Social Psychology*, ed. L Berkowitz, pp. 1–62. New York: Academic

Berkowitz L. 1984. Some effects of thoughts on antisocial and pro-social influences of media events: a cognitive-neoassociation analysis. *Psychol. Bull.* 95:410–27

Berkowitz L, Powers PC. 1979. Effects of timing and justification of witnessed aggression on the observers punitiveness. *J. Res. Personal.* 13:71–80

Blumler JG. 1985. The social character of media gratifications. In *Media Gratifications Research*, ed. KE Rosengren, LA Wenner, P Palmgreen, pp. 41–60. Beverly Hills, CA: Sage

Boerman SC, Smit EG, van Meurs A. 2011. Attention battle: the abilities of brand, visual, and text characteristics of the ad to draw attention versus the diverting power of the direct magazine context. In *Advances in Advertising Research: Breaking New Ground in Theory and Practice*, ed. S Okazaki, pp. 295–310. Wiesbaden, Ger.: Gabler Verlag

Boulianne S. 2009. Does internet use affect engagement? A meta-analysis of research. *Pol. Commun.* 26:193–211

Bradley MM. 2009. Natural selective attention: orienting and emotion. *Psychophysiology* 46:1–11

Bryant J, Miron D. 2004. Theory and research in mass communication. *J. Commun.* 54:662–704

Bryant J, Oliver MB, eds. 2009. *Media Effects: Advances in Theory and Research*. New York: Routledge. 3rd ed.

Bushman BJ. 1995. Moderating role of trait aggressiveness in the effects of violent media on aggression. *J. Personal. Soc. Psychol.* 69:950–60

Cacioppo JT, Petty RE, Feinstein JA, Blair W, Jarvis G. 1996. Dispositional differences in cognitive motivation: the life and times of individuals varying in need for cognition. *Psychol. Bull.* 119:197–253

Castells M. 2007. Communication, power and counter-power in the network society. *Int. J. Commun.* 1:238–66

Clark R. 2012. *Learning from Media: Arguments, Analysis, and Evidence*. Charlotte, NC: Inf. Age Publ.

Corbetta M, Shulman GL. 2002. Control of goal-directed and stimulus-driven attention in the brain. *Nat. Rev. Neurosci.* 3:201–15

Craig RT. 1999. Communication theory as a field. *Commun. Theory* 9:119–61

Culnan MJ, Markus ML. 1987. Information technologies. In *Handbook of Organizational Communication: An Interdisciplinary Perspective*, ed. FM Jablin, LL Putnam, KH Roberts, LW Porter, pp. 420–43. Thousand Oaks, CA: Sage

Daft RL, Lengel RH. 1986. Organizational information requirements, media richness and structural design. *Manag. Sci.* 32:554–71

Desmond RJ, Garveth R. 2007. The effects of advertising on children and adolescents. In *Mass Media Effects Research: Advances Through Meta-Analysis*, ed. R Preiss, B Gayle, N Burrell, M Allen, J Bryant, pp. 169–79. Mahwah, NJ: Erlbaum

Donsbach W. 2009. Cognitive dissonance theory—roller coaster career: how communication research adapted the theory of cognitive dissonance. In *Media Choice: A Theoretical and Empirical Overview*, ed. T Hartmann, pp. 128–49. New York: Routledge

Entman RM. 1993. Framing: toward clarification of a fractured paradigm. *J. Commun.* 43:51–58

Eveland WP, Shah DV, Kwak N. 2003. Assessing causality in the cognitive mediation model: a panel study of motivations, information processing, and learning during campaign 2000. *Commun. Res.* 30:359–86

Ferguson CJ, Kilburn J. 2009. The public health risks of media violence: a meta-analytic review. *J. Pediatr.* 154:759–63

Festinger L. 1957. *A Theory of Cognitive Dissonance*. Stanford, CA: Stanford Univ. Press

Fikkers K, Piotrowski JT, Weeda W, Vossen HGM, Valkenburg PM. 2013. Double dose: high family conflict enhances the effect of media violence exposure on adolescents' aggression. *Societies* 3:280–92

Fishbein M, Cappella JN. 2006. The role of theory in developing effective health communications. *J. Commun.* 56:S1–17

Fiske ST. 2002. Five core social motives, plus or minus five. In *Social Perception: The Ontario Symposium*, ed. SJ Spencer, S Fein, MP Zanna, JM Olson, pp. 233–46. Mahwah, NJ: Erlbaum

Früh W, Schönbach K. 1982. Der dynamisch-transaktionale Ansatz: Ein neues Paradigma der Medienwirkungen [The dynamic-transactional approach: a new paradigm of media effects]. *Publizistik* 27:74–88

Gerbner G, Gross L, Morgan M, Signorielli N. 1980. The mainstreaming of America: violence profile no 11. *J. Commun.* 30:10–29

Gonzales AL, Hancock JT. 2008. Identity shift in computer-mediated environments. *Media Psychol.* 11:167–85

Grabe S, Ward LM, Hyde JS. 2008. Role of the media in body image concerns among women: a meta-analysis of experimental and correlational studies. *Psychol. Bull.* 134:460–76

Green MC, Brock TC. 2000. The role of transportation in the persuasiveness of public narratives. *J. Personal. Soc. Psychol.* 79:701–21

Green MC, Brock TC, Kaufman GE. 2004. Understanding media enjoyment: the role of transportation into narrative worlds. *Commun. Theory* 14:311–27

Greenfield P, Farrar D, Beagles-Roos J. 1986. Is the medium the message? An experimental comparison of the effects of radio and television on imagination. *J. Appl. Dev. Psychol.* 7:201–18

Hall S. 1980. Encoding/decoding. In *Culture, Media, Language: Working Papers in Cultural Studies*, ed. S Hall, D Hobson, A Lowe, P Willis, pp. 128–38. London: Hutchinson

Hart W, Albarracin D, Eagly AH, Brechan I, Lindberg MJ, Merrill L. 2009. Feeling validated versus being correct: a meta-analysis of selective exposure to information. *Psychol. Bull.* 135:555–88

Hartmann T. 2009. *Media Choice: A Theoretical and Empirical Overview*. New York: Routledge

Harwood J. 1999. Age identification, social identity gratifications, and television viewing. *J. Broadcast. Electron. Media* 43:123–36

Holbert RL, Stephenson MT. 2003. The importance of indirect effects in media effects research: testing for mediation in structural equation modeling. *J. Broadcast. Electron. Media* 47:556–72

Holmstrom AJ. 2004. The effects of the media on body image: a meta-analysis. *J. Broadcast. Electron. Media* 48:196–217

Hornik R. 2003. *Public Health Communication: Evidence for Behavior Change*. Hillsdale, NJ: Erlbaum

Hovland CI, Janis IL, Kelley HH. 1953. *Communication and Persuasion: Psychological Studies of Opinion Change*. New Haven, CT: Yale Univ. Press

Karutz CO, Bailenson JN. 2015. Immersive virtual environments and the classrooms of tomorrow. In *The Handbook of the Psychology of Communication Technology*, ed. SS Sundar, pp. 290–310. New York: Wiley

Katz E. 1959. Mass communications research and the study of popular culture: an editorial note on a possible future for this journal. *Stud. Public Commun.* 2:1–6

Katz E, Blumler JG, Gurevitch M. 1973. Uses and gratifications research. *Public Opin. Q.* 37:509–23

Katz E, Lazarsfeld PF. 1955. *Personal Influence: The Part Played by People in the Flow of Mass Communications*. Piscataway, NJ: Trans. Publ.

Kim S. 2004. Rereading David Morley's *The "Nationwide" Audience. Cult. Stud.* 18:84–108

Klapper JT. 1960. *The Effects of Mass Communication*. Glencoe, IL: Free Press

Knobloch-Westerwick S. 2006. Mood management: theory, evidence, and advancements. In *Psychology of Entertainment*, ed. J Bryant, P Vorderer, pp. 230–54. Mahwah, NJ: Erlbaum

Knobloch-Westerwick S. 2015. *Choice and Preference in Media Use*. New York: Routledge

Krcmar M. 2009. Individual differences in media effects. In *The Sage Handbook of Media Processes and Effects*, ed. RL Nabi, MB Oliver, pp. 237–50. Thousand Oaks, CA: Sage

Lang A. 2000. The limited capacity model of mediated message processing. *J. Commun.* 50:46–70

Lazarsfeld PF, Berelson B, Gaudet H. 1948. *The People's Choice: How the Voter Makes Up His Mind in a Presidential Campaign*. New York: Columbia Univ. Press

Liebert RM, Schwartzberg NS. 1977. Effects of mass-media. *Annu. Rev. Psychol.* 28:141–73

Mangen A, Walgermo BR, Brønnick K. 2013. Reading linear texts on paper versus computer screen: effects on reading comprehension. *Int. J. Educ. Res.* 58:61–68

Mares M-L, Oliver MB, Cantor J. 2008. Age differences in adults' emotional motivations for exposure to films. *Media Psychol.* 11:488–511

Mares M-L, Sun Y. 2010. The multiple meanings of age for television content preferences. *Hum. Commun. Res.* 36:372–96

Mares M-L, Woodard E. 2005. Positive effects of television on children's social interactions: a meta-analysis. *Media Psychol.* 7:301–22

Mares M-L, Woodard EH. 2006. In search of the older audience: adult age differences in television viewing. *J. Broadcast. Electron. Media* 50:595–614

Marshall SJ, Biddle SJH, Gorely T, Cameron N, Murdey I. 2004. Relationships between media use, body fatness and physical activity in children and youth: a meta-analysis. *Int. J. Obes.* 28:1238–46

Matlin MW, Stang DJ. 1978. *The Pollyanna Principle: Selectivity in Language, Memory, and Thought*. Cambridge, MA: Schenkman

McClelland DC, Atkinson JW. 1948. The projective expression of needs: I. The effect of different intensities of the hunger drive on perception. *J. Psychol.* 26:205–22

McCombs ME, Reynolds A. 2009. How the news shapes our civic agenda. See Bryant & Oliver 2009, pp. 1–16

McCombs ME, Shaw DL. 1972. The agenda-setting function of mass media. *Public Opin. Q.* 36:176–87

McDonald DG. 2009. Media use and the social environment. In *Media Processes and Effects*, ed. RL Nabi, MB Oliver, pp. 251–68. Los Angeles, CA: Sage

McGuire WJ. 1986. The myth of massive media impact: savagings and salvagings. In *Public Communication and Behavior*, Vol. 1, ed. G Comstock, pp. 173–257. Orlando, FL: Academic

McLeod DM, Kosicki GM, McLeod JM. 2009. Political communication effects. See Bryant & Oliver 2009, pp. 228–51

McLuhan M. 1964. *Understanding Media: The Extension of Man*. London: Sphere Books

McQuail D. 2010. *McQuail's Mass Communication Theory*. London: Sage

Nathanson AI. 2001. Parents versus peers: exploring the significance of peer mediation of antisocial television. *Commun. Res.* 28:251–74

Nikkelen SWC, Valkenburg PM, Huizinga M, Bushman BJ. 2014. Media use and ADHD-related behaviors in children and adolescents: a meta-analysis. *Dev. Psychol.* 50:2228–41

O'Keefe DJ. 2003. Message properties, mediating states, and manipulation checks: claims, evidence, and data analysis in experimental persuasive message effects research. *Commun. Theory* 13:251–74

Oliver MB. 2008. Tender affective states as predictors of entertainment preference. *J. Commun.* 58:40–61

Oliver MB, Kim J, Sanders MS. 2006. Personality. In *Psychology of Entertainment*, pp. 329–41. Mahwah, NJ: Erlbaum

Oliver MB, Krakowiak KM. 2009. Individual differences in media effects. See Bryant & Oliver 2009, pp. 517–31

Paik H, Comstock G. 1994. The effects of television violence on antisocial behavior: a meta-analysis. *Commun. Res.* 21:516–46

Pearce LJ, Field AP. 2015. The impact of "scary" TV and film on children's internalizing emotions: a meta-analysis. *Hum. Commun. Res.* In press

Peter J, Valkenburg PM. 2009. Adolescents' exposure to sexually explicit internet material and notions of women as sex objects: assessing causality and underlying processes. *J. Commun.* 59:407–33

Petty RE, Cacioppo JT. 1986. The elaboration likelihood model of persuasion. In *Advances in Experimental Social Psychology*, ed. L Berkowitz, pp. 123–205. New York: Academic

Pingree RJ. 2007. How messages affect their senders: a more general model of message effects and implications for deliberation. *Commun. Theory* 17:439–61

Postmes T, Lea M, Spears R, Reicher SD. 2000. *SIDE Issues Centre Stage: Recent Developments in Studies of De-individuation in Groups*. Amsterdam: KNAW

Potter WJ. 2012. *Media Effects*. Thousand Oaks, CA: Sage

Potter WJ, Riddle K. 2007. A content analysis of the media effects literature. *J. Mass Commun. Q.* 84:90–104

Powers KL, Brooks PJ, Aldrich NJ, Palladino MA, Alfieri L. 2013. Effects of video-game play on information processing: a meta-analytic investigation. *Psychonom. Bull. Rev.* 20:1055–79

Pratto F, John OP. 1991. Automatic vigilance: the attention-grabbing power of negative social information. *J. Personal. Soc. Psychol.* 61:380–91

Prior M. 2005. News versus entertainment: how increasing media choice widens gaps in political knowledge and turnout. *Am. J. Polit. Sci.* 49:577–92

Raykov T, Marcoulides GA. 2012. *A First Course in Structural Equation Modeling*. New York: Routledge

Reber R, Schwarz N, Winkielman P. 2004. Processing fluency and aesthetic pleasure: Is beauty in the perceiver's processing experience? *Personal. Soc. Psychol. Rev.* 8:364–82

Rideout VJ, Foehr UG, Roberts DF. 2010. *Generation M2: Media in the Lives of 8- to 18-Year-Olds*. Menlo Park, CA: Kaiser Family Found.

Roberts DF, Bachen CM. 1981. Mass-communication effects. *Annu. Rev. Psychol.* 32:307–56

Rockinson-Szapkiw AJ, Courduff J, Carter K, Bennett D. 2013. Electronic versus traditional print textbooks: a comparison study on the influence of university students' learning. *Comput. Educ.* 63:259–66

Rosengren KE. 1974. Uses and gratifications: a paradigm outlined. In *The Uses of Mass Communications: Current Perspectives on Gratifications Research*, ed. JG Blumler, E Katz, pp. 269–86. Beverly Hills, NJ: Sage

Rubin A. 2009. Uses-and-gratifications perspective on media effects. See Bryant & Oliver 2009, pp. 165–84

Savage J, Yancey C. 2008. The effects of media violence exposure on criminal aggression: a meta-analysis. *Crim. Justice Behav.* 35:772–91

Scheufele DA. 1999. Framing as a theory of media effects. *J. Commun.* 49:103–22

Schramm W. 1962. Mass communication. *Annu. Rev. Psychol.* 13:251–84

Schultz D, Izard CE, Ackerman BP, Youngstrom EA. 2001. Emotion knowledge in economically disadvantaged children: self-regulatory antecedents and relations to social difficulties and withdrawal. *Dev. Psychopathol.* 13:53–67

Shah DV, Cho J, Eveland WP, Kwak N. 2005. Information and expression in a digital age: modeling Internet effects on civic participation. *Commun. Res.* 32:531–65

Sherry JL. 2001. The effects of violent video games on aggression: a meta-analysis. *Hum. Commun. Res.* 27:409–31

Shoemaker PJ. 1996. Hardwired for news: using biological and cultural evolution to explain the surveillance function. *J. Commun.* 46:32–47

Short J, Williams E, Christie B. 1976. *The Social Psychology of Telecommunications*. London: Wiley

Shrum LJ. 2009. Media consumption and perception of social reality. See Bryant & Oliver 2009, pp. 50–73

Slater MD. 2007. Reinforcing spirals: the mutual influence of media selectivity and media effects and their impact on individual behavior and social identity. *Commun. Theory* 17:281–303

Slater MD. 2015. Reinforcing spirals model: conceptualizing the relationship between media content exposure and the development and maintenance of attitudes. *Media Psychol.* 18:370–95

Slater MD, Henry KL, Swaim RC, Anderson LL. 2003. Violent media content and aggressiveness in adolescents: a downward spiral model. *Commun. Res.* 30:713–36

Slater MD, Peter J, Valkenburg PM. 2015. Message variability and heterogeneity: a core challenge for communication research. In *Communication Yearbook 39*, ed. EL Cohen, pp. 3–32. New York: Routledge

Slater MD, Rouner D. 2002. Entertainment-education and elaboration likelihood: understanding the processing of narrative persuasion. *Commun. Theory* 12:173–91

Small GW, Moody TD, Siddarth P, Bookheimer SY. 2009. Your brain on Google: patterns of cerebral activation during Internet searching. *Am. J. Geriatr. Psychiatry* 17:116–26

Smith SM, Fabrigar LR, Powell DM, Estrada M-J. 2007. The role of information-processing capacity and goals in attitude-congruent selective exposure effects. *Personal. Soc. Psychol. Bull.* 33:948–60

Snyder LB, Hamilton MA, Mitchell EW, Kiwanuka-Tondo J, Fleming-Milici F, Proctor D. 2004. A meta-analysis of the effect of mediated health communication campaigns on behavior change in the United States. *J. Health Commun.* 9:71–96

Song H, Zmyslinski-Seelig A, Kim J, Drent A, Victor A, et al. 2014. Does Facebook make you lonely? A meta analysis. *Comput. Hum. Behav.* 36:446–52

Sproull L, Kiesler S. 1986. Reducing social-context cues: electronic mail in organizational communication. *Manag. Sci.* 32:1492–512

Stoolmiller M, Gerrard M, Sargent JD, Worth KA, Gibbons FX. 2010. R-rated movie viewing, growth in sensation seeking and alcohol initiation: reciprocal and moderation effects. *Prev. Sci.* 11:1–13

Sundar SS, Jia H, Waddell TF, Huang Y. 2015. Toward a theory of interactive media effects (TIME). In *The Handbook of the Psychology of Communication Technology*, ed. SS Sundar, pp. 47–86. New York: Wiley

Swanson DL. 1987. Gratification seeking, media exposure, and audience interpretations—some directions for research. *J. Broadcast. Electron. Media* 31:237–54

Taifel H. 1978. Social categorization, social identity, and social comparison. In *Differentiation Between Social Groups: Studies in the Social Psychology of Group Relations*, ed. H Taifel, pp. 61–76. London: Academic

Taifel H, Turner JC. 1979. The social identity theory of intergroup behavior. In *Psychology of Intergroup Relations*, ed. S Worchel, WC Austin, pp. 7–24. Chicago: Nelson Hall

Tannenbaum PH, Greenberg BS. 1968. Mass communications. *Annu. Rev. Psychol.* 19:351–86

Tichenor PJ, Donohue GA, Olien CN. 1970. Mass media flow and differential growth in knowledge. *Public Opin. Q.* 34:159–70

Toffler A. 1980. *The Third Wave: The Classic Study of Tomorrow*. New York: Bantam

Valkenburg PM. 2014. *Schermgaande jeugd* [*Youth and Screens*]. Amsterdam: Prometheus

Valkenburg PM, Cantor J. 2001. The development of a child into a consumer. *J. Appl. Dev. Psychol.* 22:61–72

Valkenburg PM, Peter J. 2009. The effects of instant messaging on the quality of adolescents' existing friendships: a longitudinal study. *J. Commun.* 59:79–97

Valkenburg PM, Peter J. 2011. Online communication among adolescents: an integrated model of its attraction, opportunities, and risks. *J. Adolesc. Health* 48:121–27

Valkenburg PM, Peter J. 2013a. The differential susceptibility to media effects model. *J. Commun.* 63:221–43

Valkenburg PM, Peter J. 2013b. Five challenges for the future of media-effects research. *Int. J. Commun.* 7:197–215

Valkenburg PM, Peter J, Schouten AP. 2006. Friend networking sites and their relationship to adolescents' well-being and social self-esteem. *Cyberpsychol. Behav.* 9:584–90

Valkenburg PM, Vroone M. 2004. Developmental changes in infants' and toddlers' attention to television entertainment. *Commun. Res.* 31:288–311

Van Der Heide B, Schumaker EM, Peterson AM, Jones EB. 2013. The Proteus effect in dyadic communication: examining the effect of avatar appearance in computer-mediated dyadic interaction. *Commun. Res.* 40:838–60

Walther JB. 1992. Interpersonal effects in computer-mediated interaction: a relational perspective. *Commun. Res.* 19:52–90

Walther JB. 1996. Computer-mediated communication: impersonal, interpersonal, and hyperpersonal interaction. *Commun. Res.* 23:3–43

Walther JB, Liang YH, DeAndrea DC, Tong ST, Carr CT, et al. 2011a. The effect of feedback on identity shift in computer-mediated communication. *Media Psychol.* 14:1–26

Walther JB, Tong ST, DeAndrea DC, Carr C, Van Der Heide B. 2011b. A juxtaposition of social influences: Web 2.0 and the interaction of mass, interpersonal, and peer sources online. In *Strategic Uses of Social Technology: An Interactive Perspective of Social Psychology*, ed. Z Birchmeier, B Dietz-Uhler, G Stasser, pp. 172–94. Cambridge, UK: Cambridge Univ. Press

Webster JG. 2009. The role of structure in media choice. In *Media Choice: A Theoretical and Empirical Overview*, ed. T Hartmann, pp. 221–33. New York: Routledge

Weiss W. 1971. Mass communication. *Annu. Rev. Psychol.* 22:309–36

Wellman RJ, Sugarman DB, DiFranza JR, Winickoff JP. 2006. The extent to which tobacco marketing and tobacco use in films contribute to children's use of tobacco: a meta-analysis. *Arch. Pediatr. Adolesc. Med.* 160:1285–96

Wood W, Wong FY, Chachere JG. 1991. Effects of media violence on viewers' aggression in unconstrained social interaction. *Psychol. Bull.* 109:371–83

Yee N, Bailenson JN, Ducheneaut N. 2009. The Proteus effect: implications of transformed digital self-representation on online and offline behavior. *Commun. Res.* 36:285–312

Zillmann D. 1996. Sequential dependencies in emotional experience and behavior. In *Emotion: Interdisciplinary Perspectives*, ed. RD Kavanaugh, B Zimmerberg, S Fein, pp. 243–72. Mahwah, NJ: Erlbaum

Zillmann D, Bryant J. 1985. Affect, mood, and emotion as determinants of selective exposure. In *Selective Exposure to Communication*, ed. D Zillmann, J Bryant, pp. 157–90. Hillsdale, NJ: Erlbaum

Zillmann D, Chen L, Knobloch S, Callison C. 2004. Effects of lead framing on selective exposure to Internet news reports. *Commun. Res.* 31:58–81

Changing Norms to Change Behavior

Dale T. Miller[1] and Deborah A. Prentice[2]

[1]Graduate School of Business, Stanford University, Stanford, California 94305;
email: dtmiller@stanford.edu

[2]Department of Psychology, Princeton University, Princeton, New Jersey 08540

Annu. Rev. Psychol. 2016. 67:339–61

First published online as a Review in Advance on
August 7, 2015

The *Annual Review of Psychology* is online at
psych.annualreviews.org

This article's doi:
10.1146/annurev-psych-010814-015013

Keywords

interventions, social norms, social norm marketing, drinking behavior,
energy conservation

Abstract

Providing people with information about the behavior and attitudes of their
peers is a strategy commonly employed by those seeking to reduce behavior
deemed harmful either to individuals (e.g., high alcohol consumption) or
the collective (e.g., high energy consumption). We review norm-based interventions, detailing the logic behind them and the various forms they can
take. We give special attention to interventions designed to decrease college
students' drinking and increase environment-friendly behaviors. We identify the conditions under which norm information has the highest likelihood
of changing the targeted behavior and discuss why this is the case.

Contents

INTRODUCTION

People's behavior is greatly influenced by what they see or hear of others doing (Cialdini & Goldstein 2004, Miller & Prentice 1996). Although the powerful effect of social norms has long been known by psychologists (e.g., Asch 1955, Lewin 1943, Sherif 1937), it is only recently that interventions seeking to modify individually or collectively pernicious behavior have started to leverage normative information. This shift reflects a growing disillusionment with the capacity of factual information and economic inducements to reduce such behavior. For example, informing college students of the dangers of heavy alcohol consumption does little to reduce their drinking levels (Blane & Hewitt 1977), and providing homeowners with financial incentives for energy conservation does little to reduce home energy consumption (Epsey & Epsey 2004).

Two assumptions underlie the strategy of providing people with information about their peers in order to modify their behavior: First, accurate information about what peers or relevant others think, feel, or do is not always known or salient to people; and second, providing people with this information has the potential to alter their understanding of group norms, their own standing in the group, and the evaluative significance of the behavior in question. This altered understanding may, in turn, lead them to act differently.

TARGETING SOCIAL NORMS

The term social norm has two meanings in the context of interventions. It can refer to a common behavior or practice, as in "Most members in this community donate money to charity." It can also refer to an average outcome or output standard, as in "The median annual amount donated to charity by members of this community is $2,500." These two meanings suggest two ways that people can be more or less in step with their peers. First, people can conform to a common practice (donate to charity) or deviate from it (not donate). Second, even if people do conform to the practice, they can do so in a manner that places them nearer or further from the central tendency of their group (a high, low, or average donator). Traditional discussions of norms tend to assume that people are aware of the norm of their group and where they are in relation to it. The assumption of norm-based interventions is that people often do not know what the norm is or are mistaken about it and their relation to it. Receiving feedback as to where their actions put them in the distribution of their peers (e.g., above or below the 50th percentile) or in relation to the most common actions of their peers (e.g., in the majority or in the minority) shapes their representation of their peer group and the evaluative significance of their behavior.

INTERVENTION STRATEGIES

Researchers and practitioners have experimented with different strategies to convey distributional information in a meaningful, believable, and memorable way. These strategies fall into three main categories that vary in their commonness as a function of the behavior targeted.

Social Norms Marketing

One intervention strategy is known as social norms marketing (SNM) and has been used most commonly in attempts to reduce risky behavior, in particular college students' drinking (Burchell et al. 2013, Perkins 2014). The hallmark of this approach is the dissemination of a single factual message documenting the (high) incidence of some desirable behavior to all or at least many members of a group (e.g., college campus or neighborhood). This message can be conveyed via publicity events, t-shirts, posters, student newspapers, doorhangers, and email. An example of such a message targeting drinking among college students is "Eighty-five percent of students on our campus drink 0, 1, 2, 3 or at most 4 drinks when they party." An example of such a message that targets energy conservation is "Seventy-seven percent of your neighbors report taking shorter showers to conserve energy." This strategy is appealing in that it has the potential to disseminate the distributional information to a large number of people cheaply and efficiently. The downside is that it is scattershot and subject to misinterpretation and suspicion. Another restriction is that its effectiveness presupposes that the behavior it seeks to encourage is already highly common.

Personalized Normative Feedback

The second approach is one that aims its message at individuals, providing them with information about themselves as well as their peers. In interventions targeting alcohol consumption and other risky behavior, these interventions are termed personalized feedback interventions or personalized normative feedback (PNF) (Lewis & Neighbors 2006a, Miller et al. 2013). An alcohol-based intervention of this type first asks the members of a group or community (e.g., students at a particular college), via email or web-based means, to identify both how much they drink and how much they think their peers (more or less broadly defined) drink. As a next step, it provides members of the group with the discrepancies both between their estimates of the norm and the actual norm and between their reported level of drinking and the actual norm. An example of the feedback a student might receive is the following: "You said you drink 10 drinks per week and that you think the typical student drinks 15. The actual average is 4.6 drinks. You drink more than 80% of other college students" (Neighbors et al. 2011). This is a labor-intensive approach, but it does a better job than SNM of highlighting the implications of the distributional information for the self.

PNF interventions targeting environmental conservation behaviors typically do not collect perceptions of others from intervention participants. First, they collect each participant's rate of energy consumption, often from a utility company, and then, as a second step, present this information to the participants by mail or email along with the average usage of their peers, more or less broadly defined. An example of the feedback a homeowner might receive is "You consume more water than 60% of your ___ County neighbors" (Ferraro & Price 2013).

Focus Group Discussion

The third approach, used primarily in interventions focused on risky behavior, uses facilitator-led, live interaction groups to discuss both the misperceptions that exist about the risky practices and the cause and consequences of these misperceptions (Barnett et al. 1996, Far & Miller 2003, LaBrie et al. 2008, Reilly & Wood 2008, Schroeder & Prentice 1998, Steffian 1999). Focus group discussion (FGD) is the most labor-intensive approach of all and relies on skilled facilitators to draw out people's true attitudes and behaviors.

One challenge for norm-based interventions is ensuring that participants attend to and comprehend the information embedded in the intervention (Thombs et al. 2005). One of the rationales for using the PNF approach over the SNM approach is that the former is more likely to ensure that participants process the message of the intervention. A second challenge of norm-based intervention is perceived credibility. For example, college students are not surprisingly distrustful of an anti-drinking message that is distributed by the college administration and that contradicts their experience (Granfield 2002). The PNF approach is thought to better convince participants that the information is credible because it includes information about the source of the data it provides. The focus group approach is also able to allay credibility concerns by helping participants understand why their perceptions were incorrect.

INTERVENTIONS TO REDUCE RISKY BEHAVIOR

Norm-based interventions were developed originally to reduce the prevalence of risky behavior in situations in which people held biased perceptions of the attitudes of their peers toward this behavior. The delivery of valid information about peer attitudes and behaviors was aimed at correcting these biased perceptions. The behavior targeted most extensively by this type of intervention—and the one we focus on here—is college students' drinking behavior.

Theory of Norm-Based Interventions to Reduce College Students' Drinking

The theory of norm-based interventions is that students' drinking behavior is correlated with, and at least somewhat caused by, an exaggerated estimate of the drinking norms and that correcting students' misperceptions will curb their drinking behavior (Perkins 2003). But how influential are misperceptions, and will changing them produce an impact on behavior?

To examine the logic of norm-based interventions, consider a college where the data indicate that 7 of 10 students don't drink on most nights, yet the collective perception of students is that 7 of 10 students do drink on most nights. Why might publicizing the factual message "Seven of 10 students don't drink most nights" be expected to lower drinking? Let us begin by positing two determinants of a student's drinking level: (*a*) his or her preferred consumption rate and (*b*) his or her perception of the average consumption rate. From the fact that students generally perceive the consumption norm to be higher than their consumption level, we can assume that many moderate drinkers are not influenced by what they perceive to be the norm and instead consume at their preferred level. Correcting their perceptions of the norm and thereby showing them that their consumption level is more in step with the actual norm than they previously thought may make them feel more comfortable with their consumption level but seems unlikely to change it. The exceptions might be those moderate drinkers who, although drinking less than what they mistakenly perceived to be the norm, are still drinking more than they would like to be.

The focal participants in the intervention (in our example, the 30% of the population who are heavy drinkers) fall into two groups that vary in their potential to be influenced by a downward shift in the perception of the norm. The most receptive to change would be those who were drinking more than they wanted to because of a desire to be socially accepted. For them, learning of the actual norm should be disinhibiting and should liberate them to act on their preference to consume less. These individuals are the low-hanging fruit for norm-based interventions, and the more of them there are in the population, the more successful such interventions will be. Those heavy drinkers whose actual consumption rate is their preferred consumption rate and who previously thought that this was closer to the median rate than it is might also respond to the intervention by drinking less, but they would require more of a push. Specifically, the intervention would have to be strong enough to induce them to drink less than they would like to drink and were accustomed to drinking. Moreover, it is highly likely that these individuals would respond to such an intervention by rationalizing the meaning and relevance of the normative information and possibly by increasing their social contact with other students whose preference for alcohol consumption is similar to their own (Blanton et al. 2008). All of these responses would mute the behavioral effects of the intervention.

In summary, the potential success of a norm-based intervention depends on how norm-misperceiving students are distributed across two distinct psychological profiles. The potential for success is better the greater the number of students whose drinking behavior is preference inconsistent but is perceived to be norm consistent (i.e., students drink more than they would prefer to because they mistakenly think the behavior makes them similar to their peers).

Pluralistic ignorance. When the misperceived norm is sufficiently powerful to overcome students' more moderate drinking preferences, drinking is characterized by pluralistic ignorance (Miller et al. 2000, Prentice & Miller 1993, Suls & Green 2003): a circumstance in which most people drink heavily but assume everyone else, unlike them, is comfortable with this consumption level. When pluralistic ignorance exists, the most appropriate intervention is one that focuses not on behavioral norms but rather on attitudinal norms—that is, reports of how (un)comfortable students feel with their drinking practices, not what those practices are (Prince & Carey 2010, Schroeder & Prentice 1998). One indication that pluralistic ignorance routinely arises around drinking practices on campus is that self-other differences that emerge on measures of attitudes toward drinking tend to be larger than those that arise on measures of behavior (Borsari & Carey 2003). Students may think that their behavior differs from that of their peers, but they think that their comfort with their behavior differs much more. Of course, the fact that studies routinely find a discrepancy between perceived and actual drinking behavior suggests that situations of total pluralistic ignorance are rare on campuses.

Changing perceptions of the norm. Despite the challenges, efforts to change perceived norms often report success. This is true whether the intervention takes the form of SNM (Borsari & Carey 2003, DeJong et al. 2006, Glider et al. 2001, Gomberg et al. 2001, Haines & Spear 1996), PNF (Agostinelli et al. 1995; Collins et al. 2002; Larimer et al. 2007; Mattern & Neighbors 2004;

Neighbors et al. 2004, 2006; Walters et al. 2000), or FGD (LaBrie et al. 2008). Importantly, the test of an intervention's effectiveness in changing perceived norms is relative, not absolute. The general test is whether the perceived norm moves closer to the actual norm following the intervention and not the more conservative test of whether it converges on the actual norm. It is unclear whether this movement represents total convergence for some participants and no effect for others or partial convergence for many. It seems reasonable that for most people, their postintervention norm estimate represents a compromise between what they previously believed and what they were told was actually the case. LaBrie et al. (2008), for example, found that perceptions converged on the publicized norms but did not fully accept them.

Of course, changing norms does not necessarily change behavior. For a norm-based intervention to be successful at changing drinking behavior, the norm targeted must have evaluative significance for students. This consideration often requires a trade-off between the scope of an intervention and its impact. For example, changing the perception of the consumption level of the typical student may have little resonance with students who strongly identify with narrower groups (e.g., same-gender students, dorm mates, fellow athletes). Many investigators have targeted local norms rather than more global ones. The assumption here is that people care about some groups more than others and that it is the drinking norms of those groups about which they care most that provide the most appropriate metric for them.

Considerable research indicates that feedback on close referents has the strongest effects on behavior (Baer et al. 1991; Borsari & Carey 2003; Cho 2006; LaBrie et al. 2008; Lewis & Neighbors 2004, 2006b). For example, Lewis & Neighbors (2004) found that same-sex norms were more strongly related to personal drinking behavior than were other-sex norms. In a subsequent study, these researchers found that women who scored high on female-gender identity were especially influenced by their perceptions of female drinking norms (Lewis & Neighbors 2007). Not all evidence supports the greater influence of close referents, however. In one study using interactive PNF, LaBrie et al. (2013) found that heavy-drinking Asian male students and Greek (sorority)-affiliated female students reduced their drinking more when they were compared with typical students than with the typical Asian male or typical Greek female student.

In short, changing perceptions of the norm will not change behavior for all of the people all of the time. However, it will work for some of the people some of the time, so it is important to determine when this strategy is successful.

Effectiveness of the Norm-Based Approach to Reducing Drinking

Estimating the percentage of norm-based interventions that succeed in changing behavior is difficult because these programs are rarely evaluated in a systematic and rigorous way. Moreover, there is little consistency in the execution of the interventions, leading to disputes about which studies should and should not be included in any assessment (Perkins 2003, Wechsler et al. 2003). Restricting the focus to studies of SNM and PNF interventions that use random assignment, meaningful controls, and appear in peer-reviewed journals does not clarify the situation greatly. Some of these studies are successful (Agostinelli et al. 1995, Borsari & Carey 2003, Collins et al. 2002, DeJong et al. 2006, Glider et al. 2001, Gomberg et al. 2001, Miller et al. 2013, Neighbors et al. 2004), and others are not (Clapp et al. 2003, DeJong et al. 2009, Moreira et al. 2010, Thombs & Hamilton 2002, Werch et al. 2000).

In general, the likelihood of both Type 1 and Type 2 errors is high in these studies. On the one hand, there is no way to know that failed interventions were designed and executed effectively enough to provide the theory with a fair test. On the other hand, there is often no way to know that successful interventions succeeded because they provided normative information, as interventions typically include multiple components (Barnett et al. 2007, Carey et al. 2006). Regarding this last point, it is common for PNF interventions, in addition to highlighting normative discrepancies, to provide didactic information and encourage consideration of personal, social, financial, and even caloric costs of alcohol use (Walters & Neighbors 2005).

Mediation of behavior change by change in the normative level of consumption. Despite these challenges, a sizable body of evidence from published reports of alcohol interventions now enables us to assess the relation of changes in the perceived normative level of consumption to changes in drinking behavior. Many of these studies document that interventions produce downward changes in both perceived norms and alcohol consumption (Barnett et al. 1996, Haines & Spear 1996, Steffian 1999, Turner et al. 2008, Walters et al. 2000). Interventions that employ media campaigns are able to show parallel changes on measures of perceived norms and behaviors but typically are unable to assess what causal role norm change played in the observed behavior change. Interventions that use face-to-face or web-based interactive PNF formats, by contrast, can often conduct mediational analyses, and many of these have documented the mediational role of perceived norm change in behavior change (Borsari & Carey 2000; Carey et al. 2010; Doumas et al. 2009; LaBrie et al. 2008; Lewis & Neighbors 2007; Neighbors et al. 2004, 2006; O'Grady et al. 2011). Additional evidence that the norm-behavior link is driven by a change in the evaluative significance of the drinking norm comes from research showing that this type of intervention is particularly effective for those who report drinking for social reasons (Lee et al. 2007, Neighbors et al. 2004) and those who perceive drinking to be an integral part of student life (Crawford & Novak 2010).

Behavior change without change in the normative level of consumption. There are also cases in which norm-based interventions reduced drinking behaviors but not norm perceptions (Schroeder & Prentice 1998). One potential reason for this outcome, suggested by Nolan (2011), is that reported norm change may be constrained by the anchoring and adjustment bias. Specifically, following the intervention, people's experience might be that the norm is lower than they previously thought, but their estimate of what the new norm is may nevertheless be constrained by their previous estimate. Another possibility pertains to what the norm intervention does. Rather than relocating the norm, the effect of the intervention may be to weaken the power of the norm (Prentice 2008). The way that students code the information that others drink less than they thought may simply be that the pressure to drink is less than they thought. The perceived weakening of the norm will be especially influential for those who have been drinking more than they would like to because of their fear of social rejection (Schroeder & Prentice 1998).

Norm change without behavior change. In some cases, interventions changed perceived norms but not behavior (Bewick et al. 2000). There are various possible reasons for this outcome. First, as noted previously, many students might already have been acting independently of what they perceived to be the norm by drinking less than it prescribes. These students would have little motivation to change when they learn that the actual norm is even closer to their preferred behavior. Second, students who learn from the intervention that their preferred behavior is much more discrepant from the actual norm than they thought (i.e., they drink more) may question whether the norm carries evaluative significance for them (Blanton et al. 2008). They might, for example, accept that they were wrong about what the typical student drank but believe that they remained correct in their estimate of what those who matter drink. A third reason is that the evaluative significance of behavior may change with the change in perceived norm, but the situational presses operating on students may overwhelm these. For example, interventions that feature norms pertaining to special events such as 21st birthdays and spring breaks very often change norm perceptions but not behavior (Patrick et al. 2014, Stamper et al. 2004). It may be that social and institutional pressures to drink on these occasions are so strong (e.g., free drinks at bars on 21st birthdays) that they overwhelm the impact of the normative information. As another example of a strong situational press, DeJong et al. (2009) surmised that norm change produced by intervention is more likely to translate into behavioral changes the fewer the number of liquor stores near campus, suggesting that easy availability may dominate perceptions of drinking rates in determining drinking behavior.

Indirect effects. Thus far, we have analyzed drinking as an individual decision made by an actor who has preferences both about drinking alcohol and his or her social reputation. This analysis has neglected the impact that norm debiasing has on the behavior of those in the social environment of the at-risk individual. In fact, norm-based interventions can influence an individual's behavior directly, through their effects on his or her thoughts and perceptions, but also indirectly, through their effects on the behavior of friends, bystanders, and others in their social world.

These indirect effects stem from the fact that students drink in social settings and are supported or inhibited by the actions of others. Friends offer them drinks, tell them to slow down, encourage or discourage them to call it a night, and so on. These social behaviors, like drinking itself, depend on perceptions of the norm and therefore can be influenced by norm-based interventions. Consider, for example, the act of driving drunk, which often occurs in a social context and thus implicates bystanders who allow or encourage the individual to drive. The actions of bystanders depend, in turn, on their beliefs about the perceived commonness and appropriateness of intervening when someone is drunk. The more support people feel there is for looking out for someone who is drunk, the more willing they will be to do so (Turner et al. 2008). Indeed, studies find that students underestimate their peers' support for intervening with their drinking friends and that providing students with accurate information about the supportive actions of others increases students' willingness to undertake those actions themselves (Kenney et al. 2013, Mollen et al. 2013).

Changing the collective perception of a community of individuals can also lead to social action that, in turn, will affect individual behavior. For example, students might be more willing to support alcohol-free events on campus if their misperceptions about peer support for drinking were corrected. One example of how an SNM campaign can affect the broader social climate around alcohol use is provided by an intervention designed to reduce drinking and driving in Montana (Perkins et al. 2010). The project found that residents of the state did overestimate the prevalence of drinking and driving and mounted a campaign, using television, radio, print, and theater ads, to market accurate norms [e.g., "Most of us (4 out of 5) don't drink and drive"]. The campaign was successful in reducing norm misperception and reported prevalence of drinking and driving. Most relevant to the present discussion, the intervention increased by 16% the number of residents willing to support reducing the blood alcohol content (BAC) legal limit for drinking to 0.08, a measure that quite likely would reduce drinking-related deaths and injuries.

Beyond Drinking on Campus

As this example illustrates, alcohol use on college campuses is not the only behavioral domain in which we find systematic misperceptions of social norms. Other populations also overestimate the prevalence of drinking (Chan et al. 2007), and college students and others misperceive the prevalence of many other behaviors, including the use of tobacco (Hansen & Graham 1991) and illicit drugs (Perkins 2003), the wearing of seatbelts (Linkenbach & Perkins 2003), the practicing of safe sex (Lynch et al. 2004), bullying (Sandstrom et al. 2013), and sexual aggression (Paluck & Ball 2010). In many of these contexts, norm-based interventions have had success. Moreover, studies in these other behavioral domains provide additional insight into the dynamic nature of the behavior-change process that norm debiasing can trigger.

Consider, for example, an SNM intervention focused on seat belt use, again in Montana (Linkenbach & Perkins 2003). This three-year campaign established that although 85% of Montana drivers reported that they had buckled their seat belt the last time they drove, they estimated that only 60% of other drivers did. This campaign disseminated messages such as "Most Montanans—3 out of 4—wear seat belts" via radio, print, and public service announcements. Over the three years of the intervention, the perceptions of the actual norm became more accurate, and the number of drivers reporting wearing seat belts increased.

How might the minority (approximately 15%) of delinquent drivers have been induced to wear seat belts by the campaign? It is unlikely that prior to the campaign these non-seat-belt wearers were inhibited from wearing seat belts due to evaluative concern and that the SNM campaign was successful because it dispelled this concern. All drivers before the campaign acknowledged that the majority of drivers already wore seat belts, so it is difficult to believe anyone felt pressured into *not* wearing one. More likely, non-seat-belt wearers were simply people who preferred not to wear seat belts but who required a minimum level of perceived support to feel comfortable doing so. When these individuals saw that they were even more isolated than they thought, their increased reputational concern then dominated their preference not to wear a seat belt, and they buckled up. Alternatively, seeing the actual norm may have changed the behavior of those who already wore seat belts by making them more insistent that others (drivers and passengers) also wear seat belts. This latter, indirect effect may have been even more influential than the direct effect on the non-seat-belt wearers. In other words, it was not so much that publicizing the correct norm increased the perceived social cost that non-seat-belt wearers thought they bore, but rather that it increased the actual social cost they bore.

Correcting misperceptions about risky sexual behavior provides further insight into the role that indirect effects can have on interpersonal dynamics. Decisions about safe-sex practices are made in relationship contexts and often involve negotiations. Once individuals discover that safe-sex practices are more common than they believed, it changes the negotiation power of those who advocate for and against safe-sex practices. The ones whose preference is for unsafe sex are in a weaker position once they and their partners know that safe sex is the norm. Moreover, people are more likely to share disapproving information about a partner who refused to practice safe sex and to support authorities who advocate safe-sex practices when they recognize the support such practices have. Similarly, when college men and women learn that "Nine of 10 men stop when their partner first says no" (Bruce 2002), it may have a direct effect on the 1 man in 10 who does not stop by revealing his isolation and deviance to him. At the same time, it may have an indirect effect on his behavior by empowering women to say no to him more emphatically or to report him if he fails to take no for an answer.

Some SNM interventions explicitly target bystanders in an effort to reduce high-risk behavior indirectly by encouraging intervention (Banyard et al. 2007, Loh et al. 2005). Consider a study by Perkins et al. (2011) aimed at reducing bullying in middle schools. These researchers first assessed students' estimates of the prevalence of bullying and victimization and attitudinal support for bullying. Estimates of peer norm support for bullying behavior were found to be three to four times higher than the actual norm, which was based on self-report. The subsequent SNM campaign used posters that contained messages such as "Ninety-five percent of _____ Middle School students say students should NOT tease in a mean way, call others hurtful names, or spread unkind stories about other students" and "Most ____Middle School students (8 out of 10) think that students should tell a teacher or counselor if they or someone else are being bullied at school." The postintervention assessment showed that perceptions had become more accurate and that personal attitudes had become more anti-bullying and more pro-intervention.

In short, bystanders' willingness to intervene, whether in risky dating situations (Gidycz et al. 2011), ones involving homophobic taunts (Bowen & Bourgeois 2001), or ones involving sexist actions (Fabiano et al. 2003, Loh et al. 2005, Stein 2007), depends on their perceptions of their peers' support for such actions, support that they systematically underestimate. SNM campaigns designed to correct these misperceptions show promising results (Berkowitz 2010, Fabiano et al. 2003, Perkins 2014, Stein 2007). Moreover, research suggests that the effectiveness of these campaigns resides less in their ability to change the social costs that would-be perpetrators perceive and more in their ability to change the social costs that emboldened bystanders actually impose on perpetrators.

Summary

The verdict on the empirical effects of norm-based interventions designed to change risky behaviors is still pending. Despite the popularity of these interventions, only a small subset includes the requisite controls to permit rigorous evaluation. Examples of successful programs, including many reviewed here, provide compelling, suggestive evidence of the social-psychological processes through which this approach can be effective. However, systematic reviews of the actual effectiveness of these interventions have reached inconsistent conclusions. Tempering enthusiasm further, most of the supportive evidence rests on self-report data (for exceptions, see Johnson 2012, Neighbors et al. 2011).

INTERVENTIONS TO REDUCE CONSUMPTION OF PUBLIC GOODS

Norm-based interventions have also been deployed in an effort to reduce consumption of public goods. When it comes to public goods, perceived norms tend to be unclear or absent, rather than biased, and thus the interventions work primarily by making people more aware of their own behavior and where it falls in the distribution. To produce directional behavior change, these interventions rely on (and cultivate) people wanting to be on one side of the median more than the other. This approach has been used most extensively in interventions designed to reduce environmental harm (Abrahamse & Steg 2013, Harries et al. 2013, Iyer et al. 2006, McKenzie-Mohr et al. 2012).

Theory of Norm-Based Interventions to Reduce Environmental Harm

Norm-based interventions aimed at reducing environmental harm differ from those aimed at reducing risky behaviors in a number of important respects. For one, these interventions do not assume that there is a biased collective misperception about behavior—an overestimation or underestimation of people's environmental-conservation activities. Indeed, the information provided to people in environmental interventions tends to focus not on behavior (cf. Goldstein et al. 2008, Schultz et al. 2007) but rather on the output of behavior (e.g., kilowatt-hour use), a metric about which few people could be expected to make confident population estimates. The feedback in environmental interventions also takes a different form, focusing on people's relative standing on a consumption measure (e.g., how their weekly kilowatt use compares to that of their neighbors) rather than on their absolute discrepancy from a behavioral norm (e.g., how the number of drinks they consume per week compares to others).

If not by correcting misperceptions, how might providing people with personalized normative feedback produce aggregate behavior change? At a minimum, it must induce high users to use less. This turns out to be an elusive goal. High energy users are notoriously insensitive to other types of interventions designed to reduce their consumption, such as information campaigns, persuasive messages, and economic inducements (Abrahamse et al. 2005, Katzev & Johnson 1987). Moreover, although social pressure can change even sticky habits, the circumstances most optimal for such change to occur—specifically, high visibility of the target behavior and close contact among members of the participating group—are typically not present in the context of environmental interventions.

The theory of norm-based interventions begins with the observation that energy and other environmental resources are public goods; that is, resources from which all people benefit, whether or not they contribute (Alcott 2011). In public-goods domains, an individual's behavior has consequences not just for him- or herself, but for everyone else in the group as well, and this fact shapes the meaning of the normative information. For example, consider two individuals, one of whom learns that she uses more energy than others and another who learns that he drinks more alcohol than others. Both of these individuals have learned that they are out of step with their peers, an uncomfortable realization. However, the high energy consumer has also learned something even more threatening: She is not doing her share for the environment. She is violating not just a behavioral norm but also a good-citizenship norm. Even if she is not deeply troubled by being behaviorally out of step with others, the pressure to reciprocate the cooperativeness of her peers and do her part may be a powerful inducement to reduce her energy consumption (Alpizar et al. 2008, Bolsen 2013, Carlson 2001, Frey & Meier 2004, Shang & Crosson 2009, Strahilevitz 2003).

There is a second mechanism through which normative feedback might affect energy consumption: informational influence (Deutsch & Gerard 1955). Specifically, informing people that their neighbors use less energy will convey to people that it is possible to use less energy. As using less energy means saving money, this knowledge could conceivably increase high users' resolve to do so out of a sense of increased efficacy rather than guilt or shame. But there are a couple of reasons to doubt that the normative feedback plays a large informational role for recipients. First, research shows that providing normative information reduces energy consumption by high users more effectively when the information is presented publicly than when it is presented privately (Delmas & Lessem 2014); this finding suggests that concern with social standing is at the root of its effects. Second, as noted previously, high users have been found to be the least sensitive to variations in the cost of energy (Dolan & Metcalfe 2012), suggesting that doing the rational thing is not a high priority for them. Consistent with this evidence, normative feedback reduces the energy usage of high users even when they are not paying for their energy use (Young 2013).

The success of norm-based environmental interventions depends not just on their effectiveness with high users; they must also reinforce the behavior of low users. This, too, is a challenge, for there are at least two reasons why normative information might lead low users to increase their consumption. First, low users might simply feel uncomfortable being out of step with the behavior of their peers and wish to conform to standard practices. Although such conformity is possible in theory, it seems unlikely in practice: The behavior of low users is not conspicuously out of step, and because their actions qualify them as good—not bad—actors, low users might be motivated to maintain their status. A second, more compelling reason why feedback might induce low users to increase their consumption resides in the bivalent psychology of doing more than one's share. That is, although it is possible to see low users as good actors, it is also possible to see them as suckers, whose pro-environment actions are being exploited by free-riding neighbors (Kahan 1997). The well-documented tendency of those who discover that they are high contributors to public goods (e.g., low energy users) to reduce their contribution is known as the boomerang effect

(Mollen et al. 2013, Nolan et al. 2008). Given how powerful the fairness motive is in public-goods situations, the risk of a boomerang effect of norm-based interventions is very real. Indeed, Fischer (2008) attributed her finding of a null effect of PNF interventions on household energy use to the opposing effects of normative feedback on high and low users.

How might high contributors to a public good be made to feel less like suckers and more like good actors? Nolan et al. (2008) created one clever means to accomplish this goal: They accompanied the energy reports of low users with a positive emoticon. The presence of this happy face presumably framed low users' performance as a source of pride rather than resentment. Although there is some debate about how long this framing manipulation lasts, most large-scale interventions continue to use some means of signaling to low users that their behavior is something to feel good rather than bad about (Alcott 2011, Loock et al. 2012).

Effectiveness of the Norm-Based Approach to Reduce Environmental Harm

Current efforts to reduce environmental harm by providing normative feedback originated in a series of small field studies that used SNM and PNF (e.g., Goldstein et al. 2008, Nolan et al. 2008, Schultz et al. 2007). One study targeted towel reuse in 190 rooms of a midsize hotel in the southwestern United States (Goldstein et al. 2008). Along with encouragement to do the environmentally responsible thing ("Help save the environment") and reuse their towels, guests in one treatment condition were provided with a card that said, "Join your fellow guests in helping to save the environment. Almost 75% of our guests who are asked to participate in our new resource saving program do help by using their towels more than once." The guests receiving this normative information were 28% more likely to recycle one or more towels (an effect replicated by Schultz et al. 2008).

A second study targeted energy usage among 371 households in a California community (Nolan et al. 2008). Once a week for four weeks, participants received doorhangers that contained factual information about their neighbors' high rate (ranging from 77% to 99%) of various energy-conserving behaviors, such as taking shorter showers, turning off unnecessary lights, turning off the air conditioner at night, and using fans instead of air conditioners, along with general appeals to conserve energy. Compared to participants who did not receive the normative information, participants in the treatment condition showed a 10% decrease in kilowatt-hours used, and even after eight weeks showed a rate 7% less than control households.

The study that became the model for most of the larger-scale interventions to follow was a PNF intervention that targeted household energy usage (Schultz et al. 2007). The context for this intervention was 290 California households with visible utility meters. Researchers provided these households with various types of normative information and messages, again on doorhangers over a two-week period, and observed the effect on utility usage. In the comparative information condition, participants received information indicating where they stood (higher than average versus lower than average) in energy usage compared to their neighbors. Those who learned that they used more energy than most of their neighbors reduced their energy usage, and those who learned that they used less energy than most of their neighbors increased their energy use unless their feedback was accompanied by a smiley-face emoticon and the word "good." This information signaling approval seems to have framed their standing as an accomplishment, something to be proud of, rather than something that made them a sucker.

The success, ease, and scalability of the Schultz et al. (2007) study inspired a series of large-scale interventions that delivered personalized normative feedback about energy consumption to householders via their monthly energy bill. The first was sponsored by Opower, a publicly held company that partners with utilities around the world to promote energy efficiency. Opower began its work in 2008 by mailing home energy reports to approximately 35,000 households within the Sacramento Municipal Utility District. Twenty-five thousand ratepayers were randomly selected to receive a monthly energy report comparing their electricity consumption to the average consumption of similar homes in their community, another 10,000 households received such reports quarterly, and 50,000 served as a control group (Alcott 2011). The comparative information pointed to the average energy usage among approximately 100 neighbors with similarly sized homes that used the same energy sources (electricity only or electricity and natural gas). A further level of comparison was provided by comparing individual households to "Efficient Neighbors," defined as the lowest 20% of consumers. Households above average in consumption received a message conveying disapproval, whereas those below average in consumption received a happy face and a "good" or "great" depending on whether they fell below the 50th percentile or the 20th percentile.

The effects of the intervention were impressive. Households that had received energy reports for six months consumed 2.5% less electricity than control households. Households receiving monthly reports conserved more than those receiving quarterly reports, and high-consuming households achieved greater reduction in usage than low-consuming households. Subsequent analyses of follow-up data showed that the difference in energy consumption between treatment and control groups persisted for more than one year (Ayres et al. 2013). A comprehensive analysis of Opower interventions, encompassing 22 million utility bills from nearly 600,000 households across 12 different utility companies, determined that the implementation of Opower's home energy reports yields average energy savings of 2% (Alcott 2011, Alcott & Mullainathan 2010).

Similar studies conducted in partnership with other utility companies have reported parallel effects (Dolan & Metcalfe 2012, Ferraro & Price 2013, Loock et al. 2012). In one example, Ferraro & Price (2013) targeted 100,000 households that contracted with a water utility company in Georgia. These researchers provided ratepayers in the social comparison condition with their quarterly water usage rate and that of their neighbors. They observed a significant decrease in water usage in this condition equivalent to the decrease expected if average prices were to increase 12% to 15% per month. Ferraro et al. (2012) followed up this sample and found that those in the social comparison condition were still using less water two years later.

In summary, the evidence from norm-based interventions designed to reduce environmental harm is encouraging. Numerous small- and large-scale interventions show that providing people with information about the scope and degree of their peers' energy-related behavior can reduce their energy consumption. The magnitudes of effects vary across interventions and individual consumers, but the low cost and simple mechanics of these types of interventions make them attractive. Finding ways to strengthen the feedback and increase its salience to consumers will make norm-based interventions an even more cost-effective means of reducing energy consumption.

Whose norm is most effective? All norm-based interventions have to select a reference group to feature in the feedback. Risky behavior interventions have typically grounded their selections in social identity considerations (e.g., same-gender friends, teammates, sorority sisters). Public-goods interventions, by contrast, have focused on physical or geographical similarity—nearby residents, fellow hotel guests, etc. To use Goldstein et al.'s (2008) phrase, the greatest impact is expected to be produced by behaviors and outputs of others who share the same immediate circumstances. More generally, the question of which comparison groups have the greatest impact has generated much less attention in environmental interventions than in alcohol interventions. Studies that have manipulated the reference group generally find that the more physically or geographically close those represented in the norm are to participants, the more influence they have (Goldstein et al. 2008, Loock et al. 2012, Schultz 1999, Young 2013).

Which norm is most effective? All norm-based interventions also must select a norm to communicate. Following Cialdini et al. (1990), many researchers have distinguished between injunctive norms that characterize the prevalence of approval or disapproval of a behavior and descriptive norms that characterize the prevalence of the behavior itself. Despite much discussion in the literature about these two types of norms and their relative impact on behavior, the inconsistent operationalization of these two concepts permits few meaningful comparisons (Smith & Louis 2008). For present purposes, the most useful comparison to consider is between feedback that specifies (*a*) the commonness of particular environmental behaviors among group members and (*b*) the degree of approval among group members for those same behaviors.

One complication that arises in comparing the impact of these two types of normative feedback is that they convey information about one other (Blanton et al. 2008). That is, when interventions emphasize the high frequency of behaviors, they also imply high approval for those same behaviors, as the following examples suggest: (*a*) "Join your fellow guests in helping to save the environment. Almost 75% of guests who are asked to participate in our new resource savings program do help by using their towels more than once. You can join your fellow guests in this program to help save the environment by reusing your towels during your stay" (Goldstein et al. 2008). (*b*) "Following a recent university-wide survey, your university is pleased to report that over 65% of current students are actively reducing their consumption of bottled water" (Van der Linden 2013).

Likewise, when interventions emphasize high approval for behaviors, they also imply the high frequency of those same behaviors, as the following examples suggest: (*a*) "The vast majority of Illinois residents support energy conservation and over 90% agree that it is important for 'all Americans to make energy efficient consumption decisions'" (Bolsen 2013). (*b*) "Shoppers in this store believe that reusing shopping bags is a worthwhile way to help the environment" (De Groot et al. 2013).

Given the implicit relationship between these two types of information, it is not surprising that they are both successful at changing behavior (Abrahamse & Steg 2013, Bolsen 2013, De Groot et al. 2013, Jacobson et al. 2011). At the same time, providing both types of information can be more effective than providing either alone (Schultz et al. 2008).

The most interesting comparisons come from studies that provide information of both types and vary their consistency with one another. For example, what happens when one learns that one's peers preach one thing but practice something else? Not surprisingly, inconsistency between others' actions and expressed support produces less behavior change than does consistency (Göckeritz et al. 2010, Schultz et al. 2008, Smith & Louis 2008, Smith et al. 2012). Inconsistent information, however, does have a more positive impact than does information suggesting that peers neither support nor engage in pro-environmental activity and more impact than the absence of either type of information.

Whether it is necessary that descriptive evidence accompany injunctive evidence for behavior change to occur likely depends on the behavioral preference of the audience. If the recipient of the message is disposed to take the action, learning that others support that action—even if they don't behaviorally demonstrate that support—can be liberating (Reid & Aiken 2013, Smith & Louis 2008). For example, learning that one's peers support conservation efforts will enable one to turn down the heat without fearing social disapproval, even if no one else does the same. On the other hand, an explicitly unsupportive descriptive norm will likely undermine the effects of a supportive injunctive norm if the recipient's willingness to take the action is conditional upon the reciprocity of others (Smith et al. 2012). That others express their approval of contributing to a public good that they themselves do not contribute to is a recipe for resentment and resistance, not compliance.

When information backfires. Various types of boomerang effects are discussed in the literature. In one, conveying that a particular behavior is bad and common leads to increases in the behavior. This can happen for two different reasons. First, the reported commonness of the behavior can make it seem less inherently bad (Mollen et al. 2013). Consider an intervention that seeks to reduce premarital sex by emphasizing both its undesirability and its statistical commonness. This message could actually increase the incidence of premarital sex because the evidence that everybody is doing it undermines the credibility of the claim that it is undesirable. For this version of the boomerang effect to occur it is not necessary that the normative data compel premarital sex among those not so disposed; it is sufficient that it liberate those so disposed but previously inhibited.

Evidence of commonness can also trump evidence of undesirability in public-goods contexts. Here, people might be persuaded of the direness of the situation (e.g., pilfering petrified wood is destroying a national park, overfishing is destroying fish stocks) but nevertheless feel compelled by learning of the extent of free riding among others to free ride themselves and thereby avoid being suckers. Learning of the commonness of free riding can also liberate good actors to start free riding, as they now know that any negativity incurred by such behavior will be widely diffused (McAdams 1997). One way to address this problem is to frame the performance of low consumers as a source of pride rather than resentment. A second way to address the problem is to provide normative feedback only to high consumers.

The foregoing examples of boomerang effects emerge when people learn that an undesirable behavior is more common than they thought. These effects are most likely to occur in public-goods contexts, where free riding often leads the majority of people to engage in bad behavior. They are least likely to occur in risky-behavior contexts, where bad (risky) behavior is typically less common than people think.

Summary

In public-goods situations, people often find themselves with the unappealing choice between behaving like a fool (by failing to exploit the public good) and behaving like a knave (by exploiting it). By highlighting the commonness and desirability of nonexploitative behavior, norm-based interventions can turn fools into good actors and knaves into bad actors. The key to the success of these interventions lies in their ability to destigmatize collectively beneficial behavior by linking it to shared values. This requires not just that individuals see their own behavior as motivated by shared values but also that they see others' behavior as similarly motivated.

TOWARD A MODEL OF NORM-BASED INTERVENTIONS

The growing popularity of norm-based interventions to reduce collectively (and sometimes personally) costly behavior is a response to the failure of other intervention efforts. Programs that educate people about the riskiness of behavior through information and persuasion campaigns are stunningly ineffective (Abrahamse et al. 2005, Stern 1999). Programs that modify risky behavior through conventional carrots and sticks have also proven less than effective. For those seeking to move behavior in a positive direction, norm-based interventions are a promising alternative.

Although norm-based feedback works differently in different contexts and different populations, the goal in all cases is to change the perceived norm and therefore the evaluative significance of behavior, making a current behavior undesirable or a counterfactual behavior desirable. When feedback of this type is effective, it is because learning what others do or think makes people evaluate their own actions differently. Much of the current research on norm-based interventions focuses on how best to deliver or present the feedback. These practical considerations are undoubtedly important to the success of the interventions, but we have chosen in this review to address the more basic theoretical questions of when and why such interventions can be expected to work.

From Peer Information to Norm Change

Peer information pertaining to risky behavior is designed primarily to make people more comfortable with nonrisky behavior by establishing support for this behavior among peers. The information seeks to show people that the social pressure they feel to undertake risky behavior is illusory and that the fear they have that they will incur disapproval if they do not fully embrace risky action is unwarranted. Its goal, thus, is liberation. Most people overestimate their peers' support for risky behavior; correcting their estimates frees them to act on their less risky preferences. Even if the peer information is not fully incorporated into perceptions of the norm, perhaps because it conflicts with what people observe, the revelation that they have more allies or kindred spirits than they thought can still weaken the norm's power over them (Prentice 2008).

Peer information will have much less influence on those comfortable with high-risk behavior, for the simple reason that it is more difficult to make people feel uncomfortable doing something that they enjoy and feel comfortable doing than it is to make people feel comfortable doing something they actually want to do but don't do because of their mistaken belief that they lack peer support. For those comfortable with high-risk behavior, their comfort may owe nothing to their mistaken perception that others approve of it. Moreover, even if it does, correcting this misperception is no guarantee that the evaluative significance of the behavior will change greatly for them. The cues that supported their misperception will still exist, which, given people's resistance to viewing their own behavior as problematic, could well be sufficient for them to remain comfortable continuing doing what they have been doing. A shift in their behavior may require minimally a shift in what they actually see others do, not just in what they are told others do.

The goal of providing peer information pertaining to collectively harmful, as opposed to individually harmful, behavior is different. Here, the intervention seeks to make high consumers of public goods uncomfortable with their actions by showing them that they are not doing their fair share. In addition to this primary goal, a secondary goal is to avoid making good actors—those who are doing their share—feel like suckers. Interventions in the SNM tradition provide behavioral and/or approval information designed to change the evaluative significance of a particular discrete action, such as using a fan, reusing towels, or recycling. Although there are multiple ways this information could work, the most effective way is to establish a connection in people's minds between a value they embrace (e.g., being pro-environment, doing one's fair share) and a concrete action (e.g., reusing hotel towels) they previously had not tied to that value (McAdams 1997, Vandenbergh 2005). Establishing this connection is important because even people who care about doing their share to preserve the environment might not tie that value to taking particular actions (e.g., reusing hotel towels, using fans). The knowledge that most others engage in a behavior will have its greatest impact on those who already embrace the value that guides the action but simply had not recognized that their peers perceive the targeted action as a concrete desideratum of that value.

Interventions in the PNF tradition seek to do this and more: They use behavioral and approval information to establish the evaluative significance of particular actions and personalized feedback to motivate people to improve their own standing. The success of these interventions again rests on establishing a link between an accepted value and the target behavior; without that link, the personalized feedback loses its power. For example, if people do not see high energy use as something inconsistent with a value they care about or that others expect them to care about, showing them that they rank behind their peers on this dimension will not motivate them. It will simply signal that others are currently outperforming them on this metric.

From Norm Change to Behavior Change

Even if peer information changes the evaluative significance of behavior, will behavior change follow? Our review shows there is no guarantee, though behavior change is more likely under some conditions than others. The most fertile ground exists among those who are currently acting inconsistent with their preference due to some form of social inhibition, such as the fear that acting on their preference will make them look like a nerd or a sucker. By showing them that their preference is widely shared, the restraining force that has kept these individuals from acting on their preference is removed, and their behavior will fall in line with their preference. Thus, the more people there are who drink to excess because of a mistaken sense that others will disapprove of them if they drink more moderately, the more effective will be an intervention that highlights approval of moderate consumption. Similarly, the more people there are who resist turning down their heat for fear that doing so will make them suckers, the more effective will be an intervention that shows the commonness of this behavior.

It is a bigger challenge to induce people to act contrary to their preferences, but norm-based interventions can be effective here as well. When the context is a public-goods situation, for example, many free riders will simply be acting on their (self-interested) preference. Highlighting their lack of contribution relative to others can induce guilt or shame and thereby motivate greater contributions. The desire not to be seen as a free rider is likely more powerful than any motivation that will arise in heavy drinkers who learn that, contrary to their belief, others drink less than they do. But even here, some movement is possible.

One reason that even those comfortable with their high-risk behavior might be motivated to change stems from the fact that norm-based interventions occur in the context of broader intervention efforts. School and health authorities repeatedly tell college students about the dangers of heavy drinking, unsafe-sex practices, and any number of other risky behaviors. The principal reason these messages are ineffective is that they lack credibility: Students are distrustful of claims that behaviors that they find identity affirming (and enjoyable) are harmful, or at least as harmful as antagonistic authorities suggest they are. Discovering that their peers' behaviors are more in line with these messages than they thought serves to corroborate the authorities' message. For example, learning that most of their peers use condoms implies that their peers accept the arguments made by authorities about the importance of safe sex. Similarly, learning that most other hotel guests recycle their towels means that these other guests find the arguments for this practice made by the hotel management to be legitimate and not simply a manipulative effort to save money. Those who learn that they consume more energy than their neighbors can reasonably assume that their neighbors find the pro-environmental case to be persuasive. At the very least, the fact that there seems to be common cause between so many of their peers and authorities will increase their sense of isolation.

The process described above may seem like conventional informational influence (Deutsch & Gerard 1955), but it is importantly different. To illustrate, consider a study by Van der Linden (2013). The goal in this study was to reduce Dutch students' bottled water use, which averaged about 10 bottles per month. Participants in the experimental conditions of this study received either (a) descriptive norm information that suggested that most students were trying to reduce their bottled water usage, (b) a persuasive message that emphasized the environmental costs of bottled water and the safety of tap water, or (c) both descriptive norm information and a persuasive message. Notably, neither the descriptive norm information nor the persuasive message reduced intentions to consume bottled water when presented alone. Only when these two pieces of information were combined was there a significant decrease in behavioral intentions. What is instructive here is that if intentions were driven by informational influence, the descriptive norm alone would have been effective. The reason it was not effective is that recipients apparently knew little about the environmental argument against bottled water and therefore had difficulty knowing what significance to attach to their peers' behavior. Those who received the persuasive message making the environmental case saw the descriptive information as a referendum on that case and modified their behavior in line with the apparent coalition of fellow students and environmental authorities.

Norm-based interventions are more effective in some contexts than in others. Contexts in which there is attitudinal support but not behavioral support for the goal of the intervention will typically prove more promising than contexts in which there is neither attitudinal nor behavioral support. Highly cohesive groups or groups sharing a salient social identity also appear to be more susceptible to influence by norm-based feedback (Neighbors et al. 2004).

A final condition that boosts the effectiveness of norm-based interventions is the presence of channel factors that allow the modified psychological states of participants to convert into behavior. For example, learning that one's peers regularly use condoms may increase one's motivation to follow suit, but the ready availability of condoms will increase the likelihood that this motivation will translate into behavior. Similarly, an intention to drink less following an intervention will be more likely to translate into behavior if conditions such as alcohol-free events are in place to make that possible. Especially valuable in the context of energy conservation is ready access to capital stock, such as solar panels and energy-efficient light bulbs. Equally valuable is knowledge about steps to take or habits to form so that an increased commitment to conserve energy can translate into actual behavior (Dolan & Metcalfe 2012).

CONCLUSION

Providing people with information about the behaviors and attitudes of their peers is an increasingly common strategy for reducing behavior that is harmful to the individual or the collective. The present article has analyzed the psychological theory behind different versions of this intervention strategy and reviewed the empirical findings generated by norm-based interventions, particularly those aimed at reducing alcohol abuse and energy consumption. We expect the popularity of this intervention strategy to continue to increase and hope that consideration of the issues raised in this review will increase the sophistication and success of these interventions as well.

DISCLOSURE STATEMENT

The authors are not aware of any affiliations, memberships, funding, or financial holdings that might be perceived as affecting the objectivity of this review.

LITERATURE CITED

Abrahamse W, Steg L. 2013. Social influence approaches to encourage resource conservation: a meta-analysis. *Glob. Environ. Change* 23(6):1773–85

Abrahamse W, Steg L, Vick C, Rothengatter T. 2005. A review of intervention studies aimed at household energy consumption. *J. Environ. Psychol.* 25:273–91

Agostinelli G, Brown JM, Miller WR. 1995. Effects of normative feedback on consumption among heavy drinking college students. *J. Drug Educ.* 25:31–40

Alcott H. 2011. Social norms and energy conservation. *J. Public Econ.* 95:1082–95

Alcott H, Mullainathan S. 2010. Behavior and energy policy. *Science* 327(5970):1204–5

Alpizar F, Carlson F, Johansson-Stennman O. 2008. Anonymity, reciprocity, and conformity: evidence from voluntary contributions to a national park in Costa Rica. *J. Public Econ.* 92:1047–60

Asch S. 1955. Opinions and social pressure. *Sci. Am.* 193:31–35

Ayres I, Raseman S, Shih A. 2013. Evidence from two large field experiments that peer comparison feedback can reduce residential energy usage. *J. Law Econ. Org.* 29:992–1022

Baer JS, Stacy A, Larimer M. 1991. Biases in the perception of drinking norms among college students. *J. Stud. Alcohol* 52:580–86

Banyard VL, Moynihan MM, Plante EG. 2007. Sexual violence prevention through bystander education: an experimental evaluation. *J. Community Psychol.* 35:463–81

Barnett LA, Far JM, Maus AL, Miller JA. 1996. Changing perceptions of peer norms as a drinking reduction program for college students. *J. Alcohol Drug Educ.* 41:39–62

Barnett NP, Murphy JG, Colby SM, Monti PM. 2007. Efficacy and mediation of counselor versus computer-delivered interventions with mandated college students. *Addict. Behav.* 32:2529–48

Berkowitz AD. 2010. Fostering healthy norms to prevent violence and abuse: the social norms approach. In *The Prevention of Sexual Violence: A Practitioner's Sourcebook*, ed. KL Kaufman, pp. 147–71. Holyoke, MA: NEARI Press

Bewick BM, Trusler K, Mulhern B, Barkham M, Hill AJ. 2000. The feasibility and effectiveness of a web-based personalized feedback and social norms alcohol intervention in UK university students: a randomised control trial. *Addict. Behav.* 33:1192–98

Blane HT, Hewitt LC. 1977. *Mass Media Public Education and Alcohol: A State-of-the-Art Review*. Rockville, MD: Natl. Inst. Alcohol Abuse Alcohol.

Blanton H, Koblitz A, McCaul KD. 2008. Misperceptions about norm misperceptions: descriptive, injunctive, and affective "social norming" efforts to change behaviors. *Soc. Personal. Psychol. Compass* 2/3:1379–99

Bolsen T. 2013. A light bulb goes on: norms, rhetoric, and actions for the public good. *Polit. Behav.* 35(1):1–20

Borsari B, Carey KB. 2000. Effects of a brief motivational intervention with college student drinkers. *J. Consult. Clin. Psychol.* 68:728–33

Borsari B, Carey KB. 2003. Descriptive and injunctive norms in college drinking: a meta-analytic integration. *J. Stud. Alcohol* 64:331–41

Bowen AM, Bourgeois MJ. 2001. Attitudes towards lesbian, gay and bisexual college students: the contribution of pluralistic ignorance, dynamic social impact and contact theories. *J. Am. Coll. Health* 50(2):91–96

Bruce S. 2002. *The "A Man" campaign: marketing social norms to men to prevent sexual assault*. Rep. Soc. Norms: Work. Pap. #5. Little Falls, NJ: PaperClip Commun.

Burchell K, Rettie R, Patel K. 2013. Marketing social norms: social marketing and the "social norms approach." *J. Consum. Behav.* 12:1–9

Carey KB, Carey MP, Maisto SA, Henson JM. 2006. Brief motivational interventions for heavy college drinkers: a randomized controlled trial. *J. Consult. Clin. Psychol.* 74:943–54

Carey KB, Henson JM, Carey MP, Maisto SA. 2010. Perceived norms mediate effects of brief motivational intervention for sanctioned college drinkers. *Clin. Psychol. Sci. Pract.* 17:58–71

Carlson AE. 2001. Recycling norms. *Calif. Law Rev.* 89(5):1231–300

Chan KK, Neighbors C, Gilson M, Larimer ME, Marlatt GD. 2007. Epidemiological trends in drinking by age and gender: providing normative feedback to adults. *Addict. Behav.* 32:967–76

Cho H. 2006. Influences of norm proximity and norm types on binge and non-binge drinkers: examining the under-examined aspects of social norms interventions on college campuses. *J. Subst. Abuse* 11:417–29

Cialdini RB, Goldstein NJ. 2004. Social influence: compliance and conformity. *Annu. Rev. Psychol.* 55:591–621

Cialdini RB, Reno RR, Kallgren CA. 1990. A focus theory of normative conduct: recycling the concept of norms to reduce littering in public places. *J. Personal. Soc. Psychol.* 58:1015–26

Clapp JD, Lange JE, Russell C, Shillington A, Voas RB. 2003. A failed norms social marketing campaign. *J. Stud. Alcohol* 64:409–14

Collins SR, Carey KB, Sliwinski MJ. 2002. Mailed personalized normative feedback as a brief intervention for at-risk college drinkers. *J. Stud. Alcohol* 63:559–67

Crawford LA, Novak KB. 2010. Reactivity to conspicuousness and alcohol use among college students: the moderating effect of expectancies. *Addict. Behav.* 29:1845–49

De Groot JIM, Abrahamse W, Jones K. 2013. Persuasive normative messages: the influence of injunctive and personal norms on using free plastic bags. *Sustainability* 5:1829–44

DeJong W, Schneider SK, Towvim LG, Murthpy MJ, Doer EE, et al. 2006. A multisite randomized trial of social norms marketing campaigns to reduce college student drinking. *J. Stud. Alcohol* 67:868–79

DeJong W, Schneider SK, Towvim LG, Murthpy MJ, Doer EE, et al. 2009. A multisite randomized trial of social norms marketing campaigns to reduce college student drinking: a replication failure. *Subst. Abuse* 30:127–40

Delmas M, Lessem N. 2014. Saving power to conserve your reputations? The effectiveness of private versus public information. *J. Environ. Econ. Manag.* 67(3):353–67

Deutsch M, Gerard HB. 1955. A study of normative and informational social influence upon individual judgment. *J. Abnorm. Soc. Psychol.* 51:629–36

Dolan P, Metcalfe R. 2012. *Better Neighbors and Basic Knowledge: A Field Experiment on the Role of Non-Pecuniary Incentives on Energy Consumption*. Oxford, UK: Dep. Econ., Oxford Univ.

Doumas DM, McKinley LL, Book P. 2009. Evaluation of two web-based alcohol interventions for mandated students. *J. Subst. Abuse Treat.* 36:65–74

Epsey JA, Espey M. 2004. Turning on the lights: a meta-analysis of residential electricity demand elasticities. *J. Agric. Appl. Econ.* 36(1):65–81

Fabiano PM, Perkins WH, Berkowitz A, Lickenbach J, Stark C. 2003. Engaging men as social justice allies in ending violence against women: evidence for a social norms approach. *J. Am. Coll. Health* 52:105–12

Far J, Miller J. 2003. The small group norms challenging model: social norms interventions with targeted high risk groups. In *The Social Norms Approach to Presenting School and College Age Substance Abuse: A Handbook for Educators, Counselors, and Clinicians*, ed. HW Perkins, pp. 111–32. San Francisco: Jossey-Bass

Ferraro PJ, Miranda JJ, Price M. 2012. Persistence of treatment effects with norm-based policy instruments: evidence from a randomized environmental policy experiment. *Am. Econ. Rev.: Papers Proc.* 101(3):318–22

Ferraro PJ, Price MK. 2013. Using non-pecuniary strategies to influence behavior: evidence from a large-scale field experiment. *Rev. Econ. Stat.* 95(1):64–73

Fischer C. 2008. Feedback on household electricity consumption: a tool for saving energy? *Energy Effic.* 1:429–34

Frey BS, Meier S. 2004. Social comparisons and pro-social behavior: testing "conditional cooperation" in a field experiment. *Am. Econ. Rev.* 94:1717–22

Gidycz C, Orchowski L, Berkowitz AD. 2011. Preventing sexual aggression among college men: an evaluation of a social norms and bystander intervention program. *Violence Against Women* 17(6):720–42

Glider P, Midyett SJ, Mills-Nova B, Johannessen K, Collins C. 2001. Challenging the collegiate rite of passage: a campus-wide social marketing media campaign to reduce binge drinking. *J. Drug Educ.* 31:207–20

Göckeritz S, Schultz PW, Rednon T, Cialsinia RB, Goldstein NJ, Griskevicius V. 2010. Descriptive normative beliefs and conservation behavior: the moderating role of personal involvement and injunctive normative beliefs. *Eur. J. Soc. Psychol.* 40:514–23

Goldstein N, Cialdini RB, Griskevicius V. 2008. A room with a viewpoint: using norm-based appeals to motivate conservation behaviors in a hotel setting. *J. Consum. Res.* 35:472–82

Gomberg L, Schneider SK, DeJong W. 2001. Evaluation of a social norms marketing campaign to reduce high-risk drinking at the University of Mississippi. *Am. J. Drug Alcohol Abuse* 27:375–89

Granfield R. 2002. *Can you believe it? Assessing the credibility of a social norms campaign*. Rep. Soc. Norms: Work. Pap. #2. Little Falls, NJ: PaperClip Commun.

Haines M, Spear SF. 1996. Changing the perception of the norm: a strategy to decrease binge drinking among college students. *J. Am. Coll. Health* 45:134–40

Hansen B, Graham JW. 1991. Preventing alcohol, marijuana, and cigarette use among adolescents: peer pressure resistance training versus establishing conservative norms. *Prev. Med.* 20:414–30

Harries T, Rettig R, Studley M, Chambers S. 2013. Is social norms marketing effective? A case study in domestic electricity consumption. *Eur. J. Mark.* 47:1458–75

Iyer M, Kempton M, Payne C. 2006. Comparison groups on bills: automated personalized energy information. *Energy Build.* 38:988–96

Jacobson RP, Mortensen CR, Cialdini RB. 2011. Bodies obliged and unbound: differentiated response tendencies for injunctive and descriptive social norms. *J. Personal. Soc. Psychol.* 100:433–48

Johnson MB. 2012. Experimental test of social norms theory in a real-world drinking environment. *J. Stud. Alcohol Drugs* 73(5):851–59

Kahan DM. 1997. Social influence, social meaning, and deterrence. *Va. Law Rev.* 83:349–95

Katzev R, Johnson T. 1987. *Promoting Energy Conservation: An Analysis of Behavioral Research*. Boulder, CO: Westview

Kenney SR, LaBrie JW, Lac A. 2013. Injunctive peer misperceptions and the mediation of self-approval on risk for driving after drinking among college students. *J. Health Commun.* 18(4):459–77

LaBrie JW, Hummer JF, Neighbors C, Pederson ER. 2008. Live interactive group-specific normative feedback reduces misperception and drinking in college students: a randomized cluster trial. *Psychol. Addict. Behav.* 22:141–48

LaBrie JW, Lewis MA, Atkins DC, Neighbors C, Zheng C, et al. 2013. RCT of web-based personalized normative feedback for college drinking prevention: Are typical student norms good enough? *J. Consult. Clin. Psychol.* 81(6):1074–86

Larimer ME, Lee CM, Kilmer JR, Fabiano PM, Stark CB, et al. 2007. Personalized mailed feedback for drinking prevention among college students: one year outcomes from a randomized clinical trial. *J. Consult. Clin. Psychol.* 75:285–93

Lee CM, Geisner IM, Lewis MA, Neighbors C, Larimer ME. 2007. Social motives and the interaction between descriptive and injunctive norms in college student drinking. *J. Stud. Alcohol Drugs* 68:714–21

Lewin K. 1943. Defining the "field at a given time." *Psychol. Rev.* 50:290–310

Lewis MA, Neighbors C. 2004. Gender-specific misperceptions of college drinking norms. *Psychol. Addict. Behav.* 18:334–39

Lewis MA, Neighbors C. 2006a. Social norms approaches using descriptive drinking norms education: a review of the research on personalized normative feedback. *J. Am. Coll. Health* 54:213–18

Lewis MA, Neighbors C. 2006b. Who is the typical college student? Implications for personalized normative feedback interventions. *Addict. Behav.* 31:2120–26

Lewis MA, Neighbors C. 2007. Optimizing personalized normative feedback: the use of gender-specific referents. *J. Stud. Alcohol Drugs* 68:228–37

Linkenbach J, Perkins HW. 2003. *Most of us wear seatbelts: the process and outcomes of a 3-year statewide adult seatbelt campaign in Montana*. Presented at Natl. Conf. Soc. Norms Model, July 17, Boston, MA

Loh C, Gidycz CA, Lobo TR, Luthra R. 2005. A prospective analysis of sexual assault perpetration: Risk factors related to perpetrator characteristics. *J. Interpers. Violence* 20:1325–48

Loock CM, Landwehr J, Staake T, Fleisch E, Pentland A. 2012. The influence of reference frame and population density on the effectiveness of social normative feedback on electricity consumption. *ICIS 2012 Conf. Proc.* **http://aisel.aisnet.org/icis2012/proceedings/GreenIS/7/**

Lynch J, Mowrey R, Nesbitt G, O'Neill D. 2004. Risky business: misperceived norms of sexual behavior among college students. *NASPA J.* 42(1):21–35

Mattern JL, Neighbors C. 2004. Social norms campaigns: examining the relationship between changes in perceived norms and changes in drinking levels. *J. Stud. Alcohol* 65:489–93

McAdams RH. 1997. The origin, development, and regulation of norms. *Mich. Law Rev.* 96:338–443

McKenzie-Mohr D, Lee D, Schultz PW, Kotler P. 2012. *Social Marketing to Protect the Environment: What Works*. Thousand Oaks, CA: Sage

Miller DT, Monin B, Prentice DA. 2000. Pluralistic ignorance and inconsistency between private attitudes and public behaviors. In *Attitudes, Behavior, and Social Context: The Role of Norms and Group Membership*, ed. DJ Terry, MA Hogg, pp. 95–113. Mahwah, NJ: Erlbaum

Miller DT, Prentice DA. 1996. The construction of social norms and standards. In *Social Psychology: Handbook of Basic Principles*, ed. ET Higgins, AW Kruglanski, pp. 799–829. New York: Guilford

Miller MB, Leffingwell T, Claborn K, Meier E, Walters S, Neighbors C. 2013. Personalized feedback intervention for alcohol misuse: an update of Walters & Neighbors (2005). *Psychol. Addict. Behav.* 27:909–20

Mollen S, Rimal RN, Ruiter RAC, Jang SA, Kok G. 2013. Intervening or interfering? The influence of injunctive and descriptive norms on intervention behaviors in alcohol consumption contexts. *Psychol. Health* 28:561–78

Moreira MT, Smith LA, Foxcroft D. 2010. Social norms interventions to reduce alcohol misuse in university or college students. *Cochrane Database Syst. Rev.* 3:CD006748

Neighbors C, Dillard AJ, Lewis MA, Bergstrom RL, Neil TA. 2006. Normative misperceptions of descriptive drinking norms and temporal precedence of perceived norms and drinking. *J. Stud. Alcohol* 67:290–99

Neighbors C, Jensen M, Tidwell J, Walter T, Fossos N, Lewis MA. 2011. Social-norms interventions for light and nondrinking students. *Group Process. Intergroup Relat.* 14:651–69

Neighbors C, Larimer ME, Lewis MA. 2004. Targeting misperceptions of descriptive drinking norms: efficacy of a computer-delivered personalized normative feedback intervention. *J. Consult. Clin. Psychol.* 72:434–47

Nolan JM. 2011. The cognitive ripple of social norms communications. *Group Process. Intergroup Relat.* 14:689–702

Nolan JM, Schultz PW, Cialdini RB, Goldstein NJ, Griskevicius V. 2008. Normative social influence is under-detected. *Personal. Soc. Psychol. Bull.* 34:913–23

O'Grady MA, Cullum J, Tennen H, Armell S. 2011. Daily relationship between event-specific drinking norms and alcohol use: a four-year longitudinal study. *J. Stud. Alcohol Drugs* 72:633–41

Paluck EL, Ball L. 2010. *Social Norms Marketing Aimed at Gender-Based Violence: A Literature Review and Critical Assessment*. New York: Intl. Rescue Comm.

Patrick ME, Lee CM, Neighbors C. 2014. Web-based intervention to change perceived norms of college student alcohol use and sexual behavior on spring break. *Addict. Behav.* 39(3):600–6

Perkins HW. 2003. The emergence and evolution of the social norms approach to substance abuse prevention. In *The Social Norms Approach to Preventing School and College Age Substance Abuse: A Handbook for Educators, Counselors, and Clinicians*, ed. HW Perkins, pp. 3–17. San Francisco: Jossey-Bass

Perkins HW. 2014. Misperception is reality: the "reign of error" about peer risk behavior norms among youth and young adults. In *The Complexity of Social Norms, Computational Social Sciences*, ed. M Xenitidou, B Edmonds, pp. 11–35. Berlin: Springer-Verlag

Perkins HW, Craig DW, Perkins JM. 2011. Using social norms to reduce bullying: a research intervention among adolescents in five middle schools. *Group Process. Intergroup Relat.* 14(5):703–22

Perkins HW, Linkenbach JW, Lewis MA, Neighbors C. 2010. Effectiveness of social norms media marketing in reducing drinking and driving: a statewide campaign. *Addict. Behav.* 35:866–74

Prentice DA. 2008. Mobilizing and weakening peer influence as mechanisms for changing behavior: implications for alcohol intervention programs. In *Understanding Peer Influence in Children and Adolescents*, ed. MJD Prinstein, KA Dodge, pp. 161–80. New York: Guilford

Prentice DA, Miller DT. 1993. Pluralistic ignorance and alcohol use on campus: some consequences of misperceiving the social norm. *J. Personal. Soc. Psychol.* 64:243–56

Prince MA, Carey KB. 2010. The malleability of injunctive norms among college students. *Addict. Behav.* 35:940–47

Reid AE, Aiken LS. 2013. Correcting injunctive norms misperception motivates behavior change: a randomized controlled sun protection intervention. *Health Psychol.* 32(5):551–60

Reilly DW, Wood DM. 2008. A randomized test of small-group interactive social norms interventions. *J. Am. Coll. Health* 57(1):53–60

Sandstrom M, Makover H, Bartini M. 2013. Social context of bullying: Do misperceptions of group norms influence children's responses to witnessed episodes? *Soc. Influ.* 8(2–3):196–215

Schroeder CM, Prentice DA. 1998. Exploring pluralistic ignorance to reduce alcohol use among college students. *J. Appl. Soc. Psychol.* 28:2150–80

Schultz PW. 1999. Changing behavior with normative feedback interventions: a field experiment on curbside recycling. *Basic Appl. Soc. Psychol.* 21:25–36

Schultz PW, Khazian A, Zaleski A. 2008. Using normative social influence to promote conservation among hotel guests. *Soc. Influ.* 3(1):4–23

Schultz PW, Nolan JM, Cialdini RB, Goldstein NJ, Griskevicius V. 2007. The constructive, destructive, and reconstructive power of social norms. *Psychol. Sci.* 18:429–34

Shang J, Crosson R. 2009. Field experiments in charitable contribution: the impact of social influence on the voluntary provision of public goods. *Econ. J.* 119:1422–79

Sherif M. 1937. An experimental approach to the study of attitudes. *Sociometry* 1:90–98

Smith JR, Louis WR. 2008. Do as we say and as we do: the interplay of descriptive and injunctive group norms in the attitude-behavior relationship. *Br. J. Soc. Psychol.* 47:647–66

Smith JR, Louis WR, Terry DJ, Greenaway KH, Clarke MR, Cheng X. 2012. Congruent or conflicted? The impact of injunctive and descriptive norms on environmental intentions. *J. Environ. Psychol.* 32:353–61

Stamper GA, Smith BH, Grant R, Bogle KE. 2004. Replicated findings of an evaluation of a brief intervention designed to prevent high-risk drinking among first-year college students: implications for social norming theory. *J. Alcohol Drug Educ.* 4:53–72

Steffian S. 1999. Correction of normative misperceptions: an alcohol abuse prevention program. *J. Drug Educ.* 29:115–38

Stein J. 2007. Peer educators and close friends as predictors of male college students' willingness to prevent rape. *J. Coll. Stud. Dev.* 48:78–79

Stern P. 1999. Toward a coherent theory of environmentally significant behavior. *J. Soc. Issues* 56(3):407–24

Strahilevitz L. 2003. Social norms from close-knit groups to loose-knit groups. *Univ. Chic. Law Rev.* 70:359–72

Suls J, Green P. 2003. Pluralistic ignorance and college student perceptions of gender-specific alcohol norms. *Health Psychol.* 22:479–86

Thombs DL, Hamilton MJ. 2002. Effects of a social norm feedback campaign on the drinking norms and behavior of Division 1 student-athletes. *J. Drug Educ.* 32:227–44

Thombs DL, Ray-Tomasek J, Osborn CJ, Olds RS. 2005. The role of sex-specific normative beliefs in undergraduate alcohol use. *Am. J. Health Behav.* 29:342–51

Turner J, Perkins HW, Bauerle J. 2008. Declining negative consequence related to alcohol misuse among students exposed to a social norms marketing intervention on a college campus. *J. Am. Coll. Health* 57:85–94

Van der Linden S. 2013. Exploring beliefs about bottled water and intentions to reduce consumption: the dual effect of social norm activation and persuasive information. *Environ. Behav.* 20:1–25

Vandenbergh MP. 2005. Order without social norms: how personal norm activation can protect the environment. *Northwest. Univ. Law Rev.* 99(3):1101–66

Walters ST, Bennett ME, Miller JH. 2000. Reducing alcohol use in college students: a controlled trial of two brief interventions. *J. Drug Educ.* 30:361–72

Walters ST, Neighbors C. 2005. Feedback interventions for college alcohol misuse: what, why and for whom? *Addict. Behav.* 30:1168–82

Wechsler H, Nelson TF, Lee JE, Seibring M, Lewis C, Kelling RP. 2003. Perception and reality: a national evaluation of social norms marketing interventions to reduce college students' heavy alcohol use. *J. Stud. Alcohol* 64:484–94

Werch CB, Pappas DM, Carlson JM, DiClemente CC, Chally PS, Sinder JA. 2000. Results of a social norm intervention to prevent binge drinking among first year residential college students. *J. Am. Coll. Health* 49:85–92

Young RM. 2013. *Variations on the normative feedback model for energy efficient behavior in the context of military family housing.* PhD thesis, Univ. Md. **http://hdl.handle.net/1903/14272**

Consistency Versus Licensing Effects of Past Moral Behavior

Elizabeth Mullen[1],[*] and Benoît Monin[2],[*]

[1]School of Management, San José State University, San José, California 95192;
email: elizabeth.mullen@sjsu.edu

[2]Graduate School of Business and Department of Psychology, Stanford University, Stanford,
California 94305; email: monin@stanford.edu

Annu. Rev. Psychol. 2016. 67:363–85

First published online as a Review in Advance on
September 17, 2015

The *Annual Review of Psychology* is online at
psych.annualreviews.org

This article's doi:
10.1146/annurev-psych-010213-115120

*The authors contributed equally to this article.

Keywords

moral credentials, moral credits, compensation, balancing, identity,
self-regulation

Abstract

Why does past moral behavior sometimes lead people to do more of the
same (consistency), whereas sometimes it liberates them to do the opposite
(licensing)? We organize the literature on moderators of moral consistency
versus licensing effects using five conceptual themes: construal level, progress
versus commitment, identification, value reflection, and ambiguity. Our review reveals that individuals are more likely to exhibit consistency when
they focus abstractly on the connection between their initial behavior and
their values, whereas they are more likely to exhibit licensing when they think
concretely about what they have accomplished with their initial behavior—as
long as the second behavior does not blatantly threaten a cherished identity. Moreover, many studies lacked baseline conditions ("donut" designs),
leaving it ambiguous whether licensing was observed. And although many
proposed moderators yielded significant interactions, evidence for both significant consistency and balancing simple effects in the same study was nearly
nonexistent.

Contents

THE PUZZLE OF MORAL LICENSING

Why does past behavior sometimes lead people to do more of the same, whereas at other times it liberates them to do just the opposite? Decades of research in social psychology support the notion that individuals have a strong drive toward consistency (e.g., Beaman et al. 1983, Burger 1999, Festinger 1954, Gawronski & Strack 2012). For example, inciting people to help a little (e.g., putting a small sign in their window) causes them to help more at a later stage (e.g., display a large sign on their front lawn)—the foot-in-the-door effect (Freedman & Fraser 1966). And yet in the past 15 years [since the publication of Monin & Miller's (2001) article], numerous studies have demonstrated what seems like the reverse phenomenon: Acting in one direction enables actors to later do just the opposite. For example, getting to disagree with racist statements (Monin & Miller 2001) or express a preference to vote for Obama (Effron et al. 2009) licensed individuals to express a preference for hiring a white person for another job; getting to recall past moral actions licensed individuals to express lower prosocial intentions (Jordan et al. 2011); and getting to choose green products in an online store licensed individuals to cheat more on a subsequent task (Mazar & Zhong 2010).

Despite their recent introduction to the literature, licensing effects are now widely documented and apparently reliable, if small: A recent meta-analysis of 91 licensing studies revealed an overall 95% confidence interval for Cohen's d ranging from 0.23 to 0.38 (Blanken et al. 2015). Furthermore, when Ebersole et al. (2015) attempted to replicate the first study in this tradition (Monin & Miller 2001, study 1) across many labs and 3,134 participants, they observed a reliable licensing effect, with a 95% confidence interval for d ranging from 0.08 to 0.21. Licensing effects have also been demonstrated in naturally occurring settings (Hofmann et al. 2014) and discussed outside of psychology, in marketing (Huber et al. 2008), management (Klotz & Bolino 2013, Ormiston & Wong 2013), economics (Brañas-Garza et al. 2013; Clot et al. 2013, 2014b; Ploner & Regner 2013), nutrition (Chang & Chiou 2014, Hennecke & Freund 2014, Weibel et al. 2014), and energy policy (Jacobsen et al. 2012, Tiefenbeck et al. 2013).

Licensing:
when a positive initial behavior yields less positive target behavior than a neutral baseline condition

On the face of it, these licensing findings present a striking contradiction with the numerous demonstrations of consistency mentioned above, and this remains the largest conundrum in the emerging licensing literature. Although reviews have speculated about reasons for the divergent effects (e.g., Blanken et al. 2015, Effron & Conway 2015, Huber et al. 2008, Merritt et al. 2010, Miller & Effron 2010), only recently have authors started testing moderators to explain when past behavior produces consistency versus licensing (see **Supplemental Table**; follow the **Supplemental Material link** in the online version of this article or at **http://www.annualreviews. org**). To name just three examples, Conway & Peetz (2012) posited that recalling recent behavior leads to licensing, whereas recalling more distant behavior leads to consistency; Cornelissen et al. (2013) proposed that focusing on consequences leads to licensing, whereas focusing on rules leads to consistency; and Brown et al. (2011) suggested that licensing only occurs when the behavior being liberated is highly rationalizable. In a few years, we have gone from an unanswered question to an overabundance of sometimes conflicting answers.

The main goal of this article is to remedy this situation by reviewing these multiple proposed moderators in one place to facilitate comparison and highlight underlying themes common to seemingly disparate mechanisms. To circumscribe the problem, we focus on cases of sequential behavior in the domain of important societal values (e.g., generosity, honesty, racial tolerance, respect for the environment), sometimes referred to as moral licensing.

A COMMON FRAMEWORK FOR SEQUENTIAL BEHAVIOR PARADIGMS

We first propose a common nomenclature to facilitate comparison and integration of the papers reviewed here and to remove ambiguity in discussing findings in the rest of this article. We review others' work through this lens, substituting the authors' language with our own for uniformity.

Defining Terms in Sequential Behavior Paradigms

We call sequential behavior paradigms the experimental situations in which an individual faces a choice in the context of relevant previous behavior. This context can range from behavior that was just performed moments before to prompted recollections of past behavior. Relevance ranges from the domain specific, when the present choice is the same as one faced earlier (helping yesterday, helping today), to the global, when both choices loosely relate to the same goal of being a moral person (e.g., buying green products, not cheating). The initial behavior (or behavioral recollection/ intention) comes first in the sequence, typically constitutes the independent variable, and can be positive (e.g., disagreeing with sexist statements, engaging in prosocial behavior) or negative (e.g., cheating, harming another).[1] One methodological challenge is to ensure that participants are randomly assigned to the initial behavior and do not self-select to perform it; this is often achieved by giving participants in the positive initial behavior condition the opportunity to do an easy good deed and making sure most of them do it, while participants in a control condition are deprived of this opportunity. Increasingly authors rely on experiential recall manipulations where they simply ask participants to recall and write about a time they acted morally or immorally. Some studies also include a baseline condition with a neutral initial behavior. Monin & Miller (2001), for example, pitted an initial positive behavior (appointing a woman or African American to a position) against a baseline control (appointing a white man out of five white male candidates). Many studies,

---

[1]We omit from our analysis of sequential behavior those effects that have nothing to do with the valence of the initial behavior, such as habit or variety seeking.

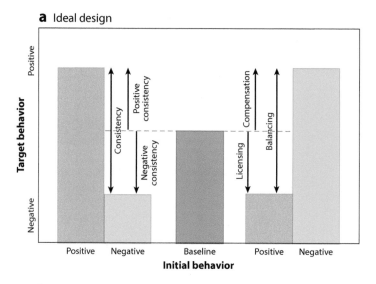

a Ideal design

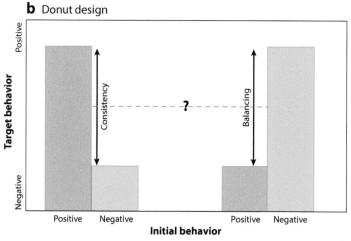

b Donut design

Figure 1

(*a*) Hypothetical outcomes of a sequential behavior paradigm in an ideal design. (*b*) In the absence of a baseline in a "donut" design, researchers cannot distinguish the contribution of licensing and compensation to any observed balancing effect.

Balancing: when an initial behavior produces the opposite in the target behavior (positive behavior decreases positivity; negative behavior increases positivity)

especially ones that involve recalling past behavior, omit the baseline control and only compare positive and negative behavior, making interpretation difficult, a point we return to below.

The target behavior (or behavioral opportunity) follows the initial behavior, serves as the dependent variable, and can also be positive (e.g., donating to charity) or negative (e.g., cheating). For the simplicity of our argument, however, we focus on whether the target behavior appears more positive (donating more, cheating less) or less positive (donating less, cheating more) than a relevant control. **Figure 1** illustrates the following potential relationships between the initial and the target behavior: consistency (positive or negative) and balancing (licensing or compensation).

MORAL CREDITS VERSUS MORAL CREDENTIALS

Some researchers (Merritt et al. 2010, Miller & Effron 2010) contrast two different forms of moral licensing: In a moral "credits" model, individuals accumulate credits in a metaphorical moral bank account and later use them to buy out of positive behavior or offset negative behavior, retaining an overall positive balance on their moral ledger despite clear withdrawals (Jordan et al. 2011, Nisan & Horenczyk 1990). By contrast, in a moral "credentials" model of licensing, the initial behavior provides a lens through which subsequent behavior is interpreted. So performing an initial moral act does not mean that one has earned the right to perform an immoral act with impunity, but instead that subsequent behavior is less likely to be interpreted as immoral (Monin & Miller 2001). As this description highlights, a credentials process is more likely at work when the motivations for the target behavior are ambiguous (e.g., racism versus pragmatism), and the initial behavior renders the suspicious motivation (here racism) less plausible. Given that most studies reviewed here were not designed to test this distinction (for an exception, see Effron & Monin 2010), we omit it from our empirical review.

The Role of Conflicting Motives

Although licensing and compensation are both instances of balancing (in different directions), it is important to distinguish them theoretically, as they likely rely on different processes. Compensation fits into a longstanding homeostatic view of self-regulation which posits that when individuals fall short of a goal, they are motivated to deploy effort to repair and compensate for this failure (e.g., guilt, Baumeister et al. 1994; self-completion, Brunstein & Gollwitzer 1996; cleansing, Tetlock et al. 2000; bolstering, Sherman & Gorkin 1980). Presumably, moral licensing is the more counterintuitive aspect of balancing, because it is less straightforward why doing the right thing could liberate people to do less good, and indeed demonstrations of licensing were rare before Monin & Miller's (2001) publication (but see Nisan 1991, Nisan & Horenczyk 1990). Although licensing is construed by some as merely the inverse of compensation (compensation involves renewed effort toward a goal, whereas licensing sometimes involves a dampening of goal striving), it can also be produced via qualitatively different psychological processes (see Moral Credits Versus Moral Credentials sidebar) (for reviews, see Effron & Monin 2010, Merritt et al. 2010, Miller & Effron 2010).

Licensing results from the fact that individuals pursue multiple, sometimes conflicting goals (e.g., to advance one's career, to be prosocial). For licensing effects to occur, there must be a conflict of motives in the target behavior (e.g., between self-interest and doing the "right" thing) that manifests as temptation or suspicion, and we distinguish temptation and suspicion cases. In the temptation case, an individual wants to do something personally beneficial (e.g., refuse to help, cheat on a test) but is torn by a conflicting motive (to be helpful, to be an honest person). In this case, prior positive initial behavior can license people to yield to temptation by adding to the positive side of the moral ledger (moral credits). In the suspicion case, the conflict is of an attributional nature (Kelley 1973): An individual wants to do something for legitimate reasons (e.g., suspend a misbehaving student) but is concerned that this choice may actually be, or appear to others to be, motivated by an illegitimate motive (e.g., racism, if the student is African American). Here, positive initial behavior can dispel causal ambiguity and reduce the potential for suspicion by making the illegitimate motive less credible (moral credentials).

Whereas we posit that either temptation or suspicion is necessary to observe licensing, neither type of conflict is required for compensation. Given that licensing and compensation potentially rely on such different processes, it is important to tease them apart, which requires including a

Compensation: when a negative initial behavior leads to more positive target behavior than a neutral baseline condition (a.k.a. cleansing)

Moral credits model: when a positive initial behavior provides credits (as in a moral bank account) that can be drawn upon to license subsequent behavior

Moral credentials model: when a positive initial behavior provides a lens through which subsequent ambiguous behavior is interpreted positively to allow licensing

Table 1 Hypothetical outcomes in the "donut" version of the sequential behavior paradigm

Initial behavior	Outcome 1	Outcome 2	Outcome 3
Positive	5	3	5
Baseline	Unknown	Unknown	Unknown
Negative	3	5	5

baseline condition. In practice, many empirical tests of sequential effects of behavior do not include a baseline condition (see **Supplemental Table**) and only contrast positive versus negative initial behavior (which only allows conclusions about balancing). We refer to such designs as "donut designs" to capture the fact that they are missing a crucial element in their middle (see **Figure 1**).[2]

We propose two explanations for the surprising prevalence of donut designs. The first, a theoretical explanation, is that authors conceive of the initial behavior manipulation as different dosages of a (unidimensional) treatment, where the "moral" condition is the high dosage and the "immoral" condition is the low dosage. With this framing, a baseline seems as unnecessary as a "medium" dosage would be to test a presumed linear effect of dosage. We propose that the dosage analogy breaks down here, as "moral" and "immoral" conditions could bring about very different psychologies relative to a baseline with no initial behavior whatsoever. A second, methodological, explanation pertains to the reliance on online studies and "recall a time" manipulations in lieu of actual behavior. In such paradigms, the easiest manipulation is to simply replace the word "moral" with "immoral" in the prompt, and to neglect the fact that this is not a neutral control. Many of the donut designs discussed below share this feature.

The Problem with Donut Designs

In the margin:

Donut design: a two-cell or 2 × 2 design that omits a baseline condition (typically compares the effect of positive versus negative initial behavior)

Positive consistency: when a positive initial behavior leads to more positive target behavior in comparison with a baseline condition (a virtuous cycle)

Negative consistency: when a negative initial behavior leads to more negative target behavior in comparison with a baseline condition (a vicious cycle)

In the case of sequential behavior paradigms, donut designs typically take the form of contrasting a positive and a negative initial behavior, with no baseline. To appreciate the problem with drawing conclusions from such a design, **Table 1** presents hypothetical outcomes of such a study, where numbers reflect means on a measure of behavior positivity (e.g., amount donated, or the number of questions on which participants did not lie). Assuming that the differences observed between these means are significant, how would we interpret these patterns in terms of consistency, licensing, or compensation? Outcome 1 strongly suggests consistency. But the absence of a baseline makes it unclear where this consistency originates. If a baseline had been added and its mean was 4 (assuming this mean is significantly different from the other two), this would suggest positive consistency and negative consistency. But a baseline at 3 would suggest instead that the effect is entirely due to positive consistency, whereas a baseline at 5 would suggest it is due to negative consistency. Outcome 2 presents the same ambiguity: It is impossible to know whether a baseline would have fallen in the middle at 4, suggesting both compensation and licensing, or might have been around 3, suggesting only compensation, or around 5, suggesting only licensing. The problem is that many authors have used such donut designs to contrast consistency and balancing, which such designs do effectively, but then have slipped to making claims about consistency versus licensing, which they are not in a position to make—because the pattern in outcome 2 could entirely be driven by compensation, with no trace of licensing. It is not even straightforward how outcome 3 should

---

[2]Although one may argue that there are cases where positive and negative initial behavior are the only options (e.g., either helping or refusing to help when one is asked for help), this ignores the fact that choice in the target behavior could have been different if no request had been formulated as the initial behavior (baseline).

be interpreted. This is typically treated as a null result, and especially in the context of testing moderators, as evidence of "no balancing" and/or "no consistency." But if we allow for potentially divergent effects for positive and negative initial behavior, such a conclusion is not warranted in the absence of a baseline. A baseline at 3, in this case, would reveal a consistency effect for the positive initial behavior and a compensation effect for the negative initial behavior—there is no strong theoretical reason for both effects to necessarily work in lockstep. Conversely, a baseline at 7 would suggest a licensing effect for the positive initial behavior and a consistency effect for the negative initial behavior. Thus, donut designs raise serious issues when interpreting results.

As noted by Blanken et al. (2014), a more subtle but equally problematic disregard of the value of the control condition is at work when researchers include a control condition in the design but do not include it in pairwise comparisons, and instead only report an omnibus F, which precludes drawing conclusions about whether any observed effect reflects compensation, licensing, or both, or when researchers do not amass sufficient statistical power to detect significant differences from the baseline. Thus, authors should include a baseline condition and ensure they have enough statistical power to test for licensing effects, and not simply report balancing as if it was evidence of licensing.

Donut Designs and Moderation

Many studies we review omit a baseline condition (see **Supplemental Table**), which poses particular challenges for the task of this article. To study the role of potential moderators of licensing versus consistency, the ideal design for the question at hand is a 2 × 2 factorial, where one variable is the prior behavior (positive versus baseline), and the other variable is the proposed moderator. Ideally, one would then demonstrate consistency and licensing within the same design by showing significant simple effects (in different directions) within the levels of the moderator, and establish the role of the proposed moderator with a significant interaction. Only such a design can reveal distinct conditions under which previous behavior leads to licensing and consistency. As we discuss below, such an ideal design is actually surprisingly rare in the literature. In summary, given their reliance on donut designs, many reported licensing effects in the literature could in fact result from compensation processes, something to keep in mind as we review findings in the rest of this article.

TESTS OF PROPOSED MODERATORS GROUPED BY FIVE THEMES

We reviewed studies proposing to test moderators of consistency and licensing. Thus, we omitted numerous published studies that have separately demonstrated consistency, licensing, or balancing without including a moderator. Also, we focused on moderation studies in which the initial behavior could be construed as having moral significance (e.g., recalling a moral behavior, imagining buying green products, expressing a preference for Obama). We did not apply the same restriction to the target behavior, though in many cases it did have moral relevance. Typical target behaviors include cheating, lying, donating, volunteering, or allocations in a dictator game.

Because investigators of moderators approach the question with such different assumptions, we could not propose a priori an overarching framework that explained even a majority of the results presented—and doing so would have required making too many unwarranted judgment calls about moderating variables not measured, manipulated, or even discussed by the original authors (e.g., whether participants construed their initial behavior as progress or commitment). Instead we have organized the reviewed papers into five themes: (*a*) level of construal, (*b*) progress versus commitment, (*c*) identity relevance, (*d*) value reflection, and (*e*) ambiguity (see **Table 2**).

Table 2 Proposed moderators of the effect of an initial behavior on a target behavior in sequential choices and examples of the studies cited. For each level of the proposed moderators, we indicate whether the model predicts balancing, consistency (C), or neither (N). See Supplemental Table for a full listing of the papers reviewed and a tabulation of the empirical support for the proposed moderators

Proposed moderator	Consistency (C)/Neither (N)	Balancing
Construal level	Abstract construal	Concrete construal
Conway & Peetz (2012)	Distant behavior (C)	Recent behavior
Cornelissen et al. (2013)	Rules (C)	Outcomes
Weibel et al. (2014)	Intentions (C)	Actions
Commitment versus progress	Commitment frame	Progress frame
Susewind & Hoelzl (2014)	Commitment (C)	Progress
Identification	High identification	Low identification
Meijers (2014)	High proenvironmentalism (N)	Low proenvironmentalism
Effron et al. (2009)	High egalitarianism (C)	Low egalitarianism
Value reflection	Value reflection	No value reflection
Joosten et al. (2014)	Nondepleted (C)	Depleted
Gneezy et al. (2012)	Costly initial act (C)	Costless initial act
Kristofferson et al. (2014)	Private initial act (C)	Public initial act
Ambiguity…		
(…of initial behavior)	Ambiguous initial behavior	Unambiguous initial behavior
Clot et al. (2013)	Paid prosocial act (N)	Unpaid prosocial act
Khan & Dhar (2006)	Mandated prosocial act (N)	Voluntary prosocial act
(… of target behavior)	Unambiguous target behavior	Ambiguous target behavior
Brown et al. (2011)	Obvious cheating (N)	Potential cheating
Effron & Monin (2010)[a]	Blatantly racist act (C)	Potentially racist act

[a] Effron & Monin (2010) pertains to judgments of third-party targets, so consistency refers to harsher judgments of the target behavior, whereas balancing refers to more lenient judgments.

From a bird's-eye view, a thread running through all these studies is the importance of whether a connection is established between one's behavior (initial or target) and one's values and identity, as a function of contextual cues or pre-existing identification. Yet upon closer examination, enough discrepancies in theoretical approaches emerge (especially regarding the meaning of identification) to prevent us from collapsing these five themes into one. We return to the commonality across themes in the Discussion section.

Level of Construal

A number of proposed moderators of consistency versus licensing boil down to whether participants are prompted to think about how their initial behavior relates to abstract values and principles (leading to consistency) or whether instead their initial behavior suggests concrete choices and tangible outcomes (leading to balancing). We briefly review construal level theory (CLT) and then describe the studies that have proposed a relevant moderator.

Construal Level Theory. CLT (Trope & Liberman 2003, 2010) begins with the notion that because people only directly experience the present time and place, they must transcend the present moment to maintain long-term goals and construct a coherent sense of identity; they do this with mental construal. High-level (abstract) construals focus on decontextualized and essential features

CLT: construal level theory

of objects based on stable, cross-situational properties, whereas low-level (concrete) construals include more specific and contextual details based on more temporary properties. High-level construals lead to a focus on reasons and superordinate goals ("Why?"), whereas low-level construals lead to a focus on specific subordinate means and subgoals ("How?"; see also Vallacher & Wegner 1987). The farther something is perceived to be from direct experience (e.g., in terms of space, time, or likelihood), the higher its level of construal.

CLT makes three predictions about the relationship between values and behavior. First, individuals behave more in line with their overarching values or identity concerns when thinking abstractly, and more in line with the feasibility constraints of performing a particular behavior when thinking more concretely (Eyal et al. 2009). Second, individuals thinking abstractly are more likely to see their behavior as reflective of their underlying personality or values. For example, individuals who refused to host a blood drive conceived of themselves as more selfish (and were more likely to refuse to help with a subsequent smaller request—a case of negative consistency) when they had first been primed with an abstract construal mindset than when primed with a concrete one (Henderson & Burgoon 2014). Thus, abstraction promotes a more coherent self-representation, which leads to more behavioral consistency. Third, CLT predicts that individuals exhibit better self-control if they adopt a higher-level construal when facing temptations about important goals, by making them weight personal values and long-term goals more than short-term gratification (Fujita et al. 2006). In summary, an abstract mindset prompts a focus on superordinate goals and values, leading to consistency, whereas a lower-level focus on actions and consequences should lead to balancing.

Abstract versus concrete construal of initial behavior. Conway & Peetz (2012) proposed that conceptual abstraction moderates whether past behavior leads to consistency or to licensing effects: Thinking of past moral behavior concretely should focus attention on the act itself, leading to balancing, whereas thinking of it abstractly should highlight the underlying reasons for the behavior (values and superordinate goals), leading to consistency. Three studies tested these predictions. In one study, participants who recalled their recent moral acts (i.e., concrete construal) reported less willingness to volunteer in the future in comparison with participants who recalled their recent immoral acts (balancing), whereas participants who recalled their moral behavior that was over a year old (i.e., abstract construal) reported more willingness to volunteer than did participants who recalled their distant immoral behavior (consistency). The balancing effect replicated in subsequent studies, but the consistency effect did not. However, because the first and third studies relied on donut designs (i.e., no baseline condition) and the second used recall of a friend's behavior as a comparison condition, it is impossible to confidently attribute this balancing pattern to licensing, compensation, or both.

Focusing on principles versus consequences. Cornelissen et al. (2013) proposed that the effects of past moral actions on future moral behavior depend on participants' broad ethical outlook. They suggested that consequentialism, because it evaluates the rightness of an act through cost-benefit analysis, allows for flexibility and trade-offs, leading to balancing, whereas deontology, with its focus on rigorous application of principles across situations, promotes consistency. In the CLT framework, an outcome focus is consistent with a more concrete representation of moral behavior, whereas a principles focus is consistent with a more abstract construal of moral behavior. In three studies (Cornelissen et al. 2013), participants with an outcome-focused mindset showed a balancing pattern, whereas those with a rule-based mindset showed a consistency pattern. For example, in study 3, participants cheated more after remembering helping than hurting someone (balancing in outcome focus), but cheated less after remembering following than breaking rules (consistency in rule focus). Moreover, in the outcome-based conditions, participants prompted to recall ethical behavior felt more moral than did participants recalling unethical behavior, and this difference predicted the difference in cheating; this mediation was not significant in the rule-based condition. Study 1 was a donut design, but a baseline condition was included in studies 2 and 3; however, it did not differ significantly from any of the four conditions in the 2 × 2 in either study, leaving it ambiguous whether the observed balancing resulted from licensing or compensation.

Intentions versus actions. The data are more ambiguous when it comes to whether participants get to talk about things they have done in the past (actions, presumably concrete) versus things they will do in the future (intentions, presumably abstract). On one hand, and consistent with the other findings in this section, Weibel et al. (2014) found that recalling completed actions leads to balancing (donut design), whereas expressing intentions of future actions leads to consistency. On the other hand, Cascio & Plant (2015) found that merely imagining future moral acts can grant one moral credits and license morally questionable behavior, so it seems that expressing intentions can sometimes lead to licensing (see also Brown et al. 2011; Clot et al. 2013, 2014a), perhaps because intentions can also be formulated in concrete terms. Thus, more research is needed to determine the conditions under which anticipated future moral acts will lead to licensing or consistency.

Summary of moderation by construal level of the initial behavior. The studies reviewed in this section converge on the conclusion that initial behavior that is construed concretely (e.g., in terms of the specifics of the act itself, or outcomes) tends to lead to balancing, whereas initial behavior that is construed abstractly (e.g., in terms of higher-order values or rules) tends to lead to consistency. Notably, despite demonstrating balancing, these studies on the whole provide little direct evidence for licensing.

Progress Versus Commitment

Fishbach and colleagues' research on the dynamics of self-regulation (Fishbach et al. 2009, 2014), and in particular their use of the distinction between highlighting (i.e., consistency) and balancing (Dhar & Simonson 1999), provides a compelling framework for understanding consistency and licensing effects. Fishbach and colleagues argue that the same movement toward a goal can be perceived either as evidence of goal progress or goal commitment, with important consequences for subsequent behavior. If individuals construe goal-consistent action as evidence of commitment to a goal, they renew their efforts toward this goal (highlighting), whereas if individuals construe it as having made progress toward a goal, they expend less effort toward this goal and instead switch to pursuing unattended goals (balancing). Using this framework, Fishbach et al. (2006) interpret the Monin & Miller (2001) licensing effect thus: "In our terms, nondiscriminatory behaviors signal that the goal is met and therefore they justify incongruent, discriminatory behavior" (p. 240).[3] However, they also argue that the Monin & Miller (2001) experiment would have yielded consistency instead of licensing if participants had connected their initial behavior with their values (". . . our analysis further implies that when individuals attribute the meaning of their initial behavior to their central values and beliefs, they are more likely to infer commitment to egalitarian values and avoid discriminatory action"; Fishbach et al. 2006, p. 240).

---

[3] Balancing in Fishbach et al.'s (2006) model best corresponds to a moral credits process (see sidebar).

Besides stable individual differences in the tendency to adopt a progress or commitment approach to self-regulation (Zhang et al. 2007), several factors influence whether the same goal-consistent actions are viewed as progress or commitment (Fishbach et al. 2009, 2014). For example, experimenters can manipulate the types of questions being asked [e.g., "To what extent do you feel committed to (feel you've made progress on) your academic tasks after studying all day?"] (Fishbach & Dhar 2005). Another factor is the salience of superordinate goals. Consistent with CLT, the degree to which individuals interpret goal-consistent actions as evidence of progress or commitment depends on whether they pay attention to the specific (concrete) action and subgoal or to the superordinate (abstract) longer-term goal. If the superordinate goal is made salient (e.g., via situational priming), sufficient goal-consistent actions signal commitment to this goal (Fishbach et al. 2009), which leads to highlighting. If the superordinate goal is not made salient, sufficient goal-consistent actions lead to balancing (Fishbach et al. 2006).

Differences in individuals' pre-existing commitment certainty also determine whether they look for evidence of commitment or progress. Individuals who are uncertain of their commitment to a goal are more likely to ask themselves about their commitment and thus, following the logic of self-perception (Bem 1972), to see movement toward the goal as evidence of commitment, leading to consistency. For novices, focusing on the ground already covered is therefore motivating (revealing a newfound commitment), whereas focusing on how much work remains to be done can be demotivating (showing how far they are from the goal). In contrast, experts or already-committed individuals are not wondering about their commitment; rather, they are concerned about making progress toward the goal. For them, focusing on the ground to be covered is more motivating (Fishbach et al. 2014, Koo & Fishbach 2008); conversely, feeling that they have made sufficient progress may allow them to temporarily turn their attention to other goals. Importantly, Fishbach and colleagues' empirical demonstrations of the interaction between commitment certainty and progress manipulations speak more to generic balancing than to licensing because they primarily rely on donut designs, and we cannot discern whether the balancing observed with high-commitment participants results from compensation, licensing, or both.

Applying the model to moral licensing. Consistent with Fishbach and colleagues' theorizing, Susewind & Hoelzl (2014) demonstrated that construing behavior as evidence of progress toward a moral value leads to balancing, whereas construing behavior as evidence of commitment to a moral value leads to consistency. In one study, participants shopped in a virtual store with a majority of green (positive initial behavior) or conventional (baseline) products and then reported their likelihood of engaging in future prosocial behaviors. In another study, students brainstormed on how to improve their own lives (baseline) or that of disabled students on campus (positive initial behavior) and then engaged in a dictator game with a random peer. In both studies, leading questions manipulated participants' focus on goal progress or commitment: When participants focused on progress, they showed a (marginal) licensing pattern, whereas when they focused on commitment, they showed a (trending) consistency pattern.

Summary of moderation by progress versus commitment. When people frame their initial behavior as reflecting commitment to their moral values, they are more likely to show consistency, whereas when they frame their initial behavior as evidence of progress toward their goal, they are more likely to exhibit balancing. There are obvious parallels between CLT (reviewed above) and Fishbach and colleagues' model: In particular, progress is often construed at a more concrete level, whereas commitment is construed at a more abstract level (see Fishbach et al. 2006). Thus, the demonstration by Weibel et al. (2014; reviewed in the Construal Level Theory section) that intentions lead to consistency, whereas completed actions lead to balancing, is consistent with

Fishbach's model: Completed actions could be construed as progress toward the goal allowing for licensing, whereas future intentions could highlight one's commitment to the goal producing consistency. The difficulty with making this parallel more broadly is that in the absence of explicit manipulations of progress versus commitment framings, it is difficult to determine whether participants in other studies construed their initial behaviors in terms of progress or commitment.

Identification

Some scholars (e.g., Meijers 2014) have argued that licensing only occurs when individuals are not particularly identified with the cause being tested by the target behavior, and that when identification is high, a positive initial behavior would have little licensing effect and could even lead to consistency.

Identification versus commitment. At first glance, the notion that highly identified individuals show less licensing than less identified individuals contradicts Fishbach and colleagues' model, which predicts that individuals confident about their commitment see movement toward the goal as progress, prompting balancing, whereas individuals less certain about their commitment see the same movement as evidence of commitment, prompting highlighting. Thus, if one equates high identification with high commitment, the two models could seem to produce diametrically opposed predictions. But a closer look reveals some important differences that may account for these divergent predictions.

First, Fishbach and colleagues' model does not make direct predictions about the difference between low- and high-commitment individuals at a particular level of progress. Instead, their model pertains to the meaning of low versus high progress for committed individuals, and the meaning of low versus high progress for uncommitted individuals, acknowledging that committed individuals likely have a higher baseline motivation regardless of progress. By choosing to focus on the effect of progress within each commitment level, Fishbach and colleagues remain relatively agnostic about the effect of commitment at each stage of progress.

Second, Fishbach compares the effects of an initial behavior for individuals "certain" of their commitment (e.g., prior donors to a cause; Koo & Fishbach 2008) and individuals who are "uncertain" (e.g., those who have never donated to the cause); the studies reviewed below instead typically rely on self-reported identification, which captures variance between people who declare caring more and people who declare caring less about a value or cause. So whereas Fishbach and colleagues posit commitment as an epistemic state (a crucial framing to explain why uncommitted individuals would be motivated to learn what their commitment is), here identification refers more to an attitudinal dimension—such that low-identification individuals might be quite certain that they do not care about an issue. Thus, the psychology attributed by Fishbach and colleagues to the uncommitted people (seeking to find out if they are committed because they aren't sure whether they value the goal) is very different from that attributed below to the low-identification people, who know full well they do not value the goal and are happy to find an excuse to slack off. This helps explain why Fishbach's model predicts consistency for low-commitment individuals, whereas the papers reviewed below predict licensing for low-identification individuals.

Third, many of the demonstrations in the commitment versus progress literature involve donut designs, which preclude isolating the role of licensing. Although the model predicts balancing for highly committed individuals, and several studies support this prediction (e.g., Finkelstein & Fishbach 2012, Koo & Fishbach 2008), it is easier to explain this balancing in terms of compensation than licensing: When highly committed individuals see that little progress is made toward the goal, they are especially motivated to increase goal-consistent actions.

Thus, Fishbach's model predicts more balancing for highly committed individuals (which could largely be driven by compensation), whereas the studies reviewed below predict that licensing is more likely to occur for low-identification actors. For example, people who strongly identify as environmentalists should be more likely to increase their goal-consistent actions when they feel they haven't done enough (compensation), but should be unlikely to purchase products they know harm the environment, no matter how many environmentally friendly behaviors (e.g., recycling) they have engaged in. In this view, it is people who do not really care about the environment (low identification) who should be all too happy to slack off if they can point to a token behavior (e.g., recycling) that they accomplished toward that goal (licensing).

Proenvironmental identity. Testing these predictions, Meijers (2014) demonstrated that participants' self-reported proenvironmental identity moderated the effect of imagining buying environmentally friendly shoes or clothing (versus control non-green products) on their subsequent expression of proenvironment emotions, concerns, and intentions. Participants who had a strong proenvironmental identity were not affected by the green purchase: They always expressed environmentally friendly intentions or concerns. But after individuals with a weaker proenvironmental identity chose the green products, they expressed lower green intentions and concerns than after buying conventional products, suggesting a licensing pattern. These findings demonstrate that when the target behavior is very explicitly a direct test of the value (e.g., rating "I would be willing to stop buying products from companies guilty of polluting the environment even though it might be inconvenient for me"), licensing occurs for low identifiers, whereas high identifiers tend to refrain from explicit violations of the value.

Similarly, Clot et al. (2014a) investigated whether proenvironmental identity interacted with imagining engaging in voluntary versus mandatory proenvironmental behaviors to influence participants' willingness to donate to an environmental charity. When the initial behavior was voluntary (instead of mandatory), high identifiers did not demonstrate licensing effects, whereas low identifiers did.

Self-reported egalitarian identity. Effron et al. (2009, study 3) showed that allowing (versus not allowing) participants an opportunity to express that they would vote for Obama in the 2008 presidential election subsequently licensed them to favor a white over an African American community organization in a resource allocation task, but only if they scored relatively higher on the modern racism scale (McConahay et al. 1981), which we translate as being lower in identification with egalitarian values. By contrast, individuals lower on the modern racism scale (i.e., higher identification with egalitarianism) showed, if anything, a marginally significant effect in the opposite direction (consistency). In other words, for participants who most identified with the value of egalitarianism, reporting their intention to vote for Obama stressed their commitment to fighting prejudice (leading to consistency), whereas for individuals less identified with egalitarianism, voting for Obama seemed good enough, leading to licensing.

Summary of the moderating effect of identity relevance. Taken together, these studies suggest that people's identification with the value or cause tested in sequential behavior paradigms moderates the effect of positive initial behavior on subsequent behavior. Particularly in domains related to morality, where one bad act can impugn one's reputation (e.g., one racist remark can severely damage one's reputation), individuals who are highly identified are unlikely to exhibit licensing effects. In contrast, low identifiers may be happy to slack off after demonstrating token commitment to the cause with their initial behavior. Indeed, in all of the studies reviewed in this section, licensing occurred among low identifiers.

Reflecting on the Values Indicated by the Initial Behavior

The next set of studies we review involves situations where individuals are prompted, or have the ability, to draw inferences about their own values or identity from their initial behavior. In these cases consistency obtains when individuals have enough self-control resources to reflect on the correspondence between their values and initial behavior or are prompted to reflect on their values because of some characteristic of the initial behavior (e.g., how costly it is, whether it is public or private).

Resource availability versus depletion. In Joosten et al.'s (2014) two studies, participants recalled a time they did something moral or immoral in their past (donut design) and then completed a task designed to deplete their self-control resources. Participants then faced a conflict between self-interest and helping others in a group task. Depleted participants were more helpful when they recalled their immoral than their moral behavior (balancing), whereas nondepleted participants were (marginally) less helpful when they recalled their immoral than their moral behavior (consistency). These findings suggest that participants must have enough self-control resources to reflect on the correspondence between their values and behaviors to produce consistency, but that they exhibit balancing when depleted.

Costliness of initial behavior. Gneezy et al. (2012) proposed that the key moderator of consistency is the costliness of the initial prosocial behavior: Costly prosocial behavior signals a prosocial identity, leading to consistency, whereas costless behavior does not, leading to no consistency. This model focuses on costliness as a necessary condition for consistency, but it is more agnostic about whether (or why) licensing should occur when no cost is incurred. In study 1 (Gneezy et al. 2012), economics students received an envelope indicating they should have received $5 for the experiment. In a control condition, participants received $5; in a costly condition, they received only $3 and were told that $2 had been deducted and given to the Make-a-Wish Foundation on their behalf; in a costless condition, they received $5 and were told that an additional $2 was given to the charity on their behalf. When later placed in a task tempting them to lie to a peer to potentially take home more money, relative to the control condition, participants lied significantly less in the costly condition and significantly more in the costless condition. Surprisingly (given that they had no say in their $2 being withheld and did not engage in any kind of actual initial behavior[4]), participants in the costly condition also rated themselves as more helpful and less selfish than participants in either of the other two conditions, and the difference in truth-telling between the costly and the costless conditions was mediated by this self-rating of prosocial identity. The authors argue that cost increases consistency by making the initial behavior seem more diagnostic about oneself, leading people to embrace the value indicated by that behavior (cf. Bem 1972, Burger 1999).

Private versus public initial behavior. Kristoferson et al. (2014) showed that another moderator of the effect of initial behavior is whether it is public or private. In their studies, individuals who agreed to sign a petition in private or to take a lapel pin home with them were more likely to agree to later donate or volunteer to help the same cause than was a baseline group with no prior behavior, suggesting consistency when the initial behavior was private—but this effect did not

---

[4]The manipulation of "costly prosocial behavior" in this study, which involves experimenters withholding promised pay from participants without their consent, is an odd fit among the type of positive initial behaviors typically used in the licensing and consistency literatures. More research is warranted to determine if participants really construe this as a donation or instead as a capricious tax imposed by an untrustworthy experimenter, and whether self-ratings as less selfish in this condition amount to a statement about the experimenter's greedy nature by comparison.

obtain when participants signed a petition in front of a group of peers or when the pin was visibly placed on their clothes (though balancing was not observed either). A private choice led individuals to reflect on their values, to embrace the identity indicated by the initial behavior, and to display consistency, whereas a public behavior seemingly did not trigger the same value reflection.[5]

Summary of the moderating effects of reflecting on the values indicated by the initial behavior. The studies reviewed above suggest that when participants can infer that their initial behavior reflects their identification with a goal or value (e.g., because it is done in private or because they had to pay a price for it), they are more likely to exhibit consistency than when this inference is harder to make (because the initial behavior is public or because participants' cognitive resources were depleted). The papers reviewed in this section were less informative when it came to predicting or explaining licensing effects, and they reported few cases of licensing.

Painted in broad brushstrokes, these findings are largely consistent with Fishbach and colleagues' model of self-regulation, which predicts highlighting (consistency) when individuals focus on whether their movement toward a goal reflects commitment. Likewise, the studies presented here report consistency when participants were in a position to infer that their initial behavior reflected deep-seated attitudes (e.g., Gneezy et al. 2012 argue that costly behavior serves as a "temporary signal to the self regarding one's prosocial identity," p. 179). These findings are also consistent with the CLT framework in that connecting one's behavior to one's values or long-term goals is a high-level construal that would lead to consistency, as observed in these studies.

Ambiguity of the Initial and Target Behaviors

The final set of studies we review reveals that the diagnosticity of a behavior (i.e., what the behavior reveals about the person performing it) and its opposite, ambiguity, moderate licensing effects. Ambiguous (i.e., less diagnostic) initial behaviors lose their ability to contribute to moral self-regard, thus inhibiting licensing effects, whereas ambiguous target behaviors facilitate licensing effects by releasing constraints on temptation or reducing suspicion.

Diagnosticity of the initial behavior. According to attribution theory (Kelley 1973) and self-perception theory (Bem 1972), external pressure to perform an initial behavior should diminish its implications for moral self-regard and thus largely rob it of its ability to yield licensing. Clot et al. (2013) asked some participants to imagine helping to clean a riverbank, manipulating whether they would be paid for their work or not. All participants then allocated money between themselves and an environmental charity. Participants in the imagined unpaid prosocial behavior condition were more likely to later keep all the money for themselves relative to a control condition (licensing), whereas there was no difference in selfishness rates between the paid prosocial behavior and the control conditions. Thus, providing a plausible external justification for the initial behavior reduced its licensing power. Similarly, Khan & Dhar (2006, study 4) found that participants who imagined performing 24 hours of community service were more likely to prefer a hedonic over a utilitarian good (licensing), but only if their community service was voluntary and not when it was an imposed penalty for a traffic violation. When the

---

[5] Greene & Low (2014) investigated whether having an audience for the target behavior (not the initial behavior) influences licensing effects. They found that participants demonstrated licensing for private but not for public unethical target behaviors. Thus, rather than leading to value reflection, the private nature of the target behavior allowed participants to act on their temptations without fear of repercussions.

initial behavior is paid or imposed instead of voluntary, it loses its ability to contribute to moral self-regard and therefore loses its ability to license.

Ambiguity of the target behavior. Diagnosticity is deeply rooted in the attributional structure of the situation, and in particular the attributional schemas attached to the moral domain (Reeder & Brewer 1979). In the case of morality (and related domains such as prejudice or the environment), this is reflected in the traditional distinction made in ethics between perfect and imperfect duties (Kant 2002, Wiltermuth et al. 2010). Imperfect duties are desirable feats for a good person—but not performing them does not impugn your morality. By contrast, perfect duties are black-and-white litmus tests, but they are asymmetrical: Someone violating a perfect duty is immoral, whereas someone respecting a perfect duty does not get much moral credit. This suggests that individuals should be particularly concerned about violating perfect duties (e.g., cheating, discriminating), but that the presence of an alternative explanation for such negative behaviors should reduce these concerns, facilitating licensing effects. The two papers reviewed below demonstrate that attributional ambiguity (i.e., multiple possible explanations) for negative target behaviors facilitates licensing effects presumably by allowing individuals to give in to temptation without damaging their moral self-image or by removing the suspicious motive from such behaviors.

Brown et al. (2011) tested whether the ease with which one can rationalize an unethical behavior determines if licensing effects occur. Participants first rated how likely they (positive initial behavior) or an acquaintance (control) would be to behave prosocially in four hypothetical moral dilemmas, and they then had an opportunity to cheat on a math test (target behavior) by failing to press the spacebar in time to prevent the correct answers to appear (from von Hippel et al. 2005). When the spacebar needed to be pressed within one second, it was easy to rationalize cheating as being too slow (high ambiguity), and participants who had expressed their prosocial intentions cheated more than participants who predicted others' prosocial behavior (licensing); but when participants had 10 seconds to press the spacebar (low ambiguity), the two conditions no longer differed. The authors argue that licensing is most effective in ambiguous situations.

Monin and colleagues (e.g., Monin & Miller 2001) typically describe licensing effects in terms of how the initial behavior changes the meaning of the target behavior for the actor (a credentials process), but documenting this construal process from the actor's perspective is methodologically challenging. A more promising approach is to use observer/judgment paradigms, where participants evaluate an actor's target behavior after the actor's initial behavior has been manipulated. The argument is that actors likely use similar processes when thinking of their own behavior, or at least they expect others to rely on similar processes when others judge them. Effron & Monin (2010) used such a third-person approach to tease apart credits and credentials (see sidebar): In study 2, participants read about a manager who did not promote black employees because he did not believe African Americans are suitable for management (blatant racism) or because he claimed that they had performed less well than others (ambiguous). This target behavior was preceded in one condition by another article detailing the manager's efforts to increase diversity at the company. Relative to a control condition, this positive initial behavior did not reduce observers' condemnation of the blatant target behavior, but it did reduce condemnation when the target behavior was ambiguous because it reduced the extent to which participants construed the actor's behavior as racial discrimination (licensing via credentials). Interestingly, when the initial behavior was in a different domain (i.e., the actor helped combat sexual harassment), it led to less condemnation of both blatant and ambiguous racist violations, but with no change in construal (licensing via credits). Although this observer methodology is a departure from the type of sequential behavior paradigms previously discussed, we posit that the attributional logic used to judge others in such contexts is the same one used by actors when they decide how to act in target situations, and in particular when they project themselves as potential observers anticipating what their target behavior would look like in light of their initial behavior.

Summary of the moderating effect of ambiguity of the behavior. In summary, licensing is inhibited when initial positive behaviors are robbed of their ability to contribute to moral self-regard due to the presence of ulterior motives for the behavior. In contrast, licensing is more likely to occur when target behaviors are ambiguous or easy to rationalize. In addition, research on third-party perceptions of others' behavior suggests that prior positive behavior can license subsequent ambiguous transgressions when that prior behavior is in the same domain (licensing via credentials) and in a different domain (licensing via credits). However, blatant transgressions can only be licensed by prior positive behavior in a different domain.

DISCUSSION

We reviewed 25 studies that proposed to test a moderator of consistency and/or licensing effects. We organized our review around five conceptual themes: construal level, progress versus commitment frame, identification, value reflection, and ambiguity, all of which influenced consistency and/or licensing effects (see **Table 2**). Our review suggests that individuals are more likely to exhibit consistency when they (*a*) think abstractly, (*b*) focus on their commitment, or (*c*) can draw inferences about their values from their initial behavior. Moreover, individuals are more likely to exhibit licensing (or at least balancing) when they (*a*) think concretely, (*b*) focus on progress made, (*c*) do not identify a priori with the value being tested by the target behavior, (*d*) face ambiguous target behaviors, or (*e*) are depleted.

Although it is easy to summarize conditions that produced licensing and consistency effects in these studies, it is more difficult to extract from this body of data a simple model predicting when consistency will occur versus balancing or licensing because of the diversity of theoretical perspectives utilized. From a bird's-eye view, it does seem that an overarching model would likely predict consistency when individuals think abstractly, focus on their commitment, and face target behaviors that are clearly tests of important values, and likely predict licensing (or at least balancing) when individuals think concretely, focus on progress made, and face ambiguous target behaviors. As soon as such an overarching model is offered, however, it becomes clear that it does not satisfactorily account for all the evidence presented in this review, let alone the numerous nonmoderated designs (excluded from our review) in the literature. Moreover, attempting to fit such an overarching model to the existing literature would require making judgment calls about variables that the researchers may not have measured, manipulated, or theorized about in their studies. For example, if we wanted to understand the Monin & Miller (2001) initial demonstrations in such a framework, would we need to assume that participants in these studies were thinking concretely, focusing on progress rather than commitment, and facing an ambiguous choice? Though it is entirely possible that this was the case, and that these experimenters stumbled upon the specific appropriate conditions to obtain the effect, it drastically reduces the falsifiability of any emerging model if most studies in the corpus require judgment calls that allow posthoc assimilation to the model.

Although the current state of the literature prevents us from proposing an overarching model of consistency and licensing effects, there are nevertheless some general conclusions that can be extracted from this review. First, the studies reviewed under the themes of construal level, progress versus commitment frame, identification, and value reflection all converge on the proposition that when individuals connect their initial behavior to their underlying values, they are more likely to behave consistently with their initial behavior. In short, researchers have made decent progress in identifying the conditions that produce consistency in sequential behavior paradigms.

Second, although accumulated demonstrations, a meta-analysis, and a recent multi-lab replication concur to support the notion that licensing effects can be reliably observed, we are arguably much less further along in determining the conditions that are optimal, or even just hospitable, for licensing to emerge. Our review reveals a list of variables that produce licensing, yet there is arguably less theoretical coherence among these variables than those we observed for consistency effects. Although this relative lack of integration among factors that produce licensing might seem reasonable given that researchers have been studying consistency effects far longer than licensing effects, we hope this review provides a starting point for increased theoretical integration moving forward.

Finally, another emerging finding of our review is that many of the proposed moderator studies do not adequately test for licensing, despite claims that they do, because the presence of balancing is not unambiguous evidence of licensing. The vast majority of papers we reviewed purporting to test a moderator in a sequential behavior paradigm report a significant interaction between the proposed moderator and whether the opportunity to perform (or recall) the initial positive behavior leads to more or less of the target behavior. However, such an interaction can be entirely driven by the cells where consistency is predicted, with no balancing in the other cells. Moreover, even if the interaction is driven in part by the cells where balancing is predicted, in the absence of a baseline condition differing significantly from the positive initial behavior condition (licensing), the observed significant balancing can result entirely from the effect of the negative initial behavior condition (compensation) – the donut design problem. Thus, observing a significant interaction is still at least two steps removed from being able to claim anything about licensing. In fact, 18 of the 25 studies we reviewed predicted that a condition should elicit consistency; of those, 83% (15 of 18) successfully demonstrated consistency (see **Supplemental Table**). All 25 studies we reviewed predicted that a condition should elicit balancing, and 84% (21 of 25) successfully demonstrated balancing. However, 7 studies (28%) utilized a donut design, leaving only 18 studies that included a design that enabled testing for licensing; of those, 12 (67%) provided evidence for licensing.

However, despite separate evidence for consistency and licensing, evidence remains elusive for the type of full crossover interaction that we called for above as the touchstone of a successful moderator. Eighteen of the 25 studies reviewed set out to demonstrate consistency and balancing in the same study (the remaining 7 only purported to turn licensing on and off—an ordinal interaction), yet even if we include "marginal" simple effects, only 4 of these 18 studies (22%) actually demonstrated both consistency and balancing, and only one (5.5%) demonstrated both effects at the conventional ($p < 0.05$) level—and it is debatable whether that study (Gneezy et al. 2012) qualifies as a sequential behavior paradigm because the initial "behavior" was a tax imposed by the experimenter (see Footnote 4). Thus, despite what a casual read of this literature might suggest, identifying a moderator that successfully flips significant consistency into significant licensing in the same sequential behavior paradigm remains an unmet challenge and is still the Holy Grail of this literature.

CONCLUSION

The past five years have seen numerous empirical attempts to elucidate why past behavior sometimes leads to licensing and sometimes to consistency. This review presents many of these findings side by side to facilitate comparison, and it utilized five overarching themes as a way of integrating the various proposed moderators under broader umbrellas. As our review makes clear, future researchers interested in disentangling licensing from compensation or consistency should consider whether individuals have an opportunity to connect their behavior to their underlying values, the extent to which individuals identify with the value a priori, and the ambiguity of the initial and target behaviors. Our review presents an initial attempt to organize and integrate the various proposed solutions to the conundrum of when initial moral behavior licenses and when it constrains subsequent behavior; if nothing else, we hope to have inspired researchers to continue chipping away at an integrative answer to this fascinating puzzle.

SUMMARY POINTS

1. The past five years have seen a dramatic increase in the number of attempts to solve the puzzle of when positive initial behavior leads to less positive behavior (licensing) versus more positive behavior (consistency).

2. Identifying moderators of consistency and licensing effects has been hindered by the profusion of theoretical approaches (with little attempt at integration) and excessive reliance on donut designs (which lack a baseline condition).

3. Licensing is most likely to occur in situations where multiple goals conflict, either actually (temptation) or potentially (suspicion). We distinguish a moral credits version of licensing, akin to a metaphorical bank account, and a moral credentials version, which reduces suspicion by interpreting later behavior in light of the former behavior.

4. Licensing is often conflated with balancing, which can result solely from compensation processes. Compensation and licensing are both elements of balancing but can be produced via different processes; thus, it is important to distinguish them theoretically and empirically by avoiding donut designs.

5. Consistency (versus licensing) is more likely to be observed when individuals think abstractly (instead of concretely), focus on commitment (instead of progress), and connect their behavior to their underlying values.

6. Individuals who strongly identify with a cause are less likely to exhibit licensing than individuals who do not identify with the cause (particularly when the target behavior is unambiguous).

7. Researchers interested in disentangling licensing from consistency should consider whether individuals have an opportunity to reflect on how their behavior relates to their underlying values, the extent to which individuals identify with the value a priori, and the ambiguity of the target behavior.

FUTURE ISSUES

1. Future studies should include a baseline condition and sufficient power to distinguish licensing effects from compensation effects in balancing paradigms.

2. Future studies should distinguish moral credits and moral credentials (for a start, see Merritt et al. 2010) and identify the conditions under which each kind of licensing prevails.

3. Future research should explore whether the ambiguity of the target behavior interacts with identification to produce licensing via different pathways. In particular, high identifiers may need credentials to engage in ambiguous, negative target behaviors, but should consistently refrain from unambiguous, negative target behaviors. In contrast, low identifiers may use credits to engage in unambiguous, negative target behaviors, whereas they may use ambiguous situations as psychological cover to act on illicit motives irrespective of their prior behavior.

4. Future research should endeavor to more clearly delineate the differential effect of commitment certainty and identification with the cause, to resolve apparent contradictions.

5. Future research should continue to explore how initial behavior relates to identity, which in turn influences licensing and consistency. Effron & Conway (2015) suggested that when initial behavior highlights a commitment to a positive identity (e.g., egalitarianism), people are more likely to behave consistently with that identity; however, when initial behavior merely allows individuals to rule out a discrediting identity (such as being a racist) rather than highlighting their commitment to a positive identity (e.g., egalitarianism), moral licensing is more likely to be exhibited. Future research should explore this possibility.

6. Large-scale replication efforts of licensing effects such as the one conducted by Ebersole et al. (2015) are encouraged to increase our confidence in effects often tested with small samples.

DISCLOSURE STATEMENT

The authors are not aware of any affiliations, memberships, funding, or financial holdings that might be perceived as affecting the objectivity of this review.

ACKNOWLEDGMENTS

The authors thank Daniel Effron, Ayelet Fishbach, Susan Fiske, and members of Benoît Monin's lab group for their helpful comments on an earlier draft of this manuscript.

LITERATURE CITED

Baumeister RF, Stillwell AM, Heatherton TF. 1994. Guilt: an interpersonal approach. *Psychol. Bull.* 115:243–67

Beaman AL, Cole CM, Preston M, Klentz B, Steblay NM. 1983. Fifteen years of foot-in-the door research: a meta-analysis. *Personal. Soc. Psychol Bull.* 9:181–96

Bem DJ. 1972. Self-perception theory. *Adv. Exp. Soc. Psychol.* 6:1–62

Blanken I, van de Ven N, Zeelenberg M. 2015. A meta-analytic review of moral licensing. *Personal Soc. Psychol. Bull.* 41:540–58

Blanken I, van de Ven N, Zeelenberg M, Meijers MH. 2014. Three attempts to replicate the moral licensing effect. *Soc. Psychol.* 45:232–38

Brañas-Garza P, Bucheli M, Paz Espinosa M, García-Muñoz T. 2013. Moral cleansing and moral licenses: experimental evidence. *Econ. Philos.* 29:199–212

Brown RP, Tamborski M, Wang X, Barnes CD, Mumford MD, et al. 2011. Moral credentialing and the rationalization of misconduct. *Ethics Behav.* 21:1–12

Brunstein JC, Gollwitzer PM. 1996. Effects of failure on subsequent performance: the importance of self-defining goals. *J. Personal. Soc. Psychol.* 70:395–407

Burger JM. 1999. The foot-in-the-door compliance procedure: a multiple-process analysis and review. *Personal. Soc. Psychol. Rev.* 3:303–25

Cascio J, Plant EA. 2015. Prospective moral licensing: Does anticipating doing good later allow you to be bad now? *J. Exp. Soc. Psychol.* 56:110–16

Chang YY, Chiou W. 2014. Taking weight-loss supplements may elicit liberation from dietary control. A laboratory experiment. *Appetite* 72:8–12

Clot S, Grolleau G, Ibanez L. 2013. Self-licensing and financial rewards: Is morality for sale? *Econ. Bull.* 33:2298–306

Clot S, Grolleau G, Ibanez L. 2014a. Do good deeds make bad people? *Eur. J. Law Econ.* doi: 10.1007/s10657-014-9441-4

Clot S, Grolleau G, Ibanez L. 2014b. Smug alert! Exploring self-licensing behavior in a cheating game. *Econ. Lett.* 123:191–94

Conway P, Peetz J. 2012. When does feeling moral actually make you a better person? Conceptual abstraction moderates whether past moral deeds motivate consistency or compensatory behavior. *Personal. Soc. Psychol. Bull.* 38:907–19

Cornelissen G, Bashshur MR, Rode J, Le Menestrel M. 2013. Rules or consequences? The role of ethical mind-sets in moral dynamics. *Psychol. Sci.* 24:482–88

Dhar R, Simonson I. 1999. Making complementary choices in consumption episodes: highlighting versus balancing. *J. Market. Res.* 36:29–44

Ebersole CR, Atherton OE, Belanger AL, Skulborstad HM, Adams RB, et al. 2015. Many Labs 3: evaluating participant pool quality across the academic semester via replication. **http://osf.io/ct89g**

Effron DA, Cameron JS, Monin B. 2009. Endorsing Obama licenses favoring whites. *J. Exp. Soc. Psychol.* 45:590–93

Effron DA, Conway PA. 2015. When virtue leads to villainy: advances in research on moral self-licensing. *Curr. Opin. Psychol.* 6:32–35

Effron DA, Monin B. 2010. Letting people off the hook: When do good deeds excuse transgressions? *Personal. Soc. Psychol. Bull.* 36:1618–34

Eyal T, Sagristano MD, Trope Y, Liberman N, Chaiken S. 2009. When values matter: expressing values in behavioral intentions for the near versus distant future. *J. Exp. Soc. Psychol.* 45:35–43

Festinger L. 1954. A theory of social comparison processes. *Hum. Relat.* 7:117–40

Finkelstein SR, Fishbach A. 2012. Tell me what I did wrong: Experts seek and respond to negative feedback. *J. Consum. Res.* 39:22–38

Fishbach A, Dhar R. 2005. Goals as excuses or guides: the liberating effect of perceived goal progress on choice. *J. Consum. Res.* 32:370–77

Fishbach A, Dhar R, Zhang Y. 2006. Subgoals as substitutes or complements: the role of goal accessibility. *J. Personal. Soc. Psychol.* 91:232–42

Fishbach A, Koo M, Finkelstein SR. 2014. Motivation resulting from completed and missing actions. *Adv. Exp. Soc. Psychol.* 50:257–307

Fishbach A, Zhang Y, Koo M. 2009. The dynamics of self-regulation. *Eur. Rev. Soc. Psychol.* 20:315–44

Freedman JL, Fraser SC. 1966. Compliance without pressure: the foot-in-the-door technique. *J. Personal. Soc. Psychol.* 4:195–202

Fujita K, Trope Y, Liberman N, Levin-Sagi M. 2006. Construal levels and self-control. *J. Personal. Soc. Psychol.* 90:351–67

Gawronski B, Strack F, eds. 2012. *Cognitive Consistency: A Fundamental Principle in Social Cognition.* New York: Guilford

Gneezy A, Imas A, Brown A, Nelson LD, Norton MI. 2012. Paying to be nice: consistency and costly prosocial behavior. *Manag. Sci.* 58:179–87

Greene M, Low K. 2014. Public integrity, private hypocrisy, and the moral licensing effect. *Soc. Behav. Personal.* 42:391–400

Henderson MD, Burgoon EM. 2014. Why the door-in-the-face technique can sometimes backfire: a construal-level account. *Soc. Psychol. Personal. Sci.* 5:475–83

Hennecke M, Freund AM. 2014. Identifying success on the process level reduces negative effects of prior weight loss on subsequent weight loss during a low-calorie diet. *Appl. Psychol. Health Well-Being* 6:48–66

Hofmann W, Wisneski DC, Brandt MJ, Skitka LJ. 2014. Morality in everyday life. *Science* 345:1340–43

Huber J, Goldsmith K, Mogilner C. 2008. Reinforcement versus balance response in sequential choice. *Mark. Lett.* 19:229–39

Jacobsen GD, Kotchen MJ, Vandenbergh MP. 2012. The behavioral response to voluntary provision of an environmental public good: evidence from residential electricity demand. *Eur. Econ. Rev.* 56:946–60

Joosten A, van Dijke M, Van Hiel A, De Cremer D. 2014. Feel good, do-good!? On consistency and compensation in moral self-regulation. *J. Bus. Ethics* 123:71–84

Jordan J, Mullen E, Murnighan JK. 2011. Striving for the moral self: the effects of recalling past moral actions on future moral behavior. *Personal. Soc. Psychol. Bull.* 37:701–13

Kant I. 2002. *Groundwork for the Metaphysics of Morals*. New Haven, CT: Yale Univ. Press

Kelley HH. 1973. The processes of causal attribution. *Am. Psychol.* 28:107–28

Khan U, Dhar R. 2006. Licensing effect in consumer choice. *J. Market. Res.* 43:259–66

Klotz AC, Bolino MC. 2013. Citizenship and counterproductive work behavior: a moral licensing view. *Acad. Manag. Rev.* 38:292–306

Koo M, Fishbach A. 2008. Dynamics of self-regulation: how (un)accomplished goal actions affect motivation. *J. Personal. Soc. Psychol.* 94:183–95

Kristofferson K, White K, Peloza J. 2014. The nature of slacktivism: how the social observability of an initial act of token support affects subsequent prosocial action. *J. Consum. Res.* 40:1149–66

Mazar N, Zhong CB. 2010. Do green products make us better people? *Psychol. Sci.* 21:494–98

McConahay JB, Hardee BB, Batts V. 1981. Has racism declined in America? It depends on who is asking and what is asked. *J. Confl. Resolut.* 25:563–79

Meijers MHC. 2014. *On justifying eco-unfriendly behaviors*. PhD thesis, Univ. Amsterdam. 158 pp.

Merritt AC, Effron DA, Monin B. 2010. Moral self-licensing: when being good frees us to be bad. *Soc. Personal. Psychol. Compass* 4:344–57

Miller DT, Effron DA. 2010. Psychological license: when it is needed and how it functions. *Adv. Exp. Soc. Psychol.* 43:115–55

Monin B, Miller DT. 2001. Moral credentials and the expression of prejudice. *J. Personal. Soc. Psychol.* 81:33–43

Nisan M. 1991. The moral balance model: theory and research extending our understanding of moral choice and deviation. In *Handbook of Moral Behavior and Development*, ed. W Kurtines, JL Gewirtz, pp. 213–49. Hillsdale, NJ: Erlbaum

Nisan M, Horenczyk G. 1990. Moral balance: the effect of prior behaviour on decision in moral conflict. *Br. J. Soc. Psychol.* 29:29–42

Ormiston ME, Wong EM. 2013. License to ill: the effects of corporate social responsibility and CEO moral identity on corporate social irresponsibility. *Pers. Psychol.* 66:861–93

Ploner M, Regner T. 2013. Self-image and moral balancing: an experimental analysis. *J. Econ. Behav. Org.* 93:374–83

Reeder GD, Brewer MB. 1979. A schematic model of dispositional attribution in interpersonal perception. *Psychol. Rev.* 86:61–79

Sherman SJ, Gorkin L. 1980. Attitude bolstering when behavior is inconsistent with central attitudes. *J. Exp. Soc. Psychol.* 16:388–403

Susewind M, Hoelzl E. 2014. A matter of perspective: why past moral behavior can sometimes encourage and other times discourage future moral striving. *J. Appl. Soc. Psychol.* 44:201–9

Tetlock PE, Kristel OV, Elson SB, Green MC, Lerner JS. 2000. The psychology of the unthinkable: taboo trade-offs, forbidden base rates, and heretical counterfactuals. *J. Personal. Soc. Psychol.* 78:853–70

Tiefenbeck V, Staake T, Roth K, Sachs O. 2013. For better or for worse? Empirical evidence of moral licensing in a behavioral energy conservation campaign. *Energy Policy* 57:160–71

Trope Y, Liberman N. 2003. Temporal construal. *Psychol. Rev.* 110:403–21

Trope Y, Liberman N. 2010. Construal-level theory of psychological distance. *Psychol. Rev.* 117:440–63

Vallacher RR, Wegner DM. 1987. What do people think they're doing? Action identification and human behavior. *Psychol. Rev.* 94:3–15

Von Hippel W, Lakin JL, Shakarchi RL. 2005. Individual differences in motivated social cognition: the case of self-serving information processing. *Personal. Soc. Psychol. Bull.* 31:1347–57

Weibel C, Messner C, Brügger A. 2014. Completed egoism and intended altruism boost healthy food choices. *Appetite* 77:36–43

Wiltermuth SS, Monin B, Chow RM. 2010. The orthogonality of praise and condemnation in moral judgment. *Soc. Psychol. Personal. Sci.* 1:302–10

Zhang Y, Fishbach A, Dhar R. 2007. When thinking beats doing: the role of optimistic expectations in goal-based choice. *J. Consum. Res.* 34:567–78

Justice and Negotiation

Daniel Druckman[1,2,3] and Lynn M. Wagner[4]

[1]School of Policy, Government and International Affairs, George Mason University, Fairfax, Virginia 22030; email: dandruckman@yahoo.com

[2]Macquarie University, Sydney, Australia

[3]University of Queensland, Brisbane, Australia

[4]International Institute for Sustainable Development, Winnipeg, Manitoba R3B 0T4, Canada; email: lynn@iisd.org

Annu. Rev. Psychol. 2016. 67:387–413

First published online as a Review in Advance on August 13, 2015

The *Annual Review of Psychology* is online at psych.annualreviews.org

This article's doi: 10.1146/annurev-psych-122414-033308

Keywords

distributive justice, equality, equity, fairness, negotiation, procedural justice, transparency

Abstract

This review article examines the literature regarding the role played by principles of justice in negotiation. Laboratory experiments and high-stakes negotiations reveal that justice is a complex concept, both in relation to attaining just outcomes and to establishing just processes. We focus on how justice preferences guide the process and outcome of negotiated exchanges. Focusing primarily on the two types of principles that have received the most attention, distributive justice (outcomes of negotiation) and procedural justice (process of negotiation), we introduce the topic by reviewing the most relevant experimental and field or archival research on the roles played by these justice principles in negotiation. A discussion of the methods used in these studies precedes a review organized in terms of a framework that highlights the concept of negotiating stages. We also develop hypotheses based on the existing literature to point the way forward for further research on this topic.

Contents

INTRODUCTION

This review examines the role played by principles of justice in negotiation. Our focus is on how justice preferences guide the process and outcome of negotiated exchanges. We are less concerned about the use of justice principles to regulate allocation decisions made by authorities or other actors charged with unilateral decision making. Focusing primarily on the two types of principles that have received the most attention, distributive justice (outcomes of negotiation) and procedural justice (process of negotiation), we introduce the topic by reviewing the most relevant experimental and field or archival research on the roles played by these justice principles in negotiation. Our coverage of the literature is broad and deep. While emphasizing more recent studies, we draw on earlier research for providing insights into the connection between justice and negotiation. The recent literature is embedded in the context of a larger body of work.

A discussion of the methods used in these studies precedes a review organized in terms of a framework that highlights the concept of negotiating stages. Following the review of relevant literature for each negotiating stage, we identify hypotheses that emerge from existing research to point the way for further studies of the relationship between justice and negotiation.

Justice principles can affect negotiation processes and outcomes in a number of ways. In negotiation simulations, subjects negotiating a contract on behalf of a homeowner and contractor, respectively, were found to be more willing to accept an agreement if they assessed the process as fair, and they reached better joint outcomes if they reported a more collaborative negotiation process (Hollander-Blumoff & Tyler 2008). In a related finding, opportunities for expression (voice) or the perception of control during a negotiation led to more positive evaluations of the decision-making process and to judgments of fairness in the outcome (Lind et al. 1990, Tyler 1987).

Similar findings are reported for cases with life and death stakes. The negotiations leading to the Rome General Peace Accords, which brought an end to a 15-year deadly conflict in Mozambique, have been held up as an example for the resolution of civil wars. The Community of Sant'Egidio, a Catholic nongovernmental organization (NGO), led the mediation efforts in these talks and fostered "a genuine political process based on dialogue between the warring factions" (Bartoli 1999, p. 265). The relationship established during the negotiations carried over into the implementation of the agreement. By contrast, many of the messages exchanged between rebels and government representatives in the talks seeking to conclude the civil war in Sierra Leone through the Abidjan Peace Agreement of 1996 were conveyed through intermediaries, public statements, and on the battlefield. Justice principles of fair play and transparency were not adhered to in the negotiation process, and the agreement failed to establish a lasting peace (Wagner & Druckman 2015).

Other examples of the role of justice come from the arenas of trade and environmental negotiations. Weaving through these negotiating processes are attempts to resolve various procedural issues. The usual result is a mix of adhering to and violating such principles as fair representation, transparency, and voluntary decision making. When these principles are satisfied, the result is often an effective agreement: Examples include the World Trade Organization talks on agricultural issues in 2004 and the Convention on Early Notification of a Nuclear Accident negotiated in 1986. When the principles are violated, the talks are less effective in producing a durable agreement: Examples include the 1990 General Agreement on Tariffs and Trade (GATT) negotiations on textiles and the 2009 Copenhagen Climate Change Conference. When some principles are satisfied while others are violated, the result is often agreements that favor only a few of the negotiating parties, as was the case with the 1992 North American Free Trade Agreement (NAFTA) and the Basel Convention on the Control of Transboundary Movements of Hazardous Wastes and Their Disposal negotiated in 1989.

Fairness. Transparency. Equality. Each of these terms is an element of a broader concept of justice. A close examination of the experiments and high-stakes negotiations discussed above reveals that justice is a complex concept, both in relation to attaining just outcomes and to establishing just processes. An understanding of the outcomes in each of these examples necessitates an appreciation of the various types of justice that could be incorporated into an outcome as well as the types of justice involved in the decision-making process.

This review of the existing literature seeks to provide such an appreciation, and in bringing together the justice literature as it relates specifically to negotiations, this article examines a topic not yet explored in the *Annual Review of Psychology*. Related reviews focus primarily on negotiation, with scant reference to justice concepts. Although the Bazerman et al. (2000) review of research on social factors that affect negotiation presents some complementary literature, its review of ethics and sacredness evaluates questions of deception in the negotiation process and the implications of negotiations for issues perceived as being taboo. Our review defines justice as a multifaceted process and outcome concept. Kelman (2006) identifies approaches to peacemaking on a larger scale, through conflict settlement, conflict resolution, and reconciliation. The Thompson et al. (2010) review examines negotiation processes and outcomes, focusing on five levels of analysis: intrapersonal, interpersonal, group, organizational, and virtual. Their study evaluates the implications of each level for integrative and distributive bargaining, which involves what the negotiators are doing at the table rather than the fundamental justice principles establishing how they have organized the talks. On the concept of justice, this article offers the first comprehensive literature review of how justice contributes to the negotiation process and acceptance of negotiated outcomes. Miller (2001) examines links among disrespect, anger, and injustice and offers a brief summary of the concepts of procedural and distributive justice, but not as they relate specifically to the negotiation context.

DISTRIBUTIVE JUSTICE AND NEGOTIATION

Distributive justice (DJ) refers to principles for allocating benefits or burdens among the members of a group or community. Four DJ principles are emphasized in the literature: equality, proportionality or equity, compensation, and need. One or more of these principles surface in the outcome of a negotiation. Perhaps the most ambitious research program on DJ in negotiation outcomes was conducted by Deutsch (1985), who investigated preferences for DJ principles in laboratory negotiation tasks. Clear findings emerged from his experiments with college students. The results, along with results from other experiments, indicated an overwhelming preference for the distributive principle of equality and, to a lesser extent, need. These findings are consistent with those obtained by a number of other investigators. Deutsch does note that the findings can be a function of the particular context of the experiments: namely, money as the resource to be distributed, a workplace as the social context, and American college students as the participants. However, he also claims that these conditions worked against a preference for egalitarianism and would seem to encourage a preference for proportionality or equity.

Yet, despite the claims for robustness of the equality preferences, Deutsch emphasizes the importance of the type of distributive system. He contrasts an egalitarian, solidarity-oriented system, characterized by positive social relations and a sense of similarity, with a meritocratic, economic-oriented system, characterized by impersonal social relations and a sense of differences. Equality is the preferred principle in the former, whereas proportionality is sought by negotiators in the latter type of social system. By taking the normative system into account, Deutsch runs into a problem. His own results, showing preferences for equality in a meritorious system, run counter to this hypothesis. Further, equality distribution preferences have been shown to correlate with higher productivity than preferences for distributions based on an equity principle (Cook & Hegtvedt 1983). The empirical results contradict expectations based on norms and raise an issue about the difference between normative and empirically based theory, which is an age-old question in this literature (cf. Rawls 1958 with Deutsch 1985 or Lind & Tyler 1988).

Deutsch's hypothesis does, however, garner support in two recent studies. Harmon & Kim's (2013) laboratory research showed that equity, rather than equality or need, is regarded as a fair DJ principle in performance-based situations in which negotiators compete for economic rewards. The Wagner & Druckman (2015) archival study of peace agreements showed that DJ principles can lead to the emergence of normative systems. They found a strong correlation between proportionality or equity and the economic component of an index of durable peace: The more central was the proportionality principle in the agreements, the more stable was the economic environment following the negotiation. Neither proportionality nor the economic component correlated with any of the parts of the durable peace index (reconciliation, security institutions, governing institutions). On the other hand, equality correlated with the other parts of the index, indicating that the noneconomic aspects of durable peace are influenced by agreements that embody this principle. Earlier research showed that positive relationships or liking (Mikula & Schwinger 1973), long-term relationships (Mikula 1980), and an emphasis on the team aspect of a relationship (Lerner 1974) led to preferences for an equality rule.

Recent results in the realm of peace agreements call attention to the instrumental value of distributive principles. Druckman & Albin (2011) found that the equality principle mediated the relationship between the intensity of the conflict environment and the durability of the peace agreements: When equality was central in the agreements, the intensity of the conflict had less influence on durability. Another study by these authors showed that equality also mediated the relationship between procedural justice (PJ) and durability: PJ increased durability when equality was central in the agreements (Albin & Druckman 2012). Despite normative systems that would seem to encourage proportionality, the peace negotiators looked forward by paving the way for a political system in which the former rebels would be treated as equal citizens of their country. Those negotiating delegations that insisted on equality provisions carved out durable agreements. Thus, distributive principles may be used in more practical or strategic and less normative ways.

These DJ findings suggest interesting issues. One is the distinction between normative and empirical approaches to the study of justice. This distinction is also a source of tension in some issue areas. For example, nonproliferation norms in arms control negotiations are viewed by developing countries as being unjust. Agreements to halt the development of nuclear technologies are seen to widen the inequality gap (Müller 2013). Another issue is the relative preferences for different DJ principles in varied contexts and situations. For example, the equality principle is essential for durable peace agreements but relatively unimportant for negotiating effective trade agreements (Albin & Druckman 2014a). These issues are discussed in the sections to follow. Similar issues arise with regard to PJ in negotiation, to which we now turn.

PROCEDURAL JUSTICE AND NEGOTIATION

Procedural justice refers to principles for guiding the negotiation process toward agreements. These principles include fair treatment and fair play, fair representation, transparency, and voluntary decisions. One or more of these principles surface during the negotiation process either positively, as, for example, more fair play or transparency, or negatively, as, for example, a lack of fair play or transparency. Positive adherence to one or more of these principles usually moves the process in the direction of agreement, whereas negative adherence often sustains impasses. An example of research that explored relationships between PJ and the negotiation process and its outcomes was conducted in two experiments by Hollander-Blumoff & Tyler (2008).

These investigators developed a simulated dispute between two lawyers representing a homeowner and contractor, respectively. The dispute was a conflict of interest over a contract for the construction of an in-ground, custom-designed swimming pool: The homeowner (contractor) desired as much (little) work as possible for as little (much) money as possible. A set of distributive issues—including various aspects of the construction and monetary value—were at stake in the negotiation. The first study focused on the distributive issues. The results showed that (*a*) the more procedurally fair the process was rated, the more willing negotiators were to accept the agreement; (*b*) the more procedurally fair the process was rated, the more that negotiators indicated they felt better and collaborated more during the process; and (*c*) negotiating dyads that indicated they were more collaborative and had good feelings during the negotiation reached better joint outcomes.

The second study introduced an integrative element to the negotiation problem. Negotiators were offered an opportunity to create extra value that had not existed in the previous version of the problem. Procedural justice influenced each of the three measures of integrative outcomes: more disclosures, higher joint outcomes, and more Pareto-optimal (most mutually beneficial) outcomes occurred for procedurally just negotiating dyads. Taken together, the two studies show that PJ influences the quality of negotiated outcomes: Greater PJ encourages agreements as well as more integrative outcomes when they are available.

Wagner & Druckman (2012) obtained similar findings in a study of 11 historical cases of agreements negotiated between governments. In addition to measures of PJ and outcomes, this study added indicators of DJ, problem-solving processes, and the durability of the agreements. These variables were coded from archival documentation about the cases. Thus, rather than the subjective questions asked in the Hollander-Blumoff & Tyler (2008) study, these investigators performed content analysis of the documents: DJ and PJ were coded in terms of principles that surface in the outcome (for DJ) or during the discussion texts (for PJ). Problem solving was measured with indicators of acknowledgment, disclosure, willingness to cooperate, and brainstorming or reframing. One of three outcome types were coded for each part of the agreement: integrative, compromise, or asymmetrical. Durability consisted of the number of years that the agreement was in force.

The key finding from this study was that problem-solving processes mediated the relationship between PJ and negotiation outcomes: When problem-solving processes were used, the outcome was more strongly influenced by the PJ principles. Specifically, more integrative outcomes emerged when problem-solving processes were set in motion by adherence to PJ principles. However, without problem solving, PJ would not lead reliably to integrative outcomes. This finding extends the Hollander-Blumoff & Tyler (2008) results in two ways. The PJ-integrative outcome relationship is shown to depend on problem solving, which is similar to their measure of disclosure. The international domain provides another context for demonstrating the role played by justice in negotiation. Similar results from the different settings bolster the case for external validity. Another finding of interest was that DJ principles were more central in durable agreements. The PJ/problem-solving/integrative outcome cluster did not relate to durability. (See Albin & Druckman 2012 for findings on the mediating effects of the DJ principle of equality on the relationship between PJ and durability.)

The DJ/PJ distinction is particularly relevant to negotiation, the one referring primarily to outcomes or allocation decisions, the other primarily to the way the process is conducted. Yet, these should not be considered as monistic formulations of justice. Indeed, combinations of principles may be relevant to particular situations. This is especially likely in complex negotiations in which different principles guide distributions on different issues. The idea of compound justice is illustrated by Zartman et al. (1996): "For example, if the two parties claim different interpretations of inequality (equity versus compensation) for different aspects of an issue (or different issues), an equality principle can be produced by offsetting one with the other" (p. 88). Similarly, violations of the PJ principles of transparency and fair representation by secret discussion among members of a small coalition may be offset by presenting a proposal for ratification by all the parties, thus satisfying the PJ principle of voluntary decisions (e.g., Quimpo 2001). The secret discussions often contribute to efficiency at the cost of representation or voice. Attempts made to reconcile these two objectives have been effective in such areas as negotiations over arms export control policy (Müller 2013). Thus, various principles may be applied in combination or sequentially to produce a fair distribution (see also Cook & Hegtvedt 1983). These examples illustrate a bridging function for justice principles, an area that has received limited attention in the research literature.

Justice principles may also serve as heuristics that are easy to implement. The DJ principles of equality and equity are generally understood and can be used to justify an allocation decision. The problem, however, is mutual acceptance of the "correct" principle: Negotiators may differ on whether the goal of negotiation is to maximize gains (preferring equity) or enhance social harmony (preferring equality). These differences can be mollified by PJ. Perceptions of fair procedures have been shown to offset perceptions of unfair outcomes and facilitate compromise (Tyler & Blader 2003). This is another example of the combined use of DJ and PJ principles. These authors also suggest a strong relationship between the types of principles. Indeed, Hauenstein et al. (2001) report an average correlation between PJ and DJ, across the 63 studies used in their meta-analysis, of 0.64.

The findings from these studies shed light on the role played by these principles in negotiation. Negotiators who view the talks as being fair or who adhere to PJ principles during the process usually engage in problem solving and attain better outcomes. It is also the case, however, that these findings were obtained from only a few studies. Further insights into the role of justice in negotiation are sought by canvassing a large empirical literature on justice in related settings. We organize the findings in terms of negotiation stages to provide analytical specificity. We generate hypotheses to be explored in laboratory and field negotiations, and we provide a basis for organizing future reviews of findings from the studies to be conducted during the next decade.

METHODOLOGY

The empirical literature on justice has consisted of both experiments and case or field studies. Both approaches have contributed to the development of theory. The complementary strengths and weaknesses of these methods (see Druckman 2005) are understood in terms of issues of causation and levels of analysis. These issues are discussed in this section.

The logic of causation guides the design of experiments. Necessary conditions include both control over the administration of independent variables (e.g., performance or relational-based task) and assessment of dependent variables (e.g., preference for a type of justice principle) as well as over the influence of possible confounding variables that threaten the validity of causal inferences. Many of the studies reviewed in this article satisfy these conditions (e.g., Deutsch 1985, Hollander-Blumoff & Tyler 2008, Harmon & Kim 2013); some studies go further by isolating mediating or moderating variables (e.g., perceptions of trust) that help to explain the independent variable–dependent variable relationship (e.g., Colquitt 2001, Hauenstein et al. 2001). Further advantages include replication and direct observation of negotiating processes. However, these internal validity strengths are gained at the cost of relevance to the complex, nonlaboratory negotiation settings in which justice plays a role before, during, and after the conclusion of negotiation. This broadened perspective is captured by case studies.

The difficulties involved in deriving causal inferences from case data are offset by wider and deeper probes of the role of justice in negotiation. Wider probes refer to an expanded portfolio of variables to analyze. Deeper probes refer to longer time periods to observe the influence of justice variables during several phases of negotiation, including postnegotiation processes. Further, historical case studies provide opportunities for comparative research. Although these strengths are gained at the cost of causal validity, some progress has been made on this front as well.

One advance has been to specify the time-ordering of variables; for example, adherence to PJ principles precedes outcomes that embody DJ principles, which leads to more or less durable implementation. Confidence in the time-ordering of the variables and a large number of cases encourages a search for mediating variables (see Albin & Druckman 2012, Chebat & Slusarczyk 2005). Another advance consists of the precautions taken to reduce the possibility of reverse causation; for example, from effective outcomes to process justice. These include developing conceptually distinct definitions of the variables, using different material for coding the justice variables, and interspersing the order of coding for the key variables such as justice and effectiveness (Albin & Druckman 2014a). A third advance is the care taken to avoid selection biases when choosing a sample of cases for analysis. This is done by drawing random or representative samples from a defined universe of cases within issue areas (e.g., trade, security, environmental negotiations). These procedures bring us closer to bridging the internal-external validity gap. The gap is reduced further when both experiments and case studies are included in a research project.

Other differences between laboratory and cases include the size of effects and levels of analysis. With regard to the former, Lind & Tyler (1988) note: "The laboratory and scenario methods used in early research may have caused us to underestimate the magnitude of PJ effects. Field research results have not only confirmed the findings of laboratory and scenario studies on PJ, but in fact have usually shown stronger PJ effects" (p. 206). This occurs, at least in part, because many of the field studies are conducted in contexts that support PJ, such as democratic institutions, and benefit from the combined effects of several independent variables operating in the same direction. Nonetheless, the correlation between PJ and DJ is consistently high across studies with varied methodologies, although there is a difference in the average size of correlations between dispute resolution and reward allocation settings (Hauenstein et al. 2001). This indicates a problem for assessing independent effects of the two types of justice, particularly when global assessments are made. It encourages the use of experimental or statistical controls in justice studies.

Laboratory research on negotiation has been conducted at a micro level, where influences are largely situational. Field and archival research has, on the other hand, construed negotiation as a process embedded in a larger domestic or international context. These macro-level variables

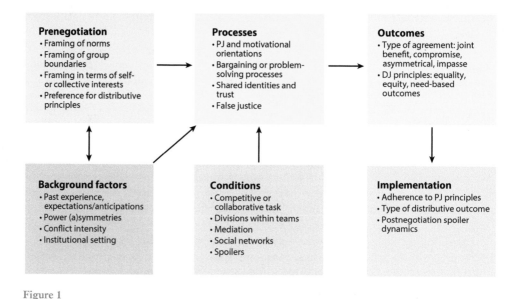

Figure 1

Justice and negotiation: a framework. Abbreviations: DJ, distributive justice; PJ, procedural justice.

are considered in our framework to be influences on justice decisions in negotiation. But the interplay between levels can also be considered as mutual influences, from negotiation to collective processes and vice versa. For example, justice principles that guide negotiated distributions may affect mobilization for collection action, which influences future negotiations (Cook & Hegtvedt 1983). But it is also the case that collective action decisions are negotiated often in large conferences involving diverse constituencies. An interesting question concerns the use of justice principles to reduce complexity and facilitate decisions in these settings. Other questions involve the path from negotiation to implementation, and some of these questions are discussed in the section on the implementation of negotiated agreements.

JUSTICE AND NEGOTIATION STAGES

The set of studies reviewed above makes a case for the importance of justice principles in negotiation. In this article, we explore further the role played by and the importance of justice principles in negotiation, drawing on literature from several social science disciplines using a variety of methodologies, including experiments and field or archival studies. But, given the limited amount of research on justice in negotiation (see Conlon 2012), we also draw on related literatures that have implications for negotiation.

The relevant literature is organized in terms of a framework that includes various parts of negotiation. These parts are depicted in **Figure 1** as boxes connected by arrows. The variables within the boxes are highlighted in the sections to follow.

The stages consist of prenegotiation, processes, outcomes, and implementation. Background factors and conditions are considered to be influences from the negotiating parties and the situations within which they negotiate. The factors in these boxes are discussed in conjunction with the stages. Each section below concludes with a summary of key points made about the role of justice in that negotiation stage and includes hypotheses to be explored in further research.

Prenegotiation

Several themes are discussed in this section in terms of their relevance to the prenegotiation stage. These include types of framing, tasks, preference for distributive principles, and anticipatory justice.

Framing. Mikula & Wenzel (2000) call attention to the importance of a shared moral community for the acceptance of justice principles. When this occurs, the principles become guides for structuring a fair process (PJ) and for agreeing on fair outcomes (DJ). Divergent perceptions of injustice can elicit social conflicts. When this occurs, justice principles become issues in negotiation. They may also be used tactically to defend positions, further exacerbating the conflict. In these situations, conflicts are resolved only when the proposed resolution leads to better outcomes for both/all parties.[1]

The concept of a shared moral community captures both shared identities and shared cognitions. These variables have been shown to influence negotiation outcomes. (See, for example, Swaab et al. 2002 on shared cognitions and Gelfand et al. 2006 on shared identities.) In an attempt to integrate these literatures, Swaab et al. (2007) showed how they interact during the process leading to integrative agreements; shared identities were both the product of, and precursor to, the development of shared cognitions. Working together, these variables increased the chances of obtaining integrative outcomes. Regarded also as components of justice, identities and cognitions may be regarded as mechanisms that explain the relationship between adherence to shared principles of justice (such as equality) and durable outcomes (see Albin & Druckman 2012).

The shared moral community argument is also similar to Tyler's (2000) discussion of the way people frame group boundaries. The wider the definition of inclusiveness, the more likely that adherence to PJ principles will contribute to favorable joint negotiation outcomes. The way that people frame their identities influences the impact of PJ on outcomes. Interestingly, perceived identities can be influenced through experimental priming. Druckman & Olekalns (2013) showed that primed shared identities influenced decisions following a negotiating crisis.

Deutsch's (1985) egalitarian/solidarity versus meritorious/economics-based distinction is similar to the distinction made by Lind & Tyler (1988) between a group value and self-interest model. An emphasis on one or the other orientation can be framed by the negotiators or third parties prior to the negotiation. Attempts to invoke shared identities place an emphasis on group values, which increase the salience of PJ principles and problem solving during the process. The cooperative context engendered by this framing may also be instrumental in creating civic values that serve to restore damaged justice and reconcile deteriorating relationships, as noted by Johnson & Johnson (2012) in their discussion of constructive controversy. A focus on self-interests orients negotiators toward allocation decisions that influence the outcome. This focus may decrease the salience of PJ in the process in favor of a competitive bargaining process. Competitive negotiators seek advantageous agreements but may also strive for fair allocations. The key point is that they approach negotiation as tacticians with an eye on the outcome rather than the process. Thus, prenegotiation framing can influence the process by orienting negotiators toward fair processes or toward advantageous (or fair) outcomes.

---

[1] Rawls (1958) distinguished between utilitarian and justice principles. He argued that unequal outcomes can be justified when benefits accrue to the entire community. The justification is bolstered when procedures used for attaining these outcomes are considered to be fair by members who share the same moral community. These circumstances, present in most democratic societies, do not vitiate the central organizing principle of equality.

Barrett-Howard & Tyler (1986) found that PJ is more important in situations in which maintaining social harmony and maximizing welfare of all group members are the goals. These are negotiating situations that may give rise to cognitive (differences over means) rather than interest (differences over ends or outcomes) conflicts. Bremer & Hammond (1977) showed that these are difficult conflicts to resolve. They did not, however, investigate the role of PJ in facilitating resolutions.

Tasks and setting. The study by Harmon & Kim (2013) on trust repair is also interesting for the prenegotiation phase. They found that trust is restored when explanations for a breech of trust were based on equity rather than equality or need. Need-based justifications were least effective, especially when the benefits accrue to the person violating the trust. This effect is mediated by perceptions of fairness. It appears that equity is regarded as a fair DJ principle in performance-based situations. Equality, on the other hand, may be the guiding principle in group solidarity situations.

A study by Cohn and colleagues (2000) showed that the dispute-resolution setting made a difference with regard to the PJ principle used to guide decisions: impartiality is more important in court-like settings, whereas voice (opportunities to be heard) is more important in settings that focus on rights and morality. Can negotiating issues be distinguished along these lines, perhaps the distinction between interests and values? This study also has implications for process: PJ considerations trump DJ in the adjudication of a rights claim (values); it was considered unjust to deny PJ to the undeserving. Further, the correlation between PJ and DJ may be somewhat stronger for dispute resolution than for reward allocation contexts: The average correlation computed across 39 dispute resolution studies was 0.72, whereas the correlation computed across 55 reward allocation studies was 0.59; the difference between these correlations is not, however, statistically significant (Hauenstein et al. 2001). Thus, the relationship between these variables is, to some extent, context specific.

Preference for distributive principles. The research reviewed by Kabanoff (1991) suggests that power differences orient parties toward the distributive principle of equity, with distributive decisions favoring the stronger party. These decisions may not be the result of a negotiation, serving to frustrate the weaker parties and leading them to withdraw from the relationship. The power differences may also preclude negotiations. One way to overcome these differences is to initiate protective contracts. Thibaut's (1968) research shows that bargainers were inclined to enter into protective contracts that insured equity (fairness) in the distribution of resources (DJ) when the conflict of interest (CI) was high. These contracts reduced the impacts of intense conflicts, defined in terms of asymmetrical power [one party could distribute resources that either favored him/herself considerably (high CI) or only slightly (low CI)]. A challenge, however, is posed to both weaker and third parties. They must persuade the more powerful parties that it is also in their interest to sign such contracts. This is more likely to occur when longer-term relational issues are at stake.

Whether achieved by contractual mechanisms or as a by-product of organizational structure, perceived power equality orients parties toward the distributive principle of equality, which usually leads to negotiation based on reciprocity. However, a lack of power differentiation may also produce overt conflict that cannot be resolved by resorting to differences in power (Kabanoff 1991). These implications are discussed further in the section on the negotiation process.

More generally, Kabanoff (1991) suggests that organizational structure influences preferences for the equality and equity principles. A preference for equality is likely in less hierarchical, more horizontal organizations; a preference for equity occurs in more hierarchical, power differentiated organizations. (See Kabanoff's 1991 figure 1 for the various combinations of structure and process.)

Structure is more influential for negotiations conducted in tightly structured organizations such as the military but less influential in loosely structured organizations such as the United Nations or other international organizations. Druckman's (2006) distinction between strong and weak cultures is relevant. Accepted institutional routines guide reward systems in strong organizational cultures; more flexible routines encourage alternative routes to advancement in weaker cultures. These structures shape distributive norms in the direction of equity for strong cultures or equality for more loosely structured organizations.

Anticipatory justice. The study by Goldman et al. (2013) on anticipatory justice is relevant in thinking about justice and prenegotiation. Anticipatory justice refers to thinking about an event that has not yet been experienced. With regard to mediation, the findings show that it is more likely to be accepted when both DJ and PJ are expected. More interesting, however, is the finding that the PJ effect depends on anticipatory DJ. Another interesting finding is that fear of the opponent (anticipated negative effects of the opponent's voice) leads to reluctance to choose mediation, and this effect depends on the anticipatory distributive injustice or costs incurred to an organization from a harmful opponent.

Summary. The review in this section highlights the influence of decisions made during the prenegotiation stage and the emergence of justice principles. With regard to PJ, the framing of group boundaries can either expand or limit the perception of inclusiveness. A broad definition of community is likely to enhance shared identities, which encourages adherence to PJ principles. The research is less clear about the mechanisms of framing or reframing. Perceptual change is a long-term process, as recognized by practitioners who design interactive problem-solving workshops (e.g., Rouhana 2000). Although progress has been made on forging collaborative relationships among adversaries in several conflict arenas, the interactive technologies have not addressed connections between cooperative motives (or shared identities) and PJ principles. Nor have justice researchers explored the impact of prenegotiation agreement on the choice of PJ principles for guiding the negotiation process. Two hypotheses are suggested for further research:

H1: Agreement on PJ principles is more likely when parties perceive shared identities or common membership in a moral community.

H2: To the extent that parties agree on PJ principles during prenegotiation, these principles will guide the negotiation process.

With regard to DJ, preferences for equality or equity principles have been shown to be influenced by the framing of the negotiation (performance or solidarity), the relative power of the parties (asymmetrical, symmetrical), and the structure of the organization in which the talks are embedded (hierarchical, horizontal): Performance (solidarity), unequal (equal) power, and hierarchical (horizontal) structures lead to equity (equality) preferences. The prenegotiation conditions that promote equality are more likely to also encourage agreement on using PJ principles to guide the process. The PJ principles then lead to equality outcomes and durable agreements, as shown by Albin & Druckman (2012) in their research on civil wars. Two hypotheses are suggested:

H3: Preferences for distributions based on the principle of equality are more likely to occur when the negotiation is framed in terms of solidarity rather than competitive performance.

H4: To the extent that parties agree on DJ principles during prenegotiation, these principles will influence preferences for certain types of outcomes.

Negotiation Processes

The discussion of processes in this section emphasizes the themes of motivational orientations and PJ, shared identification and trust, false justice, and power.

PJ and motivational orientations. The type of justice most relevant to the process of negotiation is PJ. There is an interesting parallel between the Lind and Tyler models of PJ and negotiation models. Lind & Tyler's (1988) distinction between self-interest and group value explanations for adhering to PJ principles is similar to bargaining and problem-solving approaches to negotiation. Both self-interest and bargaining focus primarily on the goal of maximizing returns for self. Both group value and problem solving focus on the goal of maintaining or improving relationships. Perhaps the key distinguishing feature for both the PJ and negotiation models is orientation toward self or other (Pruitt & Carnevale 1993). PJ judgments and negotiating behavior derive from similar sources of motivation referred to by Donohue & Hobbler (2002) as affiliation and power orientations. These parallels provide a link between justice and negotiation process. Viewed across the spectrum of negotiation stages, motivational orientations may be developed prior to negotiation, are manifest in the process as competitive or cooperative behavior, emerge as compromise or integrative agreements, and influence the durability of the agreement. This sequence is evident in the negotiation findings obtained by Hollander-Blumoff & Tyler (2008) and Wagner & Druckman (2012) discussed above.

A broad survey of the PJ literature (e.g., Tyler 2005) suggests that PJ effects on perceptions and behavior are robust across cultures and are generally noninstrumental or valued for their own sake (e.g., Machura 2003, Sugawara & Huo 1994, Wemmers et al. 1995). However, the particular PJ principle used is sensitive to the situation (Tyler 1988). Situational dimensions include type of authority encountered, formal and informal encounters, and characteristics of the experience, but also prior views and expectations, which may lead to biases (Tyler 2000).

One particular PJ principle, relevant to negotiation, is the opportunity for voice, referred to also as fair treatment. Studies by Tyler (1987) and by Lind et al. (1990) show that opportunities for expression (voice) or the perception of control over the process leads to more positive evaluations of the decision-making process and to higher fairness judgments. Interestingly, predecision voice led to higher fairness judgments than postdecision voice. More generally, opportunities for voice can ameliorate the prospect of undesirable distributive outcomes. This is often seen in electoral politics, where groups remain loyal to their candidate despite policy differences: A heretical leader is more desirable than a consistently abject alternative (see Hirschman 1970). And, as Peterson (1999) showed, opportunities for voice may have positive effects on less—but not more—intense conflicts. Voice can have the effect of either reducing or intensifying conflict depending on the sensitivity of the issues and the context in which the opinions are expressed. These robust findings on PJ effects beg the question of what accounts for them.

Tyler & Blader (2003) suggest that procedures are important because they shape peoples' social identity within groups, and these identities in turn shape values, attitudes, and behavior: Social identity may be a mediator between PJ and satisfaction or fairness judgments. The PJ feature that carries the most social-identity-relevant information is the perceived quality of interpersonal treatment, which is relevant to one's perceived status and value in the group. Tyler & Blader (2003) connect PJ to the identity literature. Implications for negotiation process may be in the realm of within-team or delegation perceptions concerning confidence in and legitimacy of the negotiating representative. These perceptions are likely to change through the course of negotiation, which is monitored by delegation members and policy makers to whom negotiators are accountable.

With regard to complex, multi-tiered negotiations between bitter adversaries, Lilja (2012) shows that there is value in developing social networks within the rebel parties. By increasing the interconnectedness of factions and thus cohesion, they become a more unified negotiating team with increased confidence in their representatives. The networks provide strong ties between individuals who control resources. Lilja's (2012) analyses suggest that the unity enhanced the team's flexibility as well as their adherence to PJ principles. This case study raises the issue of how to structure a group or delegation in order to enhance internal trust, with implications for flexibility in negotiation.

Shared identities and trust. Perhaps more important for negotiation is the extent to which the parties share an identity. Shared identities have been shown to produce improved processes and outcomes (Druckman & Olekalns 2013, Kramer et al. 1993). Thus, to the extent that PJ increases the perception of a shared identity, it should also improve the negotiation.

More broadly, shared identities are part of a cluster of covarying relationships that include PJ, trust, and problem-solving processes. Positive effects on outcomes and relationships from adhering to PJ principles may be explained by increased trust and problem-solving behavior. The Irmer & Druckman (2009) study showed that movement from calculus to identity-trust led to more comprehensive peace agreements. The Wagner & Druckman (2012) study showed that problem-solving processes mediated the relationship between PJ and integrative outcomes in historical international negotiations. The Druckman & Olekalns (2013) study showed that trust (as confidence that the other will honor commitments) propelled negotiators to continue talking in the face of a crisis even when transaction (process) costs were high. Holtz (2013) developed a model of reciprocal relations between trust and perceived justice. This model posits that the development of trust, which may form rapidly, precedes and influences employee perceptions of justice.

These studies raise questions about causal sequences among these variables: Is trust a precondition for PJ, shared identities, and problem solving? Or, does trust emerge from agreement on PJ principles and/or problem solving? If trust is a precondition, as Holtz (2013) suggests, then an early focus on creating conditions for increasing perceptions of trust would be beneficial. If, however, trust is an emergent process, as suggested by the Irmer & Druckman (2009) finding, then focusing first on establishing PJ rules would be advised. On the other hand, if the trigger is problem solving, as suggested by the Wagner & Druckman (2012) finding, then encouraging these behaviors would increase trust. It may be that the variables in this cluster are intertwined or cyclical rather than sequential. Bolstering any one of them would have ramifying effects on the others. These are issues that remain to be explored.

A related issue is the role of justice principles in trust violation and repair. Explanations for violations may be framed in terms of justice principles. Equity principles work best to repair trust when the perceived violation occurs in task performance situations. Equality is better in situations that emphasize the socioemotional aspects of relationships (Harmon & Kim 2013). Less is known about the role of PJ principles in trust repair. One issue is the extent to which PJ principles repair trust when the specific principles do not fit the situation or provide sufficient explanation for the violation.

Trust is important as well with regard to mediation. Acceptance of a mediator's suggestions has been shown to depend on the extent to which he or she is judged as being fair. Conlon et al. (1994) showed that negotiators accepted a mediator's suggestions when they perceived him or her to be fair. A suggestion to reject a compromise decision in favor of a problem-solving process was accepted after the mediator demonstrated an understanding of the compromise or equal losses outcome. That understanding enhanced perceptions of the mediator's fairness or trust that, in turn, bolstered the negotiators' willingness to take risks. The risks consisted of revealing sensitive information that aided problem solving toward integrative solutions. These mediation process variables may, however, be moderated by the parties' expectation of receiving a better outcome (Schuller & Hastings 1996).

The studies reviewed above support the idea that positive PJ perceptions are beneficial to both/all parties in negotiation: They promote shared identities and increase trust perceptions. However, it would be interesting to identify the conditions under which PJ is used instrumentally to achieve better outcomes for self, following the Lind & Tyler (1988) self-interest model of procedural justice. Relevant themes are false justice, compensatory justice, and asymmetrical power.

False justice. Despite the benefits of PJ, there is the possibility that these principles can be abused. Referring to the idea of "false consciousness," Lind & Tyler (1988) call attention to the dangers of PJ manipulation. Low-power groups can be fooled into believing that there will be distributive gains when they are given voice. This has been shown to occur at the macro, meso, and micro levels of analysis. At the macro level, politically disadvantaged groups are discouraged from mobilizing for actions that would improve their outcomes by fostering societal beliefs in the fairness of political institutions (Tyler & McGraw 1986). At the meso level, "an organization might introduce task-assignment procedures that appeared to allow workers voice prior to the allocation of task assignments when in fact the voiced preferences and values are never really considered" (Lind & Tyler 1988, p. 201). At the micro level, giving people voice in small groups may exacerbate conflict when these people fundamentally disagree (Peterson 1999). This effect was also shown to occur in attempts to negotiate peace agreements. Opportunities for voice given to rebel groups in negotiation often backfire when the agreement that emerges favors the government. Interestingly, PJ principles were adhered to even in some of the most difficult conflict environments: The correlation between PJ and conflict intensity across 16 peace negotiations was moderate (-0.49) (Druckman & Albin 2011). But, many of these cases—for example, the 1994 Rwanda negotiations—did not produce durable agreements.

Power. In asymmetrical power situations, the more powerful party prefers equitable distributions (favoring him- or herself) without alienating (disloyalty, withdrawal) less powerful parties. They may do this by espousing procedural justice, which can be used manipulatively as false justice. An exception, documented by Kapstein (2008), occurred in the Uruguay round of the GATT negotiations. In those talks, the more powerful developed countries made larger concessions than the less powerful developing countries. This was interpreted as a form of compensatory justice, which contributes to trade balance in the international system. Of interest is the question of conditions under which different types of justice principles are used in negotiation.

A key tension experienced by negotiators is between striving for equitable or equal distributive outcomes. This tension is acute when the negotiating parties are near-equals in power (Mulder 1977). The jockeying for advantage that occurs between near-equals prolongs the process and risks impasses. Both parties challenge the equity of rewards received by the "stronger" party. Both are motivated by self-interest: When PJ is motivated by self-interest, it is likely to lead to equitable distributions (to reinforce power relations). A challenge in this situation is to orient the parties toward group values: When PJ is motivated by group values, it is more likely to lead to equal distributions (to reinforce group cohesiveness). The connection between the Lind & Tyler (1988) self-interest and group values models and task or solidarity motives is made by Kabanoff (1991). He discusses the organizational designs that would balance efficiency (rewards based on performance) with cohesion or solidarity (rewards based on relationships). This balance is often achieved through negotiation processes. We know less about the possible causal sequences from motivation to PJ adherence to distributive outcomes.

Summary. In this section, we discussed the relationship between PJ and negotiation processes. The review suggests that this relationship can be understood in terms of alternative motivational orientations, trust, and power. The distinction between affiliation and power sets in motion particular negotiation processes as summarized by two hypotheses:

H1: Motivational orientations that focus on affiliation increase the likelihood of problem-solving processes.

H2: Motivational orientations that focus on power increase the likelihood of competitive bargaining processes.

These contrasting orientations can also be construed in terms of the Lind & Tyler (1988) models of PJ, referred to as group values and self-interest: An emphasis on group values is more likely to lead to problem solving, whereas a self-interested negotiator is more likely to encourage competitive bargaining. A group values emphasis strengthens group identity, with implications for both intrateam and interteam negotiations as summarized by the following hypotheses:

H3: Adherence to PJ principles with an emphasis on group values strengthens group identity, which increases trust in the team's negotiating representative.

H4: Adherence to PJ principles with an emphasis on group values increases the shared identity between the opposing representatives, leading to problem-solving processes.

A self-interest emphasis reduces group identity with implications also for intra- and interteam negotiations, as summarized by the following hypotheses:

H5: Adherence to PJ principles with an emphasis on self-interest weakens group identity, which decreases trust in the negotiating representative.

H6: Adherence to PJ principles with an emphasis on self-interest decreases the shared identity between opposing representatives, leading to competitive bargaining processes.

Another interesting relationship is between PJ and power. The review suggests that an emphasis on group values or self-interests may moderate the impact of unequal power on negotiation processes. This relationship is summarized by the following set of hypotheses:

H7: Asymmetrical power between opposing negotiating representatives enhances cooperation or competition, depending on whether negotiators emphasize group values or self-interests.

H7a: Group-value negotiators are more likely to use their power advantage to encourage adherence to noninstrumental PJ principles, which leads to problem-solving processes.

H7b: Self-interested negotiators are more likely to use their power advantage to encourage adherence to instrumental PJ principles, which leads to competitive bargaining processes.

Viewed through a PJ lens, negotiation processes are driven by the alternative orientations of group values or self-interest. The former emphasizes joint gains, whereas the latter is concerned primarily with maximizing own gains. This distinction is made also by the well-known dual-concern model of negotiation (Pruitt & Carnevale 1993) and reinforced by the relatively strong effect sizes for orientation obtained in meta-analyses of bargaining behavior (Druckman 1994). Extending the path from orientations to processes further, we can derive implications for negotiation outcomes, as discussed in the next section.

Negotiation Outcomes

Negotiation outcomes are usually considered in terms of the type of agreement, as joint benefits, compromises, or impasses (see **Figure 1**). A considerable amount of research on negotiation has focused on relationships between these outcomes and processes, such as bargaining or problem solving. Results have shown that processes influence outcomes (e.g., Hopmann 1995, Irmer & Druckman 2009, Wagner 2008). Justice provides another lens for viewing outcomes, which are considered in terms of distributional benefits (see **Figure 1**). These benefits, or DJ principles, also emerge from processes, which are construed in terms of PJ principles.

Relationships between PJ and DJ. The substantial correlations between PJ and DJ across the 63 studies analyzed by Hauenstein et al. (2001) are consistent with results on process-outcome relationships from the negotiation studies. However, the correlations are inconsistent across negotiation issue areas. Correlations among various indexes of PJ and DJ for samples of peace agreements range from 0.06 to 0.39 (see Wagner & Druckman 2015). The correlations for a sample of bilateral and multilateral trade negotiation cases range from 0.38 to 0.65 (Albin & Druckman 2014a). For a sample of arms control negotiation cases, the correlations range from 0.06 to 0.25 (Albin & Druckman 2014b), and for a sample of environmental cases, they range from 0.01 to 0.32. Thus, the strength of correlations between these variables is contingent on issue area.

A more promising line of investigation may be to consider mediating variables. As we discussed previously, PJ effects on outcomes are mediated by problem-solving processes (Hollander-Blumoff & Tyler 2008, Wagner & Druckman 2012): Adherence to PJ principles leads to integrative outcomes when negotiators engage in problem solving (versus bargaining). PJ effects on the durability of the negotiation outcome have been shown to depend on the centrality of the DJ principle of equality in the agreement (Albin & Druckman 2012): Adherence to PJ principles leads to durable outcomes when equality is emphasized in the agreement. These findings suggest that PJ/DJ relationships depend on other features of the process (bargaining and problem solving), the outcome (integrative or compromise, equality), and context (issue area). Thus, the justice variables are understood as part of a sequence of processes, outcomes, and implementation activities. These relationships have also been shown to depend on perceived time frame. Joy & Witt (1992) found that PJ and DJ are more strongly related for employees with a long-term perspective on their organization.

Another way of thinking about interactions between PJ and DJ is in terms of compensatory effects of the two types of justice. Brockner and his colleagues showed that negative effects of unfavorable outcomes, such as a small pay raise or no promotion, can be mitigated by adherence to PJ principles during the process. Indeed, the more severe the outcome, the more salient the effects of PJ (Brockner et al. 1992). Similarly, receiving favorable outcomes, such as an unexpected pay raise or promotion, can mitigate the negative effects of violations of PJ principles (Brockner & Wiesenfeld 1996). Negative events (unfair procedures, bad outcomes) seem to heighten sensitivity to the outcome received or to the procedures used to determine the outcome. More broadly, democratic political systems are based on fair procedures, particularly with regard to legal institutions. This fundamental tenet provides citizens with access to legal procedures and due process. It also cushions the disappointment of distributive losses suffered from negotiated outcomes and may avoid costly civil conflicts between groups (Tyler 1994).

Outcomes are evaluated as well in terms of perceived fairness. Interestingly, these perceptions may not be related strongly with satisfaction. Outcome fairness is based on social comparisons, whereas satisfaction is based more on the extent to which one's own outcomes correspond with expectations or preferences (Brickman 1975). There may also be a temporal effect for the relative contribution of PJ and DJ to perceptions of fairness: PJ is the stronger influence when procedural information is available before information about outcomes (van den Bos et al. 1997). Further, the fair process/fair outcome distinction depends on perceptions of authorities or institutions for process (PJ) and specific outcomes such as pay raises (DJ) (Folger & Konovsky 1989).

Impacts of DJ principles. Achieving outcomes that are "just" may fulfill a universal human desire, but as Zartman et al. (1996) indicate, the negotiating participants' interpretations of what is just are likely to vary. The different types of justice that can be represented in outcomes introduce the possibility for the creation of trade-offs, but they also present a challenge for negotiators to understand the types of just outcomes and their effects. Although equality, equity, need, and compensation are all called distributive "justice," the decision mechanisms used to reach each outcome type, the distribution accorded under each principle, and the expected outcomes from each type are different.

Proportionality (or equity) and equality have received the most attention in the DJ literature. Equitable outcomes indicate that negotiators have agreed to a distribution that is proportional to negotiators' inputs (Adams 1965, Homans 1961). By contrast, equality refers to outcomes in which there is an equal distribution of resources or burdens among the negotiators (Deutsch 1985). Thus, actors are assumed to have the same stake in the outcome, an assumption that may lead to different implications than those derived when equity is the guiding principle. A compensatory distribution of resources would involve a division that indemnifies one or more parties for undue costs or burdens (Piaget 1948). The distribution of resources based on parties' needs would signify that negotiators agreed to an outcome that assigns value in proportion to the strength of one or more party's needs (Burton 1986).

Proportional, or equitable, outcomes rely on assessments of what the relevant input (or, in Homan's 1961 terms, investments and contributions) is for a particular decision and an agreement regarding the appropriate division of rewards relative to that input. Since these assessments are made by individuals (Adams 1965), they could make room for the tradeoffs identified by Zartman et al. (1996), particularly if each negotiator values the inputs differently. Adams (1963) and others have looked into whether inputs vary based on perceptions of inequality and found that student subjects who believed they were being paid more than they deserved increased their relative inputs as a way to reduce inequities. Experiments have also revealed that the reverse may occur: Those who feel underpaid are likely to reduce their inputs. Deutsch (1985), however, critiques this theory for overlooking the interactional element of negotiations and for assuming that individuals typically try to maximize their material outcomes.

As discussed previously, the objectives of outcomes that emphasize equality and proportionality differ. Similarly, the objectives of outcomes that emphasize need also differ. Kabanoff's (1991, p. 420) observation that "equity [proportionality] was the preferred principle when productivity was emphasized, and equality was chosen when solidarity was the goal" highlights that outcome and implementation are on a continuum, where decisions at one stage can anticipate the requirements of the next. Deutsch (1985) notes that need is the prominent principle of distributive justice if fostering personal development and welfare is the primary goal of negotiation. He suggests that "caring" and "solidarity" (equality) orientations are similar and differ in similar ways from the "economic" (proportionality/equity) principle, although need is "characterized by a more direct and explicit responsibility for the fostering of the personal development and personal welfare of others in the group" (Deutsch 1985, p. 45).

These outcome-related concepts may take shape during the prenegotiation phase and influence the postnegotiation process. As negotiators develop their preference for distributive principles and assess their relevant inputs before they enter into a negotiation, implicit or explicit assumptions regarding the value of distributive outcome types are made. These concepts also indicate outcome preferences that could ensure implementation, such as convincing the other negotiator that they are receiving more than they deserved.

The concept of distributive justice also introduces a mechanism through which negotiations may become recursive in a search for justice. If parties believe they did not receive equitable distributions, they will be distressed, which in turn motivates them to try to restore equity (Walster et al. 1978). Postagreement negotiations are often stimulated by distress and by motivation for the restoration of equity.

Summary. The research on negotiated outcomes reveals that justice is a dynamic concept. It may be construed on a continuum that is set in motion by justice issues raised during the process, continuing through the outcome and to implementation activities. The relationship between justice as an outcome and the extent to which justice is involved in the procedures to reach that outcome on the one hand, and the expected type of implementation on the other, suggests a pattern of overlapping influences across negotiation stages. Some of these influences are summarized in the form of the following hypotheses:

H1: The strength of the relationship between procedural and distributive justice will vary by issue area.

H2: Equality outcomes enhance the durability of an agreement, particularly when negotiators adhere to PJ principles during the process.

H3: Adherence to PJ (DJ) principles can compensate for unfavorable distributive (procedural) outcomes.

H4: Perceived fairness is not strongly correlated with outcome satisfaction: The former is based on social comparisons; the latter is based on expectations or preferences.

H5: Equitable/proportional outcomes enhance productivity, equal outcomes enhance solidarity, and need-based outcomes enhance personal development and welfare.

Implementation of Agreements (Postnegotiation)

The discussion in this section on implementation includes considerations of both procedural and distributive justice issues.

Influence of PJ. The durability of agreements has been shown in field experiments on mediation to be influenced by PJ judgments. Pruitt and his colleagues (1990, 1993) found that long-term compliance with agreements is more strongly predicted by PJ perceptions than by joint problem-solving processes, goal achievement, or satisfaction with the agreement. Interestingly, reaching agreement or the quality of those agreements did not predict durability. Adherence to PJ principles has also been shown to increase compliance with agreements in difficult felony cases (Casper et al. 1988). These findings may be due, in part, to the positive impact of PJ on the relationship between the parties (Tyler & Blader 2003).

Postagreement negotiation processes include carrying out the terms of agreement as well as continuing negotiations over those terms, new issues that arise, or the relationship. In their discussion of intergovernmental negotiation, Spector & Zartman (2003) conceive the postagreement phase as a series of related encounters. Procedures and outcomes from one negotiation are likely to influence the next negotiation. This focus on relationships places an emphasis on a long process of reconciliation or trust building (see also Rosoux 2013). Thus, research on trust and PJ reviewed above in the section on the process is relevant as well to the postnegotiation stage. Particularly important is the cyclical idea of PJ-trust-problem solving (Holtz 2013, Wagner & Druckman 2012) and the way that PJ influences trust repair (Harmon & Kim 2013). But the path from PJ in the process to equality outcomes to durability also contributes to the success of implementing agreements (Albin & Druckman 2012). That success may, however, be challenged by groups with a political or economic interest in sustaining or escalating the conflict.

Distributive outcomes. The archival research by Druckman & Albin (2011) showed that equality outcomes (fairness) decreased the impact of intense conflicts on the durability of the agreements: For intense conflicts, an emphasis on the equality principle reduced the inverse correlation between intensity and durability. The problem, however, is to create an environment that encourages parties to desire equality outcomes. This may be more problematic in demanding social environments where conflicts are intense and relationships are deteriorating. Mittone & Ploner (2012) showed that equity rather than equality is the guiding distributive principle in these settings. But it is also the case that mediation is more likely to be used in deteriorating situations (Bercovitch & Diehl 1997). Mediators can be instrumental in moving parties to seek PJ in the process and anticipate equality as an outcome (see Goldman et al. 2013), particularly if they have a reputation for being fair (Conlon et al. 1994) or derive their authority from engaging in fair practices (Pruitt et al. 1993).

The literature on reactions to perceived inequity/inequality and on ways to restore equity/ equality is relevant. Experimental subjects generally react to restore an equilibrium by compensating the inequitably underpaid subject (Leventhal et al. 1969, Törnblom 1977). Thus, the distributive principle of compensation may replace equity in the postnegotiation period. However, when the inequity is created by chance rather than intention, compensation is not provided to restore equity (Garrett & Libby 1973, Leventhal et al. 1969). Ascription of responsibility for the inequity may be an important influence on reactions to inequity (see also Cook 1975). Another reaction to inequitable distributions is to leave the situation, which has important implications for implementing the agreement and future negotiations (Cook & Hegtvedt 1983). The issue for negotiation is whether negotiators are motivated to restore equity through compensation or to justify inequitable outcomes by believing that they are consistent with a belief in a just world (Lerner 1980; see also Kapstein 2008 on compensatory concessions from developed to developing countries in the GATT Uruguay round of trade negotiations). This issue has not benefited from research to date.

The idea of compensation to restore equity was shown to be related to age. Different DJ principles were used by children of different ages following negotiation in the study by Solomon & Druckman (1972): equity for the youngest group (7–9 years old), equality for the middle-aged group (10–12 years old), and compensation for the oldest group (13–15 years old). These differences are consistent with Piaget's (1948) stage theory of development of attitudes about resource distribution. An implication is that a compensation rule takes longer to be understood but kicks in before adulthood, suggesting that diplomats would resort to it as a mode for restoring inequity and preserving relationships.

Role of spoilers. A major problem for implementing agreements is the presence of spoilers. These are "leaders and parties who believe the emerging peace threatens their power, world view, and interests and who use violence to undermine attempts to achieve it" (Stedman 2000, p. 178). Spoilers may be inside or outside the negotiation and may have different types of goals, referred to by Stedman (2000) as limited, greedy, and total. Justice considerations come into play with regard to strategies for managing spoilers. These strategies include inducement, socialization, and coercion. Inducement may work best for spoilers with limited goals. These include a larger share of the distribution or side payments. Greedy spoilers may also be satisfied with material rewards, but care must be taken to avoid whetting their appetite for more resources. A larger problem occurs with total spoilers, whose demands are often nonnegotiable. The only option may be to resort to coercion if the spoilers' power base prevents the use of legal channels for prosecution. For each of these spoilers, a socialization strategy is appropriate but difficult to implement given the time frame needed for change to occur. A challenge is to persuade the spoilers to adhere to a common set of norms that include PJ principles. This strategy may work better for internal spoilers who are reluctant to destroy the negotiation process. The prospects of increased voice and legitimacy may satisfy their needs.

With regard to peace processes, Neu (2012) raises the dilemma of pursuing retributive justice for war criminals. Difficulties in prosecuting them increase the chances that war criminals will disrupt the process. This prospect is reduced when they are taken out of action by legal prosecution. However, it may also be the case that the groups to which the war criminals belong may rally around them and increase the intensity of protest and violence. On the positive side, such escalation of spoiler demands may serve to unite the opposing negotiating parties. They now have a shared goal of neutralizing the spoilers and a shared task of developing conflict management strategies. These cyclical action-reaction dynamics pose interesting questions for research on implementation of agreements.

Summary. The relevant research on implementation of negotiated agreements was reviewed in this section. Compliance with agreements has been shown to be influenced by PJ perceptions as well as by the distributive concepts of equality and compensation. These relationships can be understood in terms of a connected sequence of hypotheses as follows:

H1: Adherence to PJ principles leads to an emphasis on equal outcomes for the parties.

H2: PJ adherence and equal outcomes enhance the relationship between negotiating parties.

H3: Improved relationships increase the chances that the negotiating parties will comply with the terms of the agreement.

H4: Improved relationships enhance the willingness of more powerful (or advantaged) negotiating parties to offset unequal agreements through compensation during the implementation period.

Taken together, this set of hypotheses suggests the following path:

Adherence to PJ principles during the process → centrality of the equality principle in outcomes → improved relationships → compliance with the terms of agreement → use of compensatory principles to adjust unequal outcomes.

This path may also have a recursive feature by looping back to negotiation processes. Future talks between the parties may be facilitated by the strengthened relationships between them. These relationships develop in concert with adherence to PJ (process) and DJ (outcomes) principles, both of which contribute to durable agreements. However, the relationships may be threatened or strengthened by the presence of spoilers during the implementation process.

CONCLUSION: PERSPECTIVES ON JUSTICE AND NEGOTIATION

In this review, we situate justice in a broad framework of influences on and processes of negotiation (see **Figure 1**). In this concluding section, we attempt to develop implications of the review for perspectives on the topic. Two ways of construing justice variables emerge from the discussion. One consists of considering justice as part of a system of interacting variables. Another approach views justice through a chronological lens of negotiating stages. A discussion of both is followed by an attempt to provide an integration of the approaches.

A systemic approach emphasizes mutual influences of variables relevant to negotiation. This includes bidirectional effects, where justice simultaneously influences and is influenced by other variables through the course of a negotiation. An example is the way that justice covaries with motivational orientation, trust, and shared identification. A willingness to adhere to DJ or PJ principles is encouraged by a social climate in which negotiators perceive trusting relationships, share a larger professional or personal identity, and view the negotiation as a problem to be solved rather than as a contest to be won. The cyclical feature of these covarying factors is that change in any one—for example, information that violates an expectation of affective trust—reverberates through the system. This cycle links the way negotiation is conducted (PJ principles) with the principles in the outcome (DJ), relationships among the parties (trust), motivation (orientation), and social connections (shared identities). The feature of mutual influence also allows for reverse causation, for example, from justice (motivation) to motivation (justice).

The systemic idea does, however, raise questions about the interplay among these factors, for example, the difference between reinforcing effects (high trust, cooperation, and PJ lead to integrative outcomes) and offsetting effects (adherence to PJ compensates for low initial trust) or the likelihood of trumping effects (trust is a prerequisite for adherence to PJ principles). A practical question is how to set the cycle into motion. Implications for this question come from the research on prenegotiation framing and anticipatory justice, which is discussed in conjunction with the second perspective.

A different perspective is provided by situating justice concerns in a sequence of negotiation stages. Paths and cumulated effects on negotiating behavior are emphasized by this chronological perspective. Framing concerns loom large during the prenegotiation period. Of particular importance is the way that justice norms and preferences are developed in the context of structural and experiential factors. These concerns shape various aspects of the negotiation process, including decisions about PJ principles and exchange routines that emphasize bargaining or problem solving. DJ principles such as equality also come into play during the process but surface as formulae that underwrite the agreements. Adhering to these principles during the implementation phase bolsters the chances for compliance with the agreements as well as dealing with those actors intent on spoiling them. But a stage-like process also provides negotiators with experiences that shape expectations for future negotiations. The expectations in turn influence the frames that guide new rounds of negotiation.

Nonlinear (systemic) and linear (stages) approaches to theory are often considered to be alternative, even competing, conceptual vantage points. However, they may also be viewed as complementary. Both a dynamic interplay among negotiation variables and a chronological path of influences through the course of negotiation are relevant to an understanding of the role played by justice. For example, cooperative orientations that emerge from shared frames encourage adherence to PJ principles during the early days of negotiating. New information about the other's strategy or inferences about the other's intentions may provoke a reaction that reduces a willingness to abide by those principles. This development in turn reduces perceived trust, moving the talks away from agreements that embody DJ principles or an integration of needs and preferences. The systemic perspective highlights the interplay among these variables. The chronological perspective calls attention to particular variables—e.g., anticipatory justice, PJ principles, DJ principles, presence of spoilers—that set the cycles into motion. The combined perspectives may be a useful framework to guide further research about the role of justice in negotiation.

FURTHER QUESTIONS

Table 1 brings together the hypotheses developed in this literature review and can be used to develop further questions that connect the stages. For example, H1 for outcomes suggests that the relationship between procedural and distributive justice will vary by issue area: Do agreements on PJ and DJ principles have stronger influences on outcomes in certain issue areas (prenegotiation

Table 1 Hypotheses for future studies on justice and negotiation

Prenegotiation	Processes	Outcomes	Implementation
H1: Agreement on procedural justice (PJ) principles is more likely when parties perceive shared identities or common membership in a moral community. H2: To the extent that parties agree on PJ principles during prenegotiation, these principles will guide the negotiation process. H3: Preferences for distributions based on the principle of equality are more likely to occur when the negotiation is framed in terms of solidarity rather than competitive performance. H4: To the extent that parties agree on distributive justice (DJ) principles during prenegotiation, these principles will influence preferences for certain types of outcomes.	H1: Motivational orientations that focus on affiliation increase the likelihood of problem-solving processes. H2: Motivational orientations that focus on power increase the likelihood of competitive bargaining processes. H3: Adherence to PJ principles with an emphasis on group values strengthens group identity, which in turn increases trust in the team's negotiating representative. H4: Adherence to PJ principles with an emphasis on group values increases the shared identity between the opposing representatives, leading in turn to problem-solving processes. H5: Adherence to PJ principles with an emphasis on self-interest weakens group identity, which in turn decreases trust in the negotiating representative. H6: Adherence to PJ principles with an emphasis on self-interest decreases the shared identity between opposing representatives, leading in turn to competitive bargaining processes. H7: Asymmetrical power between opposing negotiating representatives enhances cooperation or competition depending on whether negotiators emphasize group values or self-interests. H7a: Group-value negotiators are more likely to use their power advantage to encourage adherence to noninstrumental PJ principles, which in turn leads to problem-solving processes. H7b: Self-interested negotiators are more likely to use their power advantage to encourage adherence to instrumental PJ principles, which in turn leads to competitive bargaining processes.	H1: The strength of the relationship between PJ and DJ will vary by issue area. H2: Equality outcomes enhance the durability of an agreement, particularly when negotiators adhere to PJ principles during the process. H3: Adherence to PJ (DJ) principles can compensate for unfavorable distributive (procedural) outcomes. H4: Perceived fairness is not strongly correlated with outcome satisfaction: The former is based on social comparisons; the latter is based on expectations or preferences. H5: Equitable/proportional outcomes enhance productivity, equal outcomes enhance solidarity, and need-based outcomes enhance personal development and welfare.	H1: Adherence to PJ principles leads to an emphasis on equal outcomes for the parties. H2: PJ adherence and equal outcomes enhance the relationship between negotiating parties. H3: Improved relationships increase the chances that the negotiating parties will comply with the terms of the agreement. H4: Improved relationships enhance the willingness of more powerful (or advantaged) negotiating parties to offset unequal agreements through compensation during the implementation period.

H1, H3, and H4)? Are power asymmetries (processes H2, H7, H7a, and H7b) related to the preferences for distribution (prenegotiation H3 and outcomes H5)? And if parties perceive shared identities or common membership in a moral community and therefore agree on PJ principles (prenegotiation H1), do they use problem-solving processes (processes H1, H4)?

SUMMARY POINTS

The key points made in this review are organized below by section.

1. **Distributive Justice (DJ) in Negotiation.** Different DJ principles are emphasized in different issue domains. For example, equality is important in securing durable peace agreements. Equity or proportionality is a preferred principle when issues of economic stability are at stake.

2. **Procedural Justice (PJ) in Negotiation.** Adherence to PJ principles encourages integrative negotiating agreements, particularly when the negotiators engage in problem solving or disclosure during the negotiating process.

3. **Methodology.** Laboratory and field research on justice are complementary research strategies. Conducted primarily at a micro level of analysis, laboratory studies provide insights into the role of justice in negotiating processes and outcomes. A focus primarily on macro-level variables in field or archival research provides insights into the influence of the institutional contexts in which negotiation occurs. A challenge for analysts is to develop methodological strategies that facilitate exploration of linkages between these levels.

4. **Prenegotiation.** Decisions made prior to negotiation influence the way negotiators discuss the issues. The framing of group boundaries influences perceptions of inclusiveness and shared identities, which in turn increase (decrease) adherence to PJ principles. Preferences for the DJ principles of equality or equity are influenced by whether the negotiation is framed as focused on building or reinforcing relationships (solidarity) or on encouraging competitive performance.

5. **Negotiation Processes.** Negotiation processes are influenced by alternative models of PJ. A group values emphasis gears the process in the direction of problem solving. PJ principles are used in noninstrumental ways. The mechanisms for this effect are strengthened intra- and interteam identity and increased trust. A focus on self-interest orients the process toward competitive bargaining. The mechanisms for this effect are weakened team identity and decreased trust. PJ principles are viewed as instrumental for achieving desired outcomes.

6. **Negotiation Outcomes.** The distinction between equal and equitable outcomes has received considerable attention in the research literature on justice. Equality is the preferred principle when the negotiation is framed in terms of solidarity. Equity is preferred when the negotiation is framed in terms of economic productivity. The former promotes group values, whereas the latter is geared toward self-interest. A third type of distribution is based on need. Emphasizing the welfare of others, this distribution compensates for losses experienced by the other negotiator. This outcome may also compensate for a lack of fairness in the negotiation process.

7. **Implementation of Agreements.** A key to the implementation of agreements is the relationship among the negotiating parties. The relationship is strengthened by adherence to PJ principles during the process and by outcomes that emphasize the distributive principle of equality. Yet despite improved relationships, an agreement can unravel when some members of negotiating delegations or third parties have incentives to spoil or undermine the implementation. Strategies for dealing with spoilers depend on the distinction between their goals as limited, greedy, or total.

8. **Conclusion.** Negotiation can be understood as a system of interacting variables. Justice perceptions influence and are influenced by relational, motivational, and identity variables. The sequential perspective used in this review provides further insights into these cyclical processes. Following a negotiation through its stages reveals how early framing encourages (or discourages) adherence to PJ principles, which in turn leads to certain types of distributive outcomes that remain in place over time or go off course through actions taken by spoilers. Systemic and sequential perspectives are shown to be complementary.

DISCLOSURE STATEMENT

The authors are not aware of any affiliations, memberships, funding, or financial holdings that might be perceived as affecting the objectivity of this review.

ACKNOWLEDGMENTS

Support for preparing this review was provided by a Swedish Research Council grant for a research project titled, "From peace negotiations to durable peace: the multiple roles of justice." Thanks go to Naomi Ellemers and Susan T. Fiske for their very valuable suggestions.

LITERATURE CITED

Adams JS. 1963. Toward an understanding of inequity. *J. Abnorm. Soc. Psychol.* 67:422–36

Adams JS. 1965. Inequity in social exchange. *Adv. Exp. Soc. Psychol.* 62:335–43

Albin C, Druckman D. 2012. Equality matters: negotiating an end to civil wars. *J. Confl. Resolut.* 56:155–82

Albin C, Druckman D. 2014a. Procedures matter: justice and effectiveness in international trade negotiations. *Eur. J. Int. Relat.* 20:1014–42

Albin C, Druckman D. 2014b. Bargaining over weapons: justice and effectiveness in arms control negotiations. *Int. Negot.* 19:426–58

Barrett-Howard E, Tyler TR. 1986. Procedural justice as a criterion in allocation decisions. *J. Personal. Soc. Psychol.* 50:296–304

Bartoli A. 1999. Mediating peace in Mozambique. In *Herding Cats: Multiparty Mediation in a Complex World*, ed. CA Crocker, FO Hampson, P Aall, pp. 245–74. Washington, DC: US Inst. Peace Press

Bazerman M, Curhan JR, Moore DA, Valley KL. 2000. Negotiation. *Annu. Rev. Psychol.* 51:279–314

Bercovitch J, Diehl PF. 1997. Conflict management of enduring rivalries: frequency, timing, and short-term impact of mediation. *Int. Interact.* 22:299–320

Bremer B, Hammond KR. 1977. Cognitive factors in interpersonal conflict. In *Negotiations: Social-Psychological Perspectives*, ed. D Druckman, pp. 70–103. Beverly Hills, CA: Sage

Brickman P. 1975. Adaptation level determinants of satisfaction with equal and unequal outcomes in skill and chance situations. *J. Personal. Soc. Psychol.* 32:191–98

Brockner J, Tyler TR, Cooper-Schneider R. 1992. The influence of prior commitment to an institution on reactions to perceived unfairness: The higher they are, the harder they fall. *Adm. Sci. Q.* 37:241–61

Brockner J, Wiesenfeld BM. 1996. An integrative framework for explaining reactions to decisions: interactive effects of outcomes and procedures. *Psychol. Bull.* 120:189–208

Burton JW. 1986. The history of international conflict resolution. In *International Conflict Resolution: Theory and Practice*, ed. EE Azar, JW Burton, pp. 40–55. Boulder, CO: Lynne Reinner Publ.

Casper JD, Tyler TR, Fisher B. 1988. Procedural justice in felony cases. *Law Soc. Rev.* 22:483–507

Chebat J-C, Slusarczyk W. 2005. How emotions mediate the effects of perceived justice on loyalty in service recovery situations: an empirical study. *J. Bus. Res.* 58:664–73

Cohn ES, White SO, Sanders J. 2000. Distributive and procedural justice in seven nations. *Law Hum. Behav.* 24:553–79

Colquitt JA. 2001. On the dimensionality of organizational justice: a construct validation of a measure. *J. Appl. Psychol.* 86:386–400

Conlon DE. 2012. Introduction to the special issue on justice, conflict, and negotiation. *Negot. Confl. Manag. Res.* 5:1–3

Conlon DE, Carnevale P, Ross WH. 1994. The influence of third-party power and suggestions on negotiation: the surface value of a compromise. *J. Appl. Soc. Psychol.* 24:1084–113

Cook KS. 1975. Expectations, evaluations, and equity. *Am. Sociol. Rev.* 40:372–88

Cook KS, Hegtvedt KA. 1983. Distributive justice, equity, and equality. *Annu. Rev. Sociol.* 9:217–41

Deutsch M. 1985. *Distributive Justice: A Social-Psychological Perspective*. New Haven, CT: Yale Univ. Press

Donohue WA, Hobbler GD. 2002. Relational frames and their ethical implications in international negotiation: an analysis based on the Oslo II negotiations. *Int. Negot.* 7:143–67

Druckman D. 1994. Determinants of compromising behavior in negotiation: a meta-analysis. *J. Confl. Resolut.* 38:507–56

Druckman D. 2005. *Doing Research. Methods of Inquiry for Conflict Analysis.* Thousand Oaks, CA: Sage

Druckman D. 2006. Uses of a marathon exercise. In *The Negotiator's Fieldbook: The Desk Reference for the Experienced Negotiator*, ed. AK Schneider, C Honeyman, pp. 645–56. Washington, DC: Am. Bar Assoc.

Druckman D, Albin C. 2011. Distributive justice and the durability of peace agreements. *Rev. Int. Stud.* 37:1137–68

Druckman D, Olekalns M. 2013. Motivational primes, trust, and negotiator's reaction to a crisis. *J. Confl. Resolut.* 57:966–90

Folger R, Konovsky MA. 1989. Effects of procedural and distributive justice on reactions to pay raise decisions. *Acad. Manag. J.* 32:115–30

Garrett J, Libby WL. 1973. Intention and chance reward allocations in the dyad as determinants of equity. *J. Personal. Soc. Psychol.* 28:21–27

Gelfand MJ, Smith V, Raver J, Nishii L, O'Brien K. 2006. Negotiating relationally: the dynamics of the relational self in negotiations. *Acad. Manag. Rev.* 31:427–45

Goldman B, Pearsall M, Shapiro D. 2013. When is mediating employee grievances chosen versus rejected as a dispute-resolution procedure: an anticipatory justice perspective. Presented at Int. Assoc. Confl. Manag., 26th, Takoma, WA

Harmon D, Kim P. 2013. Trust repair via distributive justice rationales: the contingent implications of equity, equality, and need. Presented at Int. Assoc. Confl. Manag., 26th, Takoma, WA

Hauenstein NMA, Mcgonigle T, Flinder SW. 2001. A meta-analysis of the relationship between procedural justice and distributive justice: implications for justice research. *Empl. Responsib. Rights J.* 13:39–56

Hirschman AO. 1970. *Exit, Voice, and Loyalty*. Cambridge, MA: Harvard Univ. Press

Hollander-Blumoff R, Tyler TR. 2008. Procedural justice in negotiation: procedural fairness, outcome acceptance, and integrative potential. *Law Soc. Inq.* 33:473–500

Holtz BC. 2013. Trust primacy: a model of the reciprocal relations between trust and perceived justice. *J. Manag.* 39:1891–923

Homans GC. 1961. *Social Behavior: Its Elementary Forms*. New York: Harcourt, Brace & World

Hopmann PT. 1995. Two paradigms of negotiation: bargaining and problem solving. *Ann. Am. Acad. Polit. Soc. Sci.* 542:24–47

Irmer C, Druckman D. 2009. Explaining negotiation outcomes: process or context? *Negot. Confl. Manag. Res.* 2:209–35

Johnson DW, Johnson RT. 2012. Restorative justice in the classroom: necessary roles of cooperative context, constructive conflict, and civic values. *Negot. Confl. Manag. Res.* 5:4–28

Joy VL, Witt LA. 1992. Delay of gratification as a moderator of the procedural justice-distributive justice relationship. *Group Org. Manag.* 17:297–308

Kabanoff B. 1991. Equity, equality, power, and conflict. *Acad. Manag. Rev.* 16:416–41

Kapstein EB. 2008. Fairness considerations in world politics: lessons from international trade negotiations. *Polit. Sci. Q.* 123:229–45

Kelman HC. 2006. Interests, relationships, identities: three central issues for individuals and groups in negotiating their social environment. *Annu. Rev. Psychol.* 57:1–26

Kramer RM, Newton E, Pomeranke PL. 1993. Self-enhancement biases and negotiator judgment: effects of self-esteem and mood. *Org. Behav. Hum. Decis. Proc.* 56:110–33

Lerner MJ. 1974. The justice motive: "equity" and "parity" among children. *J. Personal. Soc. Psychol.* 29:539–50

Lerner MJ. 1980. *The Belief in a Just World: A Fundamental Delusion.* New York: Plenum

Leventhal GS, Weiss T, Long G. 1969. Equity, reciprocity and reallocating rewards in the dyad. *J. Personal. Soc. Psychol.* 13(4):300–5

Lilja J. 2012. Trust and treason: social network structure as a source of flexibility in peace negotiations. *Negot. Confl. Manag. Res.* 5:96–125

Lind EA, Kanfer R, Earley PC. 1990. Voice, control, and procedural justice: instrumental and noninstrumental concerns in fairness judgments. *J. Personal. Soc. Psychol.* 59:952–59

Lind EA, Tyler TR. 1988. *The Social Psychology of Procedural Justice.* New York: Plenum

Machura S. 2003. Fairness, justice, and legitimacy: experiences of people's judges in South Russia. *Law Policy* 25:123–50

Mikula G, ed. 1980. *Justice and Social Interaction.* New York: Springer

Mikula G, Schwinger T. 1973. Liking towards one's partner and need for social approval as determinants of allocations of group rewards. *Psychol. Beiträge* 15:396–407

Mikula G, Wenzel M. 2000. Justice and social conflict. *Int. J. Psychol.* 35(2):126–35

Miller DT. 2001. Disrespect and the experience of injustice. *Annu. Rev. Psychol.* 52:527–53

Mittone L, Ploner M. 2012. Asset legitimacy and distributive justice in the dictator game: an experimental analysis. *J. Behav. Decis. Mak.* 25(2):135–42

Mulder M. 1977. *The Daily Power Game.* Leiden: Martinus Nijhoff

Müller H. 2013. Conclusion: agency is central. In *Norm Dynamics in Multilateral Arms Control: Interests, Conflicts, and Justice*, ed. H Müller, C Wunderlich, pp. 337–65. Athens: Univ. GA Press

Neu J. 2012. Pursuing justice in the midst of war: the International Criminal Tribunal for the Former Yugoslavia. *Negot. Confl. Manag. Res.* 5:72–95

Peterson RS. 1999. Can you have too much of a good thing? The limits of voice for improving satisfaction with leaders. *Personal. Soc. Psychol. Bull.* 25(3):313–24

Piaget J. 1948. *The Moral Development of the Child.* Glencoe, IL: Free Press

Pruitt DG, Carnevale PJ. 1993. *Negotiation in Social Conflict.* Pacific Grove, CA: Brooks/Cole

Pruitt DG, Peirce RS, McGillicuddy NB, Welton GL, Castrianno LM. 1993. Long-term success in mediation. *Law Hum. Behav.* 17:313–30

Pruitt DG, Peirce RS, Zubek JM, Welton GL, Nochajski TH. 1990. Goal achievement, procedural justice, and the success of mediation. *Int. J. Confl. Manag.* 1:33–45

Quimpo NG. 2001. Options in the pursuit of a just, comprehensive, and stable peace in the Southern Philippines. *Asian Surv.* 41(2):271–89

Rawls J. 1958. Justice as fairness. *Philos. Rev.* 67(2):164–94

Rosoux V. 2013. Is reconciliation negotiable? *Int. Negot.* 18:471–93

Rouhana NN. 2000. Interactive conflict resolution: issues in theory, methodology, and evaluation. In *International Conflict Resolution After the Cold War*, ed. PC Stern, D Druckman, pp. 294–337. Washington, DC: Natl. Acad. Press

Schuller RA, Hastings PA. 1996. What do disputants want? Preferences for third party resolution procedures. *Can. J. Behav. Sci.* 28:130–40

Solomon D, Druckman D. 1972. Age, representatives' prior performance, and the distribution of winnings with teammates. *Hum. Dev.* 15(2):244–52

Spector BI, Zartman IW, eds. 2003. *Getting It Done: Postagreement Negotiation and International Regimes.* Washington, DC: US Inst. Peace

Stedman SJ. 2000. Spoiler problems in peace processes. In *International Conflict Resolution After the Cold War,* ed. PC Stern, D Druckman, pp. 178–224. Washington, DC: Natl. Acad. Press

Sugawara I, Huo YJ. 1994. Disputes in Japan: a cross-cultural test of the procedural justice model. *Soc. Just. Res.* 7:129–44

Swaab R, Postmes T, Neijens P, Keirs MH, Dumay ACM. 2002. Multi-party negotiation support: the role of visualization's influence on the development of shared mental models. *J. Manag. Inform. Syst.* 19(1):129–50

Swaab R, Postmes T, van Beest I, Spears R. 2007. Shared cognition as a product of, and precursor to, shared identity in negotiations. *Personal. Soc. Psychol. Bull.* 33:187–99

Thibaut J. 1968. The development of contractual norms in bargaining: replication and variation. *J. Confl. Resolut.* 12:102–12

Thompson LL, Wang J, Gunia BC. 2010. Negotiation. *Annu. Rev. Psychol.* 61:491–515

Törnblom KY. 1977. Magnitude and source of compensation in two situations of distributive injustice. *Acta Sociol.* 20:75–95

Tyler TR. 1987. Conditions leading to value-expressive effects in judgments of procedural justice: a test of four models. *J Personal. Soc. Psychol.* 52:333–44

Tyler TR. 1988. What is procedural justice? Criteria used by citizens to assess the fairness of legal procedures. *Law Soc. Rev.* 22:301–55

Tyler TR. 1994. Governing amid diversity: the effect of fair decision-making procedures on the legitimacy of government. *Law Soc. Rev.* 28:809–31

Tyler TR. 2000. Social justice: outcome and procedure. *Int. J. Psychol.* 35(2):117–25

Tyler TR, ed. 2005. *Procedural Justice*, vols. I and II. Burlington, VT: Ashgate Publ.

Tyler TR, Blader SL. 2003. The group engagement model: procedural justice, social identity, and cooperative behavior. *Personal. Soc. Psychol. Rev.* 7:349–61

Tyler TR, McGraw KM. 1986. Ideology and the interpretation of personal experience: procedural justice and political quiescence. *J. Soc. Issues* 42:115–28

van den Bos K, Vermunt R, Wilke HAM. 1997. Procedural and distributive justice: What is fair depends more on what comes first than on what comes next. *J. Personal. Soc. Psychol.* 72(1):95–104

Wagner L, Druckman D. 2012. The role of justice in historical negotiations. *Negot. Confl. Manag. Res.* 5:49–71

Wagner L, Druckman D, .2015. Drivers of peace: the role of justice in negotiating civil war termination. Presented at Intl. Stud. Assoc. Conf., 56th, New Orleans

Wagner LM. 2008. *Problem-Solving and Bargaining in International Negotiations.* Leiden: Martinus Nijhoff Publ.

Walster E, Walster GW, Berscheid E. 1978. *Equity: Theory and Research.* Boston: Allyn & Bacon

Wemmers JA, van der Leeden R, Steensma H. 1995. What is procedural justice: criteria used by Dutch victims to assess the fairness of criminal justice procedures. *Soc. Justice Res.* 8:329–50

Zartman IW, Druckman D, Jensen L, Pruitt DG, Young HP. 1996. Negotiation as a search for justice. *Int. Negot.* 1:79–98

Stereotype Threat

Steven J. Spencer,[1] Christine Logel,[2] and Paul G. Davies[3]

[1]Department of Psychology, University of Waterloo, Waterloo, Ontario, Canada, N2L 3G1; email: sspencer@uwaterloo.ca

[2]Renison University College, University of Waterloo, Waterloo, Ontario, Canada, N2L 3G1; email: clogel@uwaterloo.ca

[3]Department of Psychology, University of British Columbia, Kelowna, British Columbia, Canada, V1V 1V7; email: paul.g.davies@ubc.ca

Annu. Rev. Psychol. 2016. 67:415–37

First published online as a Review in Advance on September 10, 2015

The *Annual Review of Psychology* is online at psych.annualreviews.org

This article's doi: 10.1146/annurev-psych-073115-103235

Keywords

stereotype threat, social identity, identity safety, stereotypes, prejudice, discrimination

Abstract

When members of a stigmatized group find themselves in a situation where negative stereotypes provide a possible framework for interpreting their behavior, the risk of being judged in light of those stereotypes can elicit a disruptive state that undermines performance and aspirations in that domain. This situational predicament, termed stereotype threat, continues to be an intensely debated and researched topic in educational, social, and organizational psychology. In this review, we explore the various sources of stereotype threat, the mechanisms underlying stereotype-threat effects (both mediators and moderators), and the consequences of this situational predicament, as well as the means through which society and stigmatized individuals can overcome the insidious effects of stereotype threat. Ultimately, we hope this review alleviates some of the confusion surrounding stereotype threat while also sparking further research and debate.

Contents

INTRODUCTION

At a recent visit to an elite college, one of the authors met two Black men who described their experience at the college. The first man, a student, told of his struggles to succeed in his chemistry class, despite studying for five hours each day. He feared that he might be misjudged based on his race, and he questioned whether he belonged at such a prestigious school. These concerns kept him from studying with other students and from asking professors for help. The second man, an administrator at the college, described his determination to excel in his position in spite of cultural stereotypes. He felt so much pressure to excel that he turned down an opportunity to participate in a day-long diversity event because he was reluctant to let his workload pile up in his absence.

The experience these men described is one that social psychologists term "stereotype threat" (Spencer et al. 1999, Steele 1997, Steele & Aronson 1995). Stereotype threat describes the situation in which there is a negative stereotype about a persons' group, and he or she is concerned about being judged or treated negatively on the basis of this stereotype. When the above men are required to perform in the negatively stereotyped domain—for example, when the student must write a chemistry test, or the administrator must give a presentation—they will be motivated to succeed for the same reasons as a White student or administrator: to meet personal standards, to impress others, and perhaps to advance their careers. Because of the stereotype about their group, however, they face extra pressure that a White student or administrator does not—pressure to avoid confirming the stereotype alleging their group's intellectual inferiority. Stereotype-threat studies have shown that this extra pressure can undermine the targeted groups' performance, making it more difficult for them to succeed than it would be for a nonstereotyped person in their position. In fact, stereotype threat can explain much of the underperformance phenomenon—the finding that minority students and women (in mathematics) tend to receive lower grades than their SAT scores would predict, as compared to their nonstereotyped counterparts (see Steele et al. 2002a, Walton & Spencer 2009). Stereotype threat also explains an important part (but not all) of the race gap in academics and the gender gap in mathematics (Walton & Spencer 2009), and it may help elucidate why minorities are underrepresented in prestigious academic programs and institutions and women are underrepresented in math and science fields (Major & O'Brien 2005, Steele 1997, Steele et al. 2002a).

Identification:
to take on a domain as being a central part of one's personal identity or self-concept

Stereotype threat can negatively affect performance in domains as diverse as negotiations (Kray et al. 2002), financial decision making (Carr & Steele 2010), golf putting (Stone et al. 1999), safe driving (Yeung & von Hippel 2008), and memory performance among older adults (Mazerolle et al. 2012). In the past, the majority of research has examined stereotype threat effects on academic performance. The theory, however, has now been extended to examine how stereotype threat is related to identity and well-being and how it is associated with feelings of belonging in various environments.

We begin by considering the sources and triggers of stereotype threat and describing common methodology used to examine stereotype threat in the lab. Next, we discuss the mechanisms through which stereotype threat undermines performance and then examine the consequences of stereotype threat—moving beyond performance decrements to investigate stereotype threat's effect on people's identification with the stereotyped domain and their well-being. We end the article by reviewing the emerging literature on how to overcome stereotype threat and by making recommendations for policymakers, educators, and individuals facing stereotype threat.

A THREAT IN THE AIR

Every individual is potentially vulnerable to stereotype threat, because every individual has at least one social identity that is targeted by a negative stereotype in some given situation.

Sources of Threat

The men described at the beginning of this article are well aware of the cultural stereotype alleging Blacks' inferior intelligence. Knowing about this stereotype, regardless of whether they believe it, they are likely to become highly skilled at reading each situation they encounter to determine whether the stereotype may be applied to them in that setting. The student, for example, may recognize this risk each time he enters a classroom or is called upon by a professor to answer a difficult question.

According to theorizing by Claude Steele and his colleagues, the targets of the threat may be largely unaware of the source of the threat (Steele 1997, Steele et al. 2002a). They posit that stereotype threat arises from any situational cue indicating that an individual is at risk of being judged in light of a negative stereotype about one of his or her social identities. Such cues may trigger stereotype threat by simply reminding targets of culturally held stereotypes. For example, gender-stereotypic advertisements can trigger stereotype threat among women facing a math test or leadership task (Davies et al. 2002, 2005). Alternatively, cues may alert targets that their group is devalued in a particular situation (Emerson & Murphy 2015, Logel et al. 2009b, Stone et al. 2012, Van Loo & Rydell 2014). Numerical imbalances in a setting, for instance, can trigger stereotype threat among women in quantitative fields and Blacks in business settings (Murphy et al. 2007, Purdie-Vaughns et al. 2008). Interpersonal interactions may also be a source of stereotype-relevant information. Prejudiced attitudes held by the high-status group may be revealed by their behavior (Emerson & Murphy 2015, Koch et al. 2014, Logel et al. 2009b) or reported by other members of the targeted group (Adams et al. 2006, Van Loo & Rydell 2014). People tend to be highly sensitive to cues indicating that one of their identities might be devalued (Purdie-Vaughns et al. 2008, Steele et al. 2002a, Wout et al. 2009), so cues do not have to be blatant in order to trigger stereotype threat. In fact, evidence suggests that both blatant and subtle cues can be harmful to performance (McGlone et al. 2006); these cues can have independent negative influences through separate mechanisms and simultaneous detrimental effects on performance (Stone & McWhinnie 2008). Thus, according to Steele's theorizing, the specific characteristics of the source and target of the threat matter less than the mere fact that the threat is in the air (Steele 1997).

> **Targets:** individuals who have negative stereotypes directed at them in a given situation

A Threat in the Lab

To examine stereotype threat in the laboratory, researchers need to recreate the circumstances of a real-world testing situation. In the real world, simply sitting down to write a test in a negatively stereotyped domain is enough to trigger stereotype threat, because the test-taker is at risk of confirming the stereotype through poor performance. Thus, real-world tests require no special instructions to trigger stereotype threat because it is commonly understood that a test in math class measures math ability, or that the SAT exams measure intellectual ability, and it is well known that women and non-Asian minorities tend to be outscored by men and Whites, respectively. Similarly, to capture stereotype threat in the lab, there is often no need to instruct participants that a test is diagnostic of the negatively stereotyped ability (e.g., Steele & Aronson 1995) or shows group differences (Spencer et al. 1999), but these superfluous instructions are often given nevertheless.

Given the prevalence of stereotype threat in traditional testing situations, researchers most often manipulate stereotype threat in the lab by reducing it for some of the participants. For example, to demonstrate stereotype-threat effects on performance, Steele & Aronson (1995) reduced threat by instructing participants that a test was *not* diagnostic of intellectual ability. Black participants who read these instructions scored equally to White students, controlling for SAT scores. However, Black participants who read instructions that the test *was* diagnostic of intellectual ability underperformed. Similarly, Spencer and colleagues (1999) reduced threat by instructing participants that a math test did not show gender differences. Women who read these instructions performed equally to men, whereas women who read instructions that the test showed gender differences underperformed.

Robustness of the Effect

How robust are the laboratory effects of stereotype threat? Stereotype-threat effects are generally robust, with moderate to small effect sizes (Flore & Wicherts 2015, Lamont et al. 2015, Nadler & Clark 2011, Nguyen & Ryan 2008, Picho et al. 2013, Stoet & Geary 2012, Walton & Spencer 2009). Meta-analyses find that the effect size of stereotype threat for women in math ranges from $d = 0.17$ to $d = 0.36$, the effect size for African Americans and Latinos on intellectual tests ranges from $d = 0.46$ to $d = 0.52$, and the effect size for age-based stereotype threat among the elderly is $d = 0.28$.

Interestingly, Nguyen & Ryan (2008) found that subtle cues triggered larger stereotype-threat effects for women in math than did blatant or moderate cues, whereas for minorities moderate cues created the largest stereotype-threat effects. These patterns, however, were reversed for strategies designed to lower stereotype-threat effects. That is, for women in math, blatant strategies aimed at eliminating threat reduced stereotype-threat effects sizes more than subtle strategies, whereas for minorities subtle strategies aimed at eliminating threat reduced effect sizes more than did blatant strategies. Nguyen & Ryan (2008) also found that stereotype-threat effects for women in math were largest among women who moderately identified with math.

A recent meta-analysis by Lamont and colleagues (2015) found some interesting moderators for age-based stereotype threat. There are strong negative stereotypes targeting older adults, which allege that memory, cognitive ability, and physical competencies progressively decline as people get older. Age-based stereotype threat has been shown by numerous researchers to cause underperformance on various cognitive and physical tasks (e.g., Thomas & Dubois 2011). Lamont and colleagues' (2015) meta-analysis of 32 articles investigating age-based stereotype threat found that older adults are particularly susceptible to underperformance when their performance is evaluated using cognitive/memory tasks rather than motor/skill-based tasks (e.g., physical competencies, driving). These researchers also discovered that age-based stereotype-threat effects were larger when the stereotype-threat manipulations were based on stereotypes rather than based on actual facts (Lamont et al. 2015).

Although all published meta-analyses have found evidence for stereotype-threat effects, the original studies by Spencer et al. (1999) and Steele & Aronson (1995) have been challenged in the literature. For example, Stoet & Geary (2012) looked at direct replications of Spencer et al. (1999) that have been published. Not surprisingly, they found that studies that used pretest covariates to reduce error in the measure of test performance created larger stereotype-threat effect sizes than the studies that did not use a covariate. As others (Sackett et al. 2004, Wicherts 2005, Yzerbyt et al. 2004) have argued, however, the use of analysis of covariance in these studies did not properly adjust the error term and may not have met all the assumptions needed for the analysis of covariance. Consequently, Stoet & Geary (2012) focused on a select group of studies (i.e., nine) that did not use pretest covariates. Despite this conservative approach, they still found evidence of a stereotype-threat effect ($d = 0.17$), but it was only marginally significant.

In their meta-analysis, Walton & Spencer (2009) were able to avoid the problems associated with using analysis of covariance. Rather than statistically controlling for pretest data when examining performance in the lab, they examined how pretest scores predicted performance in the lab and in university courses independently for stereotyped group members under high stereotype threat, stereotyped group members under low stereotype threat, and nonstereotyped group members. They found that compared to nonstereotyped group members, stereotyped group members experiencing high stereotype threat performed worse than nonstereotyped group members, but stereotyped group members experiencing low stereotype threat performed better than nonstereotyped group members. These findings held for all levels of pretest scores and for both performance in the lab and actual university grades. They found these effects for women in mathematics and for race in general performance (i.e., intellectual tests and overall grade point average).

MECHANISMS

Considering the complexity of a phenomenon such as stereotype threat, and the diversity of groups and environments that are affected, perhaps it is not surprising that stereotype-threat effects are multiply mediated. The potential intricacy of these mediational issues is captured by the work done by Shapiro and colleagues (Shapiro 2011, Shapiro & Neuberg 2007, Shapiro et al. 2013). In this section, we consider three aspects of stereotype threat that lead to underperformance: extra pressure to succeed, threats to self-integrity, and priming of stereotypes. Throughout this discussion, we focus on mechanisms that lead to underperformance because these mechanisms are among the best-understood processes in the stereotype-threat literature.

Underperformance Due to Extra Pressure to Succeed

People experiencing stereotype threat are motivated to disconfirm negative stereotypes targeting their social identity (e.g., Kray et al. 2001, 2004; Nussbaum & Steele 2007; Vandello et al. 2008) or at least to avoid confirming it (e.g., Brodish & Devine 2009; Chalabaev et al. 2012; Davies et al. 2002, 2005; Good et al. 2008; Nussbaum & Dweck 2008; Ståhl et al. 2012). This motivation to disconfirm the stereotype, or to avoid confirming it, represents a pressure to succeed that nonstereotyped individuals do not face. This pressure can undermine performance through at least three main mechanisms: mere effort, working memory depletion, and conscious attention to automatic processes.

Mere effort. People are motivated to disconfirm negative stereotypes about their group. Ironically, this motivation itself can lead to underperformance. According to a "mere effort" account of stereotype-threat effects on performance (Harkins 2006, Jamison & Harkins 2007), which builds on Zajonc's (1965) drive theory account of social facilitation, people experiencing stereotype threat are motivated to perform well in order to disconfirm the stereotype, and this potentiates the prepotent (i.e., dominant) response on a given task. On easy tasks, the prepotent response is generally correct, so extra motivation from stereotype threat tends to produce better performance (e.g., Ben-Zeev et al. 2005, O'Brien & Crandall 2003, Seibt & Forster 2004). The prepotent response, however, is often incorrect on difficult tasks, such as many academic tests. Jamison & Harkins (2007) asked participants to avoid looking at an irrelevant peripheral cue while waiting for a target to appear onscreen. Consistent with the mere effort account, participants taking an antisaccade test under stereotype threat had trouble inhibiting the prepotent tendency to look at the irrelevant cue but were quick to correct this error and look at the actual target (Jamison & Harkins 2007).

A common misconception is that stereotype threat will impair performance among targeted groups on all stereotype-relevant tasks. In reality, stereotype-threat effects are most likely to be found on tasks that are pushing the upper limit of the targets' ability. It is during these challenging tasks that the added burden of stereotype threat will interfere with performance. In fact, on tests that are well within the ability of the targeted group, the added motivation to disprove a negative stereotype targeting a social identity can actually fuel improved performance (Ben-Zeev et al. 2005, O'Brien & Crandall 2003).

Some studies have led researchers to infer the presence of physiological arousal by showing that people under stereotype threat perform better on easy tests but worse on hard tests (Ben-Zeev et al. 2005, O'Brien & Crandall 2003) and that misattribution of arousal reduces underperformance (Ben-Zeev et al. 2005). Other studies have found direct evidence for a stress response through sympathetic nervous system activation (Murphy et al. 2007), increased blood pressure (Blascovich et al. 2001), and increased cardiac output and total peripheral resistance (Mendes et al. 2002) under stereotype threat. Studies also show cardiovascular arousal (Vick et al. 2008) in response to stereotype threat. Perhaps most alarmingly, recent work by John-Henderson and colleagues (2014, 2015) found that manipulating the amount of stereotype threat experienced by their participants instigated inflammation processes associated with numerous disease processes.

Working memory depletion. Schmader and colleagues' (2008) process model explains how stereotype threat undermines performance on tasks, such as academic tests, that draw on working memory to control attention and effortfully process information (see also Schmader 2010, Schmader et al. 2009). According to this model, when a negative stereotype becomes relevant to one's performance, it triggers a physiological stress response and a monitoring process to detect self-relevant information and signs of failure. It also triggers efforts to suppress negative thoughts and feelings that result from these two processes—each of these mechanisms uses up working memory necessary for successful performance.

There is also evidence for Schmader and colleagues' (2008) proposed monitoring process, in which targets focus attention on themselves and their performance and become vigilant to detect signs of failure. Research reveals that stereotype threat can induce a prevention focus and increased performance monitoring (Beilock et al. 2006, Brodish & Devine 2009, Chalabaev et al. 2012, Kaiser et al. 2006, Murphy et al. 2007, Seibt & Forster 2004). Moreover, indirect evidence indicates that thought suppression plays a role in depleting working memory. A number of studies demonstrate negative emotions in high-threat situations, and these emotions would need to be effortfully suppressed in order to concentrate on a test: thoughts of self-doubt (Steele & Aronson 1995), negative expectancies and thoughts (Cadinu et al. 2005, Stangor et al. 1998), feelings of dejection (Keller & Dauenheimer 2003), and task-related worries (Beilock et al. 2007). Researchers have also provided direct evidence for the role of thought suppression in stereotype threat: Women about to write a high-threat math test suppressed thoughts of the stereotype, and the degree to which they suppressed the thoughts predicted the degree to which they underperformed on the test (Logel et al. 2009a).

Finally, direct evidence shows that stereotype threat reduces performance on a test of working memory capacity (Hutchison et al. 2013), and this reduced capacity mediates and moderates test performance (Régner et al. 2010, Rydell et al. 2009, Schmader & Johns 2003). These findings are further supported by indirect evidence consistent with working memory depletion (e.g., Beilock et al. 2007, Croizet et al. 2004, Inzlicht et al. 2006b, Jamison & Harkins 2007, Schmader 2010, Schmader et al. 2009).

Conscious attention to automated processes. Not all performance requires effortful processing and attentional control. For well-learned skills that do not rely heavily on working memory for successful performance, conscious attention can actually impair performance. For example, expert golf putting is hurt under stereotype threat because attention is allocated to proceduralized processes that normally run outside working memory. Giving expert golfers a secondary task to use up working memory restores performance under threat (Beilock et al. 2006). Schmader and colleagues' model suggests that the monitoring process triggered by stereotype threat undermines such automatic behaviors by making individuals more conscious of their performance and more vigilant for signs of failure, leading to a controlled rather than automated form of behavior regulation.

Underperformance Due to Threats to Self-Integrity and Belonging

In some cases, underperformance may also be explained by the actions targets take to protect their self-worth. They may self-handicap by failing to practice (Stone 2002), by reporting stress and other factors that could explain underperformance (Keller 2002, Steele & Aronson 1995), or by attempting fewer test questions (Davies et al. 2002). Self-handicapping protects the self by providing an explanation for poor performance (e.g., lack of effort) that does not reflect on ability. Targets may also lower their expectations for themselves (Cadinu et al. 2003), which may be associated with less effort.

Underperformance Due to Priming the Stereotype

Some researchers have suggested an ideomotor paradigm for stereotype-threat findings that do not require "hot" motivational processes to explain underperformance effects (for a review, see Wheeler & Petty 2001). Pointing to research showing that behavior can be a consequence of priming effects, these researchers suggest that when a stereotype becomes activated, stereotype-consistent behavior may follow automatically from that activation (e.g., Bargh et al. 1996, Dijksterhuis et al. 1998). According to the ideomotor paradigm, all individuals aware of the primed stereotypes are equally susceptible to their effects; that is, the actual relevance of the stereotype to the target is immaterial. For example, young participants primed with an elderly stereotype subsequently walk more slowly. In stark contrast to ideomotor paradigms, in stereotype-threat paradigms the relevance of the stereotype to the target is critical—only those individuals whose social identity is targeted by the stereotype are vulnerable to stereotype threat. In fact, participants in stereotype-threat paradigms for whom the primed stereotype is not relevant normally reveal a counter-stereotypic boost in their performance, a phenomenon termed "stereotype lift" (see Walton & Cohen 2003). For example, males primed with female stereotypes reveal this stereotype-lift effect in math performance (Davies et al. 2002).

CONSEQUENCES OF STEREOTYPE THREAT

Both the diversity of groups impacted by stereotype threat and the variety of domains in which stereotype threat can have its impact have been found to be more universal than originally theorized.

Consequences for Performance

Walton & Spencer (2009) summarize research on the consequences of stereotype threat in two meta-analyses, one examining 39 stereotype-threat experiments, and the other examining 3 field experiments designed to reduce stereotype threat in school settings. As in previous meta-analytic summaries of the literature (e.g., Walton & Cohen 2003), they found that stereotype threat significantly affects participants' test performance, such that people experiencing stereotype threat perform significantly worse when stereotype threat is high than when it is low. This finding holds across diverse stereotype-threat manipulations, test types, and targeted groups (e.g., African Americans, Latino Americans, Turkish Germans, and women). Walton and colleagues (2013) conservatively estimate that psychological threat accounts for 50% to 82% of the gender gap on the SAT-Math test, and it accounts for 25% to 41% of the White/Latino gap and 17% to 29% of the White/Black gap on the SAT.

Perhaps more importantly, Walton & Spencer's (2009) meta-analyses demonstrate a phenomenon they call the latent ability effect. When predicting test performance in an environment in which stereotype threat has been reduced, members of negatively stereotyped groups actually outperform nonstereotyped groups at the same level of prior performance. It is as if the members of stereotyped groups were running all of their heats at a track meet into a stiff headwind. Although they had times similar to the members of nonstereotyped groups, when they all ran the final without a headwind, the members of the stereotype group sprinted to the head of the pack. This latent ability finding suggests that if the Black student we described in this article's introduction were to take a chemistry course in an identity-safe environment in which he did not risk being judged in light of the negative stereotype about his group, he would earn better grades than a White student with the same SAT score. We return to this point in the Implications section.

Individual Difference Moderators of Performance Consequences

Individual differences tend to moderate the effects of stereotype threat on performance in one of two ways: by affecting the degree to which targets are invested in the evaluative implications of their performance, and by influencing their ability to cope with additional pressure.

One ironic and unfortunate aspect of stereotype threat is that the very people who tend to be the highest achieving and care the most are also those most affected by negative stereotypes. Students experience greater performance decrements under stereotype threat to the extent that they are identified with the stereotyped domain, because their performance in the domain is self-relevant. For instance, Whites who were threatened by the Asian positive math stereotype (Aronson et al. 1999) were found to underperform only if they were highly identified with math. In a field study, students of color who were most strongly identified with academics were more likely to withdraw from school over the course of the study (Osborne & Walker 2006). These findings may explain why disidentifying from a domain—ceasing to connect success in a domain to one's sense of self—can eliminate the negative performance consequences of stereotype threat (Steele 1997).

Similarly, people tend to be more invested in the evaluative implications of their performance to the extent that the stigmatized identity is central to their self-concept. For example, only women who were highly identified with their gender performed worse than men on a math test that was described as evaluating the abilities of women in general (Schmader 2002). People high in stigma consciousness are also especially vulnerable to underperformance in high-threat conditions because they tend to interpret more events in light of their stigmatized identity (Brown & Pinel 2003).

A clever early study on stereotype threat by Shih and colleagues (1999) demonstrated how priming individuals' social identities could either make them vulnerable to stereotype threat or shield them from the negative impact of stereotype threat. Specifically, these investigators employed female Asian American participants who have two readily available social identities with polar opposite stereotypes regarding math ability. Their Asian social identity is stereotyped as having superior math skills, whereas their female social identity is stereotyped as having inferior math skills. As predicted, Shih and colleagues (1999) discovered that priming the participants' racial identity improved their math performance, while priming their gender identity undermined their math performance.

Individual differences that affect people's vulnerability to extra pressure also affect their performance under stereotype threat. Individuals with a stronger internal locus of control (Cadinu et al. 2006), more proactive personalities (Gupta & Bhawe 2007), and higher testosterone (Josephs et al. 2003), and who are highly motivated to succeed in general, tend to underperform under high-threat conditions presumably because they "choke" under the additional pressure. In contrast, strong coping abilities are associated with resilience in the face of stereotype threat. For instance, high self-monitors, who have relatively large amounts of coping resources (Seeley & Gardner 2003), do not underperform under stereotype threat (Inzlicht et al. 2006a,b), nor do people who are high in a coping sense of humor (Ford et al. 2004). Building on the work of Schmader and colleagues (Schmader 2010; Schmader et al. 2008, 2009), Régner and colleagues (2010) discovered that individual differences in working memory can also moderate stereotype-threat effects.

Beyond Performance

Disidentification: reconceptualize the self and one's values so as to remove a domain as a self-identity and as a basis of self-evaluation

It is important to understand the consequences of stereotype threat beyond its effect on performance, because such effects are likely antecedents to withdrawal from the domain. One consequence of stereotype threat is that it fosters negative emotions in the stereotyped domain. When people complete a high-threat test, they report decreased task interest (Smith et al. 2007) and rate their experience more negatively (Adams et al. 2006) than do nontargets or targets under low-threat conditions. Stereotype threat also diminishes targets' perceptions of their own abilities in the stereotyped domain. As early as elementary school, girls report decreased math self-confidence under conditions of high threat (Muzzatti & Agnoli 2007), and as young adults, women under stereotype threat make more internal attributions for failure on a computer task than do men (Koch et al. 2008). The combination of decreased enjoyment and diminished self-confidence may explain why women experiencing stereotype threat report less interest in math and science fields and weaker leadership aspirations than men or nonthreatened women report (Davies et al. 2002, 2005).

Pronin and colleagues (2004) found that when their math-identified female participants were confronted with threatening gender stereotypes in the domain of mathematics, the women disassociated themselves from stereotypically feminine characteristics and behaviors potentially linked to math deficits. These stigmatized individuals distanced themselves from stereotypes targeting their gender identity as a means of coping with stereotype threat.

There is also evidence that the pressure of stereotype threat may lead targets to respond defensively, presumably in an effort to deflect the implications for the self and the group. People who experience stereotype threat have been shown to discount the validity of a high-threat test (Lesko & Corpus 2006), deny the importance of the domain (von Hippel et al. 2005), and question the competence of course instructors (Adams et al. 2006). These responses may be adaptive in the short term if they protect targets' self-integrity, but in the long term they may contribute to disidentification.

Stereotype threat can also undermine targets' sense of belonging, affecting their motivation and making them more likely to withdraw from the setting (Walton & Cohen 2007). In professional or academic settings, people whose groups are stereotyped or otherwise stigmatized tend to be uncertain of the quality of their social bonds. For this reason, they are especially sensitive to signs that they do not belong. Events that might seem innocuous to others, such as being left without a lab partner or receiving a disapproving glance from an instructor, may undermine targets' motivation and commitment to the domain. In one study, a manipulation designed to lead students to feel they had few friends in their field of study undermined Black students' sense of belonging and beliefs about their potential to succeed in the field (Walton & Cohen 2007). In another study, a video showing gender imbalances in a setting led women to report a decreased sense of belonging and lesser desire to participate in the setting (Murphy et al. 2007). Emerson & Murphy (2015) investigated how a company's lay theory on diversity being entity based (fixed) or incrementally based (malleable) can impact trust among women. The researchers discovered that women trusted the entity company less than the incremental company, and that this mistrust for the entity company led to disengagement among the women. Similarly, Purdie-Vaughns and colleagues (2008) found that Black professionals exposed to a corporate brochure featuring few minorities reported trust and comfort only if the company explicitly conveyed an identity-safe diversity policy.

The above research confirms how reducing concerns about belonging in potentially threatening environments can reduce vulnerability to stereotype threat and thus allow targeted individuals to perform to their full potential. Walton & Cohen (2007) and Walton and colleagues (2014)

found that increasing feelings of belonging led African Americans and women in engineering, respectively, to do much better in their university courses. Unfortunately, if targeted groups are not made to feel welcome in their university programs, chronic exposure to stereotype threat can lead those targeted students to disidentify from their programs and eventually abandon those programs of study entirely (Woodcock et al. 2012).

Consequences for Well-Being

It seems likely that the ongoing performance pressure of stereotype threat might have long-term consequences on the targets' well-being. Indeed, in research suggesting that targets have increased vulnerability to hypertension, Black students writing a high-threat test exhibited larger increases in mean arterial blood pressure than White students or Black students under little or no stereotype threat (Blascovich et al. 2001). Belonging uncertainty may further undermine health, as suggested by a large literature demonstrating the role of social support in physical health outcomes (for a review, see Cohen 2004).

Sometimes exposure to stereotype threat can even lead to behaviors that directly undermine health. For example, Guendelman et al. (2011) found that among immigrants, the pressure to fit in and avoid immigrant stereotypes led to the adoption of unhealthy eating behavior and subsequent weight gain. Similarly, Inzlicht & Kang (2010) found that stereotype threat led to depleted self-control, which in turn led to increased aggression and unhealthy eating.

Are People Aware of Their Experience of Stereotype Threat?

The two men described at the beginning of this review were clearly aware of the stereotype targeting their group, and they were concerned that they would be evaluated based on that stereotype. Although this level of awareness does not seem to be necessary for stereotype threat to occur (as we review below), at times, awareness of the experience of stereotype threat can play an important role in the mechanism that creates these effects.

Numerous lines of research have shown that targets can be consciously aware of their experience of stereotype threat: (a) In open-ended responses, Black professionals who have been exposed to threatening corporate ideology report concern about being devalued due to their racial identity (Purdie-Vaughns et al. 2008); (b) on a paper-and-pencil scale, Black students who have just written an intelligence test administered by a White experimenter report fears of being judged in light of stereotypes (Marx & Goff 2005); (c) female undergraduates in math and science report that some people believe they have weak abilities because of their gender (Steele et al. 2002b); and (d) on a scale, females who have just completed a high-threat math test report that gender stereotypes contributed to their anxiety during the test (Johns et al. 2005).

Further supporting the above findings are studies in which targets report anxiety on paper-and-pencil measures under high-threat conditions (Ben-Zeev et al. 2005, Ford et al. 2004, Osborne 2001, Spencer et al. 1999) and studies in which nonverbal behaviors reveal people are more anxious (Bosson et al. 2004) under high-threat conditions. It is not necessarily the case, however, that people are always aware of the experience of stereotype threat. White athletes fail to report anxiety when threatened with a stereotype that Whites lack natural athletic ability (Stone et al. 1999), and men do not report anxiety when threatened with an ostensible negative stereotype about affective processing (Leyens et al. 2000). One way to reconcile these mixed results is to take into account how well articulated a given stereotype is likely to be in the minds of the targets. In the studies that captured self-reports of stereotype threat and anxiety, the participants were Black students or women in mathematics. Both of these groups face stereotypes that are chronic and relatively well known and thus may be highly accessible to awareness. In contrast, studies that failed to capture self-reported anxiety involved stereotypes that are less well known or more situational in nature (e.g., White athletes and natural athletic ability, men and affective processing).

Does Stereotype Threat Explain Performance on Real-World Tests?

Some individuals have argued that the consequences of stereotype threat do not generalize from the laboratory into real-world testing situations; that is, that stereotype-threat effects do not explain actual gaps in performance between minorities and Whites, or women and men, on tests such as the SAT (Sacket et al. 2004, 2008). These individuals suggest that stereotype threat exists primarily in the laboratory, when researchers use manipulations to ensure stereotypes are especially salient (Sacket et al. 2004, 2008).

In our view, the preponderance of evidence indicates that stereotype threat is, indeed, responsible for performance decrements on real tests. In this section, we review studies that have been used as support for the argument that stereotype threat does not explain underperformance on real-world tests. To illustrate, one study found that reducing the difficulty of Graduate Record Examination (GRE) questions did not have any differential effects on test performance or on explicit indexes of stereotype threat for Black students or women (Stricker & Bejar 2004). A second study showed that performance differences between men and women, and Whites and Blacks, do not emerge only at the highest levels of difficulty on standardized tests (Cullen et al. 2004), or only among those who are highly identified with the domain (Cullen et al. 2006). Stricker & Bejar (2004) and Cullen and colleagues (2004, 2006) may have failed to replicate traditional stereotype-threat patterns in their data sets because they did not include a condition in which stereotype threat was reduced sufficiently to restore performance among targeted groups.

In one set of field studies that are impressive in their scope, researchers manipulated the placement of a demographic questionnaire on actual standardized tests taken by real test-takers—the Advanced Placement Calculus exam and one college's Computerized Placement Tests. In doing so, they tested a replication of Steele & Aronson's (1995, study 4) laboratory finding that asking the test-takers to indicate their race was enough to trigger stereotype threat on even a nondiagnostic test. Stricker & Ward (2004) moved questions about ethnicity and gender from their traditional place at the beginning of standardized tests to the end of the tests. On the basis of students' test results, they concluded that the performance of female and minority test-takers was not affected by this manipulation in any significant way—statistically or practically. Danacher & Crandall (2008) re-examined Stricker & Ward's (2004) data and concluded that the results, although small, were indeed significant in a very practical way. Inquiring about gender at the end of the test instead of in the beginning (as is traditionally done) could increase the number of US women receiving AP Calculus AB credit by more than 4,700 women every year. This finding is striking given that, unlike Steele & Aronson (1995), who showed that asking about race elicits stereotype threat on a nondiagnostic test (a low-threat situation), women taking the AP Calculus test would be well aware the test was diagnostic of math ability and thus would already be writing the test under high-threat conditions. If inquiring about gender produces performance decrements beyond those already observed in high-threat conditions, it would confirm the power of a seemingly subtle gender-identity prime.

Does Stereotype Threat Explain Performance Differences Between Groups?

As we argued in the first section of this article, because stereotype threat exists on real-world tests without explicit mention of anything about group membership or stereotypes (e.g., Smith & White 2002), the best way to manipulate stereotype threat on any given test is to reduce it for some of the participants. Next, we discuss a variety of studies that do just that, and in doing so, not only hold the promise of being able to address real-world issues of stereotype threat but also provide some of the strongest evidence for its existence.

OVERCOMING THE CONSEQUENCES OF STEREOTYPE THREAT

Having discovered that the potentially negative consequences of stereotype threat are even more far-reaching than originally believed, finding practical means for individuals to deal with this threat in the air has become a critical issue.

Interventions

Most laboratory interventions aim to reduce the pernicious effects of stereotype threat in one of three ways. The first way is to guide targets to reconstrue a potentially threatening situation as nonthreatening. The second way is to provide targets with a way to cope with the threat. The third way is to change the environment to reduce the threat itself.

Reconstrual interventions. Reconstrual interventions reduce stereotype-threat effects not by objectively changing the situation, but rather by leading participants to perceive a lower level of threat. This reduced perception of threat is then reflected in their improved performance. We have already discussed the most commonly used reconstrual method—altering the description of a test. When participants are told that the test is nondiagnostic or does not show group differences, their performance is restored. This is a simple and effective method of manipulating stereotype threat in laboratory studies and even in field studies. For example, when Good and colleagues (2008) instructed students in an actual math class that their test did not show gender differences, women's test performance increased significantly, so much so that they outperformed the men in the class.

Reconstrual of the test, however, involves an essentially false description of the test; consequently, it is not a practical method for reducing stereotype threat in the real world, and continuing to use it exclusively will not advance researchers' theoretical understanding of stereotype threat. An alternative way to change participants' perceptions of the level of threat is to have them reconstrue their experience. Guiding participants to reappraise their anxiety (Johns et al. 2008) or misattribute their arousal (Ben-Zeev et al. 2005) restores targets' performance to a low threat level. Participants may also be subtly encouraged to reconstrue the threatened identity. This may be done within the stereotyped identity by linking stereotypic traits with positive abilities (Kray et al. 2002). Alternatively, it may be done by expanding the threatened identity through a reminder of characteristics shared with the nonthreatened group (Rosenthal & Crisp 2006, Rosenthal et al. 2007, Shih et al. 1999), guiding participants to see their self-concept as composed of multiple roles and identities (Gresky et al. 2005) or leading them to individuate themselves by filling out a measure about their individual qualities (Ambady et al. 2004).

Reconstrual manipulations have also shown promise outside of the laboratory, not only in reducing underperformance but also in addressing nonperformance consequences of stereotype threat. Presenting a test as not showing gender differences significantly raised women's course grades (Good et al. 2008). Guiding Black students to reconstrue their understanding of intelligence as malleable resulted in greater enjoyment of the academic process and higher grade point averages than those in control groups (Aronson et al. 2002). Leading Black students to reconstrue experiences that could undermine their sense of belonging buffered them against daily stress and resulted in higher grade point averages (Walton & Cohen 2007). Indeed, seeing intellectual performance as something that can grow over time may be an important way to reduce stereotype threat. The "threat in the air" from stereotypes alleges that intellectual performance is both fixed and group based. Seeing intellectual performance as something that can grow and that is not limited can thus serve as an important antidote to stereotype threat.

Coping interventions. With coping interventions, the overall level of threat remains high, but it does not impact targets' task performance. For instance, participants may be given a strategy to aid them in suppressing anxious thoughts (Logel et al. 2009a) or may be instructed to practice once-susceptible test problems so that they are retrieved directly from long-term memory rather than depleting working memory (Beilock et al. 2007). Educating participants about stereotype threat, reassuring them that the stereotype is illegitimate, and guiding them to attribute any anxiety to a stereotype also results in restored performance (Johns et al. 2005).

Self-affirmation has also been shown to effectively reduce the insidious effects of stereotype threat. Participants can be guided to affirm an important value or self-attribute prior to taking a high-threat test. This self-affirmation restores self-integrity (Steele 1988), leading to improved performance (Frantz et al. 2004, Martens et al. 2006, Schimel et al. 2004). To illustrate, Sherman and colleagues (2013) conducted a field experiment in which they had minority students participate in a values affirmation writing exercise during their regular middle-school classes. Those who participated in this self-affirmation exercise earned higher grades than their fellow minority classmates who did not participate.

Mindfulness training is a coping intervention that is currently getting a lot of attention in psychology. Research has found that mindfulness exercises can alleviate working memory load, and considering the relationship between working memory and stereotype-threat effects, it should come as no surprise that mindfulness has found its way into stereotype-threat paradigms. For example, Weger and colleagues (2012) found that a simple five-minute mindfulness exercise eliminated traditional stereotype-threat effects.

Coping interventions have excellent potential to be applied to real testing situations. Until testing environments can be made identity safe, providing targets of stereotypes with coping strategies may be the best way to reduce the performance effects of stereotype threat. Some coping strategies have been highly effective. In one field study, a simple self-affirmation exercise among middle-school children was successful in closing the race gap in school performance by 40% (Cohen et al. 2006; see also Sherman et al. 2013).

Creating identity-safe environments. Although methods that intervene with the target are successful in reducing and even eliminating performance decrements, they allow the threatening environment to remain. In contrast, a third way to restore targets' performance is to alter the environment to make it identity safe. One means of doing this involves assuring individuals that their stigmatized social identities are not a barrier to success in targeted domains (Davies et al. 2005). Researchers, however, have generally created identity-safe environments by altering the interpersonal environment. This can be done by facilitating positive contact with members of the majority group (Abrams et al. 2006, Walton et al. 2014). It can also be accomplished using members of the targeted group—by providing role models of successful group members (Drury et al. 2011; McIntyre et al. 2003, 2005; Shaffer et al. 2013) or by having group members administer the test (Marx & Goff 2005, McGlone et al. 2006). Interpersonal interventions can also be employed in real-world settings. For example, a field study done with middle-school girls working in same-gender groups did not show the stereotype-threat effect on performance on a diagnostic test, and the girls' performance was mediated by accessibility of positive role models—high-performing female classmates (Pascal & Régner 2007). Another field study (Picho & Stephens 2012), found

> **Identity safety:** removing the "threat in the air" from previously threatening situations; that is, removing the risk of being reduced to a negative stereotype targeting a social identity

that female students in Ugandan coed schools were susceptible to traditional stereotype-threat effects, whereas Ugandan females in all-girl schools were not vulnerable to stereotype threat.

More recently, Walton and colleagues (2014) have used self-affirmation to convince male engineers that their female colleagues have latent ability. This intervention has successfully increased the male engineers' respect for a female colleague, a female teaching assistant, and a female research assistant who interviewed them.

IMPLICATIONS

The responsibility for counteracting stereotype threat does not rest solely on the targets' shoulders; rather, educators, researchers, and policymakers need to start taking proactive steps to remove the threat in the air.

Implications for Researchers

The study of stereotype threat to date has been a prototypical example of a scientific approach to the explication of an important social problem. Social psychologists began by identifying a social problem—the underperformance of stigmatized groups—and developing a theory to explain it. They then generated hypotheses, and through testing these hypotheses, they advanced the understanding of stereotype threat and its mechanisms and consequences. In doing so, social psychologists have developed a promising set of interventions that have been shown in the lab and in the field to reduce the negative consequences of stereotype threat.

We propose a next step, one that social scientists do not often consider: developing effective, broadly tested interventions that can provide a compelling rationale for real-world change. We believe that research on stereotype threat has reached a point that such broad-based interventions are justified. If such interventions were to hold up under widespread testing, then a compelling case could be made that changing environments to reduce stereotype threat in both educational and occupational settings is also justified.

We suggest applying the testing process used in medical research to the social sciences. In medicine, ideas are initially tested with highly controlled low-risk studies, which is analogous to our laboratory studies in the social sciences. Medical researchers take the most promising results and further test them in small clinical trials, analogous to our field interventions. In a final step, medical interventions are tested in large-scale representative clinical trials, from which conclusions can be drawn about the effectiveness, generalizability, and risks of a new treatment. We suggest that this is the step that must be added to the stereotype-threat literature. If stereotype-threat interventions are shown to be successful and low risk on a large representative sample, then policymakers will have the evidence they need to incorporate these interventions into educational curricula and testing procedures.

Implications for Policymakers

Taken together, findings on stereotype threat suggest that many of the benchmarks used to make decisions about admissions and hiring may be biased. That is, they systematically underestimate the true ability and potential of people from groups that are negatively stereotyped in intellectual settings (for a review, see Walton & Spencer 2009). To illustrate, Walton and colleagues (2013) conservatively estimate that the SAT-Math test underestimates the math ability of women by 19 to 21 points and that the SAT-Math and SAT-Reading tests underestimate the intellectual ability of African and Latino Americans by a total of 39 to 41 points for each group. Given this bias, Walton and colleagues (2013) argue that these measures, as they are, cannot be the basis for meritocratic admissions or hiring decisions. Instead, institutions must take affirmative steps to create a meritocracy. Such affirmative meritocracy first requires institutions to create identity-safe environments. Not only will reducing stereotype threat improve the performance of members of stereotyped groups, but it will do so by also unlocking latent ability that was previously hidden. Unlocking this ability will allow institutions and society as a whole to tap into unrecognized potential. Simply put, organizations that create identity-safe environments will be more productive and efficient than those that do not.

Implications for Educators

Educators can play a role in fostering identity-safe environments by applying successful interventions in their classrooms. They can teach students about stereotype threat and the illegitimacy of stereotypes alleging minorities' and women's inferior ability (Johns et al. 2005). They can encourage students to see intelligence as malleable rather than fixed (Aronson et al. 2002). Through diverse examples in class discussions, they can provide students with role models (McIntyre et al. 2003, 2005). They can communicate to their students that they are welcomed, supported, and valued, whatever their background (Davies et al. 2005). When providing critical feedback to minority students, they can emphasize their high standards and assure students that they can meet these high standards (Cohen et al. 1999).

Implications for Students

The young men described in this article's introduction were aware that they faced struggles because of negative stereotypes and were searching for tools they could use to overcome stereotype threat. In providing advice to them and to other targets, one difficulty is that many tools seem to function best without participation or awareness of the targets themselves. For example, self-affirmation, which has been shown to reduce stereotype-threat decrements in multiple studies, is not effective at restoring self-integrity among people who expect it to have such an effect (Sherman et al. 2013).

There are some active steps, however, that targets themselves can take. They can practice difficult problems so that they do not deplete as much working memory during testing situations (Beilock et al. 2007). When they feel anxious during testing situations, they can substitute an affirming or even neutral thought to aid with the suppression of concerns (Logel et al. 2009a). Evidence also suggests that some targets develop their own strategies to cope with stereotype threat. One such coping strategy is "situational disengagement" (Nussbaum & Steele 2007), in which targets temporarily disengage their self-worth from performance feedback in a particular situation, which allows them to persist longer in the domain without risking further damage to their self-worth.

SUMMARY

People experience stereotype threat when they are at risk of being judged or treated in light of a negative stereotype about one of their social identities. The extra pressure to avoid confirming the stereotype has been shown to undermine performance in negatively stereotyped domains. Stereotype threat helps explain the underperformance effect—the finding that minority students and women, as compared to their nonstereotyped counterparts, tend to receive lower grades than their SAT scores would predict.

Stereotype threat can be triggered by any cue indicating that the stereotype might be applied in a given situation. In the lab, researchers most often manipulate stereotype threat by reducing it for half of the participants, commonly by instructing participants that a test is not diagnostic of the stereotyped ability or does not show group differences.

Stereotype threat affects performance through multiple mechanisms. The extra pressure to succeed on high-threat tasks can undermine performance by potentiating the prepotent response, which is often incorrect on difficult tasks such as academic tests. Stereotype threat depletes working memory capacity, which is needed to solve difficult questions. Stereotype threat can negatively impact performance by leading people to pay conscious attention to automatic skills. Performance decrements can also be explained by actions taken to protect self-integrity (such as self-handicapping).

A series of meta-analyses show that stereotype threat undermines performance across diverse manipulations, test types, and groups, and may explain 50% to 82% of the gender gap on the SAT-Math test and 17% to 41% of the gap between non-Asian minorities and Whites on the SAT. Effects are not limited to performance, however. Stereotype threat can also lead to belonging uncertainty and withdrawal from the negatively stereotyped domain, and it may have long-term consequences for well-being.

Social psychological interventions can be effective at reducing the negative effects of stereotype threat. They may do so by guiding targets to reconstrue threatening situations as nonthreatening, providing targets with a way to cope with the threat, or ideally by changing the environment to reduce the threat itself. We recommend expanding the most effective interventions into large-scale representative clinical trials, from which policy recommendations can be made. In the meantime, we recommend organizations adopt a policy of affirmative meritocracy, in which they first create an identity-safe environment and then take performance decrements due to psychological threat into account when making selection and admission decisions.

SUMMARY POINTS

1. Stereotype threat describes the experience of being in a situation in which there is a negative stereotype targeting an individual's group, and the individual is concerned about being judged or treated negatively based on that stereotype.

2. The extra pressure to avoid confirming a negative stereotype has been shown to undermine performance in stereotype-targeted domains.

3. Stereotype threat helps explain the underperformance effect—the finding that minority students and women in mathematics, in comparison with their nonstereotyped counterparts, tend to receive lower grades than their SAT scores would predict.

4. Stereotype threat undermines performance through multiple mechanisms.

5. Beyond performance decrements, stereotype threat can also lead to belonging uncertainty and withdrawal from the negatively stereotyped domain, and it may have long-term consequences for well-being.

6. Social psychological interventions can be effective at reducing the negative effects of stereotype threat.

7. Interventions that lower stereotype threat can lead to improved performance by members of stereotyped groups.

DISCLOSURE STATEMENT

The authors are not aware of any affiliations, memberships, funding, or financial holdings that might be perceived as affecting the objectivity of this review.

LITERATURE CITED

Abrams D, Eller A, Bryant J. 2006. An age apart: the effects of intergenerational contact and stereotype threat on performance and intergroup bias. *Psychol. Aging* 21(4):691–702

Adams G, Garcia DM, Purdie-Vaughns V, Steele CM. 2006. The detrimental effects of a suggestion of sexism in an instruction situation. *J. Exp. Soc. Psychol.* 42(5):602–15

Ambady N, Paik SK, Steele J, Owen-Smith A, Mitchell JP. 2004. Deflecting negative self-relevant stereotype activation: the effects of individuation. *J. Exp. Soc. Psychol.* 40(3):401–8

Aronson J, Fried CB, Good C. 2002. Reducing the effects of stereotype threat on African American college students by shaping theories of intelligence. *J. Exp. Soc. Psychol.* 38(2):113–25

Aronson J, Lustina MJ, Good C, Keough K, Steele CM, Brown J. 1999. When white men can't do math: necessary and sufficient factors in stereotype threat. *J. Exp. Soc. Psychol.* 35(1):29–46

Bargh JA, Chen M, Burrows L. 1996. Automaticity of social behavior: direct effects of trait construct and stereotype activation on action. *J. Personal. Soc. Psychol.* 71(2):230–44

Beilock SL, Jellison WA, Rydell RJ, McConnell AR, Carr TH. 2006. On the causal mechanisms of stereotype threat: Can skills that don't rely heavily on working memory still be threatened? *Personal. Soc. Psychol. Bull.* 32(8):1059–71

Beilock SL, Rydell RJ, McConnell AR. 2007. Stereotype threat and working memory: mechanisms, alleviation, and spillover. *J. Exp. Psychol.: Gen.* 136(2):256–76

Ben-Zeev T, Fein S, Inzlicht M. 2005. Arousal and stereotype threat. *J. Exp. Soc. Psychol.* 41(2):174–81

Blascovich J, Spencer SJ, Quinn D, Steele C. 2001. African Americans and high blood pressure: the role of stereotype threat. *Psychol. Sci.* 12(3):225–29

Bosson JK, Haymovitz EL, Pinel E. 2004. When saying and doing diverge: the effects of stereotype threat on self-reported versus non-verbal anxiety. *J. Exp. Soc. Psychol.* 40(2):247–55

Brodish AB, Devine PG. 2009. The role of performance-avoidance goals and worry in mediating the relationship between stereotype threat and performance. *J. Exp. Soc. Psychol.* 45(1):180–85

Brown RP, Pinel EC. 2003. Stigma on my mind: individual differences in the experience of stereotype threat. *J. Exp. Soc. Psychol.* 39(6):626–33

Cadinu M, Maass A, Frigerio S, Impagliazzo L, Latinotti S. 2003. Stereotype threat: the effect of expectancy on performance. *Eur. J. Soc. Psychol.* 33(2):267–85

Cadinu M, Maass A, Lombardo M, Frigerio S. 2006. Stereotype threat: the moderating role of locus of control beliefs. *Eur. J. Soc. Psychol.* 36(2):183–97

Cadinu M, Maass A, Rosabianca A, Kiesner J. 2005. Why do women underperform under stereotype threat? Evidence for the role of negative thinking. *Psychol. Sci.* 16(7):572–78

Carr PB, Steele CM. 2010. Stereotype threat affects financial decision making. *Psychol. Sci.* 21(10):1411–16

Chalabaev A, Major B, Sarrazin P, Cury F. 2012. When avoiding failure improves performance: stereotype threat and the impact of performance goals. *Motiv. Emot.* 36(2):130–42

Cohen GL, Garcia J, Apfel N, Master A. 2006. Reducing the racial achievement gap: a social-psychological intervention. *Science* 313(5791):1307–10

Cohen GL, Steele CM, Ross LD. 1999. The mentors' dilemma: providing critical feedback across the racial divide. *Personal. Soc. Psychol. Bull.* 25(10):1302–18

Cohen S. 2004. Social relationships and health. *Am. Psychol.* 59(8):676–84

Croizet JC, Després G, Gauzins ME, Huguet P, Leyens JP, Méot A. 2004. Stereotype threat undermines intellectual performance by triggering a disruptive mental load. *Personal. Soc. Psychol. Bull.* 30(6):721–31

Cullen MJ, Hardison CM, Sackett PR. 2004. Using SAT-grade and ability-job performance relationships to test predictions derived from stereotype threat theory. *J. Appl. Psychol.* 89(2):220–30

Cullen MJ, Waters SD, Sackett PR. 2006. Testing stereotype threat theory predictions for math-identified and non-math-identified students by gender. *Hum. Perform.* 19(4):421–40

Danacher K, Crandall CS. 2008. Stereotype threat in applied settings re-examined. *J. Appl. Soc. Psychol.* 38(6):1639–55

Davies PG, Spencer SJ, Quinn DM, Gerhardstein R. 2002. Consuming images: how television commercials that elicit stereotype threat can restrain women academically and professionally. *Personal. Soc. Psychol. Bull.* 28(12):1615–28

Davies PG, Spencer SJ, Steele CM. 2005. Clearing the air: Identity safety moderates the effects of stereotype threat on women's leadership aspirations. *J. Personal. Soc. Psychol.* 88(2):276–87

Dijksterhuis A, Spears R, Postmes T, Stapel DA, Koomen W, et al. 1998. Seeing one thing and doing another: contrast effects in automatic behavior. *J. Personal. Soc. Psychol.* 75(4):862–71

Drury BJ, Siy JO, Cheryan S. 2011. When do female role models benefit women? The importance of differentiating recruitment from retention in STEM. *Psychol. Inq.* 22(4):265–69

Emerson KT, Murphy MC. 2015. A company I can trust? Organizational lay theories moderate stereotype threat for women. *Personal. Soc. Psychol. Bull.* 41(2):295–307

Flore PC, Wicherts JM. 2015. Does stereotype threat influence performance of girls in stereotyped domains? A meta-analysis. *J. Sch. Psychol.* 53:25–44

Ford TE, Ferguson MA, Brooks JL, Hagadone KM. 2004. Coping sense of humor reduces effects of stereotype threat on women's math performance. *Personal. Soc. Psychol. Bull.* 30(5):643–53

Frantz CM, Cuddy AJC, Burnett M, Ray H, Hart A. 2004. A threat in the computer: the race implicit association test as a stereotype threat experience. *Personal. Soc. Psychol. Bull.* 30(12):1611–24

Good C, Aronson J, Harder JA. 2008. Problems in the pipeline: stereotype threat and women's achievement in high-level math courses. *J. Appl. Dev. Psychol.* 29(1):17–28

Gresky DM, Ten E, Laura L, Lord CG, McIntyre RB. 2005. Effects of salient multiple identities on women's performance under mathematics stereotype threat. *Sex Roles* 53(9–10):703–16

Guendelman MD, Cheryan S, Monin B. 2011. Fitting in but getting fat: identity threat and dietary choices among US immigrant groups. *Psychol. Sci.* 22(7):959–67

Gupta VK, Bhawe NM. 2007. The influence of proactive personality and stereotype threat on women's entrepreneurial intentions. *J. Leadersh. Organ. Stud.* 13(4):73–85

Harkins SG. 2006. Mere effort as the mediator of the evaluation-performance relationship. *J. Personal. Soc. Psychol.* 91(3):436–55

Hutchison KA, Smith JL, Ferris A. 2013. Goals can be threatened to extinction using the Stroop task to clarify working memory depletion under stereotype threat. *Soc. Psychol. Personal. Sci.* 4(1):74–81

Inzlicht M, Aronson J, Good C, McKay L. 2006a. A particular resiliency to threatening environments. *J. Exp. Soc. Psychol.* 42(3):323–36

Inzlicht M, Kang SK. 2010. Stereotype threat spillover: how coping with threats to social identity affects aggression, eating, decision making, and attention. *J. Personal. Soc. Psychol.* 99(3):467–81

Inzlicht M, McKay L, Aronson J. 2006b. Stigma as ego depletion: how being the target of prejudice affects self-control. *Psychol. Sci.* 17(3):262–69

Jamison JP, Harkins SG. 2007. Mere effort and stereotype threat performance effects. *J. Personal. Soc. Psychol.* 93(4):544–64

John-Henderson NA, Rheinschmidt ML, Mendoza-Denton R. 2015. Cytokine responses and math performance: the role of stereotype threat and anxiety reappraisals. *J. Exp. Soc. Psychol.* 56:203–6

John-Henderson NA, Rheinschmidt ML, Mendoza-Denton R, Francis DD. 2014. Performance and inflammation outcomes are predicted by different facets of SES under stereotype threat. *Soc. Psychol. Personal. Sci.* 5(3):301–9

Johns M, Inzlicht M, Schmader T. 2008. Stereotype threat and executive resource depletion: examining the influence of emotion regulation. *J. Exp. Psychol.: Gen.* 137(4):691–705

Johns M, Schmader T, Martens A. 2005. Knowing is half the battle: teaching stereotype threat as a means of improving women's math performance. *Psychol. Sci.* 16(3):175–79

Josephs RA, Newman ML, Brown RP, Beer JM. 2003. Status, testosterone, and human intellectual performance: stereotype threat as status concern. *Psychol. Sci.* 14(2):158–63

Kaiser CR, Vick SB, Major B. 2006. Prejudice expectations moderate preconscious attention to cues that are threatening to social identity. *Psychol. Sci.* 17(4):332–38

Keller J. 2002. Blatant stereotype threat and women's math performance: self-handicapping as a strategic means to cope with obtrusive negative performance expectations. *Sex Roles* 47(3–4):193–98

Keller J, Dauenheimer D. 2003. Stereotype threat in the classroom: Dejection mediates the disrupting threat effect on women's math performance. *Personal. Soc. Psychol. Bull.* 29(3):371–81

Koch SC, Konigorski S, Sieverding M. 2014. Sexist behavior undermines women's performance in a job application situation. *Sex Roles* 70(3–4):79–87

Koch SC, Muller SM, Sieverding M. 2008. Women and computers: effects of stereotype threat on attribution of failure. *Comput. Educ.* 51(4):1795–803

Kray LJ, Galinsky AD, Thompson L. 2002. Reversing the gender gap in negotiations: an exploration of stereotype regeneration. *Organ. Behav. Hum. Decis. Process.* 87(2):386–409

Kray LJ, Reb J, Galinsky AD, Thompson L. 2004. Stereotype reactance at the bargaining table: the effect of stereotype activation and power on claiming and creating value. *Personal. Soc. Psychol. Bull.* 30(4):399–411

Kray LJ, Thompson L, Galinsky A. 2001. Battle of the sexes: gender stereotype confirmation and reactance in negotiations. *J. Personal. Soc. Psychol.* 80(6):942–58

Lamont RA, Swift HJ, Abrams D. 2015. A review and meta-analysis of age-based stereotype threat: Negative stereotypes, not facts, do the damage. *Psychol. Aging* 30(1):180–93

Lesko AC, Corpus JH. 2006. Discounting the difficult: How high math-identified women respond to stereotype threat. *Sex Roles* 54(1–2):113–25

Leyens JP, Desert M, Croizet JC, Darcis C. 2000. Stereotype threat: Are lower status and history of stigmatization preconditions of stereotype threat? *Personal. Soc. Psychol. Bull.* 26(10):1189–99

Logel C, Iserman EC, Davies PG, Quinn DM, Spencer SJ. 2009a. The perils of double consciousness: the role of thought suppression in stereotype threat. *J. Exp. Soc. Psychol.* 45(2):299–312

Logel C, Walton GM, Spencer SJ, Iserman EC, von Hippel W, Bell AE. 2009b. Interacting with sexist men triggers social identity threat among female engineers. *J. Personal. Soc. Psychol.* 96(6):1089–103

Major B, O'Brien LT. 2005. The social psychology of stigma. *Annu. Rev. Psychol.* 56(1):393–421

Martens A, Johns M, Greenberg J, Schimel J. 2006. Combating stereotype threat: the effect of self-affirmation on women's intellectual performance. *J. Exp. Soc. Psychol.* 42(2):236–43

Marx DM, Goff PA. 2005. Clearing the air: the effect of experimenter race on target's test performance and subjective experience. *Br. J. Soc. Psychol.* 44(4):645–57

Mazerolle M, Régner I, Morisset P, Rigalleau F, Huguet P. 2012. Stereotype threat strengthens automatic recall and undermines controlled processes in older adults. *Psychol. Sci.* 23(7):723–27

McGlone MS, Aronson J, Kobrynowicz D. 2006. Stereotype threat and the gender gap in political knowledge. *Psychol. Women Q.* 30(4):392–8

McIntyre RB, Lord CG, Gresky DM, Ten Eyck LL, Frye GJ, Bond CF Jr. 2005. A social impact trend in the effects of role models on alleviating women's mathematics stereotype threat. *Curr. Res. Soc. Psychol.* 10(9):116–36

McIntyre RB, Paulson RM, Lord CG. 2003. Alleviating women's mathematics stereotype threat through salience of group achievements. *J. Exp. Soc. Psychol.* 39(1):83–90

Mendes WB, Blascovich J, Lickel B, Hunter S. 2002. Challenge and threat during social interaction with white and black men. *Personal. Soc. Psychol. Bull.* 28(7):939–52

Murphy MC, Steele CM, Gross JJ. 2007. Signaling threat: how situational cues affect women in math, science, and engineering settings. *Psychol. Sci.* 18(10):879–85

Muzzatti B, Agnoli F. 2007. Gender and mathematics: attitudes and stereotype threat susceptibility in Italian children. *Dev. Psychol.* 43(3):747–59

Nadler JT, Clark MH. 2011. Stereotype threat: a meta-analysis comparing African Americans to Hispanic Americans. *J. Appl. Soc. Psychol.* 41(4):872–90

Nguyen HHD, Ryan AM. 2008. Does stereotype threat affect test performance of minorities and women? A meta-analysis of experimental evidence. *J. Appl. Psychol.* 93(6):1314–34

Nussbaum AD, Dweck CS. 2008. Defensiveness versus remediation: self-theories and modes of self-esteem maintenance. *Personal. Soc. Psychol. Bull.* 34(5):599–612

Nussbaum AD, Steele CM. 2007. Situational disengagement and persistence in the face of adversity. *J. Exp. Soc. Psychol.* 43(1):127–34

O'Brien LT, Crandall CS. 2003. Stereotype threat and arousal: effects on women's math performance. *Personal. Soc. Psychol. Bull.* 29(6):782–88

Osborne JW. 2001. Testing stereotype threat: Does anxiety explain race and sex differences in achievement? *Contemp. Educ. Psychol.* 26(3):291–310

Osborne JW, Walker C. 2006. Stereotype threat, identification with academics, and withdrawal from school: why the most successful students of colour might be most likely to withdraw. *Educ. Psychol.* 26(4):563–77

Pascal H, Régner I. 2007. Stereotype threat among schoolgirls in quasi-ordinary classroom circumstances. *J. Educ. Psychol.* 99(3):545–60

Picho K, Rodriguez A, Finnie L. 2013. Exploring the moderating role of context on the mathematics performance of females under stereotype threat: a meta-analysis. *J. Soc. Psychol.* 153(3):299–333

Picho K, Stephens JM. 2012. Culture, context and stereotype threat: a comparative analysis of young Ugandan women in coed and single-sex schools. *J. Educ. Res.* 105(1):52–63

Pronin E, Steele CM, Ross L. 2004. Identity bifurcation in response to stereotype threat: women and mathematics. *J. Exp. Soc. Psychol.* 40(2):152–68

Purdie-Vaughns V, Steele CM, Davies PG, Ditlmann R, Crosby JR. 2008. Social identity contingencies: how diversity cues signal threat or safety for African Americans in mainstream institutions. *J. Personal. Soc. Psychol.* 94(4):615–30

Régner I, Smeding A, Gimmig D, Thinus-Blanc C, Monteil JM, Huguet P. 2010. Individual differences in working memory moderate stereotype-threat effects. *Psychol. Sci.* 21(11):1646–48

Rosenthal HES, Crisp RJ. 2006. Reducing stereotype threat by blurring intergroup boundaries. *Personal. Soc. Psychol. Bull.* 32(4):501–11

Rosenthal HES, Crisp RJ, Suen MW. 2007. Improving performance expectancies in stereotypic domains: task relevance and the reduction of stereotype threat. *Eur. J. Soc. Psychol.* 37(3):586–97

Rydell RJ, McConnell AR, Beilock SL. 2009. Multiple social identities and stereotype threat: imbalance, accessibility, and working memory. *J. Personal. Soc. Psychol.* 96(5):949–66

Sackett PR, Borneman MJ, Connelly BS. 2008. High stakes testing in higher education and employment: appraising the evidence for validity and fairness. *Am. Psychol.* 63(4):215–27

Sackett PR, Hardison CM, Cullen MJ. 2004. On interpreting stereotype threat as accounting for African American–white differences on cognitive tests. *Am. Psychol.* 59(1):7–13

Schimel J, Arndt J, Banko KM, Cook A. 2004. Not all self-affirmations were created equal: the cognitive and social benefit of affirming the intrinsic (versus extrinsic) self. *Soc. Cogn.* 22(1):75–99

Schmader T. 2002. Gender identification moderates stereotype threat effects on women's math performance. *J. Exp. Soc. Psychol.* 38(2):194–201

Schmader T. 2010. Stereotype threat deconstructed. *Curr. Dir. Psychol.* 19(1):14–18

Schmader T, Forbes CE, Zhang S, Mendes WB. 2009. A metacognitive perspective on the cognitive deficits experienced in intellectually threatening environments. *Personal. Soc. Psychol. Bull.* 35(5):584–96

Schmader T, Johns M. 2003. Converging evidence that stereotype threat reduces working memory capacity. *J. Personal. Soc. Psychol.* 85(3):440–52

Schmader T, Johns M, Forbes C. 2008. An integrated process model of stereotype threat effects on performance. *Psychol. Rev.* 115(2):336–56

Seeley EA, Gardner WL. 2003. The "selfless" and self-regulation: the role of chronic other-orientation in averting self-regulatory depletion. *Self Identity* 2(2):103–17

Seibt B, Forster J. 2004. Stereotype threat and performance: how self-stereotypes influence processing by inducing regulatory foci. *J. Personal. Soc. Psychol.* 87(1):38–56

Shaffer ES, Marx DM, Prislin R. 2013. Mind the gap: Framing of women's success and representation in STEM affects women's math performance under threat. *Sex Roles* 68(7–8):454–63

Shapiro JR. 2011. Different groups, different threats: a multi-threat approach to the experience of stereotype threats. *Personal. Soc. Psychol. Bull.* 37(4):464–80

Shapiro JR, Neuberg SL. 2007. From stereotype threat to stereotype threats: implications of a multi-threat framework for causes, moderators, mediators, consequences, and interventions. *Personal. Soc. Psychol. Rev.* 11(2):107–30

Shapiro JR, Williams AM, Hambarchyan M. 2013. Are all interventions created equal? A multi-threat approach to tailoring stereotype threat interventions. *J. Personal. Soc. Psychol.* 104(2):277–88

Sherman DK, Hartson KA, Binning KR, Purdie-Vaughns V, Garcia J, et al. 2013. Deflecting the trajectory and changing the narrative: how self-affirmation affects academic performance and motivation under identity threat. *J. Personal. Soc. Psychol.* 104(4):591–618

Shih M, Pittinsky TL, Ambady N. 1999. Stereotype susceptibility: identity salience and shifts in quantitative performance. *Psychol. Sci.* 10(1):80–83

Smith JL, Sansone C, White PH. 2007. The stereotyped task engagement process: the role of interest and achievement motivation. *J. Educ. Psychol.* 99(1):99–114

Smith JL, White PH. 2002. An examination of implicitly activated, explicitly activated, and nullified stereotypes on mathematical performance: It's not just a woman's issue. *Sex Roles* 47(3–4):179–91

Spencer SJ, Steele CM, Quinn DM. 1999. Stereotype threat and women's math performance. *J. Exp. Soc. Psychol.* 35(4):4–28

Ståhl T, Van Laar C, Ellemers N. 2012. The role of prevention focus under stereotype threat: Initial cognitive mobilization is followed by depletion. *J. Personal. Soc. Psychol.* 102(6):1239–51

Stangor C, Carr C, Kiang L. 1998. Activating stereotypes undermines task performance expectation. *J. Personal. Soc. Psychol.* 75(5):1191–97

Steele CM. 1988. The psychology of self-affirmation: sustaining the integrity of the self. *Adv. Exp. Soc. Psychol.* 21:261–302

Steele CM. 1997. A threat in the air: how stereotypes shape intellectual identity and performance. *Am. Psychol.* 52(6):613–29

Steele CM, Aronson J. 1995. Stereotype threat and the intellectual test performance of African Americans. *J. Personal. Soc. Psychol.* 69(5):797–811

Steele CM, Spencer SJ, Aronson J. 2002a. Contending with group image: the psychology of stereotype and social identity threat. *Adv. Exp. Soc. Psychol.* 34:379–440

Steele J, James JB, Barnett RC. 2002b. Learning in a man's world: examining the perceptions of undergraduate women in male-dominated academic areas. *Psychol. Women Q.* 26(1):46–50

Stoet G, Geary DC. 2012. Can stereotype threat explain the gender gap in mathematics performance and achievement? *Rev. Gen. Psychol.* 16(1):93–102

Stone J. 2002. Battling doubt by avoiding practice: the effects of stereotype threat on self-handicapping in white athletes. *Personal. Soc. Psychol. Bull.* 28(12):1667–78

Stone J, Harrison CK, Mottley J. 2012. Don't call me a student-athlete: the effect of identity priming on stereotype threat for academically engaged African American college athletes. *Basic Appl. Soc. Psychol.* 34(2):99–106

Stone J, Lynch CI, Sjomeling M, Darley JM. 1999. Stereotype threat effects on black and white athletic performance. *J. Personal. Soc. Psychol.* 77(6):1213–28

Stone J, McWhinnie C. 2008. Evidence that blatant versus subtle stereotype threat cues impact performance through dual processes. *J. Exp. Soc. Psychol.* 44(2):445–52

Stricker LJ, Bejar II. 2004. Test difficulty and stereotype threat on the GRE general test. *J. Appl. Soc. Psychol.* 34(3):563–97

Stricker LJ, Ward WC. 2004. Stereotype threat, inquiring about test takers' ethnicity and gender, and standardized test performance. *J. Appl. Soc. Psychol.* 34(4):665–93

Thomas AK, Dubois SJ. 2011. Reducing the burden of stereotype threat eliminates age differences in memory distortion. *Psychol. Sci.* 22(12):1515–17

Van Loo KJ, Rydell RJ. 2014. Negative exposure: Watching another woman subjected to dominant male behavior during a math interaction can induce stereotype threat. *Soc. Psychol. Personal. Sci.* 5(5):601–7

Vandello JA, Bosson JK, Cohen D, Burnaford RM, Weaver JR. 2008. Precarious manhood. *J. Personal. Soc. Psychol.* 95(6):1325–39

Vick SB, Seery MD, Blascovich J, Weisbuch M. 2008. The effect of gender stereotype activation on challenge and threat motivational states. *J. Exp. Soc. Psychol.* 44(3):624–30

von Hippel W, von Hippel C, Conway L, Preacher KJ, Schooler JW, Radvansky GA. 2005. Coping with stereotype threat: denial as an impression management strategy. *J. Personal. Soc. Psychol.* 89(1):22–35

Walton GM, Cohen GL. 2003. Stereotype lift. *J. Exp. Soc. Psychol.* 39(5):456–67

Walton GM, Cohen GL. 2007. A question of belonging: race, social fit, and achievement. *J. Personal. Soc. Psychol.* 92(1):82–96

Walton GM, Logel C, Peach JM, Spencer SJ, Zanna MP. 2014. Two brief interventions to mitigate a "chilly climate" transform women's experience, relationships, and achievement in engineering. *J. Educ. Psychol.* 107(2):468–85

Walton GM, Spencer SJ. 2009. Latent ability: Grades and test scores systematically underestimate the intellectual ability of negatively stereotyped students. *Psychol. Sci.* 20(9):1132–39

Walton GM, Spencer SJ, Erman S. 2013. Affirmative meritocracy. *Soc. Issues Policy Rev.* 7(1):1–35

Weger UW, Hooper N, Meier BP, Hopthrow T. 2012. Mindful maths: reducing the impact of stereotype threat through a mindfulness exercise. *Conscious. Cogn.* 21(1):471–75

Wheeler SC, Petty RE. 2001. The effects of stereotype activation on behaviour: a review of possible mechanisms. *Psychol. Bull.* 127(6):797–826

Wicherts JM, Dolan CV, Hessen DJ. 2005. Stereotype threat and group differences in test performance: a question of measurement invariance. *J. Personal. Soc. Psychol.* 89(5):696–716

Woodcock A, Hernandez PR, Estrada M, Schultz P. 2012. The consequences of chronic stereotype threat: domain disidentification and abandonment. *J. Personal. Soc. Psychol.* 103(4):635–46

Wout D, Shih MJ, Jackson JS, Sellers RM. 2009. Targets as perceivers: how people determine when they will be negatively stereotyped. *J. Personal. Soc. Psychol.* 96(2):349–62

Yeung NCJ, von Hippel C. 2008. Stereotype threat increases the likelihood that female drivers in a simulator run over jaywalkers. *Accid. Anal. Prev.* 40(2):667–74

Yzerbyt VY, Muller D, Judd CM. 2004. Adjusting researchers' approach to adjustment: on the use of covariates when testing interactions. *J. Exp. Soc. Psychol.* 40(3):424–31

Zajonc RB. 1965. Social facilitation. *Science* 149:269–74

Toward a Social Psychology of Race and Race Relations for the Twenty-First Century

Jennifer A. Richeson[1] and Samuel R. Sommers[2]

[1]Department of Psychology, Department of African American Studies, and Institute for Policy Research, Northwestern University, Evanston, Illinois 60208; email: jriches@northwestern.edu

[2]Department of Psychology, Tufts University, Medford, Massachusetts 02155; email: Sam.Sommers@tufts.edu

Annu. Rev. Psychol. 2016. 67:439–63

First published online as a Review in Advance on September 11, 2015

The *Annual Review of Psychology* is online at psych.annualreviews.org

This article's doi: 10.1146/annurev-psych-010213-115115

Keywords

intergroup relations, diversity, discrimination, stereotyping and prejudice, racial identity, racial categorization

Abstract

The United States, like many nations, continues to experience rapid growth in its racial minority population and is projected to attain so-called majority-minority status by 2050. Along with these demographic changes, staggering racial disparities persist in health, wealth, and overall well-being. In this article, we review the social psychological literature on race and race relations, beginning with the seemingly simple question: What is race? Drawing on research from different fields, we forward a model of race as dynamic, malleable, and socially constructed, shifting across time, place, perceiver, and target. We then use classic theoretical perspectives on intergroup relations to frame and then consider new questions regarding contemporary racial dynamics. We next consider research on racial diversity, focusing on its effects during interpersonal encounters and for groups. We close by highlighting emerging topics that should top the research agenda for the social psychology of race and race relations in the twenty-first century.

Contents

INTRODUCTION

In the United States, one-and-a-half decades into the twenty-first century, race relations continue to be unquestionably fluid and volatile. The continuation of the troubling trend of police shootings of unarmed black people in 2014 inspired protest and the "Black Lives Matter" movement, but also backlash and counterprotest. Halfway through the second term of President Barack Obama—the first black person to hold the office—the midterm election cycle saw two Latino governors reelected and the largest black Republican delegation sent to Congress since Reconstruction. And projections continue to indicate that by the year 2050, racial minorities will comprise more than 50% of the population, a milestone that will render the United States a so-called majority-minority nation (US Census Bur. 2012).

It is in light of such developments, movements, and potential demographic shifts that we seek to review and organize the social psychological literature relevant to contemporary race relations. We begin by considering the concept of race, a discussion in which we believe psychologists too infrequently engage. We then use classic perspectives on intergroup relations to frame current understandings of race relations, before turning to a review of the effects of racial diversity on individuals and groups. Although each section includes consideration of directions for future research, we close by identifying what we believe to be essential topics for the next decade of social psychological inquiry on race and race relations.

Racial diversity: the variance in racial, ethnic, and/or cultural background of the members of a nation, community, organization, group, or dyad

CONCEPTUALIZING RACE

In order to study race relations, it is important first to consider what exactly "race" is, or at least come to some consensus regarding what we actually refer to when we use the term. Psychology, in general—and social psychology, in particular—has concerned itself with a number of questions pertaining to race. In its early days, psychology contributed to the legacy of scientific racism, offering evidence to support, if not to justify, existing racial hierarchies (see Eberhardt 2005, Metzl 2010). Other research traditions, however, sought to investigate the roots of (racial/ethnic) prejudice, including the categorization of people into different racial categories (Allport 1954, Brewer 1999, Dovidio & Gaertner 2004); potential remedies for prejudice, such as interracial contact (Pettigrew & Tropp 2006); and, more recently, psychological perspectives on racial disparities in health and well-being (Williams & Mohammed 2009; see also Mays et al. 2007). Each of these (and other) lines of research requires an understanding of who belongs in what racial group and why. Although racial categorization can seem like a relatively straightforward process, extant research highlights its complexity.

So, then, what is race? Most people think of race as a way of categorizing individuals into relatively distinct, stable, and homogenous groupings, defined largely by skin color. Indeed, we often use skin tone as a metaphor for racial category membership, echoing Dr. Martin Luther King Jr.'s famous call for judgment based on the "content of one's character," not the "color of one's skin" (ABC News 2013). Underlying this heuristic use, however, is the clear implication that the differences in skin tone (and other physical characteristics) that covary with racial categories also reflect more important innate differences. Historically, of course, these presumed biological differences were also those that justified the asserted superiority of lighter-skinned European colonizers relative to the darker-skinned native individuals (African, Asian, Indigenous American) whom they colonized (Smedley 2007). Despite such efforts to justify discrimination with appeals to biological differences between races, however, research identifies race as largely a social, rather than biological, category. Indeed, genetic studies find far more differences within traditionally defined racial groups/categories than between them (e.g., Zuckerman 1990). Nevertheless, the (mis)understanding of race as a biological reality persists among both laypeople and scientists, including psychologists (Morning 2011). In fact, it may even be resurging, especially in the natural sciences and medicine (Duster 2005, Roberts 2011).

Racial formation: the dynamic formation of racial categories and identity based on target and perceiver characteristics and embedded in socio-cultural-historical factors

Racial categorization: the process of assigning others or the self to specific or multiple racial/ethnic groups

Race as Socially Constructed and Malleable

If race is not primarily biological, then what is it? Sociologists, and more recently psychologists as well, argue that race is not simply a characteristic that people are born into. As depicted in **Figure 1**, race, at both the individual and societal levels, is largely a product of dynamic social construction. Indeed, other fields refer to "racial formation" (Omni & Winant 1994) rather than "racial categorization," recognizing that racial categories are "historically situated, context specific, and subject to processes of both resistance and reproduction" (Saperstein et al. 2013, p. 360). In other words, we don't racially categorize ourselves or others simply based on what we see—when cues regarding physiognomy shape racial categorization, they do so in concert with social norms, conventions, and even laws (Banks & Eberhardt 1998, Peery & Bodenhausen 2008). For example, the court records of states such as Virginia and Louisiana contain cases wherein individuals have petitioned to change their official racial classifications (Banks & Eberhardt 1998), typically from "nonwhite" to "white." In many instances, these individual petitioners were closer to "white" based on physical appearance, but had nevertheless been classified as "nonwhite" due to social associations with nonwhites or evidence of at least one nonwhite ancestor, no matter how distant.

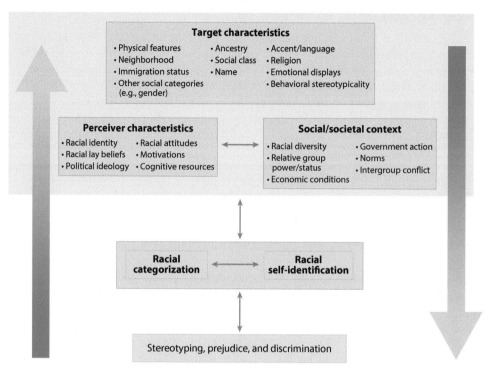

Target characteristics
- Physical features
- Neighborhood
- Immigration status
- Other social categories (e.g., gender)
- Ancestry
- Social class
- Name
- Accent/language
- Religion
- Emotional displays
- Behavioral stereotypicality

Perceiver characteristics
- Racial identity
- Racial lay beliefs
- Political ideology
- Racial attitudes
- Motivations
- Cognitive resources

Social/societal context
- Racial diversity
- Relative group power/status
- Economic conditions
- Government action
- Norms
- Intergroup conflict

Racial categorization ↔ **Racial self-identification**

Stereotyping, prejudice, and discrimination

Figure 1

Schematic of the dynamic and malleable pathways to racial categorization and self-identification. Racial categorization is shaped by both seemingly relevant (e.g., skin tone) and irrelevant (e.g., social class) target characteristics as well as by characteristics of perceivers (e.g., racial lay beliefs) and the larger social/societal context. Racial categorization and self-identification are mutually constituted but not isomorphic and are both shaped by and influence exposure to stereotyping, prejudice, and discrimination.

Additional evidence regarding the social construction of race can be gleaned from historical shifts in the number and nature of specific racial categories that have been recognized, both formally and more informally—most notably, the distinction between who is and who is not considered white (Painter 2010). For instance, Irish, Italian, and Jewish Americans were largely considered nonwhite as late as the early twentieth century; Arab Americans were often categorized as white before the terrorist attacks on September 11, 2001 (but usually considered nonwhite thereafter); and Latinos now have the opportunity to identify as white, black, or neither on official government forms, such as the US Census (Perez & Hirschman 2010). Asian Americans, interestingly, can specify discrete ethnic/national origin categories (i.e., Japanese, Filipino, Indian, etc.) as their racial designation on the Census; however, they are nevertheless clumped together as Asian for most reporting purposes. Similarly, racial categories that were readily utilized in the past, albeit sometimes only locally, have all but disappeared, such as mulatto or quadroon, while newer categories have emerged (e.g., Hapa in Hawaii; Hochschild et al. 2012). The malleability of racial categorization at the societal level may be reflected best in the decision by the US Office of Management and Budget to move from the recognition of roughly 5 mutually exclusive racial categories in 1978 to more than 100 possible racial/ethnic combinations in 2010 (Hochschild et al. 2012, Perez & Hirschman 2010).

Some of the most compelling empirical work demonstrating the dynamic social construction of race comes from sociology. For instance, in a series of papers, Aliya Saperstein and Andrew Penner have found that cues regarding status (e.g., socioeconomics, incarceration) can shape the racial category to which individuals are assigned (Freeman et al. 2011, Penner & Saperstein 2008; for a review, see Saperstein & Penner 2012). Knowing that a woman receives welfare payments makes it more likely that she will be categorized as black rather than white (Penner & Saperstein 2013). Indeed, even information regarding disease status informs racial category judgments: Knowing that someone died of cirrhosis of the liver makes it more likely that he will be categorized as American Indian (Noymer et al. 2011). Of course, consistent with the extant social-psychological research on stereotype application (see Macrae & Bodenhausen 2000), these processes are bidirectional; for instance, information about racial category membership also affects medical diagnoses (Metzl 2010). Although the flexibility of racial categorization has received less attention in social psychology, there is research to suggest that psychosocial factors such as prejudicial attitudes (e.g., Hugenberg & Bodenhausen 2004), group identification (e.g., Castano et al. 2002), stereotypes and affective orientations (e.g., Richeson & Trawalter 2005a), political ideology/affiliations (e.g., Caruso et al. 2009), and beliefs regarding the nature of race itself (Eberhardt et al. 2003, Plaks et al. 2012) can affect the racial categorization process (**Figure 1**; see Kang & Bodenhausen 2015).

Moving Beyond Either/Or Racial Categorization

It is likely no coincidence that research on the malleability of racial categorization has grown, as has the proportion of individuals who self-identify as multiracial (Gaither 2015). Specifically, members of this growing population have sparked a renewed interest in race perception, especially the categorization of people who identify as multiracial (Peery & Bodenhausen 2008). Although many studies have relied on individuals with ambiguous visual appearances as a proxy of sorts for multiracial identity (or sometimes as a set of physical cues in concert with such an identity; see Pauker et al. 2009), this work has greatly contributed to the uncovering of our assumptions about race. For instance, research on the perception of multiracial individuals has revealed that the historical convention of hypodescent—the tendency to categorize individuals with mixed racial ancestry into the socially subordinate parental race—still governs most categorization decisions (Ho et al. 2011, Peery & Bodenhausen 2008).

As this work on the perception of biracial and/or multiracial individuals continues, it will need to take care not to fall prey to the very assumptions regarding race that the work may be best positioned to disrupt—specifically, the notion that racial category membership is a matter of simple biology. For instance, what seems like a reasonable definition of "biracial" as a child of parents with different racial backgrounds actually reifies, rather than challenges, the biological understanding of race. This definition often presumes that there are two distinct biologically meaningful parental racial categories that are then passed down to biracial children. This view, then, prioritizes biology rather than the myriad cultural factors that give rise to racial identity. In addition, it ignores the historical truth that all of the racial categories that we recognize today in the United States (as well as in many other countries) are actually groupings of peoples with quite varied "racial" ancestries. It remains without question, though, that the emerging research on the perception of multiracial individuals underscores that racial categorization is far more than a simple matter of physical appearance or biology, but rather a dynamic process informed by any number of sociocultural, motivational, and cognitive factors.

Race Versus Ethnicity

We use (as others have used) the terms race and ethnicity somewhat interchangeably in this article, but it is important to note that these concepts are not always interchangeable. Some prefer to use the term ethnicity when attempting to denote cultural groupings and "race" when attempting to denote groupings defined by physical markers such as skin tone. As noted previously, however, this distinction reflects a problematic understanding of race, and thus we will not perpetuate it here. Instead, we offer the following: Ethnic categories tend to be subordinate to racial categories for the most part (except on the US Census, where it depends on racial category; Hochschild et al. 2012). Nevertheless, we agree that ethnicity does tend to refer to cultural heritage more so than does race, which instead tends to reflect sociopolitical groupings. For instance, whereas Asian American is a common umbrella or pan-ethnic racial category in the United States, it means nothing in most other countries and, importantly, little in terms of personal social identification for many individuals. Instead, the national origin of one's ancestors for Asian Americans (e.g., China, Japan) and Latinos (e.g., Mexico, Columbia) or tribal affiliation for American Indians (e.g., Choctaw, Navaho) is often a more salient source of identification and better informs people's lived experiences (Flores & Huo 2013). Moreover, although often overlooked, the racial category "black" is also composed of various ethnic subgroups in the United States (Waters 1999), including individuals from different Caribbean nations (e.g., Haiti), individuals from different African nations (e.g., Nigeria) and, of course, individuals with direct ties to chattel slavery in the United States.

The tendency to think in terms of racial rather than ethnic categories can also yield troubling forms of miscategorization. For instance, stereotypical beliefs and associations regarding Chinese Americans are often applied to all Asian Americans much as beliefs regarding Mexican Americans tend to be applied to all Latinos, to the chagrin of targets and embarrassment of perpetrators. Further, these types of categorization errors can trigger negative affect and undermine positive interracial interactions (Flores & Huo 2013, Trujillo et al. 2015). Interestingly, the use of ethnic (e.g., African American, European American), rather than racial (e.g., black, white) labels can even result in the expression of different levels of racial bias (Hall et al. 2015, Morrison & Chung 2011). Although the confusion regarding race versus ethnicity is not something that is likely to be resolved in the near future (Hochschild et al. 2012), it is nevertheless important to recognize that decisions regarding the categorization of individuals into these different racial and/or ethnic categories is multiply determined and can come with any number of unexpected downstream consequences.

Closing Thoughts

The understanding of race in the social sciences has shifted greatly over the years. Research has demonstrated quite convincingly that race is not simply a predetermined biological category, but rather is shaped by a number of sociocultural and psychological factors. Instead of modeling racial categorization as the beginning of a process that could lead to stereotyping and prejudice, therefore, this view of race reminds us that the reverse process is also occurring. In other words, stereotyping and prejudice are not solely the products of racial categorizations, but are also among their sources. Stereotypes and prejudicial attitudes help to create and sustain our beliefs about race, including who belongs in which categories. Given that the United States, like other nations, is facing dramatic changes in its racial demographic profile, social psychology should be poised to contribute to our understanding of the racial formation process, helping answer questions such as: Will the lines that separate white from nonwhite shift in the face of these changing demographics? If so, which, if any, groups will migrate from nonwhite to white? Which individuals are more likely to assert a white identity, and under what conditions will these assertions be verified by others? What new racial categories will be created and, then, contested in this new century? Only by understanding the dynamic processes through which race is perceived individually, and constructed societally and contextually, can psychological science meaningfully inform these types of pressing questions. Further, adopting a more nuanced understanding of the social construction of race allows for a more compelling understanding of the nature of prejudice—a topic to which we turn in the next section.

CLASSIC AND CONTEMPORARY THEORIES OF RACE RELATIONS

As noted previously, much of the history of social psychology is grounded in the pursuit of the roots of, and remedies for, prejudice and intergroup conflict (Allport 1954, Duckitt 2010, Paluck & Green 2009). The field has been impressively productive and largely successful in unearthing many of the cognitive and motivational underpinnings of prejudice and discrimination (for extensive treatment of this topic, see Dovidio et al. 2010). In this section, we briefly review the prevailing social psychological theories of intergroup relations, highlighting their implications for contemporary race relations, primarily in the United States.

Social identity theory: intergroup relations are shaped by cognitive and motivational processes whereby others are viewed through the lens of either ingroup or outgroup membership

Social Identity Theory

Social identity theory suggests that people sort others rapidly and with minimal effort (Allport 1954, Tajfel & Turner 1986), resulting in categories colloquially distinguished as "we" and "they" based on whether the category does or does not include the self. This basic distinction between one's ingroups and outgroups influences perception, cognition, affect, and behavior in ways that systematically produce and reinforce pervasive intergroup biases (see Brewer 1999, Dovidio & Gaertner 2010, Yzerbyt & Demoulin 2010). Specifically, classic research, often utilizing the minimal group paradigm, offers compelling evidence that merely classifying individuals into categories—even when arbitrarily assigned—is sufficient to engender bias. According to social identity theory, ingroup favoritism emerges, at least in part, because individuals are motivated to protect and affirm the self, an affordance also extended to their ingroups (Brewer 1999).

Although in part a product of evolution (Brewer 2007, Cosmides et al. 2003), ingroup favoritism is nevertheless a potent form of intergroup bias (Greenwald & Pettigrew 2014). All that is necessary to maintain, if not create, disparities in any number of outcomes is for members of the dominant, high-status group to trust, cooperate, and work for the betterment of their ingroup more than for outgroups (Brewer 2007, De Dreu 2010). Consistent with this work, white Americans have been found to reveal a preference for other white Americans both historically and in contemporary US society (Bobo et al. 2012, Duckitt 2010), especially when such preferences are assessed relatively unobtrusively (Banaji & Greenwald 2013, Crosby et al. 1980, Dovidio & Gaertner 2010). For instance, although multiply determined, white Americans continue to show a preference for living in relatively segregated neighborhoods (Bobo et al. 2012, Burrow et al. 2014). Further, as the influence of explicit racial bias seems to be on the decline in many social arenas, recent theoretical and empirical work argues that it is everyday discrimination in the form of ingroup favoritism that maintains racial disparities, for instance, in employment (DiTomaso 2013) and many legal outcomes (Sommers & Marotta 2014).

Competition over seemingly scarce resources shifts intergroup biases from ingroup favoritism to those involving the derogation of competing outgroups (Sherif et al. 1961, Stephan & Stephan 2000). Most notably, perceived threat—particularly of the loss of valued resources, whether realistic or symbolic—associated with different outgroups is thought to trigger negative intergroup reactions (Fiske et al. 2002, Riek et al. 2006, Schaller & Neuberg 2012; see also Mackie & Smith 2002). For instance, the perceived threat of disease has been found to predict heightened bias toward immigrants (Faulkner et al. 2004), the perceived threat of violence/physical danger increases antagonism toward black and Mexican Americans (Cottrell & Neuberg 2005), the potential loss of group status promotes bias toward other racial groups more generally (Blumer

1958, Craig & Richeson 2014a, Outten et al. 2012), and the perceived threat to the dominant (white) American cultural worldview can fuel a variety of racial biases (Greenberg & Kosloff 2008). Further, although often overlooked, the perceived threats associated with being outnumbered (Schaller & Abeysinghe 2006) and with past and current discrimination (Monteith & Spicer 2000) contribute to racial minorities' mistrust and negative attitudes toward the dominant racial outgroup (Terrell & Terrell 1981).

Social Categorization/Group Cognition Approach

A second major approach to intergroup relations is the social categorization/group cognition approach (Brewer 1988, Fiske 1998). Although this approach also begins with the insight that individuals carve up the social world into meaningful categories, unlike social identity theory it does not necessitate the motivational pull of ingroup bonds through social identification. Instead, this approach offers a relatively "cold" cognitive understanding of intergroup relations whereby social categorization precipitates the activation of knowledge structures regarding different groups in the form of traits (stereotypes) and attitudes (prejudice) that, in turn, shape behavior (discrimination) toward those same targets (Macrae & Bodenhausen 2000). This view understands stereotyping and prejudice as the unfortunate by-products of categorization that are best disrupted at the category activation stage, rather than attempting to suppress or correct for attitudes once activated (Bodenhausen et al. 2009).

Research in this tradition has noted the rapid, if not automatic, attention garnered by race (Ito & Bartholow 2009, Trawalter et al. 2008). Specifically, given its historical relevance to US society, race categorization seems to proceed quickly if not obligatorily. Some have even called race a basic category of person perception, much like categories with evolutionary import, such as sex and age (Fiske 1998). The evidence is clear that processes of visual attention track racial category memberships, and basic processes of face processing and evaluation are affected by race (for reviews, see Eberhardt 2005, Ito & Bartholow 2009, Kubota et al. 2012). And, of course, extant research attests to the automatic activation of racial stereotypes and evaluations that, in turn, affect behavior toward members of different racial groups (Dovidio & Gaertner 2010, Macrae et al. 1996). Some of the most compelling research in this area has demonstrated the perilous implications of automatic stereotypical associations between black men and crime (Eberhardt et al. 2004). This work, employing a variety of paradigms, finds that black men are more likely than their white male counterparts to be misperceived to be holding dangerous objects (i.e., guns versus tools; Payne 2001). Further, priming individuals with the concept of crime seems to increase the extent to which they unknowingly direct their attention toward the faces of black men and away from the faces of white men (Eberhardt et al. 2004). In other words, the social cognition view of intergroup relations has provided considerable evidence that cognition, even absent strong ingroup ties or negative intergroup attitudes, can result in the stereotyping of, and expression of discriminatory behavior toward, racial minorities.

Social Dominance Theory

A third theory of intergroup relations that is important for understanding contemporary race relations is social dominance theory (SDT; Sidanius & Pratto 2012). In short, SDT asserts that most (if not all) human societies organize themselves as group-based hierarchies, wherein members of dominant groups allocate to one another a disproportionately large share of the valued resources in the society (e.g., homes, powerful jobs/roles). SDT contends that group-based social hierarchies typically consist of three interactive systems of stratification: (*a*) an age system privileging the middle-aged over the old and young, (*b*) a patriarchal system privileging men over

---

Social categorization/group cognition approach: a perspective on intergroup relations whereby placing individuals into categories activates related knowledge structures, stereotypes, and attitudes

Social dominance theory (SDT): intergroup relations are rooted in the organization of society into group-based hierarchies with resources disproportionally controlled by dominant group members

women, and (*c*) what Sidanius and Pratto call an arbitrary set system, in which socially constructed categories, such as race, ethnicity, religion, and nationality, are hierarchically arranged. These systems of stratification, furthermore, operate on multiple levels. At the societal level, social institutions and organizations, such as police forces and other criminal justice systems, maintain and enhance the hierarchy via legitimizing myths and ideologies. These hierarchy-enhancing systems and institutions, however, are countered by competing systems and institutions designed to attenuate group-based hierarchies, for instance, human/civil rights organizations and charities. Sidanius and Pratto argue that these competing forces eventually find an equilibrium so as to maintain a stable level of social inequality.

In addition to these societal forces, both intergroup and interpersonal processes serve to support and maintain group hierarchies. Most notably, inequality breeds inequality; that is, the unequal allocation of resources often recreates itself and is typically justified by individuals as deserving. Hence, dominant groups use the resources and privileges associated with their group to perpetuate their status in ways that are largely unavailable to oppressed groups. In addition, members of subordinate groups often contribute to their groups' social location by engaging in behaviors (e.g., poor study habits, engagement in crime, poor diet) that contribute to their subordination. Indeed, considerable research suggests that many members of subordinate social groups embrace the very systems that created, maintain, and justify their subordination (Jost & Hunyady 2005).

These and other components of SDT (for a review, see Sidanius & Pratto 2012) offer an often-overlooked perspective on American race relations. For instance, SDT highlights sociostructural facets of inequality that give rise to intergroup, interpersonal, and, even, intrapersonal dynamics in support of the hierarchy. Most importantly, the SDT perspective centers the concepts of power and domination in intergroup relations, instead of the more common social-psychological focus on the attitudes, stereotypes, and emotions that perpetrators hold toward targets. Indeed, Sidanius & Pratto (2012) assert, "SDT's most important epistemological assumption is that intergroup power, not which group is liked or respected more, is what matters" (p. 429). SDT is particularly useful for capturing how dynamic systems of racial inequality are and, thus, how difficult they are to overcome. SDT, therefore, is better able to account for the persistence of racial disparities in wealth, health, and other important life outcomes than are models of intergroup relations that focus on individual-level endorsement of stereotypes or liking of different groups.

Integration of Approaches

Although we have attempted to differentiate between these prominent perspectives on intergroup relations, the approaches overlap and certainly work in concert to explain the varied psychological processes that give rise to, justify, and maintain racial discrimination. Although ingroup ties and processes of self-categorization and social identification are not essential for the activation and application of racial stereotypes, for instance, processes of self-interest certainly motivate the attitudes and behavior of both white Americans and racial minorities. Indeed, perhaps due to their relatively smaller size (Brewer 1991) and/or perceptions of common fate due to shared experiences of discrimination (Branscombe et al. 1999, Sellers et al. 1998), racial minorities often identify more strongly with their racial groups than do whites (but see Knowles et al. 2014) and sometimes even reveal greater ingroup favoritism (Mathur et al. 2010). Other research suggests, however, that racial minorities, like members of other stigmatized groups, have more ambivalent attitudes regarding their groups (Dasgupta 2004; cf. Axt et al. 2014).

It is these results, however, that remind us of the importance of intergroup power. Even if racial minorities demonstrate greater and more frequent ingroup favoritism—especially in laboratory settings—the opportunity to do so in society and in ways that disproportionately advantage members of their group are few and far between (Operario & Fiske 1998). Attention to the influence of power and status should also be brought to bear on research examining any number of intergroup processes, including intergroup emotions such as schadenfreude—the pleasure found in the misfortune of outgroups (Cikara & Fiske 2012, Leach et al. 2003)—as well as more basic processes of perception and evaluation. In general, examination of many of these processes from the perspective of racial minority and/or subordinate groups is lacking.

We also need to begin to focus our attention more squarely on relations between different racial minority groups—what we've been calling intraminority intergroup relations (Craig & Richeson 2012). Such an examination necessitates both the integration and consideration of the competing predictions of these prominent theories of intergroup relations. In other words, whereas the tenets of the theories reviewed here may apply to the dynamics of interactions among members of different minority groups, it is possible that intraminority intergroup dynamics may unfold quite differently. For instance, the common experience of racial discrimination could lead members of one racial minority group (e.g., Asian Americans) to express surprisingly positive evaluations of other racial minority groups, especially when ingroup discrimination is salient (Craig & Richeson 2012). Other research suggests, however, that racial minorities largely adopt the attitudes and behavior that white Americans direct toward racial minority outgroups, consistent with system justification theory (Jost & Hunyady 2005), especially when in the presence of whites (Shapiro & Neuberg 2008).

And, as noted previously, the social-cognition approach to stereotyping and prejudice does not require consonant ingroup ties. For instance, black Americans can harbor negative stereotypes and attitudes toward their own group, especially unconsciously (Clark & Clark 1939, Dasgupta 2004). Nevertheless, this emergent line of inquiry suggests that there is much to be gained both theoretically and practically through systematic consideration of the psychology of intergroup relations among and between members of different socially stigmatized groups, rather than assuming that the tenets of theories of intergroup relations will have similar explanatory power regardless of the status/power of the particular groups in question.

Closing Thoughts

Several prevailing theories of intergroup relations offer guidance regarding race relations in contemporary US society. Although much of the social psychology of prejudice emerged in response to ethnic/racial discrimination, conflict, and oppression (Allport 1954), research largely moved toward an examination of what may be common, if not universal, components of mind and brain that give rise to such negative intergroup biases and outcomes. This approach has been productive and insightful but has also left a number of important issues understudied, including the role of power (Sidanius & Pratto 2012), a focus on social justice rather than racial attitudes (Dixon et al. 2012), dominant group members' efforts to maintain group hierarchy (Knowles et al. 2014), and the perspective of so-called targets of prejudice (Sellers et al. 1998, Shelton 2000). Importantly, the contexts in which specific racial dynamics unfold may have been lost in the shuffle. As the racial landscape of the United States becomes more complicated and, perhaps, more pluralistic, it will be increasingly important to consider the psychology of race relations both between whites and racial minorities as well as among members of different racial minority groups.

PERCEPTIONS, OUTCOMES, AND EXPECTATIONS OF RACIAL DIVERSITY

In addition to the theoretical models of intergroup relations reviewed in the section on Classic and Contemporary Theories of Race Relations, empirical findings stemming from research focused on how individuals construe and experience racial diversity are also essential to any effort to understand race relations. During the past 10 to 15 years, considerable research has explored multiple dynamics during—and outcomes of—interracial dyadic interactions. Interestingly, during this same period, a separate line of inquiry has emerged that considers how people experience diversity at more collective levels—i.e., in work groups, companies, neighborhoods, and even societies. Both lines of work have been fruitful, revealing the potential promise and pitfalls of diversity and, further, how the effects of diversity may differ for members of dominant and subordinate racial groups.

The first question to ask in assessing how people experience diversity is what it means for an entity to be racially diverse. When this question is posed to contemporary Americans, consensus emerges: Thoughts about diversity chiefly conjure thoughts about demographic minorities such as blacks, Latinos, and Asians (Unzueta & Binning 2010). But differences emerge in the criteria used by different racial groups to assess diversity. White Americans tend to base their assessment on simple numerical representation: The higher an entity's percentage of racial minority members, the more diverse it is (Unzueta & Binning 2011). Minority individuals' perceptions of diversity are more sensitive to ingroup representation, with an entity being perceived as more diverse to the degree that members of one's own racial group are included (Bauman et al. 2014). Hence, a black perceiver is likely to view a group that is 70% white, 20% black, and 10% Asian as more diverse than is an Asian perceiver. In addition, racial minorities are more likely than whites to require diversity at both high and low levels of an organization's hierarchy in order to consider it diverse (Unzueta & Binning 2011).

Effects of Racial Diversity on Individuals

Regardless of the cues that lead individuals to construe a context as relatively diverse (or not), research suggests that the experience of diversity can engender different psychological outcomes than the experience of racial homogeneity (Crisp & Turner 2011; see **Figure 2**). So, what does racial diversity actually do? It depends on the level of analysis. Considerable research has examined the potential outcomes of increased contact between individuals of different racial backgrounds. In other words, racial diversity is thought to be important because it increases opportunities for individuals from different backgrounds to interact with and learn from one another and, in so doing, reduce the negative stereotypes and attitudes that often come from merely passively learning about each other (e.g., through media representation; Weisbuch et al. 2009). The evidence in favor of the benefits of interpersonal contact is indeed quite compelling (Brown & Hewstone 2005, Pettigrew & Tropp 2006), even when the "optimal conditions" originally outlined by Allport (1954)—equal status, cooperation, common goals, and support from relevant authorities—have not been met (see Hewstone et al. 2014). Interestingly, research finds that the effects of contact on intergroup attitudes are larger for members of majority groups than members of minority groups (Tropp & Pettigrew 2005), reflecting, again, the potential for racial diversity not only to be construed differently by members of dominant and subordinate racial groups but also to be experienced differently as a function of group status.

A great deal of recent research (for a review, see Shelton & Richeson 2006) has also focused on the dynamics of interpersonal interactions between members of dominant and minority racial groups, examining such outcomes in terms of physiology (e.g., Page-Gould et al. 2008), behavior (e.g., Dovidio et al. 2002), cognition (e.g., Richeson et al. 2003, Richeson & Shelton 2003), and affect (e.g., Pearson et al. 2008). Taken together, this body of work suggests that members of both majority and minority racial groups often enter interpersonal interactions with one another harboring concerns about prejudice (Shelton et al. 2006). Many whites are concerned about appearing prejudiced (e.g., Dunton & Fazio 1997, Richeson & Shelton 2007, Vorauer 2006); racial

National-, organizational-, neighborhood-level diversity

- Perceptions of majority versus minority group
- Diversity model/ ideology
- Intergroup threat
- Opportunities for contact

Work/small groups

Intragroup outcomes
- Cohesion
- Liking
- Trust

Intergroup outcomes
- Task performance
- Creativity

Interpersonal interactions

Concerns about prejudice
Interracial anxiety

Figure 2

Schematic of the effects of diversity at societal, group, and interpersonal levels. The benefits of diversity at each level depend, at least in part, on the perceived and actual representation of members of different groups, factors such as the prevailing models of diversity in the context, the opportunities for intergroup contact, and, of course, the management of interracial anxiety that often stems from individuals' prejudice concerns. Importantly, the outcomes of interracial contact at the interpersonal level are informed by processes that take place at the level of small groups, which, in turn, are shaped by the processes at play at larger (e.g., national, organizational, and neighborhood) levels of analysis.

minorities, by contrast, are often concerned about being the target of prejudice (i.e., experiencing prejudice) during these interactions (Mendoza-Denton et al. 2002, Shelton et al. 2005). Research suggests that both sets of concerns can increase participants' anxiety and physiological arousal (Richeson & Shelton 2007) before and during the interaction, thereby disrupting nonverbal, if not verbal, aspects of behavior (Trawalter et al. 2009). Moreover, managing these prejudice concerns seems to be quite effortful, subsequently undermining individuals' cognitive functioning (Richeson & Trawalter 2005b). In other words, individuals' concerns about prejudice often lead interracial interactions to be effortful and, as a result, experienced as less positive than same-race interactions (Toosi et al. 2012).

Interestingly, the very effort that can make these interactions less positive for individuals may actually yield relatively positive experiences for their interaction partners (Shelton & Richeson 2006). For example, Shelton and colleagues (2005) randomly assigned a sample of black participants to expect prejudice or not (control condition) prior to an interracial interaction. Results revealed that those who had been primed to expect prejudice tended to work harder during the interaction— they were more engaged than their interaction partners—and, as expected, felt more negative affect after the interaction compared with participants who had not been primed. But, examination of the experiences of these participants' white interaction partners suggests that the efforts deployed by the black participants who were primed to expect prejudice were not in vain. Indeed, these white partners reported having more positive interactions and liking their partners more than did whites who were partners of black participants in the control condition. In other words, managing prejudice concerns during interracial interactions sometimes results in divergent experiences— i.e., negative cognitive and affective outcomes for the self, but relatively positive outcomes for one's interaction partner. Hence, although interracial interactions may be experienced as more negative than same-race interactions, at least for one participant in the interaction, they may be experienced as more positive than expected for the other participant (Mallet et al. 2008), a cycle that, over time and with repeated contact, is likely to result in the emergence of more positive racial attitudes (Pettigrew & Tropp 2006).

Recent research has extended this work largely based on short, one-shot interactions between strangers but has also included the study of interracial interactions in more naturalistic contexts, such as between college roommates (Gaither & Sommers 2013, Shook & Fazio 2008, West et al. 2009). Although these encounters can be anxiety provoking and stressful (Paolini et al. 2004), they can also be beneficial for those involved (e.g., Shook & Clay 2012, Shook & Fazio 2008). Close, intimate relationships across racial lines, for instance, are thought to reduce both more explicit and automatic expressions of racial bias (Gulker & Monteith 2013, Olsson et al. 2005). Consequently, the next wave of research in the interaction domain is rightly focused on efforts to reduce individuals' apprehension regarding interracial interactions, such as by changing their lay beliefs about prejudice (Carr et al. 2012, Neel & Shapiro 2012); increasing their willingness to persist in interracial interactions, such as via the use of implementation intentions to alleviate felt anxiety (e.g., Stern & West 2014); and increasing individuals' agility navigating interracial interactions, such as by leveraging learning, rather than performance-oriented, mindsets (Goff et al. 2008, Murphy et al. 2011, Trawalter & Richeson 2006). In other words, research on interracial interaction dynamics is poised to close the gap between the largely negative outcomes of acute contact experiences and the largely positive outcomes of these same interactions over time (MacInnis & Page-Gould 2015).

Effects of Diversity in Groups

Much like research at the dyadic level, a growing body of work explores the proposition that racially diverse and racially homogeneous groups may engender different intragroup processes and outcomes. Specifically, research on diversity, broadly defined (i.e., not exclusively based on race), has largely come to the conclusion that diversity yields both negative and positive consequences (see **Figure 2**). The negative consequences tend to pertain to intragroup outcomes, often centering on group morale, with diverse groups experiencing less cohesion than homogeneous groups (e.g., King et al. 2009, Stahl et al. 2010, Thatcher & Patel 2011). By contrast, positive consequences of diversity typically pertain to differences in performance, whether in terms of creativity, problem solving, or information sharing, between diverse compared with homogenous groups (e.g., Crisp & Turner 2011, Phillips et al. 2004, Roberge & van Duck 2010). Few of these studies have focused specifically on racial diversity (cf. Cunningham, 2009, Ely et al. 2012, Herring 2009), and of those that have, even fewer have made use of experimental designs that speak to the processes by which racial diversity may be influential. In one such experiment, however, researchers charged groups with brainstorming new ideas for encouraging tourism to the United States (McLeod et al. 1996). Half of the groups consisted of all white participants and half included white, black, Latino, and Asian participants. Not only did the diverse groups generate more ideas than the homogeneous groups, but naïve coders also rated the diverse groups' suggestions as better and more practical.

The McLeod et al. (1996) study is also one of several to demonstrate divergence between individuals' perceptions of diverse groups and the actual effects of racial diversity on group performance. Specifically, white participants reported greater affinity for their group when it was racially homogeneous, but the diverse context produced superior group performance. What explains these different effects of racial diversity on intragroup outcomes (often, though not always, negative) and intergroup outcomes (often, though not always, positive)? Traditionally, many of the negative effects have been explained through a social categorization framework—the classification of group members into ingroup and outgroup interferes with group identification, commitment, and morale (see King et al. 2009, Thatcher & Patel 2011, van Knippenberg & Schippers 2007; cf. van

Dijk et al. 2012). Consistent with this view, individuals are less inclined to work in teams with members who are racially dissimilar (e.g., Hinds et al. 2000) and expect demographic similarity to reflect attitudinal similarity (Phillips & Loyd 2006).

On the other hand, the positive effects of diversity are often presumed to be due to differences in information; namely, people from demographically diverse backgrounds bring diverse perspectives that can be leveraged to obtain better task performance, compared with homogenous groups. Although there is merit to this idea (see Sommers 2006), it is not without its limitations (Sommers 2008). Most notably, this view implies a monolithic perspective for each minority racial group for whatever topic is under discussion and places the onus for the effects of diversity squarely on the shoulders of these individuals. Moreover, research suggests that demographic dissimilarity changes how majority group members process information as well. In one example, Phillips and colleagues (2006) assigned white participants to three-person groups for a decision-making task. Half the groups were homogenous (all white) and half were racially diverse. White participants assigned to diverse groups believed that more unique information had been shared than did their counterparts in homogenous groups. In other words, simply seeing that their group was racially diverse led individuals to assume that the group possessed a diversity of perspectives (Phillips et al. 2006; see also Antonio et al. 2004). These and other findings suggest, therefore, that some component of the effects of diversity reflects changes in individuals' motivational and normative concerns (Lount & Phillips 2007, Loyd et al. 2013). Further, what seem to be effects of diversity may actually be the undoing of effects of homogeneity that are detrimental to group performance (see Apfelbaum et al. 2014).

Before we close this discussion of the effects of diversity in groups, it is important to note that studies examining this issue do not tend to include groups that are racially homogenous in terms of minority individuals, thereby precluding a comparison of the effects of group diversity and homogeneity among racial minorities. Moreover, we know that the conditions that white group members might perceive as being diverse are often the very same that create token or solo status for racial minorities, leaving individuals susceptible to social identity threat effects (Steele 2010). In other words, there is every reason to believe that "diverse" groups can often be experienced as largely negative from the perspective of racial minorities. Whether such negative outcomes for the self nevertheless yield positive group outcomes, however, remains to the examined in future research. Moreover, the quite separate body of research on the experience of stigmatization, prejudice, and stereotyping needs to be integrated with this emerging and compelling research on the effects of diversity at the group level. Much as has been found within interracial dyadic interactions, racially diverse groups may also typically reveal divergent outcomes depending on the majority versus minority status of the individual group members. In order to maximize the potential benefits of diverse groups, committees, and organizations it is important to understand potential costs for members of both dominant and subordinate groups.

Models of Diversity

As the racial diversity of various societies increases, social scientists have renewed their interest in the ways in which individuals, organizations, and even nations seek to manage it (Crisp & Meleady 2012, Gaertner & Dovidio 2000). Philosophies regarding how best to manage diversity differ widely across person, group, culture, and era. Psychologists have often dichotomized these differing philosophies into colorblind (largely assimilationist) and multicultural models of diversity (see Rattan & Ambady 2013). A colorblind approach asserts that equality among and within groups is best achieved by minimizing demographic distinctions in policy setting and day-to-day interaction (see Neville et al. 2013). Dominant group members (i.e., whites) are more likely

---

Multicultural model of diversity: the perspective that racial progress is best achieved by acknowledging and, when appropriate, appreciating racial/ethnic group differences and experiences

than minority group members to endorse such a model (Ryan et al. 2010). Alas, research also links this colorblind ideology to various negative outcomes including increased prejudice among whites (Apfelbaum et al. 2012, Richeson & Nussbaum 2004) and feelings of exclusion among racial minorities (Purdie-Vaughns et al. 2008). Colorblindness has also been linked to a failure to recognize racial disparities in important life outcomes (e.g., Schofield 1986, Wolsko et al. 2000) as well as a relative insensitivity to racial discrimination (Apfelbaum et al. 2010).

A multicultural approach to diversity proposes that demographic distinctions within a group should be acknowledged and even championed. Minorities are more likely than whites to endorse this model (Verkuyten 2005), perhaps in part because of many whites' belief that their whiteness leaves them little to contribute to such a conceptualization of diversity (Plaut et al. 2011). As such, the multicultural perspective on diversity has been linked to feelings of exclusion or even threat among white individuals (Norton & Sommers 2011) as well as to increased liking for targets who fulfill existing racial stereotypes (Gutierrez & Unzueta 2010). The effects of a multicultural perspective on levels of prejudice among whites, however, is more complicated, with some research finding positive effects (Richeson & Nussbaum 2004, Wolsko et al. 2000) and other work noting that these effects are dependent on how the ideology is represented. Specifically, highlighting abstract goals of multiculturalism reduces whites' expression of racial bias, but emphasizing more concrete ways in which multiculturalism can be achieved increases bias (Yogeeswaran & Dasgupta 2014). Further, when groups are in conflict, multiculturalism can yield particularly negative intergroup outcomes (Vorauer & Sasaki 2011).

That people endorse varied ideological models of racial diversity illustrates the more general proposition that assumptions and expectations about diversity are important considerations in any effort to examine the actual effects of racial composition on cognitive, affective, and behavioral outcomes. For example, consider two individuals who both consider themselves to be proponents of racial diversity, one of whom espouses a colorblind view, and the other endorses a more multicultural perspective. Despite both seeing themselves as supportive of diversity, these individuals will likely have very different responses to specific initiatives (e.g., affirmative action, targeted recruitment, antibias training, English-only policies) put forth to promote racial cohesion (see Oh et al. 2010). Similarly, the model of diversity held by one's white coworkers, managers, and interaction partners can shape how positively or negatively racial minorities experience these contexts (Holoien & Shelton 2012, Plaut et al. 2009). Indeed, the largely colorblind model of racial diversity espoused by US Supreme Court Chief Justice John Roberts (e.g., Roberts 2007) has been cited in the rollback of various race-conscious policies, such as voluntary school desegregation plans, that many others perceive to be critical to ushering in a more egalitarian society. Last, it is entirely likely that the changing racial demographics of the country will also motivate people to rethink the models of diversity that they currently endorse (Zárate et al. 2012).

Colorblind model of racial diversity: the perspective that racial progress is best achieved by ignoring racial/ethnic categories, focusing on human similarities and sometimes promoting assimilation

Closing Thoughts

Diversity has been found to influence both interpersonal and group dynamics. There are many unanswered questions concerning the moderators and mediators of the influence of racial diversity on group performance, as well as the extent to which such effects vary by the race and status of the individuals involved. The consequences of various institutional efforts to achieve racial diversity constitute another important issue that psychologists are well equipped to address. Moreover, future research will need to integrate conclusions regarding positive performance effects for group diversity with established findings regarding the potentially negative effects "diverse" contexts can have on minority individuals by triggering social identity threat (see Steele 2010). Indeed, the very conditions that would lead many whites to identify a group as diverse are the same that can produce challenging circumstances for minorities, a conclusion that is often overlooked in discourse regarding generalized performance advantages of diversity. What is clear from the extant research, however, is that the processes by which racial diversity shapes individual and group outcomes are more varied and complex than many lay assumptions, policy initiatives, or even research paradigms suggest.

A RESEARCH AGENDA FOR THE SOCIAL PSYCHOLOGY OF RACE RELATIONS

We began this article by citing the dynamic, fluid, and somewhat volatile state of racial/ethnic relations in the United States. Even a cursory glance at the international news, however, reveals similarly complex interethnic relations in many other nations. Consider, for instance, the historic ascension of Cécile Kyenge, the first black Italian cabinet minister—both a moment of national pride and accomplishment and a catalyst for the expression of antiblack and anti-immigrant sentiment (Martin 2013). This iconic event and myriad similar events elsewhere serve as sobering reminders that race/ethnic relations are not inexorably and consistently getting better; they also underscore the potential utility of social psychological theory and research on this topic. Hence, we close by briefly identifying a number of emerging issues that we think should top the agenda for the next decade of social psychological research on race relations.

Reactions to Majority-Minority Nation Status

A profound demographic shift is underway in the United States. Indeed, racial minorities are expected to comprise more than 50% of the population by 2050 (US Census Bur. 2012). Not only does this remarkable transition to a so-called majority-minority nation reinforce the importance and relevance of studies of race and ethnic relations, it is also likely to have its own effects in need of investigation. Indeed, extant theoretical and empirical work in sociology and social psychology suggest that white individuals are likely to have largely negative reactions to this demographic change (e.g., Blumer 1958). A series of recent experiments finds that making salient the changing US racial population triggers greater prowhite/antiracial minority sentiment in both whites' explicit and more automatic attitude assessments, compared with making salient the current population, or even making salient a similar majority-minority shift in a foreign country (Craig & Richeson 2014a; see also Outten et al. 2012). Further, this population shift is perceived as a threat to whites' status in society and increases their resistance to racial diversity (Burrow et al. 2014, Danbold & Huo 2015). It also increases their endorsement of political conservatism, including (but not limited to) policies pertaining to race, such as immigration and affirmative action (Craig & Richeson 2014b). Taken together, this work underscores the possibility that rather than heralding a more tolerant and egalitarian future, the increasing diversity of a nation could actually yield more intergroup hostility.

Immigration

The rise of a so-called majority-minority United States, and similar developments in many European countries, is in part due to increases in the proportion of people in these nations who are immigrants. In the United States, for instance, the abolition of national-origin quotas in 1965 removed barriers to the immigration of people from many Latin American, Caribbean, Asian, and African countries (Lee & Bean 2012). Consequently, as of 2010, the foreign born constituted 13% of the US national population, with 53% of that group hailing from Latin

America (Grieco et al. 2012). Perhaps not surprisingly, this rise has been met with increasing consternation regarding immigration policy, concerns regarding the treatment of immigrants (especially the "undocumented"), and heated debate regarding the best approaches to promote the acculturation of new immigrants (see discussion of models of diversity in the section on Perceptions, Outcomes, and Expectations of Racial Diversity).

Social psychological research and theory should inform these pressing policy debates (see Craig & Richeson 2014c). Social psychology, for instance, could shed light on the processes through which concerns about national identity fuel anti-immigrant sentiment, which, in turn, shapes support for relevant social policies, such as those pertaining to citizenship, education, and the social safety net (see Berry 2002, Esses et al. 2010). Similarly, greater understanding of the ways in which immigrants come to racially categorize themselves (or are categorized by others) is paramount to any endeavor to promote the psychological well-being of members of this often vulnerable social group (Waters 1999).

Multiple Identities

Although some research suggests negative effects of a growing racial minority population for race relations, there is also reason to expect some movement toward a more tolerant society. For instance, the increasing racial diversity of the United States has also brought increased rates of interracial marriage, one marker of loosening racial boundaries in society (Lee & Bean 2012). Accompanying this shift is a comparable rise in the population of people that self-identifies as biracial or multiracial. In the section titled Conceptualizing Race, we considered what this may mean for our understanding of race, but it will also be critical for social psychologists to examine how this growing demographic group negotiates and maintains a healthy racial identity (Shih & Sanchez 2005), especially in the face of pressure to choose a racial category (Gaither 2015, Remedios & Chasteen 2013). Similarly, basic research examining race and race relations will need to better acknowledge the role that multiple social identities (e.g., social class, gender, sexual orientation, age, religion) play in shaping individuals' experiences and outcomes (Kang & Bodenhausen 2015). In other words, it is at the intersections of these multiple identities that "race" is created, maintained, and experienced (Sen & Wasow 2016).

Renewed Attention to Racism

Our final topic of emphasis is really a call to return to the past. It is not rare for contemporary discussions and analyses of racial bias to assert that overt forms of racism are a thing of the past. Yet, one need only scroll through the comments of almost any online article about race or racial minorities to find ample evidence that hate speech, racial slurs, and so-called old-fashioned racism are indeed alive and well. Today, the suggestion that race may have played a role in any given outcome is often met with the charge that this very suggestion itself is what is actually racist. And, the general willingness of many dominant group members to acknowledge, in abstract terms, that racial discrimination and disparities still exist often fails to be accompanied by a willingness to recognize that bias may have occurred in any one particular incident or decision (cf. Apfelbaum et al. 2010, Norton & Sommers 2011). Hence, it is important for the field to reinvest in the study of more overt forms of racial bias, such as the continued endorsement of racial stereotypes, desire for social distance (Bobo et al. 2012), and blatant dehumanization (Ktiely et al. 2015; see also Haslam 2006), as well as the reactions of both dominant and racial minority groups to evidence of these and other forms of racial bias, including collective action behavior (van Zomeren et al. 2012).

Similarly, social psychology should integrate recent research on implicit bias with more structural and cultural forms of racial bias (Adams et al. 2008, Bonilla-Silva 1997, Unzueta & Lowery 2008). For example, how else can we understand the near invisibility of American Indians in media representations, save as mascots for athletic teams (Fryberg et al. 2008)? As the racial diversity of the United States increases, members of different racial minority groups will seek greater representation and inclusion in many societal domains, including media representations. Will these efforts be embraced, ignored, or, perhaps, met with backlash? And, how will each of these responses affect the psychological health, identification, and well-being of racial minorities (Cheryan & Monin 2005)?

FINAL THOUGHTS

The twenty-first century has already presented new challenges and opportunities (e.g., multiracial identification), revealed the sustained relevance of old problems (e.g., police violence, state-sanctioned Confederate imagery), as well as brought the return of battles once thought already won (e.g., school desegregation, voting rights). Social psychology has a long and storied tradition of addressing societal issues such as these and, we believe, remains well poised to do so again in support of the development of racially diverse, yet cohesive and just, organizations, communities, and even societies. Our aim in this article, therefore, was to gather and integrate relevant research findings that are currently distributed across a variety of domains (e.g., stereotyping and prejudice, intergroup relations and interactions, diversity, social stigma) and reconnect them to the sociocultural and historical contexts in which they initially emerged, in order to focus, if not galvanize, the next decade of social psychological research on race and race relations.

DISCLOSURE STATEMENT

The authors are not aware of any affiliations, memberships, funding, or financial holdings that might be perceived as affecting the objectivity of this review.

LITERATURE CITED

ABC News. 2013. *Martin Luther King, Jr. I have a dream.* ABC video file. **http://abcnews.go.com/Politics/martin-luther-kings-speech-dream-full-text/story?id=14358231**

Adams G, Edkins V, Lacka D, Pickett K, Cheryan S. 2008. Teaching about racism: pernicious implications of the standard portrayal. *Basic Appl. Soc. Psychol.* 30:349–61

Allport GW. 1954. *The Nature of Prejudice.* Reading, MA: Perseus Books

Antonio AL, Chang MJ, Hakuta K, Kenny DA, Levin S, Milem JF. 2004. Effects of racial diversity on complex thinking in college students. *Psychol. Sci.* 15:507–10

Apfelbaum EP, Norton MI, Sommers SR. 2012. Racial color blindness: emergence, practice, and implications. *Curr. Dir. Psychol. Sci.* 21:205–9

Apfelbaum EP, Pauker K, Sommers SR, Ambady N. 2010. In blind pursuit of racial equality? *Psychol. Sci.* 21:1587–92

Apfelbaum EP, Phillips KW, Richeson JA. 2014. Rethinking the baseline in diversity research: Should we be explaining the effects of homogeneity? *Perspect. Psychol. Sci.* 9:235–44

Axt JR, Ebersole CR, Nosek BA. 2014. The rules of implicit evaluation by race, religion, and age. *Psychol. Sci.* 25:1804–15

Banaji MR, Greenwald AG. 2013. *Blindspot: Hidden Biases of Good People.* New York: Random House

Banks RR, Eberhardt JL. 1998. Social psychological processes and the legal bases of racial categorization. In *Confronting Racism: The Problem and the Response*, ed. JL Eberhardt, ST Fiske, pp. 54–75. Thousand Oaks, CA: Sage

Bauman CW, Trawalter S, Unzueta MM. 2014. Diverse according to whom? Group membership and concerns about discrimination shape diversity judgments. *Personal. Soc. Psychol. Bull.* 40:1354–72

Berry JW. 2002. A psychology of immigration. *J. Soc. Issues* 57:615–40

Blumer H. 1958. Race prejudice as a sense of group position. *Pac. Sociol. Rev.* 1:3–7

Bobo LD, Charles CZ, Krysan M, Simmons AD. 2012. The real record on racial attitudes. In *From Social Trends in American Life: Findings from the General Social Survey Since 1972*, ed. PV Marsden, pp. 38–83. Princeton, NJ: Princeton Univ. Press

Bodenhausen GV, Todd AR, Richeson JA. 2009. Controlling prejudice and stereotyping: antecedents, mechanisms, and contexts. In *Handbook of Prejudice, Stereotyping, and Discrimination*, ed. T Nelson, pp. 111–35. New York: Psychol. Press

Bonilla-Silva E. 1997. Rethinking racism: toward a structural interpretation. *Am. Sociol. Rev.* 62:465–80

Branscombe NR, Schmitt MT, Harvey RD. 1999. Perceiving pervasive discrimination among African-Americans: implications for group identification and well-being. *J. Personal. Soc. Psychol.* 77:135–49

Brewer MB. 1988. A dual process model of impression formation. In *Advances in Social Cognition*, Vol. 1, ed. T Srull, R Wyer, pp. 1–36. New York: Earlbaum

Brewer MB. 1991. The social self: on being the same and different at the same time. *Personal. Soc. Psychol. Bull.* 17:475–82

Brewer MB. 1999. The psychology of prejudice: ingroup love and outgroup hate? *J. Soc. Issues* 55:429–44

Brewer MB. 2007. The social psychology of intergroup relations: social categorization, ingroup bias, and outgroup prejudice. In *Social Psychology: Handbook of Basic Principles*, ed. AW Kruglanski, ET Higgins, pp. 695–715. New York: Guilford. 2nd ed.

Brown R, Hewstone M. 2005. An integrative theory of intergroup contact. In *Advances in Experimental Social Psychology*, ed. MP Zanna, pp. 255–343. San Diego, CA: Academic

Burrow AL, Stanley M, Sumner R, Hill PL. 2014. Purpose in life as a resource for increasing comfort with ethnic diversity. *Personal. Soc. Psychol. Bull.* 40:1507–16

Carr PB, Dweck CS, Pauker K. 2012. "Prejudiced" behavior without prejudice? Beliefs about the malleability of prejudice affect interracial interactions. *J. Personal. Soc. Psychol.* 103:452–71

Caruso E, Mead N, Balcetis E. 2009. Political partisanship influences perception of biracial candidates' skin tone. *PNAS* 106:20168–73

Castano E, Yzerbyt VY, Bourguignon D, Seron E. 2002. Who may enter? The impact of in-group identification on in-group/out-group categorization. *J. Exp. Soc. Psychol.* 38:315–22

Cheryan S, Monin B. 2005. Where are you really from? Asian Americans and identity denial. *J. Personal. Soc. Psychol.* 89:717–30

Cikara M, Fiske ST. 2012. Stereotypes and schadenfreude: behavioral and physiological markers of pleasure at others' misfortunes. *Soc. Psychol. Personal. Sci.* 3:63–71

Clark KB, Clark MK. 1939. The development of consciousness of self and the emergence of racial identification in Negro preschool children. *J. Soc. Psychol.* 10:591–99

Cosmides L, Tooby J, Kurzban R. 2003. Perceptions of race. *Trends Cogn. Sci.* 7:173–79

Cottrell CA, Neuberg SL. 2005. Differential emotional reactions to different groups: a sociofunctional threat-based approach to "prejudice." *J. Personal. Soc. Psychol.* 88:770–89

Craig MA, Richeson JA. 2012. Coalition or derogation? How perceived discrimination influences intraminority intergroup relations. *J. Personal. Soc. Psychol.* 102:759–77

Craig MA, Richeson JA. 2014a. More diverse yet less tolerant? How the increasingly-diverse racial landscape affects White Americans' racial attitudes. *Personal. Soc. Psychol. Bull.* 40:750–61

Craig MA, Richeson JA. 2014b. On the precipice of a "majority-minority" nation. Perceived status threat from the racial demographic shift affects White Americans' political ideology. *Psychol. Sci.* 25:1189–97

Craig MA, Richeson JA. 2014c. Not in my backyard! Authoritarianism, social dominance orientation, and support for strict immigration policies at home and abroad. *Polit. Psychol.* 35:417–29

Crisp RJ, Meleady R. 2012. Adapting to a multicultural future. *Science* 336:853–55

Crisp RT, Turner RN. 2011. Cognitive adaptation to the experience of social and cultural diversity. *Psychol. Bull.* 137:242–66

Crosby F, Bromley S, Saxe L. 1980. Recent unobtrusive studies of Black and White discrimination and prejudice: a literature review. *Psychol. Bull.* 87:546–63

Cunningham GB. 2009. The moderating effect of diversity strategy on the relationship between racial diversity and organizational performance. *J. Appl. Soc. Psychol.* 39:1445–60

Danbold F, Huo YJ. 2015. No longer "All-American"? Whites' defensive reaction to their numerical decline. *Soc. Psychol. Personal. Sci.* 6:210–18

Dasgupta N. 2004. Implicit ingroup favoritism, outgroup favoritism, and their behavioral manifestations. *Soc. Justice Res.* 17:143–69

De Dreu CKW. 2010. Social conflict: the emergence and consequences of struggle and negotiation. See Fiske et al. 2010, pp. 998–1023

DiTomaso N. 2013. *The American Non-Dilemma. Racial Inequality Without Racism.* New York: Russell Sage Found.

Dixon J, Levin M, Reicher S, Durrheim K. 2012. Beyond prejudice: Are negative evaluations the problem and is getting us to like one another more the solution? *Behav. Brain. Sci.* 35:411–25

Dovidio JF, Gaertner SL. 2004. Aversive racism. In *Advances in Experimental Social Psychology*, Vol. 36, ed. MP Zanna, pp. 1–52. San Diego, CA: Academic

Dovidio JF, Gaertner SL. 2010. Intergroup bias. See Fiske et al. 2010, pp. 1084–121

Dovidio JF, Hewstone M, Glick P, Esses VM, eds. 2010. *The Sage Handbook of Prejudice, Stereotyping, and Discrimination.* Thousand Oaks, CA: Sage

Dovidio JF, Kawakami K, Gaertner SL. 2002. Implicit and explicit prejudice and interracial interaction. *J. Personal. Soc. Psychol.* 82:62–68

Duckitt J. 2010. Historical overview. See Dovidio et al. 2010, pp. 29–44

Dunton BC, Fazio RH. 1997. An individual difference measure of motivation to control prejudiced reactions. *Personal. Soc. Psychol. Bull.* 23:316–26

Duster T. 2005. Race and reification in science. *Science* 307:1050–51

Eberhardt JL. 2005. Imaging race. *Am. Psychol.* 60:181–90

Eberhardt JL, Dasgupta N, Banaszynski TL. 2003. Believing is seeing: the effects of racial labels and implicit beliefs on face perception. *Personal. Soc. Psychol. Bull.* 29:360–70

Eberhardt JL, Goff PA, Purdie VJ, Davies PG. 2004. Seeing Black: race, crime, and visual processing. *J. Personal. Soc. Psychol.* 87:876–93

Ely RJ, Padavic I, Thomas DA. 2012. Racial diversity, racial asymmetries, and team learning environment: effects on performance. *Organ. Stud.* 33:341–62

Esses VM, Deaux K, Lalonde RL, Brown R. 2010. Psychological perspectives on immigration. *J. Soc. Issues* 66:635–47

Faulkner J, Schaller M, Park JH, Duncan LA. 2004. Evolved disease-avoidance mechanisms and contemporary xenophobic attitudes. *Group Process. Intergroup Relat.* 7:333–53

Fiske ST. 1998. Stereotyping, prejudice, and discrimination. In *Handbook of Social Psychology*, Vol. 2, ed. DT Gilbert, ST Fiske, G Lindzey, pp. 357–411. New York: McGraw Hill. 4th ed.

Fiske ST, Cuddy AJ, Glick P, Xu J. 2002. A model of (often mixed) stereotype content: competence and warmth respectively follow from perceived status and competition. *J. Personal. Soc. Psychol.* 82:878–902

Fiske ST, Gilbert DT, Lindzey G, eds. 2010. *Handbook of Social Psychology*, Vol. 2. Hoboken, NJ: Wiley. 5th ed.

Flores NM, Huo YJ. 2013. "We" are not all the same: consequences of neglecting national origin identities among Asians and Latinos. *Soc. Psychol. Personal. Sci.* 4:143–50

Freeman JB, Penner AM, Saperstein A, Scheutz M, Ambady N. 2011. Looking the part: social status cues shape race perception. *PLOS ONE* 6:e25107

Fryberg SA, Markus HR, Oyserman D, Stone JM. 2008. Of warrior chiefs and Indian princesses: the psychological consequences of American Indian mascots. *Basic Appl. Soc. Psychol.* 30:208–18

Gaertner SL, Dovidio JF. 2000. *Reducing Intergroup Bias: The Common Ingroup Identity Model.* Philadelphia, PA: Psychol. Press

Gaither SE. 2015. "Mixed" results: multiracial research and identity explorations. *Curr. Dir. Psychol. Sci.* 24:114–19

Gaither SE, Sommers SR. 2013. Living with an other-race roommate shapes Whites' behavior in subsequent diverse settings. *J. Exp. Soc. Psychol.* 49:272–76

Goff PA, Steele CM, Davies PG. 2008. The space between us: stereotype threat and distance in interracial contexts. *J. Personal. Soc. Psychol.* 94:91–107

Greenberg J, Kosloff S. 2008. Terror management theory: implications for understanding prejudice, stereotyping, intergroup conflict, and political attitudes. *Soc. Personal. Psychol. Compass* 2:1881–94

Greenwald AG, Pettigrew TF. 2014. With malice toward none and charity for some: ingroup favoritism enables discrimination. *Am. Psychol.* 69:669–84

Grieco EM, Acosta YD, de la Cruz PG, Gambino C, Gryn T, et al. 2012. The foreign-born population in the United States: 2010. *Am. Community Surv. Rep.* **http://www.census.gov/prod/2012pubs/acs-19.pdf**

Gulker JE, Monteith MJ. 2013. Intergroup boundaries and attitudes: the power of a single potent link. *Personal. Soc. Psychol. Bull.* 39:943–55

Gutierrez AS, Unzueta MM. 2010. The effect of interethnic ideologies of the likability of stereotypic versus counterstereotypic minority targets. *J. Exp. Soc. Psychol.* 46:775–84

Hall EV, Phillips KW, Townsend SM. 2015. A rose by any other name? The consequences of subtyping "African-Americans" from "Blacks." *J. Exp. Soc. Psychol.* 56:183–90

Haslam N. 2006. Dehumanization: an integrative review. *Personal. Soc. Psychol. Rev.* 10:252–64

Herring C. 2009. Does diversity pay? Race, gender, and the business case for diversity. *Am. Sociol. Rev.* 74:208–24

Hewstone M, Lolliot S, Swart H, Myers E, Voci A, et al. 2014. Intergroup contact and intergroup conflict. *J. Peace Psychol.* 20:39–53

Hinds PJ, Carley KM, Krackhardt D, Wholey D. 2000. Choosing work group members: balancing similarity, competence, and familiarity. *Organ. Behav. Hum. Decis.* 81:226–51

Ho AK, Sidanius J, Levin DT, Banaji MR. 2011. Evidence for hypodescent and racial hierarchy in the categorization and perception of biracial individuals. *J. Personal. Soc. Psychol.* 100:492–506

Hochschild J, Weaver V, Burch T. 2012. *Creating a New Racial Order: How Immigration, Multiracialism, Genomics, and the Young Can Remake Race in America*. Princeton, NJ: Princeton Univ. Press

Holoien DS, Shelton JN. 2012. You deplete me: the cognitive costs of colorblindness on ethnic minorities. *J. Exp. Soc. Psychol.* 48:562–65

Hugenberg K, Bodenhausen GV. 2004. Ambiguity in social categorization: the role of prejudice and facial affect in racial categorization. *Psychol. Sci.* 15:342–45

Ito AT, Bartholow BD. 2009. The neural correlates of race. *Trends Cogn. Sci.* 13:524–31

Jost JT, Hunyady O. 2005. Antecedents and consequences of system-justifying ideologies. *Curr. Dir. Psychol. Sci.* 14:260–65

Kang SK, Bodenhausen GV. 2015. Multiple identities in social perception and interaction: challenges and opportunities. *Annu. Rev. Psychol.* 66:547–74

King EB, Hebl MR, Beal DJ. 2009. Conflict and cooperation in diverse workgroups. *J. Soc. Issues* 65:261–85

Knowles ED, Lowery BS, Chow RM, Unzueta MM. 2014. Deny, distance, or dismantle? How White Americans manage a privileged identity. *Perspect. Psychol. Sci.* 9:594–609

Kteily N, Bruneau E, Waytz A, Cotterill S. 2015. The ascent of man: theoretical and empirical evidence for blatant dehumanization. *J. Personal. Soc. Psychol.* In press

Kubota JT, Banaji MR, Phelps EA. 2012. The neuroscience of race. *Nat. Neurosci.* 15:940–48

Leach C, Spears R, Branscombe NR, Doosje B. 2003. Malicious pleasure: schadenfreude at the suffering of an outgroup. *J. Personal. Soc. Psychol.* 84:932–43

Lee J, Bean FD. 2012. *The Diversity Paradox. Immigration and the Color Line in Twenty-First Century America*. New York: Russell Sage Found.

Lount RB Jr, Phillips KW. 2007. Working harder with the out-group: the impact of social category diversity on motivation gains. *Organ. Behav. Hum. Decis.* 103:214–24

Loyd DL, Wang CS, Phillips KW, Lount RB Jr. 2013. Social category diversity promotes premeeting elaboration: the role of relationship focus. *Organ. Sci.* 24:757–72

MacInnis C, Page-Gould E. 2015. How can intergroup interaction be bad if intergroup contact is good? Exploring and reconciling an apparent paradox in the science of intergroup relations. *Perspect. Psychol. Sci.* 10:307–27

Mackie DM, Smith ER. 2002. *From Prejudice to Intergroup Emotions: Differentiated Reactions to Social Groups*. Philadelphia, PA: Psychol. Press

Macrae CN, Bodenhausen GV. 2000. Social cognition: thinking categorically about others. *Annu. Rev. Psychol.* 51:93–120

Macrae CN, Stangor C, Hewstone M, eds. 1996. *Stereotypes and Stereotyping*. New York: Guilford

Mallett RK, Wilson TD, Gilbert DT. 2008. Expect the unexpected: failure to anticipate similarities leads to an intergroup forecasting error. *J. Personal. Soc. Psychol.* 94:265–77

Martin M. 2013. *Does Italy have a racism problem?* Audio file. **http://www.npr.org/2013/05/02/180570054/-does-italy-have-a-racism-problem**

Mathur VA, Harada T, Lipke T, Chiao JY. 2010. Neural basis of extraordinary empathy and altruistic motivation. *NeuroImage* 51:1468–75

Mays VM, Cochran SD, Barnes NW. 2007. Race, race-based discrimination, and health outcomes among African Americans. *Annu. Rev. Psychol.* 58:201–25

McLeod PL, Lobel SA, Cox TH Jr. 1996. Ethnic diversity and creativity in small groups. *Small Group Res.* 27:248–64

Mendoza-Denton R, Downey G, Purdie V, Davis A, Pietrzak J. 2002. Sensitivity to status-based rejection: implications for African American students' college experience. *J. Personal. Soc. Psychol.* 83:896–918

Metzl JM. 2010. *The Protest Psychosis: How Schizophrenia Became a Black Disease*. Boston: Beacon Press

Monteith MJ, Spicer CV. 2000. Contents and correlates of Whites' and Blacks' racial attitudes. *J. Exp. Soc. Psychol.* 36:125–54

Morning A. 2011. *The Nature of Race: How Scientists Think and Teach About Human Difference*. Berkeley: Univ. Calif. Press

Morrison KR, Chung AH. 2011. "White" or "European American"? Self-identifying labels influence majority group members' interethnic attitudes. *J. Exp. Soc. Psychol.* 47:165–70

Murphy MC, Richeson JA, Molden DC. 2011. Leveraging motivational mindsets to foster positive interracial interactions. *Soc. Personal. Psychol. Compass* 5:118–31

Neel R, Shapiro JR. 2012. Is racial bias malleable? Whites' lay theories of racial bias predict divergent strategies for interracial interactions. *J. Personal. Soc. Psychol.* 103:101–20

Neville HA, Award GH, Brooks JE, Flores MP, Bluemel J. 2013. Color-blind ideology: theory, training, and measurement implications in psychology. *Am. Psychol.* 68:455–66

Norton MI, Sommers SR. 2011. Whites see racism as a zero-sum game that they are now losing. *Perspect. Psychol. Sci.* 6:215–18

Noymer A, Penner AM, Saperstein A. 2011. Cause of death affects racial classification on death certificates. *PLOS ONE* 6:e15812

Oh E, Choi C, Neville HA, Anderson CJ, Landrum-Brown J. 2010. Beliefs about affirmative action: a test of the group self-interest and racism beliefs models. *J. Divers. High. Educ.* 3:163–76

Olsson A, Ebert JP, Banaji MR, Phelps EA. 2005. The role of social groups in the persistence of learned fear. *Science* 309:785–87

Omni M, Winant H. 1994. *Racial Formation in the United States: From the 1960 to the 1990s*. New York: Routledge

Operario D, Fiske ST. 1998. Racism equals power plus prejudice: a social psychological equation for racial oppression. In *Confronting Racism: The Problem and the Response*, ed. JL Eberhardt, ST Fiske, pp. 33–53. Thousand Oaks, CA: Sage

Outten HR, Schmitt MT, Miller DA, Garcia AL. 2012. Feeling threatened about the future: Whites' emotional reactions to anticipated ethnic demographic changes. *Personal. Soc. Psychol. Bull.* 38:14–25

Page-Gould E, Mendoza-Denton R, Tropp LR. 2008. With a little help from my cross-group friend: reducing anxiety in intergroup contexts through cross-group friendship. *J. Personal. Soc. Psychol.* 95:1080–94

Painter NI. 2010. *The History of White People*. New York: Norton

Paluck EL, Green DP. 2009. Prejudice reduction: What works? A review and assessment of research and practice. *Annu. Rev. Psychol.* 60:339–67

Paolini S, Hewstone M, Cairns E, Voci A. 2004. Effects of direct and indirect cross-group friendships on judgments of Catholics and Protestants in Northern Ireland: the mediating role of an anxiety-reduction mechanism. *Personal. Soc. Psychol. Bull.* 30:770–86

Pauker K, Weisbuch M, Ambady N, Sommers SR, Adams RB, Ivcevic Z. 2009. Not so black and white: memory for ambiguous group members. *J. Personal. Soc. Psychol.* 96:795–810

Payne BK. 2001. Prejudice and perception: the role of automatic and controlled processes in misperceiving a weapon. *J. Personal. Soc. Psychol.* 81:181–92

Pearson AR, West TV, Dovidio JF, Powers SR, Buck R, Henning RA. 2008. The fragility of intergroup relations: divergent effects of delayed audiovisual feedback in intergroup and intragroup interaction. *Psychol. Sci.* 19:1272–79

Peery D, Bodenhausen GV. 2008. Black + white = black: hypodescent in reflexive categorization of racially ambiguous faces. *Psychol. Sci.* 19:973–77

Penner AM, Saperstein A. 2008. How social status shapes race. *PNAS* 105:19628–30

Penner AM, Saperstein A. 2013. Engendering racial perceptions: an intersectional analysis of how social status shapes race. *Gender Soc.* 27:319–44

Perez AD, Hirschman C. 2010. The changing racial and ethnic composition of the US population: emerging American identities. *Popul. Dev. Rev.* 35:1–51

Pettigrew TF, Tropp LR. 2006. A meta-analytic test of intergroup contact theory. *J. Personal. Soc. Psychol.* 90:751–83

Phillips KW, Loyd DL. 2006. When surface and deep-level diversity collide: the effects on dissenting group members. *Organ. Behav. Hum. Decis.* 99:143–60

Phillips KW, Mannix EA, Neale MA, Gruenfeld DH. 2004. Diverse groups and information sharing: the effects of congruent ties. *J. Exp. Soc. Psychol.* 40:495–510

Phillips KW, Northcraft GB, Neale MA. 2006. Surface-level diversity and decision-making in groups: When does deep-level similarity help? *Group Process. Intergroup Relat.* 9:467–82

Plaks JE, Malahy LW, Sedlins M, Shoda Y. 2012. Folk beliefs about human genetic variation predict discrete versus continuous race categorization and evaluative bias. *Soc. Psychol. Personal. Sci.* 3:31–39

Plaut VC, Garnett FG, Buffardi LE, Sanchez-Burks J. 2011. "What about me?" Perceptions of exclusion and Whites' reactions to multiculturalism. *J. Personal. Soc. Psychol.* 101:337–53

Plaut VC, Thomas KM, Goren MJ. 2009. Is multiculturalism or color blindness better for minorities? *Psychol. Sci.* 20:444–46

Purdie-Vaughns V, Steele CM, Davies PG, Ditlmann R, Crosby JR. 2008. Social identity contingencies: how diversity cues signal threat or safety for African Americans in mainstream institutions. *J. Personal. Soc. Psychol.* 94:615–30

Rattan A, Ambady N. 2013. Diversity ideologies and intergroup relations: an examination of colorblindness and multiculturalism. *Eur. J. Soc. Psychol.* 43:12–21

Remedios JD, Chasteen AL. 2013. Finally, someone who "gets" me! Multiracial people value others' accuracy about their race. *Cult. Divers. Ethn. Minor. Psychol.* 19:453–60

Richeson JA, Baird AA, Gordon HL, Heatherton TF, Wyland CL, et al. 2003. An fMRI examination of the impact of interracial contact on executive function. *Nat. Neurosci.* 6:1323–28

Richeson JA, Nussbaum RJ. 2004. The impact of multiculturalism versus color-blindness on racial bias. *J. Exp. Soc. Psychol.* 40:417–23

Richeson JA, Shelton JN. 2003. When prejudice does not pay: effects of interracial contact on executive function. *Psychol. Sci.* 14:287–90

Richeson JA, Shelton JN. 2007. Negotiating interracial interactions: costs, consequences, and possibilities. *Curr. Dir. Psychol. Sci.* 16:316–20

Richeson JA, Trawalter S. 2005a. On the categorization of admired and disliked exemplars of admired and disliked racial groups. *J. Personal. Soc. Psychol.* 89:517–30

Richeson JA, Trawalter S. 2005b. Why do interracial interactions impair executive function? A resource depletion account. *J. Personal. Soc. Psychol.* 88:934–47

Riek BM, Mania EW, Gaertner SL. 2006. Intergroup threat and out-group attitudes: a meta-analytic review. *Personal. Soc. Psychol. Rev.* 10:336–53

Roberge M, van Dick R. 2010. Recognizing the benefits of diversity: When and how does diversity increase group performance? *Hum. Res. Manag. Rev.* 20:295–308

Roberts CJ. 2007. 551 U.S. *Parents Involved in Community Schools v. Seattle School District No. 1.* **https://www.law.cornell.edu/supct/pdf/05-908P.ZO**

Roberts D. 2011. *Fatal Invention: How Science, Politics, and Big Business Re-Create Race in the Twenty-First Century.* New York: New Press

Ryan CS, Casas JF, Thompson BK. 2010. Interethnic ideology, intergroup perceptions, and cultural orientation. *J. Soc. Issues* 66:29–44

Saperstein A, Penner AM. 2012. Racial fluidity and inequality in the United States. *Am. J. Sociol.* 118:676–727

Saperstein A, Penner AM, Light R. 2013. Racial formation in perspective: connecting individuals, institutions, and power relations. *Annu. Rev. Sociol.* 39:359–78

Schaller M, Abeysinghe AMND. 2006. Geographical frame of reference and dangerous intergroup attitudes: a double-minority study in Sri Lanka. *Polit. Psychol.* 27:615–31

Schaller M, Neuberg SL. 2012. Danger, disease, and the nature of prejudice(s). In *Advances in Experimental Social Psychology*, Vol. 46, ed. JM Olson, MP Zanna, pp. 1–54. Burlington, VT: Academic

Schofield JW. 1986. Causes and consequences of the colorblind perspective. In *Prejudice, Discrimination and Racism: Theory and Practice*, ed. S Gaertner, J Dovidio, pp. 231–53. New York: Academic

Sellers RM, Smith MA, Shelton JN, Rowley SA, Chavous TM. 1998. Multidimensional model of racial identity: a reconceptualization of African American racial identity. *Personal. Soc. Psychol. Rev.* 2:18–39

Sen M, Wasow O. 2016. Race as a "bundle of sticks": designs that estimate effects of seemingly immutable characteristics. *Annu. Rev. Polit. Sci.* 19:In press

Shapiro JR, Neuberg SL 2008. When do the stigmatized stigmatize? The ironic effects of being accountable to (perceived) majority group prejudice-expression norms. *J. Personal. Soc. Psychol.* 95:877–98

Shelton JN. 2000. A reconceptualization of how we study issues of racial prejudice. *Personal. Soc. Psychol. Rev.* 4:374–90

Shelton JN, Richeson JA. 2006. Interracial interactions: a relational approach. In *Advances in Experimental Social Psychology*, Vol. 38, ed. MP Zanna, pp. 121–81. Burlington, VT: Academic

Shelton JN, Richeson JA, Salvatore J. 2005. Expecting to be the target of prejudice: implications for interethnic interactions. *Personal. Soc. Psychol. Bull.* 31:1189–202

Shelton JN, Richeson JA, Vorauer JD. 2006. Threatened identities and interethnic interactions. *Eur. Rev. Soc. Psychol.* 17:321–58

Sherif M, Harvey OJ, White BJ, Hood WR, Sherif C. 1961. *Intergroup Conflict and Cooperation: The Robbers Cave Experiment*. Norman, OK: Univ. Book Exch.

Shih M, Sanchez DT. 2005. Perspectives and research on the positive and negative implications of having multiple racial identities. *Psychol. Bull.* 131:569–91

Shook NJ, Clay R. 2012. Interracial roommate relationships: a mechanism for promoting sense of belonging at university and academic performance. *J. Exp. Soc. Psychol.* 48:1168–72

Shook NJ, Fazio RH. 2008. Interracial roommate relationships: an experimental test of the contact hypothesis. *Psychol. Sci.* 19:717–23

Sidanius J, Pratto F. 2012. Social dominance theory. In *Handbook of Theories of Social Psychology*, Vol. 2, ed. PAM Lange, AW Kruglanski, ET Higgins, pp. 418–38. London: Sage

Smedley A. 2007. *Race in North America: Origin and Evolution of a Worldview*. Boulder, CO: Westview

Sommers SR. 2006. On racial diversity and group decision-making: identifying multiple effects of racial composition on jury deliberations. *J. Personal. Soc. Psychol.* 90:597–612

Sommers SR. 2008. Beyond information exchange: new perspectives on the benefits of racial diversity for group performance. In *Research on Managing Groups and Teams*, Vol. 11, ed EA Mannix, MA Neale, KW Phillips, pp. 195–220. Oxford, UK: Elsevier Sci.

Sommers SR, Marotta SA. 2014. Racial disparities in legal outcomes: on policing, charging decisions, and criminal trial proceedings. *Policy Insights Behav. Brain Sci.* 1:103–11

Stahl GK, Maznevski ML, Voigt A, Jonsen K. 2010. Unraveling the effects of cultural diversity in teams: a meta-analysis of research on multicultural work groups. *J. Int. Bus. Stud.* 41:690–709

Steele CM. 2010. *Whistling Vivaldi. How Stereotypes Affect Us and What We Can Do*. New York: Norton

Stephan WG, Stephan CW. 2000. An integrated threat theory of prejudice. In *Reducing Prejudice and Discrimination*, ed. S Oskamp, pp. 23–46. Hillsdale, NJ: Erlbaum

Stern C, West TV. 2014. Circumventing anxiety during interpersonal encounters to promote interest in contact: an implementation intention approach. *J. Exp. Soc. Psychol.* 50:82–93

Tajfel H, Turner JC. 1986. The social identity theory of inter-group behavior. In *Psychology of Intergroup Relations*, ed. S Worchel, LW Austin, pp. 7–24. Chicago: Nelson-Hall

Terrell F, Terrell SL. 1981. An inventory to measure cultural mistrust among Blacks. *Western J. Afr. Am. Stud.* 5:180–84

Thatcher SMB, Patel PC. 2011. Demographic faultlines: a meta-analysis of the literature. *J. Appl. Psychol.* 96:1119–39

Toosi NR, Babbitt LG, Ambady N, Sommers SR. 2012. Dyadic interracial interactions: a meta-analysis. *Psychol. Bull.* 138:1–27

Trawalter S, Richeson JA. 2006. Regulatory focus and executive function after interracial interactions. *J. Exp. Soc. Psychol.* 42:406–12

Trawalter S, Richeson JA, Shelton JN. 2009. Predicting behavior during interracial interactions: a stress and coping approach. *Personal. Soc. Psychol. Rev.* 13:243–68

Trawalter S, Todd A, Baird AA, Richeson JA. 2008. Attending to threat: race-based patterns of selective attention. *J. Exp. Soc. Psychol.* 44:1322–27

Tropp LR, Pettigrew TF. 2005. Relationships between intergroup contact and prejudice among minority and majority status groups. *Psychol. Sci.* 16:951–57

Trujillo M, Garcia RL, Shelton JN. 2015. "I thought you were Japanese": ethnic miscategorization and identity assertion. *Cult. Divers. Ethn. Minor. Psychol.* In press

Unzueta MM, Binning KR. 2010. Which racial groups are associated with diversity? *Cult. Divers. Ethn. Minor. Psychol.* 16:443–46

Unzueta MM, Binning KR. 2011. Diversity is in the eye of the beholder: how concern for the in-group affects perceptions of racial diversity. *Personal. Soc. Psychol. Bull.* 38:26–38

Unzueta MM, Lowery BS. 2008. Defining racism safely: the role of self-image maintenance on white Americans' conceptions of racism. *J. Personal. Soc. Psychol.* 44:1491–97

US Census Bur. 2012. U.S. Census Bureau projections show a slower growing, older, more diverse nation a half century from now. **http://www.census.gov/newsroom/releases/archives/population/cb12-243.html**

van Dijk H, van Engen ML, van Knippenberg D. 2012. Defying conventional wisdom: a meta-analytical examination of the differences between demographic and job-related diversity relationships with performance. *Organ. Behav. Hum. Decis. Process.* 119:38–53

van Knippenberg D, Schippers MC. 2007. Work group diversity. *Annu. Rev. Psychol.* 58:515–41

van Zomeren M, Leach CW, Spears R. 2012. Protesters as "passionate economists": a dynamic dual pathway model of approach coping with collective disadvantage. *Personal. Soc. Psychol. Rev.* 16:180–99

Verkuyten M. 2005. Ethnic group identification and group evaluation among minority and majority groups: testing the multiculturalism hypothesis. *J. Personal. Soc. Psychol.* 88:121–38

Vorauer JD. 2006. An information search model of evaluative concerns in intergroup interaction. *Psychol. Rev.* 113:862–86

Vorauer JD, Sasaki SJ. 2011. In the worst rather than the best of times: effects of salient intergroup ideology in threatening intergroup interactions. *J. Personal. Soc. Psychol.* 101:307–20

Waters MC. 1999. *Black Identities: West Indian Immigrant Dreams and American Realities.* Cambridge, MA: Harvard Univ. Press

Weisbuch M, Pauker K, Ambady N. 2009. The subtle transmission of race bias via televised nonverbal behavior. *Science* 326:1711

West TV, Shelton JN, Trail TE. 2009. Relational anxiety in interracial interactions. *Psychol. Sci.* 20:289–92

Williams DR, Mohammed SA. 2009. Discrimination and racial disparities in health: evidence and needed research. *J. Behav. Med.* 32:20–47

Wolsko C, Park B, Judd CM, Wittenbrink B. 2000. Framing interethnic ideology: effects of multicultural and color-blind perspectives on judgments of groups and individuals. *J. Personal. Soc. Psychol.* 78:635–54

Yogeeswaran K, Dasgupta N. 2014. The devil is in the details: abstract versus concrete construals of multiculturalism differentially impact intergroup relations. *J. Personal. Soc. Psychol.* 106:772–89

Yzerbyt VY, Demoulin S. 2010. Intergroup relations. See Fiske et al. 2010, pp. 1024–83

Zárate M, Shaw M, Marquez J, Biagas D. 2012. Cultural inertia: the effects of cultural change on intergroup relations and the self-concept. *J. Exp. Soc. Psychol.* 48:634–45

Zuckerman M. 1990. Some dubious premises in research and theory on racial differences: scientific, social, and ethical issues. *Am. Psychol.* 45:1297–303

Theodiversity

Ara Norenzayan

Department of Psychology, University of British Columbia, Vancouver,
British Columbia V6T 1Z4, Canada; email: ara@psych.ubc.ca

Annu. Rev. Psychol. 2016. 67:465–88

First published online as a Review in Advance on
September 17, 2015

The *Annual Review of Psychology* is online at
psych.annualreviews.org

This article's doi:
10.1146/annurev-psych-122414-033426

Keywords

atheism, WEIRD, cognition, cultural evolution, culture, gods, religion,
ritual, sacred values, secularization, supernatural beliefs, theodiversity

Abstract

Humanity is teeming with breathtaking theodiversity—in religious beliefs,
behaviors, and traditions, as well as in various intensities and forms of disbelief. Yet the origins and consequences of this diversity have received limited
attention in psychology. I first describe how evolved psychological processes
that influence and respond to cultural evolutionary trajectories generate and
channel religious diversity. Next, I explore how theodiversity in turn shapes
human psychology, and discuss three cultural dimensions of religious diversity in relation to psychological processes: (*a*) the cultural shift from small
foraging bands and their local religious practices and beliefs to large and
complex groups and their world religions, (*b*) cultural variability among
world religions, and (*c*) secularization and the ensuing cultural divide between religious and nonreligious societies and subcultures. The contributions of psychology to the scientific study of religion will increase with a
deeper understanding of theodiversity.

Contents

WHAT IS THEODIVERSITY?

Religions are, and have always been, a widespread feature of life in human societies (e.g., Bering 2011, Boyer 2001, Bulbulia 2008, Sosis & Alcorta 2003). Yet, despite their reliable recurrence across cultures and history, they are, and have always been, tremendously diverse. This theodiversity[1] can be immense. In one estimate, there are 10,000 religious traditions in the world today (Barrett et al. 2001). These traditions reflect a seemingly endless variety of beliefs, commitments, and practices that are deeply influential in the lives of practitioners of a particular tradition, and simultaneously baffling to interested observers who are looking in from the outside.

Consider beliefs about supernatural beings. At one extreme of a cultural continuum, for example, among the Hadza, a foraging group in Tanzania, one encounters Haine/Ishoko, the moon/sun god, who appears to have little or no supernatural power and dwells in indifference to human affairs (Marlowe 2010). Tuvan pastoralists in southern Siberia have beliefs about spirit masters who must be appeased with offerings when they pass through the territories they rule, but who are otherwise uninvolved in human affairs (Purzycki 2013). At the other extreme of this continuum, there is, of course, the Big God of the Abrahamic faiths who knows everything, cares deeply about how people treat each other, punishes violations of norms no matter where they occur, and instills fear and awe among adherents (Norenzayan 2013).

Theodiversity:
diversity in religious
beliefs, behaviors,
rituals, and traditions

----

[1]For an introduction to the term, and an entertaining discussion of theodiversity, see Lester (2002).

Or consider the centrality of ritualized behaviors in human group life. Ritualized behaviors are widespread in human life and are often bundled with supernatural beliefs and coopted by religions (Legare & Watson-Jones 2015, McCauley & Lawson 2002). But they also come in various intensities and varieties, making them another key driving force of theodiversity. Take, for example, the Thaipusam festival in many diasporic Tamil Hindu communities. Those who take part in the most extreme rituals, the Kavadi, engage in painful ordeals such as piercing their bodies with needles and skewers and walking barefoot for hours dragging carts hooked to their skin to reach the temple of the war god Murugan (Xygalatas et al. 2013). Other ritualized behaviors mark significant events or life cycles (Rappaport 1999) or tap an altogether different motivation—that of avoiding contamination and impurity, such as the ritual washing and cleaning found in many religions (Fiske & Haslam 1997).

Ritual: socially stipulated, causally opaque group convention

Cultural evolution: cumulative changes over time in beliefs and behaviors that often generate cultural diversity

Theodiversity has received scant attention from psychology.[2] In this article, I address this gap first by outlining two critical features of theodiversity that demand explanation and by highlighting methodological issues at the center of attempts to study theodiversity. I explore how psychological processes, responding to cultural evolutionary pressures, create and sustain theodiversity, including different shades, forms, and intensities of irreligion. I also examine how, in turn, culturally transmitted theodiversity shapes psychological outcomes. Throughout, I discuss implications for the scientific study of religion and related phenomena.

Why Theodiversity?

What can psychology contribute to the study of theodiversity to complement the contributions from anthropology, history, sociology, and religious studies? First, just as there are biological regularities underlying the great biodiversity of the planet, there are underlying psychological regularities that channel and constrain the great theodiversity in human populations. Therefore, some of the important explanations of the mental origins and contours of theodiversity, including secularization trends, can be found in psychology. Psychology also holds important clues regarding the differential cultural survival rates of religious ideas, practices, and traditions.

Second, theodiversity is crucial for a more complete understanding of the cultural history of many psychological processes. This is because human brains depend on cultural, in addition to genetic, inheritance to an extent unparalleled in other species (Richerson & Boyd 2005). One consequence is that many psychological processes are culturally variable (Heine & Norenzayan 2006, Henrich et al. 2010). A great deal of this variability has religious origins (Cohen 2015), with implications for core topics such as cooperation, self-regulation, cognitive development, perception and attention, risk-taking, prejudice, intergroup conflict, social cognition, and moral psychology. Third, some psychological barriers contribute to the cultural divides of our time—between religious and nonreligious groups as well as among rival religious groups. These divides, and the need to find ways to bridge them, motivate greater understanding of theodiversity within pluralistic societies and in regional and global conflicts (e.g., Atran 2010, Haidt 2012).

Two Features of Theodiversity

First, theodiversity is far from static. Throughout history, religious traditions are dynamically evolving in a process of cultural evolution—nongenetic, socially transmitted, cumulative changes

---

[2]Religious diversity has been the focus of rich literatures in several academic fields, including philosophy (Taylor 2007), history (Bellah 2011, Smith 1982), anthropology (Atran 2002, Boyer 2001), sociology (Berger 2014), and religious studies (Taves 2009).

in beliefs and behaviors over time (Richerson & Boyd 2005). Just in the last 200 years, several religious movements have sprung up, proliferated, and altered the cultural landscape around the world, such as the Mormon Church, the Pentecostal Church, Baha'i, Chabad-Lubavitch, Cao Dai, Shinnyo-en, and the Raelian movement, to name a few.

Second, religious ideas and practices that make up a tradition have markedly different rates of cultural survival that depend on their psychological sticking power. Almost all religious movements that have ever existed eventually succumbed to myriad internal and external threats that undermined social cohesion, demographic stability, and cultural longevity (for evidence from a historical analysis of religious communes, see Sosis 2000). One consequence of this winnowing process is that theodiversity is nonrandom: The vast majority of humanity adheres to a very few religious traditions that have come to be known as world religions (Norenzayan 2013). Christian, Muslim, Jewish, Hindu, and Buddhist practitioners, including their nonbelieving descendants, collectively account for over 93% of all human beings on the planet (Pew Res. Cent. 2012). The triple success of these world religions—their demographic growth by conversion or conquest, their high fertility rates and geographic expansion across the globe, and their historical persistence—is a fundamental feature of the world's theodiversity.

The WEIRD Challenge

Psychology has a treasure trove of methodological tools and techniques that are just beginning to be deployed to study religious cognition and behavior and their psychological antecedents and effects. But to expand and deepen psychology's contribution to the study of religion and theodiversity, the field must overcome its heavy dependence on Western, educated, industrialized, rich, and democratic (WEIRD) cultural samples that represent a thin and often unrepresentative slice of humanity (see Henrich et al. 2010b and associated commentaries). Participants in psychological studies are disproportionately from modern, industrialized societies. Of those, the overwhelming majority come from Western societies. Of those Westerners, the great majority are Americans, and of those Americans, most are university undergraduates. This sampling bias creates various and far-reaching ramifications for psychology (see Arnett 2008; Heine & Norenzayan 2006; Medin & Atran 2004; Medin et al. 2010; Nisbett 2003; Norenzayan & Heine 2005; Rozin 2007, 2009; Sears 1986). Here I concentrate on its consequences for the study of religion and theodiversity.

One unintended consequence of the narrow focus of psychology is that many aspects of human behavior that are profoundly important to people in the world are overlooked (Rozin 2007). Religion is a prime example of this, despite great interest among founders of psychology (e.g., James 1902). Most of the world is deeply religious (Pew Res. Cent. 2012), but religion rarely makes an appearance in standard psychology textbooks and, relative to its importance, is an understudied topic (Bloom 2012, Rozin 2007). As an illustration, the *Annual Review of Psychology*, in its 67-year history, has devoted only four articles to religion, two of which were published in the last four years, reflecting a recent resurgence of interest (Bloom 2012, Emmons & Paloutzian 2003, Gorsuch 1988, and the present article). (In contrast, I counted at least 18 articles in the journal devoted to some aspect of language and 7 articles on sex.)

Another side effect of the WEIRD lens is that the psychological study of religion often treats the Abrahamic religions as the culturally typical religions. But these religions, although globally successful, are cross-culturally atypical products of particular cultural evolutionary trajectories. Going further, some have argued that psychology's implicit model of religion, influenced by James's (1902) and Allport's (1950) seminal contributions, has been narrowly anchored in Protestantism, which happens to be the religious tradition from which early influential American psychologists came (Cohen 2015, Cohen et al. 2005). This home-field disadvantage (Medin et al.

2010) is compounded by the stark overrepresentation of psychology participants coming from Judeo-Christian traditions, and in particular Americans, who are disproportionately Protestant or shaped by Protestant undercurrents (Sanchez-Burks & Lee 2007, Uhlmann & Sanchez-Burks 2014).

The Definitional Challenge

Once the field transcends WEIRD sampling, the study of theodiversity can take off. Greater focus on theodiversity in turn holds the keys to the solution to another perennial methodological issue that has plagued the study of religion: the coherence of the very term religion in the humanities and social sciences (Stausberg 2010, Taves 2009). In everyday life in the Western world, we often talk about religion as if it were a unitary phenomenon that applies to people as a whole (for example, we ask, "Is she religious?"). But despite many efforts, there has been little scholarly agreement on a common definition. This is because theodiversity is itself a central characteristic of religions now and throughout history, and even within the same culture and historical period (Norenzayan 2013; see also Taves 2009 for a related but distinct account). Once we understand this, the definitional problem of religion vanishes.

Put another way, we cannot explain religion without explaining theodiversity, just as we cannot fully explain the evolution of life without explaining the evolution of biodiversity. This realization also helps solve another related puzzle: why religion often has contradictory and paradoxical consequences for human psychology. The examples are many, but here are two. For certain psychological outcomes, what kind of an afterlife people believe in (heaven or hell) is more important than whether people believe in an afterlife. In cross-national studies, and controlling for a number of factors, belief in hell is associated with reduced national crime rates, whereas belief in heaven is associated with increased crimes rates (Shariff & Rhemtulla 2012). Other studies have found that what kind of a god people believe in matters a great deal. For example, perceptions of a controlling god reduce goal pursuit and increase people's ability to resist temptations, whereas perceptions of a distant god do not have these effects (Laurin et al. 2012).

PSYCHOLOGICAL BUILDING BLOCKS OF THEODIVERSITY

For a given person to believe in a given deity or deities and engage in rituals, he or she must (a) be able to form intuitive mental representations of supernatural agents and related rituals and practices; (b) be motivated to commit to supernatural agents and rituals as real and relevant sources of meaning, comfort, and control; and (c) have received specific cultural inputs that, of all the mentally representable supernatural agents, one or more specific deities should be believed in and committed to (Norenzayan & Gervais 2013). This premise leads to the conclusion that there are core cognitive, motivational, and cultural learning mechanisms underlying theodiversity.

Cognitive Processes

Religious beliefs and practices are rooted in ordinary cognitive capacities that make them intuitive (Barrett 2004, Boyer 2001, McCauley 2011). One such cognitive frame is mind-body dualism (Bloom 2004). It appears that human brains are prepared to grasp this notion, leading to cross-cultural regularities (e.g., Chudek et al. 2014) and enabling belief in a variety of disembodied supernatural agents such as ancestor spirits, ghosts, and personal gods in a wide range of cultures (Barrett 2004, Bering 2011, Guthrie 1993). Another is a possibly domain-general teleological bias (Banerjee & Bloom 2014, Kelemen 2004). This untutored intuitive stance appears to develop

Mind-body dualism: the intuition that minds can exist separately from bodies

Teleological bias: the domain-general intuition that people, things, and events reflect purpose and design

early in childhood and is hypothesized to encourage creationist beliefs, making children and adults intuitive theists (Heywood & Bering 2014, Kelemen 2004, Kelemen & Rosset 2009). Consistent with the idea that religious belief is anchored in intuitive or System 1 cognitive processes, research shows that analytic or System 2 cognitive processes that can override or block intuitive thinking lead to the weakening of religious belief (for a review of the theory and evidence, see McCauley 2011, Norenzayan & Gervais 2013).

Anthropomorphism: the cognitive tendency to project human-like traits to the nonhuman world

Mentalizing: a suite of cognitive tendencies to detect and infer the content of other minds

Anthropomorphism is another recurrent theme in theodiversity and an idea that has a long intellectual history [Epley et al. 2007, Guthrie 1993, Hume 1956 (1757)]. The tendency to anthropomorphize the world is more pronounced under some specific conditions, namely when anthropocentric knowledge is salient, under uncertainty and explanatory gaps, and when the desire for social connection is thwarted (see Epley et al. 2007). Anthropomorphism is implicated in religious belief in two ways. People are particularly prone to projecting human-like mental states (more than physical or biological attributes) to supernatural beings. Also, the tendency to anthropomorphize is sometimes overextended to the natural world; when mountains, trees, rocks, and rivers are infused with human-like agency, the result is the animistic beliefs found in many traditional cultures (Guthrie 1993) as well as in modern-day spirituality (A. Willard & A. Norenzayan, unpublished manuscript). Although there are strong theoretical reasons to expect that cross-cultural regularities in all of these cognitive tendencies will play a role in religious thinking, the growing empirical literature remains largely confined to WEIRD samples. An important opportunity for future research is to explore the extent to which these hypothesized observations generalize.

There is also a dearth of research exploring interconnections among these cognitive tendencies. One preliminary hypothesis is that all these tendencies share a cognitive capacity for mind perception or mentalizing (Epley 2014, Waytz et al. 2010). Mentalizing enables believers to think about the mental states of supernatural beings; when they do, their projections betray an egocentric bias (Epley et al. 2009). Willard & Norenzayan (2013; see also Banerjee & Bloom 2014, Gray et al. 2010) found that mentalizing tendencies increase dualistic intuitions and to a lesser extent teleological thinking, and in turn these two tendencies increase belief in God, belief in paranormal events such as astrology, telepathy, and UFOs, and the conviction that life has meaning and purpose.

Cognitive explanations are also important for understanding rituals, another key component of many religious systems. Growing research is filling an important gap in the literature under the rubric of ritual cognition, by examining how people mentally represent, evaluate, and enact rituals (see Legare & Watson-Jones 2015, Schjoedt et al. 2013). Despite their diversity, rituals are characterized by some predictable cognitive regularities, such as repetition, redundancy, stereotypy, and causal opacity (Whitehouse 2004). Legare & Souza (2012) find that the perceived efficacy of rituals is influenced by intuitions such as repetition of procedures and number and specificity of procedural steps, independent of familiarity with the ritual content.

Two cognitive principles of magical thinking—similarity and contagion—are also rooted in intuitive processes and are important for explaining theodiversity [Nemeroff & Rozin 2000, Tylor 1974 (1871)]. The principle of similarity (the image equals the object) explains, for example, why a Buddha statue is felt to have a special connection with the real Buddha; and the principle of contagion (once in contact, always in contact) explains why the relic of a saint is believed to have healing properties. Importantly, once intuitions about supernatural beings, magic, and ritual-behavior complexes are in place, they coexist with other ordinary causal intuitions and beliefs. In other words, far from being psychologically incompatible, natural and supernatural intuitions exist in explanatory coexistence (Legare et al. 2012) in the way people make sense of the everyday world around them.

Motivational Processes

Whereas cognitive biases help explain how the diverse religious beliefs and ritual patterns are mentally represented and why they have the particular cognitive features that they do, core human motivations help explain when people come to commit to supernatural agents as potent, meaningful, and relevant to their everyday lives (see Johnson et al. 2015). There is mounting evidence that religious beliefs relieve a variety of existential anxieties (Atran 2002, Kay et al. 2009), and when these anxieties are heightened, religious beliefs are more likely to persist and spread in human minds. Cross-culturally, societies with greater existential threats, such as poverty, hunger, job insecurity, short life spans, and high infant mortality, are far more likely to be religious (Norris & Inglehart 2004). Exposure to unpredictable and potentially catastrophic natural disasters such as earthquakes similarly increases the likelihood of religiosity in a given society, controlling for a wide range of relevant demographic and economic variables (Bentzen 2013). In fact, one study found that religious commitment increased immediately after a severe earthquake even in a secularizing country such as New Zealand, but only among citizens who were directly affected by it (Sibley & Bulbulia 2012). Experimental research supports these findings. Threats to psychological control (Kay et al. 2009), predictability (Rutjens et al. 2010), social isolation (Epley et al. 2007), and immortality (Dechesne et al. 2003, Norenzayan & Hansen 2006, Vail et al. 2012) intensify commitment to personal gods who offer immortality, meaning, external control, social bonding, and stability.

Motivational biases also play a role in regulating collective rituals. Boyer & Lienard (2006) propose that many collective ritualized behaviors are intuitively compelling and likely to spread because they are rooted in a "hazard precaution" motivational psychology that is triggered when a real or symbolic threat to safety or purity is detected. Legare & Souza (2014) find evidence that randomness primes increase the perception of ritual efficacy, suggesting that the latter serves a motivational function to alleviate threats to control.

Cultural Learning Processes

Our understanding of theodiversity is incomplete without a consideration of the cultural nature of human brains, which are intensely dependent on socially transmitted information from other brains to an extent unseen in other species (Chudek et al. 2015, Richerson & Boyd 2005). Cultural learning mechanisms enable a process of cultural evolution that accumulates knowledge and know-how over generations (Tomasello 2001) and runs parallel to, and interacts with, genetic evolution (Richerson & Boyd 2005). Human beings, as cultural learners, possess a conformist bias (i.e., they selectively attend to beliefs and behaviors that are held by the majority in their group), as well as a prestige bias, which influences cultural transmission in favor of cues of perceived skill or success (Chudek et al. 2015). However, the fitness benefits of learning from others, particularly prestige-wielding individuals, are offset by learners' vulnerability to the so-called evil teacher problem, which opens the door to being duped or misinformed (Chudek et al. 2015). Human minds are therefore equipped with epistemic vigilance (Sperber et al. 2010), or a suite of preferences that guard against such manipulation. One important remedy is a tendency in cultural learners to also be sensitive to cues that a cultural model is genuinely committed to his or her advertised belief.

Therefore, when actions speak louder than words, cultural learners are more likely to be influenced by, and in turn transmit, beliefs backed up by persuasive credibility-enhancing displays (CREDs; see Henrich 2009). CREDs are hypothesized to be important in any domain of life where social influence matters. Because proselytizing religious groups spread in no small part by social influence (and not just via ancestry), these displays are likely to be important in these communities,

Credibility-enhancing displays (CREDs): extravagant, sometimes costly behaviors that cultural models display, conveying underlying beliefs to cultural learners too. The idea is that CREDs mitigate religious hypocrisy or the perceived threat of interacting with imposters who are not true believers (Norenzayan 2013). This is one explanation for why some religious groups promote restrictions on diet, dress, and sexual relations; painful rituals and fasts; and in some extreme cases even martyrdom. Such extravagant and costly behaviors have also been explained as commitment signals that promote cooperation (see Bulbulia 2008, Sosis & Alcorta 2003).

There is also growing evidence that rituals arise from the reliably developing psychological sensitivity to learn the social conventions of one's cultural group, which are also driven by cultural learning mechanisms (Legare & Watson-Jones 2015, Schjoedt et al. 2013). Consistent with this, young children are high-fidelity imitators even at the expense of personal experience or intuition (Nielsen & Tomaselli 2010). Ritual cognition is driven by conventional reasoning, which, unlike the causal reasoning that has received the bulk of attention in psychology (Legare & Souza 2012), is socially determined and causally inscrutable (Sørensen 2007).

Interacting Psychological Processes

There is much that is yet to be known. Nevertheless, taken together the psychological processes just described give us an increasingly coherent picture of how religious beliefs and practices are enabled, transmitted, and stabilized; why some elements of religions are recurrent and others culturally variable; and why some conditions foster secularization (Gervais et al. 2011, Norenzayan 2013). Cognitive tendencies have been the main focus and the source of much progress in the cognitive science of religion (Barrett 2000, Boyer 2001, Purzycki 2013, Sperber 1996), and they help explain how people mentally represent supernatural beings and shape intuitions about plausible ritual forms. Motivational biases are also crucial. They help us understand which variants of these intuitively plausible supernatural agents and rituals, in what psychological contexts, and for which individuals and groups, become relevant sources of meaning, comfort, and order (Kay et al. 2009, Norris & Inglehart 2004).

Cultural learning mechanisms explain several remaining pieces of the puzzle related to the differential spread of particular versions of religious beliefs and behaviors across cultural groups and throughout history. People selectively acquire religious beliefs and practices from the majority and from prestigious individuals in their communities, leading to cultural diversity that can persist but can also change over time when cues that trigger these mechanisms are altered (Gervais et al. 2011). CREDs help us explain why religious ideas backed up by credible displays of commitment are more persuasive and more likely to spread. In turn, we can understand why such extravagant displays are common in world religions and tied to deepening commitment to supernatural agents.

FROM SMALL GODS TO BIG GODS

Theodiversity of Supernatural Beings Across Cultures

In the Abrahamic traditions (Christianity, Islam, Judaism) and their offshoots, as well as in other world religions such as Buddhism and Hinduism, the religious group is an imagined moral community that unites large populations of strangers otherwise divided by ethnicity, geography, and language. In these communities, people are socialized to suppress selfishness in favor of broader community interests (Graham & Haidt 2010, Norenzayan 2013). But if there is one critical lesson to be taken from the ethnographic and historical record of the psychological study of religion, it is this: Even though all known societies have beliefs in gods and spirits, the linkage between religions and morality is a rather recent cultural development that is found in some places but not others.

Ethnographic observations have shown that in foraging societies, people face important cooperative challenges and possess a sophisticated set of local moral norms that apply to a wide range of domains, including food sharing, caring for offspring, kinship relations, marriage, leveling of risk, and mutual defense (Kelly 1995). Yet religion's moral scope, if any, is minimal; the gods tend to have limited omniscience and limited moral concern, and they may demand certain rituals and sacrifices but care little about how people treat each other (Boyer 2001, Marlowe 2010, Purzycki 2011, Swanson 1960). Anthropologist Frank Marlowe (2010), who has done pioneering research with the Hadza foragers of Tanzania, describes Hadza religion this way:

> I think one can say that the Hadza do have a religion, certainly a cosmology anyway, but it bears little resemblance to what most of us in complex societies (with Christianity, Islam, Hinduism, etc.) think of as religion. There are no churches, preachers, leaders, or religious guardians, no idols or images of gods, no regular organized meetings, no religious morality, no belief in an afterlife—theirs is nothing like the major religions. (p. 61)

In foraging societies, the gods are typically distant and indifferent. But as communities increase in complexity and size, the gods' powers and moral concern also become greater. For example, in his fieldwork with pastoralists among Tuvans in Siberia, Purzycki (2011) reported that local spirit masters known as *Cher eezi* are pleased by ritual offerings and are angered by the overexploitation of resources, but only of the ones that they directly oversee. They exert their powers in designated areas found in ritual cairns known as *ovaa*. *Cher eezi* do not see far and cannot intervene in distant places. Similarly, in chiefdom societies such as Fiji that exhibit a larger and more hierarchical social organization than foragers do, local supernatural beings also have some limited powers and some moral concern, though far less than the gods of world religions (McNamara et al. 2015). By the time we get to state-level societies, Big Gods predominate and religion becomes intensely intertwined with public morality (Norenzayan 2013, Roes & Raymond 2003).

From a cultural evolutionary perspective, these findings make sense. In small-scale societies, where face-to-face interactions are the norm, people build cooperative communities that draw on kin altruism, reciprocity, and a rich repertoire of local cultural norms that enforce cooperation (Henrich & Henrich 2007)—without needing to lean on watchful, interventionist gods. But as societies scale up and groups get too large, anonymity rapidly invades interactions, and free riding threatens to undermine cooperation. Similarly, societies with greater exposure to ecological threats, such as water scarcity and climatic instability, face collective action problems that, if not curbed by cultural norms, can be fatal to the survival of the group (Botero et al. 2014). These conditions therefore promote widespread belief in watchful gods and other norm-enforcing practices that contribute to maintaining large-scale prosociality (see Norenzayan et al. 2015).

Big Gods, Organized Rituals, and Parochial Prosociality

Other elements of the religious system appear to follow a similar pattern across cultures. In an analysis of an extensive cross-cultural database of the world's cultures, Atkinson & Whitehouse (2011) found that doctrinal rituals—the high-frequency, low-arousal rituals commonly found in modern world religions (Whitehouse 2004)—are associated with greater belief in Big Gods, reliance on agriculture, and societal complexity. Doctrinal rituals have many effects, among which is to deepen commitments to communities. Other rituals and practices, such as the confessional in

Catholicism, may also contribute to in-group prosociality. For example, McKay et al. (2013) found that Catholics who were led to recall a sin that was absolved by the church donated more money to the church compared to Catholics who recalled a sin that was not yet absolved. Collective action at vast scales is hard to achieve in large, complex groups, hence the importance of enshrining certain cultural norms that pertain to the entire group as metaphysically grounded sacred values (Rappaport 1999) that are divinely ordained and therefore universally applicable and non-negotiable (Norenzayan et al. 2015). This is also why the prosociality that world religions inculcate in their adherents is typically not indiscriminate, but groupish and parochial, fostering community interests in intergroup competition (Atran & Ginges 2012, Haidt 2012, Norenzayan 2013).

One of the best-documented historical case studies looks at the Abrahamic traditions that are at the extreme end of the cultural spectrum of beliefs in supernatural punishment. Textual evidence shows that even here there was a gradual cultural evolution. The Abrahamic God started off as a tribal war god with limited social and moral concern and eventually ended up as the unitary, supreme, moralizing deity of Judaism and of two of the world's largest world religions—Christianity and Islam (for an accessible summary of this evidence, see Wright 2009). Supernatural sources of public morality are also found in ancient China, Egypt, Babylon, and the Greco-Roman world (Norenzayan et al. 2015).

Hinduism, Buddhism, and Jainism, known as the karmic or dharmic world religions, also reveal a convergence between religion and public morality, although the precise psychological mechanisms are even less well understood than is the case for the Abrahamic religions and their precursors. Obeyesekere (2002) observed that the notion of rebirth is present in many small-scale societies but is originally disconnected from morality. Gradually, ideas of rebirth incorporate the idea of ethical causation across lifetimes; this sets the stage for these religious ideas to shape the cooperative sphere.

In summary—and setting aside debates about the precise causal pathways, which are currently underway (see Norenzayan et al. 2015 and associated commentaries; also see Baumard & Boyer 2013)—an important take-home point is that across the world and throughout historical time, one important source of theodiversity is a cultural gradient that goes from the human-like, morally indifferent, and limited gods of foraging societies to the all-powerful, omniscient, and moralizing Big Gods, karmic beliefs, and repetitive and extreme rituals that transmit deep faith.

THEODIVERSITY WITHIN WORLD RELIGIONS

The Abrahamic traditions, particularly Christianity and Islam and their offshoots (e.g., Mormonism, Baha'i), have a common cultural ancestry and share many commonalities. The same applies to the karmic world religions, namely Hinduism and Buddhism, and their cultural descendants (e.g., Jainism). These traditions have all been extremely successful through a combination of conversions, conquest, and demographic growth (hence their world-religion status). They inculcate intense parochial prosociality among their diverse adherents. World religions also share, to varying degrees, many pronatalist conservative values and beliefs, such as traditional gender roles, early marriage, and opposition to birth control and homosexuality (Norenzayan et al. 2015), which sustain high fertility rates and large families (Blume 2009). Nevertheless, there is breathtaking theodiversity within world religions as well.

Orthodoxy Versus Orthopraxy

All world religions fuse faith in a core set of beliefs with practices and rituals that, taken together, create large-scale moral communities (Atran & Henrich 2010, Haidt 2012, Norenzayan et al.

2015). However, world religions differ in the way they accomplish this feat of community building. Some religious traditions, such as Protestantism, privilege faith in a particular set of beliefs or dogma, referred to as orthodoxy; others, such as Judaism and Hinduism, and to a lesser extent, Catholicism, more strongly (or equally) emphasize practice, participation, and deeds, referred to as orthopraxy (Cohen 2015, Cohen et al. 2003). This divergence has wide-ranging implications for psychology and has important heuristic value in organizing many disparate findings from the cultural psychology of religion.

One such outcome is that Protestants are on average more likely than Catholics to show the fundamental attribution error (FAE), that is, the tendency to see behaviors as reflecting individual dispositions rather than social contexts and roles, a phenomenon also dubbed the fundamentalist attribution error (Li et al. 2012). This maps onto well-known cultural differences in independent versus interdependent self-construals (Markus & Kitayama 1991; see also Miller 1984 for evidence that Americans are more prone to the FAE than Hindus living in India).

This difference in emphasis also leads to important differences in moral judgment. In a now famous interview with *Playboy*, former US President Jimmy Carter confessed that he had committed adultery in his heart many times (cited in Cohen & Rozin 2001). In a series of studies, Cohen and Rozin found that this tendency to moralize thoughts is far more common among Protestants than Jews. Participants were asked questions such as whether it is morally wrong for a married man to feel lust for another woman or for a son to dislike his parents in his heart. Protestants were far harsher than Jews toward characters who had offensive thoughts even if there was no known evidence that they were behaving badly. It appears that this difference is at least partly due to Protestants' conviction that bad thoughts are likely to lead to bad behavior.

In orthodoxy, intentions are supremely important. In orthopraxy, intentions are less important than their consequences. Broadly consistent with these findings, and extending to another orthopraxic tradition, Laurin & Plaks (2014) found that Hindus were harsher than Protestants toward a person who had unintentionally done something harmful. Laurin & Plaks also found that high scores on an orthopraxy scale led to harsher moral judgment of unintended bad behavior than did high scores on an orthodoxy scale.

Yet, Protestants are less likely to moralize certain behaviors than people exposed to more orthopraxic traditions such as Catholics. Haidt et al. (1993) asked working-class and middle-class Brazilians and Americans whether it is morally wrong to behave in ways that are disgusting but harmless, such as cleaning the toilet with the national flag or eating the family dog after it was killed in a car accident. Catholic Brazilians (and particularly working-class people) found these acts morally wrong, more than Americans (and particularly middle-class people), who found these acts to be unconventional but not immoral. Although Haidt and colleagues did not specifically measure religious affiliation or involvement, their results are at least partly consistent with this framework.

The Protestant preoccupation with sinful thoughts also has implications as to whether such thoughts are channeled into creative pursuits in the form of the Freudian defense mechanism known as sublimation (Baumeister et al. 1998). In a series of experiments, Dov Cohen and his colleagues (discussed in Cohen et al. 2014; see also Kim et al. 2013) asked Protestant, Catholic, and Jewish male participants to vividly imagine being in a sexual encounter. In the experimental condition, this was an incestuous sexual encounter between a brother and a sister. In the control condition, the sister was replaced with the brother's girlfriend. Results showed that Protestants who had expressed conflicted feelings in the incest condition subsequently wrote more creative poems and designed better sculptures (as rated by independent judges). They also reported more interest in creative careers. No such effects were observed for Catholic or Jewish men. Similar cultural differences were observed when participants were instructed to suppress angry thoughts.

Orthodoxy:
a religious tradition's relative emphasis on belief, dogma, and faith

Orthopraxy:
a religious tradition's relative emphasis on practice and ritual

The role of the moral emotions in religious experiences, thoughts, and behaviors is yet another understudied topic in psychology. Empathy, compassion, guilt, shame, and pride are key emotions that are often at the center of religious narratives and experiences. Pride, for example, is discouraged in Buddhism, Christianity, and Islam and in fact is one of the seven cardinal sins in Catholicism. Yet world religious traditions differ in which particular emotions are cultivated and encouraged. In Christianity, high-intensity positive emotions such as excitement and joy are commonly celebrated ("Praise the Lord!"). In contrast, Buddhist traditions value low-intensity, calming, positive emotions such as serenity and equanimity ("Om"). This difference in emphasis is also found among Christian and Buddhist practitioners in conceptions of ideal affect (Tsai et al. 2007).

Socialization into a particular religious tradition also biases perceptual habits. This should not come as a surprise. There is now a large body of evidence showing that high-level, culturally mediated beliefs, expectations, and practices can penetrate low-level perceptual processes (e.g., Nisbett 2003, Nisbett & Miyamoto 2005). An example of such a perceptual task is the global-local task in which participants are presented with a large rectangle or square made of smaller rectangles or squares. Participants are then instructed to attend to either the global or the local shape in different sets of trials, and their response times are measured (Navon 1977). A general finding is the so-called global precedence effect, which indicates a perceptual bias toward seeing the forest before the trees, so to speak. In one Dutch study, this effect was weaker among Calvinists than among matched samples of atheists, Catholics, and Jews. In a related study, atheists who were raised Calvinist also showed reduced global precedence compared to atheists who were not raised in any religion, suggesting that these differences are already in place in early childhood (Colzato et al. 2010b). A different study found that the forest loomed even larger than the individual trees among Taiwanese Zen Buddhists compared to a matched sample of Taiwanese atheists (Colzato et al. 2010a). The fact that Calvinism dampens and Zen Buddhism accentuates this effect suggests that these differences are the result of the specific beliefs and practices embedded in these particular traditions.

The sources of these differences in perceptual habits are not very well understood. One possibility specific to Buddhism is that it encourages an intensely social orientation, for example, by offering spiritual practices that broaden the circle of compassion to all beings, and there is evidence that social orientation leads to a more holistic processing style (Nisbett & Miyamoto 2005). As to Protestantism, and Calvinism in particular, the emphasis is on individual responsibility and an inward focus (Cohen 2015), cultural traits that are known to encourage more analytic cognitive processing. Interestingly, this emphasis in traditional Calvinist upbringing goes beyond visual perception, and it has been implicated in a variety of psychological peculiarities of Calvinist-influenced American culture relative to other Western cultures, particularly in the moralization of work and the strong belief in meritocracy (for a review, see Uhlmann & Sanchez-Burks 2014).

Prosocial Behavior

Henrich et al. (2010) found that, across 15 populations of foragers, pastoralists, and horticulturalists, participation in world religions (Christianity or Islam), compared to adherence to local religions, increased prosocial behavior toward anonymous strangers in two economic games, controlling for community size, market integration, and demographic variables. The psychological literature that has examined religious influences on prosocial behavior in predominantly Christian samples is considerable and growing (Norenzayan 2013, Shariff et al. 2015). However, psychological studies of prosocial behavior among practitioners of Islam (around 1.6 billion worldwide) and among karmic religious practitioners (around 1.5 billion worldwide) are rare. One recent field study found that exposure to the Muslim call to prayer in a Moroccan city increased generosity (Aveyard 2014). In another study conducted in a Jewish context in Israel, cooperation and coordination levels measured in an economic game were found to be higher in religious kibbutzim than in secular ones, and the effect was driven by the frequency of synagogue attendance levels in the religious kibbutzim, controlling for other factors (Sosis & Ruffle 2003).

In one seminal field study with modern Hindu samples, Dimitris Xygalatas and colleagues (2013) found that participation and observation of the extreme Hindu ritual Kavadi, discussed above, increased prosocial behavior within the community. Another study found that Hindu participants in Mauritius who were randomly assigned to play a common resource pool game in a Hindu temple showed more prosocial behavior than those who played the same game in a nearby Indian restaurant (Xygalatas et al. 2013). These findings provide experimental support to the idea that karmic religions, similar to Christianity, Islam, and Judaism, also encourage prosociality.

However, given the dearth of research, we know very little about the extent to which the psychological mechanisms that are being harnessed by Hindu and Buddhist religious elements are similar to those found in populations exposed to the Abrahamic faiths, or whether they recruit novel mechanisms. For example, we do not know whether Hindus and Buddhists intuitively link karmic effects to the powers of supernatural beings, such as Hindu gods, Buddha, and Boddhisatvas (saints with supernatural powers), or whether supernatural punishment is intuitively more potent than benevolence (Johnson 2009). In addition to the powerful prosocial effects of some forms of rituals, Buddhist contemplative practices of loving kindness may also play a measurable role in well-being, social support, and connection with others (Fredrickson et al. 2008).

Karma, Fate, Immanent Justice, and the Evil Eye

A related question is whether or not the karmic beliefs found in religions such as Hinduism and Buddhism are related to beliefs about immanent justice and related system justification ideologies (Callan et al. 2006, Jost et al. 2009). Belief in a just world is the conviction that the world is fundamentally fair and that people get what they deserve (Lerner 1980). Immanent justice is the intuition that, sooner or later, misdeeds rebound in the form of misfortune. This intuition could possibly be cross-culturally widespread, although studies looking at this question are currently lacking. One series of studies with American participants found higher rates of helping others when uncertainty is high and an outcome is strongly desired (e.g., waiting for the results of a medical test), as if fate could be influenced by good deeds (Converse et al. 2012). However, one cross-cultural study found that Christian participants believed that a misfortune was fated only if it was preceded by wrongdoing in this lifetime. Hindu participants saw the same misfortune to be fated even without prior wrongdoing, consistent with the Hindu idea of ethical causation across lifetimes (Young et al. 2011). These themes offer a treasure trove of important opportunities for future research.

Parallel to the idea that misdeeds eventually cause misfortune, another magical intuition is the notion of the evil eye (Dundes 1981), or the idea that a malevolent glare or envy by others can cause misfortune. This is a widespread cultural belief throughout the Mediterranean and as far east as Central Asia, which shares some similarities with witchcraft. As a result of this belief, people in these cultures often publicly downplay their successes or good fortune, such as a successful business or the birth of a healthy child, so as not to attract the evil eye. It is also common to protect oneself with talismans representing a blue eye, also called the evil eye, when pursuing favorable goals. Currently, the psychological literature is mostly silent on the underlying psychology and impact of such beliefs and practices.

FROM BIG GODS TO NO GODS

Apatheism:
a form of irreligion characterized by indifference or apathy toward religion

Paradoxically, psychology's WEIRD lens has contributed not only to the neglect of religion, but also to its erosion as an interesting phenomenon in its own right. Secularization is not as big a topic as it should be in psychology, although it is hotly debated within history (Smith 1982), philosophy (Taylor 2007), and sociology (Berger 1999, Norris & Inglehart 2004). Yet, psychology has profound and unique insights to offer to explanations of secularization and its impact on human thought and behavior. I discuss secularization in two parts. First, I explore current hypotheses on the psychological and sociocultural conditions that give rise to various forms of disbelief. Second, I explore what we know about how secularization, in turn, affects psychological processes.

Atheodiversity

The first fact to appreciate about secularization is that its proliferation is extremely uneven across the world. Secularization has been making great inroads in most of Europe, to a lesser extent in North America, and also in places such as Australia and New Zealand. But other parts of the world, such as Africa, most of Latin America, and South Asia—all societies with high fertility rates—remain as religious as they have ever been. Nevertheless, the current worldwide prevalence of nonbelievers is unprecedented and nontrivial, numbering in the hundreds of millions. Put another way, if nonbelievers all over the world were grouped together, they would be the fourth biggest world religion (Zuckerman 2007).

Scientific understanding of the origins and consequences of disbelief is also important for public policy. Recent years have seen high-profile popular debates concerning atheism and religion and frequent clashes between the two (Atran 2010, Haidt 2012). Moreover, there is considerable evidence that where there are religious majorities, atheists are a strongly stigmatized group (Gervais & Norenzayan 2013). Therefore, the second fact to appreciate about secularization is that without understanding its causes, we could not understand the sources of this cultural divide and how to bridge it.

The third important fact about secularization is that it is not monolithic, but it reflects diverse forms of disbelief and distancing from religion. We have seen that there are distinct and converging pathways to religious beliefs, rituals, and practices, traceable to cognitive, motivational, and cultural mechanisms. These pathways, if altered, lead to various forms of disbelief:[3]

- Cognitive mechanisms are implicated in mind-blind atheism, which is associated with deficits in mentalizing that underlie a variety of intuitions that support religious belief, and to analytic atheism, in which analytic cognitive processes override or block the cognitive intuitions that anchor religious beliefs (Norenzayan & Gervais 2013).

- Motivational mechanisms are implicated in apatheism, or indifference to religion induced by the reduction of existential threats such as death, hardship, and suffering that individuals and societies may face (Kay et al. 2009, Norris & Inglehart 2004).

- Cultural learning mechanisms are implicated in inCREDulous atheism when individuals fail to witness extravagant displays of religious commitment; other cultural learning mechanisms may be at work as well, such as growing up in a culture in which the majority and the prestigious cultural models do not display religious fervor (Henrich 2009).

---

[3] So Bulbulia (2012) explores ennuitheism, or a certain boredom regarding everything religious. See also Banerjee & Bloom (2013), Geertz & Markusson (2010), and McCauley (2011) for a discussion of the importance of cultural input in the rise of disbelief and its various forms.

This atheodiversity also shows up in the rise of a new and growing demographic group in the West, the spiritual but not religious (SBNR). Gaining momentum in the secularizing world, such as in Northern Europe and the West Coast of the United States and Canada, traditional organized religion is giving way not just to varieties of disbelief, but also to an abundance of yoga studios, spiritual retreats, and healing crystals (Fuller 2001). According to a *Newsweek* poll, 30% of Americans identified as "spiritual but not religious" in 2009, up from 24% in 2005 (Princet. Surv. Res. Assoc. Int. 2009). Our understanding of the reasons behind this growing movement is rudimentary at best: Here is another opportunity for psychological research to gain insights into an important but overlooked aspect of theodiversity. In one rare study, Saucier & Skrzypińska (2006) found that religiosity and spirituality have different personality correlates. Whereas religiosity is associated with traditionalism and low openness to experience, spirituality is associated with fantasy proneness, magical ideation, and high openness to experience (see also Emmons & Paloutzian 2003).

In a recent study looking at their cognitive profile, SBNRs differed from both conventional believers and nonbelievers in exhibiting a greater endorsement of paranormal beliefs and a more experiential relationship to the divine, such as feelings of being at one with the universe. SBNRs reject the traditional religious dogmas of their cultures but accept core intuitions such as mind-body dualism, teleology, and anthropomorphism, which support a variety of supernatural beliefs and experiences (A. Willard & A. Norenzayan, unpublished manuscript). Interestingly, the spiritual experiences found among the SBNRs—such as feelings of oneness with the universe, the sense that the universe is infused with a certain life force, and an emphasis on universal compassion and love—are also recurrent themes in some of the mystical traditions of world religions as culturally diverse as Buddhist contemplative practices such as Metta and Vipassana, yoga in Hinduism, Sufi Islam, Christian mysticism, and kabbalah in Judaism. One speculation is that these experiences tap into core psychological intuitions that are stripped away from the cultural baggage inherited from their respective traditions.

In summary, religious disbelief, much like religious belief, is not a unitary phenomenon resulting from a single process. Disbelief arises from alterations of the pathways that promote religious belief and is therefore infused with different subjective qualities. Whereas mind-blind atheism does not "get" religion, apatheism and inCREDulous atheism are indifferent toward religion, and analytic atheism is skeptical of religion. These paths to disbelief are theoretically distinct but are often intertwined in the real world, such that a given individual or subculture may come to disbelief through a combination of them. Future research may discover additional pathways. Also, secularization does not always lead to disbelief, in the sense of complete absence of any supernatural beliefs; equally often, it creates ripe conditions for diverse spiritual and paranormal beliefs and practices to proliferate.

The Religious Versus Nonreligious Divide

The religious/nonreligious divide (and its close cousin, conservatism/liberalism) also plays out within nation states such as the United States, with well-known polarizing consequences that affect politics, culture, and education (Haidt 2012). Here I highlight a few core areas of psychology— parochial prosociality, fertility rates, happiness and meaning making, moral psychology, sacred values, and fate attributions—in which a religious/nonreligious divide has been found and is the hypothesized cause of particular psychological outcomes (for a broader discussion of these differences, see McKay & Whitehouse 2015; Shariff et al. 2014, 2015).

There are broad conditions that make humans a prosocial species (Keltner et al. 2014). But are religious believers generally more prosocial than nonbelievers? In sociological surveys, religious believers in the United States report more charitable giving and greater volunteerism (e.g., Brooks 2006). However, behavioral studies reveal a more nuanced picture. Religious commitment predicts prosocial tendencies best in contexts where secular institutions that encourage cooperation are weak, social monitoring is absent, reputational concerns are heightened, and the targets of prosociality are coreligionists (for reviews, see Batson et al. 1993, Norenzayan 2013). Moreover, religious commitment is an important moderator of religious priming effects. A recent meta-analysis found that religious priming increases prosocial behaviors for believers but has no average effect on nonbelievers (Shariff et al. 2015). Because the majority of psychological studies of religion and prosociality have been conducted in WEIRD contexts where the presence of secular institutions often crowds out the influence of religion, these moderating contexts have been overlooked until recently (Norenzayan et al. 2015).

Religious commitment can also be a source of happiness and a sense of meaning in life—two aspects of thriving that are increasingly at the center of attention within psychology (Keltner 2009). Past studies (predominantly conducted in the United States) have found that on average, more religious individuals are somewhat happier (Hackney & Sanders 2003). However, a growing number of cross-cultural studies suggest that religion's effect on happiness is not universal but is dependent on sociocultural and economic circumstances.

In one such study, based on a global sample of 154 nations, Diener et al. (2011) found that the religious/nonreligious divide in happiness emerges in places with high existential insecurity (poverty, high infant mortality, hunger) but disappears in wealthy and secure societies, where happiness levels are generally much higher for everyone regardless of religiosity levels. Another moderating factor is whether religiosity is normative. Gebauer et al. (2012) found in a sample of 180,000 people in 11 European nations that religiosity predicted psychological adjustment, but only in places where religiosity was culturally normative and generally valued by society; this association disappeared where the majority of the population was irreligious.

Finally, in an interesting study covering 132 nations, Oishi & Diener (2014) found that on average, individuals in poor nations were less happy but felt a stronger sense of meaning than individuals in wealthy nations. In turn, higher levels of religiosity explained the greater meaning experienced in the poorer nations. Oishi & Diener further showed that loss of meaning, but not loss of happiness, predicted the higher suicide rates in wealthier nations. Thus, when facing difficult life circumstances, happiness may not be an option, but one can still find meaning in suffering and keep on living, as Victor Frankl (1963) observed decades ago while surviving the brutality of a Nazi concentration camp. It appears that religious engagement is an important source of such sense of meaning in the face of suffering, although the reasons for this remain to be explored.

There is growing evidence that religious engagement shapes moral psychology in important ways (Haidt 2012). In a large global sample of 87 nations from the World Values Survey, Atkinson & Bourrat (2011) found that several aspects of religious commitment were associated with harsher condemnation of a range of moral transgressions, such as cheating on taxes or fare-skipping on public transport. Also, believers are more likely than nonbelievers to apply deontological, as opposed to utilitarian, considerations to many moral transgressions, such as stealing, lying, or committing treason (Piazza & Sousa 2014). Additionally, religious believers tend to ground moral judgments on a more diverse set of domains than nonbelievers. Whereas for nonbelievers morality is primarily and more narrowly about not harming, caring, and promoting fairness and justice, for believers morality also extends to loyalty to one's group, purity and sacredness, and respect for authority (Graham & Haidt 2010, Haidt 2012, Shweder et al. 1997). Religious individuals are also more likely to endorse explanations based on fate ("It was meant to happen") than the nonreligious, and this difference is statistically explained by the belief that supernatural agency controls and determines life outcomes (Norenzayan & Lee 2010), although a certain amount of belief in fate can be found even among nonbelievers (Banerjee & Bloom 2014).

Religions are also intertwined with sacred values. Unlike instrumental values that are subject to cost-benefit calculations and fall under rational actor models, sacred values are driven by emotionally loaded moral conviction and are often immune to trade-off. These relatively understudied values are better explained in terms of devoted actor models (Atran 2010, Tetlock 2003). For example, one cannot place any monetary value on one's family or community or on a national landmark that is considered a public treasure. Sacred values connected to the supernatural have measurable consequences for collective action dilemmas, such as sustainable forest management. Such an example is found among the Q'eqchi' in the highlands of Guatemala, who taboo the exploitation of certain forest species that are believed to be alive with local forest spirits (Atran et al. 2002).

Secular societies and irreligious individuals have plenty of sacred values (the national flag, the idea of democracy, a house passed down from one's ancestors for generations). However, it appears that religious conviction intensifies the tendency to see the world through a sacred lens (Sheikh et al. 2012). Why this would be is an interesting, unanswered question. One hypothesis is that imputing a divine origin to certain beliefs and behaviors that impose costs to the self but benefit the larger moral community (God forbids cheating) better insulates cooperative groups from potential defection and overexploitation, particularly under conditions of real or perceived environmental or intergroup threat (Atran 2010, Atran & Henrich 2010).

CONCLUSION

Theodiversity is to the scientific study of religion what biodiversity is to the scientific study of life on the planet. Here I have outlined underlying regularities and catalogued the landscape of theodiversity in three broad conduits, although there could be other fruitful approaches to carve this conceptual space. Despite its importance, very little of the world's theodiversity trickles into the psychological laboratory. There are fascinating and weighty questions open for study, such as sacred values, karmic beliefs, extreme rituals, mystical experiences, food taboos, witchcraft, magical thinking, religious conversion, and various forms of irreligion. But to tackle cross-culturally recurrent elements of religion, as well as plumb the depths of theodiversity, psychology must cast a wider net to capture the full range of human cultural diversity.

SUMMARY POINTS

1. Most of the world lives in overwhelmingly religious societies reflecting a great deal of theodiversity.

2. Theodiversity is rooted in and channeled by several recurrent aspects of cognition, motivation, and cultural learning processes.

3. Theodiversity can be found along at least three dimensions: as a consequence of increasing social complexity, within world religions differing in their cultural histories, and as a result of secularization in some places.

4. There is growing evidence that diversity in religious beliefs and practices, as well as secularization, has profound consequences for a wide range of psychological outcomes.

5. There are several predictable pathways to secularization, a social transformation that is gaining momentum in some parts of the world and in some subcultures.

FUTURE ISSUES

1. Explaining theodiversity calls for expanding psychology's empirical database beyond WEIRD samples.

2. There are likely additional dimensions of theodiversity that are significant for human psychology.

3. We currently know little about the psychological processes that explain beliefs and behaviors related to karma, immanent justice, witchcraft, the evil eye, and related phenomena that are widespread around the world.

4. Sacred values are an important element in moral cognition, social identity, intergroup relations, and conflict and conflict resolution.

5. The processes of secularization that generate various forms of disbelief are another important but overlooked topic in psychology.

DISCLOSURE STATEMENT

The author is not aware of any affiliations, memberships, funding, or financial holdings that might be perceived as affecting the objectivity of this review.

ACKNOWLEDGMENTS

I thank the James McKeen Cattell Fund for a generous sabbatical fellowship that supported the writing of this article. I also thank the Social Sciences and Humanities Research Council of Canada for ongoing support from a partnership grant, "The Evolution of Religion and Morality" (895-2011-1009). Finally, I thank Adam Baimel, Konika Banerjee, Adam Cohen, Nick Epley, Susan Fiske, Jon Haidt, Cristine Legare, Rick Shweder, and Doug Medin and members of the Mosaic Lab at Northwestern University for valuable comments on an earlier draft.

LITERATURE CITED

Allport GW. 1950. *The Individual and His Religion: A Psychological Interpretation*. Oxford, UK: Macmillan

Arnett J. 2008. The neglected 95%: why American psychology needs to become less American. *Am. Psychol.* 63:602–14

Atkinson QD, Bourrat P. 2011. Beliefs about God, the afterlife and morality support the role of supernatural policing in human cooperation. *Evol. Hum. Behav.* 32:41–49

Atkinson QD, Whitehouse H. 2011. The cultural morphospace of ritual form: examining modes of religiosity cross-culturally. *Evol. Hum. Behav.* 32:50–62

Atran S. 2002. *In Gods We Trust: The Evolutionary Landscape of Religion*. New York: Oxford Univ. Press

Atran S. 2010. *Talking to the Enemy: Faith, Brotherhood and the (Un)Making of Terrorists*. New York: HarperCollins

Atran S, Ginges J. 2012. Religious and sacred imperatives in human conflict. *Science* 336:855–57

Atran S, Henrich J. 2010. The evolution of religion: how cognitive by-products, adaptive learning heuristics, ritual displays, and group competition generate deep commitments to prosocial religions. *Biol. Theory* 5:18–30

Atran S, Medin D, Ross N, Lynch E, Vapnarsky V, et al. 2002. Folkecology, cultural epidemiology, and the spirit of the commons: a "garden experiment" in the Maya lowlands, 1991–2001. *Curr. Anthropol.* 43:421–50

Aveyard ME. 2014. A call to honesty: extending religious priming of moral behavior to Middle Eastern Muslims. *PLOS ONE* 9:e99447

Banerjee K, Bloom P. 2013. Would Tarzan believe in God? *Trends Cogn. Sci.* 17:7–8

Banerjee K, Bloom P. 2014. Why did this happen to me? Religious believers' and non-believers' teleological reasoning about life events. *Cognition* 133:277–303

Barrett DB, Kurian GTK, Johnson TM, eds. 2001. *World Christian Encyclopedia: Religionists, Churches, Ministries: A Comparative Survey of Churches and Religions in the Modern World*. New York: Oxford Univ. Press

Barrett JL. 2000. Exploring the natural foundations of religion. *Trends Cogn. Sci.* 4:29–34

Barrett JL. 2004. *Why Would Anyone Believe in God?* Walnut Creek, CA: AltaMira

Batson CD, Schoenrade P, Ventis WL. 1993. *Religion and the Individual: A Social-Psychological Perspective*. New York, NY: Oxford Univ. Press

Baumard N, Boyer P. 2013. Explaining moral religions. *Trends Cogn. Sci.* 17:272–80

Baumeister R, Dale K, Sommer L. 1998. Freudian defense mechanisms and empirical findings in modern social psychology: reaction formation, projection, displacement, undoing, isolation, sublimation, and denial. *J. Personal.* 66:1081–124

Bellah R. 2011. *Religion in Human Evolution*. Cambridge, MA: Harvard Univ. Press

Bentzen JS. 2013. *Origins of religiousness: the role of natural disasters*. Work. Paper 13-02, Dep. Econ., Univ. Copenhagen, Copenhagen, Den. **http://papers.ssrn.com/sol3/papers.cfm?abstract_id=2221859**

Berger P. 1999. *The Desecularization of the World: Resurgent Religion and World Politics*. Grand Rapids, MI: Ethics Policy Cent.

Berger P. 2014. *The Many Altars of Modernity: Toward a Paradigm for Religion in a Pluralist Age*. Boston, MA: Walter de Gruyter

Bloom P. 2004. *Descartes' Baby*. New York: Basic Books

Bloom P. 2012. Religion, morality, evolution. *Annu. Rev. Psychol.* 63:179–99

Blume M. 2009. The reproductive benefits of religious affiliation. In *The Biological Evolution of Religious Mind and Behavior*, ed. E Voland, W Schiefenhovel, pp. 117–26. Berlin: Springer-Verlag

Botero CA, Gardner B, Kirby KR, Bulbulia J, Gavin MC, Gray R. 2014. The ecology of religious beliefs. *PNAS* 111:16784–89

Boyer P. 2001. *Religion Explained*. New York: Basic Books

Boyer P, Lienard P. 2006. Why ritualized behavior? Precaution systems and action parsing in developmental, pathological and cultural rituals. *Brain Behav. Sci.* 29:595–650

Brooks AC. 2006. *Who Really Cares: The Surprising Truth About Compassionate Conservatism*. New York: Basic Books

Bulbulia J. 2008. Free love: religious solidarity on the cheap. In *The Evolution of Religion: Studies, Theories and Critiques*, ed. J Bulbulia, S Richard, R Genet, E Harris, K Wynan, C Genet, pp. 153–60. Santa Margarita, CA: Collins Found.

Bulbulia J. 2012. Ennuitheism. In *Science and the World's Religions*, Vol. 3: *Religions and Controversies*, ed. W Wildman, P McNamara, pp. 165–94. Santa Barbara, CA: Greenwood

Callan MJ, Ellard JH, Nicol JE. 2006. The belief in a just world and immanent justice reasoning in adults. *Personal. Soc. Psychol. Bull.* 32:1646–58

Chudek M, MacNamara R, Birch SA, Bloom P, Henrich J. 2014. *Developmental and cross-cultural evidence for intuitive dualism*. Work. Pap., Dep. Psychol., Univ. Br. Columbia. **http://www2.psych.ubc.ca/~henrich/pdfs/ChudekEtAl_InutiveDualism_WorkingPaper_June2014.pdf**

Chudek M, Muthukrishna M, Henrich J. 2015. Cultural evolution. In *Handbook of Evolutionary Psychology*, Vol. 2, ed. DM Buss. Hoboken, NJ: Wiley. In press

Cohen AB. 2015. Religion's profound influences on psychology: morality, intergroup relations, self-construal, and enculturation. *Curr. Dir. Psychol. Sci.* 24:77–82

Cohen AB, Hall DE, Koenig HG, Meador KG. 2005. Social versus individual motivation: implications for normative definitions of religious orientation. *Personal. Soc. Psychol. Rev.* 9:48–61

Cohen AB, Rozin P. 2001. Religion and the morality of mentality. *J. Personal. Soc. Psychol.* 81:697–710

Cohen AB, Siegel PR, Rozin P. 2003. Faith versus practice: different bases for religiosity judgments by Jews and Protestants. *Eur. J. Soc. Psychol.* 33:287–95

Cohen D, Kim E, Hudson N. 2014. Religion, the forbidden, and sublimation. *Curr. Dir. Psychol. Sci.* 23:208–14

Colzato LS, Hommel B, van den Wildenberg WPM, Hsieh S. 2010a. Buddha as an eye opener: a link between prosocial attitude and attentional control. *Front. Psychol.* 1:156

Colzato LS, van Beest I, van den Wildenberg WPM, Scorolli C, Dorchin S, et al. 2010b. God: Do I have your attention? *Cognition* 117:87–94

Converse BA, Risen JL, Carter TJ. 2012. Investing in karma: when wanting promotes helping. *Psychol. Sci.* 23:923–30

Dechesne M, Pyszczynski T, Arndt J, Ransom S, Sheldon KM, et al. 2003. Literal and symbolic immortality: the effect of evidence of literal immortality on self-esteem striving in response to mortality salience. *J. Personal. Soc. Psychol.* 84(4):722–37

Diener E, Tay L, Myers DG. 2011. The religion paradox: If religion makes people happy, why are so many dropping out? *J. Personal. Soc. Psychol.* 101:1278–90

Dundes A. 1981. *The Evil Eye: A Casebook*. Madison: Univ. Wisc. Press

Emmons RA, Paloutzian RF. 2003. The psychology of religion. *Annu. Rev. Psychol.* 54:377–402

Epley N. 2014. *Mindwise: Why We Misunderstand What Others Think, Believe, Feel, and Want*. New York: Knopf

Epley N, Converse BA, Delbosc A, Monteleone GA, Cacioppo JT. 2009. Believers' estimates of God's beliefs are more egocentric than estimates of other people's beliefs. *PNAS* 106:21533–38

Epley N, Waytz A, Cacioppo JT. 2007. On seeing human: a three-factor theory of anthropomorphism. *Psychol. Rev.* 114:864–86

Fiske AP, Haslam N. 1997. Is obsessive-compulsive disorder a pathology of the human disposition to perform socially meaningful rituals? Evidence of similar content. *J. Nerv. Ment. Dis.* 185:211–22

Frankl VE. 1963. *Man's Search for Meaning: An Introduction to Logotherapy*. New York: Wash. Sq. Press

Fredrickson BL, Cohn MA, Coffey KA, Pek J, Finkel SM. 2008. Open hearts build lives: Positive emotions, induced through loving-kindness meditation, build consequential personal resources. *J. Personal. Soc. Psychol.* 95:1045–62

Fuller RC. 2001. *Spiritual But Not Religious: Understanding Unchurched America*. New York: Oxford Univ. Press

Gebauer JE, Sedikides C, Neberich W. 2012. Religiosity, social self-esteem, and psychological adjustment: on the cross-cultural specificity of the psychological benefits of religiosity. *Psychol. Sci.* 23:158–60

Geertz AW, Markusson GI. 2010. Religion is natural, atheism is not: on why everybody is both right and wrong. *Religion* 40:152–65

Gervais WM, Norenzayan A. 2013. Religion and the origins of anti-atheist prejudice. In *Intolerance and Conflict: A Scientific and Conceptual Investigation*, ed. S Clarke, R Powell, J Savulescu, pp. 126–45. Oxford, UK: Oxford Univ. Press

Gervais WM, Willard A, Norenzayan A, Henrich J. 2011. The cultural transmission of faith: why innate intuitions are necessary, but insufficient, to explain religious belief. *Religion* 41:389–410

Gorsuch RL. 1988. Psychology of religion. *Annu. Rev. Psychol.* 39:201–21

Graham J, Haidt J. 2010. Beyond beliefs: Religions bind individuals into moral communities. *Personal. Soc. Psychol. Rev.* 14:140–50

Gray K, Jenkins AC, Heberlein AS, Wegner DM. 2010. Distortions of mind perception in psychopathology. *PNAS* 108:477–79

Guthrie SE. 1993. *Faces in the Clouds: A New Theory of Religion*. New York: Oxford Univ. Press

Hackney CH, Sanders GS. 2003. Religiosity and mental health: a meta-analysis of recent studies. *J. Sci. Study Religion* 42:43–55

Haidt J. 2012. *The Righteous Mind: Why Good People Are Divided by Politics and Religion*. New York: Pantheon Books

Haidt J, Koller S, Dias M. 1993. Affect, culture, and morality, or is it wrong to eat your dog? *J. Personal. Soc. Psychol.* 65:613–28

Heine SJ, Norenzayan A. 2006. Toward a psychological science for a cultural species. *Perspect. Psychol. Sci.* 1:251–69

Henrich J. 2009. The evolution of costly displays, cooperation and religion: credibility enhancing displays and their implications for cultural evolution. *Evol. Hum. Behav.* 30(4):244–60

Henrich J, Ensminger J, McElreath R, Barr A, Barrett C, et al. 2010a. Markets, religion, community size, and the evolution of fairness and punishment. *Science* 327(5972):1480–84

Henrich J, Heine SJ, Norenzayan A. 2010b. The weirdest people in the world? *Behav. Brain Sci.* 33:61–83

Henrich J, Henrich N. 2007. *Why Humans Cooperate: A Cultural and Evolutionary Explanation.* New York: Oxford Univ. Press

Heywood BT, Bering JM. 2014. Meant to be: how religious beliefs and cultural religiosity affect the implicit bias to think teleologically. *Religion Brain Behav.* 4:183–201

Hume D. 1956 (1757). *The Natural History of Religion.* London: Black

James W. 1902. *The Varieties of Religious Experience: A Study in Human Nature.* New York: Longmans, Green & Co.

Johnson DDP. 2009. The error of God: error management theory, religion and the evolution of cooperation. In *Games, Groups and the Global Good,* ed. SA Levin, pp. 169–80. Berlin: Springer-Verlag

Johnson KA, Li YJ, Cohen AB. 2015. Fundamental motives and the varieties of religious experience. *Religion Brain Behav.* 5:197–261

Jost JT, Kay AC, Thoristtodor H. 2009. *Social and Psychological Bases of Ideology and System Justification.* New York: Oxford Univ. Press

Kay AC, Whitson JA, Gaucher D, Galinsky AD. 2009. Compensatory control achieving order through the mind, our institutions, and the heavens. *Curr. Dir. Psychol. Sci.* 18(5):264–68

Kelemen D. 2004. Are children "intuitive theists"? *Psychol. Sci.* 15:295–301

Kelemen D, Rosset E. 2009. The human function compunction: teleological explanation in adults. *Cognition* 111:138–43

Kelly RL. 1995. *The Foraging Spectrum: Diversity in Hunter-Gatherer Lifeways.* Washington, DC: Smithson. Inst. Press

Keltner D. 2009. *Born to Be Good: The Science of a Meaningful Life.* New York: Norton

Keltner D, Kogan A, Piff PK, Saturn S. 2014. The sociocultural appraisals, values, and emotions (SAVE) framework of prosociality: core processes from gene to meme. *Annu. Rev. Psychol.* 65:425–60

Kim E, Zeppenfeld V, Cohen D. 2013. Sublimation, culture, and creativity. *J. Personal. Soc. Psychol.* 105:639–66

Laurin K, Kay AC, Fitzsimons GM. 2012. Divergent effects of activating thoughts of God on self-regulation. *J. Personal. Soc. Psychol.* 102:4–21

Laurin K, Plaks JE. 2014. Religion and punishment: opposing influences of orthopraxy and orthodoxy on reactions to unintentional acts. *Soc. Psychol. Personal. Sci.* 5:835–43

Legare CH, Evans EM, Rosengren KS, Harris PL. 2012. The coexistence of natural and supernatural explanations across cultures and development. *Child Dev.* 83:779–93

Legare CH, Souza AL. 2012. Evaluating ritual efficacy: evidence from the supernatural. *Cognition* 124:1–15

Legare CH, Souza AL. 2014. Searching for control: priming randomness increases the evaluation of ritual efficacy. *Cogn. Sci.* 38:152–61

Legare CH, Watson-Jones RE. 2015. The evolution and ontogeny of ritual. In *Handbook of Evolutionary Psychology,* Vol. 2, ed. DM Buss, pp. 829–47. Hoboken, NJ: Wiley

Lerner MJ. 1980. *The Belief in a Just World: A Fundamental Delusion.* New York: Plenum Press

Lester T. 2002. Oh gods! *The Atlantic Monthly,* February. **http://www.theatlantic.com/magazine/archive/2002/02/oh-gods/302412/**

Li YJ, Johnson KA, Cohen AB, Williams MJ, Knowles ED, Chen Z. 2012. Fundamental(ist) attribution error: Protestants are dispositionally focused. *J. Personal. Soc. Psychol.* 102:281–90

Markus HR, Kitayama S. 1991. Culture and the self: implications for cognition, emotion, and motivation. *Psychol. Rev.* 98(2):224–53

Marlowe FW. 2010. *The Hadza: Hunter-Gatherers of Tanzania.* Berkeley: Univ. Calif. Press

McCauley RN. 2011. *Why Religion Is Natural and Science Is Not.* New York: Oxford Univ. Press

McCauley RN, Lawson ET. 2002. *Bringing Ritual to Mind: Psychological Foundations of Cultural Forms.* Cambridge, UK: Cambridge Univ. Press

McKay R, Herold J, Whitehouse H. 2013. Catholic guilt? Recall of confession promotes prosocial behaviour. *Religion Brain Behav.* 3:201–9

McKay R, Whitehouse H. 2015. Religion and morality. *Psychol. Bull.* 141:447–73

McNamara RA, Norenzayan A, Henrich J. 2015. Supernatural punishment, in-group biases, and material insecurity: experiments and ethnography from Yasawa, Fiji. *Religion Brain Behav.* In press. doi:10.1080/2153599X.2014.921235

Medin DL, Atran S. 2004. The native mind: biological categorization and reasoning in development and across cultures. *Psychol. Rev.* 111(4):960–83

Medin DL, Bennis WM, Chandler M. 2010. Culture and the home-field disadvantage. *Perspect. Psychol. Sci.* 5:708–13

Miller JG. 1984. Culture and the development of everyday social explanation. *J. Personal. Soc. Psychol.* 46:961–78

Navon D. 1977. Forest before trees: the precedence of global features in visual perception. *Cogn. Psychol.* 9:353–83

Nemeroff C, Rozin P. 2000. The making of the magical mind. In *Imagining the Impossible: Magical, Scientific, and Religious Thinking in Children*, ed. K Rosengren, C Johnson, P Harris, pp. 1–34. Cambridge, UK: Cambridge Univ. Press

Nielsen M, Tomaselli K. 2010. Overimitation in Kalahari Bushman children and the origins of human cultural cognition. *Psychol. Sci.* 21:729–36

Nisbett RE. 2003. *A Geography of Thought.* New York: Free Press

Nisbett RE, Miyamoto Y. 2005. The influence of culture: holistic versus analytic perception. *Trends Cogn. Sci.* 9:467–73

Norenzayan A. 2013. *Big Gods: How Religion Transformed Cooperation and Conflict.* Princeton, NJ: Princeton Univ. Press

Norenzayan A, Gervais WM. 2013. The origins of religious disbelief. *Trends Cogn. Sci.* 17:20–25

Norenzayan A, Hansen IG. 2006. Belief in supernatural agents in the face of death. *Personal. Soc. Psychol. Bull.* 32:174–87

Norenzayan A, Heine SJ. 2005. Psychological universals: What are they and how can we know? *Psychol. Bull.* 135:763–84

Norenzayan A, Lee A. 2010. It was meant to happen: explaining cultural variations in fate attributions. *J. Personal. Soc. Psychol.* 98:702–20

Norenzayan A, Shariff AF, Gervais WM, Willard A, McNamara RA, et al. 2015. The cultural evolution of prosocial religions. *Behav. Brain Sci.* **http://dx.doi.org/10.1017/S0140525X14001356.** In press

Norris P, Inglehart R. 2004. *Sacred and Secular: Religion and Politics Worldwide.* Cambridge, UK: Cambridge Univ. Press

Obeyesekere G. 2002. *Imagining Karma: Ethical Transformation in Amerindian, Buddhist, and Greek Rebirth.* Berkeley: Univ. Calif. Press

Oishi S, Diener E. 2014. Residents of poor nations have a greater sense of meaning in life than residents of wealthy nations. *Psychol. Sci.* 25:422–30

Pew Res. Cent. 2012. *The global religious landscape.* Rep., Dec. 18. **http://www.pewforum.org/2012/12/18/global-religious-landscape-exec/**

Piazza J, Sousa P. 2014. Religiosity, political orientation, and consequentialist moral thinking. *Soc. Psychol. Personal. Sci.* 5:334–42

Princet. Surv. Res. Assoc. Int. 2009. *Newsweek poll: a post-Christian nation?* Retrieved May 29, 2014. **http://www.psrai.com/filesave/0904%20top%20w%20methodology.pdf**

Purzycki BG. 2011. Tyvan cher eezi and the socioecological constraints of supernatural agents' minds. *Religion Brain Behav.* 1(1):31–45

Purzycki BG. 2013. The minds of gods: a comparative study of supernatural agency. *Cognition* 129:163–79

Rappaport RA. 1999. *Ritual and Religion in the Making of Humanity.* Cambridge, UK: Cambridge Univ. Press

Richerson PJ, Boyd R. 2005. *Not by Genes Alone: How Culture Transformed Human Evolution.* Chicago: Univ. Chicago Press

Roes FL, Raymond M. 2003. Belief in moralizing gods. *Evol. Hum. Behav.* 24(2):126–35

Rozin P. 2007. Exploring the landscape of modern academic psychology: finding and filling the holes. *Am. Psychol.* 62:751–66

Rozin P. 2009. What kind of empirical research should we publish, fund, and reward? A different perspective. *Perspect. Psychol. Sci.* 4:435–39

Rutjens BT, Van Der Pligt J, Van Harreveld F. 2010. Deus or Darwin: randomness and belief in theories about the origin of life. *J. Exp. Soc. Psychol.* 46(6):1078–80

Sanchez-Burks J, Lee F. 2007. Culture and workways. In *Handbook of Cultural Psychology*, Vol. 1, ed. S Kitayama, D Cohen, pp. 346–69. New York: Guilford

Saucier G, Skrzypińska K. 2006. Spiritual but not religious? Evidence for two independent dimensions. *J. Personal.* 74:1257–92

Schjoedt U, Sørensen J, Nielbo KL, Xygalatas D, Mitkidis P, Bulbulia J. 2013. Cognitive resource depletion in religious interactions. *Religion Brain Behav.* 3:39–55

Sears D. 1986. College sophomores in the laboratory: influences of a narrow database on social psychology's view of human nature. *J. Personal. Soc. Psychol.* 51:515–30

Shariff AF, Piazza J, Kramer SR. 2014. Morality and the religious mind: why theists and non-theists differ. *Trends Cogn. Sci.* 18(9):439–41

Shariff AF, Rhemtulla M. 2012. Divergent effects of belief in heaven and hell on national crime rates. *PLOS ONE* 7:e39048

Shariff AF, Willard AK, Andersen T, Norenzayan A. 2015. Religious priming: a meta-analysis with a focus on prosociality. *Personal. Soc. Psychol. Rev.* In press

Sheikh H, Ginges J, Coman A, Atran S. 2012. Religion, group threat and sacred values. *Judgm. Decis. Mak.* 7:110–18

Shweder RA, Much NC, Mahapatra M, Park L. 1997. The "big three" of morality (autonomy, community, and divinity), and the "big three" explanations of suffering. In *Morality and Health*, ed. A Brandt, P Rozin, pp. 119–69. New York: Routledge

Sibley CG, Bulbulia J. 2012. Faith after an earthquake: a longitudinal study of religion and perceived health before and after the 2011 Christchurch New Zealand earthquake. *PLOS ONE* 7(12):e49648

Smith JZ. 1982. *Imagining Religion: From Babylon to Jonestown*. Chicago: Univ. Chicago Press

Sørensen J. 2007. *A Cognitive Theory of Magic*. Lanham, MD: AltaMira

Sosis R. 2000. Religion and intra-group cooperation: preliminary results of a comparative analysis of utopian communities. *Cross-Cult. Res.* 34:70–87

Sosis R, Alcorta C. 2003. Signaling, solidarity, and the sacred: the evolution of religious behavior. *Evol. Anthropol.* 12:264–74

Sosis R, Ruffle BJ. 2003. Religious ritual and cooperation: testing for a relationship on Israeli religious and secular kibbutzim. *Curr. Anthropol.* 44:713–22

Sperber D. 1996. *Explaining Culture: A Naturalistic Approach*. Oxford, UK: Wiley-Blackwell

Sperber D, Clément F, Heintz C, Mascaro O, Mercier H, et al. 2010. Epistemic vigilance. *Mind Lang.* 25:359–93

Stausberg M. 2010. Prospects in theories of religion. *Method Theory Study Religion* 22:223–28

Swanson GE. 1960. *The Birth of the Gods*. Ann Arbor: Univ. Mich. Press

Taves A. 2009. *Religious Experience Reconsidered: A Building-Block Approach to the Study of Religion and Other Special Things*. Princeton, NJ: Princeton Univ. Press

Taylor C. 2007. *A Secular Age*. Cambridge, MA: Belknap

Tetlock PE. 2003. Thinking about the unthinkable: coping with secular encroachments on sacred values. *Trends Cogn. Sci.* 7:320–24

Tomasello M. 2001. *The Cultural Origins of Human Cognition*. Cambridge, MA: Harvard Univ. Press

Tsai JL, Miao F, Seppala E. 2007. Good feelings in Christianity and Buddhism: religious differences in ideal affect. *Personal. Soc. Psychol. Bull.* 33:409–21

Tylor EB. 1974 (1871). *Primitive Culture: Researches into the Development of Mythology, Philosophy, Religion, Art and Custom*. New York: Gordon

Uhlmann EL, Sanchez-Burks J. 2014. The implicit legacy of American Protestantism. *J. Cross-Cult. Psychol.* 45:991–1005

Vail KE, Arndt J, Abdollahi A. 2012. Exploring the existential function of religion and supernatural agent beliefs among Christians, Muslims, atheists, and agnostics. *Personal. Soc. Psychol. Bull.* 38(10):1288–300

Waytz A, Gray K, Epley N, Wegner DM. 2010. Causes and consequences of mind perception. *Trends Cogn. Sci.* 14:383–88

Whitehouse H. 2004. *Modes of Religiosity: A Cognitive Theory of Religious Transmission*. Walnut Creek, CA: AltaMira

Willard A, Norenzayan A. 2013. Cognitive biases explain religious belief, paranormal belief, and belief in life's purpose. *Cognition* 129:379–91

Wright R. 2009. *The Evolution of God*. New York: Little, Brown & Co.

Xygalatas D, Mitkidis P, Fischer R, Reddish P, Skewes J, et al. 2013. Extreme rituals promote prosociality. *Psychol. Sci.* 24:1602–5

Young MJ, Morris MW, Burrus J, Krishnan L, Regmi MP. 2011. Deity and destiny: patterns of fatalistic thinking in Christian and Hindu cultures. *J. Cross-Cult. Psychol.* 42:1032–55

Zuckerman P. 2007. Atheism: contemporary numbers and patterns. In *The Cambridge Companion to Atheism*, ed. M Martin, pp. 47–65. Cambridge, UK: Cambridge Univ. Press

Materialistic Values and Goals

Tim Kasser

Department of Psychology, Knox College, Galesburg, Illinois 61401; email: tkasser@knox.edu

Annu. Rev. Psychol. 2016. 67:489–514

First published online as a Review in Advance on August 13, 2015

The *Annual Review of Psychology* is online at psych.annualreviews.org

This article's doi: 10.1146/annurev-psych-122414-033344

Keywords

money, well-being, prosocial behavior, consumer psychology, economic psychology

Abstract

Materialism comprises a set of values and goals focused on wealth, possessions, image, and status. These aims are a fundamental aspect of the human value/goal system, standing in relative conflict with aims concerning the well-being of others, as well as one's own personal and spiritual growth. Substantial evidence shows that people who place a relatively high priority on materialistic values/goals consume more products and incur more debt, have lower-quality interpersonal relationships, act in more ecologically destructive ways, have adverse work and educational motivation, and report lower personal and physical well-being. Experimentally activating materialistic aims causes similar outcomes. Given these ills, researchers have investigated means of decreasing people's materialism. Successful interventions encourage intrinsic/self-transcendent values/goals, increase felt personal security, and/or block materialistic messages from the environment. These interventions would likely be more effective if policies were also adopted that diminished contemporary culture's focus on consumption, profit, and economic growth.

Contents

I. MEASUREMENT AND CONCEPTUALIZATION OF MATERIALISM

The exorbitant cornucopia of consumerism that characterizes the twenty-first century may lead some to conclude that materialism is a relatively recent development in human experience. Yet in every historical age and corner of the world, philosophers and religious leaders, economists and politicians, and playwrights and novelists have identified materialism, greed, avarice, and financial self-interest as basic human characteristics. Many have decried a focus on money and possessions in life, claiming that a materialistic outlook undermines deep spirituality, satisfying relationships, and much else that makes life worth living (for a review, see Belk 1983). Others, in contrast, have proposed that economic and social systems that encourage this very human desire hold the most promise for maximizing material wealth (Smith 1776/1976) and individual freedom (Rand 1967).

Despite its prominent place in human experience, the scientific study of materialism long languished on the sidelines in psychology; the scant attention it did receive came primarily from psychodynamic and humanistic/existential theorists (e.g., Fromm 1976). Eventually, in the mid-1980s and early 1990s, consumer researchers and psychologists began conducting quantitative, empirical projects on materialism, developing tools to measure the construct and theories about its nature.

The earliest sophisticated attempt to measure materialism (Belk 1985) conceived of the construct as a trait composed of three facets: possessiveness, nongenerosity, and envy. More recent theoretical statements have proposed that materialism is an aspect of identity (Dittmar 2008, Shrum et al. 2013). Most empirical research on materialism, however, has followed Richins & Dawson (1992) and Kasser & Ryan (1993, 1996) by measuring and conceiving of materialism as a value or goal that reflects the extent to which an individual believes that it is important to acquire money and possessions, as well as to strive for the related aims of an appealing image and high status/popularity, both of which are frequently expressed via money and possessions.[1] Understanding materialism as a value/goal allows researchers to investigate hypotheses about both a person's relatively stable disposition toward materialism (as is shown next and in Section II) and what occurs when materialistic values/goals are momentarily activated in a person's mind (as is shown in Section III).

Probably the most widely used device to assess materialism at a dispositional level is Richins & Dawson's (1992) Material Values Scale (MVS; for a revised, shortened scale, see Richins 2004). The MVS consists of three subscales: the centrality of acquisition to a person's life (e.g., "I like a lot of luxury in my life") and the beliefs that acquisition provides happiness ("I'd be happier if I could afford to buy more things") and signifies success (e.g., "The things I own say a lot about how well I'm doing in life"). Variations on this measure have been used in many studies and have inspired materialism measures for children and adolescents (e.g., Goldberg et al. 2003, Kasser 2005, Opree et al. 2011). Another widely used means of assessing materialistic aims is the Aspiration Index (AI; Kasser & Ryan 1993, 1996), on which participants rate the importance of a variety of goals. Materialism is assessed by calculating the relative centrality (Rokeach 1973) of extrinsic goals for financial success ("I will be financially successful"), image ("My image will be one others find appealing") and popularity ("I will be admired by many people") in comparison to nonmaterialistic goals. Other value- and goal-based approaches in this tradition ask study participants to rank-order guiding principles in life (Kasser & Ryan 1993, 1996) or to rate how well self-generated personal strivings help them progress toward more or less materialistic possible futures (Sheldon & Kasser 1995, 1998).

Value and Goal Systems

Since Rokeach's (1973) publication of *The Nature of Human Values*, most value researchers have agreed that any particular value is part of a larger, dynamic system. Schwartz's (1992) work, conducted in dozens of nations around the world, shows that values are organized in a circular, or "circumplex," fashion, such that every value is consistent with some values, in conflict with other values, and orthogonal to still other values. Thus, if materialism is indeed a value, it should have a predictable place in the human value system.

Burroughs & Rindfleisch (2002) were the first to explore this issue empirically. They administered Schwartz's value survey, along with the MVS and supplemental assessments of religious, family, and community values, to 373 US adults. Multidimensional scaling analyses yielded the results presented in **Figure 1**; values nearby each other are psychologically consistent, those opposite each other are in conflict, and those approximately 90° apart are orthogonal. As predicted, materialism fell within the cluster of self-enhancement values for power and achievement; it was also nearby values for hedonism and stimulation. At the same time, materialism stood in relative conflict with collective or self-transcendent values for religiosity, benevolence, family, community, universalism, and conformity. Such results support the age-old critique that materialism orients people toward superficial satisfactions and conflicts with caring about the broader world, one's family, and/or religious pursuits. Studies in Turkey, Canada, and Germany have yielded parallel findings, particularly regarding the positive association of materialism with self-enhancement values (Karabati & Cemalcilar 2010, Kilbourne et al. 2005).

---

[1]Materialism has another standard meaning in philosophy, i.e., the belief that all of the world can be explained through recourse to tangible matter and objective laws. The current review does not consider this form of materialism, nor does it focus on the distinction between "having" and "being" (Van Boven & Gilovich 2003), a conceptualization focused on how one chooses to spend one's money rather than on the desire for money and possessions per se.

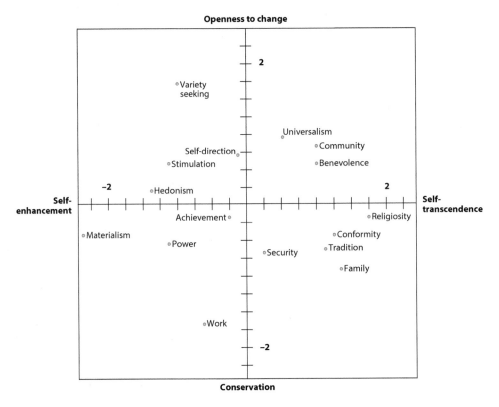

Figure 1

Results of multidimensional scaling analyses representing the relative compatibility and conflict of materialism with other values in the Schwartz value model and with additional values for community, family, and religiosity (from Burroughs & Rindfleisch 2002). Adapted with permission from the University of Chicago Press, ©2002 by *Journal of Consumer Research*.

Grouzet et al. (2005) reported similar findings when 1,854 undergraduates from 15 cultures rated the importance of goals on the AI. **Figure 2** shows the results of circular stochastic modeling analyses conducted on these data. The extrinsic goals of financial success, image, and popularity clustered tightly together in all 15 samples assessed; financial success was also relatively compatible with hedonism, as Burroughs & Rindfleisch (2002) reported. Also consistent with previous findings, the importance placed on these three extrinsic goals stood in relative opposition to community, affiliation, and self-acceptance goals; financial success was also in relative conflict with spirituality goals. One advantage of the circular stochastic modeling procedure Grouzet et al. used is that it provides point estimates reflecting (in this case) where on the circumference of a circle a particular value lies relative to other values; the more consistent two values are, the more similar are their respective point estimates, whereas the more in conflict two values are, the closer to 180° apart are their point estimates. The point estimates of Grouzet et al. (2005) showed, for example, that financial success goals are 33° from image and 46° from hedonism but 192° opposed to community feeling and 143° opposed to spirituality. Such results again corroborate the long-standing notion that a life focused around money is relatively compatible with pursuing one's image and sensual pleasure but relatively difficult to reconcile with being generous and focused on a spiritual life.

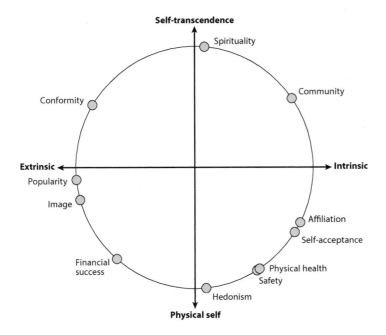

Figure 2

Results of circular stochastic modeling analyses representing the relative compatibility of extrinsic, materialistic goals for financial success, image, and popularity and their relative compatibility and conflict with other goals (from Grouzet et al. 2005). Adapted with permission from the American Psychological Association.

Future Research

Researchers use many materialism measures besides the MVS and the AI, and although diversity of measurement has advantages, many studies use single-item measures or measures with unknown or questionable psychometric properties. A systematic and critical empirical review of materialism measures would help determine which have the strongest psychometric properties; further work on the MVS may also be warranted, as its purported three-factor structure does not always emerge (e.g., Richins & Chaplin 2015). More research is also needed to understand if the meaning of materialism changes across cultures. Consider for example that Grouzet et al.'s (2005) point estimates suggested that financial success is somewhat more compatible with image aspirations in wealthier (27°) than poorer (48°) nations, but somewhat more compatible with safety aspirations in poorer (49°) than in wealthier (71°) nations. Thus, in wealthy nations, financial success aspirations are colored more by the style of one's clothes and handbags, whereas the same goals are more closely tied to survival in poorer nations. Further research is necessary to explore more fully such differences, as well as others that might emerge from cross-cultural research.

Researchers' over-reliance on self-report scales is another major limitation of the literature. Given that social desirability biases may influence self-reporting of materialism (Mick 1996, Solberg et al. 2004), researchers could use and improve upon the implicit methods that exist to measure materialism (Chaplin & John 2007, Schmuck 2001, Solberg et al. 2004). Methods could also be developed to assess the presence of materialistic values in natural language, newspaper articles, politicians' speeches, advertising messages, etc.

Finally, work is needed to explore further materialism's relationship to other values, to traits, and to identity. Although materialism's place in the human value/goal system seems fairly stable, some discrepancies between **Figures 1** and **2** are notable (i.e., materialism's relationship to conformity and to self-direction/self-acceptance values). In addition, given that materialism has been conceived as a trait (Belk 1985), that trait and value/goal measures of materialism correlate positively (see Kasser & Ahuvia 2002), and that materialism is consistently negatively correlated with agreeableness and openness to experience (e.g., Otero-López & Villardefrancos 2013, Roberts & Robins 2000), more work is needed to determine the interrelationships between these conceptualizations of the construct. Further, if materialism is an aspect of identity (Shrum et al. 2013), narrative, psychobiographical, and single-case methods might prove useful.

II. CORRELATES OF DISPOSITIONAL MATERIALISM

If materialism is a value/goal with a particular set of relations to other aims in the human value/goal system, then the pattern of materialism's relationships to other psychological constructs should depend on whether materialism is compatible or in conflict with those other constructs [see, e.g., Schwartz's (1992) discussion of sinusoidal patterns]. Specifically, materialism should correlate positively with experiences, attitudes, and behaviors relevant to amassing wealth and possessions, to being concerned about image and popularity, and to pursuing hedonistic pleasures, as these aims are relatively consistent with materialistic values and goals (see **Figures 1** and **2**). At the same time, materialism should correlate negatively with experiences, attitudes, and behaviors relevant to prosocial, community, and other self-transcendent concerns, and, perhaps to a lesser extent, with personal growth/self-acceptance strivings, as these aims stand in relative conflict with materialistic pursuits.

The literature reviewed below on the correlates of dispositional materialism provides substantial support for these general claims.

Financial and Consumption Attitudes and Behaviors

Hypotheses derived from the circumplex models suggest that the priority people place on materialism should be positively associated with consuming at high rates, particularly when consuming might help build status and an image that others will applaud. Indeed, compared to individuals who do not care much about materialistic values/goals, individuals who prioritize materialistic values/goals are rather "loose" with their money, as they have worse money management skills (Donnelly et al. 2012, 2013) and more gambling problems (Carver & McCarty 2013); they also endorse attitudes and engage in behaviors that are less thrifty and create more debt (Richins 2011, Watson 2003). A recent meta-analysis (Dittmar et al. 2014) also showed relatively strong positive associations between materialism and compulsive consumption problems (see **Figure 3**), suggesting that materialism is associated with difficulty holding back one's desires to buy stuff.

Dispositional materialism is also positively associated with consumption-relevant behaviors and attitudes that are flavored by hedonism, image, and status values. For instance, Dittmar et al.'s (2014) meta-analysis revealed that materialism scores were positively correlated with engaging in risky health behaviors (see **Figure 3**); such behaviors not only often involve consumption (of cigarettes, alcohol, etc.) but also often have strong hedonistic components. Likewise, materialism is positively associated with attitudes and behaviors relevant to image, including strong concerns for fashion and clothing (Kamal et al. 2013, Workman & Lee 2011), and positive attitudes toward, and intentions to get, cosmetic surgery (Henderson-King & Brooks 2009). Status concerns are also notable in the motives of people scoring high in materialism, as such individuals typically report wanting to make money for reasons such as to have a house and cars that are better than those of their neighbors (Srivastava et al. 2001).

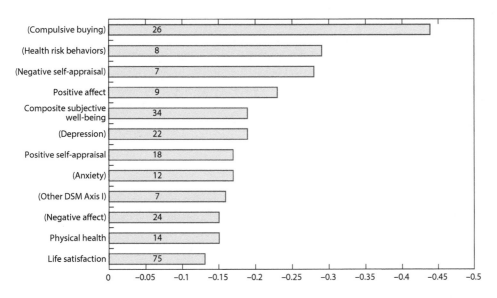

Figure 3

Summary of meta-analytic findings representing the strength of relationships between materialism and various types of well-being (based on table 6 of Dittmar et al. 2014). Note: All forms of well-being in this figure are coded so that a negative correlation indicates that lower well-being is associated with higher materialism; types of well-being that have been reverse coded are in parentheses. Measures that assess materialist values and beliefs (e.g., the Material Values Scale) were used as the reference category for comparing the sizes of these different correlations, and the correlations are based on analyses in which the type of materialism measure was also entered as a factor. The number of samples used to calculate the strength of each relationship (i.e., the k) is indicated by the number within its respective bar. Abbreviation: DSM, *Diagnostic and Statistical Manual of Mental Disorders*.

Social Attitudes and Behaviors

Because materialistic aims stand in relative conflict with values/goals for benevolence, family, affiliation, and community (see **Figures 1** and **2**), hypotheses derived from the circumplex models would suggest that materialism is associated with more interpersonal problems and with negative social attitudes toward other people. Indeed, compared to those low in materialism, people high in materialism often get caught in vicious cycles of loneliness (Pieters 2013), have an anxious attachment style (Norris et al. 2012), and have more difficulty balancing family and work commitments (Promisio et al. 2010). Further, materialism is associated with shorter (Kasser & Ryan 2001) and lower-quality interpersonal relationships (as rated by their friends and family; Solberg et al. 2004). Carroll et al.'s (2011) study investigating the materialism of married couples found that, despite the benefits one might assume would result from sharing similar values, couples who both scored high in materialism reported lower marital quality than did couples with only one materialistic partner; couples who were both low in materialism reported the highest levels of marital quality.

Materialism is also associated with treating other people in more self-serving ways. For example, compared to those low in materialism, those high in materialism score lower in empathy (Sheldon & Kasser 1995) and score higher in narcissism (Kasser & Ryan 1996), Machiavellianism (McHoskey 1999), and the affective and interpersonal aspects of psychopathy (Foulkes et al. 2014). They also engage in fewer prosocial behaviors (such as volunteering and helping others; Briggs et al. 2007, Sheldon & Kasser 1995) and more antisocial behaviors (Cohen & Cohen 1996, Kasser

& Ryan 1993, McHoskey 1999). In business settings, materialism is negatively correlated with caring about corporate social responsibility (Kolodinsky et al. 2010) and positively correlated with interpersonally deviant workplace behaviors (Deckop et al. 2015). Materialism scores also predict more competitive (and less cooperative) behavior in the Prisoner's Dilemma Game, even when playing with friends (Sheldon et al. 2000). Finally, people high in materialism have a stronger social dominance orientation, hold more prejudicial beliefs about out-group members (Duriez et al. 2007), and are less concerned about the egalitarian aspects of democracy (Flanagan et al. 2005) compared to people low in materialism.

Ecological Attitudes and Behaviors

Because concerns about the health of our planet are reflected in self-transcendent values/goals for universalism and community feeling, hypotheses derived from the circumplex models in **Figures 1** and **2** suggest that materialism should be associated with caring less about ecological sustainability. As predicted, people who strongly endorse materialistic values/goals engage in fewer environmentally beneficial behaviors and have higher ecological footprints (Brown & Kasser 2005, Richins & Dawson 1992) than those who place a low priority on materialism; they also behave more greedily and less sustainably in forest management dilemma games (Sheldon & McGregor 2000). Hurst et al.'s (2013) recent meta-analysis of this literature found modest but consistent negative associations between materialism and both ecological attitudes ($r = -0.22$ across eight studies) and behaviors ($r = -0.24$ across nine studies).

Educational and Job Motivation

Researchers have also explored how materialism predicts motivational outcomes in work and educational settings. Given that money can increase how much people engage in particular behaviors (although not necessarily the quality of that engagement; Jenkins et al. 1998), and given that materialistic values are consistent with the achievement values frequently encouraged in work and educational settings (see **Figures 1** and **2**), materialism might be positively associated with work and educational outcomes. On the other hand, because external rewards such as money and grades typically undermine intrinsic motivation (Deci et al. 1999), and because intrinsic motivations are reflected in the self-direction and self-acceptance goals that conflict somewhat with materialistic goals (see **Figure 2** in particular), a materialistic focus might be negatively associated with motivation in work and educational domains. The latter hypothesis has more support at present. When employees strongly endorse materialistic values/goals, they report more burnout as well as lower job and career satisfaction (Deckop et al. 2010, Vansteenkiste et al. 2007a). Further, compared to those who do not much care about materialism, children who prioritize materialistic aims report higher performance goals and lower mastery goals for their schoolwork, reflecting an orientation toward extrinsic rather than intrinsic motives for learning; they also have worse learning outcomes (Ku et al. 2012, 2014).

Personal Well-Being

Since the publication of the earliest studies showing that materialism is negatively associated with personal well-being (Belk 1985; Cohen & Cohen 1996; Kasser & Ryan 1993, 1996; Richins & Dawson 1992), and since Kasser's (2002a) review of that literature, dozens more empirical investigations have replicated this finding. Dittmar et al. (2014) recently reported a comprehensive meta-analysis of this literature, examining 749 effects from 258 independent samples (many unpublished) covering all parts of the populated world. A modest negative correlation ($r = -0.15$, 95% CI: -0.18 to -0.13) was found between materialism and well-being, but additional analyses showed that the size of this association depended on the ways that materialism and well-being were each measured. Regarding materialism measures, correlations were generally stronger for multidimensional scales (such as the MVS and the AI) that assessed the full array of materialistic aims than for single-item scales or scales focused solely on money. Regarding well-being, as can be seen in **Figure 3**, materialism had consistent, negative associations with a wide array of well-being measures (including risky behaviors, self-image, affect, and both subjective and physical well-being), with the size of these effects varying from $r = -0.44$ to $r = -0.13$.

The conclusions drawn from these types of cross-sectional studies are complemented by studies that have used longitudinal and national time-series designs. Over time frames ranging from 6 months to 12 years, college students, emerging adults, and adults who reduced the priority they placed on materialism reported increases in well-being (Hope et al. 2014, Kasser et al. 2014). Nation-level studies conducted in Norway (Hellevik 2003) and the United States (Twenge et al. 2010) also found that increases over time in national levels of citizens' materialism correlated with decreases over time in national levels of citizens' well-being.

Attempts to understand when and why materialism correlates negatively with well-being have spawned several theories and empirical investigations. Space limitations preclude a full overview here, but Dittmar et al.'s (2014) meta-analysis did explore numerous potential moderators and mediators of this relationship.

In terms of moderators, Dittmar et al. (2014) found that the negative associations between materialism and well-being were generally robust across study, sample, and cultural characteristics, with only 7 of the 25 moderators examined yielding significant effects. Even in cases where significant moderation was revealed, the results showed that the negative relationship between materialism and well-being weakened rather than disappeared. For example, materialism had a somewhat weak, but still significantly negative, relationship with well-being (*a*) in samples that were relatively young, had many males, and were composed of many students and practitioners of business and law; and (*b*) in nations that were more economically unequal, had faster economic growth, and deprioritized cultural values for enjoyment and pleasure. Dittmar et al. (2014) interpreted the overall pattern of moderation findings as providing little support for (*a*) an environmental congruence hypothesis claiming that materialism does not hurt well-being if people work or live in contexts that support materialistic values (see Kasser & Ahuvia 2002, Vansteenkiste et al. 2006) and (*b*) a goal-attainment hypothesis claiming that materialism does not hurt well-being if people succeed in their materialistic goals (see Martos & Kopp 2012, Niemiec et al. 2009; although see Nickerson et al. 2003 for mixed results).

In terms of the mediation of the relationship between materialism and well-being, Dittmar et al. (2014) tested two theories. No support was found for the hypothesis that materialism causes dissatisfaction with one's financial life that, in turn, causes decreases in general well-being (although see Sirgy et al. 2012). Support was forthcoming for the explanation derived from self-determination theory (Deci & Ryan 2000, Kasser 2002a) that when people prioritize materialistic values/goals, they experience relatively low satisfaction of psychological needs for autonomy (feeling free), competence (feeling efficacious), and relatedness (feeling connected). This low level of need satisfaction, in turn, leads to low levels of well-being (see Ryan & Deci 2001).

This need-based explanation is quite consistent with hypotheses derived from the circumplex models in **Figures 1** and **2**. The intrinsic goals for self-acceptance, affiliation, and community feeling that are represented in the eastern portion of **Figure 2** have long been described as those whose pursuit helps satisfy these three psychological needs (Kasser & Ryan 1996). Thus, as materialism becomes more important to individuals, intrinsic goals either are "crowded out" [to use

Frey & Oberholzer-Gee's (1997) wonderful phrase], leading people to deprioritize such aims in life, or are experienced as being in conflict with materialistic pursuits (Burroughs & Rindfleisch 2002). Either way, lower need satisfaction would result as the quality of one's interpersonal relations declines, as one spends less time pursuing "something bigger" than one's self, and as one's motives are increasingly driven by status and rewards rather than freedom and interest (for further discussion, see Kasser 2002a).

Future Research

Although the data reviewed in this section suggest that researchers can be confident that materialism is detrimental for people's financial and consumption behavior, interpersonal relationships, treatment of our planet, work and educational motivation, and personal well-being, the processes underlying many of these associations remain unclear. As just discussed, there is growing support for a need-based explanation of the negative relationship between materialism and well-being. Further, investigators have started to explore the pathways through which materialism is positively correlated with compulsive consumption (e.g., Donnelly et al. 2013, Richins 2011). That said, the relationship between materialism and many of the other variables discussed above requires substantial further investigation to clarify the mechanisms involved. Particularly vexing is the question of why people persist at materialistic values/goals when such pursuits are associated with personally unhelpful outcomes. As discussed in Section IV, experiences of insecurity/threat and ongoing modeling of materialism each lead people to prioritize materialism; do they also explain why people maintain a value/goal orientation that yields little long-term satisfaction?

Improvements in study designs are also warranted. Many of the studies reviewed above assess outcomes with retrospective self-report surveys. More compelling designs would utilize diary reports of objective behaviors, reports of peers, and/or observations of study participants in the laboratory or in natural settings; such methods could be applied to many of the types of behaviors discussed above (i.e., financial, ecological, educational, etc.). Greater variety in the types of samples utilized is also needed. Although some studies have investigated materialism in children and in less economically developed nations, such studies are underrepresented in the literature. More studies that use prospective and longitudinal designs would be useful, as would studies with experimental designs. Indeed, as discussed in Section III, experiments that momentarily activate materialistic values/goals hold substantial promise for better understanding dynamics relevant to these aims, as do experiments that test interventions to reduce materialism (see Section IV).

III. THE MOMENTARY ACTIVATION OF MATERIALISM

Although most research on materialism has operationalized the construct as a dispositional, individual-difference variable, a fundamental theoretical assumption underlying the circumplex models presented in **Figures 1** and **2** is that each of these values/goals is present, at least to some extent, in all people, because they represent fundamental motivations basic to all humans (Grouzet et al. 2005, Schwartz 1992). As such, even though a particular person may not place a high priority on a particular aim (such as materialism) at a dispositional level, that aim is nonetheless present within his/her psyche. If this is true, then that aim can be momentarily activated and should influence that individual's behavior soon after activation.

Maio et al. (2009) took this idea a step further by arguing that if a particular value/goal is activated at a moment in time, the circumplex arrangement of values/goals suggests that two predictable sets of effects should ensue. First, activation of a value/goal should increase behaviors and attitudes that reflect the values/goals that are consistent with the activated value/goal; this can be called a bleed-over effect. Second, activation of a value/goal should suppress behaviors and attitudes that reflect the values/goals that are in conflict with the activated value/goal; this can be called a seesaw effect. Applied to **Figure 2**, this argument suggests that momentary activation of financial success goals should (at least temporarily) increase people's attitudes and behaviors relevant to the acquisition of not only money and possessions, but also image, popularity, and hedonism goals, as these goals are compatible with financial success aims. At the same time, the activation of financial success goals should suppress people's valuing of the intrinsic goals that lie on the opposite side of the circumplex, thereby decreasing people's focus on community feeling, affiliation, and self-acceptance.

A small but growing body of experimental studies supports these hypotheses, yielding many findings that parallel those reported above for studies of dispositional materialism.

Overview of Activation Findings

Several studies have supported the bleed-over effect by using experimental manipulations that activate materialism in ways that many people encounter in their day-to-day lives. For instance, viewing movies (e.g., *Wall Street*) and advertisements with materialistic themes increases materialistic and appearance-related concerns (Ashikali & Dittmar 2012, Shrum et al. 2011), relative to viewing control stimuli. Being referred to as a "consumer" rather than a "citizen" causes study participants to have more positive implicit evaluations of the self-enhancing values with which materialism is consistent (Bauer et al. 2012). Thinking of one's own time (versus another person's time) in terms of money leads people to report that economic criteria are particularly important in their decision-making (Pfeffer & Devoe 2009). And viewing faint (versus blurred) images of $100 bills increases people's endorsement of free-market economic systems (Caruso et al. 2013). Each of these studies supports the proposition that a materialistic prime causes a shift toward greater concern with topics, values, self-concepts, and economic systems that reflect the values/goals that **Figures 1** and **2** suggest are compatible with materialistic concerns.

The kinds of seesaw effects that Maio et al.'s (2009) logic predicts are also notable in the activation literature, particularly for outcomes that reflect the prosocial behaviors and attitudes reflected in universalism values and community feeling goals. For instance, after being primed with materialistic (versus control) images or thoughts, people report a higher social dominance orientation (Caruso et al. 2013) and behave more selfishly in community (Frey & Oberholzer-Gee 1997) and environmentally relevant (Bauer et al. 2012) resource dilemmas. Several studies also show that momentarily activating materialism (versus other topics) causes people to be less likely to help others and to donate money (Roberts & Roberts 2012, Vohs et al. 2006, Wierzbicki & Zawadzka 2014). Such results occur even in children as young as 5 years old (Gasiorowska et al. 2012) and may be due to the belief that money issues should play a key role in one's decisions (Pfeffer & Devoe 2009).

Interpersonal behaviors are also suppressed by the activation of materialism. Vohs et al. (2006) reported a series of studies demonstrating that exposure to materialistic (versus neutral) primes causes people to prefer to be self-sufficient and to distance themselves from others. And in one telling study (Goldberg & Gorn 1978), 4- and 5-year-old children who watched a program with two commercials for a particular toy (versus no commercials) later chose to play with the toy by themselves rather than with their friends in a sandbox.

Motivation for academic behavior is also affected by activating materialistic values/goals. Framing a task as concerning extrinsic (rather than intrinsic) goals caused decreased depth of processing, persistence, and performance (Vansteenkiste et al. 2004). Similarly, Chinese students shifted toward a performance orientation (and away from a mastery orientation) after a materialistic (versus no) prime, and British students gave up more quickly on a puzzle after a materialistic (versus affiliative) prime (Ku et al. 2014).

Some evidence also suggests that materialistic primes affect well-being outcomes. For instance, priming extrinsic (versus intrinsic) values decreases motivation to engage in the health-promoting behavior of exercise (Vansteenkiste et al. 2007b). Although Solberg et al. (2004) did not find immediate effects on well-being after materialistic primes, Bauer et al. (2012) reported that viewing advertisements of luxury consumer goods (versus neutral images) caused increases in negative affect. Further, thinking about one's time as money (versus control procedures) caused increased feelings of impatience, decreased happiness from leisure-time activities on the Internet, and decreased pleasure from listening to a song (Devoe & House 2012).

Future Research

The literature on the momentary activation of materialistic values/goals is clearly in its infancy, but its importance should not be underestimated. First, using many of the same types of outcomes that have been studied in correlational research, these findings provide some experimental evidence pointing to the possibility that a focus on materialistic values causes some of the same deleterious outcomes reviewed in Section II. Second, taken as a group, these studies provide further evidence that materialism is a value/goal with a predictable set of relations to other values/goals in the human motivational system. Without the kinds of predictions derived from the models in **Figures 1** and **2**, and from Maio et al.'s (2009) theoretical insights, the studies reviewed above could seem like a miscellany of unrelated findings. But by understanding materialism's relative place in the value/goal system, it becomes sensible that the momentary activation of materialism not only increases concerns for money, image, and status, but also suppresses prosocial and proenvironmental behavior, interpersonal connections, educational motivation, and personal well-being.

As research unfolds in the years to come, a few issues are worthy of consideration. First, might the well-known undermining effect of intrinsic motivation by financial and other extrinsic rewards (Deci et al. 1999) be understood from a value/goal conflict perspective? Perhaps rewards momentarily activate the materialistic values/goals in the western portions of **Figures 1** and **2**, thereby suppressing the kinds of intrinsic motivations represented in self-direction and self-acceptance pursuits. Second, although there are a few inklings of the mediational processes involved when materialistic values/goals are momentarily activated (e.g., Pfeffer & DeVoe 2009), substantially more work is required to understand exactly how activation causes bleed-over and seesaw effects. Third, in life outside of the laboratory, people rarely experience only a single exposure to any particular set of stimuli, much less to the materialistic stimuli so common in consumer culture. As such, more externally valid designs would explore the effects of frequent exposures to materialistic stimuli (both in and out of focal awareness).

A final, crucial methodological issue concerns the use of control groups that are neutral with regard to values/goals. Some experimental studies have compared behaviors or attitudes of people exposed to a materialistic prime with people exposed to a prime that might have momentarily activated some other value/goal, such as community feeling or spirituality. Although such designs are appropriate when researchers are interested in studying the overall dynamics of the value/goal system, they make it difficult, if not impossible, to know conclusively what effects drove the observed results. For example, imagine a study in which the experimental group is primed with stimuli relevant to materialistic values/goals and the control group is primed with stimuli relevant to universalism values/goals. If the group primed with materialistic stimuli donates less to charity than does the control group, this effect could be due to materialism's suppression of prosocial behaviors (i.e., a seesaw effect), to universalism's activation of prosocial behaviors (i.e., a bleed-over effect), or to both effects working together. Thus, when researchers want to isolate materialism's effects, a control group that is neutral with regard to values/goals should be included in the study design.

IV. WAYS TO DECREASE MATERIALISM

The literature reviewed thus far suggests that a variety of detrimental outcomes are associated with, and perhaps caused by, a relatively high prioritization of materialistic values/goals. Although both the historical record and the theoretical assumptions underlying the circumplex models of values/goals suggest that materialistic values will probably never be excised from the human psyche, it is possible that people could focus less on materialistic pursuits. How, then, to decrease materialism?

Overview of Materialism-Reduction Strategies

Crompton & Kasser (2009) and Kasser (2011a,b) presented three sets of strategies to decrease materialistic, extrinsic values/goals. These strategies are not only supported by empirical and theoretical work, but are also flexible enough to be applied at many levels, ranging from therapeutic and community interventions to broader policies and practices.

The first set of strategies involves activating and encouraging the values/goals that stand in relative opposition to materialistic values/goals. As reviewed above, when people focus on materialistic values/goals, they tend to deprioritize behaviors and attitudes associated with the intrinsic and self-transcendent values/goals on the opposite side of the value/goal circumplex (see **Figures 1** and **2**). But the converse is also true: To the extent people prioritize intrinsic and self-transcendent values/goals for community, for connection with others, and for their own personal growth, they tend to place less priority on materialistic values/goals. As such, interventions and policies that activate and encourage intrinsic and self-transcendent aims not only should support the attitudes and behaviors consistent with those healthier aims (i.e., the bleed-over effect), but should also reap the additional benefit of suppressing materialistic values/goals (i.e., the seesaw effect).

A second set of strategies involves attempts to reduce the extent to which people are exposed to and affected by messages in their social surroundings suggesting that money, possessions, status, and image are important values/goals to pursue. Numerous studies show that exposure to materialistic messages causes people to prioritize these values/goals. For instance, individuals report relatively high materialism scores when their parents espouse materialistic values (Goldberg et al. 2003, Kasser et al. 1995) or engage in materialistic parenting practices (Richins & Chaplin 2015), when they experience peer pressure concerning materialism (Banerjee & Dittmar 2008), and when they were raised in an overall materialistic milieu (Ahuvia & Wong 2002). Materialistic values are also relatively high when students pursue academic topics that encourage materialistic values (Sheldon & Krieger 2004) and when people live in wealthy neighborhoods that model materialistic values (Zhang et al. 2014). Television use is also positively correlated with materialism (Good 2007, Nairn et al. 2007, Schor 2004, Sirgy et al. 1998); indeed, longitudinal (Opree et al. 2014), quasi-experimental (Brand & Greenberg 1994), and experimental (Shrum et al. 2011) studies all support the conclusion that exposure to materialistic (versus non-materialistic) messages through this medium can cause increases in materialism. At a broader societal level, increases in the materialism of American youth from 1976–2007 (of the sort represented in **Figure 4**) are predicted by increases in the percentage of the US Gross Domestic Product that was due to advertising expenditures (Twenge & Kasser 2013). Finally, when people live under capitalistic economic systems that are more competitive, deregulated, and free-market oriented (versus more

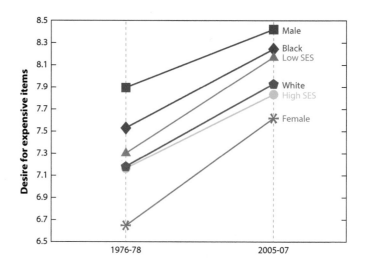

Figure 4

Increases in the desire of US youths for expensive items from 1976–78 to 2005–07, across socioeconomic status (SES), gender, and race (from Twenge & Kasser 2013). Adapted with permission from Sage Publications.

regulated and cooperative), they more strongly endorse materialistic and self-enhancing values for money, power, status, and the like (see Kasser 2011c, Kasser et al. 2007, Kilbourne et al. 2009, Schwartz 2007). Materialism can therefore be decreased by removing materialistic messages from the environment, by reducing people's exposure to those messages, and/or by providing people with strategies to diminish the effect of those messages when they are encountered.

A third set of strategies involves helping people to feel less insecure, threatened, and worried about their ability to satisfy their physical and psychological needs. Multiple types of data show that threat and insecurity cause people to place a relatively high priority on materialistic values/goals. For instance, high levels of materialism are associated with experiential avoidance (Kashdan & Breen 2007), motivations and self-presentational strategies designed to overcome feelings of incompetence and insecurity (Christopher et al. 2005, Christopher & Schlenker 2004, Srivastava et al. 2001), and dreams of falling and death (Kasser & Grow Kasser 2001). Materialistic values, goals, and behaviors increase as a result of threat-inducing experimental manipulations involving hunger (Briers et al. 2006), uncertainty (Chang & Arkin 2002), social exclusion (Twenge et al. 2007), physical pain (Zhou et al. 2009), thoughts of death (Kasser & Sheldon 2000), and concerns about economic insecurity (Sheldon & Kasser 2008). People with family histories characterized by cold, inconsistent, and/or controlling parental styles, by parental divorce, by food insecurity, and by economic stress also place a relatively high priority on materialistic values [Allen & Wilson 2005, Cohen & Cohen 1996, Kasser et al. 1995, Richins & Chaplin 2015, Rindfleisch et al. 1997; see also the life history methods advocated by Moschis 2007 and used in numerous studies (e.g., Nguyen et al. 2009)]. Materialism is also increased by threats induced at broader societal levels, including recent political and economic turmoil (Ger & Belk 1996) and economic stress, instability, and disconnection (Abramson & Inglehart 1995, Twenge & Kasser 2013). If these threats can be reduced, or if people can learn to respond to these threats differently, materialism should decline.

In sum, efforts to decrease materialism should be successful to the extent that they activate and encourage intrinsic and self-transcendent values/goals, reduce exposure (or the effects of exposure) to societal models of materialistic values, and/or increase a sense of felt security and safety. The next section discusses some of the interventions that have been shown to reduce materialism and explains how their effectiveness can be understood as consistent with these strategies. Some broader policies that could utilize these strategies are then briefly mentioned.

Interventions to Decrease Materialism

Several studies have directly shown that when people are led to focus on intrinsic and self-transcendent values/goals, they shift away from materialistic values. For example, Weinstein et al. (2009) conducted four laboratory studies in which participants reported their aspirations after being exposed to scenes or objects that either reflected nature (thereby activating a self-transcendent value) or scenes or objects that were human-made. To the extent people became immersed in the nature stimuli, they deprioritized extrinsic aspirations and increased the value they placed on intrinsic aspirations. Environmental norms also mitigate the tendency to behave in more materialistic and greedy ways after thinking about one's own death (Fritsche et al. 2010). Similar results occur when spiritual or religious values are activated. For instance, recalling a spiritual event decreases materialistic desires (Stillman et al. 2012), and reading an essay that reviews evidence supporting the existence of the afterlife decreases people's greedy behaviors after thinking about death (Dechesne et al. 2003). Lekes et al. (2012) conducted one of the more ambitious studies examining the potential benefits of activating intrinsic values. Undergraduates selected their two most important intrinsic values and then wrote brief essays about the importance of these values in their lives. Doing so led to immediate increases in well-being compared to the control group members, who focused on everyday topics such as cooking dinner. Over the next month, participants in the experimental group were sent weekly emails reminding them of their chosen intrinsic values, providing them with quotes expressive of intrinsic values, and inviting them to reflect on their intrinsic values; subjects in the control group received parallel emails. Participants in the intrinsic reflection group who reported deep engagement with the exercises shifted toward intrinsic and away from extrinsic aspirations, with consequent benefits for their well-being; engagement in the control exercises yielded no such changes.

Interventions that improve people's feelings of security also cause decreases in materialism. For instance, adolescents whose self-esteem was temporarily boosted became less materialistic soon afterward (Chaplin & John 2007). Similarly, thinking about high-quality interpersonal relationships shifts people away from materialistic, extrinsic goals (Clark et al. 2011, Sheldon & Kasser 2008); nostalgic recollections also decrease people's attachment to money, apparently because such recollections typically involve memories of positive interpersonal activities (Lasaleta et al. 2014). Having the opportunity to deeply consider one's own death also reduces materialism. In contrast to the effects that typically occur when people undergo a standard mortality salience manipulation (Arndt et al. 2004), when people reflect on their own death in a deep, involved manner (Cozzolino et al. 2004) or on a daily basis (Lykins et al. 2007), they shift away from extrinsic, materialistic values and toward more intrinsic values. The fact that similar shifts occur after near-death experiences (Ring 1984) and as a result of posttraumatic growth (Tedeschi & Calhoun 2004) suggests that deep consideration of one's own death may impel people to view their lives in ways that lead them to reject materialistic values/goals.

Indeed, inward reflection in and of itself shifts people away from materialistic values/goals. For example, merely reconsidering one's ratings on the AI causes people to less strongly prioritize extrinsic goals and more strongly prioritize intrinsic goals (Sheldon et al. 2003). Gratitude reflections also produce declines in materialistic values/goals (Lambert et al. 2009). Further, when individuals who participated in a meditation program became more mindful, they also reported smaller gaps between their current and desired financial situation; this, in turn, benefitted their well-being (Brown et al. 2009).

Interventions with adults can also help children become less susceptible to consumer culture's influences. Children's materialistic values are less affected by exposure to advertising when their parents use an active style that critiques commercials and when they involve their children in discussions about family consumption decisions (Buijzen & Valkenburg 2005). Experimental evidence also shows that when adults make factual (e.g., "Those commercials are intended to sell") or evaluative ("These commercials are stupid") comments while watching advertisements with children, the children report more negative attitudes toward the commercials, with consequent reductions in their expressed desire for the product advertised (Buijzen 2007). Kasser et al. (2014) combined these techniques with other materialism-reduction strategies in an in-depth intervention with adolescents and their parents. Participants were randomly assigned either to a no-treatment control group or to an established financial planning program that met for three, 3-hour group sessions. The program critiqued consumer culture and attempted to decrease the influence of its messages (via discussions of the power and purpose of advertising); it also attempted to activate intrinsic values by encouraging value reflection, by facilitating discussions about the importance of sharing one's money (i.e., universalism and community values/goals), and by helping participants develop value-based plans for their money. Materialism was measured before the intervention and again ~2 months and ~10 months after it ended. Latent growth curve analyses showed that, compared to adolescents in the control group, those in the intervention group decreased in materialism over time, a trend still evident ~10 months after the intervention ended. What's more, those adolescents who began the study high in materialism and who received the intervention showed sustained increases in self-esteem over time, whereas their counterparts in the control group experienced decreases in self-esteem.

Future research. Although support is accumulating for the materialism-reduction strategies articulated in this section, the studies reviewed above suffer from numerous weaknesses. First, most involved brief, one-off interventions, with only a handful (Brown et al. 2009, Kasser et al. 2014, Lekes et al. 2012) endeavoring to implement interventions that might lead to sustained changes in materialism; more studies of this latter type are needed. Second, most of the interventions have been conducted with samples that are rather financially privileged. Would these interventions be effective among individuals who are experiencing substantially more economic stress? Third, the exact processes responsible for the beneficial effects of some interventions remain unknown. For example, why do the various reflection interventions lead people to orient away from materialism? Does reflection diminish feelings of insecurity in the same way that mindfulness helps decrease the experiential avoidance (Hayes et al. 2012) known to be associated with materialism (Kashdan & Breen 2007)? Does reflection help people orient their lives around an organismic valuing process that recognizes how well intrinsic and self-transcendent values/goals succeed in promoting health and well-being (see Kasser 2002b, Sheldon et al. 2003)? Understanding such mediational processes could lead to the development of even more effective interventions.

Policies to Decrease Materialism

The evidence reviewed above suggests that materialistic values/goals can become less important when people orient their lives around intrinsic and self-transcendent values/goals, try to shield themselves (and their children) from the messages of consumer culture, and/or engage in activities that help increase felt security. Ultimately, however, individual-level attempts to orient away from

Table 1 Policy proposals to diminish materialism and their relevance to materialism-reduction strategies

Policy proposal	Relevance to strategies
Replace or supplement existing measures of progress that are primarily economic (e.g., Gross National Product, consumer confidence) with alternative measures (e.g., Gross National Happiness Index, Well-Being Index, and Human Development Index). Such measures can be used at national, regional, or local levels (as is already the case in Bhutan and the US city of Seattle)	Would diminish the modeling of materialistic values/goals by governments and encourage pursuit of intrinsic/self-transcendent values/goals; might also promote felt security if progress on alternative measures improves
Repeal existing tax deductions for business advertising expenses; instead, tax advertising and marketing expenses at a 10% "value pollution" rate, using the resulting revenue to fund programs that promote intrinsic/self-transcendent values/goals and felt security	Would penalize efforts to promote materialistic values/goals, thereby potentially diminishing their presence in the environment; if revenue were used for the proposed purpose, would encourage intrinsic/self-transcendent values/goals and promote felt security
Ban advertisements in schools, on school buses, and in learning materials	Would diminish modeling of materialistic values/goals
Remove advertising from public spaces (as has been done in São Paulo, Brazil and Grenoble, France)	Would diminish modeling of materialistic values/goals
Ban advertising targeted at children (as has been done in Brazil, Sweden, Norway, and Quebec, and as is being recommended by the United Nations Special Rapporteur on Cultural Rights)	Would diminish modeling of materialistic values/goals; might promote felt security of children (who would no longer be manipulated by advertisers)
Empower localities so they can refuse to allow certain corporations to operate in their areas	Would diminish the power of purveyors of materialistic values/goals; might promote felt security
Pass amendments that differentiate the constitutional rights of persons from the constitutional rights of corporations	Would diminish the power of those who purvey materialistic values/goals
Reinstate requirements that corporations balance attempts to maximize financial profit with community responsibility	Would diminish the power of those who purvey materialistic values/goals and would encourage them to pursue intrinsic/self-transcendent values/goals

materialistic values/goals will be hampered to the extent that people are frequently encouraged by their peers, employers, media, and government to focus on materialistic values, and to the extent that the economic system under which they live suggests that possessions, profit, and economic growth are crucially important aims. Materialistic values/goals would be more likely to decline if the culture and economy promoted feelings of security rather than threat, and if intrinsic and self-transcendent values/goals were encouraged more than materialistic aims.

Cultural and economic shifts of these sorts will require broader policy changes. **Table 1** reviews a number of policies that hold promise for decreasing materialism; it also explains how each policy is relevant to the materialism-reduction strategies articulated in this section. Given space limitations for the current review, and given that these policy suggestions have not yet been subjected to nearly as much empirical scrutiny as have person-level interventions to decrease materialism, I offer just one comment regarding them. (Readers interested in other policy suggestions are referred to Kasser 2011a,b.)

Psychologists and other academics are often reticent about, and rarely rewarded for, investigating topics of a politically sensitive nature and then writing about the societal implications of their findings (Hoffman 2015, Kasser & Kanner 2004). Nonetheless, research is clearly needed to inform effective policy-making so as to reduce materialism and the personal, social, and ecological ills associated with it. For example, one proposal mentioned in **Table 1** that has gained some traction concerns the use of alternative indicators of national progress (e.g., Bates 2009, Diener &

Seligman 2004) to replace dominant measures such as Gross National Product. Gross National Product clearly privileges materialistic values over other values, as it increases whenever money changes hands, even when that money is used to purchase antidepressants, clean up toxic waste, build prisons, go to war, etc. The proposed alternative indicators, in contrast, typically focus on intrinsic and self-transcendent values/goals by directly assessing well-being, interpersonal connections, the health of one's community and natural environment, etc. Social scientists have been at the forefront of efforts to design such alternative indicators, and they could contribute further by asking questions such as: How do people behave in laboratory simulations where one or another type of indicator is used as a measure of "success"? What factors would increase the likelihood that politicians actually would use the alternative indicators in their decision-making? What types of interventions would be most effective in raising a community's standing on alternative indicators? Similar sets of research questions could be asked about all of the other policies described in **Table 1** (see, e.g., Kunkel et al. 2004 for numerous research questions relevant to advertising aimed at children).

V. CONCLUSION

In closing, I hope that readers take the following three points from this review.

First, although materialism may have trait-like and identity-like features, I hope to have shown the usefulness of considering materialism as a set of values/goals with particular dynamic relations to the other aims in the human value/goal system. I believe that this means of conceptualizing the construct provides the best way of integrating the diverse array of findings that have been reviewed here, including the associations of materialism with one's debt levels, treatment of other people and the planet, health behavior, and personal well-being, among others variables.

Second, I hope readers see that although it may be easy to believe that research on materialism mostly concerns the study of materialistic individuals who strongly prioritize such aims in life, a more useful, and, I think, more accurate attitude is to recognize that all of us have materialistic tendencies. These tendencies can be activated in a particular moment, enhanced when we see them modeled in society, and brought on by temporary or chronic feelings of threat or insecurity. As such, researchers need to ask not only, "Who is materialistic?" but also "When are people materialistic?"

Third, given that materialism is not likely to disappear from the human psyche, given the ills associated with it, and given how much contemporary culture encourages people to pursue materialistic values/goals, I believe the most important question for materialism researchers to confront in the coming years is the following: "How can people create lives, organizations, economies, and societal structures that acknowledge humans' materialistic tendencies but that do not allow those tendencies to run rampant over other valuable aims in life?"

SUMMARY POINTS

1. Materialistic aims are a fundamental part of human value/goal systems; they concern becoming wealthy, obtaining possessions, presenting an appealing image, and being of high status.

2. Materialistic aims are in relative conflict with self-transcendent and intrinsic values/goals that concern having good interpersonal relationships, helping the world be a better place, growing as a person, and being spiritual.

3. Meta-analytic results document that to the extent people prioritize materialistic aims, they report higher levels of compulsive consumption, lower personal well-being, more physical health problems, and more ecologically destructive attitudes and behaviors.

4. To the extent people prioritize materialistic aims, they also consume more and incur more debt, have lower-quality interpersonal relationships, treat other people in less caring ways, and have adverse educational and occupational motivation.

5. Momentarily activating materialistic aims increases concerns for psychologically compatible values (e.g., money, image, status) and suppresses concerns for the intrinsic and self-transcendent aims that are in psychological conflict with materialism (including prosocial and proenvironmental behavior, interpersonal connections, educational motivation, and personal well-being).

6. Interventions to reduce materialism are effective when they activate and encourage intrinsic and self-transcendent values/goals, reduce exposure (or the effects of exposure) to societal models of materialistic values, and/or increase a sense of felt security and safety.

7. Numerous policy approaches could reduce materialism by increasing the extent to which cultures and economies promote feelings of security rather than threat, and by encouraging intrinsic and self-transcendent values/goals rather than materialistic aims.

FUTURE ISSUES

1. Although materialism can be validly measured with self-report instruments, the field would benefit from the development of implicit measures of materialism and means of coding materialistic values/goals in natural language, politicians' speeches, life narratives, etc.

2. Substantially more research on materialism is needed that utilizes samples of children and people from economically developing cultures and that uses prospective, longitudinal, and experimental designs.

3. Although the mediators of the negative relationship between materialism and well-being are fairly well documented, research has yet to definitively reveal the processes that explain the relationships between materialism and other problematic outcomes (e.g., compulsive consumption, ecologically damaging behaviors).

4. Further research is required to understand the reasons why people continue to prioritize materialistic values/goals even when such aims bring little satisfaction.

5. To increase the external validity of research on the activation of materialistic aims, studies need to expose participants to materialistic stimuli more frequently (as opposed to only once or twice).

6. Most studies that have attempted to reduce materialism involve brief interventions that likely have short-lasting effects; more in-depth interventions are needed to test if longer-lasting reductions in materialism can occur.

7. The development and implementation of policies to decrease materialism will be facilitated if researchers study and write about broader, macro-oriented topics such as advertising to children and alternative indicators of progress.

8. A crucial question for researchers to consider is how people can create lives, organizations, economies, and societal structures that acknowledge humans' materialistic tendencies but that do not allow those tendencies to run rampant over other valuable aims in life.

DISCLOSURE STATEMENT

The author is not aware of any funding or financial holdings that might be perceived as affecting the objectivity of this review. That said, the author does sit on the boards of directors of two not-for-profit organizations (the Campaign for a Commercial-Free Childhood and the Center for a New American Dream) whose work is directly relevant to reducing materialism in society.

LITERATURE CITED

Abramson PR, Inglehart R. 1995. *Value Change in Global Perspective*. Ann Arbor: Univ. Mich. Press

Ahuvia AC, Wong NY. 2002. Personality and values based materialism: their relationship and origin. *J. Consum. Psychol.* 12:389–402

Allen MW, Wilson M. 2005. Materialism and food security. *Appetite* 45:314–23

Arndt J, Solomon S, Kasser T, Sheldon KM. 2004. The urge to splurge: a terror management account of materialism and consumer behavior. *J. Consum. Psychol.* 14:198–212

Ashikali E-M, Dittmar H. 2012. The effect of priming materialism on women's responses to thin-ideal media. *Br. J. Soc. Psychol.* 51:514–33

Banerjee R, Dittmar H. 2008. Individual differences in children's materialism: the role of peer relations. *Personal. Soc. Psychol. Bull.* 34:17–31

Bates W. 2009. Gross national happiness. *Asian-Pac. Econ. Lit.* 23:1–16

Bauer M, Wilkie JEB, Kim JK, Bodenhausen GV. 2012. Cuing consumerism: Situational materialism undermines personal and social well-being. *Psychol. Sci.* 23:517–23

Belk RW. 1983. Worldly possessions: issues and criticisms. *Adv. Consum. Res.* 10:514–19

Belk RW. 1985. Materialism: trait aspects of living in the material world. *J. Consum. Res.* 12:265–80

Brand JE, Greenberg BS. 1994. Commercials in the classroom: the impact of Channel One advertising. *J. Advert.* 34:18–21

Briers B, Pandelaere M, Dewitte S, Warlop L. 2006. Hungry for money: The desire for caloric resources increases the desire for financial resources and vice versa. *Psychol. Sci.* 17:939–43

Briggs E, Landry T, Wood C. 2007. Beyond just being there: an examination of the impact of attitudes, materialism, and self-esteem on the quality of helping behavior in youth volunteers. *J. Nonprofit Public Sector Mark.* 18:27–45

Brown KW, Kasser T. 2005. Are psychological and ecological well-being compatible? The role of values, mindfulness, and lifestyle. *Soc. Indic. Res.* 74:349–68

Brown KW, Kasser T, Ryan RM, Linley AP, Orzech K. 2009. When what one has is enough: mindfulness, financial desire discrepancy, and subjective well-being. *J. Res. Personal.* 43:727–36

Buijzen M. 2007. Reducing children's susceptibility to commercials: mechanisms of factual and evaluative advertising interventions. *Media Psychol.* 9:411–30

Buijzen M, Valkenburg PM. 2005. Parental mediation of undesired advertising effects. *J. Broadcast. Electron. Media* 49:153–65

Burroughs JE, Rindfleisch A. 2002. Materialism and well-being: a conflicting values perspective. *J. Consum. Res.* 29:348–70

Carroll JS, Dean LR, Call LL, Dean M. 2011. Materialism and marriage: couple profiles of congruent and incongruent spouses. *J. Couple Relatsh. Ther.: Innov. Clin. Educ. Interv.* 10:287–308

Caruso EM, Vohs KD, Baxter B, Waytz A. 2013. Mere exposure to money increases endorsement of free-market systems and social inequality. *J. Exp. Psychol.: Gen.* 142:301–6

Carver AB, McCarty JA. 2013. Personality and psychographics of three types of gamblers in the United States. *Int. Gambl. Stud.* 13:338–55

Chang L, Arkin RM. 2002. Materialism as an attempt to cope with uncertainty. *Psychol. Mark.* 19:389–406

Chaplin LN, John DR. 2007. Growing up in a material world: age differences in materialism in children and adolescents. *J. Consum. Res.* 34:480–93

Christopher AN, Morgan RD, Marek P, Keller M, Drummond K. 2005. Materialism and self-presentational styles. *Personal. Individ. Differ.* 38:137–49

Christopher AN, Schlenker BR. 2004. Materialism and affect: the role of self-presentational concerns. *J. Soc. Clin. Psychol.* 23:260–72

Clark MS, Greenberg A, Hill E, Lemay EP, Clark-Polner E, et al. 2011. Heightened interpersonal security diminishes the monetary value of possessions. *J. Exp. Soc. Psychol.* 47:359–64

Cohen P, Cohen J. 1996. *Life Values and Adolescent Mental Health*. Mahwah, NJ: Erlbaum

Cozzolino PJ, Staples AD, Meyers LS, Samboceti J. 2004. Greed, death, and values: from terror management to transcendence management theory. *Personal. Soc. Psychol. Bull.* 30:278–92

Crompton T, Kasser T. 2009. *Meeting Environmental Challenges: The Role of Human Identity*. Godalming, UK: WWF-UK

Dechesne M, Pyszczynski T, Arndt J, Ransom S, Sheldon KM, et al. 2003. Literal and symbolic immortality: the effect of evidence of literal immortality on self-esteem striving in response to mortality salience. *J. Personal. Soc. Psychol.* 84:722–37

Deci EL, Koestner R, Ryan RM. 1999. A meta-analytic review of experiments examining the effects of extrinsic rewards on intrinsic motivation. *Psychol. Bull.* 125:627–68

Deci EL, Ryan RM. 2000. The "what" and "why" of goal pursuits: human needs and the self-determination of behavior. *Psychol. Inq.* 11:227–68

Deckop JR, Giacalone RA, Jurkiewicz C. 2015. Materialism and workplace behaviors: Does wanting more result in less? *Soc. Indic. Res.* 121:787–803

Deckop JR, Jurkiewicz CL, Giacalone RA. 2010. Effects of materialism on work-related personal well-being. *Hum. Relat.* 63:1007–30

Devoe SE, House J. 2012. Time, money and happiness: How does putting a price on time affect our ability to smell the roses? *J. Exp. Soc. Psychol.* 48:466–74

Diener E, Seligman MEP. 2004. Beyond money: toward an economy of well-being. *Psychol. Sci. Public Interest* 5:1–31

Dittmar H. 2008. *Consumer Culture, Identity and Well-Being: The Search for the "Good Life" and the "Body Perfect."* Hove, UK: Psychol. Press

Dittmar H, Bond R, Hurst M, Kasser T. 2014. The relationship between materialism and personal well-being: a meta-analysis. *J. Personal. Soc. Psychol.* 107:879–924

Donnelly G, Iyer R, Howell RT. 2012. The Big Five personality traits, material values, and financial well-being of self-described money managers. *J. Econ. Psychol.* 33:1129–42

Donnelly G, Ksendzova M, Howell RT. 2013. Sadness, identity, and plastic in over-shopping: the interplay of materialism, poor credit management, and emotional buying motives in predicting compulsive consumption. *J. Econ. Psychol.* 39:113–25

Duriez B, Vansteenkiste M, Soenens B, De Witte H. 2007. The social costs of extrinsic relative to intrinsic goal pursuits: their relation with social dominance and racial and ethnic prejudice. *J. Personal.* 75:757–82

Flanagan C, Gallay LS, Gill S, Gallay E, Naana N. 2005. What does democracy mean? Correlates of adolescents' views. *J. Adolesc. Res.* 20:193–218

Foulkes L, Seara-Cardoso A, Neumann CS, Rogers JSC, Viding E. 2014. Looking after number one: associations between psychopathic traits and measures of social motivation and functioning in a community sample of males. *J. Psychopathol. Behav. Assess.* 36:22–29

Frey B, Oberholzer-Gee F. 1997. The cost of price incentives: an empirical analysis of motivation crowding out. *Am. Econ. Rev.* 87:746–55

Fritsche K, Jonas E, Kayser DN, Koranyi N. 2010. Existential threat and compliance with pro-environmental norms. *J. Environ. Psychol.* 30:67–79

Fromm E. 1976. *To Have or to Be?* New York: Harper & Row

Gasiorowska A, Zaleskiewicz T, Wygrab S. 2012. Would you do something for me? The effects of money activation on social preferences and social behavior in young children. *J. Econ. Psychol.* 33:603–8

Ger G, Belk RW. 1996. Cross-cultural differences in materialism. *J. Econ. Psychol.* 17:55–77

Goldberg ME, Gorn GJ. 1978. Some unintended consequences of TV advertising to children. *J. Consum. Res.* 5:22–29

Goldberg ME, Gorn GJ, Peracchio LA, Bamossy G. 2003. Understanding materialism among youth. *J. Consum. Psychol.* 13:278–88

Good J. 2007. Shop' til we drop? Television, materialism and attitudes about the natural environment. *Mass Commun. Soc.* 10:365–83

Grouzet FME, Kasser T, Ahuvia A, Fernandez-Dols JM, Kim Y, et al. 2005. The structure of goal contents across 15 cultures. *J. Personal. Soc. Psychol.* 89:800–16

Hayes SC, Strosahl KD, Wilson KG. 2012. *Acceptance and Commitment Therapy: The Process and Practice of Mindful Change.* New York: Guilford. 2nd ed.

Hellevik O. 2003. Economy, values, and happiness in Norway. *J. Happiness Stud.* 4:243–83

Henderson-King D, Brooks KD. 2009. Materialism, sociocultural appearance messages, and paternal attitudes predict college women's attitudes about cosmetic surgery. *Psychol. Women Q.* 33:133–42

Hoffman AJ. 2015. Isolated scholars: making bricks, not shaping policy. *Chron. High. Educ.* 50(22):A48

Hope NH, Milyavskaya M, Holding AC, Koestner R. 2014. Self-growth in the college years: Increased importance of intrinsic values predicts resolution of identity and intimacy stages. *Soc. Psychol. Personal. Sci.* 4:705–12

Hurst M, Dittmar H, Bond R, Kasser T. 2013. The relationship between materialistic values and environmental attitudes and behaviors: a meta-analysis. *J. Environ. Psychol.* 36:257–69

Jenkins GD, Mitra A, Gupta N, Shaw JD. 1998. Are financial incentives related to performance? A meta-analytic review of empirical research. *J. Appl. Psychol.* 83:777–87

Kamal S, Chu S-C, Pedram M. 2013. Materialism, attitudes and social media usage and their impact on purchase intention of luxury fashion goods among American and Arab young generations. *J. Interact. Advert.* 13:27–40

Karabati S, Cemalcilar Z. 2010. Values, materialism, and well-being: a study with Turkish university students. *J. Econ. Psychol.* 31:624–33

Kashdan TB, Breen WE. 2007. Materialism and well-being: experiential avoidance as a mediating mechanism. *J. Soc. Clin. Psychol.* 26:521–39

Kasser T. 2002a. *The High Price of Materialism.* Cambridge, MA: MIT Press

Kasser T. 2002b. Sketches for a self-determination theory of values. In *Handbook of Self-Determination Research*, ed. EL Deci, RM Ryan, pp. 123–40. Rochester, NY: Univ. Rochester Press

Kasser T. 2005. Frugality, generosity, and materialism in children and adolescents. In *What Do Children Need to Flourish? Conceptualizing and Measuring Indicators of Positive Development*, ed. K Moore, LH Lippman, pp. 357–73. New York: Springer Sci. Bus. Media

Kasser T. 2011a. Values and human wellbeing. Commissioned paper for the Bellagio Initiative: the future of philanthropy and development in the pursuit of human wellbeing. **http://www.bellagioinitiative.org/wp-content/uploads/2011/10/Bellagio-Kasser.pdf**

Kasser T. 2011b. Ecological challenges, materialistic values, and social change. In *Positive Psychology as Social Change*, ed. R Biswas-Diener, pp. 89–108. New York: Springer Sci. Bus. Media

Kasser T. 2011c. Capitalism and autonomy. In *Human Autonomy in Cross-Cultural Context: Perspectives on the Psychology of Agency, Freedom, and Well-Being*, ed. VI Chirkov, RM Ryan, KM Sheldon, pp. 191–206. Dordrecht: Springer

Kasser T, Ahuvia AC. 2002. Materialistic values and well-being in business students. *Eur. J. Soc. Psychol.* 32:137–46

Kasser T, Cohn S, Kanner AD, Ryan RM. 2007. Some costs of American corporate capitalism: a psychological exploration of value and goal conflicts. *Psychol. Inq.* 18:1–22

Kasser T, Grow Kasser V. 2001. The dreams of people high and low in materialism. *J. Econ. Psychol.* 22:693–719

Kasser T, Kanner AD. 2004. Where is the psychology of consumer culture? In *Psychology and Consumer Culture: The Struggle for a Good Life in a Materialistic World*, ed. T Kasser, AD Kanner, pp. 3–7. Washington, DC: Am. Psychol. Assoc.

Kasser T, Rosenblum KL, Sameroff AJ, Deci EL, Ryan RM, et al. 2014. Changes in materialism, changes in psychological well-being: evidence from three longitudinal studies and an intervention experiment. *Motiv. Emot.* 38:1–22

Kasser T, Ryan RM. 1993. A dark side of the American dream: correlates of financial success as a central life aspiration. *J. Personal. Soc. Psychol.* 65:410–22

Kasser T, Ryan RM. 1996. Further examining the American dream: differential correlates of intrinsic and extrinsic goals. *Personal. Soc. Psychol. Bull.* 22:280–87

Kasser T, Ryan RM. 2001. Be careful what you wish for: optimal functioning and the relative attainment of intrinsic and extrinsic goals. In *Life Goals and Well-Being: Towards a Positive Psychology of Human Striving*, ed. P Schmuck, KM Sheldon, pp. 116–31. Göttingen, Ger.: Hogrefe & Huber

Kasser T, Ryan RM, Zax M, Sameroff AJ. 1995. The relations of maternal and social environments to late adolescents' materialistic and prosocial values. *Dev. Psychol.* 31:907–14

Kasser T, Sheldon KM. 2000. Of wealth and death: materialism, mortality salience, and consumption behavior. *Psychol. Sci.* 11:348–51

Kilbourne WE, Dorsch MJ, McDonagh P, Urlen B, Prothero A. 2009. The institutional foundations of materialism in Western societies: a conceptualization and empirical test. *J. Macromarketing* 29:259–78

Kilbourne W, Grunhagen M, Foley J. 2005. A cross-cultural examination of the relationship between materialism and individual values. *J. Econ. Psychol.* 26:624–41

Kolodinsky RW, Maden TM, Zisk DS, Henkel ET. 2010. Attitudes about corporate social responsibility: business student predictors. *J. Bus. Ethics* 91:167–81

Ku L, Dittmar H, Banerjee R. 2012. Are materialistic teenagers less motivated to learn? Cross-sectional and longitudinal evidence from the United Kingdom and Hong Kong. *J. Educ. Psychol.* 104:74–86

Ku L, Dittmar H, Banerjee R. 2014. To have or to learn? The effects of materialism on British and Chinese children's learning. *J. Personal. Soc. Psychol.* 106:803–21

Kunkel D, Wilcox BL, Cantor J, Palmer E, Linn S, et al. 2004. *Report of the APA Task Force on Advertising and Children*. Washington, DC: APA. **http://www.apa.org/pubs/info/reports/advertising-children.aspx**

Lambert NM, Fincham FD, Stillman TF, Dean LR. 2009. More gratitude, less materialism: the mediating role of life satisfaction. *J. Posit. Psychol.* 4:32–42

Lasaleta JD, Sedikides C, Vohs KD. 2014. Nostalgia weakens the desire for money. *J. Consum. Res.* 41:713–29

Lekes N, Hope NH, Gouveia L, Koestner R, Philippe FL. 2012. Influencing value priorities and increasing well-being: the effects of reflecting on intrinsic values. *J. Posit. Psychol.* 7:249–61

Lykins ELB, Segerstrom SC, Averill AJ, Evans DR, Kemeny ME. 2007. Goal shifts following reminders of mortality: reconciling posttraumatic growth and terror management theory. *Personal. Soc. Psychol. Bull.* 33:1088–99

Maio GR, Pakizeh A, Cheung W-Y, Rees KJ. 2009. Changing, priming, and acting on values: effects via motivational relations in a circular model. *J. Personal. Soc. Psychol.* 97:699–715

Martos T, Kopp MS. 2012. Life goals and well-being: Does financial status matter? Evidence from a representative Hungarian sample. *Soc. Indic. Res.* 105:561–68

McHoskey JW. 1999. Machiavellianism, intrinsic versus extrinsic goals, and social interest: a self-determination theory analysis. *Motiv. Emot.* 23:267–83

Mick DG. 1996. Are studies of dark side variables confounded by socially desirable responding? The case of materialism. *J. Consum. Res.* 23:106–19

Moschis GP. 2007. Life course perspectives on consumer behavior. *J. Acad. Market. Sci.* 35:295–307

Nairn A, Ormrod J, Bottomley P. 2007. *Watching, Wanting and Wellbeing: Exploring the Links*. London: Natl. Consum. Counc.

Nguyen HV, Moschis GP, Shannon R. 2009. Effects of family structure and socialization on materialism: a life course study in Thailand. *Int. J. Consum. Stud.* 33:486–95

Nickerson C, Schwarz N, Diener E, Kahneman D. 2003. Zeroing in on the dark side of the American dream: a closer look at the negative consequences of the goal for financial success. *Psychol. Sci.* 14:531–36

Niemiec CP, Ryan RM, Deci EL. 2009. The path taken: consequences of attaining intrinsic and extrinsic aspirations in post-college life. *J. Res. Personal.* 43:291–306

Norris JI, Lambert NM, DeWall CN, Finchman FD. 2012. Can't buy me love? Anxious attachment and materialistic values. *Personal. Individ. Differ.* 53:666–69

Opree SJ, Buijzen M, van Reijmersdal EA, Valkenburg PM. 2011. Development and validation of the Material Values Scale for Children (MVS-c). *Personal. Individ. Differ.* 51:963–68

Opree SJ, Buijzen M, van Reijmersdal EA, Valkenburg PM. 2014. Children's advertising exposure, advertised product desire, and materialism: a longitudinal study. *Commun. Res.* 41:717–35

Otero-López JM, Villardefrancos E. 2013. Five-factor model personality traits, materialism, and excessive buying: a mediational analysis. *Personal. Individ. Differ.* 54:767–72

Pfeffer J, DeVoe SE. 2009. Economic evaluation: the effect of money and economics on attitudes about volunteering. *J. Econ. Psychol.* 30:500–8

Pieters R. 2013. Bidirectional dynamics of materialism and loneliness: not just a vicious cycle. *J. Consum. Res.* 40:615–31

Promisio MD, Deckop JR, Giacalone RA, Jurkiewicz CL. 2010. Valuing money more than people: the effects of materialism on work-family conflict. *J. Occup. Organ. Psychol.* 83:935–53

Rand A. 1967. *Capitalism: The Unknown Ideal.* New York: Signet

Richins ML. 2004. The Material Values Scale: measurement properties and development of a short form. *J. Consum. Res.* 31:201–19

Richins ML. 2011. Materialism, transformation expectations, and spending: implications for credit use. *J. Public Policy Mark.* 30:141–56

Richins ML, Chaplin LN. 2015. Material parenting: how the use of goods in parenting fosters materialism in the next generation. *J. Consum. Res.* 41:1333–57

Richins ML, Dawson S. 1992. A consumer values orientation for materialism and its measurement: scale development and validation. *J. Consum. Res.* 19:303–16

Rindfleisch A, Burroughs JE, Denton F. 1997. Family structure, materialism, and compulsive consumption. *J. Consum. Res.* 23:312–25

Ring K. 1984. *Heading Toward Omega: In Search of the Meaning of the Near-Death Experience.* New York: Morrow

Roberts BW, Robins RW. 2000. Broad dispositions, broad aspirations: the intersection of personality traits and major life goals. *Personal. Soc. Psychol. Bull.* 26:1284–96

Roberts JA, Roberts CF. 2012. Money matters: Does the symbolic presence of money affect charitable giving and attitudes among adolescents? *Young Consum.* 13:329–36

Rokeach M. 1973. *The Nature of Human Values.* New York: Free Press

Ryan RM, Deci EL. 2001. On happiness and human potential: a review of research on hedonic and eudaimonic well-being. *Annu. Rev. Psychol.* 52:141–66

Schmuck P. 2001. Intrinsic and extrinsic life goals preferences as measured via inventories and priming methodologies: mean differences and relations with well-being. In *Life Goals and Well-Being: Towards a Positive Psychology of Human Striving*, ed. P Schmuck, KM Sheldon, pp. 132–47. Göttingen, Ger.: Hogrefe & Huber

Schor JB. 2004. *Born to Buy: The Commercialized Child and the New Consumer Culture.* New York: Scribner

Schwartz SH. 1992. Universals in the content and structure of values: theory and empirical tests in 20 countries. In *Advances in Experimental Social Psychology*, vol. 25, ed. M Zanna, pp. 1–65. New York: Academic

Schwartz SH. 2007. Cultural and individual value correlates of capitalism: a comparative analysis. *Psychol. Inq.* 18:52–57

Sheldon KM, Arndt J, Houser-Marko L. 2003. In search of the Organismic Valuing Process: the human tendency to move towards beneficial goal choices. *J. Personal.* 71:835–69

Sheldon KM, Kasser T. 1995. Coherence and congruence: two aspects of personality integration. *J. Personal. Soc. Psychol.* 68:531–43

Sheldon KM, Kasser T. 1998. Pursuing personal goals: Skills enable progress, but not all progress is beneficial. *Personal. Soc. Psychol. Bull.* 24:1319–31

Sheldon KM, Kasser T. 2008. Psychological threat and extrinsic goal striving. *Motiv. Emot.* 32:37–45

Sheldon KM, Krieger LS. 2004. Does legal education have undermining effects on law students? Evaluating changes in motivation, values, and well-being. *Behav. Sci. Law* 22:261–86

Sheldon KM, McGregor H. 2000. Extrinsic value orientation and the tragedy of the commons. *J. Personal.* 68:383–411

Sheldon KM, Sheldon MS, Osbaldiston R. 2000. Prosocial values and group assortation in an *N*-person prisoner's dilemma. *Hum. Nat.* 11:387–404

Shrum LJ, Lee J, Burroughs JE, Rindfleisch A. 2011. An online process model of second-order cultivation effects: how television cultivates materialism and its consequences for life satisfaction. *Hum. Commun. Res.* 37:34–57

Shrum LJ, Wong N, Arif F, Chugani SK, Gunz A, et al. 2013. Reconceptualizing materialism as identity goal pursuits: functions, processes, and consequences. *J. Bus. Res.* 66:1179–85

Sirgy MJ, Lee D-J, Kosenko R, Meadow JL, Rahtz D, et al. 1998. Does television viewership play a role in the perception of quality of life? *J. Advert.* 27:125–42

Sirgy MJ, Gurel-Atay E, Webb D, Cicic M, Husic M, et al. 2012. Linking advertising, materialism, and life satisfaction. *Soc. Indic. Res.* 107:79–101

Smith A. 1776 (1976). *An Inquiry into the Nature and Causes of the Wealth of Nations.* New York: Random House

Solberg EC, Diener E, Robinson MD. 2004. Why are materialists less satisfied? In *Psychology and Consumer Culture: The Struggle for a Good Life in a Materialistic World*, ed. T Kasser, AD Kanner, pp. 29–48. Washington, DC: Am. Psychol. Assoc.

Srivastava A, Locke EA, Bartol KM. 2001. Money and subjective well-being: It's not the money, it's the motives. *J. Personal. Soc. Psychol.* 80:959–71

Stillman TF, Fincham FD, Vohs KD, Lambert NM, Phillips CA. 2012. The material and immaterial in conflict: Spirituality reduces conspicuous consumption. *J. Econ. Psychol.* 33:1–7

Tedeschi RG, Calhoun LG. 2004. Post-traumatic growth: conceptual foundations and empirical evidence. *Psychol. Inq.* 15:1–18

Twenge JM, Baumeister RF, DeWall CN, Ciarocco NJ, Bartels JM. 2007. Social exclusion decreases prosocial behavior. *J. Personal. Soc. Psychol.* 92:56–66

Twenge JM, Gentile B, DeWall CN, Ma DS, Lacefield K, Schurtz DR. 2010. Birth cohort increases in psychopathology among young Americans, 1938–2007: a cross-temporal meta-analysis of the MMPI. *Clin. Psychol. Rev.* 30:145–54

Twenge JM, Kasser T. 2013. Generational changes in materialism and work centrality, 1976–2007: associations with temporal changes in societal insecurity and materialistic role-modeling. *Personal. Soc. Psychol. Bull.* 39:883–97

Van Boven L, Gilovich T. 2003. To do or to have? That is the question. *J. Personal. Soc. Psychol.* 85:1193–202

Vansteenkiste M, Duriez B, Simons J, Soenens B. 2006. Materialistic values and well-being among business students: further evidence for their detrimental effect. *J. Appl. Soc. Psychol.* 36:2892–908

Vansteenkiste M, Matos L, Lens W, Soenens B. 2007b. Understanding the impact of intrinsic versus extrinsic goal framing on exercise performance: the conflicting role of task and ego involvement. *Psychol. Sport Exerc.* 8:771–94

Vansteenkiste M, Neyrinck B, Niemiec CP, Soenens B, De Witte H, Van den Broeck A. 2007a. On the relations among work value orientations, psychological need satisfaction, and job outcomes: a self-determination theory approach. *J. Occup. Organ. Psychol.* 80:251–77

Vansteenkiste M, Simons J, Lens W, Sheldon KM, Deci EL. 2004. Motivating learning, performance and persistence: the synergistic effects of intrinsic goal contents and autonomy-supportive contexts. *J. Personal. Soc. Psychol.* 87:246–60

Vohs KD, Mead NL, Goode MR. 2006. The psychological consequences of money. *Science* 31:1154–56

Watson JJ. 2003. The relationship of materialism to spending tendencies, saving, and debt. *J. Econ. Psychol.* 24:723–39

Weinstein N, Przybylski AK, Ryan RM. 2009. Can nature make us more caring? Effects of immersion in nature on intrinsic aspirations and generosity. *Personal. Soc. Psychol. Bull.* 35:1315–29

Wierzbicki J, Zawadzka AM. 2014. The effects of the activation of money and credit card versus that of activation of spirituality—which one prompts pro-social behaviours? *Curr. Psychol.* doi: 10.1007/s12144-014-9299-1

Workman JE, Lee S-H. 2011. Materialism, fashion consumers and gender: a cross-cultural study. *Int. J. Consum. Stud.* 35:50–57

Zhang JW, Howell R, Howell C. 2014. Living in wealthy neighborhoods increases material desires and maladaptive consumption. *J. Consum. Cult.* doi: 10.1177/1469540514521085

Zhou X, Vohs KD, Baumeister RF. 2009. The symbolic power of money: reminders of money alter social distress and physical pain. *Psychol. Sci.* 20:700–6

Beyond Work-Life "Integration"

Joan C. Williams,[1] Jennifer L. Berdahl,[2]
and Joseph A. Vandello[3]

[1]Center for WorkLife Law, University of California, Hastings College of the Law,
San Francisco, California 94102; email: williams@uchastings.edu

[2]Sauder School of Business, University of British Columbia, Vancouver,
British Columbia V6T 1Z2

[3]Department of Psychology, University of South Florida, Tampa, Florida 33620

Annu. Rev. Psychol. 2016. 67:515–39

First published online as a Review in Advance on
October 6, 2015

The *Annual Review of Psychology* is online at
psych.annualreviews.org

This article's doi:
10.1146/annurev-psych-122414-033710

Keywords

work-family, work-life, conflict, enrichment, balance, gender, motherhood,
social class, masculinity

Abstract

Research on the work-family interface began in the 1960s and has grown
exponentially ever since. This vast amount of research, however, has had
relatively little impact on workplace practice, and work-family conflict is at
an all-time high. We review the work-family research to date and propose
that a shift of attention is required, away from the individual experience of
work and family and toward understanding how identity and status are defined at work. Several factors enshrine cherished identities around current
workplace norms. The work devotion schema demands that those who are
truly committed to their work will make it the central or sole focus of their
lives, without family demands to distract them. Importantly, the work devotion schema underwrites valued class and gender identities: Work devotion
is a key way of enacting elite class status and functions as the measure of a
man—the longer the work hours and higher the demand for his attention, the
better. Advocating change in the way work is done and life is lived meets resistance because it places these cherished identities at risk. Resistance to these
identity threats keeps current workplace norms in place. This is why even
the business case—which shows that current practices are not economically
efficient—fails to persuade organizations to enact change. What is needed
now is sustained attention to the implicit psychological infrastructure that
cements the mismatch between today's workplace and today's workforce.

Contents

INTRODUCTION

The study of the work-family interface can be traced back to at least the 1960s (e.g., Goode 1960, Kahn et al. 1964), but research on the topic has seen explosive growth since the 1980s. Demographers have documented several trends that frame the field. First is the shift away from the breadwinner-homemaker family: In roughly 70% of American families with children, all adults are in the labor force (Williams & Boushey 2010). The second demographic shift is the sharp rise in men's participation in family work: Men's household contributions doubled between 1965 and 2000, mostly due to increases in men's time spent providing child care (Bianchi et al. 2000). Both trends pull in the direction of greater gender equality.

The workplace has not kept up with these trends. Although families have shifted toward equal parenting, the workplace pulls them in the opposite direction. For professionals, the rise in over-work leads to neo-traditional families, in which the father typically has the "big job" while the mother's workforce participation is curtailed to support his. Less privileged workers often face just-in-time schedules that change daily and weekly, often with little notice (Lambert et al. 2014), requiring low-wage workers to make brutal trade-offs between supporting their families and caring for them.

The classic tool for persuading businesses to adopt new practices is to demonstrate their bottom-line economic benefits, also known as "the business case." After 25 years of demonstrating the business case for family-friendly work practices, however, businesses have not been persuaded to adopt them. A key—but little examined—question is why. The answer requires attention to questions that have rarely been posed in the psychological literature on the work-family interface: how fundamental social identities and statuses are forged on the job. Sociologists have chiefly explored this psychological issue. The vast majority of studies in the psychology literature on work and family have focused on the individual experience (Casper et al. 2007), sometimes on what organizations can do to help individuals, but not on organizational and social contexts that define their experiences. We believe this is why, to quote Ellen Kossek and colleagues, "Work-family researchers have not made a significant impact in improving the lives of employees relative to the amount of research that has been conducted" (Kossek et al. 2011a, p. 353). Our hypothesis is that identities constructed around the ideal worker norm (Williams 2000) and the work devotion schema (Blair-Loy 2003), combined with gendered identities regarding masculinity and motherhood, have made the business case impossible to hear and time and career norms extraordinarily resistant to change. What's needed now is sustained attention to the hidden psychological infrastructure that cements the mismatch between today's workplace and today's workers.

BRIEF OVERVIEW OF SIX MAJOR STRAINS OF WORK-FAMILY RESEARCH

Industrial-Organizational Psychology

The bulk of research on the work-family interface has been in industrial-organizational (I/O) psychology. The primary focus of this research has been on the individual experience of work-family conflict, its correlates, and refining tools of measurement (e.g., Masuda et al. 2012). A notable and important exception is the growing literature on informal organizational support and workplace cultures (e.g., Hammer et al. 2011, Swanberg et al. 2011). Measures of work-family culture and perceptions of informal managerial support can be more important than formal policies on employee affective and behavioral outcomes (Behson 2005). Hammer and colleagues (2011), for instance, designed a supervisor-training program intended to increase family-friendly culture. The training program was effective (increasing job satisfaction, reducing turnover intentions) for employees high in work-family conflict but actually counterproductive for employees with low work-family conflict, which may explain why movements toward family-friendly work cultures are hard to sustain.

Social Psychology

Until recently, experimental social psychologists have been little engaged in the work-family field: a 2007 review found that only 2% of work-family studies used experimental designs (Casper et al. 2007). Most salient are the studies on the maternal wall and the flexibility stigma in the *Journal of Social Issues* and on redesigning and redefining work in *Work and Occupations* (all coedited by Joan C. Williams). These studies demonstrated the nature and extent of discrimination against working mothers, the flexibility stigma to caregiving fathers, and how work norms and structures are hostile to or supportive of balancing work and family. Like I/O psychology, the focus of this research has been at the individual level of analysis, but social identities and cultural norms inform its theorizing.

Survey Research

A third important arena of work-family scholarship consists of survey-based studies documenting the rise of workplace flexibility policies. A crucial resource for both scholars and advocates is the Study of the Changing Workforce database of the Families and Work Institute (Aumann et al. 2011, Bond et al. 2002). This work documents the rise in organizations' adoption of a canonical array of flexibility policies that include telecommuting, flextime (the ability to change starting and stopping times), compressed workweeks (working full time hours in less than five days a week), and reduced hours arrangements. The steady rise in the adoption of such policies ended with the Great Recession of 2008. As of 2010, many organizations were reducing or eliminating flexibility policies, with the largest drops in flextime (SHRM 2010). Post-recession, no increase occurred except in ad hoc telecommuting (Kossek et al. 2014).

The Business Case

A fourth key area of research documents the business case for workplace flexibility. For a good recent summary, see the pamphlet that prominent work-life scholars wrote for the Society for Human Resource Management (Kossek et al. 2014). Work-family conflict costs employers in decreased job satisfaction and commitment from their employees (Kossek & Ozeki 1998), more frequent absenteeism and intentions to quit, greater attrition, and lower job performance and career success (Anderson et al. 2002). Effective flexibility policies enable employers to attract and retain from a much broader talent pool than do time norms that artificially privilege breadwinners married to homemakers (e.g., Kelly et al. 2008, Kossek & Michel 2010). Longitudinal studies document that work-family conflict predicts physical and mental health deterioration over time (e.g., Goodman & Crouter 2009, Van Steenbergen & Ellemers 2009), further costing employers in absenteeism, productivity, and health insurance. Many studies report business benefits of restructured work, including improved recruiting and productivity and decreased turnover intentions and absenteeism (Kelly et al. 2008, Kossek et al. 2006, Moen et al. 2011).

Action Research

A fifth strain of work-family research was founded in the 1990s by Lotte Bailyn's *Breaking the Mold: Women, Men, and Time in the New Corporate World* (1993). Bailyn's "action research" involves working with companies to design, study, and document a workplace intervention. Bailyn's collaborative interactive action research (CIAR) model reflected a dual agenda combining the goals of increasing the retention and advancement of women with improved business performance. The CIAR model involved intensive interventions designed to question the gendered assumptions that shape organizational time norms and uncover ways in which overwork leads to poor planning, decreased productivity, and other organizational detriments. Bailyn's 2002 coauthored book describes a number of interventions, some of which proved sustainable and some of which did not (Bailyn et al. 2002). More recent action research projects bump up the level of rigor, relying on randomized control experimental designs (Kelly et al. 2014), discussed below.

Cultural Comparisons

A final growing area of scholarship examines public policy in cross-cultural context, documenting that the United States has the fewest work-family reconciliation policies of any developed country and the longest work hours (OECD 2014). Jody Heymann's (2013) path-breaking work documented that the United States stands alone among developed nations for its lack of paid maternity leave. Janet Gornick and Marcia Meyers' (2003) work highlights how many fewer family supports exist in the United States than in Europe, where families benefit from such policies as paid parental leaves as long as six months (US paid parental leave: 0 weeks), a minimum of four weeks paid vacation (US minimum paid vacation: 0 weeks), shorter average workweeks (down to 35 hours/week in France), the right to have one parent work part time until the youngest child is age 12, part-time equity (proportional pay for part-time work), high-quality subsidized child care, the right to request a flexible schedule, and limits on mandatory overtime. American parents "are squeezed for time and pay a comparatively higher penalty for working reduced hours" than parents in most other developed countries (Gornick & Meyers 2003, p. 58).

THE INDIVIDUAL EXPERIENCE OF WORK AND FAMILY

With that brief overview, we now turn to a closer examination of work-family research in psychology. The field has grown exponentially since the 1960s. A PsycINFO search on the topic reveals a handful of publications in the 1960s leading up to almost 2,000 in the first decade of the twenty-first century. This literature has benefited from many review essays and meta-analyses (e.g., Allen et al. 2012, Amstad et al. 2011, Bianchi & Milkie 2010, Butts et al. 2013, Byron 2005, Eby et al. 2005, Ford et al. 2007, Kossek & Ozeki 1998, Maertz & Boyar 2011, McNall et al. 2010, Michel et al. 2011). By far the most common approach to the study of work and family has been to view them as conflicting domains, referred to as work-family conflict or work-family interference. As we will see, that is only one of the theoretical takes on the work-family interface. This review makes no attempt to summarize every study, or even every theme explored in various studies, but instead sketches a basic background to provide a springboard to defining a way forward for work-family research.

Work-Family Conflict

The theoretical foundations for the conflict perspective on work and family can be traced to the scarcity hypothesis (Goode 1960), which proposes that time and energy are limited, finite resources, and to Robert Merton's role conflict hypothesis, which proposes that people sometimes face conflict among their multiple social roles (Merton 1949). These models were applied to work-family studies in the 1970s, in important early work (Kanter 1977, Pleck 1977, Rapoport & Rapoport 1971) acknowledging the existence of dual-career families and the overlap and conflict between work and family roles. Overall, early research on work and family presented a bleak picture. For instance, conflict theory (Greenhaus & Beutell 1985) proposed that work and family were incompatible domains due to their competing responsibilities. Early research on work and family almost exclusively examined negative outcomes of attempts to combine them, particularly for women and their families. Perspectives that allowed for the possibility of role enhancement would come later.

The framing of work and family as oppositional forces highlighted the need to consider the direction of conflict, from work to family and from family to work. From a scarcity perspective, work-family conflict might be expected to have different directions for women and men due to traditional gender roles. Traditional caregiving roles expect women to devote relatively more attention to family (Eagly 1987), suggesting work should be a greater source of conflict for women than men. Conversely, because of traditional breadwinner roles (Zuo 2004), men's conflicts might be expected to have their source in the home (see Gutek et al. 1991). Indeed, though the earliest studies usually failed to consider the direction or flow of conflict, by 1984 researchers began to explore family-to-work spillover (Crouter 1984) or family interference with work (FIW, as opposed to work interference with family, WIF). Empirical work has shown that FIW and WIF have distinct antecedents and outcomes (e.g., Frone et al. 1992, Kossek & Ozeki 1998), that rates of self-reported WIF are substantially higher than rates of FIW (Bellavia & Frone 2005), and that sex is only weakly correlated with FIW and WIF (Byron 2005).

By the early 2000s a wide range of studies and several meta-analyses had documented high levels of individual work-family conflict, with negative consequences at work and at home. After 2000 a new perspective became influential: that work and family can enrich, as well as deplete, one another.

Work-Family Enrichment

In 2001, Rosalind Chait Barnett and Janet Shibley Hyde posited an "expansionist" theory: that multiple roles can be beneficial (Barnett & Hyde 2001). This perspective was consistent with earlier work by Catherine Kirchmeyer (1993), designed to reassure employers that women's (and men's) nonwork commitments did not make them less desirable workers, a finding that was duplicated in a more recent study (Allis & O'Driscoll 2007). Another early study documented the benefits of multiple roles for managerial women: This early literature clearly was intended to counter the common contention that working mothers hurt children, families, and themselves (Ruderman et al. 2002). Meanwhile, Joe Grzywacz, Leslie Hammer, and their coauthors explored the theme of positive spillover (e.g., Grzywacz & Marks 2000, Hammer et al. 2005). Other authors explored work-family enhancement (Ruderman et al. 2002), work-family facilitation (Hill et al. 2007, Tompson & Werner 1997, Wayne et al. 2004), and work-family enrichment (Greenhaus & Powell 2006). All of these constructs, the distinctions among which "are not always clear," articulate the mutual benefit of integrating work and family and "the perspective that combining multiple roles can result in beneficial outcomes for the individual" (Allen 2012, p. 1170).

As with work-family conflict research, enrichment studies have examined the direction of the flow of benefit, from work to family and vice versa. The past decade has seen many attempts to review and assess the state of research on work-to-family and family-to-work enrichment (Greenhaus & Powell 2006, Grzywacz et al. 2007, McNall et al. 2010). As early as 2001, scholars recognized that work-family spillover could simultaneously be enriching and depleting (Rothbard 2001). A review by Greenhaus & Powell (2006) found that the 15 studies measuring both work-family conflict and work-family enrichment reported low correlations between them. Heavy investment in work or family roles has a surprisingly small effect on the experience of conflict (Byron 2005); work-family conflict and enrichment are not simple opposites (Allen 2012). For example, in their study of legal secretaries, Weer and colleagues (2010) found that work interference with family diminished employees' work capacity while family-to-work enrichment did not compensate for the diminished capacity. In other words, one's participation in family produces positive spillover to the workplace, but this positive spillover does not compensate for the conflict the workplace introduces for the family, resulting in lower overall job performance.

LIMITATIONS OF THE INDIVIDUAL FOCUS

Absence of Context

In the flurry of definition, direction, and measurement of constructs, something was gained, but something was lost: the focus on work-family conflict as a structural problem. Some recent studies do not focus on workplace interventions at all. A notable example advocates making families happier by urging employees to talk more with their partners about the good things that happened to them at work. The same study proposes that employers should produce more positive affect at work that will spill over at home (Culbertson et al. 2012), which seems too vague a prescription for employers to implement. Indeed, many of the interventions proposed in the work-family literature propose organizational interventions that would leave the workplace-workforce mismatch intact. Examples include proposals to enhance work-family enrichment by creating opportunities for professional development (Molino et al. 2013).

An encouraging recent trend is research that aims to measure organizational culture (Allen 2001, Behson 2005). Much of this work considers the specific aspects of culture, such as work-family climate (Paustian-Underdahl & Halbesleben 2014), work-family culture (Thompson et al. 1999), and supervisor support (Hammer et al. 2011). These studies take a crucially important step in the direction of looking at how workplace ideals are constructed on the job, abandoning the tight focus on individuals' experience of the work-family interface.

Yet much of the research on work-family enrichment is headed in an ever-more-individualistic direction, as evidenced by the recent fascination with the dispositional factors that correlate with work-family conflict (e.g., Wayne et al. 2004). To quote the ever-insightful Joseph Grzywacz and Dawn Carlson, "[v]iewing work-family balance as an individual-level problem borders on victim blaming" for a "challenge [that] itself is the consequence of demographic transitions in the workforce and the American family, and transitions in how work is performed" (Grzywacz & Carlson 2007, p. 458). Although it is no doubt interesting that work-family conflict correlates with neuroticism, negative affect, low self-efficacy (Allen et al. 2012), a preoccupied attachment style (Sumer & Knight 2001), and the Big Five (Michel et al. 2011), and it is mitigated by positive thinking (Rotundo & Kincaid 2008), surely the takeaway is not that employers should address the sky-high levels of work-family conflict among US workers by hiring only the well-adjusted and cheery or that society can rest assured that people end up where they deserve. Plugged into current work structures, the well adjusted and cheery are likely to become neurotic, negatively affective, low in self-efficacy, and subject to negative thinking.

Erasing Gender

In addition, some studies often ignore gender in ways that end up mixing apples and oranges. Although Barnett's expansionist theory focused on countering the "separate spheres" assumption that working women hurt both themselves and their families, family-to-work enrichment studies have not distinguished between a dual-career husband's support for his working wife and a homemaker's kudos to her breadwinning husband; rather, both are captured in a single measure of partner support (Ferguson et al. 2012, Greenhaus & Powell 2006, Grzywacz & Marks 2000). This erasure of gender is troubling given findings that spousal support is particularly important for working wives, even more important than supervisor support (Lee et al. 2014, Wayne et al. 2006), and that wives provide more emotional support for husbands than vice versa (Greenberger & O'Neil 1993). By neglecting gender, family-to-work enrichment measures inadvertently embrace, as uncontroversial and untroubling, some key aspects of male privilege within families.

An excellent critique—tellingly written by Canadians, not Americans—advocates integrating gender more thoroughly, and in a more sophisticated way, into work-family research (Korabik et al. 2008). It pinpoints some of the ways that gender effects are overlooked when researchers use highly gendered categories without acknowledging the key role played by gender: studies of part- versus full-time work and of job categories that are heavily male or female, samples that are heavily skewed toward men or women, or analyses of the impact of egalitarian attitudes on the work-family interface without differentiating between men and women. A meta-analysis of 61 studies found no overall gender differences in either work interference with family or family interference with work (Byron 2005), yet one wonders what is getting bleached out in the wash. For example, one study found that men with egalitarian attitudes experience more family interference with work than women with egalitarian attitudes and than men with traditional ones (Korabik et al. 2008).

Ignoring Class

Similarly, inattention to class sometimes shapes the field in disturbing ways. The clearest example is that some researchers' insistence on shifting from the term "work-life balance" to "work-life integration" inadvertently embeds a series of class-based assumptions. Studies of nonelite Americans report that they emphatically do not want a work life that pervades their home life. Jessi Streib's study of cross-class marriages found that although spouses who grew up in white-collar households typically exhibit work devotion and prefer work deeply integrated into their lives, spouses from blue-collar childhoods distance their identity from work and create clearer boundaries between their work and home lives; these findings echo prior studies (Streib 2015). Blue-collar men's identities are intertwined with being a good provider, and often they see their jobs as a means to an end—to support their families—rather than a totalizing identity (Williams 2010). Thus, one study found that although physicians worked all of the time, emergency medical technicians took pride in putting limits on their overtime shifts for the good of their families (Shows & Gerstel 2009). Shifting to the terminology of "work-family integration" implicitly takes sides in this debate and embeds the expectation that work will be ever present in the life of every responsible worker. That is why we do not use the term.

A subtler example concerns findings about whether limiting work hours correlates with work-family conflict (Wayne et al. 2004). The important work of Jerry Jacobs and Kathleen Gerson (Jacobs & Gerson 2004) documenting the time divide—that in the United States, high-income workers work too many hours while low-income workers have trouble getting enough hours of work to pay the bills—shows that a measure seeking a simple correlation between work hours and work-family conflict or enrichment is doomed to fail. At a deeper level, the failure to connect work-family facilitation/enrichment/spillover findings with the extensive literature on class would be a loss for both fields, because the work-to-family enrichment measure offers a profound message: It holds the potential to show, with all the precision of measurement I/O psychology offers, precisely how a lack of class and gender privilege makes people unhappy.

BEYOND THE INDIVIDUAL EXPERIENCE OF WORK AND FAMILY

Prior authors have called for changes in work-family scholarship, and the response has been mixed. We echo one persistent critique, first articulated as early as 1990 (Zedeck & Mosier 1990), and encourage work-family scholars to move beyond their focus on the individual experience of work-family conflict and enrichment toward an analysis of social context (e.g., Eby et al. 2005, Zedeck 1992). In 2007, Casper and colleagues noted that work-family research should make "greater use of longitudinal and experimental research designs, gather more multisource data, and move beyond the individual level of analysis," as well as adopt "more diverse conceptions of family" and study workers in occupations other than nonmanagerial or professional positions (p. 28).

New Methods

Some researchers have answered the call for new methodologies, notably Gerstel & Clawson's (2001) elegant multisource study, which combined in-depth interviews, survey data, and an analysis of union contracts. Less effective have been calls to shift from cross-sectional to longitudinal studies in order to gain a better understanding of causation (Allen 2012) and calls for less reliance on single-report, self-report survey data (Greenhaus & Parasuraman 1999, Zedeck 1992). As of 2007, most studies were still cross-sectional (89%) and correlational (89%), and 77% of studies used only one data collection method (Casper et al. 2007). With some notable exceptions, that remains the case today; however, longitudinal studies have begun to emerge (e.g., Goodman & Crouter 2009, Hall et al. 2010, Hammer et al. 2005, Nohe et al. 2015, Radcliffe & Cassell 2014, Van Steenbergen & Ellemers 2009). Given that one-shot survey studies are so much easier and cheaper than longitudinal or multisource studies, their persistence will remain a fact of life in the context of ever-increasing research funding shortages and intense pressures to publish more and faster; longitudinal studies take time and can be expensive. If the field begins to place high value on longitudinal multisource studies, higher-quality research allowing for more in-depth and causal temporal analysis may become more common.

Diversified Samples

On the other hand, work-family researchers have responded admirably to the call to diversify their samples. Although 95% of work-family research has been based on US or British samples (Kossek et al. 2011b), recent studies have explored work-family enrichment in China (Kwan et al. 2010, Siu et al. 2010) and India (Bhargava & Baral 2009), positive spillover in Australia (Haar & Bardoel 2008), the relationship of spillover and sleep quality in Canada (Williams et al. 2006), stress reduction in Germany (Hartung & Hahlweg 2011), work-home conflict and facilitation in Norway (Innstrand et al. 2010), negative effects of work on home life and positive effects of home life on work in South Africa (Rost & Mostert 2007), and work-family facilitation in Albania (Karatepe & Bekteshi 2008), to name a few. Ollier-Malaterre and colleagues (2013, p. 433) point out the various ways in which such studies "conceptualize national context as dynamic rather than static and as heterogeneous rather than homogeneous."

Some fascinating findings are emerging from these studies. One example: Koreans who feel close to their families feel they need to work more to reward their family members for their emotional support (Lee et al. 2011). Another example: Indians report the same level of work-family enrichment regardless of their marital or parental status, presumably because mothers are not assumed to be sole suppliers of children's needs but rather have extended family networks (Bhargava & Baral 2009). An important finding from a recent cross-cultural study of national paid-leave policies and work-family conflict was that paid-leave policies had only modest effects on work-family conflict (Allen et al. 2014), which is troubling, given the nigh-exclusive focus on paid leave among advocates of work-family policy in the United States. An interesting transnational research question is whether less workaholic countries show more work interference with family than family interference with work, as US samples do (Allen 2012).

One review focused on studies in sociology and demography noted that, whereas research before 2000 focused almost exclusively on whites, research on low-income families and families of color increased after 2000 (Bianchi & Milkie 2010). In I/O psychology, startlingly few studies include American nonwhites—a significant oversight because the few studies that exist suggest substantial racial differences. One found a larger gender difference in both family-to-work and work-to-family spillover among Latinos than among whites or blacks (Roehling et al. 2005). Another found that white mothers experience more negative spillover from family to work than black mothers do (Dilworth 2004, p. 256).

Equally exciting are the new studies that address calls by several scholars to examine working-class jobs (Casper et al. 2007, Heymann et al. 2002), such as studies of hourly workers as opposed to professionals, including studies of legal secretaries (Weer et al. 2010), blue-collar workers (Berdahl & Moon 2013, Rost & Mostert 2007), nurses in Italy (Russo & Buonocore 2012), and hotel workers in Albania (Karatepe & Bekteshi 2008). Other studies explore the impact of unions on the work-life interface of unionized workers (e.g., Berg et al. 2014). No doubt the most influential studies of hourly workers are those examining just-in-time scheduling by Susan Lambert (e.g., Lambert 2008) and Julia Henly (e.g., Henly et al. 2006). Their studies document the harsh impact on workers of just-in-time schedules that change from day to day and week to week, often with as little as three days' notice. Such schedules impose costs on employers that are typically overlooked, notably turnover that reaches as high as 500% a year (Lambert 2008).

Organizational Intervention Studies

"To assume that individual-level work-family relationships translate into system-level change is thus far unsubstantiated" (Grzywacz et al. 2007, p. 560) and is probably unwarranted. Studies are needed that "design organization-wide interventions to avoid or mitigate [work-family conflict]" (Maertz & Boyar 2011, p. 87). Though relatively few and far between, some excellent studies of organization-wide interventions have shed light on how policies can be designed and implemented to help employees balance their work and home lives (Kelly & Moen 2007; Kelly et al. 2011, 2014; Perlow 2012). These organizational intervention studies involve top-down initiatives that enable employees to flexibly manage their work schedules. Studies to document the business case for flexibility have debunked concerns about its cost and disruption to business. We review these studies as examples of what research could look like moving forward to effect real understanding and change, and then we consider social norms that stand in the way of changing how work gets measured and done.

As noted, Lotte Bailyn started doing intervention studies in the 1990s. More recent is Leslie Perlow's study of consultants at the Boston Consulting Group (BCG) (Perlow 2012). Perlow identified that the reason BCG consultants were experiencing such high work-family conflict and burnout was not so much their long hours and travel, but rather the unpredictability of their schedules: People could not make personal plans. Working with a single BCG team, Perlow gave them a collective goal of scheduling predictable time off (PTO). Each team member got one night "off" starting at 6:00 PM for a defined and predictable unit of time each week. "Off" meant no work, no phone, no email, etc. The team would need to have a weekly meeting (with mandatory attendance) for 30 minutes to talk about the calendar for whose night off would take place when and to review whether people took their night off, and if not, what to do differently next time so they did. The intervention was so successful that BCG has rolled out PTO to more than 2,000 teams in 32 offices with 30 facilitators in 14 countries.

Additional intervention studies reflect the work of Erin Kelly, Phyllis Moen, and their coauthors documenting the benefits of a results-only work environment (ROWE) model of scheduling and accomplishing work (Bloom & Roberts 2015, Hammer et al. 2011, Kelly et al. 2011, Moen et al. 2011). ROWE was developed and implemented at the corporate headquarters for Best Buy. Unlike most flexible work arrangements targeted at individual workers, ROWE attempted to change the corporate culture by making flexibility the norm. The culture change was intended to destigmatize the choice to work remotely or in nontraditional hours. Studies of the ROWE model showed that it decreased work-family conflict, negative spillover (Kelly et al. 2011), and turnover (Moen et al. 2011).

The gold standard for this kind of research are the intervention studies by led by Erin Kelly, Phyllis Moen, Ellen Kossek, and Leslie Hammer, financed by the Work, Family, and Health Network funded by the National Institutes of Health. These studies rely on randomized control trials (Kelly et al. 2014). One such study, performed in the informational technology department of a Fortune 500 company, combined supervisor-support training (Kossek et al. 2011a) with increased worker schedule control. The intervention showed significant, although modest, improvements in work-family conflict and family time adequacy, and larger shifts in schedule control and perceived supervisor support for work-life balance (Kelly et al. 2014).

These studies reinforce earlier findings that demonstrate how organizational culture, practices, and policies can affect work-family conflict. McNall and colleagues (2011) showed that high perceived organizational support is associated with high levels of work-family enrichment regardless of low core self-evaluations (Greenhaus & Powell 2006), indicating the importance of organizational support and the conceptual limits of focusing on dispositional characteristics of the individual worker. A perception of supervisor and coworker support is particularly beneficial in reducing work-family conflict (Grzywacz & Marks 2000, Kossek et al. 2011a), as are family-supportive mentoring programs (de Janasz et al. 2013). Combining supervisor support with schedule control and family-friendly work policies is especially effective (Kelly et al. 2011). And consistent with Leslie Perlow's study of a major consulting firm, team aspects of organizational culture have been shown to be associated with work-family enrichment insofar as team resources can be deployed in the interest of allowing individuals increased flexibility (Hunter et al. 2010).

Value incongruence between individuals and organizations is also associated with greater work interference with family (Perrewe & Hochwarter 2001). To the extent that employees perceive organizations as family supportive, they increase affective commitment. Understanding the impact of informal organizational resources on employee perceptions allows for deeper understanding of the reciprocal relationship between work-to-family enhancement and employee affective commitment to the organization (Wayne et al. 2013).

The Flexibility Stigma and the Business Case

Simple surveys documenting the availability of flexible work options gloss over the important issue of whether organizations stigmatize those who use them. Studies find mixed evidence on the effect of common work-life policies on workers' perceived schedule control (Kelly et al. 2008, Kossek & Michel 2010). Both qualitative and quantitative studies have consistently reported that professionals with flexible work arrangements are viewed as time deviants who are marginalized (e.g., Epstein et al. 1999, Glass 2004, Leslie et al. 2012). Christened the usability problem by Susan Eaton (Eaton 2003), this flexibility stigma deeply flaws many, or most, existing flexibility programs (Williams et al. 2013). Quantitative studies confirm workers' fears. Those who take leaves or use flexible work practices experience slowed wage growth (Coltrane et al. 2013, Glass 2004), earn fewer promotions, have lower performance reviews (Judiesch & Lyness 1999), and are perceived as less motivated and dedicated to work (Rogier & Padgett 2004) than those who conform to the ideal-worker template.

The flexibility stigma literature from experimental social psychology needs to be integrated with studies from I/O psychology on family-supportive workplace cultures to assess which flexibility policies are window dressing and stigmatized and which are embraced and usable. Also important are studies of what Ellen Kossek and colleagues have called the implementation gap (Kossek et al. 2011a). The question is whether the flexibility stigma represents a policy implementation gap or whether it also (or instead) represents resistance within the organization to changing the time norms that frame the identities of powerful actors whose personal and professional identities were forged on the anvil of work devotion.

What matters is whether time norms are changed. Leslie Perlow and Erin Kelly differentiate between accommodation policies that plunk down flexible work arrangements in an environment where the norm of work devotion remains unchanged and the work redesign model, in which workplace norms are changed for everyone without linking the change specifically to work-family issues—arguing instead that the new model responds to business needs (Perlow & Kelly 2014). Examples of work redesign are the interventions of Kelly and her colleagues and of Bailyn and Perlow's PTO.

In addition, new organizations are emerging that make work-life balance integral to their business models. A 2015 study identifies over 40 organizations with new business models for practicing law in ways that offer better work-life balance for lawyers—many of them men who want to work a flexible 50-hour week rather than being "always on" (Williams et al. 2015b). Other "new models" have been identified elsewhere (Schulte 2014). It would be fascinating to have studies comparing family supportiveness of the workplace cultures of these new models with the cultures of more traditional organizations.

The fact that these new models have acted on the business case for workplace flexibility makes it all the more striking that more traditional organizations remain unimpressed. This highlights an important issue: Why has extensive documentation of the business case failed to persuade most organizations to initiate meaningful change? A related question is why even successful interventions, with thoroughly documented business benefits, remain fragile flowers: Bailyn and her team mention several successful interventions that were nonetheless abandoned (Bailyn et al. 2002). More dramatic is that Best Buy eliminated ROWE when a new CEO decided he needed all hands on deck, despite rigorous academic research documenting its business benefits (Kelly et al. 2011, Moen et al. 2011, Ressler & Thompson 2008).

Perhaps what is needed is a more rigorous business case (Correll et al. 2012). But businesses typically do not require regression analysis before making decisions. We propose that what is needed is not simply more evidence or more rigor but a different conversation—one that explores the psychological investments in cherished identities.

THE WAY FORWARD

We need to direct our attention to the social norms and workplace structures that have proved remarkably resilient in the face of widespread demands for change. We propose that what is required is a merging of the individual and contextual lenses of analysis to understand how social norms and identities incentivize individual behavior. Social norms are the "soft tissue" of organizational life, enacted through micro social processes that can eclipse concerns about the organizational bottom line. Social identity concerns deflect attention away from rational metrics of production—and indeed may cloud people's ability to differentiate between identity performance and a rational assessment of the effectiveness of existing work practices. The way forward in work-family research requires a sustained focus on identity. Sociologists look at social structures, psychologists look at individual behavior; identity connects the two.

This discussion begins with an assessment of which identities people perform at work: the good worker, the good man, the good woman, and the good person. Our chief focus is on professionals, as the norms of work devotion (Blair-Loy 2003) that fuel extreme work hours and the exponential pay that comes with them (Cha & Weeden 2014) are most intense in this demographic. Professionals are also most influential in shaping workplace policies and norms.

The way forward for work-family research suggests five new kinds of studies: (*a*) studies that explore the intertwining of work devotion with workers' sense of themselves as moral people; (*b*) studies that explore work as a masculinity contest in which hours worked become the measure of a man; (*c*) studies that explore the tug-of-war among women, as ideal-worker mothers judge mothers who take leave and use workplace flexibility as bad workers—and those mothers judge ideal-worker mothers as bad mothers; (*d*) studies that explore how work devotion is a way of enacting professional-managerial class status; and (*e*) studies that explore a new business case for redefining the ideal worker, focused not on the costs of failing to retain women, but instead on the inefficiencies and costs that ensue when work becomes a masculinity contest.

The Good Worker: Work as a Moral Act

People whose identities have developed around the norm of work devotion have deep investments in proving—to others, but perhaps more importantly, to themselves—that redefining the ideal worker norm is infeasible. Identity threat research documents how vigorously people resist threats to the identities around which they have forged their lives (Branscombe et al. 1999). The ideal worker norm is just such an identity. Identities framed around work devotion may well exercise an additional hold because people who live up to them have to make painful sacrifices in order to do so (Blair-Loy 2003). Those who make themselves always available for work do so at the cost of "missing their children's childhoods," to quote the cliché, among other things. If work could be organized differently, does that mean their sacrifice was unnecessary? Women face unsettling considerations. A mother who devotes herself first and foremost to work may be an ideal worker— but is she a bad mother? A psychologically healthy woman in this situation will have a lot invested in convincing both herself and others that she had no alternative. Both the personal sacrifices demanded by the work devotion schema, and the conflict between the ideal worker and the ideal mother, make the identity threat posed by demands to change the organization of work too threatening to countenance. Thus the ideal worker norm may well be even stickier than are other fundamental social norms.

Assessing the extent to which the work devotion schema defines a given workplace will be an important direction for future research on the success and failure of organizational policies and social practices around work and family. Some important recent research has begun to examine the centrality of work and family to people's identities (Greenhaus et al. 2012, Ng & Feldman 2008); also useful in this context is work on the life roles salience scale (e.g., Cinamon & Rich 2002). Although this recognition of identity in shaping work hours and the work-life interface is a welcome sign, these studies treat work centrality as an individual difference variable rather than a gendered cultural norm. When cultural expectations to work are strong (as they are for men), relationships between individual difference variables (in attitudes, values, and personality) and work behaviors might be expected to be attenuated. This may help explain why work and family centrality predict women's work hours but not men's (Greenhaus et al. 2012). Similarly, Ng & Feldman (2008) unexpectedly found that career satisfaction and educational level were more strongly related to work hours for women than for men. In essence, the male norm of work devotion may trump individual attitudes about the centrality of work.

The Good Man: Work as a Masculinity Contest

Mary Blair-Loy observes that elite men's jobs revolve around the work devotion schema, which communicates that high-level professionals should "demonstrate commitment by making work the central focus of their lives" and "manifest singular 'devotion to work,' unencumbered with family responsibilities" (Blair-Loy & Wharton 2004, pp. 151, 153). Extreme schedules, inflexible schedules, and chaotic last-minute schedules that require constant adaptation and availability to work are a way of enacting masculinity (Ely & Meyerson 2000).

Cynthia Fuchs Epstein and her coauthors found that, among corporate lawyers, overwork was seen as a heroic activity—a way of measuring masculinity without a ruler (1999). The next year,

Marianne Cooper's study of Silicon Valley engineers closely observed how working long hours turns computer keyboarding into a manly test of physical endurance (Cooper 2000). "There's a kind of machismo culture among the young male engineers where you just don't sleep," one father confided. "He's a real man; he works 90-hour weeks. He's a slacker; he works 50 hours a week" (p. 382), another engineer explained. Said yet another, "I really feel like it is kind of a machismo thing; I'm tough. I can do this. Yeah, I'm tired, but I'm on top of it. . . . The people who conspicuously overwork are guys, and I think it's usually for the benefit of other guys" (p. 384). Seven years after that, Pamela Stone quoted a woman saying that her department was "really dominated by these young guys who wanted to be hotshot litigators," noting that part-time employment and job sharing "just wasn't in their realm of reality" (Stone 2007, p. 86).

An insightful study is Katherine Kellogg's investigation of a mandated reduction in work hours among surgical residents in Boston; it demonstrated how masculine work culture resists even mandated changes. Kellogg documented the tremendous resistance to the new rule, which provided that surgical residents could work no more than 80 hours a week, a sharp decrease from their traditional 120-hour workweeks. Virtually all of the "attendings" (senior doctors) opposed the new rule, she found—despite the fact that it offered them concrete advantages in terms of work-life balance. She also documents why: Older surgeons had built their identities around an "iron man" model of the surgeon as the top-of-the-macho-hospital heap, lording it over not only nondoctors but also over nonsurgeon doctors by enacting the role of "action-oriented male heroes who singlehandedly perform death-defying feats, courageously acting with certainty in all situations" (Kellogg 2011, p. 51). These iron men viewed the need for sleep as a weakness, and valued "living at the hospital" as a manly badge of honor. They derided reformers who sought to comply with the new rules as "weak," "softies," "part-timers," "wusses," "pantywaists," and "girls" (p. 135).

If long hours, and the exponential income benefits that follow them, are the measure of a man, men will find themselves under strong pressure to intensely devote themselves to work. Indeed, existing studies suggest that men face a stark choice. If they conform to the breadwinner role, having children helps them at work—after all, they have a family to support (Cuddy et al. 2004, Fuegan et al. 2004). But men who do not make themselves always available to work often face harsh interpersonal penalties. Studies on the flexibility stigma found that men who took family leave, requested a flexible schedule, or even just made their caregiving responsibilities salient on the job encountered a serious stigma because they were seen as too feminine or not man enough (Berdahl & Moon 2013, Rudman & Mescher 2013, Vandello et al. 2013). This flexibility stigma for men is a penalty for gender deviance; serious organizational penalties follow (Butler & Skattebo 2004). If work is a masculinity contest in which outing oneself as not 100% devoted to work can cause a severe loss of status, no wonder most men keep quiet and conform. A recent study found that men experience work-family conflict to the same extent as women but tend to cope in ways that permit them to "pass" as ideal workers, even as they take more time off work than work devotion suggests they should (Reid 2015).

The identity threat perspective also offers insight into the sharp increase in the wage premium for overwork (Cha & Weeden 2014), which is largest in professional-managerial jobs. Before women entered elite jobs in large numbers, no wage premium existed for working 50+ hours/week (overwork). In recent decades, such a premium has arisen—and all but offsets the convergence in the educational levels of men and women. The overvaluation of work hours in excess of 50 hours/week is not justified economically, but it is part and parcel of the work-as-a-masculinity-contest dynamics in which hours have become the measure of a (elite) man.

Viewing work as a masculinity contest can also help explain why work-life initiatives often are supported at the top but are undermined by middle management (Hochschild 1997). Although masculinity is precarious for most men (Vandello et al. 2008), men in the middle tend to hold on tightest to traditions of manliness (Berdahl 2007, Munsch 2015). Men on the top can afford to take on feminine traits without losing face (think of Brad Pitt, with babies hanging from every limb). So can low-status men, who are out of the "game." But middle-status men tend to hold on for dear life—they are so close, after all, to the measure of a man. This may explain the persistent pattern of middle-level managers' resistance to work-life initiatives. More research could help unpack this dynamic and how to interrupt it.

Another promising avenue for study is the shift in ideals of fatherhood, away from "set-piece fatherhood"—the good dad as someone who shows up to the school play and other special events (Hochschild 1989)—to the involved father as someone who participates in his children's daily care (Aumann et al. 2011). This is commonly understood to be a generational shift; it would be nice to know whether it is true. A recent study interviewed baby boomer men who left traditional law firms to found their own new models of legal practice that allow them more participation in family life (Williams et al. 2015b); this study suggests that new ideals of fatherhood are not limited to millennial men. Studies on the "new" dad would be welcome (e.g., Humberd et al. 2015).

A final promising avenue of research for which psychologists are well suited concerns how one goes about changing time norms when work is a masculinity contest. Kellogg's (2011) study of surgeons highlights two important ingredients. The first is a way that men with alternate visions of what it means to be a "real man" can begin to align with women to gel resistance to the dominant narrative. The second is that reformers articulate their alternate vision as an alternate vision of manliness. Kellogg's reformers countered the traditional narrative of the surgeons as "working machines" who "don't eat and don't sleep" with a new narrative of surgeons who were "well-organized" and "efficient" workers who "know how to prioritize tasks" in order to hand off patient care efficiently to the "night floats" who take over and allow the surgical residents to go home (Kellogg 2011, p. 161). Reformers, like those who opposed them, used masculine metaphors: They spoke of chief residents as coaches rather than commanders, of interns as rookies rather than beasts of burden. Too often, work-life reformers have used the language of femininity, for example by linking the work-life reform with the need to revalue traditionally devalued "invisible work" (of relationship building, team building, etc.) (Bailyn et al. 2002). Doing so dooms reform efforts. The key is to make explicit that this is a contest between two different visions of what it means to be a man.

The Good Woman: Work as a Moral Hazard

All women face a clash of social ideals: The ideal worker is always available to the employer, and the ideal woman is always available to her family (Kobrynowicz & Biernat 1997). This is a situation fraught with potential for identity threat. Field studies have shown that working women who forego having children experience the highest levels of mistreatment from their coworkers (Berdahl & Moon 2013), consistent with experimental research documenting that women who do not become mothers are seen as competent but cold (Cuddy et al. 2004).

Experimentalists have also documented the negative judgments made about the competencies of working women who have children: Women appear to be damned if they do and damned if they don't. A vignette study of normative discrimination against mothers presented mothers who were indisputably competent and committed to their work and found that women—not men—tended to dislike those mothers and held them to higher performance standards (Benard & Correll 2010). The authors suggest that identity threat explains the female subjects' hostility to the working mother: "People perceive similar, highly successful others as threatening to one's self-concept when that person's success seems unattainable" (Benard & Correll 2010, p. 623). This is an example of what has been called the tug-of-war among women, when gender bias against women fuels conflicts among women (Williams & Dempsey 2014).

This tug-of-war helps explain the persistent reports of older women judging younger women for having kids, or advising them not to avail themselves of flexible schedules or other family-friendly options such as stop-the-tenure-clock policies. One study found that single women work the highest levels of unpaid overtime of any group (Trades Union Congr. 2008). This helps explain the backlash against family-friendly policies by single women, who protest that they get left holding the bag when mothers (and, increasingly, fathers) leave for child-care reasons. "I worked full time my whole career" is a common refrain among older women with and without children. The message: I performed as an ideal worker, which is why I succeeded professionally.

This identity is often sharply contested by younger women with statements such as, "I don't want someone else to raise my children"—direct statements about who's a good mother and who isn't. In this context, older women's insistence that "I just did what this job requires" is another instance in which any challenge to work devotion is interpreted by ideal workers as a personal attack. Interestingly, a parallel tug-of-war is emerging among men. Younger men's insistence that a good father is involved in the daily care of his children articulates an attack on the older, absent breadwinners as "bad fathers" (e.g., Humberd et al. 2015). In this highly fraught atmosphere, reimaging workplace ideals becomes too personally threatening.

The Good Person: Work Devotion as a "Class Act"

"The work devotion schema articulates a moral imperative," notes Mary Blair-Loy (2003, p. 22). Michèle Lamont's study confirms that ambition and a strong work ethic are "doubly sacred" for professional-managerial men "as signals of both moral and socioeconomic purity" (Lamont 2012, p. 85). Hard work and competence were seen by the elite American men (but not the French ones) Lamont interviewed as a central component of moral character: "A strong work ethic continues to be read as a guarantee of moral purity. Hard work and competence are equated with moral superiority, especially if they result in professional success" (Lamont 2012, p. 40). Ambition, too, is seen as a sign of character by professional-managerial American men, but not by blue-collar men, who tend to see it as a form of narcissism (Williams 2010).

Work devotion intertwines moral purity with elite status. It's a class act; a way of signaling and enacting privileged status (Williams 2010). Fifty years ago, Americans signaled class by displaying their leisure (think bankers' hours, 9:00 AM to 3:00 PM). At present, elites display their extreme schedules to establish how important they are—and how virtuous, given how very, very hard they work. Thus, Kellogg's surgeons scornfully decried new work rules limiting the hours of surgical residents to 80 a week, with explicit statements that work should be the central focus of one's life ("Surgery shouldn't be part of what you do. It should be all of what you do"; Kellogg 2011, p. 68) and that reformers who wished to follow the new rules were degrading surgery into a blue-collar job ("Residents would develop a shift-worker mentality rather than an ethic of commitment to the patient"; p. 4).

Blair-Loy (2003) draws parallels between the words bankers use to describe their work—"complete euphoria" or "being totally consumed"—and Emile Durkheim's classic account of a religious ceremony among Australian natives. Work devotion, like many forms of religion, provides moral credentialing through a totalizing experience. "Holidays are a nuisance because you have to stop working," one banker told Blair-Loy. "I remember being really annoyed when it was Thanksgiving. Damn, why did I have to stop working to go eat a turkey? I missed my favorite uncle's funeral, because I had a deposition scheduled that was too important" (Blair-Loy 2003, p. 34). Identity threat, again: Once someone has missed a favorite uncle's funeral, that individual has a substantial investment in the belief that this is the only way to be a true professional—and not (just) because work devotion is the measure of a man, but because it is a method of moral credentialing. (That speaker, in fact, was a woman.) The assumption that the work role is the key axis of identity is epitomized by the classic cocktail party question, "What do you do?" Asked this question at a reunion, one blue-collar guy leaned his head aggressively toward the questioner and stated, "I sell *toilets*" (Williams 2010, p. 185).

The convergence of so many powerful social forces—gender, class, and morality—fuels a "devotion to work that borders on addiction," notes Marianne Cooper (2000, p. 395) in her study of Silicon Valley workers. She quotes one engineer who admitted, "I was just anxious as hell unless I was working." Ultimately, it took him "years and 12-step programs" to cure his addiction (p. 389). These and other emotional dimensions of work have been oddly understudied by work-family researchers.

Why the Business Case Fails to Persuade

The business case for workplace flexibility has been documented over and over again for decades. Some have argued that the problem is the lack of causal studies rigorously linking workplace flexibility with enhanced recruitment, productivity, and worker engagement, and decreased turnover, absenteeism, and health insurance costs (Correll et al. 2014). Yet the need for rigorous double-blind studies, itself, is telling. Businesses typically do not insist on double-blind levels of rigor before making a business decision. The fact that the most rarefied academic-level data would be required to convince businesses highlights the profound resistance with which workplace flexibility proposals are met—resistance fueled by identity threat.

The way forward points to quite different sorts of studies. A new business case would shift attention away from the costs imposed on organizations by their failure to attract and retain women and would focus instead on the costs imposed by treating work as a forum for moral, gender, and class identity contests. Cooper's study points the way: "Remarkably, poor planning is reinterpreted as a test of will, a test of manhood for a team of engineers" (2000, p. 389), she notes, commenting that failure to delegate was tolerated or even admired. "They have no idea how to delegate," one engineer told her, because the need to work long hours made delegation counterproductive to ledger masculinity (Cooper 2000, p. 388). Working oneself so hard as to undermine productivity also was an accepted practice: "The managers have no idea what an altered state they are in all the time while they are managing these guys," noted another engineer (p. 389). Similarly, Kellogg (2011) found that the iron man mentality made surgeons who live for the OR (operating room) scornful of follow-ups with patients (or indeed scornful of talking with patients at all), apt to wear surgical scrubs outside the hospital (which signals work devotion but compromises sterility), and, of course, utterly exhausted (which leads to medical mistakes and malpractice lawsuits).

Other promising lines of inquiry would examine resistance to the business case. One coauthor has spent a lot of time trying to persuade businesses of its validity, only to be met (not invariably, but persistently) with a sentiment that "my business is different"—unique in some way. Again, the insistence on totally precise and rigorous real-time information of a type not typically demanded in other business contexts signals a deep level of resistance. It would be helpful to better understand this dynamic. Another avenue might be to abandon the business case for the moral imperative of equal opportunity and making life manageable and fulfilling for workers and their families. Just as we do not argue against child labor or slavery with a business case, but consider these practices to violate incontrovertible human values, perhaps we should also not rely on a business case to argue against inhumane and discriminatory work norms that hurt employees and their families. The recent sharp shift in business ethics concerning highly unstable just-in-time schedules for hourly workers offers hope. Once *The New York Times* got interested in covering the havoc wreaked on workers' lives by unstable hours, businesses abruptly began to treat scheduling as a corporate responsibility, such that first Starbucks and then Walmart announced a shift to more stable schedules (Kantor 2014, Lobosco 2015). Of course, it has always been easier to change workplace norms that do not threaten the identities of the (mostly) men at the top of organizations (Ely & Meyerson 2000), as evidenced by Robin Ely and Debra Meyerson's influential study of an organizational change initiative that reformed workplace norms for blue-collar offshore oil platform workers (Ely & Meyerson 2010).

CONCLUSION

Today's workplace remains a relic of the past. This review attempts to detail psychological processes that have made this workplace remarkably resistant to adaptation to the modern workforce. All too often, the ideal worker is still defined as someone always available for work, despite the fact that today only 20% of American families are breadwinner-homemaker families (Cohn et al. 2014). At various points in their lives, most workers have responsibility to care for children, elders, and/or ill or disabled partners or other family members.

We propose that organizational change to reshape workplace time norms for professionals has been stalled by two psychological processes. The first is that critical social identities are forged on the job: core identities of what it means to be a good worker, a good man or woman, and a good person. The second, resulting from the first, is that any proposal to redefine work is profoundly threatening to people whose identities have been forged around the old way of doing it. These psychological processes need to be studied by psychologists. Until they are, the work-family field will have far less impact than it should in helping to update the twenty-first century workplace to the twenty-first century workforce.

DISCLOSURE STATEMENT

The authors are not aware of any affiliations, memberships, funding, or financial holdings that might be perceived as affecting the objectivity of this review.

ACKNOWLEDGMENTS

Many thanks to Tammy Allen, Lotte Bailyn, Erin Kelly, and Ellen Kossek for their close attention to prior drafts of this article. Their comments have vastly improved it; mistakes, of course, are ours. Thanks, too, to Jessica Lee, Katherine Logan, Hilary Hardcastle, and Sanaz Rizlenjani for their help in preparing this article. We regret that limited space for references did not allow us to cite all relevant publications in this review.

LITERATURE CITED

Allen TD. 2001. Family supportive work environments: the role of organizational perceptions. *J. Vocat. Behav.* 58:414–35

Allen TD. 2012. The work and family interface. In *The Oxford Handbook of Organizational Psychology*, ed. SWJ Kozlowski, pp. 1163–98. New York: Oxford Univ. Press

Allen TD, Johnson RC, Saboe KN, Cho E, Dumani S, Evans S. 2012. Dispositional variables and work-family conflict: a meta-analysis. *J. Vocat. Behav.* 80:17–26

Allen TD, Lapierre LM, Spector PE, Poelmans SAY, O'Driscoll M, et al. 2014. The link between national paid leave policy and work-family conflict among married working parents. *Appl. Psychol.* 63:5–28

Allis P, O'Driscoll M. 2007. Positive effects of nonwork-to-work facilitation on well-being in work, family and personal domains. *J. Manag. Psychol.* 23:273–91

Amstad FT, Meier LL, Fasel U, Elfering A, Semmer NK. 2011. A meta-analysis of work-family conflict and various outcomes with a special emphasis on cross-domain versus matching domain relations. *J. Occup. Health Psychol.* 16:151–69

Anderson SE, Coffey BS, Byerly RT. 2002. Formal organizational initiatives and informal workplace practices: links to work-family conflict and job-related outcomes. *J. Manag.* 28:787–810

Aumann K, Galinsky E, Matos K. 2011. *The New Male Mystique*. New York: Fam. Work Inst.

Bailyn L. 1993. *Breaking the Mold: Women, Men, and Time in the New Corporate World*. New York: Free Press

Bailyn L, Rapoport R, Fletcher JK, Pruitt BH. 2002. *Beyond Work-Family Balance: Advancing Gender Equity and Workplace Performance*. San Francisco: Jossey-Bass

Barnett RC, Hyde JS. 2001. Women, men, work and family. *Am. Psychol.* 56:781–96

Behson SJ. 2005. The relative contribution of formal and informal organizational work-family support. *J. Vocat. Behav.* 66:487–500

Bellavia GM, Frone MR. 2005. Work-family conflict. In *Handbook of Work Stress*, ed. J Barling, EK Kolloway, MR Frone, pp. 113–48. Thousand Oaks, CA: Sage

Benard S, Correll SJ. 2010. Normative discrimination and the motherhood penalty. *Gender Soc.* 24:616–46

Berdahl JL. 2007. Harassment based on sex: protecting social status in the context of gender hierarchy. *Acad. Manag. Rev.* 32:641–58

Berdahl JL, Moon SH. 2013. Workplace mistreatment of middle class workers based on sex, parenthood, and caregiving. *J. Soc. Issues* 69:341–66

Berg P, Kossek EE, Misra K, Belman D. 2014. Work-life flexibility policies: Do unions affect employee access and use? *Ind. Labor Relat. Rev.* 67:111–37

Bhargava S, Baral R. 2009. Antecedents and consequences of work-family enrichment among Indian managers. *Psychol. Stud.* 54:213–25

Bianchi SM, Milkie MA. 2010. Work and family research in the first decade of the 21st century. *J. Marriage Fam.* 72:705–25

Bianchi SM, Milkie MA, Sayer LC, Robinson JP. 2000. Is anyone doing the housework? U.S. trends and gender differentials in domestic labor. *Soc. Forces* 79:191–228

Blair-Loy M. 2003. *Competing Devotions: Career and Family Among Women Executives*. Cambridge, MA: Harvard Univ. Press

Blair-Loy M, Wharton AS. 2004. Mothers in finance: surviving and thriving. *Ann. Am. Acad. Polit. Soc. Sci.* 596:151–71

Bloom N, Roberts J. 2015. A working from home experiment shows high performers like it better. *Harvard Bus. Rev.*, Jan. 23

Bond T, Thompson C, Galinsky E, Prottas D. 2002. *Highlights of the National Study of the Changing Workforce*. New York: Fam. Work Inst.

Branscombe NR, Ellemers N, Spears R, Doosje B. 1999. The context and content of social identity threat. In *Social Identity: Context, Commitment, Content*, ed. N Ellemers, R Spears, B Doosje, pp. 35–58. Oxford, UK: Blackwell Sci.

Butler AB, Skattebo A. 2004. What is acceptable for women may not be for men: the effect of family conflicts with work on job-performance ratings. *J. Occup. Organ. Psychol.* 77:553–64

Butts MM, Casper WJ, Yang TS. 2013. How important are work-family support policies? A meta-analytic investigation of their effects on employee outcomes. *J. Appl. Psychol.* 98:1–25

Byron K. 2005. A meta-analytic review of work-family conflict and its antecedents. *J. Vocat. Behav.* 67:169–98

Casper WJ, Eby LT, Bordeaux C, Lockwood A, Lambert D. 2007. A review of research methods in IO/OB work-family research. *J. Appl. Psychol.* 92:28–43

Cha Y, Weeden KA. 2014. Overwork and the slow convergence in the gender gap in wages. *Am. Sociol. Rev.* 79:457–84

Cinamon RG, Rich Y. 2002. Profiles of attribution of importance to life roles and their implications for the work-family conflict. *J. Couns. Psychol.* 49:212–20

Cohn D, Livingston G, Wang W. 2014, April 8. After decades of decline, a rise in stay-at-home mothers. Washington, DC: Pew Res. Cent. **http://www.pewsocialtrends.org/2014/04/08/after-decades-of-decline-a-rise-in-stay-at-home-mothers/**

Coltrane S, Miller EC, DeHaan T, Stewart L. 2013. Fathers and the flexibility stigma. *J. Soc. Issues* 69:279–302

Cooper M. 2000. Being the "go-to guy": fatherhood, masculinity, and the organization of work in Silicon Valley. *Qual. Sociol.* 23:379–405

Correll S, Kelly E, O'Connor LT, Williams JC. 2014. Redesigning, redefining work. *Work Occup.* 41:3–17

Crouter AC. 1984. Spillover from family to work: the neglected side of the work-family interface. *Hum. Relat.* 37:425–42

Cuddy AJC, Fiske ST, Glick P. 2004. When professionals become mothers, warmth doesn't cut the ice. *J. Soc. Issues* 60:701–18

Culbertson SS, Mills MJ, Fullagar CJ. 2012. Work engagement and work-family facilitation: making homes happier through positive affective spillover. *Hum. Relat.* 65:1155–77

de Janasz S, Behson SJ, Jonsen K, Lankau MJ. 2013. Dual sources of support for dual roles: how mentoring and work-family culture influence work-family conflict and job attitudes. *Int. J. Hum. Resour. Manag.* 24:1435–53

Dilworth JL. 2004. Predictors of negative spillover from family to work. *J. Fam. Issues* 25:241–61

Eagly AH. 1987. *Sex Differences in Social behavior: A Social-Role Interpretation.* Hillsdale, NJ: Erlbaum

Eaton SC. 2003. If you can use them: flexibility policies, organizational commitment and perceived performance. *Ind. Relat.* 42:145–67

Eby LT, Casper WJ, Lockwood A, Bordeaux C, Brinley A. 2005. Work and family research in IO/OB: content analysis and review of the literature (1980–2002). *J. Vocat. Behav.* 66(1):124–97

Ely RJ, Meyerson DE. 2000. Theories of gender in organizations: a new approach to organizational analysis and change. *Res. Organ. Behav.* 22:103–51

Ely RJ, Meyerson DE. 2010. An organizational approach to undoing gender: the unlikely case of offshore oil platforms. *Res. Organ. Behav.* 30:3–34

Epstein CF, Seron C, Oglensky B, Saute R. 1999. *The Part-Time Paradox: Time Norms, Professional Life, Family and Gender.* London: Routledge

Ferguson M, Carlson D, Zivnuska S, Whitten D. 2012. Support at work and home: the path to satisfaction through balance. *J. Vocat. Behav.* 80:299–307

Ford MT, Heinen BA, Langkamer KL. 2007. Work and family satisfaction and conflict: a meta-analysis of cross-domain relations. *J. Appl. Psychol.* 92(1):57–80

Frone MR, Russell M, Cooper ML. 1992. Antecedents and outcomes of work-family conflict: testing a model of the work-family interface. *J. Appl. Psychol.* 77:65–78

Fuegan K, Biernat M, Haines E, Deaux K. 2004. Mothers and fathers in the workplace: how gender and parental status influence judgments of job-related competence. *J. Soc. Issues* 60:737–54

Gerstel N, Clawson D. 2001. Unions' responses to family concerns. *Soc. Probl.* 48:277–98

Glass JL. 2004. Blessing or curse? Work-family policies and mother's wage growth over time. *Work Occup.* 31:367–94

Goode WJ. 1960. A theory of role strain. *Am. Sociol. Rev.* 25:483–96

Goodman WB, Crouter AC. 2009. Longitudinal associations between maternal work stress, negative work-family spillover, and depressive symptoms. *Fam. Relat.* 58:245–58

Gornick JC, Meyers MK. 2003. *Families That Work: Policies for Reconciling Parenthood and Employment.* New York: Russell Sage Found.

Greenberger E, O'Neil R. 1993. Spouse, parent, worker: role commitments and role-related experiences in the construction of adults' well-being. *Dev. Psychol.* 29:181–97

Greenhaus JH, Beutell NJ. 1985. Sources of conflict between work and family roles. *Acad. Manag. Rev.* 10:76–88

Greenhaus JH, Parasuraman S. 1999. Research on work, family, and gender: current status and future directions. In *Handbook of Gender and Work*, ed. GN Powell, pp. 391–412. Thousand Oaks, CA: Sage

Greenhaus JH, Peng AC, Allen TD. 2012. Relations of work identity, family identity, situational demands, and sex with employee work hours. *J. Vocat. Behav.* 80:27–37

Greenhaus JH, Powell GN. 2006. When work and family are allies: a theory of work-family enrichment. *Acad. Manag. Rev.* 31:72–92

Grzywacz JG, Carlson DS. 2007. Conceptualizing work-family balance: implications for practice and research. *Adv. Dev. Hum. Resour.* 9:455–71

Grzywacz JG, Carlson DS, Kacmar KM, Wayne JH. 2007. A multi-level perspective on the synergies between work and family. *J. Occup. Organ. Psychol.* 80:559–74

Grzywacz JG, Marks NF. 2000. Reconceptualizing the work-family interface: an ecological perspective on the correlates of positive and negative spillover between work and family. *J. Occup. Health Psychol.* 5:111–26

Gutek BA, Searle S, Klepa L. 1991. Rational versus gender role explanations for work-family conflict. *J. Appl. Psychol.* 76:560–68

Haar JM, Bardoel EA. 2008. Positive spillover from the work-family interface: a study of Australian employees. *Asia Pac. J. Hum. Resour.* 46:275–87

Hall GB, Dollard MF, Tuckey MR, Winefield AH, Thompson BM. 2010. Job demands, work-family conflict, and emotional exhaustion in police officers: a longitudinal test of competing theories. *J. Occup. Organ. Psychol.* 83:237–50

Hammer LB, Cullen JC, Neal MB, Sinclair RR, Shafiro MV. 2005. The longitudinal effects of work-family conflict and positive spillover on depressive symptoms among dual-earner couples. *J. Occup. Health Psychol.* 10:138–54

Hammer LB, Kossek EE, Bodner T, Anger K, Zimmerman K. 2011. Clarifying work-family intervention processes: the roles of work-family conflict and family supportive supervisor behaviors. *J. Appl. Psychol.* 96:134–50

Hartung D, Hahlweg K. 2011. Stress reduction at the work-family interface: Positive parenting and self-efficacy as mechanisms of change in Workplace Triple P. *Behav. Modif.* 35:54–77

Henly JR, Shaefer HL, Waxman E. 2006. Nonstandard work schedules: employer- and employee-driven flexibility in retail jobs. *Soc. Serv. Rev.* 80:609–34

Heymann J. 2013. *Children's Chances: How Countries Can Move from Surviving to Thriving.* Cambridge, MA: Harvard Univ. Press

Heymann J, Boynton-Jarrett R, Carter P, Bond JT, Galinsky E. 2002. *Work-Family Issues and Low-Income Families.* New York: Ford Found.

Hill EJ, Allen S, Jacob J, Bair AF, Bikhazi SL, et al. 2007. Work-family facilitation: expanding theoretical understanding through qualitative exploration. *Adv. Dev. Hum. Resour.* 9:507–26

Hochschild A. 1989. *The Second Shift: Working Parents and the Revolution at Home.* New York: Penguin

Hochschild A. 1997. *The Time Bind: When Work Becomes Home and Home Becomes Work.* New York: Metropolitan/Holt

Humberd B, Ladge JJ, Harrington B. 2015. The "new" dad: navigating fathering identity within organizations. *J. Bus. Psychol.* 30:249–66

Hunter EM, Perry SJ, Carlson DS, Smith SA. 2010. Linking team resources to work-family enrichment and satisfaction. *J. Vocat. Behav.* 77:304–12

Innstrand ST, Langballe EM, Espnes GA, Aasland OG, Falkum E. 2010. Work-home conflict and facilitation across four different family structures in Norway. *Community Work Fam.* 13:231–49

Jacobs JA, Gerson K. 2004. *The Time Divide: Work, Family, and Gender Inequality.* Cambridge, MA: Harvard Univ. Press

Judiesch MK, Lyness KS. 1999. Left behind? The impact of leaves of absence on managers' career success. *Acad. Manag. J.* 42:641–51

Kahn RL, Wolfe DM, Quinn R, Snoek JD, Rosenthal RA. 1964. *Organizational Stress.* New York: Wiley

Kanter RM. 1977. *Work and Family in the United States: A Critical Review and Agenda for Research and Policy.* New York: Russell Sage Found.

Kantor J. 2014. Working anything but 9 to 5. *New York Times,* Aug. 13. **http://www.nytimes.com/interactive/2014/08/13/us/starbucks-workers-scheduling-hours.html**

Karatepe OS, Bekteshi L. 2008. Antecedents and outcomes of work-family facilitation and family-work facilitation among frontline hotel employees. *Int. J. Hosp. Manag.* 27(4):517–28

Kellogg KC. 2011. *Challenging Operations: Medical Reform and Resistance in Surgery.* Chicago: Univ. Chicago Press

Kelly EL, Kossek EE, Hammer LB, Durham M, Bray J, et al. 2008. Getting there from here: research on the effects of work-family initiatives on work-family conflict and business outcomes. *Acad. Manag. Ann.* 2:305–49

Kelly EL, Moen P. 2007. Rethinking the clockwork of work: why schedule control may pay off at work and at home. *Adv. Dev. Hum. Resour.* 9:487–506

Kelly EL, Moen P, Oakes JM, Fan W, Okechukwu C, et al. 2014. Changing work and work-family conflict: evidence from the work, family, and health network. *Am. Sociol. Rev.* 79:485–516

Kelly EL, Moen P, Tranby E. 2011. Changing workplaces to reduce work-family conflict: schedule control in a white-collar organization. *Am. Sociol. Rev.* 76:265–90

Kirchmeyer C. 1993. Nonwork-to-work spillover: a more balanced view of the experiences and coping of professional women and men. *Sex Roles* 28:531–52

Kobrynowicz D, Biernat M. 1997. Decoding subjective evaluations: how stereotypes provide shifting standards. *J. Exp. Soc. Psychol.* 33:579–601

Korabik K, McElwain A, Chappell DB. 2008. Integrating gender-related issues into research on work and family. In *Handbook of Work-Family Integration: Research, Theory, and Best Practices*, ed. K Korabik, DS Lero, DL Whitehead, pp. 215–32. Amsterdam: Academic

Kossek EE, Baltes BB, Matthews RA. 2011a. How work-family research can finally have an impact in organizations. *Ind. Organ. Psychol.: Perspect. Sci. Pract.* 4:352–69

Kossek EE, Baltes BB, Matthews RA. 2011b. Innovative ideas on how work-family research can have more impact. *Ind. Organ. Psychol.: Perspect. Sci. Pract.* 4:426–32

Kossek EE, Hammer LB, Thompson RJ, Burke LB. 2014. *Leveraging Workplace Flexibility for Engagement and Productivity*. SHRM Found. Eff. Pract. Guidel. Ser. Alexandria, VA: SHRM Found.

Kossek EE, Lautsch BA, Eaton SC. 2006. Telecommuting, control, and boundary management: correlates of policy use and practice, job control, and work-family effectiveness. *J. Vocat. Behav.* 68:347–67

Kossek EE, Michel JS. 2010. Flexible work schedules. In *APA Handbook of Industrial and Organizational Psychology*, Vol. 1, ed. S Zedeck, pp. 535–72. Washington, DC: Am. Psychol. Assoc.

Kossek EE, Ozeki C. 1998. Work-family conflict, policies, and the job-life satisfaction relationship: a review and directions for organizational behavior-human resources research. *J. Appl. Psychol.* 83:139–49

Kwan HK, Mao Y, Zhang H. 2010. The impact of role-modeling on protégés' personal learning and work-family enrichment. *J. Vocat. Behav.* 77(2):313–22

Lambert SJ. 2008. Passing the buck: labor flexibility practices that transfer risk onto hourly workers. *Hum. Relat.* 61:1203–27

Lambert SJ, Fugiel PJ, Henly JR. 2014. *Precarious Working Schedules Among Early-Career Employees in the US: A National Snapshot*. Chicago: EINet, School Soc. Serv. Admin., Univ. Chicago

Lamont M. 2012. *Money, Morals, and Manners: The Culture of the French and American Upper-Middle Class*. Chicago: Univ. Chicago Press

Lee E-S, Chang JY, Kim H. 2011. The work-family interface in Korea: Can family life enrich work life? *Int. J. Hum. Resour. Manag.* 22:2032–53

Lee NY, Zvonkovic AM, Crawford DW. 2014. The impact of work-family conflict and facilitation on women's perceptions of role balance. *J. Fam. Issues* 35:1252–74

Leslie LM, Manchester CF, Park T, Mehng SA. 2012. Flexible work practices: a source of career premiums or penalties? *Acad. Manag. J.* 55:1407–28

Lobosco K. 2015. Walmart's other promise to workers: better schedules. *CNN Money*, Feb. 19. **http://money.cnn.com/2015/02/19/news/companies/walmart-wages-schedules/**

Maertz CP, Boyar SL. 2011. Work-family conflict, enrichment, and balance under "levels" and "episodes" approaches. *J. Manag.* 37:68–98

Masuda AD, McNall LA, Allen TD, Nicklin JM. 2012. Examining the constructs of work-to-family enrichment and positive spillover. *J. Vocat. Behav.* 80:197–210

McNall LA, Masuda AD, Shanock LR, Nicklin JM. 2011. Interaction of core self-evaluations and perceived organizational support on work-to-family enrichment. *J. Psychol.* 145(2):133–49

McNall LA, Nicklin JM, Masuda AD. 2010. A meta-analytic review of the consequences associated with work-family enrichment. *J. Bus. Psychol.* 25:381–96

Merton RK. 1949. *Social Theory and Social Structure*. New York: Free Press

Michel JS, Clark MA, Jaramillo D. 2011. The role of the Five Factor Model of personality in the perceptions of negative and positive forms of work-nonwork spillover: a meta-analytic review. *J. Vocat. Behav.* 79:191–203

Moen P, Kelly E, Hill R. 2011. Does enhancing work-time control and flexibility reduce turnover? A naturally occurring experiment. *Soc. Probl.* 58:69–98

Molino M, Ghislieri C, Cortese CG. 2013. When work enriches family life: the meditational role of professional development opportunities. *J. Workplace Learn.* 25:98–113

Munsch CL. 2015. *Transformations in masculinity and homophobia*. Presented at Intl. Conf. on Masculinities: Engaging Men and Boys for Gender Equity, March 5–8, New York, NY

Ng TWH, Feldman DC. 2008. Long work hours: a social identity perspective on meta-analysis data. *J. Organ. Behav.* 29:853–80

Nohe C, Meier LL, Sonntag K, Michel A. 2015. The chicken or the egg? A meta-analysis of panel studies of the relationship between work-family conflict and strain. *J. Appl. Psychol.* 100:522–36

OECD (Organ. Econ. Coop. Dev.). 2014. Average annual hours actually worked per worker [data set]. Paris: OECD. **http://stats.oecd.org/index.aspx?DataSetCode=ANHRS**

Ollier-Malaterre A, Valcour M, den Dulk L, Kossek EE. 2013. Theorizing national context to develop comparative work-life research: a review and research agenda. *Eur. Manag. J.* 31:433–47

Paustian-Underdahl SC, Halbesleben JRB. 2014. Examining the influence of climate, supervisor guidance, and behavioral integrity on work-family conflict: a demands and resources approach. *J. Organ. Behav.* 35:447–63

Perlow LA. 2012. *Sleeping with Your Smart Phone: How to Break the 24/7 Habit and Change the Way You Work*. Cambridge, MA: Harvard Bus. Rev. Press

Perlow LA, Kelly EL. 2014. Toward a model of work redesign for better work and better life. *Work Occup.* 41:111–34

Perrewe PL, Hochwarter WA. 2001. Can we really have it all? The attainment of work and family values. *Curr. Dir. Psychol. Sci.* 10:29–33

Pleck JH. 1977. The work-family role system. *Soc. Probl.* 24:417–27

Radcliffe LS, Cassell C. 2014. Resolving couples' work-family conflicts: the complexity of decision making and the introduction of a new framework. *Hum. Relat.* 67:793–819

Rapoport R, Rapoport R. 1971. *Dual-Career Families*. Baltimore, MD: Penguin Books

Reid E. 2015. Embracing, passing, revealing and the ideal worker image: how people navigate expected and experienced professional identities. *Organ. Sci.* **http://dx.doi.org/10.1287/orsc.2015.0975**

Ressler C, Thompson J. 2008. *Why Work Sucks and How to Fix It*. New York: Penguin

Roehling PV, Jarvis LH, Swope HE. 2005. Variations in negative work-family spillover among white, black, and Hispanic American men and women. *J. Fam. Issues* 26:840–65

Rogier SA, Padgett MY. 2004. The impact of utilizing a flexible work schedule on the perceived career advancement potential of women. *Hum. Resour. Dev. Q.* 15:89–106

Rost I, Mostert K. 2007. The interaction between work and home of employees in the earthmoving equipment industry: measurement and prevalence. *SA J. Ind. Psychol.* 33:54–61

Rothbard NP. 2001. Enriching or depleting? The dynamics of engagement in work and family roles. *Adm. Sci. Q.* 46:655–84

Rotundo DM, Kincaid JF. 2008. Conflict, facilitation, and individual coping styles across the work and family domains. *J. Manag. Psychol.* 23:484–506

Ruderman MN, Ohlott PJ, Panzer K, King SN. 2002. Benefits of multiple roles for managerial women. *Acad. Manag. J.* 45:369–86

Rudman LA, Mescher K. 2013. Penalizing men who request a family leave: Is flexibility stigma a femininity stigma? *J. Soc. Issues* 69:322–40

Russo M, Buonocore F. 2012. The relationship between work-family enrichment and nurse turnover. *J. Manag. Psychol.* 27:216–36

Schulte B. 2014. *Overwhelmed: Work, Love, and Play When No One Has the Time*. New York: Sarah Crichton Books

Shows C, Gerstel N. 2009. Fathering, class, and gender: a comparison of physicians and emergency medical technicians. *Gender Soc.* 23:161–87

SHRM (Soc. Hum. Resour. Manag.). 2010. 2010 employee benefits: examining employee benefits in the midst of a recovering economy. **http://www.shrm.org/research/surveyfindings/articles/documents/10-0280%20employee%20benefits%20survey%20report-fnl.pdf**

Siu O, Lu J, Brough P, Lu C, Bakker A, et al. 2010. Role resources and work-family enrichment: the role of work engagement. *J. Vocat. Behav.* 77:470–80

Stone P. 2007. *Opting Out? Why Women Really Quit Careers and Head Home.* Berkeley: Univ. Calif. Press

Streib J. 2015. *The Power of the Past: Understanding Cross-Class Marriages.* New York: Oxford Univ. Press

Sumer HC, Knight PA. 2001. How do people with different attachment styles balance work and family? A personality perspective on work-family linkage. *J. Appl. Psychol.* 86:653–63

Swanberg JE, McKechnie SP, Ojha MU, James JB. 2011. Schedule control, supervisor support and work engagement: a winning combination for workers in hourly jobs? *J. Vocat. Behav.* 79:613–24

Thompson CS, Beauvais LL, Lyness KS. 1999. When work-family benefits are not enough: The influence of work-family culture on benefit utilization, organizational attachment, and work-family conflict. *J. Vocat. Behav.* 54:392–415

Tompson HB, Werner JM. 1997. The impact of role conflict/facilitation on core and discretionary behaviors: testing a mediated model. *J. Manag.* 23:583–601

Trades Union Congr. 2008. Single women in their thirties do more unpaid overtime than anyone else. London: TUC. **http://www.tuc.org.uk/equality-issues/childcare/equal-pay/single-women-their-30s-do-more-unpaid-overtime-anyone-else**

Vandello JA, Bosson JK, Cohen D, Burnaford RM, Weaver JR. 2008. Precarious manhood. *J. Personal. Soc. Psychol.* 95:1325–39

Vandello JA, Hettinger VE, Bosson JK, Siddiqi J. 2013. When equal isn't really equal: the masculine dilemma of seeking work flexibility. *J. Soc. Issues* 69:303–21

Van Steenbergen EF, Ellemers N. 2009. Is managing the work-family interface worthwhile? Benefits for employee health and performance. *J. Organ. Behav.* 30:616–42

Wayne JH, Casper WJ, Matthews RA, Allen TD. 2013. Family-supportive organization perceptions and organizational commitment: the mediating role of work-family conflict and enrichment and partner attitudes. *J. Appl. Psychol.* 98(4):606–22

Wayne JH, Musisca N, Fleeson W. 2004. Considering the role of personality in the work-family experience: relationships of the Big Five to work-family conflict and facilitation. *J. Vocat. Behav.* 64:108–30

Wayne JH, Randel AE, Stevens J. 2006. The role of identity and work-family support in work-family enrichment and its work-related consequences. *J. Vocat. Behav.* 69:445–61

Weer CH, Greenhaus JH, Linnehan F. 2010. Commitment to nonwork roles and job performance: enrichment and conflict perspectives. *J. Vocat. Behav.* 76:306–16

Williams A, Franche R-L, Ibrahim S, Mustard C, Layton FR. 2006. Examining the relationship between work-family spillover and sleep quality. *J. Occup. Health Psychol.* 11:27–37

Williams JC. 2000. *Unbending Gender: Why Family and Work Conflict and What To Do About It.* New York: Oxford Univ. Press

Williams JC. 2010. *Reshaping the Work-Family Debate: Why Men and Class Matter.* Cambridge, MA: Harvard Univ. Press

Williams JC, Blair-Loy M, Berdahl JL. 2013. Cultural schemas, social class, and the flexibility stigma. *J. Soc. Issues* 69:209–34

Williams JC, Boushey H. 2010. Three faces of work-family conflict: the poor, the professionals, and the missing middle. San Francisco: Univ. Calif. Hastings Coll. Law, Cent. WorkLife Law. **http://www.worklifelaw.org/pubs/ThreeFacesofWork-FamilyConflict.pdf**

Williams JC, Dempsey R. 2014. *What Works for Women at Work: Four Patterns Working Women Need to Know.* New York: NYU Press

Williams JC, Phillips K, Hall ER. 2015a. Double jeopardy: gender bias against women in STEM. San Francisco: Univ. Calif. Hastings Coll. Law, Cent. WorkLife Law. **http://www.toolsforchangeinstem.org/tools/double-jeopardy-report**

Williams JC, Platt A, Lee J. 2015b. Disruptive innovation: new models of legal practice. San Francisco: Univ. Calif. Hastings Coll. Law, Cent. WorkLife Law. **http://worklifelaw.org/new-models-report/**

Zedeck S, ed. 1992. *Work, Families, and Organizations: Frontiers of Industrial and Organizational Psychology*, Vol. 5. San Francisco: Jossey-Bass

Zedeck S, Mosier KL. 1990. Work in the family and employing organization. *Am. Psychol.* 45:240–51

Zuo J. 2004. Shifting the breadwinning boundary: the role of men's breadwinner status and their gender ideologies. *J. Fam. Issues* 25:811–32

Vocational Psychology: Agency, Equity, and Well-Being

Steven D. Brown[1] and Robert W. Lent[2]

[1] School of Education, Loyola University Chicago, Chicago, Illinois 60611;
email: sbrown@luc.edu

[2] College of Education, University of Maryland, College Park, Maryland 20742;
email: boblent@umd.edu

Annu. Rev. Psychol. 2016. 67:541–65

First published online as a Review in Advance on
October 2, 2015

The *Annual Review of Psychology* is online at
psych.annualreviews.org

This article's doi:
10.1146/annurev-psych-122414-033237

Keywords

career adaptability, self-efficacy, work volition, social class, STEM
participation, work well-being

Abstract

The present review organizes the vocational psychology literature published
between 2007 and 2014 into three overarching themes: Promoting (*a*) agency
in career development, (*b*) equity in the work force, and (*c*) well-being in
work and educational settings. Research on career adaptability, self-efficacy
beliefs, and work volition is reviewed in the agency section, with the goal
of delineating variables that promote or constrain the exercise of personal
agency in academic and occupational pursuits. The equity theme covers research on social class and race/ethnicity in career development; entry and
retention of women and people of color in science, technology, engineering, and math (STEM) fields; and the career service needs of survivors of
domestic violence and of criminal offenders. The goal was to explore how
greater equity in the work force could be promoted for these groups. In
the well-being section, we review research on hedonic (work, educational,
and life satisfaction) and eudaimonic (career calling, meaning, engagement,
and commitment) variables, with the goal of understanding how well-being
might be promoted at school and at work. Future research needs related to
each theme are also discussed.

Contents

INTRODUCTION

Many schemes have been used to organize prior reviews of the vocational psychology literature. To fashion a framework for this review, we began by searching the tables of contents of six journals that are exclusively or largely devoted to vocational psychology and career development (*Career Development Quarterly, Journal of Career Assessment, Journal of Career Development, Journal of Vocational Behavior, Journal of Counseling Psychology,* and *The Counseling Psychologist*). The time frame for this search (2007–2014) was set to dovetail with the last *Annual Review of Psychology* examination of the vocational psychology literature (Fouad 2007).

A frequency count of theories, constructs, and populations revealed that two theoretical perspectives, person-environment (P-E) fit and social cognitive career theory (SCCT), had received the bulk of research attention during the review period. The P-E fit perspective hypothesizes that the degree of match (or fit) between person characteristics (e.g., interests, work values, personality, abilities) and characteristics of the work environment is an important predictor of work satisfaction, performance, and tenure. SCCT focuses on the roles of person characteristics (e.g., self-efficacy beliefs, outcome expectations, goals) and contextual factors (e.g., supports, barriers) in educational and work interest development, choice making, satisfaction, and performance. Career construction theory, which emphasizes the ways in which people help to author their own work lives in relation to environmental (e.g., family, role model) influences, had also received favorable attention as a practice framework, though less vigorous empirical activity, with the notable exception of recent research on the career adaptability construct. A few other conceptual frameworks, such as the psychology of working perspective, which is concerned with the work participation of underserved and understudied workers, also stimulated valuable discussion and some inquiry during the review period.

In terms of constructs, we noted that the following had received concentrated research attention since 2007: self-efficacy beliefs, career adaptability, career exploration and decision making, career and educational barriers and supports, work and well-being, work volition, career aspirations, work transitions, work-family conflict and enhancement, vocational calling, interests, and personality. A variety of population segments (and individual difference variables) had been studied, with a focus on such dimensions as race, ethnicity, gender, sexual orientation, social class, and disability; children and adolescents; prisoners and ex-offenders; and domestic violence survivors. International samples were also included more frequently than in prior years, marking an important new era in vocational psychology research.

In conducting our analysis of journal content, we realized that much of the recent literature can be organized around three overarching themes that reflect the social justice zeitgeist of contemporary vocational psychology: promoting agency in career development, equity at work, and well-being in occupational and educational settings. It can be argued that these three themes form a cogent narrative for the field at present, along with a meaningful framework for integrating much research on its theories, constructs, and populations of interest. Although a good deal of valuable research on more traditional vocational psychology topics (e.g., interest measurement, career decision making) was generated during the review period, our goal is to focus more selectively on work that is emerging from newer as well as ongoing conceptual streams and that reflects the field's concerns with a variety of contemporary social issues. We also seek a balance between topics that have received a good deal of research during the review period and topics that have received more limited inquiry but are relevant to vocational psychology's understanding of agency, equity, or well-being. Given space considerations, in many instances, we cite only a few studies as examples of larger bodies of research.

The first theme (agency) includes research on career adaptability, self-efficacy beliefs, and work volition. The second theme (equity) encompasses (*a*) the career development of underserved youth; (*b*) the science, technology, engineering, and math (STEM) entry and retention of women and people of color; and (*c*) the career experiences and service needs of domestic abuse survivors and criminal justice populations. Although these groups have received varying levels of attention in the literature, their inclusion in this review reflects the field's increasing emphasis on persons who often face significant impediments to their work participation or career advancement. The third theme (well-being) involves research on both hedonic and eudaimonic well-being in educational settings and in the workplace. Hedonic well-being includes such affective outcomes as job and academic satisfaction. Coverage of eudaimonic well-being focuses on topics, such as meaning and calling, that capture ways in which people achieve a sense of growth and fulfillment at school and work. Our review concludes with an outline of several directions for future inquiry on agency, equity, and well-being in the context of academic and work settings.

AGENCY: MECHANISMS OF SELF-DIRECTION IN CAREER DEVELOPMENT

In this section, we highlight research involving constructs that, theoretically, enable people to exercise agency in their career development and to adapt well to their vocational options. At the same time, these research streams often point to contextual (e.g., social and economic) variables that may either maximize or hinder the exercise of agency in career pursuits.

Adaptability

Career adaptability refers to "the readiness to cope with the predictable tasks of preparing for and participating in the work role and with the unpredictable adjustments prompted by changes in work and working conditions" (Savickas 1997, p. 254). Adaptability is a central construct of career construction theory. Though it has been operationalized in a variety of ways (e.g., Rottinghaus et al.

2012), most recent research on the construct has used the Career Adapt-Abilities Scale (CAAS). Savickas & Porfeli (2012) described the development and initial psychometric examination of the scale, which was studied within a remarkable multicountry collaborative project.

Factor structure and correlates of adaptability. The CAAS consists of four 6-item scales, each corresponding to the conceptual dimensions of career adaptability: career (*a*) concern (an orientation toward planning for the future), (*b*) control (tendencies toward conscientiousness and organization), (*c*) curiosity (willingness to explore how one fits into the work world), and (*d*) confidence (self-efficacy regarding one's problem-solving capabilities). Confirmatory factor analysis of the CAAS has supported a hierarchical latent structure, with each of the primary four dimensions loading on a higher-order adaptability factor (Savickas & Porfeli 2012). CAAS total and subscale scores have been found to relate to a wide array of career and noncareer variables, such as vocational identity (Porfeli & Savickas 2012), job and life satisfaction (Maggiori et al. 2013), and Big Five personality factors (van Vianen et al. 2012). Hamtiaux et al. (2013) found evidence of convergent validity between the CAAS and an alternative measure of adaptability.

Model tests and developmental considerations. Several studies have tested theoretical models of how career adaptability functions in relation to other variables. For example, Guan et al. (2013) examined career adaptability relative to the job search process in Chinese university graduates, finding that career adaptability was associated with more favorable appraisals of job search self-efficacy which, in turn, predicted later employment status and aspects of fit to the new work environment. In a study of Serbian business students, Tolentino et al. (2014) found that career adaptability was related to entrepreneurial career intentions through entrepreneurial self-efficacy, particularly among participants with exposure to a family business. Other studies have reported that career adaptability partially mediated the relation of personality factors to work engagement (Rossier et al. 2012) and explained unique variance in career satisfaction and self-rated performance beyond personality factors (Zacher 2014a).

A few investigations have examined aspects of change or malleability in career adaptability. In a longitudinal study of Australian workers, Zacher (2014b) found that age, education, future temporal focus, and certain personality dimensions predicted change in one or more of the four dimensions of career adaptability over time. In a quasi-experimental study with Dutch university graduates, Koen et al. (2012) offered training designed to promote career adaptability. Relative to a control group, they found that those receiving training exhibited positive change on three of the four adaptability dimensions. A six-month follow-up indicated that, among those who subsequently found employment, participants who had received adaptability training fared better than controls on indicators of employment quality (e.g., higher job satisfaction, lower turnover intentions).

In sum, the recent literature on career adaptability, particularly that involving the CAAS, is remarkable both in the amount of research generated in a short time and in the breadth of variables to which adaptability has been related. A useful future research direction might include study of how adaptability functions relative to preparation for, or adaptation to, work transitions. For example, might higher levels of career adaptability promote more thorough preparation for work changes (e.g., via anticipatory marshaling of coping resources or proactive skill updating) or more resilience (e.g., quicker recovery) when adverse work events occur? It may also be useful to clarify the types of criterion variables that career adaptability should, theoretically, explain. Such added theoretical precision may help to target particularly salient questions (e.g., what is the role of career adaptability relative, say, to social support and other psychosocial resources in the process and aftermath of work changes?).

Self-Efficacy

In this section, we discuss findings on self-efficacy and related social cognitive variables in relation to a broad array of educational and work topics. In later sections, we highlight inquiry on social cognitive variables specifically within the context of STEM domains as well as in relation to well-being outcomes.

Self-efficacy, interest, and choice. One of the more active areas of career self-efficacy inquiry has involved tests of social cognitive career theory's interest and choice models (Lent et al. 1994). In brief, these models hypothesize that career-relevant interests are largely a function of self-efficacy (beliefs about personal capabilities) and outcome expectations (beliefs about the consequences of actions), in particular performance domains (e.g., science, arts). People are likely to make educational and occupational choices that are consistent with their interests, self-efficacy, and outcome expectations, particularly if their preferred options are accompanied by favorable environmental conditions (e.g., adequate supports, minimal barriers). Sheu et al. (2010) reported a meta-analysis of data from 45 independent samples that had tested versions of the SCCT choice model. The results were reported separately by Holland themes (Holland 1997), which group people and environments into six primary types: (*a*) realistic (e.g., preference for mechanical, manual, and physical tasks), (*b*) investigative (e.g., preference for scientific and mathematical activities), (*c*) artistic (e.g., preference for artistic and creative activities), (*d*) social (e.g., preference for helping and teaching people), (*e*) enterprising (e.g., preference for selling, leading, managing, and persuading people), and (*f*) conventional (e.g., preference for an ordered work environment and engaging in detailed business tasks).

Sheu et al. (2010) found that the choice model generally fit the data well across Holland themes, though self-efficacy (confidence in successfully completing theme-related tasks) tended to contribute to the prediction of choice goals more indirectly, through outcome expectations (expected outcomes of engaging in theme-related tasks) and interests, than directly. In addition, contextual supports and barriers generally produced more reliable indirect paths to choice goals, via self-efficacy and outcome expectations, than direct ones. These findings suggest a nuanced interplay among person and contextual variables in the career choice process. For example, contextual supports and barriers (e.g., the presence or absence of mentors or financial resources) may bolster or temper self-efficacy and outcome expectations, which in turn may reshape interests and goals. Although Sheu et al.'s (2010) path analysis was based on cross-sectional data, several longitudinal studies have supported many of the hypothesized temporal linkages among the social cognitive variables, including the paths from self-efficacy to outcome expectations, interests, and goals (e.g., Lent et al. 2008, 2010).

Self-efficacy, performance, and persistence. The relations of self-efficacy and other social cognitive variables to performance outcomes has been a topic of interest to researchers in educational and organizational psychology as well as vocational psychology, with some studies specifically aimed at testing SCCT's performance model, which posits that academic and occupational performance (indicators of success) and persistence result from the interplay among ability or past performance, self-efficacy, outcome expectations, and performance goals.

Wright et al. (2013) examined the role of self-efficacy in relation to college students' performance and persistence behavior. They found that, controlling for gender, ethnicity, first-generation status, and prior performance, self-efficacy regarding academic capabilities was a good predictor of students' academic success as well as of their likelihood of remaining in college beyond their first semester. Cupani & Pautassi (2013) examined the relations of social cognitive variables to the academic performance (math grades) of Argentinian high school students. Consistent with hypotheses, numeric ability was linked to performance both directly and indirectly through math self-efficacy. Stronger self-efficacy and outcome expectations were each associated with more ambitious performance goals, which in turn predicted better performance. Unexpectedly, however, ability was negatively associated with outcome expectations.

Two meta-analyses assessed the SCCT performance model during the period examined in this review. In the first meta-analysis, support was found for the joint roles of ability and self-efficacy relative to college academic outcomes (Brown et al. 2008). Measures of ability and high school performance predicted college grades both directly and indirectly through self-efficacy; however, the relation of ability/past performance to persistence was fully mediated by self-efficacy. Performance goals contributed to the prediction of persistence but not of grades.

In the second meta-analysis, Brown et al. (2011) tested the performance model in the context of work performance. As in the academic performance meta-analysis, goals did not explain unique variance in performance beyond that explained by self-efficacy and cognitive ability. It was also found that conscientiousness, a personality factor, was linked to performance both directly and indirectly, via self-efficacy. Thus, performance may profit not only from cognitive ability and technical skills but also from self-efficacy and conscientiousness, which enable workers to leverage their talents. Other work using longitudinal designs has tended to support the roles of goals and self-efficacy as antecedents of career performance (Abele & Spurk 2009) as well as hypothesized reciprocal links between self-efficacy and performance (Spurk & Abele 2014).

Self-efficacy, process behaviors, and the socioeconomic context. Many studies have examined self-efficacy and other social cognitive variables in relation to process aspects of career development (Lent & Brown 2013), that is, agentic behaviors, such as decision making or job seeking, that people employ to achieve their educational and occupational objectives across varied performance domains and often in the face of obstacles (e.g., economic limitations, work-family conflict). Gibbons & Borders (2010) studied the college-going expectations of racially diverse and economically challenged middle schoolers whose parents had not attended college. They found that students' college-related self-efficacy and outcome expectations were predicted by perceived barriers (e.g., financial limitations, lack of role models) and social supports relative to college attendance; self-efficacy and outcome expectations were, in turn, predictive of students' intentions to attend college. In a study of high school students in a high-poverty rural area, Ali & Saunders (2009) found that students' self-efficacy (related to educational and job-finding skills) and outcome expectations (related to career decision making) predicted their level of career aspirations beyond social supports and economic variables.

Dahling et al. (2013) examined the job search goals of unemployed workers in the context of financial strain and regional unemployment rates. They found that self-efficacy and outcome expectations were each positively related to search goals. Financial strain had a direct, negative relation with job search self-efficacy and indirect, negative relations (via self-efficacy) with job search outcome expectations and search goals, particularly under conditions of high regional unemployment.

Most of the process-oriented research on social cognitive variables has involved career decision-making self-efficacy in student samples. Mirroring findings on content aspects of career choice (i.e., goals to pursue particular career paths, such as science), research has shown that intention to engage in career exploration or decision-making activities is well predicted by career decision self-efficacy and outcome expectations. For example, Huang & Hsieh (2011) found that Taiwanese college students' self-efficacy and outcome expectations mediated the relation of family socioeconomic status (SES) to career exploration intentions. Self-efficacy and goals were each found to account for unique variance in Australian high school students' career planning behavior, both in cross-sectional (Rogers et al. 2008) and longitudinal studies (Rogers & Creed 2011). In a recent meta-analysis, Choi et al. (2012) reported that career decision self-efficacy is related strongly and negatively with career indecision. In sum, self-efficacy has been linked to greater career exploration and job search intentions, more engagement in the career planning process, and lower levels of career indecision.

Self-efficacy sources and interventions. Researchers have also examined the learning experiences that are assumed to give rise to self-efficacy and outcome expectations. Thompson & Dahling (2012) found that the primary sources of efficacy information (e.g., performance accomplishments, vicarious learning) were, as hypothesized, related to college students' self-efficacy and outcome expectations across Holland themes. They also found that the paths from gender and perceived social status to self-efficacy and outcome expectations were partly mediated by the sources of self-efficacy in certain Holland themes, suggesting that gender and socioeconomic privilege predict exposure to learning experiences that, in turn, help to shape career-relevant self-efficacy and outcome expectations.

Tokar et al. (2007) found that the paths from gender to the sources of efficacy information were partly mediated by conformance with gender role norms in particular Holland's themes associated with gender-typed choices. These results suggest the interplay among person variables and socially mediated learning experiences that help to perpetuate the status quo. For example, women tend to receive more exposure to learning experiences that promote efficacy at social than at realistic activities, along with encouragement to conform to gender role norms. Career-relevant choices may thus become constrained in part through an environmental shaping process that fosters internalized beliefs about personal efficacy and the range of acceptable occupational options for one's sex.

Several researchers have designed and tested educational or counseling methods to help promote beneficial efficacy beliefs. For example, Betz & Borgen (2009) compared the effects of two online career exploration systems with undecided college freshmen. Both systems were associated with significant increases in career decision self-efficacy and decidedness about college majors. Positive changes in career decision self-efficacy and related outcomes (e.g., vocational identity) have been reported with other online (Tirpak & Schlosser 2013) and career course (Scott & Ciani 2008) interventions as well. (For a review of research on interventions and experimental studies relative to change in self-efficacy and other social cognitive constructs, see Sheu & Lent 2015.)

Work Volition

Work volition has been defined as "the perceived capacity to make occupational choices despite constraints" (e.g., Jadidian & Duffy 2012, p. 155). Volition is a key notion in the psychology of working perspective (Blustein 2006, Blustein et al. 2008). Blustein (2006) argued that, given their life circumstances (e.g., income, race/ethnicity, availability of resources), many people are not sufficiently privileged to make unencumbered work choices or to work in their ideal careers. Thus, extant theories that emphasize agency may be less relevant to those with less privilege. Two specific hypotheses about the role of work volition in the occupational choice and attainment process have been suggested: (*a*) A negative relationship exists between work volition and the number of constraints that people encounter, and (*b*) the relationship between agentic-like career variables (e.g., self-efficacy beliefs, goals) and choices is moderated by work volition (e.g., the path from self-efficacy to goals in the SCCT choice model should be weaker for those with less volition and stronger for those with more volition) (Duffy et al. 2014b).

Relative to the first hypothesis, statistically significant but small negative relations of work volition to career barrier perceptions have been found in student (Duffy et al. 2012b) and adult (Duffy et al. 2012c) samples, suggesting that those with a greater sense of control over their work lives tend to perceive somewhat fewer hurdles to their occupational progress. In a study testing the second hypothesis among undergraduate science majors, Duffy et al. (2014b) found that volition did not moderate self-efficacy/outcome expectation or self-efficacy/goal relations in the SCCT choice model. That is, these relations were comparable regardless of level of volition. Other research has found work volition to relate strongly to career decision self-efficacy (Duffy et al. 2012b, Jadidian & Duffy 2012) and moderately to academic satisfaction (Jadidian & Duffy 2012) in college students. Duffy and colleagues found that, controlling for self-efficacy, work volition explained unique variance in the job satisfaction of employed workers (Duffy et al. 2013c) and the life satisfaction of unemployed workers (Duffy et al. 2013b).

On balance, this modest set of findings suggests that perceptions of control over one's work life may contribute directly to broad affective outcomes but do not moderate paths in the SCCT choice model. Although further construct validity data are needed, the work volition measure appears to represent a generalized sense of efficacy, or agency, in the career domain (Brown 2015). Like career adaptability, work volition may translate or "carry" the effects of personality traits into the career domain. Because predictors tend to produce larger relations with criterion variables to the extent that they are well matched with them in terms of content, context, and level of specificity (Ajzen 1988), work volition may improve upon nondomain-specific personality indices in predicting career-relevant outcomes. By the same token, work volition may account for unique variance beyond more task-specific measures of self-efficacy in predicting overall job and life satisfaction because it may better match the latter at a global (versus specific) level of measurement.

EQUITY: SOCIAL JUSTICE IN CAREER DEVELOPMENT

A commitment to social justice is a central value of vocational psychology science and practice (Blustein 2006). In this section, we review research on the career development of persons who are underrepresented in particular career paths (women and most racial/ethnic minority groups in STEM fields) or who often face substantial hurdles in educational and occupational settings (e.g., underserved youth, survivors of domestic violence).

Educational and Occupational Attainment and Success of Underserved Youth

Much has been written about how experiences associated with poverty (e.g., lack of financial resources, under-resourced schools, lack of role models, neighborhood violence) can severely limit the types of occupations available to and attainable by poor youth as they grow into adulthood (e.g., Arbona 2000). Youth growing up under lower socioeconomic conditions tend to have disproportionately lower rates of occupational attainment compared to more affluent youth (Natl. Cent. Educ. Stat. 2002). Poor youth of color may experience additional sociopolitical barriers to occupational attainment (e.g., structural racism and discrimination), compounding the long-term effects of poverty on occupational attainment (e.g., Blustein 2006). In this section, we review vocational psychology research on the linkage of poverty and race to occupational attainment.

Socioeconomic status and occupational attainment. Research has explored the direct and mediated effects of SES (usually indexed by some combination of parents' education, occupation, and income) on educational or occupational aspirations or expectations. Aspirations reflect the amount of education or level of occupational attainment adolescents hope to attain (under ideal conditions). Expectations involve the educational or occupational level that adolescents expect to achieve (under current conditions). Although aspirations are frequently not realized, higher aspirations are associated with more favorable occupational outcomes, perhaps in part because low aspirations prompt avoidance of educational experiences that can facilitate higher attainment (Howard et al. 2011). Both aspirations and expectations have been found to predict educational and occupational attainment (with educational attainment also predicting later occupational attainment; Lee & Rojewski 2009, Mello 2008). It is, therefore, important to understand the pathways through which they operate.

Several studies (Ali & Sanders 2009, Garriott et al. 2013, Navarro et al. 2007) used SCCT (Lent et al. 1994) to explore the relations of social class to educational or occupational expectations. Both Garriott et al. (2013) and Navarro et al. (2007) found that the relation of social class to math/science goals (expectations, or intentions, to take math courses) was completely mediated by past performance in math classes, which in turn had positive relations with mathematics self-efficacy. Math self-efficacy then predicted intentions. Garriott et al. (2013) found that math outcome expectations also predicted course-taking intentions among prospective first-generation college students, but Navarro et al. (2007) did not find such a link in a sample of Mexican American eighth-graders. Ali & Sanders (2009) found that SES and vocational/educational self-efficacy and outcome expectations each contributed to the prediction of occupational aspirations among rural adolescents, but they did not test for possible mediation effects.

Two other studies employing adolescent samples reported that academic ability and achievement mediated the relationship between SES and occupational expectations. Cochrane et al. (2011) found that the SES–occupational expectation relationship was mediated by scores on a test of vocational aptitude, whereas Schmitt-Wilson (2013) found that the relationship was mediated by academic achievement and by parent and student educational expectations. That is, SES positively predicted academic achievement and parents' educational expectations, parental expectations positively predicted student educational expectations, and student educational achievement and expectations positively predicted students' occupational expectations.

The importance of parental educational expectations and adolescent school achievement was underscored in a 34-year longitudinal analysis of data collected from a British cohort born in 1970 (Ashby & Schoon 2010). Parent educational expectations when participants were 16 years old related to concurrent levels of students' career aspirations and school achievement. Career aspirations and school achievement then predicted occupational status when participants were 34 years old. SES accounted for about 25% of the variance in parent educational expectations. In a longitudinal analysis of a national database in the United States, Ling & O'Brien (2013) found that, among non-college-bound youth, high school educational attainment predicted adult job attainment, stability, and quality. Number of jobs held and hours worked in high school were the only other variables that predicted adult job stability and quality.

Some scholars have criticized traditional SES indicators based on parents' education, occupation, and income as failing to capture the psychological aspects of social class (e.g., Diemer & Ali 2009, Fouad & Brown 2000). They have argued that measures of perceived social status will account for more variance in vocational and educational outcomes than do traditional indicators. Several studies have recently explored perceived social status in the vocational psychology literature. Matheny & McWhirter (2013) reported that the relation of SES to career decision-making self-efficacy beliefs was mediated by perceived social status. Thompson & Dahling (2012) found that the relation of perceived social status to self-efficacy beliefs and outcome expectations was mediated by learning experiences. These results suggest that adolescents with lower social class backgrounds may perceive that they have lower social status (e.g., less power to affect their lives and less access to resources), which is associated with differential access to learning experiences that underlie decisional and occupationally relevant self-efficacy and outcome expectations.

In sum, findings suggest that social class may limit the occupational attainment of children and adolescents growing up in low-SES families in part via several intervening variables, including (*a*) parental educational expectations; (*b*) adolescent educational expectations, school achievement, and aptitude; and (*c*) academic and subject matter self-efficacy beliefs and outcome expectations. Each of these variables suggests avenues for intervention to promote the educational and occupational expectations (and later attainment) of poor youth. Adolescent perceptions of power and resources (perceived social status) may also mediate between social class and these other outcomes and, thus, provide another potential target for intervention.

Race/ethnicity and occupational attainment. The educational and occupational aspirations and expectations of youth of color have also received concerted research attention in recent years, with a particular focus on variables that may mediate or mitigate the effects of racism and discrimination on educational and occupational behavior. Three major types of variables, sometimes studied in the context of SCCT, tended to receive the bulk of the attention: (*a*) supports and barriers; (*b*) racial/ethnic identity and social political development (SPD); and (*c*) acculturation, enculturation, and related variables (e.g., Anglo versus Mexican orientation).

Three studies (Ali & Menke 2014, Irvin et al. 2012, McWhirter et al. 2007) explored racial/ethnic differences in perceptions of barriers between students of color and white high school students. All three reported that Latino high school students reported more barriers to pursuing postsecondary education than did white students, especially barriers related to parent support and expectations, separation from family, and inadequate preparation (McWhirter et al. 2007). Irvin et al. (2012) found that African American high school students perceived more barriers than did their white, but not Latino, counterparts. Despite the imbalance in barrier perceptions, the Latino students in Ali & Menke's (2014) study reported stronger vocational/educational self-efficacy beliefs and similar levels of aspirations relative to white students, suggesting that they may not have perceived the barriers to be insurmountable. Ojeda & Flores (2008), however, found that the perception of barriers accounted for unique variance (beyond gender, generational level, and parents' education) in Mexican American high school students' aspirations. Thompson (2013) reported that perceptions of ethnic discrimination and classicism correlated negatively with coping efficacy beliefs in a sample of Native American college students.

In terms of supports, Gibbons & Borders (2010) reported that both parent and teacher supports related positively to the college-going self-efficacy beliefs of seventh-graders who were prospective first-generation college students. Perry et al. (2010) found that both teacher and parent career support related to the amount of career planning engaged in by urban (mostly minority) high school students. Career planning, in turn, related positively to school grades via school engagement. In other words, students who engaged in career planning were also more engaged in school and displayed higher levels of school achievement, a set of findings that has important implications for the role of career planning activities in school achievement.

Ethnic identity, defined as identification with one's ethnic group and participation in shared cultural activities (Phinney 1996), has long been assumed to play a positive role in the career development of racial/ethnic group members. Although Byars-Winston et al. (2010) found that ethnic identity did not contribute to the prediction of STEM goals of college students of color, Tovar-Murray et al. (2012) found that ethnic identity interacted with experiences of racism-related stress to predict levels of career aspirations in African American college students. Specifically, racism-related stress was associated positively with career aspirations when ethnic identity was well defined, but negatively among those with a less integrated identity, suggesting that ethnic identity may serve as a protective factor in the context of racism-related stress.

Another potential protective factor studied during the review period was SPD, which is seen as an internal resource that marginalized individuals can draw on to cope with inequality. SPD is hypothesized to consist of (*a*) motivation to change sociopolitical inequalities and (*b*) development of a positive self-definition in the context of oppression (Diemer et al. 2009). Research with poor youth of color has demonstrated that SPD accounts for unique variance in occupational expectations (Diemer & Hsieh 2008) and that SPD, along with academic achievement in the tenth grade, predicted adult (age 26) occupational attainment via tenth- and twelfth-grade occupational expectations (Diemer 2009). These findings suggest that interventions that aid children of color in developing positive ethnic identities and SPD beliefs may promote persistence in the face of adversity, yielding (along with school achievement) more positive vocational expectations and, in the case of SPD, increased occupational attainment.

The roles of acculturation (orientation to host culture) and enculturation (orientation to home culture) have also been studied relative to the career development of people of color in the United States. Several studies found that orientation to Anglo culture (acculturation), though not to Mexican culture (enculturation), accounted for unique variance in the educational goals (Flores et al. 2006) and educational aspirations and expectations (Flores et al. 2008) of Mexican American high school students. Both types of cultural orientation explained variance in college self-efficacy, though only Anglo orientation contributed to prediction of outcome expectations in Mexican American college students (Ojeda et al. 2011). Chen & Fouad (2013) found that Asian American college students' intentions to pursue advanced degrees were predicted by enculturation (but not acculturation), academic achievement, and the value of honoring one's parents. Thus, the role of acculturation and enculturation may depend on the racial/ethnic group and the criterion of interest.

Other studies have suggested that achievement motivation (Caldwell & Obasi 2010), autonomous motivation (i.e., engaging in school work out of a desire to learn rather than due to coercion; Close & Solberg 2008), and autonomy support (i.e., receiving support from teachers for autonomously motivated school behaviors; Kenny et al. 2010) may also relate to the academic performance and self-efficacy beliefs of urban high school students and college students of color. Caldwell & Obasi (2010) reported that achievement motivation and valuing of education added uniquely to the prediction of academic performance in African American college students. Close & Solberg (2008) found that autonomous motivation was linked to grades obtained by urban freshmen and sophomore high school students via academic self-efficacy beliefs, whereas Kenny et al. (2010) found that autonomy support from teachers was related to levels of achievement motivation displayed by urban high school students.

In sum, findings suggest that students of color often perceive more barriers to educational and occupational attainment than do white students. On the other hand, several types of factors, such as parent and teacher supports, robust ethnic and sociopolitical identities, and autonomous and achievement motivation, may potentially facilitate career development in the face of barriers. Acculturation to mainstream culture may also aid some groups (e.g., Mexican Americans) but not others (e.g., Asian Americans) in fostering positive educational expectations. Each of these potential protective factors is theoretically amenable to intervention and deserves further research attention.

STEM Entry and Retention of Women and People of Color

Federal policy makers have raised repeated concerns about the supply of workers available to enter STEM careers. The problem is perceived as a general supply-demand issue as well as a social justice matter in that women and particular racial/ethnic groups continue to be underrepresented in STEM educational and occupational paths. Vocational psychology research has, therefore, focused on factors that predict initial interest and choice, as well as persistence, in STEM pursuits, particularly over the lengthy period of educational preparation prior to career entry wherein earlier math and science choices and performances tend to grant (or inhibit) access to later STEM options.

Person and contextual variables. Several investigators have focused on person-level variables, such as interests, that may promote or deter selection of STEM options. Iskander et al. (2013) examined archival data from the American College Testing (ACT) program over a 30-year period on expressed interest patterns, ACT scores, gender, and intended college majors or careers. Results confirmed a significant discrepancy in the number of male and female students expressing interest in engineering majors and careers. However, they also found that female students with interests in STEM fields tend to be well prepared academically, based on their ACT scores. This is a positive sign given that sustained STEM pursuits require ability and skill development beyond interests alone.

Moakler & Kim (2014), employing a large national database on college freshmen, reported that students were more likely to choose STEM majors if they had strong confidence in mathematics (a variable conceptually related to self-efficacy) and parents in STEM occupations. It is possible that these parents provided their children with greater access to efficacy-relevant learning experiences (e.g., role modeling, performance opportunities) related to STEM careers. Reflecting prior trends, female students were less likely than males to choose STEM majors. Of course, once women select STEM majors, they often must still contend with a host of contextual challenges to their persistence. Morganson et al. (2010) studied the use of social coping (e.g., actively seeking social support) among women and men in computer science classes. Women reported engaging in more social coping, which differentially predicted their college major commitment and persistence intentions.

Other research has focused on contextual variables that may enable or discourage interest and involvement in children's STEM pursuits. Ing (2014), using data from a large-scale longitudinal study, examined the role of parent behavior relative to STEM outcomes in middle school and high school students. She reported that, controlling for gender, ethnicity, and parent educational level, parents' intrinsically oriented motivational practices, such as conveying the importance of math along with high expectations regarding effort and success, encouraged growth in students' math performance and STEM persistence between the seventh and twelfth grades. In addition, levels of seventh-grade achievement and growth over time in math achievement forecast STEM persistence. Fouad et al. (2010) developed a multidimensional measure of contextual supports and barriers to pursuing STEM educational and career options. They did not find significant gender differences in overall supports or barriers, though interesting variations were observed in support and barrier perceptions as a function of educational level (e.g., students generally perceived more math-related barriers and fewer supports with increasing education).

Model tests. The above studies focused mainly on individual person or contextual variables, often without explicit theoretical grounding. By contrast, the studies in this subsection involved fuller sets of person and contextual variables, typically using SCCT as a conceptual base. For example, Garriott et al. (2014) examined the role of parent support (e.g., encouragement to do well in math) along with math/science-based sources of efficacy information as precursors of math/science interests in a sample of high school students of color. They found that parent support was positively related to most of the efficacy sources and that two of the sources, performance accomplishments and vicarious learning, uniquely predicted math/science self-efficacy, which was, in turn, linked to interest.

Several other studies have tested SCCT's models with the addition of a variety of variables designed to tap gender-related, cultural, or socioeconomic aspects of the STEM environment.

Deemer et al. (2014) conceptualized stereotype threat as a type of contextual barrier to women's pursuit of STEM options. They studied a sample of female undergraduate students in science classes and found that stereotype threat (operationalized as perceptions of gender stereotypes regarding science activities) was negatively related to science-related choice goals via self-efficacy beliefs and intentions to pursue undergraduate research activities. That is, stereotype threat was associated with diminished self-efficacy beliefs and research intentions, which in turn predicted weaker science goals.

Flores et al. (2010) examined the relations of contextual-cultural variables (e.g., Anglo and Mexican orientation), self-efficacy, and interests to the career choice goals of Mexican American college students regarding Holland's realistic (e.g., mechanical-technical) and investigative (e.g., scientific-mathematic) themes. Byars-Winston et al. (2010) assessed the context in terms of perceptions of campus climate and included two cultural orientation variables (ethnic identity and other-group orientation) in a sample of racial-ethnic minority science and engineering majors. Garriott et al. (2013) studied the linkage of social class to math/science goal intentions in a racially diverse, mostly female sample of high school students participating in a college preparation program. Navarro et al. (2007) included social class, along with Anglo and Mexican cultural orientation, in their model predicting the math/science goals of Mexican American middle school students. Garriott et al. (2013) and Navarro et al. (2007) also included other measures of social supports and/or barriers as well as efficacy-based learning sources (e.g., performance accomplishments).

Despite the number and variety of their predictors, and the complexity of their findings, at least two general patterns are evident regarding the above studies. First, the authors generally reported indications of good overall model-data fit of the SCCT variations, though not all social cognitive variables explained unique predictive variance in every study. Second, contextual and culture-specific variables generally related to math/science interests and choices indirectly, through social cognitive person variables, supporting the view that the latter are informed by and help to mediate the effects of more distal person, contextual-cultural, and learning experience variables. Although it is important to devote more research to the presumed temporal ordering of these variables, a few longitudinal studies have yielded theory-consistent findings in samples of students underrepresented in STEM fields (e.g., Lent et al. 2010, Navarro et al. 2014).

Researchers have also examined whether SCCT's interest and choice models fit the data differentially as a function of gender or race/ethnicity. Findings generally suggest invariance of fit across gender and race/ethnicity in samples of undergraduate STEM majors (Flores et al. 2014; Lent et al. 2011a, 2013) and in middle school students (Navarro et al. 2007). The cultural generality of the models has also been examined in international samples, with findings showing adequate model-data fit across gender in South Korean (Kim & Seo 2014) and Spanish (Inda et al. 2013) engineering students. In a study of female engineers in the United States, Singh et al. (2013) found that training and development experiences at work (conceptualized as contextual supports that inform self-efficacy and outcome expectations) predicted job attitudes both directly and through outcome expectations. Job attitudes (satisfaction and organizational commitment), in turn, strongly predicted turnover intentions (i.e., more favorable attitudes were associated with less turnover intent).

Collectively, the findings in this section point to the importance of environmentally mediated experiences that can be marshaled via interventions to attract more women and students of color to, and to encourage their persistence within, STEM fields. In addition, these findings point to the mechanisms through which contextual supports, barriers, and learning experiences may operate relative to STEM participation (i.e., by promoting favorable self-efficacy and outcome expectations).

Promoting Work Participation of Survivors of Domestic Violence and Criminal Offenders

The vocational needs of two groups that have previously been understudied by vocational researchers—survivors of domestic violence and criminal offenders—received long overdue attention during the period this review examined.

Domestic abuse can have a significant impact on the economic well-being of survivors and their families via lost hours and wages, underemployment and unemployment, and hindered educational attainment (Chronister et al. 2012). Several qualitative studies documented the barriers to occupational and educational attainment experienced by domestic abuse survivors (e.g., Brown et al. 2009, Chronister et al. 2008), and one intervention showed promising results. The Advancing Career Counseling and Employment Support for Survivors of Domestic Violence (ACCESS) program has been found to relate to gains in career search self-efficacy and critical consciousness beliefs (Chronister & McWhirter 2006, Davidson et al. 2012) and reductions in career barriers, anxiety, and depression (Davidson et al. 2012). Chronister & McWhirter (2006) suggested that it is essential to help domestic abuse survivors develop a critical understanding of the power dynamics in their lives and a renewed sense of control and responsibility (critical consciousness), although the hypothesis has not received direct testing in career intervention research. Chronister et al. (2012) described how the ACCESS program was incorporated into a comprehensive, collaborative partnership with a domestic abuse service agency. Further research is needed to assess the employment outcomes of ACCESS participants.

A number of factors have been identified that place criminal offenders at high risk for recidivism, including employment problems associated with a lack of job skills, experience, and networks; limited education; substance abuse history; and employers' attitudes and willingness to hire ex-offenders (Brown 2011). One study (Fitzgerald et al. 2013) tested the effectiveness of a modified version of ACCESS (Chronister & McWhirter 2006) versus a treatment-as-usual control with a sample of male inmates who were within six months of release. Compared with controls, ACCESS participants showed greater increases in career search self-efficacy and perceived problem-solving abilities at post-treatment and one-month follow-up. No follow-up data on recidivism or employment rates were reported. Varghese (2013) proposed an integrative framework for directing interventions aimed at job attainment and stability needs. Research is needed on the efficacy of this model in promoting occupational outcomes as well as reducing recidivism.

WELL-BEING: POSITIVE ADAPTATION TO SCHOOL AND WORK SETTINGS

Vocational psychology has long been concerned with factors that promote well-being in educational and work settings. In this section, we focus on two different perspectives on well-being. The hedonic perspective defines well-being in terms of the presence of positive affect (e.g., happiness, satisfaction) and the absence of negative affect (e.g., sadness). The eudaimonic perspective equates well-being with living a good or meaningful life. Our discussion of the hedonic perspective focuses on educational and job satisfaction as well as the relationships of academic and job satisfaction to life satisfaction. Our coverage of the eudaimonic perspective includes research on selected variables that may index personal growth, meaning, and healthy engagement in work.

Hedonic Well-Being: Job, Academic, and Life Satisfaction

A number of studies over the period of this review were derived from Lent & Brown's (2006, 2008) SCCT model of work satisfaction, an adaptation of SCCT aimed at explaining the ways in which social, cognitive, trait, and behavioral variables contribute to affective outcomes in academic and work settings. Tests of the full model have generally reported that it provided good overall fit to the data, but support for specific paths in the model has been less consistent. For example, self-efficacy has been found to relate to academic satisfaction directly in some studies (e.g., Flores et al. 2014, Lent et al. 2012) or only indirectly via goal progress in others (e.g., Hui et al. 2013, Singley et al. 2010). Environmental supports (e.g., perceived organizational support, goal or role support; Buyukgoze-Kavas et al. 2014, Lent et al. 2011b, Singley et al. 2010) and positive affectivity (Buyukgoze-Kavas et al. 2014, Lent et al. 2011b) have also been linked consistently to academic or job satisfaction in model tests.

Findings have largely supported the hypothesized relationship between academic/work and life satisfaction (Ojeda et al. 2011, Lent et al. 2011b, Sheu et al. 2014). However, one longitudinal study found that the relationship between domain and life satisfaction was largely unidirectional (from academic to life satisfaction; Lent et al. 2012) rather than reciprocal, as had been hypothesized. These findings suggest that domain satisfaction may be an important source of life satisfaction for many persons and that interventions designed to promote satisfaction in career-relevant domains may have valuable implications for overall life satisfaction.

As noted previously, work volition has also received attention in the job and life satisfaction literatures. This research has shown that work volition may have a direct relation to the job satisfaction of employed workers (Duffy et al. 2013c) and the life satisfaction of unemployed workers (Duffy et al. 2013b). The research has also identified some interesting moderator effects of volition. Duffy et al. (2013b) found that perceived organizational support was more strongly related to job satisfaction among those with lower versus higher volition. Dik & Hansen (2011) also demonstrated that a volition-like variable (perceived control over the work environment) moderated the relationship between P-E congruence and job satisfaction. However, the moderator relationship was opposite to what might be expected on the basis of the psychology of working framework—the relationship was stronger under conditions of low perceived work control than under conditions of high control. Thus, P-E fit may be more, rather than less, important to the job satisfaction of those with low work volition, who may perceive that they have fewer alternative work options if things do not work out as planned.

Eudaimonic Well-Being: Calling, Meaning, Commitment, and Engagement

A number of studies have also focused on elements of eudaimonic well-being in the context of educational and vocational functioning. Such research emphasizes school and work as contexts for actualizing personal potential or growth, seeking life meaning and purpose, or doing good (e.g., helping others) versus feeling good. In many cases, research has focused on eudaimonic variables in relation to hedonic or other, more distal outcomes rather than as ends in themselves.

Calling: Definitions and measures. A good deal of recent eudaimonic research in vocational psychology has involved the concept of vocational calling, which Dik & Duffy (2009) defined as "...a *transcendent summons*, experienced as originating beyond the self, to approach a particular life role in a manner oriented toward demonstrating or deriving a *sense of purpose or meaningfulness* and that *holds other-oriented values and goals* as primary sources of motivation" (p. 427; italics added for emphasis). This is a complex definition that contains three relatively distinct elements: (*a*) the sense that one has been compelled by external forces, such as a supreme being, to select a particular life role (usually considered as a vocational path); (*b*) the expectation that one derives purpose or meaning from engaging in this role; and (*c*) the added requirement that the role involves service to others. Although the prior literature contains numerous variables that resemble the latter two elements (e.g., altruistic work values), the transcendent summons element is, arguably, the core and most distinctive aspect of calling.

Dik et al. (2012) developed a set of measures, the Calling and Vocation Questionnaire (CVQ) and the Brief Calling Scale (BCS), to capture the three elements of calling, both in terms of whether they are experienced as present in people's work lives and whether they are actively seeking them. These investigators reported that the transcendent summons, purposeful work, and prosocial orientation features constitute relatively distinct calling dimensions. The CVQ combines them into two 12-item scales reflecting, respectively, the presence of, and search for, calling. The BCS consists of two 2-item scales that measure an overall sense of calling that one has either attained (e.g., "I have a calling to a particular kind of work") or that one is seeking (e.g., "I am trying to figure out my calling in my career"). The presence and search scales of the CVQ and BCS scales were shown to interrelate strongly and to correlate, to varying degrees, with a variety of vocational (e.g., work hope) and nonvocational (e.g., meaning in life) criteria. Their relations to life satisfaction were nonsignificant.

Duffy et al. (2012a) also assessed calling in terms of the degree to which persons are "living a calling" in their current work (i.e., the work one does is congruent with one's calling). This measure produced stronger relations with job satisfaction than did the BCS presence of calling scale. Alternative calling measures have been developed that tap aspects of calling that are similar to (e.g., transcendent guiding force, service to others) and somewhat distinct from (e.g., sense of P-E fit, passion for one's work) those on the Dik-Duffy measures (Hagmaier & Abele 2012, Praskova et al. 2014). These measures offer a variety of ways to index calling, and their additional elements raise interesting questions about the essence of the construct. In particular, must one perceive a transcendent summons to have a calling? Or is the essential feature engagement in work for which one feels a strong sense of passion, P-E fit, or fulfillment of altruistic values? If the latter, then what is gained by defining calling in terms of externally impelled work behavior?

Calling in relation to work meaning, commitment, and other outcomes. Most of the recent research on calling in vocational psychology has involved the measures developed by Dik, Duffy, and their colleagues. In a review, Duffy & Dik (2013) concluded that calling, particularly when measured as lived calling, has been related to greater levels of career maturity, career commitment, work meaning, and job satisfaction as well as to more general outcomes (e.g., global life meaning, life satisfaction). Beyond establishing bivariate relations, researchers have been exploring mediators and moderators of calling-criterion relations. For example, Duffy et al. (2011a) found that the relation of calling to academic satisfaction in college students was mediated by career decision self-efficacy and work hope. Other cross-sectional studies have found that the relation of calling to job satisfaction in employed adults was mediated by career commitment (Duffy et al. 2011b) or by both career commitment and work meaning (Duffy et al. 2012a, 2013a). A few studies have examined calling-criterion relations longitudinally and have found that the predominant temporal paths tend to be from other variables—such as life meaning (Duffy et al. 2011c) or career commitment, work meaning, and job satisfaction (Duffy et al. 2014a)—to calling, though some reciprocal paths from calling to criterion variables (e.g., work and life meaning) have also been found (Duffy et al. 2014a,c).

Work meaning as an alternative to calling. The above findings suggest that the perception of calling is associated with a greater sense of work meaning and career commitment and that these latter variables may either be antecedents of calling or may mediate the relation of calling to more distal (e.g., job satisfaction) outcomes. It may, therefore, be useful to study such variables in their own right. Steger et al. (2012) developed a measure of work meaning (the Work and Meaning Inventory) that taps the extent to which one sees one's work as meaningful (e.g., offering the experience self-understanding, purpose, personal growth, and benefit to the greater good). This measure correlated strongly with measures of calling as well as with career commitment and job satisfaction. It was also found to predict job and life satisfaction and work absences beyond the effects of calling.

Steger et al. (2013) found that work meaning correlated strongly with work engagement and modestly with (trait) positive affect. They also reported that work meaning moderated the relation of positive affect to work engagement: When work was perceived as less meaningful, workers with high versus low levels of positive affect were more strongly engaged in their work. However, when work was seen as more meaningful, those with high and low levels of positive affect did not differ in work engagement. Thus, work meaning may compensate for low positive affect as a source of work engagement. Adopting a psychology of working perspective, Allan et al. (2014) found a small but significant relation between work meaning and social class, with persons of higher (versus lower) social class reporting more work meaning. This link was mediated by work volition and financial constraints, suggesting that the control and resources conferred by social class may differentially promote (or constrain) the pursuit of personally meaningful work.

In sum, research on eudaimonic variables has been a fertile topic of career inquiry in recent years. Findings suggest that the relation of calling to criterion variables, such as job satisfaction and work engagement, is typically mediated by (and, in some instances, may be a reflection of) work meaning and other variables (e.g., career commitment). Whether calling offers unique predictive value, therefore, remains an open empirical question. The response to this question may require further conceptual clarity regarding what calling is (and is not) and added research on the incremental validity of transcendent summons relative to work meaning, passion, virtuous motives, P-E fit perceptions, and other variables that are sometimes considered a part of (and sometimes apart from) calling. The issue is not whether some persons view their work in spiritual terms but rather how this perception translates into work-relevant outcomes.

Work meaning represents another potentially fruitful path for research on eudaimonic well-being, either in combination with or apart from calling. Yet it, too, may raise some interesting, and potentially controversial, issues. For example, to what extent is work meaning (and other aspects of eudaimonic well-being, such as personal growth and self-actualization) enabled by social class, volition, or work conditions that favor self-expression or goal choice? Must meaningful work serve the greater good? Or does it simply lie in the eye of the beholder; for example, can the self-absorbed and antisocial also find meaning in their work? In other words, what does it mean to have work meaning, and who gets to have it?

SUMMARY AND FUTURE DIRECTIONS

We reviewed the recent literature in vocational psychology (2007–2014) within the three overarching themes of agency, equity, and well-being. Although these themes do not reflect the only ways in which the literature could have been organized, they do convey a sense of the field's renewed vitality and commitment to promoting optimal educational and work functioning, even in the midst of uncertain or unfavorable environmental conditions. We think the findings reviewed herein offer several useful insights and directions for future research, both within and across the three themes.

The research reviewed under the agency and equity themes highlights the critical role of educational achievement in the occupational expectations and attainments of college-bound and non-college-bound youth. Educational achievement was also shown to be a critical mediating pathway that explained, in part, the positive link between SES and occupational expectations and attainment. The research also suggests some pathways that might promote greater academic achievement of poor youth and youth of color, or that may operate in concert with academic performance to promote increased levels of occupational expectations and attainment. For instance, research on the SCCT academic performance model suggests two variables that are important to academic achievement—academic ability/past performance and self-efficacy beliefs. Academic ability was found to relate to performance both directly and indirectly by informing students' academic self-efficacy beliefs. Thus, efforts to promote self-efficacy beliefs that are optimistic yet commensurate with students' academic talents may foster increased academic performance.

Other variables were also found to be predictive of academic achievement either directly or via indirect pathways. These included parental expectations and support. Parent educational expectations were important predictors of student occupational expectations and, in one case, actual occupational attainment via their relations to students' educational expectations and achievement. Parent support seemed to operate primarily as a source of efficacy information. SPD also showed promise as a means of promoting occupational expectations and attainments of poor youth of color via its relation to educational expectations and school performance. One intriguing finding suggested that engaging in career development activities may have a positive bearing on educational performance via greater school engagement. Many of these predictors of academic achievement are, theoretically, relatively malleable. The next step is to translate them into empirically testable interventions.

The findings regarding STEM interests and choice intentions also point to the role of contextual factors and learning experiences (e.g., achievement opportunities, models) that can inform the design of interventions to attract more women and students of color to, and encourage their persistence within, STEM fields. These findings also suggest the mechanisms through which such interventions may operate. For example, providing social encouragement, exposure to relevant models, assistance in interpreting performance feedback, or barrier-coping methods (e.g., social coping) may promote STEM participation and persistence, at least in part by nurturing favorable self-efficacy beliefs and outcome expectations.

Research on educational and job satisfaction in the vocational psychology literature did not appear to substantially advance what was already known about the relations of perceived organizational support, goal progress, and positive affectivity to the experience of satisfaction in academic and work settings. However, research using the SCCT satisfaction model suggested how these variables may operate together and, in particular, how goal progress might be facilitated (e.g., via promotion of task and goal-related self-efficacy beliefs and supports). Such variables provide potential targets for efforts to enhance academic and work satisfaction. An understudied part of the SCCT model is the hypothesis that work-role salience, or importance, may moderate the relation of job and life satisfaction. That is, the path from job to life satisfaction may be stronger to the extent that work is perceived as a central feature of one's personal identity. This suggests that efforts to promote job satisfaction may carry over into enhanced life satisfaction for persons with greater psychological investment in the work role, provided of course that future research supports the moderator hypothesis.

Several new or updated vocational constructs, including career adaptability, work volition, and calling, have potentially important implications for efforts to facilitate agency, equity, and well-being. These constructs have generated impressive amounts of research over a short period, no doubt aided by the availability of new measures for assessing them. At this stage, research on these constructs might benefit from more precise theoretical overlays. For example, adaptability research might be aided by the provision of more specific hypotheses about the criterion variables with which adaptability should (and should not) relate and about the mediators and moderators of these relations. For example, do more highly career-adaptable persons engage in more activities designed to prepare for untoward work events, and are they more resilient in bouncing back when such events occur? Likewise, research on calling may profit from theoretical efforts to differentiate it from conceptually similar or overlapping constructs. For example, is transcendent summons necessary to define calling? If so, what is its unique predictive value (and for whom)? If not, then how does calling differ from such concepts as work meaning, work passion, altruistic value fulfillment, or perceptions of ideal P-E fit?

Research on work volition to this point calls into question the assumption that extant vocational theories may be less relevant to, or predictive of, important career outcomes among poor and marginalized persons (Blustein 2006). The psychology of working perspective suggests that persons who feel little control over their work lives (e.g., due to prevailing social and economic conditions) will consequently feel constrained in the occupational choice process. However, the limited research that is available suggests that persons who feel little volition in their work lives may benefit more than those with greater volition from efforts to help them find good-fitting work environments. This may be due, in part, to the limited alternative job options perceived by those with low volition. Thus, contrary to assumptions, the well-being of those with low rather than high volition might be particularly aided by efforts to promote P-E fit and access to supportive work organizations. It is possible that, paradoxically, such activities may be less useful for people who perceive greater flexibility to change jobs when things do not work out as expected.

Though still in its early stages, vocational psychology research on survivors of domestic violence and criminal offenders has yielded some promising findings and warrants additional research attention. Such research may profitably focus on whether theory-based interventions are associated with improved employment rates and other indices of employment success (job satisfaction, life satisfaction, income, and tenure). Follow-up recidivism rates also need to be examined in intervention research with offenders/ex-offenders.

In sum, this has been a ripe period in the history of vocational psychology, with research moving beyond the field's traditional comfort zone and, increasingly, into topics that reflect wider concerns with social justice, diversity, and promotion of optimal functioning under nonoptimal conditions. Further inquiry on these topics will be aided by conceptual statements that more clearly specify the nature and function of particular constructs. In addition, the translation of findings into practice will require more design and testing of theory-based interventions. Newer approaches, such as career construction theory and the psychology of working perspective, offer added possibilities for studying variables and conditions that both allow and constrain the exercise of agency in school and work contexts. We anticipate that agency, equity, and well-being will receive sustained inquiry from vocational researchers in the years ahead, and that this inquiry will ultimately equip career practitioners with new and refined tools for serving a wider range of students and clients.

DISCLOSURE STATEMENT

The authors are not aware of any affiliations, memberships, funding, or financial holdings that might be perceived as affecting the objectivity of this review.

LITERATURE CITED

Abele AE, Spurk D. 2009. The longitudinal impact of self-efficacy and career goals on objective and subjective career success. *J. Vocat. Behav.* 74:53–62

Ajzen I. 1988. *Attitudes, Personality, and Behavior.* Stony Stratford, UK: Open Univ. Press

Ali SR, Menke KA. 2014. Rural Latino youth career development: an application of social cognitive career theory. *Career Dev. Q.* 62:175–86

Ali SR, Sanders JL. 2009. The career aspirations of rural Appalachian high school students. *J. Career Assess.* 17:172–88

Allan BA, Autin KL, Duffy RD. 2014. Examining social class and work meaning within the psychology of working framework. *J. Career Assess.* 22:543–61

Arbona C. 2000. The development of academic achievement in school aged children: precursor to career development. In *Handbook of Counseling Psychology*, ed. SD Brown, RW Lent, pp. 270–309. New York: Wiley. 3rd ed.

Ashby JS, Schoon I. 2010. Career success: the role of teenage career aspirations, ambition value, and gender in predicting adult social status and earnings. *J. Vocat. Behav.* 77:350–60

Betz NE, Borgen FH. 2009. Comparative effectiveness of CAPA and FOCUS online: career assessment systems with undecided college students. *J. Career Assess.* 17:351–66

Blustein DL. 2006. *The Psychology of Working: A New Perspective for Career Development, Counseling, and Public Policy*. Mahwah, NJ: Erlbaum

Blustein DL, Kenna AC, Gill N, Devoy JE. 2008. The Psychology of Working: a new framework for counseling practice and public policy. *Career Dev. Q.* 56:294–308

Brown C. 2011. Vocational psychology and ex-offenders' reintegration: a call for action. *J. Career Assess.* 19:333–42

Brown C, Trangsrud HB, Linnemeyer RM. 2009. Battered women's process of leaving: a 2-year follow-up. *J. Career Assess.* 17:439–56

Brown SD. 2015. On statistical wizardry, construction proliferation, and other challenges for our science. *Couns. Psychol.* 43:614–28

Brown SD, Lent RW, Telander K, Tramayne S. 2011. Social cognitive career theory, conscientiousness, and work performance: a meta-analytic path analysis. *J. Vocat. Behav.* 79:81–90

Brown SD, Tramayne S, Hoxha D, Telander K, Fan X, Lent RW. 2008. Social cognitive predictors of college students' academic performance and persistence: a meta-analytic path analysis. *J. Vocat. Behav.* 72:298–308

Buyukgoze-Kavas A, Duffy RD, Guneri OY, Autin KL. 2014. Job satisfaction among Turkish teachers: exploring differences by school level. *J. Career Assess.* 22:261–73

Byars-Winston A, Zalapa J, Howard C, Davis D. 2010. Influence of social cognitive and ethnic variables on academic goals of underrepresented students in science and engineering: a multiple-groups analysis. *J. Couns. Psychol.* 57:205–18

Caldwell T, Obasi EM. 2010. Academic performance in African American undergraduates: effects of cultural mistrust, educational value, and achievement motivation. *J. Career Dev.* 36:348–69

Chen YL, Fouad NA. 2013. Asian American educational goals: racial barriers and cultural factors. *J. Career Assess.* 21:73–91

Choi BY, Park H, Yang E, Lee SK, Lee Y, Lee SM. 2012. Understanding career decision self-efficacy: a meta-analytic approach. *J. Career Dev.* 39:443–60

Chronister KM, Harley E, Aranda CL, Barr L, Luginbuhl P. 2012. Community-based career counseling for women survivors of intimate partner violence: a collaborative partnership. *J. Career Dev.* 39:515–39

Chronister KM, Linville D, Kaag KP. 2008. Domestic survivors' access of career counseling services: a qualitative investigation. *J. Career Dev.* 34:339–61

Chronister KM, McWhirter EH. 2006. An experimental examination of two career interventions for battered women. *J. Couns. Psychol.* 53:151–64

Close W, Solberg VS. 2008. Predicting achievement, distress, and retention among lower-income Latino youth. *J. Vocat. Behav.* 72:31–42

Cochrane DB, Wang EW, Stevenson SJ, Johnson LE, Crews C. 2011. Adolescent occupational aspirations: test of Gottfredson's theory of circumscription and compromise. *Career Dev. Q.* 59:412–27

Cupani M, Pautassi RM. 2013. Predictive contribution of personality traits in a sociocognitive model of academic performance in mathematics. *J. Career Assess.* 21:395–413

Dahling JJ, Melloy R, Thompson MN. 2013. Financial strain and regional unemployment as barriers to job search self-efficacy: a test of social cognitive career theory. *J. Couns. Psychol.* 60:210–18

Davidson MM, Nitzel C, Duke A, Baker CM, Bovaird JA. 2012. Advancing career and employment support for survivors: an intervention evaluation. *J. Couns. Psychol.* 59:321–28

Deemer ED, Thoman DB, Chase JP, Smith JL. 2014. Feeling the threat: stereotype threat as a contextual barrier to women's science career choice intentions. *J. Career Dev.* 41:141–58

Diemer MA. 2009. Pathways to occupational attainment among poor youth of color: the role of sociopolitical development. *Couns. Psychol.* 37:6–35

Diemer MA, Ali SR. 2009. Integrating social class into vocational psychology: theory and practice implications. *J. Career Assess.* 17:247–65

Diemer MA, Hsieh C. 2008. Sociopolitical development and vocational expectations among lower-SES adolescents of color. *Career Dev. Q.* 56:257–67

Diemer MA, Hsieh C, Pan T. 2009. School and parental influences on sociopolitical development among poor adolescents of color. *Couns. Psychol.* 37:317–44

Dik BJ, Duffy RD. 2009. Calling and vocation at work: definitions and prospects for research and practice. *Couns. Psychol.* 37:424–50

Dik BJ, Eldridge BM, Steger MF, Duffy RD. 2012. Development and validation of the Calling and Vocation Questionnaire (CVQ) and Brief Calling Scale (BCS). *J. Career Assess.* 20:242–63

Dik BJ, Hansen JC. 2011. Moderation of P-E fit–job satisfaction relations. *J. Career Assess.* 19:35–50

Duffy RD, Allan BA, Autin KL, Bott EM. 2013a. Calling and life satisfaction: It's not about having it, it's about living it. *J. Couns. Psychol.* 60:42–52

Duffy RD, Allan BA, Autin KL, Douglass RP. 2014a. Living a calling and work well-being: a longitudinal study. *J. Couns. Psychol.* 61:605–15

Duffy RD, Allan BA, Dik BJ. 2011a. The presence of a calling and academic satisfaction: examining potential mediators. *J. Vocat. Behav.* 79:74–80

Duffy RD, Bott EM, Allan B, Autin KL. 2014b. Exploring the role of work volition within social cognitive career theory. *J. Career Assess.* 22:465–78

Duffy RD, Bott EM, Allan B, Torrey CL. 2013b. Examining a model of life satisfaction among unemployed adults. *J. Couns. Psychol.* 60:53–63

Duffy RD, Bott EM, Allan BA, Torrey CL, Dik BJ. 2012a. Perceiving a calling, living a calling, and job satisfaction: testing a moderated, multiple mediator model. *J. Couns. Psychol.* 59:50–59

Duffy RD, Bott EM, Torrey CL, Webster GW. 2013c. Work volition as a critical moderator in the prediction of job satisfaction. *J. Career Assess.* 21:20–31

Duffy RD, Diemer MA, Jadidian A. 2012b. The development and initial validation of the Work Volition Scale—Student Version. *Couns. Psychol.* 40:291–318

Duffy RD, Diemer MA, Perry JC, Laurenzi C, Torrey CL. 2012c. The construction and initial validation of the Work Volition Scale. *J. Vocat. Behav.* 80:400–11

Duffy RD, Dik BJ. 2013. Research on calling: What have we learned and where are we going? *J. Vocat. Behav.* 83:428–36

Duffy RD, Dik BJ, Steger MF. 2011b. Calling and work-related outcomes: career commitment as a mediator. *J. Vocat. Behav.* 78:210–18

Duffy RD, Douglass RP, Autin KL, Allan BA. 2014c. Examining predictors and outcomes of a career calling among undergraduate students. *J. Vocat. Behav.* 85:309–18

Duffy RD, Manuel RS, Borges NJ, Bott EM. 2011c. Calling, vocational development, and well being: a longitudinal study of medical students. *J. Vocat. Behav.* 79:361–66

Fitzgerald EL, Chronister CM, Forrest L, Brown L. 2013. OPTIONS for preparing inmates for community reentry: an employment preparation intervention. *Couns. Psychol.* 41:990–1010

Flores LY, Navarro R, DeWitz SJ. 2008. Mexican American high school students' post-secondary educational goals: applying social cognitive career theory. *J. Career Assess.* 16:489–501

Flores LY, Navarro RL, Lee HS, Addae DA, Gonzalez R, et al. 2014. Academic satisfaction among Latino/a and white men and women engineering students. *J. Couns. Psychol.* 61:81–92

Flores LY, Ojeda L, Huang Y, Gee D, Lee S. 2006. The relation of acculturation, problem-solving appraisal, and career decision-making self-efficacy to Mexican American high school students' educational goals. *J. Couns. Psychol.* 53:260–66

Flores LY, Robitschek C, Celebi E, Andersen C, Hoang U. 2010. Social cognitive influences on Mexican Americans' career choices across Holland's themes. *J. Vocat. Behav.* 76:198–210

Fouad NA. 2007. Work and vocational psychology: theory, research, and applications. *Annu. Rev. Psychol.* 58:543–64

Fouad, NA, Brown MT. 2000. The role of race and social class in development: implications for counseling psychology. In *Handbook of Counseling Psychology*, ed. SD Brown, RW Lent, pp. 379–408. New York: Wiley. 3rd ed.

Fouad NA, Hackett G, Smith PL, Kantamneni N, Fitzpatrick M, et al. 2010. Barriers and supports for continuing in mathematics and science: gender and educational level differences. *J. Vocat. Behav.* 77:361–73

Garriott PO, Flores LY, Martens MP. 2013. Predicting math/science career goals of low-income prospective first generation college students. *J. Couns. Psychol.* 60:200–9

Garriott PO, Flores LY, Prabhakar B, Mazzotta EC, Liskov AC, Shapiro JE. 2014. Parental support and underrepresented students' math/science interests: the mediating role of learning experiences. *J. Career Assess.* 22:627–41

Gibbons MM, Borders LD. 2010. Prospective first-generation college students: a social-cognitive perspective. *Career Dev. Q.* 58:194–208

Guan Y, Deng H, Sun J, Wang Y, Cai Z, et al. 2013. Career adaptability, job search self-efficacy and outcomes: a three-wave investigation among Chinese university graduates. *J. Vocat. Behav.* 83:561–70

Hagmaier T, Abele AE. 2012. The multidimensionality of calling: conceptualization, measurement and a bicultural perspective. *J. Vocat. Behav.* 81:39–51

Hamtiaux A, Houssemand C, Vrignaud P. 2013. Individual and career adaptability: comparing models and measures. *J. Vocat. Behav.* 83:130–41

Holland JL. 1997. *Making Vocational Choices: A Theory of Vocational Personalities and Work Environments*. Odessa, FL: Psychol. Assess. Resour. 3rd ed.

Howard KAS, Carlstrom AH, Katz AD, Chew AY, Ray GC, et al. 2011. Career aspirations of youth: untangling race/ethnicity, SES, and gender. *J. Vocat. Behav.* 79:98–109

Huang J, Hsieh H. 2011. Linking socioeconomic status to social cognitive career theory factors: a partial least squares path modeling analysis. *J. Career Assess.* 19:452–61

Hui K, Lent RW, Miller MJ. 2013. Social cognitive and cultural orientation predictors of well-being in Asian American college students. *J. Career Assess.* 21:587–98

Inda M, Rodríguez C, Peña JV. 2013. Gender differences in applying social cognitive career theory in engineering students. *J. Vocat. Behav.* 83:346–55

Ing M. 2014. Can parents influence children's mathematics achievement and persistence in STEM careers? *J. Career Dev.* 41:87–103

Irvin MJ, Byun SY, Meece JL, Farmer TW, Hutchins BC. 2012. Educational barriers of rural youth: relation of individual and contextual difference variables. *J. Career Assess.* 20:71–87

Iskander ET, Gore PJ, Furse C, Bergerson A. 2013. Gender differences in expressed interests in engineering-related fields ACT 30-year data analysis identified trends and suggested avenues to reverse trends. *J. Career Assess.* 21:599–613

Jadidian A, Duffy RD. 2012. Work volition, career decision self-efficacy, and academic satisfaction: an examination of mediators and moderators. *J. Career Assess.* 20:154–65

Kenny MF, Walsh-Blair LY, Blustein DL, Bempechat J, Seltzer J. 2010. Achievement motivation among urban adolescents: work hope, autonomy support, and achievement-related beliefs. *J. Vocat. Behav.* 77:205–12

Kim MS, Seo YS. 2014. Social cognitive predictors of academic interests and goals in South Korean engineering students. *J. Career Dev.* 41:526–46

Koen J, Klehe U, Van Vianen AE. 2012. Training career adaptability to facilitate a successful school-to-work transition. *J. Vocat. Behav.* 81:395–408

Lee IH, Rojewski JW. 2009. Development of occupational aspirations: a piecewise latent growth model of selected influences. *J. Vocat. Behav.* 75:82–90

Lent RW, Brown SD. 2006. Integrating person and situation perspectives on work satisfaction: a social-cognitive view. *J. Vocat. Behav.* 69:236–47

Lent RW, Brown SD. 2008. Social cognitive career theory and subjective well-being in the context of work. *J. Career Assess.* 16:6–21

Lent RW, Brown SD. 2013. Social cognitive model of career self-management: toward a unifying view of adaptive career behavior across the life span. *J. Couns. Psychol.* 60:557–68

Lent RW, Brown SD, Hackett G. 1994. Toward a unifying social cognitive theory of career and academic interest, choice, and performance. *J. Vocat. Behav.* 45:79–122

Lent RW, Lopez FG, Sheu H, Lopez AM. 2011a. Social cognitive predictors of the interests and choices of computing majors: applicability to underrepresented students. *J. Vocat. Behav.* 78:184–92

Lent RW, Miller MJ, Smith PE, Watford BA, Lim RH, et al. 2013. Social cognitive predictors of adjustment to engineering majors across gender and race/ethnicity. *J. Vocat. Behav.* 83:22–30

Lent RW, Nota L, Soresi S, Ginevra MC, Duffy RD, Brown SD. 2011b. Predicting the job and life satisfaction of Italian teachers: test of a social cognitive model. *J. Vocat. Behav.* 79:91–97

Lent RW, Sheu H, Gloster CS, Wilkins G. 2010. Longitudinal test of the social cognitive model of choice in engineering students at historically black universities. *J. Vocat. Behav.* 76:387–94

Lent RW, Sheu H, Singley D, Schmidt JA, Schmidt LC, Gloster CS. 2008. Longitudinal relations of self-efficacy to outcome expectations, interests, and major choice goals in engineering students. *J. Vocat. Behav.* 73:328–35

Lent RW, Taveira MC, Lobo C. 2012. Two tests of the social cognitive model of well-being in Portuguese college students. *J. Vocat. Behav.* 80:362–71

Ling TJ, O'Brien KM. 2013. Connecting the forgotten half: the school-to-work transition of noncollege-bound youth. *J. Career Dev.* 40:347–67

Maggiori C, Johnston CS, Krings F, Massoudi K, Rossier J. 2013. The role of career adaptability and work conditions on general and professional well-being. *J. Vocat. Behav.* 83:437–49

Matheny J, McWhirter EH. 2013. Contributions of social status and family support to college students' career decision self-efficacy and outcome expectations. *J. Career Assess.* 21:378–94

McWhirter EH, Torres DM, Salgado S, Valdez M. 2007. Perceived barriers and post-secondary plans in Mexican American and white adolescents. *J. Career Assess.* 15:119–38

Mello ZR. 2008. Gender variation in developmental trajectories of educational and occupational expectations and attainment from adolescence to adulthood. *Dev. Psychol.* 44:1069–80

Moakler MJ, Kim MM. 2014. College major choice in STEM: revisiting confidence and demographic factors. *Career Dev. Q.* 62:128–42

Morganson VJ, Jones MP, Major DA. 2010. Understanding women's underrepresentation in science, technology, engineering, and mathematics: the role of social coping. *Career Dev. Q.* 59:169–79

Natl. Cent. Educ. Stat. 2002. *Digest of Education Statistics. Table 6. Percent of Population 3 to 34 Years Old Enrolled in School, By Age Group: April 1940 to October 2001.* Washington, DC: US Dep. Educ.

Navarro RL, Flores LY, Lee H, Gonzalez R. 2014. Testing a longitudinal social cognitive model of intended persistence with engineering students across gender and race/ethnicity. *J. Vocat. Behav.* 85:146–55

Navarro RL, Flores LY, Worthington RL. 2007. Mexican American middle school students' goal intentions in mathematics and science: a test of social cognitive career theory. *J. Couns. Psychol.* 54:320–35

Ojeda L, Flores LY. 2008. The influence of gender, generation level, parents' educational level, and perceived barriers on the educational aspirations of Mexican American high school students. *Career Dev. Q.* 57:84–95

Ojeda L, Flores LY, Navarro RL. 2011. Social cognitive predictors of Mexican American college students' academic and life satisfaction. *J. Couns. Psychol.* 58:61–71

Perry JC, Liu X, Pabian Y. 2010. School engagement as a mediator of academic performance among urban youth: the role of career preparation, parental career support, and teacher support. *Counsel. Psychol.* 38:269–95

Phinney JS. 1996. When we talk about American ethnic groups, what do we mean? *Am. Psychol.* 51:918–27

Porfeli EJ, Savickas ML. 2012. Career Adapt-Abilities Scale–USA Form: psychometric properties and relation to vocational identity. *J. Vocat. Behav.* 80:748–53

Praskova A, Hood M, Creed PA. 2014. Testing a calling model of psychological career success in Australian young adults: a longitudinal study. *J. Vocat. Behav.* 85:125–35

Rogers ME, Creed PA. 2011. A longitudinal examination of adolescent career planning and exploration using a social cognitive career theory framework. *J. Adolesc.* 34:163–72

Rogers ME, Creed PA, Glendon AI. 2008. The role of personality in adolescent career planning and exploration: a social cognitive perspective. *J. Vocat. Behav.* 73:132–42

Rossier J, Zecca G, Stauffer SD, Maggiori C, Dauwalder J. 2012. Career Adapt-Abilities Scale in a French-speaking Swiss sample: psychometric properties and relationships to personality and work engagement. *J. Vocat. Behav.* 80:734–43

Rottinghaus PJ, Buelow KL, Matyja A, Schneider MR. 2012. The Career Futures Inventory–Revised: measuring dimensions of career adaptability. *J. Career Assess.* 20:123–39

Savickas ML. 1997. Career adaptability: an integrative construct for life-span, life-space theory. *Career Dev. Q.* 45:247–59

Savickas ML, Porfeli EJ. 2012. Career Adapt-Abilities Scale: construction, reliability, and measurement equivalence across 13 countries. *J. Vocat. Behav.* 80:661–73

Schmitt-Wilson S. 2013. Social class and expectations of rural adolescents: the role of parental expectations. *Career Dev. Q.* 61:226–39

Scott AB, Ciani KD. 2008. Effects of an undergraduate career class on men's and women's career decision-making self-efficacy and vocational identity. *J. Career Dev.* 34:263–85

Sheu H, Chong SS, Chen H, Lin W. 2014. Well-being of Taiwanese and Singaporean college students: cross-cultural validity of a modified social cognitive mode. *J. Couns. Psychol.* 61:447–60

Sheu H, Lent RW. 2015. A social cognitive perspective on career intervention. In *APA Handbook of Career Intervention*, Vol. 1, ed. PJ Hartung, ML Savickas, WB Walsh, pp. 115–28. Washington, DC: Am. Psychol. Assoc.

Sheu H, Lent RW, Brown SD, Miller MJ, Hennessy KD, Duffy RD. 2010. Testing the choice model of social cognitive career theory across Holland themes: a meta-analytic path analysis. *J. Vocat. Behav.* 76:252–64

Singh R, Fouad NA, Fitzpatrick ME, Liu JP, Cappaert KJ, Figuereido C. 2013. Stemming the tide: predicting women engineers' intentions to leave. *J. Vocat. Behav.* 83:281–94

Singley DB, Lent RW, Sheu HB. 2010. Longitudinal test of the social cognitive model of academic and life satisfaction. *J. Career Assess.* 18:133–46

Spurk D, Abele AE. 2014. Synchronous and time-lagged effects between occupational self-efficacy and objective and subjective career success: findings from a four-wave and 9-year longitudinal study. *J. Vocat. Behav.* 84:119–32

Steger MF, Dik BJ, Duffy RD. 2012. Measuring meaningful work: the Work and Meaning Inventory (WAMI). *J. Career Assess.* 20:322–37

Steger MF, Littman-Ovadia H, Miller M, Menger L, Rothmann S. 2013. Engaging in work even when it is meaningless: positive affective disposition and meaningful work interact in relation to work engagement. *J. Career Assess.* 21:348–61

Thompson MN. 2013. Career barriers and coping efficacy among Native American students. *J. Career Assess.* 21:311–25

Thompson MN, Dahling JJ. 2012. Perceived social status and learning experiences in social cognitive career theory. *J. Vocat. Behav.* 80:351–61

Tirpak DM, Schlosser LZ. 2013. Evaluating FOCUS-2's effectiveness in enhancing first-year college students' social cognitive career development. *Career Dev. Q.* 61:110–23

Tokar DM, Thompson MN, Plaufcan MR, Williams CM. 2007. Precursors of learning experiences in social cognitive career theory. *J. Vocat. Behav.* 71:319–39

Tolentino LR, Sedoglavich V, Lu VN, Garcia PM, Restubog SD. 2014. The role of career adaptability in predicting entrepreneurial intentions: a moderated mediation model. *J. Vocat. Behav.* 85:403–12

Tovar-Murray D, Jenifer ES, Andrusyk J, D'Angelo R, King T. 2012. Racism-related stress and ethnic identity as determinants of African American college students' career aspirations. *Career Dev. Q.* 60:254–62

van Vianen AE, Klehe U, Koen J, Dries N. 2012. Career Adapt-Abilities Scale—Netherlands Form: psychometric properties and relationships to ability, personality, and regulatory focus. *J. Vocat. Behav.* 80:716–24

Varghese FP. 2013. Vocational interventions with offenders: interdisciplinary research, theory, and integration. *Couns. Psychol.* 41:1011–39

Wright SL, Jenkins-Guarnieri MA, Murdock JL. 2013. Career development among first-year college students: college self-efficacy, student persistence, and academic success. *J. Career Dev.* 40:292–310

Zacher H. 2014a. Career adaptability predicts subjective career success above and beyond personality traits and core self-evaluations. *J. Vocat. Behav.* 84:21–30

Zacher H. 2014b. Individual difference predictors of change in career adaptability over time. *J. Vocat. Behav.* 84:188–98

Causal Inference in Developmental Origins of Health and Disease (DOHaD) Research

Suzanne H. Gage,[1,2] Marcus R. Munafò,[1,2] and George Davey Smith[1]

[1]MRC Integrative Epidemiology Unit (IEU) at the University of Bristol, Bristol BS8 2BN, United Kingdom; email: kz.davey-smith@bristol.ac.uk

[2]UK Center for Tobacco and Alcohol Studies, School of Experimental Psychology, University of Bristol, Bristol BS8 1TU, United Kingdom

Annu. Rev. Psychol. 2016. 67:567–85

First published online as a Review in Advance on October 6, 2015

The *Annual Review of Psychology* is online at psych.annualreviews.org

This article's doi:
10.1146/annurev-psych-122414-033352

Keywords

DOHaD, causal inference, instrumental variable, negative control, cross-contextual comparison, twin study

Abstract

Studies of the developmental origins of health and disease (DOHaD) often rely on prospective observational data, from which associations between developmental exposures and outcomes in later life can be identified. Typically, conventional statistical methods are used in an attempt to mitigate problems inherent in observational data, such as confounding and reverse causality, but these have serious limitations. In this review, we discuss a variety of methods that are increasingly being used in observational epidemiological studies to help strengthen causal inference. These methods include negative controls, cross-contextual designs, instrumental variables (including Mendelian randomization), family-based studies, and natural experiments. Applications within the DOHaD framework, and in relation to behavioral, psychiatric, and psychological domains, are considered, and the considerable potential for expanding the use of these methods is outlined.

Contents

INTRODUCTION

The developmental origins of health and disease (DOHaD) hypothesis proposes that the environment individuals experience in utero and during early development can affect their health and susceptibility to disease over the rest of their life. A long lineage can be traced for DOHaD (Kuh & Davey Smith 2004), but contemporary interest increased following work from David Barker and colleagues in the mid-1980s that suggested that early-life nutrition is associated with cardiovascular disease risk in later life (Barker 1995, Barker & Osmond 1986, Fall et al. 1995). The concept that early-life experiences have long-term effects is not new to psychology. From imprinting in Lorenz's geese (Lorenz 1935) to the long-term effects of trauma on little Albert (Watson & Rayner 1920), theories conceptually similar to the DOHaD hypothesis have played a key role in psychological research over the preceding century. Understanding these relationships is important, since elucidating the mechanisms by which early-life experiences can affect adult physical and mental well-being will identify potentially important targets for intervention to prevent adverse outcomes from occurring, many years before they are likely to do so.

A substantial body of evidence supports the DOHaD hypothesis. Barker and colleagues' original series of papers presented evidence of associations between low birth weight and a number of offspring health outcomes, including risk of coronary heart disease and stroke (Barker 1997), hypertension (Barker & Martyn 1997), and type 2 diabetes (Hales & Barker 1992). These studies were originally considered under the umbrella term of the fetal origins of adult disease (FOAD) because the major focus was on the role of the intrauterine environment on later offspring outcomes, but the concept was later extended to include other aspects of developmental plasticity, including the early postnatal period and possible preconceptual and intergenerational influences (Davey Smith 2012a). Since the initial papers were published, low birth weight has also been shown to be associated with offspring obesity (Eriksson et al. 2015), depression (Van Lieshout & Boylan 2010), and intelligence (Eryigit Madzwamuse et al. 2015). However, studies to date have for the most part been conducted using observational data; therefore, although they provide suggestive evidence that these developmental influences affect later outcomes, they are limited in terms of providing strong enough evidence for a causal interpretation to be drawn.

The purpose of this review is to describe the limitations of traditional methods for assessing associations in observational studies and inferring causality, and to provide an introduction to alternative approaches to fashioning and analyzing data sources that can help in this regard.

Although DOHaD is the main lens through which these questions are discussed, we extend it to consider development and health more generally, as there are other time periods that are likely to be critical for later physical and mental health, such as adolescence, for which the same issues apply.

Problems with Observational Studies

When considering the impact of an exposure on an outcome, the strongest evidence of a causal association comes from experimental designs, in particular randomized controlled trials (RCTs), in which individuals are randomly assigned to either an exposure condition or a control condition and then followed up to ascertain differential incidence of the outcome between the two groups. However, the use of an experimental design is not possible when it is unethical or impractical either to give or to withhold a particular exposure. For example, when the exposure in question might only have an effect after many years, such RCTs would be prohibitively expensive and impractical to run. Therefore, in order to attempt to ascertain causation in these circumstances, observational data must be interrogated. Without the ability to randomize people, associations seen between an exposure and outcome in observational data could be due to a number of possibilities aside from a causal association between the two. These possibilities include confounding, reverse causation, and various biases that could distort the underlying association (Davey Smith & Ebrahim 2002).

Confounding. If other differences exist between those who experience the exposure and those who do not, any association seen could be due to these confounding factors. Adjustment must be made in analyses for all potential confounders. However, statistical adjustment will usually be incomplete: Not only must all the confounders be measured, but confounders must suffer from no measurement error for such adjustments to successfully account for confounding (Phillips & Davey Smith 1992). Unmeasured confounding factors and measurement error (due to either technical issues or temporal variation in a factor assessed only once) in assessed confounding factors leads to residual confounding even when confounders have apparently been statistically controlled for in the analysis (Davey Smith & Phillips 1992, Fewell et al. 2007). For this reason, residual confounding can never be completely ruled out in observational studies.

Reverse causation. When assessing observational data, it is challenging to ascertain the direction of causation, even when there is a temporal gap between exposure and outcome. Pre-existing symptoms of the outcome that influence the exposure could generate the observed associations. For example, observational evidence has shown that alcohol consumption is associated with mortality in a J-shaped curve, with those who drink nothing at all showing worse outcomes than those who drink a small amount. It has been suggested that this association might be seen because some nondrinkers stop drinking due to ill health; the drinking behavior is a consequence of the increased risk, rather than the other way round (Liang & Chikritzhs 2013).

Selection bias. Estimates seen in observational studies can be affected by selection bias because of how participants are recruited into a study or how data from participants are collected. For example, certain types of people might be more likely to be lost to follow-up in longitudinal studies. If loss to follow-up is related to two or more variables, then the available sample is, in effect, stratified by whether follow-up was successful or not, which generates associations between these variables in the available dataset even when associations do not exist in the underlying population and could change the strength and even direction of associations that do exist (Ebrahim

& Davey Smith 2013). This is a form of collider bias (Cole et al. 2010)—a family of biases that can distort observational estimates of exposure effects—that has perhaps been underappreciated in the literature until recently.

Misclassification can occur when participants are incorrectly assigned to an exposure or outcome category due to imprecise data collection methods, and if this is differential (e.g., degree of misclassification of outcome relates to the exposure), it can distort exposure-outcome associations. Self-report measures might not adequately capture variables when participants might want to hide their use of a substance (e.g., smoking during pregnancy). Such information biases may particularly influence case-control studies when retrospective reporting of exposures occurs after the outcome condition has developed (Rothman et al. 2008).

The usual approach to attempting to mitigate the potential biases above is to use statistical methods aimed at removing or minimizing them. However, statistical analyses necessarily require assumptions to be made about the data, and these may be (and indeed probably usually are) unjustified. Moreover, statistical adjustments can lead to overconfidence in the robustness of findings—the commonly used term that factors have been statistically controlled for gives a sense of this—and result in the literature containing many associations that are overinterpreted in terms of causal evidence (Davey Smith & Ebrahim 2001). As with residual confounding, attempted statistical adjustment to account for potential biases has serious limitations.

In this review, we discuss improving causal inference through alternative approaches to conventional statistical adjustment methods. Ways of assembling and analyzing data can strengthen such inference, and triangulating evidence from multiple independent sources can provide more reliable evidence for causation than would a single approach. In lieu of experimental designs, which are typically not ethical or practical, a far stronger foundation for this literature can be built through identifying study designs that reveal bias, confounding, or reverse causality, or are better protected from these than conventional approaches, and applying these to questions related to the DOHaD hypothesis (Richmond et al. 2014).

METHODS FOR CAUSAL INFERENCE

Below we describe methods from epidemiological studies that attempt to address problems of confounding, reverse causation, and bias at the design stage of a study rather than rely on statistical methods after data collection. We argue that such methods allow for stronger causal inference and have the potential to provide much stronger evidence to elucidate the mechanisms that might underlie the associations between developmental experiences and adult physical and mental health. **Table 1** summarizes these methods.

Table 1 Description of the methodologies reviewed

Technique	Summary
Negative control	Exposures or outcomes with similar confounding but no plausible biological connection are identified to ascertain whether associations are likely to be causal or due to confounding.
Cross-contextual	Two populations with differing confounding structures are sampled and associations are compared between them.
Instrumental variable analysis	Unconfounded proxies are found for exposures of interest (e.g., genetic variants in Mendelian randomization).
Family studies	Assumptions are made about shared genetic and environmental factors in comparisons of related pairs of individuals.

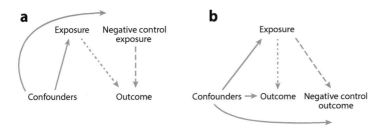

Figure 1

Schematic representations of (*a*) negative control exposure and (*b*) negative control outcome. Confounding is the same for the exposure or outcome and its negative control. However, there is no causal association between (*a*) the negative control exposure and the outcome of interest or (*b*) the exposure of interest and the negative control outcome. The dashed line represents the negative control analysis, and the dotted-and-dashed line represents the association under interrogation.

Negative Controls

When assessing an observational association, one cannot be certain whether the association being seen is due to residual confounding. One method to examine this possibility is to compare the association of interest with that of another related association but for which there is no biologically plausible mechanism for causation. This is known as a negative control design and was developed in the economics and econometrics literature (DiNardo & Pischke 1997, Oosterbeek 1997). The negative control analysis will have either the same exposure or the same outcome as in the main analysis of interest but will replace either the exposure or the outcome with a negative control in order to uncover potential unobserved or unaccounted-for confounding or bias. A suitable negative control should be subject to the same confounding structure as the association of interest. Associations between the exposure and outcome of interest are then compared to those between the negative control exposure and the outcome of interest, or the exposure of interest and the negative control outcome. If the association seen between the exposure and outcome is of a larger magnitude than the association between the exposure and the negative control, this would contribute positively to an evaluation of the strength of evidence for a causal association between the exposure and outcome of interest. If, however, the association seen between the two is due to confounding, then a similar association is likely to be seen in both the analysis of interest and the negative control analysis, in which there is no biologically plausible mechanism for causation (Davey Smith 2008, 2012b; Lipsitch et al. 2010). **Figure 1** shows an example of a negative control exposure and a negative control outcome design.

The rationale behind negative control designs is that the inspection of analyses that utilize negative control exposures or outcomes—which are likely to share similar confounding with the exposure or outcome of interest—can help strengthen causal inference. For example, consider maternal smoking during pregnancy, which researchers have hypothesized may cause offspring depression through a direct intrauterine effect. A plausible negative control exposure in this situation is paternal smoking during pregnancy, where no substantial intrauterine biological effect will occur, but confounding factors are likely to be similar. Researchers can also investigate the relationships between an exposure and a negative control outcome. The negative control outcome should be influenced by similar confounding and other biases as would be seen for the outcome of interest but would be unlikely to be caused by the exposure. For example, as smoking has similar associations with both suicide and homicide mortality, this casts doubt on smoking causing suicide; although apparently plausible causal biological mechanisms exist that can be advanced to explain the smoking-suicide association, the same is not the case for the smoking-homicide association (Davey Smith et al. 1992).

Negative control exposures. Negative control exposures have been used in studies trying to assess the potential causal effects of periconceptual folate or folic acid supplementation. Given the established causal association between inadequate periconceptual folate status and neural tube defects (Pitkin 2007), randomized trials deliberately withholding advice to take periconceptual folate supplements from the control group would be unethical, so trials aimed at evaluating the effect on other outcomes are unlikely to be undertaken. The observational associations seen between lack of folate supplement use and other outcomes such as increased rates of autism spectrum disorders or slower language development could be due to residual confounding from socioeconomic position or health-adverse maternal behaviors in general (Davey Smith 2008). In order to strengthen causal inference with regard to maternal periconceptual folate supplementation and autism, one study examined the association between fish oil supplements and autism in the same sample (Suren et al. 2013), since the use of fish oil supplements and the use of folic acid supplements were similarly socially patterned with respect to potential confounders such as parental characteristics. A robust inverse association was identified between the use of folic acid supplements and the subsequent risk of autism spectrum disorder. However, there was little evidence of an association between the use of fish oil supplements and autism spectrum disorder. The difference between these two results provides evidence that residual confounding from maternal health-related behaviors or social circumstances more generally is not leading to the observed association between maternal folate and autism spectrum disorders.

Similarly, another study assessed the association between folate supplementation and language delay (Roth et al. 2011). This group used a four-category exposure measure of "no supplement," "supplements other than folic acid," "only folic acid," and "folic acid plus other supplements." The authors found that there was little evidence of an association between supplements not containing folic acid and later language delay, compared to the baseline of "no supplement use," despite the similar associations with confounding factors shown for the different supplements. However, an inverse association was seen for both of the groups in which the different supplements included folic acid. This provided further evidence that the association seen with folate supplementation could be a protective one and not simply due to residual confounding—although of course causation is still not in any sense proven.

As already introduced above, a now widely used negative control exposure for studies investigating effects thought to occur in utero is to examine the same association for exposures in fathers, rather than mothers, since a direct intrauterine effect will not occur in the former case (Davey Smith 2008). Brion and colleagues found that maternal macronutrient and energy intake during pregnancy predicted later offspring dietary intake, whereas paternal nutrition during the partner's pregnancy did not. They concluded that this provides some evidence that maternal intake during pregnancy could program later offspring appetite (Brion et al. 2010a). Conversely, associations between maternal or paternal smoking and later offspring blood pressure were similar, suggesting that the association seen is unlikely to be due to an intrauterine effect and could indicate that residual confounding affects the associations (Brion et al. 2007).

Negative control outcomes. Negative control outcomes use broadly the same principles as negative control exposures. An outcome variable is selected that is unlikely to be caused by the exposure of interest.

An example of negative control outcomes is taken from studies of hormone replacement therapy (HRT). Many early studies found evidence that HRT was associated with lower mortality from cardiovascular disease. In the late 1980s, Petitti and colleagues similarly found evidence that HRT was associated with lower mortality from cardiovascular disease, a result they described as "suggestive." However, they conducted a further analysis to assess rates of mortality from accidents, suicide, and homicide in women using HRT compared to those not using it, in whom there is no plausible biological mechanism (Petitti et al. 1986, 1987). They found evidence that HRT was associated with lower rates of these forms of mortality as well and suggested that this finding indicated that at least some of the differences in outcomes seen between HRT users and nonusers were likely to be due to lifestyle, socioeconomic, behavioral, and related differences. As was later borne out by RCTs, the observational evidence suggesting that HRT substantially reduced the risk of cardiovascular mortality was indeed spurious (Lawlor et al. 2004).

Limitations. The use of negative controls can provide useful evidence of residual confounding if similar associations are seen for the negative control exposure or in the negative control outcome. However, if associations are not similar between the association of interest and that seen in the negative control, this is not of course definitive proof of causation, as the association of interest could still be confounded by other factors that are not shared with the negative control or could be subject to bias. The technique is also inappropriate if there might be a plausible biological mechanism that affects the negative control. For example, paternal smoking during pregnancy could conceivably affect the developing fetus via the effects of environmental tobacco smoke exposure (Taylor et al. 2014), although the association with outcomes of interest would still be expected to be attenuated relative to associations observed with maternal smoking during pregnancy.

Cross-Contextual Comparisons

Cross-contextual comparisons operate on the opposite principle to negative control methods. These designs look for similar associations in very different populations (typically across different countries). If the same association between exposure and outcome is seen in populations in which the underlying confounding structures are very different, the association provides stronger evidence of causality. It would mean that if the association were due to residual confounding, it would have to be from different sources in the different populations, which is not likely. **Figure 2** illustrates this concept.

One way this design has been utilized is by comparing birth cohorts in different countries. Brion and colleagues (2011) used the Avon Longitudinal Study of Parents and Children (ALSPAC) birth cohort based in the United Kingdom, and the Pelotas cohort based in Brazil, to assess the causal effects of breastfeeding on various outcomes. Whereas breastfeeding in the United

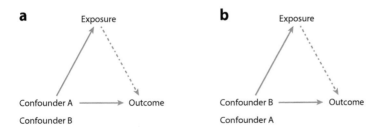

Figure 2

Schematic representations of a cross-contextual design. The exposure and outcome should be equivalent across the different contexts, but the confounding structure should not. Here, confounder A affects the relationship in context (*a*) but not in context (*b*). The reverse is true for confounder B.

Kingdom is associated with higher socioeconomic position, healthier diet, and lower levels of maternal smoking, the same social patterning of breastfeeding behavior did not exist at the time the Brazilian cohort was established. The authors found that in the ALSPAC cohort, breastfeeding was associated with lower offspring body mass index and blood pressure, but these inverse associations were not seen in the Pelotas cohort. The authors used this divergence in cross-contextual findings to provide suggestive evidence that many of the associations seen in observational studies in Western countries between breastfeeding and various outcomes are likely to be due to residual confounding. Some evidence indicated that the association between breastfeeding and IQ might be causal, and indeed this has been supported by results from an RCT conducted in Belarus (Kramer et al. 2007, Patel et al. 2014) and from further recent evidence from a different wave of the Pelotas cohort studies in Brazil (Victora et al. 2015).

A second example of cross-contextual comparison is the examination of cohorts in which the patterning of an exposure has changed over time. For example, breastfeeding was not strongly socially patterned in the United Kingdom in the 1920s. Martin and colleagues (2007) compared bottle-fed and breastfed infants in the Boyd-Orr Survey of Diet and Health; the infants were born in the 1920s and 1930s and surveyed between 1937 and 1939 and again between 1997 and 1998. The authors found that breastfeeding in the 1920s was associated with upward social mobility (i.e., moving from a lower- to a higher-occupational social class from childhood to adulthood). Critically, breastfeeding was not associated with indicators of socioeconomic position such as household income. Since confounding structures have changed over time, consistency in associations of breastfeeding with offspring health outcomes at different time points increases confidence that these associations are causal in nature.

Conversely, if associations change over time, this suggests that the association may not be causal. Consider one example of this in cannabis research. Some evidence indicates that cannabis use during adolescence could be damaging to later mental health due to changes that occur in the endocannabinoid system during this period of development (Rubino & Parolaro 2008, Trezza et al. 2008). Levels of tetrahydrocannabinol (THC) and other cannabinoids in street cannabis have changed substantially since investigations into the association between cannabis and psychosis were first conducted (Mehmedic et al. 2010). If the nature of the association between cannabis and psychosis is a biological effect of THC, it might be expected that associations between cannabis and psychosis would be stronger in more recent cohort studies than in earlier ones. However, the association between cannabis use and psychosis was first reported in a cohort measured in the 1960s (Zammit et al. 2002), which was before levels of THC are thought to have increased (King et al. 2004), and the size of the point estimates in individual studies has not increased in a systematic way since then. A recent case-control study suggested that skunk cannabis (which is high in THC but has little cannabidiol) is associated with hospitalization for first-episode psychosis, but hash cannabis (with equivalent levels of THC and cannabidiol) is not (Di Forti et al. 2015). Although this could provide evidence in support of an effect of cannabis strength on the risk of psychosis, an alternative explanation might be that people at a higher risk of psychosis for other reasons are self-selecting to an extreme end of cannabis use distribution and are switching to stronger strains as they become available (Gage et al. 2015).

Limitations.   When conducting such cross-contextual studies, it is important to ascertain whether relevant differences exist in confounding structure between the two populations being compared. If similar confounders in both contexts could be driving the association seen, then the comparison is inappropriate. Also, the exposure and outcome variables being compared need to be harmonized across the cohorts in order to be directly comparable. When an exposure has changed over time, a number of other variables might have also changed, which could confound the association.

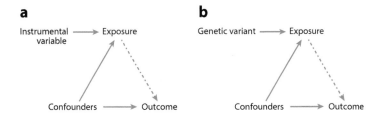

a

Instrumental variable ⟶ Exposure

Confounders ⟶ Outcome

b

Genetic variant ⟶ Exposure

Confounders ⟶ Outcome

Figure 3

Schematic representations of (*a*) an instrumental variables analysis and (*b*) a Mendelian randomization analysis. The instrument or genetic variant is associated with the exposure of interest, but not with the confounding variables associated with the exposure and outcome. The instrument is associated with the outcome only via its association with the exposure of interest.

Instrumental Variable Analyses

Another method to help strengthen causal inference in observational data was conceived in the econometrics literature. Instrumental variable analyses use a proxy variable (known as an instrumental variable or instrument) in place of the exposure of interest. If an appropriate instrument can be identified, it should in principle allow for causal interpretation from observational data. However, the proposed instrument must satisfy three assumptions to be a valid instrumental variable. First, it should be robustly associated with the exposure of interest. Second, it should not associate with potential confounding factors, either known or unknown, that can bias naïve observational associations. Third, it should not directly affect the outcome of interest (Angrist & Pischke 2009). A diagram of these requirements is shown in **Figure 3a**.

One study used a short-lived policy change, which had unintended consequences, in an instrumental variable design. In Sweden, a law was introduced that substantially increased access to strong beer by those under 21 in some regions but not other regions. This policy change was used as a proxy for in utero alcohol exposure. Critically, the participants in the study were conceived prior to the policy being introduced; thus, the pregnancies were not due to an increase in unplanned pregnancies resulting from risky sexual behaviors following increased alcohol consumption. The study indicated that children born to mothers under 21 who were pregnant for the longest period during the policy change (5 to 8.5 months) had lower earnings and wages, were more likely to be unemployed, and had higher welfare dependency rates compared to cohorts from other parts of Sweden or those people born to mothers pregnant in the regions in which policy change occurred but in utero just before or just after this change (Nilsson 2014).

Limitations. The principal limitation of instrumental variable methods is the challenge of identifying valid instruments that are genuinely not associated with potential confounders and not subject to reverse causality. Critically, it is not possible to definitively test the validity of putative instruments because unmeasured confounders may be operating.

Mendelian Randomization

Mendelian randomization is a type of instrumental variable analysis that uses genetic variants as unconfounded proxies (i.e., instruments) for the exposure of interest (Burgess et al. 2015). Due to the random nature of inheritance of genetic information, it can be reasonably assumed that we inherit each variant (for the most part) independently from other genetic variants and from environmental factors, meaning such variants are unlikely to be associated with potential confounding factors. Also, because our genomes are determined at conception, associations between genetic variants and outcomes cannot be due to reverse causation. Therefore, if a genetic variant is robustly associated with an exposure of interest, it could potentially be used in a Mendelian randomization experiment (Davey Smith 2010, Davey Smith & Ebrahim 2003). This concept is illustrated in **Figure 3b**. With regard to developmental outcomes, single nucleotide polymorphisms (SNPs) or genetic risk scores have already been identified via genome-wide association studies for use as proxies for exposures such as smoking or drinking during pregnancy or for maternal body mass index.

A genetic variant has been identified that robustly correlates to smoking heaviness in daily smokers (Ware et al. 2012). Located in the *CHRNA5-A3-B4* gene cluster, on chromosome 15, rs1051730 and rs16969968 are in perfect linkage disequilibrium and can be treated as interchangeable. Each additional copy of the minor (T) allele is associated with one extra cigarette smoked per day in smokers (Thorgeirsson et al. 2008), accounting for ~1% of the variation in cigarette consumption in daily smokers (Ware et al. 2011) and ~4% of levels of cotinine, the primary metabolite of nicotine and a more precise biomarker of exposure (Keskitalo et al. 2009, Munafò et al. 2012). The variant has also been shown to associate with lack of ability to give up smoking during pregnancy, which is crucial for investigating developmental outcomes (Freathy et al. 2009). This variant has been used in a number of Mendelian randomization designs, including as a proxy for fetal exposure to cigarette smoke. Tyrrell and colleagues (2012) have shown that variation at this locus not only predicts an increased likelihood to continue smoking during pregnancy, but also a larger number of cigarettes per day in pregnant women who continue to smoke. The authors performed a meta-analysis of 14 studies, comprising 26,241 women. Of those who smoked beyond the first trimester during pregnancy, each additional copy of the rs1051730 T allele, associated with increased smoking, was associated with a 20-g reduction in offspring birth weight. Conversely, the authors found little evidence of differences in birth weight by genotype in nonsmokers. Given the genotype's lack of association with factors that usually confound observational associations such as age, socioeconomic position, and occupation, and the lack of possibility of reverse causation in this type of design, this study provides much stronger evidence of causation than is possible from observational designs.

Genetic variants have also been identified that predict alcohol use (Enomoto et al. 1991). Although one variant is only prevalent in East Asian populations, there are also variants present in Western populations that can be used as a proxy for exposure to alcohol during pregnancy. As previously noted, many observational studies have suggested that the association between alcohol use and many outcomes is J-shaped, indicating that those who drink a small amount have better outcomes than those who do not drink at all. However, drinking behavior is highly socially patterned, so residual confounding could well still be affecting these findings. For example, Kelly and colleagues (2012) reported that low levels of maternal alcohol consumption in pregnancy (one to two drinks per week or per occasion) were associated with reduced behavioral difficulties and hyperactivity in offspring at age 5 years. However, data from the same study indicated that similar associations were observed for tobacco use and maternal socioeconomic position. Never-drinking mothers and those who did not drink during pregnancy were more likely to smoke and more likely to have never worked or to have been unemployed long term in comparison with light drinkers (see **Figure 4**). Also, reverse causation is harder to rule out in this context as people may have stopped drinking due to ill health, which might not be adequately captured in the collected data. Zuccolo and colleagues (2013) found evidence that a genotype associated with lower alcohol consumption or abstinence during early pregnancy was associated with offspring academic achievement at age 11, which suggests that alcohol exposure in utero is causally associated with lower offspring educational outcomes. However, these investigators found no strong evidence of an association with childhood IQ at age 8, although the statistical power was lower for this analysis.

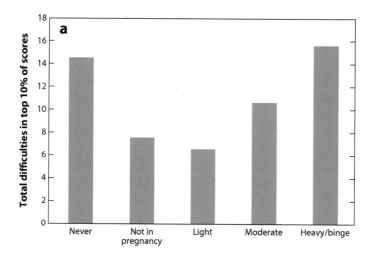

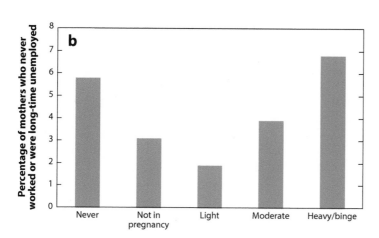

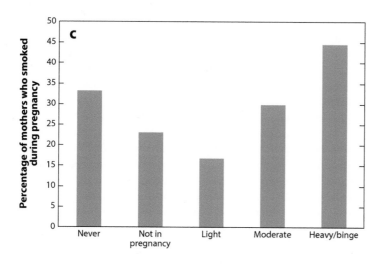

Figure 4

Association of
mother's drinking
status during
pregnancy with
(*a*) offspring
behavioral
difficulties,
(*b*) maternal
employment history,
and (*c*) maternal
smoking. Figure
based on data from
Kelly et al. (2012).

Genetic variants that predict adiposity have been used as a proxy for maternal body mass index in order to ascertain the potential programming effect of prenatal maternal obesity on offspring outcomes. Lawlor and colleagues (2008) found little evidence that maternal genotype predicted offspring fat mass by age 9 to 11 years, after adjustment for offspring genotype (which is important when there could be a direct effect of offspring genotype on the outcome of interest). This finding suggests that the association between maternal and offspring adiposity may not operate via the prenatal environment.

Limitations. Mendelian randomization is an inappropriate study design in a number of circumstances. Most obviously, it is not possible to use the design if there is no genetic variant yet identified that is robustly associated with the exposure of interest. For example, although cannabis use is known to be heritable, genome-wide association studies have not yet identified any variants robustly associated with cannabis use phenotypes. Given that the associations between variants and exposures of interest are often of modest size, large samples are required for adequate power to undertake such study designs, which means that consortia are often necessary. This can lead to heterogeneous measures of the outcome as studies are combined. The most fundamental limitation relates to when a genetic variant has a direct pleiotropic effect (whereby a gene influences more than one phenotype) on the outcome of interest as well as on the exposure, as this can lead to spurious associations. Some genetic variants are in linkage disequilibrium, meaning they are more likely to be inherited together, which can generate biases similar to those seen for pleiotropy. Methods to evaluate and account for such reintroduced confounding for pleiotropy or linkage disequilibrium are discussed elsewhere (Bowden et al. 2015, Davey Smith & Hemani 2014). If the sample contains two or more ancestrally different populations, associations between genetic variants and outcomes could be due to population stratification rather than to a causal effect of the exposure on the outcome. These issues can be addressed through study designs that utilize ancestrally similar samples and by using principal components analysis to correct for stratification and account for ancestry (Davey Smith & Hemani 2014).

Family Design Techniques

The use of genetically related pairs or groups of individuals can mean that potential confounding from genetics and shared environments (the latter referring to factors that are the same for both siblings when they grow up together) are less plausible explanations of observed associations (Davey Smith 2008, D'Onofrio et al. 2014). Twin and sibling designs have been used for many years, and a number of different possible designs exist for such studies. The classic twin study design compares monozygotic and dizygotic twin pairs in order to separate additive genetic influence (correlated at 1.0 in monozygotic twins and 0.5 in dizygotic twins), shared environment influence (correlated in both types of twins at 1.0), and nonshared environment influence (not correlated in either type of twins) (Davey Smith 2011).

If pairs of monozygotic twins reared together are discordant for the exposure of interest, they can be used as ideally matched pairs in a case-control study. Any association seen will not be due to confounding from genetic factors and will not be due to confounding from shared environmental factors. However, this design cannot rule out the impact of nonshared environmental confounders. It is also important to consider that the intrauterine environment of a twin is not the same as that of a singleton pregnancy, and this could mean results from such studies are less easily generalizable. Other designs using genetically related individuals include those with sibling or cousin pairs, which remove the shared intrauterine environment but do not account for all genetic variation.

Twin studies have been used to investigate aspects of the DOHaD hypothesis (D'Onofrio et al. 2014). For example, Class and colleagues (2014) used a sibling comparison design approach to disentangle genetic and environmental effects on associations between fetal growth and psychiatric and socioeconomic problems. They found that within sibling pairs, lower birth weight predicted autism spectrum disorder and attention-deficit/hyperactivity disorder. However, when they assessed associations with suicide attempt and substance use, these associations were fully attenuated in sibling comparison models where the sibling differed in his or her substance use, suggesting that residual confounding may have been responsible for associations seen in more traditional cohort designs in which nonrelated individuals were sampled.

Another study used dizygotic twins to investigate whether exposure to testosterone in utero increases the risk of attention-deficit/hyperactivity disorder and autism spectrum disorder (Attermann et al. 2012). The sex of the participants' cotwin was used as a genetic proxy for exposure to testosterone, as a male cotwin would increase the female twin's exposure to prenatal testosterone. However, sex of the cotwin should not be confounded with other genetic or environmental factors. The authors found that having a male cotwin was associated with a reduction in risk of attention-deficit/hyperactivity disorder and autism spectrum disorder in the female twin, opposite to what had been predicted. They concluded that this finding could be due to parental reporting bias or unmeasured variables still confounding the association.

Limitations. Different limitations exist depending on the type of twin or family study design employed. Most notably, finding monozygotic twins discordant on the exposure of interest is not trivial, which can make these studies challenging to conduct or result in studies being underpowered. The potential lack of generalizability due to different intrauterine experiences for twin versus singleton births can also limit the impact of some of these study designs, particularly when assessing exposures occurring prenatally.

Natural Experiments

Occasionally, situations will arise whereby unusual circumstances can provide insights that observational studies cannot. One such event was the Dutch Hunger Winter of 1944–1945. Toward the end of World War II, a Nazi blockade led to a severe food shortage in the Netherlands, where civilians were subjected to rations equivalent to less than 500 calories per day. Pregnancies that occurred during this period represent a rare opportunity to experimentally investigate the impact of severe calorie restriction upon offspring outcomes.

Early studies using the cohort found an association between conception during the height of the famine and neural tube defects (spina bifida and anencephaly) in comparison with the background rate of such disorders in the Dutch population (Brown & Susser 1997). When the cohort was older, an association with schizophrenia was also assessed, which found the cumulative risk of schizophrenia between ages 24 and 48 years to be double that of unaffected comparison cohorts and of those exposed to the famine during other periods of gestation (Hoek et al. 1998). This finding was replicated in another natural experiment that was possible after a famine in China brought about by the Great Leap Forward period of social and economic upheaval. Although caloric intake data were not available for this cohort, it was still possible to assess the impact of famine during conception on the risk of later schizophrenia. The impacts of severe caloric restriction in this very culturally different cohort were largely similar to those seen in the Netherlands (Song et al. 2009).

Limitations. Such extreme events as famine may have other consequences that could confound associations. For example, prenatal stress is likely to have been much higher during these periods than surrounding times. However, in the Dutch study it was possible to compare with cohorts in other areas of the Netherlands that had moderate levels of starvation and similar experiences of war, but not quite the extreme caloric deprivation experienced in the most affected areas. Differential associations were still seen when using these cohorts as a control group, which suggests that other factors such as stress and the experience of wartime are unlikely to account for the results (Brown & Susser 2008).

CONCLUSION

The approaches described in this review represent a number of different ways in which study design and broad analytical methods can be used to allow for stronger causal inferences than are provided by conventional statistical adjustments. Negative control designs identify an exposure or outcome where no association is predicted but a similar confounding structure is shared with the main association of interest. This can help rule out residual confounding as an explanation for the association of interest. Cross-contextual studies compare associations between two populations in which underlying confounding structures are likely to be very different, thus lessening the likelihood of associations being due to confounding. Instrumental variable analyses identify an unconfounded proxy for the exposure of interest and assess the association between that and the outcome to remove the effect of unmeasured confounding. A specific version of this, Mendelian randomization, utilizes genetic variants as the proxy variables, which can also rule out reverse causation because genes are determined at conception. Family-based studies use shared genetic and environmental characteristics to generate highly matched case-control studies. Other methods can also be used in specific circumstances (for example, see the sidebar on In Vitro Fertilization Variation).

Although none of these techniques represents a panacea and each has its own strengths and weakness, they can be used in conjunction with each other to provide an overall evaluation of the support for putative causal associations seen in observational data. Combining these different designs in a single report assessing one research question from a variety of angles can be particularly effective. For example, Brion and colleagues (2010b) combined cross-contextual and negative control designs to assess associations between maternal smoking and child psychological problems.

They found that maternal smoking during pregnancy was associated with greater offspring externalizing and peer problems in cohorts in Brazil and the United Kingdom, despite the different social patterns of smoking during pregnancy in the two countries. The authors also showed that associations between maternal smoking and offspring conduct problems were stronger than those between paternal smoking and the same problems (although statistical evidence was weak in one cohort). By combining these study designs, the findings become much more compelling than they would alone.

The different approaches that use study design to leverage stronger causal inference each rely on specific assumptions, which may not be valid. Critically, however, they rely on different assumptions. The triangulation of evidence from these different methods is therefore a powerful tool, and arguably a much more reliable approach to causal inference than statistical adjustment for imprecisely measured confounders, which are likely to constitute only some of the confounding factors that plague naïve observational epidemiology. Many methods are particularly well suited to the study of the developmental origins of health and disease, and a number of examples exist of the application of these methods to better understand the causal effects of intrauterine exposures to substances such as tobacco and alcohol on offspring developmental outcomes.

The tools necessary to implement these methods are becoming increasingly widely available. Access to datasets from large cohort studies across different countries is increasing, and a growing number of genetic variants associated with exposures of interest, such as tobacco and alcohol use, are being identified via genome-wide association studies. The potential for the application of these methods is therefore growing rapidly and offers great promise for future DOHaD research. A few key considerations can contribute to the robust triangulation of evidence, such as ensuring that variables across studies are meaningfully and harmoniously coded and scaled to allow direct comparison across designs. Consideration of the magnitude of effect of a hypothesized dose-response relationship across different study durations can provide stronger evidence in support of causation. For example, exposure differences in RCTs are likely to be of much shorter duration than those in cohort studies, and in Mendelian randomization studies, exposures are likely to be longer than in either RCT or cohort studies (as they may be present from soon after conception); therefore, the magnitude of the observed effect size would be expected to differ across these studies if associations were causal and showed dose response.

Critical periods should also be considered when triangulating the findings from different study designs, which is particularly relevant for DOHaD research. A risk factor may have an effect on an outcome only during a specific period of pregnancy, and if different studies measure variables at slightly different times, the timing rather than a lack of a causal association could be the reason for inconsistent results. Finally, multiple hypotheses may explain observed associations, and therefore applying principles of inference to the best explanation (Lipton 2004) and considering possible sources of bias will be important when attempting to triangulate results across different designs (Richmond et al. 2014).

DISCLOSURE STATEMENT

The authors are not aware of any affiliations, memberships, funding, or financial holdings that might be perceived as affecting the objectivity of this review.

ACKNOWLEDGMENTS

We thank Neil Davies for helpful comments on an earlier draft of this review, and Rebecca Richmond and Gemma Sharp for initial comments. All authors work within the MRC Integrative

Epidemiology Unit, supported by the Medical Research Council (MC_UU_12013/1, MC_UU_12013/6) and the University of Bristol. S.H.G. and M.R.M. are members of the UK Center for Tobacco and Alcohol Studies, a UKCRC Public Health Research: Center of Excellence. We gratefully acknowledge funding from the British Heart Foundation, Cancer Research UK, the Economic and Social Research Council, the Medical Research Council, and the National Institute for Health Research, under the auspices of the UK Clinical Research Collaboration.

LITERATURE CITED

Angrist JD, Pischke J-S. 2009. *Mostly Harmless Econometrics: An Empiricist's Companion*. Princeton, NJ: Princeton Univ. Press

Attermann J, Obel C, Bilenberg N, Nordenbaek CM, Skytthe A, Olsen J. 2012. Traits of ADHD and autism in girls with a twin brother: a Mendelian randomization study. *Eur. Child Adolesc. Psychiatry* 21:503–9

Barker DJ. 1995. Fetal origins of coronary heart disease. *BMJ* 311:171–74

Barker DJ. 1997. Intrauterine programming of coronary heart disease and stroke. *Acta Paediatr.* 423:178–83

Barker DJ, Martyn CN. 1997. The fetal origins of hypertension. *Adv. Nephrol. Necker Hosp.* 26:65–72

Barker DJ, Osmond C. 1986. Infant mortality, childhood nutrition, and ischaemic heart disease in England and Wales. *Lancet* 1:1077–81

Bowden J, Davey Smith G, Burgess S. 2015. Mendelian randomization with invalid instruments: effect estimation and bias detection through Egger regression. *Int. J. Epidemiol.* 44:512–25

Brion MJ, Lawlor DA, Matijasevich A, Horta B, Anselmi L, et al. 2011. What are the causal effects of breastfeeding on IQ, obesity and blood pressure? Evidence from comparing high-income with middle-income cohorts. *Int. J. Epidemiol.* 40:670–80

Brion MJ, Leary SD, Smith GD, Ness AR. 2007. Similar associations of parental prenatal smoking suggest child blood pressure is not influenced by intrauterine effects. *Hypertension* 49:1422–28

Brion MJ, Ness AR, Rogers I, Emmett P, Cribb V, et al. 2010a. Maternal macronutrient and energy intakes in pregnancy and offspring intake at 10 y: exploring parental comparisons and prenatal effects. *Am. J. Clin. Nutr.* 91:748–56

Brion MJ, Victora C, Matijasevich A, Horta B, Anselmi L, et al. 2010b. Maternal smoking and child psychological problems: disentangling causal and noncausal effects. *Pediatrics* 126:e57–65

Brown AS, Susser ES. 1997. Sex differences in prevalence of congenital neural defects after periconceptional famine exposure. *Epidemiology* 8:55–58

Brown AS, Susser ES. 2008. Prenatal nutritional deficiency and risk of adult schizophrenia. *Schizophr. Bull.* 34:1054–63

Burgess S, Timpson NJ, Ebrahim S, Davey Smith G. 2015. Mendelian randomization: Where are we now and where are we going? *Int. J. Epidemiol.* 44:379–88

Class QA, Rickert ME, Larsson H, Lichtenstein P, D'Onofrio BM. 2014. Fetal growth and psychiatric and socioeconomic problems: population-based sibling comparison. *Br. J. Psychiatry* 205:355–61

Cole SR, Platt RW, Schisterman EF, Chu H, Westreich D, et al. 2010. Illustrating bias due to conditioning on a collider. *Int. J. Epidemiol.* 39:417–20

D'Onofrio BM, Class QA, Lahey BB, Larsson H. 2014. Testing the developmental origins of health and disease hypothesis for psychopathology using family-based quasi-experimental designs. *Child Dev. Perspect.* 8:151–57

Davey Smith G. 2008. Assessing intrauterine influences on offspring health outcomes: Can epidemiological studies yield robust findings? *Basic Clin. Pharmacol. Toxicol.* 102:245–56

Davey Smith G. 2010. Mendelian randomization for strengthening causal inference in observational studies: application to gene × environment interactions. *Perspect. Psychol. Sci.* 5:527–45

Davey Smith G. 2011. Epidemiology, epigenetics and the "gloomy prospect": embracing randomness in population health research and practice. *Int. J. Epidemiol.* 40:537–62

Davey Smith G. 2012a. Epigenesis for epidemiologists: Does evo-devo have implications for population health research and practice? *Int. J. Epidemiol.* 41:236–47

Davey Smith G. 2012b. Negative control exposures in epidemiologic studies. *Epidemiology* 23:350–51; author reply 351–52

Davey Smith G, Ebrahim S. 2001. Epidemiology—is it time to call it a day? *Int. J. Epidemiol.* 30:1–11

Davey Smith G, Ebrahim S. 2002. Data dredging, bias, or confounding. *BMJ* 325:1437–38

Davey Smith G, Ebrahim S. 2003. "Mendelian randomization": Can genetic epidemiology contribute to understanding environmental determinants of disease? *Int. J. Epidemiol.* 32:1–22

Davey Smith G, Hemani G. 2014. Mendelian randomization: genetic anchors for causal inference in epidemiological studies. *Hum. Mol. Genet.* 23:R89–98

Davey Smith G, Phillips AN 1992. Confounding in epidemiological studies: why "independent" effects may not be all they seem. *BMJ* 305:757–59

Davey Smith G, Phillips AN, Neaton JD. 1992. Smoking as "independent" risk factor for suicide: illustration of an artifact from observational epidemiology? *Lancet* 340:709–12

Di Forti M, Marconi A, Carra E, Fraietta S, Trotta A, et al. 2015. Proportion of patients in south London with first-episode psychosis attributable to use of high potency cannabis: a case-control study. *Lancet Psychiatry* 2:233–38

DiNardo JE, Pischke JS. 1997. The returns to computer use revisited: Have pencils changed the wage structure too? *Q. J. Econ.* 112:291–303

Ebrahim S, Davey Smith G. 2013. Should we always deliberately be non-representative? *Int. J. Epidemiol.* 42:1022–26

Enomoto N, Takase S, Yasuhara M, Takada A. 1991. Acetaldehyde metabolism in different aldehyde dehydrogenase-2 genotypes. *Alcohol. Clin. Exp. Res.* 15:141–44

Eriksson JG, Sandboge S, Salonen M, Kajantie E, Osmond C. 2015. Maternal weight in pregnancy and offspring body composition in late adulthood: findings from the Helsinki Birth Cohort Study (HBCS). *Ann. Med.* 47:94–99

Eryigit Madzwamuse S, Baumann N, Jaekel J, Bartmann P, Wolke D. 2015. Neuro-cognitive performance of very preterm or very low birth weight adults at 26 years. *J. Child Psychol. Psychiatry* 56:857–64

Fall CH, Osmond C, Barker DJ, Clark PM, Hales CN, et al. 1995. Fetal and infant growth and cardiovascular risk factors in women. *BMJ* 310:428–32

Fewell Z, Davey Smith G, Sterne JA. 2007. The impact of residual and unmeasured confounding in epidemiologic studies: a simulation study. *Am. J. Epidemiol.* 166:646–55

Freathy RM, Ring SM, Shields B, Galobardes B, Knight B, et al. 2009. A common genetic variant in the 15q24 nicotinic acetylcholine receptor gene cluster (*CHRNA5-CHRNA3-CHRNB4*) is associated with a reduced ability of women to quit smoking in pregnancy. *Hum. Mol. Genet.* 18:2922–27

Gage SH, Munafò MR, MacLeod J, Hickman M, Davey Smith G. 2015. Cannabis and psychosis. *Lancet Psychiatry* 2:380

Gaysina D, Fergusson DM, Leve LD, Horwood J, Reiss D, et al. 2013. Maternal smoking during pregnancy and offspring conduct problems: evidence from 3 independent genetically sensitive research designs. *JAMA Psychiatry* 70:956–63

Hales CN, Barker DJ. 1992. Type 2 (non-insulin-dependent) diabetes mellitus: the thrifty phenotype hypothesis. *Diabetologia* 35:595–601

Hoek HW, Brown AS, Susser E. 1998. The Dutch famine and schizophrenia spectrum disorders. *Soc. Psychiatry Psychiatr. Epidemiol.* 33:373–79

Kelly YJ, Sacker A, Gray R, Kelly J, Wolke D, et al. 2012. Light drinking during pregnancy: still no increased risk for socioemotional difficulties or cognitive deficits at 5 years of age? *J. Epidemiol. Community Health* 66:41–48

Keskitalo K, Broms U, Heliovaara M, Ripatti S, Surakka I, et al. 2009. Association of serum cotinine level with a cluster of three nicotinic acetylcholine receptor genes (*CHRNA3/CHRNA5/CHRNB4*) on chromosome 15. *Hum. Mol. Genet.* 18:4007–12

King L, Carpentier C, Griffiths P. 2004. *EMCDDA Insights: An Overview of Cannabis Potency in Europe.* Luxembourg: Eur. Monit. Cent. Drugs Drug Addict.

Kramer MS, Matush L, Vanilovich I, Platt RW, Bogdanovich N, et al. 2007. Effects of prolonged and exclusive breastfeeding on child height, weight, adiposity, and blood pressure at age 6.5 y: evidence from a large randomized trial. *Am. J. Clin. Nutr.* 86:1717–21

Kuh D, Davey Smith G. 2004. The life course and adult chronic disease: an historical perspective with particular reference to coronary heart disease. In *A Life Course Approach to Chronic Disease Epidemiology*, ed. D Kuh, Y Ben-Shlomo, pp. 15–37. Oxford, UK: Oxford Univ. Press. 2nd ed.

Lawlor DA, Davey Smith G, Ebrahim S. 2004. Socioeconomic position and hormone replacement therapy use: explaining the discrepancy in evidence from observational and randomized controlled trials. *Am. J. Public Health* 94:2149–54

Lawlor DA, Timpson NJ, Harbord RM, Leary S, Ness A, et al. 2008. Exploring the developmental overnutrition hypothesis using parental-offspring associations and FTO as an instrumental variable. *PLOS Med.* 5:e33

Liang W, Chikritzhs T. 2013. Observational research on alcohol use and chronic disease outcome: new approaches to counter biases. *Sci. World J.* 2013:860915

Lipsitch M, Tchetgen Tchetgen E, Cohen T. 2010. Negative controls: a tool for detecting confounding and bias in observational studies. *Epidemiology* 21:383–88

Lipton P. 2004. *Inference to the Best Explanation.* London/New York: Routledge. 2nd ed.

Lorenz K. 1935. Der Kumpan in der Umwelt des Vogels. *J. Ornithol.* 83:137–213

Martin RM, Goodall SH, Gunnell D, Davey Smith G. 2007. Breast feeding in infancy and social mobility: 60-year follow-up of the Boyd Orr cohort. *Arch. Dis. Child* 92:317–21

Mehmedic Z, Chandra S, Slade D, Denham H, Foster S, et al. 2010. Potency trends of Δ9-THC and other cannabinoids in confiscated cannabis preparations from 1993 to 2008. *J. Forensic Sci.* 55:1209–17

Munafò MR, Timofeeva MN, Morris RW, Prieto-Merino D, Sattar N, et al. 2012. Association between genetic variants on chromosome 15q25 locus and objective measures of tobacco exposure. *J. Natl. Cancer Inst.* 104:740–48

Nilsson JP. 2014. *Alcohol availability, prenatal conditions, and long-term economic outcomes.* Work. Pap., Inst. Int. Econ. Stud., Stockholm Univ.

Oosterbeek H. 1997. Returns from computer use: a simple test on the productivity interpretation. *Econ. Lett.* 55:273–77

Patel R, Oken E, Bogdanovich N, Matush L, Sevkovskaya Z, et al. 2014. Cohort profile: the Promotion of Breastfeeding Intervention Trial (PROBIT). *Int. J. Epidemiol.* 43:679–90

Petitti DB, Perlman JA, Sidney S. 1986. Postmenopausal estrogen use and heart disease. *N. Engl. J. Med.* 315:131–32

Petitti DB, Perlman JA, Sidney S. 1987. Noncontraceptive estrogens and mortality: long-term follow-up of women in the Walnut Creek Study. *Obstet. Gynecol.* 70:289–93

Phillips AN, Davey Smith G. 1992. Bias in relative odds estimation owing to imprecise measurement of correlated exposures. *Stat. Med.* 11:953–61

Pitkin RM. 2007. Folate and neural tube defects. *Am. J. Clin. Nutr.* 85:285–88S

Rice F, Harold GT, Boivin J, Hay DF, van den Bree M, Thapar A. 2009. Disentangling prenatal and inherited influences in humans with an experimental design. *PNAS* 106:2464–67

Richmond RC, Al-Amin A, Davey Smith G, Relton CL. 2014. Approaches for drawing causal inferences from epidemiological birth cohorts: a review. *Early Hum. Dev.* 90:769–80

Roth C, Magnus P, Schjolberg S, Stoltenberg C, Suren P, et al. 2011. Folic acid supplements in pregnancy and severe language delay in children. *JAMA* 306:1566–73

Rothman K, Greenland S, Lash TL. 2008. *Modern Epidemiology.* Philadelphia, PA: Lippincott Williams & Wilkins

Rubino T, Parolaro D. 2008. Long lasting consequences of cannabis exposure in adolescence. *Mol. Cell. Endocrinol.* 286:S108–13

Song S, Wang W, Hu P. 2009. Famine, death, and madness: schizophrenia in early adulthood after prenatal exposure to the Chinese Great Leap Forward Famine. *Soc. Sci. Med.* 68:1315–21

Suren P, Roth C, Bresnahan M, Haugen M, Hornig M, et al. 2013. Association between maternal use of folic acid supplements and risk of autism spectrum disorders in children. *JAMA* 309:570–77

Taylor AE, Davey Smith G, Bares CB, Edwards AC, Munafò MR. 2014. Partner smoking and maternal cotinine during pregnancy: implications for negative control methods. *Drug Alcohol Depend.* 139:159–63

Thapar A, Rice F, Hay D, Boivin J, Langley K, et al. 2009. Prenatal smoking might not cause attention-deficit/hyperactivity disorder: evidence from a novel design. *Biol. Psychiatry* 66:722–27

Thorgeirsson TE, Geller F, Sulem P, Rafnar T, Wiste A, et al. 2008. A variant associated with nicotine dependence, lung cancer and peripheral arterial disease. *Nature* 452:638–42

Trezza V, Cuomo V, Vanderschuren LJ. 2008. Cannabis and the developing brain: insights from behavior. *Eur. J. Pharmacol.* 585:441–52

Tyrrell J, Huikari V, Christie JT, Cavadino A, Bakker R, et al. 2012. Genetic variation in the 15q25 nicotinic acetylcholine receptor gene cluster (*CHRNA5-CHRNA3-CHRNB4*) interacts with maternal self-reported smoking status during pregnancy to influence birth weight. *Hum. Mol. Genet.* 21:5344–58

Van Lieshout RJ, Boylan K. 2010. Increased depressive symptoms in female but not male adolescents born at low birth weight in the offspring of a national cohort. *Can. J. Psychiatry* 55:422–30

Victora CG, Horta BL, Loret de Mola C, Quevedo L, Pinheiro RT, et al. 2015. Association between breast-feeding and intelligence, educational attainment, and income at 30 years of age: a prospective birth cohort study from Brazil. *Lancet Glob. Health* 3:e199–205

Ware JJ, van den Bree MB, Munafò MR. 2011. Association of the *CHRNA5-A3-B4* gene cluster with heaviness of smoking: a meta-analysis. *Nicotine Tob. Res.* 13:1167–75

Ware JJ, van den Bree MB, Munafò MR. 2012. From men to mice: *CHRNA5/CHRNA3*, smoking behavior and disease. *Nicotine Tobacco Res.* 14:1291–99

Watson JB, Rayner R. 1920. Conditioned emotional reactions. *J. Exp. Psychol.* 3:1–14

Zammit S, Allebeck P, Andreasson S, Lundberg I, Lewis G. 2002. Self reported cannabis use as a risk factor for schizophrenia in Swedish conscripts of 1969: historical cohort study. *BMJ* 325:1199

Zuccolo L, Lewis SJ, Davey Smith G, Sayal K, Draper ES, et al. 2013. Prenatal alcohol exposure and offspring cognition and school performance. A "Mendelian randomization" natural experiment. *Int. J. Epidemiol.* 42:1358–70

From Brain Maps to Cognitive Ontologies: Informatics and the Search for Mental Structure

Russell A. Poldrack[1] and Tal Yarkoni[2]

[1]Department of Psychology, Stanford University, Stanford, California 94305;
email: poldrack@stanford.edu

[2]Department of Psychology, University of Texas at Austin, Austin, Texas 78712;
email: tyarkoni@utexas.edu

Annu. Rev. Psychol. 2016. 67:587–612

First published online as a Review in Advance on
September 21, 2015

The *Annual Review of Psychology* is online at
psych.annualreviews.org

This article's doi:
10.1146/annurev-psych-122414-033729

Keywords

neuroimaging, neuroinformatics, ontologies, meta-analysis, classification,
cognition

Abstract

A major goal of cognitive neuroscience is to delineate how brain systems
give rise to mental function. Here we review the increasingly large role
informatics-driven approaches are playing in such efforts. We begin by reviewing a number of challenges conventional neuroimaging approaches face
in trying to delineate brain-cognition mappings—for example, the difficulty
in establishing the specificity of postulated associations. Next, we demonstrate how these limitations can potentially be overcome using complementary approaches that emphasize large-scale analysis—including meta-
analytic methods that synthesize hundreds or thousands of studies at a
time; latent-variable approaches that seek to extract structure from data in
a bottom-up manner; and predictive modeling approaches capable of quantitatively inferring mental states from patterns of brain activity. We highlight the underappreciated but critical role for formal cognitive ontologies
in helping to clarify, refine, and test theories of brain and cognitive function.
Finally, we conclude with a speculative discussion of what future informatics
developments may hold for cognitive neuroscience.

Contents

INTRODUCTION

One of the central goals of cognitive neuroscience is to understand how brain systems give rise to cognitive functions, which raises a critical question: What are the cognitive processes that we aim to understand? To grasp the importance of this question, consider an analogy from the field of molecular biology. A central question for this field is how genes are translated into proteins, and answering this question requires a systematic description of the genes and the proteins that are being related. Fortunately for molecular biologists, a number of databases describe all of the proteins and genes that have been discovered across a wide range of species. These databases ground the concepts that researchers in the domain are studying in a set of objective definitions, allowing different researchers to be sure that they are talking about the same thing. For example, researchers may describe the object of their study as "DARPP-32," but by providing an accession number in the UniProt database, one could easily ensure that the protein under investigation is the same as one named "protein phosphatase 1 regulatory subunit 1B" in another paper.

By comparison, cognitive neuroscience is awash in a sea of conflicting terms and concepts. William Uttal (2001) summed up this problem clearly in his well-known critique of neuroimaging, *The New Phrenology*:

> Unlike lepidopterists, who have the relatively simple task of gathering and classifying butterflies, psychologists have few such convenient physical anchors. Organizing the myriad proposed psychological components—"butterflies"—of our minds has been and is one of the great unfulfilled challenges of our science. Indeed, it is not only unfulfilled; it has not, in my opinion, been adequately engaged. Rather, hypothetical psychological constructs are invented ad lib and ad hoc without adequate consideration of the fundamental issue of the very plausibility of precise definition. (p. 90)

In this article, we outline how the field of cognitive neuroscience has begun to address this challenge through the use of tools adapted from the field of biomedical informatics. First we address two fundamental challenges that face the enterprise of cognitive neuroscience. One challenge centers on the difficulty in isolating specific mental functions using psychological tasks. Even if this challenge is solved, a second, deeper problem arises in the establishment of selective mappings between brain systems and mental functions. We argue that the standard approach to neuroimaging is fundamentally unable to deliver such selective mappings.

Second, we discuss how large-scale databases enable more powerful analyses to address these challenges. In addition to reviewing conventional benefits of conducting analyses at scale—for example, aggregating over hundreds or thousands of studies at a time allows estimation of associations with a precision that individual studies typically cannot—we focus on novel inferences that are only possible using such large-scale data. We demonstrate how large-scale databases can help quantify the true specificity of hypothesized structure-function associations by zooming out from a single brain circuit or experimental contrast to survey an entire complex landscape of many-to-many mappings between psychological and neural processes. We review data-driven approaches that leverage the scale and breadth of such databases to identify latent components of brain activity and cognitive function, and we illustrate how predictive modeling techniques can combine with large-scale databases to support novel quantitative approaches to the decoding of mental states from brain activity.

Finally, we discuss how formal ontologies hold an important key to better describing the structure of the mind and its relation to the brain. We describe the Cognitive Atlas project, which aims to develop a formal ontology for cognitive neuroscience. We conclude by highlighting some of the future directions that we foresee for the field of cognitive neuroinformatics.

Decoding: the use of neuroimaging data to classify mental activity

Ontology: a formal description of the concepts assumed to exist within a particular domain, and their relationships

INFERENTIAL CHALLENGES FOR NEUROIMAGING

The development and widespread application of modern functional neuroimaging methods such as functional magnetic resonance imaging (fMRI) have long offered the tantalizing promise that researchers might one day understand how large-scale patterns of brain activity map onto specific mental states or processes. This promise has already been partly realized by the discovery of numerous brain-cognition associations over the past two decades [e.g., the existence of brain regions that preferentially process certain classes of perceptual stimuli, or the increase in activation of a "default mode network" (Raichle et al. 2001) when people are engaged in undirected mental activity]. However, it has also become increasingly clear that numerous inferential challenges threaten the broad goal of attaining a comprehensive understanding of the joint structure of the mind and brain using functional neuroimaging techniques. Many of these inferential threats are statistical or methodological in nature (e.g., low statistical power, preprocessing and registration problems) and are outside the scope of this review. However, a number of threats stem from very basic conceptual challenges that we believe remain widely underappreciated within the neuroimaging community. Here we discuss two such challenges: first, the difficulty of isolating cognitive functions, and second, the difficulty in establishing specific mappings between brain and behavior.

Isolating Cognitive Functions

In principle, identifying the neural substrates of specific cognitive functions using functional neuroimaging would appear to be conceptually straightforward. According to the classical subtraction logic that underlies much of neuroimaging research (Poldrack 2010), it should be possible to identify the neural correlates of specific processes by contrasting experimental conditions that are carefully selected to vary with respect to only a key process of interest. This is sometimes referred to as the assumption of pure insertion in reference to the idea (originally attributed to Donders;

cf. Sternberg 1969) that one can theoretically add a discrete processing step to an existing task without meaningfully altering the remaining set of processes. For example, by contrasting a condition in which participants passively view visual stimuli with a condition in which participants press a button whenever a new stimulus appears (while holding presentation duration constant across both conditions), one might perhaps be able to cleanly isolate the neural processes associated with planning and executing a motor response.

In practice, of course, things are more complicated. In particular, the logic of cognitive subtraction is notoriously fragile in the face of real-world psychological tasks (e.g., Egeth et al. 1972, Friston et al. 1996, Jennings et al. 1997). For one thing, the assumption of pure insertion is demonstrably false in many, and perhaps most, cases. Even a simple manipulation of motor responding is unlikely to cleanly isolate motor processes as intended because the requirement to make a motor response is all but guaranteed to change the way participants deploy attention to the visual stimuli (e.g., it may induce top-down biasing of early visual activity in a proactive effort to identify stimulus changes as soon as they occur—something that would be unlikely during passive viewing). Consistent with this, both behavioral (Egeth et al. 1972) and neuroimaging (Jennings et al. 1997) studies have shown interactions between task performance (response times and activation, respectively) and response sets. The same fragility is likely to be true for most other experimental approaches as well. For example, parametric designs (in which a single task parameter is varied, such as memory load) rely on a similar pure modulation assumption (Poldrack 2010); that is, that the only change occurring is that of the specific parameter being modulated. Parametric increases in working memory load influence not only working memory–related circuits but also motivational and attentional circuits (e.g., as the number of encoded items in a Sternberg task increases, some participants may begin to experience negative emotion due to their inability to perform the task), violating the pure modulation assumption.

Although these problems with the isolation of specific processes using subtractive designs are widely known, it remains common in the neuroimaging literature to conflate experimental manipulations with the specific cognitive functions that are putatively manipulated. The cautions of Chronbach & Meehl (1955) against conflating latent constructs with operational measures appear to have been largely forgotten. For example, a search of PubMed reveals more than 1,800 papers whose title or abstract includes the phrase "working memory task." It may not register to most of those authors that in using this term (rather than a more descriptive term such as "Sternberg item recognition task" or "delayed response task"), they are making a theoretical claim that the task in question provides a way to isolate a specific mental process called working memory. This becomes particularly problematic when the mappings between constructs and tasks come into question. For example, 99 abstracts in PubMed include the phrase "N-back working memory task," even though the construct validity of the N-back task as a measure of working memory has come into serious question (Kane et al. 2007). As we discuss further below, this is a perfect recipe for conceptual confusion.

Establishing Specificity

Even if we suppose, for the sake of argument, that it were possible to employ manipulations in neuroimaging experiments that completely uphold the subtractive assumptions, we would still face the equally daunting problem of establishing the specificity of brain-behavior associations. Suppose we found a 100% pure task of working memory that reliably activated lateral prefrontal brain regions when scanned with fMRI. Would we be entitled to conclude that we have established the cognitive function of lateral prefrontal cortex (LPFC)? No. What such a finding would establish is only that working memory engagement is a sufficient condition for activation of LPFC. It would not support the opposite inference—namely, that if LPFC is active, working memory processes must be engaged. The latter inference is invalid because there could in principle be many other psychological processes that also activate LPFC but have little to do with working memory. This difficulty in probabilistically inferring mental function from observed brain activity has been dubbed the problem of reverse inference in the cognitive neuroscience literature (Poldrack 2006, 2011). Formally, the reverse inference problem involves inferring the likelihood of engagement of a particular mental process MP from a particular activation A (which could be a single region or pattern across regions). This can be obtained using Bayes' rule (Poldrack 2006),

$$P(MP|A) = \frac{P(A|MP) * P(MP)}{P(A)},$$

given some prior $P(MP)$ on the likelihood of the mental process being engaged and a base rate $P(A)$ for the activation in question. The utility of framing the reverse inference problem in terms of Bayesian inference is that it makes clear that the added value of any activation in identifying the underlying mental process (i.e., the difference between the prior and the posterior probability) is a function of the likelihood of activation in the specific condition relative to the base rate of activation in that region. Regions that are more active across all psychological functions will provide less support for any specific reverse inference.

Alternatively, one can describe these inferential challenges in terms of necessary and sufficient conditions. The reason that randomized, controlled experimentation is widely hailed as the gold standard in science is that it can support strong conclusions about causal sufficiency. For example, suppose we experimentally manipulate the nature of the stimuli during a working memory task—presenting, say, faces in one condition and words in another—and observe that the face condition is associated with widespread changes in inferotemporal and frontal brain activity, and also with longer behavioral reaction times. We would be able to definitively conclude that the experimental manipulation we introduced is causally sufficient to produce both the neural and the behavioral changes we observed. However, we cannot conclude the opposite—that engagement of those specific cognitive processes is necessary to produce that specific activation or behavioral response.

To see this, consider an example from psychology. Suppose subjects perform a working memory task with two conditions that vary in putative working memory load, and they tend to respond more slowly in the high-load condition. It might be natural in such a case to say that increased working memory processing is the cause of subjects' slowed responses. But now suppose that the same subjects also perform a visual discrimination task involving two conditions that differ only in the physical size of the on-screen stimuli. Further, suppose that the subjects tend to respond more slowly in the small-stimulus condition. Surely, in this case, few psychologists would want to conclude that slowed responses to smaller visual stimuli must at least partly reflect increased working memory load! What this example illustrates is that claims that seem perfectly reasonable in one context—for example, that increased reaction time in a working memory task reflects increased working memory load—often depend critically on tacit background assumptions that are not part of the formal inference. If the context changes, one may then have to invoke a completely different set of putative causes for the same observable outcome. Unless the background conditions thought to differentiate between different contexts can be explicitly modeled, it is not clear how one might quantitatively infer which particular set of causes was responsible for a given outcome.

Relatedly, we also cannot easily draw causal conclusions about the relationship between brain activity changes and behavioral changes. When one observes correlated neural and behavioral changes that make intuitive sense, it can be tempting to interpret the former as the cause of the latter. However, the fact that all behavioral changes must derive from some neural changes does not mean that they must derive from the particular neural changes one happens to observe in any given study. For example, the fact that increases in frontal activity are consistently associated with longer reaction times does not entail that the former cause the latter. It is conceivable that frontal increases are the result rather than the cause of variations in reaction time, simply reflecting the fact that participants are processing information for a longer period of time on trials when they take longer to respond (cf. Yarkoni et al. 2009). Indeed, one underappreciated implication of the fact that the blood-oxygen-level-dependent (BOLD) signal sums approximately linearly over time (Dale & Buckner 1997) is that any increase in the duration of local processing in a region—no matter what its cause may be—is likely to produce a corresponding increase in observed brain activity. Such examples underscore a major challenge to efforts to map the structure of human cognition using neuroimaging because many of the brain-behavior mappings researchers have drawn in the literature are based largely on observation of concomitant neural and behavioral changes.

Annotation:
the description of relationships between a dataset and other concepts or datasets

THE BENEFITS OF LARGE-SCALE INFORMATICS APPROACHES

Importantly, the inferential challenges discussed in the previous section are not intrinsic to cognitive neuroscience or functional neuroimaging but simply reflect pragmatic constraints on what one can expect to achieve in any single study. The problem of reverse inference, for instance, arises not because it is fundamentally impossible to infer mental states from brain states, but rather because it is very difficult to contrast a sufficient number of experimental conditions to justify strong claims about the specificity of any individual mapping. It may be feasible to make much more circumscribed claims that are conditioned on specific background conditions (cf. Hutzler 2014, Klein 2012, Machery 2014)—for example, that conditional on doing a reading task, some pattern of activity implies orthographic decoding. Similarly, the uncertainty surrounding which cognitive process deserves credit for the effect of a particular experimental task on brain activity is attributable to the impracticality of using dozens of different tasks in every study in order to isolate a specific process by converging operations (Garner et al. 1956). Fortunately, both of these limitations can be ameliorated by scaling up one's investigation to simultaneously consider the results of many different studies. In this section, we discuss a number of ways that existing and emerging informatics platforms can help map the structure of human cognition in novel ways and on an unprecedented scale.

Large-Scale Meta-Analytic Structure-to-Function Mapping

One of the first informatics-driven advances in researchers' ability to map brain-cognition relationships was the development of new statistical methods and software packages for fMRI meta-analysis and the creation of associated coordinate databases such as BrainMap (Laird et al. 2005), Brede (Nielsen et al. 2004), and SumsDB (Dickson et al. 2001). The BrainMap database, for example, currently contains over 100,000 activation coordinates from over 2,600 fMRI studies that span diverse cognitive domains. All experimental contrasts are annotated with key metadata (e.g., sample size, clinical populations) and coded along key dimensions (e.g., stimulus modality, task type). Drawing on such databases and tools, researchers have conducted hundreds of fMRI meta-analyses on topics ranging from single-word reading (Turkeltaub et al. 2002) to rectal distension in irritable bowel syndrome (Tillisch et al. 2011). By aggregating across dozens, and in some cases hundreds, of fMRI studies, such meta-analyses have been able to overcome the sensitivity limitations associated with many primary fMRI studies (Wager et al. 2007) and provide highly robust estimates of the neural correlates of relatively specific cognitive tasks.

Despite their enormous impact on the field, however, conventional meta-analytic approaches also have important limitations. One is their lack of scalability: Because manual annotation and verification of published articles is a time-consuming process, existing coordinate databases such as BrainMap are no longer able to keep up with the growth of the primary literature (cf. Derrfuss & Mar 2009). Thus, as time goes on, it becomes increasingly difficult for investigators to conduct comprehensive meta-analysis of the literature, even in relatively circumscribed domains. A second problem is that conventional meta-analysis approaches, which focus on identifying the brain regions consistently activated by particular cognitive tasks or processes, do not help address the long-standing problem of reverse inference. Consider, for example, the challenge of determining what cognitive function(s) the human anterior insula supports. Individual fMRI studies have implicated this region in the processing of pain (Wager et al. 2004), interoceptive awareness (Critchley et al. 2004), error monitoring (Klein et al. 2007), sustained attention (Dosenbach et al. 2006), phonological processing (Wise et al. 1999), salience (Wiech et al. 2010), and numerous other processes—and this variety is recapitulated in an equally broad range of meta-analyses that also report anterior insula activation, such as studies of empathy (Fan et al. 2011), subsequent memory (Kim 2011), and working memory (Owen et al. 2005), among others. Although such findings convincingly demonstrate that many different kinds of tasks reliably activate the anterior insula, they provide relatively little insight into what the specific function of the anterior insula (or any other region) might be.

In work that addresses both the scalability and inferential limitations of conventional meta-analysis, Yarkoni et al. (2011) recently introduced a novel framework called Neurosynth that supports large-scale synthesis of fMRI data using a fundamentally different approach. Instead of relying on careful manual annotation of studies, this approach emphasizes automation and scale—effectively trading quality for quantity. Neurosynth uses relatively simple text mining and computational linguistics methods to automatically extract both reported activations and semantic annotations from published articles (see **Figure 1**). Although the data extracted from any individual study are highly susceptible to error and lack corresponding metadata (e.g., one cannot even reliably determine whether a particular activation represents an increase or decrease in blood flow), the high degree of automation enables Neurosynth to grow in stride with the primary literature at virtually no cost. Consequently, the Neurosynth database has now eclipsed BrainMap in size, with over 10,000 studies and 360,000 discrete activations represented. In keeping with a philosophy of data sharing, reproducibility, and open science, the entire database is made freely available to the community without any use restrictions or requirements of coauthorship.

The relatively comprehensive coverage of the Neurosynth database opens the door to novel kinds of inference—particularly those focused on quantifying the specificity of brain-cognition associations. In an emblematic recent study, Chang and colleagues (2013) used Neurosynth to quantitatively decode the psychological processes associated with different sectors of the human insula, including the aforementioned anterior sector. The availability of a relatively comprehensive cross-section of the fMRI literature enabled the authors to quantify not only which kinds of tasks tend to consistently produce anterior insula activity (nearly all of them), but also which processes were most likely to activate the region—thereby providing a measure of specificity that individual fMRI studies or meta-analysis studies focused on experimental comparisons could not (**Figure 2**). These investigators demonstrated that the anterior insula is maximally associated with higher cognitive processes such as task-switching and response inhibition, which suggests that its frequent presence in other kinds of tasks may reflect a fundamental role in basic goal-directed cognitive processes necessary for all kinds of complex cognition (for further discussion, see Chang et al. 2013).

The entire Neurosynth codebase has been released under a permissive software license and an interactive web portal (**http://www.neurosynth.org**) has been developed to facilitate community adoption of such methods. The Neurosynth website makes it possible, for example, to obtain

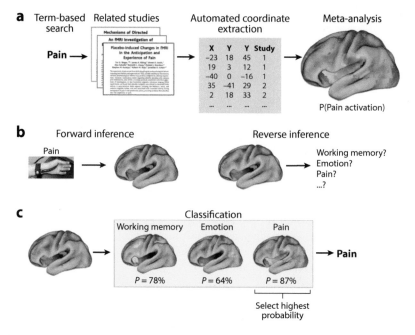

Figure 1

An overview of the Neurosynth project. (*a*) Neurosynth involves the automated extraction of activation coordinates from published papers; these coordinates can be used to perform a meta-analysis to identify regions associated with the presence of specific terms in publications. (*b*) Forward inference involves estimation of the likelihood of activation given the presence of a term, whereas reverse inference involves estimation of the likelihood of presence of a term given activation in each voxel. (*c*) Neurosynth can be used to predict which of a set of terms is most likely to be present in a paper, given a particular activation pattern. Figure adapted with permission from Yarkoni et al. (2011).

whole-brain reverse inference maps for concepts such as reward, episodic memory, or response inhibition, or to generate a rank-ordered list of the psychological concepts most strongly associated with activation at any location in the brain (**http://www.neurosynth.org/locations**). Most recently, a real-time web interface was introduced to support the kind of open-ended decoding functionality employed by Chang et al. (2013); this interface enables other researchers to perform near-instantaneous quantitative reverse inference on uploaded whole-brain statistical maps. Although the results of such analyses have a number of important limitations (discussed below), they nevertheless represent a significant advance over the largely qualitative interpretations that have historically dominated discussion sections in fMRI articles (cf. Poldrack 2006). Notably, the analyses support inferences that are based on interpretation of whole-brain patterns of activity rather than isolated brain regions, and by virtue of relying on an automated analysis of the literature as a whole, they are less susceptible to various cognitive biases known to affect research results (e.g., the tendency to preferentially focus on studies that converge with one's preferred theoretical position).

Functional Parcellation and the Search for Latent Structure

An analysis of the latent structure of the neuroimaging data provides a second, and very different, way of approaching the search for mental structure and determining whether and how the brain

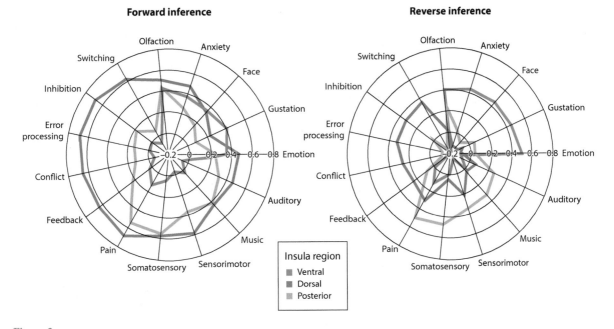

Figure 2

Results of large-scale forward-inference and reverse-inference analyses of insula function in the Neurosynth database. Whereas the dorsal anterior insula (blue) is consistently activated by a broad range of tasks in the forward-inference analysis, the reverse-inference analysis reveals it to be preferentially associated with higher cognitive functions. Figure adapted with permission from Chang et al. (2013).

carves the joints of mental function. There is a long history of using statistical methods to try to parcellate the brain into functional units based on correlated activity or connectivity patterns. Early reports that widely distributed networks of brain regions often modulate in concert (e.g., Biswal et al. 1995) quickly led to a diversity of large-scale efforts aimed at extracting a comprehensive set of networks, parcels, or components that capture the dynamics of brain activity—for example, by using clustering techniques to identify locally homogeneous sets of voxels (Craddock et al. 2012, Gordon et al. 2014), or by using matrix factorization methods such as independent components analysis (Beckmann & Smith 2004) to find low-rank approximations to high-dimensional connectivity data (for a review, see Varoquaux & Craddock 2013). Although such efforts were initially focused solely on the neurobiological level of analysis, researchers soon recognized their potential utility as bridges between brain-based network analysis and cognitive function. In an influential example, Smith et al. (2009) mapped a set of components extracted from activation coordinates in the BrainMap database onto the domains of tasks used in the associated studies, uncovering a set of plausible mappings between neural networks and psychological functions. **Figure 3** presents a similar analysis performed on the Neurosynth database.

It is also possible to work in the opposite direction, starting with a decomposition of the psychological space and assessing its relationship to brain activity. Poldrack et al. (2012) first performed topic modeling on the text from the Neurosynth database using a technique known as latent Dirichlet allocation (Blei et al. 2003). This method defines a probabilistic generative model for text that involves first sampling from a set of topics and then sampling words according to their probability under the selected topic. Given a set of documents, the latent topics are inferred using Bayesian estimation, which provides a set of weights for each term and each document in

Figure 3

Multivariate meta-analysis identifies mappings between neural activation and psychological function. The MELODIC tool was used to perform probabilistic independent components analysis (ICA) on 9,721 images from the Neurosynth database (Beckmann & Smith 2004). The slice maps show voxels that were significantly associated with each of the top six components (red-orange, positive association; blue, negative association). Polar plots show the relative association between each component and selected latent topics from the database (cf. Poldrack et al. 2012) and demonstrate that most ICA components showed relatively selective associations with cognitive topics.

Component 1

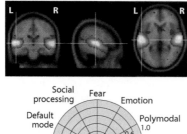

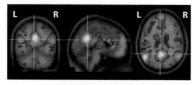

Component 2

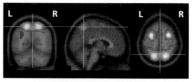

Component 3

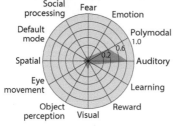

Component 4

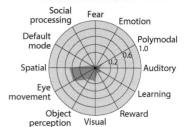

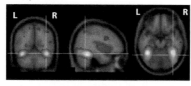

Component 5

Component 6

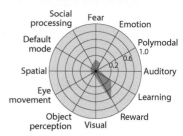

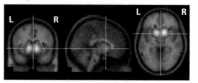

relation to each of the topics. Separate analyses were performed limiting the text to terms related to either psychological functions or brain disorders. These weights were then used to generate maps showing which regions were statistically associated with loading on each topic (referred to as topic maps). The topics identified using this technique generated plausible sets of cognitive terms and related maps (e.g., one topic had as its top terms "narrative," "discourse," "comprehension," "memory," and "discourse processing" and was associated with activation across the left hemisphere language network; another topic's top terms were "auditory," "perception," "hearing," "attention," and "listening" and was associated with activation in bilateral auditory cortices). More recently, Yeo and colleagues (2014) used a more sophisticated hierarchical topic model to extract a set of cognitive components that jointly explain the covariance structure between both cognitive tasks and brain activity, thus attempting to formalize the intuitive idea that the mapping between neural activity in individual brain regions and cognitive tasks may be best described hierarchically (i.e., lower-level units are repeatedly configured into higher-level circuits).

Decoding Mental Structure

A third way to approach the challenge of inferring mental structure from neurobiological data is in terms of prediction: Given a neuroimaging dataset, we wish to make the most accurate prediction possible regarding which mental processes are engaged. The coordinate-based approaches described above have been surprisingly successful at making predictions about broad categories, but they generally lack the detailed process-level annotation or the subject-level neuroimaging data necessary to make much more specific predictions. An alternative approach has been to apply machine learning classification and decoding techniques (Haynes & Rees 2006, Norman et al. 2006) to smaller datasets—for example, to try to determine which of several classes of pictures or words a subject is currently viewing (e.g., Mitchell et al. 2003, Cox & Savoy 2003). The earliest work in this domain focused primarily on decoding of specific stimulus or task features within a single individual, but subsequent work has shown that one can decode large-scale psychological functions from fMRI data in a way that generalizes across individuals (Mourão-Miranda et al. 2005, Shinkareva et al. 2008, Wager et al. 2013). However, the high decoding accuracies frequently reported in such studies also belie their highly constrained nature: It is much easier to correctly classify subjects' mental states when there are only a handful of possible candidates (e.g., discriminating faces versus houses as opposed to discriminating all possible classes of objects) (cf. Hutzler et al. 2014, Klein 2012, Machery 2014). Thus, the major open challenge is to combine the respective strengths of these two decoding approaches, with the goal of eventually generating highly accurate, yet relatively unconstrained, predictions about people's mental states.

Although unconstrained decoding of mental states currently lies more in the realm of fiction than of science, promising incipient efforts have been made. One recent line of work focuses on reconstructing subjects' experience of a broad range of stimuli under relatively naturalistic conditions—often including identification of previously unseen stimuli. For example, Kay and colleagues (2008) used novel encoding models to accurately identify which of 120 natural images subjects were viewing. More recent studies have used similar approaches to reconstruct movie clips from visual cortex activation (Nishimoto et al. 2011) or apply semantic labels to thousands of objects and actions (Huth et al. 2012). Related work has used large-scale models of semantic structure to decode the identity of words and pictures from brain images (Mitchell et al. 2008). Although such studies remain constrained to one particular modality, their use of generative encoding models that can identify entirely new objects represents an important advance over older approaches that discriminate between a small, fixed set of alternatives.

In a different line of work using subject-level data from eight different tasks, Poldrack and colleagues (2009) examined whether it was possible to decode which task an individual was engaged in from their brain activity pattern, using a neural network classifier trained on other individuals. These investigators found that it was possible to decode these tasks with greater than 80% accuracy and that the underlying structure of the trained neural network provided insights into the clusters of tasks that engaged similar neural patterns. Subsequent work using the OpenfMRI database has shown that it is possible to decode a much larger number of tasks; for example, Poldrack et al. (2013) found that it was possible to obtain greater than 50% accuracy at classifying between 26 different task contrasts from this database. Interestingly, this classification accuracy could be obtained even when the dimensionality was greatly reduced using independent components analysis (reaching asymptote around 100 dimensions), which suggests that it primarily reflects the balance between large-scale neural systems rather than fine-grained patterns of activity. Further analysis of the confusion matrix showed that in many cases, similar tasks from different studies were systematically confused by the classifier, which suggests that it was tapping into general cognitive features of those tasks rather than specifics of the particular design.

A more demanding question is whether it is possible to predict the psychological processes underlying the task rather than the task identity. This question has also been addressed in a number of recent studies. Koyejo & Poldrack (2013) used data from the OpenfMRI database that had been annotated manually to specify the putative psychological processes engaged by each of the 26 task contrasts, with the goal of predicting psychological processes rather than task labels. Because many of the contrasts were thought to isolate multiple psychological functions, the authors used multilabel classifiers that have the ability to predict the presence of multiple processes for any particular dataset. They found that it was possible to predict many of the psychological processes with relatively high accuracy, particularly for those processes that occurred relatively often within the database (and thus had more data available for training). In similar work, Schwartz and colleagues (2013) used the OpenfMRI database to decode task features (such as the stimulus modality and nature of the response) and showed similarly strong classification for these features. These studies provide the proof of concept that it should be possible to accurately decode the psychological building blocks of a task from their associated activation patterns.

Limitations of Large-Scale, Brain-Based Approaches

The results described above highlight the utility of large-scale, brain-based approaches in discovering interesting relations between psychological functions and brain systems. However, such approaches also have important limitations. Some of these limitations are primarily technical in nature and reflect current methodological weaknesses that are likely to be overcome in the future via introduction of other novel approaches and informatics platforms. For example, one general problem for virtually all extant meta-analytic databases is the lack of psychologically detailed annotations. This weakness is most prominent in the case of Neurosynth, where data are automatically extracted using relatively simple heuristics that cannot readily identify key metadata fields (e.g., sample size, direction of experimental contrast); however, even when neuroimaging studies are manually curated, as in the BrainMap database, annotations are largely focused on task-level descriptions rather than underlying psychological processes (e.g., knowing that an N-back paradigm with face stimuli was used in an experiment does not directly convey whether psychological processes such as active maintenance of information, familiarity detection, phonological rehearsal, and so on, are involved in carrying out the task). We discuss potential solutions to this problem in the next section.

Another technical limitation is that virtually all existing meta-analytic approaches rely on the analysis of discrete coordinates reported in published articles rather than continuous whole-brain statistical maps. Coordinate-based meta-analysis is demonstrably inferior to image-based meta-analysis because it unnecessarily discards the vast majority of usable information in the original maps, thereby reducing sensitivity and typically precluding the estimation of continuous effect sizes (Salimi-Khorshidi et al. 2009). In the hopes of facilitating a shift to image-based approaches, investigators are currently working to address this limitation by creating a centralized online repository of whole-brain statistical maps. NeuroVault (**http://www.neurovault.org**) is a new platform that allows researchers to quickly upload and annotate their images, which facilitates rapid dissemination and interactive visualization of statistical maps and eventually will support more powerful meta-analytic syntheses (Gorgolewski et al. 2014).

Finally, limitations are inherent in fMRI as an imaging methodology. In particular, the temporal resolution of fMRI limits the ability to identify dynamic changes in the millisecond time scale, whereas this is exactly the time scale over which most psychological processes occur. Thus, fMRI maps should be viewed as a composite of all activity occurring during a particular episode of mental activity. To the degree that different psychological functions are distinguished by different dynamic combinations of a common set of processing functions on this short time scale, then it may not be possible to disentangle these using fMRI.

In contrast to these purely technical challenges, other limitations of the approaches discussed above are inherent to any effort to approach mind-brain mapping from a purely neurobiological perspective—that is, by seeking first to identify the "right" functional units at the level of the brain and then to map the revealed structures onto psychological processes. Perhaps the most pressing problem is that a model developed to achieve statistical or theoretical parsimony strictly at a single level of description (e.g., to find the optimal parcellation of functional brain networks given some fixed statistical loss criterion) is not guaranteed to map cleanly onto other levels of description (e.g., cognitive processes). In fact, it almost assuredly will not. For instance, it is exceedingly unlikely that there is any single brain region, cluster, or network that corresponds neatly to high-level psychological concepts such as episodic recall, working memory, or phonological rehearsal (in much the same way that one would not expect to find a single gene, protein, or neuron type that isomorphically maps onto such high-level concepts). The central question that then arises is what one ought to do in cases where well-established psychological and biological structures do not seem to map well onto one another. For instance, if there is no obvious biological entity that maps cleanly onto the psychological concept of working memory, should we jettison working memory from our psychological models in favor of other psychological constructs?

The answer to this question is neither straightforward nor unequivocal. On the one hand, all else being equal, we believe that a model of psychological processes that also maps systematically onto known biological structures is strongly preferable over one that does not—often even when there are other grounds to prefer the latter. For example, suppose that a psychological model with one free parameter captures 92% of the variance in some target behavior, whereas a different model with eight free parameters captures 93%. In such a case, it would seem both theoretically and statistically advisable to favor the simpler model over the more complex because the additional seven parameters add little incremental value to the behavioral prediction. Yet if the parameters of the more complex model were to each map very cleanly onto well-delineated biological variables, whereas the single-parameter model correlated very diffusely and nonspecifically with brain activity (as it almost certainly must), we argue that the more complex model is probably more scientifically useful. In this sense, biological discoveries can and should inform the continual revision of psychological theories.

At the same time, we recognize that there may be many cases in which there just isn't any psychologically tractable model available that simultaneously respects theoretical constraints from both psychology and biology. For example, there is no guarantee that there is any viable replacement for the concept of working memory that would both (*a*) map cleanly onto underlying biological structures and (*b*) remain sufficiently compact and psychologically interpretable to be useful in practice. Would it be advantageous to eliminate a high-level term such as working memory from our scientific lexicon if the only way to cover approximately the same territory with a biologically detailed model is to introduce a large disjunctive set of of separate mechanisms? This question largely echoes earlier criticisms of reductionism (Fodor 1974); that is, the mere fact that a "fuzzy" higher-level description can in principle be replaced by a lower-level description does not mean that the lower-level description will necessarily be more useful in practice. Ultimately, the question will rest on whether such a new framework is more scientifically productive than the current framework, which is unanswerable until the new framework is proposed and tested.

Unfortunately, we know of no algorithmic way to distinguish cases in which a psychological concept has outlived its utility from those in which a concept simply lacks any viable biologically inspired replacement but remains useful. In practice, this is a problem that researchers may always have to navigate on a case-by-case basis, and disagreements between researchers will certainly arise in the process. We argue strongly, however, that informatics-driven methodologies can make it much easier to navigate this problem. In the next section, we discuss ongoing efforts to develop formal cognitive ontologies that can help clarify conceptual definitions, distinguish genuine substantive disagreements from pointless terminological disputes, and generate new ways of studying and thinking about causal relationships within and between different levels of description.

TOWARD A COGNITIVE ONTOLOGY

The Need for Formal Representations

We argue above that the question, "What are the parts of the mind?" cannot be successfully addressed strictly through a bottom-up perspective that first asks, "What are the functional units of the brain?" and only then seeks to map the resulting components onto the psychological space (cf. Price & Friston 2005). But we have also suggested that simply inverting this process and adopting a purely top-down approach—that is, taking well-established psychological constructs such as working memory and seeking their underlying neural substrates—is not likely to prove much more fruitful. Aside from the methodological and conceptual problems with such an approach discussed in the previous sections (e.g., the problem of reverse inference), there is an arguably even more fundamental problem, which is that psychologists rarely agree on the meaning of the constructs under investigation. For example, definitions of the term working memory include:

- "The manipulation and use of information [in short-term memory] to guide behavior" (Larocque et al. 2014);
- "Working memory involves the process of active maintenance of a limited amount of information" (Jeneson & Squire 2012);
- "A hypothetical cognitive system responsible for providing access to information required for ongoing cognitive processes" (Wilhelm et al. 2013); and
- "Working memory subsumes the capability to memorize, retrieve and utilize information for a limited period of time" (Rottschy et al. 2012).

This diversity of views may reflect what Walter Mischel (2008) has called the "toothbrush problem" in psychology: "Psychologists treat other peoples' theories like toothbrushes—no self-respecting person wants to use anyone else's." With such divergent definitions of constructs (and equally divergent tasks used to measure them), how can we expect to find consistent mappings between mental constructs and brain systems?

Of course, it is hardly surprising that disagreements should arise over how to delineate and describe an organ as complex as the human mind. And there is nothing intrinsically wrong with having a diversity of opinions. The concern, however, is that psychologists do not seem to have well-established procedures for effectively resolving such differences. For instance, how should we determine whether working memory is best defined in terms of maintenance and manipulation of information in a short-term memory buffer, or in terms of the ability to flexibly recruit other cognitive resources in support of current goals? Should the label working memory apply solely to a central executive mechanism, or should it also encompass slave systems such as the phonological loop and visuospatial sketchpad, as in Baddeley's (1992) influential model? The textbook approach to such disputes is to devise a critical experiment that can offer definitive evidence in favor of one theory over another. But in practice, it is exceedingly difficult to identify real-world cases in which a critical experiment has actually prompted the abandonment of a theory (cf. Greenwald 2012).

We suggest that much of the difficulty in resolving theoretical differences is due to the informal nature of most theoretical claims. At present, no unifying framework allows researchers to represent their theories and definitions in a structured, formal way; although formalization will not resolve differences on its own, it makes differences clearer and thus more amenable to testing. Until recently, there was no resource we know of that allowed one to easily determine which cognitive processes the Sternberg task invokes, what clinical conditions are associated with impairments of grammar learning, or what set of mental states can be considered instances of emotion. We believe the development of a formal framework for specifying relationships between psychological concepts and tasks would substantially advance our ability to map the structure of human cognition and its underlying neurobiological bases. Notably, there is considerable precedent for such a development in other biomedical fields, where formal ontologies have played a critical role in facilitating hypothesis testing and scientific exploration alike.

Formal Ontologies as a Potential Solution

One of the most basic questions that is raised by cognitive neuroscience (and that one might reasonably expect psychologists to be able to answer) is, "What are the parts of the mind?" If one had asked this question of a psychologist in the eighteenth century, an answer would have been quickly forthcoming in the form of a list of mental faculties, which were adopted by the earliest "brain mapping" researchers (i.e., phrenologists) as the basis for their structure-function mapping. However, today virtually no psychologists would have an answer to this question. The closest that one might come would be to examine the index of a cognitive psychology textbook, but one would quickly find that there is no systematic description of how psychologists currently characterize the structure of the mind. Given that the goal of cognitive neuroscience is to map mental functions onto brain systems, this poses a fundamental problem.

Compare this situation to a similar question in biology, "What are all of the biological functions that occur within a cell?" As recently as the 1990s, one would have been similarly challenged to find a systematic answer to this question. However, in the late 1990s a group of biologists and informatics experts developed a consortium (called the Gene Ontology Consortium) that began to develop a formal knowledge base (or ontology) to represent the state of current knowledge regarding the structure and function of biological systems (Ashburner et al. 2000). Today, one can visit the Gene Ontology website (**http://www.geneontology.org**) and obtain a comprehensive formal description of cellular components, biological processes, and molecular functions.

What Is an Ontology?

The term ontology is used here to refer to an "explicit specification of a conceptualization" (Gruber 1993) or more generally as a formal description of a knowledge structure; this usage of the term, which arises from computer science, is related to but distinct from the usage of the term in philosophy, where it often refers to the entities that are postulated by a particular theory (Quine 1948) or more generally to the nature of existence. At its base, a formal ontology specifies the entities that exist within a domain along with the relations between those entities (Bard & Rhee 2004). For example, within the Gene Ontology, the entity "rough endoplasmic reticulum" has the relation "is-a" to the entity "endoplasmic reticulum" (**Figure 4**), meaning that the former is agreed upon to be a particular kind of the latter.

The Gene Ontology currently has entries for more than 26,000 biological processes, nearly 10,000 molecular functions, and more than 3,600 cellular components (and it is only one of many ontologies that have been developed within the bioinformatics community to describe various levels of biological function and structure). Given that each of these entries was manually curated, this represents a massive investment of human time. Why would researchers put so much time and effort into doing this? We review below several important benefits (for others, see Bard & Rhee 2004, Bodenreider & Stevens 2006, Rubin et al. 2008).

Controlled vocabulary with unique identifiers. The establishment of an agreed-upon ontology provides researchers in the field with a controlled vocabulary for the description of biological entities, each of which has a unique identifier (e.g., the identifier for endoplasmic reticulum is GO:0005789). This provides a machine-readable way to describe each entity, which can remain consistent even if the field decides to change the name of the entity. It also provides a means to link between different databases, which has proven remarkably powerful in biomedical informatics (Bard & Rhee 2004).

Framework for annotation. One of the most important aspects of the ontology is that it provides a framework through which to relate the ontology entities to other types of data, which in the context of bioinformatics is referred to as annotation. Gene Ontology entities are annotated by associating them with specific gene products (proteins or RNAs). The Gene Ontology annotation database currently has over two million annotation entries, which reflect many different types of evidence relating specific entities to specific gene products. For example, a search for annotations of the entity "endoplasmic reticulum" identified 119,040 entries involving 74,239 proteins across all species. The availability of a database of these annotations has enabled a number of new tools for understanding biological data. Most important, it has provided the ability to assess, for any specific set of genes, which entities in the ontology are likely to be "enriched" for that set of genes, thus providing insights into the larger biological context for the experiment (Rhee et al. 2008).

Inferring relations. Ontologies are generally specified using formal knowledge representation systems, or ontology languages, such as the Ontology Web Language. Once specified this way, formal reasoning systems can be used to infer relations between entities that are not explicitly specified in the ontology. For example, if we know that rough endoplasmic reticulum is a kind of endoplasmic reticulum and that endoplasmic reticulum is a kind of cytoplasmic part, we can infer that rough endoplasmic reticulum is a kind of cytoplasmic part.

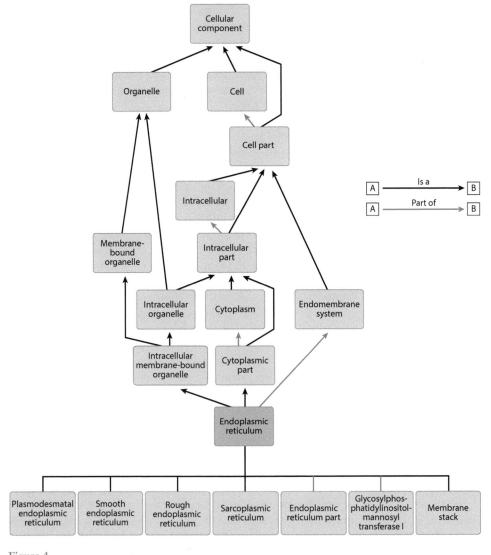

Figure 4

An example of entities and relations within the Gene Ontology. This chart (generated using the QuickGO browser: **http://www.ebi.ac.uk/QuickGO**) shows the relations of the term "endoplasmic reticulum"; different possible relations between entities are denoted using different line styles.

A Pragmatic Approach to Ontology Building

An important consideration when developing a formal ontology of mental processes is that psychological processes are inherently "fuzzier," or less structured, than biological processes. In many biomedical domains, the basic units of analysis correspond to well-defined physical entities and are not up for serious debate. For example, it's highly unlikely that 10 or 20 years hence, geneticists will decide that they were wrong all along about the nucleotide bases that make up the human genome and will move to eliminate all talk of cytosine, guanine, adenine, and thymine from the lexicon. In contrast, major psychological concepts appear to fall in and out of favor with some regularity—typically without having been demonstrably refuted by any critical experiment (Greenwald 2012). More generally, it is not clear that a question such as what are the fundamental building blocks of human cognition admits of a clear-cut answer in the same way that one can unambiguously identify the letters of the human genome. Is working memory a more basic concept than executive control or cognitive control? Does it make sense to speak of perception as a basic concept, or is that a purely extensional definition that is best ignored in favor of individual sensory systems such as vision and audition? Will concepts such as love and hate find their place in a formal ontology of the mind, or are they merely folk psychological abstractions to be abolished as science progresses, in the way that some philosophers once envisioned (Churchland 1981)?

The critical point here is not just that no consensus presently exists on such questions; it is that the questions very likely admit of no single right answer. There is little reason to suppose that the extremely complex and high-dimensional structure of human cognition can be neatly reduced to a much lower-dimensional, "human-readable" description without substantial loss of fidelity. Nor is it clear what criteria one could use to unambiguously distinguish between good and bad models. Should researchers privilege theoretical parsimony, such that a good model is one that maps well onto theoretical entities identified by prior scientific investigation (e.g., nodes in a cognitive ontology should strive to attain a one-to-one mapping with neurobiological structures)? Or should they favor statistical parsimony, such that if two models explain the same amount of behavioral variance, the simpler one is to be preferred, even if the more complex one maps more sensibly onto underlying biological entities? The answer will undoubtedly depend on individual researchers' goals and preferences.

Importantly, however, the principled absence of a single unassailable description of the structure of human cognition does not diminish the need for a formal ontology of psychological processes. If anything, the contrary is true. Many of the theoretical disputes that arise in psychology are, we submit, driven to a large extent by tacit differences in terminology that ramify as substantive disagreements. For example, in the personality literature, researchers have long debated whether the "fundamental feature" of extraversion is reward sensitivity, positive affect, or sociability (Ashton et al. 2002; Lucas & Diener 2001; Lucas et al. 2000, 2008; Smillie et al. 2012). In our view, it is not clear that there is a definitive answer to this question. It may well be that different research communities are simply applying the label extraversion to different (though partly overlapping) behaviors—in which case there would be no more utility in trying to determine what the "true" definition of extraversion is than in trying to arbitrate between two formal color standards that disagree as to whether aquamarine is a shade of blue or of green. The ability to formally clarify and translate between different lexica would thus be a major boon to theoreticians.

From a purely pragmatic standpoint, one can think of a good ontology as a kind of universal language that dramatically reduces the likelihood of miscommunication between researchers by enabling statements to be defined in more formal and less ambiguous terms, even when the mapping between terms and their referents is still not perfect. At their best, good ontologies can serve as sophisticated inference engines capable of informing and even answering certain kinds of questions that the unaided human mind is known to have trouble with—for example, by identifying when two terms are being used interchangeably, when a single term is being used in multiple conflicting ways, when a relationship between two concepts is likely to exist even though one has not yet been reported, and when the putative nomological network (Chronbach & Meehl 1955) of a given concept contains internal inconsistencies.

The Cognitive Atlas

The success and broad utility of biomedical ontologies such as the Gene Ontology inspired the question of whether it would be possible to address the problems described above by developing

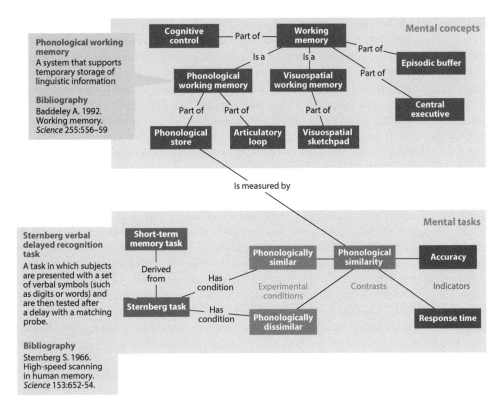

Figure 5

A schematic example of the Cognitive Atlas representation of Baddeley's (1992) working memory theory. (*Top panel*) A representation of the concepts underlying the working memory theory. (*Bottom panel*) An example of a task measuring one of these concepts.

a formal ontology of mental processes and tasks, which led to the establishment of the Cognitive Atlas (**http://www.cognitiveatlas.org**) (Poldrack et al. 2011). The broad goal of the Cognitive Atlas is to serve as an open collaborative knowledge base for psychological science. It is meant to capture two primary forms of knowledge. First, it aims to define psychological constructs in order to provide consensus definitions that can serve as the basis for accurate scientific communication and discussion. A fundamental distinction made within the Cognitive Atlas is between mental concepts, which refer to putative but unobservable psychological processes or structures, and mental tasks, which are the objective operations used to measure those putative constructs (see **Figure 5**). This distinction follows the previously noted admonition by Chronbach & Meehl (1955) regarding the separation of latent constructs and the operations used to measure them. Second, the project aims to establish a knowledge base of the relations within and between mental tasks and mental concepts. In a sense, it is these relations that form a major part of the basis for psychological theories. For example, Baddeley's (1992) theory of working memory could be specified in terms of a set of concepts (e.g., phonological loop, acoustic store, and central executive), a set of relations between these concepts (e.g., acoustic store is part of phonological loop), and relations to tasks (e.g., the acoustic store is measured by the comparison of acoustically similar versus dissimilar words on a short-term memory task).

Within the Cognitive Atlas, mental tasks are described in terms of three primary features: (*a*) conditions (which specify different conditions of measurement), (*b*) contrasts (which specify either comparisons between conditions or relationships with continuous variables), and (*c*) indicators (which specify variables that are measured within the task; these could reflect behavioral, neural, or other physiological measurements). In order to capture the relations between tasks and concepts, a novel ontological relationship (measured-by) was defined that denotes the fact that a specific concept is measured by a specific task. Importantly, concepts are not related to the overall representation of a task but rather to specific contrasts. This design decision recognizes the subtractive/contrastive logic of psychological measurement: researchers are typically interested in comparisons between conditions that vary in some specific set of putative mental processes rather than in the value of a specific indicator. For example, the concept of the phonological loop might be measured by the contrast of phonologically similar versus dissimilar items on the Sternberg delayed recognition task. Other contrasts within the task could be related to other mental concepts; for example, the contrast between target-present and target-absent probe trials might be thought to reflect some aspect of decisional processes rather than measuring working memory.

The description of tasks within the Cognitive Atlas is relatively abstract and does not include specific aspects of the stimuli, responses, or instructions for the task. A parallel effort, known as the Cognitive Paradigm Ontology (or CogPO) (Turner & Laird 2012), is developing the means to describe tasks in more detail. Ultimately it should be possible to link these two ontologies in order to span directly from psychological processes outlined in the Cognitive Atlas to detailed operational descriptions of tasks. This would allow the proper annotation of cases in which specific task implementation details are critical determinants of the psychological processes that are engaged (e.g., changes in the architecture of task switching in relation to the amount of time available for preparation prior to switching) (Rogers & Monsell 1995).

FUTURE DEVELOPMENTS

The projects outlined above represent the first steps in the development of a cognitive neuroinformatics that can support strong inferences regarding the relation between brain systems and psychological functions. What new advances will the next few years bring? In a short review several years ago (Yarkoni et al. 2010), we briefly considered the question, What will cognitive neuroscience look like 10 years from now? Some of the developments we anticipated at the time included fully automated quantitative mapping between cognitive and neural states; intelligent preprocessing and analysis pipelines that evaluate local data in relation to global databases; integration of neuroimaging databases with other kinds of data, for example, functional genomic repositories; introduction of centralized neuroimaging data repositories; and integration of formal ontologies and formal method descriptions into fMRI analysis software. Now, five years on (and halfway through our earlier forecast horizon), we are more optimistic than ever about the prospects for a cumulative, integrative, informatics-driven science of the human mind/brain. A number of the developments we anticipated five years ago already have realized implementations that we discuss above (e.g., centralized data repositories such as OpenfMRI and NeuroVault, and the ability to instantly decode maps uploaded to NeuroVault using Neurosynth). Others are in very early stages of development. And then, of course, there are other important emerging projects that we did not anticipate at all five years ago. Here we outline a few recent developments of particular interest.

Toward open, standardized, and centralized data sharing. The benefits of cognitive ontologies to scientific discovery become most apparent when applied at scale. A critical component of ongoing and future efforts will therefore be the centralized aggregation and organization of neuroimaging and psychology data. Currently, major ongoing efforts are directed at developing machine-readable standards for representing neuroimaging data (e.g., the Neuroimaging Data

Model; **http://www.nidm.nidash.org/**); creating reproducible, shareable, open-source analysis pipelines (e.g., the Nipype framework; Gorgolewski et al. 2011); and the establishment of open resources for the sharing of both raw fMRI datasets (e.g., OpenfMRI; Poldrack et al. 2013) and statistical images (e.g., NeuroVault; **http://www.neurovault.org**). Some work has started to combine these datasets with ontologies of psychological processes (e.g., Poldrack et al. 2012), but the rapid development and growth of these databases will likely enable much more powerful analyses in the future.

Crowdsourced annotation. Despite the recent successes of the automated meta-analysis approaches discussed above, it is clear that careful human consideration and annotation of neuroimaging data remain critical components of most investigations and are unlikely to be replaced by machine learning approaches soon. We suggest that the next wave of advances in the area of neuroimaging meta-analysis may result from successful hybridization of manual and automated approaches, particularly from the development of user-friendly crowdsourcing interfaces that allow researchers to easily apply their expertise to manual curation of communal databases. A promising prototype is Brainspell (**http://www.brainspell.org**), a website that allows users to manually validate, annotate, and tag all data presently in Neurosynth—potentially providing all of the benefits of manual curation for substantially less effort than full manual entry would require. An ongoing challenge, however, is to develop effective incentives for participation in such efforts. One largely unexplored approach in this area is the kind of "gamification" successfully achieved in other domains using platforms such as Foldit (Khatib et al. 2011) and EyeWire (**http://www.eyewire.org**).

Using ontologies to resolve psychological debates. One of the greatest promises of a comprehensive formal ontology of cognitive processes lies in the potential to develop a kind of formal inferential engine that enables researchers to compute well-defined operations over its nodes and relationships, thereby informing, and in some cases even resolving, ongoing theoretical debates. For example, in the Cognitive Atlas a measured-by relationship is defined that indicates that a given task contrast (e.g., the high- versus low-load conditions on the Sternberg item recognition task) depends critically on a particular psychological concept (e.g., working memory). In the future, we could define a comparison operation that takes two concepts as input and returns separate lists of all known task contrasts that (*a*) tap both constructs and (*b*) tap only one of the constructs. Further, we could define additional operations such as similarity or difference that take two lists of contrasts (or concepts) and return either quantitative metrics of similarity (e.g., based on computing the similarity of two nodes' local neighborhood or network structure parameters) or a list of concepts (or tasks) that maximally distinguishes the two inputs. Given such a platform, it could conceivably turn out, for example, that whether the episodic buffer is or is not a central part of working memory is largely a definitional matter: Two researchers might each feed in a list of what they consider to be critical working memory tasks only to find that they are talking past each other, inasmuch as the disagreement is purely extensional (i.e., there is no implied contradiction in which other latent concepts working memory is linked to but only in how broadly the label is applied to individual tasks).

Similarly, when genuine substantive disagreements between theories exist, a formal ontology of cognition could help focus attention appropriately. For example, there is debate in the executive function literature over whether performance on tasks requiring suppression of a prepotent or ongoing response in favor of a different response requires an active inhibitory process or whether it instead can rely solely on competitive inhibition within a network (Munakata et al. 2011, Aron et al. 2004). Each of these theories makes different predictions regarding the similarity (i.e., covariance) of both behavioral and neural activation patterns across a large number of tasks. Given an appropriate annotation of a sufficiently large dataset, one could directly assess which of these theories provides a better fit to the observed data (e.g., using analogs to structural equation modeling) and also potentially demonstrate which specific set of concepts needs to be experimentally compared in order to most powerfully assess the specific theoretical debate.

A unified, interoperable ecosystem. Perhaps the most promising development of the coming years will be the increasing convergence and interoperability between diverse resources for informatics-driven investigation of the human mind/brain. We anticipate the relatively near-term emergence of a unified, interoperable ecosystem made up of dozens of individual services that all loosely follow the same standards and protocols, enabling researchers to construct automated pipelines that easily integrate currently disparate resources. Optimistically, we predict that within a few years, researchers will be able to easily (i.e., without requiring advanced technical skills) upload raw data they have acquired and annotated to centralized platforms that run state-of-the-art cloud-based processing and analysis pipelines; interactively explore the results of such analyses via rich, user-friendly web interfaces that include extensive literature-based quantitative interpretation and allow easy piping to other third-party services; and use ontology-driven inference engines to conduct sophisticated, highly customized meta-analyses that draw on thousands of datasets acquired and deposited using similar platforms.

CONCLUSION

The field of cognitive neuroscience faces a number of daunting challenges in its attempt to understand the relation between brain systems and psychological functions. We have argued that the most commonly used approaches in cognitive neuroscience are fundamentally unable to identify the kind of selective associations between neural structure and psychological function that are the presumed goal of the field, but that this question can be profitably addressed using informatics approaches that employ large-scale databases and formal ontologies. We predict that such approaches will become increasingly common in psychology, as they have in biology, and that this will provide a new pathway toward discoveries regarding how neural computations give rise to mental life.

DISCLOSURE STATEMENT

The authors are not aware of any affiliations, memberships, funding, or financial holdings that might be perceived as affecting the objectivity of this review.

ACKNOWLEDGMENTS

The work described here was supported by NIMH grants R01MH082795 (to R.A.P.) and R01MH096906 (to T.Y.) and by the James S. McDonnell Foundation and Laura and John Arnold Foundation (to R.A.P.). Thanks to Tim Bayne, Patrick Bissett, Chris Gorgolewski, Colin Klein, Sanmi Koyejo, Mac Shine, and Vanessa Sochat for helpful comments on this manuscript.

LITERATURE CITED

Aron AR, Robbins TW, Poldrack RA. 2004. Inhibition and the right inferior frontal cortex. *Trends Cogn. Sci.* 8:170–77

Ashburner M, Ball CA, Blake JA, Botstein D, Butler H, et al. 2000. Gene ontology: tool for the unification of biology. The Gene Ontology Consortium. *Nat. Genet.* 25:25–29

Ashton MC, Lee K, Paunonen SV. 2002. What is the central feature of extraversion? Social attention versus reward sensitivity. *J. Personal. Soc. Psychol.* 83:245–52

Baddeley A. 1992. Working memory. *Science* 255:556–59

Bard JBL, Rhee SY. 2004. Ontologies in biology: design, applications and future challenges. *Nat. Rev. Genet.* 5:213–22

Beckmann CF, Smith SM. 2004. Probabilistic independent component analysis for functional magnetic resonance imaging. *IEEE Trans. Med. Imaging* 23:137–52

Biswal B, Yetkin FZ, Haughton VM, Hyde JS. 1995. Functional connectivity in the motor cortex of resting human brain using echo-planar MRI. *Magn. Reson. Med.* 34:537–41

Blei D, Ng A, Jordan M. 2003. Latent Dirichlet allocation. *J. Mach. Learn. Res.* 3:993–1022

Bodenreider O, Stevens R. 2006. Bio-ontologies: current trends and future directions. *Brief Bioinform.* 7:256–74

Chang LJ, Yarkoni T, Khaw MW, Sanfey AG. 2013. Decoding the role of the insula in human cognition: functional parcellation and large-scale reverse inference. *Cereb. Cortex* 23:739–49

Chronbach LJ, Meehl PE. 1955. Construct validity in psychological tests. *Psychol. Bull.* 52:281–302

Churchland PM. 1981. Eliminative materialism and the propositional attitudes. *J. Philos.* 78:67–90

Cox DD, Savoy RL. 2003. Functional magnetic resonance imaging (fMRI) "brain reading": detecting and classifying distributed patterns of fMRI activity in human visual cortex. *NeuroImage* 19:261–70

Craddock RC, James GA, Holtzheimer PE 3rd, Hu XP, Mayberg HS. 2012. A whole brain fMRI atlas generated via spatially constrained spectral clustering. *Hum. Brain Mapp.* 33:1914–28

Critchley HD, Wiens S, Rotshtein P, Ohman A, Dolan RJ. 2004. Neural systems supporting interoceptive awareness. *Nat. Neurosci.* 7:189–95

Dale AM, Buckner RL. 1997. Selective averaging of rapidly presented individual trials using fMRI. *Hum. Brain Mapp.* 5:329–40

Derrfuss J, Mar RA. 2009. Lost in localization: the need for a universal coordinate database. *NeuroImage* 48:1–7

Dickson J, Drury H, Van Essen DC. 2001. "The Surface Management System" (SuMS) database: a surface-based database to aid cortical surface reconstruction, visualization and analysis. *Philos. Trans. R. Soc. B* 356:1277–92

Dosenbach NUF, Visscher KM, Palmer ED, Miezin FM, Wenger KK, et al. 2006. A core system for the implementation of task sets. *Neuron* 50:799–812

Egeth H, Marcus N, Bevan W. 1972. Target-set and response-set interaction: implications for models of human information processing. *Science* 176:1447–48

Fan Y, Duncan NW, de Greck M, Northoff G. 2011. Is there a core neural network in empathy? An fMRI based quantitative meta-analysis. *Neurosci. Biobehav. Rev.* 35:903–11

Fodor JA. 1974. Special sciences (or: the disunity of science as a working hypothesis). *Synthese* 28:97–115

Friston KJ, Price CJ, Fletcher P, Moore C, Frackowiak RS, Dolan RJ. 1996. The trouble with cognitive subtraction. *NeuroImage* 4:97–104

Garner WR, Hake HW, Eriksen CW. 1956. Operationism and the concept of perception. *Psychol. Rev.* 63:149–59

Gordon EM, Laumann TO, Adeyemo B, Huckins JF, Kelley WM, Petersen SE. 2014. Generation and evaluation of a cortical area parcellation from resting-state correlations. *Cereb. Cortex.* doi: 10.1093/cercor/bhu239

Gorgolewski K, Burns CD, Madison C, Clark D, Halchenko YO, et al. 2011. Nipype: a flexible, lightweight and extensible neuroimaging data processing framework in Python. *Front. Neuroinform.* 5:13

Gorgolewski KJ, Varoquaux G, Rivera G, Schwartz Y, Ghosh SS, et al. 2015. NeuroVault.org: a web-based repository for collecting and sharing unthresholded statistical maps of the human brain. *Front. Neuroinform.* 9:8

Greenwald AG. 2012. There is nothing so theoretical as a good method. *Perspect. Psychol. Sci.* 7:99–108

Gruber T. 1993. A translation approach to portable ontology specifications. *Knowl. Acquis.* 5:199–220

Haynes JD, Rees G. 2006. Decoding mental states from brain activity in humans. *Nat. Rev. Neurosci.* 7:523–34

Huth AG, Nishimoto S, Vu AT, Gallant JL. 2012. A continuous semantic space describes the representation of thousands of object and action categories across the human brain. *Neuron* 76:1210–24

Hutzler F. 2014. Reverse inference is not a fallacy per se: Cognitive processes can be inferred from functional imaging data. *NeuroImage* 84:1061–69

Jeneson A, Squire LR. 2012. Working memory, long-term memory, and medial temporal lobe function. *Learn. Mem.* 19:15–25

Jennings JM, McIntosh AR, Kapur S, Tulving E, Houle S. 1997. Cognitive subtractions may not add up: the interaction between semantic processing and response mode. *NeuroImage* 5:229–39

Kane MJ, Conway ARA, Miura TK, Colflesh GJH. 2007. Working memory, attention control, and the *N*-back task: a question of construct validity. *J. Exp. Psychol.: Learn. Mem. Cogn.* 33:615–22

Kay KN, Naselaris T, Prenger RJ, Gallant JL. 2008. Identifying natural images from human brain activity. *Nature* 452:352–55

Khatib F, Cooper S, Tyka MD, Xu K, Makedon I, et al. 2011. Algorithm discovery by protein folding game players. *PNAS* 108:18949–53

Kim H. 2011. Neural activity that predicts subsequent memory and forgetting: a meta-analysis of 74 fMRI studies. *NeuroImage* 54:2446–61

Klein C. 2012. Cognitive ontology and region- versus network-oriented analyses. *Philos. Sci.* 79:952–60

Klein TA, Endrass T, Kathmann N, Neumann J, von Cramon DY, Ullsperger M. 2007. Neural correlates of error awareness. *NeuroImage* 34:1774–81

Koyejo O, Poldrack RA. 2013. *Decoding cognitive processes from functional MRI.* Presented at NIPS Workshop Mach. Learn. Interpret. Neuroimaging, Dec. 5–10, Lake Tahoe, CA

Laird AR, Lancaster JL, Fox PT. 2005. BrainMap: the social evolution of a human brain mapping database. *Neuroinformatics* 3:65–78

Larocque JJ, Lewis-Peacock JA, Postle BR. 2014. Multiple neural states of representation in short-term memory? It's a matter of attention. *Front. Hum. Neurosci.* 8:5

Lucas RE, Diener E. 2001. Understanding extraverts' enjoyment of social situations: the importance of pleasantness. *J. Personal. Soc. Psychol.* 81:343–56

Lucas RE, Diener E, Grob A, Suh EM, Shao L. 2000. Cross-cultural evidence for the fundamental features of extraversion. *J. Personal. Soc. Psychol.* 79:452–68

Lucas RE, Le K, Dyrenforth PS. 2008. Explaining the extraversion/positive affect relation: Sociability cannot account for extraverts' greater happiness. *J. Personal.* 76:385–414

Machery E. 2014. In defense of reverse inference. *Br. J. Philos. Sci.* 65:251–267

Mischel W. 2008. The toothbrush problem. *APS Obs.* 21:11

Mitchell TM, Hutchinson R, Just MA, Niculescu RS, Pereira F, Wang X. 2003. Classifying instantaneous cognitive states from fMRI data. *AMIA Annu. Symp. Proc.* 2003:465–69

Mitchell TM, Shinkareva SV, Carlson A, Chang KM, Malave VL, et al. 2008. Predicting human brain activity associated with the meanings of nouns. *Science* 320:1191–95

Mourão-Miranda J, Bokde ALW, Born C, Hampel H, Stetter M. 2005. Classifying brain states and determining the discriminating activation patterns: Support Vector Machine on functional MRI data. *NeuroImage* 28:980–95

Munakata Y, Herd SA, Chatham CH, Depue BE, Banich MT, O'Reilly RC. 2011. A unified framework for inhibitory control. *Trends Cogn. Sci.* 15:453–59

Nielsen FA, Hansen LK, Balslev D. 2004. Mining for associations between text and brain activation in a functional neuroimaging database. *Neuroinformatics* 2:369–80

Nishimoto S, Vu AT, Naselaris T, Benjamini Y, Yu B, Gallant JL. 2011. Reconstructing visual experiences from brain activity evoked by natural movies. *Curr. Biol.* 21:1641–46

Norman KA, Polyn SM, Detre GJ, Haxby JV. 2006. Beyond mind-reading: multi-voxel pattern analysis of fMRI data. *Trends Cogn. Sci.* 10:424–30

Owen AM, McMillan KM, Laird AR, Bullmore E. 2005. *N*-back working memory paradigm: a meta-analysis of normative functional neuroimaging studies. *Hum. Brain. Mapp.* 25:46–59

Poldrack RA. 2006. Can cognitive processes be inferred from neuroimaging data? *Trends Cogn. Sci.* 10:59–63

Poldrack RA. 2010. An exchange about localism. In *Foundational Issues in Human Brain Mapping*, ed. SJ Hanson, M Bunzl, pp. 147–60. Cambridge, MA: MIT Press

Poldrack RA. 2011. Inferring mental states from neuroimaging data: from reverse inference to large-scale decoding. *Neuron* 72:692–97

Poldrack RA, Barch DM, Mitchell JP, Wager TD, Wagner AD, et al. 2013. Toward open sharing of task-based fMRI data: the OpenfMRI project. *Front. Neuroinform.* 7:12

Poldrack RA, Halchenko YO, Hanson SJ. 2009. Decoding the large-scale structure of brain function by classifying mental states across individuals. *Psychol. Sci.* 20:1364–72

Poldrack RA, Kittur A, Kalar D, Miller E, Seppa C, et al. 2011. The Cognitive Atlas: toward a knowledge foundation for cognitive neuroscience. *Front. Neuroinform.* 5:17

Poldrack RA, Mumford JA, Schonberg T, Kalar D, Barman B, Yarkoni T. 2012. Discovering relations between mind, brain, and mental disorders using topic mapping. *PLOS Comput. Biol.* 8:e1002707

Price C, Friston K. 2005. Functional ontologies for cognition: the systematic definition of structure and function. *Cogn. Neuropsychol.* 22:262–75

Quine WV. 1948. On what there is. *Rev. Metaphys.* 2:21–38

Raichle ME, MacLeod AM, Snyder AZ, Powers WJ, Gusnard DA, Shulman GL. 2001. A default mode of brain function. *PNAS* 98:676–82

Rhee SY, Wood V, Dolinski K, Draghici S. 2008. Use and misuse of the gene ontology annotations. *Nat. Rev. Genet.* 9:509–15

Rogers RD, Monsell S. 1995. Costs of a predictable switch between simple cognitive tasks. *J. Exp. Psychol.: Gen.* 124:207–31

Rottschy C, Langner R, Dogan I, Reetz K, Laird AR, et al. 2012. Modelling neural correlates of working memory: a coordinate-based meta-analysis. *NeuroImage* 60:830–46

Rubin DL, Shah NH, Noy NF. 2008. Biomedical ontologies: a functional perspective. *Brief Bioinform.* 9:75–90

Salimi-Khorshidi G, Smith SM, Keltner JR, Wager TD, Nichols TE. 2009. Meta-analysis of neuroimaging data: a comparison of image-based and coordinate-based pooling of studies. *NeuroImage* 45:810–23

Schwartz Y, Thirion B, Varoquaux G. 2013. *Mapping paradigm ontologies to and from the brain.* Presented at NIPS Workshop Mach. Learn. Interpret. Neuroimaging, Dec. 5–10, Lake Tahoe, CA

Shinkareva SV, Mason RA, Malave VL, Wang W, Mitchell TM, Just MA. 2008. Using fMRI brain activation to identify cognitive states associated with perception of tools and dwellings. *PLOS ONE* 3:e1394

Smillie LD, Cooper AJ, Wilt J, Revelle W. 2012. Do extraverts get more bang for the buck? Refining the affective-reactivity hypothesis of extraversion. *J. Personal. Soc. Psychol.* 103:306–26

Smith SM, Fox PT, Miller KL, Glahn DC, Fox PM, et al. 2009. Correspondence of the brain's functional architecture during activation and rest. *PNAS* 106:13040–45

Sternberg S. 1969. Memory-scanning: mental processes revealed by reaction-time experiments. *Am. Sci.* 57:421–57

Tillisch K, Mayer EA, Labus JS. 2011. Quantitative meta-analysis identifies brain regions activated during rectal distension in irritable bowel syndrome. *Gastroenterology* 140:91–100

Turkeltaub PE, Eden GF, Jones KM, Zeffiro TA. 2002. Meta-analysis of the functional neuroanatomy of single-word reading: method and validation. *NeuroImage* 16:765–80

Turner JA, Laird AR. 2012. The cognitive paradigm ontology: design and application. *Neuroinformatics* 10:57–66

Uttal W. 2001. *The New Phrenology: The Limits of Localizing Cognitive Processes in the Brain.* Cambridge, MA: MIT Press

Varoquaux G, Craddock RC. 2013. Learning and comparing functional connectomes across subjects. *NeuroImage* 80:405–15

Wager TD, Atlas LY, Lindquist MA, Roy M, Woo CW, Kross E. 2013. An fMRI-based neurologic signature of physical pain. *N. Engl. J. Med.* 368:1388–97

Wager TD, Lindquist M, Kaplan L. 2007. Meta-analysis of functional neuroimaging data: current and future directions. *Soc. Cogn. Affect. Neurosci.* 2:150–58

Wager TD, Rilling JK, Smith EE, Sokolik A, Casey KL, et al. 2004. Placebo-induced changes in fMRI in the anticipation and experience of pain. *Science* 303:1162–67

Wiech K, Lin CS, Brodersen KH, Bingel U, Ploner M, Tracey I. 2010. Anterior insula integrates information about salience into perceptual decisions about pain. *J. Neurosci.* 30:16324–31

Wilhelm O, Hildebrandt A, Oberauer K. 2013. What is working memory capacity, and how can we measure it? *Front. Psychol.* 4:433

Wise RJ, Greene J, Büchel C, Scott SK. 1999. Brain regions involved in articulation. *Lancet* 353:1057–61

Yarkoni T, Barch DM, Gray JR, Conturo TE, Braver TS. 2009. Bold correlates of trial-by-trial reaction time variability in gray and white matter: a multi-study fMRI analysis. *PLOS ONE* 4:e4257

Yarkoni T, Poldrack RA, Nichols TE, Van Essen DC, Wager TD. 2011. Large-scale automated synthesis of human functional neuroimaging data. *Nat. Methods* 8:665–70

Yarkoni T, Poldrack RA, Van Essen DC, Wager TD. 2010. Cognitive neuroscience 2.0: building a cumulative science of human brain function. *Trends Cogn. Sci.* 14:489–96

Yeo BTT, Krienen FM, Eickhoff SB, Yaakub SN, Fox PT, et al. 2014. Functional specialization and flexibility in human association cortex. *Cereb. Cortex.* doi: 10.1093/cercor/bhu217

Modular Brain Networks

Olaf Sporns[1,2] and Richard F. Betzel[1]

[1]Department of Psychological and Brain Sciences, Indiana University, Bloomington, Indiana 47405; email: osporns@indiana.edu

[2]Indiana University Network Science Institute, Indiana University, Bloomington, Indiana 47405

Annu. Rev. Psychol. 2016. 67:613–40

First published online as a Review in Advance on September 21, 2015

The *Annual Review of Psychology* is online at psych.annualreviews.org

This article's doi:
10.1146/annurev-psych-122414-033634

Keywords

connectome, clustering, functional connectivity, graph theory, hubs, resting state

Abstract

The development of new technologies for mapping structural and functional brain connectivity has led to the creation of comprehensive network maps of neuronal circuits and systems. The architecture of these brain networks can be examined and analyzed with a large variety of graph theory tools. Methods for detecting modules, or network communities, are of particular interest because they uncover major building blocks or subnetworks that are particularly densely connected, often corresponding to specialized functional components. A large number of methods for community detection have become available and are now widely applied in network neuroscience. This article first surveys a number of these methods, with an emphasis on their advantages and shortcomings; then it summarizes major findings on the existence of modules in both structural and functional brain networks and briefly considers their potential functional roles in brain evolution, wiring minimization, and the emergence of functional specialization and complex dynamics.

Contents

INTRODUCTION

Behavior and cognition are associated with neuronal activity in distributed networks of neuronal populations and brain regions. These brain networks are linked by anatomical connections and engage in complex patterns of neuronal communication and signaling. In recent years, the convergence of two major scientific developments has prompted a new network-based perspective on brain function (Bressler & Menon 2010, Bullmore & Sporns 2009, Park & Friston 2013, Sporns 2014, Sporns et al. 2004). On the one side, improved capabilities in brain imaging and recording have provided new ways to measure the brain's anatomical (structural) as well as dynamic (functional) connections. These developments have given rise to the emerging field of brain connectivity (Jirsa & McIntosh 2007, Sporns 2011). On the other side, the availability of increasingly complex data in the social, technological, and biological sciences has led to the development of new tools and methods for representing and analyzing networks, giving rise to the new discipline of network science (Börner et al. 2007). The network science of the brain, or network neuroscience, is still a very recent endeavor, and new observational techniques and analytic methods (Rubinov & Sporns 2010) are continually emerging. Here we provide a survey of the state of the art in both methods and principal findings in a particularly active area of network neuroscience: modular brain networks.

Network: a set of elements (nodes) and the pairwise interactions (edges) among those elements

Structural and Functional Brain Networks

Data about relations between elements, for example, connections among brain regions, can be summarized and represented as a set of nodes and edges forming a network (**Figure 1a**). The construction of brain networks begins with the collection of observational data on how brain regions, neuronal populations, or neurons are connected. A major distinction is that between

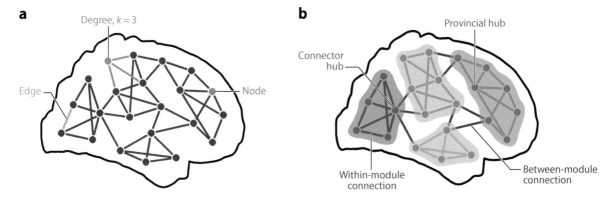

Figure 1

Schematic diagram of a brain network introducing basic terminology. (*a*) Networks consist of nodes and edges. The node degree corresponds to the number of edges that are attached to each node. (*b*) Networks can be decomposed into communities or modules. Connections (edges) are either linking nodes within modules or between modules. Highly connected nodes are hubs, and they either connect primarily with other nodes in the same community (provincial hub) or with nodes that belong to different communities (connector hub).

structural and functional networks. Structural networks correspond to a pattern of anatomical connections, summarizing synaptic links between neurons or projections among brain regions. Most relevant for studies of the human brain are large-scale networks of interregional pathways that link cortical and subcortical gray matter regions, which taken together form the human connectome (Sporns 2013, Sporns et al. 2005). In contrast, functional networks are assembled from estimates of statistical dependencies between neuronal or regional time series data (Friston 2011). Although many different measures of functional connectivity exist (Smith et al. 2011), most human neuroimaging studies currently employ Pearson cross-correlations of hemodynamic or electrophysiological time courses. Unlike large-scale structural networks (which are thought to be stable on shorter timescales of seconds to minutes), functional networks are highly variable, exhibiting spontaneous dynamic changes during rest (Hutchison et al. 2013) as well as characteristic modulations in different task conditions (Cole et al. 2014).

Network Analysis and Modularity

Modules are encountered across a broad range of networks. They may correspond to groups of individuals in social networks, ensembles of interacting proteins, or coregulated genes in cellular networks. In this article, the term module refers exclusively to building blocks in the organization of brain networks; this usage of the term is distinct from concepts like modularity of mind in cognitive theory (Fodor 1983). Modules in networks, generally speaking, correspond to clusters of nodes that are densely connected, also called network communities (**Figure 1*b***). Modules derive from a decomposition of the network into subcomponents that are internally strongly coupled, but externally only weakly coupled. This near-decomposability has long been regarded as a hallmark of complex systems (Simon 1962). Importantly, modules can be detected in a purely data-driven way, based only on the topology of the network, and understanding which nodes belong to which modules can yield important insights into how networks function. Although network modules seem to be easy to define, their detection presents significant obstacles and is subject to several misinterpretations and biases.

Module: a subnetwork of densely interconnected nodes that is connected sparsely to the rest of the network

Modularity: the scoring of a partition according to whether the internal densities of its modules are greater or less than the expected density

Outline of Article

First, we survey various methods for detecting modules in brain networks, evaluate their advantages and shortcomings, and discuss some practical issues. We then review the evidence for the existence of modules in both structural and functional brain connectivity data sets. Finally, we briefly consider the potential functional roles of modules from a variety of perspectives, including brain evolution, wiring minimization, and the emergence of functional specialization and complex dynamics.

METHODS FOR MODULE DETECTION

The notion of module detection refers to a collection of methods used to uncover a network's latent community structure. Most of the methods covered in this section use only the information encoded in a network's connectivity matrix to assess whether or not a network has modules/communities, and, if so, to which module each node should be assigned (for an encyclopedic review of many different approaches to module detection in networks, see Fortunato 2010). The terms community and module both refer to subnetworks that are embedded within a larger network and will be used interchangeably. A related term is partition, which refers to any division of network elements into communities. Although most module detection methods yield nonoverlapping communities, in which each network node belongs to one and only one module, it is possible in principle to partition a network into communities that overlap.

Community structure: a partition that induces the division of a network into modules, usually such that no modules overlap

Community detection: a set of tools used for identifying a network's community structure based on its topology

Modularity maximization: a set of community detection methods aimed at uncovering partitions that maximize the modularity quality function

Modularity Maximization

A method for community detection that is widely applied in the detection of brain modules is known as modularity maximization. This method aims to partition a network's nodes into K nonoverlapping communities, $C_1, \ldots C_K$, so as to maximize the modularity quality function, Q (Newman & Girvan 2004). Conceptually, a partition is considered high quality (and hence achieves a greater Q score) if the communities it defines are more internally dense than would be expected by chance. The partition that achieves the greatest value of Q, then, is taken to be a good estimate of a network's community structure. This intuition can be formalized as

$$Q = \frac{1}{2m} \sum_{ij} [a_{ij} - p_{ij}] \delta(\sigma_i, \sigma_j).$$

In this expression, a_{ij} represents the number of links between nodes i and j. The term p_{ij} stands in for the expected number of links according to a null model, whose precise form is left up to the user. The de facto null model is one that preserves each node's degree but otherwise allows connections to be formed at random. For an undirected network, this model gives an expected weight of $p_{ij} = \frac{k_i k_j}{2m}$, where $k_i = \sum_j a_{ij}$ is a node's degree and $2m = \sum_{ij} a_{ij}$ is the total number of connections in the network. The Kronecker delta function, $\delta(\sigma_i, \sigma_j)$, which is equal to unity when nodes' community assignments, denoted by $\sigma_i \in \{1, \ldots, K\}$, are the same and is zero otherwise, ensures that contributions to Q come only from the $\{i, j\}$ where $\sigma_i = \sigma_j$, i.e., from pairs of nodes assigned to the same community. Whereas this description of Q is suitable for undirected networks, the form of the quality function Q can be easily adapted to work for weighted and directed networks (Leicht & Newman 2008).

The process of optimizing Q is known as modularity maximization and presents a challenge, because it is computationally intractable to exhaustively search the space of all possible partitions, even for small networks. To this end, many heuristics have been proposed to uncover partitions with large Q scores, with the hope of approximating the partition corresponding to the global maximum Q. These methods include divisive algorithms (Girvan & Newman 2002), spectral decomposition (Newman 2004), extremal optimization (Duch & Arenas 2005), greedy algorithms (Blondel et al. 2008, Clauset et al. 2004), and simulated annealing (Guimera & Amaral 2005), among others.

Partition degeneracy: the tendency for community detection algorithms to uncover partitions of nearly identical quality that nonetheless induce very different modules

Modularity Maximization in Signed Networks

In human neuroimaging, functional brain networks are commonly estimated from the signed correlation matrix, r_{ij}, of hemodynamic time series. This matrix is often converted to a sparse positive-only matrix (amenable to standard graph analysis) by applying a threshold to retain coefficients $r_{ij} \geq \tau$. However, weak and negative correlations may reflect neurobiologically relevant patterns, in which case the thresholding step can offer only a partial view of the topology. In order to retain negative correlations and still use modularity maximization to define communities, the definition of a community must be slightly reformulated. In the context of signed networks, communities can be thought of as groups of nodes that are internally positively correlated but externally anticorrelated. The standard modularity function can be adapted and made consistent with this intuition by separately modeling the contributions of positive and negative correlations. To calculate such a modularity, it is useful to first define the matrices r_{ij}^+ and r_{ij}^-, which contain only positive and negative correlation coefficients, respectively, and satisfy the expression $r_{ij} = r_{ij}^+ - r_{ij}^-$. The positive (+) and negative (−) modularities are then given by

$$Q^{\pm} = \frac{1}{2m^{\pm}} \sum_{ij} [r_{ij}^{\pm} - p_{ij}^{\pm}] \delta(\sigma_i, \sigma_j).$$

These signed modularities can be scaled and combined to represent the total modularity of the system (Gómez et al. 2009, Rubinov & Sporns 2011, Traag & Bruggeman 2009). The simplest formulation is

$$Q = \frac{2m^+}{2m^+ + 2m^-} Q^+ - \frac{2m^-}{2m^+ + 2m^-} Q^-.$$

Here the positive modularity, Q^+, which represents the excess of positive correlation coefficients within modules, serves to increase the total modularity. The negative modularity, Q^-, which represents the excess of negative coefficients within modules, acts to decrease total modularity.

It is useful to note that, again, the precise form of the null model, $p_{ij}^{\pm}$, was left unspecified. Typically its value is given by the familiar expression $p_{ij}^{\pm} = \frac{k_i^{\pm} k_j^{\pm}}{2m^{\pm}}$, though some authors have proposed alternative models that may be more compatible with the Pearson correlation measure (Bazzi et al. 2014, MacMahon & Garlaschelli 2015).

Methodological Issues and Extensions of Modularity Maximization

Despite its widespread use, modularity maximization (and in some cases the enterprise of community detection, more generally) encounters a number of shortcomings that limit its practical applicability. Some of these shortcomings are mainly conceptual and relate to how one interprets the estimated community structure obtained by modularity maximization. In other cases, they represent fundamental limits of the measure itself.

Degenerate partitions. As a network's size and its number of communities increase, the number of partitions that achieve a near-maximal Q grows exponentially, leading to a degeneracy of high-quality partitions (Good et al. 2010). This degeneracy becomes especially problematic if the partitions are dissimilar to one another. In that case it becomes difficult to choose a single ("best") representative partition. In fact, this is an issue shared by quality functions other than Q, some of which will be discussed in later sections. The issue may be addressed by expressing the optimal partition not as a single "best" partition but as a meaningful average across multiple near-optimal partitions, and by treating nodes' community affiliations as fuzzy variables (Bellec et al. 2010, Rubinov & Sporns 2011) or characterizing them by probabilistic clustering (Hinne et al. 2014), rather than as hard assignments. Some practical guidelines for obtaining a consensus partition are discussed below.

Resolution limit and multiresolution modularity. Another methodological issue facing modularity maximization is that, under certain conditions, it may be impossible to detect communities below a certain scale (size), even if those communities are otherwise well defined (e.g., internally maximally dense). This problem is called the resolution limit of modularity (Fortunato & Barthelemy 2007) and arises from a trade-off between the number of communities into which a network is partitioned and the Q value associated with those partitions. At some optimal number of communities, this trade-off achieves a peak corresponding to the partition with the maximum value of Q. The location of this peak, however, is a consequence of how Q is formally defined and may not reflect the network's true community structure. In practical terms, the resolution limit implies that the communities obtained by simply maximizing modularity may contain several smaller and better-defined communities.

To circumvent the resolution limit issue, a number of multiresolution techniques have been proposed (Arenas et al. 2008, Reichardt & Bornholdt 2006). These techniques incorporate resolution parameters into the Q measure that can be tuned to uncover communities of different sizes. In the formulation of Reichardt & Bornholdt (2006), for example, the resolution parameter, γ, scales the importance of the null model:

$$Q(\gamma) = \frac{1}{2m} \sum_{ij} [a_{ij} - \gamma p_{ij}] \delta(\sigma_i, \sigma_j).$$

When $\gamma < 1$, larger communities are resolved, whereas $\gamma > 1$ yields more communities containing fewer nodes. It is important to note, however, that varying γ only makes it possible to detect communities of different sizes; it does not solve the issue of the resolution limit (Lancichinetti & Fortunato 2011). That is, for any value of γ, the resolution limit still exists, and at that level it remains impossible to detect communities of certain sizes.

A number of methods to choose the resolution parameter have been proposed. Many modularity maximization techniques contain a stochastic element, so that their output varies from run to run, as is the case for the method of Blondel et al. (2008) or simulated annealing. This means that in practice these algorithms should be run multiple times, thereby generating an ensemble of high-quality partitions. One suggested method for choosing γ takes advantage of the variability within a partition ensemble, reporting community structure at the value of γ at which partitions are most similar to one another (Bassett et al. 2013). The similarity of two partitions can be computed, for example, as the normalized mutual information, the Jaccard index, or the Rand index. However, because the precise values of these similarity measures are often difficult to interpret, it is good practice to use the z-scores, rather than the raw scores, of these measures (Traud et al. 2011). Alternative approaches for choosing γ include cross-validation using metadata or domain-specific knowledge. For example, Betzel et al. (2013) identified multiscale modules from brain structural networks, reporting the resolution at which the structural modules were most similar to brain functional connectivity. Alternatively, detailed comparison to an appropriately constructed null

---

Resolution limit: a shortcoming of the modularity function that under certain conditions prevents it from detecting small modules

Resolution parameter: a parameter that tunes the size and number of communities obtained from modularity maximization

model can be used to select the γ at which community structure deviates most from what would be expected under the null model (Traag et al. 2014). In general, although many older studies of brain networks have not explicitly considered the resolution limit inherent in Q, it is now increasingly clear that exploring a range of γ values yields a more comprehensive view of a network's modular organization.

Multiresolution, multislice modularity. Brain networks are most often analyzed as single-slice networks, or snapshots, providing a picture of how one single instance of a network is configured. Although this approach may be appropriate in cases in which brain networks reflect static arrangements of nodes and edges (as in many anatomical networks or longtime averages of resting-state functional networks), it fails to capture situations in which the research objective is to compare modularity in networks collected across multiple time points, many individual participants, or different experimental conditions. A number of studies have begun to investigate multislice representations of brain networks (Bassett et al. 2011, 2013, 2015; Cole et al. 2014) in which multiple instances of a single network (a slice) form a multislice stack. If the connectivity in a single-slice network is encoded in the matrix, a_{ij}, the connectivity of a multislice network is given by a_{ijs}, where the additional subscript, s, indexes slices.

Given a series of network slices, it might be interesting to characterize community structure across slices. A naïve way to accomplish this is to maximize the modularity of each slice independently. This comparison, however, requires matching communities across slices, a process that often leads to ambiguities. An alternative approach for finding communities in multislice networks (Mucha et al. 2010) consists of introducing a coupling parameter that links corresponding nodes across slices and then using a quality function that extends $Q(\gamma)$ multislice networks. The new quality function reads

$$Q(\gamma, \omega) = \frac{1}{2\mu} \sum_{ijsr} [(a_{ijs} - \gamma_s p_{ijs}) \delta(\sigma_{is}, \sigma_{js}) + \delta(i, j) \cdot \omega_{jrs}] \delta(\sigma_{is}, \sigma_{jr}).$$

The expression $(a_{ijs} - \gamma_s p_{ijs}) \delta(\sigma_{is}, \sigma_{js})$, with the exception of the slice subscript, s, corresponds to the summand in the single-slice version of multiscale modularity. The additional term, $\delta(i, j) \cdot \omega_{jrs}$, defines the strength of coupling of nodes between slices. The other delta function, $\delta(\sigma_{is}, \sigma_{jr})$, ensures that the $\{i, j, r, s\}$ that fall outside of communities are not counted in the total summation.

One of the advantages of this method is that community labels are consistent across slices. In other words, nodes assigned to some community C, irrespective of the slice in which they appear, all reference the same community, which makes matching communities across slices unnecessary. As with multiscale modularity, there is the issue of how one should choose the parameters $\{\gamma, \omega\}$. The choice is nontrivial and as yet there is no clear method for doing so. Bassett et al. (2013) advocated making detailed comparisons to null models (e.g., coupling node i to $j \neq i$ across slices) and focusing on the $\{\gamma, \omega\}$ pair corresponding to the maximum difference between some measure—e.g., the quality of the partition $Q(\gamma, \omega)$—taken on the real community structure and the same measure taken on the communities obtained from the null model.

Participation coefficient. Once a network has been partitioned into modules, individual network nodes can be classified based on how they are embedded within and between communities. Two measures that have proven fruitful in this endeavor are a node's participation coefficient and the z-score of its within-community degree (Guimera & Amaral 2005). The participation coefficient, p_i, expresses the degree to which a node's connections are distributed across communities. If its value is close to unity, the node's connections fall uniformly across all communities; if its value is close to zero, most of its connections fall within a single community. The z-score of a node's

Multislice network: a representation of a network as a series of slices, in which each slice represents a separate observation of the network

Participation coefficient: a measure that quantifies how evenly or unevenly a node's connections are distributed across a set of modules

within-community degree, z_i, expresses the number of connections a node makes to other nodes in the same community in terms of standard deviations above or below the mean. Positive z-scores indicate that a node is highly connected to other members of the same community; negative z-scores indicate the opposite.

Random walk:
a traversal over a
network where each
step from one node to
another is randomly
chosen

Guimera & Amaral (2005) suggested that nodes' functional roles could be gleaned from the combination of p_i and z_i. The first distinction is between nodes that serve as hubs and those that are considered part of the network's periphery (nonhubs). Intuitively, hub nodes make disproportionately more connections to nodes within their own module compared to peripheral nodes, and therefore correspond to nodes with the highest z_i. Hub nodes can be further classified according to the magnitude of their participation coefficient. As the value of p_i increases from zero to unity, a node's connections are distributed more uniformly across modules. The smallest participation coefficients identify provincial hubs whose connections are largely restricted to their own module. At the opposite extreme are kinless hubs, with connections in virtually all modules. Intermediate participation coefficients highlight connector hubs, whose links fall between a few different modules.

An appealing aspect of assigning roles to nodes based on module partitions is that this approach can be applied to both structural and functional networks, and it can reveal which nodes are especially important for maintaining intermodule communication. Alternative ways to express the relations of nodes across multiple modules include the measurement of regional connection diversity (analogous to the entropy of the node's module-by-module connection strengths), which can also be adapted for use with signed networks (Rubinov & Sporns 2011).

Alternatives to Modularity Maximization

Though modularity maximization is the most common method for identifying a network's communities, there are a multitude of alternative techniques. These alternatives present attractive opportunities for network neuroscience; however, only a subset has so far been applied to brain data. Here we review some of them.

Distance-based modules. One of the simplest methods for detecting modules in complex networks is to extend distance-based clustering techniques to be compatible with network data (Hastie et al. 2009). This method assumes that network nodes can be embedded in a high-dimensional space and that modules correspond to clusters near one another in that space. How distance in that space is measured is flexible, though one common choice is to set the distance of node i to j equal to $d_{ij} = 1 - J_{ij}$, where $J_{ij} = \frac{|a_i \cap a_j|}{|a_i \cup a_j|}$ is the Jaccard index and a_i is the connectivity profile of node i (i.e., the set of all other nodes it is connected to). In this case, the greater the overlap in nodes' connectivity profiles, the closer they will be to one another. Given the complete set of pairwise distance relationships, modules can then be recovered using standard distance-based algorithms such as k-means or hierarchical agglomerative clustering. Although this process is simple, and deterministic in the case of hierarchical clustering, its definition of a community as a spatial cluster diverges from the intuition (inherent in modularity maximization) of communities as defined by internally dense connectivity.

Infomap. Another interesting class of community detection methods is grounded in information theory (Aldecoa & Marin 2011, Ronhovde & Nussinov 2009). The most commonly used is the Infomap algorithm (Rosvall & Bergstrom 2008), which casts community detection in terms of the path that a random walker traces as it hops from node to node, using connections as pathways to traverse the network. A random walk on a network defines a Markov chain whose states correspond to the network's nodes, where the transition probability from node i to j is given by $\pi_{i \to j} = \frac{a_{ij}}{k_i}$. If a random walker makes L steps, the sequence of nodes it visits is given as $X = \{x_1, \ldots, x_L\}$, where $x_t \in \{1, \ldots, N\}$ is the node the walker visits at step t of the walk.

The aim of Infomap is to describe an infinite-length walk as succinctly as possible. A naïve approach would be to assign each node a name, with the shortest names reserved for the nodes that are visited most frequently. This strategy is usually suboptimal: Because each node needs a unique name to unambiguously describe the walk, the description tends to be long. The random walk can be described more succinctly by taking into account regularities in the process that generated X. Networks with communities, for example, introduce biases in random walks. If a walker starts in a community, it will likely dwell inside that community for many steps due to the preponderance of within-community connections. A more efficient description of the random walk takes this bias into account by using two separate lists of names: One list assigns communities unique names, whereas the other list is a reusable set of names reserved for nodes within communities. Using these lists along with an indicator that tells when the walker is entering a new community, one can describe the random walk much more efficiently (Rosvall et al. 2009). This intuition forms the basis of the Infomap algorithm. The same way modularity maximization uses Q to score the quality of a partition, Infomap scores partitions by their description length; the optimal partition is the one that can compress the description of a random walk by the greatest amount.

Block model: model-based community detection method whose parameters are selected to maximize the likelihood that the model generated an observed network

Block models. Community detection can also be recast as a statistical inference problem by fitting what are known as block models to network data (Carrington et al. 2005, Hastings 2006). A block model is an example of a network generative model, which makes assumptions about the process underlying a network's formation and estimates the likelihood that this process generated the network. In the simplest case, block models assume that all connections are made independent of one another, and that the probability of a connection forming between nodes i and j depends only on the communities σ_i and σ_j to which those nodes are assigned. Usually these community assignments and the intercommunity connection probabilities θ_{rs}, where r and s are different communities, are unknown and treated as free parameters. The aim of block modeling, then, is to reverse engineer the generative model by estimating those parameters for which the likelihood that the resulting block model generated a given network is maximized.

It may seem that the added complication of having to estimate θ in addition to nodes' community assignments (not to mention the fact that the number of communities usually has to be specified ahead of time) makes block modeling unattractive. However, block modeling actually offers more flexibility than other community detection methods, because it can identify more diverse architectures than the standard community definition of internally dense and externally sparse groupings of nodes. These architectures include core-periphery and bipartite organizations. As an example, consider the following intercommunity connection probability matrix:

$$\theta = \begin{bmatrix} 0.8 & 0.2 \\ 0.2 & 0.8 \end{bmatrix}.$$

If we generated synthetic networks using this matrix as a template, we would expect that virtually any community detection method would be able to resolve the two communities, given that the two communities are clearly defined through their internally dense connections.

Contrast this with another example of a network with a dense core and sparse periphery:

$$\theta = \begin{bmatrix} 0.8 & 0.2 \\ 0.2 & 0.1 \end{bmatrix}.$$

In this case, the first group is still community-like, but nodes in the second group are more likely to make connections to nodes in the first group than to nodes in their own group. Approaches such as modularity maximization or Infomap, if applied to synthetic networks generated using this set of parameters, would fail to deliver anything resembling the matrix θ. A block model, instead, easily detects this type of organization. In general, block models can be used to detect more varied types of communities than most other methods because the definition of communities is not prespecified, but rather inferred from the network data and encoded in the elements of θ.

Overlapping communities. All the community detection methods that have been reviewed to this point partition networks into nonoverlapping communities. An alternative set of methods returns overlapping communities, so that nodes can be affiliated with more than one subnetwork simultaneously. Clique percolation is one of the earliest methods for identifying overlapping communities (Palla et al. 2005). This method is based on the intuition that communities tend to be comprised of cliques, that is, fully connected subgraphs. To identify communities, all cliques of a fixed size k must first be enumerated, and a clique adjacency matrix is constructed. Two cliques are considered adjacent if they share $k - 1$ nodes. Communities correspond to the connected components of the clique adjacency matrix. Because nodes can participate in multiple cliques, mapping the communities from the clique level back to the node level may result in nodes being assigned to multiple communities.

Another set of methods for detecting overlapping communities involves transforming a network into its corresponding line graph. Nodes in a line graph represent connections in the original network. Line graph nodes are connected to one another if the corresponding connections share a node in the original network. For example, if $\{b, i\}$ and $\{i, j\}$ are edges in some network, they would be linked in that network's line graph because they are both incident on node i, whereas $\{b, i\}$ and $\{j, k\}$ would not. There exist several similar approaches for using a network's line graph to obtain overlapping communities. The simplest approach is the one advocated by Evans & Lambiotte (2009), which assigns weights to the connections via a normalization step and then applies nonoverlapping community detection methods (e.g., modularity maximization) to the resulting line graph's connectivity matrix. When the resulting edge communities are mapped back to nodes, nodes may have multiple community affiliations.

A second approach for clustering a network's line graph, proposed by Ahn et al. (2010), weights line graph connections according to their similarity (Jaccard index). Line graph nodes are aggregated into communities using agglomerative hierarchical clustering, and the hierarchical tree is cut at a level that maximizes the partition density quality function, which is the average density of connections within communities, weighted by the size of each community. Interestingly, partition density does not suffer from a resolution limit.

Independent component analysis. In the neuroimaging literature, an important technique for uncovering communities from functional data is independent component analysis (ICA) (Beckmann & Smith 2005, McIntosh & Mišić 2013). ICA assumes that voxels' time series are linear combinations of a smaller set of archetypical time series. Unlike the similar technique of principal component analysis, in which the archetypes are both spatially and temporally independent, ICA yields archetypes that are maximally independent in one or the other domain. If one specifies spatial independence, the result is a loading of voxels onto minimally overlapping spatial archetypical patterns, which can be interpreted as communities. Interestingly, the patterns obtained from clustering or performing community detection on functional magnetic resonance imaging (fMRI) functional connectivity networks are often quite similar to those obtained with ICA (Bellec et al. 2010, Power et al. 2011, Yeo et al. 2011). In contrast to network-based approaches to modularity,

ICA requires the user to select a desired number of components (i.e., a model order) and provides no information about how these components are related (e.g., through between-module connections).

Practical Issues in Module Detection

To this point we have discussed a number of popular community detection methods, emphasizing those that have been applied to brain data. In doing so, we necessarily omitted many methods that may yet prove useful in network neuroscience, including several based on random walks (Delvenne et al. 2010, Pons & Latapy 2005), belief propagation (Zhang & Moore 2014), and phase synchronization (Boccaletti et al. 2007). This section is concerned with practical issues related to community detection (see example in **Figure 2**), specifically the choice of method for module detection, and with the significance and robustness of module partitions.

Choice of method. The choice of method for detecting communities first depends on how network communities are conceptualized. Are communities taken to be groups of tightly connected nodes? Do they represent groups with similar connectivity profiles? Can nodes belong to more than one community? Another factor influencing the choice of method is the nature of the neurobiological data and the empirical question that is being explored. For example, signed correlation matrices derived from functional connectivity may require approaches that can deal with signed connections (unless only positive connections are deemed of interest). Similarly, a research question dealing with the time evolution of networks strongly suggests multislice approaches. These conceptual data- and research-driven considerations motivate the use of certain methods while excluding others and should be carefully examined before beginning community detection.

An important factor for choosing a method is how well community detection algorithms perform in identifying planted communities in synthetic benchmark networks. A benchmark network usually contains multiple clusters of nodes that can be made more or less community-like by tuning a parameter that controls the ratio of within-cluster to between-cluster connections. The best benchmark networks also incorporate as many properties of real-world networks as possible, for example, heterogeneous degree distributions and communities of different sizes (Lancichinetti et al. 2008). Several recent studies have undertaken the task of benchmarking community detection methods, including many of those surveyed here (Danon et al. 2005, Lancichinetti et al. 2009). Interestingly, these studies report a stratification of community detection methods, with some clearly outperforming others in terms of both computational complexity and the ability to successfully identify communities in benchmark networks. The more recent study (Lancichinetti et al. 2009) found that Infomap, a modularity maximization algorithm (Blondel et al. 2008) and a multiresolution algorithm that maximizes a quality function similar to Q (Rondhove & Nussinov 2009), performed the best across all test cases. (The algorithm by Blondel et al. returns a hierarchy of communities; the lowest level of hierarchy—i.e., the smallest communities—was used to benchmark the algorithm.) It should be noted that the benchmark networks used in these tests lacked some important features typically found in real-world networks (e.g., hierarchical communities).

Consensus communities. Given that different methods have sometimes complementary strengths or weaknesses, it may be advantageous to combine the outputs of multiple methods (or multiple runs of a single method to address degeneracy of module partitions) to obtain average or consensus communities. One approach for doing so is to generate and iteratively cluster a network's association matrix through a process called consensus clustering. Given an ensemble of partitions acquired from several community detection methods (or multiple runs), the association

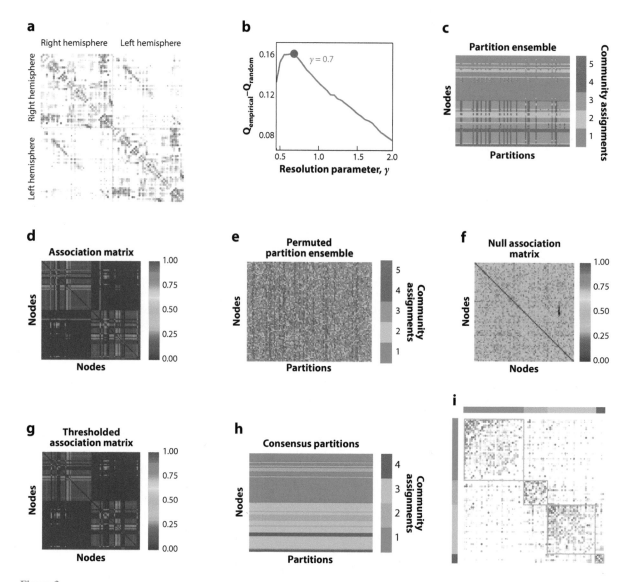

Figure 2

Illustration of multiscale modularity maximization for a structural (diffusion spectrum imaging) brain network (*a*). The size and brightness of connections indicate the number of subjects for which a connection is present and the log-transformed weight of that connection, respectively. For this network and for 20 random networks (rewired to preserve degree sequence), we maximized modularity using the Louvain algorithm (Blondel et al. 2008) and varied the resolution parameter from $\gamma \in [0.5, 2.0]$ in increments of 0.05. As a function of γ, we obtained the mean modularity for the empirical and randomized networks, $Q_{empirical}$ and Q_{random}. To report community structure, we chose the scale of γ at which the quality of empirical partitions exceeded that of random partitions by the greatest amount (*b*). At this scale ($\gamma = 0.7$) we further examined 100 partitions of the empirical network (*c*), which revealed that nodes' community assignments were inconsistent. To resolve this variability, we performed consensus clustering, following Bassett et al. (2013) and Lancichinetti & Fortunato (2012). We constructed the association matrix (*d*) counting the number of times that node pairs were assigned to the same community. We generated many realizations of null partition ensembles by randomly permuting the columns of the partition ensemble matrix (*e*) and constructed null association matrices (*f*). We thresholded the empirical association matrix (*g*), retaining only elements greater than the maximum value of any null association matrix. We then reclustered the thresholded matrix to obtain consensus communities (*h*). Finally, we visualized community structure by reordering the connectivity matrix so that nodes in the same community would be next to one another (*i*).

matrix is an $n \times n$ matrix whose element t_{ij} counts the number of times that nodes i and j are assigned to the same community across the full ensemble. To obtain consensus communities, one can simply recluster the consensus matrix using the same community detection algorithms that generated the original ensemble of partitions. To amplify the contribution of node pairs that are consistently assigned to the same community while silencing those that are not, researchers often impose a threshold on the consensus matrix prior to reclustering, setting any elements $t_{ij} < \tau$ equal to zero. Lancichinetti & Fortunato (2012) advocated exploring a range of thresholds, because smaller or larger values of τ may produce correspondingly larger or smaller consensus communities. Alternatively, one can choose τ in a data-driven way by comparison with a postoptimization null model. Bassett et al. (2013) suggested setting the threshold equal to the maximum value of a randomized association matrix, t_{ij}^{r}, constructed by permuting the node order of each partition in the ensemble and generating an association matrix from the randomized partitions. In any case, the partitions obtained after reclustering the thresholded consensus matrix are usually more similar to one another than are the partitions used as input, and they often converge into a single consensus partition. Another approach that does not require thresholding involves finding the partition that maximizes the modularity $Q = \sum_{ij} [t_{ij} - t_{ij}^{r}] \delta(\sigma_i, \sigma_j)$, where t_{ij}^{r} is the mean association weight across an ensemble of randomized association matrices. As an alternative to consensus clustering, one can also calculate, for every partition in an ensemble, its mean similarity with respect to all other partitions and choose as the consensus partition the one with greatest average similarity (Doron et al. 2012).

Statistical significance and robustness. Once a network's community structure has been estimated, there remain some challenging technical and theoretical questions. For instance, how "good" do the communities have to be before we can confidently say that a system is modular? It is important to remember that most module detection methods will converge on module partitions even for random networks.

There are multiple ways of addressing this question. One approach consists of comparing the quality of the community structure estimated from the empirical network with the same measure made on an ensemble of totally random networks (e.g., preserving the degree sequence of the original network, but otherwise randomizing the placement of connections). For example, comparison of the estimate Q for the empirical network to $\langle Q_{\text{random}} \rangle$ and $\langle Q_{\text{random}}^{2} \rangle - Q_{\text{random}}^{2}$ obtained from an ensemble of random networks can yield a z-score, $Q_z = \frac{Q - \langle Q_{\text{random}} \rangle}{\sqrt{\langle Q_{\text{random}}^{2} \rangle - Q_{\text{random}}^{2}}}$. There are some issues with this approach, as certain classes of networks can be more modular than chance without possessing any true community structure (e.g., lattice networks), whereas there are networks with a clear community structure but whose overall Q is not statistically different than chance (Karrer et al. 2008). Nonetheless, Q_z can provide some general indication as to whether a system is, indeed, modular.

Another approach, known as robustness testing, entails adding a small amount of noise to the community detection process to induce change in a network's community structure (Gfeller et al. 2005, Karrer et al. 2008, Wu & Huberman 2004). Intuitively, the estimates of community structure for networks with well-defined communities will be similar both pre- and postperturbation, whereas networks with ill-defined or brittle communities are more likely to experience larger changes in their estimated community structure or in the quality of communities following the perturbation. The perturbations can be subtle—e.g., rewiring a small fraction of connections, adding noise to the network's edge weights, shuffling edge weights, changing by a small amount the scale of a resolution parameter, or using an altogether different quality function. This approach has a number of downsides. For instance, it requires that the community detection process be repeated multiple times for each perturbation tested, which may be time consuming. It also introduces several free parameters, such as the number of edges to be rewired, the nature of the noise added to the edge weights, or the amount of variation in the resolution parameter. Despite these issues, robustness testing represents a powerful method for teasing apart the aspects of a network's community structure that are fragile in the presence of noise.

The approaches described above entail comparing estimates of a network's community structure to estimates made on a null (or noisy) model in an effort to determine whether those communities are statistically significant or robust to perturbations. Another set of methods attempts to detect ab initio only the most statistically significant communities. One such method is OSLOM (Order Statistics Local Optimization Method) (Lancichinetti et al. 2011), which scores communities based on how likely it is to find a community with similar properties in a random network with no community structure (Lancichinetti et al. 2010). OSLOM identifies significant communities using a growing-pruning model in which a community's statistical significance is assessed after both adding new nodes and pruning existing ones. Because communities are detected using only local information, this method does not suffer from a resolution limit, and it also allows for communities to overlap. OSLOM is also unique in that it can detect no communities in the event that no possible grouping results in a statistically significant community. This is the outcome one would expect if OSLOM were given a totally random network as its input. OSLOM also makes another unique contribution, in that it detects communities using only the local properties of a network. Other approaches, like modularity maximization, pursue global optimization strategies; this entails that, if new nodes were added to a given network, the overall community structure would likely change, whereas with OSLOM this is typically not the case.

EVIDENCE FOR MODULES IN BRAIN NETWORKS

The focus of the previous section was on the methods and technical challenges associated with detecting communities in complex networks. We now turn to a brief review of the empirical evidence for modularity in brain networks.

Brain Networks in Model Organisms

Significant evidence for modularity in neural systems comes from the anatomical neural networks of model organisms such as the nematode *Caenorhabditis elegans* and various mammalian species. Brain networks of model organisms are generally mapped using various techniques, including reconstruction from serially sectioned electron micrographs (White et al. 1986) or the aggregation of data from anatomical tract-tracing experiments (Kötter et al. 2004, Markov et al. 2014, Oh et al. 2014, Scannell et al. 1995, Stephan et al. 2001).

The neuronal network of *C. elegans* contains more than 300 neurons and several thousand electrical and chemical synapses. Since its reconstruction in the early 1980s (White et al. 1986), this network has been the subject of many graph-theoretical analyses (Varshney et al. 2011), including several that have attempted to elucidate its division into communities. These studies have employed a wide range of methods for uncovering *C. elegans*' community structure, including modularity maximization (Bassett et al. 2010, Sohn et al. 2011, Towlson et al. 2013), simulated annealing (Sohn et al. 2011), divisive algorithms (Towlson et al. 2013), and spectral decomposition (Jarrell et al. 2012, Pan et al. 2010, Sohn et al. 2011) as well as stochastic block models (Pavlovic et al. 2014), Infomap, and link-clustering (Jarrell et al. 2012). Despite the varied approaches to community detection, the results of these analyses largely converge in that the resulting communities resemble, at some level, the functional organization of the *C. elegans'* nervous system. For example, Jarrell et al. (2012) analyzed the subnetwork of neural circuitry and musculature involved in mating. Among the communities uncovered in this analysis were groups of sensory neurons and interneurons for detecting the mate's vulva and initiating a motor response, along with another group of mostly motor neurons associated with locomotion. Analyses of the complete *C. elegans* network have reported similar results, with communities revealing known functional groups (Pan et al. 2010, Sohn et al. 2011) or novel network properties, such as cores (Pavlovic et al. 2014), the roles of hub nodes (Towlson et al. 2013), and the hierarchical organization of communities nested within communities (Bassett et al. 2010, Sohn et al. 2011).

Similarly, meta-analytic cortical networks for both the cat and the macaque (Felleman & van Essen 1991, Scannell et al. 1995) have been described as modular by Hilgetag et al. (2000). These early analyses predated the Q quality function, so the authors developed their own module detection approach called optimal set analysis (OSA). When applied to the cat cortical network, OSA returned four prominent clusters corresponding to visual, auditory, frontolimbic, and somatosensory areas. Corresponding clusters were detected in the macaque cortex, with the visual cluster subdivided into dorsal and ventral streams. Using the cat data set, Zamora-Lopez et al. (2010) discovered that a small number of hub regions extend connections across community boundaries to other hub regions, forming a higher-level community situated on top of the four communities detected by Hilgetag et al. (2000). Confirming these earlier findings, de Reus & van den Heuvel (2013) have described specific patterns of directed connections that interlink hubs and network communities in cat cortex.

More recently, using a different macaque data set, researchers have detected a slightly different set of communities using modularity maximization and taking the partition with the highest Q (Harriger et al. 2012, Modha & Singh, 2010). These communities were largely the same as in Hilgetag et al. (2000), though the frontolimbic community was now fractured into two communities. Using yet another (incomplete) macaque data set, Goulas et al. (2015) maximized Q (again treating the partition with the highest Q as the optimal partition), which returned five communities, corresponding roughly to parieto-motor, occipito-temporal, temporal, frontal, and somato-motor communities. Anatomical modules that map onto functionally related network nodes have also been identified in the *Drosophila* (Shi et al. 2015), mouse (Wang et al. 2012), and rat (Bota et al. 2015) brain. In general these studies, together with community analyses of the cellular network of *C. elegans*, support the notion that brain networks are organized into communities whose boundaries largely agree with known functional subdivisions.

Despite their generally converging results, these efforts also have shortcomings. Nearly all of these references optimized single-scale modularity to uncover communities, reporting only the partition corresponding to the observed maximum Q. Given the resolution limit associated with Q and the near-degeneracy of solutions, future studies would benefit from performing detailed comparisons against null models, expressing communities not as hard assignments but as fuzzy assignments over an ensemble of partitions, or testing the robustness of the observed communities to network perturbations.

It is interesting to note that most of the studies discussed here report communities whose members (neurons or brain regions) are spatially contiguous. In other words, nodes assigned to communities are not only densely connected, but also spatially proximal to one another. On the one hand, spatial contiguity is consistent with the hypothesis that neural systems attempt to reduce total metabolic and material cost by preferentially forming short-range connections, a well-documented aspect of the *C. elegans* nervous system (Chen et al. 2006, Cherniak et al. 2004, Nicosia et al. 2013). Indeed, the spatial compactness of anatomical communities may reflect an evolutionary drive to place functionally related neural elements near one another, thereby reducing the total cost of wiring. On the other hand, a system that strictly minimizes wiring cost will tend to form a geometric lattice, which can give the impression of comprising communities because it possesses a greater Q score than chance, although in fact it has no true community structure (Henderson & Robinson 2013, Samu et al. 2014). If this is the case, then observed communities may be a reflection of spatial clustering and not functional relatedness of neurons.

Thus, a network's spatial embedding can confound the interpretation of its communities. In effect, it introduces ambiguity about the process under which the communities were generated: Does the density of internal connections reflect spatial or functional relationships? If one is using modularity maximization for community detection, this issue can in part be addressed by modifying the connectivity null mode, p_{ij}, so that the expected density of connections depends on distance (Expert et al. 2011). Maximizing such a quality function returns communities whose internal density of connections exceeds what is expected given not only the nodes' degrees but also the internode distances within those communities.

So far, the majority of network studies in animal models have focused on anatomical connectivity. The availability of large-scale cellular-resolution recording methods will soon provide data sets that are amenable to the detection of functional modules in dynamic brain activity. For example, clusters of highly correlated brain regions can be derived from optical recordings of neural activity (Ahrens et al. 2013) or from spike time series on multielectrode arrays (Shimono & Beggs 2015). In general, network-based module detection methods are important tools for dimension reduction and compact descriptions of functional neuronal assemblies in animal recordings.

Human Brain Networks

Unlike the anatomical networks discussed in the previous section, networks of the human brain are estimated noninvasively, usually using MRI technology. The indirect manner in which these data are acquired raises questions about the sensitivity and reliability with which human brain networks can be mapped, issues that are extensively covered in the extant neuroimaging literature. Nonetheless, the fact that neuroimaging can be performed in vivo on cognitively engaged individuals makes these methods indispensable for investigating how human brain networks relate to brain function and behavior. Here we briefly review what has been learned to date about the modular organization of the human brain. We will leave aside an extremely active research area focusing on disturbances of modular organization in the context of clinical disorders (Alexander-Bloch et al. 2012, Fornito et al. 2015), because even a cursory overview of this topic is far beyond the scope of the present article.

Anatomical networks. Despite considerable methodological differences, human brain networks share many of the same properties with those of model organisms, including community structure. The study by Hagmann et al. (2008), one of the first to note this, used spectral decomposition to maximize Q, which yielded six spatially contiguous communities: two positioned medially over the posterior cingulate cortex and precuneus and two pairs of bilaterally symmetric communities centered on the frontal and temporoparietal cortex. Highly connected brain regions situated along the midline formed links to multiple communities and served as connector hubs, whereas regions within the more lateral communities maintained most of their connections within their own community, thus forming provincial hubs. These results were expanded upon in recent work showing that hub regions, in particular those that are densely interconnected as part of the human brain's anatomical rich club, are located at the interface of many functional resting state networks and may play an important role in regulating information flow (van den Heuvel & Sporns 2011,

Wiring cost: the material and metabolic expenditure associated with supporting an organism's neural wiring

2013). As in analyses of modules in model organisms, findings from human studies again indicate a close correspondence of membership in structural modules with functional relations expressed across different domains of behavior and cognition.

As noted above, Q suffers from a resolution limit, the effects of which can be partially mitigated by exploring the range of communities encountered upon varying a resolution parameter. Two recent papers examined the multiscale organization of human anatomical networks by varying the resolution parameter in the multiscale modularity generalization (Lohse et al. 2014) and by recasting community detection in terms of a random walker moving over the network at different timescales (Betzel et al. 2013). Both studies reveal interesting community-level organization at multiple scales. Lohse et al. (2014) found that community radius, a measure of the spatial compactness of communities, increased the community size, a relationship that would be absent in a network with inefficient spatial embedding. Furthermore, they demonstrated that the way specific variables fluctuated as a function of the resolution parameter was useful for identifying whether a subject was diagnosed with schizophrenia or was part of a control population. Betzel et al. (2013) detected communities by maximizing the partition stability quality function (Delvenne et al. 2010) and looked for the resolution parameter for which the relationship between the structural communities was most predictive of brain functional connectivity. Interestingly, the scale at which this relationship peaked was far from the default scale, further motivating the exploration of multiscale community structure.

Functional networks. Community detection can be readily applied to brain functional networks, though some care must be taken in matching the community detection method to the method used for estimating functional connections. For example, if a functional network is estimated using full (Pearson) or partial correlation as the measure of connectivity, then there may be many connections with negative weights. Very few community detection methods, other than the signed variant of Q, are capable of dealing with negative edge weights. Although most studies remove negative correlations (by thresholding) from the analysis, it should be noted that this step may inadvertently discard neurobiologically relevant information. Alternative non-negative measures of functional connectivity like coherence or mutual information allow the use of any community detection method that can handle weighted connections.

Numerous studies have shown that the brain is organized into clusters or modules of functionally interconnected regions (Meunier et al. 2009b) with reproducible boundaries and that resolve subject-specific aspects of the brain's intrinsic functional organization (Laumann et al. 2015). One of the best examples of community structure in brain functional networks (Power et al. 2011) extracted communities from resting-state fMRI data and, using a map of task-based activations, mapped these communities to cognitive/behavioral function. An outstanding feature of this study is its use of multiple methods for detecting communities (Infomap and modularity maximization). Comparison of these methods showed significant agreement but also small differences in partitions obtained using Infomap versus those obtained using modularity maximization. Analysis of the relation between network communities and cognitive/behavioral function revealed some interesting features of communities obtained from functional brain networks that were not usually present in structural brain networks. In functional networks, connections correspond to statistical relationships between brain regions rather than physical linkages, and therefore carry no direct metabolic or material cost. Thus, there is no obvious penalty to forming strong long-distance functional connections. Accordingly, many of the communities observed in brain functional networks are spatially distributed. For example, Power et al. (2011) identify large communities corresponding to the default mode network and to the frontoparietal control, dorsal attention, and ventral attention networks, each of which are made up of multiple spatially remote components.

FUNCTIONAL MODULES ACROSS THE HUMAN LIFESPAN

Modules in functional brain networks are thought to represent groups of brain regions that are collectively involved in one or more cognitive domains. A number of recent studies have presented evidence suggesting that the brain becomes increasingly less modular (i.e., less segregated) with age. Meunier et al. (2009a) compared groups of younger and older adults, using single-scale modularity maximization to discover modules for both groups. The older group formed fewer modules containing groups of brain regions that, in the younger group, had formed distinct modules. Corroborating these results, Geerligs et al. (2015) compared populations of young and old participants, reporting a decrease in modularity, Q, driven by decreased internal connectivity within control, default mode, and somatomotor modules along with increased intermodule connections. Two recent studies have tracked the modularity of functional brain networks continuously with age. Chan et al. (2014) used communities defined in an earlier study (Power et al. 2011) and reported an overall decrease in segregation with age, an effect driven by both association and sensorimotor systems. Concurrently, and using a different definition of communities (Yeo et al. 2011), Betzel et al. (2014) reported decreased modularity with age in modules associated with cognitive control and attention.

Another study, rather than directly measuring functional connectivity, relied on a meta-analytic approach for building brain coactivation maps (Crossley et al. 2013). In this case, the authors used the thousands of images detailing the foci of task-based brain activations available in the database BrainMap (Laird et al. 2005), along with the conditions under which those activations were reported. Regions that became active under similar task conditions across a range of tasks were considered adjacent to one another in a coactivation network. This network is different from most functional networks in that the connections represent coactivation rather than correlations among time courses, and in that the data are derived from task-evoked rather than resting brain activity. Modularity maximization yielded four communities corresponding to four behavioral domains: emotion, perception, action, and mixed. A parallel analysis carried out on a resting-state functional connectivity network revealed similar communities, confirming earlier work on the similarity of task-evoked and resting brain networks (Smith et al. 2009).

These studies demonstrate that module detection is important for mapping the basic functional organization of resting and task-evoked connectivity. Going beyond these relatively static descriptions of functional brain modules, modularity can also reveal characteristic changes in functional networks in the course of changes in an individual's cognitive state (Andric & Hasson 2015, Godwin et al. 2015) or with aging (see sidebar Functional Modules Across the Human Lifespan). Such changes in network architecture have also been documented over the course of a motor learning paradigm (Bassett et al. 2011, 2013). In the first of these studies (Bassett et al. 2011), subjects were asked to respond to particular visual stimuli with a specific motor action. The researchers repeated this analysis three times over the course of three days. Subjects were also scanned during the task, which allowed the authors to extract hemodynamic time courses from different brain regions and to construct functional brain networks. Each scan session was divided into a series of nonoverlapping blocks, and for each block a functional brain network was constructed. Rather than estimating community structure for each block independently, the authors made use of the multiscale, multislice variant of Q, which allowed them to track the affiliation of brain regions to specific modules over the course of time. Using a novel measure called flexibility, which counts the number of times that a node changes its module affiliation from one slice to the next, the authors discovered that with practice, flexibility varied. From the first experimental session to the second, flexibility increased on average, whereas the opposite was true moving from the second to the third session. Interestingly, flexibility was also predictive of the overall learning rate. In general, subjects whose community structures were more flexible over time (brain regions moved between modules) learned at a greater rate than those whose flexibility was low (brain region community assignments were relatively static across time).

In a second study (Bassett et al. 2013) using a similar learning paradigm, the authors investigated which brain regions were flexible and which were not. What they found was a relatively inflexible set of core regions, comprised mostly of visual and sensorimotor areas, which formed cohesive modules that were relatively fixed over time. Higher-order association areas tended to be more promiscuous, in the sense that they changed their module allegiance more often. These observations support the notion that the brain exhibits a kind of core-periphery organization. Importantly, static estimates of community structure are incapable of revealing this type of organization, which can only be revealed by examining the time evolution of communities.

Evolvability: the capacity of a system to generate useful variation that promotes adaptive evolution through natural selection

FUNCTIONAL ROLES OF MODULES

Modularity is a general hallmark of complex biological systems. Potential functional roles of modules have been considered across multiple different biological domains, from evolution and development to metabolism and information processing. Here we outline potential roles for modular brain networks in promoting evolvability, conserving wiring cost, and in creating specialized information and complex dynamics.

Evolution and Development

An important idea in evolutionary theory is that modularity in the organization of biological systems confers significant advantages in an evolutionary setting, by supporting adaptability and robustness and thus increasing the system's evolvability (Kirschner & Gerhart 1998). From an evolutionary perspective, uniformly strong interdependence of biological processes may be undesirable, because changes to single components would tend to have widespread (and generally maladaptive) consequences. Keeping the system largely compartmentalized would limit the interdependence of processes that are part of different modules and thus promote greater resilience in the context of continuous genetic and developmental changes. Modularity has also been demonstrated to promote adaptation and increase flexibility in response to a changing environment (Kashtan & Alon 2005, Kashtan et al. 2007). In the face of unpredictable endogenous or exogenous changes, swapping or rearranging maladaptive modules is less costly than redesigning the entire system. In a similar vein, Ellefsen et al. (2015) demonstrated that modular brain networks can help prevent catastrophic forgetting, that is, the loss of a previously learned skill upon learning a new one.

A second benefit of modular organization is increased robustness in response to sudden perturbations. In modular system architectures, the effects of local perturbations remain largely confined to the module within which they originate (and this is used for detecting modules with methods like Infomap). In a sense, modules allow a system to buffer the effects of randomly introduced fluctuations. These fluctuations may be internally generated (e.g., stochastic noise in neural activity) or externally triggered (e.g., as a result of environmental stimulation). In genetics, such external fluctuations could relate to the effects of cryptic genetic variation, which uncovers novel phenotypes under conditions of environmental change (Gibson & Dworkin 2004), thus potentially promoting increased robustness. Taken together, there are many reasons to view modularity as essential for the generation of stable heritable variation and for the emergence of new solutions to unanticipated changes in the environment.

Hierarchical modularity: organization of a module into submodules, of submodules into sub-submodules, and so on

Criticality: state situated between complete randomness and order, a hallmark of which is the absence of a characteristic scale of description

Conservation of Wiring Cost

The evolutionary and developmental benefits of modular organization beg the question of how or why modularity itself evolved. Clune et al. (2013) have argued that the adaptive advantages of modularity, for example, in yielding a more flexible system design, may not be sufficiently strong or direct to explain the modularity currently observed in biological organisms. Instead, they argue that modularity has evolved as a by-product of strong selection pressure on reducing the cost of connections in networks. Indeed, the notion that wiring cost is a major constraint on the layout of (structural) brain networks has a long history in neuroscience. Wiring cost has many dimensions, from the physical volume occupied by the wiring, to the processing cost imposed by conduction delays, to the metabolic cost of supporting neuronal processes and synapses (Bullmore & Sporns 2012). Modular architectures can help conserve wiring cost if modules are spatially compact, as indeed appears to be the case for modules in most, if not all, structural brain networks. The role of cost conservation in generating modular brain architectures has also been demonstrated in an analysis of the anatomical networks of *C. elegans* and the macaque cerebral cortex (Chen et al. 2013). In addition to the spatial layout of nodes, specific functional constraints, for example, on the network's processing efficiency, were found to be important as well, supporting the idea that brain network topology is shaped by a trade-off between spatial and functional factors (Bullmore & Sporns 2012).

Information and Complex Dynamics

Another driving force for the emergence of modular organization in brain networks may be related to neural processing that is specialized and unfolds on multiple timescales. In molecular regulatory pathways, modularity has been shown to promote specialization (Espinosa-Soto & Wagner 2010), and it has been suggested that the persistence of modular organization cross-linked by long-distance weak ties is crucial for preserving functional specialization in brain networks (Gallos et al. 2012). Modular organization of brain networks shapes how information is distributed and processed: Regions that are functionally close and tend to share information are members of the same cluster or module. Modular networks allow for richer patterns of distribution of information than systems that are nonmodular. In a computational modeling study, Yamaguti & Tsuda (2015) have shown that evolutionary algorithms that aim to maximize bidirectional information transmission between neuronal populations favor the emergence of modular structures.

Modularity has a major role in constraining the dynamics of neural activity as well. For example, modular networks give rise to more complex dynamics than random networks (Sporns et al. 2000), and they promote metastability (Wildie & Shanahan 2012) and synchronizability (Arenas et al. 2006) as well as the separation of timescales (Pan & Sinha 2009). These effects are particularly evident in networks that exhibit hierarchical modularity, i.e., are characterized by the existence of modules-within-modules across multiple spatial scales (Kaiser et al. 2010). Network models suggest that hierarchical modularity is an important structural ingredient for enabling the dynamic regime of criticality (Rubinov et al. 2011), which is characterized by spontaneous and persistent fluctuations, long transients following perturbations, and high information transfer. The importance of modular brain networks for shaping brain dynamics is a strong motivation for ongoing empirical work examining changes in modularity associated with disturbances of brain function in clinical disorders (Fornito et al. 2015).

CONCLUSION

In this article, we provided an overview of methods for detecting modules in brain network data as well as a brief survey of studies that have examined modules in the structural and functional connectivity of animal and human brains and have illuminated their many potential functional roles. Module detection requires appropriate use of network and statistical tools and should avoid known confusions and biases, while including an assessment of the statistical significance and robustness of network partitions. Despite great heterogeneity in methods and statistical practices, virtually all studies across all species support the existence of modules in both structural and functional brain networks. Theoretical work points to the importance of modules for promoting stability and flexibility, conserving wiring cost, and enabling complex neuronal dynamics. As analytic methods mature and richer brain network data become available, the topic of modular brain networks will likely continue to evolve for many years to come.

SUMMARY POINTS

1. Modularity is a key characteristic of structural and functional brain networks across species and scales.

2. The most widely applied method for module detection, modularity maximization, is subject to several biases and limitations that can and should be addressed through modifications in optimization and statistical techniques.

3. Important extensions to modularity maximization include the application of multislice approaches that can detect variations of modular organization across subjects or time points.

4. Alternative approaches like clique percolation, block modeling, and detection of overlapping communities offer attractive opportunities for more detailed analyses of brain networks.

5. Anatomical modules generally reflect functional associations among neurons and brain regions.

6. Structural modules are often spatially compact, whereas functional modules can be more widely distributed and fluctuate in relation to cognitive states.

7. Modular organization may confer increased robustness and more flexible learning, help to conserve wiring cost, and promote functional specialization and complex brain dynamics.

FUTURE ISSUES

1. Sophisticated applications of community detection methods to brain data sets will uncover network modules with increasing emphasis on their significance and robustness.

2. Overcoming the resolution limit will allow mapping network modules across several scales and spatial resolutions.

3. Significant attention will be devoted to untangling the contributions of spatial embedding and functional specialization to the definition of network communities.

4. Multislice functional network approaches will reveal characteristic changes in modular architecture across time, for example, in the course of task performance and learning.

5. Module detection methods applied to cellular-resolution data from high-density functional recordings and/or microscale reconstructions of neuronal circuits will be instrumental for defining anatomical and functional microcircuits.

DISCLOSURE STATEMENT

The authors are not aware of any affiliations, memberships, funding, or financial holdings that might be perceived as affecting the objectivity of this review.

ACKNOWLEDGMENTS

The authors thank Santo Fortunato for reading a draft of this manuscript and providing comments and useful suggestions. O.S. was supported by the JS McDonnell Foundation (22002082) and the National Institutes of Health (R01 AT009036-01). R.F.B. was supported by the National Science Foundation/Integrative Graduate Education and Research Traineeship Training Program in the Dynamics of Brain–Body–Environment Systems at Indiana University (0903495).

LITERATURE CITED

Link-clustering algorithm for obtaining an estimate of a network's overlapping community structure.

Ahn YY, Bagrow JP, Lehmann S. 2010. Link communities reveal multiscale complexity in networks. _Nature_ 466(7307):761–64

Ahrens MB, Orger MB, Robson DN, Li JM, Keller PJ. 2013. Whole-brain functional imaging at cellular resolution using light-sheet microscopy. _Nat. Methods_ 10(5):413–20

Aldecoa R, Marin I. 2011. Deciphering network community structure by surprise. _PLOS ONE_ 6(9):e24195

Alexander-Bloch A, Lambiotte R, Roberts B, Giedd J, Gogtay N, Bullmore E. 2012. The discovery of population differences in network community structure: new methods and applications to brain functional networks in schizophrenia. _Neuroimage_ 59(4):3889–900

Andric M, Hasson U. 2015. Global features of functional brain networks change with contextual disorder. _Neuroimage_ 117:103–13

Arenas A, Díaz-Guilera A, Pérez-Vicente CJ. 2006. Synchronization reveals topological scales in complex networks. _Phys. Rev. Lett._ 96:114102

Arenas A, Fernández A, Gómez S. 2008. Analysis of the structure of complex networks at different resolution levels. _New J. Phys._ 10(5):053039

Bassett DS, Greenfield DL, Meyer-Lindenberg A, Weinberger DR, Moore SW, Bullmore ET. 2010. Efficient physical embedding of topologically complex information processing networks in brains and computer circuits. _PLOS Comp. Biol._ 6(4):e1000748

An important technical paper highlighting many useful guidelines for modularity maximization.

Bassett DS, Porter MA, Wymbs NF, Grafton ST, Carlson JM, Mucha PJ. 2013. Robust detection of dynamic community structure in networks. _Chaos_ 23(1):013142

Bassett DS, Wymbs NF, Porter MA, Mucha PJ, Carlson JM, Grafton ST. 2011. Dynamic reconfiguration of human brain networks during learning. _PNAS_ 108(18):7641–46

Bassett DS, Yang M, Wymbs NF, Grafton ST. 2015. Learning-induced autonomy of sensorimotor systems. _Nat. Neurosci._ 18:744–51

Bazzi M, Porter MA, Williams S, McDonald M, Fenn DJ, Howison SD. 2014. Community detection in temporal multilayer networks, and its application to correlation networks. arXiv:1501.00040 [physics.soc-ph]

Beckmann CF, DeLuca M, Devlin JT, Smith SM. 2005. Investigations into resting-state connectivity using independent component analysis. *Philos. Trans. R. Soc. B* 360(1457):1001–13

Bellec P, Rosa-Neto P, Lyttelton OC, Benali H, Evans AC. 2010. Multi-level bootstrap analysis of stable clusters in resting-state fMRI. *Neuroimage* 51(3):1126–39

Betzel RF, Byrge L, He Y, Goñi J, Zuo XN, Sporns O. 2014. Changes in structural and functional connectivity among resting-state networks across the human lifespan. *Neuroimage* 102(2):345–57

Betzel RF, Griffa A, Avena-Koenigsberger A, Goñi J, Hagmann P, et al. 2013. Multi-scale community organization of the human structural connectome and its relationship with resting-state functional connectivity. *Netw. Sci.* 1(3):353–73

Blondel VD, Guillaume JL, Lambiotte R, Lefebvre E. 2008. Fast unfolding of communities in large networks. *J. Stat. Mech. Theor. Exp.* 2008(10):P10008

Boccaletti S, Ivanchenko M, Latora V, Pluchino A, Rapisarda A. 2007. Detecting network modularity by dynamical clustering. *Phys. Rev. E* 75(4):045102

Börner K, Sanyal S, Vespignani A. 2007. Network science. *Annu. Rev. Inform. Sci. Technol.* 41(1):537–607

Bota M, Sporns O, Swanson LW. 2015. Architecture of the cerebral cortical association connectome underlying cognition. *PNAS* 112(16):E2093–101

Bressler SL, Menon V. 2010. Large-scale brain networks in cognition: emerging methods and principles. *Trends Cogn. Sci.* 14(6):277–90

Bullmore ET, Sporns O. 2009. Complex brain networks: graph theoretical analysis of structural and functional systems. *Nat. Rev. Neurosci.* 10(3):186–93

Bullmore ET, Sporns O. 2012. The economy of brain network organization. *Nat. Rev. Neurosci.* 13(5):336–49

Carrington PJ, Scott J, Wasserman S, eds. 2005. *Models and Methods in Social Network Analysis.* New York: Cambridge Univ. Press

Chan MY, Park DC, Savalia NK, Petersen SE, Wig GS. 2014. Decreased segregation of brain systems across the healthy adult lifespan. *PNAS* 111(46):E4997–5006

Chen BL, Hall DH, Chklovskii DB. 2006. Wiring optimization can relate neuronal structure and function. *PNAS* 103(12):7423–28

Chen Y, Wang S, Hilgetag CC, Zhou C. 2013. Trade-off between multiple constraints enables simultaneous formation of modules and hubs in neural systems. *PLOS Comp. Biol.* 9(3):e1002937

Cherniak C, Mokhtarzada Z, Rodriguez-Esteban R, Changizi K. 2004. Global optimization of cerebral cortex layout. *PNAS* 101(4):1081–86

Clauset A, Newman MEJ, Moore C. 2004. Finding community structure in very large networks. *Phys. Rev. E* 70(6):066111

Clune J, Mouret JB, Lipson H. 2013. The evolutionary origins of modularity. *Proc. R. Soc. B* 280(1755):20122863

Cole MW, Bassett DS, Power JD, Braver TS, Petersen SE. 2014. Intrinsic and task-evoked architectures of the human brain. *Neuron* 83(1):238–51

Crossley NA, Mechelli A, Vertes PE, Winton-Brown TT, Patel AX, et al. 2013. Cognitive relevance of the community structure of the human brain functional coactivation network. *PNAS* 110(28):11583–88

Danon L, Díaz-Guilera A, Duch J, Arenas A. 2005. Comparing community structure identification. *J. Stat. Mech. Theor. Exp.* 9:P09008

de Reus MA, van den Heuvel MP. 2013. Rich club organization and intermodule communication in the cat connectome. *J. Neurosci.* 33(32):12929–39

Delvenne JC, Yaliraki SN, Barahona M. 2010. Stability of graph communities across time scales. *PNAS* 107(29):12755–60

Doron KW, Bassett DS, Gazzaniga MS. 2012. Dynamic network coordination of interhemispheric coordination. *PNAS* 109(46):18661–68

Duch J, Arenas A. 2005. Community detection in complex networks using extremal optimization. *Phys. Rev. E* 72(2):027104

Ellefsen KO, Mouret JB, Clune J. 2015. Neural modularity helps organisms evolve to learn new skills without forgetting old skills. *PLOS Comp. Biol.* 11(4):e1004128

Espinosa-Soto C, Wagner A. 2010. Specialization can drive the evolution of modularity. *PLOS Comp. Biol.* 6(3):e1000719

Evans TS, Lambiotte R. 2009. Line graphs, link partitions, and overlapping communities. *Phys. Rev. E* 80(1):016105

Expert P, Evans TS, Blondel VD, Lambiotte R. 2011. Uncovering space-independent communities in spatial networks. *PNAS* 108(19):7663–68

Felleman DJ, van Essen DC. 1991. Distributed hierarchical processing in the primate cerebral cortex. *Cereb. Cortex* 1(1):1–47

Fodor JA. 1983. *The Modularity of Mind: An Essay on Faculty Psychology*. Cambridge, MA: MIT Press

Fornito A, Zalesky A, Breakspear M. 2015. The connectomics of brain disorders. *Nat. Rev. Neurosci.* 16(3):159–72

Fortunato S. 2010. Community detection in graphs. *Phys. Rep.* 486(3):75–174

Fortunato S, Barthelemy M. 2007. Resolution limit in community detection. *PNAS* 104(1):36–41

Friston KJ. 2011. Functional and effective connectivity: a review. *Brain Connect.* 1(1):13–36

Gallos LK, Makse HA, Sigman M. 2012. A small world of weak ties provides optimal global integrations of self-similar modules in functional brain networks. *PNAS* 109(8):2825–30

Geerligs L, Renken RJ, Saliasi E, Maruits NM, Lorist MM. 2015. A brain-wide study of age-related changes in functional connectivity. *Cereb. Cortex.* 25(7):1987–99

Gfeller D, Chappelier JC, De Los Rios P. 2005. Finding instabilities in the community structure of complex networks. *Phys. Rev. E* 72(5):056135

Gibson G, Dworkin I. 2004. Uncovering cryptic genetic variation. *Nat. Rev. Genet.* 5(9):681–90

Girvan M, Newman MEJ. 2002. Community structure in social and biological networks. *PNAS* 99(12):7821–26

Godwin G, Barry RL, Marois R. 2015. Breakdown of the brain's functional network modularity with awareness. *PNAS* 112(12):3799–804

Gómez S, Jensen P, Arenas A. 2009. Analysis of community structure in networks of correlated data. *Phys. Rev. E* 80(1):016114

Good BH, de Montjoye YA, Clauset A. 2010. Performance of modularity maximization in practical contexts. *Phys. Rev. E* 81(4):046106

Goulas A, Schaefer A, Margulies DS. 2015. The strength of weak connections in the macaque cortico-cortical network. *Brain Struct. Funct.* 220:2939–51

Guimerà R, Amaral LAN. 2005. Functional cartography of complex metabolic networks. *Nature* 433(7028):895–900

Hagmann P, Cammoun L, Gigandet X, Meuli R, Honey CJ, et al. 2008. Mapping the structural core of human cerebral cortex. *PLOS Biol.* 6(7):e159

Harriger L, van den Heuvel MP, Sporns O. 2012. Rich club organization of macaque cerebral cortex and its role in network communication. *PLOS ONE* 7(9):e46497

Hastie T, Tibshirani R, Friedman J. 2009. *The Elements of Statistical Learning*, Vol. 2. New York: Springer

Hastings MB. 2006. Community detection as an inference problem. *Phys. Rev. E* 74(3):035102

Henderson JA, Robinson PA. 2013. Using geometry to uncover relationships between isotropy, homogeneity, and modularity in cortical connectivity. *Brain Connect.* 3(4):423–37

Hilgetag CC, Burns GA, O'Neill MA, Scannell JW, Young MP. 2000. Anatomical connectivity defines the organization of clusters of cortical areas in the macaque and the cat. *Philos. Trans. R. Soc. B* 355(1393):91–110

Hinne M, Ekman M, Janssen RJ, Heskes T, van Gerven MAJ. 2014. Probabilistic clustering of the human connectome identifies communities and hubs. *PLOS ONE* 10:e0117179

Hutchison MR, Womelsdorf T, Allen EA, Bandettini PA, Calhoun VD, et al. 2013. Dynamic functional connectivity: promise, issues, and interpretations. *Neuroimage* 80:360–78

Jarrell TA, Wang Y, Bloniarz AE, Brittin CA, Xu M, et al. 2012. The connectome of a decision-making neural network. *Science* 337(6093):437–44

Jirsa VK, McIntosh AR, eds. 2007. *Handbook of Brain Connectivity*, Vol. 1. Berlin: Springer

Kaiser M, Hilgetag CC, Kötter R. 2010. Hierarchy and dynamics in neural networks. *Front. Neuroinform.* 4:112

Karrer B, Levina E, Newman MEJ. 2008. Robustness of community structure in networks. *Phys. Rev. E* 77(4):046119

An encyclopedic reference on community detection algorithms.

Kashtan N, Alon U. 2005. Spontaneous evolution of modularity and network motifs. *PNAS* 102(39):13773–78

Kashtan N, Noor E, Alon U. 2007. Varying environments can speed up evolution. *PNAS* 104(34):13711–16

Kirschner M, Gerhart J. 1998. Evolvability. *PNAS* 95(15):8420–27

Kötter R. 2004. Online retrieval, processing, and visualization of primate connectivity data from the CoCoMac database. *Neuroinformatics* 2(2):127–44

Laird AR, Lancaster JJ, Fox PT. 2005. BrainMap: the social evolution of a human brain mapping database. *Neuroinformatics* 3(1):65–78

Lancichinetti A, Fortunato S. 2009. Community detection algorithms: a comparative analysis. *Phys. Rev. E* 80(5):056117

Lancichinetti A, Fortunato S. 2011. Limits of modularity maximization in community detection. *Phys. Rev. E* 84:066122

Lancichinetti A, Fortunato S. 2012. Consensus clustering in complex networks. *Sci. Rep.* 2:336

Lancichinetti A, Fortunato S, Radicchi F. 2008. Benchmark graphs for testing community detection algorithms. *Phys. Rev. E* 78(4):046110

Lancichinetti A, Radicchi F, Ramasco JJ. 2010. Statistical significance of communities in networks. *Phys. Rev. E* 81(4):046110

Lancichinetti A, Radicchi F, Ramasco JJ, Fortunato. 2011. Finding statistically significant communities in networks. *PLOS ONE* 6(4):e18961

Laumann TO, Gordon EM, Adeyemo B, Snyder AZ, Joo SJ, et al. 2015. Functional system and areal organization of a highly sampled individual human brain. *Neuron* 87(3):657–70

Leicht EA, Newman MEJ. 2008. Community structure in directed networks. *Phys. Rev. Lett.* 100(11):118703

Lohse C, Bassett DS, Lim KO, Carlson JM. 2014. Resolving anatomical and functional structure in human brain organization: identifying mesoscale organization in weighted network representations. *PLOS Comp. Biol.* 10(10):e1003712

MacMahon M, Garlaschelli D. 2015. Community detection for correlation matrices. *Phys. Rev. X* 5:021006 [physics.data-an]

Markov NT, Ercsey-Ravasz MM, Ribeiro Gomes AR, Lamy C, Magrou L, et al. 2014. A weighted and directed interareal connectivity matrix for macaque cerebral cortex. *Cereb. Cortex* 24:17–36

McIntosh AR, Mišić B. 2013. Multivariate statistical analysis for neuroimaging data. *Annu. Rev. Psychol.* 64:499–525

Meunier D, Achard S, Morcom A, Bullmore E. 2009a. Age-related changes in modular organization of brain functional networks. *Neuroimage* 44(3):715–23

Meunier D, Lambiotte R, Fornito A, Ersche KD, Bullmore ET. 2009b. Hierarchical modularity in human brain functional networks. *Front. Neuroinform.* 3:37

Modha DS, Singh R. 2010. Network architecture of the long-distance pathways in the macaque brain. *PNAS* 107(30):13485–90

Mucha PJ, Richardson T, Macon K, Porter MA, Onnela JP. 2010. Community structure in time-dependent, multiscale, and multiplex networks. *Science* 328(5980):876–78

Newman MEJ. 2004. Fast algorithm for detecting community structure in networks. *Phys. Rev. E* 69(6):066133

Newman MEJ, Girvan M. 2004. Finding and evaluating community structure in networks. *Phys. Rev. E* 69(2):026113

Nicosia V, Vértes PE, Schafer WR, Latora V, Bullmore ET. 2013. Phase transition in the economically modeled growth of a cellular nervous system. *PNAS* 110(19):7880–85

Oh SW, Harris JA, Ng L, Winslow B, Cain N, et al. 2014. A mesoscale connectome of the mouse brain. *Nature* 508(7495):207–14

Palla G, Derényi I, Farkas I, Vicsek T. 2005. Uncovering the overlapping community structure of complex networks in nature and society. *Nature* 435(7043):814–18

Pan RK, Chatterjee N, Sinha S. 2010. Mesoscopic organization reveals the constraints governing *Caenorhabditis elegans* nervous system. *PLOS ONE* 5(2):e9240

Pan RK, Sinha S. 2009. Modularity produces small-world networks with dynamical time-scale separation. *Europhys. Lett.* 85:68006

A general method for obtaining consensus communities through iterative thresholding and reclustering of association matrices.

OSLOM method for detecting statistically significant communities.

A multilayer analog of the standard single-layer modularity quality function.

Seminal work in which the modularity quality function was first formalized.

Clique percolation algorithm for obtaining overlapping community structure.

Park HJ, Friston K. 2013. Structural and functional brain networks: from connections to cognition. *Science* 342(6158):1238411

Pavlovic DM, Vértes PE, Bullmore ET, Schafer WR, Nichols TE. 2014. Stochastic blockmodeling of the modules and core of the *Caenorhabditis elegans* connectome. *PLOS ONE* 9(7):e97584

Pons P, Latapy M. 2005. Computing communities in large networks using random walks. In *Computer and Information Sciences—ISCIS 2005*, ed. P Yolum, T Güngör, F Gürgen, C Özturan, pp. 284–93. Berlin: Springer

Power JD, Cohen AL, Nelson SM, Wig GS, Barnes KA, et al. 2011. Functional network organization of the human brain. *Neuron* 72(4):665–78

Reichardt J, Bornholdt S. 2006. Statistical mechanics of community detection. *Phys. Rev. E* 74(1):016110

Ronhovde P, Nussinov Z. 2009. Multiresolution community detection for megascale networks by information-based replica correlations. *Phys. Rev. E* 80(1):016109

Rosvall M, Axelsson, Bergstrom CT. 2009. The map equation. *Eur. Phys. J. Special Top.* 178(1):13–23

Rosvall M, Bergstrom CT. 2008. Maps of random walks on complex networks reveal community structure. *PNAS* 105(4):1118–23

Rubinov M, Sporns O. 2010. Complex network measures of brain connectivity: uses and interpretations. *Neuroimage* 52:1059–69

Rubinov M, Sporns O. 2011. Weight-conserving characterization of complex functional brain networks. *Neuroimage* 56(4):2068–79

Rubinov M, Sporns O, Thivierge JP, Breakspear M. 2011. Neurobiologically realistic determinants of self-organized criticality in networks of spiking neurons. *PLOS Comp. Biol.* 7(6):e1002038

Samu D, Seth AK, Nowotny T. 2014. Influence of wiring cost on the large-scale architecture of human cortical connectivity. *PLOS Comp. Biol.* 10(4):e1003557

Scannell JW, Blackmore C, Young MP. 1995. Analysis of connectivity in the cat cerebral cortex. *J. Neurosci.* 15(2):1463–83

Shih CT, Sporns O, Yuan SL, Su TS, Lin YJ, et al. 2015. Connectomics-based analysis of information flow in the *Drosophila* brain. *Curr. Biol.* 25(10):1249–58

Shimono M, Beggs JM. 2015. Functional clusters, hubs, and communities in the cortical microconnectome. *Cereb. Cortex* 25:3743–57

Simon HA. 1962. The architecture of complexity. *Proc. Am. Philos. Soc.* 106:467–82

Smith SM, Fox PT, Miller KL, Glahn DC, Fox PM, et al. 2009. Correspondence of the brain's functional architecture during activations and rest. *PNAS* 106(31):13040–45

Smith SM, Miller KL, Salimi-Khorshidi G, Webster M, Beckmann CF, et al. 2011. Network modeling methods for fMRI. *Neuroimage* 54(2):875–91

Sohn Y, Choi MK, Ahn YY, Lee J, Jeong J. 2011. Topological cluster analysis reveals the systemic organization of *Caenorhabditis elegans* connectome. *PLOS Comp. Biol.* 7(5):e1001139

Sporns O. 2011. *Networks of the Brain*. Cambridge, MA: MIT Press

Sporns O. 2013. The human connectome: origins and challenges. *Neuroimage* 80:53–61

Sporns O. 2014. Contributions and challenges for network models in cognitive neuroscience. *Nat. Neurosci.* 17(5):652–60

Sporns O, Chialvo DR, Kaiser M, Hilgetag CC. 2004. Organization, development, and function of complex brain networks. *Trends Cogn. Sci.* 8(9):418–25

Sporns O, Tononi G, Edelman GM. 2000. Theoretical neuroanatomy: relating anatomical and functional connectivity in graphs and cortical connection matrices. *Cereb. Cortex* 10(2):127–41

Sporns O, Tononi G, Kötter R. 2005. The human connectome: a structural description of the human brain. *PLOS Comp. Biol.* 1:e42

Stephan KE, Kamper L, Bozkurt A, Burns GA, Young MP, Kötter R. 2001. Advanced database methodology for the Collation of Connectivity data on the Macaque brain (CoCoMac). *Philos. Trans. R. Soc. B* 356(1412):1159–86

Towlson EK, Vértes PE, Ahnert SE, Schafer WR, Bullmore ET. 2013. The rich club of the *C. elegans* neuronal connectome. *J. Neurosci.* 33(15):6380–87

Traag VA, Bruggeman J. 2009. Community detection in networks with positive and negative links. *Phys. Rev. E* 80(3):036115

Application of Infomap and modularity maximization to functional brain networks to uncover modules.

Infomap algorithm for uncovering nonoverlapping community structure based on a random walk over a network.

Traag VA, Krings G, Van Dooren P. 2014. Significant scales in community structure. *Sci. Rep.* 3:2930

Traud AL, Kelsic ED, Mucha PJ, Porter MA 2011. Comparing community structure to characteristics in online collegiate social networks. *SIAM Rev.* 53(3):526–43

van den Heuvel MP, Sporns O. 2011. Rich-club organization of the human connectome. *J. Neurosci.* 31(44):15775–86

van den Heuvel MP, Sporns O. 2013. An anatomical substrate for integration among functional networks in human cortex. *J. Neurosci.* 33(36):14489–500

Varshney LR, Chen BL, Paniagua E, Hall DH, Chklovskii DB. 2011. Structural properties of the *Caenorhabditis elegans* neuronal network. *PLOS Comput. Biol.* 7(2):e1001066

Wang Q, Sporns O, Burkhalter A. 2012. Network analysis of corticocortical connections reveals ventral and dorsal processing streams in mouse visual cortex. *J. Neurosci.* 32(13):4386–99

White JG, Southgate E, Thomson JN, Brenner S. 1986. The structure of the nervous system of the nematode *Caenorhabditis elegans. Philos. Trans. R. Soc. B* 314(1165):1–340

Wildie M, Shanahan M. 2012. Metastability and chimera states in modular delay and pulse-coupled oscillator networks. *Chaos* 22(4):043131

Wu F, Huberman BA. 2004. Finding communities in linear time: a physics approach. *Eur. Phys. J. B* 38(2):331–38

Yamaguti Y, Tsuda I. 2015. Mathematical modeling for evolution of heterogeneous modules in the brain. *Neural Netw.* 62:3–10

Yeo BTT, Krienen FM, Sepulcre J, Sabuncu MR, Lashkari D, et al. 2011. The organization of the human cerebral cortex estimated by intrinsic functional connectivity. *J. Neurophys.* 106(3):1125–65

Zamora-Lopez G, Zhou C, Kurths J. 2010. Cortical hubs form a module for multisensory integration on top of the hierarchy of cortical networks. *Front. Neuroinform.* 4:1

Zhang P, Moore C. 2014. Scalable detection of statistically significant communities and hierarchies using message passing for modularity. *PNAS* 111(51):18144–49

RELATED RESOURCES

Andrea Lancichinetti Personal Site
C++ code for performing consensus clustering, generating synthetic benchmark graphs, and assessing the statistical significance (c- and b-scores) of communities obtained from any community detection method **https://sites.google.com/site/andrealancichinetti/software**

Brain Connectivity Toolbox
MATLAB toolbox of many useful graph theoretic functions, including single-slice, multiscale modularity maximization **http://www.brain-connectivity-toolbox.net/**

BrainMap
Searchable repository of activation foci coordinates from functional neuroimaging studies **http://brainmap.org/**

CFinder
JAVA code for running clique percolation; analysis can be performed using GUI or command line **http://www.cfinder.org/**

Infomap
C++ code for running Infomap (can be performed locally or using online applet); also features useful tool for visualizing communities and their evolution (alluvial flow generator) **http://www.mapequation.org/**

Louvain algorithm

C++ code (with MATLAB MEX files) for performing modularity maximization using the Louvain algorithm **https://sites.google.com/site/findcommunities/**

Network Community Toolbox

MATLAB toolbox for performing community detection, obtaining consensus communities, and assessing the statistical significance of communities **http://commdetect.weebly.com/**

OSLOM

C++ code for finding statistically significant overlapping communities **http://www.oslom.org/**

Sequential Sampling Models in Cognitive Neuroscience: Advantages, Applications, and Extensions

B.U. Forstmann,[1] R. Ratcliff,[2] and E.-J. Wagenmakers[3]

[1]Amsterdam Brain and Cognition Center, University of Amsterdam, 1018 WS Amsterdam, The Netherlands; email: buforstmann@gmail.com

[2]Department of Psychology, Ohio State University, Columbus, Ohio 43210

[3]Department of Methodology, University of Amsterdam, 1018 WV Amsterdam, The Netherlands

Annu. Rev. Psychol. 2016. 67:641–66

First published online as a Review in Advance on September 17, 2015

The *Annual Review of Psychology* is online at psych.annualreviews.org

This article's doi: 10.1146/annurev-psych-122414-033645

Keywords

diffusion decision model, information accumulation, decision making, response time, speed-accuracy trade-off, drift rate

Abstract

Sequential sampling models assume that people make speeded decisions by gradually accumulating noisy information until a threshold of evidence is reached. In cognitive science, one such model—the diffusion decision model—is now regularly used to decompose task performance into underlying processes such as the quality of information processing, response caution, and a priori bias. In the cognitive neurosciences, the diffusion decision model has recently been adopted as a quantitative tool to study the neural basis of decision making under time pressure. We present a selective overview of several recent applications and extensions of the diffusion decision model in the cognitive neurosciences.

Contents

INTRODUCTION

Every day, people make thousands of small decisions. Many of these decisions are trivial (e.g., what pair of socks to wear or what TV series to watch), many are to some degree automatic (e.g., how to greet your colleague in the morning or what word to type next in an email), but all of them are made under time pressure. One simply cannot take hours to ponder over what pair of socks to wear or how to greet a colleague: After some deliberation, a decision needs to be made based on the data at hand. Consequently, most real-life decisions are composed of two separate decisions: first the decision to stop deliberating and act, and then the decision or act itself.

The decision to stop deliberating and act is not straightforward, because it involves a balance between two opposing forces. On the one hand, the quality of decision making improves when it is based on more information; on the other hand, decisions are only acceptable when they are timely. In psychology, this balance is known as the speed-accuracy trade-off, a trade-off that affects basketball players, honeybees, and even acellular organisms such as slime molds (Latty & Beekman 2011).

Several models have been developed to account for the speed-accuracy trade-off and explain how people and animals make decisions under time pressure. The most popular class of models assumes that the decision maker accumulates noisy samples of information from the environment until a threshold of evidence is reached. Such accumulation-to-threshold models are known as sequential sampling models.

Sequential sampling models have been developed in mathematical psychology ever since the 1960s (e.g., Stone 1960). Over the course of several decades, researchers began to understand

Speed-accuracy trade-off: the universal finding that response time can be shortened at the expense of a higher error rate

the benchmark phenomena that underlie decision making under speed stress, and the models became increasingly sophisticated to account for these findings (Luce 1986, Townsend & Ashby 1983). In the early 1990s, it became clear that one particular sequential sampling model—the diffusion decision model (DDM)—stood out as the effective standard model (see sidebar Fitting the Diffusion Decision Model to Data) in the field.

Even though the DDM had been successful as a mathematical process model that accounted for the speed and accuracy of decision making under a wide variety of circumstances, initially its domain of application remained relatively limited. Around the turn of the century, this state of affairs changed radically when it became apparent that the DDM not only accounted for observed behavior but also provided an explanation for some of the general dynamics of single-cell firing rates in monkeys. In the following years, neuroscientists have applied and extended the DDM, and presently it provides a point of departure for many modeling attempts in both low-level and high-level cognitive neuroscience.

As we intend to demonstrate, the ever-increasing interest in applying and extending the DDM in the domain of speeded decision making is motivated by the growing realization that a quantitative approach can greatly help guide empirical work and deepen our understanding of cognition (Forstmann & Wagenmakers 2015).

The outline of this article is as follows. The first section provides historical context and outlines the current standard form of the DDM; the second section lists the advantages of using the DDM for both experimental psychology and cognitive neuroscience; the third section provides an overview of DDM applications in cognitive neuroscience, focusing on low-level neural firing rates in monkeys and on high-level brain imaging techniques in humans; and the fourth section outlines recent extensions and exciting new developments. A brief summary of the most important points concludes the article.

SEQUENTIAL SAMPLING MODELS

People often need to make decisions based on information that unfolds over time. An example of this is the idealized work process of a police detective solving a homicide: Following a state of confusion and uncertainty, informative cues become available over time that allow the detective to reduce the uncertainty and hopefully solve the case. However, the decision-making process can be sequential even when all of the information is immediately available. For instance, a chess player contemplating a particular move has all the information available, in the sense that the environment will not offer any more cues as time progresses: All the information is contained in

Diffusion decision model (DDM): a model of speeded decision making in which noisy information is accumulated over time until a threshold of evidence is reached

RDK: random dot
kinematogram

Response time (RT):
the time between
stimulus onset and
response execution in a
decision-making task
performed under
substantial time
pressure

the configuration of the pieces on the board, which can be perceptually encoded at a glance. The problem for the chess player is that mental capacity is limited, and the relevant information can only be extracted and processed piecemeal. Hence, the sequential nature of decision making is a fundamental property of the human nervous system, reflecting its inability to process information instantaneously.

To understand the dynamics of decision making, most studies focus on simple, repeatable choice problems with just two alternatives. For instance, participants in lexical decision are confronted with letter strings that have to be classified as a word (e.g., mango) or a nonword (e.g., drapa); participants in the moving dots task are confronted with a random dot kinematogram (RDK) and have to judge whether a subset of dots move to the left or to the right. The elementary nature of these tasks makes it possible to collect thousands of decisions for a single participant in a single session, providing rich data for modeling. Traditionally, the measures of interest are the response times (RTs) for correct responses and for error responses, the distributions of RTs, and the proportion of correct responses. Note that the simplicity of the tasks does not preclude errors; when participants are instructed to respond quickly, errors inevitably arise, and a participant may well classify drapa as a word.

The data from these elementary decision-making tasks reveal several law-like patterns that any model of decision making should try to account for. Some of these law-like patterns are trivial (e.g., mean RT is shorter for easy stimuli than it is for hard stimuli; increasing speed stress shortens mean RT but increases the proportion of errors), but others are not. For instance, (a) mean RT is proportional to RT standard deviation (Wagenmakers & Brown 2007); (b) manipulations that increase the speed of correct responses also increase the speed of error responses; (c) RT distributions are right-skewed, and this skew increases with task difficulty; and (d) for difficult tasks, mean error RT is often slower than mean correct RT, but this pattern can be reversed by speed stress (e.g., Wagenmakers et al. 2008; for a description of these and other law-like patterns see Brown & Heathcote 2008, Carpenter 2004, Luce 1986, Mulder et al. 2012, Ratcliff 2002, Ratcliff & McKoon 2008, Van Ravenzwaaij et al. 2011).

Sequential sampling models come in various forms. The general idea is that evidence is gradually accumulated and each response (e.g., word/nonword, left/right) is represented by a separate decision boundary. However, the models differ according to whether there are one or two counters and whether the counters are independent; whether they are assumed to be leaky; or whether they exert a top-down influence on the accumulation process. Responses can be determined by an absolute evidence rule (i.e., two fixed thresholds, one for each counter) or a relative evidence rule (one threshold on the difference in accumulated activation; e.g., Bogacz et al. 2006, Ratcliff & Smith 2004, Teodorescu & Usher 2013).

One famous class of sequential sampling models consists of accumulator models (e.g., Van Zandt et al. 2000, Vickers & Lee 1998). A prototypical accumulator model has independent counters and an absolute evidence response rule. Here we focus on a different class of sequential sampling models, which assumes a relative evidence rule: A response is initiated as soon as the difference in evidence accumulated exceeds a prespecified criterion. For discrete evidence accumulation, this account is known as a random walk model; for continuous evidence accumulation, the process is known as a diffusion process.

Interdisciplinary History

The history of random walk models dates back to the early days of probability theory, when much effort was devoted to problems related to gambling. In a famous problem known as the gambler's ruin, two gamblers, A and B, play a sequence of independent games against each other. Each gambler has a (possibly different) starting capital, and every game has a fixed chance p of being won by gambler A. Every time one of the gamblers wins a game, the winner obtains one unit of the other player's capital; the process continues until one of the gamblers is bankrupt (Carazza 1977, Feller 1968). Provided the two starting capitals and the chance p, what is the probability that A goes bankrupt? And what is the expected number of games until this happens? (For answers, readers are referred to Feller 1968.)

The temporal flow of capital in the gambler's ruin process can be represented as a random walk with two absorbing boundaries; whenever a boundary is reached, this signifies that one of the gamblers is bankrupt. Parameter p represents the drift of the process; when $p > 1/2$, the noisy process will tend to drift toward the bound associated with gambler B's bankruptcy.

In the continuous limit of small stakes and with p close to 1/2, the process is known as Brownian motion or Wiener diffusion process. This process was proposed to explain the movement of physical particles influenced by many molecular collisions (e.g., Einstein 1905; for a visual demonstration, see **http://en.wikipedia.org/wiki/Brownian_motion**). The experimental verification of this explanation helped confirm the existence of molecules and atoms, and it earned Jean Perrin the 1926 Nobel Prize in Physics. In mathematics, the Wiener diffusion process is a prototypical example of a stochastic differential equation (e.g., Smith 2000) with applications in finance, heat flow, and fluid dynamics.

The random walk process is also of considerable interest to statisticians, partly because it is related to sequential analysis; data come in over time and the statistician has to determine when to stop collecting data and make a decision. The sequential analyses initiated by Alan Turing famously helped break the German enigma code, expediting the end of World War II (Good 1979). At about the same time, Abraham Wald proposed the sequential probability ratio test (SPRT; e.g., Wald & Wolfowitz 1948). In the SPRT, each incoming datum is transformed into a log likelihood ratio that quantifies the relative evidence for one hypothesis versus another; the likelihood ratios are added as the data flow in, and the process halts as soon as a predetermined level of evidence is reached. The appeal of this procedure is that it is optimal in the sense that it achieves the fastest mean decision time for a given accuracy (Bogacz et al. 2006). For applications in neuroscience, the optimality of the SPRT is an attractive property, because evolutionary pressures and reinforcement learning mechanisms may have shaped neurons to process information near-optimally, given their innate limitations (Ma et al. 2006).

In psychology, the interest in random walk models started with Stone (1960) and was followed by major contributions from Laming (1968) and Link & Heath (1975). The early models, however, did not account for the relative speed of error RTs across all experimental scenarios. To account for all of the data, the early models needed to be expanded, and this resulted in the model that is the current standard: the DDM.

Current Standard Form: The Diffusion Decision Model

The DDM (e.g., Ratcliff 1978, Ratcliff & McKoon 2008, Voss et al. 2013) assumes that dichotomous decisions are based on the accumulation of noisy evidence, commencing at the starting point and terminating at a decision threshold that is associated with a particular decision or choice. **Figure 1** represents an application of the model to the RDK task. The figure demonstrates that the diffusion process is inherently noisy, causing the choices to be error prone and the RTs to be variable.

The model structure shown in **Figure 1** provides a unified account of the psychological mechanisms that underlie both RTs and the probabilities with which responses are chosen. The model has four key parameters. First, drift rate represents the average amount of evidence accumulated

SPRT: sequential probability ratio test

Drift rate: parameter in the diffusion decision model that quantifies the information used in the accumulation process

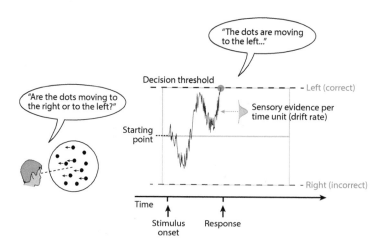

Figure 1

Schematic representation of the diffusion decision model. Figure adapted with permission from Mulder et al. (2012).

per unit time, and it is an index of task difficulty or subject ability. Second, boundary separation represents the level of caution; increasing boundary separation results in fewer errors (because of the reduced impact of the within-trial diffusion noise) but at the cost of slower responding. Hence, boundary separation implements the speed-accuracy trade-off. Third, the starting point reflects the a priori bias or preference for one or the other choice alternative. Fourth, nondecision time is an additive lag parameter that measures the time for peripheral processes such as encoding a stimulus, transforming the stimulus representation into a decision-related representation, and executing a response. Consequently, the total time for a response is the time to diffuse from starting point to boundary, plus the nondecision time.

In addition to the four key parameters, the DDM features three across-trial variabilities in drift rate, starting point, and nondecision time. Without across-trial variability in any of these, and with boundaries equidistant from the starting point, the model would predict the distributions of RTs for correct and error responses to be identical. However, with across-trial variability in drift rate, the model predicts errors to be slower than correct responses because of probability mixtures of processes with different times and accuracies. For example, for a larger drift rate in the mixture, accuracy will be higher and RT slower for both correct and error responses; for a lower drift rate, accuracy will be lower and RTs longer. Therefore, there will be a smaller number of fast errors and a higher number of slow errors from this mixture (relative to correct responses), leading to slower errors relative to correct responses (for further explanation, see Ratcliff 1978; Ratcliff & McKoon 2008, figure 4). With across-trial variability in the starting point, the model predicts errors to be faster than correct responses (e.g., Ratcliff & Rouder 1998, figure 2; Wagenmakers et al. 2008). When a process starts near the correct response boundary there will be few errors and they will be slow, because the process has to travel a long distance to reach the error boundary. When a process starts near the error boundary there will be more errors and they will be fast, because the process only has to travel a short distance to reach the error boundary. Both patterns are found in the data (with a crossover sometimes so that fast errors occur in easy conditions and slow errors in difficult conditions), and the model explains why these patterns occur. A mixture of starting points gives fast errors overall.

Equipped with these parameters, the DDM provides an excellent account of the law-like patterns observed across virtually all speeded RT tasks. For instance, the DDM accounts for the relationship between mean RTs and the probabilities of the choices (errors and correct responses), including how these covary with stimulus difficulty. In addition, the DDM accounts for the shapes of RT distributions and for how these change as a function of experimental conditions.

Based on a superficial analysis, a skeptic may argue that the excellent fit of the DDM is achieved partly because its parameters make it highly flexible; in other words, the model may be overparameterized and immune to empirical falsification. A deeper analysis, however, shows this concern to be without merit (Wagenmakers 2009). First, experimental designs usually feature multiple conditions, and this allows the model parameters to be constrained in meaningful ways; for instance, only the drift rate parameter is allowed to vary with stimulus difficulty, and only the boundary separation parameter is allowed to vary across conditions with different levels of speed stress. Such constraints severely limit the model's flexibility. Second, Ratcliff (2002) has demonstrated by simulations how the DDM fails to account for fake but plausible data patterns. Third, typical experimental designs allow the model parameters to be adequately recovered. Finally, tests of specific influence show that manipulations of psychological processes affect the associated parameters; for instance, a manipulation of task difficulty mostly affects the drift rate parameter, and a manipulation of speed stress mostly affects the boundary separation parameter (e.g., Voss et al. 2004).

ADVANTAGES OF THE DIFFUSION DECISION MODEL

The DDM can be considered a dynamic version of signal-detection theory (SDT; Gold & Shadlen 2007, Ratcliff 1978, Wagenmakers et al. 2007). In SDT, the decision maker is assumed to assess the diagnosticity of a single sample of information; in the DDM, the decision maker draws a sequence of samples, adding their diagnostic values until a threshold amount of evidence is reached. Thus, like SDT, the DDM allows one to disentangle estimates of ability (i.e., that which is not under strategic control: d' in SDT versus drift rate in DDM) from estimates of criteria settings (i.e., that which is under strategic control: c in SDT versus boundary separation and starting point in DDM). Unlike SDT, however, the DDM considers not only response proportion but also the shapes of RT distributions, both for errors and correct responses. This has the advantage of finding invariance in evidence used in a decision when speed or accuracy settings are manipulated; in contrast, SDT analyses find that evidence changes when accuracy is stressed.

Below we discuss the advantages that the DDM has to offer, both for the analysis of choice behavior and for cognitive neuroscience.

Advantages for the Analysis of Choice Behavior

At its core, a DDM analysis allows researchers to decompose observed choice behavior into its constituent cognitive processes. By simultaneously taking into account both response accuracy and response latency, the model addresses the speed-accuracy trade-off and allows an assessment of individual ability that is not contaminated by differences in threshold settings or in the speed of peripheral processes unrelated to the decision-making process itself (Wagenmakers et al. 2007). This decomposition makes it possible to evaluate the adequacy of verbal theories such as the global slowing hypothesis of aging, which effectively states that the effect of aging is to decrease drift rate. The decomposition also facilitates the use of the DDM as a cognitive psychometric tool (Riefer et al. 2002, Vandekerckhove et al. 2011) to pinpoint the cognitive processes that are dysfunctional in clinical populations, for instance, in patients with aphasia, hypoglycemia, dysphoria, attention deficit hyperactivity disorder (ADHD), dyslexia, and anxiety disorders.

One criterion for a model's usefulness is whether it does more than simply reiterate what can be obtained from traditional analyses. Below we describe a number of recent DDM applications and highlight how some of these have provided new insights into cognition, individual differences, and differences among subject groups. In other cases, however, the model only provides obvious results. But even in this case, the model still integrates the three dependent variables—accuracy and the shapes of correct and error RT distributions—into a common theoretical framework that provides a mechanistic explanation for the observed data. This stands in contrast to the commonly used hypothesis-testing approaches that are mute on the psychological processes that produce behavior, usually focusing only on accuracy or mean correct RT as the dependent variable. In some cases, separate statistical analyses of each variable tell the same empirical story, but in other cases they are inconsistent. A model-based approach helps resolve such inconsistencies.

Aging. The application of the diffusion model to studies of aging has been especially successful, producing a novel view of the effects of aging on cognition. The general finding in the literature was that older adults are slower than young adults (but not necessarily less accurate) on most tasks, and this has been interpreted as a decline with age in all or almost all cognitive processes. However, application of the DDM showed that this interpretation is generally not correct (Ratcliff et al. 2007b, and references therein). For example, Ratcliff et al. (2010) tested old and young adults on numerosity discrimination, lexical decision, and recognition memory. What they found is that older adults had slower nondecision times and set wider boundaries, but their drift rates were not lower than those of young adults. In contrast, large age-related declines in drift rate have been found in other tasks, such as associative recognition and letter discrimination (Ratcliff et al. 2011, Thapar et al. 2003).

Working memory and IQ. Schmiedek et al. (2007) analyzed data from eight choice RT tasks (including verbal, numerical, and spatial tasks) from Oberauer et al. (2003). They found that drift rates in the diffusion model mapped onto working memory, speed of processing, and reasoning ability measures (all measured by aggregated performance on several tasks).

Similarly, the DDM analyses from Ratcliff et al. (2010, 2011) showed that drift rate varied with IQ (by as much as 2:1 for higher versus lower IQ participants), but boundary separation and nondecision time did not. Note that this is the opposite of the pattern for aging.

Clinical populations. Research on psychopathology and clinical populations commonly uses two-choice tasks to investigate processing differences between patients and healthy controls. For instance, highly anxious individuals show enhanced processing of threat-provoking materials, a pattern that is found reliably only when two or more stimuli are competing for processing resources. White et al. (2010) recently challenged this resource competition account. They conducted a lexical decision experiment with single words (i.e., without resource competition) that included threatening and control words; using a DDM decomposition, they found a consistent processing advantage for threatening words in highly anxious individuals, whereas traditional comparisons showed no significant differences. Because the diffusion model makes use of both RT and accuracy data, it can better detect differences among subject populations than RT or accuracy alone.

In a similar vein, studies of depression have sometimes found mixed patterns of results. In general, depressive symptoms are closely linked with abnormal emotional processing: Whereas nondepressed people have a positive emotional bias, clinical depression is accompanied by a negative emotional bias, and dysphoria is accompanied by evenhandedness (i.e., no emotional bias). However, studies using item recognition and lexical decision tasks often fail to produce significant results. White et al. (2009) used the DDM to examine emotional processing in dysphoric and nondysphoric college students to examine differences in memory and lexical processing of positive and negative emotional words, which were presented among many neutral filler words. They found positive emotional bias in drift rates for nondysphoric subjects and evenhandedness for dysphoric subjects. As before, this pattern was not apparent with comparisons of RTs or accuracy, consistent with previous null findings.

Another study examined the effects of aphasia in a lexical decision task for which the neurolinguistic patients showed exaggerated RTs. A DDM decomposition revealed that both decision and nondecision processes were compromised, but the quality of information processing (i.e., drift rate) did not differ much between patients and controls (Ratcliff et al. 2004a). It is unclear how a traditional statistical analysis could have arrived at a similar insight.

Miscellaneous. Ratcliff & Van Dongen (2009) looked at effects of sleep deprivation using a numerosity discrimination task; Van Ravenzwaaij et al. (2012) looked at the effects of alcohol consumption using a lexical decision task; and Geddes et al. (2010) looked at the effects of reduced blood sugar using a numerosity discrimination task. The main result of all of these studies was a reduced drift rate but with either small or no effect on boundary separation and nondecision time.

By way of contrast, in studies of cognitive development, younger children show larger boundary separation and longer nondecision times than do older children (Ratcliff et al. 2012). Other experiments have found drift rates to be lower for ADHD and dyslexic children relative to normal controls (for ADHD, see Mulder et al. 2010; for dyslexia, see Zeguers et al. 2011). The above applications demonstrate how a comprehensive DDM decomposition of observed choice behavior yields deeper conclusions and insights than traditional methods of analysis.

Advantages for Cognitive Neuroscience

The DDM advantages are particularly acute for the field of model-based cognitive neuroscience, a nascent discipline that combines insights and measurement tools from experimental psychology, mathematical psychology, and neuroscience (Forstmann et al. 2011, Forstmann & Wagenmakers 2015). **Figure 2** shows each discipline's primary concern with the cognitive process and how formal models can act as a hub that connects the contributions of the separate disciplines.

A DDM decomposition allows cognitive neuroscientists to associate brain measurements with specific cognitive processes instead of behavioral data. This comes with a number of advantages. First, the DDM decomposition can confirm that a particular manipulation is selective or process-pure; for instance, a manipulation of task difficulty is process-pure when it selectively affects drift rate. When task difficulty is manipulated across blocks, however, other processes such as boundary separation could also be affected. Second, even when a manipulation is not process-pure, a DDM decomposition allows the researcher to isolate and focus on the contribution of the process of interest. In the example above, brain measurements (e.g., fMRI contrasts) may reflect the impact of changes in both drift rate and boundary separation; yet, the DDM parameter estimates can be used to disentangle the joint impact of the two processes and to associate the brain measurements with the process of interest (e.g., drift rate). Finally, the DDM decomposition facilitates an individual differences analysis; for instance, people with relatively large changes in drift rate may show more pronounced activation in frontoparietal network areas, suggesting that these areas are important for stimulus processing.

In addition, as we will outline below in more detail, the DDM has stimulated the development of quantitative models for neural processes. This work suggests that the processes that drive observed choice behavior are qualitatively similar to those that describe the behavior of individual neurons.

Model-based cognitive neuroscience: interdisciplinary field that studies cognition by combining insights and models from mathematical psychology with measurement tools from neuroscience

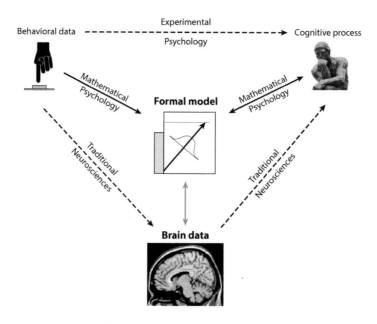

Behavioral data

Experimental
Psychology

Cognitive process

Mathematical
Psychology

Formal model

Mathematical
Psychology

Traditional
Neurosciences

Traditional
Neurosciences

Brain data

Figure 2

The model-in-the-middle approach unites the separate disciplines of experimental psychology, mathematical psychology, and cognitive neuroscience in the common goal of understanding human cognition. The red double-headed arrow indicates the reciprocal relation between measuring the brain and modeling behavioral data. Figure adapted with permission from Forstmann et al. (2011).

THE DIFFUSION DECISION MODEL IN COGNITIVE NEUROSCIENCE: APPLICATION

To bridge the gap between neural process and observed choice behavior, it is helpful to model and estimate the intermediate latent psychological processes. The DDM constitutes an important general framework to understand how neurons process information and how brain activation gives rise to choice and action. Nevertheless, there remains a vast divide between neurons and choice, and one of the main unsolved challenges is to provide a unified account of both low-level and high-level brain processes and of how these determine choice behavior.

Below we first discuss the application of the DDM in low-level neuroscience and single-cell recordings in monkeys, and then turn to the application of the DDM in high-level neuroscience and brain measurements in humans. Due to space limitations, our review is necessarily selective.

Application in Low-Level Cognitive Neuroscience: Neural Firing Rates and Single-Cell Recordings in Monkeys

Single-cell recording: recordings of spiking activity for individual neurons as measured for instance in monkeys and rats

LIP: lateral intraparietal cortex

One of the main reasons for the current popularity of diffusion models in neuroscience is the possibility to observe the behavior of single neurons of monkeys (and occasionally rats) performing simple decision-making tasks such as the RDK. Hanes & Schall (1996) made one of the first connections between theory and single-cell recording data, which was subsequently taken up in work by Shadlen and colleagues (e.g., Gold & Shadlen 2001). As shown in **Figure 3**, the key finding is that the firing rates of single cells in decision-related areas increase to a maximum that is independent of both the speed and the difficulty of the decision. These decision-related areas include the lateral intraparietal cortex (LIP; see Roitman & Shadlen 2002, Shadlen & Newsome

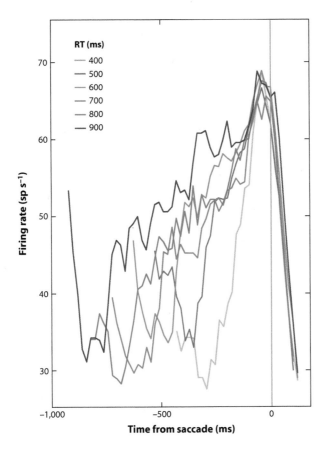

Figure 3

Immediately before monkeys execute a saccade, all trials reach a stereotyped firing rate. This dynamic is consistent with that of a diffusion model with evidence accumulation to a fixed threshold. Abbreviation: RT, response time. Figure adapted with permission from Gold & Shadlen (2007).

1996), the frontal eye field (FEF; see Ferrera et al. 2009, Hanes & Schall 1996), and other parts of the prefrontal cortex and the superior colliculus (SC; Ding & Gold 2012; Horwitz & Newsome 1999; Ratcliff et al. 2003a, 2007a). These results dovetail nicely with models that assume gradual accumulation of evidence up to a fixed decision criterion.

There is debate about where exactly the accumulation takes place, but it is clear that (at least) LIP, FEF, and SC form part of a circuit that is involved in implementing oculomotor decisions in monkeys performing simple decision-making tasks. The above studies generally support the notion that decision-related information flows from LIP to FEF and then to SC just prior to a decision.

This domain benefits from an abundance of recent high-quality reviews (Ding & Gold 2012; Glimcher 2003; Gold & Shadlen 2001, 2007; Schall 2001, 2013; Shadlen & Kiani 2013) that show a variety of approaches but mainly focus on the accumulation of evidence up to a decision criterion. In addition, a number of articles present explicit neurobiological models that assume that evidence is gradually accumulated over time; here, evidence is conceptualized as activity in populations of neurons associated with a specific choice alternative (Boucher et al. 2007; Ditterich 2006; Gold & Shadlen 2001, 2007; Hanes & Schall 1996; Platt & Glimcher 1999; Purcell et al. 2010; Ratcliff et al. 2003a; Roitman & Shadlen 2002; Shadlen & Newsome 2001).

The proposed neurobiological models fall into several classes: Some models assume accumulation of a single evidence quantity that can take on positive and negative values (as is consistent with the DDM; Gold & Shadlen 2000, 2001; Ratcliff 1978; Ratcliff et al. 1999, 2003a; Smith 2000); others assume that evidence is accumulated in separate accumulators corresponding to separate choice alternatives (Churchland et al. 2008, Ditterich 2006, Ratcliff et al. 2007a, Usher & McClelland 2001). In this latter class of models, accumulation in separate accumulators can be independent or interactive—so that as evidence grows in one accumulator, it inhibits evidence accumulation in the other accumulator. These two classes of models largely mimic each other at a behavioral level (Ratcliff 2006, Ratcliff & Smith 2004).

In one innovative application, Purcell et al. (2010) used real neural firing rate data as the input for a range of different sequential sampling models of decision making in a visual search task. The models they examined involved independent accumulation models with decay, inhibition, and a gating mechanism (i.e., activity had to be greater than some base level to be involved in the decision). The modeling results revealed that models that included decay or gating provided an excellent account of the observed RT distributions. In the model proposed by Purcell et al. (2010), the stimulus is directly tied to the decision-making mechanism without the involvement of an intermediate short-term memory representation. For highly overtrained monkeys, this is likely appropriate.

E pluribus unum. The modeling efforts for single neurons raise an important question: If single neurons act as noisy evidence accumulators, how does this determine the behavior of a large pool of neurons? In other words, do the properties of an individual neuron scale up to determine the dynamics of the neural population?

This question was recently addressed by Zandbelt et al. (2014), who examined a number of models in which individual neurons act as single redundant accumulators that together constitute a neural ensemble. The decision rule is that when some proportion of neurons from the ensemble have reached their criterion, the decision is made. They found that, under general conditions, the behavior of such a system was relatively insensitive to ensemble size. This suggests that a single diffusion process (used in modeling at the behavioral level) might be implemented in hardware as a combination of multiple accumulators.

Another attempt to bridge the gap from neuron to ensemble comes from modeling efforts that relate diffusion models to models based on spiking neurons (e.g., Deco et al. 2013, Roxin & Ledberg 2008, Wong & Wang 2006). Roxin and Ledberg examined models in which separate populations of spiking neurons are assumed to represent the two choices. They show that such models can be reduced to a one-dimensional model that is similar but not identical to the standard DDM (their model involves nonlinearity). Wong and Wang present a spiking neuron model and then reduce it to a two-variable model with self-excitation and inhibition. Their approximation is similar to the leaky competing accumulator model (Usher & McClelland 2001). Wang's modeling approach has had a wide range of applications (Wang 2008). Unfortunately, the Wang model is relatively complex, and at this point it is not possible to use it to fit data. However, its strength is that it takes seriously the relationship between neural processes, including synaptic currents, the behavior of neurotransmitters, membrane voltages, etc.

Smith (2010) suggested a different approach. He made an explicit connection between diffusion processes at a macro behavioral level and Poisson shot noise processes at a slightly abstract neural level. The shot noise process describes the cumulative effects of time-varying events (i.e., action potentials) that arrive according to a Poisson process. Smith showed that the time integral of such Poisson shot noise pairs follows an integrated Ornstein-Uhlenbeck process, whose long timescale statistics are very similar to those assumed in the standard DDM.

Single-cell recordings and bias effects. In a two-alternative task, bias toward one or the other alternative can be induced by instructions, by varying the relative proportions of occurrence, or by asymmetric rewards. Such bias can be modeled within the DDM framework in two ways. First, the starting point of the process can be moved nearer the boundary that represents the preferable alternative. Alternatively, the zero point of the drift rate (i.e., the drift criterion) can be altered by increasing drift rates toward the preferred boundary and decreasing drift rates to the nonpreferred boundary (Leite & Ratcliff 2011, Mulder et al. 2012, Ratcliff 1985, Ratcliff & McKoon 2008, Ratcliff & Smith 2004, Starns et al. 2012, Wagenmakers et al. 2007).

In human decision making it is clear that changing the relative proportion of occurrence brings about a change in the starting point of the decision process. This is evident from changes not only in accuracy and mean RT (Mulder et al. 2012), but also in the shape of RT distributions. If the starting point moves nearer one boundary, the RT distribution for that response shifts to lower values. In contrast, if the drift criterion changes, the leading edge of the RT distribution does not change very much (see Ratcliff & McKoon 2008 for a detailed discussion).

Hanks et al. (2011) presented single-cell recording data and human data from the motion discrimination task. They used their conclusions from the human data to support a drift criterion interpretation, but they did not examine RT distributions nor perform the critical test. Their results conflict with the conclusions from Ratcliff & McKoon (2008), who presented data from a bias manipulation in the motion discrimination task and found strong evidence for a change in starting point. For the monkey data, the initial firing rates differed as a function of bias, with an increase in firing rate for neurons corresponding to the more likely decision. Hanks et al. interpreted this as a change in drift rate, but it could also be the way the system changes the starting point of activity in the decision process. Again, explicit modeling of accuracy and RT distributions would make this finding clear.

Single-cell recordings and sequential dependencies. Gold et al. (2008) examined sequential dependencies in a motion discrimination task and found evidence for changes in LIP neuron firing rates, which they interpreted as changes in the drift criterion. In human data, Ratcliff et al. (1999) found that sequential effects were best modeled as changes both in the starting point and in the drift criterion. Again, explicit modeling of the behavioral data would clarify the interpretation of this finding.

Single-cell recordings and trade-off effects. Two recent studies have attempted to manipulate speed-accuracy settings in monkeys (Hanks et al. 2014, Heitz & Schall 2012; see Cassey et al. 2014 for a critique). One immediate problem is that it is extremely difficult to get monkeys to exercise caution and to slow down responding based on rewards in the same way as humans do. This means that monkey must be trained to delay, something that Heitz & Schall accomplished using explicit deadline cutoffs. In the Hanks et al. study, the monkeys naturally produced fast responses; to make the total time of the trial the same for fast and slow responses, the monkeys had to be trained to respond more slowly by using time delays following the response. To move the monkeys back to a speed regime, one of them needed an additional manipulation in which stimulus presentation duration was reduced.

Perhaps the main lesson from this experiment is that it is difficult to get monkeys to adopt different speed-accuracy regimes (see also Cassey et al. 2014). This contrasts with humans: Young adults find it easy to adopt different regimes, whereas older adults require some training, but once reassured that fast responses are acceptable or even desirable, they are able to switch between regimes on a block-by-block basis (Ratcliff et al. 2001, 2003b, 2004).

Surprisingly, both the Hanks et al. (2014) and Heitz & Schall (2012) studies found that the firing rate threshold did not change with speed-accuracy instructions, a finding that seems to

Functional magnetic
resonance imaging
(fMRI): popular
brain-imaging
technique used to
locate brain areas that
are relatively active
during task
performance

contradict the results of human studies that suggest a change in decision boundaries. However, the results for monkeys showed changes in the starting level of activity, with a higher level for the speed regime. This is consistent with a dual racing accumulator model in which changes in starting point are identical to changes in boundary settings (Forstmann et al. 2008, Ratcliff & Smith 2004).

Heitz & Schall (2012) also found a reduction of peak activity in the accuracy regime relative to the speed regime. Hanks et al. (2004) proposed a model in which a boost is added to the drift rate in a diffusion model in the speed regime. However, there is the question of whether monkeys and humans perform the tasks in the same way. This can be examined using RT distributions. In the Heitz & Schall study, the RT distributions for the speed and accuracy regimes hardly overlap. This is inconsistent with most human studies that use instructions (and not time deadlines or signals; e.g., Ratcliff 1988, 2006), in which RT distributions overlap to a great degree (Ratcliff et al. 2001, 2003b, 2004b). The relationship between speed and accuracy manipulations in humans and monkeys is not yet settled (Cassey et al. 2014).

In general, much work in the animal area is limited by the lack of explicit modeling of behavioral data featuring a thorough quantitative analysis of accuracy as well as the shapes of RT distributions for correct and error responses. If sequential sampling models such as the DDM were fit to the data, this would increase the confidence in the theoretical link between behavior and neural processes (e.g., Purcell et al. 2010, Ratcliff et al. 2007b).

In sum, the application of sequential sampling models in the arena of low-level cognitive neuroscience opens up exciting new prospects. Instead of considering only behavioral data, researchers could test the models on additional findings such as neural firing rates. These data add useful constraints and allow a deeper understanding of the computational mechanisms that ultimately produce overt decisions. The work in this new area can be improved further by rigorous modeling of the behavioral data to confirm the validity of more qualitative conclusions.

Application in High-Level Cognitive Neuroscience: Measuring Human Brain Activity

The application of sequential sampling models in low-level cognitive neuroscience comes with several challenges. For instance, it can be unclear whether monkeys and human carry out an experimental task in the same way (Hawkins et al. 2015), compromising the extent to which neural firing rate results in monkeys generalize to humans. Furthermore, neural firing rates are measured in a select subset of neural structures, making it difficult to assess the network dynamics among larger structures such as frontal cortex, premotor cortex, and the basal ganglia. These challenges can be addressed by using methods from high-level cognitive neuroscience.

Magnetic resonance imaging. In recent years, studies using functional magnetic resonance imaging (fMRI) have started to correlate parameter estimates from sequential sampling models to the blood-oxygen-level dependent signal obtained from fMRI experiments in perceptual decision making. **Figure 4** summarizes the results of these efforts. The summary includes results from seven fMRI studies focusing on evidence accumulation, two studies on decision thresholds, five studies on starting point bias, one study on drift rate bias, and one study on nondecision time (Mulder et al. 2014).

Figure 4 shows the relevance of a large variety of brain areas. Several global patterns emerge. First, individual differences in the accumulation of evidence are mainly associated with regions belonging to the frontoparietal network (top row of **Figure 4**). Second, individual differences in adjusting response thresholds are associated with a frontobasal ganglia network. Third, a more complex pattern arises for choice bias, which is associated with individual differences in both

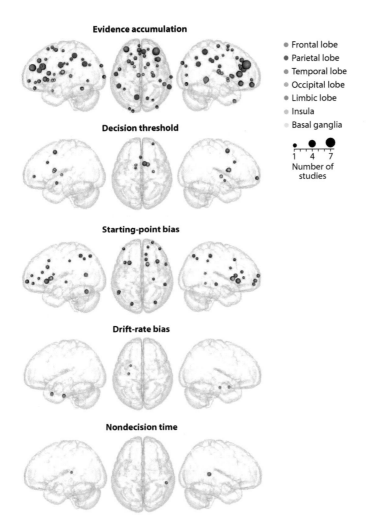

Figure 4

Summary of peak coordinates reported in functional magnetic resonance imaging (fMRI) studies that correlate blood-oxygen-level-dependent activation with parameter estimates from sequential sampling models. The size of each sphere is proportional to the number of studies that reported a specific region of interest. Only studies reporting whole-brain analyses were included. Figure adapted with permission from Mulder et al. (2014).

the frontoparietal and the frontobasal ganglia networks. There is only weak evidence for the involvement of brain regions in individual differences in nondecision time.

Electroencephalography. A growing number of studies has started to use sequential sampling models in combination with human neurophysiology measurement techniques such as electroencephalography (EEG). The main advantage of these techniques is their high temporal resolution, an advantage that is particularly pronounced for the study of speeded RT tasks.

Philiastides et al. (2006) used multivariate pattern analysis to derive spatiotemporal profiles of activity that could discriminate between relevant stimulus categories (i.e., face versus car) and between different levels of difficulty (i.e., image phase coherence). The results revealed an early

Electroencephalography (EEG): popular method for measuring electrical activity along the scalp, used to study the temporal aspects of information processing in the brain

(170 ms) and a late (300 ms) event-related potential (ERP) component that were predictive of decision accuracy. In a later study, Ratcliff et al. (2009) showed that within each stimulus coherence level, higher late-component amplitudes were associated with higher DDM drift rates. Hence, this study demonstrated that, for nominally identical stimuli, the amplitude of a single-trial EEG component can be used to measure and predict the quality of information processing.

Other model-based EEG work has tried to elucidate the temporal dynamics of decision making. Van Vugt et al. (2012) employed an EEG experiment to disentangle stimulus- and response-locked processes using an RDK task. They applied a general linear model comparable to event-related fMRI designs including a set of stimulus- and response-locked regressors. Their results revealed spectral changes primarily in the theta band (4–8 Hz), a frequency band associated with cognitive control processes (Cohen 2014). Importantly, changes in the theta band matched the dynamics (i.e., the ramping temporal profiles) of evidence accumulation during the decision process. These results are broadly consistent with recent work showing that weighting discrete stimuli presented in a series and as an input to the accumulation process fluctuated in accordance with delta band (1–3 Hz) oscillations (Wyart et al. 2012).

In another EEG study, Cavanagh et al. (2011) used theta power to quantify trial-to-trial fluctuations in activation of the medial prefrontal cortex (mPFC). They found that an increase in activation of the mPFC—a brain structure thought to be involved in effortful control over behavior—was associated with an increase in the DDM boundary separation parameter. They argued that mPFC signals response conflict and acts in concert with structures in the basal ganglia to increase the response threshold, slowing down response execution and hence creating more time for information accumulation.

Similarly, Boehm et al. (2014) had participants perform an RDK task either under speed stress or under accuracy stress. Trial-by-trial fluctuations in the adjustment of response thresholds under speed stress correlated with single-trial amplitudes of the contingent negative variation (CNV), a slow cortical potential that occurs whenever a stimulus prompts a participant to perform a task. Based on their results, Boehm et al. (2014) concluded that the CNV might reflect adjustments of response caution, which serve to prepare the system for action and facilitate quick decision making.

Taking a different approach, Bode et al. (2012) examined how neural activity preceding the stimulus affects the later decision process. They used a multivariate pattern classification approach to decode choice outcomes in a perceptual decision task from spatially and temporally distributed patterns of brain signals. Interestingly, in addition to decoding choice outcomes based on pre- and poststimulus activity, the authors were able to show that the past history of choices primed the decision process on subsequent trials. More concretely, a DDM decomposition revealed that the starting point of the evidence accumulation process was shifted toward the previous choice, thereby biasing the choice process.

In sum, recent work in high-level cognitive neuroscience has employed the DDM decomposition methodology and related the estimated parameters to brain measurements involving fMRI and EEG; these applications have been varied, concerning individual differences, theta power for specific brain structures, and more generally the construction of spatiotemporal profiles of brain activity. We expect this area of research to continue its ongoing expansion in the near future.

THE DIFFUSION DECISION MODEL IN COGNITIVE NEUROSCIENCE: EXTENSIONS

In this section, we show how the basic framework of the DDM has recently been extended to account for more complicated phenomena in decision making and their neural underpinnings.

Extension to Multi-Alternative Decisions

There is a developing interest in multi-alternative decision-making paradigms such as those concerning visual search (Basso & Wurtz 1998, Purcell et al. 2010), motion discrimination (Ditterich 2010, Niwa & Ditterich 2008), and other more behavioral tasks (Leite & Ratcliff 2010, Ratcliff & Starns 2013). Also, confidence judgments in decision and memory involve multi-alternative decision making (Pleskac & Busemeyer 2010, Ratcliff & Starns 2013, Van Zandt 2002; see also the next section). Many of these approaches compare a variety of competing models, and conclusions about what architectures are most promising are just being reached.

Compared to the present volume of work on two-choice decision making, only a modest amount of research has aimed at modeling both RT and choice proportions in multi-alternative decisions and confidence judgments. It is clear that the two-choice DDM cannot be simply extended to tasks with three or more choice alternatives. However, models with racing accumulators can be naturally extended by adding accumulators for each additional choice. Some models with racing accumulators become standard diffusion models when the number of choices is reduced to two.

Extension to Confidence Judgments

The psychological literature has a long tradition of using confidence judgments to better understand decision making and cognition. Probably the main domain of application of confidence judgments has been memory research (e.g., Egan 1958, Murdock 1974). In this line of research, subjects are often asked to respond on an ordinal many-point scale (e.g., a six-point scale ranging from "very sure" for one choice to "very sure" for the other choice).

In the past there have been several attempts to model the response confidence and response latency jointly (e.g., Murdock & Anderson 1975, Vickers 1979), but recently researchers have proposed more detailed models. Because the confidence choice is an explicit decision, the models have different decision boundaries for each choice.

Sequential sampling models for confidence. In order to model confidence judgments in recognition memory tasks, Ratcliff & Starns (2013) proposed a multiple-choice diffusion decision process with separate accumulators of evidence for the different confidence choices. The accumulator that first reaches its decision boundary determines which choice is made. Five algorithms for accumulating evidence were compared and one of them was successful, in the sense that it produced proportions of responses for each of the choices and full RT distributions for each choice that closely matched empirical data. Within this algorithm, an increase in the evidence in one accumulator is accompanied by a decrease in the others, so that the total amount of evidence in the system is constant. This is one way in which the two-choice DDM can be generalized to multi-alternative decisions (see also Audley & Pike 1965).

Application of the model to experimental data uncovered a relationship between the shapes of z-transformed receiver operating characteristics (z-ROC) and the behavior of RT distributions. For low-proportion choices, the RT distributions were shifted by as much as several hundred milliseconds relative to high-proportion choices. This behavior and the shape of z-ROC functions were both explained in the model by the behavior of the decision boundaries.

Ditterich (2010) argued that behavioral data alone would not be sufficient to discriminate among a number of different multi-alternative models. However, Ratcliff & Starns (2013) applied the decision model to a three-choice motion discrimination task in which one of the alternatives was the correct choice on a low proportion of trials. Like the shifts for the confidence judgment data, the RT distribution for the low-probability alternative was shifted relative to the higher-probability alternatives. The diffusion model with constant evidence accounted for shifts in the RT distribution better than a competing class of models.

Confidence judgments in animals. The animal domain and the human domain have different definitions or measures of confidence. In the animal domain the definition seems to depend on the amount of accumulated evidence: the more the evidence accumulated, the more confident the response. By contrast, in the human domain the measure seems to depend on an explicit choice on a scale, usually among a relatively small number of alternatives. Thus, in the human case, a commitment to a level of confidence is made. Humans find it easy to make decisions on such scales, but it is likely very difficult to train animals to make such judgments. To assess confidence in animals a different kind of task is employed, in which the animals are rewarded for correct choices and are offered smaller rewards if they opt out of the task.

Kepecs et al. (2008) performed an odor discrimination task in which stimuli were mixtures of two odors. Confidence was identified based on distance from the decision boundary and modeling was based only on accuracy. In a delayed version of the task, rats were more likely to move to the next trial without waiting for a reward when the stimulus was more ambiguous. However, this study only reported and modeled accuracy, although there was some discussion of evidence accumulation models.

Kiani et al. (2014) used a more explicit opt-out task in which, on some trials, monkeys could explicitly opt for a lower-value reward rather than risking zero reward. In the experiments, responses were given after a delay so that activity in the LIP neurons was maintained until the signal to respond, at which point a decision criterion was reached. When recordings were made in the area of LIP corresponding to the opt-out responses, there was no strong evidence of accumulation to a criterion for these decisions. This means that decisions can be made both when activity in a neural population reaches a decision criterion and when it does not.

Extension to Value-Based Decision Making

Recent work by Krajbich et al. (2010) set out to understand the role of visual fixation in value-based decision making. In an elegant design, they let people choose between options associated with different subjective values (e.g., a picture of a candy bar versus a picture of an apple) while tracking their eye movements. An extended version of the DDM linking choice preference to eye fixations was fit to the eye fixation data. The results show that this extended DDM in which fixations are involved in the value integration process could provide an excellent fit to the data, providing a new link between fixation and choice data. Interestingly, the duration of fixation was predictive of the choice as well as choice biases.

Extension to Changes of Mind

Resulaj et al. (2009) proposed another interesting extension of the DDM, trying to model how participants change their mind during decision making. Recall that the DDM proposes that a decision is initiated as soon as the accumulated evidence reaches a response boundary. Resulaj et al. challenged this assumption by showing that the simple formalism of the DDM fails to explain what happens when people change their mind. In their study, people had to make a decision about the directionality of a centrally positioned RDK stimulus by moving a handle to a leftward or rightward response location. Changes in the movement trajectories of the handle revealed that people occasionally changed their mind. The DDM extension of Resulaj et al. allows information that is already in the perceptual processing pipeline to influence and possibly overrule the initial decision.

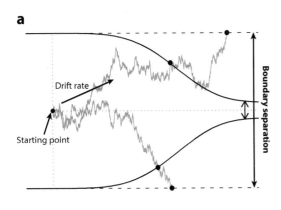

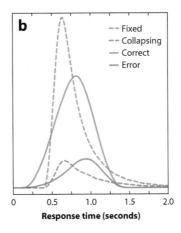

Figure 5

A standard fixed-bound diffusion decision model (DDM) versus a collapsing-bound DDM. (*a*) The DDM
with fixed (*dashed*) or collapsing (*solid*) response boundaries. Models with collapsing boundaries can
terminate the evidence accumulation process earlier than models with fixed boundaries, resulting in faster
decisions. (*b*) The ways in which the models lead to different predictions for response time distributions,
particularly in the tails. Figure adapted with permission from Hawkins et al. (2015).

Extension to Dynamic Thresholds

One of the most popular extensions of the DDM introduces the idea of thresholds or response
boundaries that are collapsing instead of fixed (see **Figure 5**). The core idea of this extension
is that decisions are based on less and less evidence as time passes; in other words, the decision
maker grows increasingly impatient (Bowman et al. 2012, Ditterich 2006, Drugowitsch et al. 2012,
Thura et al. 2012; but see Hawkins et al. 2015).

A different implementation of collapsing-bound models is through a rising urgency signal that
is parameterized in a so-called gain parameter. This gain parameter increases with the duration
of the decision (Churchland et al. 2008, Cisek et al. 2009, Ditterich 2006, Thura et al. 2012).

Importantly, the fixed- and collapsing-bound models make different predictions for the shape
of RT distributions of correct and error responses (**Figure 5b**). Hawkins et al. (2015) exploited
these differential predictions by fitting data from both humans and nonhuman primates using
different versions of the DDM. The results showed that whereas there is occasional evidence for
a collapsing-bound DDM, this model outperformed the fixed-bound DDM only under certain
circumstances, mostly for monkeys and after extensive practice.

CONCLUDING COMMENTS

The last 15 years have witnessed an explosion of interest in sequential sampling models such as
the DDM. This interest was initially fueled by the realization that sequential sampling models
provide a principled and plausible account of the macrolevel dynamics of the behavior of single
cells. Currently this interest has shifted somewhat, and many applications in high-level cognitive
neuroscience use models such as the DDM to decompose performance into its constituent psychological processes, such that brain measurements may be connected not to observed behavior,
but to specific latent processes of interest.

Another recent shift in interest is evident from research efforts that aim to extend the DDM to
novel tasks and new dependent variables, and to probe its adequacy under a set of circumstances

that had not been originally considered. New applications and extensions of the DDM now appear on a regular basis, and they constitute one of the most exciting recent trends in the neuroscience of speeded decision making. The work described here is a testament to the symbiosis that is slowly arising between mathematical psychology and cognitive neuroscience; this symbiosis and the accelerated development of quantitative models for brain and behavior hold much promise for the future.

SUMMARY POINTS

1. The DDM provides an excellent account of the law-like patterns observed across virtually all speeded RT tasks.

2. The DDM accounts for the relationship between mean RTs and the probability of choices (errors and correct responses) in both healthy and diseased populations.

3. One of the main reasons for the current popularity of diffusion models in neuroscience is the behavior of single neurons of monkeys (and occasionally rats) performing simple decision-making tasks.

4. In addition, fMRI and EEG data show specific neural patterns related to DDM model parameters, thereby offering the promise of a mechanistic understanding of latent cognitive processes.

5. Extensions of the DDM include multiple-choice behavior, confidence judgments, value-based decision making, and dynamic decision thresholds.

6. A DDM decomposition of choice performance provides numerous benefits, both for a purely behavioral analysis and for a model-based cognitive neuroscience approach.

FUTURE ISSUES

1. How do people set and adjust criteria for response caution? The speed with which people achieve relatively stable criteria suggests that they bring to bear substantial prior knowledge.

2. To what extent can the DDM prove useful in examining deficits in various neuropsychological disorders?

3. How can the DDM be extended to more complex and multistage decision making?

4. What exactly is the relation between latent processes in the DDM and key structures in the human brain (e.g., control structures in the basal ganglia and structures that support working memory processes in the frontal cortex)?

5. How can we build truly integrated models of decision making, that is, models that include knowledge of how motor processes are implemented in motor cortex and the oculomotor system?

6. To what extent can the DDM be applied to more deliberate economic decision making?

7. Will the DDM be able to quantitatively account for choice behavior in groups of animals?

8. To what extent can the DDM be used to jointly model behavioral and neuroscience data pertaining to clinical populations?

DISCLOSURE STATEMENT

The authors are not aware of any affiliations, memberships, funding, or financial holdings that might be perceived as affecting the objectivity of this review.

ACKNOWLEDGMENTS

We would like to thank Martijn Mulder, Leendert van Maanen, and Guy Hawkins for valuable discussions. This research line is financially supported by the European Research Council (B.U.F., E.-J.W.), the Dutch Research Foundation NWO (B.U.F.), and the National Institute of Aging (R.R.; grant R01-AG041176).

LITERATURE CITED

Audley RJ, Pike AR. 1965. Some alternative stochastic models of choice. *Br. J. Math. Stat. Psychol.* 18:207–25

Basso MA, Wurtz RH. 1998. Modulation of neuronal activity in superior colliculus by changes in target probability. *J. Neurosci.* 18:7519–34

Bode S, Sewell DK, Lilburn S, Forte JD, Smith PL, Stahl J. 2012. Predicting perceptual decision biases from early brain activity. *J. Neurosci.* 32:12488–98

Boehm U, Van Maanen L, Forstmann B, Van Rijn H. 2014. Trial-by-trial fluctuations in CNV amplitude reflect anticipatory adjustment of response caution. *NeuroImage* 96:95–105

Bogacz R, Brown E, Moehlis J, Holmes P, Cohen JD. 2006. The physics of optimal decision making: a formal analysis of models of performance in two-alternative forced choice tasks. *Psychol. Rev.* 113:700–65

Boucher L, Palmeri TJ, Logan GD. 2007. Inhibitory control in mind and brain: an interactive race model of countermanding saccades. *Psychol. Rev.* 114:376–97

Bowman NE, Kording KP, Gottfried JA. 2012. Temporal integration of olfactory perceptual evidence in human orbitofrontal cortex. *Neuron* 75:916–27

Brown SD, Heathcote A. 2008. The simplest complete model of choice response time: linear ballistic accumulation. *Cogn. Psychol.* 57:153–78

Carazza B. 1977. The history of the random-walk problem: considerations on the interdisciplinarity in modern physics. *Riv. Nuovo Cimento Ser. 2* 7:419–27

Carpenter RHS. 2004. Contrast, probability, and saccadic latency: evidence for independence of detection and decision. *Curr. Biol.* 14:1576–80

Cassey P, Heathcote A, Brown SD. 2014. Brain and behavior in decision-making. *PLOS Comput. Biol.* 10:e1003700

Cavanagh JF, Wiecki TV, Cohen MX, Figueroa CM, Samanta J, et al. 2011. Subthalamic nucleus stimulation reverses mediofrontal influence over decision threshold. *Nat. Neurosci.* 14:1462–67

Churchland AK, Kiani R, Shadlen MN. 2008. Decision-making with multiple alternatives. *Nat. Neurosci.* 11:693–702

Cisek P, Puskas GA, El-Murr S. 2009. Decisions in changing conditions: the urgency-gating model. *J. Neurosci.* 29:11560–71

Cohen MX. 2014. A neural microcircuit for cognitive conflict detection and signaling. *Trends Neurosci.* 37:480–90

Deco G, Rolls ET, Albantakis L, Romo R. 2013. Brain mechanisms for perceptual and reward-related decision-making. *Prog. Neurobiol.* 103:194–213

Ding L, Gold JI. 2012. Neural correlates of perceptual decision making before, during, and after decision commitment in monkey frontal eye field. *Cereb. Cortex* 22:1052–67

Ditterich J. 2006. Evidence for time-variant decision making. *Eur. J. Neurosci.* 24:3628–41

Ditterich J. 2010. A comparison between mechanisms of multi-alternative perceptual decision making: ability to explain human behavior, predictions for neurophysiology, and relationship with decision theory. *Front. Neurosci.* 4:184

Proposed a competing nonstochastic model for decision making.

Drugowitsch J, Moreno-Bote R, Churchland AK, Shadlen MN, Pouget A. 2012. The cost of accumulating evidence in perceptual decision making. *J. Neurosci.* 32:3612–28

Egan JP. 1958. *Recognition memory and the operating characteristic.* USAF Oper. Appl. Lab Tech. Note AFCRC-TN-58-51, Hear. Commun. Lab., Indiana Univ., Bloomington, IN

Einstein A. 1905. Über die von der molekularkinetischen Theorie der Wärme geforderte Bewegung von in ruhenden Flüssigkeiten suspendierten Teilchen. *Ann. Phys.* 17:549–60

Feller W. 1968. *An Introduction to Probability Theory and Its Applications.* New York: Wiley

Ferrera VP, Yanike M, Cassanello C. 2009. Frontal eye field neurons signal changes in decision criteria. *Nat. Neurosci.* 12:1458–62

Forstmann BU, Dutilh G, Brown S, Neumann J, von Cramon DY, et al. 2008. Striatum and pre-SMA facilitate decision-making under time pressure. ***PNAS*** **105:17538–42**

Forstmann BU, Wagenmakers EJ, eds. 2015. *An Introduction to Model-Based Cognitive Neuroscience.* New York: Springer

Forstmann BU, Wagenmakers EJ, Eichele T, Brown S, Serences J. 2011. Reciprocal relations between cognitive neuroscience and cognitive models: opposites attract? *Trends Cogn. Sci.* 6:272–79

Geddes J, Ratcliff R, Allerhand M, Childers R, Wright RJ, et al. 2010. Modeling the effects of hypoglycemia on a two-choice task in adult humans. *Neuropsychologia* 24:652–60

Glimcher PW. 2003. The neurobiology of visual-saccadic decision making. *Annu. Rev. Neurosci.* 26:133–79

Good IJ. 1979. Studies in the history of probability and statistics. XXXVII. A.M. Turing's statistical work in World War II. *Biometrika* 66:393–96

Gold IJ, Law C-T, Connolly P, Bennur S. 2008. The relative influences of priors and sensory evidence on an oculomotor decision variable during perceptual learning. *J. Neurophysiol.* 100:2653–68

Gold IJ, Shadlen MN. 2000. Representation of a perceptual decision in developing oculomotor commands. *Nature* 404:390–94

Gold IJ, Shadlen MN. 2001. Neural computations that underlie decisions about sensory stimuli. *Trends Cogn. Sci.* 5:10–16

Gold IJ, Shadlen MN. 2007. The neural basis of decision making. *Ann. Rev. Neurosci.* 30:535–74

Hanes DP, Schall JD. 1996. Neural control of voluntary movement initiation. ***Science*** **274:427–30**

Hanks T, Kiani R, Shadlen MN. 2014. A neural mechanism of speed-accuracy tradeoff in macaque area LIP. *eLife* 3:e02260

Hanks TD, Mazurek ME, Kiani R, Hopp E, Shadlen MN. 2011. Elapsed decision time affects the weighting of prior probability in a perceptual decision task. *J. Neurosci.* 31:6339–52

Hawkins GE, Forstmann BU, Wagenmakers EJ, Ratcliff R, Brown SD. 2015. Revisiting the evidence for collapsing boundaries and urgency signals in perceptual decision making. ***J. Neurosci.*** **35:2476–84**

Heitz RP, Schall JD. 2012. Neural mechanisms of speed-accuracy tradeoff. *Neuron* 76:616–28

Horwitz GD, Newsome WT. 1999. Separate signals for target selection and movement specification in the superior colliculus. *Science* 284:1158–61

Kepecs A, Uchida N, Zariwala HA, Mainen ZF. 2008. Neural correlates, computation and behavioural impact of decision confidence. *Nature* 455:227–31

Kiani R, Corthell L, Shadlen MN. 2014. Choice certainty is informed by both evidence and decision time. *Neuron* 84:1329–42

Krajbich I, Armel C, Rangel A. 2010. Visual fixations and the computation and comparison of value in simple choice. *Nat. Neurosci.* 13:1292–98

Laming DRJ. 1968. *Information Theory of Choice-Reaction Times.* London: Academic

Latty T, Beekman M. 2011. Speed-accuracy trade-offs during foraging decisions in the acellular slime mould *Physarum polycephalum. Proc. R. Soc. B* 278:539–45

Leite FP, Ratcliff R. 2010. Modeling reaction time and accuracy of multiple-alternative decisions. *Atten. Percept. Psychophys.* 72:246–73

Leite FP, Ratcliff R. 2011. What cognitive processes drive response biases? A diffusion model analysis. *Judgm. Decis. Mak.* 6:651–87

Link SW, Heath RA. 1975. A sequential theory of psychological discrimination. *Psychometrika* 40:77–105

Showed that increased activity in a cortico-basal ganglia network is associated with interindividual differences in response caution.

Proposed a connection between diffusion processes and buildup of activity in neurons involved in decision making.

Tested one of the most popular dynamic-threshold extensions of the DDM in both humans and nonhuman primates.

Luce RD. 1986. *Response Times*. New York: Oxford Univ. Press

Ma WJ, Beck JM, Latham PE, Pouget A. 2006. Bayesian inference with probabilistic population codes. *Nat. Neurosci.* 9:1432–38

Mulder MJ, Bos D, Weusten JMH, van Belle J, van Dijk SC, et al. 2010. Basic impairments in regulating the speed-accuracy tradeoff predict symptoms of attention-deficit/hyperactivity disorder. *Biol. Psychiatry* 68:1114–19

Mulder MJ, van Maanen L, Forstmann BU. 2014. Perceptual decision neurosciences—a model-based review. *Neuroscience* 277:872–84

Mulder MJ, Wagenmakers EJ, Ratcliff R, Boekel W, Forstmann BU. 2012. Bias in the brain: a diffusion model analysis of prior probability and potential payoff. *J. Neurosci.* 32:2335–43

Murdock BB. 1974. *Human Memory: Theory and Data*. Potomac, MD: Erlbaum

Murdock BB, Anderson RE. 1975. Encoding, storage, and retrieval of item information. In *Information Processing and Cognition: The Loyola Symposium*, ed. RL Solso, pp. 145–94. Hillsdale, NJ: Erlbaum

Niwa M, Ditterich J. 2008. Perceptual decisions between multiple directions of visual motion. *J. Neurosci.* 28:4435–45

Oberauer K, Süß H-M, Wilhelm O, Wittmann WW. 2003. The multiple faces of working memory: storage, processing, supervision, and coordination. *Intelligence* 31:167–93

Philiastides MG, Ratcliff R, Sajda P. 2006. Neural representation of task difficulty and decision making during perceptual categorization: a timing diagram. *J. Neurosci.* 26:8965–75

Platt M, Glimcher PW. 1999. Neural correlates of decision variables in parietal cortex. *Nature* 400:233–38

Pleskac TJ, Busemeyer J. 2010. Two-stage dynamic signal detection: a theory of confidence, choice, and response time. *Psychol. Rev.* 117:864–901

Purcell BA, Heitz RP, Cohen JY, Schall JD, Logan GD, Palmeri TJ. 2010. Neurally constrained modeling of perceptual decision making. *Psychol. Rev.* 117:1113–43

Ratcliff R. 1978. A theory of memory retrieval. *Psychol. Rev.* 85:59–108

Ratcliff R. 1985. Theoretical interpretations of speed and accuracy of positive and negative responses. *Psychol. Rev.* 92:212–25

Ratcliff R. 1988. Continuous versus discrete information processing: modeling the accumulation of partial information. *Psychol. Rev.* 95:238–55

Ratcliff R. 2002. A diffusion model account of response time and accuracy in a brightness discrimination task: fitting real data and failing to fit fake but plausible data. *Psychon. Bull. Rev.* 9:278–91

Ratcliff R. 2006. Modeling response signal and response time data. *Cogn. Psychol.* 53:195–237

Ratcliff R, Cherian A, Segraves M. 2003a. A comparison of macaque behavior and superior colliculus neuronal activity to predictions from models of simple two-choice decisions. *J. Neurophysiol.* 90:1392–407

Ratcliff R, Childers R. 2015. Individual differences and fitting methods for the two-choice diffusion model of decision making. *Decision* 2:237–79

Ratcliff R, Hasegawa YT, Hasegawa YP, Smith PL, Segraves MA. 2007a. Dual diffusion model for single-cell recording data from the superior colliculus in a brightness-discrimination task. *J. Neurophysiol.* 97:1756–74

Ratcliff R, Love J, Thompson CA, Opfer J. 2012. Children are not like older adults: a diffusion model analysis of developmental changes in speeded responses. *Child Dev.* 83:367–81

Ratcliff R, McKoon G. 2008. The diffusion decision model: theory and data for two-choice decision tasks. *Neural Comput.* 20:873–922

Ratcliff R, Perea M, Colangelo A, Buchanan L. 2004a. A diffusion model account of normal and impaired readers. *Brain Cogn.* 55:374–82

Ratcliff R, Philiastides MG, Sajda P. 2009. Quality of evidence for perceptual decision making is indexed by trial-to-trial variability of the EEG. *PNAS* 106:6539–44

Ratcliff R, Rouder JN. 1998. Modeling response times for two-choice decisions. *Psychol. Sci.* 9:347–56

Ratcliff R, Smith PL. 2004. A comparison of sequential sampling models for two-choice reaction time. *Psychol. Rev.* 111:333–67

Ratcliff R, Starns JJ. 2013. Modeling confidence judgments, response times, and multiple choices in decision making: recognition memory and motion discrimination. *Psychol. Rev.* 120:697–719

Reviewed fMRI studies that used a model-based cognitive neuroscience approach to perceptual decision making.

Used multivariate pattern analysis to derive spatiotemporal activity profiles that could discriminate between relevant stimulus categories and between different levels of difficulty.

Introduced the DDM for RT distributions and accuracy, with application to recognition memory.

Reviewed DDM modeling, data, and applications.

Ratcliff R, Thapar A, McKoon G. 2001. The effects of aging on reaction time in a signal detection task. *Psychol. Aging* 16:323–41

Ratcliff R, Thapar A, McKoon G. 2003b. A diffusion model analysis of the effects of aging on brightness discrimination. *Percept. Psychophys.* 65:523–35

Ratcliff R, Thapar A, McKoon G. 2004b. A diffusion model analysis of the effects of aging on recognition memory. *J. Mem. Lang.* 50:408–24

Ratcliff R, Thapar A, McKoon G. 2007b. Application of the diffusion model to two-choice tasks for adults 75–90 years old. *Psychol. Aging* 22:56–66

Ratcliff R, Thapar A, McKoon G. 2010. Individual differences, aging, and IQ in two-choice tasks. *Cogn. Psychol.* 60:127–57

Ratcliff R, Thapar A, McKoon G. 2011. Effects of aging and IQ on item and associative memory. *J. Exp. Psychol.: Gen.* 140:464–87

Ratcliff R, Van Dongen HPA. 2009. Sleep deprivation affects multiple distinct cognitive processes. *Psychon. Bull. Rev.* 16:742–51

Ratcliff R, Van Zandt T, McKoon G. 1999. Connectionist and diffusion models of reaction time. *Psychol. Rev.* 106:261–300

Introduced a DDM change-of-mind extension allowing information in the perceptual processing pipeline to influence and possibly overrule the initial decision.

Resulaj A, Kiani R, Wolpert DM, Shadlen MN. 2009. Changes of mind in decision-making. *Nature* 461:263–66

Riefer DM, Knapp BR, Batchelder WH, Bamber D, Manifold V. 2002. Cognitive psychometrics: assessing storage and retrieval deficits in special populations with multinomial processing tree models. *Psychol. Assess.* 14:184–201

Roitman JD, Shadlen MN. 2002. Response of neurons in the lateral interparietal area during a combined visual discrimination reaction time task. *J. Neurosci.* 22:9475–89

Roxin A, Ledberg A. 2008. Neurobiological models of two-choice decision making can be reduced to a one-dimensional nonlinear diffusion equation. *PLOS Comput. Biol.* 4:e1000046

Schall JD. 2001. Neural basis of deciding, choosing and acting. *Nat. Rev. Neurosci.* 2:33–42

Schall JD. 2013. Macrocircuits: decision networks. *Curr. Opin. Neurobiol.* 23:269–74

Schmiedek F, Oberauer K, Wilhelm O, Süß H-M, Wittmann W. 2007. Individual differences in components of reaction time distributions and their relations to working memory and intelligence. *J. Exp. Psychol.: Gen.* 136:414–29

Shadlen MN, Kiani R. 2013. Decision making as a window on cognition. *Neuron* 80:791–806

Shadlen MN, Newsome WT. 1996. Motion perception: seeing and deciding. *PNAS* 93:628–33

Shadlen MN, Newsome WT. 2001. Neural basis of a perceptual decision in the parietal cortex (area LIP) of the rhesus monkey. *J. Neurophysiol.* 86:1916–36

Smith PL. 2000. Stochastic dynamic models of response time and accuracy: a foundational primer. *J. Math. Psychol.* 44:408–63

Smith PL. 2010. From Poisson shot noise to the integrated Ornstein-Uhlenbeck process: neurally principled models of diffusive evidence accumulation in decision-making and response time. *J. Math. Psychol.* 54:266–83

Starns JJ, Ratcliff R, McKoon G. 2012. Evaluating the unequal-variability and dual-process explanations of zROC slopes with response time data and the diffusion model. *Cogn. Psychol.* 64:1–34

Stone M. 1960. Models for choice reaction time. *Psychometrika* 25:251–60

Teodorescu AR, Usher M. 2013. Disentangling decision models: from independence to competition. *Psychol. Rev.* 120:1–38

Thapar A, Ratcliff R, McKoon G. 2003. A diffusion model analysis of the effects of aging on letter discrimination. *Psychol. Aging* 18:415–29

Outlined one of the first models to implement principles from the neuroscience of decision making in a formal psychological model.

Thura D, Beauregard-Racine J, Fradet CW, Cisek P. 2012. Decision making by urgency gating: theory and experimental support. *J. Neurophysiol.* 108:2912–30

Townsend JT, Ashby FG. 1983. *Stochastic Modeling of Elementary Psychological Processes.* London: Cambridge Univ. Press

Usher M, McClelland JL. 2001. The time course of perceptual choice: the leaky, competing accumulator model. *Psychol. Rev.* 108:550–92

van Ravenzwaaij D, Brown S, Wagenmakers EJ. 2011. An integrated perspective on the relation between response speed and intelligence. *Cognition* 119:381–93

van Ravenzwaaij D, Dutilh G, Wagenmakers EJ. 2012. A diffusion model decomposition of the effects of alcohol on perceptual decision making. *Psychopharmacology* 219:1017–25

van Vugt MK, Simen P, Nystrom LE, Holmes P, Cohen JD. 2012. EEG oscillations reveal neural correlates of evidence accumulation. *Front. Neurosci.* 6:106

Van Zandt T. 2002. Analysis of response time distributions. In *Stevens' Handbook of Experimental Psychology*, Vol. 4: *Methodology in Experimental Psychology*, ed. JT Wixted, H Pashler, pp. 461–516. New York: Wiley. 3rd ed.

Van Zandt T, Colonius H, Proctor RW. 2000. A comparison of two response time models applied to perceptual matching. *Psychol. Bull. Rev.* 7:208–56

Vandekerckhove J, Tuerlinckx F. 2007. Fitting the Ratcliff diffusion model to experimental data. *Psychon. Bull. Rev.* 14:1011–26

Vandekerckhove J, Tuerlinckx F. 2008. Diffusion model analysis with MATLAB: a DMAT primer. *Behav. Res. Methods* 40:61–72

Vandekerckhove J, Tuerlinckx F, Lee MD. 2011. Hierarchical diffusion models for two-choice response times. *Psychol. Methods* 16:44–62

Vickers D. 1979. *Decision Processes in Visual Perception*. New York: Academic

Vickers D, Lee MD. 1998. Dynamic models of simple judgments. I: Properties of a self-regulating accumulator module. *Nonlinear Dyn. Psychol. Life Sci.* 2:169–94

Voss A, Nagler M, Lerche V. 2013. Diffusion models in experimental psychology: a practical introduction. *Exp. Psychol.* 60:385–402

Voss A, Rothermund K, Voss J. 2004. Interpreting the parameters of the diffusion model: an empirical validation. *Mem. Cogn.* 32:1206–20

Voss A, Voss J. 2007. Fast-dm: a free program for efficient diffusion model analysis. *Behav. Res. Methods* 39:767–75

Voss A, Voss J. 2008. A fast numerical algorithm for the estimation of diffusion-model parameters. *J. Math. Psychol.* 52:1–9

Wabersich D, Vandekerckhove J. 2014. Extending JAGS: a tutorial on adding custom distributions to JAGS (with a diffusion model example). *Behav. Res. Methods* 46:15–28

Wagenmakers EJ. 2009. Methodological and empirical developments for the Ratcliff diffusion model of response times and accuracy. *Eur. J. Cogn. Psychol.* 21:641–71

Wagenmakers EJ, Brown S. 2007. On the linear relation between the mean and the standard deviation of a response time distribution. *Psychol. Rev.* 114:830–41

Wagenmakers EJ, Ratcliff R, Gomez P, McKoon G. 2008. A diffusion model account of criterion shifts in the lexical decision task. *J. Mem. Lang.* 58:140–59

Wagenmakers EJ, van der Maas HL, Grasman RP. 2007. An EZ-diffusion model for response time and accuracy. *Psychon. Bull. Rev.* 14:3–22

Wald A, Wolfowitz J. 1948. Optimum character of the sequential probability ratio test. *Ann. Math. Stat.* 19:326–39

Wang XJ. 2008. Decision making in recurrent neuronal circuits. *Neuron* 60:215–34

White C, Ratcliff R, Vasey M, McKoon G. 2009. Dysphoria and memory for emotional material: a diffusion model analysis. *Cogn. Emot.* 23:181–205

White CN, Ratcliff R, Vasey MW, McKoon G. 2010. Using diffusion models to understand clinical disorders. *J. Math. Psychol.* 54:39–52

Wiecki TV, Sofer I, Frank MJ. 2013. HDDM: Hierarchical Bayesian estimation of the drift-diffusion model in Python. *Front Neuroinform.* 7:14

Wong KF, Wang XJ. 2006. A recurrent network mechanism of time integration in perceptual decisions. *J. Neurosci.* 26:1314–28

Wyart V, de Gardelle V, Scholl J, Summerfield C. 2012. Rhythmic fluctuations in evidence accumulation during decision making in the human brain. *Neuron* 76:847–58

Zandbelt B, Purcell BA, Palmeri TJ, Logan GD, Schall JD. 2014. Response times from ensembles of accumulators. *PNAS* 111:2848–53

Zeguers MHT, Snellings P, Tijms J, Weeda WD, Tamboer P, et al. 2011. Specifying theories of developmental dyslexia: a diffusion model analysis of word recognition. *Dev. Sci.* 14:1340–54

RELATED RESOURCES

Fast-dm-30 documentation
http://www.psychologie.uni-heidelberg.de/ae/meth/fast-dm/
This website provides detailed information on how to use Fast-dm to fit the DDM to data.

HDDM 0.5.3 documentation
http://ski.clps.brown.edu/hddm_docs/
This website provides detailed information on how to use HDDM to fit the DDM to data. The HDDM program is supported by an active mailing list of core users.

Ratcliff & McKoon
http://star.psy.ohio-state.edu/coglab/
This website contains information about all aspects concerning the DDM.

Society for Mathematical Psychology
http://mathpsych.org/
The latest DDM developments are presented at the annual meeting of the Society for Mathematical Psychology.

Evidence-Based Practice: The Psychology of EBP Implementation

Denise M. Rousseau[1] and Brian C. Gunia[2]

[1]Heinz College of Public Policy, Information, and Management and Tepper School of Business, Carnegie Mellon University, Pittsburgh, Pennsylvania 15213; email: denise@cmu.edu

[2]Carey Business School, Johns Hopkins University, Baltimore, Maryland 21202-1099; email: brian.gunia@jhu.edu

Annu. Rev. Psychol. 2016. 67:667–92

First published online as a Review in Advance on September 11, 2015

The *Annual Review of Psychology* is online at psych.annualreviews.org

This article's doi: 10.1146/annurev-psych-122414-033336

Keywords

evidence-based practice, decision supports, evidence appraisal, critical thinking, protocols and checklists, practice-oriented evidence

Abstract

Evidence-based practice (EBP) is an approach used in numerous professions that focuses attention on evidence quality in decision making and action. We review research on EBP implementation, identifying critical underlying psychological factors facilitating and impeding its use. In describing EBP and the forms of evidence it employs, we highlight the challenges individuals face in appraising evidence quality, particularly that of their personal experience. We next describe critical EBP competencies and the challenges underlying their acquisition: foundational competencies of critical thinking and domain knowledge, and functional competencies such as question formulation, evidence search and appraisal, and outcome evaluation. We then review research on EBP implementation across diverse fields from medicine to management and organize findings around three key contributors to EBP: practitioner ability, motivation, and opportunity to practice (AMO). Throughout, important links between psychology and EBP are highlighted, along with the contributions psychological research can make to further EBP development and implementation.

Contents

INTRODUCTION

Strive to do the best imperfect human beings can do.

—Harris (2012), p. 13

Evidence-based practice (EBP) is a disciplined approach to decision making and action, the hallmark of which is attention to evidence quality and the use of the best available evidence. Its goals are to improve the results of professional decisions and to increase the use of practices that lead to desired outcomes while eliminating dysfunctional practices. All professions engaged in EBP make some use of scientific evidence and methodologies, reflecting the premise that science can improve outcomes through a better understanding of the world (e.g., Melnyk & Fineout-Overholt 2011, Miller 2004, Wells & Miranda 2006).

However, EBP is implemented to different degrees within professions and even within the same organization (Ferlie et al. 2006, Melnyk et al. 2012). This review examines research on the implementation and effective use of EBP. In doing so, we describe the psychological factors underlying its implementation and their ties to EBP's professional and organizational supports. We begin by describing EBP, its background, and the elements that comprise it. We then review research on its implementation across various domains, from medicine to management. The review addresses three key contributors to EBP: practitioner ability, motivation, and opportunity (AMO). The AMO framework highlights important links between EBP and psychology. The review then addresses EBP effectiveness research and trends apparent in EBP implementation. It concludes with a discussion of how psychological research can contribute to the further development and implementation of EBP.

WHAT IS EVIDENCE-BASED PRACTICE?

EBP involves conscientious, explicit, and judicious use of the best available evidence in making decisions (Sackett 2000). Individuals, both laypeople and professionals, typically use some form of evidence in making decisions—if only their past experience. EBP raises the issue of what that evidence is and, in particular, how strong it might be (Barends et al. 2014, Sackett 2000). Evidence-based practitioners seek to improve the quality of the evidence used and condition their decisions and practices on the confidence that the evidence warrants. Importantly, effective EBP requires a commitment to continuous practice improvement and lifelong learning (Straus et al. 2005).

The Background of EBP

EBP originated in medicine in the 1980s, with the goal of promoting the more systematic use of scientific evidence in physician education and clinical practice (Barends & Briner 2014). It arose out of recognition that physicians had tended to prioritize tradition and personal experience, giving rise to troubling variation in treatment quality. Underlying this issue was the tendency for medical schools to teach their own specific approaches to clinical problems, without clear (or at least explicit) links to scientific evidence. This approach to professional education has three problems. First, in fields with rapid advances in research, practices can go out of date quickly (Weber 2009), and educators may lag in updating course content (Rousseau 2006). Second, practices taught in professional education can vary widely in their scientific support, with some unsupported by any scientific evidence (Barends & Briner 2014). Third, professionals faced with novel or unfamiliar situations can lack the ability to access relevant new evidence (Barends & Briner 2014).

EBP has since become a movement in fields as diverse as nursing (Melnyk et al. 2012), conservation (Pullin et al. 2004), psychotherapy (Goodheart et al. 2006), and management (Rousseau 2012). Recently, the EBP movement has tended to move beyond its original focus on the education of individual practitioners and toward addressing the practices of organizations and professions (Dogherty et al. 2013, Stevens 2013). At the same time, EBP has become part of popular culture. The TV series *House*, for example, showcased an iconoclast physician who used research findings and clinical data to save at least one life within one television hour. The TV series *Lie to Me* purported to use scientific evidence on facial expressions to aid law enforcement. Exercise studios tout "evidence-based fitness." As a movement, EBP is indicative of the social trend tracing to at least the age of Enlightenment to ground action in reason and empiricism rather than tradition or authority.

Primary Types of Evidence Used in EBP

As a discipline, EBP involves a mindful integration of both scientific evidence and local evidence. When available, scientific evidence is seen as a critical contributor to effective practice. In nature conservation, for example, evidence-based decision making stands in contrast to decision making based on anecdote and habitat management handbooks (Pullin et al. 2004). In fields from medicine to management, EBP has led to greater attention to the critical appraisal and synthesis of existing research to identify what is known or unknown about effective practice (Sackett 2000, Tranfield et al. 2003). Still, EBP is not limited to scientific evidence, but also incorporates local or situational information, stakeholder concerns, and practitioner judgment and experience. Rather than a narrow focus on scientific research, a focus on evidence directs attention to the quality of the available information and knowledge, the various forms it can take, and the way people use it in decision making and action. The term "practice" refers to the entire decision-making process: before, during, and after.

Scientific evidence enters EBP in several ways. At least in EBP fields, it now informs the content of practitioners' professional education. At the same time, practitioners need to learn how to acquire scientific evidence pertinent to their professional practice (Sackett 2000). These skills permit them to use scientific evidence to stay current and address new questions that arise as their careers progress. Accessing scientific evidence is still not enough, however. Practitioners need to evaluate its quality, a task many find challenging (Scurlock-Evans et al. 2014). The quality of a particular research study (or an entire body of research) depends on the type of question being answered (Petticrew & Roberts 2003). If the practitioner wonders whether a practice or intervention works as intended (e.g., Can training reduce staff dissatisfaction? Does it increase compliance with patient care protocols?), quality depends on whether the available evidence employs sufficient controls to rule out competing explanations (e.g., randomization and control groups). If the question is how particular kinds of employees are likely to feel about a new way of working, quality depends on the representativeness of the populations studied and the relevance of the assessments employed. Thus, in contrast to critiques of EBP as overly valuing randomized controlled trials (RCTs; e.g., Webb 2001), the diversity of possible practice questions necessitates methodological pluralism (e.g., O'Neill et al. 2014). Nonetheless, EBP does presume that, for a given question, some available evidence may be of better quality than other evidence, and practitioners need to be able to assess evidence quality.

Scientific evidence relevant to practice is also subject to evidence synthesis, where researchers and sometimes practitioners collaborate to evaluate the implications of a body of evidence to a particular practice question (Haynes 2001). Practitioners in many fields can now access evidence summaries related to their practice via such online sources as the Cochrane Library (for health care) and the Campbell Library (for education, criminology, social work, and social science generally). Such summaries make EBP easier. Nonetheless, practitioners need to pay careful attention to the quality of evidence on which such summaries are based. Summaries based on low-quality evidence can lead to the use of ineffective or dysfunctional practices. Practices based on low-quality evidence may ultimately be overturned by better-quality research, as in the case of the now-refuted use of hormone replacement therapy for postmenopausal women (Guyatt et al. 2008). Luckily, some useful standards exist for determining which scientific findings to export to organizations and how (Fiske & Borgida 2011).

EBP also makes use of local evidence regarding the circumstances and setting in which practice occurs. Local evidence takes the form of diagnostic information that practitioners obtain from patients (human or animal) and clients (individual, family, firm, etc.; Goodheart et al. 2006, Groopman 2008) as well as organizational facts and indicators (Kovner et al. 2009). Local evidence also includes situational factors such as constraints (e.g., time and resources) and contingencies (e.g., risks) as well as observed practice outcomes (Kovner et al. 2009, Lambert 2010, Nutt 1999). Importantly, outcome assessment is needed to evaluate whether an application of scientific evidence is working.

Local evidence is also essential in EBP because the available scientific evidence in most fields is limited relative to the array of problems practitioners may face. Although no one knows the true percentage of professional practices that have been validated by scientific study, one commentator estimated it to be 25% in medicine (Goodman 1998), and it is probably lower in other fields. Practices that have not been studied scientifically need not be ineffective, however; they simply lack affirmative evidence. In the absence of scientific evidence, local evidence provides a necessary basis for action, recognizing that much remains unknown and much of what we "know" may turn out to be incorrect, ineffective, or even harmful. The failure of once-popular programs such as Scared Straight, formerly believed to reduce juvenile delinquency (Petrosino et al. 2013), and science-informed recommendations overturned by new evidence (e.g., to eat breakfast in order to avoid weight gain; Mekary & Giovannucci 2014) have raised awareness that knowledge requires frequent reevaluation and testing.

Attention to differences in the quality of local evidence has led to the development of integrated organizational databases (e.g., "big data" linking clinical and financial data in healthcare or diverse functions in business; Davenport et al. 2010). Nevertheless, little consensus exists on the quality criteria to apply to local evidence. Reliability and validity certainly contribute, but other criteria, such as timeliness for specific decisions or usefulness to particular stakeholders, may contribute as well (Davenport et al. 2010, Staubus 1999). Independent outsiders, such as auditors, may help to assess the quality of local evidence (Cokins et al. 2008).

Finally, local evidence is important when practitioners confront novel circumstances such as previously unknown diseases or the advent of disruptive innovations, because historical evidence is less likely to apply. In these circumstances, practitioners may need to learn by doing; that is, by experimenting with alternative courses of action and evaluating the results (Weick & Sutcliffe 2011). Local evidence gathered via pilot tests and experiments may be critical • to solving novel problems.

Stakeholder perspectives constitute additional forms of evidence. Attending to stakeholder concerns, interests, and points of view has been characterized as a professional or even ethical obligation of EBP (Rousseau 2012, Sackett 2000). For example, physicians often weigh patient preferences and family concerns alongside scientific evidence when devising a treatment plan (Straus et al. 2005). Stakeholder perspectives tend to be decision specific and include client or family preferences, community or regulatory concerns, or the interests of an organization's employees, managers, and shareholders (Baba & HakemZadeh 2012). These perspectives play varying roles in EBP depending on the profession, with a more consistent role in clinical disciplines, such as medicine (Sackett 2000) and psychology (Am. Psychol. Assoc. 2006), than in broad fields, such as management, that are buffeted by a wide variety of incentives, regulatory pressures, and other contextual factors (Ghoshal 2005). Nonetheless, considering stakeholder perspectives can help balance immediate situational pressures and the narrowing of judgment that decision makers face under stress (cf. Heath & Heath 2012, Yates & Potworowski 2012). Stakeholder considerations can introduce multiple objectives into professional decisions, calling attention to trade-offs and optimizations where cost and human well-being or short- and long-term goals are concerned, helping to generate more integrative decisions (Heath & Heath 2012). Explicit attention to multiple objectives when framing decisions helps resolve some ambiguities that decision makers routinely face (Heath & Heath 2012). Last, stakeholders (e.g., employees, patients) are sources of outcome assessments when scientific and local evidence are applied.

A final, critical source of evidence is professional experience. Like all forms of evidence, EBP practitioners must appraise the quality and relevance of their own experience to the situation at hand (Barends & Briner 2014, Thyer 2002). Similarly, if considered, the experience of others, from consultants to in-house experts, must also be appraised. In reality, however, appraising individual experience is problematic.

Psychologists are of two minds about the value of experience for decision making. One research stream substantiates the fallibility of experience-based decisions due to cognitive biases and processing limitations—factors that even sustained practice cannot easily overcome (Dawes 2008, Kahneman 2011). In contrast, another stream focuses on domain-specific expertise, where experts including firefighters and nurses quickly and accurately draw from experience to recognize and respond to new situations, tapping extensive domain-specific expertise using automatic pattern recognition (Salas et al. 2009).

A weak link between experience and decision quality has been reported in areas as diverse as medical diagnosis (Camerer & Johnson 1991), professional software design (Sonnentag 1998), and management (March 2010). A systematic review of 62 published studies found that the quality of care physicians provided tended to decline as their years of experience increased (Choudhry et al. 2005) due to less up-to-date factual knowledge and lower adherence to professional standards and guidelines. Nonetheless, Hay et al. (2008) noted that physicians' confidence in their effectiveness increases with experience even when they do not track their patients' outcomes. Likewise, in clinical psychology, the ability to make correct diagnoses does not appear to improve with experience, as even relatively simple statistical models objectively outperform the most experienced practitioners (Clement 2013, Dawes et al. 1989).

One reason these issues persist is that professionals often "obtain little to no information about the accuracy of their predictions" (Dawes et al. 1989, p. 1671); in other words, opportunities for feedback are often rare. Gigerenzer (2014) notes that heuristics validated by feedback, like the gaze heuristic that both pilots and ballplayers use for positioning, can be reliably applied intuitively as well as systematically. On the other hand, professionals may not always seek out feedback regarding their judgments even when it is available (Lambert 2010). Indeed, the effectiveness of "intuitive" or fast decisions appears to depend on learning from feedback, which in turn requires feedback that is prompt, information rich, and consistent (Kahneman & Klein 2009). Few, if any, of these conditions exist in the context of practice in fields such as psychotherapy or management. One issue the present review raises is the effects EBP might have on the practitioner's ability to learn from experience, a matter research has not yet addressed.

The complicated link between experience and effectiveness means that individuals may have a hard time appraising their own judgment. More difficult still may be appraising the experience of others, since individuals tend to overweight their own opinions (Soll & Larrick 2009). The tendency toward confirmation bias means that individuals are likely to find support for their own judgments, experiencing little uncertainty while acting on their intuitions (Morewedge & Kahneman 2010). Aggravating such difficulties is the tendency of both laypeople and experts to use less information in their decisions than they recognize (Fischoff 2013). Indeed, a narrowing of focus may impair the use of any form of evidence—one motivation behind the development of EBP decision supports.

Decision Supports in EBP

Decision supports refer to tools, rubrics, and processes that aid human information processing by overcoming the limits of human judgment and memory, reducing the effect of distractions, and integrating expertise (Simon 1990, 1996). These supports, inspired by the difficulties practitioners face in using large amounts of information, take many forms in EBP, applicable in some cases to problem solving generally and in others to specific circumstances.

Checklists and protocols derived from scientific and local evidence provide guidelines for action under specific circumstances (Gawande 2010), increasing the regular use of effective practices. Other forms of information-gathering routines, such as those used by physicians to assess patient vital signs and history, aid general problem solving, as when assessment routines help physicians avoid the temptation to stop searching prematurely (Groopman 2008). Similarly, decision rubrics that guide information gathering help reduce the tendency to focus on only a small portion of the evidence (Larrick 2009). Rubrics can take the form of logic models (e.g., inputs→throughputs→outputs) to guide decision making and problem solving generally (Goodman 1998, Zanardelli 2012) or provide criteria such as the CAMEL (capital adequacy, asset quality, management, earnings, and liability) framework for the specific problem of evaluating loans (Heath et al. 1998). Supports also exist to help practitioners appraise the quality and relevance of scientific evidence (e.g., Downs & Black 1998). Nonetheless, there are two critical requirements for EBP-related decision supports to work well: (*a*) practitioners need to understand the quality of the evidence on which the supports are based in order to use them appropriately, and (*b*) supports need to be updated regularly as new evidence emerges (Knaapen 2013).

In fields where domain or technical knowledge is critical to high-quality decisions (e.g., medicine), decision supports typically are not meant for standalone use. Checklists and guidelines are approximates (cf. Simon 1990), rough blueprints to guide thinking and action (Gawande 2010). They do not generally substitute for education and training; instead, they require that the user be trained in both their appropriate use and underlying evidence. Training aids the user in balancing fidelity to the guidelines with flexibility in the face of practice conditions (Gawande 2010, Sewell et al. 2011). Without such training, practitioners may apply guidelines to incorrect situations or slavishly follow their recommendations in the face of contradictory local evidence (Gawande 2010). Even without special training, patient care protocol use (a form of guideline) has been found to improve the uptake of EB practice in critical care settings (Sinuff et al. 2013), although staff in those settings may already have considerable professional education.

Specific decision processes may also help in the acquisition and effective use of evidence (Rousseau 2012). The cardinal issue perspective (Yates & Potworowski 2012), for example, may aid group decision making, where relevant evidence is distributed and stakeholders have diverse interests. Likewise, decision reviews, which seek to introduce new information and perspectives before a decision is finalized, may help to identify biases and permit reconsideration. Groopman (2008, pp.185–86) describes the practice of having several doctors independently read X-rays and record their findings into a database each day. After-actions reviews help workgroups learn and improve practice by evaluating decisions, projects, or interventions immediately after they occur (Ellis & Davidi 2005, Salas et al. 2008). The use of decision aids and systematic decision processes appears to increase with a field's involvement in EBP, particularly via the efforts of institutions that incorporate EBP into their mission (e.g., the Agency for Healthcare Research and Quality National Guideline Clearinghouse in the United States and the National Clinical Guideline Center in the United Kingdom). In sum, decision supports come in many forms and help with many aspects of EBP, but practitioners need to use them thoughtfully in order to improve decisions and practice outcomes.

EXISTING RESEARCH ON EVIDENCE-BASED PRACTICE IMPLEMENTATION

This section reviews research on the implementation of EBP. Extensive research on this topic exists for professions with substantial EBP experience, particularly medicine, nursing, and allied health fields such as clinical psychology. Because EBP is a form of goal-related behavior, we organize our review using an integration of Ajzen's (1991) theory of planned behavior and Vroom's (1964) theory of workplace behavior. The integrated ability, motivation, opportunity (AMO) framework is useful for describing workplace-related behavior (e.g., Hughes 2007, Petty & Cacioppo 1986). This framework helps to shed light on why people do or do not adopt EBP as a function of their ability, motivation, and opportunities to engage in EBP-related activities.

Ability to Practice

Effective use of EBP requires the individual to possess both foundational and functional competencies. Foundational competencies are general skills and knowledge required to engage in all aspects of EBP. Functional competencies are specific skills and knowledge related to discrete EBP activities, such as evidence search and critical appraisal.

EBP's foundational competencies include the capacity for critical thinking and the domain or technical knowledge acquired through education and practice experience in a particular field (Sackett 2000). Critical thinking is the intellectually disciplined process of actively and skillfully conceptualizing, analyzing, evaluating, and synthesizing information as a guide to belief and action (Facione & Facione 2008, Profetto-McGrath 2005). It reflects the capacity for higher-order thinking, including reflection on one's own thinking and experience, evaluation of information, and hypothetical thinking about alternatives. Because an individual's observations and mental models can be somewhat inaccurate or incomplete, practitioners who can attend to discrepancies and alternative mental models are better able to search and make sense of a problem space. Because individuals appear to have difficulty employing more than one mental model at a time, however, the ability to consider multiple mental models requires individuals to adopt a critical standard to avoid merely accepting the first mental model that provides a minimally satisfactory answer (Simon 1990). In effect, critical thinking imposes standards on one's thinking in order to reduce bias and distortion and increase the completeness of available information. Thus, it is likely to aid the EBP process of asking practice-related questions and adapting evidence to practice (Profetto-McGrath 2005).

Critical thinking is positively related to academic performance (Kowalski & Taylor 2009). Denney (1995) observed that it appears to increase with age, at least among educated people. Some evidence from nursing suggests that training in thinking processes can enhance critical thinking (e.g., Allen et al. 2004). Conversely, when individuals are busy or otherwise overloaded cognitively, their ability to think critically can be impaired (Bittner & Gravlin 2009). Low levels of critical thinking correspond to naïve realism (Lilienfeld et al. 2008), where individuals unreflectively accept an initial mental model triggered by an experience as if there were no error in perception. Insufficient critical thinking is associated with a preference for intuitive decisions (Dawes 2008) and a preference for intuition over scientific evidence (cf. Highhouse 2008, Lilienfeld et al. 2008).

Another foundational competency for EBP is domain or technical knowledge—i.e., specific knowledge and procedural skills related to a professional practice area, corresponding to the psychological construct of expertise (Ericsson & Lehmann 1996). Important in its own right for attaining and sustaining a successful professional career, domain knowledge also facilitates the critical thinking underlying EBP, and the two may be mutually reinforcing (Bailin 2002). Specifically, domain knowledge helps practitioners recognize incomplete information, evaluate evidence quality, and interpret new evidence (Ericsson & Lehmann 1996). More generally, domain knowledge provides the mental models that can facilitate appropriate inferences regarding problems and helps practitioners judge the relevance of evidence.

As a field adopts EBP, the domain knowledge that practitioners develop can evolve. Importantly, widespread adoption of EBP increases the likelihood that practitioners will have been disabused of inaccurate beliefs, especially when learners can think critically (Kowalski & Taylor 2009). For example, criminal justice professionals might begin to recognize that innocent people sometimes confess to crimes (Howard-Jones 2014). Given individuals' strong tendency to accept their initial mental model, evidence-based domain knowledge increases the likelihood that an initial mental model represents an accurate understanding of a problem. In sum, foundational competencies such as domain knowledge are broad skills necessary to excel as a practitioner, especially an EB practitioner.

EBP's core functional competencies are associated with obtaining and applying the best available evidence and are supported by the foundational competencies above. Individuals with strong functional skills are able to follow the core steps of EBP evidence use: ask, acquire, appraise, apply, and assess (Sackett 2000). More generally, practitioners need to be able to identify their information needs as they arise, translate them into potentially answerable questions, and acquire the evidence needed to answer them. Practitioners must then critically evaluate evidence quality and applicability and use the highest-quality evidence to inform their actions.

Asking. Fundamental to formulating a question amenable to obtaining evidence is the aptitude for organizing problems that are ill structured, that is, subject to several interpretations or involving choices that are difficult to specify (Chi et al. 1988). To ask tractable questions, practitioners must structure their thinking. Structured thinking enables them to ask questions for diagnosis (What is happening?), challenge assumptions (Is what I know true?), plan interventions (How can we induce change?), or assess risk (How certain is it that if we do X we get Y?). Asking such questions amounts to recognizing that uncertainty or ambiguity exists and can lead to the realization that adequate evidence is available or that search is needed. The way a question is formulated impacts the process of acquisition or search. EBP question formulation often entails the use of templates that structure the question in order to facilitate search. In health care, PICO (population, intervention, comparison, outcome) is a common question framework (Richardson et al. 1995) and has been adapted for use in other domains such as management (Rousseau & Barends 2011) and speech therapy (Schlosser et al. 2007).

Acquiring. Acquiring scientific evidence typically entails a search process (Kaplan Jacobs et al. 2003), commonly via online databases, a capability increasingly incorporated into professional education and development (Rousseau & Barends 2011, Straus et al. 2005). This competency varies not only with education and training but also with EBP support from the practitioner's work setting (e.g., access to librarians or search tools).

The extent of a field's EBP-related knowledge determines whether evidence exists in the form of systematic reviews and evidence summaries (Melnyk et al. 2004). Considerable attention has been devoted to the methodology of systematic reviews and evidence summaries in order to enhance their quality (Haynes 2001, Tranfield et al. 2003). Yet, their availability tends to be greater in fields with longer EBP experience, increasingly via new information technologies (e.g., smartphone apps for medical specialties; Heneghan & Badenoch 2006).

Less systematic attention has been given to the acquisition of local, stakeholder, or experiential evidence, although gathering these forms of evidence is typically an important part of the EBP diagnostic process via interviews, focus groups, etc. Acquisition can also entail running local experiments and using in-house databases for monitoring outcomes (Davenport et al. 2010, Kovner et al. 2009). As in the case of scientific evidence, the ability to acquire local evidence depends on the abilities of the practitioner (e.g., analytical; Davenport et al. 2010) as well as local infrastructure such as high-quality data and control systems (Davenport et al. 2010) and senior leadership support for data acquisition (Kovner et al. 2009).

Appraising. As noted, practitioners often have difficulty appraising evidence quality (Scurlock-Evans et al. 2014), finding appraisal more difficult than acquisition (McCluskey & Lovarini 2005). For scientific evidence, this difficulty persists despite the existence of systematic reviews because many reviews fail to qualify their conclusions on the basis of evidence quality (Berkman et al. 2013). A systematic review of training in critical appraisal concluded that the appraisal skills of undergraduates improved more than those of medical residents (Norman & Shannon 1998), possibly due to the latter group's prior training or busy schedules and weak compliance.

Guidelines and checklists for appraising research quality improve the accuracy of scientific evidence appraisals (e.g., Downs & Black 1998, Sackett 2000). In contrast, little guidance currently exists for appraising local evidence, practitioner experience, or stakeholder perspectives, leaving such appraisals up to individual judgment.

Applying. Having high-quality evidence is not equivalent to having answers. Practitioners have to interpret the available evidence for their own situations. When existing evidence does not correspond to the situations practitioners confront, EBP becomes more difficult (Feinstein & Horwitz 1997, Goodman 1998). Additionally, the published scientific evidence on interventions may not be detailed enough to guide actual use. Glasziou et al. (2008) reviewed 80 studies chosen for their importance to evidence-based medicine and found that clinicians could reproduce the particular intervention in only half.

Practitioners often need to adapt evidence from the simpler controlled conditions of scientific research to the more complicated conditions of practice. Alternatively, the best available evidence may come from an altogether different field or discipline; for example, patient safety practitioners learn from airline safety research (Denham et al. 2012) and veterinarians regularly adapt findings from human medicine (e.g., Roudebush et al. 2004). Scholars have noted that transferring knowledge between disciplines may require a different paradigm than creating new knowledge (Watson & Hewett 2006), however, and it also may require different practitioner skills.

Assessing. Once an action has been taken based on evidence, it is necessary to evaluate the outcome. However, meaningful outcome assessment requires the practitioner to prepare in advance by obtaining a relevant and reliable baseline measure (e.g., pre- and posttest measures of rates of infection, customer complaints, employee satisfaction or retention). The need for assessment applies both in the application of scientific evidence and in circumstances in which the practitioner made a decision when scientific or local evidence regarding a problem was unavailable. In the latter case, the practitioner can rely only on the last step of the EBP process: assessing the outcome. By providing the practitioner with feedback in the latter case, this last phase of the EBP process permits valid learning to occur based on experience. Overall, functional competencies allow practitioners to engage in all relevant aspects of EBP, from asking questions to assessing outcomes.

Measuring functional competencies. The importance of assessing EBP proficiency is demonstrated by performance variability in fields that lack standards and required competencies, such as fingerprinting and criminal profiling (Lilienfeld & Landfield 2008). In contrast, more than 100 instruments exist to evaluate the functional competencies of medical students and postgraduate trainees (Shaneyfelt et al. 2006), although less attention has been given to how to best help practitioners acquire these specific skills. The Fresno test, which assesses performance of each component of EBP rather than relying on self-reports, is widely used in evaluation (McCluskey & Bishop 2009). As EBP becomes more sophisticated within a given discipline, additional functional skills may become important, including participation in research (e.g., Scurlock-Evans et al. 2014). At the same time, training in evidence acquisition and use is not likely to lead to actual behavior change unless individuals are motivated to do so (McCluskey & Lovarini 2005).

Motivation to Practice

Motivation, the drive to engage in a certain behavior, is a function of three individual beliefs (Ajzen 1991). Behavioral beliefs represent a favorable or unfavorable attitude toward the behavior, perceived behavioral control reflects an individual's belief that he or she is capable of the behavior, and normative beliefs reflect perceived social norms regarding the commonality of the behavior. The individual's intention to perform a behavior generally is expected to be strongest when all three beliefs are high (Ajzen 1991).

Behavioral beliefs reflect the extent to which a behavior is seen as beneficial. The appeal of EBP has been linked to beliefs in its benefits (Aarons 2004). Practitioners who possess EBP-related knowledge are more likely to see it as beneficial (e.g., Jette et al. 2003, Melnyk et al. 2004). Where introduction of EBP economically or psychologically costs the practitioner in some fashion, it is more likely to be resisted (Ajzen 1991). Simply stopping a non-evidence-based practice tends to be more difficult than replacing it with an evidence-based practice that brings the user benefits (Bates et al. 2003). For example, managers tend to resist following structured hiring practices that simply reduce their control over who gets hired (Bozionelos 2005).

Such costs to the practitioner often make higher-level intervention and more complex implementation processes necessary to effect a transition to EBP (Bates et al. 2003). Having an EBP mentor increases perceived benefits, knowledge, and practice of EBP (Melnyk et al. 2004). Ties to favorable EBP opinion leaders outside the organization also increase the perceived benefits of EBP and increase people's openness to innovation, a disposition that contributes to positive EBP attitudes (Aarons 2004). Older practitioners who came of age before EBP tend to be more skeptical and have different notions of evidence than younger practitioners (Aarons & Sawitzky 2006), which may contribute to the finding that experience is negatively related to guideline compliance (Choudhry et al. 2005). Whatever their source, then, behavioral beliefs that EBP is beneficial contribute to its active adoption.

Perceived behavioral control reflects confidence in one's ability to manifest a behavior. As a form of self-efficacy, perceived behavioral control has been linked to EBP behaviors (Beidas & Kendall 2010, Salbach et al. 2007). Given that EBP involves self-directed, lifelong learning (Sackett 2000), self-efficacy is an essential component of effective EBP application. Evidence concerning the effectiveness of self-efficacy training programs on EBP is mixed. Some EBP training programs have been shown to increase EBP-related self-efficacy (Kiss et al. 2010, Salbach et al. 2007), whereas others increase EBP skill without any change in self-efficacy (e.g., Spek et al. 2013). Education in EBP does typically increase student knowledge and self-perceived skills (e.g., Haas et al. 2012). Ongoing supervisory support following EBP training appears to heighten these effects (Beidas & Kendall 2010). In sum, perceived behavioral control is often related to training and support that shape practitioners' abilities, thus promoting their self-efficacy as EB users.

Normative beliefs reflect the extent an individual believes that a specific behavior is normal or common within a reference group. Behaviors seen as normal, in turn, are more likely to be adopted by others (Ajzen 1991). Faced with uncertainty, for example, professionals tend to rely upon existing norms (Montgomery & Oliver 1996), which may or may not support EBP. Such norms can reflect an individual's education and training as well as the education and training of coworkers. In workgroups with shared beliefs that EBP is difficult, an individual is less likely to perceive EBP as normative (Dalheim et al. 2012).

EBP-related norms, as well as other motivational beliefs, are shaped by broad organizational and/or institutional cultures. When first adopted within a field, EBP's emphasis on scientific evidence and evidence quality can seem to dismiss practice experience. In its early years, for example, evidence-based medicine's protocols and guidelines were ridiculed as "cookbook medicine" (LaPaige 2009). In the same way, EBP's introduction can initially threaten a practitioner's professional identity (e.g., "You think police are corrupt"; Sherman 2002) or a manager's sense of self as a competent decision maker (Highhouse 2008). A particularly important countervailing force is leadership support, which helps to legitimate EBP and explain its complementarity with practitioner experience (Melnyk et al. 2004, 2012). Similarly, the support of professional peers encourages the uptake of innovations generally, and EBP in particular (Ferlie et al. 2006), as do the views of pro-EBP opinion leaders (Soumerai et al. 1998).

Structural arrangements can also shape beliefs in the commonality of EBP. For example, roles that encourage practitioners to participate in or conduct their own research promote pro-EBP norms (Kothari & Wathen 2013, Melnyk & Fineout-Overholt 2011). Such norms are more likely to be weak or absent when leaders and peers reject EBP or other situational supports are absent. Lastly, research on the diffusion of innovation has suggested that members of a profession may not fully adopt new norms and transition to new practices for a generation (Rogers 1995), and such generational differences may characterize EBP. In sum, normative beliefs trace to an array of organizational and/or institutional factors and can exert a strong influence on the decision to engage in EBP.

Opportunity to Practice

Opportunity to practice refers to perceptions regarding the support that the practice context provides for engaging in EBP. Having the ability and motivation to engage in EBP is less likely to lead to actual behavior unless individuals also experience the opportunity to practice (Jette et al. 2003). A sense that practice conditions interfere with EBP is often referred to as the "reality of practice" (Mantzoukas 2008, Novotney 2014). The opportunity to practice EBP is linked to on-the-job autonomy and flexibility (Belden et al. 2012). Time pressure is negatively related to EBP (Dalheim et al. 2012, Jette et al. 2003) and increases reliance on intuition (Klein et al. 2001). Lack of authority to act on evidence creates another barrier (Dalheim et al. 2012).

Complexity and variability in practice conditions also impose perceived barriers. Facing multiple interrelated problems rather than only one (e.g., a depressed alcoholic patient versus simply a depressed patient) can make it difficult for practitioners to fit the evidence to practice conditions. Additionally, the opportunity to practice can be constrained by large heterogeneous caseloads, limiting the accessibility of relevant evidence and decision supports (Hoagwood et al. 2001), and by a lack of supervisory support (Hoagwood et al. 2001; Melnyk et al. 2004, 2012). A particularly important factor in the opportunity to practice is psychological safety, the shared belief among workgroup members that the setting is safe for risk taking. Psychological safety increases the likelihood of engaging in the experiential learning needed to adapt EBP to the work setting (Tucker et al. 2007).

The perceived barriers imposed by practice conditions can change as practitioners gain experience with EBP. More-skilled practitioners perceive fewer barriers to practice than do less-skilled practitioners (Melnyk et al. 2004), suggesting a link between EBP self-efficacy and perceived opportunities to practice. Experience with EBP can help individuals and their organizations learn to adapt evidence to practice and develop decision supports that ease evidence use (Zanardelli 2012). Barriers to EBP practice may thus be especially salient in EBP's initial implementation phases. Wright (2013) observed that volunteers given release time and mentoring still had problems obtaining research articles and often felt they lacked both the time and work space to reflect on, process, and use the information obtained. Such problems may stem from a lack of autonomy, high workloads, and low skill in searching and reflection. Swain et al. (2010) found that 80% of mental health agency sites that used an implementation toolkit along with EBP consultants or trainers were able to sustain EBP after two years, though effects varied with the availability of financing, training, and leadership support. Qualitative research on factors facilitating the expansion of EBPs suggests that leadership support, the involvement of other specialties in EBP, and demands from an organization's performance management system affect perceived opportunities for EBP (Tierney et al. 2014).

Institutional supports beyond the work setting can provide infrastructure that increases perceived EBP opportunity. The development of online search portals and research databases (e.g., the Cochrane Library) has advanced professionals' access to scientific research over the past decade. In the early years of EBP, information in such databases was largely limited to questions about what works. In recent years, systematic reviews using new approaches have emerged that address a broader array of questions including cost-effectiveness, risks associated with interventions, and implementation concerns (Lavis et al. 2005). This expansion of review topics is aided by the development of practice-oriented research investigating the practice conditions that serve as EBP barriers and facilitators (Castonguay et al. 2013). In sum, we now have a good understanding of the factors that increase opportunity to practice, as well as the fact that, without the opportunity to practice, the ability and motivation to practice may not be enough.

EVIDENCE FOR EVIDENCE-BASED PRACTICE EFFECTIVENESS

EBP's guiding principle is to rely on high-quality evidence rather than tradition or authority. This means that collecting evidence on the effectiveness of EBP is essential. Although we attempt an overview of the evidence amassed to date, a full review is beyond our scope. Additionally, our review reveals that evaluating EBP effectiveness is no easy matter, so much more evidence remains to be gathered.

In evaluating EBP, it is important to first recognize that the differences between practice conditions and the conditions under which the original evidence was obtained can have serious implications. It is widely recognized that effect sizes from controlled studies tend to decline in field applications; situational demands, problem complexity, and individual practitioner differences all play a role (Weisz et al. 2013).

Studies of EBP effectiveness differ considerably in focus and operationalization. EBP has been operationalized variously as adherence to guidelines and checklists (Haynes et al. 2009), training in evidence search (Coomarasamy & Khan 2004), avoidance of dysfunctional practices (Ziewacz et al. 2011), and effects of evidence-based interventions under real-world conditions (Michelson et al. 2013). Local evidence such as patient data is one source of effectiveness criteria, researcher-generated assessments another.

Decision supports such as guidelines have shown widely beneficial effects as an indicator of EBP. For example, documentation of nursing interventions based on evidence guidelines was positively associated with home-care patients' health (Doran et al. 2014). The use of checklists has been found to improve uptake of EBPs and produce greater fidelity in their application (Arriaga et al. 2013), resulting in improved outcomes (Gawande 2010, Haynes et al. 2009).

When effectiveness is operationalized in terms of the impact of specific practices, evaluation studies refer to them as including "evidence-based," "evidence-informed," or "best" practices. It is important to closely examine studies of so-called best practices because that label is sometimes misleadingly applied to popular practices lacking an evidence base (Marchington & Grugulis 2000). In the case of evidence-based best practices, these refer both to discrete interventions, such as cognitive behavioral therapy for obsessive-compulsive disorder (Hofmann & Smits 2008), and bundles of mutually supportive practices, as in adult offender rehabilitation (Cullen 2013). In investigating the effects of discrete practices, it is important to consider the conditions of their use in order to gauge whether co-occurring factors influence these effects. Studies of discrete practices in isolation may be misleading if their success is tied to bundles of mutually reinforcing practices. For example, although criminal justice research in the late twentieth century commonly concluded that rehabilitation of criminals did not work, a fresh look at the evidence revealed that a systematic approach using a combination of practices led to a high success rate (Cullen 2013). Sets of practices including treatments tailored to offenders' demographic and risk characteristics, for example, were broadly effective. Whether as single practices or bundles, such interventions typically are evaluated using various forms of controlled designs, with usual treatment or care as the comparison. Such evaluations form the basis of meta-analyses and systematic reviews to synthesize findings for practitioners, e.g., the meta-analysis of studies contrasting RCTs of EBPs with usual care (e.g., youth psychotherapy; Weisz et al. 2013). Although effect sizes of EBP are widely found to be greater than usual care, cost and effort are considerations in justifying change (Weisz et al. 2013). Additionally, as Weisz and colleagues noted, studying usual care is valuable in understanding its conditions and which of its features already work. Some of its features might become EBPs if studied more systematically.

Intervention compliance (i.e., the fidelity with which EBPs are followed) is another concern when evaluating EBP effectiveness. The effects of fidelity differ from those of implementation. The former reflect controllable compliance with practice requirements, whereas the latter refer to the circumstances of implementation beyond the practitioner's control (e.g., treatment volume). Drops in effect sizes from research studies to field applications can be due to either (Weisz et al. 2013).

Evaluation of both EBP itself and fidelity is essential because a bandwagon effect has led many organizations to adopt the label "evidence based" while ignoring its key tenets. For example, insurance companies and regulators sometimes impose "evidence-based" reimbursement schedules that are founded on out-of-date or low-quality evidence (Steinberg & Luce 2005). In other instances, organizations may attempt to confer legitimacy to programs and policies by invoking the label of EBP (Jacobs & Manzi 2013) or mandate compliance with guidelines that are based on weak evidence (Knaapen 2013). Creating guidelines from weak evidence is a form of early overadoption because it occurs in advance of good evidence and risks undermining belief in EBP's benefits, thereby creating reservations and resistance (Ferlie et al. 2006). Organizations that seek legitimacy from EBP without making a substantive commitment to its tenets tend to share one feature: They fail to square their purportedly evidence-based practices with local evidence. As noted, local evidence is needed to evaluate whether intended effects actually occur and how they impact stakeholders. A full evaluation of EBP, then, must recognize several complexities and controversies, but careful study does begin to suggest that EBP can improve practice in several ways.

CRITICISMS OF EVIDENCE-BASED PRACTICE

Like any new idea implying fundamental change, EBP has its critics. Many criticisms have been debunked on the basis of underlying misinformation or misunderstandings (Gibbs & Gambrill 2002, Lilienfeld 2014), whereas other criticisms have proven more substantial. We summarize the former first. A common claim is that EBP represents a one-size-fits-all approach to practice decisions. Successful adoptions of EBP, however, have shown that EBP instead involves substantial adaptation of evidence to fit with local conditions and practitioner judgment (Lilienfeld et al. 2013). Additionally, the claim that EBP stifles innovation does not appear to be supported, as reviews describe how EBP helps diffuse effective new practices that might otherwise have spread more slowly (Grol & Grimshaw 2003, Lilienfeld et al. 2013). In contrast to the claim that EBP relies solely or primarily on RCTs, its review syntheses and evidence summaries incorporate the diverse array of studies relevant to practice questions (Lilienfeld et al. 2013, Petticrew & Roberts 2003). In this regard, EBP has also led to new forms of research, often descriptive in nature, to provide more readily useable evidence to practitioners (e.g., Woolf 2008).

At present, other criticisms appear to have more support. First, despite its emphasis on improving the decisions professionals make, EBP is criticized for its heavy reliance on human judgment. As Knaapen (2013) describes in her study of guideline development, evidence search and guideline creation are not automated processes. The choice of which evidence to use may still be influenced by a decision maker's biases and political interests. Certain evidence may be preferred because of its implications for practice or action (Revkin 2014). The potential political and judgmental influences on evidence choice, however, raise concerns that EBP does not, or perhaps cannot, provide a fully rational basis for action, which points to the importance of ongoing EBP evaluation.

Second, the guidelines that began as supports for EBP can become ends in themselves. Authorities may demand that guidelines be written when scientific evidence does not exist or is relatively weak (Knaapen 2013). Such demands can result in guidelines based purely or primarily on opinion. Transparency regarding the search and selection criteria used in guideline development provides some protection from arbitrariness, as does the regular evaluation of outcomes resulting from their use. Conversely, one danger in opaque guidelines is that they can undermine the decision processes they were originally intended to support. The routine use of checklists in aviation, for example, has revealed that their effectiveness can be impeded by memory problems and workarounds. For guidelines and other decision supports to be effective, they need to be evidence based and integrated into the sociotechnical system in which the practitioner works (Degani & Wiener 1990). We regard these and other criticisms of EBP as important areas for future EBP research.

PATTERNS OBSERVED IN EVIDENCE-BASED PRACTICE RESEARCH

Our review of research on EBP implementation leads us to describe a number of broad patterns we observe in the literature. These patterns highlight both lessons learned from the past and important issues to investigate in the future.

Practitioners Need Guidelines for Appraising All Forms of Evidence

Appraising the quality of local evidence, stakeholder concerns, and practitioner judgment remains difficult. As noted, EBP's initial (~1990s) focus on scientific evidence has broadened to take ongoing practice evaluation, local evidence, and stakeholder perspectives more seriously. How practitioners should evaluate these forms of evidence, however, remains largely ignored. The development of guidelines for appraising the quality of non-science-based evidence is particularly important given the limited availability of scientific knowledge in some domains. In addition to needing frameworks to evaluate whatever kinds of evidence they use, practitioners need to learn how to make decisions effectively when evidence is limited or absent.

Both Top-Down and Bottom-Up EBP Implementation Occurs

EBP typically evolves over the course of its implementation. From a top-down perspective, the initial emphasis tends to be on formal programs for developing individual practitioner knowledge and skills, particularly regarding the use of scientific evidence. If sustained, engagement in EBP tends to lead to greater codification of decisions and practices where high-quality information is available. As EBP becomes even more widespread, collectives, such as professional groups, tend to advocate for greater use of guidelines, perhaps reflecting the greater capacity of collectives than individuals for overcoming decision-making biases (Heath et al. 1998). As practice outcomes become more salient, stakeholder demands for accountability can promote a transparency that improves both the quality of individual practice decisions and the available evidence (Dogherty et al. 2013). In addition, as a field's use of EBP evolves, new resources and supports emerge; institutional supports such as training programs and summaries of preappraised scientific evidence, for example, create further opportunities and reduce barriers for practice.

From a bottom-up perspective, opportunities for practitioners to engage in EBP increase both as they become more skilled and as EBP becomes more familiar to the people with whom they work closely. Similarly, as work groups address recurrent problems through evidence-based routines and guidelines, more time becomes available to seek proactive solutions for novel problems (Goodman & Rousseau 2004). These are just a few examples of the general point that EBP implementation is a long-term developmental process involving both bottom-up and top-down components.

Effective EBP Implementation Requires Evidence-Based Change Management

As noted, the successful implementation of EBP requires the adoption of a constellation of new tools, practices, and behaviors. In other words, it involves organizational change and benefits from effective change management. Some efforts to implement EBP, such as the proliferation of guidelines without appropriate training and support, have not fully recognized the need for change management, prompting the same kinds of implementation barriers observed for other organizational changes (Goodman & Rousseau 2004, Shortell et al. 2007). These barriers are surmountable, however, as attention to organizational variables, such as leader support and organizational climate, contributes to effective EBP implementation across fields (Aarons & Sawitzky 2006, Sherman 2002). Practitioners can learn from past implementation successes and failures. Interventions targeting the development of leader and practitioner commitment to EBP are particularly likely to help (Aarons 2006, Wakefield et al. 2003).

EBP Creates New Knowledge

EBP has prompted more attention among scientists to synthesis and conditions of use. Synthesis involves both integrating findings across research areas and transforming information into intervention guidelines. For example, more than 50 elements in various EBP protocols for children with anxiety were effectively synthesized to 7 key elements (exposure, cognitive restructuring, modeling, etc.; Chorpita et al. 2011). Additionally, many of the problems that practitioners face across disciplines have commonalities, allowing evidence-based, problem-specific guidelines to be used in multiple professions (Thyer 2002). Although new processes may be needed to test the applicability of guidelines across practice domains, such synthesis offers the potential for accelerating the transition of science-based knowledge into practice across professions (Watson & Hewett 2006).

EBP has also led to a new kind of research, prompted by increased collaboration between producers and users of evidence. Practice-oriented research examines the application of scientific evidence in everyday clinical practices. For example, it investigates how much an intervention's effectiveness depends on practitioners' compliance with its specific features. Practice research has led to some important findings, e.g., that tight control over blood pressure is important to diabetics' health, whereas tight control over blood glucose is not (Giménez-Pérez et al. 2005). Such findings help practitioners direct patients' health management efforts.

Another area of practice research concerns the practice conditions that can facilitate or impede the effective use of EBP. For example, physicians who are aware of research highlighting the dangers of overprescribing antibiotics might still tend to overprescribe to patients at risk for infections. Practice-oriented research (e.g., Kumar et al. 2003) has shown that physicians do so with patients they are unable to follow up. This research led to the development of a blood test to determine on the spot whether antibiotics were appropriate (Aabenhus et al. 2014). Such research makes it easier for practitioners to act on and comply with evidence-based practices and guidelines (Castonguay et al. 2013). In doing so, research can help resolve some of the uncertainty that emerges when translating scientific evidence into practice and help overcome practitioners' skepticism of academically oriented research (Lilienfeld et al. 2013). Practice-oriented research is part of a zeitgeist anticipated by Simon (1996) in his book *The Sciences of the Artificial*, which explicated how theory and practice can be considered together to generate both better-informed science and more effective practice. Given institutional constraints in both academia and the professions, we encourage systematic study of the conditions that facilitate or impede practice-oriented research.

FUTURE RESEARCH

Many issues surrounding EBP could benefit from additional research. The first issue that we note here concerns practitioner judgment, an area in which research has raised more questions than answers. EBP advocates argue that the strength of EBP is the complementarity between judgment and systematically gathered evidence, with neither replacing the other (Sackett 2000). As noted, however, practitioner knowledge and effectiveness in several EBP fields do not seem to improve with experience (Choudhry et al. 2005, Clement 2013, Dawes 2008). Yet we do not know how evidence based the practice of these practitioners has been. Since experience coupled with feedback can lead to improved performance, the expanded use of outcome assessment and feedback in EBP as well as its impact on practitioner judgment over time warrant study to evaluate the effect of feedback on the knowledge and effectiveness of individual practitioners as well as their organizations. In sum, it would be helpful to better understand the conditions under which feedback increases the complementarity between professional judgment and systematically gathered evidence.

We also need to better understand how practitioners can make high-quality decisions under uncertainty. It is ironic that EBP calls attention to indeterminancy, i.e., the unknowns and uncertainty characterizing many real-world situations. Strictly speaking, incompleteness characterizes almost all knowledge—from human medicine, to veterinary science, to clinical psychology, to management. Indeterminacy in the context of EBP can result from gaps in the evidence base (Knaapen 2013), existing evidence that does not specifically address the current situation (Goodman 1998), or an imperfect mastery of available evidence (Groopman 2008, p. 152). Langer's (1989) research suggests that incomplete knowledge is not a void about which nothing can be said, however. Rather, identifying unknowns can help to make decisions more mindful. Psychological research could focus more attention on how decision makers and practitioners might cope with indeterminacy more effectively. Research is also needed on decision making under circumstances of true novelty: a previously unknown disease, a drastic change in climate, or a set of challenging conditions with unknown interactions (e.g., patients with complex diagnoses). Trial and error (or learning by doing) has been suggested as an appropriate response to these "unknown unknowns," and organizational researchers have begun to look at how people do that (Weick & Sutcliffe 2011). Nevertheless, much remains unknown about how to cope effectively with true novelty.

Psychological research is needed to better develop tools that can overcome the limitations of human judgment. Fields using EBP have increasingly adopted decision supports despite relatively little psychological research to inform their features, structure, modality, or delivery. As Heath and colleagues (1998) have noted, organizations may do a better job of debiasing decisions than individuals can. Attention to decision-making practices used in organizations provides opportunities for psychologists to investigate the routines and protocols that can improve decision quality (e.g., Mannes et al. 2014). In sum, it would be helpful to know more about the potentially beneficial connections between psychological research and the decision supports, tools, and routines that facilitate EBP.

EBP research is increasingly focusing on levels of analysis higher than the individual (Stevens 2013). For example, our review of the existing empirical literature highlights the critical importance of leadership support and psychological safety to EBP's effectiveness in organizations. Many other organizational differences may also contribute to EBP's effectiveness, e.g., the magnet status of hospitals (Melnyk et al. 2004). However, systematic organization-level research on factors that facilitate or impede EBP is limited. One important condition that research might consider is the uniformity of the problems or patient conditions that an organization faces. Hospitals with higher volumes of patients with certain conditions, for example, tend to be more effective in treating them than hospitals with lower volumes (Halm et al. 2002), perhaps in part because the former more often have established evidence-based protocols for their treatment. Similar effects of problem familiarity may be important in other applications of EBP. Thus, understanding organization-level contributors to EBP remains a priority.

Research is also needed to advance understanding on the role of professions in encouraging EBP. Professions provide both the training and the infrastructure that facilitate practice, and they contribute to the formation of professional identities that incorporate systematic use of evidence and attention to its quality. Indeed, professions could contribute to the diffusion of EBP in multiple ways, shaping practitioners' knowledge base, providing them with tools (e.g., preappraised evidence, summaries, and guidelines), and cultivating their professional identities as evidence-based practitioners. The last may be particularly important, as identities can help individuals persist at difficult behaviors in unsupportive environments (Trope & Liberman 2010). Specifically, identity leads to the pursuit of specific goals that sustain the identity, and contribute to what Thompson & Bunderson (2003) have referred to as an ideological contract, a mental model regarding a valued aspect of people's employment. Professions that cultivate EBP-supportive identities in their members may be more likely to foster EBP despite challenges in local organizational conditions. At this point, however, these possibilities are just that; further psychological research could greatly enhance our understanding of how professions influence EBP.

A final, fruitful research area is the complex relationship between values and EBP. Critics have argued that EBP is not entirely evidence based; rather, it involves the commitment to a particular set of values (e.g., rationality, empiricism, and transparency; Webb 2001). This claim raises important research questions that have received scant attention. First and most obviously, which values contribute to practitioners' adoption and use of EBP? Which values contribute to its rejection? Research that tackles these questions could study individuals engaged in the EBP process or whole disciplines that have collectively embraced or resisted EBP. Second, how do a practitioner's values interact with the evidence during an evidence-based decision? Do particular values lead to the use of particular evidence? How do values adjudicate when the evidence is contested? How do values contribute to the trade-offs that practitioners must make between evidence high in internal versus external validity? Finally, research could fruitfully investigate the opposite causal path: the influence of EBP on values. Empirical research on value-based decisions (e.g., the choice between honesty and deception) has grown exponentially in the past few decades (Tenbrunsel & Smith-Crowe 2009). How has the evidence contributed to our understanding of values? Finally, can evidence really change values, or are values somehow resistant to evidence (Skitka et al. 2005)? These and many other questions about the complex relationships between values and evidence await future research.

CONCLUSION

EBP has emerged in diverse fields over the past 30 years. Good evidence indicates that effective EBP adoption depends on the ability, motivation, and opportunity of the individual practitioners involved and the support their professions and work settings provide. At the same time, experience with EBP highlights the critical contributions psychology has made and still needs to make so that the growing body of available evidence can be mindfully used and so practitioners can respond mindfully even when evidence is absent.

SUMMARY POINTS

1. Originating in medicine but now used across numerous professions, evidence-based practice (EBP) is an approach to professional practice that focuses practitioner attention on evidence quality in decision making and action.

2. Specifically, EBP calls on practitioners to identify the evidence underlying their decisions, to improve the quality of that evidence where possible, and to condition their decisions and practices on the confidence that the evidence warrants.

3. Evidence-based decisions involve a mindful integration of both scientific evidence (e.g., research studies) and local evidence (e.g., situational assessments), often with the help of decision supports.

4. Practitioners tend to implement EBP when they have the ability (foundational and functional competencies), motivation (behavioral beliefs, perceived behavioral control, and normative beliefs), and opportunity (support that overcomes barriers) to do so.

5. Evaluating the effectiveness of EBP is complicated and requires additional research, but the existing research suggests that EBP improves practice outcomes across an array of fields.

6. Although several criticisms of EBP have been debunked, others (e.g., the continuing reliance on human judgment) highlight important issues that should be taken seriously.

7. A holistic look at EBP research reveals several patterns that can meaningfully guide EBP implementation across fields (e.g., both top-down and bottom-up implementation occurs).

8. At the same time, a holistic examination of EBP research reveals several gaps that would very much benefit from future research (e.g., the role of human values in evidence-based decisions).

FUTURE ISSUES

1. What criteria are most appropriate for appraising the quality of the various forms of local evidence that practitioners may use?

2. Given institutional constraints in both academia and the professions, what conditions are likely to facilitate or impede additional practice-oriented research?

3. Under what conditions can feedback increase the complementarity between professional judgment and systematically gathered evidence?

4. How can evidence-based decision makers best cope with conditions of true novelty (e.g., unknown unknowns)?

5. How can EBP research harness psychological findings to develop decision supports, tools, and routines that support EBP?

6. Which features of organizations, as a whole, tend to facilitate or impede EBP?

DISCLOSURE STATEMENT

The authors are not aware of any affiliations, memberships, funding, or financial holdings that might be perceived as affecting the objectivity of this review.

ACKNOWLEDGMENTS

We thank Eric Barends, Richard Larrick, Scott Lilienfield, and Maria Tomprou for their insightful feedback. We appreciate the support an H.J. Heinz II Professorship provided in the writing of this review.

LITERATURE CITED

Aabenhus R, Jensen J, Jørgensen KJ, Hróbjartsson A, Bjerrum L. 2014. Biomarkers as point-of-care tests to guide prescription of antibiotics in patients with acute respiratory infections in primary care. *Cochrane Database Syst. Rev.* 11:CD010130

Aarons GA. 2004. Mental health provider attitudes toward adoption of EBP: the EBP Attitude Scale (EBPAS). *Mental Health Serv. Res.* 6:61–74

Aarons GA. 2006. Transformational and transactional leadership: association with attitudes toward evidence-based practice. *Psychiatr. Serv.* 57(8):1162–69

Aarons GA, Sawitzky AC. 2006. Organizational culture and climate and mental health provider attitudes toward evidence-based practice. *Psychol. Serv.* 3(1):61–72

Ajzen I. 1991. The theory of planned behavior. *Organ. Behav. Hum. Decis. Process.* 50:179–211

Allen GD, Rubenfeld MG, Scheffer BK. 2004. Reliability of assessment of critical thinking. *J. Prof. Nurs.* 20:15–22

Am. Psychol. Assoc. 2006. Evidence-based practice in psychology. *Am. Psychol.* 61:271–85

Arriaga AF, Bader AM, Wong JM, Lipsitz SR, Berry WR, et al. 2013. Simulation-based trial of surgical-crisis checklists. *N. Engl. J. Med.* 368:246–53

Baba VV, HakemZadeh F. 2012. Toward a theory of evidence based decision-making. *Manag. Decis.* 50:832–67

Bailin S. 2002. Critical thinking and science education. *Sci. Educ.* 11:361–75

Barends EG, Briner RB. 2014. Teaching evidence-based practice: lessons from the pioneers. An interview with Amanda Burls and Gordon Guyatt. *Acad. Manag. Learn. Educ.* 13:476–83

Barends EG, Rousseau DM, Briner RB. 2014. *Evidence-Based Management.* Amsterdam: Cent. Evid.-Based Manag.

Bates DW, Kuperman GJ, Wang S, Gandhi T, Kittler A, et al. 2003. Ten commandments for effective clinical decision support: making the practice of evidence-based medicine a reality. *J. Am. Med. Inform. Assoc.* 10:523–30

Beidas RS, Kendall PC. 2010. Training therapists in evidence-based practice: a critical review of studies from a systems-contextual perspective. *Clin. Psychol. Sci. Pract.* 17(1):1–30

Belden CV, Leafman J, Nehrenz G, Miller P. 2012. The effect of evidence based practice on workplace empowerment of rural registered nurses. *Online J. Rural Nurs. Health Care* 12(2):64–76

Berkman ND, Lohr KN, Morgan LC, Kuo TM, Morton SC. 2013. Interrater reliability of grading strength of evidence varies with the complexity of the evidence in systematic reviews. *J. Clin. Epidemiol.* 66(10):1105–17.e1

Bittner NP, Gravlin G. 2009. Critical thinking, delegation, and missed care in nursing practice. *J. Nurs. Admin.* 39:142–46

Bozionelos N. 2005. When the inferior candidate is offered the job: the selection interview as a political and power game. *Hum. Relat.* 58:1605–31

Camerer CF, Johnson EJ. 1991. The process-performance paradox in expert judgment: How can experts know so much and predict so badly? In *Toward a General Theory of Expertise: Prospects and Limits*, ed. A Ericsson, J Smith, pp. 342–64. New York: Cambridge Univ. Press

Castonguay LG, Barham M, Lutz W, McAleavy A. 2013. Practice-oriented research. *Bergin and Garfield's Handbook of Psychotherapy and Behavior Change*, ed. MJ Lambert, pp. 85–133. Hoboken, NJ: Wiley. 6th ed.

Chi MTH, Glaser R, Farr MJ. 1988. *The Nature of Expertise*. Hillsdale, NJ: Erlbaum

Chorpita BF, Daleiden EL, Ebesutani C, Young J, Becker KD, et al. 2011. Evidence-based treatments for children and adolescents: an updated review of indicators of efficacy and effectiveness. *Clin. Psychol. Sci. Pract.* 18:153–72

Choudhry NK, Fletcher RH, Soumerai SB. 2005. Systematic review: the relationship between clinical experience and quality of health care. *Ann. Intern. Med.* 142:260–73

Clement P. 2013. Practice-based evidence: 45 years of psychotherapy's effectiveness in a private practice. *Am. J. Psychother.* 67:23–46

Cokins G, Euske KJ, Millush G, Nostrom P, Vercio A. 2008. Let's certify the quality of a manager's information. *Strateg. Finance* 90:39–45

Coomarasamy A, Khan KS. 2004. What is the evidence that postgraduate teaching in evidence based medicine changes anything? A systematic review. *Br. Med. J.* 329(7473):1017–22

Cullen FT. 2013. Rehabilitation: beyond nothing works. In *Crime and Justice in America: 1975–2025*, ed. M Tonry, pp. 299–376. Chicago: Univ. Chicago Press

Dalheim A, Harthug S, Nilsen RM, Nortvedt MW. 2012. Factors influencing the development of evidence-based practice among nurses: a self-report survey. *BMC Health Serv. Res.* 12:367

Davenport TH, Harris JG, Morison R. 2010. *Analytics at Work: Smarter Decisions, Better Results*. Boston: Harvard Bus. Press

Dawes RM. 2008. Psychotherapy: the myth of expertise. *Navigating the Mindfield: A User's Guide to Distinguishing Science from Pseudoscience in Mental Health*, ed. SO Lilienfeld, J Ruscio, SJ Lynn, pp. 311–44. Amherst, NY: Prometheus Books

Dawes RM, Faust D, Meehl PE. 1989. Clinical versus actuarial judgment. *Science* 31:1668–74

Degani A, Wiener E. 1990. *Human factors of flight-deck checklists: the normal checklists*. NASA Contract. Rep. 177549, Natl. Aeronaut. Space Admin., Moffett Field, CA. **http://www.ntrs.nasa.gov/archive/nasa/casi.ntrs.nasa.gov/19910017830.pdf**

Denham CR, Sullenberger CB III, Quaid DW, Nance JJ. 2012. An NTSB for health care—learning from innovation: debate and innovate or capitulate. *J. Patient Saf.* 8(1):3–14

Denney NW. 1995. Critical thinking during the adult years: Has the developmental function changed over the last four decades? *Exp. Aging Res.* 21:191–207

Dogherty EJ, Harrison MB, Graham ID, Vandyk AD, Keeping-Burke L. 2013. Turning knowledge in action at the point-of-care: the collective experience of nurses facilitating the implementation of evidence-based practice. *Worldviews Evid.-Based Nurs.* 10(3):129–39

Doran D, Lefebre N, O'Brien-Pallas L, Estabrook CA, White P, et al. 2014. The relationship among evidence-based practice and client dyspnea, pain, falls, and pressure ulcer outcomes in the community setting. *Worldviews Evid.-Based Nurs.* 11:274–83

Downs SH, Black N. 1998. The feasibility of creating a checklist for the assessment of the methodological quality both of randomised and non-randomised studies of health care interventions. *J. Epidemiol. Community Health* 52:377–84

Ellis S, Davidi I. 2005. After-event reviews: drawing lessons from successful and failed experience. *J. Appl. Psychol.* 90:857–71

Ericsson KA, Lehmann AC. 1996. Expert and exceptional performance: evidence of maximal adaptation to task constraints. *Annu. Rev. Psychol.* 47:273–305

Evans JST, Handley SJ, Harper CNJ, Johnson-Laird PN. 1999. Reasoning about necessity and possibility: a test of the mental model theory of deduction. *J. Exp. Psychol.* 25:1495–513

Facione NC, Facione PA. 2008. *Critical Thinking and Clinical Judgment in the Health Sciences—An International Teaching Anthology.* Millbrae, CA: Calif. Acad.

Feinstein AR, Horwitz RI. 1997. Problems in the "evidence" of "evidence-based medicine." *Am. J. Med.* 103:529–35

Ferlie E, Fitzgerald L, Wood M, Hawkins C. 2006. The nonspread of innovations: the mediating role of professionals. *Acad. Manag. J.* 48:117–34

Fischoff B. 2013. For those condemned to study the past. In *Judgment and Decision-Making*, ed. B Fischoff, pp. 50–64. New York: Earthscan

Fiske ST, Borgida E. 2011. Best practices: how to evaluate psychological science for use by organizations. *Res. Organ. Behav.* 31:253–75

Gawande A. 2010. *The Checklist Manifesto: How to Get Things Right.* New York: Metrop. Books

Ghoshal S. 2005. Bad management theories are destroying good management practices. *Acad. Manag. Learn. Educ.* 4:75–91

Gibbs L, Gambrill E. 2002. Evidence-based practice: counterarguments to objections. *Res. Soc. Work Pract.* 12:452–76

Gigerenzer G. 2014. *Risky Savvy: How to Make Good Decisions.* New York: Viking

Giménez-Pérez G, Caixas A, Giménez-Palop O, González-Clemente JM, Mauricio D. 2005. Dissemination of "patient-oriented evidence that matters" on the Internet: the case of type 2 diabetes treatment. *Diabet. Med.* 22:688–92

Glasziou P, Meats E, Heneghan C, Shepperd S. 2008. What is missing from descriptions of treatment in trials and reviews? *Br. Med. J.* 336(7659):1472–74

Goodheart CD, Kazdin AE, Sternberg RJ. 2006. *Evidence-Based Psychotherapy: Where Practice and Research Meet.* Washington, DC: Am. Psychol. Assoc.

Goodman PS, Rousseau DM. 2004. Organizational change that produces results: the linkage approach. *Acad. Manag. Exec.* 18(3):7–21

Goodman RM. 1998. Principles and tools for evaluating community-based prevention and health promotion programs. *J. Public Health Manag. Pract.* 4(2):39–47

Grol R, Grimshaw J. 2003. From best evidence to best practice: effective implementation of change in patients' care. *Lancet* 362(9391):1225–30

Groopman J. 2008. *How Doctors Think.* Boston: Mariner

Guyatt GH, Oxman AD, Vist GE, Kunz R, Falck-Ytter Y, et al. 2008. GRADE: an emerging consensus on rating quality of evidence and strength of recommendations. *Br. Med. J.* 336:924–26

Haas LM, Peterson D, Lefevbre R, Varvek D. 2012. Evaluation of the effects of an evidence-based practice curriculum on knowledge, attitudes, and self-assessed skills and behaviors in chiropractic students. *J. Manip. Physiol. Ther.* 35:701–9

Halm EA, Lee C, Chassin MR. 2002. Is volume related to outcome in health care? A systematic review and methodologic critique of the literature. *Ann. Intern. Med.* 137:511–20

Harris DA. 2012. *Failed Evidence: Why Law Enforcement Resists Science.* New York: NYU Press

Hay MC, Weisner TS, Subramanian S, Duan N, Niedzinski EJ, Kravitz RL. 2008. Harnessing experience: exploring the gap between evidence-based medicine and clinical practice. *J. Eval. Clin. Pract.* 14:707–13

Haynes AB, Weiser TG, Berry WR, Lipsitz SR, Breizat AHS, et al. 2009. A surgical safety checklist to reduce morbidity and mortality in a global population. *N. Engl. J. Med.* 360(5):491–99

Haynes RB. 2001. Of studies, summaries, synopses, and systems: the "4S" evolution of services for finding current best evidence. *Evid.-Based Ment. Health* 4(2):37–38

Heath C, Larrick RP, Klayman J. 1998. Cognitive repairs: how organizations compensate for the shortcomings of individual learners. *Res. Organ. Behav.* 20:1–37

Heath D, Heath D. 2012. *Decisive: How to Make Better Decisions in Life and Work.* New York: Crown

Heneghan C, Badenoch D. 2006. *Evidence-Based Medicine Toolkit.* Malden, MA: Blackwell. 2nd ed.

Highhouse S. 2008. Stubborn reliance on intuition and subjectivity in employee selection. *Ind. Organ. Psychol.* 1:333–42

Hoagwood KE, Burns BJ, Kiser L, Ringeisen H, Schoenwald SK. 2001. Evidence-based practice in child and adolescent mental health services. *Psychiatr. Serv.* 52:1179–89

Hofmann SG, Smits JA. 2008. Cognitive-behavioral therapy for adult anxiety disorders: a meta-analysis of randomized placebo-controlled trials. *J. Clin. Psychiatry* 69:621–32

Howard-Jones PA. 2014. Neuroscience and education: myths and messages. *Nat. Rev. Neurosci.* 15:817–24

Hughes J. 2007. The ability-motivation-opportunity framework for behavior research in IS. In *Proc. 40th Hawaii Int. Conf. Syst. Sci.*, IEEE Comput. Soc., Washington, DC

Jacobs K, Manzi T. 2013. Modernisation, marketisation and housing reform: the use of evidence based policy as a rationality discourse. *People Place Policy Online* 7(1):1–13

Jette DU, Bacon K, Batty C, Carlson M, Ferland A, et al. 2003. Evidence-based practice: beliefs, attitudes, knowledge, and behaviors of physical therapists. *Phys. Ther.* 83:786–805

Kahneman D. 2011. *Thinking, Fast and Slow*. New York: Macmillan

Kahneman D, Klein G. 2009. Conditions for intuitive expertise: a failure to disagree. *Am. Psychol.* 64:515–26

Kaplan Jacobs S, Rosenfeld P, Haber J. 2003. Information literacy as the foundation for evidence-based practice in graduate nursing education: a curriculum-integrated approach. *J. Prof. Nurs.* 19:320–28

Kiss TL, O'Malley M, Hendrix TJ. 2010. Self-efficacy-based training for research literature appraisal: a competency for evidence-based practice. *J. Nurses Staff Dev.* 26(4):170–77

Klein G, Orasanu J, Salas E. 2001. Taking stock of naturalistic decision-making. *J. Behav. Decis. Mak.* 14:331–52

Knaapen L. 2013. Being "evidence-based" in the absence of evidence: the management of non-evidence in guideline development. *Soc. Stud. Sci.* 43:681–706

Kothari A, Wathen N. 2013. A critical second look at integrated knowledge translation. *Health Policy* 109:187–91

Kovner AR, D'Aquila R, Fine D. 2009. *Evidence-Based Management in Healthcare*. Chicago: Health Admin. Press

Kowalski P, Taylor AK. 2009. The effect of refuting misconceptions in the introductory psychology class. *Teach. Psychol.* 36(3):153–59

Kumar S, Little P, Britten N. 2003. Why do general practitioners prescribe antibiotics for sore throat? Grounded theory interview study. *Br. Med. J.* 326(7381):138–43

Lambert MJ. 2010. *Prevention of Treatment Failure: The Use of Measuring, Monitoring, and Feedback in Clinical Practice*. Washington, DC: APA Books

Langer EJ. 1989. *Mindfulness*. Reading, MA: Addison-Wesley

LaPaige V. 2009. Evidence-based decision-making within the context of globalization: a "Why-What-How" for leaders and managers of health care organizations. *Risk Manag. Healthc. Policy* 2:35–46

Larrick RP. 2009. Broaden the decision frame to make effective decisions. In *Handbook of Principles of Organizational Behavior*, ed. EA Locke, pp. 461–80. Chichester, UK:Wiley. 2nd ed.

Lavis J, Davies H, Oxman A, Denis JL, Golden-Biddle K, Ferlie E. 2005. Towards systematic reviews that inform health care management and policy-making. *J. Health Serv. Res. Policy* 10(Suppl. 1):35–48

Lilienfeld S. 2014. Evidence-Based Practice: The misunderstandings continue: A recent essay displays startling misconceptions regarding science and therapy. *The Skeptical Psychologist Blog*, Jan. 27. **https://www.psychologytoday.com/blog/the-skeptical-psychologist/201401/evidence-based-practice-the-misunderstandings-continue**

Lilienfeld SO, Landfield K. 2008. Science and pseudoscience in law enforcement. A user-friendly primer. *Crim. Justice Behav.* 35:1215–30

Lilienfeld SO, Lohr JM, Olatunji BO. 2008. Encouraging students to think critically about psychotherapy: overcoming naïve realism, in teaching critical thinking. In *Psychology: A Handbook of Best Practices*, ed. DS Dunn, JS Halonen, RA Smit, pp. 267–71. Oxford, UK: Wiley-Blackwell

Lilienfeld SO, Ritschel LA, Lynn SJ, Cautin RL, Latzman RD. 2013. Why many clinical psychologists are resistant to evidence-based practice: root causes and constructive remedies. *Clin. Psychol. Rev.* 33:883–900

Mannes AE, Soll JB, Larrick RP. 2014. The wisdom of select crowds. *J. Personal. Soc. Psychol.* 107:276–99

Mantzoukas S. 2008. A review of evidence-based practice, nursing research and reflection: leveling the hierarchy. *J. Clin. Nurs.* 17:214–23

March J. 2010. *The Ambiguities of Experience*. Ithaca, NY: Cornell Univ. Press

Marchington M, Grugulis I. 2000. "Best practice" human resource management: perfect opportunity or dangerous illusion? *Int. J. Hum. Resour. Manag.* 11:1104–24

McCluskey A, Bishop B. 2009. The Adapted Fresno Test of competence in evidence-based practice. *J. Contin. Educ. Health Prof.* 29:119–26

McCluskey A, Lovarini M. 2005. Providing education on evidence-based practice improved knowledge but did not change behaviour: a before and after study. *BMC Med. Educ.* 5:40

Mekary RA, Giovannucci E. 2014. Belief beyond the evidence: using the proposed effect of breakfast on obesity to show 2 practices that distort scientific evidence. *Am. J. Clin. Nutr.* 99:212–13

Melnyk BM, Fineout-Overholt E. 2011. *Evidence-Based Practice in Nursing & Healthcare: A Guide to Best Practice*. Philadelphia: Lippincott Williams & Wilkins

Melnyk BM, Fineout-Overholt E, Fischbeck Feinstein N, Li H, Small L, et al. 2004. Nurses' perceived knowledge, beliefs, skills, and needs regarding evidence-based practice: implications for accelerating the paradigm shift. *Worldviews Evid.-Based Nurs.* 1(3):185–93

Melnyk BM, Fineout-Overholt E, Gallagher-Ford L, Kaplan L. 2012. The state of evidence-based practice in US nurses: critical implications for nurse leaders and educators. *J. Nurs. Adm.* 42(9):410–17

Michelson D, Davenport C, Dretzke J, Barlow J, Day C. 2013. Do evidence-based interventions work when tested in the "real world"? A systematic review and meta-analysis of parent management training for the treatment of child disruptive behavior. *Clin. Child Fam. Psychol. Rev.* 16:18–34

Miller JD. 2004. Public understanding of, and attitudes toward, scientific research: what we know and what we need to know. *Public Underst. Sci.* 13:273–94

Montgomery K, Oliver AL. 1996. Responses by professional organizations to multiple and ambiguous institutional environments: the case of AIDS. *Organ. Stud.* 17:649–71

Morewedge CK, Kahneman D. 2010. Associative processes in intuitive judgment. *Trends Cogn. Sci.* 14(10):435–40

Norman GR, Shannon SI. 1998. Effectiveness of instruction in critical appraisal (evidence-based medicine) skills: a critical appraisal. *Can. Med. Assoc. J.* 158:177–81

Novotney A. 2014. Educating the educators. *Monit. Psychol.* 45:48–51

Nutt PC. 1999. Surprising but true: Half the decisions in organizations fail. *Acad. Manag. Exec.* 13(40):75–90

O'Neil M, Berkman N, Hartling L, Chang S, Anderson J, et al. 2014. *Observational Evidence and Strength of Evidence Domains: Case Examples*. Rockville, MD: Agency Healthc. Res. Qual.

Petrosino A, Buehler J, Turpin-Petrosino C. 2013. Scared Straight and other juvenile awareness programs for preventing juvenile delinquency: a systematic review. *Campbell Syst. Rev.* 9:5. doi: 10.4073/csr.2013.5

Petticrew M, Roberts H. 2003. Evidence, hierarchies, and typologies: horses for courses. *J. Epidemiol. Community Health* 57:527–29

Petty RE, Cacioppo JT. 1986. *Communication and Persuasion: Central and Peripheral Routes to Attitude Change*. New York: Springer-Verlag

Profetto-McGrath J. 2005. Critical thinking and evidence-based practice. *Prof. Nurs.* 21:364–71

Pullin AS, Knight TM, Stone DA, Charman K. 2004. Do conservation managers use scientific evidence to support their decision-making? *Biol. Conserv.* 119:245–52

Revkin AC. 2014. How "solution aversion" and global warming prescriptions polarize the climate debate. *New York Times*, Nov. 10. **http://www.dotearth.blogs.nytimes.com/2014/11/10/how-solution-aversion-and-global-warming-prescriptions-polarize-the-climate-debate/?_r=0**

Richardson W, Wilson M, Nishikawa J, Hayward R. 1995. The well-built clinical question: a key to evidence-based decisions. *ACP J. Club* 123:A12–13

Rogers EM. 1995. *Diffusion of Innovations*. Free Press: New York

Roudebush P, Allen TA, Dodd CE, Novotny BJ. 2004. Application of evidence-based medicine to veterinary clinical nutrition. *J. Am. Vet. Med. Assoc.* 224:1766–71

Rousseau DM. 2006. Is there such a thing as "evidence-based management"? *Acad. Manag. Rev.* 31:256–69

Rousseau DM, ed. 2012. *Oxford Handbook of Evidence-Based Management*. New York: Oxford Univ. Press

Rousseau DM, Barends E. 2011. Becoming an evidence-based manager. *Hum. Resour. Manag. J.* 21:221–35

Sackett DL. 2000. *Evidence-Based Medicine*. New York: Wiley

Salas E, Klein C, King H, Salisbury M, Augenstein JS, et al. 2008. Debriefing medical teams: 12 evidence-based best practices and tips. *Jt. Comm. J. Qual. Patient Saf.* 34:518–27

Salas E, Rosen MA, DiazGranados D. 2009. Expertise-based intuition and decision-making in organizations. *J. Manag.* 36:941–73

Salbach NM, Jaglal SB, Korner-Bitensky N, Rappolt S, Davis D. 2007. Practitioner and organizational barriers to evidence-based practice of physical therapists for people with stroke. *Phys. Ther.* 87:1284–303

Schlosser RW, Kuhl R, Costello J. 2007. Asking well-built questions for evidence-based practice in augmentative and alternative communication. *J. Commun. Disord.* 40:225–38

Scurlock-Evans L, Upton P, Upton D. 2014. Evidence-based practice in physiotherapy: a systematic review of barriers, enablers and interventions. *Physiotherapy* 100:208–19

Sewell M, Adebibe M, Jayakumar P, Jowett C, Kong K, et al. 2011. Use of the WHO surgical safety checklist in trauma and orthopaedic patients. *Int. Orthop.* 35:897–901

Shaneyfelt T, Baum KD, Bell D, Feldstein D, Houston TK, et al. 2006. Instruments for evaluating education in evidence-based practice: a systematic review. *JAMA* 296:1116–27

Sherman LW. 2002. Evidence-based policing: social organization of information for social control. In *Crime and Social Organization*, ed. E Waring, D Weisburd, pp. 217–48. New Brunswick, NJ: Trans. Publ.

Shortell SM, Rundall TG, Hsu J. 2007. Improving patient care by linking evidence-based medicine and evidence-based management. *JAMA* 298(6):673–76

Simon HA. 1990. Invariants of human behavior. *Annu. Rev. Psychol.* 41:1–20

Simon HA. 1996. *The Sciences of the Artificial.* Cambridge, MA: MIT Press. 3rd ed.

Sinuff T, Muscedere J, Adhikari NK, Stelfox HT, Dodek P, et al. 2013. Knowledge translation interventions for critically ill patients: a systematic review. *Crit. Care Med.* 41:2627–40

Skitka LJ, Bauman CW, Sargis EG. 2005. Moral conviction: another contributor to attitude strength or something more? *J. Personal. Soc. Psychol.* 88:895–917

Soll JB, Larrick RP. 2009. Strategies for revising judgment: how (and how well) people use others' opinions. *J. Exp. Psychol.: Learn. Mem. Cogn.* 35:780–805

Sonnentag S. 1998. Expertise in professional software design: a process study. *J. Appl. Psychol.* 83:703–15

Soumerai SB, McLaughlin TJ, Gurwitz JH, Guadagnoli E, Hauptman PJ, et al. 1998. Effect of local medical opinion leaders on quality of care for acute myocardial infarction: a randomized controlled trial. *JAMA* 279:1358–63

Spek B, Wieringa-de Waard M, Lucas C, van Dijk N. 2013. Teaching evidence-based practice (EBP) to speech-language therapy students: Are students competent and confident EBP users? *Int. J. Lang. Commun. Disord.* 48:444–52

Staubus G. 1999. *The Decision Usefulness Theory of Accounting: A Limited History.* Oxford, UK: Routledge

Steinberg EP, Luce BR. 2005. Evidence based? Caveat emptor! *Health Aff.* 24(1):80–92

Stevens K. 2013. The impact of evidence-based practice in nursing and the next big ideas. *Online J. Issues Nurs.* 18(2):4

Straus SE, Richardson WS, Glasziou P, Haynes RB. 2005. *Evidence-Based Medicine: How to Practice and Teach EBM.* Edinburgh: Elsevier. 3rd ed.

Swain K, Whitley R, McHugo GJ, Drake RE. 2010. The sustainability of evidence-based practices in routine mental health agencies. *Community Ment. Health J.* 46(2):119–29

Tenbrunsel AE, Smith-Crowe K. 2009. Ethical decision-making: where we've been and where we're going. *Acad. Manag. Ann.* 2:545–607

Thompson JA, Bunderson JS. 2003. Violations of principle: ideological currency in the psychological contract. *Acad. Manag. Rev.* 28:571–86

Thyer BA. 2002. Evidence-based practice and clinical social work. *Evid.-Based Ment. Health* 5:6–7

Tierney S, Kislov R, Deaton C. 2014. A qualitative study of a primary-care based intervention to improve the management of patients with heart failure: the dynamic relationship between facilitation and context. *BMC Fam. Pract.* 15(1):153

Tranfield D, Denyer D, Smart P. 2003. Towards a methodology for developing evidence-informed management knowledge by means of systematic review. *Br. J. Manag.* 14(3):207–22

Trope Y, Liberman N. 2010. Construal-level theory of psychological distance. *Psychol. Rev.* 117:440–63

Tucker AL, Nembhard IM, Edmondson AC. 2007. Implementing new practices: an empirical study of organizational learning in hospital intensive care units. *Manag. Sci.* 53:894–907

Vroom VH. 1964. *Work and Motivation*. New York: Wiley

Wakefield J, Herbert CP, Maclure M, Dormuth C, Wright JM, et al. 2003. Commitment to change statements can predict actual change in practice. *J. Contin. Educ. Health Prof.* 23(2):81–92

Watson S, Hewett K. 2006. A multi-theoretical model of knowledge transfer in organizations: determinants of knowledge contribution and knowledge reuse. *J. Manag. Stud.* 43:141–73

Webb SA. 2001. Some considerations on the validity of evidence-based practice in social work. *Br. J. Soc. Work* 31:57–79

Weber B. 2009. Daniel C. Tosteson, longtime dean who reshaped Harvard Medical School, dies at 84. *New York Times*, June 3. **http://www.nytimes.com/2009/06/03/education/03tosteson.html**

Weick KE, Sutcliffe KM. 2011. *Managing the Unexpected: Resilient Performance in an Age of Uncertainty*. New York: Wiley

Weisz JR, Kuppens S, Eckshtain D, Ugueto AM, Hawley KM, Jensen-Doss A. 2013. Performance of evidence-based youth psychotherapies compared with usual clinical care: a multilevel meta-analysis. *JAMA Psychiatry* 70:750–61

Wells KB, Miranda J. 2006. Promise of interventions and services research: Can it transform practice? *Clin. Psychol. Sci. Pract.* 13(1):99–104

Woolf SH. 2008. The meaning of translational research and why it matters. *JAMA* 299:211–13

Wright N. 2013. First-time knowledge brokers in health care: the experiences of nurses and allied health professionals of bridging the research-practice gap. *Evid. Policy* 9:557–70

Yates JF, Potworowski G. 2012. Evidence-based decision management. See Rousseau 2012, pp. 198–222

Zanardelli J. 2012. At the intersection of the academy and practice at Asbury Heights. See Rousseau 2012, pp. 559–79

Ziewacz JE, Arriaga AF, Bader AM, Berry WR, Edmondson L, et al. 2011. Crisis checklists for the operating room: development and pilot testing. *J. Am. Coll. Surg.* 213:212–17

Scientific Misconduct

Charles Gross

Department of Psychology and Neuroscience Institute, Princeton University, Princeton, New Jersey 08544; email: cggross@princeton.edu

Annu. Rev. Psychol. 2016. 67:693–711

First published online as a Review in Advance on August 13, 2015

The *Annual Review of Psychology* is online at psych.annualreviews.org

This article's doi:
10.1146/annurev-psych-122414-033437

Keywords

scientific misconduct, fabrication, falsification, plagiarism

Abstract

Scientific misconduct has been defined as fabrication, falsification, and plagiarism. Scientific misconduct has occurred throughout the history of science. The US government began to take systematic interest in such misconduct in the 1980s. Since then, a number of studies have examined how frequently individual scientists have observed scientific misconduct or were involved in it. Although the studies vary considerably in their methodology and in the nature and size of their samples, in most studies at least 10% of the scientists sampled reported having observed scientific misconduct. In addition to studies of the incidence of scientific misconduct, this review considers the recent increase in paper retractions, the role of social media in scientific ethics, several instructional examples of egregious scientific misconduct, and potential methods to reduce research misconduct.

Contents

INTRODUCTION

Over the past few decades, there has been an apparent outbreak in scientists behaving very badly. One such case is that of Dutch social psychologist Diederik Stapel, who fabricated more than 50 influential studies, usually "finding" things that academic liberals wanted to believe, including that dirty environments encouraged racism, that eating meat made people selfish, and that power had a negative effect on morality. His studies elevated his status to that of a superstar and dean before some of his students finally turned him in (Bhattacharjee 2013). Then there is the case of Eric Poehlman, a University of Vermont medical scientist who published 10 reports containing fabricated patients and data to support his claim of metabolic changes in menopausal women. Poehlman defrauded the government of $2.9 million in grants and became the first US scientist jailed for scientific fraud (Dalton 2005).

In this review, we consider the incidence of scientific misconduct and what might be done about it. We use the latest National Institutes of Health (NIH) and National Science Foundation (NSF) definitions of scientific misconduct as consisting of fabrication, falsification, and plagiarism. Fabrication is making up data or results. Falsification is manipulating research materials, equipment, or processes, or changing data or results. Plagiarism is the appropriation of another person's ideas, processes, results, or words without giving appropriate credit (NSF 1996, ORI 2011).

Research misconduct does not include honest errors or differences of opinion. Under the federal (NIH and NSF) definitions, it also does not include more general offenses, such as misuse of funds, sexual abuse, or discrimination. Furthermore, other dubious behaviors of a scientist that are more difficult to assess, such as in the determination of authorship or in the responsible mentoring of students, are excluded.

SCIENTIFIC MISCONDUCT IN THE PAST

Scientific misconduct is not a recent phenomenon simply tied to some decline of morality or increased competition for tenure and research funds. Rather, accusations of scientific misconduct, sometimes well supported, pepper the history of science, from the Greek natural philosophers onward.

Ptolemy of Alexandria (90–168), the greatest astronomer of antiquity, has been accused of using (without attribution) observations of his predecessor Hipparchus of Rhodes (~162–127 BCE), who in turn used much earlier Babylonian observations as if they were his own (Newton 1977; cf. Neugebauer 1875). Isaac Newton used "fudge factors" to better fit data to his theories (Kohn 1986, Westfall 1973). Gregor Mendel, in his work with crossing pea plants, reported near-perfect ratios, and therefore statistically very unlikely ones. The high unlikelihood of getting exact ratios was first pointed out by Ronald A. Fisher, the founder of modern statistics and one of the founders of population genetics, when he was still an undergraduate at Cambridge University in 1911 (Franklin et al. 2008). Though Charles Darwin has been cleared of accusations of stealing the idea of natural selection from Alfred Russell Wallace, he seems to have only reluctantly credited some of his predecessors (Eisley 1979, Gross 2010). Robert A. Millikan, in his measurement of the charge of an electron, which led to his Nobel Prize in Physics in 1923, failed to report unfavorable data (Kohn 1986; cf. Goodstein 2010). Incidentally, Millikan also failed to give coauthorship to his student Harvey Fletcher, whose work was crucial to the discovery (Kohn 1986), but in those days—as still today—this was not scientific misconduct as defined by the NIH and NSF. William T. Summerlin at Memorial Sloan-Kettering faked a skin transplantation experiment in 1974 with the help of a black marker pen (Hixson 1976), giving rise to the term "paint the mouse" as a synonym for scientific misconduct.

The first formal discussion of scientific misconduct is Charles Babbage's *Reflections on the Decline of Science in England, and on Some of Its Causes* (1970/1830). Babbage held Newton's chair at Cambridge and made major contributions to the development of computers ("difference machines," "analytical engines") and to astronomy, mathematics, and many other fields. He distinguished "several species of impositions that have been practiced in science...hoaxing, forging, trimming and cooking" (p. 174). An example of hoaxing would be the Piltdown Man (discovered in 1912 and exposed in 1953): Parts of an ape skull and a human skull were put together, supposedly to represent a "missing link" (Weiner 1955). Hoaxes are intended to expose naïveté and credulousness and to mock pseudowisdom. A more recent brilliant hoax that drew a flurry of attention in the academic world was Alan Sokal's article in *Social Text* (1996), in which he purported to argue that "physical reality...is at bottom a social and linguistic construct" (p. 217).

Unlike hoaxes, the other impositions distinguished by Babbage are carried out to advance the perpetrator's scientific career. Forging, which Babbage thought rare, is making up results, today called fabrication. Trimming consists of getting rid of outliers to decrease the variance and make the results look better. Cooking is the selection of data. Trimming and cooking fall under the modern rubric of falsification.

ORIGINS OF UNITED STATES GOVERNMENT INVOLVEMENT

Around 1980, several cases of egregious scientific misconduct were extensively publicized. One was the case of John Long. While working at Massachusetts General Hospital, Long apparently made a major advance in studying Hodgkin's disease by developing four lines of tissue culture cells from Hodgkin's disease tumors, enabling the disease to be studied in detail. However, Long's colleagues eventually discovered that three of the lines were from a healthy monkey and the fourth from a normal human (Wade 1981). A second case was that of Vijay R. Soman, a promising Yale University assistant professor of medicine who working on anorexia nervosa. Twelve of Soman's papers eventually had to be retracted, ending his research career and seriously sullying that of his mentor and protector. (This case is sufficiently instructive that I return to it in detail below.) These and other cases spurred US Representative Al Gore, who was then chairman of the Investigations and Oversight Subcommittee of the House Science and Technology Committee, to hold hearings on "Fraud in Biomedical Research" on March 31 and April 1, 1981 (US House Rep. 1981). This marked the beginning of the US federal government's involvement in scientific misconduct.

Gore began the hearings by noting, "We need to discover whether recent incidents [of data falsification] are merely episodes that will drift into the history of science as footnotes, or whether we are creating situations and incentives . . . that make such cases as these the tip of the iceberg" (US House Rep. 1981, p. 1). The first witness was Philip Handler, president of the National Academy of Sciences, who made it clear that he found "little pleasure and satisfaction in testifying" because in his view the problem had been "grossly exaggerated in the full, and occasionally fulsome treatment that it has had in the press" (US House Rep. 1981, p. 10). He contended, "The matter of falsification of data . . . need not be a matter of general societal concern. It is, rather, given the size of the total research effort, a relatively small matter which . . . is normally effectively managed by . . . the scientific community itself" (pp. 10–11). Handler added, "None of us know the real magnitude of the problem that concerns you. Nor can we" (p. 11). Yet he went on to say, "The number of untoward incidents involving fraud or falsification of data is remarkable, not so much for the fact that they occur, but for the fact that they occur so very rarely" (p. 13). As to what should be done about the problem of falsification in science, Handler said, "We would much prefer that the institutions within which science is conducted be responsible for their own affairs, that is, the universities, research institutes, etcetera" (p. 50).

The next witness was Donald S. Fredrickson, director of the NIH. He opined, "I think cases of downright fraud in science have always been quite rare . . . I don't know whether scientific fraud in less spectacular forms occurs more frequently today than it has in the long history of science" (US House Rep. 1981, p. 26). Gore found it quite "perplexing" that the witnesses claimed "that the problem of fraud is essentially a private one that should be dealt with by the informal codes of the scientific community and that fraud was not an important ethical problem that should worry those of us charged with the public trust" (p. 111). Another member of the committee was "taken somewhat aback by the chastisement of the committee for being presumptuous enough to even have the hearing at all" (p. 154).

On both days of the hearings, witnesses made it clear—somewhat to the committee's surprise—that neither the government nor most institutions that conduct scientific research had any formal and public procedures for dealing with scientific misconduct. In the years after the hearings, cases of misconduct continued to surface, and Congress continued to be interested. In 1985, Congress passed the Health Research Extension Act, which required the Secretary of Health and Human Services to issue a regulation requiring applicant or awardee institutions to establish "an administrative process to review reports of scientific fraud" and "report to the Secretary any investigation of alleged scientific fraud which appears substantial"; the Act also required the NIH director to establish a process for receiving and responding to reports from institutions (Goodstein 2010, p. 59). Four years later, the Office of Scientific Integrity (OSI) within the NIH was established. The OSI's mission was to protect the integrity of scientific research by investigating scientific fraud (Goodstein 2010). In 1992, the OSI moved out of the NIH and became the Office of Research Integrity (ORI) within the Public Health Service. The NSF created a similar Office of the Inspector General.

The OSI and Office of the Inspector General definitions of misconduct gradually became more specific and uniform until 2000, when the Office of Science and Technology Policy in the Office of the President set out the federal government definitions given in the second paragraph of the present review.

The NIH and NSF now require all institutions that apply for research support to have a set of procedures for dealing with allegations of scientific misconduct. These are usually available on each institution's website. Very briefly, the typical drill is that after an allegation is made to a university departmental chair or dean, an inquiry is set up to determine if a formal investigation is warranted. If it is, a small committee of faculty members from other departments carries out the investigation. During both phases, the accused scientist is given opportunities to respond, and all proceedings are supposed to be completely confidential. The investigating committee is given full access to all computer disks, unpublished data, and notes from research supported by the federal government, as all such material legally is the property of the federal government, which vests its control in the university. Specific time limits are usually set for each stage of the process.

If the investigation finds misconduct, the university can take a variety of possible actions, ranging from removal of the scientist from the particular project and withdrawal of published papers to firing. The ORI or an equivalent federal agency then conducts it own investigation. The agency has the power to deny, for a specific period or forever, future research funds and study section memberships. Federal prosecution for misuse of research funds can occur as well. Partial or total secrecy is usually attempted until after the federal investigation is completed, although earlier leaks to newspapers sometimes occur.

Using the representative University of Maryland procedures, Shamoo & Resnik (2003) estimate that if all deadlines are met and no "hitches" occur, the internal university process should take approximately 10 months, excluding the time for possible appeal at the university level and then the ORI deliberations and possible appeal from their decisions. This seems like an underestimate. In the recent case of Harvard Professor Marc Hauser's misconduct in connection with a small number of studies in comparative cognition, the investigation took three years and the ORI deliberations another two. Yet there do not appear to have been any hitches, delays, or appeals, and the Harvard committee is reported to have met diligently and often (Gross 2012). Sometimes this process of investigating scientific conduct is even more prolonged: In the well-publicized and complex case of Margot O'Toole, Thereza Imanishi-Kari, and David Baltimore, the dispute was not resolved until 10 years later (by the end of which Baltimore was president of Caltech, where today he is the Robert A. Millikan Professor of Biology) (e.g., Judson 2004, Kevles 1998, Sarason 1993).

INCIDENCE OF MISCONDUCT TODAY

A very low incidence of scientific fraud was claimed not only by über establishment figures Handler and Fredrickson but also by the usually acute founder of the modern sociology of science, Robert Merton, who thought scientific fraud to be "extremely infrequent" (Merton 1957, p. 651). In the decades since Gore asked whether the well-publicized examples of scientific misconduct starting in the 1970s were just a few bad apples or the tip of the iceberg, a number of attempts have been made to answer this question. Studies began asking scientists at every level in a variety of fields, and under the cover of anonymity, whether they themselves had engaged in fabrication, falsification, or plagiarism or had direct evidence of such scientific misconduct by others. Although the results were variable and involved different survey response rates and methodologies, the overall picture is disturbing.

In a large and pioneering survey of science graduate students and faculty at 99 universities, ethicist and biology historian Judith Swazey and colleagues found that 44% of students and 50% of faculty had knowledge of two or more types of misconduct, broadly defined; approximately 10% had observed or had direct knowledge of fabrications of data (Swazey et al. 1993). The International Society of Clinical Biostatistics surveyed its membership and found that 51% of the respondents knew of at least one fraudulent project in the previous 10 years (Ranstam et al.

2000). Of 549 biomedical research students at the University of California, San Diego, 11% said they had firsthand knowledge of scientists intentionally altering or fabricating data for purposes of publication (Kalichman & Friedman 1992). In a similar survey, 9% of biological and medical postdoctoral fellows at the University of California, San Francisco, said they had observed scientists altering data, and 3% admitted to having fabricated data (Eastwood et al. 1996). The American Association for the Advancement of Science surveyed a random sample of its members, and 27% of the respondents said they believed they had encountered or witnessed fabricated and falsified or plagiarized research over the previous 10 years, with an average of 2.5 examples (Titus et al. 2008). In a study carried out by the Gallup Organization for the ORI, of 2,212 researchers receiving NIH research grants, 210 reported instances of federally defined misconduct over a three-year period, of which 60% were fabrication or falsification and 36% plagiarism. Noting that 155,000 personnel receive research support, the authors suggest that under the most conservative assumptions, a minimum of 2,325 possible acts of research misconduct occur in a year (Wells 2008). Finally, in a meta-analysis of 18 studies, 2% of scientists admitted to fabricating or falsifying data, and 14% had observed other scientists doing the same (Fanelli 2009).

Retractions of Published Papers

Further insights into the incidence of scientific misconduct come from studies of retractions of published scientific articles. A particularly strong examination of this phenomenon is that of Fang et al. (2012). Unlike previous studies of retraction (e.g., Grieneisen & Zhang 2012, Nath et al. 2006, Steen 2011, Wagner & Williams 2011), Fang and colleagues explored the reason for the retraction if none was mentioned in the retraction notice, as was often the case. Among their sources for the reason for a retraction were reports from ORI, blogs such as Retraction Watch (**http://retractionwatch.com**; see below), news media, and other pubic records. Their review of 2,047 retractions of biomedical articles indicated that only 23% were due to error, whereas 67% were attributed to some type of misconduct such as fraud or suspected fraud (43%), duplicate publication (14%), and plagiarism (10%) (see figure 1 in Fang et al. 2012). The most common nonmisconduct errors that led to retractions were laboratory errors, analytical errors, and irreproducible results (Casadevall et al. 2014).

Fang et al. (2012) found a tenfold increase in retractions for fraud or suspected fraud since 1975. The rates of retraction varied across academic disciplines, with cell biology and oncology being on the high end and sociology and political science on the low end (Margraf 2015). Presumably, this reflects that criteria are more objective and the medical consequences of error more serious in cell biology and oncology than in sociology and political science. The incidence of retractions in psychology was intermediate (Margraf 2015).

Considerable variation exists in geographic origins, with the United States, Germany, Japan, and China responsible for three-quarters of the cases of fraud or suspected fraud; in comparison with other countries, China and India accounted for more cases of duplicate publication and plagiarism (Fang et al. 2012). The authors note several cases of fraudulent articles that were never retracted and suggest this indicates that the number of retractions is an underestimate of the incidence of fraud. Fang et al. (2012) and others (e.g., Steen 2011) have noted a correlation between the impact factor of a journal and the number of retractions for fraud or suspected fraud.

There are a several possible reasons why the marked increase in the incidence of retractions in the past 10 years may not have been primarily due to an increase in scientific misconduct (Fanelli 2013, Steen et al. 2013). First, although the number of retracted journal articles has grown, the number per retracting journal has not. Second, the frequency of finding of misconduct by OSI has not increased. Third, retractions for plagiarism and duplicate publication are a relatively new practice and thereby enhance the contemporary rate of retraction. Finally, and most likely to be the primary reason for the increase, is the greater scrutiny by editors and reviewers, who also have more of a tendency to look into the past papers of an author found guilty of misconduct.

Retracted papers continue to be cited even after their retractions (see, e.g., Budd et al. 1998, Grieneisen & Zhang 2012). Eighteen percent of authors of retracted papers continue to cite them, and of these, less than 5% mention that the papers were retracted (Madlock-Brown & Eichmann 2015). In addition to self-citation, a reason for the continued citing of retracted papers may be that the majority of citations in the literature seem to derive from secondary sources, not from the original paper (Broadus 1983, Siskin & Roychowdhury 2006), and therefore the citer often may not know of the retraction.

Role of Social Media

Social media has entered the world of scientific ethics, and there are now blogs that deal with possible scientific misconduct. Among the early blogs was Retraction Watch (**http://retractionwatch. com**), founded in August 2010 by science writers and editors Ivan Oransky and Adam Marcus to publicize and comment on retractions of scientific papers. They note that many retractions and the reasons for them remain buried in obscurity and say they view tracking retractions as a window into the scientific process.

Another new postpublication review is PRE: Peer Review Evaluation, whose stated purpose is to support publishers in promoting trust and transparency related to peer review. They say they hope to provide information on a journal's peer review practices, such as the number of rounds of review an article went through and what roles the editors played.

One blog devoted to scientific misconduct is Aubrey Blumsohn's Scientific Misconduct Blog (**http://scientific-misconduct.blogspot.com**), which began in July 2006. It includes links to a number of other blogs that include discussions of scientific misconduct as well as many topics related to academic and big pharma life and ethics. Some of these blogs specialize in the postpublication discussion of papers, something like a very critical lab meeting on problematic research practices or obvious misconducts.

Another example of postpublication peer review is PubPeer (**http://www.blog.pubpeer.com**). Recently, PubPeer was sued by a cancer scientist at Wayne State University, who claimed he lost a prospective tenured position at the University of Mississippi as a result of anonymous comments in PubPeer that suggested misconduct in his research (Servick 2014).

One blog devoted to scientific misconduct (sciencefraud.org, which is no longer active) had the unusual opportunity to examine the effects of Internet publicity (Brookes 2014). From July to December 2012, this blog site received and published 274 anonymous emails claiming data integrity problems, most of which were in biomedical journals. In January 2013, legal threats forced the closure of this site, but an additional 233 anonymous emails claiming integrity problems were submitted and could not be published. Brookes (2014) found no differences in the characteristics of the 274 "public" cases and the 223 unpublished "private" cases submitted between November 2012 and January 2013. He then examined whether papers in the two groups (*a*) were retracted, (*b*) had errata published, or (*c*) had no action taken. He found that in comparison with the private set, the public set had a rate of retractions that was 6.5 times higher and a rate of corrections that was 7.7 times higher. Overall, some kind of corrective action was taken on 23% of the publicly discussed papers as opposed to 3.1% of the private, nondiscussed papers. These findings suggest the value of Internet publicity for greater scientific integrity.

Similar to the growth in postpublication review blogs has been the increased use of laboratory websites for the critique of published papers. This use of the Internet is analogous to posting the results of a lab meeting critique of a published paper.

WHO ARE THE MISCREANTS?

Scientists guilty of misconduct have been found in many fields and at different levels in universities and research institutions; their social and educational backgrounds vary. There appear to be no systematic empirical studies of the characteristics of perpetrators of scientific misconduct and no good evidence for any common characteristics. However, there does seem to be a modal scientist whose misdeeds in science are well publicized in *The New York Times*, *Science*, and *Nature* and in books on the subject (e.g., Broad & Wade 1982, Goodstein 2010, Judson 2004). This scientist is a bright and ambitious young man working in an elite institution in a rapidly moving and highly competitive branch of modern biology or medicine, where results have important theoretical, clinical, or financial implications. He has been mentored and supported by a senior and respected establishment figure who is often the coauthor of many of his papers but may have not been closely involved in the research.

The following sections give examples of two well-publicized cases that fit this stereotype. They are probably not typical of the entire of sample of scientists engaged in misconduct, but they are instructive because they involve senior US scientists and distinguished US institutions; therefore, they may indicate some of the problems that government and research institutions are struggling with in maintaining scientific integrity. These cases have also, presumably, spurred the recent attempts of federal government agencies and research institutions to reduce scientific misconduct.

The Case of Vijay Soman

The story of Vijay Soman began on November 9, 1978, when a young Brazilian physician, Helena Wachslicht-Rodbard, who was working in the laboratory of Jesse Roth, chief of the diabetes branch of the National Institute of Arthritis, Metabolism and Digestive Diseases at the NIH, submitted a paper on insulin binding in patients with anorexia nervosa to the prestigious *New England Journal of Medicine* (*NEJM*). The paper, with Roth as coauthor, showed that insulin receptors in blood cells of patients with anorexia nervosa bound more insulin than normal. Editor Arnold Relman sent it to two referees, one of whom recommended rejection, so a third referee was called in. After two and a half months, the editor wrote Rodbard that two of the referees were favorable and one recommended rejection. He also wrote that the paper could be acceptable after minor revisions.

Unknown to Rodbard, the negative reviewer had been Philip Felig, an endowed professor at Yale School of Medicine, vice chairman of the Department of Medicine, and chief of endocrinology research. Felig gave Rodbard's paper to an assistant professor in his laboratory, Vijay Soman, who had been supposedly working on the identical subject as that of the paper. Shortly after receiving Rodbard's paper, Felig sent off a paper on the same subject, with Soman as coauthor, to the *American Journal of Medicine*.

Ironically, the Soman-Felig manuscript was send to Roth for review, and Roth passed it on to Robard. To quote Broad & Wade (1982, p. 165), "She was aghast. Here was her paper, complete with verbatim passages . . . and even a formula she had devised." Comparing the content and typeface of the submitted paper with that of the negative review, she realized that Felig had written the negative review. She immediately wrote to *NEJM* Editor Relman, accusing Felig and Soman of "plagiarism, of conflict of interest in reviewing her paper and of trying to slow down the acceptance of her work" (Broad & Wade 1982, p. 166).

In late February of the next year, Relman called Felig to discuss the conflict of interest charges, and Felig claimed (incorrectly) that their work had been completed before the Rodbard paper arrived. In any case, Relman then published the Rodbard-Roth paper in the *NEJM*. A week later, Felig and Roth (grade-school buddies from Brooklyn) got together at the NIH and compared the two manuscripts. Felig agreed that there was a minor plagiarism problem and said he would (*a*) refer in the Rodbard-Roth paper in the Soman-Felig manuscript, (*b*) delay publishing theirs so Rodbard would have priority, and (*c*) not publish it at all if there were any "legitimate" questions about the independence of Soman's work. Returning to New Haven, Felig confronted Soman, who confessed to have used Rodman's paper in writing his own, but Felig saw enough of Soman's notes to satisfy himself that Soman had done the work on their paper.

Meanwhile, Rodbard had come to believe that beyond the plagiarism, the Soman-Felig study had been entirely fabricated on the basis of her study. Roth didn't accept this view, told Felig so, and pressured Rodbard not to pursue the issue. Rodbard then wrote to Robert Berliner, dean of Yale School of Medicine, and demanded an investigation to establish the authenticity of the data in the Soman-Felig paper, giving a number of cogent reasons for this in addition to the plagiarism. For example, neither the hospital nor the collaborating psychotherapists were identified, and the author seemed unfamiliar with the methodology. If such an investigation was not undertaken, Rodbard threatened to denounce the Soman-Felig paper at an upcoming meeting of the American Federation of Clinical Research. The requested investigation, or audit, is unusual in the world of academic research. A mutually agreed auditor, Joseph E. Rall, Roth's boss at the NIH, was chosen as the auditor to examine Soman's data.

In the interim, two major developments occurred in the career trajectories of Rodbard and Felig in July 1979. First, Rodbard quit research at the NIH to take a residency in internal medicine. Second, Felig was offered and accepted the prestigious Bard professorship and chairmanship of Columbia University's Department of Medicine, a post he planned to take up in June 1980. In January he took Soman to Columbia and recommended he be made an assistant professor. In the same month, the Soman-Felig paper, which Felig had agreed to hold back until the audit was complete, was published in the *American Journal of Medicine*. Rall, the prospective auditor, had been too busy, so the agreed-upon audit had never been carried out.

Rodbard continued to demand that Roth get another auditor. In February, the new auditor, Jeffrey Flier, an assistant professor at Harvard Medical School (now dean), examined the data that formed the bases of Soman's paper. Soman soon confessed to "fudging" and fabricating data but said that Felig didn't know about it. Soman said, "He'd been under great pressure to publish as soon as possible to obtain priority" (Broad & Wade, p. 173). Upon hearing Soman's confession, the Yale Department of Medicine chairman told Soman that "his best choice was to resign and give up research" (Broad & Wade 1982, p. 174). At that point, the only excuse Soman gave for his misconduct was that it was his "fate" (Broad & Wade, p. 174). He disappeared into India a few weeks later.

Felig thereupon retracted the disputed article with Soman, which he had published in violation of the agreement with Rodbard. Because of Rodbard's continued charges about data fabrication by Felig's laboratory, Yale called in another auditor, Jerrold Olefsky, then of University of Colorado, to examine all of Soman's 14 publications dealing with insulin receptors. Of them, Olefsky could find data supporting only two. Felig had coauthored 10 of the remaining papers. Yale retracted the 12 papers by the end of May. In August 1980, Columbia asked Felig to resign from his new post as Bard Professor and chair of the Department of Medicine.

Yale rehired Felig as a tenured full professor but not to his original endowed chair. He was found not guilty of fraud by an NIH investigating committee, and his major NIH grant was renewed. A few years later he left Yale to work briefly for Sandoz, a major pharmaceutical company, and is now in private practice in New York. Apparently, he has disappeared from the biomedical scene and no longer publishes or attends the major meetings he had attended in the past.

Rodbard is now in private practice as an endocrinologist in the Washington, DC area and is active in clinical research. She is past president of the American College of Endocrinology, past president of the American Association of Clinical Endocrinologists, a Master of the American College of Endocrinology (an average of only two are so honored every year), and a Fellow of the American College of Physicians. She has been consistently listed in Best Doctors in America and Best Doctors in Washington, DC. Under the name H.W. Rodbard, she is listed in Pub Med as having authored or coauthored 49 clinical endocrinology papers since she left the NIH to enter private practice. [This (abbreviated) account of the story of Vijay Soman is based on Altman (1980), Broad (1980), Broad & Wade (1982), Hunt (1981), and H.W. Rodbard (personal communication).]

The Case of John R. Darsee

The next case is again about the fall of a promising young man protected by a senior figure, this time at Harvard Medical School. In 1979, John R. Darsee, after a brilliant five-year research and clinical career at Emory University, joined Eugene Braunwald's large cardiac research laboratory at Harvard. Braunwald held the hoary chair of Professor of Theory and Practice of Physic at Harvard and was chairman of Medicine and physician-in-chief at both the Brigham and Women's and Beth Israel hospitals. In 1979, Braunwald had over 800 papers listed in PubMed and more than $3.3 million in NIH funding.

Darsee went to Harvard as an NIH postdoc and was slated for a faculty appointment at Harvard Medical School. In two years at Harvard, he published over 100 abstracts and papers (Broad 1983a,b). Braunwald often called Darsee "one of the most outstanding of the 130 research fellows he has trained, more than 40 of whom are now full professors, department chiefs, or directors of academic cardiology divisions" (Knox 1983, p. 1799).

Several of Darsee's lab colleagues had been suspicious of his prodigious output. For example, he claimed "to have done some complicated long-term dog experiments . . . spanning up to six weeks and involving indwelling intracoronary pressure transducers, ultrasonic crystals, and meticulous sterile techniques [which] no one in the laboratory could remember seeing" (Knox 1983, p. 1802). Finally, in May 1981, some of his coworkers went to Robert Kloner, their immediate supervisor, and suggested that Darsee had faked the data for an abstract that he was about to send off. When Kloner confronted Darsee and asked to see the raw data, Darsee started taking a "hemodynamic reading off a dog in an experiment and as the chart paper came out, he marked it day 1, day 2 and so forth, making it look as though the data had been taken over the course of several days" as several colleagues "watched in awe" (Broad 1982a, p. 479). When later confronted by Kloner, Darsee admitted his misconduct but called it a single foolish act performed because he had thrown away the real raw data (Culliton 1983b). Kloner reported this to Braunwald, who initiated an investigation of Darsee's work. As a result of this inquiry, the abstract was never sent out and Darsee's NIH postdoc and his Harvard appointments were terminated, but the NIH was not informed of his fabrications.

Yet Darsee continued his active cardiac research in the lab. He was paid from private funds controlled by Braunwald and continued to publish many abstracts and papers, most of them coauthored by Kloner or Braunwald. Braunwald apparently trusted Darsee in spite of his recently demonstrated misconduct (Braunwald 1992). Darsee wrote Braunwald that his single misdeed "should be considered in the context of the 'laboratory environment,' which he characterized as bristling with envy, spite, spying, and even sabotage directed toward him . . . as such a hard worker, meticulous scientist, and lone wolf" (Knox 1983, p. 1803).

At this time Braunwald's laboratory in Brigham and Women's Hospital was participating in an NIH-sponsored multi-institutional study of drug treatment for heart attacks. When the data from the different institutions were compared, the Harvard data, collected by Darsee, were different from those of the other labs. When challenged, Darsee could not support his claims. Harvard and the NIH set up formal committees to investigate these discrepancies.

In January 1981, the Harvard committee revealed multiple fabrications by Darsee. In March, the NIH committee reported "extensive irregularities" in five papers authored by Darsee, Kloner, and Braunwald and suggested one cause was insufficient supervision by Braunwald (Broad 1982b). The NIH required Brigham and Women's Hospital to return $122,371 in research funds designated for their part of the study, which apparently marked the first time that money had to be returned to the NIH because of fraud.

In response to the implication of the NIH report that his lax supervision had contributed to Darsee's behavior, Braunwald defended his practices and declared, "I had gotten a bum rap" (Culliton 1983b, p. 31). In an apparent effort to counter the implication that he was responsible for Darsee's misconduct at Harvard, Braunwald then reviewed some of Darsee's papers from Emory and reported his concerns about their integrity to both the NIH and Emory. An Emory investigation concluded that only 2 of the 10 papers published by Darsee from Emory were valid, and of 45 abstracts, only 2 stood up to scrutiny. The investigating committee viewed many of the publications as fiction and noted that some mentioned collaborators who did not exist.

Darsee left Harvard and obtained a clinical position at a Schenectady hospital. He issued the following statement: "I am asking for forgiveness for whatever I have done wrong and want to contribute to the medical system" (Culliton 1983b, p. 35). He excused his behavior in a letter: "I had too much to do, too little time to do it...I had not taken a vacation, sick day or even a day off from work for six years. I had put myself on a track that I hoped would allow me to have a wonderful academic job" (Knox 1983, p. 1805). [This account is based on Broad (1982a,b, 1983a,b); Broad & Wade (1982); Culliton (1983a,b,c); Knox (1983); Moran (1985).] In 1984, New York State revoked Darsee's license to practice medicine. He appears to be currently practicing internal medicine in Indianapolis (**https://www.doximity.com/pub/john-darsee-md**).

In spite of the considerable publicity (e.g., the references cited in the previous paragraph) about Darsee's fraudulent publications, these publications continued to be cited in a positive fashion with no mention of fraud (Kochan & Budd 1992, Moran 1985). From 1982 to 1990, only 5.7% of 256 citations to Darsee acknowledged fraud. The continued citation of retracted articles is a more general phenomenon (Madlock-Brown & Eichmann 2015).

Walter Stewart and Ned Feder, two NIH scientists, used the Darsee issue to inquire into the roles of coauthors, editors, and referees in Darsee's publications. They examined 109 of Darsee's papers, abstracts, and chapters, which had a total of 47 coauthors at Emory and Harvard, approximately half junior and half senior, the latter including departmental chairs and full professors (Stewart & Feder 1987). They were not concerned with Darsee's science or his fraud. They were only concerned with the papers themselves—with "lapses in generally accepted standards" (p. 207) for publication, such as internal errors (major and minor), inconsistencies in numerical values within the papers and with previous publication, lack of controls, inadequately presented data, unsupportable claims, honorary authorship, repeated publication of the same data without acknowledgment, and similar flaws that "should have been detected by any competent scientist who read the papers carefully" (Boffey 1986), let alone their coauthors (Boffey 1986, Mervis 1986, Stewart & Feder 1987).

They unsuccessfully submitted a draft of their paper to *Nature* in 1983 and to *Cell* in 1985, "and the two journals were bombarded with more than 20 letters and memorandums, some 150 typed pages in all, from lawyers for the scientists accused of misdeeds"; most of the correspondence originated from the lawyers for Braunwald, probably the most eminent of the scientists involved (Boffey 1986; N. Feder, personal communication). They also submitted their paper to another 14 journals, none of which were interested in publishing it (Boffey 1986).

In letters to some of Darsee's Emory and Harvard coauthors, Stewart and Feder inquired about apparent flaws in their papers with Darsee. In September 1983, Lester Salans, chief of the National Institute of Infectious Diseases, wrote Stewart that he and Feder did "not have the authority to act on behalf of NIH or to utilize official time and/or with the aid of NIH resources, including NIH stationery" (N. Feder, personal communication). According to Feder, "This was the first of many episodes in which NIH officials challenged the legitimacy of our examination of the practices of Darsee's coauthors, as well as the legitimacy of our subsequent public comments, spoken and in print, on these practices" (N. Feder, personal communication).

Eventually, *The New York Times*, under a Freedom of Information Act request, obtained a copy of the article, along with its voluminous legal history, from the NIH and published an account (Boffey 1986). Soon afterward *Nature* published a toned-down version of the paper, i.e., one in which the editors had made changes without the authors' permission (Stewart & Feder 1987). In the same issue of *Nature*, Braunwald (1987) answered Stewart and Feder. In his long reply in *Nature*, Braunwald concentrated on defending his lab and characterized the admitted errors in the various papers he coauthored with Darsee as either Darsee's fault or trivial.

Their work on Darsee was only the beginning of Stewart and Feder's long, distinguished, and sometimes controversial career of exposing scientific misconduct. The other issues they were active on included the O'Toole, Imanishi-Kari, and Baltimore controversy discussed below, the Gallo case on priority for the discovery of HIV, and the phenomenon of NIH grantees receiving huge fees from drug companies. For these and similar activities, they were subjected to many years of harassment and threats to stop their investigations by their NIH bosses. Near the end of their government career, Stewart and Feder invented a plagiarism-detecting computer program and used it to file a 1,400-page report accusing the best-selling Lincoln historian Stephen Oates of massive plagiarism. This led the NIH to close their lab, seize their files, and transfer them to positions that were incompatible with misconduct investigations (Hilts 1993a). Stewart went on a 33-day hunger strike in protest, but to no avail. Many scientists defended them, including Margot O'Toole, who said, "But when all the critics are silenced, who will be left to dissent?" (O'Toole 1993).

In 2007, Feder left the NIH to continue his work on scientific misconduct at the private Project on Government Oversight (POGO) (Feder 2012). Accounts of Stewart and Feder's campaign against scientific misconduct can be found in Boffey (1986); Feder (2008, 2012, personal communication); Grossman (1993); Hoke (1993, 1995a); Monastersky (2008); Powledge (1987); Sarasohn (1993); Wade (1988); Wadman (2008).

PREVENTION OF SCIENTIFIC MISCONDUCT

In the previous sections, we presented data on the incidence and characteristics of scientific misconduct. We also recounted two case histories in two leading biomedical research facilities; the case histories suggest that some institutional structures may foment scientific misconduct. In this final section, we consider ways that scientific misconduct might be reduced.

Whistle-Blowing

Fabrication and falsification of scientific data can be uncovered in a variety of ways. One way is through referees or readers identifying internal contradictions and inconsistencies with previous papers from the same lab. Another way is through the detection of previously published or apparently doctored figures. An unusual way, as in the case of Helena Wachslicht-Rodbard, is by discovering plagiarism of one's own work and detecting the similarity of fonts in a referee report with those in a submitted paper. However, most detection of scientific misconduct appears to come from laboratory colleagues: from students, peers, technicians, and supervisors of the miscreant (Shamoo & Resnik 2003).

The individual making the accusation of possible misconduct is often termed a whistle-blower, especially if he or she is not the senior member of the research unit. Even if the whistle-blowing turns out to be justified, the consequences for the whistle-blowers are often disastrous in terms of their income, research, personal relations at work, and future in science, as has been repeatedly related (e.g., Alford 2002, D'Angelo 2012, Hilts 1993b, Lock et al. 2001, Martin 2013, Penslar 1995, Rivlin 2004).

The plight of the whistle-blowing junior scientist was widely publicized in the case of Margot O'Toole versus Thereza Imanishi-Kari. The case, which began in 1986, continued for over ten years and, *inter alia*, involved Congress, the Secret Service, fraud-busters Feder and Stewart, and the resignation of Nobel Laureate David Baltimore as president of Rockefeller University (see, e.g., Kevles 1998; Judson 2004; O'Toole 1991, 1993; Sarasohn 1993). O'Toole, a postdoc working in the laboratory of Imanishi-Kari, questioned the latter's data in a paper about genes that are involved with the immune system of mice; the paper was coauthored by Imanishi-Kari and Baltimore. Independent of whether O'Toole's accusations were valid and whether Imanishi-Kari's treatment of data was sloppy, fraudulent, or neither, it was clear that Baltimore, the senior scientist, treated O'Toole's stubborn skepticism with inappropriate arrogance, intolerance, and brutality. Baltimore eventually apologized to O'Toole: "I commend Dr. O'Toole for her courage . . . and I regret and apologize for my failure to act vigorously enough in my investigation of her doubts" (Hilts 1991).

Perhaps partially as a result of this incident, the ORI began to systematically investigate the consequences of whistle-blowing for the whistle-blower. In 1995, the ORI reported that "over 60% of whistleblowers suffered at least one negative consequence, such as being pressured to withdraw their allegation, being ostracized by colleagues, suffering a reduction in research support, or being threatened with a lawsuit. Over 10% noted significant negative consequences, such as being fired or losing support" (Lubalin et al. 1995, p. 51). The ORI then issued to institutions receiving NIH funds a detailed set of guidelines on protecting whistle-blowers against retaliation (ORI 1995). These guidelines provide specific and detailed procedures for investigating any claims by whistle-blowers of retaliation for their actions.

However, if retaliation of whistle-blowing is validated, the recommendations as to what to do next are rather vague: The deciding official shall determine what remedies are appropriate to satisfy the institution's regulatory obligation to protect whistle-blowers. The deciding official shall, in consultation with the whistle-blower, take measures to protect or restore the whistle-blower's position and reputation, including making any public or private statements, as appropriate. In addition, the deciding official may provide protection against further retaliation by monitoring or disciplining the retaliator (ORI 1995).

However, in the typical case of whistle-blowing in a research laboratory, these elaborate protections against retaliation may be of little value to whistle-blowers. For example, if the whistle-blowers are graduate students or postdocs and if and their evidence eventually is accepted, their supervisor is likely to leave and their lab likely to be closed, leaving the whistle-blowers without facilities, financial support, mentoring, or even a project; in addition, whistle-blowers sometimes are forced to endure the obloquy of other members of the department (e.g., Couzin 2006).

Because whistle-blowing by members of a laboratory is a major weapon against research misconduct, it would seem important to encourage such behavior rather than punishing it. For example, if the whistle-blower is a graduate student in good standing, he or she might be guaranteed financial support, laboratory facilities, and a mentor until he or she receives a degree. Postdocs or technicians might be insured a paid position for a year or two, until they obtain other support. More generally, the institution should commit to preventing whistle-blowing from resulting in career destruction, whatever the level of the whistle-blower.

Of course, premature, inadequately justified, unjustifiable, and/or inappropriately carried out whistle-blowing can be a disaster for all involved. There are a number of good and cautious guides to whistle-blowing (see, e.g., Gunsalus 1998 and other articles in the same issue; Hoke 1995b, Rennie & Gunsalus 2008).

Responsible Conduct of Research Courses

As a result of the scientific misconduct scandals and hearings in the late 1980s, the federal government has been increasingly involved in requiring education in the responsible conduct of research (RCR). As of 2011, the NIH has required that all trainees, fellows, participants, and scholars receiving support through any NIH training, career development award, research education grant, and dissertation research grant must receive instruction in responsible conduct of research (NIH 2009).

Similarly, the NSF requires each institution that applies for financial assistance to describe in its grant proposal a plan to provide appropriate training and oversight in the responsible and ethical conduct of research to undergraduate students, graduate students, and postdoctoral researchers participating in the proposed research project (NSF 2009).

The NIH and NSF provide detailed guidelines for the development of institutional RCR courses that have been developed over the past 20 years. These courses cover:

1. conflict of interest—personal, professional, and financial;
2. policies regarding human subjects, live vertebrate animal subjects in research, and safe laboratory practices;
3. mentor/mentee responsibilities and relationships;
4. collaborative research, including collaborations with industry;
5. peer review;
6. data acquisition and laboratory tools—management, sharing, and ownership;
7. research misconduct and policies for handling misconduct;
8. responsible authorship and publication; and
9. the scientist as a responsible member of society, contemporary ethical issues in biomedical research, and the environmental and societal impacts of scientific research.

The strongly recommended format for RCR courses is small-group discussion of case studies. A semester-long series of meetings (or at least eight contact hours) is recommended over a more compressed schedule. Online courses are not normally an acceptable substitute. Faculty and mentors are encouraged to participate as "discussion leaders, speakers, lecturers, and/or course director" on a rotational schedule to insure "full faculty participation" (NIH 2009).

Participation should occur at least once at every career level from undergraduate to faculty, at a frequency of no less than every four years. Detailed instructions for proposing and reporting on RCR implementation are available for each type of instructional and individual award.

Excellent print and online materials are available for such RCR courses [e.g., Macrina (2005), Natl. Acad. Sci. (2009), Penslar (1995), Shamoo & Resnik (2003), Steneck (2007)]. The ORI has produced a virtual experience interactive learning simulation program entitled *The Lab: Avoiding Research Misconduct*. In this sophisticated simulation, class participants assume different roles, such as that of graduate student or principal investigator, and are required to decide how to handle possible research misconduct. In my experience, students quickly get emotionally and intellectually involved in dealing with this case of research misconduct. Training is also available for RCR course leaders, such as workshops offered at the Poynter Center for the Study of Ethics and American Institutions at Indiana University in Bloomington.

To determine whether US research institutions are meeting federal government requirements for RCR instruction, Resnik & Dinse (2012) conducted a national survey of 200 such institutions. Of the 144 institutions that responded to the survey, all had an RCR program, which was required either of federally mandated individuals (48%) or of everyone involved in research (52%).

RCR courses usually end with student evaluations. A meta-analysis of 26 evaluations suggested that case-based discussion was preferred over lectures, and stand-alone courses were preferred over embedded ones (Antes et al. 2009). An ORI panel suggested that most of the usual topics in an RCR course were favorably judged; among the ones that were the least so were (*a*) detailed philosophical or historical issues in ethics, (*b*) financial matters, and (*c*) health and safety (**http://www.ori.hhs.gov/rcr-objectives-introduction-0**).

I have taught an RCR course a number of times since 2006. The courses have met for six three-hour weekly sessions and have generally followed the NIH guidelines. Discussion has worked best with 15 participants, usually graduate students along with a few other participants. One very successful variation was to invite two different faculty members to every session. The differences between the faculty members, and between the faculty members and the students, on such topics as authorship, mentoring, and personal use of laboratory facilities were surprising and, I think, instructive to all.

There does not seem to be any good evidence that RCR courses make scientific misconduct less likely to occur or even that the courses change attitudes toward fabrication, falsification, and plagiarism. However, it is my strong feeling, and that of the faculty and student participants, that the vigorous class discussions are valuable in raising consciousness; that is, in increasing sensitivity, empathy, understanding, and awareness on a number of major issues in the life of a research scientist. These issues involve mentoring, authorship, and reviewing as well as the ethical implications of research, conflict of interest, and ownership of data (for a review of studies of the effect of RCR courses, see Kligyte et al. 2008).

The Role of Publication Number

A common response to incidents of scientific misconduct is a call to de-emphasize the quantity of publications—as opposed to their quality—as an important criterion for appointments, promotions, tenure, prizes, and membership in honorific organizations. A number of elite institutions have made gestures in this direction by considering as few as two to five papers (of the applicant's choice) in tenure decisions. Nominations to the National Academy of Sciences require a maximum of ten papers. The emphasis placed on the impact factor of the journal in which an article is published has also been criticized.

Data Recording and Data Sharing

In the past decade, there has been a new development in the handling of data that has been termed "a marriage of word processing and software command scripts" (Clearbout & Karrenback 1992). In this marriage, all data from an experiment, all experimental parameters, and all programs used to analyze the data are stored in an organized fashion so that, for example, pushing a button attached to a figure will yield access to the data and the analysis and programs that are the basis of the published figure. This idea of "reproducible research" derives from the computational and computer science community, and it is applicable to any branch of science (Wandell et al. 2015; **http://reproducibleresearch.net/bibliography/**). For example, in primate field biology, perhaps on the other end of the dimension from computational neuroscience, Tomasello & Call (2011) have advocated for the recording, in an accessible form, of videos in all primate field studies.

The widespread adoption of reproducible research tools would be valuable for many purposes. For the individual investigator, it would provide a permanent, accessible history of his or her own data for further analysis, communication, and publication. For collaborators, it would provide a common core of information. For members of the laboratory, it would provide the opportunity to find out what their colleagues have been doing as well as a platform for internal laboratory discussion and critique before the presentation and publication stages. For journals, it would provide tools that would enable all authors to submit all data, all experimental parameters, and all programs used to analyze the data for examination by the journal referees and, if the paper is accepted, by the entire scientific community. With modern technology, this process represents a small fraction of the cost of acquiring and analyzing the original data; the cost is comparable to the publication fee or the incremental cost of printing a color figure. Twenty years ago, 132 of 850 journals surveyed had already required deposition of sequence or structure data in a data bank and deposition or sharing of research results upon request (McCain 1995).

Reproducible research practices cannot eliminate outright fabrication and falsification of data. But widespread adoption of these practices would certainly radically reduce the type of scientific misconduct described in this review, and would promote the sharing of methods and data across large and distributed research communities.

DISCLOSURE STATEMENT

The author is not aware of any affiliations, memberships, funding, or financial holdings that might be perceived as affecting the objectivity of this review.

ACKNOWLEDGMENTS

Thanks for generous help from Drs. Ned Feder and Helena Wachslicht-Rodbard and, on data sharing, from Dr. Brian Wandell. Some of the material in this article appeared in Gross (2012).

LITERATURE CITED

Alford CF. 2002. *Whistleblowers: Broken Lives and Organizational Power.* Ithaca, NY: Cornell Univ. Press

Altman LK. 1980. Columbia's medical chief resigns; ex associate's data fraud at issue. *New York Times*, Aug. 9

Antes AL, Murphy ST, Waples EP, Mumford MD, Brown RP, et al. 2009. A meta-analysis of ethics instruction effectiveness in the sciences. *Ethics Behav.* 19:379–402

Babbage C. 1970 (1830). *Reflections on the Decline of Science in England.* New York: Kelley

Bhattacharjee Y. 2013. The mind of a con man. *New York Times Magazine*, April 26

Boffey P. 1986. Major study points to faulty research at two universities. *New York Times*, April 22

Braunwald E. 1987 On analyzing scientific fraud. *Nature* 325:215–16

Braunwald E. 1992. Cardiology: the John Darsee experience. In *Research Fraud in the Behavioral and Biomedical Sciences*, ed. DJ Miller, M Henson, pp. 55–79. New York: Wiley

Broad WJ. 1980a. Imbroglio at Yale (I): emergence of a fraud. *Science* 210(4465):38–41

Broad WJ. 1980b. Imbroglio at Yale (II): a top job lost. *Science* 210(4466):171–73

Broad WJ. 1982a. Harvard delay in reporting fraud. *Science* 215:478–82

Broad WJ. 1982b. Report absolves Harvard in case of fakery. *Science* 215:874–76

Broad WJ. 1983a. Fraud in science taints the high and mighty. *New York Times*, March 20

Broad WJ. 1983b. Notorious Darsee case shakes assumptions about science. *New York Times*, June 14

Broad WJ, Wade N. 1982. *Betrayers of the Truth*. New York: Simon & Schuster

Broadus RN. 1983. An investigation of the validity of bibliographic citations. *J. Assoc. Inf. Sci. Technol.* 34:132–35

Brookes PS. 2014. Internet publicity of data problems in the bioscience literature correlates with enhanced corrective action. *Peer J.* 2:e313

Budd JM, Sievert M, Schultz TR. 1998. Phenomena of retraction: reasons for retraction and citations to the publications. *JAMA* 280:296–97

Casadevall A, Steen RG, Fang FC. 2014. Sources of error in the retracted scientific literature. *FASEB J.* 28:3847–55

Clearbout J, Karrenbach M. 1992. *Electronic Documents Give Reproducible Research a New Meaning*. Stanford, CA: Stanford Explor. Proj. **http://sepwww.stanford.edu/doku.php?id=sep:research:reproducible:seg92**

Couzin J. 2006. Truth and consequences. *Science* 313:1222–26

Culliton BJ. 1983a. Fraud inquiry spreads blame. *Science* 219:937

Culliton BJ. 1983b. Coping with fraud: the Darsee case. *Science* 220:31–35

Culliton BJ. 1983c. NIH to review Emory in Darsee case. *Science* 220:1029

D'Angelo J. 2012. *Ethics in Science*. Boca Raton, FL: CRC Press

Dalton R. 2005. Obesity expert owns up to million-dollar crime. *Nature* 434:424

Eastwood S, Derish P, Leash E, Ordway S. 1996. Ethical issues in biomedical research: perception and practices of postdoctoral research fellows responding to a survey. *Sci. Eng. Ethics* 2:89–114

Eisley L. 1979. *Darwin and the Mysterious Mr. X*. New York: Dutton

Fanelli D. 2009. How many scientists fabricate and falsify research? A systematic review and meta-analysis of survey data. *PLOS ONE* 4:e5738

Fanelli D. 2013. Why growing retractions are (mostly) a good sign. *PLOS Med.* 10:e1001563

Fang FC, Steen RG, Casadevall A. 2012. Misconduct accounts for the majority of retracted scientific publications. *PNAS* 109:17028–33

Feder N. 2008. *Ethical Problems at NIH—The Struggle Continues*. Washington, DC: Proj. Gov. Overs. **http://www.pogo.org/about/press-room/releases/2008/ph-iis-20081024.html**

Feder N. 2012. *Project on Government Oversight*. Washington, DC: Proj. Gov. Overs. **http://www.pogo.org/about/board-staff/staff-profiles/ned-feder.html**

Franklin A, Edwards AWF, Fairbanks DJ, Hartl DL, Seidenfeld T. 2008. *Ending the Mendel-Fisher Controversy*. Pittsburgh, PA: Univ. Pittsburgh Press

Goodstein DL. 2010. *On Fact and Fraud: Cautionary Tales from the Front Lines of Science*. Princeton, NJ: Princeton Univ. Press

Grieneisen ML, Zhang M. 2012. A comprehensive survey of retracted articles from the scholarly literature. *PLOS ONE* 7:e68397

Gross CG. 2010. Alfred Russell Wallace and the evolution of the human mind. *Neuroscientist* 16:496–507

Gross CG. 2012. Disgrace: on Marc Hauser. *The Nation*, Jan. 9–16

Grossman R. 1993. Machine designed to find plagiarism winds up wrecking inventors' careers. *Chicago Tribune*, May 13

Gunsalus CK. 1998. How to blow the whistle and still have a career afterwards. *Sci. Eng. Ethics* 4:51–63

Hilts PJ. 1991. Nobelist apologizes for defending research paper with faulty data. *New York Times*, May 4

Hilts PJ. 1993a. Institutes of Health close fraud investigation unit. *New York Times*, May 5

Hilts PJ. 1993b. Ideas & Trends: why whistle-blowers can seem a little crazy. *New York Times*, June 13

Hixson J. 1976. *The Patchwork Mouse*. New York: Doubleday

Hoke F. 1993. HHS pressed to reverse whistleblowers' reassignment. *The Scientist*, June 28

Hoke F. 1995a. On their own: Stewart and Feder persist with misconduct inquiries. *The Scientist*, Feb. 6

Hoke F. 1995b. Veteran whistleblowers advise other would-be "ethical resisters" to carefully weigh personal consequences before taking action. *The Scientist*, May 5

Hunt M. 1981. A fraud that shook the world of science. *New York Times Magazine*, Nov. 1

Judson HF. 2004. *The Great Betrayal: Fraud in Science*. Orlando, FL: Harcourt

Kalichman MW, Friedman PJ. 1992. A pilot study of biomedical trainees' perceptions concerning research ethics. *Acad. Med.* 67:769–75

Kevles DJ. 1998. *The Baltimore Case: A Trial of Politics, Science, and Character*. New York: Norton

Kligyte V, Marcy RT, Sevier ST, Godfrey ES, Mumford MD. 2008. A qualitative approach to Responsible Conduct of Research (RCR) training development: identification of metacognitive strategies. *Sci. Eng. Ethics* 14:3–31

Knox R. 1983. The Harvard fraud case: Where does the problem lie? *JAMA* 249:1797–99, 1802–7

Kochan CA, Budd JM. 1992. The persistence of fraud in the literature: the Darsee case. *J. Am. Soc. Inf. Sci.* 43:488–93

Kohn A. 1986. *False Prophets*. Oxford, UK: Blackwell

Lock S, Wells F, Farthing F. 2001. *Fraud and Misconduct in Biomedical Research*. London: BMJ Books. 3rd ed.

Lubalin JS, Ardini ME, Matheson JL. 1995. *Consequences of Whistleblowing for the Whistleblower in Misconduct in Science Cases*. Washington, DC: Res. Triangle Inst. **https://ori.hhs.gov/sites/default/files/final.pdf**

Macrina FL. 2005. *Scientific Integrity*. Herndon, VA: ASM Press

Madlock-Brown CR, Eichmann D. 2015. The (lack of) impact of retraction on citation networks. *Sci. Eng. Ethics* 21:127–37

Margraf J. 2015. Zur Lage der Psychologie. *Psychol. Rundsch.* 66:1–30

Martin B. 2013. *Whistleblowing: A Practical Guide*. Sparsnäs, Sweden: Irene Publ.

McCain K. 1995. Mandating sharing: journal policies in the natural sciences. *Sci. Comm.* 16:403–31

Merton RK. 1957. Priorities in scientific discovery: a chapter in the sociology of science. *Soc. Rev.* 22:635–59

Mervis J. 1986. Study sharpens debate on role of co-authors. *The Scientist*, Nov. 17

Monastersky R. 2008. NIH punished scientist who had called for open records. *The Chronicle of Higher Education*, Oct. 22

Moran NC. 1985. Report of ad hoc committee to evaluate research of Dr. John R. Darsee at Emory University. *Minerva* 23:276–305

Nath SB, Marcus SC, Druss BG. 2006. Retractions in the research literature: misconduct or mistakes? *Med. J. Aust.* 185:152–54

Natl. Acad. Sci. 2009. *On Being a Scientist: A Guide to Responsible Conduct in Research*. Washington, DC: Natl. Acad. Press

Neugebauer O. 1875. *A History of Mathematical Astronomy*. Berlin: Springer

Newton RR. 1977. *The Crime of Claudius Ptolemy*. Baltimore, MD: Johns Hopkins Univ. Press

NIH (Natl. Inst. Health). 2009. *Update on the Requirement for Instruction in the Responsible Conduct of Research*. Bethesda, MD: NIH. **http://grants.nih.gov/grants/guide/notice-files/NOT-OD-10-019.html**

NSF (Natl. Sci. Found.). 1996. *Research Misconduct*. Arlington, VA: NSF. **https://www.nsf.gov/oig/resmisreg.pdf**

NSF (Natl. Sci. Found.). 2009. *Responsible Conduct of Research (RCR)*. Arlington, VA: NSF. **http://www.nsf.gov/bfa/dias/policy/rcr.jsp**

O'Toole M. 1991. The whistle-blower and the train wreck. *New York Times*, April 12

O'Toole M. 1993. Silencing the dissenters: an unwise, ignominious move. *The Scientist*, May 17

ORI (Off. Res. Integr.). 1995. *ORI Guidelines for Institutions and Whistleblowers: Responding to Possible Retaliation Against Whistleblowers in Extramural Research*. Rockville, MD: US Dep. Health Human Serv. **http://ori.hhs.gov/guidelines-whistleblowers**

ORI (Off. Res. Integr.). 2011. *Definition of Research Misconduct*. Rockville, MD: US Dep. Health Human Serv. **http://ori.hhs.gov/definition-misconduct**

Penslar RL. 1995. *Research Ethics*. Bloomington: Indiana Univ. Press

Powledge T. 1987. Stewart-Feder (finally) in print. *The Scientist*, Feb. 9

Ranstam J, Buyse M, George SL, Evans S, Geller NL, et al. 2000. Fraud in medical research: an international survey of biostatisticians. *Control. Clin. Trials* 21:415–27

Rennie D, Gunsalus CK. 2008. What is research misconduct? In *Fraud and Misconduct in Biomedical Research*, ed. S Lock, F Wells, F Farthing, pp. 29–52. London: BMJ Books. 4th ed.

Resnik DB, Dinse GE. 2012. Do U.S. research institutions meet or exceed federal mandates for instruction in responsible conduct of research? A national survey. *Acad. Med.* 87:1237–42

Rivlin S. 2004. *Scientific Misconduct and Its Cover-Up*. Boca Raton, FL: BrownWalker

Sarasohn J. 1993. *Science on Trial*. New York: St. Martin's Press

Servick K. 2014. Researcher files lawsuit over anonymous PubPeer comments. *Science*. **http://news.sciencemag.org/scientific-community/2014/10/researcher-files-lawsuit-over-anonymous-pubpeer-comments**

Shamoo AE, Resnik DB. 2003. *Responsible Conduct of Research*. New York: Oxford Univ. Press

Siskin M, Roychowdhury V. 2006. Do you sincerely want to be cited? Or: Read before you cite. *Significance* 3:179–81

Sokal AD. 1996. Transgressing the boundaries: toward a transformative hermeneutics of quantum gravity. *Soc. Text* 46/:217–52

Steen RG. 2011. Retractions in the scientific literature: Do authors deliberately commit research fraud? *J. Med. Ethics* 37:113–17

Steen RG, Casadevall A, Fang FC. 2013. Why has the number of scientific retractions increased? *PLOS ONE* 8:e68397

Steneck NH. 2007. *ORI Introduction to the Responsible Conduct of Research*. Washington, DC: US Gov. Print. Off.

Stewart WW, Feder N. 1987. The integrity of the scientific literature. *Nature* 325:207–14

Swazey JP, Anderson MS, Louis KS. 1993. Ethical problems in academic research. *Am. Sci.* 81:542–53

Titus SL, Wells JA, Rhoades LJ. 2008. Repairing research integrity. *Nature* 19:453:980–82

Tomasello M, Call J. 2011. Methodological challenges in the study of primate cognition. *Science* 334:1227–28

US House Rep. 1981. Fraud in biomedical research. Hearings before Committee on Science and Technology. *Subcomm. Investig. Overs., 97th Congr.*, 1st sess. Washington, DC: US Gov. Print. Off.

Wade N. 1981. A diversion of the quest for truth. *Science* 211:1022–25

Wade N. 1988. Ideas & Trends: looking hard at science's self-scrutiny. *New York Times*, Aug. 21

Wadman M. 2008. Department of beams in the eye. *Nature News Blog*, Oct. 23. **http://blogs.nature.com/news/2008/10/department_of_beams_in_the_eye.html**

Wagner E, Williams P. 2011. Why and how do journals retract articles? An analysis of Medline retractions 1988–2008. *J. Med. Ethics* 37:567–70

Wandell BA, Rokem A, Perry LM, Schaefer G, Dougherty RF. 2015. Data management to support reproducible research. arXiv:1502.06900

Weiner JS. 1955. *The Piltdown Forgery*. London: Oxford

Wells JA. 2008. *Final Report: Observing and Reporting Suspected Misconduct in Biomedical Research*. Washington, DC: Gallup Org. **http://ori.hhs.gov/sites/default/files/gallup_finalreport.pdf**

Westfall RS. 1973. Newton and the fudge factor. *Science* 179:751–58

The Council of Psychological Advisers

Cass R. Sunstein

Harvard Law School, Harvard University, Cambridge, Massachusetts 02138;
email: csunstei@law.harvard.edu

Annu. Rev. Psychol. 2016. 67:713–37

First published online as a Review in Advance on
September 21, 2015

The *Annual Review of Psychology* is online at
psych.annualreviews.org

This article's doi:
10.1146/annurev-psych-081914-124745

Keywords

behavioral economics, nudge, default rules, social norms

Abstract

Findings in behavioral science, including psychology, have influenced policies and reforms in many nations. Choice architecture can affect outcomes even if material incentives are not involved. In some contexts, default rules, simplification, and social norms have had even larger effects than significant economic incentives. Psychological research is helping to inform initiatives in savings, finance, highway safety, consumer protection, energy, climate change, obesity, education, poverty, development, crime, corruption, health, and the environment. No nation has yet created a council of psychological advisers, but the role of behavioral research in policy domains is likely to grow in the coming years, especially in light of the mounting interest in promoting ease and simplification ("navigability"); in increasing effectiveness, economic growth, and competitiveness; and in providing low-cost, choice-preserving approaches.

Contents

INTRODUCTION

Many nations have some kind of council of economic advisers. Should they also have a council of psychological advisers (Schwartz 2012, Thaler 2012)? Perhaps some already do. Consider four initiatives from the United States:

1. In 2010, the Federal Reserve Board adopted a regulation to protect consumers from high bank overdraft fees (12 C.F.R. § 205.17; Fed. Reserve Syst. 2009). The regulation forbids banks from automatically enrolling people in overdraft protection programs; instead, customers have to sign up (Willis 2013). In explaining its action, the Board observed that studies have shown that "consumers are likely to adhere to the established default rule, that is, the outcome that would apply if the consumer takes no action" (Fed. Reserve Syst. 2009, p. 59038). The Federal Reserve Board also referred to the phenomenon of unrealistic optimism, suggesting that consumers might well underestimate the likelihood that they would not overdraw their accounts (Fed. Reserve Syst. 2009, p. 59044).

2. In 2014, the Food and Drug Administration (FDA) proposed to revise its nutrition facts panel, which can be found on almost all food packages. Aware that it was obliged to identify the market failure that the regulation would address, the FDA stated that the new label could "assist consumers by making the long-term health consequences of consumer food choices more salient and by providing contextual cues of food consumption" (US FDA 2014a, p. 6). The FDA noted that the "behavioral economics literature suggests that distortions internal to consumers (or internalities) due to time-inconsistent preferences, myopia or present-biased preferences, visceral factors (e.g., hunger), or lack of self-control, can also create the potential for policy intervention to improve consumer welfare" (US FDA 2014a, p. 6).

3. In 2010, the Environmental Protection Agency (EPA) and the Department of Transportation (DOT) adopted aggressive fuel economy standards for motor vehicles. Most of the benefits of such standards come from economic savings for consumers, which raises a puzzle:

Why can't consumers choose fuel-efficient cars if they want? In answering that question, the government invoked behavioral research suggesting that "consumers appear not to purchase products that are in their economic self-interest" (US EPA & US DOT 2010, p. 25510). It offered a catalog of hypotheses based on psychological research:

    a. Consumers might be myopic and hence undervalue the long term.

    b. Consumers might lack information or a full appreciation of information even when it is presented.

    c. Consumers might be especially averse to the short-term losses associated with the higher prices of energy-efficient products relative to the uncertain future fuel savings, even if the expected present value of those fuel savings exceeds the cost (the behavioral phenomenon of "loss aversion").

    d. Even if consumers have relevant knowledge, the benefits of energy-efficient vehicles might not be sufficiently salient to them at the time of purchase, and the lack of salience might lead consumers to neglect an attribute that it would be in their economic interest to consider.

4. In 2014, the FDA proposed to assert authority over a range of tobacco products. In explaining its action, it emphasized that there are "opportunities for regulation of tobacco products to enhance social welfare for the population at large. Time inconsistency exists when consumers use lower rates of discount for consequences far in the future than for consequences close to the present. Time-inconsistent consumers make current decisions that they would not make from the perspective of their future selves" (US FDA 2014b, p. 10). The FDA added, "Consumers may suffer from time-inconsistent behavior, problems with self-control, addiction, and poor information, which prevent them from fully internalizing the benefits of reducing tobacco use" (US FDA 2014b, p. 15).

The above examples should make clear the significant role that psychological research has played in important policy domains in the United States. Initiatives based on psychological research enlist tools such as default rules, simplification, disclosure, and social norms, and they can be found in areas that involve fuel economy, energy efficiency, environmental protection, health care, education, financial products, smoking, and obesity. The Consumer Financial Protection Bureau, created in 2010, is particularly interested in using psychological research to protect consumers in financial markets (consider its mantra—"Know before you owe"). Psychological findings, and behavioral science more generally, have become an important reference point for policymaking in the United States.

In 2010, the United Kingdom created the Behavioural Insights Team, with the specific goal of incorporating an understanding of human psychology into policy initiatives. On its website (**http://www.behaviouralinsights.co.uk/about-us**), the organization states:

> We coined the term "behavioral insights" in 2010 to help bring together ideas from a range of inter-related academic disciplines (behavioural economics, psychology, and social anthropology). These fields seek to understand how individuals take decisions in practice and how they are likely to respond to options. Their insights enable us to design policies or interventions that can encourage, support and enable people to make better choices for themselves and society.

The Team uses behavioral insights to promote initiatives in numerous areas, including smoking cessation, energy efficiency, organ donation, consumer protection, tax compliance, and compliance strategies in general. The Team has enlisted the acronym "EAST" to capture its approach: easy, attractive, social, and timely (**http://www.behaviouralinsights.co.uk/ publications/east-four-simple-ways-to-apply-behavioural-insights/**).

The results of the Team's work include many substantial successes (for a catalog, see **http://www.behaviouralinsights.co.uk/publications**). For example, (*a*) a psychologically informed approach increased tax payment rates from delinquent taxpayers by over 5 percentage points, (*b*) a message designed to prompt people to join the Organ Donor Registry added 100,000 people to the Registry in a single year, and (*c*) automatically enrolling individuals in pension schemes has increased savings rates for those employed by large firms in the United Kingdom from 61% to 83%. In 2014, the Team moved from the Cabinet Office to become a partly privatized joint venture, a self-described "social purpose company" owned by the government, the Team's employees, and Nesta (an innovation charity). Other nations have expressed keen interest in the work of the Team, and its operations have significantly expanded. The idea of "nudge units," or behavioral insights teams, is receiving worldwide attention.

In Germany, Australia, Denmark, Sweden, Canada, Singapore, Israel, the Netherlands, South Korea, and Mexico, among other countries, psychological insights have been enlisted in discussions of environmental protection, financial reform, energy policy, corruption, and consumer protection. In 2014, the United States created a behavioral insights team of its own, called the White House Social and Behavioral Sciences Team. It is run by the White House Office of Science and Technology Policy and is engaged in a range of projects designed to test the effects of various policies, with close reference to psychological research.

Behavioral science has drawn considerable (and growing) attention in Europe more broadly. For example, a European Commission report, *Green Behavior*, enlists behavioral science to outline policy initiatives to protect the environment (Eur. Comm. 2012; **http://www.inudgeyou. com/resources**). The Organisation for Economic Development and Cooperation (OECD) has published a Consumer Policy Toolkit that recommends a number of initiatives rooted in behavioral findings (OECD 2010). In the European Union, the Directorate General for Health and Consumers has also shown the influence of psychology and behavioral economics (DG SANCO 2010). Private organizations, notably including the European Nudge Network, are producing creative and imaginative uses of behavioral insights to promote a variety of environmental, health-related, and other goals (see **http://www.inudgeyou.com/resources**, **http://www.greenudge.no/en/**). Emphasizing relevant psychological work, Singapore has initiated a large number of reforms in this domain (Low 2011).

There has been particular interest in using the relevant research in the areas of poverty and development (Banerjee & Duflo 2012, Mullainathan 2007), with considerable attention from the World Bank. Behaviorally informed approaches might help combat corruption and inefficiency and make existing programs more effective, in part by combating low take-up rates and improving well-motivated but counterproductive initiatives that are not alert to human psychology (cf. Mullainathan & Shafir 2013).

A central reason for the mounting influence of psychology is that it has complemented, and in some ways complicated, the conventional emphasis on the importance of material incentives. No one denies that actual and perceived costs and benefits matter. But the word "perceived" is important; it is necessary to understand how people will actually respond to material incentives. Sometimes their responses surprise policymakers. If people do not pay attention to an incentive, it may have little or no impact, even if it is large in economic terms (cf. Chetty et al. 2012), and inertia, inattention, and procrastination might render an incentive irrelevant. Consider, for example, the fact that large numbers of people do not refinance their mortgages, even though they have a great deal to gain from doing so (Keys et al. 2014).

Officials are increasingly aware that they should explore the importance of the social environment, sometimes described as "choice architecture" (Thaler & Sunstein 2008). Even when the material incentives seem small or nonexistent, changes in choice architecture can have large effects on outcomes (Thaler & Sunstein 2008, Wansink 2014). Suppose, for example, that healthy foods are made easily accessible. If so, people are more likely to choose them. According to one study, making food more difficult to reach (as, for example, by varying its proximity by 10 inches or altering the serving utensil) produces an 8% to 16% decrease in intake (Rozin et al. 2011). This finding has implications for the problem of childhood obesity, which is, in part, a product of the easy availability of unhealthy foods (Wansink 2014). What is easily available and what commands attention also matter for policies involving smoking, alcohol abuse, and even happiness, which has also been receiving significant official attention (Dolan 2014). Subjective well-being very much depends on social design (Dolan 2014). There are implications for discrimination and inequality as well. When job candidates are evaluated together rather than independently, the incidence of sex discrimination is reduced, thus suggesting the possibility of nudges that would reduce discrimination of diverse kinds (Bohnet et al. 2012).

Psychologically informed initiatives often have major consequences. For example, automatic enrollment in savings programs can have far larger effects than significant economic incentives—a clear testimonial to the potential power of choice architecture and its occasionally larger effect than standard economic tools (Chetty et al. 2012). If people are asked to sign self-report forms at the beginning rather than at the end—an especially minor change—the incidence of honesty might increase significantly (Shu et al. 2012). Default rules can have a substantial impact in the environmental area, with large effects on public health (Sunstein & Reisch 2014). Obesity can be significantly reduced by nudges (Wansink 2014); consider the notion that "[b]ecoming slim by design is easier than trying to become slim by willpower" (p. 1). There is even a possibility of increasing happiness "by design," at least if we focus on the overriding importance of where our attention is directed (Dolan 2014).

The catalog of potentially effective choice-preserving interventions, which is large and growing, includes (*a*) default rules (such as automatic enrollment in various programs involving education, health, food, and savings); (*b*) simplification (perhaps radical) of existing requirements; (*c*) insistence on active choosing; (*d*) reminders (e.g., by email or text message); and (*e*) priming (perhaps by emphasizing a relevant feature of the situation or some aspect of people's identity) (for a longer list, see Freedom-Preserving Tools or "Nudges" sidebar). Favoring some mandates (e.g., fuel economy standards) or instituting bans on psychological or behavioral grounds is also possible if the welfare calculus so suggests (Bubb & Pildes 2014, Sunstein 2014).

A great deal remains to be learned, especially about the effects of reforms on large populations, across cultures, and on potentially distinctive subpopulations. One of the most important developments in recent years has been the emphasis on rigorous testing of policies to identify their effects. The use of randomized controlled trials at official levels is growing (Sunstein 2013a), and such trials are often essential for policymaking. At present, the findings from psychological research suggest:

1. Default rules are an especially promising tool, combining effectiveness with preservation of freedom of choice.
2. In some cases, required active choosing may be preferable to default rules insofar as it counteracts the problem of inertia while also responding to the risk that policymakers may err if they rely on default rules.
3. Simplification often pays large dividends, in part because it reduces burdens on people's bandwidth (Mani et al. 2013, Mullainathan & Shafir 2013), potentially increasing uptake of

FREEDOM-PRESERVING TOOLS OR "NUDGES"

1. Establishing default rules (e.g., automatic enrollment in programs, including education, health, savings)
2. Simplifying and easing of current requirements (in part to promote take-up)
3. Requiring active choosing (requiring people to make an explicit choice)
4. Prompting choice (people are asked a question without having to answer)
5. Simplifying active choosing (asking people whether they want to choose or instead to rely on a default rule)
6. Enhancing or influencing active choosing (e.g., asking people to choose but using order effects or loss aversion to influence choices; alternatively, enlisting authority to influence people)
7. Making contexts or policies easily navigable, with pointers and guides
8. Providing reminders or accessible counts and accounts (e.g., by email or text message, as for overdue bills; reminder apps; health-related wristbands, watches, or apps)
9. Priming (perhaps by emphasizing a relevant feature of the situation, such as its effect on an individual's future self, or an aspect of people's identity, such as their inclination to be honest)
10. Eliciting implementation intentions or commitments (e.g., "Do you plan to vote?")
11. Anchoring (starting with certain figures, e.g., "Do you want to give $200 to this charity?")
12. Using social norms (emphasizing what most people do, e.g., "Most people plan to vote," "Most people pay their taxes on time," or "Most people are eating healthy these days")
13. Ordering effects (e.g., what people see first on a website or in a room; asking people to sign forms on the first page)
14. Enlisting loss aversion (e.g., "You will lose X dollars if you do not use energy conservation techniques," or alternatively, and a bit beyond a nudge, a small tax (e.g., a five-cent tax for plastic grocery bags)
15. Increasing ease/convenience (e.g., making low-cost options or healthy foods visible)
16. Framing (e.g., "90% fat-free" versus "10% fat"; loss frame versus gain frame)
17. Providing disclosures (as in calorie counts or traffic light systems for food)
18. Issuing warnings, graphic or otherwise (as for cigarettes—might counteract optimistic bias)
19. Providing literal or figurative speed bumps or cooling-off periods (as for waiving rights)
20. Using formal precommitment strategies (as in Save More Tomorrow)
21. Offering automatic enrollment with precommitment (e.g., automatic enrollment in Save More Tomorrow)
22. Using visual effects, colors, picture, signs, noises, fonts (e.g., to promote highway safety or attention to one's future self, as in virtual aging through online programs)
23. Decreasing vagueness and ambiguity through the use of plain language (e.g., MyPlate, not Food Pyramid)
24. Attracting or reducing attention, including through drawing attention to certain product attributes or through product placement (e.g., through cafeteria design)
25. Using moral suasion, increasing fun, or triggering a sense of responsibility
26. Using checklists (as for doctors or administrators)
27. Reducing paperwork (including prepopulation or elimination of forms)
28. Giving comparative information (to overcome comparison friction)
29. Informing people of the nature and consequences of their own past choices ("midata")
30. Jointly rather than separately evaluating goods/people (to help reduce discrimination)
31. Structuring choices (as through pointers or eliminating rarely chosen options)

important programs and reducing serious burdens on ordinary people (especially—but not only—the poor).

4. Policymakers can fruitfully enlist social norms in the service of public goals, because people are more likely to engage in desirable behavior if they are informed that most people engage in desirable behavior.

5. Disclosure can be helpful, but only if it is psychologically informed (Loewenstein et al. 2014b).
6. Cognitive accessibility (sometimes described as salience) greatly matters, in part because people have limited attention (Dolan 2014).

Notwithstanding the lessons learned from psychological research, it is important to acknowledge that the idea of a council of psychological advisers, or of psychologically informed policymaking, might produce political concern, possibly even alarm. Indeed, prominent uses of behavioral science have sometimes proved controversial (Rebonato 2012, Sunstein 2013a). The goal of increasing simplification and navigability is unlikely to raise serious concerns, but any form of paternalism might run into real objections (for very different perspectives, see Conly 2012, Rebonato 2012). As discussed below, transparency and openness are exceedingly important. The idea of behaviorally informed policymaking also raises significant institutional challenges. The relevant concerns and issues of paternalism and institutional design are briefly explored in the section titled Politics, Paternalism, and Institutional Design (see also Rebonato 2012, Thaler & Sunstein 2008).

DEFAULT RULES

In many contexts, policymakers can promote social goals with sensible default rules that preserve freedom of choice and that avoid the cost, rigidity, and potential unintended harmful consequences of coercive approaches, such as mandates and bans (Sunstein & Reisch 2014, Thaler & Sunstein 2008). Because of their unique importance, I devote special attention to default rules here (for interesting applications, see Dolan 2014, Wansink 2014).

Automatic Enrollment and Default Rules: Examples

Savings. Many people do not save enough money for retirement. What can be done? In the United States, the default rule has long been nonenrollment in pension plans; employers have asked employees whether they want to opt in, and the number of employees who enroll has often been low (Gale et al. 2009, Madrian & Shea 2001). In response, many employers have changed the default to automatic enrollment, by which employees are enrolled unless they opt out. The results have been dramatic. With an opt-out design, many more employees enroll than with an opt-in design (Chetty et al. 2012, Gale et al. 2009), even when opting out is easy. Automatic enrollment has increased the anticipated savings for all groups, in particular Hispanics, African Americans, and women (Chiteji & Walker 2009, Orszag & Rodriguez 2009, Papke et al. 2009). As noted, default rules can have much larger effects than significant tax incentives (Chetty et al. 2012), which is a genuine puzzle from the perspective of standard economics but a far less surprising finding from the standpoint of psychology.

Drawing on these findings, the Pension Protection Act of 2006 {Pension Protection Act of 2006, Pub. L. No. 109–280, 120 Stat. 780 [codified in scattered sections of 26 and 29 U.S.C. (2012)]} encourages employers to adopt automatic enrollment plans through a series of steps. In explicit recognition of the behavioral research, President Obama directed the Internal Revenue Service (IRS) and the Treasury Department to undertake initiatives to make it easier for employers to adopt such plans (IRS 2009, Obama 2009a). As a result of both private and public action—informed by psychological research—automatic enrollment in pension plans (along with automatic escalation, sometimes under the rubric of "Save More Tomorrow") has been growing rapidly (Benartzi 2012, Benartzi & Thaler 2013).

Many other nations are using automatic enrollment in pension plans. In 2007, New Zealand introduced the idea of "KiwiSaver," whose principal feature is automatic enrollment. Within four years, the result of the initiative was to increase pension coverage by nearly 50 percent (Lunn 2014). As noted, similar success has been found in the United Kingdom, and Denmark has also experienced substantial increases as a result of automatic enrollment (Chetty et al. 2012).

Green energy. Many people have been interested in increasing consumers' use of green energy—energy sources that do not significantly contribute to air pollution, climate change, and other environmental problems. Although such energy sources are available in many places, relatively few choose them [notwithstanding the fact that in response to questions, many say that they would do so, as noted by Pichert & Katsikopoulos (2008)]. The point certainly holds in Germany (Pichert & Katsikopoulos 2008). However, two communities in that nation have long shown strikingly high levels of green energy use—in a recent period, well over 90%—in dramatic contrast to the level of participation in green energy programs in other German towns, which in the relevant time period was approximately 1% (Pichert & Katsikopoulos 2008). The reason for the difference is that in the two communities with 90% participation, individuals are automatically enrolled in green energy programs and must opt out if they choose not to participate.

In many contexts, environmental and energy-related goals could be, and to some extent are being, promoted through green default rules (Sunstein & Reisch 2014). For example, a double-sided printing default rule for printers is likely to save a great deal of paper and indeed to have a larger effect than a significant tax on paper use (for citations and discussion, see Sunstein & Reisch 2014).

Health care. In an important provision, the Affordable Care Act requires employers with more than 200 employees automatically to enroll employees in health care plans—but it also allows employees to opt out {Pub. L. No. 111–148, 124 Stat. 119 [2010] [codified in scattered sections of 26 and 42 U.S.C. (2012)]}. This provision will not be in force without implementing regulations, but the expectation is that they will appear in 2015 or 2016. When employers automatically enroll employees, there is far less pressure on healthcare.gov and other mechanisms by which people might comply with the insurance requirement (known as the individual mandate) on their own.

Consumer rights. In a number of areas, policymakers have attempted to protect consumer rights through the regulation of default rules. Recall the action of the Federal Reserve Board that forbade automatic enrollment in overdraft protection programs (Willis 2013). Under the Credit Card Accountability Responsibility and Disclosure Act of 2009, companies are forbidden to impose fees on cardholders who go over their credit limit unless cardholders agree to opt in to authorize that practice (Willis 2013). In Europe, Article 22 of the 2011 Consumer Rights Directive explicitly bans the use of prefilled boxes in online payment forms: "If the trader has not obtained the consumer's express consent but has inferred it by using default options which the consumer is required to reject in order to avoid the additional payment, the consumer shall be entitled to reimbursement of this payment" (Eur. Parliam. & Counc. Eur. Union 2011, p. L304/81; Lunn 2014).

School meals. Under federal law, poor children are eligible for free lunches and breakfasts at school. Unfortunately, many poor families fail to sign up for the relevant programs, perhaps because of the burdens involved in doing so—a special problem in light of what researchers describe as the limited cognitive bandwidth of the poor (Mani et al. 2013, Mullainathan & Shafir 2013). In response, the National School Lunch Act authorizes and promotes direct certification of eligibility, thus reducing complexity and providing a form of automatic enrollment (Healthy, Hunger-Free Kids Act of 2010; **http://www.fns.usda.gov/school-meals/healthy-hunger-free-kids-act**){Pub. L. No. 111–296, 124 Stat. 3183 [codified in scattered sections of 42 U.S.C. (2012)]}.

Under the program, children who are eligible for benefits under certain programs are directly eligible for free lunches and free breakfasts and hence do not have to fill out additional applications (**http://www.fns.usda.gov/school-meals/healthy-hunger-free-kids-act**). In 2011, the US Department of Agriculture (USDA) issued an interim final rule that provided school meals for up to 270,000 children (USDA 2011a). The total number of school children now enrolled in the direct certification program exceeds two million (**http://www.fns.usda.gov/direct-certification-national-school-lunch-program-state-implementation-progress-school-year-2012**).

Risks of Default Rules

It should be accepted that default rules can be badly chosen or misused by both private and public institutions. A central question—at the intersection of psychology, economics, and policy—is whether the relevant rule is one that informed individuals would select (Sunstein 2015b). But that question might not be easy to answer, and some choice architects might not even ask it. Both standard economics and psychology identify reasons that markets might produce harmful default rules, at least when they are not visible or easily accessible to consumers. Self-interested actors might promote default rules that benefit them rather than choosers, and such rules might nonetheless "stick." As a result, people might experience serious welfare losses. Companies might enroll consumers in programs that do not suit their interests, and governments might do the same.

REQUIRING ACTIVE CHOOSING

Public officials and outside observers sometimes do not like default rules because they might not fit diverse situations or might be harmful or even manipulative (Rebonato 2012). We need to learn much more about people's reactions to such rules (Brehm & Brehm 1981, Loewenstein et al. 2014a). To the extent that the concerns are warranted, policymakers should consider a different approach: Avoid any default rule, and prompt or require active choices (Carroll et al. 2009, Sunstein 2013b).

Active choices, which ask or require people to select among various options rather than be defaulted into an alternative, result in far higher levels of savings than a default rule that requires people explicitly to opt in (Carroll et al. 2009). With respect to savings and health care, for example, an employer might reject both opt out and opt in and simply require employees to indicate their preferences. Such an approach should have significant results. If inertia and procrastination are playing a significant role, then active choosing may be better than opt in. In such circumstances, active choosing increases the likelihood that people will end up with their preferred outcomes. For that reason, there is a strong psychological argument for requiring active choosing (Sunstein 2015a).

Active choosing may also be favored over opt in when public officials lack relevant information. In such circumstances, the chosen default rule might prove to be damaging (Rebonato 2012; Sunstein 2013b, 2015a). When the default rule is no better than a guess, it might lead people in the wrong direction. The same point argues against a default rule when self-interested private groups have managed to call for it even though it is not in the interest of those on whom it is imposed (Rebonato 2012).

Active choosing might also be better than opt in when the members of a relevant group are highly diverse and thus a single approach will not fit their variable situations. In such contexts, a default rule might also be harmful because the power of inertia, or the force of suggestion, may mean that many people will end up in a situation that is not in their interest. In addition, active choosers take responsibility for their choices, and their sense of responsibility might have significant effects on their own future (for example, in making them more committed to taking care of their health) and also on family members (to whom it might greatly matter, for example in the context of end-of-life care, that the relevant decision is made actively rather than passively).

It is also true that active choosing can have significant disadvantages. Active choosing may impose unjustified or excessive burdens in situations that involve unfamiliarity or great complexity, so that people lack information or experience (Sunstein 2013b, Thaler & Sunstein 2008). These burdens should not be underestimated; they can take a serious toll (Mani et al. 2013, Mullainathan & Shafir 2013). Such burdens include not only the time (and potentially resources and emotion) required for people to obtain relevant information and to make the choice, but also the resources that must be expended to ensure that they actually make it. As compared with a default rule, active choosing increases the costs of decisions, possibly significantly. Active choosing also might increase errors, possibly significantly, in unfamiliar and confusing areas. In such situations, opt in or opt out might produce better outcomes for people.

When public officials have good reason for confidence that a particular default rule will fit with the informed preferences of the relevant group, and thus promote its interests, it may be preferable to select that default rule rather than to require active choosing (Sunstein 2015b). Personalized default rules, by virtue of their accuracy, are especially promising on this count.

SIMPLIFICATION

A great deal of psychological work demonstrates that complexity can have harmful effects (including indifference, delay, and confusion), potentially reducing compliance or decreasing the likelihood that people (including the poor) will benefit from various policies and programs (Mullainathan & Shafir 2013). Complex forms can be especially troublesome on this count—a point that is often insufficiently appreciated by policymakers, who can frequently achieve their substantive goals through simplification.

Consider two examples, both with significant policy implications. (*a*) Simplification of a complex form for financial assistance for college can have the same effect, in terms of increasing program participation, as a significant boost in economic incentives—in the thousands of dollars (Bettinger et al. 2009). (*b*) Homeowners can save a great deal of money by refinancing their mortgage to obtain a lower interest rate, but in the United States, $5.4 billion has been recently lost as a result of the failure to refinance, largely because of the psychological burden imposed on homeowners by the relatively complex requirements (Keys et al. 2014).

A particular area for further study involves the effects of cognitive load, which imposes a kind of bandwidth tax that has particularly harmful effects on poor people (Mani et al. 2013, Mullainathan & Shafir 2013). Although the US Paperwork Reduction Act of 1995 was designed to reduce form-filling burdens, policymakers have only recently identified the connection between those burdens and the bandwidth problem. If psychologically informed policymakers can increase participation in important programs through simplifying paperwork requirements, or even achieve the same goals that would otherwise be achieved only through large expenditures, there is a clear advantage to simplification (Mullainathan & Shafir 2013, Sunstein 2013a). In a related vein, when people stand to gain significant amounts of money from redeeming coupons or certificates, they are unrealistically optimistic about the likelihood that they will take the trouble to mail in the relevant forms; the only intervention that appears to work is to make redemption easier (Tasoff & Letzler 2014). As the authors put it, "Everyone believes in redemption," but whether people will actually seek redemption depends on whether it is simple for them to do so (Tasoff & Letzler 2014).

In recognition of the underlying psychological and behavioral research, the US government has taken a number of steps toward simplifying and shortening the Free Application for Federal

Student Aid (FAFSA), reducing the number of questions and allowing electronic retrieval of information (OMB 2010). In addition, a special initiative permits online users to transfer data previously supplied electronically in their tax forms directly into their FAFSA applications. These steps are intended to simplify the application process for financial aid and thus to increase access to college; such steps are enabling many students to receive aid for attending college when they previously could not do so. A great deal remains to be done to simplify FAFSA; a very short form, perhaps just two pages or less, might be sufficient. Related steps might be taken in many other domains, especially those designed to help poor people, where well-intended and seemingly innocuous paperwork burdens can be counterproductive (Mullainathan & Shafir 2013). Prepopulation of forms may seem technical, but it could have big benefits.

In 2011, the Office of Management and Budget drew on psychological research in calling for simplification of programs, focusing in particular on small business and benefit programs (Sunstein 2011a). The request drew attention to the potential harms of complexity (in the context of financial products, see Bar-Gill 2012), noting that the process of renewing or applying for benefits can be time-consuming, confusing, and unnecessarily complex, thus discouraging participation and undermining program goals. Agencies sometimes collect data that are unchanged from prior application forms; in such circumstances, they might be able to use, or give people the option to use, prepopulated electronic forms (Sunstein 2011a).

And indeed, imperfect take-up of existing benefit programs, including those that provide income support, is partly a product of behavioral factors such as procrastination and inertia (Keys et al. 2014; cf. Mullainathan & Shafir 2013, Tasoff & Letzler 2014). It follows that efforts to increase simplicity, including automatic enrollment, may have substantial benefits (Mullainathan & Shafir 2013). In the United Kingdom, significant results have been obtained in increasing the payments of fines, largely by making it easier and more convenient for people to do so and by sending reminders by telephone and text (Lunn 2014).

The UK's Office of Gas and Electricity Markets (OFGEM) has undertaken a number of initiatives to simplify regulatory burdens on both industry and consumers. In the aftermath of the deregulation of energy markets, many consumers made poor choices, which in some cases resulted in costly tariffs imposed by incumbent suppliers (Lunn 2014). The OFGEM initiatives propose to simplify how energy retailers provide information about rate tariffs to consumers, with the goal of enhancing and informing consumer choice (Lunn 2014).

SOCIAL NORMS AND CONFORMITY

Because the behavior of others provides information about what is normal or appropriate, individuals might well imitate that behavior (Cialdini et al. 2006). In fact, social norms can operate as the equivalent of defaults, with observed choices spurring imitative behavior (Huh et al. 2014).

If, for example, people learn that they are using more energy than similarly situated others, their energy use may decline—reducing pollution as well as consumers' costs. The same point applies to health-related behavior. It has long been understood that people are more likely to engage in healthy behavior if they live with or work with others who so engage. The behavior of relevant others can provide valuable information about sensible or appropriate courses of action. Informational cascades are a possible consequence as people rely on, and thus amplify, the informational signals produced by the actions of predecessors (Hirshleifer 1995). Similarly, those actions can provide information about what others will approve and disapprove.

Psychological research suggests that efforts to use social comparisons can alter decisions and significantly reduce economic and environmental costs. In the private sector, these points are being put to creative use. Opower, an American company that makes impressive use of behavioral economics, specializes in providing people with social comparisons, above all through its innovative Home Energy Report. Opower's endeavors have had a major effect. More than four million households now receive Home Energy Reports, and people are saving hundreds of millions of dollars as a result (see **http://www.opower.com** for details).

These points have implications for many domains. For example, social norms can be enlisted in efforts to increase tax collection and to reduce violations (Hallsworth et al. 2014). In the first of two careful experiments from the UK Behavioural Insights Team, Hallsworth and colleagues sent letters to more than 100,000 citizens in 2011. All of the letters noted that the recipients had not yet made correct tax payments, but different versions of follow-ups were sent. The first said, "Nine out of ten people pay their taxes on time." The second version said, "Nine out of ten people in the UK pay their taxes on time." The third stated, "Nine out of ten people in the UK pay their taxes on time. You are currently in the very small minority of people who have not paid us yet." The fourth did not refer to social norms, but added, "Paying tax means we all gain from vital public services" such as the National Health Service, roads, and schools.

The letters were exceedingly effective. Overall, those who received one of these letters were nearly four times more likely to pay their tax bill than those who did not. The most effective letter was the third: In less than a month, it produced $3.18 million in additional revenue. If that letter had been used across the entire sample, it is estimated that it would have produced an additional $18.9 million.

Hallsworth and colleagues' second experiment involved nearly 120,000 taxpayers and more than one dozen different letters. Some of the letters referred to a general norm about existing practices: "The great majority of people in the UK pay their tax on time." Other letters were more specific: "The great majority of people in your local area pay their tax on time" or "Most people with a debt like yours have paid it by now" (Hallsworth et al. 2014).

Some of the letters referred to what people in the United Kingdom think taxpayers should do: "The great majority of people agree that everyone in the UK should pay their tax on time," or "Nine out of ten people agree that everyone in the UK should pay their tax in time." Some of the letters emphasized that people could save money by paying now rather than later: "We are charging you interest on this amount."

With this experiment, Hallsworth and colleagues replicated their earlier finding: "Norm" messages have a large impact. Finally, highlighting a penalty that would increase over time made it more likely that people would pay. Within a period of about three weeks, Hallsworth and colleagues were able to generate approximately $15.24 million in additional tax revenue. Note that letters of this sort are not expensive to produce and send, so the benefits of the intervention are easily justified. In other contexts, reminders have had significant effects, and they appear to work best if they are personalized (Lunn 2014).

An understanding of social norms and conformity also helps to explain political polarization in a way that can be relevant to political actors of all kinds. For example, social psychologists have explored the phenomenon of group polarization, which means that people in deliberating groups tend to end up in a more extreme point in line with their predeliberation tendencies (Sunstein 2009). If members of one like-minded group (say, people who are left of center) speak only with one another, and if members of another like-minded group (say, people who are right of center) speak only with one another, severe divisions might be expected. An understanding of group polarization thus casts light on political divisions in many democracies. It also helps explain why some groups become quite extreme and even prone to violence (Hardin 2002).

The implications for the problem of groupthink, understood in the light of recent psychological findings, help to show how institutions can elicit, or fail to elicit, important information (Sunstein

& Hastie 2015). A pressing challenge is to devise strategies, especially—but not only—within governments to prevent polarization and herding (Sunstein & Hastie 2015).

DISCLOSURE

Actually Informing Choice

Examples. In numerous cases, disclosure requirements have been psychologically informed, especially since the early 2000s. Central examples include legislative efforts to require disclosure of the potential savings from energy efficiency and of information that bears on health. Some disclosure initiatives have drawn directly from psychology and behavioral science, emphasizing the importance of plain language, clarity, and simplicity, and of ensuring that any advice is actionable. But in the disclosure area in particular, existing knowledge is inadequate, and many gaps remain to be filled (Bubb 2014, Loewenstein et al. 2014b).

Nutrition. In the domain of nutrition, a number of disclosure requirements are in place. For example, in 2011 the USDA issued a final rule requiring provision of nutritional information to consumers with respect to meat and poultry products. Under the rule, nutrition facts panels containing information about calories and total and saturated fats must be provided on the labels of such products (9 C.F.R. § 317.309).

The rule reflects an understanding of the importance of the framing. If a product includes a percentage statement such as 80% lean, it must also include the fat percentage. This requirement should prevent the confusion that can result from selective framing; a statement that a product is 80% lean, standing by itself, makes leanness salient and may therefore be misleading. As noted, and more important still, the FDA has proposed new rules to govern nutrition facts panels, and those rules explicitly refer to the behavioral literature, which informs the content of the proposals (US FDA 2014a).

Credit cards and consumer financial protection. Behavioral science played a role in informing the Credit Card Accountability, Responsibility, and Disclosure Act of 2009 (Credit CARD Act of 2009) {Pub. L. No. 111–24, 123 Stat. 1734 [2009] [codified in scattered sections of 15 and 16 U.S.C. (2012)]}, which is designed in large part to ensure that credit card users are adequately informed. Among other things, the Credit Card Act of 2009 prohibits an increase in annual percentage rates without 45 days' notice, prohibits the retroactive application of rate increases to existing balances, and requires clear notice of the consumer's right to cancel the credit card when the annual percentage rate is raised.

Evidence suggests that the Credit Card Act of 2009 has saved US consumers an estimated $12 billion annually. Moreover, one small nudge—requiring disclosure of the interest savings from paying off balances in 36 months rather than making only minimum payments—has saved consumers an estimated $170 million annually (Agarwal et al. 2014).

More generally, the US government's Consumer Financial Protection Bureau has a central goal of designing disclosure policies that will actually inform choices, as captured in the slogan "Know before you owe." The Consumer Financial Protection Bureau has taken steps to simplify disclosures for student loans, credit cards, and mortgages. In the process, it has taken careful account of psychological and behavioral research about the harmful effects of complexity (Lunn 2014).

Health care. The Patient Protection and Affordable Care Act of 2010 {Affordable Care Act of 2010; Pub. L. No. 111–148, 124 Stat. 119 [2010] [codified in scattered sections of 26 and 42 U.S.C. (2012)]} contains a large number of disclosure requirements designed to promote accountability and informed choice with respect to health care. Indeed, the Affordable Care Act is, in significant part, a series of disclosure requirements, many of which are meant to inform consumers and to do so in a way that is alert to findings from psychological research. Under the Affordable Care Act, for example, a restaurant that is part of a chain with 20 or more locations doing business under the same name is required to disclose calories on the menu board (for a discussion of the empirical complexities and the mixed evidence about the effects of disclosures, see Loewenstein et al. 2014b). Such restaurants are also required to provide in a written form (available to customers upon request) additional nutrition information pertaining to total calories and calories from fat, as well as amounts of fat, saturated fat, cholesterol, sodium, total carbohydrates, complex carbohydrates, sugars, dietary fiber, and protein.

Similarly, section 1103 of the Affordable Care Act calls for "[i]mmediate information that allows consumers to identify affordable coverage options." It requires the establishment of an Internet portal for beneficiaries to find information about affordable and comprehensive coverage options, including information about eligibility, availability, premium rates, cost sharing, and the percentage of total premium revenues spent on health care rather than on administrative expenses.

Implementing a provision of the Affordable Care Act, the Department of Health and Human Services (HHS) finalized a rule to require insurance companies to provide summaries of relevant information to prospective customers in clear, plain language. The rule mandates the provision of basic information, including the annual premium, the annual deductible, a statement of services that are not covered, and a statement of costs for going to an out-of-network provider (Healthcare.gov 2011).

Smart disclosure. In the United States, psychologically informed initiatives have focused on the idea of smart disclosure, which is designed to help consumers know about their own choices (Kamenica et al. 2011). Smart disclosure is based on the understanding that it can be costly for consumers to obtain that information, in part as a result of inertia; it helps if information is made available in downloadable, machine-readable formats (Sunstein 2011b). In the United Kingdom, the "midata" initiative aspires to give consumers more access to their consumption data, with the goal of allowing members of the public to analyze their data via software applications and to use the analysis to improve their decision-making (Lunn 2014; **https://www.gov. uk/government/policies/providing-better-information-and-protection-for-consumers/ supporting-pages/personal-data**). Under the UK Enterprise and Regulatory Reform Act 2013, the government has the authority to compel businesses to release consumer data; to date this has not been done, and the government is hoping for businesses to release their data voluntarily.

It should be clear from this brief survey that the recent disclosure requirements are wide-ranging. Although such approaches have considerable promise, the jury is still out on their effects (Bubb 2015, Loewenstein et al. 2014b).

How, not only whether. As psychologists have emphasized, disclosure as such may not be enough; regulators should devote care and attention to how, not only whether, disclosure occurs (Loewenstein et al. 2014b). Clarity and simplicity are often critical. If disclosure requirements are to be helpful, they must be designed to be sensitive to how people actually process information.

A good rule of thumb is that disclosure should be concrete, straightforward, simple, meaningful, timely, and salient. If the goal is to inform people about how to avoid risks or to obtain benefits, disclosure should avoid abstract statements (such as, for example, of "healthy eating" or "good diet") and instead clearly identify the steps that might be taken to obtain the relevant goal (by specifying, for example, what specific actions parents might take to reduce the risk of childhood obesity).

In 2010, the HHS emphasized the importance of clarity and cognitive accessibility in connection with its interim final rule entitled "Health Care Reform Insurance Web Portal Requirements," which "adopts the categories of information that will be collected and displayed as Web portal content, and the data we will require from issuers and request from States, associations, and high risk pools in order to create this content" (US Dep. HHS 2010) (for the web portal, see **http://www.healthcare.gov/**). The preamble to the interim final rule is behaviorally informed in the sense that it is directly responsive to how people process information:

> In implementing these requirements, we seek to develop a Web site (hereinafter called the Web portal) that would empower consumers by increasing informed choice and promoting market competition. To achieve these ends, we intend to provide a Web portal that provides information to consumers in a clear, salient, and easily navigated manner. We plan to minimize the use of technical language, jargon, or excessive complexity in order to promote the ability of consumers to understand the information and act in accordance with what they have learned . . . [W]e plan to provide information, consistent with applicable laws, in a format that is accessible for use by members of the public, allowing them to download and repackage the information, promoting innovation and the goal of consumer choice. (US Dep. HHS 2010, p. 24471)

If not carefully designed, disclosure requirements can produce ineffective, confusing, and potentially misleading messages. Psychologically informed approaches are alert to this risk and suggest possible improvements. For instance, automobile manufacturers are currently required to disclose the fuel economy of new vehicles as measured by miles per gallon (MPG). This disclosure is useful for consumers and helps to promote informed choice. As the EPA has emphasized, however, MPG is a nonlinear measure of fuel consumption (US EPA 2009). Consider the fact that an increase from 10 to 20 MPG produces more savings than an increase from 20 to 40 MPG, and an increase from 10 to 11 MPG produces savings almost as high as an increase from 34 to 50 MPG. Many consumers do not understand this point and tend to interpret MPG as linear with fuel costs (see Larrick & Soll 2008).

A closely related finding is that because of misunderstandings about the MPG measure, consumers tend to underestimate the cost differences between low-MPG vehicles and tend to overestimate the cost differences between high-MPG vehicles (Allcott 2011). Recognizing the imperfections and potentially misleading nature of the MPG measure, and referring to the psychological literature, the Department of Transportation and EPA chose a new label to respond to the psychological and behavioral research (US EPA 2009).

This approach calls for disclosure of annual gasoline costs, and it also requires a clear statement about anticipated fuel savings (or costs) over a five-year period (compared to the average vehicle). The statement of fuel savings (or costs) should simultaneously help counteract confusion over the MPG measure and inform consumers of the economic effects of fuel economy over a relevant time period (US EPA 2009).

In a related vein, and informed by psychological research, the USDA has abandoned its food pyramid, which was used for years as the central icon to promote healthy eating. The food pyramid has long been criticized as insufficiently informative; it does not offer people with any kind of clear path with respect to a healthy diet. According to one critical account, "Its meaning is almost completely opaque . . . To learn what the Food Pyramid has to say about food, you must be willing to decipher the Pyramid's markings . . . The language and concepts here are so hopelessly abstracted from people's actual experience with food ... that the message confuses and demoralizes" (Heath & Heath 2010, pp. 61–62).

Aware of these objections, and after an extended period of deliberation, the USDA (2011b) replaced the Food Pyramid with a new, simpler icon (a food plate named MyPlate) consisting of a plate with clear markings for fruits, vegetables, grains, and protein. MyPlate is accompanied by straightforward guidance, including, "Make half your plate fruits and vegetables," "Drink water instead of sugary drinks," and "Switch to fat-free or low-fat (1%) milk." This approach has the key advantage of informing people what to do if they seek to have a healthier diet.

The tendency toward unrealistic optimism (Bar-Gill 2012, Sharot 2011) may lead consumers to downplay or neglect information about statistical risks associated with a product or an activity. If they do, there is a psychological argument for a more graphic kind of disclosure, designed to make the risks associated with the product less abstract and more vivid and salient. For example, the Family Smoking Prevention and Tobacco Control Act of 2009 {Smoking Prevention Act; Pub. L. No. 111–31, 123 Stat. 1776 [codified at 21 U.S.C. 301 et seq. (2012)]} requires graphic warnings with respect to the risks of smoking tobacco, and the FDA finalized such warnings for public comment, with vivid and even disturbing pictures of some of the adverse outcomes associated with smoking. The compulsory warnings were invalidated in court (on free speech grounds), but the government has issued its own graphic warnings, which may well be having significant effects.

Psychology, Spurring Competition

Straightforward and simple disclosures should facilitate comparison shopping and hence competition. Drawing on social science research, the US Treasury Department's account of financial regulation emphasizes the value of requiring that "communications with the consumer are reasonable, not merely technically compliant and nondeceptive. Reasonableness includes balance in the presentation of risks and benefits, as well as clarity and conspicuousness in the description of significant product costs and risks" (US Dep. Treas. 2009, p. 64). The Treasury Department's analysis goes on to say that one goal should be to

> harness technology to make disclosures more dynamic and adaptable to the needs of the individual consumer.... Disclosures should show consumers the consequences of their financial decisions.... [The regulator] should mandate or encourage calculator disclosures for mortgages to assist with comparison shopping. For example, a calculator that shows the costs of a mortgage based on the consumer's expectations for how long she will stay in the home may reveal a more significant difference between two products than appears on standard paper disclosures. (US Dep. Treas. 2009, p. 65)

Similarly, the US Consumer Financial Protection Bureau is authorized to ensure that "consumers are provided with timely and understandable information to make responsible decisions about financial transactions" {Dodd-Frank Act 2010; Dodd-Frank Wall Street Reform and Consumer Protection Act, Pub. L. No. 111–203, 124 Stat. 1376 [2010] [codified in scattered sections of the U.S.C. (2012)]}. The Bureau is also authorized to issue rules that ensure that information is "fully, accurately, and effectively disclosed to consumers in a manner that permits consumers to understand the costs, benefits, and risks associated with the product or service, in light of the facts and circumstances" (Dodd-Frank Act 2010, 12 U.S.C. § 5532). Note that new technologies make it possible to inform consumers of their own choices and usages, an approach that may be especially important when firms have better information than consumers do about such choices and usages.

The Bureau is authorized to issue model forms with "a clear and conspicuous disclosure that, at a minimum—(A) uses plain language comprehensible to consumers; (B) contains a clear format and design, such as an easily readable type font; and (C) succinctly explains the information that must be communicated to the consumer" (Dodd-Frank Act 2010, 12 U.S.C. § 5532). In addition, the director of the Bureau is required to "establish a unit whose functions shall include researching, analyzing, and reporting on ... consumer awareness, understanding, and use of disclosures and communications regarding consumer financial products or services" and "consumer behavior with respect to consumer financial products or services, including performance on mortgage loans" (Dodd-Frank Act 2010, 12 U.S.C. § 5493).

In the same general vein, the Department of Labor issued a final rule requiring disclosure to workers of relevant information in pension plans. The rule is designed to require clear, simple disclosure of information about fees and expenses and to allow meaningful comparisons, in part through the use of standard methodologies in the calculation and disclosure of expense and return information (29 C.F.R. § 2550.404a-5).

A final rule of the Department of Education promotes transparency and consumer choice with respect to for-profit education by requiring institutions to provide clear disclosure of costs, debt levels, graduation rates, and placement rates (US Dep. Educ. 2010a). The rule states that relevant institutions must disclose, among other things, the occupations that the program prepares students to enter, the on-time graduation rate for students completing the program, the tuition and fees charged to students for completing the program within a normal time, the placement rate for students completing the program, and the median loan debt incurred by students who completed the program. These disclosures must be included in "promotional materials [the institution] makes available to prospective students" and be "[p]rominently provide[d] ... in a simple and meaningful manner on the home page of its program Web site" (34 C.F.R. § 668.6; US Dep. Educ. 2010b).

As noted, a great deal of work remains to be done on disclosure polices and in particular on when they are likely to be effective (Bubb 2015). But it is clear that disclosures that are attuned to how people process information are far more likely to succeed than those that are not (Bubb 2015, Loewenstein et al. 2014b).

ATTENTION AND COGNITIVE ACCESSIBILITY

Psychological research suggests that it is often possible to promote policy goals by triggering people's attention and making certain features of a product or a situation more accessible to consumers. As a simple example of the importance of cognitive accessibility, consider alcohol taxes. There is evidence that when alcohol taxes are specifically identified in the posted price, increases in such taxes have a larger negative effect on alcohol consumption than when they are applied at the register (Chetty et al. 2009, Finkelstein 2009). Of course incentives matter, but in order for them to matter, people must pay attention to them (Dolan 2014). Sensible policies, especially those that involve disclosure, are highly attentive to the importance of cognitive accessibility.

With respect to smoking prevention, for example, triggering attention to adverse health effects is a central purpose of disclosure requirements. In the context of smoking, graphic warnings are designed for immediate cognitive accessibility. Similarly, the US Occupational Safety and Health Administration has issued a regulation requiring chemical manufacturers and importers to prepare labels for hazardous chemicals that include pictograms and signal words that can be easily understood by workers (29 C.F.R. §§ 1910, 1915, 1926). Well-designed labels trigger attention; they make relevant factors salient to those who will see them.

Or consider the area of energy efficiency. The energy paradox refers to the fact that some consumers do not purchase energy-efficient products even when it is clearly in their economic interest to do so. Empirical work suggests that nonprice interventions can alter decisions and significantly reduce electricity use by making the effects of energy use more accessible. Evidence indicates that such interventions can lead to private as well as public savings (Howarth et al. 2000). Consider, for example, the fact that energy costs are generally visible only once a month, when people are presented with the bill. Efforts to increase the cognitive accessibility of such costs, by displaying them in real time, can produce significant savings.

POLITICS, PATERNALISM, AND INSTITUTIONAL DESIGN

Policymakers work, of course, amid political constraints. While behavioral insights teams, using psychology, are increasingly popular (and have been created in the United States, the United Kingdom, and Germany, among others), no nation currently has a self-described council of psychological advisers, and at least one reason is political: Some citizens would be acutely suspicious of, and probably even alarmed by, the very idea. Is such a council helping government to manipulate its citizens by exploiting human psychology to steer them in what it considers to be the right direction? Does government have any business using psychology to manipulate people (Rebonato 2012)? In some nations, including the United States, policies that incorporate psychology and behavioral economics have sometimes been controversial and have triggered adverse political reactions, in part because of the fear of manipulation on the government's part (Sunstein 2013a). In many nations, active discussions are underway about whether use of the relevant research might be threatening to liberty or self-government.

Campaigns and Governance

In political campaigns, of course, the key goal is to convince people to vote for one's candidate, and on that count, the use of psychology is well established, not least as part of get-out-the-vote-strategies (Nickerson & Rogers 2010). We know, for example, that if people are asked to describe their implementation intentions (their specific plans to execute their goals), they are more likely to act as planned, and if the identity of people is triggered (for example, as voters), they are more likely to act in accordance with that identity (Nickerson & Rogers 2010). In campaigns, most observers agree that it is legitimate to try to persuade people, and to date, the use of psychological research has not created serious negative reactions. Modern campaigns sometimes do have something like a council of psychological advisers, whether or not its members include people with psychological training, and any candidate would be well advised to be informed by psychological research.

In actual governing, however, the use of psychology can be more controversial, and the public reaction has sometimes been more skeptical. In the United States, the United Kingdom, and Germany, for example, some critics have wondered whether the use of psychology and behavioral science, and the idea of nudging, might count as an objectionable interference with freedom and dignity and might show a kind of disrespect for citizens.

Problems, Not Theories

One lesson for policymakers is that it is generally best if psychologically informed approaches are problem driven and concrete rather than theory driven and abstract. In other words, it is preferable to begin not with high-level theory but rather with identifiable problems—for example, waste, fraud, corruption, health care, obesity, poverty, consumer protection, crime, and pollution—and to consider which tools might help to reduce them. Social scientists, and academics more generally, often focus on the development and testing of theories and on the generation of interesting and original ideas. In government, that approach is (to say the least) not ideal. In all probability, a council of psychological advisers with that orientation would be promptly disbanded. It is far better to focus on current policies that are hurting people, or not helping them, and to see how such policies might be improved—or better still to identify serious problems that citizens are now facing and to see how those problems might be addressed.

When a context is difficult to navigate, a reform that increases navigability is a good idea (Norman 2013). Increased navigability, and decreased confusion, should not be controversial. If a nation faces a problem of low participation rates in pension plans, automatic enrollment is a potential solution, and it does not much matter whether psychology lies behind the policy. If the problem is one of low take-up, simplification ought not to be especially troubling (Tasoff & Letzler 2014). If the goal is to help poor people to become self-sufficient, a focus on cognitive or bandwidth limits, and on the adverse effects of programs that strain those limits, might move policy in better directions (Mullainathan & Shafir 2013). With respect to healthy diets, a disclosure requirement that informs consumers is far better than one that confuses them; the fact that psychological research helps to explain and clarify consumer reactions is not a problem. (It is important to note that those nations that have some kind of nudge unit, or behavioral insight team, do include people who have psychological or behavioral training and who are able to bring that training to bear.)

It is necessary, of course, for any uses of psychology—for example, to inform default rules or disclosure requirements—to be open and transparent rather than covert and hidden. In democratic societies, citizens are entitled to know what their government is doing and why. In the United States, for example, uses of behavioral science have been open and subject to public scrutiny, usually through the official process for obtaining public comment (Sunstein 2013a).

Paternalism and Psychology

In some nations, approaches might be highly controversial if and because they are paternalistic (Rebonato 2012). (Not incidentally, the diverse reactions to paternalistic approaches, across nations, might themselves be subject to empirical research, including psychological research; some nations, such as Denmark and Singapore, appear far more comfortable with paternalism than others, such as the United States and Germany.) But as we have seen, many psychologically informed policies are intended simply to help to make life more easily navigable, and there is nothing paternalistic about that. Indeed, increased navigability is a large goal of many recent reforms. Consider, for example, the rejection of the confusing Food Pyramid and efforts to make regulations simple to understand. Insofar as the goal is to increase navigability, paternalism need not be involved in any way (Norman 2013).

It is true that some people, including the present author, have defended forms of libertarian paternalism (Thaler & Sunstein 2008), which preserve freedom of choice while also steering people in a certain direction. Examples include disclosure of information, warnings, and default rules, all of which allow people to go their own way (see also sidebar Freedom-Preserving Tools or "Nudges"). A reasonable debate is certainly possible with respect to that form of paternalism (Rebonato 2012, Sunstein 2013a). If the goal is simply to protect human welfare, there may even be a credible argument for coercive paternalism (Conly 2012), and libertarian paternalism, which can produce significant benefits at low cost, often has strong welfarist justifications.

Much could be said on this topic (for detailed discussion, see Conly 2012). Two central points favor libertarian paternalism over libertarianism. The first is that decades of work in psychological and behavioral sciences have shown that on occasion, human beings do err, reducing their own well-being in the process (Kahneman 2011, Thaler & Sunstein 2008). If, for example, people suffer from "present bias," or display unrealistic optimism (Sharot 2011) or procrastinate, their lives might be improved or perhaps even saved by helpful information, warnings, reminders, or default rules. Impressed by the psychological findings, some people have argued for coercive paternalism on the ground that it can improve people's welfare and even their autonomy (Bubb & Pildes 2014, Conly 2012). But it is not necessary to go so far as to urge that freedom-preserving approaches can be helpful.

The second and more fundamental point is that some form of choice architecture is unavoidable (Thaler & Sunstein 2008; cf. Norman 2013), and hence both private and public sectors are likely be nudging people even if they claim not to be doing so. Those in the private sector are frequently aware of that fact, and whether or not they consciously invoke psychological research, their choices about order, colors, sizes, noise, and placement will reflect at least implicit psychological judgments. For example, Wansink (2014) has demonstrated that the order in which cafeterias display items affects choices. If the government issues forms, discloses information, or maintains the website, it will be creating choice architecture and thus influencing what people will do. Those who purport to reject libertarian paternalism must grapple with the extent to which social influences, and perhaps certain forms of paternalism, are inevitably in place (Conly 2012, Thaler & Sunstein 2008). If choice architecture is inevitably in place, and if it nudges, it is useful to wish it away.

To be sure, it would be possible for a government to attempt to minimize the number of nudges (Glaeser 2006, Rebonato 2012). Should it? The answer ought to depend on judgments about both welfare and autonomy. At the very least, there is a strong argument that soft forms of paternalism often promote welfare and that autonomy is not jeopardized (Sunstein 2013a). To be sure, manipulation should be avoided, and transparency is exceedingly important. People should not be deceived or fooled. To make sensible evaluations, it is best to investigate particular initiatives and details rather than to proclaim in the abstract (Conly 2012). A testing question is: Of the psychologically informed policies cataloged here, which, exactly, are objectionable as illegitimate paternalism? Another testing question: Who would prefer a policy that pays no attention to the psychology of the people it is supposed to benefit?

Institutional Design

Institutional questions must also be addressed. We could imagine a system in which existing officials and institutions use an understanding of psychological findings. For example, the relevant research could be enlisted by those involved in environmental protection, in health care, or in combatting infectious diseases and obesity. Officials with well-established positions—like my own as Administrator of the White House Office of Information and Regulatory Affairs, from 2009 to 2012—might be expected to use that research, at least on occasion. If such officials have genuine authority, they might be able to produce significant reforms simply because they are not akin to a mere research arm or a think tank but on the contrary have line authority. This was the essential pattern during the first term of the Obama Administration.

A different approach would be to create a new institution—a behavioral insights team, a nudge unit, or something akin to a council of psychological advisers. The advantage of such an approach is that it would have a dedicated team that would be specifically devoted to the relevant work. If the team could conduct its own research, including randomized controlled trials, it might be able to produce important findings (as has in fact been done in the United Kingdom, and similar efforts are underway elsewhere). The risk of creating such a team is that it could be akin to an academic adjunct, with no ability to initiate real reform. Authority greatly matters. In this domain, one size does not fit all, and different nations can reasonably make different choices. But it is noteworthy that many nations (as noted, the United States, the United Kingdom, and Germany are prominent among them) have concluded that it is worthwhile to have a dedicated team. Of course the two approaches might be complementary.

WELL BEYOND INCENTIVES

Many officials are aware that if the goal is to alter behavior, it is best to alter material incentives. When the price of a certain activity increases, there will usually be less of that activity. But psychologists have shown that for material incentives to work, the incentives have to attract people's attention, and to make policies sensibly, policymakers have to combine an understanding of incentives with an appreciation of human complexity, the power of nudges, and the nature and inevitability of choice architecture. Sometimes people's responses are quite different from what was anticipated (Loewenstein et al. 2014b)—often in degree, and sometimes even in direction.

An understanding of human behavior helps to uncover a series of new tools. It also shows the great importance of increased simplification and (perhaps above all) navigability (cf. Norman 2013). There is no substitute for empirical testing, and we should expect a significant increase in randomized controlled trials in the coming decades. We may not see nations creating councils of psychological advisers, but all over the world, governments will enlist psychological findings, and behavioral science more generally, in the interest of achieving policy goals.

SUMMARY POINTS

1. Psychological research is having a large and growing impact on public policy in the United States, the United Kingdom, Denmark, Germany, Canada, Mexico, and many other nations.

2. Default rules can have important effects on social outcomes while preserving freedom of choice.

3. Simplification often pays large dividends, in part because it reduces burdens on people's limited bandwidth, potentially increasing uptake of important programs and reducing serious burdens on ordinary people (especially, but not only, the poor).

4. People are far more likely to engage in a certain behavior if they believe that other people are engaging in that behavior.

5. Disclosure can be a valuable, low-cost, regulatory strategy, but it must be attuned to how people process information, and we need to learn far more about its actual effects.

6. Cognitive accessibility (sometimes described as salience) greatly matters to social outcomes, in part because people have limited attention; relevant areas include health, crime prevention, and highway safety.

7. Important questions have been raised about the relationship between the uses of psychology and paternalism; one answer is that such uses should generally preserve people's freedom of choice.

DISCLOSURE STATEMENT

The author is not aware of any affiliations, memberships, funding, or financial holdings that might be perceived as affecting the objectivity of this review.

ACKNOWLEDGMENTS

I am grateful to Nicholas Epley for valuable comments and to Richard Thaler for many years of discussion. A few sections of this review draw on Cass R. Sunstein, *Empirically Informed Regulation*, 78 U. Chic. L. Rev. 1349 (2011), and readers might consult that essay for some relevant details.

LITERATURE CITED

Agarwal S, Chomsisengphet S, Mahoney N, Stroebel J. 2014. *Regulating consumer financial products: evidence from credit cards*. SSRN. **http://ssrn.com/abstract=2330942**

Allcott H. 2011. Consumers' perceptions and misperceptions of energy costs. *Am. Econ. Rev.* 101(3):98–104

Banerjee A, Duflo E. 2012. *Poor Economics*. New York: PublicAffairs

Bar-Gill O. 2012. *Seduction By Contract*. New York: Oxford Univ. Press

Benartzi S. 2012. *Save More Tomorrow: Practical Behavioral Finance Solutions to Improve 401(k) Plans*. New York: Portfolio/Penguin

Benartzi S, Thaler R. 2013. Behavioral economics and the retirement savings crisis. *Science* 339:1152–53

Bettinger EP, Long BT, Oreopoulos P, Sanbonmatsu L. 2009. *The role of simplification and information in college decisions: results from the H&R Block FAFSA experiment*. Work. Pap. 15361, Natl. Bur. Econ. Res., Cambridge, MA. **http://www.nber.org/papers/w15361**

Bohnet I, Bazerman M, Van Gean A. 2012. When performance trumps gender bias: joint versus separate evaluation. HKS Work. Pap. RWP12-009. **http://papers.ssrn.com/sol3/papers.cfm?abstract_id=2087613**

Brehm JW, Brehm R. 1981. *Psychological Reactance: A Theory of Freedom and Control*. Mahwah, NJ: Erlbaum

Bubb R. 2015. TMI? Why the optimal architecture of disclosure remains TBD. *Mich. Law Rev.* 113(6). **http://repository.law.umich.edu/mlr/vol113/iss6/13**

Bubb R, Pildes R. 2014. How behavioral economics trims its sails and why. *Harv. Law Rev.* 127:1593–678

Carroll GD, Choi JJ, Laibson D, Madrian BC, Metrick A. 2009. Optimal defaults and active decisions. *Q. J. Econ.* 124(4):1639–74

Chetty R, Friedman J, Leth-Petersen S, Nielsen T, Olsen T. 2012. *Active versus passive decisions and crowdout in retirement savings accounts: evidence from Denmark*. Work. Pap. 18565, Natl. Bur. Econ. Res., Cambridge, MA. **http://www.nber.org/papers/w18565**

Chetty R, Looney A, Kroft K. 2009. Salience and taxation: theory and evidence. *Am. Econ. Rev.* 99(4):1145–77

Chiteji N, Walker L. 2009. Strategies to increase the retirement savings of African American households. See Gale et al. 2009b, 10:231–60

Cialdini RB, Demaine LJ, Sagarin BJ, Barrett DW, Rhoads K, Winter PL. 2006. Managing social norms for persuasive impact. *Soc. Influ.* 1(1):3–15

Conly S. 2012. *Against Autonomy*. Cambridge, UK: Cambridge Univ. Press

Dir. Gen. Health Consum. (DG SANCO). 2010. *Consumer Behaviour: The Road to Effective Policy-Making*. Brussels: DG SANCO. **http://ec.europa.eu/consumers/docs/1dg-sanco-brochure-consumer-behaviour-final.pdf**

Dolan P. 2014. *Happiness By Design*. London: Hudson Str. Press

Eur. Comm. 2012. *Science for Environment Policy, Future Brief: Green Behavior*. Brussels: Eur. Comm. **http://ec.europa.eu/environment/integration/research/newsalert/pdf/FB4_en.pdf**

Eur. Parliam., Counc. Eur. Union. 2011. Directive 2011/83/EU of the European Parliament and of the Council of 25 October 2011 on consumer rights. *Off. J. Eur. Union* 54(L 304):64–88

Fed. Reserve Syst. 2009. Electronic fund transfers; final rule. *Fed. Regist.* 74:59033–54

Finkelstein A. 2009. E-ZTax: tax salience and tax rates. *Q. J. Econ.* 124(3):969–1010

Gale W, Iwry J, Walters S. 2009a. Retirement savings for middle- and lower-income households: the Pension Protection Act of 2006 and the unfinished agenda. See Gale et al. 2009b, 2:11–27

Gale G, Iwry JM, John DC, Walker L, eds. 2009b. *Automatic: Changing the Way America Saves*. Washington, DC: Brookings Inst. Press

Glaeser E. 2006. Paternalism and psychology. *Univ. Chic. Law Rev.* 73:133–56

Hallsworth M, List J, Metcalfe R, Vlaev I. 2014. *The behavioralist as tax collector: using natural field experiments to enhance tax compliance*. Work. Pap. 20007, Natl. Bur. Econ. Res., Cambridge, MA. **http://www.nber.org/papers/w20007**

Hardin R. 2002. The crippled epistemology of extremism. In *Political Extremism and Rationality*, ed. A Breton, G Galeotti, P Salmon, R Wintrobe, pp. 3–22. Cambridge, UK: Cambridge Univ. Press

Healthcare.gov. 2011. *Providing clear and consistent information to consumers about their health insurance coverage*. Baltimore, MD: CMS.gov. **https://www.cms.gov/CCIIO/Resources/Fact-Sheets-and-FAQs/labels08172011a.html**

Heath C, Heath D. 2010. *Switch: How to Change Things When Change Is Hard*. New York: Broadway Books

Hirshleifer D. 1995. The blind leading the blind: social influence, fads, and informational cascades. In *The New Economics of Human Behavior*, ed. M Tommasi, K Ierulli, pp. 188–215. Cambridge, UK: Cambridge Univ. Press

Howarth RB, Haddad BM, Paton B. 2000. The economics of energy efficiency: insights from voluntary participation programs. *Energy Policy* 28(6–7):477–86

Huh YE, Vosgerau J, Morewedge C. 2014. Social defaults: Observed choices become choice defaults. *J. Consum. Res.* 41:741–57

Kahneman D. 2011. *Thinking, Fast and Slow*. New York: Farrar, Straus & Giroux

Kamenica E, Mullainathan S, Thaler R. 2011. Helping consumers know themselves. *Am. Econ. Rev.* 101(3):417–22

Keys BJ, Pope DG, Pope JC. 2014. *Failure to refinance*. NBER Work. Pap. 20401, Natl. Bur. Econ. Res., Cambridge, MA. **http://www.nber.org/papers/w20401**

Intern. Revenue Serv. (IRS). 2009. *Retirement & Savings Initiatives: Helping Americans Save for the Future*. Washington, DC: IRS. **http://www.irs.gov/pub/irs-tege/rne_se0909.pdf**

Larrick R, Soll JB. 2008. The MPG illusion. *Science* 320:1593–94

Loewenstein G, Bryce C, Hagmann D, Rajpal S. 2014a. *Warning: You are about to be nudged*. Work. Pap., SSRN. **http://papers.ssrn.com/sol3/papers.cfm?abstract_id=2417383**

Loewenstein G, Sunstein CR, Golman R. 2014b. Disclosure: Psychology changes everything. *Annu. Rev. Econ.* 6:391–419

Low D. 2011. *Behavioural Economics and Policy Design: Lessons from Singapore*. Singapore: World Sci. Publ.

Lunn P. 2014. *Regulatory Policy and Behavioural Economics*. Paris: OECD Publ.

Madrian BC, Shea DF. 2001. The power of suggestion: inertia in 401(k) participation and savings behavior. *Q. J. Econ.* 116(4):1149–87

Mani A, Mullainathan S, Shafir E, Zhao J. 2013. Poverty impedes cognitive function. *Science* 341:976–80

Mullainathan S. 2007. Psychology and development economics. In *Behavioral Economics and Its Applications*, ed. P Diamond, H Vartiainen, pp. 85–113. Princeton, NJ: Princeton Univ. Press

Mullainathan S, Shafir E. 2013. *Scarcity: Why Having So Little Means So Much*. New York: Times Books

Nickerson DW, Rogers T. 2010. Do you have a voting plan? Implementation intentions, voter turnout, and organic plan making. *Psychol. Sci.* 21(2):194–99

Norman D. 2013. *The Design of Everyday Things*. New York: Basic Books

Obama B. 2009a. *Weekly Address: President Obama Announces New Initiatives for Retirement Savings*. Washington, DC: White House Off. Press Secr. **http://www.whitehouse.gov/the_press_office/Weekly-Address-President-Obama-Announces-New-Initiatives-for-Retirement-Savings**

OECD (Organ. Econ. Coop. Dev.). 2010. *Consumer Policy Toolkit*. Paris: OECD. **http://www.oecd.org/sti/consumerpolicy/consumerpolicytoolkit-9789264079663-en.htm**

OMB (Off. Manag. Budg.). 2010. *Information Collection Budget of the United States Government*. Washington, DC: OMB. **http://www.whitehouse.gov/sites/default/files/omb/inforeg/icb/icb_2010.pdf**

Orszag PR, Rodriguez E. 2009. Retirement security for Latinos: bolstering coverage, savings, and adequacy. See Gale et al. 2009b, 8:173–98

Papke LE, Walker L, Dworsky M. 2009. Retirement savings for women: progress to date and policies for tomorrow. See Gale et al. 2009b, 9:199–230

Pichert D, Katsikopoulos KV. 2008. Green defaults: information presentation and pro-environmental behaviour. *J. Environ. Psychol.* 28:63–73

Provides an overview of what is known, and what is not known, about the effects of disclosure requirements.

Provides an empirical treatment of how green default rules have very large effects on social outcomes.

Rebonato R. 2012. *Taking Liberties: A Critical Examination of Libertarian Paternalism*. London: Palgrave Macmillan

Rozin P, Scott S, Dingley M, Urbanek JK, Jiang H, Kaltenbach M. 2011. Nudge to nobesity I: Minor changes in accessibility decrease food intake. *Judgm. Decis. Mak.* 6(4):323–32

Schwartz B. 2012. Move over economists: We need a council of psychological advisers. *The Atlantic*, Nov. 12. http://www.theatlantic.com/politics/archive/2012/11/move-over-economists-we-need-a-council-of-psychological-advisers/265085/

Sharot T. 2011. *The Optimism Bias: A Tour of the Irrationally Positive Brain*. New York: Knopf

Shu L, Mazar N, Gino F, Ariely D, Bazerman M. 2012. Signing at the beginning makes ethics salient and decreases dishonest self-reports in comparison to signing at the end. *PNAS* 109(38):15197–200

Sunstein CR. 2009. *Going to Extremes*. New York: Oxford Univ. Press

Sunstein CR. 2011a. *Memorandum for Chief Information Officers: Minimizing Paperwork and Reporting Burdens*. Washington, DC: OMB

Sunstein CR. 2011b. *Memorandum for the Heads of Executive Agencies and Departments: Informing Consumers Through Smart Disclosure*. Washington, DC: OMB

Sunstein CR. 2013a. *Simpler*. New York: Simon & Schuster

Sunstein CR. 2013b. Deciding by default. *Univ. PA Law Rev.* 162(1):1–57

Sunstein CR. 2014. *Valuing Life: Humanizing the Regulatory State*. Chicago: Univ. Chicago Press

Sunstein CR. 2015a. Active choosing or default rules? A dilemma for policymakers. *Behav. Sci. Policy* 1(1):29–34

Sunstein CR. 2015b. *Choosing Not to Choose*. London: Oxford Univ. Press

Sunstein CR, Hastie R. 2015. *Wiser: Getting Beyond Groupthink to Smarter Decisions*. Cambridge, MA: Harvard Bus. Sch. Press

Sunstein CR, Reisch L. 2014. Automatically green: behavioral economics and environmental protection. *Harvard Environ. Law Rev.* 38:127–58

Tasoff J, Letzler R. 2014. Everyone believes in redemption: nudges and overoptimism in costly task completion. *J. Econ. Behav. Organ.* 107A:107–22

Thaler RH. 2012. Watching behavior before writing the rules. *New York Times*, July 7. http://www.nytimes.com/2012/07/08/business/behavioral-science-can-help-guide-policy-economic-view.html

Thaler RH, Sunstein CR. 2008. *Nudge*. New Haven, CT: Yale Univ. Press

USDA (US Dep. Agric.). 2011a. Direct certification and certification of homeless, migrant and runaway children for free school meals. *Fed. Regist.* 76:22785–802

USDA (US Dep. Agric.). 2011b. *Dietary Guidelines 2010: Selected Messages for Consumers*. Washington, DC: USDA. http://choosemyplate.gov/food-groups/downloads/MyPlate/SelectedMessages.pdf

USDA (US Dep. Agric.) 2013. Direct Certification in the National School Lunch Program: State Implementation Progress, School Year 2012-2013: Report to Congress. http://www.fns.usda.gov/direct-certification-national-school-lunch-program-state-implementation-progress-school-year-2012

US Dep. Educ. 2010a. Program integrity issues. *Fed. Regist.* 75:66832–975

US Dep. Educ. 2010b. *Department of Education Establishes New Student Aid Rules to Protect Borrowers and Taxpayers*. Washington, DC: US Dep. Educ. http://www.ed.gov/news/press-releases/department-education-establishes-new-student-aid-rules-protect-borrowers-and-tax

US Dep. HHS (Health Hum. Serv.). 2010. Health care reform insurance web portal requirements. *Fed. Regist.* 75:24470–82

US Dep. Treas. 2009. *Financial Regulatory Reform: A New Foundation*. Washington, DC: Dep. Treas. http://www.treasury.gov/initiatives/wsr/Documents/FinalReport_web.pdf

US EPA (Environ. Prot. Agency). 2009. Fuel economy labeling of motor vehicles: revisions to improve calculation of fuel economy estimates. *Fed. Regist.* 74:61537–55

US EPA (Environ. Prot. Agency), US DOT (Dep. Transp.). 2010. Light-duty vehicle greenhouse gas emission standards and corporate average fuel economy standards. *Fed. Regist.* 75:25323–728

US FDA (Food Drug Admin.). 2014a. *Preliminary Regulatory Impact Analysis: Nutrition Facts/Serving Sizes*. Washington, DC: US FDA. http://www.fda.gov/downloads/Food/GuidanceRegulation/GuidanceDocumentsRegulatoryInformation/LabelingNutrition/UCM385669.pdf

US FDA (Food Drug Admin.). 2014b. *Deeming Tobacco Products to be Subject to the Food, Drug, and Cosmetic Act, as Amended by the Family Smoking Prevention and Tobacco Control Act; Regulations Restricting the Sale and Distribution of Tobacco Products and Required Warning Statements for Tobacco Product Packages and Advertisements.* Washington, DC: US FDA. **http://www.fda.gov/downloads/AboutFDA/ ReportsManualsForms/Reports/EconomicAnalyses/UCM394933.pdf**

Wansink B. 2014. *Slim By Design.* New York: William Morrow

Willis LE. 2013. When nudges fail: slippery defaults. *Univ. Chic. Law Rev.* 80:1155–229

RELATED RESOURCES

Federal Reserve Board Requirements for Overdraft Services
12 C.F.R. § 205.17
Federal Trade Commission Use of Prenotification Negative Option Plans
16 C.F.R. § 425 (2013)
Occupational Safety & Health Administration Occupational Safety and Health Standards
29 C.F.R. § 1910 (2013)
Occupational Safety & Health Administration Occupational Safety and Health Standards for Shipyard Employment
29 C.F.R. § 1915 (2013)
Occupational Safety & Health Administration Safety and Health Regulations for Construction
29 C.F.R. § 1926 (2013)
US Department of Agriculture Nutrition Label Content
9 C.F.R. § 317.309 (2013)
US Department of Agriculture Reporting and Disclosure Requirements for Programs that Prepare Students for Gainful Employment in a Recognized Occupation
34 C.F.R. § 668.6 (2013)
US Department of Labor Fiduciary Requirements for Disclosure in Participant-Directed Individual Account Plans
29 C.F.R. § 2550.404a-5 (2013)

Cumulative Indexes

Contributing Authors, Volumes 57–67

Cole SW, 60:501–24
Cole SW, 66:733–67
Collins LM, 57:505–28
Collins W, 60:631–52
Coltheart M, 62:271–98
Conger RD, 58:175–99
Connor-Smith J, 61:679–704
Cook TD, 60:607–29
Coplan RJ, 60:141–71
Cosmides L, 64:201–29
Craighead W, 65:267–300
Crano WD, 57:345–74
Crosby FJ, 57:585–611
Csibra G, 66:689–710
Cudeck R, 58:615–37
Curran PJ, 62:583–619
Curry SJ, 60:229–55

D

Davey Smith G, 67:567–85
Davies PG, 67:415–37
de Waal FB, 59:279–300
Deary IJ, 63:453–82
den Nieuwenboer NA, 65:635–60
D'Esposito M, 66:115–42
Diamond A, 64:135–68
Dickel N, 62:391–417
Diefendorff JM, 61:543–68
Dijksterhuis A, 61:467–90
Dishion TJ, 62:189–214
Donnellan M, 58:175–99
Dotsch R, 66:519–45
Druckman D, 67:387–413
Dunkel Schetter C, 62:531–58
Dunlop BW, 65:267–300
Dunlosky J, 64:417–44
Dupré KE, 60:671–92

E

Eby LT, 61:599–622
Echterhoff G, 63:55–79
Ehrhart MG, 64:361–88
Einarsson E, 61:141–67
Eisenberger NI, 66:601–29
Elliot AJ, 65:95–120
Emberson LL, 66:349–79
Emery NJ, 60:87–113
Erez M, 58:479–514
Erickson KI, 66:769–97

Evans GW, 57:423–51
Evans JS, 59:255–78
Everitt BJ, 67:23–50

F

Fairchild AJ, 58:593–614
Farah MJ, 63:571–91
Federico CM, 60:307–37
Federmeier KD, 62:621–47
Fingerhut AW, 58:405–24
Finniss DG, 59:565–90
Fivush R, 62:559–82
Floresco SB, 66:25–52
Forstmann BU, 67:641–66
Fouad NA, 58:543–64
Fox NA, 66:459–86
French DC, 59:591–616
Frese M, 66:661–87
Fried I, 63:511–37
Friedman HS, 65:719–42
Frith CD, 63:287–313
Frith U, 63:287–313
Fritz MS, 58:593–614
Fuligni AJ, 66:411–31
Furman W, 60:631–52

G

Gage SH, 67:567–85
Gaissmaier W, 62:451–82
Gallistel C, 64:169–200
Gallo LC, 62:501–30
Gazzaniga MS, 64:1–20
Geisler WS, 59:167–92
Gelfand MJ, 58:479–514
Gelman SA, 60:115–40
Gervain J, 61:191–218
Gifford R, 65:541–79
Gigerenzer G, 62:451–82
Glover LR, 66:53–81
Glück J, 62:215–41
Goldin-Meadow S, 64:257–83
Golomb JD, 62:73–101
Gonzalez CM, 59:329–60
Goodman GS, 61:325–51
Gorman-Smith D, 57:557–83
Gosling SD, 66:877–902
Gould E, 61:111–40
Graham JW, 60:549–76
Graham S, 65:159–85

Green DP, 60:339–67
Griffiths TD, 65:743–71
Gross C, 67:693–711
Gross JJ, 58:373–403
Grotevant HD, 65:235–65
Grusec JE, 62:243–69
Gunia BC, 61:491–515
Gunia BC, 67:667–92
Gunnar MR, 58:145–73

H

Hall RJ, 61:543–68
Hampson SE, 63:315–39
Han S, 64:335–59
Hardt O, 61:141–67
Harring JR, 58:615–37
Haslam N, 65:399–423
Hauser M, 61:303–24
Hawkins EH, 60:197–227
Healey MP, 59:387–417
Heatherton TF, 62:363–90
Heine SJ, 60:369–94
Hen R, 57:117–37
Hennessey BA, 61:569–98
Henry D, 57:557–83
Hensch TK, 66:173–96
Herek GM, 64:309–33
Higgins E, 59:361–85
Hirst W, 63:55–79
Hodgkinson GP, 59:387–417
Hollins M, 61:243–71
Holsboer F, 61:81–109
Holyoak KJ, 62:135–63
Horn EE, 65:515–40
Hornsey MJ, 65:461–85
Huston AC, 61:411–37
Hwang E, 61:169–90
Hyde J, 65:373–98

I

Iacoboni M, 60:653–70
Irwin MR, 66:143–72
Ising M, 61:81–109
Iyer A, 57:585–611
Izard CE, 60:1–25

J

Jetten J, 65:461–85

Johnson EJ, 60:53–85
Jonides J, 59:193–224
Jost JT, 60:307–37
Judge TA, 63:341–67
Juvonen J, 65:159–85

K

Kammeyer-Mueller JD,
  63:341–67
Kang SK, 66:547–74
Kaplan RM, 64:471–98
Kassam KS, 66:799–823
Kasser T, 67:489–514
Keen R, 62:1–21
Keil FC, 57:227–54
Keith N, 66:661–87
Kelley K, 59:536–63
Kelloway E, 60:671–92
Kelman HC, 57:1–26
Kelso E, 66:277–94
Keltner D, 65:425–60
Kern ML, 65:719–42
Kilduff M, 64:527–47
Kim HS, 65:487–514
Kingdom FA, 59:143–66
Kish-Gephart JJ, 65:635–60
Kitayama S, 62:419–49
Kitayama S, 64:335–59
Knobe J, 63:81–99
Kogan A, 65:425–60
Koob GF, 59:29–53
Kopp CB, 62:165–87
Kornell N, 64:417–44
Kounios J, 65:71–93
Kraiger K, 60:451–74
Kramer AF, 66:769–97
Kraus N, 67:83–103
Kruglanski AW, 58:291–316
Kurzban R, 66:575–99
Kutas M, 62:621–47

L

Lagnado D, 66:223–47
Lakin J, 64:285–308
Langdon R, 62:271–98
Le Moal M, 59:29–53
Leary MR, 58:317–44
Lee H, 64:445–69
Lent RW, 67:541–65

Leonardo ED, 57:117–37
Lerner JS, 66:799–823
Leuner B, 61:111–40
Leventhal EA, 59:477–505
Leventhal H, 59:477–505
Levin HS, 65:301–31
Levine EL, 63:397–425
Lewis RL, 59:193–224
Li X, 65:301–31
Li Y, 66:799–823
Lieberman MD, 58:259–89
Lievens F, 59:419–50
Liu Z, 66:631–59
Loewenstein G, 59:647–72
Logel C, 67:415–37
Loken B, 57:453–85
Lord RG, 61:543–68
Loughnan S, 65:399–423
Lowenstein AE, 62:483–500
Lustig CA, 59:193–224

M

Macey WH, 64:361–88
MacKenzie SB, 63:539–69
MacKinnon DP, 58:593–614
MacKinnon DP, 62:299–329
Maguire EA, 67:51–82
Maher CP, 61:599–622
Mahon BZ, 60:27–51
Maier MA, 65:95–120
Manuck SB, 65:41–70
Mar RA, 62:103–34
Markus H, 65:611–34
Martin A, 58:25–45
Martin C, 61:353–81
Mashek DJ, 58:345–72
Masicampo EJ, 62:331–61
Mason W, 66:877–902
Masten AS, 63:227–57
Mather M, 67:213–38
Matthews KA, 62:501–30
Matzel LD, 64:169–200
Maxwell SE, 59:536–63
Mayer JD, 59:507–36
Mays VM, 58:201–25
McAdams DP, 61:517–42
McArdle JJ, 60:577–605
McCaffery JM, 65:41–70
McDermott JM, 65:235–65
McGaugh JL, 66:1–24
McIntosh AR, 64:499–525

McKay R, 62:271–98
McLemore KA, 64:309–33
Meaney MJ, 61:439–66
Mechoulam R, 64:21–47
Meck WH, 65:743–71
Medin DL, 66:249–75
Meece JL, 57:487–503
Mehler J, 61:191–218
Mende-Siedlecki P, 66:519–45
Mermelstein RJ, 60:229–55
Mesquita B, 58:373–403
Metzger A, 57:255–84
Milad MR, 63:129–51
Miller DT, 67:339–61
Miller GE, 60:501–24
Miller MI, 66:853–76
Mills KL, 65:187–207
Mišic B, 64:499–525
Monin B, 67:363–85
Moore K, 59:193–224
Moors A, 67:263–87
Mori S, 66:853–76
Morris MW, 66:631–59
Morris R, 59:451–75
Morris RG, 61:49–79
Morrison C, 59:55–92
Moscovitch M, 67:105–34
Mukamel R, 63:511–37
Mullen E, 67:363–85
Mulliken GH, 61:169–90
Munafò MR, 67:567–85

N

Nadel L, 67:105–34
Nader K, 61:141–67
Nagayama Hall GC, 60:525–48
Napier JL, 60:307–37
Narayan AJ, 63:227–57
Nee D, 59:193–224
Nesbit JC, 61:653–78
Nichols S, 63:81–99
Niedenthal PM, 63:259–85
Norenzayan A, 67:465–88
Northoff G, 64:335–59
Norton ES, 63:427–52
Norton MI, 60:475–99

O

Ochsner KN, 58:373–403

Ogle CM, 61:325–51
Oishi S, 65:581–609
ojalehto bl, 66:249–75
Olivola CY, 66:519–45
Olson BD, 61:517–42
Oppenheimer DM, 66:277–94
Orehek E, 58:291–316
Owen AM, 64:109–33
Ozer DJ, 57:401–21

P

Palmer SE, 64:77–107
Paluck EL, 60:339–67
Park DC, 60:173–96
Parker LA, 64:21–47
Parker SK, 65:661–91
Peissig JJ, 58:75–96
Penn DC, 58:97–118
Pennington BF, 60:283–306
Peplau L, 58:405–24
Peter J, 67:315–38
Pettersson E, 65:515–40
Pettigrew TF, 67:1–21
Phelps EA, 57:27–53
Phillips DA, 62:483–500
Phillips L, 59:477–505
Phillips L, 65:611–34
Piff PK, 65:425–60
Pine DS, 66:459–86
Pittman TS, 59:361–85
Ployhart RE, 65:693–717
Podsakoff NP, 63:539–69
Podsakoff PM, 63:539–69
Poldrack RA, 67:587–612
Posner MI, 58:1–23
Postle BR, 66:115–42
Povinelli DJ, 58:97–118
Powers A, 67:239–61
Prakash R, 66:769–97
Pratte MS, 63:483–509
Preacher KJ, 66:825–52
Prentice DA, 67:339–61
Price DD, 59:565–90
Prislin R, 57:345–74
Proctor RW, 61:623–51

Q

Qiu A, 66:853–76
Quas JA, 61:325–51
Quevedo K, 58:145–73

Quirk GJ, 63:129–51

R

Rabinowitz AR, 65:301–31
Ratcliff R, 67:641–66
Rausch JR, 59:536–63
Rauschecker AM, 63:31–53
Raver C, 66:711–31
Recanzone GH, 59:119–42
Ressler K, 67:239–61
Reuter-Lorenz P, 60:173–96
Revenson TA, 58:565–92
Rhodes G, 57:199–226
Richeson JA, 67:439–63
Rick S, 59:647–72
Rilling JK, 62:23–48
Rissman J, 63:101–28
Robbins P, 63:81–99
Robbins TW, 67:23–50
Roberts RD, 59:507–36
Roediger III HL, 59:225–54
Rosati AG, 66:321–47
Rothbart MK, 58:1–23
Rousseau DM, 67:667–92
Rubin KH, 60:141–71
Ruble DN, 61:353–81
Rünger D, 67:289–314
Ryan A, 65:693–717

S

Sackett PR, 59:419–50
Salmon DP, 60:257–82
Salthouse T, 63:201–26
Sammartino J, 64:77–107
Samuel AG, 62:49–72
Sanchez JI, 63:397–425
Sandler I, 62:299–329
Sanfey AG, 62:23–48
Santos LR, 66:321–47
Sargis EG, 57:529–55
Saribay S, 59:329–60
Sarkissian H, 63:81–99
Sasaki JY, 65:487–514
Sasaki Y, 66:197–221
Saturn SR, 65:425–60
Schippers MC, 58:515–41
Schloss KB, 64:77–107
Schmidt AM, 61:543–68
Schneider B, 64:361–88
Schoenfelder EN, 62:299–329

Schooler JW, 66:487–518
Schultz W, 57:87–115
Scott RM, 67:159–86
Seyfarth RM, 63:153–77
Shadish WR, 60:607–29
Shamsudheen R, 66:689–710
Shanks DR, 61:273–301
Sharma S, 67:239–61
Shaywitz BA, 59:451–75
Shaywitz SE, 59:451–75
Sherman DK, 65:333–71
Sherry DF, 57:167–97
Shevell SK, 59:143–66
Shi J, 65:209–33
Shiffrar M, 58:47–73
Shors TJ, 57:55–85
Shukla M, 66:349–79
Sincharoen S, 57:585–611
Skinner EA, 58:119–44
Skitka LJ, 57:529–55
Slater J, 67:83–103
Sloman SA, 66:223–47
Smallwood J, 66:487–518
Smetana JG, 57:255–84
Snyder DK, 57:317–44
Sobel N, 61:219–41
Sommers SR, 67:439–63
Sommers T, 63:81–99
Spencer SJ, 67:415–37
Sporer AK, 60:229–55
Sporns O, 67:613–40
Stanton AL, 58:565–92
Staudinger UM, 62:215–41
Stephens NM, 65:611–34
Sternberg RJ, 65:1–16
Stewart MO, 57:285–315
Stickgold R, 57:139–66
Stone AA, 64:471–98
Strunk D, 57:285–315
Stuewig J, 58:345–72
Sue S, 60:525–48
Sunstein CR, 67:713–37
Sutter ML, 59:119–42

T

Tangney J, 58:345–72
Tarr MJ, 58:75–96
Tasselli S, 64:527–47
Teki S, 65:743–71
Tennen H, 58:565–92
Thau S, 60:717–41

Thompson LL, 61:491–515
Tipsord JM, 62:189–214
Todorov A, 66:519–45
Tolan PH, 57:557–83
Tomasello M, 64:231–55
Tong F, 63:483–509
Tooby J, 64:201–29
Treviño L, 65:635–60
Trickett EJ, 60:395–419
Tsai KM, 66:411–31
Turk-Browne NB, 62:73–101
Turkheimer E, 65:515–40
Tyler TR, 57:375–400

U

Uleman JS, 59:329–60
Uskul AK, 62:419–49

V

Vaish A, 64:231–55
Valdesolo P, 66:799–823
Valkenburg PM, 67:315–38
van IJzendoorn MH, 66:381–409
van Knippenberg D, 58:515–41
Vandello JA, 67:515–39

Varnum ME, 64:335–59
Vogeley K, 64:335–59
Vohs KD, 62:331–61
Voss MW, 66:769–97
Vu KL, 61:623–51

W

Wagenmakers E, 67:641–66
Wagner AD, 63:101–28
Wagner LM, 67:387–413
Walker BM, 58:453–77
Walker MP, 57:139–66
Walther JB, 67:315–38
Walumbwa FO, 60:421–49
Wanberg CR, 63:369–96
Wandell BA, 63:31–53
Wang J, 61:491–515
Wang M, 65:209–33
Wang S, 61:49–79
Ward J, 64:49–75
Watanabe T, 66:197–221
Weber TJ, 60:421–49
Weinman J, 59:477–505
Welsh DP, 60:631–52
Werker JF, 66:173–96

West SA, 66:575–99
Wexler BE, 64:335–59
Whisman MA, 57:317–44
Williams JC, 67:515–39
Williams KD, 58:425–52
Winne PH, 61:653–78
Winocur G, 67:105–34
Winter DA, 58:453–77
Wolchik SA, 62:299–329
Wolf M, 63:427–52
Wood J, 61:303–24
Wood W, 67:289–314

Y

Yarkoni T, 67:587–612
Yeatman JD, 63:31–53
Yeshurun Y, 61:219–41
Yousafzai AK, 66:433–57

Z

Zane N, 60:525–48
Zhang T, 61:439–66
Zimmer-Gembeck MJ,
    58:119–44

Article Titles, Volumes 57–67

Combination Psychotherapy and
    Antidepressant Medication Treatment for
    Depression: For Whom, When, and How   W Craighead,   65:267–300
                                          BW Dunlop

Family/Marital Therapy

Current Status and Future Directions in
    Couple Therapy   DK Snyder,   57:317–44
                                          AM Castellani,
                                          MA Whisman

Adult Clinical Neuropsychology

Neuropsychological Assessment of Dementia   DP Salmon, MW Bondi   60:257–82
Sport and Nonsport Etiologies of Mild
    Traumatic Brain Injury: Similarities and
    Differences   AR Rabinowitz, X Li,   65:301–31
                                          HS Levin

Child Clinical Neuropsychology

Relations Among Speech, Language, and
    Reading Disorders   BF Pennington,   60:283–306
                                        DV Bishop

Social Psychology

Social Cognition

Social Cognitive Neuroscience: A Review of
    Core Processes   MD Lieberman   58:259–89

Social Psychology of Attention, Control, and Automaticity

Goals, Attention, and (Un)Consciousness   A Dijksterhuis, H Aarts   61:467–90
The Science of Mind Wandering: Empirically
    Navigating the Stream of Consciousness   J Smallwood,   66:487–518
                                          JW Schooler
Automaticity: Componential, Causal, and
    Mechanistic Explanations   A Moors   67:263–87

Inference, Person Perception, Attribution

Partitioning the Domain of Social Inference:
    Dual Mode and Systems Models and Their
    Alternatives   AW Kruglanski,   58:291–316
                                          E Orehek

Spontaneous Inferences, Implicit Impressions,
    and Implicit Theories   JS Uleman, S Saribay,   59:329–60
                                        CM Gonzalez

Environmental Psychology

Community Psychology

Psychology and Culture

Cross Country or Regional Comparisons

Subcultures Within Countries

Organizational Psychology or Organizational Behavior

Work Motivation

Organizational Groups and Teams

Leadership

Vocational Psychology: Agency, Equity,
and Well-Being   SD Brown, RW Lent   67:541–65

Health Psychology

Bringing the Laboratory and Clinic to the
Community: Mobile Technologies for
Health Promotion and Disease Prevention   RM Kaplan, AA Stone   64:471–98
The Neuroendocrinology of Social Isolation   JT Cacioppo,   66:733–67
                                                    S Cacioppo,
                                                    JP Capitanio,
                                                    SW Cole

Psychobiological Mechanisms (Psychophysiology, Psychoimmunology and Hormones, Emotion, Stress)

Health Psychology: Developing Biologically
Plausible Models Linking the Social World
and Physical Health   GE Miller, E Chen,   60:501–24
                                                    SW Cole
Physical Activity and Cognitive Vitality   R Prakash, MW Voss,   66:769–97
                                                    KI Erickson,
                                                    AF Kramer

Personality and Coping Styles

Personality and Coping   CS Carver,   61:679–704
                                                    J Connor-Smith
Personality, Well-Being, and Health   HS Friedman, ML Kern   65:719–42

Adjustment to Chronic Diseases and Terminal Illness

Health Psychology: Psychological Adjustment
to Chronic Disease   AL Stanton,   58:565–92
                                                    TA Revenson,
                                                    H Tennen

Health Promotion and Disease Prevention

Health Psychology: The Search for Pathways
Between Behavior and Health   H Leventhal,   59:477–505
                                                    J Weinman,
                                                    EA Leventhal,
                                                    L Phillips

Causal Inference in Developmental Origins of
Health and Disease (DOHaD) Research   SH Gage, MR Munaò,   67:567–85
                                                    G Davey Smith

Health and Social Systems

The Case for Cultural Competency in
Psychotherapeutic Interventions   S Sue, N Zane,   60:525–48
                                                    GC Nagayama Hall,
                                                    LK Berger